The New Companion to Scottish Culture

The New Companion to Scottish Culture

Edited by David Daiches

Polygon
Edinburgh

First published under the title
A Companion to Scottish Culture
in 1981 by Edward Arnold (Publishers) Ltd.

Revised and updated version published by
Polygon, 22 George Square,
Edinburgh, EH8 9LF.

Set in 9 on 10 pt Perpetua
by ROM-Data Corporation Ltd.,
Falmouth, Cornwall

Printed and bound in Great Britain by
Page Bros, Norwich

British Library Cataloguing in Publication Data

New Companion to Scottish Culture
2 Rev.ed
 I. Daiches, David
941.1

ISBN 0 7486 6148 4

The Publisher acknowledges subsidy from
the Scottish Arts Council towards the publication
of this volume.

Preface

The object of this work is to provide a compendium of information about all significant aspects of Scottish culture. The chief problem in compiling it was to define the word 'culture'. The more my advisers and I considered the problem the more widely we were inclined to define it, and in the end it emerged that virtually all aspects of life, work, play and imagination were included in the definition, which embraced subjects ranging from children's street games to portrait painting, from eating habits to marriage customs, from the Paisley shawl to the Scottish Enlightenment.

The aim, then, is to cover all these varied aspects of Scottish culture throughout history with articles on both movements, institutions and individuals. Although this is intended as a work of reference, I have not made any attempt to impose a uniform, impersonal style on contributors, who have been encouraged to present their material in their own natural style and from their own point of view. Total impersonality is neither possible nor desirable in these matters; liveliness and a sense of coming to terms with a living and sometimes changing subject seem to me to be of the first importance. I hope the articles gathered here will be read, not just 'looked up', and that they will prove stimulating as well as informative.

I am very conscious of the gaps which are inevitably to be found in a work with this comprehensive aim and I can only plead that one could talk for ever (as we very nearly did) about what to cover and that to make sure that no gaps were left would mean the indefinite postponement of the completion of the work. There is also the point that those surveys of activities and institutions that run up to the present become out of date in their later phases with every month that passes between the completion of the article and the publication of the book. The longer we delayed completion, in a search for total coverage, the more acute this problem could become.

Nevertheless this work will, I hope, fill a long-felt want— the first reference work to cover most if not all of the significant aspects of Scottish life, thought and imagination throughout history.

I must express my thanks to the many scholars who have assisted me with advice and encouragement, especially to Professor Geoffrey Barrow on historical matters, Professor Ian Finlay on art, Professor Derick Thomson on Gaelic literature, Dr Donald Low on literature in English and Scots and on the general bibliography, Professor Roy Campbell on economic history, Professor Frederick Rimmer and Mr Francis Collinson on music, and the School of Scottish Studies of Edinburgh University on a range of subjects. If I were to add the names of all the other colleagues, friends and well-wishers who have helped in one way or another the list would take up many pages, so I hope they will not mind if I simply make this blanket acknowledgement. I must also thank the publishers for their patience and helpfulness, and I should like to mention especially Mr John Davey, although he is no longer a member of the firm, for the scheme was originally his brain-child and it was his enthusiasm in its early stages that enabled it to get off the ground.

David Daiches
1980

Note to New Edition

Almost as soon as the first edition of this book went to press I became aware of important omissions, and in the years that followed its publication more have been brought to my attention. The passage of time has also brought new developments in many of the subjects treated, so that some topics require expansion. Again, the amount of new scholarship in almost every area of Scottish culture, in the last thirteen years has been formidable, and this makes necessary significant additions to the reading lists. All this adds up to the need for the present revision. I am most grateful to Professor Ian Campbell for the active part he has played in identifying the areas to which new attention must be paid, to David M. Bennie for the revised bibliography and to all those who produced additions and revisions in record time. And I must pay special tribute to Clare Lawler for organizing the revisions with such efficiency and enthusiasm.

David Daiches
March, 1993.

A

Aberdeen. Between 2000 and 1800 BC a great wave of the Beaker Folk, with their brachycephalous heads, invaded and settled the hinterland of Aberdeen. The physical type of the Beaker Folk remains dominant in the area to this day. The Beaker Folk became the peasants of the region. As a royal burgh Aberdeen was established by the kings of the Canmore dynasty and peopled by Normans and Flemings, whose task was to act as a catalyst to the regional economy. Robert the Bruce and his army, 'tattered and rent', came to Aberdeen after Methven to be sheltered and re-shod. In gratitude, Bruce afterwards gave Aberdeen its extensive Freedom Lands, the conversion of which from craggy heath to flourishing farmlands astonished outside observers like Lord Cockburn.

The sense of regional identity has been powerfully reinforced by Aberdeen's two universities, King's College (founded 1494) and Marischal College (1593) which remained completely separate until the Fusion of 1860. They created the urbane atmosphere which the boy Byron found congenial in the last decade of the eighteenth century. Still in the city then was James Beattie, poet of 'The Minstrel', from whom Byron derived the rhyme-scheme of 'Childe Harold'. By the time Dr Johnson visited Aberdeen in 1773 it was already changing from a mercantile to a manufacturing city and building in the bright, hard stone which gave it the cachet of 'the Granite City'.

In Johnson's day it was famed for 'Aberdeen stockings' which were marketed by Aberdeen merchants, but actually made on the smallholdings of Aberdeenshire. The stocking frames of Nottingham and the onset of the industrial revolution ended that era. Hundreds of smallholdings became uneconomic and were merged together. Great numbers of rural families migrated to the town, where papermaking, textile factories and ship-building boomed. Between 1755 and 1801 the population rose from 15,750 to 26,992.

In the next three decades there was a quite unprecedented decennial increase of 29.6, 25.7, and 29.5 per cent respectively, and by 1841 the population was 63,262. Yet the vast bulk of the incomers were natives of the region. As late as 1851 it was found that out of a population of 72,000 fewer than 20,000 were derived from outside the city or the county. The town was thus far more homogeneous in its make-up than any of the other developing industrial centres in Scotland.

Pressure of population compelled the physical re-making of the city. By an engineering feat, which had its parallel in Newcastle about the same time, an artificial highway was constructed to leap over two enclosing hollows and link the ancient town to an extensive plain to the west, where layouts resembling the Edinburgh New Town were envisaged. Another great new highway to the north was planned at the same time. Thus Union Street and King Street were created. Native architects of outstanding gifts, Archibald Simpson (1790–

1847) and John Smith (1781–1832) demonstrated that the fine grey granite from Rubislaw, which was now being quarried and dressed with a skill unknown since the monumental art of ancient Egypt, could be employed for public and domestic buildings of neo-classic splendour.

The period from 1801 to 1850 thus became Aberdeen's architectural golden age. Victorian over-elaboration in the latter half of the century infringed some canons of good taste, but the granite craftsmanship remained high, and the legacy to the modern city forms the basis of over six notable conservation areas. From an earlier period Aberdeen retains medieval treasures like the Brig o'Balgownie (1329) over the river Don, St Machar's Cathedral (1424), the seven-arched Bridge of Dee (1527), King's College Chapel and its famous Crown Tower (1500–1504) while the University village of Old Aberdeen (from 1494–1892 a burgh in its own right), with buildings of the Georgian period in the main, has been lovingly preserved and restored.

All down its history the port of Aberdeen, carved out the hard way from a delta and almost land-locked lagoon at the mouth of the River Dee, has linked the city with the seven seas. Trade with the Baltic has been continuous since the thirteenth century. In 1882 Aberdeen entered the trawling industry and in a short time became the third fishing port in the UK. In the 1970s North Sea oil transformed the harbour once again.

Despite North Sea oil, however, despite the tides of industrial change that have swept over Aberdeen since 1800, it is probably the most stubbornly provincial city in Britain. The imaginative literature of Aberdeen for the past century has been dominated by a single theme—a single myth if you like in the deep psychological sense—a passion for the land. It motivated a long line of novels: William Alexander's *Johnny Gibb of Gushetneuk*, Ian Macpherson's *Shepherd's Calendar*, Lewis Grassic Gibbon's *Sunset Song*, Nan Shepherd's *Quarry Wood*, and more recent novels by Jessie Kesson and David Toulmin, together with John R. Allan's superb *Farmer's Boy*. In poetry Charles Murray, John C. Milne and Flora Garry have illuminated the same obsessive concern.

This is explained by history. In the first half of the nineteenth century Aberdeen's home counties of Aberdeen, Banff and Kincardine were known as Poor Man's Country because, despite the slaughter of small-holdings, there still remained such a balance of small, medium-sized and large farms that it was possible for the son of a peasant, either to inherit a father's tenancy, or by hiring himself to larger farms and scraping and saving his fees for half a lifetime to buy himself into a holding of his own. It became the way-of-life ideal for whole generations of northeast folk to inherit or acquire 'a placie' of their own. Since the overwhelming majority of Aberdonians are of farming stock the death of the family farm system became the inevitable subject of imaginative drama, which fed also on the folk literature of the Bothy Ballad, a uniquely northeast genre.

To a very much lesser degree fishing has inspired local or incoming poets: e.g. George Bruce, Burns Singer, Peter Buchan. Musically Aberdeen has an honourable history ranging down from its Renaissance Sang Schule to its eighteenth-century Musical Society and issuing today in a multiplicity of choral and orchestral organizations. Aberdeen's theatre is now civically owned.

Like Edinburgh, Aberdeen has happily escaped so far the orgy of demolition and redevelopment which has devastated Glasgow and Dundee. Limited damage may be done in certain city-centre areas, but on the whole its impregnable Granite City skeleton has resisted the brash developer. The continuing rapport between Aberdeen and the hinterland which has so largely peopled its existing stock is another safeguard for the future. Granite is no longer used as a building material, but its contribution to the character of the city will be with us for as long as anyone can foresee.

C. Graham

Adam, Robert and James (1728–1792, 1730–1794), were the two most famous sons of William Adam, himself a talented architect and entrepreneur who died in Edinburgh in 1748. All four of his sons were interested in architecture and the contribution of the eldest, John Adam (1721–1792), to Scottish building and gardening was an important if neglected one. It was John who held the family together after 1748, ensuring the continuity of their various government posts, particularly within the Board of Ordnance, and gave sufficient financial backing for both Robert and James to undertake their Grand Tours in 1754–58 and 1760–63. These Italian sojourns were of crucial importance in the establishment of the Adam style.

Before Robert Adam's departure for Rome in 1754, his architectural work was largely limited to finishing off designs begun or proposed by his father. Of these Dumfries House, designed in 1747, begun in 1754, was perhaps the most considerable and successful, making a firm break with the baroque tradition of his father. In addition, his work at Fort George, Inverness, one of the post '45 rebellion forts, gave him a thorough grounding in the mechanics of architecture and functional design. Its lessons were never forgotten.

Adam travelled to Rome via Paris, Genoa and Florence. In his passion to acquire the reputation of a fashionable connoisseur he neglected Paris, a misjudgement that he never put right and one that later cut him off from the style Louis Seize. In Rome he sought with iron dedication to draw himself, in both senses of the word, into a classical style. To this end he studied drawing, especially under the French expatriate C. L. Clérisseau, and the more imaginative interpretation that might be wrung from ancient architecture offered by the brilliant etcher and popularizer Piranesi. The proof of his assiduity, if not of his genius, is shown in *The Ruins of the Palace of Emperor Diocletian at Spalatro* which he published after his return to London in 1764. In this dramatic bid for fame and employment

he was successful, and virtually overnight marked himself out as a man of immense classical knowledge matched by ingenuity and architectural skill. In finishing this book, he was assisted by James, who had followed him to Italy in 1760 and succeeded in the employment of Clérisseau with whom he ultimately quarrelled.

In London, Adam set up in Lower Grosvenor Street (later 13, Albemarle Street), and it may legitimately be claimed that for the decade following 1765, he dominated British architecture with his Adam style. This was a personal mixture which combined with an unsurpassed splendour of material the whole gamut of styles he had found in classical architecture, and expressed it not only architecturally but especially in the decorative arts. It is no generalization that Adam could turn from designing a door handle to a ducal castle with ease and no flagging of inspiration. To accomplish this Adam employed a considerable office, housed in the Adelphi in London, as well as being connected through his brothers John and William with an infinite and interlocking variety of commercial concerns for building. In all of this James Adam played a full but shadowy part, concerned perhaps more with theory—the introduction to *The Works in Architecture of Robert and James Adam* of 1773 was probably his—and perhaps with the incursions into town planning and speculative building. His unsuccessful project for the altar screen at King's College, Cambridge, of 1769, does prove however his independent existence as a designer.

Adam is perhaps most easily understood in his domestic work, in the town and country houses he built or remodelled, and frequently decorated from top to toe. The most distinguished of these was Kedleston, Derbyshire, begun as an early commission in 1760, where its owner was struck 'all of a heap with wonder and amaze' at the sight of Adam's innovatory designs. It was followed by the crucial patronage of the Duke and Duchess of Northumberland for whom he worked at Syon House, Alnwick Castle, Hulne Abbey, and Northumberland House in London. Their wealth and position in eighteenth-century society gave Adam his ideal opportunity. The Glass Drawing Room from Northumberland House, now in the Victoria and Albert Museum, and the contrasting styles of the Hall and Long Gallery at Syon, showed Adam's talents to the full.

Against this talent must be placed his important contribution to public building and town planning, of which the ill-fated Adelphi (brothers) was typical. This was an attempt to lay out a whole quarter of London beside the Thames with a variety of houses and commercial property, indeed to supply London with the grandeur denied by official patronage and to which public funds would not run. It failed through its very scale—too much for the resources of any family—and its trail of debt and opprobrium followed the Adam brothers to the grave. James Adam was not a great deal more fortunate in his speculative building in Portland Place in the 1770s and Fitzroy Square in c. 1790. It was only in Edinburgh that Adam attracted the right sort of public patronage and his work in Charlotte Square, the Register House and Edinburgh University, showed his capacity to compose in the restrained monumentality of

Neoclassicism. His scheme for the Bridges area of Edinburgh repeated the size of the Adelphi venture and landed both Robert and James in a further financial crisis.

Both Robert and James Adam are posthumously associated more often with interior decoration than architecture. While it is very clear that the Adam practice was prepared to take in anything and that many of Adam's commissions—Bowood, Saltram, Osterley, Harewood, Newby—were a remodelling, often of contemporaries' work, both brothers were fully alive to the intellectual problems of pure architecture. Their philosophy was set out in the introductory essay to *Works in Architecture*, undoubtedly written by James, and more tangibly expressed in the buildings of the 1780s. In these, there was a deliberate simplification of the forms of the earlier Adam style which brought it more closely in line with the current Neoclassic trend. But more intriguing was Adam's attempt to combine the seemingly irreconcilable of the Classical and Gothic, and create a form that can only be called Picturesque. Its most outstanding example is Culzean Castle in Ayrshire of 1773–90, and the style itself steps less out of architecture and more from the large number—over a thousand—of watercolours and drawings he carried out in the decade of 1780.

On Adam's death in 1792 and on that of James two years later, the whole Adam style and reputation fell into immediate and profound disrepute. No doubt to the nineteenth century Adam appeared to personify the insincerity and capriciousness of the previous century. But this was not all, and much of the vituperative character of the abuse undoubtedly arose from Adam's sheer genius and moreover from his own appreciation of it—'I think it is not amiss for a man to have a little glisk of that infinite merit he is possess'd of.'

A. A. Tait

Agriculture, it has been said, was basic to the history of Scotland to a greater degree than for most other countries. To this extent Scottish culture and agriculture are, if not identical, at least inseparable. It is now known that what a previous generation called 'rude stone implements', shaped stones of unknown use from Shetland and Orkney, are the shares of ploughs or 'ards' that were at work in the most northerly parts of Britain in the Bronze Age or even earlier. They tilled the soil for three types of grain, hulled and naked barley and emmer, a kind of wheat, which were harvested with sickles of flint and bronze and reaping knives of stone, or probably plucked by the roots if long straw was required for thatching. Even then fields could be dyke-enclosed, and sheep and cattle served domestic purposes, providing meat and milk, clothing, bones for tools and horns for containers. There is almost no time over the last 3,500 years or more when agriculture can really be called primitive and lacking sophisticated tools like the plough, which has been seen as one of the keys to civilization.

Some wooden plough parts have also been found in Shetland bogs, and others in southwest Scotland, the latter dated by the radiocarbon technique to 80 BC and 400 BC. The whole plough was easily light enough to carry across a shoulder, and two small oxen with wooden yokes could pull it, as they did for the monks of Celtic Scotland in later monastic times. In the Romano-British period, first to third century AD, iron ploughshares first appeared, along with two new crops, rye and oats, which latter became such a staple of the diet that Samuel Johnson referred to it as a food for men in Scotland and for horses in England.

As yet, coulters were unknown, but they were certainly in use on the rich abbey lands of southern Scotland by early medieval times, on types of ploughs that may have been brought from France. Some of them had small pebbles inserted into their timbers to prevent wear. The first illustrations of iron coulters, along with shares, are on fourteenth-century Dumfriesshire grave slabs. With coulters and shares went mouldboards that turned a substantial furrow, and these mark the new, big-scale, organized farming tradition that came to Scotland with the spread of monasteries in the twelfth century. It is only necessary to look at a map of monastic Scotland to see where the best farming land lies.

From the twelfth century Scotland began to know both the feudal order and continental monasticism. Parishes were formed, and conditions became more settled. In the Northern Isles, the feudal form of tenure prevailed from an earlier period. Whatever the way in which society was organized, however, and whether the land was under lay or Church ownership, everyone had to eat and the lords and abbots wanted some surplus besides. Indeed the feudal system was as much a means of mobilizing resources as it was a legal concept. Bearing in mind the undrained land, the limited range of equipment, most of it worked by hand or foot—only the plough and sometimes the sled, cart, or very rarely the four-wheeled wagon were horse or ox-drawn—there were serious limits to the amount of farming improvement that could be done, and income for both estates and state was limited accordingly. It is little wonder that James VI had a description of the isles of Scotland carried out about 1577–95, for the revenue from the uncultivated resources of hill and moor, loch and river in the Highlands and Islands, as well as in the Borders and Galloway, and the produce of cattle and sheep and feral or semi-feral goats (about 50,000 goat- and kid-skins a year were exported in the seventeenth century), was of as much importance as what was produced by the Lowland tillers of the soil. No doubt the natural income of the higher-lying and remoter areas, as managed by the chiefs, gave an economic base on which art forms such as carved tombstones and also bardic traditions could be developed. Later came the decorated powder-horns and targes, the basket-hilted swords, the pistols, and even the piobaireachd, a special form of bagpipe music devised in the 1600s. For such 'higher' forms of culture, economic continuity is a necessary base.

In the Highlands and Lowlands alike, limitations due to the nature of the environment, the range of available tools, and the restricted storage space in the thatched, cruck-framed and turf-, stone- or wicker-walled buildings, meant that farming was everywhere carried on in the form of *runrig*, whereby the tenants in a settlement group worked the land jointly. The cultivators did not have their ground blocked out in separate croft or farm units, but each worked ridges or parts of ridges of land intermingled with those of his neighbours, sometimes reallocated by lot to the tenants at regular intervals, and intermingled too with stretches of stony or boggy country that was of use for nothing but the grazing of tethered animals and the mowing of meadow hay. A dyke or turf wall cut off each community from the moor and rough grazing beyond, and from the hills where the summer grazings and shieling-huts lay. From the rougher areas around these farming villages was dug the turf that was used to roof and wall the houses, to build enclosure dykes, to serve as bedding in the byre and an element in compost middens, and sometimes as the fuel if peat and tree branches were scarce. The best land, or infield, nearest the houses, got all the manure and was cropped with bere (barley) or oats without much rest. Rougher or more distant land, the outfield, was manured by folding stock on it, then cropped with oats to exhaustion before being left to recover. The origins of this joint farming, *runrig* form of land use have not been exactly ascertained but may go back at least to the twelfth century. By the sixteenth century, *runrig* (or *rundale*) was established as a term for the joint use of land by tenant communities.

The working of the ground was also marked by the shared use of the plough and its draught animals, which could number eight or more oxen. The medieval Pleugh Sang tells of a team of eight oxen, with names like Brandie, Cromack, Hakey, Humby, Garie, with up to 25 workers present, some tending the plough and the team, others taking care of the sowing and harrowing. Since an Act of James I in 1424 laid down that every man of simple estate who worked as a labourer should have half an ox in the plough or else should dig seven feet square of earth each day, it is theoretically possible for the plough team to have been shared among 16 tenants. Conjoint use of the draught animals and sometimes the plough was a feature of the *runrig* community.

At the same time, not all land was cultivated in *runrig*. From Orkney to the Borders there were farms held in units of individual ownership, as former monastic farms or mains farms, kept by the owner of the land in his own hands. These were usually on the richer soils, for example in the wheat-growing areas of the east coast, where seaweed manure was plentiful and ports for exporting the grain were convenient. Wheat was a cash crop, sold for profit, so the bread of all but the richer classes was of oatmeal and beremeal, not wheat-flour, with the occasional exception of festival days. On such farms, though the ground was still divided into strips, and ploughed in the characteristic ridge and furrow form, nevertheless these strips could be blocked into groups, and not divided between many people. Such farms were the centres of improvement and innovation from the late seventeenth century onwards.

For centuries, change was limited in degree, but there was no stagnation. The process of settlement expansion was perva-sive and ceaseless. The cutting of peat for fuel could clear ground for grazing or even cultivation, and forests also were eroded. In the long perspective of time, the adoption and spread of new plough-types can be observed, and even though older varieties remained in use in the Highlands and Islands, they too could be adapted. The old Highland spade was elab-orated into the *cas chrom*, possibly during the seventeenth century, a bigger and more specialized instrument that could lever out stones as well as dig the ground. To many such changes the term indigenous development may be given, mark-ing the unsung and little-recorded internal dynamics of the *runrig* communities, unaffected by inventions or innovations from outside.

But the approach of the Union of 1707 brought an increase in tempo. Till the 1690s, writings on agriculture are negligi-ble. There then appeared James Donaldson's *Husbandry Anatomiz'd* and Lord Belhaven's *The Countrey-Man's Rudiments*. Andrew Fletcher of Saltoun, Mackintosh of Borlum, the sixth Earl of Haddington, Barclay of Urie, Grant of Monymusk and many others, then and later, responded to the mood of Europe and sowed the first seeds of the agricultural revolution. The shape of the future was laid down. Belhaven gave for the first time an outline of the ideal layout of farm buildings, arranged around a square with a central midden—an arrangement which became widespread later. Liming of the outfield, especially in lime-rich districts where coal could be got to burn it, led to much land improvement and by the 1760s farms were begin-ning to stand, as new and individual units, separated by dykes from their neighbours, on such improved outfield land. Parlia-mentary legislation in 1695 made possible the division of commonties and the separating into grouped blocks of ridges belonging to different proprietors. The stage was thus set in the late seventeenth century for the subsequent abolition of *runrig*—though its traces remain still in the Highlands and Lowlands—and the general enclosing and blocking out of farms into the units with which we are familiar today.

Enclosing with stone dykes began around the laird's grazing parks in Galloway already before 1684, under the stimulus of the cattle trade with England. It was the spread of such grazing enclosures that sparked off the Levellers' Rising of 1724 be-cause small tenants were evicted to make room for them. The enclosing of arable fields first took place on the mains farms and bigger farms, allowing innovations or experiments in cropping techniques and stock-breeding (because animals could be left separate from each other) to be tried. The widespread enclosure of ordinary tenants' holdings, accompa-nied by subdivision into fields surrounded by ditch and hedge, dyke and later stob-and-wire fences, sometimes did not hap-pen till well through the nineteenth century.

The beginnings of the mechanization of farming go back to the 1760s. From this decade comes the swing-plough patented by James Small the Berwickshire ploughwright. It could be drawn by two horses instead of the draught teams of up to ten or twelve for the 'old Scotch' plough that preceded it, and the man between the stilts controlled the pair. The earlier plough needed both a ploughman and a helper to control the team.

The new plough brought savings in both animal- and man-power at a time when the old farming villages and cot-towns, with their labour surpluses, were vanishing from the face of the improving landscape. A second major innovation of the 1780s was the world's first successful threshing machine. The speed at which it spread throughout the country gives some indication of the almost desperate need for it, for as crops improved both in quality and in acreage it was becoming more difficult to process them with the old hand-operated flails. Mills became standard items of barn equipment, and alongside the barns there appeared their motive-power, dams and water-wheels, or the open or covered horse-walks, often in themselves of a fine architectural quality.

By 1800 a great many elements of modern farming practice were present: individual farms with enclosed fields, new farm buildings and steadings where cattle could be overwintered on turnips, hay and straw in good byres, and where the barns contained mills. The first all-iron swing plough was to appear in 1803–4, made by the firm of Gray of Uddingston, near Hamilton. The technological back-up to the farming industry had begun.

With all these and other improvements, a fundamental problem remained—that of speeding up the harvesting of the cereal crops. In northeast Scotland, this was solved for a time by a changeover from the sickle to the scythe as the main harvesting tool; in the south, groups of migrant shearers, first from the Highlands and then from Ireland, were depended on for reaping the grain from the late seventeenth century till the second half of the nineteenth century. Both sickle and scythe are slow tools and urgent efforts were being made to mecha-nize the reaping process. The inhibiting factor, however, was drainage. For centuries, the old Scotch plough had been putting up the land surface in ridges and furrows, whose corrugations remain on the lower slopes of the Pentland Hills and elsewhere. This was a practical means of achieving surface drainage, but the up and down surface was very inconvenient for machinery. It was only after the 1830s that systematic drainage with tiles laid below the ploughing depth led to a levelling of the cultivated surface. This was why reaping machinery, though experi-mented with from 1805, was not widely adopted till after 1850. Patrick Bell, from Auchterhouse in Angus, produced the world's first effective reaper in 1828, and this machine may well be regarded as the basis for a harvesting revolution, just as underground drainage brought a landscape revolution, and gave the landscape of Scotland the face it has at the present day.

The spread of the reaping machine, and later the binder and combine harvester, of which the first example, a Clayton, reached Scotland in 1932, completes the harvesting story; but as long as horses were needed in the draught, farmers could not cut down to any great extent on manpower. This had to wait till the coming of the tractor, effectively between the two World Wars, and the mechanized farmer came to view the horse, his old faithful standby, as 'the poorest motor ever built. He eats 12,000lb of food a year. He eats the whole output of five acres.' The tractor and the machinery it can operate represent another farming revolution.

Agriculture long remained one of the country's major in-dustries, even though two-thirds of the total land area consists of hill, heather, and deer forest. Intensive mechanization at most levels—milking machinery, bulk handling of grain, po-tato planting and gathering machinery, hay and straw balers, mechanical grabs and hoists, silos etc.—means that much of the work can be done with the minimum of manpower, in wage terms now an expensive item. The effect of the wide-spread use of machinery has led to some erosion of the formerly strongly marked regional characteristics of farming. Sheep remain on the hills; dairy cattle in the hinterlands of the main towns and cities provide their populations with milk and dairy products; wheat and barley, with a decreasing acreage of oats, characterize the eastern Lowlands; soft-fruit farming in Angus supplied till recently the jam factories of Dundee; glasshouses and tomatoes cluster, though dwindling in num-ber, in Lanarkshire; and market gardening marks the country east of Edinburgh. But present regional variations are perhaps more the result of economic incentives. There is no longer any need for the ploughwright to adapt his products to suit the soil types on the farms where they are used, for power rules, more than finesse of the old kind, when the farmer and his men knew the land intimately through foot and arm, at all seasons.

In a sense, the wheel has come full circle. In the days of *runrig* farming villages, even though the specific forms of land use were closely dependent on their environment, neverthe-less the form of organization was common to much of Europe. Subsequently individual units, the farms we now know, be-came the basis of farming, and Scotland forged ahead with a kind of revolution that was more all-embracing than in almost any other country, leaving a remodelled landscape and a range of new farm buildings, few of which are over 200 years old. It produced Small's swing plough, Meikle's threshing mill, and Bell's reaper, all of which had a considerable influence on the agriculture of other countries. Now farming can no longer go its own way solely in relation to local circumstances. Farmers must think of Europe, of outside economic tendencies. We have become part of Europe again.

Joining the EC has had powerful consequences. Over-pro-duction in many European countries has led to substantial farming changes. Subsidised crops like rape flourish, swedes and turnips for animal fodder have been replaced by smaller garden-type turnips for urban housewives, grown in often de-stoned fields. Set-aside policies mean that many fields lie uncropped, with farmers being compensated for not using them. Alternative forms of land-use, including forestry on good lowland arable, are having to be implemented. Farmers stand in the midst of a new European revolution, and the name of the survival game is diversification.

A. Fenton

Alasdair Mac Mhaighstir Alasdair / Alexander MacDon-ald (*c.* 1695–*c.*1770). The '45 Rising can be seen as a great political and social watershed in Gaelic Scotland. Alasdair Mac Mhaighstir Alasdair belongs vitally to both the old and the new worlds: he anticipates the divide and he carries the virtues of the old world with him into the new. He is deeply knowledgeable in the Gaelic literary tradition, and can use and adapt the classical metres and the folk-tale runs; he echoes the anonymous songs and the seventeenth-century poets and the MacMhuirich bardic poets; he is said to have been skilled in the old script. But he can experiment and borrow, inventing the *Celòl-mór* metre, adapting old and contemporary themes in topographical and 'Nature' poetry, and using English borrowings with humour and verve. He is perhaps the most vital and exciting poet in the history of Scottish Gaelic.

Mac Mhaighstir Alasdair was born *c.*1695. We know little of his early career. He is said to have been a student at Glasgow University, and an early marriage to Jane MacDonald of Dalness (a family with strong literary interests) may have interrupted his University career. By 1729 he was a teacher and catechist at Islandfinnan, and he was still in the employment of the SPCK in 1744, but by then his son Ranald was deputizing for him in the school at Corryvullin in Ardnamurchan. In 1741 he published for the SPCK a Gaelic-English Vocabulary, the first such to be printed. Sometime in the early '40s he turned Catholic, and for some time before Prince Charlie's arrival in 1745 he was moving about stirring up support for the Rising, not least by his songs. He held a Captain's commission in the prince's army, fought in various campaigns and was in the march to Derby. We have parts of an English journal which he communicated to Bishop Forbes, author of *The Lyon in Mourning*, and there can be little doubt that he was the author of the *Journal and Memoirs of P—C—Expedition into Scotland etc. 1745–6* (Lockhart Papers, Vol. II (1817)). A form of words used there may suggest that he also took part in the '15 Rising. He was a first cousin of Flora MacDonald and close to the Clanranald chiefs.

It is doubtful if any of his early verse survives. The extant verse seems to fall into three periods: (1) before 1744, (2) 1744–49, (3) post 1749. From the first period we have his seasonal poems in praise of summer and winter, probably dating from close to 1740, other topographical poems, especially 'Allt an t-Siùcair' / 'Sugar Brook', a poem about the Gaelic language and one about his poetic art ('The Author's Entreaty to the Muses'), and the vivid love poem in pibroch metre 'Moladh Mòraig' / 'Praise of Morag', together with the scurrilous and less interesting 'Dispraise' of the same lady. There can be no doubt that he knew both the moralistic nature poetry of the sixteenth and seventeenth century Gaelic tradition, and James Thomson's *Seasons*. He follows neither slavishly, and in his 'Song to Summer' and the 'Sugar Brook' particularly achieves descriptions and evocations of season and place that are full of closely observed detail, linguistic and metrical exuberance and skill, and amused observation. In his seasonal poems as in other types he started a vogue that lasted most of the century, and influenced Donnachadh Bàn (q.v.) among others. His nature poems are celebrations. He is clearly captivated by the fecundity of nature, its continual movement and variety, and he creates an impression of teeming life, moving from trees to plants, to birds, to fish, to animals, to

flowers, then cutting back to pick up some facet he had omitted, and thus reducing the effect of catalogue. The senses of sight and hearing are those most used. His 'Praise of Morag' has a similar linguistic exuberance, and great rhythmic vitality, combined with fun and sensuousness. His 'Entreaty to the Muses' shows that he was very much a conscious man of letters as well as a natural bard.

Into the second period there falls the greater part of his exhortatory and political verse. These poems, centred on the '45 and its aftermath, have an interesting emotional and intellectual range. Some are frankly propagandist. They are the equivalent of the old *brosnachadh catha* or battle incitement, and once at least echo the MacMhuirich *brosnachadh* for Harlaw (1411). Others take their place in a more political setting: an optimistic invitation to the Campbells to support the Prince, the celebration of victories in the campaign, satire and vituperation of the Hanoverian royal family, as where King George is addressed as a cannibal from Deutschland (*A chanibal Dhuidsich*). The political argument is sometimes clinched with a telling Biblical analogy, and there is much evangelical fervour in these songs, but at other times the political argument is more straightforward, though often conducted in urgent rhythmical phrases and singing metres (as in 'A Song made in 1746'). The standpoint can be a clan one or a Gaelic nationalist one, Scottish, British or European (exceptionally). Among the post-Rising satires is the lengthy poetic pamphlet 'An Airce' / 'The Ark', in which, in close on 400 lines, he produces a Ragman's Roll of prominent Argyll folk who had opposed the Jacobite cause, and who now fail to win a place in the new Ark. He has, probably from this period also, some lewd and clever satire of individuals and groups, as in the song describing an outbreak of 'the clap' in Ardnamurchan. But sometimes, as in a 1747 poem about the Disclothing Act, a tired disillusion begins to show:

> Let me not enjoy wearing my plaid,
> enjoy my health, and also my body,
> if I am not willing to give them in sacrifice
> in the cause of the king and of justice.

Despite this tiring, and the physical hardships of the post-Rising years, Mac Mhaighstir Alasdair's largest single work, and his most striking, was still to come: the *Birlinn* or Galley of Clanranald. It may have been composed partly in Canna and partly in South Uist. Like Donnachadh Bàn he reserved his greatest praise-poem not for an individual but for a symbol. In his case it was a symbol of hardihood and courage, of the glorious fight against odds. Or so it may seem to us now. But if such ideas were in the poet's mind he did not spell them out. He uses once again objective, detailed description, and even when this has a large element of the fantastic in it, it is rigidly controlled, in terms of language and metre. Unlike Donnachadh Bàn there are human *dramatis personae* in this poem, the crew members who are described acutely, and they remain germane to the action when the galley runs into the epic storm. He remembered the tradition of rhythmical descriptive 'runs' that decorate some of the Gaelic folk-tales, and in fact a version of 'Cath Finntrágha' / 'The Battle of Ventry' survives in the poet's hand, in the National Library of Scotland. He used some other traditional material, especially in the Ship's Blessing, and drew on his own earlier poem 'Iorram Cuain' / 'Oar Song'. From these ingredients, and his imagination, he made a hard, clear, many-faceted intellectual and poetic diamond.

    D. S. Thomson

Alexander, Sir William (1580–1640) was of Highland descent, claiming to trace his ancestors back to the Lord of the Isles who married a daughter of Robert II, the name MacAlastair being Anglicized to Alexander when the family received grants of the lands around Menstrie. Alexander became a powerful and influential politician. He played a small part in that unfortunate enterprise (the consequences of which are still with us), the final stages of the colonization of Northern Ireland by indigent Scots. A more important benefaction to Alexander was the gift and grant of the Canadas, including Nova Scotia and New-foundland, as a result of which he devised a scheme whereby Nova Scotia would be colonized by baronetcies, the baronets to be enfeoffed on the esplanade of Edinburgh Castle. Unfortunately, the French conquest of Canada rendered the baronetcies worthless, and the Nova Scotia barons rounded on Alexander when they found they could neither claim their six square miles of territory nor recover the £150 they had paid for it.

From Charles I, Alexander received permission to manufacture 'turners' or 'black farthings', which merely stoked inflation and soon lost their face value, causing him to be disliked by ordinary people. He became Secretary of State for Scotland in 1630, then Lord Alexander of Tullibody, Viscount Stirling, an extraordinary judge of the Court of Session, and Earl of Stirling and Visount Canada in quickly succeeding years. In 1640, however, he died in disillusioned poverty, possibly one of the most disliked men in Scotland.

His earliest verse was published under the title *Aurora*, the poems in it were probably written soon after leaving Glasgow University, when Alexander travelled on the Continent with the Earl of Argyle. The *Aurora* sonnets reflect popular interest in the form created by Wyatt and Surrey, though Alexander lacked the imaginative gifts of these English contemporaries.

Alexander concentrated his main formal effort on four large-scale 'monarchicke' tragedies, *Darius, Croesus, The Alexandrean* and *Julius Caesar*, dealing for the most part with the 'falls of princes'. Their flavour can perhaps be appreciated by one stanza, which declares:

> Our painted pleasures but apparel pain:
>   We spend our days in dread, our lives in dangers,
> Balls to the stars, and thralls to Fortune's reign,
>   Known unto all, yet to ourselves but strangers.

These unactable plays were followed by a more or less unreadable poem *Doomsday* (1614). In his old age, Alexander published his collected works under the title *Recreations of the Muses* (1637).

An anonymous contemporary wrote an unpleasant epitaph on him, describing Alexander as:

> A vain, ambitious flattering thing,
> Late secretary for a king;
> Some tragedies in verse he pen'd,
> At last he made a tragic end.

    M. Lindsay

Angus, Marion (1866–1946), the daughter of a United Presbyterian Minister, was born in Arbroath. On her father's death she moved to Aberdeen with her invalid mother, and eventually made her home in a cottage at Hazelhead.

She was over 50 when she began writing, during the next 30 years producing several books of verse. Her best lyrics are in Scots, although her most frequently anthologized poem, 'Alas! Poor Queen', is in English. Within a somewhat narrow tradition, when able to resist the fashionable trafficking with elves and fairies common among Scottish writers in the 1920s, she struck an original note, telling:

> Of joyful tears unwept,
>   Of tenderness unwist
> Of lovers lips unkissed
>   And promises unkept.

Her fellow poetess Helen Cruickshank relates how in 1931 she arranged a meeting between the young W. H. Auden, then teaching at Larchfield, Helensburgh, and the elderly Marion Angus, who was wintering in the town. He came to tea several times and read his poems to her: 'Yards and yards of them, not one line of which I could understand. But I thought to myself, *Is this the new poetry? It sounds like a voice from another planet?*' These must surely have been interesting tea parties!

    M. Lindsay

Architecture and Sculpture, Medieval. The essential Scottishness of Scottish medieval architecture is an elusive quality that is by no means readily or easily identifiable. Indeed, one of the more popular beliefs surrounding this subject is a modest and slightly perverse conviction that most of the chief characteristics of Scottish medieval buildings, and especially such artistic merit that they possess, are ultimately of foreign inspiration, if not actually of foreign workmanship. Certainly, from the twelfth century onwards, during the high and late Middle Ages, the various phases of international Romanesque, Gothic and Renaissance architectural styles penetrated Scotland to a greater or lesser degree, arriving here either directly from the European continent or *via* England, Ireland or Scandinavia. These styles were themselves grafted on to a native rootstock, which already contained significant elements derived from Hiberno-Saxon, Pictish and Norse sculptural and building traditions.

It is also self-evident that Scotland experienced in some measure the general underlying social and political conditions of feudal western Europe which gave rise to a good deal of church- and castle-building in the twelfth and thirteenth centuries, and, in the later Middle Ages, to the increasingly fashionable endowment of chantries, collegiate churches and the production of private funerary monuments, in addition to other symbols of personal, status-conscious display. As in other medieval realms, the chronology, form and amount of this architectural activity were closely linked to the needs and fortunes—both realized and expected—of the clients, as well as being a reflection of the competence of their craftsmen. Herein, perhaps, lies part of the explanation for both the idiosyncratic and the cosmopolitan features of these branches of Scottish medieval art.

It has long been recognized that the fully developed Romanesque style came to be firmly established in Scotland only by about the middle of the twelfth century (Plate 1), and the succeeding phases of Transitional and First Pointed (or Early English) Gothic period-styles might thus be on occasion a generation or so later than their British and European counterparts. Few of the major works erected in these styles, even including the far-distant cathedral of St Magnus in the Norse earldom of Orkney, show a significant native admixture in their Anglo-Norman, mainly Durham-style patterns of plan-form, applied mouldings and sculptured decoration. Such regional or provincial variations that have so far been identified may be largely attributable to external cultural influences, as in the case of the two important monastic houses on Iona, which bear distinct Irish affinities.

From about the turn of the fourteenth century, however, the conventional labels of 'Decorated' and 'Perpendicular' Gothic become increasingly less appropriate to the dating and appreciation of the details and structural systems employed in the later phases of medieval Scots Gothic. For arguably the only convincing examples of each of these styles as overall building systems are to be found in the abbey-church of Melrose where they appear to be roughly contemporary and to represent the work, or at least the influence of different schools of craftsmanship and design in northern France and northern England respectively. Elsewhere, individual features such as a traceried window here, a moulded doorway there, or even the open-work crown of a church-tower seem to represent the more customary and slightly random application of details casually borrowed from the southern kingdom and further afield. In other words, few of these salient and incidental architectural trimmings are without continental or British parallels of some sort, but that is not necessarily to imply a direct and deliberate importation of foreign ideas and practitioners in every case.

Whatever the ultimate source and character of the more superficial decorative treatment, however, a native building idiom emerged in the later Middle Ages, and especially from the later fourteenth century onwards. In many respects it represented a return to the relatively low, massive and heavy modes of the Romanesque and Transitional styles, and involved the extensive use of building-stone for slab-roofing and tunnel-vaulting, which was generally of an arch-pointed kind and occasionally incorporated applied surface-ribs. Such a form of construction was usually associated with low thick walls and closely-spaced buttresses, while it also imposed some limitations on roof-spans and on the sizes of voids generally. This structural system can be seen to best effect in a number of small—and perhaps deliberately intimate—rural collegiate churches situated up and down the country, but it would be a mistake to characterize late medieval ecclesiastical building wholly in these limited terms. For where social requirements were backed by available funds for large-scale enterprises the buildings were altogether more ambitiously conceived and were executed along more internationally familiar lines. In scale and general character at least, few of the prestigious burgh churches of the later Middle Ages would look out of place in a contemporary English setting, St Michael's Parish Church at Linlithgow being a particularly good case in point.

Much the same unevenness in form and quality can be observed in late medieval decorative sculpture. It is found at its refined royal best in parts of Linlithgow Palace, for example, but in buildings of more humble status one may occasionally detect a vernacular touch in the simplified, coarse, oddly proportioned or even slightly overdone treatment of figures and foliage. Foreign exemplars can again be more readily discovered than validated. Even the exotic sculptural detail and the slightly unusual plan of Sir William Sinclair's fantastic chapel at Roslin may conceal a greater indigenous element than has usually been accepted, although the overall effect of the crowded decoration is undeniably similar to that of later buildings in the Iberian peninsula.

Heraldic sculpture was on the whole noticeably late in arriving in the country. Appropriately enough, the late four-teenth-century phase of Dundonald Castle, centre of the Kyle estates of the Stewart family, was one of the first Scottish buildings to incorporate carved stone armorials actually within its fabric, some of which clearly marked the family's attainment of royal power in 1371. Earlier manifestations of sculptured heraldry can, however, be claimed for a group of effigial monuments that are charged with variants of the Menteith armorial, and are to be found at Inchmahome Priory and St Mary's Church, Rothesay.

These particular effigies can also be regarded as geographical outliers and perhaps precursors of a distinctive style of monumental sculpture that came to be produced by several different schools of stone-carving in the west Highlands and Islands during the later Middle Ages. A recent study of the numerous grave-slabs, effigies and free-standing crosses (Plate II) in this area has confirmed an earlier verdict that their elaborate decorative motifs are derived principally from Romanesque art. The style, in the words of Steer and Bannerman (*Late Medieval Monumental Sculpture in the West Highlands*, 1977, p. 4), 'is Celtic only in the sense that it was produced by Celtic craftsmen and displays certain inherited qualities, such as a fondness for interlacing and the elaborate use of ornament to produce a rich spread of decoration'. It has also been suggested that production was largely initiated on Iona under the patronage of the Clan Donald, Lords of the Isles, in the fourteenth century, and at the hands of stone-carvers who were probably of Irish descent.

The commissioning of these funerary monuments by lay clients as well as ecclesiastics can be seen as part of a widespread trend which in England was reflected mainly in the creation of brasses and alabaster effigies. The practice also coincided with the heyday of the chantry movement which has certainly left permanent architectural traces in the same province at, for example, Oronsay Priory and Killean in Kintyre. But, considering the personal wealth and faith that the carved memorials undoubtedly represent, one of the most striking and special features of the phenomenon (apart from their sheer numbers) is that, with a few notable exceptions, there is a curious lack of correspondence between the decoration of the monuments and that of the architecture. This dichotomy in the stone-carver's art is especially marked in numerous cases where the monuments occur in the vicinity of small churches that are of relatively crude workmanship, slightly stunted growth, and conspicuously lacking in any form of adornment.

Contemporary secular buildings were generally of a plain and massive kind, with a strong vertical emphasis, and offered comparatively little scope for decorative embellishment. Superior carved treatment was mainly reserved for maximum effect around the entrances and in the principal public apartment, the great hall (Plate III). Whatever the external guise of the building, the internal arrangements tended to follow the conventional medieval plan found elsewhere in the British Isles, except that the residential quarters were most frequently at first-floor level and above, the ground floor usually being set aside for cellarage and services. Other distinctive features that afforded some domestic comfort and protection against the Scottish climate emerged more clearly in the later Middle Ages, and among these can be singled out the relatively lavish provision of fireplaces, which necessarily resulted in an intricate network of mural flues. Such feats of constructional ingenuity combined with a preference for building in stone, which was so abundantly available and so splendidly and confidently used, go some way towards epitomizing the emergent Scottish tradition. For timber-framing practices, which were confined to the burghs and to rural or ancillary buildings of low rank, never seem to have achieved a comparable level of proficiency and importance, although the roof-structures of some major churches bespeak the endurance of a carpentry tradition of no mean standard throughout the Middle Ages.

The tower-house in all its several forms was the most widely adopted house type, and found acceptance with all grades of landowners in late medieval Scotland, as it also did quite noticeably in Ireland and Northumberland. To what extent its design was influenced by the massive keeps of Anglo-Norman and Angevin England, and indeed the date of the earliest Scottish towers, may long remain a matter of debate. Suffice it to say that there are no clear parallels for northern English keeps of the Norham Castle variety. Otherwise, however, prior to about 1300, Scottish castellar construction generally adhered to the pattern and typology of both earth-and-timber and stone-built castles in England, although there was sometimes a time-lag in their appearance north of the Border.

Island-refuges and some fairly basic types of enclosure-castle that have so far been identified mainly in the western half of the country may represent a more distinctively Scottish contribution to the history of British medieval fortification. In a very loose sense they may also be ultimately derived from Prehistoric and Dark Age building-practices, especially since a number of the earlier sites have themselves revealed evidence of occupation in the Middle Ages.

The variety and style of many aspects of Scottish medieval architecture and sculpture thus arise from a fusion of several different traditions, in which the elements of continuity and adaptation cannot always be distinguished precisely. On the other hand, the actual quality of the workmanship is often more clearly related to the available patronage, which the greater landowners, including the Crown and the religious orders, were in the best position to provide. These same groups were also the first to adopt any desirable changes in current fashion, and their more impressive and manageable designs often furnished the models from which succeeding generations of lesser builders copied. The overall geographical distribution of major medieval monuments reflects a similar pattern. Even where they occur, for military or spiritual reasons, in remote and less well favoured parts of the country, castles and religious houses normally commanded the resources of a sizeable estate, and frequently stand close to the principal demesne. In a society whose economy outside the major burghs was based disproportionately on landed wealth it is thus not surprising to find that the more fertile and prosperous agricultural lands such as the Lothians and the Merse, parts of Clydesdale and the southwest, Fife, Tayside and Strathmore, together with the Laigh of Moray, have bequeathed some of the finest and most densely distributed remains of Scottish medieval architecture.

G. P. Stell

Architecture in the Nineteenth and Twentieth Centuries.

Nineteenth-century architecture has long been associated with the revival of past styles. Too often this has been allowed to obscure the inventiveness and originality of the work of many nineteenth-century architects faced as they were with unprecedented demands on their skills in absorbing the new technologies of building and in responding to the rapid social changes of the Victorian age.

The early years of the nineteenth century saw a marked change in the practice of architecture. The 'gentleman architect' and the 'builder architect' of the eighteenth century gave way to a new breed of professional architect. This new professionalism found its way to Scotland at the hands of young Scots who served their time as apprentices in London offices. William Burn, for example, worked in the office of that arch-professional, Sir Robert Smirke. When Burn returned to his native Edinburgh and set up in practice, he embraced many of the lessons he had learned in Smirke's London office.

These changes were consolidated in Scotland with the founding of the Architectural Institute of Scotland in 1840, only five years after the formation of the Institute of British Architects in London.

This professionalism had grown amongst the rising generation of young architects, many of them the sons of builders, who established their reputations in the large city building programmes that went ahead rapidly at the end of the Napoleonic Wars. In rural Scotland aristocratic patronage still held sway for much of the nineteenth century, but in the towns and cities the new industrialists and merchants and their institutions were the major force in creating this new type of architect.

One of the most striking features of nineteenth-century Scottish architecture is the way in which regional character was sustained throughout the period. This was due in part to the continued use of local materials, but also to the regional divisions in architectural practice. In the capital, Edinburgh, there were a few eminent architects whose work was to be found throughout Scotland, but this was the exception. The architects of Glasgow, Dundee, Aberdeen and Edinburgh seldom worked in each other's territory.

Between 1815 and the mid century the volume of new housing in the cities was prodigious. The innovations were largely in the boldness of their layouts, while the style of individual buildings still clung to the classical precedents of the eighteenth century. Experiments in style were carried out mainly in public buildings where the Greek style predominated for secular buildings and Gothic for ecclesiastical.

Thomas Hamilton's success in the competition for a monument to Robert Burns at Alloway (1818), where he produced an exquisitely refined version of the Athenian Monument of Lysicrates to celebrate a poet whose debt to Greece was almost nil, is one of the puzzles of architectural history.

However, in spite of this unlikely beginning, the Greek Revival became firmly established in Scotland and persisted well after it had gone out of fashion south of the border.

In their designs for public buildings, William Playfair and William Burn in Edinburgh, Archibald Simpson in Aberdeen and William Stark in Glasgow all wrestled with the adaptation of that most unyielding of precedents, the Greek temple. Thomas Hamilton can perhaps be credited with its most skilful and dramatic interpretation in the former Royal High School in Edinburgh (1825–29). Hamilton, who, like many Greek revivalists, had never made the journey to Greece, used elements gleaned from the pages of Stuart and Revett's *Antiquities of Athens*. He blended these into one of the most powerfully composed versions of ancient Greek architecture to be found in Scotland. To achieve this heroic effect, however, he had to conceal the boys' lavatories beneath the entrance stairways and snake the flues across the building so that the chimney pots were out of sight.

In Scotland, as in England, Gothic had a special authority in the field of church building. But north of the border it was treated with caution as there was more than a hint of unwelcome Roman Catholicism associated with the style.

Gothic with a strong castellated element, was, however, increasingly fashionable as the 'picturesque' country house

ideal spread from England. Robert Adam boosted this fashion in the later years of the eighteenth century with such buildings as Culzean and Seton Castles, although his interiors remained classical in spite of the castellated exteriors.

The building of Abbotsford (1816–23) in its clumsy castellated Gothic style and Sir Walter Scott's enthusiasm for the Border abbeys did much to make Gothic more acceptable as a style in Scotland.

The fierce moral tone of Pugin's advocacy, in his famous books, of Gothic as Christian architecture had little impact. But slowly and surely the Gothic revival moved into a more serious phase where greater attention was paid to archaeological correctness and sound constructional principles.

John Ruskin's lectures in Edinburgh in 1853 did, however, produce a marked shift of emphasis in the revival. The most extreme reaction to Ruskin's approach was taken by F.T. Pilkington in his designs for churches. Pilkington used vigorous polychromy, stumpy polished shafts and stiff-leaf ornament in an attempt to interpret Ruskin's admiration for Northern Italian Gothic. In a much more gentle way, Ruskin's emphasis in his lectures on variegated sky-lines, bay windows and prominent steeply pitched roofs finally extinguished that love of classical order which had been the guiding principle in Scotland since the middle of the eighteenth century.

Domestic architecture in the mid century was to be given a fresh impetus by the publication in 1848–52 of Billings's *Baronial and Ecclesiastical Antiquities of Scotland*. It was not a scholarly work, but its seductive engravings of sixteenth and seventeenth-century baronial architecture reminded architects of this important legacy of noble architecture which had no counterpart in England.

David Bryce and other Victorian architects picked from this rich quarry details which adorned their rather overblown baronial country houses. The royal seal of approval was given to this style in the building of Balmoral in 1853–8. Balmoral is an unspectacular example of this style, but it was a model which carried all the status and sentiment associated with Scottish country life.

Building in the cities remained unaffected by this revived national style. Commercial and institutional architecture still adhered to classical models and quietly absorbed the new technologies of nineteenth-century building without disturbing its sense of stylistic propriety. The radical technology of the Crystal Palace had its impact in Scotland in the iron-fronted buildings of commercial streets and the elegant Kibble Palace in the Botanic Gardens in Glasgow. More typical of the age, however, is the way in which this elegant technology is wrapped in the formal stone facade of the Royal Scottish Museum in Edinburgh.

In the second half of the nineteenth century in England, William Morris and his followers were showing architects the common sense and beauty to be found in vernacular architecture, and emphasizing above all its Englishness. Arts and Crafts ideals gradually seeped into Scotland, resulting in renewed interest in craftsmanship and the search for a less self-conscious style of Scottish architecture. The publication of MacGibbon and Ross's epoch-making *Castellated and Domestic Architecture of Scotland* in 1887–92 made available to architects and their patrons a scholarly work where the layouts and subtleties of plan were explored and details of the Scottish vernacular tradition were explained and illustrated.

The master of this tradition in Scotland was Sir Robert Lorimer, although many other architects subsequently followed his lead in the search for a Scottish architecture. Even the famous Glasgow School relied heavily on this tradition, although continental Art Nouveau with its characteristic attenuation and whiplash forms was also an ingredient in the work of Charles Rennie Mackintosh, James Salmon and other Glasgow architects at the turn of the century. Salmon's remarkable Lion Chambers in Glasgow of 1905 was one of the first buildings in Britain to use the Hennebique system of reinforced concrete construction imported from France, but still his intentions were to reinterpret 'the Scottish style of the old rough-cast castle'.

At the beginning of the twentieth century architects had at their disposal both the reinforced concrete and steel frame, and they frequently took advantage of them, but the outward appearance seldom gives a hint of their use. Large Edwardian commercial buildings were still generally clothed in stone and decked out in a variety of classical detail. In the hands of a master such as Sir J.J. Burnet they frequently displayed a powerful sense of grandeur and style.

For the Edwardian architect, the 'classical language' seemed to offer a coherent language of expression which could give order and stature to these increasingly large buildings. The Arts and Crafts ideal was never able to offer an alternative model for large city buildings. Both the Arts and Crafts tradition and revived classicism survived the First World War and continued, albeit in rather a lame way, well into the 1930s.

The Schools of Architecture were, however, by this time full of students thirsting for the introduction of the new functional and undecorated continental modernism of Le Corbusier and Walter Gropius. In spite of this, the number of examples built in Scotland before the Second World War were few. Some patrons were willing to experiment in the design of their private houses, and the rather more flashy world of the cinema and the 'road house' often show the streamlined style of the period.

After the Second World War, what had been an avant-garde movement before the war now became the orthodox style of the new social architecture. Housing, schools, hospitals and above all the Scottish New Towns show no trace of the old tradition. In spite of the continued use of certain traditional Scottish building techniques such as harling, the images were international and the regional character of Scottish architecture that had survived until 1939 was swept aside.

More was built in Scotland in the post-war years than at any other time in its history, but as to its quality, the public were less and less convinced as time went on. The destruction of many of the city centres in the interests of comprehensive development gave rise to concern that the character of Scottish towns and cities might be lost forever.

In the 1960s the conservation movement grew rapidly, sometimes spurred on by local battles over a single building, but often activated by threats to whole areas of the environment both in the towns and cities and in rural areas. The listing of historic buildings and the delineation of conservation areas greatly helped to turn the tide, and the increasing power of planning legislation forced architects to respect and pursue a more sympathetic attitude to the existing environment.

Since the late 1960s attempts to rekindle a national style of architecture have not been successful. The demise of Modernism and the advent of Post-Modernism has licensed, as in other European countries, the indiscriminate use of historical architectural motifs for superficial effect. No coherent Scottish style has emerged despite a self-conscious search by many architects and critics. More characteristic of the architecture of these decades has been the grafting of Baronial, Glasgow School and Art Deco decorative features on to otherwise Modernist buildings.

M. Higgs

Art in the Christian Celtic Era. The impact of Christianity on art in what is now Scotland at first was imperceptible. North of Hadrian's Wall the Romans had had a precarious hold, and the change to the new faith under Constantine here left no visible mark. First news of a Christian mission is in the fifth century, when Ninian, a disciple of St Martin of Tours, came to Whithorn in Galloway; but the mission which he founded is commemorated only in a few stones, some with incised crosses or with Latin inscriptions crudely done. Those may be seen both at Whithorn and at Kirkmadrine nearby. They include stones with the *Chi-Rho* monogram, symbol of the early Christians, derived from the first letters of the Greek rendering of the name of Christ. Ninian's famed church at Whithorn, Candida Casa, would be a very simple structure.

In the following century missions began to come to Scotland from Ireland, and this is the route by which the new art forms eventually made their way. Columba, when he set up his monastery on Iona, no more enlisted masons or sculptors in his service than Ninian had done; but as a dedicated copier of the gospels, he himself and his brother monks took the first steps towards the art of the Irish gospel-book, which in a couple of centuries would develop into the supreme achievement of the Christian Celtic artist. In Columba's time the scribe's main contribution to this achievement is the evolution of the beautiful script known as 'Celtic half-uncial', together with bold initial letters derived from Coptic manuscripts which came into their hands. Multiplication of gospel-books was vital to the spread of the Church, and it formed part of a monk's duties to spend time in copying gospels and psalters. His growing delight in his work soon led to perfection of technique and gradually to embellishment.

Scotland shared this important late phase of Celtic art with Ireland and Northumbria. The Celtic Church was always inspired by a sense of mission and perpetual movement characterized it. Its missions went as far afield as Iceland in the north, Switzerland and Italy in the south, and everywhere the eclectic Celt borrowed from the cultures of the countries where he went. His artists took motifs and ideas from Saxon, from Norseman, from the Mediterranean and the Middle East and wove them into concepts Celtic in feeling and significance. What part Scotland specifically played in this is impossible to say. Certainly it did not possess the many diligent scriptoria of Ireland. Yet one of the earlier masterpieces, the Book of Durrow in Dublin, is generally attributed to the Northumbrian school, and as Lindisfarne was an Iona foundation the Scots of Dalriada can claim a certain responsibility for such Hiberno-Saxon work. And that is not all. The Durrow animal symbols of the Evangelists seem to be indebted to Anglo-Saxon jewellery, and those jewellers in turn must have been inspired by the animal symbols of the Picts. So that even manuscripts which at no time were worked upon north of Hadrian's Wall are products of a culture which embraced Scotland, and it may be accepted that the monks of Iona and other communities from the Hebrides to Melrose were familiar with gospel-books of ever-increasing beauty.

The vellum surface and the ease of decorating it with coloured inks presented the artist-monks with an exciting new dimension. That they would set out the Latin on the page with a script in faultless taste was predictable. The brilliance and abundance of their imaginative response to the opportunity made possible a new chapter in Celtic art and gave it a special place in the history of religious art. Output was prodigious. Many examples have survived, but the vast majority of them are preserved in libraries where relatively few people see them: cathedral libraries in this country and abroad, and in the many great Irish foundations such as St Gall in Switzerland and Bobbio in Italy. As it happens, the two best known, the Book of Lindisfarne in the British Library and the Book of Kells in the Library of Trinity College, Dublin, can be claimed as coming directly within the sphere of Scottish influence.

The Book of Lindisfarne is credited to Eadfrith of Lindisfarne before his accession as bishop in AD 698; and, as Nordenfalk notes, Eadfrith was trained in the tradition of Columban book-decoration, a tradition which had dwindled after the defeat of the Columban cause at the Synod of Whitby. The result of Whitby is reflected in those beautiful pages, for example in the classical layout of the canon-tables, even more in the iconography of the Evangelists, derived from Byzantine ivories. Mirroring Celtic tradition though it does, there are subtle differences in the Book of Lindisfarne which betray that Eadfrith was an Anglo-Saxon. It is otherwise with the supreme example of the gospel-books, the Book of Kells. This appears to have been begun in the scriptorium of Iona itself just before the great Viking descent of AD 807, and when the monks fled to Kells they must have taken the manuscript with them and completed it there. Byzantine influence is much less evident in the Kells Evangelist figures. They seem much more part of the decorative settings. Figures in the picture of the Arrest of Christ (fol. 114) are so treated that the draperies move with a Celtic rhythm, and the hair of Christ is an interlace pattern. Nothing is more splendid than the Incarnation initial page (fol.

34). It might be called the reincarnation of La Tène art. Not only are the devices and motifs reborn on the vellum, but the ancient spirit springs alive in every turn of the pen or brush. Celtic art is often compared with music, and here is a complex piece of orchestration in which the intricacies add up to a symphonic poem which is deeply moving. In a sense, this page is a key to Celtic symbolism over the centuries, for the recognizable Christian content is borne on a tide of emotive colour and movement, and the delight of the artist in his pious work is eloquent. This is not the place to speculate on the union between pagan beliefs and Christian faith as revealed in this era of Celtic art, but the Book of Kells more than any other gospel-book makes nonsense of the charge that the Celt was merely a decorative artist. Moreover, the techniques employed are as accomplished as any in the history of painting. It should be remembered the scribe had to prepare the page by setting out a controlling grid of lines with mathematical precision by means of rule and compass, and that the result relies on instrumental mastery and rigid discipline as much as does any musical work. Finally, this great book disposes of any suspicion that Scotland was merely a bridge between Irish culture to the west and Anglo-Saxon to the south. Masterpieces do not appear out of thin air, and if Iona was capable of this achievement there must have been a substructure of high capability to support it.

The original contribution of the Picts to Iron-Age art (q.v.) is described elsewhere. In the Christian period they continued to be accomplished stone sculptors, but they were influenced much less by Irish art than by Anglo-Saxon. Around the eighth century their symbol-stones underwent a change. The cross in relief appears, though still accompanied by symbols. Possibly this is a result of the invitation from the king, Nechton, to the abbot Ceolfrith of Monkwearmouth and Jarrow, to send not only religious teachers but also architects to build him a church in the Roman manner, an event which took place about 710 AD. The new slabs with crosses were not just monoliths, but were given a more or less rectangular shape to accommodate the cross, which is modelled on Anglo-Saxon originals. Interlacing of very elaborate nature covers the surface of the cross. A feature of much interest is the relief carving of warriors or huntsmen, both mounted and on foot, and the horses in particular are executed deftly and with spirit. Stags and hounds also appear. The sculptors had lost none of their old ability to interpret living creatures, and some of the old tricks of stylization persist into. Some have tried to read Christian meanings into the hunting and battle scenes, but they may be spontaneous recordings of events. This is certainly the case with that monument unlike all others, Sueno's Stone at Forres, with a battle scene which has been compared with an Assyrian relief. The largest distribution of cross-slabs, however, is in southern Pictland, in Strathmore. The Department of the Environment has assembled splendid collections in the small museums at Meigle and St Vigeans, yet many slabs remain *in situ*, for example at Glamis, Aberlemno and Eassie. This is the region where the Picts came into conflict with the invading Northumbrians, therefore where southern influence made the greatest impact, but cross-slabs are also distributed far to the north and beyond Inverness. An imported feature of the slabs is the monsters, probably allegorical creatures from the bestiaries, and this theory is strengthened by the appearance of angels or seraphim, as at Eassie. An outstanding Pictish piece dating from the eighth century or just after is the tomb-shrine known as the St Andrews Sarcophagus, the central panel of which carries a representation of David in a style strongly classical in feeling.

It has been argued that Pictish crosses influenced the Irish school which produced the magnificent high-crosses of the eighth and following centuries. This seems doubtful, if only because the few Scottish high-crosses are later than the earlier Irish ones, implying a west-east traffic. The main Scottish examples are the St Martin's and St John's crosses on Iona (the latter in fragments, but a replica has been erected in recent years), and the Kildalton cross on Islay. In common with Irish high-crosses, they are of 'wheel' form: that is, a wheel or nimbus connects the cross members. Five bosses mark the focus of the St Martin's cross, thought by some to represent metal rivets in wooden crosses which preceded the stone ones, later perhaps symbolizing the Stations of the Cross. Smaller bosses and a panel of vine-scrolls occupy the shaft of the cross. On its reverse side it displays figure sculpture, including the Virgin and Child with angels. In this it deviates from the Irish crosses, which never show the Virgin, and since she also appears in the Book of Kells (fol. 7v) it has been suggested there may have been a painting of her on the island, possibly a Byzantine ikon. The multiplication of figure sculpture on those crosses is typical of a later phase, as earlier monuments show a preference for abstract designs, conforming to the aversion for the human form dating from pagan times, but also reminding us of the Judaistic origin of Irish Christianity. The Kildalton cross is less lofty but no less beautiful. Traditionally there were many more high-crosses in western Scotland, in and around Dalriada, and especially on Iona.

One great cross which is outside the Irish and Pictish forms is at Ruthwell, near Dumfries, re-erected in the well of the little church there. Probably seventh-century, it is purely Anglian, the figure sculptures markedly hellenistic. It carries not only a Latin inscription but a poem on Calvary in Anglian runes.

Metal, favourite medium of expression of the Iron-Age artist, offered new opportunities in Christian times. The Church came to be the chief patron, and the larger monasteries would have their workshops and bronze-smiths. Their needs were shrines or cases for precious gospel-books, reliquaries, chalices—Columba sought a chalice for every church—bells and shrines to contain them, croziers and processional crosses, and the output from the seventh century to the early Middle Ages must have been enormous. In Ireland a fair number have been preserved. Scotland had only a fraction of the monasteries, and those were vulnerable to Viking raids. Much Scottish metalwork may have come from Irish workshops. This could be true of the Monymusk reliquary in the National Museum of Antiquities. Basically, it is a little box cut from solid wood in

the shape of a hip-roofed oratory such as the holy men of the early Church lived and worshipped in, and the wood is protected by plates of bronze and silver. On the silver are delicately chased zoomorphic patterns, and there are settings for enamels and semi-precious stones. It is a choice little object, though too small to have contained the *Cathach* of Columba, as tradition maintained it did. It had a hereditary keeper, an abbot, who was required to do service for it to the king by carrying it around the army before a battle. In the Book of Kells the Temple of Jerusalem is portrayed in the shape of this sort of reliquary. The date is around 700.

The hoard of seventh and eighth-century silver discovered in 1958 on St Ninian's Isle in Shetland was buried under the remains of a Pictish church, probably to save it from raiders. It shows the Picts were familiar with sophisticated techniques. Certainly some of the objects are imports, among them a fine sword-pommel from the south; but the presence of an unfinished chape from a scabbard, with several completed chapes, may indicate the presence of a worker in precious metals on the island. It has been suggested some of the bowls in the hoard come from the same workshop as the Monymusk reliquary. But the bulk of early silverwork in Scotland, that is of the seventh and eighth centuries, probably took the form of brooches. These reveal the persisting tradition of La Tène culture. Two great silver brooches inlaid with gold found at Rogart in Sutherland indicate skills and taste of a high order, and the supreme example of such work in Scotland is the Hunterston brooch, like the Rogart brooches in the National Museum. It is of silver with intricate filigree work on a background of gold. It may have a Northumbrian origin, but there are signs of Celtic influence; and as a fragment of another such brooch, perhaps even finer, was dug up as far north as Caithness hints, superb jewellery may have been at least worn all over Scotland.

The cult of fine metalwork, notably ecclesiastical metalwork, persisted right into the Middle Ages. Celtic Church traditions were carried on by the Culdees even after the twelfth century, among them the old forms of church furniture. Bells once owned by holy men were preserved with much care, and indeed may still be seen in a niche in a little church in Inverness-shire, and some were protected in ornate shrines. Two twelfth-century examples survive in Scotland: the Guthrie and the Kilmichael-Alassary shrines, now in the National Museum. Both are of bronze. The applied figures are romanesque in style, but there is still a faint echo of Hiberno-Saxon tradition in the surface decoration. Then again, the old croziers, their crooks quite different from crooks of croziers of the Roman Church, were passed on from generation to generation, their importance marked by the richness of the cases made to contain them. The one Scottish example of the group, the crozier or 'quigrich' of St Fillan, dating perhaps from the eleventh century, has a splendid silver-gilt case made about the fourteenth. Unlike Irish cases such as the Clonmacnoise, with its Celto-Scandinavian decoration, it scarcely seems Celtic at all apart from the shape of the crook and the presence of a comb or crest. The word 'quigrich' means a stranger, and there has been speculation about a possible foreign origin; but a treasured crozier is not likely to have been sent abroad to have a case fitted, and the case may have been done by a Continental craftsman working in Scotland. The custodians of the relic since 1487 have been the Dewars of Strathfillan, and when one of them emigrated to Canada he took it with him. However, it was brought back and acquired by the National Museum in 1876.

Scotland remained a Celtic kingdom until the reign of Malcolm III (Canmore) in the eleventh century. He knew the English court, and when he married the daughter of Edward the Confessor, Margaret, the doom of the Columban Church became inevitable. He and his queen were buried not on Iona, but in Dunfermline. Although the Culdees kept the old forms in being, they were a dwindling sect, and the cultural traditions which Scotland had shared with Ireland and the rest of the Celtic world were driven out by Saxon and Norman ways or lingered on only in the west, whose chiefs were far from the new seats of power and could not nourish adequately the few seeds of Celtic art which still lay dormant in their territories. The only fostering ground was the Lordship of the Isles. The Lords of the Isles were constantly in revolt against the kings of Scotland, but their domain straddled the Irish Sea and the past to which they were loyal was Celtic; with an element of Norse. The Lordship is symbolized, in a way, by a relic familiar to visitors to Dunvegan Castle in Skye, the Macleod Cup. It is a wooden mether mounted in silver and embellished with gilding and *niello*, and a Latin inscription relates it to one John Macguire and adds the date 1493. Macguire is mentioned in the *Annals of the Four Masters*, and the mounts of the cup suggest Irish metalwork of the period just after the Anglo-Norman invasion. There is little evidence of native creative craftsmanship in the west during this period, although two carved whalebone boxes in the National Museum do seem to indicate it had not completely disappeared. They are known as the Fife and Eglinton caskets.

I. Finlay

Art Galleries *see* Museums and Art Galleries

Art, Iron-Age.
In the Iron Age, Scotland as we know it now was very much an outlier of western Europe. The dominant people were Celts, and waves of them crossed into Britain, some direct from Gaul and some by way of Ireland, bringing with them the elegant art-form known as La Tène. It achieved its finest manifestations in metalwork. The Celts were ruled by a warrior-aristocracy, therefore their art tended to find expression in weapons and armour, in horse-furniture and in personal ornaments.

Around the third century BC powerful tribes from Gaul penetrated as far as Yorkshire, and they seem to have brought their 'Marnian' culture into southern Scotland. Among the most notable evidence of this is a bronze pony-cap from Torrs, Kirkcudbrightshire, once in Scott's collection at Abbotsford

but now in the National Museum of Antiquities in Edinburgh. It dates from about 200 BC. Its bold relief decoration in *repoussé* is typical of La Tène art, and may be compared with several splendid finds from England, now in the British Museum. This is British La Tène art at its best, and the climax of the style, the chief characteristic of which is assymetrical, restless patterns, the antithesis of classical Mediterranean art. It is a mistake, however, to think of it as merely ornamental or as wayward, or to conclude that because it it is not representational it has no significant content or message. Those strange, rhythmic patterns had meaning enough, even if we never succeed fully in deciphering them.

Before examining their significance and the techniques involved, reference to a few Scottish examples of this art may be useful. One of the loveliest is a gold ornament found in Peeblesshire, at Cairnmuir. It is a ring-like ornament, with bold, plastic modelling, intricate detail contrasting with plain surfaces, and we know it to be a terminal from a torc or neck-piece because a complete torc in the same style turned up at Snettisham in Norfolk. It is a product of the first century BC. It is remarkably sophisticated, both technically and aesthetically, and reflects a culture in which both ostentation and taste were determining factors, certainly not a barbarian culture. We have to rely on Roman commentators, but on the whole they complement the evidence of surviving art. The Celtic aristocracy was prideful, quarrelsome, but had qualities which even Romans admired. They in turn admired and copied features of Roman life; but in northern Britain, by contrast with Gaul, art retained its anti-classical spirit and spoke its own language of symbol. This occurs even on small personal ornaments, such as brooches and pins, many of which have been found in Scotland. Warlike the northern tribes were, but the art evidence suggests it is quite wrong to think there was nothing but hordes of untutored savages beyond Hadrian's or even Antonine's Wall.

The most impressive ornaments worn by those northern Celts perhaps are the bronze collars. The finest from a Scottish site comes from Lochar Moss, Dumfriesshire. It is classified as a 'beaded torc', because it comprises in part beads ingeniously strung on an iron rod square in section to prevent them rotating. There is a marvellous balance between strength and delicacy, and the same is seen in another collar, found in Roxburghshire. Some may hold that sophisticated finds such as these from the south of Scotland are strays and do not reflect the accomplishments of the area, but there is no good reason to suppose so. Welsh-speaking Strathclyde extended right up to Dumbarton. The warrior-chieftains from Galloway to Lothian would garb themselves much like those of Anglesey, and so the bronze scabbard from Mortonhall, Edinburgh, is no stray either. Like others from British and Irish sites, it is an accomplished piece of metal-working. Ornament is limited to three areas: hilt, a central ring for the baldric support, and chape of curious form, and the nice sense of balance and restraint recalls the taste of the Japanese master-metalworkers.

One class of metalwork objects unparalleled outside Scotland is the group of massive bronze armlets apparently produced exclusively beyond Forth and Tay. They are barbaric in their bold design, trapping light and shade in their flanges. A flawed casting in the National Museum shows how the armlets were processed, for the finished piece is smoothed to a fine surface usually enhanced by a beautiful green patina like that of a Chinese bronze. Some, such as the examples from Castle Newe and Drummond Castle in the British Museum, are picked out with yellow and red enamels. Although analysis of the metal suggests a period after Roman occupation of the south, there is an element of La Tène feeling in those armlets, which is interesting because they come from the territory of the Picts.

Some branches of insular Iron-Age art are represented in Scotland poorly or not at all. Only one of the group of British bronze mirrors was found in Scotland, at Balmaclellan in Kirkcudbrightshire. It may be an import from southwest England, where the school of mirror-workers seems to have been concentrated, but on the other hand it is much inferior aesthetically to mirrors such as those from Birdlip or Desborough, which rival anything in this field achieved in ancient China.

Most of the metal-working skills in which the Celt excelled seem to have been known in Scotland. Casting has been mentioned, so has the beating up of sheet bronze in the *repoussé* process. The smiths were equally at home with chasing and engraving. Enamelling is of course another art, but associated with metal-working, and the Greek Philostratus described how the Celts heated colours on metal so that they fused and adhered to the surface. Most Scottish Iron-Age examples of enamel decoration, for example the bridle-bit from Birrenswark, are not elaborate; but the magnificent patera from West Lothian in the National Museum, the body and handle enriched with glowing reds, greens and blues, is a tantalizing pointer to the skills once present, skills later lost. The method here is that known as *champlevé*, involving tracing outline patterns on the surface and digging these out into compartments, which are filled with the powdered enamels.

It will be noted that those high artistic skills serve mainly one social class, the warriors and leaders. Helmets, swords, harness-mounts and other horse-furniture are necessary and functional, but they transcend mere function and become the insignia of rank. The artist himself, like the poet, was a person of importance who helped to build and maintain the reputations of rulers, and his status was considerable. Consequently a purely domestic art like pottery reached no great heights. This is not true of the Continental Celts, who produced some beautiful ceramic wares, so no doubt living conditions in Scotland were much simpler.

Among ancient peoples religion sometimes rivalled kings and princes in patronage of the arts, but not among the Celts. In the Rhineland and Gaul there was a certain amount of religious sculpture, some of it sinister, but Celtic deities were strange presences in the oak groves, difficult to materialize in wood or stone. The influence of Roman anthropomorphism does not seem to have penetrated much beyond the Solway, so that those half-classical god figures found in Gaul and even England are not found in the north. Nor is there anything like the Turoe stone in Ireland which speaks the same baffling symbol language as other stones of the kind in Brittany and Germany. It is only in the Pictish territories that stone sculpture had a place in Scotland. However, the Pictish achievement is unique and consistently excels Celtic sculpture elsewhere aesthetically.

The Iron Age is usually reckoned to end with the first century AD, so that what are termed the Class I sculptured stones of Pictland, dated between the sixth and eighth centuries hardly seem to qualify, but the culture which produced these monuments is in fact a carry-over from the Iron Age. The Class I stones are monoliths on which devices are carved in shallow relief. On a high proportion of them there are abstract symbols done with much precision and artistry, symbols which are open to various interpretations. They appear to have some kind of tribal or totemistic meaning. There were probably schools of artists working under chieftainly or maybe druidical patronage, and it is significant that the distribution of the earlier stones is mainly in the northeastern region, from Easter Ross to Aberdeenshire. This was the main area of Pictish power, with the royal seat reputedly at Inverness. Here Columba is said to have gone to confront King Brude or Bridei in the sixth century.

Another feature of the earlier stones is their animal carvings. They too appear to have a symbolic purpose, and they are contemporary with the abstract signs. The animals are incised, outline drawings. Although they are stylized, they possess the most arresting spontaneity and are evidently done by men who were close observers of their subjects and familiar with their movements. Among the most celebrated examples are the bull-carvings excavated at Burghead in Morayshire, possibly the best of which is in the British Museum. Burghead must have been the centre of a cult of this animal involving sacrifices. In the Inverness Museum is a magnificent wolf, found at Ardross. Its sense of loping movement is superb. No less superb is the eagle from the Broch of Burrian, in Orkney; and but for the weathering of the surface the boar on the roadside stone at Knocknagael, near Inverness, could be classed with them. A feature of all such animals is the rendering of what are called the joint-spirals, elaborations of joint and shoulder muscles which can be matched in animal sculptures in Celtic Europe, for example on the little carving of the boar-god of Euffigneix in the Musée National at St Germain. Here is evidence of ancient Iron-Age tradition, however it may have been transmitted. It has been argued such animals were borrowed from gospel-books such as the Book of Durrow, but the naive animals of those books could never have become the living creatures of the Pictish monuments which, it becomes obvious, were the originals. It has been suggested that the scribes of the gospel-books used as models the animals of Saxon metalwork such as those found in the Sutton Hoo hoard, the Saxon jeweller having bent Pictish naturalism to suit his needs.

It remains to examine briefly the significance of this Iron-Age art. Is it, as claimed earlier, more than mere decoration? Is its message for the society which produced it in any degree comparable with what is conveyed through the arts of the

Mediterranean civilizations? First, it tells us a great deal about the Celts. Its appeal is emotional rather than intellectual, yet it is calculated; its precision and control are as evident as are those same elements in classical art. That it was established in early Scotland is important, therefore, to an understanding of Scottish history. Its message is baffling, certainly, for we have no obvious clue to its symbol language, but it had perhaps a close affinity to the rhetoric so prized by the Celts everywhere. Moreover, this poetic symbolism attained its peak in insular Celtic art. The differences and similarities between the style of the La Tène finds in southern Scotland and the nature of Pictish art are also important in a study of the society of early Scotland.

I. Finlay

Ayton, Sir Robert (1570–1638) was a descendant of an old Fife land-owning family sprung illegitimately from the Royal Stewart line. He was born at Kinaldie, Fife, and graduated at St Andrews. He studied law in Paris and held various ambassadorial and court offices, the most important being his secretaryship to James's Queen, Anne of Denmark and later to Queen Henrietta Maria. He wrote in Scots, English, Latin, Greek and French. His Scots poems, dating from the 1580s and written as part of a sequence with his fellow students Alexander and Craig, reflect the influence of the work of Alexander Scott. Ayton is very much a transitional poet, the most successful of that group who, after 1603, found it desirable to change over from writing Scottish poetry in Scots to writing it in English. In his mature work in English, small though it is in bulk, he moves away from the openness of the Elizabethan lyric towards the new metaphysical manner, combining forceful language with the use of irony and paradox and the employment of elaborate intellectual conceits. Several of Ayton's lyrics are to be found in most Scottish anthologies, the temper of them being reflected in 'The Exercise of Affection'

> Methinks a wise man's actions should be such
> As always yield to reason's best advice,
> Now for to love too little, or too much,
> Are both extremes, and all extremes are vice.
>
> Yet have I been a lover by report,
> Yea, I have died for love as others do.
> But praised be God, it was in such a sort,
> That I revived within an hour or two.

Some of his Latin verses were included in Johnson's *Delitiae Poetae Scotorum*. James Watson, in his anthology *A Choice Collection of Comic and Serious Scots Poems* (Part III, 1711), credited Ayton with a poem beginning

> Should old acquaintance be forgot
>   And never thought upon,
> The flames of love extinguished,
>   And freely passed and gone?
>
> Is thy kind heart now grown so cold
>   In that loving breast of thine

> That thou canst never once reflect
>   On old-lang-syne?

It therefore appears that Ayton thought out, or at least first set down on paper, the phrase that was to inspire Burns to write the world's greatest parting song more than a century and a half later.

M. Lindsay

B

Bagpipes, Highland. Air is fed from the mouth to a bag operated by the elbow which supplies the chanter and two or (nowadays) three drones. The chanter is conical and encloses a single reed, and uses an open fingering system which means the sound is continuous. Complex 'grips' or decorations give the impression of repeated notes and variations in volume, as well as pointing the rhythm. A syllabic notation known as *canntaireachd* was developed uniquely for bagpipe music and is still in use.

There is no evidence to prove that the highland bagpipes were in use before the 15th century, but they were clearly well established as military instruments by the mid-16th century.

Bagpipes, Cauld-Wind. The name refers to the fact that air from a bellows is cold unlike air from the mouth. The term is applied to a variety of bellows-blown pipes including the Lowland bagpipe with cylindrical chanter producing a sweet tone, similar to the Northumbrian pipes. The Border pipes with three drones and conical bore chanter were used by town pipers for reveilles and curfews, probably from the late 16th century on. Pastoral pipes have an open chanter using soft reeds allowing for extension of the range by overblowing.

See **Pibroch, Music in the Lowlands.**

Ballads, The. 'There was never ane o my sangs prentit till ye prentit them yoursel, and ye hae spoilt them awthegither. They were made for singing an no for readin: but ye hae broken the charm noo, and they'll never be sung mair.'

This rebuke was administered by Margaret Laidlaw, the mother of the Ettrick Shepherd, to Sir Walter Scott, through whose agency the most familiar versions of the Scots classic ballads were to become known to the world: so much so that 'Border ballad' and 'Scots ballad' have become for people at large almost synonymous terms. Like Burns before him, Scott set up what was virtually a personal folksong workshop—William Motherwell referred to it somewhat caustically as 'the alembic established at Abbotsford for the purification of

Ancient Song'—and the ballads that passed through it were almost invariably 'improved', not always to their advantage. Scott's work in the field of ballad-editing played—like his novels—a significant part in the growth of European Romanticism, and at home generations of Scottish school-children have been introduced to their country's ballad heritage through his Minstrelsy, or anthologies based on it. Nevertheless, Scott's role in our convoluted ballad history is a much more complex one than might appear at first sight; it is necessary to get it into focus, and to do this we must examine Margaret Laidlaw's remark, quoted above, in a little more detail.

Her forthright words serve to remind us that the ballads are essentially folk*songs*, linked by countless ties to others of the species, and that without the reshapings and recreations of oral tradition they would not possess their characteristic qualities and identity. Not a few are living and evolving folksongs, and some excellent specimens of these have been collected from singers young and old in the last two or three decades. The most prolific ballad-zone of Britain is and seems always to have been not the Borders but the northeast—Aberdeenshire, Banff, Moray and the Mearns—and at the beginning of this century the Buchan dominie Gavin Greig (in collaboration with the Rev. Duncan of Lynturk) gathered a harvest there that one can truthfully call a 'burstin' kirn': about 3,050 folksong texts and 3,100 records of tunes, one of the largest and most important folksong collections in the world. This included hundreds of versions of classic ballads, 84 of which came from a single informant, Bell Robertson (who was however not a singer and could only recite what she had heard). The ballads in the Greig-Duncan collection were edited by Alexander Keith, and published by the Buchan Club in 1925.

And what, it may be asked, do we actually mean by ballad? Although the word has often been used to denote a fairly wide range of song-poetry, ballad, for present purposes, means a song-poem belonging to the high 'caste' of narrative folksong which Professor Francis James Child admitted to his great thesaurus *English and Scottish Popular Ballads*; it means the 'big ballad' or (*Scotice*) 'muckle sang', which has often been regarded as the aristocrat of the folksong world—more by scholars, needless to say, than by the egalitarian clan of ordinary folksingers. In his excellent short study *The Ballads*, M.J.C. Hodgart warns us that the 'Child' ballads 'are as hard to define as they are easy to recognize. They are anonymous, narrative poems, nearly always written down in short stanzas of two or four lines. They are distinguished from all other types of narrative poetry by a peculiar and effective way of telling their stories. They deal with one single situation and deal with it dramatically, beginning "in the fifth act" and there is a high proportion of dialogue to stage-direction.' (The reference is to Thomas Gray's celebrated remark about Child Maurice that 'it begins in the fifth act of the play'. It was this ballad which had earlier given John Home the idea for his play *Douglas*.) 'They are not only anonymous but also impersonal: the storyteller does not intrude his personality, and there is no moralizing or didacticism.' To this we may add Professor

Gordon H. Gerould's admirably concise definition: 'a ballad is a folksong that tells a story with stress on the crucial situation, tells it by letting the action unfold itself in event and speech, and tells it objectively with little comment or intrusion of personal bias.'

After the foundation of the School of Scottish Studies in 1951, systematic collecting with tape-recorders began in the northeast; the School's research workers were looking for everything that came under the general heading of oral tradition, but priority was naturally given to these same classic or 'Child' ballads. This led in 1953 to the discovery in Aberdeen of the great Jeannie Robertson (1908-1975), a singer widely regarded—by scholars, as well as by the 'folk' public—as the finest modern exponent of traditional ballad-singing. (This was the singer of whom Alan Lomax wrote that she was 'a monumental figure of world folksong', and of whom A.L. Lloyd remarked that she was 'a singer sweet and heroic'.) Jeannie was, however, only one of a sizeable company of singers who turned out to have good versions of classic ballads. Others were found all over the Lowlands, and even in parts of the still Gaelic-speaking Highlands. We can claim with confidence, therefore, that the great stream of Scots traditional balladry is still flowing strongly, and that Hogg's mother was luckily wrong when she averred that they would 'never be sung mair'.

She was also wrong, of course, when she thought of the ballads as never having been printed before. Ever since the invention of cheap printing, broadside versions of the ballads had been travelling all over the country, and many of the variants current among non-literate singers had undoubtedly reached them from printed sources. (Scotland has prided itself, since the Reformation, on being the most literate nation in Europe, and although this idea is part of the national myth, there must have been in most parishes individuals who were ready and willing to interpret the hieroglyphics of print for the benefit of non-literate singers.) Not only the sometimes gormless reworkings of hack writers employed by the broadside printers but even the sophisticated (if not always felicitous) re-touchings and tintings of learned antiquarian poet-editors became tributaries of the main stream of oral tradition. The result was a situation aptly described by Alan Lomax when he was assembling documentation for the Scottish album (vol. VI) of the Columbia World Library of Folk and Primitive Music:

> The Scots have the liveliest folk tradition of the British Isles, but paradoxically it is the most bookish. Everywhere in Scotland I collected songs of written or bookish origin from country singers, and, on the other hand, I constantly encountered bookish Scotsmen who had good traditional versions of the finest folksongs. For this reason I have published songs which show every degree and kind of literary influence.

The most famous single figure in Scotland's ballad history is a bookish lady who read Ossian and wrote verses—this was Anna Gordon, better known as Mrs Brown of Falkland (1747–1810). Anna was the daughter of the Professor of Humanity at

King's College, Aberdeen, and the wife of a Kirk of Scotland minister, and also the source-singer of priceless oral versions of classic ballads. Child gave every ballad version preserved by her a place in his canon; 20 of her versions are his A or primary texts, and four his B texts. It has lately been argued by Dr David Buchan in *The Ballad and the Folk* (London, 1972) that Mrs Brown was able to recreate her ballads at every singing, using techniques similar to those employed by the Yugoslav epic singers investigated by Milman Parry and Albert Lord. A discussion of this still highly controversial subject will be found in my article 'The Ballad, the Folk and the Oral Tradition' in *The People's Past*, a symposium edited by Edward J. Cowan (Edinburgh, 1980). Suffice it to say here that Mrs Brown does not seem to me by any means a unique figure, in spite of the excellence of the ballad versions she preserved; she is rather an outstanding exemplar of a *type* of creative literate folksinger which is one of the most characteristic types of folksinger on the Scottish scene, and one which certainly did not die out during the course of the nineteenth century.

The first traditional singer to record his entire repertoire for the School of Scottish Studies was Willie Mathieson, a septuagenarian retired farm servant who had devoted much spare time throughout his life to collecting songs. In his kist, which he transported from farm to farm when he got a new fee, were three large ledger books full to overflowing with songs of all kinds, from classic ballads through lyric-lovesongs to place-name rhymes and bairn songs. Willie had either collected songs on the spot from his fellow ploughmen, or had diligently followed up his informants by correspondence. He had also tried his hand at versifying, and one of the poems which he wrote down alongside ballads and bothy songs was a moving elegy for his dead wife. Willie Mathieson was quite capable of discoursing knowledgeably about different 'weys' of a ballad, and he would often quote 'what Gavin thocht aboot it'—giving the great collector his first name, in familiar Scots style—but the ballads, especially the tragic love ballads, were closer to him (and 'truer') than they could possibly be to the mere scholar; when he referred to Barbara Allen's callous cruelty to her luckless lover on his death-bed, he would shed tears.

Willie was one of a long and distinguished line of Aberdeenshire singer-collectors. In a letter to the Aberdeen antiquary William Walker, written in 1895, Professor Child expressed the opinion: 'The original derivation of many of the ballads cannot be determined, but that the best Scottish ballads are from the north, there can be no doubt.' As recent collecting amply confirms, the northeast continues to maintain its supremacy, but in recent years a great deal of fascinating material has come to light in east-central Scotland: the Dunkeld-Blairgowrie area, and Strathmore. Quite apart from geographical locations, however, intensive and highly productive research has been conducted among social groups hardly, if at all, investigated by earlier collectors, and concentrated field-work has succeeded in revealing part at least of the treasure that had previously lain unworked among the camps and on the stamping grounds of the Scots tinkers (or 'travellers').

It should be stressed, of course, that many of the ballads which we have been brought up to regard as distinctively Scottish have relatives in many other countries. Gavin Greig put it well when he remarked of the Aberdeenshire balladry that 'it connects at every point with the world beyond "the bonnie Buchan borders". Our folksong like our language has endless affinities, and together they become the twin handmaidens of ethnology.' Of the international ballads with world-wide ramifications the best known is *Lord Randal* (No. 12 in Child's great thesaurus), the ballad of the false 'true-love' who poisons her lover with 'eels boiled in broo'.

I've been awa courtin'; mither, mak my bed soon,
For I'm sick at the heart, and I fain wad lie doon.

Scott's much anthologized version is the most familiar to us, but the ballad has been reported in communities all over Europe; it first appears in Italy in 1629, and it may well have spread to the north from the Mediterranean world. (Other ballads have crossed and re-crossed the seas lying between Scotland and Scandinavia.) Versions of *Lord Randal* collected in many different languages exhibit the most striking correspondences of stanza to stanza, the sequence of questions and answers being often virtually identical, and this means that the ballad—which has obviously struck a deep shaft into human consciousness everywhere—has travelled, and crossed language-boundaries, not just as a narrative story-line (folktale fashion) but as a structured poetic artefact. This phenomenon is surely not the least among the many mysteries of human artistic creation.

The Scots ballads have relations, therefore, which in some cases can be traced quite literally to the ends of the earth, but there has been—and still is—a remarkable consensus of opinion among folklorists and literary critics that Scottish produce 'bears the gree'. I have space for only one quotation, which must stand for many In *The Kenyon Review* of Winter 1954, in an article on 'The Language of Scottish Poetry', the American critic Stanley Hyman referred to

> a folk literature unsurpassed by any in the world, the Scottish popular ballads ... . If we seek language that is simple, sensuous, and passionate, a corpus of more than a dozen tragic Scottish ballad texts constitutes almost a classic tradition. I think of 'The Wife of Usher's Well', 'The Twa Sisters', 'Edward', 'Clerk Saunders', 'Sir Patrick Spens', 'Johnie Cock', 'Mary Hamilton', 'The Bonny Earl of Murray', 'Child Maurice', 'Young Waters', 'The Baron of Brackley', 'Lamkin', 'The Cruel Mother', 'The Twa Corbies', and 'The Daemon Lover'. Alongside these there is a body of Scottish folk song and rhyme in other forms that adds up to as rich a poetic heritage as any we know.

If we accept these golden opinions, we are still left with the question, 'Why *are* the Scots ballads so good?'—and this brings us curvetting back to Sir Walter Scott, that canny heritor of a highly idiosyncratic national-cultural patrimony. In the same article already quoted, Hyman speaks more harshly of Scott's smoky 'alembic' than Motherwell cared to do—'the worst fouler of the nest was certainly Scott', etc.—but in retrospect Scott's services seem vastly to outweigh his demerits; he is, in fact—with Mrs Brown of Falkland—one of the two most interesting practitioners of that singular folk-literary collaboration which has been such a constant feature of Scots song tradition. If we are to press for an answer to the question at the beginning of the paragraph, part of it must surely lie in this recurrent fruitful cross-fertilization, which has operated at every stage of ballad creation and recreation.

Another part of the answer to the question undoubtedly resides in the nature of 'ballad-Scots', the idiom in which these song-makers were operating—a flexible formulaic language which grazes ballad-English along the whole of its length, and yet is clearly identifiable as a distinct folk-literary lingo. Gavin Greig paid tribute to the 'simple, clear and dignified' language of the older classic ballads found in Aberdeenshire, and the curious 'bilingualism in one language' which greatly extends its range demonstrably makes it a much suppler instrument than the often rather wooden 'ballad-English'. Yet one of the major influences in the shaping of ballad-Scots, as we know it in the finest eighteenth and nineteenth-century texts, undoubtedly came to us from the south. It was the coming of the New Testament 'in Inglis tung', and then the mighty power and authority of the whole King James's Bible, which played a vital part in stabilizing ballad-Scots, and facilitating a resourceful creative 'togetherness': a sort of chemical fusion of two distinct but related ballad languages. In the folk field, as well as in the less sure-footed literary Lallans, Scots may be said to 'include English, and go beyond it'.

H. Henderson

Banking. One of the great achievements of Scottish culture has lain in her contribution to the evolution of banking. It began simultaneously with the Scottish Enlightenment, and indeed may fairly be regarded as a facet of that flowering. Through the generations between the 1740s and the 1850s the Scots pioneered over an astonishing range. Their innovations included banking on the limited liability principle, the early adoption of and generalizing of their note issues to the point at which gold and silver virtually disappeared from Scotland, the elaboration of an agency/branch system, the invention of the cash credit (later to become the overdraft), and the vigorous development of deposits attracted by the payment of interest. Scottish bankers conducted experiments in exchange stabilization (made between Edinburgh and London). They were among the first to adapt the joint-stock principle to banking. Very early they developed the practice among banks of being willing, in times of stress, to hold one another's notes, a principle now being applied by central banks in the international field. Scotland also began the Savings Bank movement.

These initiatives, accompanied by a strong sense of practicality and credit-worthiness, placed the banks of a tiny country in the forefront in Europe and the world. They were the product of Scotland's situation and culture: a literate population, though initially poor and remote from the commercial heartland of Europe, could, through its ethos and education, thus generate a remarkable system.

So confident were the native protagonists of Scottish banking that, as with Presbyterian principles of Church government in the seventeenth century, they wished to see the Scottish system of banking extended to England in the nineteenth. Domestically the competition and conflicts between the Scottish banks are of great interest. In particular the interplay of banking initiative between Edinburgh, the traditional capital of the east, and Glasgow, the commercial capital of the west, produced a paradigm apparent elsewhere, as in the United States.

After 1850 it was, of course, impossible for Scotland to maintain its ascendancy in banking innovation. Yet the Scottish system affords an excellent opportunity to trace the behaviour of a community of bankers, small enough to be encompassed, but important enough to be interesting, as they reacted first to the challenges of high Victorian prosperity and then to the period of wars and depression between 1914 and 1945. The English system moved in the Scottish direction as England took up the Scottish examples of the joint-stock principle, the branch system and the payment of interest on deposits. In the new age of banking giants the Scottish chartered banks could at first hold their own, for they were large even by English standards. But of course the greater size of the English economy meant that, in this respect, as mergers proceeded in England, the Scots could not maintain their relative position. Yet the behaviour of the Scottish banks in this period has its own interest. The system by the later nineteenth century was highly developed, with elaborate rules of procedure and a strict, hierarchical structure. There was a considerable air of complacency and perhaps a growing rigidity. There was also, uncharacteristically, irresponsible behaviour: it was in this phase of security and respectability that there occurred the extraordinary incident of the failure of the City of Glasgow Bank, one of the most astonishing examples of bad banking management on record.

The most recent phase is concerned with the recovery from war after 1945, and the very rapid changes that have taken place since 1958. The story is less complicated than in earlier times in terms of the number of firms, for the amalgamation movement was to reduce the Scottish clearing banks to three. But in terms of function a new complexity has developed. The old classic activities of the banks as short-term lenders have been diversified as new quasi-banking rivals multiplied, and as the control of the economy by the Bank of England and the Treasury became more complete and more demanding. From 1945 the Scottish banks were called upon, after a long period of sound but unexacting business, to renew themselves, reviving the flexibility and inventiveness for which they were so rightly admired in their great years of initiative before 1850. It was a Scottish bank that led the way to the acquisition of hire-purchase companies and so to other subsidiaries; the Scots also invented the notion so far at least as Britain was concerned, of a non-banking holding company as the means of integrating a banking group. The world's first Institute of Bankers had been formed in Scotland as early as 1875, reflecting a concern with professional education. Trained young bankers have been exported all over the world, many of them rising to top positions and extending Scottish usages and outlook.

S.G. Checkland

'Bardic Verse / Poetry' is a term used by Gaelic scholars for most of this century as a technical description, and like 'skaldic poetry' refers to an esoteric kind of verse. The bardic poet was a trained professional, and there were many grades of poet, the bard being in early times a lowly grade, and mainly a metrical technician, while the *fili* was in addition a scholar and also at times a seer. In the Dark Ages and in early medieval times the functions of the bard were eulogy, incitement to battle, and satire. But by the twelfth century the *fili* had begun to intrude on the bard's territory, taking over some of his subject matter, especially praise-poetry, and using the bardic metres. There is good evidence that at this time also the *fili* began to acquire land and property, commercial power and social position.

An elaborate order of poets, with professional requirements in terms of knowledge and technique, implies training arrangements. It is thought that the bardic schools, as distinct from the law and monastic schools, came into being in the twelfth century. At this time the Irish Annals begin to record the deaths of members of prominent bardic families e.g. in 1139 that of an Ó Dálaigh called Cú Chonnacht na Scoile (i.e. C. of the School); this was probably an early bardic school. Two of Cú Chonnacht's great-grandsons were famous poets in the thirteenth century, and one of these, Muireadhach Albanach (Scottish Muireadhach) was the founder of the premier bardic family in Scotland.

The bardic office was normally hereditary, as were other offices of a professional and/or artistic kind. Great networks of these hereditary families came to be set up, often straddling differing sectors, taking in especially the Church. The more prominent bardic families ran their own bardic schools, and some of the handbooks they used have survived: the syntactical and the metrical tracts which prescribed the linguistic and technical usages that were permissible. But we have good evidence of amateurs making similar poetry, as in the love-poems of a Countess of Argyll and the satires of a Campbell of Glenorchy. Our most important manuscript anthology of bardic verse is the sixteenth-century Book of the Dean of Lismore.

The best-known hereditary bardic families in Scotland are those of the MacEwens in Lorn, the Ó Muirgheasáins in Mull and Skye and the MacMhuirichs or descendants of Muireadhach Albanach. This latter family, which we may take as a brief case-study, produced poets from the thirteenth century to the eighteenth, and in 1800 Lachlan MacMhuirich claimed to be eighteenth in descent from Muireadhach. We know of members of the family as holders of land, poets and ecclesiastics, at many points throughout these six centuries. A good number of Muireadhach's poems survive, including one addressed to Alun, the Earl of Lennox who died c. 1217, and one addressed to Amhlaoibh, probably Alun's son. In this second poem,

Muireadhach complains about the kind of land Amhlaoibh had given him, on Loch Lomondside, and threatens to go back to Ireland. He reminds Amhlaoibh of his famous and generous ancestors.

By 1411, however, we find a MacMhuirich poet described as poet to MacDonald of the Isles, and composing a battle incitement before Harlaw. His name was Lachlann Mor, and it is probably his grandson who appears in a charter of 1485 as 'Lacclannus Mac Muirghich Archipoeta'. A group of poems refer to the murder of John of the Isles's son in 1490, and the subsequent forfeiture of the Lordship. One of these is by a John MacMhuirich who was Dean of Knoydart, and he is possibly the author of two other poems, also in the Dean of Lismore's manuscript, one being a poem of courtly love. This John MacMhuirich was dead by 1510, but a namesake appears in rental rolls in Kintyre from 1505 to 1541, being called Johannes McMurech Albany, which suggests that he was the chief poet of his line, and incidentally affirms his descent from Muireadhach Albanach.

This John MacMhuirich was probably the last poet to hold office and land in Kintyre. We next find the bardic family in the service of MacDonald of Clanranald, holding bardic lands in South Uist in particular. The earliest representative there is Niall Mor MacMhuirich, author of a fine love-poem *Soraidh slán don oidhche a-réir* (Fairwell for ever to last night), and a satire on the bagpipes. The two main seventeenth-century bards of this family are Cathal and Niall (the younger), who wrote elegies, eulogies and salutations, religious verse, political poems and satire, drawing on their wide knowledge of historical and legendary lore, upholding the honour and primacy of the MacDonald confederacy, showing an awareness of national issues, conducting an internal dialogue about their poetic art, and reflecting on the changes in society, especially as they affect the relationship between poet and patron. Their poetry has a clear MacMhuirich stamp, in spite of the rules and regulations that govern it, and it is not difficult to distinguish it from the more severely genealogical work of the MacEwen bards for example.

A little of the flavour of this verse may be sensed in the following medley of quotations in translation, but none of its technical ornateness is conveyed:

apple-blossom from the Islay soil, salmon from a nook in Kintyre.

From the boundary of Ross to the Rhinns of Islay, it was his hereditary right to protect them, from the land of Lewis to the sea of Man they flock to him whose royal blood is lively, forceful ...

The gentle, noble Conchobhar, because of jealousy which caused instability, killed at drinking the sons of Uisneach: a story from which Ireland brought forth her sorrows.

Their garments were not concealed from the poets, nor their steeds nor their golden goblets.

[the sound of the pipes] like a scraggy cow coming into lush pasture ... like a fart from the black Devil's bottom.

The race of Colla did not make a practice of having no man of knowledge among them until now ... their nobles take the wrong turning and go astray
D.S. Thomson

Barrie, Sir James Matthew (1860–1937), the son of a weaver, was born in Kirriemuir, Forfarshire, and educated at Glasgow Academy, Dumfries Academy and Edinburgh University. From boyhood his ambition was to become a writer. He joined the staff of the *Nottingham Journal* in 1883, and moved to London two years later, having established a connection with several papers there. During his journalistic years a sketch appeared in the *British Weekly, When A Man's Single*, and two other series of sketches were published, *Auld Licht Idylls* (1888), and *A Window in Thrums* (1889), Thrums being Barrie the writer's name for his birthplace. His first novel, *The Little Minister*, was published in 1891.

In 1894 he married Mary Ansell, an actress, and they settled in Kensington. Three more novels followed: *Margaret Ogilvy and Her Son* (1896), a curious dissection of his mother as a son-driver towards the great goal of success and the wearing out of a dutiful daughter too devout to stand up for herself; *Sentimental Tommy* (1896) and *Tommy and Grizel* (1900).

Though it had been preceded by *Walker, London* (1892) and *The Professor's Love Story* (1895) a dramatized version of *The Little Minister* (1898) was his first real stage success, eventually netting him £80,000. He therefore abandoned novel-writing to concentrate on writing for the stage. The sentimental comedy *Quality Street* (1901) was followed by *The Admirable Crichton* (1902) and by what many still regard his greatest work, *Peter Pan* (1904), the story of the boy who did not want to grow up. While it undoubtedly reflects the psychological difficulties from which its author suffered, and its unintended sexual overtones, particularly in the stage directions, make us smile today, on the level of children's entertainment, dealing with a phase through which all healthy children pass, it has survived the test of time. Its place in the mythology of the British child is attested by the statue which Barrie caused to be set up in Kensington Gardens, where this creature of his fancy had his home.

In the ensuing years, famous actors and actresses vied with each other for new Barrie parts. Many other West End successes were to follow, including *What Every Woman Knows* (1808), *The Old Lady Shows Her Medals* (1917), *Dear Brutus* (1917), *Mary Rose* (1920) and *The Boy David* (1936), the latter, based on a biblical subject, a less successful vehicle for Barrie's neatly tailored sentiment and hampered by a transvestite title part.

In 1909 the childless Barrie and his wife were divorced. He moved to the Adelphi, where one of his neighbours was Shaw. In 1913 he was made a baronet and in 1922 he received the Order of Merit. Edinburgh and St Andrews made him LL D

and as Lord Rector of St Andrews he delivered a once famous lecture on *Courage*. Oxford and Cambridge made him D Litt.

As a novelist, Barrie has all the faults of sentimentality associated with the Kailyard School, to which he originally belonged. Only occasionally does he manage to rise above the falsification of whimsy, the make-believe phantasy of evasion, turning his characters into caricatures. It must, however, be said in fairness that in relation to such other Kailyard writers as Maclaren or Crockett, Barrie's fiction shows a far more confident sense of style, whatever one may think of the content.

Style also characterizes the construction and the writing in his plays. He exercised a command over language in the theatre much greater than that which he possessed in handling it in the more inert form of fictional prose. His characters come alive and sustain credibility within his own terms of reference. He was also an expert constructor of plots in an age when theatre audiences were unwilling to accept the dramatic equivalent of the ragged edges of life, as they do so much more readily today.

Apart from the special circumstances that keep *Peter Pan* alive, only one other Barrie play still stands up fully to scrutiny on the late twentieth-century stage, *The Admirable Crichton*. It amusingly portrays the super-butler who, when family and domestic staff are wrecked on an island, becomes a virtual dictator because of his inherent ability, only to revert to his original status once a rescue has been carried out. Barrie's sense of the limiting dimensions of late Victorian and Edwardian class structure shows most strongly in this play, although by implication he seems to come down on the side of the domestics. From the moment its exposition is complete, the plot is entirely predictable; yet a certain charm of phrase and a continuous supply of well-turned wit keep it alive through periodic revival. In a sense, too, it suggests, very faintly, the influence of Shaw, and also looks forward to the work of Bridie.
M. Lindsay

Bell, Alexander Graham (1819–1905) is credited with having made the first telephone transmission in 1875. Son of educationalist Alexander Melville Bell, he was educated in Edinburgh and London but emigrated to Canada at the age of twenty-three. Like his father, he worked initially in speech education and this led to experiments with sound. His telephone was patented in America in 1876.
P. Ingalls

Bells. Scotland's quadrangular hand bells are among the oldest in Europe. They are made of sheet iron, folded, lapped and rivetted, or of cast bronze. The former date from the 8th century and are closely associated with the Iona missions to the Picts. The latter are c. 9th century and three of them can each sound three distinct notes of different pitch depending upon which face is struck by the iron clapper. Their functions included healing, exorcism, banishing, gathering the faithful and giving warning. Keepers of the bells were known as dewars (hence the surname), and the function still survives in unbroken succession.

    J. Purser

Bilingual Policy. In 1975, following regional reorganization and the setting up of an all-purpose local authority for the Outer Isles, that body, symbolically named Comhairle nan Eilean, announced its intention to pursue a bilingual policy within its area. This decision was facilitated by the prior decision to set up a Bilingual Research and Development Project in the Outer Isles, and this came into being in 1975 also, with funding from the Scottish Education Department and the local authority, and with close links with Jordanhill College of Education. The Bilingualism Project has now been at work for three years (1978), working closely with 20 Primary Schools, preparing material and getting some of this published in book form, some in the form of video-tape, slides etc. It is a cardinal principle of this educational project that a balanced fluency should be achieved in both languages by the end of the Primary school course, and to this end the use of Gaelic as a medium for teaching various subjects is encouraged. The main weakness of the scheme to date seems to be that there is not adequate provision (if there is any) for making Gaelic-speaking children literate in Gaelic first. Perhaps there will be some improvement in this respect as the scheme progresses. It has been recently announced (Summer, 1978) that a modest start is to be made with a similar scheme in Skye (in the Highland Region), and in the second triennium of the Project it is hoped to extend the scheme to other schools in the Outer Isles.

The Outer Isles Council or Comhairle began by stating that it would extend the use of Gaelic in the area under its jurisdiction. It has increased the use of Gaelic in office business, both oral and written, introduced more public signs in Gaelic, uses bilingual cheque-forms, has advertised local elections in Gaelic (which was unfortunately none too readable) and has made provision for simultaneous translation in its planned Council chambers. But a Consultative document issued in December 1977 seemed to withdraw from the brink of various bold decisions, and the use of Gaelic in minutes, reports, advertising and public signs is now subject to a moratorium, its use in public meetings is still restricted, and it is confessed that many appointments of staff without Gaelic fluency will continue to be made. The difficulties are genuine, and improvement must be awaited with patience. The climate for Gaelic in public business has been greatly improved by the Comhairle's initiative.

In the event of a Scottish Assembly, and later a Scottish Parliament, coming into being, the SNP has a comprehensive policy for extending the use of Gaelic in public life, including the use of the language in a range of ceremonial and practical contexts, in Assembly/Parliament, the Civil Service, Government agencies, road signs, education and so on. The implementing of these proposals, together with the technical and research back-up envisaged, would help the Outer Isles policy powerfully, and extend a reasonable degree of Gaelic usage much more widely.

(The above late 1970s account mingles optimism and caution. From a 1993 standpoint, the bilingual policy of the Western Isles Council can be seen to have lacked full commitment, especially at the educational level, and the 1991 Census shows a sharp decline in Gaelic usage by children. The accessibility and attraction of English-language television is a relevant factor here. But the provision of Gaelic books and teaching aids has continued. From the middle and late 1980s Gaelic-medium schools have been seen as the better alternative, and their number is growing in the Highland region and in the Western Isles. A more widely-spread Gaelic nursery school movement is intended to feed into the system. Significant Government funding of Gaelic TV may also help. Interest in learning Gaelic has grown significantly over the last two decades, but we still await the stimulus of a Scottish Parliament.)

    D.S. Thomson

Blake, George (1893–1961) a Greenock man, went to Glasgow University where he read law, but got caught up by the 1914–18 war. He was wounded at Gallipoli and invalided out of the army. After a spell of journalism on Neil Munro's *Glasgow Evening News* he went to London in 1923 to edit the popular literary weekly, *John O'London's*. In 1925 he became editor of the *Strand Magazine*. He was instrumental in founding The Porpoise Press, the publishers of Neil Gunn's first novel. It was later incorporated in the publishing house of Faber, of which Blake became a director in 1930. Two years later he returned to Scotland and settled in Helensburgh until the 1939–45 war took him to London and the Ministry of Information. His last years were spent in Glasgow, in a flat in Queen Margaret Drive.

Of all the Scottish Renaissance writers, Blake is the only novelist of the older generation who faced up to the values and dilemmas of industrial society. He also showed an acute awareness of the social niceties founded on class distinctions separating the men and women of his time. This reflects in the worker/boss relationships in his best known novel *The Shipbuilders* (1935), a brilliant fictional realization of the disasters that all but overcame Clydeside before and after the Slump.

His sequence of novels depicting the lives of successive generations centred in Garvel (his fictional name for his native town) is a splendid achievement worthy of reissue (and, incidently, a gift to the creators of television family epics): *The Constant Star* (1945), *The Westering Sun* (1946) and *The Valiant Heart* (1946).

Occasionally Blake's styles incline to be slip-shod; but he knew central Scotland and its people, and the complex industrial forces that shaped it. These he writes of always with an eloquent impact.

In addition to his fiction, he chronicled the development of the Clyde in *Down to the Sea* (1937), and the fascination of the growth of the Clyde Estuary as a pleasure ground in *The Firth of Clyde* (1952).

M. Lindsay

Bloodfeud, The, is normally regarded as a feature of early medieval society. In fact, its survival can be detected in many parts of northern Europe in the late medieval and early modern period. Scotland is a notable example of this survival, and Scottish evidence provides a wealth of detailed insight into the working of the feud.

That evidence shows that while it is correct to see Scotland as a feuding society, it is wrong to see it as a lawless one. It forces a rethink about contemporary attitudes to justice, for feud, as social anthropologists have demonstrated, includes within it justice as well as bloodshed. Its success depended on two things: first, that most people wanted peace and security, not disruption and violence, as James VI himself pointed out in *Basilikon Doron*; and second, that its justice depended not on retributive or deterrent punishment, but on the principle of compensation to those wronged. In the early Middle Ages, compensation was assessed on a rigid and limited tariff, based on the seriousness of the injury and the status of the injured. By the sixteenth century, this had developed into a much more flexible and realistic assessment of the effect of crime on individuals; unmarried daughters got more compensation than sons, and younger sons more than the heir, for example. There was now an impressive degree of social concern and sophisticated thought about the problem of criminal liability. The great advantage of compensation over deterrent, in a highly localized society, was that it offered much better hopes of restoring peace after feud, for the wronged party was satisfied in real terms, far more meaningful than the purely psychological satisfaction of seeing a criminal locked up or dangling from the end of a rope.

The kin remained, as it had always been, fundamental to the justice of the feud; they retained their legal responsibility for bringing criminals to justice. In practice, however, either kin or lord could act in the case of feud to impose settlement, this being a recognized obligation of lordship. Many such settlements succeeded very well, for local lords had an immediate power far greater than the dictates of a court remote in Edinburgh. That success explains why this justice survived. Another crucial reason for its survival was that the crown underwrote this justice, for it was very much in the crown's interests to strengthen and supplement local means of control. Naturally there was a demand for royal justice; then as now, higher courts of appeal had their necessary place. But royal justice was on the whole forced out of a monarchy whose own policy was to keep justice as far as possible in the localities. James I, famed for his interest in justice, concentrated on effective local justice; almost two centuries later, James VI was doing the same thing.

The decline of the bloodfeud came about not because of royal policy, but because the lawyers, as well as the crown, took up the justice of the feud, and in the end transformed it into legal procedure in the courts. The emergence of a professional lay lawyer class, firmly established in Edinburgh by the end of the sixteenth century, forecast the victory of professionalism over amateurism. Moreover, Calvinist emphasis on punishment of crime as sin against God rather than offence against a human, clashed fundamentally with the justice of the feud. In the seventeenth century, the bloodfeud and its justice finally died out. As it did, lawyer-historians, with conscious pride in their modern system of law, began to emphasize the violence and not the justice of the feud. Yet the long history of the bloodfeud is an impressive reminder of a kind of justice which had provided one effective answer to the perennial problem of crime.

J. Wormald

Borders, The. The Scottish Border country is rich in history, natural and human resources, and literary associations. Its inhabitants have a sense of shared cultural identity which sets them apart from the rest of the Scottish Lowlands and overrides more local diversities; this cohesion is perhaps more noticeable in the central parts of the Borders than the eastern and western extremities. In comparison with those travellers who cross the border from the south at Berwick upon Tweed or over the flat fields north of Carlisle, those who enter Scotland at the Carter Bar in the heart of the Cheviot Hills pass into a strikingly different landscape. The ecological transition is matched by other reflections of culture whose roots lie deep in the history of the Borders and its people.

As a term 'the Borders' is generally used in Scotland to refer to the former counties of Dumfries, Roxburgh, Berwick, Selkirk, and Peebles. The first three march with the English counties of Cumberland and Northumberland, whose northern parts are also known as the Border(s), usually in the singular form. Selkirk and Peebles are included by reason of their common geographical likeness and historical experience. The Local Government Act of 1974 established a new administrative Border Region comprising the districts of Roxburgh, Berwickshire, Ettrick and Lauderdale, and Tweeddale, excluding Dumfries which fell into the Dumfries and Galloway Region. However, the traditional usage persists in all but official contexts: though the habit may tend to weaken in Dumfriesshire, especially away from the border itself, the people who live in these five Scottish counties still call themselves Borderers.

The actual boundary between Scotland and England today runs northeast for some 70 miles as the crow flies, from the inner end of the Solway Firth to the mouth of the River Tweed; its true length is 108 miles. From Gretna, famous for its marriage-house for runaway couples bent on Scots marriage by declaration, the border follows the line of the River Sark, River Esk, and Liddel Water to Kershopefoot; then by the Kershope Burn and the hills enclosing Liddesdale on the south, to run for some 35 miles along the spine of the Cheviot Hills before turning north at the root of the Cheviot itself. It meets the south bank of the Tweed near Carham, about 4 miles above

Coldstream where another one-time toll-house and marriage-house, though less famous, stands at the Scottish end of the bridge spanning the river. The border then follows the Tweed to some 3 miles above the town of Berwick, where it crosses the river and runs north and east to the coast at Lamberton, whose toll-house is now gone, like the old Scots marriage law whose purposes it formerly also served.

The Scottish Borders, though containing vast stretches of rugged hills and desolate moorland as on the English side, also encompass sheltered valleys of high fertility and great beauty, watered by the river systems of Eskdale and Liddesdale to the west, and of Teviotdale and Tweeddale to the east. The principal tributaries of the Teviot include the Borthwick, Ale, Jed and Kale Waters; of the Tweed, the Manor, Gala, Yarrow, Ettrick, and Leader Waters, the Teviot (which joins the Tweed at Kelso), and the Rivers Eden, Blackadder, and Whiteadder draining the southern Lammermuirs. Their names and those of the peeltowers, castles, and battlefields past which they run reverberate in history, legend, and Border ballad.

Till after the Union of the Crowns (1603) that history is one of violence and warfare counterbalanced only by the foundation of the medieval abbeys and their stabilizing influence. The conflict of native Celt and Roman is strikingly epitomized on the summit of Ruberslaw near Hawick, where the rectangular vallum of a Roman signal station has been crushingly imposed on the concentric circular ditches of a native hill fort, giving the hill an oddly serrated crest clearly visible from the A68, which for long stretches follows the line of the Roman road from Hadrian's Wall in Northumberland to Newstead (Castra Trimontium) by the Eildon Hills (reputedly split in three by the astrologer Michael Scott, *c*. 1175–1234), and so to the Forth-Clyde Antonine Wall. In the centuries after the Romans withdrew, the region was invaded by Picts from the north of Scotland and Angles from oversea. The patterns of settlement and alliance which eventually developed into the kingdoms of Strathclyde and Northumbria were continuously disturbed by skirmishes and war, often on a local family and tribal level, and later flurried also by Viking marauders; but gradually they assumed a national character as the Scottish and English kings contended for the prize of the Merse, the broad rich acres of the lower Tweed Valley. By the Treaty of York (1237) what is substantially the line of the present border was formally recognized, though historians detect the underlying pattern a century earlier, while in the later Middle Ages further adjustments were made. These included the transfer of Berwick to England and the settlement of the Bateable Lands in 1552 by assigning the parishes of Kirkandrews to England and Canonbie to Scotland. In 1286 the death of Alexander III and the determination of Edward I to unite Scotland with England turned the Borders once more into a battlefield and harrying-ground. The major battles of Halidon Hill (1333), Otterburn (1388), Flodden (1513), Solway Moss (1542), Ancrum Moor (1545), and the Redeswire Raid (1575) were complemented by fighting between the great Border families, often over cattle reiving. In the fifteenth and sixteenth centuries the Borders, divided into three Marches, were administered by Wardens appointed by the Scottish and English kings; but the region was rarely at peace till the seventeenth century, which later saw the Covenanting times and the Battle of Philiphaugh (1645) near Selkirk where Leslie defeated Montrose. These centuries also brought about the destruction of the Border Abbeys, the twelfth-century creations of David I—Kelso (founded by Tironensians from France, 1126), Melrose (Cistercians from Rievaulx, 1136), Jedburgh (Augustinians from Beauvais, 1138), and Dryburgh (Premonstratensians from Alnwick, 1140), perhaps the loveliest of these ruins in its peaceful natural setting, and the burial place of Sir Walter Scott. Repeatedly damaged by English armies in the sixteenth century especially, there was often little enough left for the Reformers to attack and destroy.

The Union of 1603 made it possible to dismantle the castles and their garrisons, and by the Union of 1707 the inhabitants of the Borders had at last become accustomed to more peaceful ways. New prosperity followed the eighteenth-century farming improvements, while the nineteenth century saw the rise of the tweed and hosiery industries and the expansion of manufacturing towns.

By the beginning of the twentieth century the Borders enjoyed a stable mixed economy, renowned for the quality of its hill-farm sheep, store cattle, the oats, barley, and root crops of the Merse, and Border woollens. In the second half of the century this last industry declined with the advent of man-made fibres and low-cost foreign competition; but new light industries, including electronics and plastics, have been introduced. Tourism has also expanded, with trout and salmon fishing (q.v.), pony-trekking, and the historical and literary associations of the Scott country as particular attractions, including the Common Ridings (q.v.) which commemorate the old battles and affrays.

Sir Walter Scott (1771–1832) was himself largely responsible for collecting and kindling an interest in the history and traditions of the Borders. Oral literature has rarely found as dramatic or poignant expression as in those ballads which celebrate the exploits of Border heroes, villains, and lovers; Kinmont Willie and Johnnie Armstrong; Jamie Telfer; the Elliots, Douglases, Humes and Percys; the bold Buccleuch, head of the powerful Scott family; Wat Scott of Harden and the line of Branxholm; Edom o' Gordon who saw ill dooms in the bonny face of a girl who met death on his spear; the lady gay whose brothers and lover fought and were slain in the dowie dens of Yarrow. From the Borders too come those remarkable ballads of magic and fairyland, *Thomas the Rhymer* and *Tam Lin*; even for these as for the historical ballads one can today trace the topography of the events they retell.

The other literary associations of the Borders are numerous. Apart from Scott and his circle, most notably James Hogg the Ettrick Shepherd (1770–1835) and such visitors as Burns and the Wordsworths, the list includes the Subtle Doctor Duns Scotus (?1265–1308), born at Duns; James Thomson (1700–48), poet of *The Seasons*, born at Ednam; John Leyden (1775–1811), Orientalist, poet, folklorist, and physician, born at Denholm; Sir James Murray (1837–1915), editor of the Oxford English Dictionary, born at Denholm; Andrew Lang (1844–1912), man of letters and folklore theorist, born at Selkirk; and John Buchan (1875–1940), historian, novelist, and statesman, whose family ties with Peeblesshire influenced the choice of themes and settings for much of his fiction.

S.F. Sanderson

Boswell, James (1740–95), 'the Shakespeare of Biographers' (Macaulay)—but also autobiographer, essayist, polemicist and writer on general subjects. The discovery in this century of his long-lost private papers has both completely altered his place in literary history and made it possible to explore the context of his *Life of Johnson* (1791) more thoroughly than that of any other literary text. The Boswell archives, now at Yale after many vicissitudes, form perhaps the most valuable collection of eighteenth-century personal documents ever discovered. They record the private emotions and intimate thoughts of an upper-class Scot during more than 30 years—the obsessional conflict with his father which prefigured in life the intensified Oedipus-complexes of later Scottish fiction (*Weir of Hermiston*, by R.L. Stevenson (q.v.); *The House with the Green Shutters*, by G.D. Brown (q.v.)); his penchant for the company of the abnormal and the grotesque, evidenced in his many interviews with condemned criminals on the eve of their execution; his varied sexual experience ranging from the grossest whoremongering to a largely happy marriage; his reaction against the narrow, utility-minded, bigoted past; his love and hate for his native land; the pull of Europe and a wider cosmopolitanism; an almost Gascon ancestor-worship; extrovert euphoria alternating with a paralysing melancholia. True, Boswell was an eccentric, in temperament the reverse of 'Normal'; yet at the same time he was a representative figure, in that he experienced day by day and year by year the most typical conflicts of what, with all its limitations, was Scotland's greatest century. If there really is a 'Caledonian antisyzygy', then Boswell was its living exemplar.

Born in Edinburgh, the son of Alexander Boswell of Auchinleck in Ayrshire, who as a judge of the Court of Session was entitled to be called Lord Auchinleck, Boswell was educated at a private school, by tutors, and at the Universities of Edinburgh, Glasgow and Utrecht, where he studied law, 'passing advocate' in 1766. His studies were interrupted by picaresque forays, first towards London (2 visits, 1760 and 1762–63—the latter amusingly written up in the best-selling *London Journal* (ed. F.A. Pottle, 1950)), then towards Europe (1764–66), including Corsica (1765), where he sought out General Paoli, the elected 'general of the people', in the same way as he had earlier impressed himself on both Voltaire and Rousseau. On his return to Britain, his advocacy of the islanders' cause, culminating in the *Account of Corsica* (1768) and *Essays in Favour of the Brave Corsicans* (1769) made him a worthy member of that distinguished band of British writers (e.g. Byron, George Orwell) who have actively championed European freedom-fighters. From 1776 onwards his Tory principles did not prevent him from supporting the American

Revolution. Though he made frequent visits from 1768 to 1784 to his beloved London, to see Johnson, for most of his adult life his base was in Scotland. Called to the English bar in 1786 he was Recorder of Carlisle from 1788 to 1790, residing mainly in London from 1789. To his great chagrin, he failed in his ambition to represent Ayrshire in the Commons.

From the Scottish point of view the most engrossing of the published journals are *Boswell in Search of a Wife*, 1766–69 (ed. F. Brady and F.A. Pottle, 1957), which tells of his gradual discovering and testing of the penniless cousin whom he married, and *Boswell for the Defence*, 1769–1774 (ed. W.K. Wimsatt and F.A. Pottle, 1960), revealing the life of a busy young Edinburgh advocate from the inside, whose championship of the underdog did little to further his career. *Boswell: the Ominous Years*, 1774–1776 (ed. C. Ryskamp and F.A. Pottle, 1963) and *Boswell in Extremes* (ed. C.M. Weiss and F.A. Pottle, 1970) mark the beginning of his recognition that he will never be a worldly success, document how his moods swing more absolutely than ever before between exuberance and despair, and contain some of the best London scenes in the record. With *Boswell Laird of Auchinleck*, 1778–1782 (ed. J.W. Reed and F.A. Pottle, 1977) the interest shifts again to Scotland, with the stress on the strains and consolations of marriage and the last bickerings with his father and stepmother. *The Applause of the Jury*, 1782–1785 (ed. I. S. Lustig and F. A. Pottle, 1981) and other journals still to appear in the Trade Edition reveal on the one hand his deepening unhappiness and decay; on the other, the details of the composition of the *Life of Johnson*.

The *Life of Johnson* is not simply written-up journal: that accounts for less than half of the whole. The work shows great power of interpretation, condensation, and structuring. Remarks, conversations, and whole scenes are subtly altered and reshaped in the interests of his ideal, and Boswell took this creativity into life itself, organizing confrontations between Johnson and formidable opponents with all the skill of a theatrical impresario. The result is a remarkable synthesis of art and science, inspiration and scholarship. *The Journal of a Tour to the Hebrides* (made with Dr Johnson in 1773) (1785) is as vivid as the Life, and second only to it in popularity. But Boswell's miscellaneous writings should not be forgotten—his youthful correspondence with the Hon. Andrew Erskine (1763), the allegorical Spanish tale *Dorando* on the complicated legal issues of the Douglas Cause (1767), and 70 essays entitled *The Hypochondriack* (1777–83) for *The London Magazine* (ed. Margery Bailey, 2 vols. 1928; selected, as *Boswell's Column*, 1951), which include authoritative presentations of depression and melancholia amid a plethora of general reflections. He also published pamphlets on current Scottish political and constitutional issues, and wrote copiously for magazines and newspapers from 1758 onwards. Some works planned but never executed testify to the ambivalence of this Anglophile— a 'Dictionary of Words Peculiar to Scotland' (1769), 'A Life of Thomas Ruddiman' (1773), 'A History of James IV of Scotland' (1773), 'A Novel on Sir Alexander MacDonald' (1773), 'A History of Edinburgh' (1774), 'A Life of Lord Kames' (1775), 'A Life of Sir Alexander Dick' (1777), 'A

History of the Civil War in Great Britain in 1745 and 1746' (1777), an edition of 'The Autobiography of Sir Robert Sibbald' (1778), 'A Collection of Feudal Tenures and Charters of Scotland' (1791). He loved Scottish music, and delighted to set his own words to both Scottish and English tunes.

T. Crawford

Bremner, Robert (*c*.1713–1789), music publisher, in business in Edinburgh, 1754–61; moved business to London, 1762; died Kensington, London, 12 May.

Bremner was Scotland's first music publisher in the modern commercial sense; previous music-publishing in Scotland had been undertaken with town-council patronage, or as a piece of composer's private enterprise. Bremner was original in studying sales markets, viewing publishing as a means of making money rather than gaining kudos.

He was notably successful. His first issues were reprints of McGibbon's *Scots Tunes*, a parish-church choir manual, tutors for thorough-bass, harpsichord, and cittern, two books of Scots songs and one of folk-fiddle variations, and the Earl of Kelly's *Six Overtures op. 1*. It was probably this last—the first Mannheim-style orchestral music to be printed in Britain—which emboldened him to transfer his business to London in 1762.

Bremner maintained links with Edinburgh after his departure south. He kept his Edinburgh shop on under a manager, was Kelly's exclusive publisher up to 1769, and during the 1770s issued much chamber music by the German-Scottish composer Schetky. By his death he was the richest music publisher in Britain.

D. Johnson

Brewing. In a country famed for its whisky it is perhaps not surprising that the traditions and history of Scotland's other drink—beer—have been so little regarded. Brewing is just as ancient as distilling, and in the Lowlands was—and remains—very important both in terms of output and the size of business units. Certainly, since the seventeenth century the brewing industry in Scotland has provided a useful barometer of general economic progress—or the lack of it. In social terms too beer has almost always been as important as spirits. Scots are still among the world's leading beer drinkers, especially of lager, which for peculiar historical reasons as much as popular taste accounts for about half the sales.

Before the eighteenth century brewing was a widespread domestic craft. The city of Aberdeen had no fewer than 144 brewers in 1693, while there were over 500 in Fife. The houses of the gentry had their own breweries: a splendid example, refurbished by the laird, can be seen at Traquair House, Peeblesshire, its product being a traditional, Scottish strong ale. Not all beers were so palatable, however, for one English observer noted that even the ale drunk by 'the better sort of Citizens' was so bad that it would 'distemper a Stranger's body'.

Despite problems of local and national taxation (notably the hated Malt Tax instituted under the Union of 1707, but later amended) larger mass-production breweries were established in increasing numbers after the middle of the eighteenth century. Among the more important firms were John and Robert Tennent of Wellpark Brewery, Glasgow (*c*. 1745), and William Younger of Holyrood in Edinburgh (1749). From the outset these family firms were brewers of consequence—and it is no accident that they ultimately came to dominate the Scottish trade during the early nineteenth century. Significantly, in the classic Industrial Revolution period Scottish brewing expanded rapidly along parallel paths: numerous breweries were built in country towns, while in the cities much larger units began to emerge. The size of a brewery more often than not reflected the size of its local market. Edinburgh became the focus of this rapidly expanding trade—partly a reflection of good water and grain supplies in its Lothian hinterland. Elsewhere Alloa, Falkirk and Glasgow were important brewing centres. Such was the rate of expansion that by 1800 there were over 200 breweries and output was 400,000 barrels paying £75,000 in excise. The principal products of the age were table beer and strong ale, though quantities of porter based on English and Irish recipes were also brewed.

In general Scottish brewing techniques before 1850 differed significantly from those elsewhere, particularly in malt mashing (using equipment known as a sparger) and in fermentation at lower temperatures than was the practice south of the Border. The usual brewhouse was a large, three-storey building, entered from a courtyard, around which were grouped maltings, copperage, cellar, stables and a counting house or office. Brewers often maintained close contact with the countryside, for the industry was still essentially seasonal, and availability of raw materials reflected harvest yields and grain prices. Many of the tasks in and around the brewery were actually akin to those on the farm. Additionally, the industry relied heavily on horse transport well into the railway age.

The expansion of the Scottish brewing industry in the latter half of the nineteenth century far outstripped its earlier growth. Brewing benefited from rapid advances in science and technology, especially a deeper understanding of the chemical processes involved in brewing. These advances—in Scotland as elsewhere—could best be exploited by increased production. The trend after 1850 was therefore toward larger breweries in traditional centres like Edinburgh, Alloa and Glasgow. Improved technology raised the capital threshold of entry to the industry, although for old-established firms, like Younger and Tennent, the increased volume of profits which typified much of the period to 1914 allowed for higher investment in new plant and techniques. Capital in the Scottish industry rose from £600,000 in 1850 to over £6 million in 1900. This growth was accompanied by dramatic structural change, for the number of breweries fell from 220 in 1860 to 125 in 1900. Despite falling numbers several new and important firms, like that of William McEwan in Edinburgh, sprang into being, especially during the 'Brewery Boom' of the 1880s and 1890s. Peak production for the period of 2.2 million barrels was reached in 1899.

Notable product changes also occurred in the later Victorian era, when there was a swing in public taste from heavy to light ales. Scottish brewers took the lead in this respect for experimentation in the brewery science of the day was essentially concerned with low-temperature fermentation and cooling—in which the Scots had considerable experience. Perhaps the most famous product was pale ale—marketed worldwide to expatriate Scots in India and other far-flung outposts of Empire. During the 1880s lager brewing was pioneered in Scotland by Tennent in Glasgow and Jeffrey in Edinburgh. Lager ultimately became very popular among Scottish beer drinkers.

Rationalization after 1914 greatly altered the character of the trade as the number of breweries continued its steady decline. By 1930 there were 45 at work, with an output of 1.3 million barrels. A sign of the times—and a pointer to the future—was the formal linking in 1931 of William Younger and William McEwan, the two leading firms, in a new combine known as Scottish Brewers.

Amalgamation was common after 1945, and by the 1960s most of the smaller firms had been absorbed by larger counterparts. Brewing ceased in many historic centres, such as Aberdeen, Ayr, Dalkeith, Dundee and Falkirk. While in Edinburgh, Glasgow and Alloa brewing continues in large, integrated plants owned by Scottish & Newcastle, Tennent-Caledonian, and Allied Brewers; smaller traditional breweries survive in Alloa, Dunbar and Slateford (Edinburgh). Moreover, several successful micro-breweries have been set up, the most northerly being in Orkney.

Despite a market dominated by powerful multi-nationals, the Scottish brewing industry maintains its own distinctive products and marketing arrangements. As a result of recommendations by the Clayson Committee in 1973, Scottish licensing was liberalised, bringing dramatic changes in drinking habits and greater improvements to pubs. Consumer demand played an important part in the resurgence of traditional cask-conditioned or real ales, with a growing number of outlets offering some fine Scottish ales as an alternative to kegs. By accident, rather than design, the story of brewing has moved full circle since the seventeenth century, when domestic brewers and publicans produced their own distinctive ales for local customers and passing travellers.

I. Donnachie

'Bridie, James' *see* **Mavor, O.H**.

British Language, The. The Brittones, the Celtic people of Britain south of the Forth and Clyde in the Roman period, spoke the 'P-Celtic' language called British (*see* Pictish Language), which developed in the sixth century into Welsh, Cornish, and in southern Scotland and northern England into Cumbric, an early northern dialect of Welsh. The chief centre of power after the Romans left was the kingdom of Strathclyde, the Clyde valley (Cumbric *Strat Clut*), but others were Gododdin and Rheged; their respective capitals were Dumbarton, Edinburgh (*Din kidyn*), and probably Carlisle. Cumbric was spoken throughout these regions, but died out in Gododdin after the occupation by the Angles, but perhaps not wholly in Strathclyde till the eleventh century, after its final absorption by the Gaelic Scots, though it may have lingered in parts of Cumberland as late as the early twelfth.

We have no texts written in British or even Cumbric. Our exiguous sources for the language are as follows. First, place-names, whether in early documents or still surviving. British examples in Roman sources are *Dēva*, 'The Goddess', the Kirkcudbrightshire Dee, and *Maporiton*, 'The Ford of the Son', not identifiable. Names at least as old as the Cumbric period are Pencaitland, Melrose, Lanark, Pennersax, Penpont, and Ochiltree, from Cumbric Penn *Cētlann*, Melros, Lannerch, Penn er Sachs, Penn Pont and Ucheldrev, respectively 'The Hill of the Copse', 'The Bare Moor', 'The Glade', 'The Englishman's Hill', 'Bridgend', and 'The High Village'.

Second, British and Cumbric personal names in the fifth to seventh-century Latin inscriptions of the region. For example, Brigomaglos at Chesters on Hadrian's Wall, in an inscription of perhaps the late fifth century, the name which appears later in Welsh as Briafael; or the princely brothers Nudos and Dumnogenos, Welsh Nudd and Dyfnien, in a fine inscription of the early or middle sixth century near Yarrow.

Third, Cumbric personal names in early Latin historical documents such as genealogies like that of the kings of Strathclyde down to 872, or in Lives of the Saints, or in early Welsh tradition. For example, Riderch or Rederech, king of Strathclyde about 600, 'The Very Conspicuous'; Talhaern *Tataguen*, a probably Cumbrian poet of the sixth century, 'Iron Brow, Father of Inspiration'; or St Kentigern, a Norman spelling for Cumbric Contigern, 'Houndlike Lord'.

Fourth, some very old heroic poems emanating from Rheged and Gododdin, the originals of which are believed by many scholars to date from the end of the sixth century, but which now survive only in later Welsh versions. One of these, the *Gododdin*, contains nearly 1,500 lines. The Cumbric originals are not likely to have differed very greatly in language from the surviving Welsh ones.

Last, three legal terms, the only recorded Cumbric common nouns, in a Latin text probably of the early eleventh century, 'The Laws between the Britons and the Scots' (i.e. the Gaelic Scots and Strathclyde Britons). These are *galnes*, Welsh *galanas*, 'blood-fine'; *mercheta*, a payment to the overlord on the marriage of a daughter (Welch *merch*); and *kelchyn*, an impost perhaps originally paid at the time of a royal visit (Welsh *cylch*).

K. Jackson

Broadcasting and Scottish Culture. The role of broadcasting in the Scottish cultural scene is bedevilled by a lack of any sense of direction, and by a number of paradoxes. As individuals, Scots have played as essential a role in the development of

British broadcasting as they did in the formation and adminis-tration of the British Empire. John Reith was undoubtedly the animator and architect of broadcasting through an institution inspired by a sense of public responsibility—a model imitated in many parts of the world. John Logie Baird's daemonic drive gave impetus to television, even if he led it into a technical dead-end. Despite this and much else, Scotland has contrib-uted relatively little to the evolution of whatsoever art forms there may be in broadcasting, either in the United Kingdom as a whole, or within Scotland itself. There has been a tendency to turn, not just inwards, but backwards—a tendency which has led to self-indulgent sentimentality, or to a chip-on-the-shoulder feeling that Scotland was not being treated fairly by the United Kingdom broadcasting institutions. There are many reasons why Scotland has not played a more positive role in evolving a distinctive form of broadcasting for itself or, within the wider field, the development of something which could be recognized clearly as a Scottish programme.

As elsewhere in Britain, broadcasting in Scotland started with local stations, Glasgow in March 1923, and Aberdeen six months later. Within days of its opening, Glasgow broadcast the first transmission of an opera in Britain by the simple expedient of placing a microphone in front of the stage of the Coliseum Theatre. For most of the period up to the start of the regional scheme in 1930, the four Scottish stations of the BBC (Edinburgh and Dundee were in operation by late 1924) en-couraged local speakers and artists and broadcast largely locally originated programmes. The whole atmosphere was that of a church soiree—an improving chat and a little 'respectable' entertainment. A glance at the *Radio Times* for the first two or three years is indicative. On a Monday afternoon from Aber-deen dance music from a local store, and in the evening a talk on 'Feminine Topics'. From Glasgow the same evening a Dr Pio del Fratre gives a talk *in Italian*, followed by excerpts from Rutland Boughton's 'The Immortal Hour' performed by the Station Orchestra and Singers, and later a talk on eighteenth-century Russian Literature. Whilst technically adventurous, these stations experimented little with ideas. The Scottish content—a minor part of their output—was almost exclu-sively in the presentation of popular and nostalgic traditional material, with Burns, Scott and Stevenson as the high peaks. Even contemporaries such as Bridie and Joe Corrie had estab-lished their reputations elsewhere and were 'acceptable'. This contrasts with the position in Belfast which did much to evolve truly radio drama leading to such seminal work as 'The Flowers Are Not For You To Pick'.

Two points are to be noted from these first seven years of Scottish broadcasting. The first is that there was little attempt to create an all-Scotland service. Although the four stations did interchange programmes, they normally took the London pro-gramme when not doing one of their own. The second point is that from an early stage they did contribute to the UK 'Network' material, not necessarily Scottish, that would have general appeal. For instance the famous talk by Father Ronald Knox, in which he had a mock news report about a revolution in Trafalgar Square, and which alarmed many listeners in much

the same way as did the later Orson Welles broadcast, was originated in the Edinburgh studios. In a way the early days of broadcasting in Scotland were characterized both by a respect-able timidity, and by a wide catholicity of output. Aberdeen might well broadcast the tea-dance from Watt and Grant's Restaurant, and an elocutionist reading 'A Lum Hat Wantin' a Crown', but it also saw no reason why it should not put on scenes from *Macbeth*, or a talk by a local academic on the influence of the Crusades on Dante.

The coming of the Regional scheme in the 1930s introduced a lasting dichotomy of purpose and outlook which has been the bugbear of Scottish broadcasting ever since. The aim of the Regional scheme was primarily to improve audience coverage by the use of a small number of high-power transmitters, instead of increasing the number of local stations, and to provide two programmes throughout the whole United King-dom. The 'National' Programme was to be the main instrument of information and education, and to carry the prestige programmes in music and drama. The 'Regional' programme could be fractionated with each region at times providing its own programmes; but when it was not originat-ing a programme of its own, the London network programme was the almost invariable alternative.

The argument which developed in the early 1930s was about what should be the role of the regions within this scheme. At that time broadcasting had developed few stan-dards of its own. The programmes, whether as talks, as music, as drama or as light entertainment were almost entirely judged by prevailing outside standards. The philosophy of the BBC was, therefore, to put 'the best' of what was available in each field on the air. Because there was a concentration of talent and facilities in London, this led to a concept of centralization. The whole of this process is detailed by Asa Briggs in the second volume of his *History of Broadcasting in the United Kingdom* (Part III, Chapter 3). The concomitant of this centralization of 'the best' was that the role of the regions was to concentrate on what was peculiar to themselves and their audiences. In the case of the English Regions this did lead to a specialization on programmes which were still of general interest, for instance in Manchester on features, and later in Bristol on natural history. In the case of the National Regions it led to a concen-tration on their nonexportable traditional cultures.

The highlights of Scottish programming were 'From A' the Airts' and similar reflections of traditional folk culture, to-gether with some emphasis on religious programming, and material for farming, fishing and Gaelic interests which could not be covered from network sources. All this may have been well and conscientiously done, but it reinforced the tendency of Scottish broadcasters to look inwards and backwards, ac-cepting conformity to the established rather than developing the full potential of the new medium. There were two excep-tions to this. One was that for largely technical reasons, Aberdeen remained largely autonomous and outside the re-gional scheme, and it was also fortunate in having as its chief members of staff two outstanding creative broadcasters—Moultrie Kelsall and Alan Melville. As a result its actual output was large, varied and original. The other exception was 'The March of the '45', perhaps the most outstanding programme of the period not originated in London. This was written and produced by D.G. Bridson in Manchester, but with a major section produced by Gordon Gildard in Scotland. Together Bridson and Gildard produced an epic which was conceived entirely in radio terms, and whose fame and impact lasted for some 20 years. But it must be noted that whilst Scotland contributed enormously to the success of this production—on an essentially Scottish theme—its concept and script came from Manchester.

By the start of the 1939 war, whilst the scale of Scottish broadcasting had increased, and whilst technical efficiency was as good as anywhere, the inward looking of most productions had given little encouragement to new thinking. Even though the BBC Scottish Orchestra under Ian Whyte was well established, it was not of symphonic proportions and concentrated largely on the small corpus of 'Scottish Music'.

During the war, the reduction of services meant that activities within Scotland were severely limited. War News reporting expanded under A.P. Lee and Robert Dunnett. Kathleen Garscadden indefatigably maintained output for Children's Hour. Moultrie Kelsall, back from television, Farquharson Small, and for a short time Eric Fawcett, loaned from the Variety department at Bangor, maintained a small number of programmes in their respective fields for the network, but there was no 'opting-out', and thus the number of purely Scottish programmes (Gaelic, piping and religious services) was kept to a very low level. Scotland's main contribution to the broadcasting scene during the war was the introduction of two short breakfast-time programmes, 'Up in the Morning Early' a series of healthy physical exercises, and 'Lift Up Your Hearts' a short devotional programme—perhaps a broadcast equivalent of *mens sana in corpore sano*.

The future balance between the regions and London was much debated in some of the back-rooms of the BBC during 1943 and 1944 (Asa Briggs, vol. IV, Part II, Chapter 3) with the old arguments about 'quality' and 'local concern' being reiterated. The outcome was a decision essentially to return to the pre-war situation as soon as possible. This led to what, in retrospect, was the golden age of Scottish radio between 1947 and 1955. Producers, such as Robert Kemp and A.P. Lee in the features field, originated many programmes firmly based in Scotland, but of a quality which made them almost invariably acceptable to the network. George Bruce and Robin Richardson were responsible for a wide range of programmes reflecting the arts and traditional writing, and James Crampsey was doing a similar job in drama. His production of an adaptation of Lewis Grassic Gibbon's *The Scots Quair* became a classic example of forceful radio production, but despite this flowering of production expertise, it was rarely expansive. The titles of major series are indicative, 'The Annals of Scotland' and 'Scottish Heritage'. Again Scotland was not only looking inwards, but looking backwards. Except in some of the work of the documentary producers there was no sense of challenge, but rather a cry to 'preserve' the Scottish heritage.

The rise of television after the mid 1950s, with its capturing of the public interest, its absorption of facilities and money, and its winning over of the ambitions of most younger producers, made the 1960s a period of retreat for radio. However, in music the BBC Scottish Symphony Orchestra, at full size and reinvigorated under Norman Del Mar and his successors, considerably extended its repertoire whilst continuing to include a percentage of music by Scottish composers; and there was also an increase in the broadcasting of chamber music and recitals together with encouragement for young composers and performers. In features, A.P. Lee and John Gray continued the documentary tradition and contributed fairly consistently to the networks. They also encouraged Scottish writers by the maintenance of a high level of short stories—an area properly used as 'Nursery slopes'. Nevertheless during this period in general the output was piecemeal and pedestrian.

The reorganization of 'Broadcasting in the Seventies'—a restructuring of the BBC's radio operations—meant that Scottish output for Scotland was, for technical reasons, concentrated on Radio 4—essentially the talk and middle-brow service. This encouraged an attitude both inside and outside the BBC that it was only programmes of this nature which truly reflected Scotland. There was a further complication in that the development of 'stranded' programmes on this network—(e.g. 'the World at One' 'Analysis') made it very difficult for the Scottish producer to contribute a single programme as had been the custom previously, and the Scottish contributions to the general network output declined. At the same time the programmes to which the majority of listeners tuned—Radios 1 and 2, had little Scottish identity, and it was not until the arrival of the commercial local radios that popular radio acquired this dimension.

Throughout the 1970s the BBC in Scotland made sporadic attempts to come to terms with some of these questions facing it in radio, and in 1978 it was decided to depart from the concept of concentrating on a Scottish equivalent of Radio 4, and taking advantage of certain wavelength changes start a full and separate Radio Scotland service catering for a wider audience. These changes were resented by many, and within two years the bulk of Radio Scotland's output was again of the Radio 4 nature. Though there were programmes aimed at the Radio 1 and 2 audiences the best of the output was in the familiar vein of nostalgia. Billy Kay's *Odyssey* series was outstanding among these.

The pattern of Scottish radio—and television—and its reflection of Scottish culture has been complicated by the increasing emphasis in the output on news and 'topicality'. This stresses the inward-looking view and those aspects of Scottish life which are of import only to Scotland, and are unlikely to commend themselves to network. The concentration of effort and resources on such programmes tended to be at the expense of trying to develop the creative use of the medium. Despite this, and largely due to the work of Stewart Conn and the late Gordon Emslie, in radio there was throughout the 1970s an encouragement of play-writing often venturing to the frontiers of the medium. A considerable amount of Stewart Conn's most interesting work has been on Radio 3, and has not had the attention it deserves within Scotland. Writers who have been encouraged and developed during the period include Robert Nye, Tom Leonard, Menzies McKillop—all of them willing to experiment. Earlier and an outstanding experimentalist but of rather uneven work was the late Betty Clark; still earlier one can cite John Keir Cross, Jessie Kesson and John Wilson. An encouraging development has been the production by Radios Clyde and Forth of effective radio-features in the classic style but closely linked to their own service areas. The best of these have gained wide recognition and UK awards.

BBC Television came to Scotland in 1952, to be followed within five years by STV and within ten by Grampian Television. To begin with, the BBC programmes were the London-originated network. As facilities became available local production grew—largely sport and religion—as outside broadcasts. Within the studio, other than an over-ambitious attempt to do a play *The Boy David*, the output tended to be restricted to current-affairs magazine, an occasional arts magazine, and conventional light entertainment exemplified by 'The Kilt is My Delight'. From the middle 1960s as better studio facilities became available BBC Scotland television drama developed along three lines. Firstly there was the 'hosting' of programmes, that is the provision of facilities for London-based productions. This led to the 'Classic' series, and gave the technical crews the challenge of working to network standards from which they profited greatly. There was however much less to encourage Scots-based actors and writers, and 'hosting' because the source of a 'chip-on-the-shoulder' attitude towards London—a feeling that it would have been better to give the money to Scotland and let them make their own mistakes in learning. Secondly there were the occasional obviously 'Scottish' productions, Bridie, etc. Thirdly and in some ways most important there was a development of the straightforward action thriller in the Buchan tradition, and this strand has continued through culminating in a number of successful programmes of this type in the late 1970s, e.g. *Running Blind*. The brunt of maintaining the production of drama in Scotland during the fairly lean years of the 1960s was borne by Pharic MacLaren almost single-handed. It was not until the middle of the 1970s that the department expanded under Roderick Graham, one of the few Scots who returned after successfully establishing himself in London. A number of writers resident in Scotland can be identified with the steadily increasing output. Initially the late Eddie Boyd, who more than most mastered the art of dialogue for radio and television combined with the ability to engender suspense; Jack Gerson and Tom Wright who both evidenced a consistency of craftsmanship in television writing otherwise much lacking in Scotland. The ubiquitous Cliff Hanley was able to indulge in a strain of self-mockery which otherwise was rare. Scottish writers living outside Scotland and more often contributing to network include Bill Craig and the late Jack Ronder.

The best of television drama clearly recognizable as 'Scottish' was the effective production by Pharic MacLaren of *Sunset Song* echoing the earlier dominance of this work in radio, and the subsequent adaptation of Lewis Grassic Gibbon's *Clay, Smeddum and Greenden. Smeddum*, for many, is the best single offering to have come out of any Scottish TV Studio. There was also James MacTaggart's production of George Mackay Brown's *The Orkney Trilogy*. James MacTaggart, more than any other producer, mastered the new technology without letting it become 'gimmicky'. Although his main work lies outside Scotland, MacTaggart more than any other individual can be described as having made a Scottish contribution to television as an art. His early death was a loss of the first magnitude. Alongside the successful thrillers such as *Running Blind* and *The Omega Factor* BBC Scotland has made a number of well received children's and family serials such as *Huntingtower* and *Eagle of the Ninth*. But here again there is a return to the past and the safety of non-controversial established work. Scotland itself has almost never attempted controversial plays dealing with current political themes. When they have been done it has been by London-based units albeit with the producer an exiled Scot.

Since the start of Grampian in 1962, the two commercial companies operating entirely in Scotland have commanded on average at least half the viewing audience. Because of the different structure of commercial television, in many ways Scottish Television and Grampian have been able to identify themselves much more with their audiences than has the BBC in Scotland. This has been particularly true in their catering for the general audience. Although often mentioned disparagingly, STV's early 'One o'Clock Gang' responded to, and captured one strand of popular west-central Scottish culture as no other programme has ever done. In a corresponding fashion Grampian's 'Bothy Ballads' programmes responded to a strong strain in the northeast. As in so much Scottish broadcasting, both shows were a re-serving of existing material and in due course ran out of steam. They did not provide foundations for new material or new talent.

Grampian, a small company, has been limited by facilities from attempting drama, though it has to its credit some very good features. STV has tried various forms of drama at different times, and should be given more credit than it usually gets for having evolved and sustained a regular series 'Garnock Way'. To achieve the higher peaks of television as an art depends on a structure of prosaic craftsmanship. This is provided by 'Garnock Way'. Too often in Scotland in the arts there is a feeling that we should attempt only the heights without first crossing the foothills. As with the BBC, STV has dramatized many of the classics—e.g. *Flight of the Heron* again revealing the obsession with the established archetype rather than pioneering. Even the successful *Jean Brodie* of 1977 is a near period piece and adaptation. But the range of STV's drama output in the final years of the 1970s has been broadening and acquiring a polish which achieved more network showings.

It is possible to mention Gaelic Broadcasting only briefly, since it has always been on a small scale, and in the main directed towards the preservation of the language and the existing culture. In the BBC Fred Macaulay has encouraged a considerable degree of experimentation in radio, and pioneered certain strands of light entertainment in television. Grampian deserve some praise for their provision of a Gaelic cartoon programme for children. The arguments about how much Gaelic broadcasting should be provided are complex and often emotive. It should be possible to increase the output in radio, although possibly by reducing the options for the other listeners; television is a more difficult matter. But inevitably the role of broadcasting as regards Gaelic culture is unlikely to be other than at best aiding preservation. Regardless of the degree of subsidization, a population of less than 100,000 Gaelic speakers scattered over a large geographic area cannot hope to provide the material for a sustained television output that would not be highly repetitious and bear little comparison with alternative material. The tragedy for Gaelic is that if there is to be television at all for the essentially Gaelic areas then it will be very largely non-Gaelic television.

Overall, in the 1970s the Scottish broadcasting institutions tended to put most of their effort and resources into the production of current affairs and topical programmes. This is the field in which it is most difficult to look outwards and contribute to the networks, and easiest to look inwards. Even though it may have been unintentional, the greatest effects of Scottish broadcasting on Scottish culture may well have been its effect on the political scene, by making the audience more aware of potential political needs and differences, and through the rise of investigative journalism less willing to accept the existing operations of society, and, by the emphasis of 'the Scottish viewpoint' canalizing resentment against London. Whether all this has been of benefit to Scotland or otherwise is a matter for political decision. Scottish broadcasting may well have performed a useful role in 'preserving' some aspects of the precedent culture; it has done little to develop a Scottish culture consonant with the medium. The audience, used to a prolific supply of technically high-standard programmes from the networks, has demanded too much from the native output. Comparisons are always drawn with the facilities and range of the UK networks, and there is a feeling that Scotland should be able to emulate these in all respects. It would have been better if those concerned with broadcasting in Scotland had made their comparisons with Eire or Austria, nations of a more comparable size and whose audiences frequently took their programmes from richer neighbours with a common language. It is unlikely that the Scottish audience would ever be satisfied with a broadcast service on the scale of that in Eire, and derived purely from their own resources. The BBC, and to a lesser extent the commercial companies, in catering for Scotland's needs have sought to compromise between a number of conflicting aims, and have fallen between a number of stools. Until the institutions, and their governing bodies such as the Broadcasting Council for Scotland, take a clearer stand on the principal issues, the lack of such leadership is likely to mean that broadcasting in Scotland is weak, unadventurous and limited.

Both Scottish Television and Grampian retained their franchises in the renewals of 1981 and 1993, their fundamental structure unchanged. The renewal of the BBC Charter in 1996 may result in changes in the BBC.

Scotland has not been immune to the moves towards a market-led more materialistic society in the latter years of the twentieth century, and this has been very much reflected in the broadcast media. Increasingly throughout the 1980s, financial considerations, a need to sell or co-produce major programmes, and a market-dominated response to a belief in public demand, have altered the perceptions of both programme makers and the public at large. Together with this has been a steady if slow increase in the use of satellite broadcasting, and to a lesser extent cable. At the same time the use of the domestic video cassette recorder (VCR) has grown hugely, both in the hire of pre-recorded programmes from the many libraries and also in the use of VCRs for time shift. A close inspection of the shelves of any video library would reveal next to no material of Scottish origination. Therefore, especially in television, the normal viewing of the average Scot has included less material of, and about, Scotland.

This is, however, the negative side of the picture. In contrast, there are positive aspects. As regards television there has been an increase in quantity, and an improvement in technical quality, of much of the news and current affairs programming both on the BBC and the commercial stations. This has certainly contributed to, even if not designedly so, the sense of identity and differentiation from England which grew throughout the decade.

To a lesser extent the same principle applies to programmes about the arts, though these are increasingly moved to late night off-peak transmissions. Coverage of the Edinburgh Festival, and to a smaller degree the Glasgow Mayfest, has increased and in many ways acquired a more Scottish nature. Of interest was the emergence in 1992 of 'Festival FM', a short-term radio operation set up to cover the Edinburgh Festival. A similar ad hoc radio coverage of Mayfest had already been in operation, rather differently, for two years.

Scottish Television scored a considerable success with their *Taggart* detective series, a derivative perhaps of the already mentioned Scots penchant for a well-told adventure story. The soap *Take the High Road* has become a firm part, not only of the fare for Scottish audiences, but of many other outlets. If not quite in the top class of soaps, it has acquired a gloss and competence it lacked earlier, and does present credible Scottish characters and situations.

BBC Scotland had a *succes d'éstime* with *Tutti Frutti* and has developed with more success the Rab C. Nesbitt comedy series, producing what might be described as the Scots successor to Alf Garnett. Whilst this blunt, often foul-mouthed, character has acquired a considerable cult following and is a good example of black alternative comedy, it is questionable whether such a stereotype of the urban Scot is a desirable image, any more than the Harry Lauder image.

BBC Radio in the 1980s mounted the monumental and admirable 26-part series on the history of Scottish music and its Edinburgh-based radio drama department acquired one of Europe's most advanced stereo studios as a result of the refurbishing of the Edinburgh headquarters, maintaining a very high level of output, including George Rosie's *The Blasphemer*.

Indeed it is in radio that the biggest changes, and potentially the most important cultural changes, began to occur during the 1980s.

The Radio Authority, having established its own identity following the break-up of the IBA showed considerable concern in developing small scale stations in Scotland, though regrettably ceased to have a permanent officer in Scotland. This included the inception of Heartland FM based in Pitlochry and initially serving a population of some 5,000 weekends only. All the programming is done by volunteers and the station has a programme balance which it can well claim corresponds to the culture of Highland Perthshire. There has also been a considerable use of Restricted Service Licences (RSLs) which permit a low-powered short term operation, and this has great potential especially for rural areas. Towards the end of the period under review, the Radio Authority began to re-advertise the local radio franchises, and it is likely that in many cases the AM and FM frequencies would be separated. In turn this could lead to an increase in truly locally based speech programmes. But there is also the danger that it might lead to purely automated music stations. The BBC, however, began to cut back on the scale of its local operations.

The two most significant developments in broadcasting affecting Scottish culture were undoubtedly the rise of Gaelic television boosted by more than £9 million of government money. Against most expectations this, amongst other activities, gave rise to the first Gaelic soap *Machair* which was not only a programme of high standards with a strong verisimilitude—eclipsing BBC's *Strathblair*—but to a great extent solved the bilingual problems and made, when required, subtitling acceptable.

The other potentially important development was the establishment of the well-funded Film and Television School based in Napier and Dundee Universities.

The future of Scottish broadcasting and the extent to which it has a positive part in the evolution of Scottish culture is still on a knife-edge in the early 1990s. The dynamism of many individual producers has to be set against low morale in the big organizations, uncertain of their future, and the increasing internationalization of the 'market'.

J. Gray

Brown, George Douglas (1869–1902), poor, illegitimate, hypersensitive to the sneers (real or imagined) of his native Ochiltree, grew up with an understandably bitter view of Scotland in the closing years of the nineteenth century. Lucky in his local schoolmasters, heroically supported through long years of university education by his mother, he passed triumphantly through a classics degree at Glasgow, and rather less successfully at Oxford, where his studies were interrupted by his mother's last illness. He disappeared into literary London: essays, odd-jobs for publishers, an immature boy's novel (*Love and a Sword*, by 'Kennedy King') supported him while he mentally composed and refined the novella which grew into his only major production, *The House with the Green Shutters*

(1901). Professedly anti-romantic, determined to show the 'Scot malignant' in a contrived counterblast to the sentimentalized but popular 'kailyard' fiction of the time, Brown's lonely masterpiece suffers from flaws of obvious overstatement: its tragic form, derived from the author's classical studies, sometimes shows uneasily through the surface: the characteristics are overdrawn frequently to the point of parody: for all this, its power is extraordinary, now as well as at the time it was produced.

The House with the Green Shutters concerns itself with Barbie, a backwater in the southwest suspiciously like his native town, yet representative of his view of rural Ayrshire. At first glance it could be any one of the sleepy hollows dreadfully familiar then (and not altogether forgotten today) from the kailyard romancers. Yet while Brown cleverly gives his scene surface familiarity, the predictable cast of local figures—ministers, dominie, provost, man of business, local boy going to university for a meteoric career, returned prodigal—are wicked inversions of their worthy prototypes and overturn sharply the all-too-predictable plots and situations of the kailyard. Each character is corrupt, worthless, outwardly fairly normal, corrupt at heart and often seething with envy and perverted spite. Born into this town, its chief characters the gossiping 'bodies' who form the chorus to the tragedy, John Gourlay has little chance of success. Brutalized by his domineering father, whose carting business has made him rich enough to build the new house with the green shutters which dominates Barbie, young Gourlay's progress through school and university is far from the kailyard success-story. He fails to make good—rather he drinks, idles, is expelled, faces his father in a drunken stupor and kills him.

The book is rescued from melodrama or mere parody by inversion, by the close observation of the changes sweeping across rural Ayrshire (and by extension, rural Scotland) during the time of the book's action. Change brings 'progress', most notably in the form of the railway, and carting (and John Gourlay) are ruined. Old institutions die, and the new ones evolve slowly and unsatisfactorily. Brown is content to expose the weaknesses of the existing institutions and the greed and self-interest of the improvers—his positive philosophy or 'message' is confined to exhortations, feebly made, to charity. The bad are judged, the weak destroyed. The good are merely suggested, or simply omitted. Above all, the women in this book are a horrendous group. Barbie, Brown was to admit, had 'too much black for the white in it', but it had the crude anger of a man writing about the injustices of his youth, and writing against a falsified view of his country which he considered even worse than Barbie. With experience, he might have written very much more subtle and balanced later novels. But this is mere speculation.

His achievement in puncturing the kailyard myth, in recreating life in rural Scotland with extraordinarily vivid writing, is considerable. The novel's overall impression is still compelling and vivid, and suggests that Brown's untimely death in 1902 robbed Scotland of a formidable observer and commentator for a century of change.

I. Campbell

Bruce, George (b. 1909). His relatives and ancestors were connected with the fishing industry in the northeast of Scotland, and he himself was born and schooled at Fraserburgh, from where he progressed to Aberdeen University. From 1933 to 1946 he taught English. He then joined the BBC as General Programmes Producer, Aberdeen, but increasingly came to be concerned with the output of programmes relating to the arts. Ten years later he moved to Edinburgh as Talks Producer. For more than 20 years he established a tradition of responsible seriousness in the broadcast treatment of important Scottish issues and experiences other than news, a tradition unfortunately dissipated on his departure. He retired from the BBC in 1970 and took up the work of a freelance broadcaster and critic.

His poetry draws much of its strength and imagery from the way of life of his native airt. His language is always spare and precise:

> That which I write now
> Was written years ago
> Before my birth
> In the features of my father ...
> Not I write
> But perhaps, William Bruce,
> Cooper ...

The poet's words become:

> ... the paint
> Smeared upon
> The inarticulate.

His awareness of the world and its concerns outside Scotland, and of the relationship of Scotland to them, is movingly celebrated in his poem 'A Gateway to the Sea', one of the finest anyone has written using the town of St Andrews as its *point de départ*. Though a poet with a markedly personal style, Bruce does not use a loud voice, and is content to be something of an isolated figure. Yet no other poet has reflected so fully the ethos of at least one fundamental aspect of Scottish life and the Scottish character: that of the qualities of the fishermen as individualists in an increasingly collectivist world.

His later work applies the same technique of sparseness to a wider range of human interests, as in his poem 'Laotian Peasant Shot', deriving from a horrifying image of the television screen. His *Collected Poems* appeared in 1970, but this did not mark the end of his productivity. His late collection *Perspectives* (1987) reflects his experiences as a lecturer in the United States and Australia, and also contains an amusing pseudo-lament for the much-heralded demise of the Scots tongue.

He edited an anthology, *The Scottish Literary Revival* in 1968, and was one of the co-editors of several of the editions of the occasional anthology *Scottish Poetry*; and more recently, editor (with Rennie) of the anthology *The Land Out There* (1991). He was made OBE in 1984, having received a D Litt. from the College of Wooster, United States of America in 1977.

M. Lindsay

Bryce, David (1803–76). Many Victorian architects were plagued by doubts that they might be failing to produce an original architecture which was truly representative of their age. Surely no such doubts ever crossed the mind of David Bryce. He was the archetypal confident and successful Victorian architect, no theoretician but a sound pragmatist. More than 200 buildings are known to have been designed by Bryce, many of them lavish even by Victorian standards.

Bryce was born in 1803, the son of an Edinburgh builder. After attending the Royal High School, he worked for his father but left in 1825 to become a pupil of William Burn, one of the emerging talents of the Edinburgh architectural scene. Bryce's talents developed rapidly and in 1841 he became Burn's partner. By 1844, when Burn moved to London, Bryce had virtual control of all the Scottish work. The partnership came under severe strain with the building of Dalkeith Chapel (1845) and was finally dissolved in 1850.

Although Bryce's fame rests on his fulsome version of the Scottish baronial style, many of his city buildings were classical in inspiration. The former British Linen bank, St Andrew's Square (1846–51) is a grand palazzo-style design with a giant Corinthian order marching across the facade. His most prominent classical design in Edinburgh is the Bank of Scotland on the Mound (1864–71), where he recased Robert Reid's modest building in a flamboyant essay in the Roman Baroque style. Less grand, but still imposing, is the former Union Bank, 62–6 George Street (1874) with its long palazzo façade.

From Burn, Bryce had learnt the techniques of planning the complicated layouts of Victorian country houses. He quickly became the unrivalled master in this field in Scotland, mingling the forms of seventeenth-century Scottish and sixteenth-century French architecture. Time has not dealt kindly with many of his grandest houses. Panmure House, Angus (1852) where he used a version of the Scottish Jacobean style was blown up in 1955. Kinnaird Castle (1854) where he employed the French chateaux style was gutted by fire in 1921, and restored on more modest lines. Blair Castle, which he remodelled between 1870–72, survives intact, with its full display of bartizan towers, crenellations, crow-stepped gables and dramatic corbelling.

To our eyes, accustomed as they are to the austere modern style, these houses may seem overblown and vulgar. To their Victorian owners they exactly captured that image of grandeur and extravagance which was so much a part of nineteenth-century country life.

Bryce's masterpiece is surely Fettes College (1864–70). A well arranged symmetrical plan is orchestrated into one of the most fanciful of versions of French Gothic architecture. Bryce was once described as a 'gruff, forthright, tenacious professional with no particular charm'. Few would guess this when they catch a distant glimpse of the fairy tale silhouette of Fettes.

M. Higgs

Buchan, John (1st Baron Tweedsmuir) (1875–1940), a Borderer by extraction, was born in Perth on 26 August, a son of the Manse. In 1876, the Buchan family moved to Pathhead, Fife, and in 1888 to Glasgow. Buchan attended Hutcheson's Grammar School in that city, completing his education at Glasgow University and Brasenose College, Oxford. From 1899 to 1901, he worked on the *Spectator*, and in 1901 was called to the Bar at the Middle Temple. From 1901 to 1903 he was in South Africa, on Lord Milner's staff. From 1903 to 1906, back in England, he worked again for the *Spectator* and at the Bar. In 1907, he married Susan Grosvenor, a partner in the publishing firm of Thomas Nelson and Son, with which, until he resigned in 1929, he thus became involved. He was adopted as Unionist candidate for Peebles and Selkirk in 1911.

During the First World War he visited the Western Front for the *Times* newspaper in 1915 and the following year became a Major in the Intelligence Corps, attached to GHQ, France. From 1917–18 he became Director of Information, and Director of Intelligence at the Ministry of Information. During this period Buchan was also the author of *Nelson's History of the War* (1915–1919).

From 1919 he worked for Reuters, first as a Director, then, in 1923 as Chairman, visiting Canada and the United States in 1924. From 1927 to 1935 he was Member of Parliament for the Scottish Universities; in 1933 and 1934, High Commissioner to the General Assembly of the Church of Scotland, and in 1935 he was created Baron Tweedsmuir of Elsfield, the year in which he also became Governor-General of Canada.

As a novelist, Buchan began his writing career in the Scott-Stevenson-Munro vein with a Border tale, *John Burnet of Barnes* (1898, reprinted 1978). Burnet is modelled on Stevenson's Alan Breck Stewart, and even the chapter headings are reminiscent of *Kidnapped*—'How I ride to the South', 'I Fall in with Strange Friends', and so on.

Later historical novels included *The Path of the King* (1921), which deals with the 'tragically fated' Lovells, and another probing history's shadows, *Midwinter* (1923), which traces imaginatively the 'missing' years in Boswell's knowledge of Johnson's life. *Witch Wood* (1927), Buchan's own favourite, is a study of religious intolerance in which Montrose makes an appearance.

Buchan's wide popular acclaim, however, was achieved with his adventure stories, or 'shockers' as he called them. The best-loved are the tales involving Richard Hannay and include *The Thirty-Nine Steps* (1915), where the Kinlochrannoch chase in *Kidnapped* is emulated; *Greenmantle* (1916), *Mr Standfast* (1919) and *The Island of Sheep* (1936).

Another common-sense hero, Dickson McCunn, presented himself in *Huntingtower* (1922) and tramped through adventures in terrains as widely separated as Glasgow's Gorbals and the imaginary Central European country of Evallonia before bowing out in *The House of the Four Winds* (1935).

In some respects Buchan's most interesting hero is Edward Leithan, whose first full-length appearance was in the Highland poaching tale *John MacNab* (1925). He perhaps reflected something of Buchan's own emotional reserve in *Sick Heart River* (1941), set in Canada, and Buchan's last novel.

Though fluent and easily readable, Buchan's novels are not without serious flaws. Few of his characters are wholly convincing, and many of them regularly indulge in adventuring for adventuring's sake, as if life were a kind of protracted dangerous sport. Often, too, they seem to be upholding values that are positively objectionable outside the conventions of romancing.

Yet for Buchan, the barrister, politician, statesman and Governor-General of Canada, writing was but one facet of a long, full and successful life chronicled in *Memory Hold-the-Door* (1940), an autobiography that tells plenty about the public man but little about the private.

With Buchan, the last connection between the historical novel and anything that might be considered literature was severed. What followed has been, in the Stevenson sense, 'the merest slap-dash commercial tusherie'. Buchan's two biographical studies *Montrose* (1928) and *Sir Walter Scott* (1932) are both warmly perceptive and sympathetic, and retain their interest well.

M. Lindsay

Buchanan, Dugald (1716-1768), native of Strathyre, Perthshire, employed in later life as schoolmaster and catechist at Kinloch Rannoch. In young manhood, Buchanan experienced a turbulent religious conversion which he chronicled in a Diary somewhat reminiscent of Bunyan's *Grace Abounding to the Chief of Sinners*. He became the outstanding Gaelic poet of the evangelical movement of the eighteenth century, though his extant compositions number only those eight which he personally saw through the press in 1767, while supervising the publication of the first Scottish Gaelic translation of the New Testament.

Geographically and educationally, Buchanan's experience straddled two cultures, and his spiritual songs owe at least as much to the writings of the English puritans as to any native exemplars. In particular, the influence of Isaac Watts's hymns and Young's *Night Thoughts* is obvious. At the same time, he responded to prevailing vogues and long-standing ideals in the native culture, writing, for example, as other Gaelic poets had done, a seasonal poem, but making it clear that, for him, winter is symbolic of the physical decay and death which all men must face. He also writes his own 'heroic' poem, but upholds the moral and spiritual champion against the ideal of the military hero so long lauded in Gaelic tradition, and so forcibly extolled by the contemporary Mac Mhaighstir Alasdair.

Buchanan's verse is part and parcel of his function as a religious teacher; it is overtly designed to persuade, and most of the pieces contain a direct appeal to the hearer. 'Fulangas Chriosd' is an easily memorizable synopsis of the Gospel story for people who as yet had no translation of the Scriptures in their own tongue. 'Là a' Bhreitheanais' is his longest and most ambitious composition, a dramatic portrayal of the cosmic upheaval and moral crisis of the Day of Judgment, drawn mainly from the apocalyptic sections of the Bible, but with recurring echoes of the *Night Thoughts*. 'An Claigeann' is a meditation on the *memento mori* theme, incorporating a gallery of vignettes in which Buchanan puts across some pointed social comment.

As a versifier, Buchanan was a fastidious craftsman: there is a tradition that he spent a sleepless night agonizing over the choice of one word in 'An Claigeann'. There is an orderly progression of thought in all his songs, and his verses are more rigorously pared and polished than those of most of his Gaelic contemporaries. Even for readers out of sympathy with their presuppositions and their strong evangelistic thrust, Buchanan's poems are rewarding for their varied and clear-sighted use of imagery, drawn mainly from the immediate environment of his Perthshire audience.

The most notable of Buchanan's successors as evangelical poets, some of them far exceeding his output in bulk, though seldom equalling his technical competence, were the Rev. James MacGregor (1759-1830), the Rev. John MacDonald of Ferintosh (1779-1849), the Rev. Peter Grant of Strathspey (1783-1867) and John Morison of Harris (1790-1852).

K. D. MacDonald

Buchanan, George (1506-1582), humanist and reformer. Born at Moss, near Killearn, Stirlingshire, Buchanan was sent by his uncle to the University of Paris in his fourteenth year and spent two years there studying Latin, returning to Scotland on his uncle's death in 1522. In 1523 he took part in the Regent Albany's abortive military expedition against England. Early in 1525 he went to St Andrews University where he took his BA degree. At St Andrews he studied with the historian and philosopher John Major or Mair (1470-1550) and he followed Major back to Paris in 1526. For two years of 'hard struggle and untoward fortune' he was at the Scots College in Paris, graduating MA in 1528. He stayed in Paris, lecturing at the College of Sainte Barbe and then acting as tutor to the young Earl of Cassilis, until 1535, when he (with Cassilis) returned to Scotland, where he became tutor to the child Lord James Stewart, natural son of James V, thus for the first time coming into contact with Court circles. The king encouraged him to attack the Franciscans in his savagely satirical Latin poem *Franciscanus*, which brought him into trouble with the ecclesiastical authorities. He was imprisoned as a heretic but escaped to England and thence proceeded to Paris, going on to Bordeaux where he became professor at the new College of Guyènne, a centre of humanistic Latin study. At Bordeaux he wrote his two Latin biblical dramas *Jephthes* and *Baptistes*, high points in humanist Latin literature. (The former has been admirably rendered into Scots by the modern poet Robert Garioch.) In 1547 he went to Portugal, where he spent five years at the University of Coimbra. Here he produced his Latin version of the Psalms as well as a certain amount of secular Latin poetry, some of it erotic, based on classical models. He was imprisoned for heresy by the Inquisition but was soon released and left for England in 1552. He returned to France in 1553 and stayed two years in Paris as professor at the Collège Boncourt. From 1555 to 1561 he was tutor to the 12-year-old

son of the Comte de Brissac. During this period he wrote *De Sphaera*, a Latin poem explaining and elaborating the Ptolemaic theory (in its latest form before it succumbed to the Copernican). Among other Latin poems he wrote at this period is his Epithalamium on the marriage of the Dauphin with Mary of Scotland in 1558 and his elegy on the death of King Francis II (as the Dauphin had become) in 1560. He returned to Scotland soon after, about the same time as Queen Mary did.

Buchanan tutored the young widowed Queen and they read together in the evenings. She rewarded him with a pension of £500 Scots from the lands of the Abbey of Crossraguel in Ayrshire. In spite of his ardent support of the cause of religious reform, his relations with the Catholic Queen at this time were cordial. He became Principal of St Leonard's College, University of St Andrews, in 1566 and held the post until 1570. He wrote a Latin poem on the birth of James VI in 1566 (in which he implied the view he was to express vigorously in his *De Jure Regni apud Scotos* that kings exist by the will and for the good of the people) and, the last poem expressing friendly relations with the Queen, one on the baptism of the infant that December. The murder of Darnley in 1567 (in which Buchanan saw Mary as implicated) and Mary's marriage to Bothwell in 1567 turned Buchanan into an implacable foe of the Queen. He was in England in 1568 with the Regent Moray and the King's Commissioners testifying against her. His Latin polemic against Mary, generally known simply as the *Detectio*, has all the bitterness of humanist controversy coupled with a feeling of personal moral outrage. Buchanan also wrote two pamphlets in Scots in support of the King's party *Admonitioun to the trew Lordis* and *Chamaeleon*, which show him using Scots with a studied Ciceronian eloquence.

Buchanan became tutor to the young James VI: he was now elderly and in ill health and his royal pupil was in his fourth to his twelfth year. He seems to have been a strict but effective teacher: James later said of somebody else that 'he ever trembled at his approach, it minded him so of his pedagogue.' But he turned the king into a good Latin scholar and a considerable craftsman with words in several languages. Buchanan also held the post of Keeper of the Privy Seal until 1578.

Buchanan's two most important prose works (in Latin) were his *De Jure Regni apud Scotos*, a learned argument for the accountability of monarchs to the people which aroused furious hostility among royalists, and his *Rerum Scoticarum Historia*, which is chiefly interesting now in the parts which deal with his own time. He told the truth as he saw it without fear or favour and was said to have said of the work on his deathbed, when a friend suggested that the king would be offended with it, 'Tell me, man, giff I have tauld the treuthe.' He died in Edinburgh and was buried in Greyfriar's Churchyard.

Buchanan is the greatest of the Scottish humanists, who was throroughly at home in the Latin language and culture revived by European humanism. His passionate espousal of the Reformation meant that his humanism lacked the tolerant, uncensorious irony with respect to the relation between the classical and the Christian tradition that many pre-Reformation humanists showed. The short-lived attempt to revive a

Scoto-Latin culture made by Thomas Ruddiman and Robert Freebairn in the early eighteenth century looked back in some ways to Buchanan (whose *Opera Omnia* Ruddiman edited and printed) but, being Jacobite-oriented, lack altogether Buchanans Presbyterian democratic feeling. *See also* Scottish Literature 1700–1800 and Humanism.

D. Daiches

Burnet, Gilbert (1643–1715) was the son of a Royalist, an Episcopalian lawyer who became a judge. His mother was a sister of Johnston of Warriston, a Covenanting leader. Burnet was born in Edinburgh, and educated at Aberdeen and Amsterdam. He became successively Episcopalian minister at Saltoun and Professor of Divinity in Glasgow, when he was offered, but declined, a Scottish bishopric. He took a vigorous part in the controversies of the times, endeavouring to bring about a reconciliation between Episcopacy and Presbyterianism. In London, he attracted the attention of Charles II, from whom he received various preferments; but he lost the king's favour on account of a critical letter addressed to the monarch. He was out of sympathy with the policies pursued by James II and VII and in 1687 went to Holland, where he became an adviser of the Prince of Orange. He returned with William to England at the revolution of 1688 and was made Bishop of Salisbury. A moderate who hated Episcopalian oppression as much as he disliked Covenanting stubbornness, he somewhat unfairly earned the dislike of both sides and, in the end, also that of King William.

Burnet's works include a *Vindication of the Authority, Constitution and Laws of the Church and State in Scotland* (1672), a *History of the Reformation* (1679–1714), two biographies, and an essay, still not devoid of interest, on the biographer's art. His most important production was his *History of My Own Times* published posthumously in 1723. His strength of character and firmness of his belief in his own opinions is evident throughout, but the prose is vigorous and the portraits of Charles II and Lauderdale, and his descriptions of the execution of Montrose and the muddle and duplicity that resulted in the massacre of Glencoe, vividly memorable.

M. Lindsay

Burnet, Sir John James (1857–1938). John Burnet Senior of Glasgow (1814–1 901) was a skilful and eclectic architect, who established a sound reputation with such buildings as the Stock Exchange (1875–77) in the Ruskinian Gothic style and St Jude's Church, Woodlands Gate (1874–76) in the French Gothic style and the Clydesdale Bank, St Vincent Place (1870–23) in the Italian palazzo manner.

His youngest son John James was to outshine him and secure a reputation in Scotland as well as in England for his bold classicism in both the academic Beaux Arts manner and the vigorous free-style version.

John James was born in 1857 and attended various schools in Glasgow. He spent two years in his father's office, but in 1874 finally persuaded his father to send him to study in Paris at the Ecole des Beaux Arts, where for three years he was a student in the atelier of Jean-Louis Pascal.

With his successful design in 1878 for the Fine Art Institute Building, Sauchiehall Street, his Glasgow practice was established. During the 1890s a remarkable group of buildings was to emerge from Burnet's office. Charing Cross Mansions (1890–91) is a vigorous exercise in the French Renaissance of the sixteenth century, while his banking hall for the Savings Bank, Ingram and Glassford Streets (1895–96) is a confident design in the newly fashionable Beaux Arts manner.

In 1896 he made his first visit to America, where Beaux Arts classicism was the height of fashion, notably the designs of McKim, Mead and White.

At the turn of the century he could still produce the serene academic classicism of the Elder Library, Govan (1901) as well as the striking Chicago style used in McGeogh's Warehouse, West Campbell Street (1905–6).

In 1905 Burnet moved to London, mainly to carry out the commission for the Edward VII Galleries at the British Museum (1904–14), another superb essay in academic classicism.

Although his office continued to work in Scotland, the major work now appeared in England and the quality of the Scottish work declined as it tried to grapple with the new dogmas of international modernism.

Honours were heaped on him. Knighted in 1914, he received the Gold Medal of the RIBA in 1923. He retired in 1935 settling in Edinburgh, and died there in 1938.

It was said that in his retirement 'he had no profession and no recreation, nothing of interest for him to turn to, no hobbies of any kind. He passed through life with one all-absorbing interest which burned him dry'. It was this 'absorbing interest' which gave Glasgow some of its most beautiful Edwardian buildings.

M. Higgs

Burns, Robert (1759–1796), the national bard, centre of a world cult celebrated by the consumption of sacred food (haggis) and drink (whisky) on his birthday (25 January). Burns's poems have been translated into 25 languages and have become best-sellers in the Soviet Union in the versions of Samuel Marshak, and others. From his own lifetime to the mid-nineteenth century and beyond, middle and upper-class admirers cast him in the mould of the 'heaven-taught ploughman' who owed everything to inspired natural genius, and until the 1890s he was valued mainly as a precursor of Wordsworth and the individualist, expressionist side of Romanticism. The Centenary Edition of W. E. Henley and T. F. Henderson (4 vols., 1896) did much to further the now standard picture of a personality divided between satire and sentimentality, explosive vernacular and insipid English, vigorous bawdry and pietistic moralizing, who was prevented from writing sustained poetry of the very highest sort because the linguistic and intellectual contradictions of his milieu made a satisfactory integration impossible.

Yet for almost 200 years the ordinary people of lowland Scotland have taken him to themselves. His life-long struggle to educate himself (parallelled in the life of many a 'lad o' pairts'), the torturing flesh which yet gave rise to some of the best love-songs ever written, his attacks on hypocrisy and religious humbug, his forthright plebeian democracy, his unique fusion of his folk inheritance with Augustan literary culture and Enlightenment ethics—all these have commended him to successive generations of stay-at-homes and emigrants. Perhaps the most acute remark on Burns's personality is Byron's: 'What an antithetical mind!—tenderness, roughness—delicacy, coarseness—sentiment, sensuality—soaring and grovelling, dirt and deity—all mixed up in that one compound of "inspired clay" ' (*Journal*, 13 Dec. 1813). It was the contradictoriness which has made it possible for his works, and his myth, to find favour with so many different types of Scot.

From his mother Agnes Broun (1732–1820) and her female servants and relatives he derived a wide knowledge of traditionary tales, proverbs; folk ballads and popular lyrics, which he later increased from oral manuscript and printed sources; while his father, the struggling tenant farmer William Burnes (1721–1784) introduced him to the Bible, moderate theology, and the impulse towards the concerns of the intellect. When Robert was six, his father and four neighbours employed a young man trained for the ministry to teach their children. After his tutor left the district in 1768, the father himself took on his sons' education, and continued it during their labours on the farm. When Burns's sporadic formal education ceased in 1775, he had had a grounding in mensuration and surveying, and been introduced to French and even, however slightly, to Latin. In the 20 years that were left to him he never ceased to extend his acquaintanceship with Enlightenment culture and with English poets, novelists and essayists.

Though as a boy he had read Hamilton of Gilbertfield's *Wallace* and some of Allan Ramsay's poems, it was not until he came across the Scots poems of Robert Fergusson (q.v.) in 1784 that he became aware of the full possibilities of Scots as a creative medium. Fergusson's poetry was a catalyst, fusing with English influences and the extraordinary events of his own life to produce his own very individual contribution. Ayrshire was a stronghold of last-ditch Calvinism in the Church disputes of the eighteenth century, and Burns found in vernacular measures and traditions the perfect instruments for his 'priest-skelpin' turns against the ministers and elders of the Auld Licht persuasion. By mid 1786 amorous entanglements had made it almost impossible for him to continue in and around Mauchline, and he seriously considered emigration to Jamaica. But the huge success of his carefully chosen selection of 34 poems (excluding epigrams and other brief rhymes), the famous Kilmarnock edition of July 31, led him to change his plans. 28 November saw him in the capital, to arrange for an Edinburgh edition (published 17 Apr., 1787). He was the social sensation of the year. Tours of the Borders and the Highlands followed, and he spent much of the first three months of 1788 in Edinburgh. Later in 1788 he acknowledged his previous irregular marriage with Jean Armour, and combined his lease of Ellis-

land farm in Dumfriesshire with a minor job in the Excise from September 1789. In November 1791 he moved to Dumfries as a full-time exciseman. The most fruitful events of the Edinburgh period were his meetings with enthusiasts like the antiquarian David Herd who took folksongs and ballads seriously, and James Johnson, the engraver and music publisher, whose collection *The Scots Musical Museum* (6 vols., 1787-1803) printed both words and music. From the second volume (1787) until 1796 Burns was the main driving force; to the *Museum*, and to George Thomson's more genteel *Select Collection of Original Scotish [sic] Airs* (5 vols., 1793–1818), he contributed some 250 songs wholly or partly of his own composition, and many others collected in a 'folkloristic' spirit. Burns performed his excise duties faithfully, although his outspoken support of the French Revolution caused some trouble with his superiors (the Excise Board investigated his loyalty Dec. 17th Jan. 1793) and made him unpopular with the local establishment. He often got drunk, but his early death was not due to alcoholism but to a rheumatic heart condition—aggravated by the treatment prescribed by his doctors—bathing in the Solway.

Burns's place in world literature rests on the 34 poems of the Kilmarnock edition; on *Holy Willie's Prayer*, perhaps the finest concentrated satire ever written, and that most vigorous and joyous expression of 'humanity's unofficial self' (George Orwell), *The Jolly Beggars*; on his masterpiece of comic narrative, *Tam o' Shanter*; and on the songs, unique fusions of words and tunes, of inherited tradition and individual modification. Each of his best works has its own unity of the particular and the general. Drawing together the local and the national, the international and the universal, Burns was at one and the same time a master of colloquial language and inherited poetic diction; the impressionist of a popular tradition who yet produced bounding lines as clear and definite as the arguments of that other great Scot of his century, David Hume (q.v.); a poet of the great commonplaces; and a shrewd and forceful thinker expressing the ideas which grip ordinary men and women in an age of revolution and social change.

T. Crawford

C

Calderwood, David (1575–1650) was born at Dalkeith and educated in Edinburgh. He became minister of Crailing, Roxburghshire in 1604, and opposed James VI's ideas on Episcopalian worship. He had to flee to Holland, where his controversial assault upon Episcopacy, *The Altar of Damascus*, was published in 1621. He returned to Scotland in 1625 after

Charles I's accession, and embarked on the writing of his *History of the Kirk of Scotland*. It was published in an abridged form in 1646, and in its final form between 1641 and 1949. Calderwood's *History* lacks the calm judgement of that of his Episcopalian rival and contemporary, Spottiswoode, but contains vivid passages, including his description of the death of Knox.

M. Lindsay

Callanish, Isle of Lewis. The standing stones at Callanish were part of one of the great ceremonial centres of early prehistoric Scotland. They dominate a ridge of rock above Loch Roag on the west coast of Lewis, and there are several small stone circles around the head of the loch. Callanish itself is unique, for it consists of a circle with rows of stones leading out from the circle to the cardinal points of the compass; a double row or 'avenue' some 82m long to the north and single rows to the south, east and west. The central circle is not only 5m in diameter, but its thirteen tall pale monoliths surround a single giant, almost 5m high and a small stone tomb.

The tomb was only discovered in 1857 when a thick layer of peat was stripped from the site, and it was assumed that the tomb was an afterthought, added to an existing sacred site. Modern excavations have shown that the tomb was in fact part of the original design of the stone setting, and that both date to around 3000 BC. This has a bearing on the interpretation of the site, for very few people can have gathered within the central circle itself, its small area restricted even further by the cairn of stones over the tomb. The stone rows may have played an essential role in organising, perhaps even separating, the bulk of the people attending ceremonies here. The nature of these ceremonies is a matter for speculation, but the presence of this ritual complex on the west coast of Lewis suggests that there was a flourishing and well organized population to build and sustain it.

Both the design of the tomb and the type of pottery found are related to contemporary society in Orkney rather than to local Hebridean fashions. They may reflect an early use of the western seaways that were to become so important in later times. The spread of ideas throughout Scotland, even before 3000 BC, implies considerable knowledge of boats and seamanship, and voyages were aided by a comparatively mild climate. Both skin boats and log boats are likely to have been used, the latter more for local traffic and skin boats for longer sea voyages.

Impressive though Callanish is, it is not an ideal monument on which to base any arguments about the possible astronomical prowess of its builders. It appears to demonstrate an interest in the four cardinal points, but, as the ridge on which it stands is aligned north-south, the arrangement of the stone rows may be no more than the result of a desire for symmetry.

A. Ritchie

Calvinism labels the form of Protestant theology and Church order which derives from the Swiss Reformation in the sixteenth century and was shaped chiefly by John Calvin (1509–1564), the Reformer of Geneva. The Calvinist (or 'Reformed') movement was distinct both from the Lutheran in Germany and the Anglican in England. It spread to various parts of Europe, established itself especially firmly in Holland and Scotland, and had a powerful influence also in England, America and the British colonies. In Scotland it took a particular Presbyterian form, and the Church of Scotland is regarded as the mother-church of English-speaking Presbyterianism.

Calvin's theology particularly emphasized the glory, majesty and sovereignty of God; the 'total depravity' of man which vitiates even the greatest human achievements; forgiveness through Jesus Christ as the only means of reconciliation with God; the futility of any religion which men might work out for themselves; the authority of the Bible; and the need to govern both Church and society according to God's law. John Knox (c. 1514–1572), the leader of the Scottish Reformation, was deeply influenced by Calvin, and all these notes were struck in *The Scots Confession* which he drew up, with others, in 1560.

As time passed, Calvinism hardened into a more rigid and all-embracing system of belief and practice. This is reflected in *The Westminster Confession*, drawn up in the 1640s, which became the official standard of belief of the Scottish Church. One theme, already present in Calvin, but now given fresh prominence, was 'double predestination': by an inscrutable decree of God, each individual is marked from all eternity either as 'elect', in which case he will be saved through Christ, or as 'reprobate', in which case he will be justly damned for his sins. The intention of this teaching was positive—to encourage the faithful to put their trust in God's irrevocable decision in their favour. But it could lead both to the kind of hypocrisy pilloried by Burns in *Holy Willie's Prayer* and to agonizing fear in those who felt uncertain of their own election. Along with this developed the idea of 'limited atonement': Christ had not died 'for all', but only for the elect. At the same time his death tended to be interpreted in terms of 'penal substitution': he had borne the punishment imposed by God for sin. In this same period in the seventeenth century Calvinism took the form of 'Federal Theology', centred on the theme of God's 'covenant' (in Latin, *foedus*: hence 'federal'). Adam in Paradise had broken the 'covenant of works' by his disobedience; in Christ the 'covenant of grace' replaced it. The notion of 'covenant' was applied politically as well as theologically, notably in the *National Covenant* of 1638 and the *Solemn League and Covenant* of 1643, and underlies the later political theory of the 'social contract'. The 'covenant' tended however to be interpreted as a 'contract', offered by God upon certain conditions, such as repentance and obedience; and this could lead both to despairing uncertainty in those who were unsure if they fulfilled the conditions and to an unattractive excess of (often censorious) confidence in those who were certain that they had 'struck hands with God'.

The frequently stark and intolerant outlook which these developments encouraged did not, however, go unchallenged in Scotland. In the 1720s the 'Marrow-men' attacked the 'conditionality' of the 'covenant of grace'; the eighteenth-century Seceders criticized the use of secular power to maintain orthodox religion and the 'persecuting principles' they found in the *Westminster Confession;* the idea that Christ's death was a punishment was opposed by men like Thomas Erskine and John McLeod Campbell in the early nineteenth century. Many of these were driven out of the Church of Scotland, but would now be generally held to have been right. Nor did the Church of Scotland generally push its Calvinism to the extremes of the English Baptist 'Hyper-Calvinists' of the eighteenth century. In that period, indeed, the Church was largely dominated by the 'Moderates', whose loyalty to the *Confession* was somewhat diluted by the new climate of their time. The last 100 years have brought a considerable further softening of the old rigidities, though the *Westminster Confession* still remains the official standard of belief both of the Church of Scotland and of the Free Church. The Church of Scotland requires of its ministers only a general adherence to the 'fundamental doctrines of the Christian faith contained in the *Confession*', not to every point of it, and attempts have been made in recent years to relegate the *Confession* even from this status.

The main lines of Calvin's teaching have nonetheless etched themselves deeply on Scottish life and culture, and their influence remains powerful, if diffuse, even today. It naturally tended to stress authority, obedience and responsibility; the careful use of resources; the discipline of work; the importance of education and understanding; the intellect rather than the imagination; simplicity rather than the ornate and decorative. Its sense of the majesty of God and of human frailty and sinfulness predisposed to an attitude more douce than exuberant, more reverent, or even fearful, than cheerfully confident, before a God more easily associated with the stern implacability of the divine decrees than with the love of the heavenly Father. In justice to Calvin himself it must be said that his theology was by no means as lopsided as some later Calvinism made it. Further, some of the austere features commonly associated with Scottish Calvinism owe less to Calvin or the Scots Reformers than to other factors—the poverty of the country, the bitter religious and political conflicts of the seventeenth century, and not least the influence of English Puritanism in that same era. (The barrenness of Presbyterian worship for centuries, brought about by the abandoning of set liturgies, and even of such set forms as the Lord's Prayer and the Apostles' Creed, reflected Puritanism rather than Calvinism.) But the interaction between Calvinism and these other forces, and the part played by Calvinism itself, cannot be overlooked in any analysis of the elusive Scottish national soul.

A. I. C. Heron

Campbell, Thomas (1777-1844) was the son of a 67-year-old Glasgow business man. After graduating at Glasgow University, Campbell acted as a tutor in Mull, an experience which inspired his love of Highland scenery. He then set about studying law at Edinburgh, but abandoned this course when, at the age of 21, his poem *The Pleasures of Hope* (1799) achieved

a wide measure of popularity, giving to the national folk-memory the often inaccurately quoted:

> 'Tis distance lends enchantment to the view,
> And robes the mountain in its azure hue.

A similarly half-remembered quotation comes from his poem 'The Beech-Trees' Petition'—'Spare, wood-man, spare the beechen tree'—while Campbell (and not, as sometimes believed, Byron) declared: 'Now Barabbas was a publisher'.

Later long poems included *Gertrude of Wyoming* (1809), *O'Connor's Child* (1809) and *Theodoric* (1824). All of them, like most early nineteenth-century novels in verse, are now little read. But such ballads as 'Lord Ullin's Daughter', 'Hohenlinden' and his stirring war-song 'Ye Mariners of England' keep his name alive. Two of his lyrics, 'Florine' (set by the Scottish composer F. G. Scott) and 'How delicious is the winning/Of a kiss at love's beginning' are regularly anthologized.

From 1803 until his death in Boulogne, where he had gone in search of health, Campbell lived in London, working as an editor and critic. His prefatory essay to *Specimens of the British Poets* (1819) is a good example of his fairness and critical balance. His most important prose work is his *Annals of Britain*, dealing with the earlier years of the reign of George III.

He was three times elected Lord Rector of Glasgow University, on one occasion defeating Sir Walter Scott. Buried in Westminster Abbey, his statue is one of the 12 adorning George Square, Glasgow. A *Life*, together with some of his letters, was issued by W. Beattie in 1849.

M. Lindsay

Caraid nan Gaidheal ('Friend of the Highlanders') (1783–1862), popular sobriquet of the Rev. Norman MacLeod, native of Morvern, and minister, successively, of Campbeltown, Campsie and St Columba Gaelic Church, Glasgow. He initiated the tradition of creative prose-writing in Scottish Gaelic, chiefly through his contributions to the periodicals *An Teachdaire Gaelach* (1829–31), *Cuairtear nan Gleann* (1840–43), both edited by himself, and *Fear-Tathaich nam Beann* (1848–50), edited by his son-in-law, Archibald Clerk.

Aware of a new Gaelic reading public nurtured by the Gaelic Schools Societies since 1811 and the General Assembly's schools since 1824, and doubtless influenced by the example of English periodicals, especially *Blackwood's Magazine*, MacLeod aimed to provide both spiritual edification and secular instruction for his fellow Highlanders. His two anthologies for use in schools, *Co'chruinneachadh* (1828) and *Leabhar nan Cnoc* (1834), are weightily homiletic in character, but his writings in the periodicals range more widely in content and presentation. He uses the dialogue form to introduce his rustic readers to current affairs, new developments, and distant and exotic places. There are spoof letters to the editor, in which Highlanders record their impressions of the urban industrial society to which increasing numbers of them were now emigrating. Indeed, the abiding worth of this section of his

writings inheres largely in its portrayal of the cultural dislocation which Gaelic-speaking Highlanders experienced in the
late eighteenth and early nineteenth centuries.

Caraid nan Gaidheal has also had a seminal influence as the
pioneer of short-story writing in Gaelic. His efforts in this
genre, most of them marked by a facile romanticism and
heavily larded with pathos, obviously draw some of their
inspiration from Dickens as well as from MacLeod's own
experience of industrial Glasgow, where disease was rife and
child mortality commonplace. His stories are thus very much
of their period, with the exception of one, 'Crotachan na
Beinne', which, as a psychological study, has had no real
successors in Gaelic until recent times.

Macleod's prose style has had a dominating influence on
Gaelic writing which is still not altogether spent. It is formal
and heavily gilded, modelled to a great extent on the Gaelic
translation of the Bible, completed in 1801. In the dialogues
and 'letters', he achieves a lighter touch, though even there the
attempts at humour are somewhat contrived and cumbersome.
For all that, he can, on occasion, write with animation and
pace, as, for example, in the Tiree man's account of his first
train journey. A substantial collection of his most representative pieces, edited by Archibald Clerk, was published
posthumously in 1867 under the title *Caraid nan Gaidheal*.
Among MacLeod's contemporaries, mention should be made
of John MacKenzie, whose major prose work was *Eachdraidh
a' Phrionnsa* (1844), an account of the '45 Rebellion, and
Lachlan Maclean, who in 1837 published *Adhamh agus Eubh*, a
quixotic attempt to prove that Gaelic was the original language
of mankind.

Caraid nan Gaidheal's innovating work was reinforced and
extended by further developments in the later part of the
nineteenth century. The publication of J .F. Campbell's *Popular Tales of the West Highlands* (1860–62) conferred on oral
Gaelic material the prestige of the printed page, and the
proliferation of Highland societies in southern towns and cities
created a demand for Gaelic entertainment. This demand was
in part met by writers who published volumes of sketches,
dialogues and readings for public performance. Prominent
among these was Henry Whyte, who published *The Celtic
Garland* (1881), *Leabhar na Céilidh* (1898), and two volumes of
Naidheachdan Firinneach (1905, 1906). Somewhat similar material was provided by John MacFadyen in *An t-Eileanach*
(1890) and *Sgeulaiche nan Caol* (1902); and by K. W. Grant in
Aig Tigh na Beinne (1911). Gaelic essay-writing was also further
developed, in formal and erudite style by Donald MacKinnon,
whose pieces first appeared in the periodical *An Gaidheal*
(1871–77); in lighter and more whimsical vein by Donald
MacKechnie, whose volume *Am Fear-Ciùil* appeared in 1904,
and Donald Lamont, who from 1907 onwards contributed
entertaining pieces with a light leavening of moralizing to the
Church of Scotland magazine *Life and Work*.

    K.D. MacDonald

Carlyle, Alexander (1722–1805), nicknamed 'Jupiter' because

of his stately appearance, was the son of the minister of
Cummertrees, Dumfriesshire. He was educated at Edinburgh,
Glasgow and Leyden Universities, and on entering the Church
became minister of Inveresk, near Edinburgh, where he remained throughout his long career. When his brother
clergyman the Reverend John Home was attacked for writing
the play of *Douglas*, Carlyle forced the narrower brethern to
weaken their opposition to the theatre. He was a frequenter of
literary company both in London and in Edinburgh.

Of his two Swiftian pamphlets, the more pungent is 'An
Argument to Prove that the Tragedy of 'Douglas' ought to be
publicly burnt by the Hands of the Hangman' (1757). He left
behind him an autobiography, edited by Hill Burton in 1860
and published under the title of 'Memoirs'. These reflect not
only 'Jupiter' Carlyle's shrewd understanding of character,
but his sheer enjoyment of life.

    M. Lindsay

Carlyle, Thomas (1795–1881) resists easy summing up. The
prophet of silence left too many volumes, too many magnificent letters, found a successful and important 'voice' for too
many of his contemporaries, to be brushed aside or forgotten,
yet he is difficult to pin down to one 'important' facet. The
friend of Dickens and Browning, Forster and Tennyson, Carlyle along with his gifted wife Jane held court in their Chelsea
home for several decades after they moved to London in 1834;
then the 'Sage of Chelsea' was almost 40, and it is both easy
and dangerous to overlook the importance of his youth and
early manhood in a Scotland still in an intellectual flurry as the
'Golden Age' of the Enlightenment changed and redefined
itself, as the age of Hume gave way to the age of Scott and the
Edinburgh Reviewers. Already well known in writing circles
before Victorian literature as we know it began (indeed before
Victoria came to the throne), an important translator and early
critic of German literature, author of the brilliant and provocative fantasia *Sartor Resartus* (1833), a radical social critic
sharply attacking the 'mechanism' of his age, and a historian of
growing power, the angular but compelling Scot who moved
into London literary and intellectual circles in the 1830s owed
a great deal to his Ecclefechan upbringing and his Edinburgh
education.

*The French Revolution, Chartism, Past and Present, Heroes and
Hero-Worship, Latter-Day Pamphlets, Oliver Cromwell, Frederick the
Great* made him famous throughout the world. His conversational powers were rightly renowned and visitors to Chelsea
copied his *bons mots* for posterity. To many of his readers he
embodied the heroic power he so much wished to find in his
own age. He possessed the intelligence to read widely, absorb
the many currents of his time, see the strains which rapid
change had caused in his society, and to produce in vivid prose
(heavily influenced by German, and by the pulpit oratory he
had known in his youth) analyses which sharply attacked the
root causes of decay in his time, and laid bare the shams and
hypocrisies he saw in his age.

Sartor appeared more than 30 years before the end of *Fred-*

erick, and the spread of dates should caution the critic who sees too much of a unity in his extraordinary output of influential and justly famous work. We are not talking about the same author at the beginning as at the end of the sequence, nor is he talking about the same Great Britain. The times through which Carlyle lived gave him a rich source of material, of course, but he saw things from different angles with passing years, and with changing circumstances. The intolerant social critic of the 1860s, advocating the use of force to make workers return to their work and quell rebellion, is far from the polished ironist of 'Signs of the Times' and the other influential enquiries of the 1820s and 1830s. Yet they share a common driving force: Carlyle's philosophical position.

Bred in a liberal Calvinist family, Carlyle naturally felt a vacuum when he gave up at university the stated ambition of his parents that he should enter the Church. The vacuum he filled first with important and very professionally performed scientific study, and then with the 'New Heaven' and 'New Earth' he found in Goethe and the other Germans. From the Germans came ideas sufficiently close to the discarded ideals of childhood Ecclefechan for him to reconstruct a new, workable, yet familiar philosophy. The result, marvellously transformed in *Sartor*, is a strongly defined and sometimes over-simplified message which he communicated with great skill to great numbers of his bewildered contemporaries. He preached the humility to admit the existence of a God, or the possibility of one: also, he insisted on the importance of seeing a holier and deeper significance to life than the scientific, industrial, utilitarian or economic analyses common in his time. He urged employers to treat workers as human beings, governments to treat populations on those terms and not as mere pawns. He urged workers to work, and to treat work as a sacred duty. He urged everyone to look for heroes, God-appointed strong men who crop up in the pages of history (particularly the areas of history which fascinated Carlyle) and justify their activities by their very evident success. Every age, in Carlyle's analysis, should find its God-sent heroes, and obey them. Unfortunately, Carlyle recognized no hero in his own age: his analyses of Victorian Britain were rarely other than negative or gloomy, and became more so as time passed. His destructive criticism was rightly celebrated, but his constructive suggestions were fewer and more generalized: important as they were, improved education, and assisted emigration, seemed tame beside the vividness of his attacks on his age. The real positive thrust of his message was less obvious, but more important. He was preaching (literally) a spiritual rebirth, after which a rearrangement and improvement of society would be possible.

Though not himself a regular churchgoer or orthodox Christian in the usual sense, Carlyle preached a most attractive message, in a blazing style which gave it a wider acceptance than is readily explainable today. At his best (arguably in *The French Revolution*) he achieves a prose which works in large related sections to manipulate the reader's response in a manner which is irresistible. The profusion of reprints and cheap editions testifies to the effect it had in his century.

His marriage to Jane Welsh was crucial to his success.

Deeply in love, temperamentally prone to frequent quarrel, they spurred on each others' exceptional creative talents. Jane's talent lay in conversation, in friendship, in correspondence: the labour of editing the Carlyles' correspondences is revealing an extraordinary width of friendship and interest, but also a remarkable talent in letter-writing. Jane died in 1866, Thomas in 1881, and the intervening years saw almost no large-scale creative work apart from the letters. In the years following Jane's death he achingly relived their years together in a series of extraordinary *Reminiscences* of Jane, his early years, and their early friendships. Raw-nerved, edgy, seemingly chaotic, these sketches were dashed off in the first months of loneliness and grief, yet a sure controlling artistic instinct makes them shapely, and a marvellously complete autobiography. Carlyle had a photographic memory and in reading the *Reminiscences* today one has a documentary picture of life in a crucial period of both British and Scottish history.

Carlyle, sage, prophet, survivor—human being—lived through these times, and his work survives him. After long neglect, republication and re-editing is slowly revealing the width of his interests, the sources of his ideas, the secrets of his style and his effect on his contemporaries. No assessment of Victorian Britain, and certainly no assessment of nineteenth-century Scotland, can be complete without him.

I. Campbell

Carver, Robert (c. 1484–c. 1567) was a canon of the Augustinian Abbey of Scone as well as being attached to the Chapel Royal at Stirling. Perhaps the greatest of Scotland's composers, his surviving compositions (five masses and two motets) are in a single manuscript, partly written in his own hand. *Dum Sacrum Mysterium* is a ten part mass almost mediaeval in style and symbolism, the ten parts representing the nine orders of angels joined by mankind to complete the heavenly chorus. This and the nineteen part *O Bone Jesu* use a Scottish technique known as Cant Organe, in which neighbouring chords alternate, the voices changing places with a freedom that allows for many dissonances and parallel fifths and octaves. *O Bone Jesu* is a supreme masterpiece of the Renaissance, possibly commissioned by James IV as a penitential prayer to atone for his involvement in the death of his father. The contrast of vast chordal textures, subtly varied, with the more elaborate and intimate sections of part writing is immensely impressive. His other motet, *Gaude Flore Virginali*, is a work of restrained but harmonically adventurous beauty depicting the seven joys of the Holy Virgin. The *L'Homme Armee* mass is the only insular mass to use this tune, which it incorporates at various speeds, drawing from it to form complex decorative passages. It was perhaps inspired by the example of Dufay whose mass on the same tune Carver copied into his book. His command of continental structural imitation is movingly displayed in the bleak closing Agnus Dei of the 5-part mass, *Fere Pessima*. The late four part mass, *Pater Creator Omnium* shows the restraining influence of reformist ideals.

J. Purser

Castles and Fortified Houses. Scottish castles, like Scottish lairds, appear in many different shapes and sizes, some more characteristic than others. Indeed, the earliest castles stand a good chance of escaping recognition altogether, except by archaeologists, for they were constructed not of stone and lime, but of earth, clay, timber and other perishable materials which have often left only indistinct traces on today's landscape. Such were the 'motte-and-bailey' castles erected throughout southern and eastern Scotland during the twelfth and thirteenth centuries by immigrant Anglo-Norman barons, and by the king himself at important centres like royal burghs and residences.

As the landowning aristocracy became better established, however, they began to build in hewn stone, and the great majority of castles erected during the later Middle Ages were constructed of this material. Like their earth and timber prototypes, these castles most frequently took the form of a defensive enclosure, the living space being completely surrounded by a stout curtain-wall which could be entered only by means of a fortified gateway. Many of these castles were quite small, the owner's family and household being accommodated in buildings ranged round the inside of the curtain-wall. Larger fortresses, however, such as Edinburgh and Stirling, incorporated free-standing buildings, and in addition to the main enclosure, or courtyard, there might be one or more outer baileys containing ancillary structures. In some cases the curtain itself was punctuated by towers, which served both as strongpoints and auxiliary dwelling-quarters; good examples of these can be seen at the late thirteenth-century castles of Caerlaverock and Kildrummy.

There was nothing distinctively Scottish about these castles, which were essentially local manifestations of widely prevailing types of western European fortification. During the fifteenth and sixteenth centuries, however, something approaching a national style of military architecture appeared, following the adoption by the Scottish baronage of a more compact variety of fortified residence known as the tower-house. Not, of course, that castles of this type were peculiar to Scotland, but in no other country, except perhaps Ireland, was their popularity so widespread and lasting.

It is not difficult to understand the attractions of the tower-house in a society which was both economically depressed and politically unstable. Essentially a self-contained residence housing a series of rooms placed one above the other, it was at once cheap to build and easy to defend. At the same time the plan-form was flexible enough to suit most tastes and pockets, taking in at one end of the scale the simple four-square tower of the bonnet laird and at the other the elaborately constructed stronghold of the greater baron. The tower-house also struck a sensible balance between the competing claims of comfort and defence, being designed not as a base for strategic warfare but as a private dwelling-house defensible against local assault.

It was this practical, if at times somewhat incongruous, combination of domestic and military attributes that continued to give the Scottish fortified house of the later sixteenth and seventeenth centuries its distinctive character. Traditional structural devices, such as the barrel-vault and turnpike-stair, were retained, but wall-thicknesses were reduced to allow of larger rooms within, and more and bigger windows were provided. Iron yetts, gun-ports, angle-turrets and battlemented wall-walks, while outwardly making a brave show of defence, were now valued chiefly as status symbols, and military effectiveness took second place to decorative effect. The same taste for embellishment is reflected in the popularity of armorial panels, commemorative inscriptions, carved pediments, painted ceilings and decorative plasterwork. Indeed, the finest buildings of this Scottish Baronial school, such as Amisfield Tower and Craigievar Castle, exhibit a profusion of ornamental detail hitherto unparalleled in the country's domestic architecture.

In many of these buildings the layout followed that of the late medieval tower-house, the L- or Z-plan frequently being chosen in preference to the simple rectangle. As standards of accommodation improved, however, it became necessary to incorporate more rooms, which could be done only by extending the building horizontally. This development, coupled with the introduction of Renaissance ideas of symmetry and the final abandonment of defensive precautions, eventually brought design into line with the emerging architecture of the classical country house.

J.G. Dunbar

Catholicism since the Reformation. For nearly a quarter of a century after the Reformation Parliament of 1560 religion in Scotland hung upon politics, with hopes or fears related to what France, England, or Spain might do. The balance of power in the country favoured the Protestant cause which had also more energetic and purposeful leadership. Effective organization was absent on the Catholic side. Some of the bishops had become Protestant; others went abroad, like James Beaton, archbishop of Glasgow. John Hamilton, archbishop of St Andrews, was entangled in his family's political manoeuvres, but, when hanged at Stirling in 1571, died 'as he had lived', in the words of a Protestant chronicler, 'ane obstinat papist'.

There was no counter-Reformation programme in Scotland until after 1622. A small band of Scottish Jesuits did what it could; one of them, John Ogilvie (canonized 1976) was hanged in Glasgow in 1615. A few members of the clergy worked on for a time with difficulty, including the Dominican, John Black, murdered with Riccio in 1566; the Benedictine, Abbot Quintin Kennedy; Franciscans; some diocesan priests, but without central direction. Catholic apologists wrote from the continent, notably Ninian Winzet, formerly schoolmaster in Linlithgow, who laid the foundations at Ratisbon of a Scottish Benedictine Congregation in Germany. Exiled Scots developed other bases abroad in which priests would be trained for work at home; colleges at Douai, Paris, Rome, joined in 1627 by the Scots College in Madrid (now, since 1771, in Valladolid.). Some exiles, like the Jesuit John Hay, made reputations as scholars.

After 1622 Scottish Catholics were under the authority of the Roman Congregation for the Propagation of the Faith ('Propaganda'), set up to direct missionary effort throughout the world. Inevitably Scotland was one of the least of its interests; nevertheless, by varying supplies of men and money it contributed to the survival of a native Scottish Catholicism, especially in the Hebrides and in parts of Inverness-shire, Banffshire and Aberdeenshire, with smaller pockets farther south. Irish Gaelic-speaking priests reclaimed parts of what were virtually ecclesiastical deserts in the Highlands and Islands. The colleges abroad, Jesuits, and various Orders maintained a slender supply of priests throughout the seventeenth century. They were based sometimes on great houses whose owners, for example Gordons or Maxwells, remained Catholic. Some endured great hardship, living rough to avoid risking the ruin of the people whom they served. A number suffered imprisonment for lengthy periods, including two superiors of the Mission, both converts to Catholicism: William Ballantyne, who had studied at Edinburgh University, and Thomas Nicolson, sometime student in Aberdeen and professor in Glasgow University.

Nicolson, as Vicar-Apostolic (1695–1718) was the first episcopally ordained Scottish superior since the extinction of the old hierarchy. Scottish Catholics remained under Vicars-Apostolic until the restoration of regular diocesan structures in 1878. After 1688 they were compromised by involvement in Jacobite plots, and weakened also by internal dissensions, for example about Jansenism. Nicolson achieved the establishment of a training centre in Glenlivet in 1717 which, with a similar college in the Gaelic west, produced 'heather priests' throughout the eighteenth century.

There were bonds between Scots Catholics and their Protestant compatriots which would grow after the Jacobite collapse. Father Thomas Innes (1674–1744), who helped Ruddiman to catalogue ancient manuscripts in the Advocates Library, published in London in 1729 his *Critical Essay on the Northern Parts of Britain or Scotland*. His cooperation with other scholars set a pattern maintained later by such men as Bishop John Geddes (1735–99), contributor to the *Encyclopedia Britannica*, leading member of the Society of Antiquaries of Scotland, friend of Robert Burns; and Bishop James Kyle (1788–1869), whose assistance is frequently acknowledged in printed editions of historical records. Dr Alexander Geddes, cousin of the bishop, was a stormy petrel whose biblical scholarship was ahead of his time.

By 1800 there were about 30,000 Roman Catholics in Scotland. They had been led firmly, if conservatively, for over 30 years by Bishop George Hay (1729–1811) and had proved their loyalty in the French wars. Hay, once Protestant medical student in Edinburgh, was known widely for his *Treatise on Miracles* (1775), a reply to Hume; and for three books, *The Sincere Christian*, *The Devout Christian*, *The Pious Christian*, which were translated into various languages. He had published also an edition of the Bible in English. The college in Glenlivet had been moved by him to Donside and in 1829, year of the Catholic Emancipation Act, would be united with its Gaelic counterpart as St Mary's College, Blairs, near Aberdeen, housing an important collection of books and archives later transferred to Edinburgh—the books to the National Library, the archives to Columba House, Drummond Place.

Bishops Hay and Geddes (and others) had administered the Lowland parts of Scotland, including the northeast. The Gaelic west was under separate Vicars-Apostolic. It suffered heavy emigration as a result of Jacobite failure, Clearances, and potato famine in the 1840s. Settlers, accompanied by their priests, established Gaelic-speaking Catholic communities in Ontario and the Maritime Provinces of Canada. At home Robert Menzies, priest in charge of Highlanders in Edinburgh, published a handbook of doctrine in Gaelic in 1781, and in 1785 *Leanmhuin Chriosd ann Ceithear Leabhraichann*, a version of *The Imitation of Christ*. The traditional culture of Gaelic Catholics is well represented in Alexander Carmichael's *Carmina Gadelica*, and by Father Allan Macdonald of Eriskay (1859–1905). A Scots Gaelic translation of the New Testament, from Strathglass, was published in Aberdeen, with episcopal approval, in 1875.

The huge Irish influx caused by famine strained the resources of native Catholicism desperately in mid-nineteenth century. Establishment of an episcopal hierarchy in 1878 brought greater order and peace into a Church divided between a large new industrial proletariat and a traditional, mainly rural community, with a slight aristocratic crust, partly convert. Energies went into building churches and schools, the latter brought into the state system by the Education (Scotland) Act of 1918. Slowly immigrants have been assimilated into the Scottish nation, whose separate identity was witnessed to at the Second Vatican Council by the presence of eight bishops. For a fuller account of the place of Roman Catholicism during the last century the reader is referred to *Modern Scottish Catholicism*, ed. David McRoberts (Burns, Glasgow 1979).

A. Ross

Celtic Languages were once spoken over wide areas of Europe, including most of France, much of Germany, and parts of Spain and Italy. They are now mainly confined to Britain and Ireland, apart from Breton, spoken in Brittany. These languages fall into two main divisions (1) Brythonic, which includes Welsh, Breton and Cornish (the latter existing only in a revived form) (2) Goedelic, which includes Scottish Gaelic, Irish and Manx (the latter existing only in a revived form). Within this division, Scottish Gaelic and Manx form an Eastern Gaelic grouping. One of the distinctions between these two main groupings is in their treatment of the Indo-European labio-velar guttural (qu-), which often appears as *p* in Brythonic and *c* in Goedelic (e.g. penn: cenn/ceann 'head'), and though the importance of this one distinction is exaggerated, it has given rise to the labels P-Celtic and Q-Celtic for Brythonic and Goedelic respectively. These are insular-Celtic labels (there were both -*p*- and -*q*- forms in Gaulish).

One or more Celtic languages have been spoken in Scotland throughout the entire Christian era, and their legacy can be seen plainly, especially in the toponymy of the country. There is less than total agreement as to the datings and the natures of the earliest Celtic settlements in the country, but one early one which took place no later than the first century BC was that of a people of Hallstatt antecedents, who came to Scotland via Southern England (using these names in their modern senses) and settled especially between the Firth of Forth and the Moray Firth. Another group of Celtic settlers had their main colony in Yorkshire, but spilled over into southern Scotland. And shortly before the start of the Christian era there was another migration of Celts, this time of La Tène antecedents, to north-western and northern Scotland (the broch-builders). But some archaeologists would place the earliest Celtic settlement some centuries earlier than the dates suggested for any of these.

We have no evidence that any of these pre-Christian settlements were made by Celts who spoke a Goedelic (i.e. ancestral Gaelic) language, though there may have been pockets of such. But we have strong evidence that the early settlers used a Brythonic (i.e. ancestral Welsh) language.

When we emerge from the uncertainties of prehistory to the relative illumination of the Dark Ages, and consider the country we now know as Scotland over the period from the fourth century AD to the ninth, a complex picture emerges. But one of the things we can confidently say about this Scotland is that it was predominantly Celtic, although it must have carried the cultural marks of Roman settlement in the south, was yielding ground in both the southeast and the southwest to Anglian, and had newly been infiltrated in the north and west by the Norse raiders and settlers. In this period Celtic Scotland comprises three separate components: (1) the British territories (2) the Pictish territories (3) the Gaelic territories.

(1) In the southwest there were two British/Brythonic kingdoms which formed part of the extensive British-speaking region known as Cumbria (which extended from the Clyde to the Ribble): these were Reget (later spelt Rheged) which straddled the present border in the west, and Strathclyde to the north of that kingdom (with its political capital at Dumbarton and its ecclesiastical capital at Glasgow). The other large British kingdom was that of the Votadini (as Latin writers called them) or the Gododdin. Their territory extended from the head of the Firth of Forth to the Wear in Co. Durham, and included Lothian and part of Peeblesshire, Selkirkshire and Roxburghshire. The same or a related people inhabited what may have been a small separate kingdom at the northern end of this region, the territory known as Manaw Gododdin, whose name survives in the modern names Slamannan and Clackmannan. The earliest literary work composed in Scotland, the *Gododdin*, is concerned with this people and kingdom, and is composed in the British language (q.v.) which is the ancestor of Welsh. It is thought that this language may have survived in Scotland as late as the eleventh century.

(2) When we come to the Pictish language(s) (q.v.) we are indeed on unsure ground, but there can be no doubt that there was an important Celtic element in this/these. The best-attested location of the Picts is between the Forth and Moray Firths, and to the east of Druim Alban, and this is the territory of these two main Pictish peoples, the Caledonii/Caledones and the Maeatae. It is also the territory marked by the heaviest concentration of names containing the element *pit* or *pett*, and of sculptured stones bearing Pictish symbols. But it is more satisfactory to refer to this area as the heartland of the Picts, or the territory of the later historical Picts, for the Picts are certainly to be found farther afield, e.g. in the north of Scotland and in the northern isles, and probably in Skye and the northwestern seaboard, perhaps even in the Outer Isles. Pictish seems to have consisted of two quite different elements, one being non-Indo-European and the other a more primitive form of P-Celtic (or Brythonic) than was spoken in the British territories in the south of Scotland and parts of England and Wales. It is necessary to have the Celtic hypothesis to explain the presence of P-Celtic place names in this whole Pictish territory, and necessary to have the non-Indo-European hypothesis to explain their low frequency. The Pictish inscriptions, mostly in a late variety of Ogam script, are thought to be relatively late (eighth century), and though they use two Gaelic words, *maqq* ('mac') and *crroscc* ('cross'), their main content has not yet been understood, and is thought to be expressed in the non-Indo-European component of Pictish, perhaps surviving as a ritual language.

(3) We have no firm evidence of when the Gaelic-speaking Scots first settled in Scotland, and the nearness of the country to Ireland makes it probable that there was some mutual migration. In 297 AD, however, the orator Eumenius, as part of his panegyric on the Emperor Constantius Augustus, says that the Britons (referring to the Roman province in the south of Scotland) are accustomed to Picti and Hiberni as enemies. Ammianus Marcellinus says that in the year 360 AD tribes of Scotti and Picti had broken the truce and were ravaging those parts of Roman Britain in the neighbourhood of the walls, and Ammianus has a reference to Pecti and Scotti harassing the Britons in 365 AD (see W. J. Watson, CPNS, 59). Our first historical view of the Scots or Gaels in Scotland is as allies of the Picts against the Romans. With this situation we should probably link the substantial Irish or Scottic settlement in South Wales (Dyfed) and in Cornwall, and the quartering of two Roman legions on the Welsh border, interpreted by the Welsh historian J. E. Lloyd as a defence against both the disaffected Britons of Wales and the invaders from Ireland (*A History of Wales* I, p. 82). It seems likely that there was already considerable Gaelic settlement in western Scotland before the time of Fergus mac Eirc (late fifth century AD, the time that is usually regarded as that of the historic founding of Dalriada, and John Bannerman argues a similar conclusion on the basis of an analysis of the early saga and historical traditions regarding the early settlers there (see especially *Studies in the History of Dalriada*, p. 122 ff.). A not unlikely interpretation of these movements is that they had by the late fifth century reached the point at which it was politically realistic for Fergus to move the main seat of his dynasty from Ireland to Scotland. And following a similar line of thought, Columba may be thought to have established a powerful base in Dalriada, in the middle

of the sixth century, because of a spectacular build-up of population and power there.

It may be that the relatively rapid infiltration of Pictland by the Gaels owed much to such a prolonged history of settlement, and also to a context of alliance against the Romans. There was conflict also, whether with the Britons of Manaw (as in a battle won by the Scots in 538), or those of Strathclyde (the battle of Strathcarron c. 643), or with the Picts (as when Aedan was defeated at Circinn in the late sixth century). There was a prolonged dynastic rivalry between the reigning families of the Scots and the Picts, and also intermarriage. But long before the kingdoms of the Picts and Scots became united, in 843, there were substantial Gaelic settlements in Pictland, as evidenced by the reference to Athfoithle 'New Ireland' (i.e. Atholl) in the Annals of Ulster (AD 739).

These various Celtic settlements have left substantial evidence 'on the ground' in the form of place names. A disentangling of the various British or Cumbric layers of names has not been achieved, and there seems to be much common ground between Cumbric and Pictish naming elements. Among the commonest Cumbric place-name elements are *penn* 'head, end', *pren* 'tree' and *tref* 'steading, village, settlement', Ochiltree comes from *Ucheldrev* 'high village' and Pencaitland from a triple compound *penn* + *cēd* 'wood' + *llann* 'enclosure'. By contrast, *pit* 'piece, portion of land', and *carden* 'brake, thicket' are almost totally confined to Pictland. And a few other elements are found both in Pictland and in the southern kingdoms, as *pert* 'copse' (as in Perth, Mill of Pert in Forfar), *lannerch* 'clearing', (as in Lanark and Lendrick in Angus), *pevr* 'bright, radiant' (as in Peffer in the Lothians and Strathpeffer in Ross-shire) and *aber* 'confluence' (as in Aberdeen, Lochaber, and Abercarf in Lanark). These are the elements with the widest distribution, though only a small selection of the P-Celtic elements found in place names in the areas concerned. A closer glance, however, at the commonest of these elements, *pit*, sounds a warning. *Pit* is Pictish, and its affinities are with P-Celtic, but in the vast majority of cases it is compounded in place names with Gaelic words, and the names are constructed according to Gaelic rules, as in *Pitcarmick* 'Cormac's portion', *Pittentagart* 'the priest's portion' and *Pett in Mulenn* 'the mill's portion', the latter two incorporating the Gaelic definite article as well as common Gaelic nouns. A similar comment can be made about a number of the *tref* names in Pictland, e.g. *Fintry*, whose first element is the Gaelic adjective *finn* 'fair, white'. Many of these hybrid names must have been given when Gaelic and Pictish/Cumbric were being spoken side by side, or in a Gaelic context which had accommodated Pictish and/or Cumbric loans.

Gaelic has by far the longest history in Scotland of continuing use both as a spoken language and as a medium for the naming of places. One of the oldest place-name elements is *sliabh* 'hill, high ground, rough grazing', which we can see being introduced at two separate bridgeheads: Kintyre/Islay/Arran and the Rhinns of Galloway. Other early Gaelic elements are *carraig* 'rock' (Carrick etc.), *cill* 'church etc.' (often combined with saints' names, as in Kilbride,

Kildonan) and *neimhidh* (Old Irish *nemed*, 'sacred, sacred place') as in Rosneath. But the two naming elements which illustrate the blanketing of Scottish terrain with Gaelic names are *baile* 'steading, township, village' and *achadh* 'field'. Such evidence of Gaelic place-name distribution shows us that Gaelic at one time or another was used over almost the whole of Scotland (Lothian being the region least affected).

By the eleventh century Cumbric/British and Pictish were either dead or moribund, and Gaelic had come to its peak in terms of expansion. The situation did not remain stable for long. The Anglian linguistic invasion began to gain ground especially from the twelfth century and by c. 1300 English or Scots was probably the usual language of land-owning classes in Strathclyde, Central Scotland and the east coast north to Buchan, while it had gained ground strongly in the trading burghs generally. Gaelic would have continued for some time to be the language of other classes. But from the thirteenth century onwards there has been a slow contraction of the area of Gaelic speech. Some of this contraction is relatively recent, for Gaelic was spoken in Galloway and Carrick into the seventeenth century (and possibly the eighteenth), in Angus and on Loch Lomondside into the nineteenth, in Donside and Deeside into the twentieth, and both in Deeside and in many places in Perthshire, Morayshire, and the east Highlands generally it has weakened or disappeared in recent living memory. At the 1971 Census there were just under 90,000 Gaelic speakers in Scotland, and this figure, for the first time this century, showed a rise, which is to be explained by the substantial body of learners of Gaelic in recent decades. The areas of greatest native Gaelic strength are the Outer Isles, with parts of Skye, parts of Islay, and the northwest coast from Kintail to Durness. Gaelic, since the eighteenth century, has also had a colonial off-shoot in Nova Scotia, but this is largely undifferentiated from Scottish Gaelic.

There has been very little carry-over of vocabulary from the earlier Celtic languages used in Scotland, to Gaelic. There is a small number of British loanwords, the most used being *monadh* 'mountain, moor', and as small a number of Pictish (the impolite *pit* being the best example). But it is very likely that aspects of Gaelic syntax, such as the preference for analytic verbal constructions of the type *tha e a' tighinn*, show either the influence of British/Cumbric/Pretenic Pictish on Gaelic or the influence of an early substratum on all these languages. And such processes never entirely stop, so that Scots and English as spoken in Scotland also show influence from these Celtic languages spoken so long and so widely in the country.

D. S. Thomson

Celtic Plainchant. The 13th century Inchcolm Antiphoner and Sprouston Breviary contain chants in honour of Celtic saints Columba and Kentigern respectively. The former contains unique material, some of it probably originating in Iona and composed as early as the 7th century. The close structural links between music and text are typical of early Hiberno-Latin styles. The music is tuneful, makes use of a wide vocal range, and is frequently highly patterned. The chants for St Kentigern are likewise tuneful and wide-ranging but have yet to be checked for concordances.

J. Purser

Chalmers, Thomas (1780–1847), one of the outstanding Scottish Church leaders of the nineteenth century who more than any other single individual altered the course of his country's ecclesiastical history. Born at Anstruther into a merchant family, he entered St Andrews University as a student at the early age of 11 years. His early career as a student in Arts and Divinity, as assistant to the Professor of Mathematics, and as minister of the parish of Kilmenny, shows him to be one of exceptional ability and 'supremely bent on achieving what to him was the most desirable of all goals, literary distinction and the plaudits of the learned'.

A religious crisis in his life about 1810, transforming him into an enthusiastic evangelical, had a profound effect on his preaching, made him an ardent advocate of foreign missions, and an exponent of self-help as the surest remedy against pauperism. His ever-widening reputation secured for him the presentation to the Tron Kirk, one of the largest churches in Glasgow, where over four years his sermons brought him universal acclaim as a popular preacher confronting in the pulpit the practical problems of a fast-developing city in times of increasing material wealth. As a pastor he devoted himself to the welfare of the people of the parish, sought to provide for their religious needs, especially those of the poor and the lower working classes and their children, and thereby to make his ministry an instrument of spiritual and social benefit. Simultaneously, he was emerging on the national scene as the potential leader of the evangelical party.

To obtain fuller scope for his pastoral work he was instrumental in securing the erection of the new parish of St John's, where he confidently attempted from 1819 to 1823 to combat the twin evils of the contemporary fast-developing industrial society, poverty and irreligion, by establishing an effective all-embracing parochial ministry exercised by minister, elders and deacons. St John's provided the base for a social experiment which involved pastoral oversight of virtually every aspect of the life of the parish aimed at eliminating poor relief (except for the truly needy) by encouraging independence, self-reliance and self-help. In recent years Chalmers's methods have come under criticism, but in its day his social reform plan was claimed to have in its success exceeded Chalmers's own hopes and he should at least be given credit for tackling a prevailing problem even if today he may justly be accused of seeking to apply outdated remedies for unprecedented conditions.

To the surprise of all who knew the man and his ministry, Chalmers, seemingly at 'the zenith of his usefulness to the Church', accepted appointment to the Chair of Moral Philosophy in the United College in the University of St Andrews with a view to pursuing among other objectives his interest in political economy, stimulated by his work in Glasgow and his extensive enquiry into the system of poor relief in England, and in the hope of being able from a professorial chair to exercise a more extensive Christian ministry. At St Andrews, by his evangelical role rather than on account of the originality of his lecturing, he exerted a profound effect on undergraduates, many of whom either entered the ministry or went as missionaries overseas. From this time dates his interest in the wider work of the Church and in particular in its General Assemblies, to which as an elder he was annually elected by the Burgh of Anstruther. His translation to the Chair of Divinity in Edinburgh University in 1828 widened still further the scope of his influence. After the chilly reception afforded his *Political Economy in connection with the Moral State and Moral Prospects of Society*, he concentrated his attention on his theological and allied writings which, despite contemporary success, made no lasting contribution to their subject.

Voluminous as his publications were and continuous throughout his life, it was as the emerging leader of the evangelical party within the Church that he was to exercise the deepest influence. Upholding on the one hand the principle of an established Church, and advocating on the other the abolition of the legal disabilities of dissenters in England and evangelicals in Scotland, he was forced in time to make a painful choice. In the Ten Years' Conflict leading to the Disruption of the Church in Scotland in 1843, he played a dominant role in seeking to secure for the Church freedom from those legal ties that were held to obstruct her progress and prevent her in the eyes of evangelicals from meeting satisfactorily the needs and challenges of the rapidly changing face of Scotland. Pressure of events, political and social as well as ecclesiastical, probably drove him further than he would have desired. The attempted and at one time fully expected solution, viz. the replacing of the established Church by a national Free Church of Scotland with congregations and schools in every parish, which might have justified so much zeal and a measure of sacrifice, was not, however, accomplished. In time the offending obstacles in the established Church, such as patronage, were largely removed. The Free Church as a separate thriving institution, adorned with many distinguished evangelical preachers, literary and theological scholars, profoundly affected Scottish life in many parishes for nearly 100 years and was largely the creation of Thomas Chalmers. Nevertheless, at the same time it introduced into the Scottish ecclesiastical scene an element of contentiousness similar to that that was scarcely ever absent from Chalmers's extraordinary life.

J. K. Cameron

Chambers, William and Robert, (1800–1883; 1802–1871) publishers and authors. Born in Peebles, the brothers moved to Edinburgh with the family when still very young and each established himself, at first very humbly, as a bookseller in the city when still in his teens. They were both eager readers and as small boys in Peebles had stored their minds with the books in the town's small circulating library and the articles in the

Encyclopaedia Britannica which their father had bought. William branched out from bookselling into printing, and in 1821 the brothers produced their first periodical, *Kaleidoscope*, or *Edinburgh Literary Amusement*, which ran only until January 1822. William printed it and Robert wrote most of it. The brothers were responsive to the popular educational movement of the 1820s and this led them to a number of enterprises notably the production of Chambers's *Edinburgh Journal* (later *Chambers' Journal of Literature, Science and the Arts*) which rapidly reached an unprecedented circulation of 50,000 copies. Robert in particular amassed enormous quantities of information which he proceeded to pour out in vivid and lively prose not only in essays for the *Journal* and elsewhere but also in encyclopaedias, dictionaries and other works of reference. Among these are the *Cyclopaedia of English Literature* (1842–44), written largely by Robert himself, which remained a standard work well into the twentieth century, *Biographical Dictionary of Eminent Scotsmen* (1833–35), *Popular Rhymes of Scotland* (1826), *Songs of Scotland Prior to Burns* (1862) and *Domestic Annals of Scotland* (1859–61). His *Life of Robert Burns* (1851), as revised by William Wallace in 1896, is still an authoritative work, while his *Traditions of Edinburgh* (1824) remains invaluable to any historian of the city. Perhaps Robert's most remarkable work was *Vestiges of the Natural History of Creation*, published anonymously in 1843–46, which created a sensation by developing arguments from geology for something like a Darwinian view of the development of the earth and its inhabitants. Seven volumes of Robert's *Select Writings* were published in 1847. W. and R. Chambers, the publishing firm founded by the brothers, still flourishes, and is best known for its dictionaries.

D. Daiches

Chartism. Following closely upon the revival of a reform agitation in England came the re-emergence in Scotland in 1838 of a popular movement for the reform of parliament by means of an extended franchise, annual parliaments elected by secret ballots, a more equal distribution of seats, payment of MPs and the end of property qualifications. The movement build upon the strong radical traditions that dated back to the notorious trials of the 1790s, and many old middle-class radicals, who had campaigned with the Whigs to achieve the first Reform Act of 1832, reappeared at public meetings. It reflected the disenchantment of many with the activities of the Whig governments and disappointment at the failure of an extended franchise to bring the rapid achievement of middle-class aims. This new campaign, coming as it did at a time of rising unemployment and weak trade unionism, produced a response among the working class. It particularly attracted those urban craftsmen who had for long been feeling the impact of industrialization, with its erosion of craft traditions, new patterns of work and general undermining of the status and independence of the artisan. Meetings were held and committees formed throughout the country to demand the implementation of the 'People's Charter', and at least three newspapers promoted the cause. Tensions existed from the start between

extremists and moderates. On the extreme wing was Dr John Taylor, editor of the *New Liberator* and an associate of Feargus O'Connor, while more moderate figures, like John Fraser in Edinburgh and Abram Duncan in Glasgow, reflected the majority views of the Scottish branches by aligning with Thomas Attwood and the middle-classed Birmingham movement. At an early stage some sections of the Scottish movement repudiated the use of violence to achieve their end and committed themselves firmly to a 'moral and constitutional agitation'. In practice, however, no group in Scotland was seriously contemplating violent action and the divisions of opinion were largely about language, tone and personalities rather than about actual tactics.

Chartism quickly became a real political force in Scotland with, by the start of 1839, around 80 local associations, a flourishing press and a network of itinerant lecturers. Delegates were sent to national conventions in London and Birmingham, where they were concerned to dissociate the Scottish movement from the fiery language of the 'physical force men', especially from the proposed general strike and 'sacred month' of agitation. As a means of exerting pressure, Scottish activists tended to prefer exclusive dealing, the boycotting of non-radical shopkeepers and abstention from highly-taxed items, such as alcohol.

It was a measure of the success of the movement that the *Scottish Chartist Circular*, first issued in September 1839 under the editorship of the handloom weavers' leader William Thomson, had, in its first year, a weekly circulation of over 22,000. It sought to create a unifying focus for the various associations but quickly came under attack from those who believed in the tactic of 'peaceably if we may, forcibly if we must'. There was objection to the petitioning approach advocated by the *Circular* and by the short-lived Central Committee for Scotland. While there can have been no more than a tiny handful in Scotland who seriously considered arming for revolution, an astonishing amount of verbiage was expended in debating whether or not the reform associations should renounce the right to use violence. In many ways, the endless debates on the issue did little more than fill a vacuum of inactivity. However, while undoubtedly a majority of the leadership stressed their respectability and 'moral suasion' was constantly proclaimed, violent outbreaks, such as the Newport 'Rising' in Wales tended to revitalize the Scottish movement and to bring in new members. Also, extremists like George Julian Harney, whose 'savage harangues' terrified the moderates, found ready audiences in Scotland in 1840.

While the leadership debated tactics, for many of the working class the chartist movement offered, not some rather distant political reform, but an opportunity to assert a class identity through their own organizations. From the political movement there grew cooperative societies, social clubs and, most significantly, chartist churches and schools, where the social control and middle-class domination of orthodox churches could be avoided. Lay-preachers went so far as to offer marriage, baptism and communion in such chartist churches. These spread to many towns and for long remained the most vital part of the movement. The schools included evening classes, libraries, debating societies and Sunday schools for adults and children. Moral improvement through temperance reform was another cause that attracted many of the same people who were involved in chartism, though, inevitably, it provided yet another point of dissension.

A further assertion of chartist independence from middle-class domination or control came with the adoption of a policy of disrupting meetings of the Anti-Corn-Law League, although many leading reformers had in fact been founders of the agitation against the Corn Laws in Scotland. By 1841 the tone of much of Scottish chartism was firmly against class collaboration with chartist candidates standing in the general election of that year in opposition to both Whigs and Tories. O'Connor made a triumphant Scottish tour. Nonetheless, bitter personal and ideological divisions continued to weaken the movement. Within a year most chartist newspapers had disappeared, funds were low and, although some chartist activists did seek to give leadership in the industrial troubles that arose during the economic depression of 1842, there was a lack of coordination in what was done. By the end of that year, only a small number of local organizations remained, though the ideas and the class consciousness continued to flourish in those working-class communities where chartist churches contributed to the creation of a distinct class identity.

Only when missionaries from south of the Border undertook tours were there moments of enthusiasm and activity among the chartists after 1842. Even 1848 brought only a slight, short-lived revival. On these occasions there was clear evidence of the continuing existence of a network of small chartist associations in towns and villages throughout the country and a visit of Bronterre O'Brien or Ernest Jones could still pack halls in the 1850s. A variety of alternative radical campaigns did by then however offer other centres of interest to the politically aware, while improved economic conditions alleviated some working-class discontents. The ideas lingered on and some of the supporters of chartism were to influence many of a younger generation.

W. H. Fraser

Children's Games—full of rhymes and tunes—must be the only well left of an oral tradition like the ballads. Not many years ago I found that the jumping ropes even kept alive the ballad of the 'Cruel Mother', calling her the 'Green Lady'.

There was a lady dressed in green
  Puir ludo lydo
There was a lady dressed in green
Down at the greenwood side O!

Verses tell the story. 'She had a baby in her arms', 'She stuck a penknife in its heart', 'She took a cloth to wipe the blood', 'The more she wiped the more it bled', 'There came a knocking at the door ...'

'There were two policemen at the door
Down at the greenwood side O!

'What did you do to your baby last night?' 'I stuck a penknife in its heart ...'

They took her to the jail and hung her on a nail
Down at the greenwood side O!

That was the end of the lady in green
Puir ludo lydo Iydo
That was the end of the lady in green
Down at the greenwood side O!

For long enough the three places for playing were the street, the back-green and the school playground. Though 'bools' still show up in the 'boolie season' you no longer see laddies in the street knuckling 'glessies' or 'dollickers'. Not with fast cars flashing past. 'Girds' and 'peeries' are alike impossible. But in quieter back-streets the traditional games flourish as much as ever.

On pavements there the lassies get down on their hands and knees—the first hint of spring—to chalk their peeverie beds.

Nowadays 'Aeroplane Beds' seem the rage but 'Plain Beds' hold their own—with the peever skiffing for 'Oneie' 'Twoie' 'Threeie' 'Fourie' 'Fiveie' and 'Sixie'.

And how about 'Tig' and 'Hide-and-Seek?' Over two dozen different games of tig—*Chainie Tig, Hospital Tig, Shadow Tig* ...

As for Hide-and-Seek, Hessy or Hideie-Go without a doubt the classic game is *Kick-the-Can* just as *Hal-a-levoy* is the top game for laddies while the favourite mixed game is *Catch-a-Kiss, Kissie-Catch, Catch-Kissie, Kissie-Catchie or Catchie-Kissie!*

Before a game can start sides have to be chosen, and 'Chapping-out Rhymes' help to decide. *One Potato, Two Potato, Queen, Queen, Caroline* ... there are hundreds of them.

Eentie teentie teen tie tithery mithery bamfileerie
  Hover-dover—you are out!

And skipping is endlessly rich in chants, rhymes and songs. For 'Plain Skipping' alone, never mind 'French Ropes' or 'German Ropes'. The most popular tunes are *Down in the Valley where the Green Grass Crows, I'm a Little Orphan Girl, Grannie in the Kitchen, I've a Sweetheart in America, I'm the Monster of Loch Ness* ...

But 'Bumps' or 'Fierys' is the skipping game most chosen. In plain skipping—your feet off the ground—the rope turns once but in bumps it makes a swift double turn. Where the words are stressed—that's where the skipper bumps.

Rabbie Burns was born in *Ayr*
Now he's in Trafalgar *Square*
If you want to see him *there*
Jump on a bus and skip the *fare*.

Next we come to games using a 'stottie ba'—games that only stone-and-lime or streets paved with Caithness flagstones could inspire. The oldest rhyme here is 'One Two Three a-Leerie' where you stot the ball on the ground, but stotting smartly against a tenement or playground wall—'Single Ballie' or 'Double Ballie'—is much more in favour.

Plainie, clappie
Rollie-pin, to backie
Right hand, left hand
High si-toosh, low si-toosh
Telephone the answer
Touch my heel, touch my toe
Through ye go, big birly-O!

Last but not least the playground delights in its Singing Games, the best-known being:

The wind, the wind, the wind blows high
The snow comes falling from the sky
Marion Dickson says she'll die
For the want of the golden city

She is handsome, she is pretty
She is the girl of the golden city
She is handsome, one two three
Come and tell me who shall be ...

Every school or street prefers its own variation, and since children are realists we sometimes hear:

She is ugly, she is pretty
She is the witch of the tin-can city.

And the old ring-games keep to the fore. *Poor Tommy is Dead, Here's a Poor Widow, In and Out the Dusting Bluebells, The Big Ship Sails through the Eely-Alley-O ...*

On the mountain stands a lady
Who she is I cannot tell
All she wants is gold and silver
All she wants is a nice young man
So call in ...

With the variation

On the mountain stands a castle
With its owner Frankenstein
And his daughter, Pansy Potter
She's my only Valentine
So call in ...

Scottish children, for their happiness, are clearly best left to their own devices. In the classroom they put up with a whole fandangle, outside of it, in the playground they can dance their own picture of things.

This way Valerie, that way Valerie
This way Valerie—all day long!
That way Valerie, this way Valerie
That way Valerie—all day long!
Shortman's Lizzie, Shortman's Lizzie
Shortman's Lizzie—all day long!
Here comes another one, just like the other one
Here comes another one—all day long!

J. T. R. Ritchie

Church before 1560, The. Christianity in southern Scotland appears to have been part of the legacy of the Romans. They left some kind of organized base which made possible the celebrated missionary work of such men as Ninian, perhaps Patrick (and through him certainly Columba), Kentigern and Cuthbert. This was a long story over three centuries *c.*400— *c.*700 AD, which left Scotland with its gallery of sainted heroes and an amalgam of Irish and Roman religious traditions of Church organization. By about 750 the areas of modern Scotland then occupied by the Scots, Picts, Britons and English all supported a Christian clergy, and civilization had sufficiently advanced for artists to be employed to produce sculptures of stunning quality on Christian themes and probably also the famous illuminated gospel-book now known as the *Book of Kells.*

The occupation of the Western and Northern Isles by pagan Norwegian settlers from about 800 led to the detaching of these areas politically from Scotland until 1266 and 1468–69 respectively; but the new master race soon adopted Christianity and thereafter kept abreast culturally with the rest of Europe, even if linked for centuries more influentially with Norway and Ireland than with mainland Scotland. There until the late eleventh century the organized Church necessarily became more limited in its activities for a time while a general sense of the importance of family interests over religious ones led to a secularization of much Church property.

Then for about four centuries from the time of Queen Margaret (d.1093) the clergy of Scotland shared with the Western Church as a whole under papal leadership in an urge to have 'liberty' in managing the affairs of their Church as their own. In truth they never succeeded in eliminating altogether what was now regarded as the separable 'lay' interest of king and landed magnates. It was indeed with the enthusiastic support of such influential people (especially King David I, 1124–53) that new material resources were made available for a major spiritual revival. There emerged an elaborate system of diocesan administration under the bishops with priests dispersed in a network of parishes, and there was experimentation on a hugely expensive scale with the newly fashionable international orders of monks and friars. Not only did the clergy come to control endowments in land on a very large scale: they also came to be entitled to an income from teinds, which amounted to the vast sum of one-tenth of the nation's produce and profit each year. It is no wonder that by the later Middle Ages the clergy, though a comparatively small group, were able to pay two-fifths of national taxation.

Much effort was now needed to manage this property and income. Monasteries and bishops required agricultural tenants on their lands and employed tradesmen of all kinds. Thus the Church contributed materially to the economic development of the country, especially in sheep-farming, coal-mining and trading in general. More connected with religion was the use made of the wealth thus received or generated for elaborate building projects on a hitherto unprecedented scale. There were by the twelfth century more than a thousand parish churches to be maintained. In addition great churches and residential buildings were now thought necessary to accommodate communities at cathedrals and in monasteries. The thirteenth century was a period of especially ambitious projects, though rebuilding was continuous until the fifteenth. It was conspicuous expenditure which must surely reflect the spiritual values of the age: the daily prayers of respected clergy in splendid surroundings were important.

But the clergy were involved in many other activities. At the 'tradesman' level were the bulk of parish priests, who had been trained locally just enough to be entrusted with cure of souls, but who spent most of their time as farmers of their glebes. Much more 'professional' were the more highly trained clergy employed in Church administration at deanery, archdeaconry and diocese levels. Similar men are often found exercising their expertise in the households of prelates and lay magnates, and more importantly in the service of the central government, in council and parliament, and in diplomatic work. There were many openings too for careers in the law, whether locally as notaries available for all kinds of transaction or as practitioners in the many Church courts which offered justice to the whole community. And there was a great variety of educational, medical and welfare services in which clergy were involved. The Church was only partly concerned with religion.

Until 1472 there was no archbishop in Scotland, so that most of the bishops came equally and directly under Rome in a way that was unique in the Western Church. In consequence Scots were often obliged to travel on business to the papal court, and the more ambitious clergy regularly obtained papal backing for their careers. This applies particularly to those who went to universities abroad from the mid twelfth century onwards. The leading Scottish clergy therefore were characteristically well travelled and well informed on continental affairs and intellectual developments. New ideas and new books were quickly known in Scotland, and the clergy were well equipped to draw attention regularly to external standards of thought and conduct. With their monopoly of clerical skills and their elitist but unifying Latin culture they played a large share in holding the diverse parts of Scotland together. Both as historians and as framers of current policy they were central to national development.

But the late fifteenth century brought a resurgence of lay desire to control Church resources once again more openly for secular advantage. As the Church lost its vaunted 'liberty' many 'professional' clergy lost respect for failing to protest. At the same time there was a somewhat hectic descent into religiosity arising from a much increased enthusiasm among the laity for endowing the perpetual celebration of masses for souls in purgatory. Too many of the 'tradesmen' clergy were now involved in a practice which came to be questioned by thoughtful and opportunist reformers alike. Very few in Scotland had listened to the followers of John Wyclif early in the fifteenth century: the Church was then serving satisfactory purposes. But once the clergy generally were in disrepute it was to be different with John Knox.

D. E. R. Watt

Church after 1560, The. The sanction by Parliament in 1560 of Reformed doctrine together with the abolition of the authority, jurisdiction, and worship of the Roman Church, provided legal recognition of the ecclesiastical changes that had been taking place in various parts of the country in the preceding years, particularly in the east-coast burghs. There reformed congregations had already been organized with the cooperation of the civil authorities. A long way had yet to be traversed and many difficulties encountered before a Reformed Church of Scotland was secured. Foremost amongst these difficulties was the failure of Church and the State to agree on the relations that should obtain between them and consequently on the form of ecclesiastical polity—a failure that brought with it intense political strife.

During the uncertain years of Mary's unhappy reign, the reformers set about radical reorganization of the Church largely on the lines of continental reformed Protestantism as these were concurrently being followed in France. Congregations with kirk sessions and ministers or readers were organized in the parishes; provincial synods and general assemblies were held and implicitly recognized by the State; and ecclesiastical jurisdiction maintained despite the fact that parliament had not accepted the *First Book of Discipline* drawn up towards the close of 1560. Nevertheless, five superintendents had been appointed in accordance with its recommendations.

During the reign of James VI (1567–1625) the requirements of the monarchy for strengthening and of the Church for financial provision and security led to various attempts to introduce a form of episcopal government, which were for a time abandoned in favour of a reformed or presbyterian polity, but which were effected in 1610. King James VI's policy of bringing the Church's ceremonial practices and administrative structure into conformity with those of the Church in England was carried further by Charles I. As a result of his ill advised attempts to introduce a liturgy and canons without securing the cooperation of the Church in its General Assemblies, the king found himself in open conflict with his Scottish people. They were, in fact, coming to a greater realization of the political as well as the religious consequences of the union of the crowns, and at the same time were nursing deep-seated suspicion, indeed fear and hatred, of all that savoured of Roman Catholicism. Opposition to the royal ecclesiastical policy was symbolized in the signing of the National Covenant in 1638 by nobles, barons, burgesses and ministers who united in defence 'of the True Reformed Religion and of our Liberties, Laws and Estates'. In the Church it took the form of violently rejecting episcopacy in favour of the presbyterian polity of earlier years usually associated with Andrew Melville. Fundamental in the Church's opposition was its adherence to the notion of an independent jurisdiction exercised nevertheless in cooperation with the civil authorities. King Charles regarded the Covenanters (q.v.) as rebels. Civil war ensued. The king's political opponents in England and the Covenanters in Scotland were encouraged to look upon each other as allies in their political and ecclesiastical aspirations. The ensuing cooperation led in the religious field to Scottish participation in the drawing up of the Confession of Faith and the Shorter and Larger Catechisms by the Westminster Assembly of Divines. These documents embodying a rigorous Calvinism (q.v.) were later adopted by General Assemblies and had a profound and enduring effect upon the theological complexion of Scottish life.

The bitter strife that followed the execution of the king is as much part of political as of ecclesiastical history. It had the effect of drawing much of the Church's attention to its relations with the State and of emphasizing ecclesiology at the expense of other aspects of doctrine central to reformed Christianity. Still it has often been highlighted as 'the heroic period in the history of national Church' and has left its mark on national literature and character.

The Restoration brought no permanent settlement of the Church's polity. King Charles was bent on establishing a form of Church government that was 'most suitable to monarchial government and most complying with the public peace and quiet of the kingdom'. That meant the acceptance of the royal supremacy in all things and the reintroduction of episcopacy. The form of polity containing both episcopal and presbyterian elements which emerged might, in calmer times and at the hands of more skillful advocates, have been a success. Instead repression and rebellion left as an inheritance to the Scottish people a bitter detestation, as much political as religious, of episcopacy.

The Revolution settlement and the slow emergence of a more tolerant attitude secured a brighter future for the Church now recognized by Parliament as presbyterian. 'Moderation', King William informed the General Assembly, 'is what religion enjoins, neighbouring Churches expect of you, and we recommend to you'. And 'Moderation' became the dominant characteristic for the next 150 years. Those who hankered for the Puritanism of the covenanting period, who rebelled against the more liberalizing tendencies in philosophy and theology that were beginning to show themselves in 'the Church by Law Established', and who saw in the operation of the revived Patronage Act of 1712 the source of all their ills, found themselves compelled to secede and set up rival voluntary congregations, remaining Calvinist in doctrine and presbyterian in polity. They formed, however, a distinct minority.

Throughout the eighteenth century the Church increasingly came under the direction of intellectual leaders influenced by the Enlightment such as William Robertson (1721–1793), Principal of Edinburgh University. The relaxation of the strictly held Calvinist theology was not easily accomplished. But the General Assembly grew weary of heresy trials. Towards the end of the century Hugh Blair (1718–1800), one of the ministers of Edinburgh whose sermons were translated into a number of European languages and were read by Johnson 'with more than approbation', was encouraging his congregation to 'cultivate humanity' and to remember 'the natural equality of men'. In St Andrews George Hill (1750–1819), the successor of Robertson as leader of the Moderates, upheld 'extensive information and enlightened criticism' as the 'handmaids of religion'.

Not all in the Church, however, were upholders of Moderatism, later described by its detractors as a kind of 'spiritual frost'. A renewed emphasis on spiritual experience, which can be traced to the rise of Pietism on the Continent, had profoundly affected England and was in the first half of the nineteenth century making considerable headway in Scotland. Changes in economic and political life brought about in part by the new industrialism were also affecting the life of the Church. Evangelicals under the leadership of Thomas Chalmers (q.v.) found themselves, in their plans for ecclesiastical development, thwarted by the operation of the Patronage Act and the decisions of the civil courts, and brought about the Disruption of the Church (q.v.) in 1843. They formed the Free Church of Scotland with the express purpose of replacing the Established Church; rival congregations were set up in every parish and an extensive building operation undertaken throughout the land to provide churches supported on a voluntary but national basis. But the Church of Scotland more than weathered the storm. The Patronage Act was abolished and efforts to secure disestablishment failed. In 1900 the majority of the Free and seceding Churches came together to form the United Free Church, which has been described as 'strong, high principled, enterprising, generous ... loyal to the past but alive to the present, doing splendid work in theology, preaching and pastoral care'.

The changing conditions of the early twentieth century brought about by the Great War and the industrial unrest challenged the necessity of an independent witness extravagant in manpower and financial resources, and led to the union of the United Free Church with the Church of Scotland in 1928. The way had been prepared by Parliament's recognition in the Declaratory Acts of the Church's inherent and independent jurisdiction. The work of Churches, which had extended through overseas missions into almost all parts of the world, was severely checked by the Second World War. Since then the Church has been challenged by a new tide of secularism, and has found it necessary greatly to reduce the number of its congregations. Despite this fact and the increasing dependence upon the voluntary resources of the people which the union entailed, the Church has sought to maintain its national responsibility and has given strong support and valued leadership to contemporary movements towards a more extensive cooperation among Churches of all denominations.

See also Catholicism since the Reformation.

J. K. Cameron

Clans. Members of the Highland clans, in the days of their greatest influence, were bound together by one or both of the ties mentioned in the succinct words of an Act of James VI's Parliament in 1587—'be pretence of blude or place of thair duelling'.

The clan (Gaelic *clann*—children) was primarily a family, and in theory at least the chief was the father of it. After him came his immediate kin, consisting of younger brothers and uncles and junior branches who had been given part of the ancestral lands to maintain themselves. As feudal practice became merged with the old patriarchal system, this widening ancestral lands to maintain themselves. As feudal practice became merged with the old patriarchal system, this widening 'family' was further extended to include all those living on the chief's lands who acknowledged his authority and accepted his protection. Most of them were people of native birth and ancestry, and in some clans both chief and clan would be of mainly Scottish stock; but as new leaders came in they too would form a powerful nucleus round which men would gather. Besides Norse and Irish incomers, between the eleventh and fourteenth centuries displacements caused by rebellion, and the victory of the Bruce party over those who supported Balliol and the Comyns, brought men of Norman blood (Gordon and Fraser), Bretons (Stewart), and Flemings (Murray and Sutherland) into the Highland area. Frequent intermarriage both in and outside the family group set up a complicated web of relationships which further strengthened the clan, and made it hard to tell whether kinship was real or fancied.

Chiefship was not 'elective', but the old method of choosing the most suitable leader in peace and war from a limited family group lingered on, particularly in the west. The Macleans bypassed the nearest heir in James IV's time, and so did the MacDonalds of Clanranald in the next reign—both sanctioned by charters from the crown. The succession of an eldest son had obvious advantages, and if he was too young or otherwise unfit a 'tutor' could be appointed to lead the clan and administer the lands. Branch families held their lands by inheritance, and could give long-term feus or 'tacks' to substantial tenants, with shorter leases for lesser men; and there were occasions when these 'cadets' advised and even restrained their chief when he seemed to be acting against the best interests of the clan.

Surnames are sometimes thought to be the hallmark of the clans, but these were not in general use in the Highlands before the seventeenth century. Allan Cameron of Lochiel, who died in 1647, was known to his contemporaries as Allan macDonald Dubh, and his father as Donald Dubh macDonald vicEwen; such patronymic styles preserve a pedigree of several generations, and are still common in verbal tradition and everyday use. When surnames came to be required for legal documents, some took the name of their chief or a recognized variant of it, some 'froze' a patronymic form, and some names reflected occupations or personal characteristics, with the result that the same surname often figures among the followers of more than one chief.

As the royal power spread, chiefs were increasingly held responsible for the good conduct of their people; by the end of the sixteenth century, they had become answerable not only for their own tenants, but also for kinsmen living under other feudal superiors—who in turn could and sometimes did appeal to their distant chief for justice. As a chief's power depended on the number of his followers, pacts and alliances were common, and great confederacies were formed like the Lordship of the Isles and the Clan Chattan; but this could widen feuds as well as settle quarrels. Events of violence inevitably gain undue prominence in the records of a central government trying to curb disorder, and some of the worst atrocities were committed under colour of commissions from the king and privy council. For the gentler arts of peace one must turn to the poetry, songs and chronicles passed on by word of mouth, hear the music of the harp and bagpipe, or see the work of craftsmen carved in stone. The clan system—if such a word can properly be used of such a diverse structure—eventually fell before the impact of outside social and economic forces. The end was hastened, but not caused, by the clans' part in the civil wars of the seventeenth and eighteenth centuries, when such irregular forces could be used to support or to disrupt the state. The Jacobite risings of 1715 and 1745 did not find all the clans on one side, but the threat was strong enough to ensure that no government would dare to risk a repetition.

Modern clan societies, which lay more stress on surnames than their ancestors did, try to keep alive some of the pride and friendship of a kin-based society, and help to unite those of Highland descent throughout the world.

R. W. and J. M. Munro

Clarsach. This Gaelic term is now widely used to describe a variety of Celtic triangular-framed harps of varying size. The world's oldest depictions of triangular-framed harps are Pictish and date from as early as the 8th century. They may have been strung with horse-hair, and some depictions indicate a much larger harp than the seven or eight strings accommodated on the stone would imply. The Queen Mary and Lamont harps are the earliest (15th century) surviving instruments. They had about thirty metal strings which would have been plucked with the fingernails. Gut-strung harps played with the flesh are referred to from the 16th century. A variety of tunings was used, including overlapping tunings, and a small part of the repertoire survives in early 17th century transcriptions for lute, and in late 18th century sources. A clarsach player is known as a 'clarsair'.

J. Purser

Clearances, The. The word is usually reserved in Scottish historiography for the transfer and removals of Highland population by landowners in and after the 1790s. This specific use ignores the fact that considerable transfer of lowland population also took place in the course of the adoption of 'improvement' from 1770 onwards. It also adds confusion by mixing the transfer of tenants to new areas with their total expulsion from the area.

The early transfers of Highland population were responses to the idea of economic improvement of the late eighteenth century. They can be understood only in the light of a land law which provided very little in the way of tenant right. From the early seventeenth century Highland chiefs had been behaving as if they were also owners of the clan land. The law accepted this claim. As a result it was legally possible for chiefs or landowners to rearrange the holdings of their tenants as they wished, though before the '45 rebellion such actions were restrained by the need to keep the confidence of the clan and its military strength. After the '45 the deliberate attack of the British Parliament on the concept of chieftainship and, in some cases, the exile of the chiefs, hastened the change of chief into simple landowner, though many continued to exercise clan authority profitably in the raising of regiments for government service.

The landowners, often with government encouragement, made various attempts to bring into action new resources to enlarge the narrow base of the Highland economy. The main items in this policy were the linen industry, fishing, kelp manufacture and sheep. All but sheep proved, in the long run, unsuccessful. In the later eighteenth century the rapid growth of Highland population, in spite of bouts of emigration, brought an urgency to the search for new resources, as did the local famines which struck the Highlands area with increasing force in the late eighteenth and early nineteenth century. Unfortunately, whereas linen, fishing and kelp were all labour-intensive activities, sheep farming not only used very little labour directly but could not, on a large scale, be combined with the existing pattern of settlement, and it was on a large scale only that it was really profitable. It also required farming capital beyond the capacity of the existing peasantry. So where this type of farming came in, the sheep farm tended to be in the hands of a Lowland farmer, and to require not only the rough hill pastures of the old farming but also the better valley land on which the previous tenants had grown their cereal crops. Since the eighteenth century all recommendations for improvement had considered that the population, which at the time all wished to retain, would be of greater economic use on the coast than inland. So policy was to shift the population to the coast and to encourage it to mix farming with other activities. The inland area could then be used for sheep farming which would bring in a large rent.

The conspicuous adherent of this policy in the early nineteenth century was the vast Sutherland estate, where many of the big inland straths were 'cleared' for sheep and the bulk of the population placed on the coast to engage in fishing and in 'industries' that were to be developed with the aid of the wealth of the Marquis of Stafford's English estates. In the long run these developments were not economically successful, and in the short run the resentment created against the landowner was intense. In some particular cases, since the estate unwisely allowed some of its sub-factors to receive leases of the new sheep farms, the removals were carried through in a hurry before new holdings and houses on the coast were ready. Accusations of brutality were particularly made against Patrick Sellar, and though these were not proved in court they have entered into the popular image of these clearances.

The Sutherland estate had expected the peasantry to benefit from the changes in increased income and also in 'habits of industry'. Probably the material standard of living did improve, but the cultural shock and the failure of the new ventures to prosper largely nullified these benign but autocratic intentions. Other Highland landowners had not the same financial resources as the Sutherland estate, and many other 'clearances' were less public-spirited in interest and sometimes remarkably unfeeling in the way they were carried out. Most of them involved the decision to remove people totally from the land, and there are graphic descriptions of the grief and dismay this could cause. After the failure of the potato crop in 1846 the view that the population of the Highlands was too great for the resources, which had been gaining ground for 20 years, became generally accepted, and from then on in most parts there was pressure by landowners on the tenantry to leave, even where there were not clearances. The Sutherland estates also exercised such pressure on the cottars and endeavoured to prevent crofter holdings from being effectively subdivided by the presence of married sons on their parents' holding. Highland population fell steadily from the 1841 census until in 1951 it was back almost exactly to the level of 1755, though in a different pattern of settlement. It is not possible to say what proportion of the population loss, which was of course much larger than the actual fall in numbers (for the rate of natural increase was high), was due to voluntary movement away, and what to involuntary.

The resentment and land hunger of the crofters was not satisfied by the fall of population especially since by the second half of the nineteenth century much of the best land was included within sheep farms. Eventually disturbances in Skye in the early 1880s, always an area of resistance, over demands for enlarged holdings led to the focusing of public attention on the situation, the establishment of a royal commission under Lord Napier and Ettrick to investigate crofting and finally, in 1886, a major change in the law which gave the remaining peasantry a privileged position in law of secure tenure and controlled low rents. This did not prevent the crofting population from suffering considerable economic hardship at times, nor has it meant that crofts could be found for all that would wish to have them, but it made further clearance impossible. In any case by the 1880s much of the sheep farming had ceased to be profitable and there was less pressure on landowners to clear. On the other hand the possible use of the upper grounds as deer forest and the rents sport could command, made the return of sheep farmland to crofting unattractive to them. Land hunger therefore continued.

The strength of feeling over 'clearances' has owed much to the cultural, and, often, religious gulf between landowner and peasantry. It is noticeable that it was absentee landowners against whom feeling was strongest. Much of what at various times has been said about particular heartless episodes has not stood up well to investigation and is better evidence of the resentment the whole movement caused than of the actual events. There have developed a series of historical myths about the series of events: that the motive behind all clearance was simply greed on the part of landowners, that the condition of the peasantry before, in some eighteenth-century golden age, was good and its economic support adequate, that all clearances were accompanied with brutality and the burning down of houses of the people, that all emigration was the result of clearance, and that there were clearances for the purpose of creating deer forests. The story is a sorry enough one of economic failure, social inadequacy, class gulf and the harshness of concepts of property to make the myths an unnecessary elaboration.

　　R. Mitchison

Clearances, Verse of the. The Highland Clearances, one of the most emotive and searing movements in the history of Gaelic Scotland, fit into a wider Scottish, British and indeed larger pattern. They were preceded by the abortive military risings of 1715 and 1745, and by the repressive measures that followed these: the partial military occupation of the Highlands, the proscription of arms and Highland dress and the pipes, and the emasculation of the clan system. The clan chief became a landlord, and began to identify with other landlords not of his race or culture. Meantime the industrial revolution and the creation of an urban proletariat stimulated the demand both for labour and for manufactured clothing for an industrial populace, and from these economic stimuli, and the greed of those who had control of the land, there came the rise of sheepfarming and the clearance of the former tenantry. The Blackface and Cheviot sheep were already being introduced into Perthshire in the 1760s, while sheepfarming on a large scale appears in Mull and Ardgour and Lochaber and Glenelg and Sutherland towards the end of the eighteenth century.

　　Though there were earlier movements of population consequent on the introduction of sheep, the main clearances took place in the nineteenth century, e.g. in Sutherland in the first two decades, in South Uist and in Park, Lewis, in the 1820s and 1830s, in Skye about the same time. These movements were naturally referred to in song, both anonymous and of known authorship. Duncan Ban Macintyre comments on this in his 'Oran nam Balgairean', saying that 'every customary practice in the Highlands has changed, and become so unnatural'; Ailean Dall MacDougal in 'Oran nan Ciobairean Gallda' 'Song of the Lowland Shepherds' concentrates on the shepherds; John Maclean of Tiree shows us the Gaelic emigrant adjusting to life on the Nova Scotian terrain. John MacLachlan of Rahoy sings of the desolation and bitterness of the Morven clearances, William Livingstone of the Islay ones, John Smith of the clearances of Uig, Lewis, Mary Macpherson of those of Skye. In these latter instances, from the second half of the nineteenth century, the poets become involved in the struggle for rights of land tenure: this is the most militant phase, contrasting vividly with the resignation of much of the earlier clearance verse.

　　Naturally there is a good deal of nostalgia in this verse, but the best of it has some realistic description of what the new landscape had become, and brings some political penetration and moral indignation to bear on the events and on the motives of individuals and governments. Probably the most powerful poets involved were John Smith, especially in his 'Spiorad a' Charthannais' / 'The Spirit of Kindliness', and William Livingstone, e.g. in 'Fios thun a' Bhàird' / 'A message to the Poet', but the most popular was Mary Macpherson or Màiri Mhor nan Oran, of Skye, and a few of her songs are still sung with great

acceptance. In general the verse associated with the Clearances is of interest mainly for its social and historical comment or for its attraction as song.

　　D. S. Thomson

Coal Industry, The. Coal has been mined on an economic scale in Scotland since at least the thirteenth century, the earliest sites being close to the Forth, such as the estates of Newbattle Abbey. After the Reformation exploitation of the easily accessible seams gradually intensified, the fuel finding a ready outlet in Edinburgh ('auld Reekie') and through seasale. (Scotland exported coal to both the Continent and subsequently Ireland, but quantities became substantial only in the nineteenth century. Before this, competition from Newcastle severely limited the Scottish share of the North Sea trade.) Most mines long remained small and technically backward, though notable exceptions exist. Sir George Bruce's colliery at Culross was widely famed around 1600 and saw possibly the earliest British example of the employment of the Egyptian wheel in mining. It was visited by John Taylor, the 'water poet', and probably by James VI in 1617.

　　During the eighteenth century coal extraction expanded markedly in response to growing demand from a rising urban population and a widening circle of coal-using industries. Accurate output figures are not available until 1854, but production probably increased from under 400,000 tons in 1700 to almost 2 million tons in 1800. Traditionally related industries such as salt distillation continued to consume much inferior coal, but increasingly from 1750 the rising tide of industrialization brought new and more insistent demands. The most momentous was iron-making, following the introduction of coke-smelting to Scotland in 1760 by Carron Company. By 1808 the iron industry alone accounted for at least 250,000 tons of coal. Technologically, too, Scots coal mining made many advances during this century, though it remained well behind England's great northern coalfield. Steam pumping was introduced from England in c. 1719 and although the diminutive average size of Scottish enterprises initially curtailed its applicability, there are known to have been 70 to 80 steam engines at Scots collieries by 1800. Horse waggonways improved the surface transport of the largest concerns from 1722 onwards, whilst the best equipped mines had by the Napoleonic Wars installed underground railways and steam winding. Longwall extraction, brought to Carron's mines by Shropshire colliers, was already spreading. Among the key entrepreneurs in these developments were the Clerks of Penicuik—especially Sir John II (1676–1755), Sir James (d. 1782) and John Clerk of Eldin (1728–1812), the ninth Earl of Dundonald (1748–1831), the Cadell family of Grange, Dr John Roebuck (1718–94), Robert Reid Cuninghame of Auchenharvie (d. 1812) and William Dixon (1753–1824). Robert Bald (1776–1861), who published his *General View of the Coal Trade of Scotland* in 1808, may be regarded as the first great professional Scottish expert on mining. By the early nineteenth century the more substantial concerns were generally owned by iron masters (a trend which was consolidated after 1828 with the coming of the hot-blast) while the traditional estate mine declined rapidly in relative importance.

Great changes also occurred in social structure. The increased demand for coal (at times almost a 'famine' in Edinburgh) intensified the already existing labour shortage and called in question the institution of collier serfdom. This peculiar system, based on an amalgam of estate custom and certain Acts of the Scottish Parliament (notably the Act of 1606), had attempted to stamp out labour poaching and desertion and had the effect of tying mine employees to their masters for life. Scottish jurists tended to defend this adscription and periodic challenges to it in the Court of Session seldom succeeded. It was mainly the hope (especially by the new coal and iron companies) that a free labour market would encourage better recruitment that led to the eventual abolition of mining bondage. Emancipation was accomplished by Acts of 1775 and 1799, but such was the lingering stigma of slavery that labour remained scarce until the immigration of the Irish eased the situation from c. 1820. The underground employment of females, chiefly as coal 'bearers' in the geologically difficult edge seams adjoining the Firth of Forth persisted until 1 March 1843, despite the trenchant criticism of Robert Bald. The Mines Act of 1842 provided for the end of this pernicious system, though the measure was not welcomed by all the beneficiaries because of the fear of lower family earnings resulting.

The nineteenth and early twentieth centuries witnessed an unprecedented growth in coal production and the emergence of powerful dynasties of iron—and coalmasters (e.g. the Dixons and especially the Bairds of Gartsherrie) who dominated the industry. Output was 7.4 million tons in 1854 and thereafter rose steadily (discounting a few checks) to reach an all-time peak of 42.5 million tons in 1913. The labour force grew commensurately from around 40,000 in 1866 to a summit of just under 150,000 (coal miners exclusively) in 1921. Scotland was always a long way behind England's great northern coalfield as a producer, and was overtaken by Wales in 1878 and Yorkshire in 1913, but she nevertheless survived as a very important field until quite recent times. Indeed, in the history of machine mining Scotland can claim to have been in the British vanguard, forced as she was by thin seams to explore more cost-effective methods. Where Britain as a whole cut scarcely 1 per cent of her coal mechanically in 1900 and only 8 per cent in 1913, the figures for Scotland were 3 and 22 per cent respectively—and the Scottish percentage exceeded 50 as early as 1927.

The Scottish coal industry produced some notable miners' leaders from the mid-nineteenth century (e.g. Alexander McDonald, 1821–1881) but achieved a national union linked to the English miners only in 1894. McDonald played a creditable part in securing safer working conditions and represented the miners in the enquiry into Scotland's worst pit disaster at Blantyre (22 October 1877: 207 deaths). Quite apart from its wider political aims, local union activity was frequently a vital element in the life of what were often very isolated mining communities.

In common with most British coalfields production stagnated in the inter-war years and slumped from the 1950s, as the state forced through pit closures in the now nationalized industry. During the past decades oil and natural gas have monopolized government fuel policies and in a market of fierce price competition coal has been given little protection. By 1993 only two Scottish collieries were fully operational in the public sector. The total number of coal miners was 1,350 and even some of these jobs were under threat.

Baron F. Duckham

Cockburn, Henry (1779–1854), born in Edinburgh and raised in what he called 'the last purely Scotch age', became a Whig and a lawyer, like his lifelong friend Francis Jeffrey. Early training in debate in the Academical and Speculative Societies helped to make him an accomplished speaker. As an advocate, he was noted for his skill in pleading, especially when defending unpromising clients. With the establishment of the Jury Court in Scotland in 1816, his professional practice flourished. He became Solicitor-General for Scotland in 1830, helping Jeffrey, who was Lord Advocate, to draft the Scottish Reform Act, and in 1834 was raised to the bench with the judicial title of Lord Cockburn. In later life, he was a respected Circuit Judge and passionate Edinburgh conservationist. The Cockburn Association, dedicated to preserve the best in Edinburgh's architecture and civic amenities, is named after him.

Cockburn had considerable literary ability, and in particular great flair for writing about people and places. From about 1821 he kept a journal, in which he recorded his reminiscences and impressions of the changing social scene; but although he prepared a fair copy of the earlier part of this, he held back from publishing it. The only general work of any length which he brought out was his *Life of Jeffrey* (1852), a fairly conventional biography of 'the greatest of British critics', which includes lengthy extracts from Jeffrey's letters. 'These letters', Cockburn notes modestly, 'will probably be deemed the only valuable part of the work'. But in fact the liveliest passages in the *Life of Jeffrey* are character-sketches of prominent late eighteenth-century Scotsmen, taken from Cockburn's own journal.

Following hints which he had left them, Cockburn's executors published in 1856 a somewhat bowdlerized text of the earlier part of his journal, which deals with the period 1779–1830, under the title *Memorials of his Time*. This book proved very popular, particularly in Cockburn's native city. In 1874 a new edition appeared, along with Cockburn's *Journal*, a continuation of the *Memorials* which brings the narrative down to the year of his death. Finally, there was published in 1888 *Circuit Journeys*, based on Cockburn's diary as a Judge on Circuit in the period 1837–54.

The best of Cockburn is to be found in *Memorials of his Time* and in *Circuit Journeys*. In the former, he writes vividly of Edinburgh life in the 1780s and 1790s, evoking distinctively Scottish personalities and customs in a manner which combines acute perception with informality and a relaxed style. His pen-portraits of *literati* and of legal figures are masterly—perhaps indeed the outstanding examples of character-writing in the entire Scottish tradition—and Stevenson was to send from the South Seas for a copy of *Memorials*, with its powerful character-sketch of Lord Braxfield, while working on *Weir of Hermiston*. But the book is more than a gallery of portraits and caricatures. By subtly varied means, Cockburn succeeds in conveying the differences in outlook between generations, and the way in which one century passed into the next. He is especially informative about the troubled, questioning mood of the 1790s and the impact of the French revolution in Scotland. 'Everything rung, and was connected with the Revolution in France; which, for above 20 years, was, or was made, the all in all. Everything, not this or that thing, but literally everything, was soaked in this one event.'

Circuit Journeys, by contrast, is a product of the railway age and of Cockburn's travels from Edinburgh to every part of Scotland. As in *Memorials*, he displays freshness of observation, humanity, and wit. Part of his purpose is to record changes in Scottish legal practice, but he writes about many other subjects as well: the whole amounts to a remarkably comprehensive yet entertaining record of social change in the early Victorian period.

D. A. Low

Comedy and Comedians. The demise of music-hall and variety theatre, throughout the sixties and seventies, attributed mainly to the advent of television, led the Scottish comedy scene to adapt to the changing public and commercial demands of the seventies and eighties; by developing three divergent, yet often inter-related, sectors.

Comedy on television and radio. Few of the 'stand-up' comedians of the variety era were able to make the transition to television successfully, due in some respect to the less theatrical nature of T.V. performance, the artistic restrictions imposed on their material, and a certain reluctance by national broadcasting to accept regional comedy, particularly the idiosyncratic and parochial humour of the traditional stand-up comic. With few exceptions, namely Lex McLean, Jack Milroy and Johnny Beattie, the major contributions to television comedy in Scotland were comedy-actors, ably supported by a highly-talented, if frequently unacclaimed, group of comedy writers.

The highly successful *One O'Clock Gang* (Larry Marshall, Charlie Sim, Dorothy Paul, Jimmy Nairn) on STV, the quick-fire repartee of 'Francie and Josie' (Rikki Fulton, Jack Milroy) and the T.V. adaptions of Neil Munro's *Para Handy Tales as The Vital Spark* (Roddy McMillan, Walter Carr, John Grieve, Alex McAvoy) were the major outlets of Scottish T.V. comedy during the sixties and seventies with the occasional guest appearance by stand-up comics (Chic Murray, Jimmy Logan, Johnny Beattie etc) on variety or chat shows.

A lengthy hiatus developed in T.V. comedy output, *The Stanley Baxter Picture Show* and *Scotch and Wry* (Rikki Fulton)

being notable exceptions, until the introduction of BBC Scotland's comedy unit (Colin Gilbert and Philip Differ) which helped launch a plethora of popular radio and T.V. comedy institutions: *Naked Radio*, and later *Naked Video* shows (Gregor Fisher, Tony Roper, Elaine C. Smith), whose ranks eventually produced Rab C. Nesbitt, and two of the most successful comedy writers of the eighties, Ian Pattison and Tony Roper. Credit must also be given to *City Lights* (Gerard Kelly), *2000 Not Out* (Craig Ferguson); *Absolutely* (Jack Docherty, Moray Hunter, Gordon Kennedy, Pete Baikie) and *Scotland the What* both showing a less Glasgow-dominated sense of humour.

Stand-up comedy. The old music-hall stand-up comic tradition did in fact survive, in many respects, within the growing social club circuit which developed during the seventies and had peaked by the mid-eighties. Inheriting a fine legacy of comedy tradition, and more than a few jokes (!), from the comedy stand-up masters of the past, Harry Gordon, Jimmy Neil, and the legendary Chic Murray (considered by many modern comics to be the 'Godfather' of the modern style of 'observational, off-the-wall humour'), the club-comics developed the ten minute 'front-of-curtain' spot into a fully-fledged forty-five minute act in its own right. Their public popularity eventually led, in some cases, to an acceptance within the wider entertainment faculty, but the artistic elitism was still in effect against the 'pub-comic'. During the seventies and eighties they became the stalwarts of the pantomime, summer-season, and social club circuit, with acts like Johnny Beattie, Hector Nicol, Glen Daly, Clem Dane, Andy Cameron, Alan Stewart, Janet Brown, Dean Park, and Jack Milroy, helping to maintain a fine tradition of Scottish mainstream comedy.

The alternative comedy scene. The seventies produced a new popular comedy scene, much of it stemming initially from the sixties folk music fraternity. Often politically and socially-oriented, a new breed (in an old tradition) of singer/songwriter/storytellers emerged headed by Matt McGinn, Hamish Imlach, Danny Kyle, and Billy Connolly. Their contribution to the future development of a new, Scottish comedy identity was frowned upon by the entertainment and media establishment (due more to their irreverence rather than their 'offensiveness', which was highly over-stated). Once again, public popularity won the day, and their controversial stance was eventually legitimized by their commercial acceptability. Billy Connolly, in particular, achieved international recognition; setting a fine example to a new comic generation.

The rise in the eighties of London's 'alternative' comedy scene prompted a wide range of new comedians to follow suit: Arnold Brown, Craig Ferguson, Victor and Barry (Forbes Masson and Alan Cumming). The Merry Mac Fun Co., and the Alexander Sisters (Lynn Ferguson and Carolyn Bonnyman) being the first wave. Much of the second-wave was centred, initially, around a comedy co-operative *The Funny Farm* (later an STV stand-up comedy series) and included Stu Who?, Fred McAulay, Bruce Morton and Parrot. The public and media acceptance of the alternative comedy scene has slowly achieved a partial merging of the alternative and mainstream groupings, with comedians successfully crossing from both sides of the barriers. New club comics, like Joe Camay, Tracey Dean, Nikki Allen and Gary Moir are helping to build the respective differences.

Unfortunately, the rapid growth of comedy venues in London, and many other English cities, has not been echoed in Scotland. However, the inauguration of an international comedy festival in 1993 in Edinburgh will hopefully encourage and enthuse new Scottish comedy talent to maintain the unique comedy tradition established by a small, but persistent comedy community.

Stu Who?

Common Riding ceremonies and festivities are a notable event in the life of many towns and burghs throughout Lowland Scotland, and especially in the Border districts. Held mainly in June or July, they originate in the ancient custom of 'Riding the Marches' of the burgh's common lands once a year; but other customs have accreted to this, some from traditional May and midsummer festivals and fairs, more from twentieth-century revivalist innovations such as the inauguration of Civic Weeks, the crowning of Summer Queens, and the enactment of historical pageants.

The rights of burgesses to graze cattle and sheep, cut peats, excavate building stone, etc. on the common land were jealously preserved. Some of the Royal Burgh charters state that the king himself had perambulated the marches of the lands he was donating; thereafter a deputation of burgesses annually walked or rode round the march stones, trees, burns and other boundary marks to ensure that no encroachments or alienation of land had taken place. Transmission of knowledge of the marks was often reinforced by the custom of 'dumping' younger burgesses against the march stones or on the ground at boundary junctions: the High Constables of Holyrood, dressed in business suits, may still be seen ceremonially swinging new colleagues against the 'bumping tree' in the palace grounds.

In some places the custom of riding the marches annually was dying out by the nineteenth century, in many it was abandoned during World Wars I and II. But there were spasmodic revivals at the end of the nineteenth century and between the wars. Most Border burghs re-established Common Riding festivals in the 1950s, while some which have no common land, and thus no Common Riding tradition, instituted festivals modelled on those of their neighbours. Though details differ from burgh to burgh, especially the names of the office-bearers, certain common elements may be observed in contemporary celebrations. A Standard-Bearer is elected, young, unmarried, and of good repute. This is his title in Selkirk, but he is also often called the Cornet (e.g. Annan, Hawick, Sanquhar), the Jethart Callant (Jedburgh), the Braw Lad (Galashiels), the Duns Reiver, the Kelso Laddie, and so forth. There is usually a Cornet's Lass and supporting bodyguard, sometimes known as Right-hand and Left-hand Men. On the Sunday preceding the Riding, the Kirking of the Cornet takes place in the parish church. On the appointed day there is the Bussing of the Standard (when the flag is usually decorated with ribbons), the Provost or Burgh Officer reads a proclamation calling on the burgesses to ride the marches, and the cavalcade sets off on its mission, which may be spread over more than one day and include ceremonial visits to local lairds or meetings with the Standard-Bearers of other burghs. When the circuit is completed the Standard-Bearer reports publicly that all is in order, and sometimes is required formally to sign the burgh map.

Though many features of present-day Common Riding festivals are of recent innovation, the celebrations serve to reaffirm a sense of civic community, solidarity, and pride which is deeply rooted in history and legend, particularly in those Border burghs whose memories of Flodden Field and the Redeswire Raid are woven into a romantic tapestry along with the Eildon Tree, the Covenanters, the Incorporations of Weavers, Souters, Tailors and Hammermen, and the traditional cry of 'Safe oot an' safe in' to the Standard-Bearer's retinue.

S. F. Sanderson

Communications, 1650–1850. The development of communications in Scotland makes a slow and almost imperceptible start in the first half of the seventeenth century. When the curtain rises on any attempt to portray the position as it existed about this date, the scene is indeed bleak and cheerless. It is true that in the immediate neighbourhood of the larger towns or cities, particularly along the east coast, some effort had been made to mark out, if not construct, rudimentary roads for pedestrian and horse traffic, but for the rest and throughout by far the greater part of the land, the ways which men followed, had they urgent need to move from place to place, were little more than paths which necessity had traced out marked only by the footsteps of the beasts that travelled along them. During the first half of the century responsibility for such road construction or maintenance as existed rested with the local Justices of the Peace while legislation in the latter half made tenants of land liable for annual work with horse and cart to the same end. Such obligations were however commonly commuted for money payments so small as to make only a negligible impact even in days of cheap labour. So matters rested till the first quarter of the eighteenth century and only then at length did signs appear of the great surge forward in road-making and bridge-building which was to take place during the next 100 years and more.

Measures for the pacification of the Highlands after the Risings of 1715 and 1719 had met with little success and in 1724 George Wade, the real pioneer of Highland roadbuilding, came to Scotland charged with the duty of reporting on and effecting measures required to bring lasting peace to the Highlands, a duty, which he was to continue to perform for the next 15 years. Wade was first and foremost a soldier, always conscious of the duty of checking or forestalling potential insurrection, but even he recognized increasingly the value of his roads in opening up the country for civilian as well as military traffic. His total achievement as a road and bridge-maker using a purely military force of 300 to 500 men working from May to October each year was probably very close to the figure of 250 miles recorded on his great bridge over the Tay at Aberfeldy. The main roadmaking work covered the years till 1736. The principal roads made during these 12 years were from Inverness to Fort William following the south side of Loch Ness; from Inverness by Drumochter Pass to Dunkeld; from Fort Augustus by Corrieyairack to Dalwhinnie and from Dalnacardoch by Tummel Bridge to Crieff. There was also a subsidiary road from Fort Augustus to Bernera opposite Skye, but this must have been somewhat rudimentary, for in 1803 Thomas Telford described it as 'just the vestiges of a military road'. In addition 40 stone bridges were constructed including major ones over the Spean and the Tay. Only in places have the routes used by Wade been used for the roads of today. From Dalnacardoch to Aberfeldy the modern road follows Wade's line pretty closely while the road from Fort Augustus by the Pass of Corrieyairack though no longer in general use remains largely as he made it. Of Wade's major bridges only that over the Tay at Aberfeldy is still in use.

The road system to which Wade's name is popularly applied embraces many roads which were made by the army long after Wade's death in 1748, but some of these were planned by him, and though he did not live to see them made it is neither unnatural nor unfitting that the name of the pioneer should in this way be perpetuated. Wade was succeeded in 1740 as Commander-in-Chief in Scotland by General Clayton and for the next 50 years the extension of the military roads in the Highlands was carried on more or less continuously by a succession of Military Commanders. These military roads included a road from Stirling to Crieff and one from Dumbarton to Inveraray. The Rising of 1745 called a brief halt to road work, but it was soon resumed with renewed vigour and purpose, and about 1767 it was estimated that 858 miles of military road nearly all in the Highlands had been completed. These roads had been made largely by unskilled labour, many of them hurriedly, and in the circumstances it was inevitable that the cost of their repair and upkeep was rapidly increasing. The employment of military labour on the roads ceased after 1790 and thereafter all the repair work was carried out by civilian labourers working for a daily wage. By now the extent of military roads in the Highlands had far passed its peak.

Enthusiasm for military road construction was rapidly waning as memories of 1745 became increasingly dim and only some 600 miles were still in some sort of repair. Three main lines of road were still in being. From Callander a road led by Lochearnhead to Tyndrum where it joined another which came up Loch Lomond and so by Arrochar and Inveraray to Dalmally. From the junction at Tyndrum the road led on over the Black Mount to Fort William, Inverness and Fort George. From Inverness a second road went by Aviemore and Blair Atholl to Dunkeld and Crieff. The third main road ran from Fort George by Grantown and the Upper Don to Braemar, Glenshee, Blairgowrie and Perth. The total sum spent on military roads between the start of Wade's work and the end of the century was over £300,000 and reading the somewhat confused records of the times it is impossible to avoid the conclusion that much of this was ultimately wasted. As to the country north of Inverness, George Dempster of Skibo described this in 1795 as 'accessible only for goats and garrons'.

In the opening years of the nineteenth century there took place that further surge forward which was within a short space of time to transform Scottish and particularly Highland communications virtually out of all recognition. The factors which brought this about were many and complex. The 50 years and more since Culloden had brought great changes to the Highlands. The enlightened work of the Commissioners on the forfeited estates had, in the absence of the old lairds and chieftains, brought many changes, nearly all for the good. The abolition of what were known as the Heritable Jurisdictions had struck a heavy blow at the prestige of the Highland Chieftains. The latter in turn sought to compensate themselves for loss of prestige by financial gain. This led in many cases to action against the tacksmen, hitherto as the largest tenants, the lynch-pin of the social structure of many a Highland estate.

Improved farming methods brought farmers, mainly sheep men, from the south of Scotland to exploit the hill grazing. This in turn often meant the end of common grazing rights hitherto enjoyed by small tenants, while restricting the amount of employment available in the glens. All this meant over-population and turned the thoughts of many to emigration. This in fact took place on a large scale in the later years of the century, threatening recruitment for the Highland Regiments which had come to be the elite of the army and the pride of the country. All these factors—and the list is far from exhaustive—caused alarm to the Government and the growing realization that Scotland and particularly the Scottish Highlands from being a potential source of sedition had come to be a peaceful but distressed area calling aloud for attention. The anxieties and perplexities of politicians at Westminster were reinforced by the reports of travellers and social reformers of all types attracted to the Scottish Highlands in search of an answer for problems easy to see but hard to resolve. The diagnoses pronounced were as numerous and as varied as the cures suggested. While the doctors disagreed the patient suffered. Yet in their prescriptions one ingredient was common to nearly all. The past half century of work and expenditure on making and maintaining military roads in the Highlands had reached the point where it was no longer relevant; but whether for farming, fishing, industry or the ordinary needs of a peaceful society, roads suited for these purposes were needed. If they achieved nothing more they would give work, hope and livelihood to thousands and would surely check the insidious flow of emigrant ships. So by different paths and with hesitant steps the planners had come to stand at last on common ground.

In June 1803, following detailed reports on the position in

the Highlands, two parallel Commissions were set up by the Government, one to build Highland roads and bridges on a scale far beyond anything yet attempted, the other to build the Caledonian Canal. Each Committee was happy in having the services of Thomas Telford, son of a Dumfriesshire shepherd and now a prominent civil engineer, John Rickman, Clerk to the House of Commons and as such a civil servant of the highest quality, and James Hope, an eminent Edinburgh lawyer. These three, happily spared to see the completion of their labours, carried for over 20 years a burden which must at times have seemed almost insupportable. The magnitude of the problems involved was at first hardly realized. Money was scarce, tools were primitive and there were few with experience of road or bridge building on a large scale. As to the Caledonian Canal, this was pioneer work of a vast order.

It had been realized from the first that the huge expenditure on the canal must be met wholly by the government, but as regards the work on the roads and bridges it was decided that they must be shared equally between the landed proprietors and the Commissioners. This latter decision involved legal, financial and practical problems of the greatest intricacy. The scarcity of money in 1803 would have rendered the task almost impossible, but happily this was surmounted with the help of the Bank of Scotland, which agreed to advance the half share payable by landowners in return for bonds or other guarantees amply secured. While Telford dealt with technical and engineering problems of great complexity, Hope wrestled with legal and financial problems from his Edinburgh office and Rickman in London acted as Secretary to the Commissioners directing and keeping from confusion the whole vast undertaking.

Applications for new roads poured in from all parts of the Highlands. When the legal complications involved in securing the share payable by the applicants had been solved, the detailed contracts were drafted by Telford and then advertised. Offers to undertake the work came from all quarters, some from local landowners, a few from genuine contractors with at least some knowledge of road work, but many from men without knowledge, experience or resources. Some offers were much too high, others absurdly low. To Hope fell the delicate task of keeping a fair balance between the interests of local proprietors who wished low offers to be accepted and those of the Commissioners who would thus almost inevitably be landed with bankrupt contractors, unpaid workmen and all the trouble and cost of re-advertising. Meantime Telford and his surveyors spent countless days inspecting lines of proposed road in all the Highland Counties and some of the Islands, meeting and dealing with technical problems towards the solution of which no precedents were available. The Commissioners wisely insisted on guarantees for the satisfactory completion of the contracts. This entailed much correspondence and many perplexities for Hope and travail for nearly all concerned. Contractors constantly failed and went bankrupt leaving work incomplete and men unpaid. The motives of proprietors in applying for new roads were in nearly every case disinterested. No payments were allowed for land taken for road or bridge construction and in fact few such claims were ever put forward.

An accurate survey of Scotland was sorely needed but completely absent. Happily Aaron Arrowsmith was then engaged on a survey of England. Helped by earlier surveys by General Roy, John Ainslie and others, Arrowsmith set to work on a Scottish survey which was finally completed in 1809 at a cost of over £2,000.

The first contracts entered into were for roads from Fort William to Arisaig and through Glengarry to the head of Loch Hourn. In each case Perth contractors, Dick & Readdie, undertook the work at too low a figure. Inexperience, bad weather and the knowledge that they were working at a loss weighed heavily against them. On the verge of bankruptcy they struggled on and at length threw up the contracts leaving men and other debts unpaid. The work which was to be finished in 1806 dragged on till 1812. Time and, in the case of the Arisaig road, money had been spent far in excess of expectations; but two much-needed roads had at last been opened, while already the Glengarry road was in constant use by cattle drovers from Skye and for timber for the Caledonian Canal.

The varied troubles which afflicted all concerned in Arisaig and Glengarry could be paralleled in scores of cases all over the Highlands. By 1812, 40 contracts were under way and there were many more to come. Men were at work on roads in South Argyll, by Loch Laggan, on the north side of Loch Ness, between Fort Augustus and Fort William and in Moidart. Roads were being built too from Dingwall to Loch Carron and Loch Alsh, from Dingwall to Wick and Thurso, in Arran, Islay, Jura and Skye. The three contracts reported in 1806 had grown by 1816 to a total of 120 and Hope could claim a large share of the credit that despite all the complexities caused by incompetence, insolvency and in some cases, dishonesty, all had up to that date been accomplished—and that without litigation. More than £450,000 had been expended, just over £200,000 having been provided by local contributions and the remainder by the Commissioners. 875 miles of road had up till then been made and 11 large bridges had been built, besides many hundreds of smaller ones included in the road contracts. Year by year the average number of men employed in roadmaking and repairing was 2,700 with a maximum number in one year of over 3,500. The total loss suffered by guarantors was estimated at £34,000, but was believed to be in fact nearer double that figure.

Telford's initial report on the state of communications in the Highlands in 1802 had emphasized the lack of bridges. Wade's bridges with the exception of those over the Tay at Aberfeldy and the Spean had all been small. The Spey and the Tay were unbridged in their lower reaches while many rivers were completely unbridged. An incomplete bridge over the Spey at Fochabers was completed at an early stage in the work of the Commissioners while a bridge over the Tay at Dunkeld built by Telford was finished in 1809. In general, bridges, unless very large, were included in road contracts, two bridges to a mile of road being recognized as an average requirement. Competent masons or contractors with experience in bridge-building were far to seek and Telford in his bridge contracts stipulated that the bridge must be maintained for three years against any but quite abnormal floods. A real but unexpected hazard arose from the floating of timber. In the early part of the nineteenth century the floating of large logs either in rafts or as single units on some of the biggest Scottish rivers was a common practice. Danger to incomplete bridges from this source first became apparent on the Dee in 1809. This danger was narrowly averted but three years later a bridge nearing completion at Potarch on the same river was totally destroyed while timber floating caused acute anxiety over Lovat Bridge on the Beauly. High water in the winter of 1818 caused further damage while in 1829 huge floods destroyed large bridges at Fochabers, Ballater and Forres, and others on the Findhorn, the Dee and the Upper Spey. Even today the rains which fell during the night of 2–3 August 1829 are remembered as among the most grievous natural disasters suffered by the Highland counties.

While the building of the new roads was steadily gathering momentum, events in the Great Glen between Inverness and Fort William were moving fast. Within a few days of the passing of the Act of Parliament which set up the Commission for the building of the Caledonian Canal, the Commissioners had met and Telford had been appointed engineer to the great undertaking. Since the whole cost of the canal was to be met by the government the legal and financial problems seemed likely to be much smaller than in the case of the roads but the technical problems were infinitely greater. Telford's detailed plans for the canal were soon approved, while stores of tools and oatmeal for the workmen were accumulated at Inverness at the east end and Corpach at the west. The labour force grew fast but with constant fluctuations. Many of the men came from the western Highlands and the Islands where the claims of fishing, peat-cutting, harvesting and potato-lifting competed with canal work. The average number at work seems to have varied between 700 and 900, rising to 1,200 to 1,400 in the summer. The wage of the common labourer was 1s. 6d. a day while those accustomed to canal work earned 1s. 8d. to 2s. 0d. Cutting in the great peat moss near Corpach had been let at the rate of 2½d. a yard, while rock-blasting was paid at the rate of 2s. 6d. a cubic yard, the men supplying the powder. The work was pushed on with energy, and before the canal project was 10 years old John Rickman in London was able to report to the Commissioners a highly satisfactory measure of progress.

When in 1821 John Rickman was reviewing the work on the roads, then all but completed, it seemed that they and the canal had run a neck-and-neck race. A small but steadily increasing amount of shipping was using the canal, if not throughout its length, at least to Fort Augustus. But in fact all was not well with the canal, and the date for final completion ever receded. Wages and costs of all sorts were rising alarmingly. The original plan had provided for a minimum depth of 20 feet but as costs rose the depth aimed at was progressively reduced. Even this was made difficult by dredging problems on the shallow Loch Oich, and before the canal was finally

opened to traffic the depth had dwindled to twelve feet. Even on this much reduced basis, many years of effort, of mishap and of frustration lay ahead. If the failure of the canal as a commercial enterprise must be acknowledged so must the grandeur of its conception and the unique quality of its original construction. If Wade's great bridge at Aberfeldy remains a memorial to a great road pioneer so the canal remains a memorial to a great engineer.

While the making of the Caledonian Canal captured the imagination of the public to a unique degree, it was by no means the only canal project put forward or actually put in hand in the last years of the eighteenth and the early years of the nineteenth centuries. There were many such projects in all parts of Scotland very many of which can only be described as fantastic. The most practical and important were the Crinan Canal completed in the early years of last century and the Forth & Clyde Canal both helped by loans from the Commissioners on the Forfeited Estates who had received large sums from Highland and other proprietors on the return to them of estates which had in very many cases been greatly improved.

Postal Services. South of the Border some form of postal service, mainly for the use of the Crown, had existed during at least the latter half of the sixteenth century but so far as Scotland is concerned there are few signs of such a service before the very end of the century, and the year 1603 may be said to mark the start of Scotland's postal history. In that year King James VI went south to rule the United Kingdom from London and postal stages were fixed between Berwick and Edinburgh as an extension of the Great North Road from London. The Postmasters at these points were obliged to keep three good horses and to forward letters to the next post at 6 m.p.h. in summer and 5 m.p.h. in winter. There is evidence that it was intended to extend a similar service at least over part of southern Scotland, but as late as 1656 with the exception of a post from Edinburgh to Portpatrick it was agreed that no part of the country needed or could support a horse post. These very early posts were almost entirely for Crown or military use, but the need for a civilian post was coming to be recognized and in 1662 the first rates for posts in Scotland were fixed. In addition the cities of Edinburgh, Glasgow and Aberdeen had private and burgh posts and had acquired at least by use and custom some rights to messenger services between the cities. The Post Offices of England and Scotland were united in 1711, considerations of financial need, expediency and hard common sense dictating this union, as four years earlier they had dictated the Union of the Parliaments.

Until 1715, with the exception of the extension to Edinburgh of the Great North Road, Scotland's mail was carried everywhere on foot, but in that year a horse post between Edinburgh and Glasgow was initiated to do the journey in 10 hours in summer and 12 in winter while in 1716 a temporary horse post was instituted to take military dispatches from Perth to Inverness. Meantime the growth of the network of foot-posts is shown by the fact that the 34 post-towns recognized as such in 1708 had grown by 1715 to 60. The amount of use coming to be made of these civilian postal services in important centres is shown by the fact that in the last eight months of 1734 a total of 2,450 letters passed through the hands of the Post Master at Inveraray, the centre of the great Argyll Estates.

Until past the middle of the eighteenth century the main postal routes linking the chief centres of population with Edinburgh served fairly adequately the postal needs of the country. Cross-posts from one country town to another were favoured neither by the geography of much of Scotland nor by the fact that the postal charge on a letter was fixed by the total distance the letter covered in transit. This clearly favoured the retention of Edinburgh as a centre where the charge was reckoned and marked on the letter. Yet despite all the inefficient and archaic practices under which it laboured the postal network was steadily spreading out, and by the middle of the eighteenth century, posts went from Inverness to Fort Augustus and Fort William, to Wick, Thurso and Kirkwall, to Cromarty and to Skye. Postal links, too, were shortly to be forged with Kyle of Lochalsh and Poolewe, and also with the fishing station at Ullapool where the men of the fishing fleet and their masters waited impatiently for letters from home, for sailing instructions or for news of the peripatetic herring shoals. With the opening years of the nineteenth century the work of the road and canal builders under Telford and his colleagues meant increased calls for postal services and, as the work on the roads and bridges progressed, new or improved routes came into being to carry foot, horse and ultimately coach traffic. While the early postal services were mostly on foot a steady transition to horse posts was in very many cases forced on the Post Office by the growing interest in the French War and the increasing demand for newspapers, copies of Acts of Parliament and army reports. Indeed on the east side of the country and especially on the route to Aberdeen the growing weight of the mail was making it abundantly clear that nothing short of mail coaches could meet the demand.

Mail coaches had been tentatively introduced in England in 1782 and had proved a complete success. Four years later they were introduced on the route between London and Edinburgh and soon after on the Glasgow route. Rates of travel in the early days were only 7 or 8 m.p.h. but with improved roads this speed was soon bettered and by 1830 speeds of 10 m.p.h. were being regularly maintained over long distances on the main routes. A change of horses every 10 miles was called for, and mail contractors found that they had to keep a horse for every mile of road worked by them. At first mail coaches were exempt from Turnpike tolls but this led to bitter resentment and at length the Post Office was forced to accept liability for tolls in return for an extra ½d. on each letter carried by coach. It was to prove a poor bargain.

While postal services were thus being extended and improved on the Scottish mainland the people of the Islands joined the queue of applicants. Rudimentary posts to Orkney and Shetland were among the first to achieve some betterment but soon Lewis, the Outer Hebrides and Skye got better posts, the latter pleading the importance of the trade in black cattle, herrings and kelp. With improved posts between towns and villages came a change in the postal picture within the towns themselves. As early as 1772 it had been established by the Courts that full postage paid on a letter covered its delivery to the recipient. This had been widely ignored and for many years the actual receipt of a letter by the addressee in towns and villages depended on the enterprise of the latter in collecting it, or at best, on the good nature of the Post Master. Such an obvious gap in the postal service inspired one Peter Williamson to set up a private enterprise by means of which letters could be delivered within the limits of Edinburgh for the price of 1d. each. The service prospered greatly for 20 years and was then taken over by the Post Office, the eventual outcome being that in nearly all the towns of Scotland and very many rural districts centred on the villages letters and parcels came to be delivered at first for 1d. in addition to the normal postal charge on the item in question and later free of extra charge.

Postal rates paid on letters had long been regarded almost entirely as a source of revenue, a steadily increasing sum being exacted each year from the Post Office by the Exchequer. The needs of the Treasury in the long war-time years about the turn of the century and rising costs of all kinds meant increased postal charges. In 1782 the cost of a letter between Edinburgh and London was 7d. but by 1801 this had risen to 11d. and before the Napoleonic Wars ended the cost was 1s. 1½d. At that time it would have seemed inconceivable to those in charge of Post Office affairs that a penny would one day carry a letter to and from any part of the United Kingdom; but in fact, the idea that postage was primarily a public service and only incidentally a source of revenue was steadily gaining ground and before many years had passed the apparent miracle had come about.

So, as the nineteenth century neared its mid-term, Scotland with new roads, bridges and canals stood poised, ready to move forward into a new era in which steam was to be the motive power of railways, ships and industry, the whole stimulated and vitalized by the boon of Penny Post.

A. R. B. Haldane

Communist Party. The Communist Party of Great Britain (CPGB) was founded in 1920 and wound up at its 43rd Congress in 1991. It became the Democratic Left, although one seceding minority retained the original name while another became the Communist Party of Scotland. Earlier splits had produced a New Communist Party and a Communist Party of Britain (CPB), the latter comprising supporters of the *Morning Star* (begun 1966; formerly the *Daily Worker*, founded 1930), which, until a division over the CPGB's adherence to 'Eurocommunism' in the mid-1980s, had been regarded as the Party's daily newspaper. The CPGB had a much greater influence on twentieth-century Scottish history than is generally recognised.

In the aftermath of the Russian revolution of 1917, Communist parties affiliated to the Third International (1919–1943) were formed all over the world. In Britain, events in Scotland, particularly on 'Red Clydeside', were significant in creating the circumstances which made such a party possible. The well-documented discussions between the Paisley-born engineer, William Gallacher, and Bolshevik leaders in Moscow in 1920, provide an insight into the optimistic internationalism and sharp political debate which informed this period of labour history. In the second half of 1920 and early 1921 a number of socialist parties, militant shop stewards and others formed the CPGB. Small though it was, it reflected working-class aspirations for a socialist alternative to war and social deprivation; and disillusionment with existing labour leaderships.

Scots such as Gallacher (1881–1965), Arthur MacManus (1889–1927), Tom Bell (1882–1944), Bob Stewart (1877–1973) and J. R. Campbell (1894–1969) played key roles in the party's early years. But the leading Marxist from 'Red Clydeside' refused to join. John Maclean (1879–1923) thought the Party had been created without a sound foundation of Marxist education. In Glasgow he tried to form a Scottish Communist Party and (in 1923) a Scottish Workers Republican Party. The latter had some appeal but did not survive.

Parts of the 'Celtic fringe', along with East London, provided the most fertile soil for the CPGB. The heavy industrial areas of west central Scotland were significant, as were the coalfields of Fife and Lanarkshire. In the latter a communist trade union, the United Mineworkers of Scotland (1929–1936), even proved a brief possibility. And the Scottish mineworkers supplied key party militants such as Abe (1896–1975) and Alex (1904–1967) Moffat and Michael McGahey (b. 1925). West Fife was the only constituency in Britain to return a Communist MP (Gallacher) at two successive general elections (1935, 1945).

The Party's lack of success at parliamentary elections is one reason why its role has been underestimated. Two of the main areas of power were Lumphinnans in Fife and Vale of Leven in Dunbartonshire. Right up to the Party's demise, local personalities, notably in Fife, were still able to win council seats in its name.

A key early episode was the defeat of the general strike, and the miners' lockout, of 1926, widely seen as the result of betrayal of the TUC. Ian MacDougall's *Militant Miners* (1981) gives a good picture of the active role of Party members in the localities (in this case Fife), but this can be contrasted with the CP's lack of clear *political* leadership, and its subsequent inability to give consistent theoretical guidance on how to create new leadership in the labour movement. Many of the recruits gained by the example provided by local activists in 1926, were soon lost.

MacDougall has also used oral history to good effect in accounts of the struggle against unemployment—*Voices from the Hunger Marches* (2 vols, 1990, 1991)—and the fight against fascism in Spain—*Voices from the Spanish Civil War* (1986). These were causes in which the CP played a leading organizational role, inspiring support. The Scottish Hunger Marches

were led by a Party member and former follower of John Maclean, Harry McShane (1891–1988). He resigned from the Party in the early 1950s.

Many from the Party intelligentsia went on to play important roles in cultural and intellectual life. Recruitment amongst the middle classes had not been a feature of the Party in Scotland which was regarded much more as a source of its working-class praetorian guard. Nevertheless Kenneth (later Sir Kenneth), Alexander (b. 1922) was one of those who left after Hungary, later chairing the Highlands and Islands Development Board and serving as Principal of Stirling University. Others who resigned were a former foreign editor of the party's *Daily Worker*, Malcolm MacEwen (b. 1911)—son of the Scottish nationalist leader of the 1930s, Sir Alexander MacEwen and Victor Kiernan (b. 1913), an Englishman, but the only member of the influential group of 'British Marxist historians' to make his career in Scotland—at Edinburgh University—or to write effectively on Scottish history.

Hugh MacDiarmid (1892–1978), who joined the party in the 1930s and left again because of its opposition to Scottish nationalism, rejoined in the aftermath of the Hungarian episode. For good or ill, MacDiarmid has come to dominate debates about twentieth-century Scottish culture. His Stalinism (he styled himself a 'Stalinist-Leninist') remains the least analysed aspect of his career. Amongst other Scottish literary figures, involved at some point with the Party were Lewis Grassic Gibbon (1901–1935), and James Barke (1905–1958).

A major blow to the party in the industrial sphere after 1956, was the loss of miners' leader Lawrence Daly (b. 1924), who attempted to form his own Fife Socialist League. Briefly successful, it was to prove a conduit through which Party support ebbed away, in what had been one of its most loyal working-class bases.

Scotland, however, provided the Party with its general secretaries in its declining years: Edinburgh's John Gollan (1911–1977) from 1956 to 1975, whose *Scottish Prospect* (1948) was a well-researched argument for devolution; and Glasgow's Gordon McLennan (b. 1924) from 1975 to 1989; with influential trade unionists, particularly Aberdeen's James Milne (1921–1986), general secretary of the Scottish TUC from 1975 to 1986; and with some of its best orators. McGahey, then President of the Scottish miners and national NUM Vice-President, could still, during the 1984–85 miners' strike, sound like a traditional fire-breather; temporarily he seemed to recapture the ferocious reputation he perhaps unjustifiably earned in the strikes of 1972 and 1974 which helped unseat Edward Heath's Tory government. Yet, he now supported the ultra-moderate 'Euro' wing of the party and was known to oppose the militancy in the strike of NUM President Arthur Scargill, a former ally.

The divorce between militant trade union rhetoric and a growing movement towards political respectability was also evident in the Communist shop stewards who led the famous Upper Clyde Shipbuilders' 'work-in' in 1971–72. James Reid (b. 1932), a former Young Communist League National Secretary, hoped that, in Scotland at least, there was still force in the idea that a reputation for responsible industrial militancy would lead to parliamentary success. Students made him their rector at Glasgow University from 1971 to 1974, but his rejection by the Clydebank electorate in 1974 was followed by his disgruntled departure from the Party; and his subsequent unpopularity with former supporters when he became a columnist for the tabloid press.

The first attempt at a posthumous historical assessment of the CPGB was Willie Thompson's *The Good Old Cause* (1992). Written by a Scot, it sometimes elides empathy into apology, but it provides a critical starting point and describes Scotland and Wales as 'the heartlands of British communism'.

   T. Brotherstone

Connery, Sean, is undoubtedly the most famous living Scotsman. Born in 1930, his early careers in the Royal Navy, as a bodybuilder and an artist's model, led eventually to steady work in stage and screenacting. Although his early roles are largely unmemorable he shot into the limelight when cast as secret agent James Bond in the film *Dr No*. The film brought him instant stardom and over five sequels Connery's star status grew and, despite appearing in a variety of other roles, he became closely identified with the character of Bond. In 1971 Connery retired from Bond-age (despite a brief return in 1983) and developed his skills as a character actor in Hollywood. While the quality of the films varied, Connery managed to maintain his broad audience appeal and, after winning an Oscar for 1987's *The Untouchables*, became firmly established as both a powerful actor and a major movie star.

   D. Bruce

Conservation. The importance of concern for the environment and the man-made heritage has really only won wide popular support during the final quarter of the 20th century. In the Highlands, there was never any shortage of space, discarding worn-out furniture and out-dated vehicles and farm implements in the open air worried no one, until tourism became a major Scottish industry. In the Lowlands, industrial development proceeded at such a land-despoiling pace that there was neither time nor economic occasion to consider its effect on the environment.

While it is true that systematic town and village planning was carried out by a few enlightened landowners in the eighteenth Century—notably at Inveraray (the Argyll family); Eaglesham (the Eglintons); and, on a smaller scale at Luss, Loch Lomond (the Colquhouns)—few people saw the need for organized conservation. The mediaeval nucleus of Glasgow disappeared in the 19th Century (the destruction of the ancient university being the most serious loss), just as the Blythswood early 19th-century Glasgow style has partly disappeared in our own day (although now it is the subject of mandatory facade retention), in the 1950s and 60s pressure for high-rise office development.

The first practical conservationist who was not himself an interested party was undoubtedly Lord Cockburn (q.v.), who died in 1854. He had set about the City Fathers of Edinburgh with such gusto in his pamphlet *The Best Ways of Spoiling the Beauty of Edinburgh* (1849), that in 1875, Scotland's first Civic Society, The Cockburn Association came into being to commemorate his efforts and to act as a continuing watchdog body on behalf of the citizens of the Capital. It still flourishes, as The Cockburn Association and Edinburgh Civic Trust.

Edinburgh, however, remained something of a special case and it was many years before further similarly motivated societies came into being. Among comparatively early societies, still surviving were the St Andrews Preservation Trust Limited (1938), the Crail Preservation Society (1952), and a similar society in Elgin, founded in 1945.

In 1931 The National Trust for Scotland was established, with objectives similar to those of The National Trust for England and Wales (1895). Like its English counterpart, the National Trust for Scotland is incorporated by an Act of Parliament. It is dependent for its financial support upon legacies, donations and member subscriptions presently numbering around 237,000. It is recognized as a charity for tax exemption purposes, and enjoys certain privileges under various Finance Acts as regards death duties.

It administers some properties covering about 97,000 acres, including landscapes of outstanding natural beauty, on behalf of the nation. Great houses in its care include The Binns (West Lothian), Brodick Castle (Isle of Arran), Crathes Castle (Kincardineshire), Culzean Castle (Ayrshire), Falkland Palace, Hill of Tarvit and Kellie Castle (Fife), the Castle of Drum, Castle Fraser, Leith Hall, Craigievar Castle and Haddo House (Aberdeenshire) and House of Dun (Angus). Acquired more recently with assistance from the National Heritage Memorial Fund are Fyvie Castle (Aberdeenshire) and Charles Rennie Mackintosh's Hill House (Helensburgh, Dunbartonshire).

It also has in its care several noteworthy gardens, some associated with great houses, others, like Inverewe in Wester Ross, conserved in its own right. Among the mountainous tracts of Scotland the National Trust owns on behalf of the nation, are the Pass of Glencoe and the mountain group known as The Five Sisters of Kintail, as well as the estate of Torridon in Wester Ross. The islands of St Kilda and Fair Isle are in its care, as are the historical sites of Bannockburn, Killiecrankie, Glen Finnan and Culloden. Its properties with literary associations include the birthplaces of Barrie at Kirriemuir, Carlyle in Ecclefechan and Hugh Miller in Cromarty. It owns Burns's Bachelors' Club at Tarbolton and Soutar Johnnie's house in Kirkoswald, Ayrshire.

Under a Revolving Fund, originally of £100,000, it has carried out the restoration of groups of small houses, the properties being bought, restored and resold. The most notable groups are perhaps those in Culross in Fife and at Dunkeld, Perthshire. For this work the Trust was awarded the European Prize for the Preservation of Ancient Monuments given by the FVS Foundation of Hamburg in 1976.

Broadly speaking, the National Trust for Scotland's main

task thus is to own and maintain buildings and land on behalf of the Scottish people. But there has also been increasing concern over a wide range of other environmental issues since mandatory planning was introduced, and the planners turned their attention to such problems as the renewal of city and town centres, many of which contained important buildings. Government statutory listing was introduced in Scotland between 1969 and 1971, the idea being that buildings of outstanding architectural or historic interest would be listed, after investigation by experts, in consultation with Local Authorities in these categories.

Category A: Buildings of national or more than local importance, either architectural or historic or fine little-altered examples of some particular period or style.

Category B: Buildings of primarily local importance or major examples of some period or style which may have been somewhat altered.

Category C(S): Good buildings which may be considerably altered, other buildings which are fair examples of their period, or in some cases buildings of no great individual merit which group well with others in categories A or B.

In 1953 the Historic Buildings Council for Scotland was set up by the Government to administer Government grants for listed buildings, recommended by a Council appointed by the Secretary of State for Scotland who himself makes the grants. Its powers over the years have remained unaltered, especially since the passing of the Civic Amenities Act of 1967, since incorporated in the Town and Country Planning Act Scotland 1972. This created Conservation Areas of group importance, the best of which could be designated as outstanding. Buildings not individually listed in Conservation Areas are now offered similar protection to their listed neighbours, to ensure that if new constructions were to be erected they would be of a suitable matching standard. In addition, Government grant-assistance is now available for the carrying out of Town Schemes, the purpose of which is to achieve practical group conservation in an urban context in partnership with local authorities. Government assistance to churches still in use for worship became possible for the first time in 1978.

A decade after the creation of the Civic Trust in London in 1957 by the Rt Hon. Duncan Sandys (later Lord Duncan Sandys), the Scottish Civic Trust was set up in Glasgow in May 1967 under the Chairmanship of a former Secretary of State for Scotland, the Rt Hon. Viscount Muirshiel. Its roles were: to encourage the growth of responsible local Civic and Amenity Societies (there were 27 in 1967 and currently about 150 in existence, from Shetland to the Borders); to report with suitable recommendations to the Planning Authorities on applications to demolish or radically alter listed buildings, and if necessary, oppose such demolition or alteration proposals at Public Inquiries (though negotiation to achieve pragmatic compromise has been and remains, one of the Trust's most important tasks); to encourage high standards in the planning of new development and building construction; and to assist in the carrying through of such environmental schemes as might seem necessary or desirable.

Under this last heading, the most extensive has been the Trust's work (with the Edinburgh Architectural Association) in the voluntary survey and the International Conference of June 1970, leading to the setting up of Edinburgh New Town Conservation Committee, under a full-time Director, with funds provided by both Central and Local Authorities.

A similar role was undertaken by the Trust in connection with the model 18th-century industrial village of New Lanark, on the Clyde, set up by David Dale and developed by his son-in-law Robert Owen. It has since become an award-winning success story, achieving world-wide recognition and a large number of visitors throughout each year.

In 1970, the Trust undertook a large-scale voluntary 'clean-up' project, 'Facelift Glasgow', for the local authority, over a period of five years, thus helping to provide some stimulus towards the remarkable Glasgow environmental 'renaissance'which has transformed the fabric of the City. Its achievements were recognized by the record number of Europa Nostra Awards secured in 1991, and by the results of the Scottish Civic Trust 25th Anniversary Glasgow Award Scheme 1992. The Trust also provided the Scottish Secretariat for European Architectural Heritage Year 1975, when Scotland completed a record number of projects out of the United Kingdom total.

The Trust has been concerned, in partnership with local authorities, with regeneration schemes at Lesmahagow and Newmilns. Since 1990, it has operated a Buildings at Risk service on behalf of Historic Scotland (the built heritage division of the Scottish Office was thus re-named in 1990 when it became an agency).

Other bodies which owe their inception wholly or partly to the Scottish Civic Trust include the Scottish Environmental Education Committee, the Scottish Churches Architectural Trust and the Glasgow West Conservation Trust.

In recent years the Buildings Preservation Trust movement has developed in Scotland. Twelve independent Building Preservation Trusts now operate throughout Scotland. They work on the revolving fund principle, pioneered by the National Trust for Scotland's 'little houses' scheme. By these means, buildings of interest having an otherwise uncertain future are acquired and restored, using funds obtained from a variety of private, charitable and public sources, any profit from eventual sale being applied to further restoration projects.

A national voluntary body that also concerned itself with the pressure of modern development upon good historic architecture is the Architectural Heritage Society of Scotland, founded in 1956 (as the Scottish Georgian Society) with its headquarters in Edinburgh. It acts as an effective pressure group, often in conjunction with other bodies, to arouse public interest, to contribute to scholarship and specially to care for the future of historic architecture throughout Scotland.

Since 1964, the Scottish Wildlife Trust has operated in a similar manner with regard to the conservation of animals and birds. In 1991, the Nature Conservancy Council's Scottish office and the Countryside Commission for Scotland (founded in 1968) were amalgamated in a single body, as the Scottish

Natural Heritage, with wide advisory and executive powers concerning the natural heritage. Operating mainly in the urban context, there is also the Royal Fine Art Commission for Scotland, founded in 1927. It has a full-time secretary but honorary commissioners act in an advisory capacity, commenting upon the architectural effects of new buildings, mainly in relation to the urban environment. Unfortunately, it is an organization that lacks body as the ungainly design offered for the Skye Bridge (against its recommendation) will testify for generations to come.

In some respects the planning laws of Scotland, like those of the United Kingdom as a whole, win the admiration of many other countries. Local Authorities have implemented or encouraged outstanding conservation work. Where serious environmental losses do still occur, the fault is sometimes due to a failure of the Central or Local Authority to make use of the powers at its disposal, often because it lacks either the necessary political muscle or will, or the resources to bear any resulting financial burden. With so much of the Scottish urban heritage now 100 to 200 years old, the need for money to be spent on its conservation is bound to increase, if we are not to lose much that is both irreplaceable and a major tourist economic asset.

At a time when the architectural profession is suffering from the effects of world recession, distinguished voices are sometimes raised suggesting that conservation has gone far enough and is now stultifying modern development. Such scarcely disinterested cries of distress should be resisted. The same financial constraints that restrict the scope of conservation too often limit the design quality of new buildings with a resultant deterioration of the urban environment, creating the widespread public concern of which HRH Prince of Wales has been a mouthpiece.

A well organized, well informed and vocally effective voluntary amenity lobby is one of the most effective democratic lines of defence against any hesitancy on the part of our administrators to use their full powers to protect the environment and the heritage, and to speak out against wrongly sited or inadequate new design. Only when all aspects of the environment become a vote-catching issue in elections are fully adequate measures for its safeguarding likely to become politically acceptable. That day may not be too far distant.

M. Lindsay

Conservatives and Conservatism in Scotland.

Disraeli claimed that he was a Conservative to 'preserve all that is good in our Constitutions' and a Radical to 'remove all that is bad'. This rhetorical embodiment of the philosophical basis of Conservatism highlights the dilemma faced by Scottish Conservatives today: defending what is good and removing what is bad, is not only subjective but may result in conflict between those values and institutions which are distinctly Scottish and those which are English or British.

Conservatism in Scotland has had much in common with its English counterpart but it has also had some distinct features.

The ideology of Conservatism owes more to Unionism in Scotland than has ever been the case in England and the levels of public support for the party have often diverged on either side of the border. These differences reflect the different contexts in which Conservatives and Conservatism operate. Unionism has had a number of threads: constitutional conservatism, patriotism, anti-immigrant, Scottish particularism, social and economic moderation. Modern Conservatism has retained many of these features but greater emphasis is now placed on free-market ideas and less emphasis on Scottish particularism.

In its original form at the end of the nineteenth century, Scottish Unionism meant support for the Union with Ireland. In time, it has come to mean strong support for the Anglo-Scottish Union and opposition to any measure perceived as weakening it. This change occurred gradually and came about in reaction to the changing agenda of Scottish politics rather than to any conscious effort by the party.

The importance of Unionism was made clear in 1912 when the Conservatives adopted the name Scottish Unionist Party and only changed it to the Scottish Conservative and Unionist Party in 1965. In its earlier form it came to be associated with opposition to Irish Catholic demands for Irish unity and independence. This was soon translated into opposition to Irish Catholic immigration into the west of Scotland. Familial and political links between Protestants in the north of Ireland and Scotland played a significant part in reviving the fortunes of Scottish Conservatism. The influx of Irish immigrants to west-central Scotland gave Unionism a populist, anti-immigrant appeal. Fears that the indigenous population might be 'swamped' and that the national culture obliterated has been a theme of right-wing parties throughout Europe. In Scotland, this anti-Irish feature aided the party electorally, projecting itself as protecting Scotland from an 'alien culture'. Its Scottish particularism had a more positive aspect. The party played a significant part in maintaining and developing a distinct pattern of Scottish central administration through the establishment and growth of the Scottish Office.

The appeal of the earlier version of Unionism allowed the Conservatives to win support amongst a broad spectrum of Scottish society, including amongst sections of the recently enfranchised working classes. In turn, this support made Scottish Conservatives aware of wider concerns and interests in Scottish society and may partly explain the party's often moderate position on social and economic issues.

Figures such as Sir John Gilmour, Walter Elliot, Noel Skelton and John Buchan helped shape the ideology and image of the party in the earlier part of the twentieth century. Each projected a distinctly Scottish dimension to their politics as well as stressing the merits of Britain and the Empire. Support for moderate policies and state intervention was an added dimension. The nature of modern Scottish politics—its institutional structures most notably—were shaped in the inter-war period largely by the Unionists.

The 1955 election marked the apogee in support for the party when it achieved 50.1 per cent of the popular vote cast—the only political party to win a simple majority since full adult enfranchisement in Scotland. The party's success probably owed at least as much to the lack of third party support, post-war economic recovery; a perception that Labour was more centralist as to anything the party may have been doing. A degree of complacency and a lack of vitality was evident in the period after 1945. A number of forces led to a decline in its support: secularisation and the decreasing salience of the Irish question in Scottish politics; the failure of the party to modernise in the manner that occurred in England after the 1945 election; a gradual decline in Scottish support for the Union and Britain, and in more recent years the move to the right particularly under Mrs Thatcher, and a growing perception amongst Scots that the Conservatives were unsympathetic to the Scottish dimension.

The beginning of a long and fairly steady decline began at the 1959 election. By the mid-1960s, the need for modernisation in Scotland was felt necessary in some quarters, including parts of the leadership, though this was strongly resisted by the party faithful. Under Sir John George's chairmanship, the party underwent a series of reforms, including the change of name to incorporate Conservative into its title after an absence of over fifty years and attempts were made to encourage candidates to contest local elections under the party banner. However, apart from organisational reforms and the name change, there was little else that changed. From Heath's leadership through to the Thatcher years, the attempts to modernise the Scottish party often had their source outside Scotland. The party's membership showed the kind of resistance to the British leadership's demands for change, which the Scottish electorate showed to the policies of Conservative Governments from 1970 onwards. Heath's attempt to revive the party north of the border included a brief flirtation with support for a weak measure of home rule. Thatcher's attempts involved urging her radical agenda on a reluctant Scotland. The former found opposition within the Scottish party while the latter discovered strong opposition amongst the Scottish electorate.

During the 1980s, support for the Scottish dimension became almost synonymous with support for a Scottish Parliament and the party's opposition to this deprived it of what in former times had been a popular strand in its ideology. The strands in Conservative ideology which had provided a wide coalition of support earlier in the century, were either inappropriate in Scottish society in the 1980s or were less evident in the party's message.

The 1987 election saw the party record its worst showing in Scotland when it won only ten of Scotland's seventy-two Parliamentary seats with 24 per cent of the vote. Eleven seats were lost as compared with the previous election. The image of the party, as in some way 'anti-Scottish', played a major part in the defeats, with perceptions of Mrs Thatcher and the imposition of the poll tax contributing to this. Mrs Thatcher's Conservatism involved preserving the constitutional arrangements affecting Scotland while Scots wanted a measure of self-government and those policies she pursued as a Radical,

to 'remove all that was bad', included many which Scots disliked and even abhorred.

The 1992 election saw little evidence of a Conservative recovery. The party won only 11 seats with 25.7 per cent of the vote, despite the relative popularity of John Major and the decision to replace the poll tax. The precarious position of the party of Government in Scotland remained, as it had been throughout the 1980s, the main focus of Scottish politics.

J. Mitchell

Covenanters, The. The origins of the covenanting movement lie in the ill-conceived policies consistently pursued by Charles I after his accession in 1625. An Act of Revocation designed to aid the finances of Church and crown enraged magnates who resented a loss of the teinds which they possessed, while taxation, which also affected the burghs, and the use of bishops as royal advisers constituted further grievances. The introduction of a prayer book acted as a catalyst and led, after rioting, to the organization of committees to receive petitions against what was conceived to be the arbitrary use of royal authority.

The result was the National Covenant of 1638 which by its emphasis upon measures to be taken in 'free assemblies and in parliaments' presaged the condemnation of the office of bishop in 1638, and demands in 1641 for a parliament free of royal influence. These two causes, the triumph of presbyterianism and the establishment of constitutional monarchy, proved incompatible and led to opposition to covenanting policies. Nevertheless, support for presbyterianism was sufficiently widespread to permit its extension and this, in time, enabled the revolution to be secured through alliance with the English parliamentarians.

The Solemn League and Covenant of 1643 clarified the situation, but the extent of opposition can be overstressed. The defeat of Montrose's rising in support of Charles at Philiphaugh in 1645 was predictable but it denied to the Scots the opportunity of implementing the Solemn League. Even so, the king's downfall had been achieved and thereafter new attitudes appeared on how the divergent interests of the two covenants could be reconciled. The Engagement of 1647 between king and magnates while seeking presbyterian unity was primarily designed to safeguard the authority of the magnates—hence the implacable opposition of the General Assembly.

The Engagement, and the military defeat for its supporters at Preston in 1648, shattered the unity of the covenanting movement. If the aim of the subsequent oligarchy of lairds and ministers was to produce a God-fearing nation, enforcement of the Covenant remained their primary objective and recognition of Charles II was made conditional on its acceptance. All this made hostilities with Cromwell inevitable. Defeat at Dunbar in 1650 ended the theocratic experiment and although its exponents produced the Remonstrance in which they declared the 'mother sin of this nation ... to be the backslydinge breache of covenant', support was forthcoming for a new coalition of former Engagers and supporters of Montrose in a series of resolutions—hence their new name of Resolutioners. This unity proved to be transitory as subjugation followed defeat of a Scottish army at Worcester in 1651.

The character of the struggle changed at this juncture. The military occupation limited the pretensions of both parties who, deprived of political power, struggled for dominance in the Church. The Resolutioners in contrast to their opponents, who after their protest against the Resolutions in the General Assembly in 1651 were termed Protesters, became less committed to the covenants. Nevertheless, commitment to presbyterianism remained paramount. The Restoration thus found presbyterians divided and this aided the reimposition of episcopacy which royal autocracy favoured. This solution was accepted by the magnates and even by a majority of Resolutioner ministers, but a minority along with the Protesters remained intransigent and by 1663 some 270 ministers had left the Established Church. Many sympathizers, especially in the southwest, followed their example and thereafter worshipped at secret conventicles. Enforced conformity was attempted, but military repression led to resistance which manifested itself in the Pentland Rising of 1666.

Conciliatory policies were adopted after the rising had been crushed at Rullion Green. Of those pursued, accommodation, which advocated subjection of bishops to a triennial synod, was unattainable and toleration as proferred in indulgences of 1669 and 1672 proved initially more promising. The indulgences, however, split the conventiclers and bitterness against the indulged increased as repression was reimposed with the arrival of a 'Highland Host' in the southwest in 1678. The murder of Archbishop Sharp by a group of conventiclers hastened the inevitable conflict which erupted with the defeat of Claverhouse at Drumclog, but it ended in disaster for the opposition at Bothwell Bridge in 1679.

Dissension among the conventiclers came to a head before the battle, one party reserving judgement on the indulgences for a free General Assembly while another stressed their abhorrence of the indulged and their disapproval of royal authority. The ensuing rout widened the divisions between these two parties. Concession and repression had broken the covenanting movement and the majority of dissenters thereafter advocated presbyterianism without the covenants. Anti-erastianism was discredited, and the party which maintained this attitude—the Covenanters or Cameronians as they were to be called after their leader Richard Cameron—could no longer validly claim to represent the presbyterian conscience. The intensity of their conviction was expressed, nevertheless, in various manifestos, but after the death of Cameron in a skirmish and the execution of Donald Cargill, the 'Remnant' was no longer an active opposition and congregations resembled praying societies. Even so, the council, faced with further presbyterian opposition created by the Test and Succession Acts of 1681, pursued increasingly hostile policies designed to crush both presbyterians and Cameronians. The revival of field preaching and the arrival in 1683 of James Renwick as minister to the 'Remnant' brought redoubled efforts which culminated in the 'killing times' when refusal to renounce the Apologetical Declaration of 1684, in which the Cameronians had denied royal authority, carried a sentence of death. Presbyterians as such were seldom executed but policies for their extirpation were avidly pursued.

On the surface these persecutions were successful and most flocks were driven back to their parish churches. Coercion had become the mainstay of the Established Church and when this was removed by Acts of Indulgences of 1687 designed by James VII to aid his fellow Catholics the presbyterians were poised to press their claims for establishment at the Revolution of 1688. With this effected by 1690, many of the Cameronians returned to the presbyterian fold leaving their societies numerically weak and with little cohesion. Without ministers, since the execution of Renwick, the Covenanters might have gradually withered away, but there were some within their ranks who were determined to maintain the Covenants and their claims to be the 'True Church of Scotland', and, although remaining a small insignificant sect, emerged in 1743 as the Reformed Presbyterian Church.

I.B. Cowan

Crafts. 'Craftsmanship' is often used by copywriters to describe products hot off industrial conveyor belts, as such craftsmen and women in Scotland are taking shelter under a different umbrella—the Applied Arts. The term serves them well, as the crafts are produced by skilful control of tools and materials, applied to creative ideas.

Craftsmen seem always to have been subject to the variable demands of their markets. Traditionally, those in agricultural communities bought their cloth, clothes and furniture from local workshops. They thrived until railways and the Industrial Revolution gave consumers a wider choice. City-based workshops had a longer life not only because there were potentially more buyers with greater wealth, but also because of apprenticeship systems which ensured a continuity of skills and a greater ability to produce bespoke products for a fashion-conscious clientele.

In the 1970s, Government-funded encouragement led to the establishment of many factory-based craft businesses, with an emphasis on production techniques, financial planning and marketing. Several firms started to mass-produce glassware, ceramic tableware and jewellery and continue to be important employers, particularly in the Highlands and Islands. Professionally-organized annual trade fairs were started to link craftsmen and retailers, helping to generate orders for home and export markets. In the '80s, however, the crafts in Scotland as elsewhere, started to divide into distinct market sectors—wholesale/retail; art; architecture.

Several thousand design graduates, self-taught and bench-trained craftsmen set up as sole proprietors of full-time businesses in Scotland from 1970–90. Earning a living from craftwork has never been an easy option, and to gain any extra support, craftsmen have had to adopt the business skills promoted by government agencies. As a result, craftsmen in Scotland have been somewhat more market-oriented and perhaps less adventurous than those in the South. Those most ambitious aim for profit and tend to be production-minded and oriented towards tourist markets. 'Life-stylers', on the other hand, the bane of accountants and the taxman, often produce innovative work. Somewhere between these two extremes, the majority of craftsmen survive by producing work on both a speculative and commissioned basis. As competitors for a tiny market share, they compromise a fiercely independent and individual group.

It was a serious blow to the growing confidence of these small crafts firms when a mysterious perverseness on the part of the Scottish Office led to the virtual withdrawal of Government support in 1991. Both the crafts division of the Scottish Development Agency/and the training and technical resources at Highland Craftpoint were closed down. The Scottish Craft Centre, a craftsman's cooperative retail outlet, had already shut its doors in 1990 after 41 years in business. Ironically, while craftsmen in Scotland were told to make do with an annual trade fair, the Treasury continued to support a wide range of crafts activity in England and Wales. As of April 1993, however, a change of mind has meant that the crafts are to be encouraged once again, this time under the aegis of the Scottish Arts Council, with formal linkages to the Crafts Council in London.

Scottish strengths during the past two decades include ceramics, jewellery/silversmithing and most of the textile crafts, tapestry weaving, hand weaving and knitting, handframe knitwear, silkscreen printing and embroidery. The high quality of this work is due in large to standards set by the four Scottish art colleges, and the Scottish College of Textiles in Galashiels, which has fed an impressive number of its graduates into industrial production throughout the UK.

Public venues such as Aberdeen Art Gallery, Edinburgh City Art Centre and Kelvingrove in Glasgow, have a key role in mounting regular exhibitions of craftwork. While the Royal Scottish Academy declines to include the applied arts in its annual shows, commercial galleries such as The Open Eye and the Scottish Gallery in Edinburgh regularly exhibit craftwork alongside painting and sculpture. The Royal Museum of Scotland has inherited a major collection of contemporary craft work purchased by the Scottish Development Agency (SDA) in the 1980s which, added to its own collection, should create a valuable historical resource. Another fine collection at Paisley Art Gallery and Museum features British studio pottery and Paisley shawls. Museum shops, however, tend to be disappointing.

One of the earliest forms of consumer protection in the UK is the hallmarking of precious metals, dating from 1457. There were enough gold and silversmiths in Edinburgh in 1525 to form a trade guild and by 1750, many silversmiths worked in small burghs such as Tain, Wick, Banff, Elgin, Montrose, Ayr and Greenock as well as in the main cities. Each had its own hallmark. In 1836, however, a law required all Scottish silver to be marked in Edinburgh or Glasgow. The 1841 census records 641 goldsmiths, silversmiths and jewellers in Scotland, evidence of considerable custom from churches and private clients. When assaying ceased at Glasgow in 1963, the Edinburgh Assay Office became the sole source of a Scottish hallmark, a symbolic Edinburgh Castle. There are now some 200 jewellery and silversmithing workshops, many started by art college graduates. Yet commemorative silverware commissions remain rare and there is still much evidence of playing safe. However, it augers well that the experimental work of Scottish students has for several years taken many of the major prizes in national design competitions.

Glass is an expensive craft to practice, and there are only a few successful businesses in blown glass and in the more traditional area of paperweight manufacture. Recently, stained-glass artists have been invited by architects to work to challenging briefs, achieving a national lead in the field. The resulting works are to be found not only in churches but also in offices, universities and shopping centres. Engraved glass, another area in which Scottish craftsmen excel, is commissioned mainly for special presentations. The best of this work demonstrates fine drawing in combination with engraving skills, although the lead crystal blanks, for use in this process, are mainly imported.

Today a number of craftsmen develop their skills in a more scientific direction and become conservationists, servicing both museum and private collections. Scotland pioneered the wide dissemination of information on conservation of both buildings and objects and through the SDA (now SE), has done much to generate work for architects and the 180 crafts businesses listed in the *Scottish Conservation Directory*.

It has never been a smooth ride, but craftsmen can be more optimistic. Public enthusiasm for long-dead skills generated by *Antiques Roadshow* may be mostly about the prices present-day owners might fetch at auction, but it does craftsmen no harm to have experts glowingly praise qualities of past craftsmanship. It is encouraging too that art galleries find it commercially sound to exhibit craftwork with sculpture and painting. European markets are opening and innovative crafts firms have survived a recession. Perhaps the most exciting development is the scope now being given to craftsmen to contribute to the built environment. Local authorities and architects are commissioning original works in a variety of media for new buildings and public sites, giving more people an opportunity to experience at first hand the visual and tactile qualities of art, applied.

S. Smith

Cricket undoubtedly came to Scotland from England and most probably was introduced in the early 1700s by military forces stationed in towns such as Kelso, Edinburgh, Glasgow, Stirling, Perth and Aberdeen, all areas where early records of the game are known.

This is certainly true for Perth where soldiers were recorded as playing on the North Inch about 1750 and later in 1812. James Hogg, in a novel published in 1824, suggests that the game was practised in Edinburgh by 1705 and it is known that Glasgow University students were playing by 1790.

The *Caledonian Mercury* reports the two earliest known matches; the first in 1785 at Shaw Park, Alloa and the second in 1789 at Aberdeen. Shaw Park was the home of The Earl Cathcart who, with several relatives, played in the game. A painting by David Allan of the Cathcart family shows the game as a background. In the second match Col. Charles Lennox (later Duke of Richmond) scored a century. Here we had men of rank and property bringing the game north and it is clear that those matches were reported because of the social standing of the players.

But others of lesser degree, such as the textile workers in the Border towns, papermakers in Penicuik, ironworkers in Coatbridge and excisemen in the northeast were coming north and establishing the game in their regions of employment.

Schoolmasters brought the game into schools, particularly in the Edinburgh area. Engravings of the High Schools of Edinburgh (1819) and Leith (1820) show pupils carrying bats and the game was played from the beginning at residential schools such as Loretto (1825), Merchiston (1833), and Glenalmond (1842).

Gradually clubs appeared, the earliest known being at Kelso, who possess a Minute Book dating from 1821. Perth can claim the first external club match in 1826 against a local military team on the North Inch whilst the Edinburgh Brunswick, in spite of the lack of railway transport, travelled to play the Western on Glasgow Green in 1830.

In 1832 several wealthy men formed the Grange Club which played on a private field in the Grange district of Edinburgh and in 1834 they engaged as groundsman and coach John Sparks, a prominent English cricketer, thus becoming the first Scottish club to play on their own ground and engage a professional. In 1836 they moved to a better field at Grove Street and quickly established themselves as one of the strongest clubs in the country.

In 1849 they brought the famous All-England XI to Grove Street to play a 20 which included players from Grange, Perth, Glasgow Albyn and the Garrison. In the second innings Charles Lawrence of Perth took all 10 wickets. This match firmly established the game in Scotland for it created so much interest that thereafter clubs sprang up all over the country. In the west Clydesdale and later Drumpellier and the West of Scotland were soon staging similar matches on their own grounds whilst Kelso and Perth, using public parks, were equally active.

The spreading of the railway systems (the first Edinburgh-Glasgow line opened in 1842) allowed clubs to widen their fixture cards and then in 1872 the first East and West Elevens were selected to open the Grange's present ground at Raeburn Place.

The first Scottish Cricket Union was formed in 1877 only to collapse in 1883 when a dissatisfied Grange, having withdrawn, put forward proposals which would authorize them, aided by two elected representatives from the other clubs, to take over the main duties attempted by the Union. At this time Grange with a great playing strength, a fine field in Edinburgh and a high social standing wielded such an influence that they were able to persuade a majority of the Union clubs to agree to this mandate with the result that from 1884 to 1907 Grange acted as the administrators of the game in Scotland, arranging international matches and chairing an annual meeting of club representatives in Edinburgh.

Inevitably this single-club domination met with opposition which came to a head in the early 1900s and Grange, who incidentally had found the organizing of international games an expensive duty, gave way to join with other clubs to form the present Union in 1908.

The new Union soon had to establish its authority by firmly rapping a few knuckles but has now survived two wars and can fairly claim to have raised the quality of its representative teams by the policy of arranging more matches against County and touring teams. Several of its choices, which include a Test captain, have been playing successfully in English County teams.

A. M. C. Thorburn

Crofting is a form of small-holding agriculture confined to the seven Crofting Counties and the *c.* 17,700 crofts are holdings with a rental of £100 or less or of 30 ha. or lesser extent, recorded in the Crofters Commission Register. Ninety-five per cent of all crofts are tenanted and more than 95 per cent of all working units (individual crofts or groups of crofts worked by the same person) are part-time holdings requiring less than 250 standard man-days input of labour. The total extent of land in crofting tenure is 734,000 ha. or 22 per cent of the agricultural land of the Highlands and Islands, the bulk of it on infertile and poorly drained soils.

The origin of the crofts can be traced to the period of agricultural improvement of the late eighteenth and early nineteenth centuries. During this period, the arable and pasture land on certain multiple-tenancy farms or on farms held by tacksmen with sub-tenants was lotted in unenclosed small-holdings and the rough pasture or shieling grounds of these farms was shared by tenants of these lots as common grazings with grazing rights or *soumings* expressed as the number of breeding cows, breeding ewes and *followers* (young cattle and sheep) which might be pastured by each tenant. In areas with machair plains, as in the southern Hebrides, the arable land was often shared in a number of non-contiguous, unfenced strips. The sharing of land resources engendered a distinctive communal spirit in these crofting communities.

These divided farms became known as crofting townships and the crofts were usually laid out in long rectangular lots, running from the moorland to the coast or from the hillside to the river in valley locations. The houses and outbuildings were sited on the individual lots, often in a regular line. The characteristic crofting landscape is a planned entity, deliberately created for economic reasons; the earliest crofting townships may well be those created on the Argyll estates *c.* 1786 to exploit resources of seaweed but the system spread and small lots, generally without leases and too small for subsistence, were created to fulfil the main economic objective of the estates, the manufacture of kelp or the prosecution of sea fisheries.

Kelp manufacture proved ephemeral, and from 1815 to

1830, first cattle and then kelp prices fell drastically and the estate rentals were no longer secure. The introduction of sheep led to certain crofting townships being cleared of their tenantry: the potato famine of 1847–50 led to further evictions. During the clearances (q.v.), further crofts were established on the poorer coastal peninsulas or on interior moorlands. Growing pressure of population on the remaining croft land led to local unrest in the 1870s and the establishment of a Royal Commission of Inquiry into crofting. The ensuing Crofters Holdings (Scotland) Act of 1886 gave all crofters security of tenure, rights to bequeath their tenancy and to receive compensation for improvements on renouncing their holdings and the Crofters Commission was set up in 1886 to determine fair rents and draw up grazing regulations. A subsequent Royal Commission was set up in 1892 to identify land which might form new crofts or be suitable for the extension of existing townships. Over 2,600 new crofts were created, over 5,000 crofts enlarged and more than 19,000 ha. of arable land and 250,000 ha. of pasture were added to the crofting lands between 1897 and 1939, and the lands lost to small tenants during the nineteenth century were virtually returned.

From 1954, with the re-establishment of the Crofters Commission charged with regulating and developing crofting and major assistance from the Department of Agriculture and Fisheries and the North of Scotland College of Agriculture, apportionments of common land, undersowing of arable land and stock and pasture improvements have taken place and crofter housing has been renewed or greatly improved. No comprehensive, detailed statistics reflecting these developments exist, but a study of change in certain South Uist townships between 1957 and 1976 showed that of the 108 legal crofts, 74 working units in 1975 had declined to 65 in 1976, the average size of the units had increased from 19 to 22 ha. and the average number of breeding cows had increased from 3.6 to 5.1 per working unit.

The map broadly depicts the distribution of the contemporary crofting lands, crofts and working units in 1977. Almost two-thirds of all crofts are located on islands: the remainder are almost equally divided between the north and west and east coasts and their hinterlands, with a distinctly lesser distribution in West Inverness and Argyllshire. In parts of Caithness and in Orkney, crofts are often small farms without common grazing but whose low rental qualified for inclusion under the Crofters Act of 1886. The average croft today is a small-holding with some 4 ha. of crops and grass and grazing rights on 30 ha. of common grazing, a stock of 4 breeding cows, and 20 ewes with the tenant in regular employment. Store cattle and wedder lambs are the main product.

With progressive depopulation and the gradual increase of employment in services, the number of active crofters has declined and the Crofters Commission statistics on working units do not wholly reflect considerable informal sub-letting of land nor the decline in intensity of land use often reducing the role of the croft to the grazing of a small sheep flock. The majority of active crofters are above 45 years of age; the younger age groups are little represented in crofting so that the future survival of numerous individual small-holdings is uncertain. On the other hand, through amalgamation of crofts through assignments, bequests, purchase of improvements and sub-letting, a small but significant group of larger working units is growing with active, enterprising crofters using modern equipment building up stocks of over 30 breeding cows. The Crofting Reform (Scotland) Act of 1976 now confers on the tenant the right to purchase his croft, a measure which may well lead to the development of activities other than agriculture on some crofts. These include participation in the benefits of tourism. Crofting is not static but still evolving.

J. B. Caird and A. Fenton

Cults, Literary. 'Scotland has long gloried in the fame of her divinest son'. The words come from the *Edinburgh Evening Courant* of 27 January 1816, reporting an historic Burns Supper attended by Walter Scott, Francis Jeffrey, 'Christopher North', George Thomson the publisher of many of Burns's songs, and other prominent men of the time. James Hogg had been invited, too, and Scott thought there must have been 'a snow storm in the headlands' to have kept him away. The Burns Cult was gathering force.

It began in 1786 with the publication of *Poems, Chiefly In The Scottish Dialect* at Kilmarnock. Burns's earliest readers delighted in his work, and beyond Ayrshire, Henry Mackenzie summed up what many people wanted to believe in describing the poet in *The Lounger* as 'this Heaven-taught ploughman'. Primitivism, or faith in natural, untaught genius as both the condition and rare source of the highest artistic excellence, thrived in eighteenth-century Edinburgh, a city much given to theorizing; hence the still continuing excitement over James Macpherson's claims to have discovered and translated fragments of ancient Gaelic poetry. Burns seemed to meet all of the requirements of this pre-existing cult. The title page of the Kilmarnock edition even carried this verse:

> The Simple Bard, unbroke by rules of Art,
> He pours the wild effusions of the heart:
> And if inspir'd, 'tis Nature's pow'rs inspire;
> Her's all the melting thrill, and her's the kindling fire.

Burns's fame was assured, but not long after his death in 1796 he was criticized on various grounds. Because of the French war, the period was one of intense political sensitivity. Some were quick to suggest that towards the end of his life the poet had flirted irresponsibly with 'jacobin' or revolutionary ideas. To this political point was added the imputation, based upon nothing more substantial than gossip and a clumsily worded obituary notice, that he had lived dissolutely and died of drink. Finally, the poems which had made his name did not seem to have been followed up in the manner Mackenzie and others had hoped they would be. Instead, Burns had devoted his later years to song-writing, an activity which was not well publicized or understood.

Thus the first efforts to honour the poet's memory were made against a background of denigratory talk and whispered criticism. What took place was not an underground campaign, or even in its early stages a deliberately concerted movement; but Burns had championed the common man and liberal ideals, and in some places, and on the part of certain individuals, there was a connection with Foxite and similar political anniversary celebrations. Appropriately, the practice of holding an annual Supper on or near the poet's birthday began in the west of Scotland. The first Burns Clubs to be formally constituted were Greenock (1801), Paisley (1805), and Kilmarnock (1808), followed in 1812 by Dunfermline. In 1811, William Peebles, who had been mocked by Burns in no fewer than three satires, attacked the Greenock Burns Club in ragged, scornful verse. Understandably enough, he could not tolerate the idea of Burns having become a kind of national hero:

> To the great bard, erect a Bust:
> Nor is this all: from age to age,
> As for a monarch, hero, sage,
> Let anniversaries repeat
> His glories, celebrate a fete
> Imbibe his spirit, sing his songs,
> Extol his name, lament his wrongs,
> His death deplore, accuse his fate.
> And raise his name far above the great.
> What call you this? Is it Insania?
> I'll coin a word, 'tis Burnomania.
> His Greenock friends we therefore dub
> The Annual Burnomanian Club.

But 'Burnomania' had come to stay, and the poet was indeed a national hero of a special kind. It can be argued that the reasons had much to do with Scotland's frustrations and tangled cultural history, that the nation needed such a figure as Burns. However, Burns's communicative flair and mastery of sentiment should not be overlooked. Unlike many poets, he had written simply and directly, of love and the human comedy, while in both his poems and songs he showed his love of Scotland. His way of summing up the plight of the poor and underprivileged earned him his standing as spokesman for ordinary folk everywhere. Moreover, in an age of progressive industrialization, which brought constant movement from the land to towns and cities, his rural writings were deeply appealing; as was his evocation of a Scotland they seemed to have known in youth to emigrants and exiles. By 1859, the centenary of his birth, the habit of meeting to honour the name of Burns and all that he stood for had spread to many countries overseas.

In the twentieth century that habit has continued to thrive, supported by the far-flung international Federation of Burns Clubs, and by the continuing popularity of the poet's work, especially 'Tam o' Shanter', a handful of other poems, and a number of songs. Burns is part of the Scottish image the world over. Yet for this very reason some reaction was inevitable. The Burns movement has had its critics, and none more eloquent than Hugh MacDiarmid, who wrote in *A Drunk Man Looks At The Thistle* (1926):

No' wan in fifty kens a wurd Burns wrote

> But misapplied is a'body's property,
> And gin there was his like alive the day
> They'd be the last a kennin' haund to gi'e—
> Croose London Scotties wi' their braw shirt fronts
> and a' their fancy freen's, rejoicin'
> That similah gatherings in Timbuctoo,
> Bagdad—and Hell, nae doot—are voicin'
> Burn's sentiments o' universal love,
> In pidgin' English or in wild-fowl Scots,
> And toastin' ane wha's nocht to them but an
> Excuse for faitherin' Genius wi' *their* thochts.

To MacDiarmid it appeared that

> As Kirks wi' Christianity hae dune,
> Burns Clubs wi' Burns—wi' a' thing it's the same,
> The core o' ocht is only for the few,
> Scorned by the mony, thrang wi'ts empty name.

There is a MacDiarmid cult, but MacDiarmid was essentially an élitist thinker, like Ezra Pound, poles apart in outlook from Burns. Despite the range of his gifts and achievement, it does not seem likely that he will ever have the popular following of Burns.

A minor but characteristic and persistent cult is that of William McGonagall, Dundee weaver, or, as he styled himself on broadsheets 'Sir William Topaz McGonagall, Poet and Tragedian, Knight of the White Elephant, Burma', as Awful or Enjoyable Bad Poet, whose verses—especially those on the Tay Bridge Railway disaster—are frequently reprinted.

Prose has not produced any cult on the Burnsian scale, but Scott's novels (very notably), Stevenson's *Kidnapped and Treasure Island*, and Lewis Grassic Gibbon's *Sunset Song*, have all attracted devotees.

D. A. Low

Cunninghame Graham, Robert Bontine (1852–1936), was the son of the Laird of Gartmore and grandson of Robert Graham (1735?–1797?), one time Member of Parliament for Stirlingshire, and Rector of Glasgow University, remembered today for his lyric 'If doughty deeds my lady please'. In 1796 Robert Graham altered the family name, adding the then hyphenated Cunninghame.

R.B. Cunninghame Graham was born in London, three-quarters descended from noble Scottish blood, one quarter from Spanish. Brought up by his Spanish grandmother, Spanish was the first language he learned. He was educated at Harrow, an experience that left him with a vigorous dislike of the English public-school system, and by the time he was 17 he had already travelled in South America. He married a Chilean poetess, Gabriela de la Belmondière, in 1879, and five years later inherited the family estates, only to find them hopelessly overburdened with debts. He therefore sold Gartmore and settled on the small estate of Ardoch, Dunbartonshire, on the River Clyde.

His entry into politics began with his election for northwest

Lanarkshire in 1886, a seat he held until 1892. He described his years in the House as enduring 'the concentrated idiocy of the Asylum for Imbeciles at Westminster'. With Keir Hardie he founded the Scottish Labour Party, and was imprisoned in 1887 for his part in the 'Bloody Sunday' Trafalgar Square riots of 13 November. In 1897 he made an exploratory journey to Morocco, resulting in several of his finest short stories and the book *Mogreb-el-Acksa* (1898). This was the first of many journeys to the then lesser known countries, especially those in South America. He was, indeed, an incorrigible traveller in the tradition of Charles Doughty and Robert Burton, though he put his experiences to greater literary use. *El Rio de la Plata* (1914) is his testimony to his South American journeys.

His best stories are to be found in *Thirteen Stories* (1900), *Success* (1902), *Faith* (1909), *Hope* (1911), *Charity* (1912), and *Scottish Stories* (1914). His strength as a story-teller lay in his relentless portrayal of his characters, usually against a vividly but economically etched colourful background, in situations pursued to their logical end. Sentimentality was no part of his style, as the grim humour of his much-anthologized Scottish story 'Beattock for Moffat' illustrates.

His other books include several biographies, the most important being *Doughty Deeds* (1925), a study of his famous ancestor. In 1928 he became the first President of the Scottish National Party.

A passionate champion of the underdog, a man of flamboyant style and a rapier wit—'I sometimes wish I could believe in religion, for if I did I could be sure that Gladstone is in hell'—he was the friend of Morris, Wells, Beerbohm, Whistler and Shaw. The great Irish dramatist used his friend's aphorism 'I *never* withdraw', made in the House of Commons, as 'I *never* apologize' in *Arms and the Man*.

Several biographies have been produced, *Don Roberto* (1937) by A.J. Tchiffely being the most colourful. Currently, the most up-to-date is *Cunninghame Graham: A Critical Biography* by Cedric Watts and Laurence Davies (1979). There have also been several reprints of selections of his stories, including *Beattock for Moffat and the Best of R.B. Cunninghame Graham* (1979). Under the editorship of Professor John Walker recent American reprints of his work include *The South and North American Sketches of R.B. Cunninghame Graham* (two volumes) and *An Annotated Bibliography of Works on Cunninghame Graham*.

M. Lindsay

Curling is a game played on ice by rinks, or teams, of four players, each of whom throws two large, heavy, polished, handled stones along a sheet of ice. The object is to place more of one's rink's stones closer to the 'tee', or centre, of a 12-foot circle, (the 'house'), marked on the ice, than the nearest stone of the opposing rink. A game consists of 'ends': each end is completed when all 16 stones have been thrown. Thus it is only possible for one rink to score at each end.

The 'skip', or captain, of each rink directs the play. Originally on natural outdoor ice it was necessary to sweep snow and other debris from the path of a running stone. This used to be done with a bunch of broom. Straw besoms and latterly horsehair or nylon brushes replaced this. It has been found that hard sweeping of the ice in front of a running stone can cause it to travel up to 15 feet further than an unswept stone. Moreover, the curler imparts a rotation to the stone as he delivers it, which causes it to deviate from a straight course to one side or the other, in the manner of lawn bowls. Sweeping affects the degree to which this occurs. Thus all members of a rink participate, often energetically, in every stone of the game.

Despite some scholarly disagreement the received view is that curling is of Scottish origin. In any event it was in the Lowlands of Scotland that the game evolved from a rough trial of strength with huge misshapen boulders to the elegant and skilful game of today. It was from Scotland that it has spread to the colder parts of the New World, Europe, and the Antipodes.

Curling used to be a game of the winter, played for a few days, or at most weeks, only on natural ice, on lochs, rivers, and specially constructed shallow ponds. Nowadays there are ice rinks in most parts of Scotland and the season occupies not only the whole winter but borrows the end of the autumn and the beginning of spring as well. In fact at Aviemore Ice Rink there is a midsummer bonspiel.

The game was formerly organized on a parochial and democratic basis; laird played with tenant, lord with cottar; and skill, not rank, determined the order of play. Each parish had its own rules. For instance, in most parts of southwest Scotland a rink consisted of seven, eight, or nine curlers, each throwing a single stone; whereas in Edinburgh and district four men playing two stones each was the custom; and the rules as to Sweeping varied considerably.

With the improvement in communications at the beginning of the nineteenth century curlers were beginning to travel further in pursuit of competition. By 1838 it had become necessary to impose order on diversity and the Royal Caledonian Curling Club was formed to unite curlers into 'one brotherhood of the rink and regulate by rules the ancient Scottish game of curling'. From that time it has been the 'Mother Club' of curling and has legislated for, and promoted, the game by organizing local and national competitions. The largest of these—the Grand Match between the south and north of Scotland; involving about 3,000 curlers, on one of the large lochs in Central Scotland is planned each year, but such is the Scottish climate that it seldom takes place. Other competitions abound, however, in the various ice rinks, and there is seldom a week in which a keen curler cannot find an excellent competition in some part of Scotland.

D. B. Smith

D

Dance. There are three forms of dance which are uniquely Scottish. These may be called (after the dancer or combination of dancers): solo, couple, and set dances, all of which have Scottish and general European antecedents.

Little is known about the pre-Renaissance dancing of Scotland, although there are indications that many current steps and figures have their origins in both the medieval Lowlands and Highlands.

Except for reels and twosomes all of what is termed Highland dancing falls into the category of solo dancing. In Scottish solo dancing, little attention is paid to the pattern on the floor, while importance is placed upon the precise execution of intricate footwork. In their early forms, dance steps were either characterized by the rhythm of the feet treading the floor (as in hornpipes and modern tap-dancing), or by hopping on one foot while the other is moved to predetermined positions (setting or capering).

Two of the most noted solo dances are the Fling and the Sword Dance. Before the nineteenth century, the word 'fling' was used to denote a particular step. In 1805, however, we find the earliest unambiguous reference to a distinct form of dance known as the Fling. Its steps, which are also used for setting in appropriate places in couple and set dances, are characterized by the kicking of the free foot into the air (hence fling). The number and combination of fling steps is almost infinite and was not regulated or standardized until the foundation of the Scottish Official Board of Highland Dancing (SOBHD), in 1953. At present the Fling consists of four to eight steps, each with a descriptive name in the Lowland tongue (shedding, shaking, rocking, etc.) or in Gaelic (ceum coisiche, leum a trasd, etc.).

The fling steps, when they first appear in documented sources, are described as taught by the dancing masters who were greatly influenced by the Continental ballet. As a result, the steps of the modern Fling (and almost all Scottish Dancing) are described and taught in the rigid terms of the ballet positions.

The Sword Dance (Gille Callum), as danced over a sword and not with the dancer holding one, is first alluded to in the mid eighteenth century, with its tune first referred to in 1734 (published in 1768). The first example of a description appears in 1881. Other solo dances, still popular, include character or occupational dances (jigs, hornpipes, etc.), the Seann Truibhas, and nationals (the Scottish Lilt, Wilt Thou Go to the Barracks Johnny, The Earl of Errol, etc.).

After 1800, couple or round-the-room dances were popular throughout the western world. Many of the early dances of this period used the step-step-step-hop pattern of the Scottish strathspey and reel time skip-change-of-step (ceum siubhail). On the Continent, these are known as ecossaises or schottisches (the latter reimported into Scotland). Later the waltz, never as popular in Scotland as in England and on the Continent, came in with other couple dances, whose descendants are now known in Scotland and England as 'Old Time Dances'! These nineteenth-century dances include: schottisches, barn dances, and sequenced polkas and waltzes. This tradition has continued unbroken into the present, modified by different popular forms from an international dance repertoire set to Scottish traditional music.

The earliest forms of set dances featured ring and chain formations and their related figures. The modern dance form with the oldest known source is the Highland Reel. It consists of a chain or reel figure made up of three or more dancers in a line, who alternate dancing a figure-of-eight pattern around each other (the hay) and setting (the caper). Evidence of circle dances appears in children's games and early quadrilles.

The ring and chain dances both gave way to the longways set of two facing lines (men on one side, facing women on the other, or alternating men and women on each side). The sets were for 'as many as will', limited only by the size of the room or the stamina of the musicians. The modern set is usually limited to four couples dancing eight repetitions of the music with 24 to 40 measures per repetition usually. These are called 'country dances' from the French 'contra' referring to the opposing lines of dancers. As evidenced by John Playford's *Dancing Master* of 1651, there were many of these country dances still popular which dated back to the beginning of the seventeenth century, as indicated by their tunes and titles.

From the time of Playford until the reign of the Georges (I to IV) there was a social division between the different styles of country dancing. The courts of Scotland and England introduced country dances as 'licht' (second-best and not serious) dances, usually reserved for the end of the evening's dancing. Later country dances were moved into the repertoire of the main part of the evening, where they almost replaced the minuet (which gave way to the waltz in the nineteenth century). When the country dances became the popular dances of the courts, they became more rigid in form and footwork, giving rise to the later tradition, kept alive by the country gentry and burghal middle class, through the itinerant dancing masters. At the same time both the steps and figures were danced in a more open form by the lower classes. Each of these two styles of dancing supplied the other with ideas, because of the democratic nature of a predominantly rural Scotland without a resident court. Court dances and fashions, in modified forms, influenced the dancing of the countryside and the indigenous rural forms influenced the steps and figures of the court.

In the nineteenth century, the longways set was supplanted in most of Europe by the new quadrilles and couple dances (waltz and polka). In Scotland, the country dances lived on in the burgh and countryside until the First World War, after which they rapidly began to decline. During this period, the longways set was augmented by new figures and formations. The old round reel reappeared as a quadrille in such popular dances as the Scottish Eightsome Reel and the foreign La Russe. The Swedish progression of couples facing couples round the room gave rise to the Scottish versions of The Circassian Circle, La Tempete, The Dashing White Sergeant, and Waltz Country Dance.

The decline of Scottish country dancing had been early identified in the middle of the nineteenth century and by 1881 James Stewart Robertson had founded the Highland Reel and Strathspey Society. This was followed by numerous efforts and publications aimed at keeping both Highland and country dancing alive. In Glasgow, in 1913, the late Dr Jean Milligan founded the Beltane Society to revive country dancing. In 1923, Mrs Stewart of Fasnacloich, assisted by Lord James (later Duke of Atholl) and Dr Milligan, founded the (now Royal) Scottish Country Dance Society (RSCDS). This Society selected the period 1860 to 1880 as the golden age of country dancing and attempted to resurrect its style while publishing dances from living memory to manuscripts dating back to the mid seventeenth century. The work of the Society has been augmented by the efforts to the English Folk Dance and Song Society (EFDSS), the Imperial Society of Teachers of Dance (ISTD), the British Association of Teachers of Dance (BATD), and the Scottish Official Board of Highland Dancing (SOBHD)—founded in 1953 to save Highland dancing. An associated benefit of the Society's work is in its network of branches and affiliated groups throughout the world, bringing Scottish culture to both the Scot and the scotophile.

At the same time, the Society in Scotland speaks with less authority than overseas. Here it is used mostly as a reference, guide and a source of dances, as there is still a non-literate tradition of country dances and dancing, alive and somewhat unaffected by the Society's ballroom style.

Today there is both a living and a written and oral tradition supporting the three forms of Scottish dance. Solo dancing, published and taught by the Society but specifically within the domain of the Scottish Official Board of Highland Dancing, is covered under the area of Highland dancing. Solo dancing along with the Highland Reel and Reel of Tulloch is very much a part of the Highland gatherings, both for purposes of demonstration and competition. The Scottish Official Board of Highland Dancing is constantly revising its syllabus to provide for more dances and more steps to existing dances.

Couple dances are danced as 'old time dances' at ceilidhs, weddings and in dancing clubs, the Gay Gordons being the most popular.

Country dancing organizations are not just resurrecting and republishing the old dances but are encouraging the devising and publication of new ones. Well known in this field are: James B. Cosh, John Drewry, and the late Hugh Foss. The Royal Scottish Country Dance Society published the Reel of the Fifty-first Division, its first modern dance in traditional style, just after the Second World War and has continued to publish more of these modern devisings. The Scottish Dance Archives acts as a clearing-house both for its own and privately published dances.

The interest in Scottish dancing has affected interrelated areas of Scottish culture, such as history, folk tales, songs, and especially music. The country dance bands, besides playing well known traditional reels, jigs, and strathspeys, have adapted other Scottish musical forms to the dance idiom as well as composed new tunes. This has aided in the preservation and performance of the traditional music of the pipes and fiddle, along with the more modern piano and accordion.

R. N. Goss

Dark Ages. The Dark Ages covers the period between the departure of the Romans in the 4th century and the accession of Malcolm Canmore in the 11th. 'Scotland' in the fifth century could not be said to exist.

503 is the traditional date for the arrival of the Scots under Fergus mac Erc in Argyll. Almost certainly however a continuous movement of people between Ireland and Scotland had been taking place for generations. Already in existence were the Pictish kingdoms of the east and north. In the west lay the kingdom of Strathclyde ruled by the descendants of Coel Hen (Old King Cole of later legend), a dynasty possibly established by the Romans as a buffer state for their northern frontier. South again around the Solway Firth lay the kingdom of Rheged, and in Lothian the land of the Gododdin. These kingdoms had much more to worry them than the fledgling kingdom of Dalriada. In the east the young Anglian kingdom of Northumbria, fuelled by migration from the continent was pushing west and north. The clash gave rise to Scotland's oldest poem, Aneirin's 'Y Gododdin' commemorating the heroic defeat of the men of Gododdin at 'Catraeth' by the Angles at the end of the 6th century. Rheged and Gododdin fell before the Anglian advance and the kingdom of Northumbria at the height of its glory controlled all of southern Scotland apart from Strathclyde.

In 685 at the battle of Nechtansmere (Dunnichen) the Northumbrian hegemony was ended by the Picts. The Picts under Onuist rose to prominence before the twin pressures of Dalriada, its links with Ireland broken by military defeat in the mid 7th century, and the Vikings, led to the union of Picts and Scots under Kenneth mac Alpin in 843. Strathclyde too was to suffer greatly at the hands of the Vikings and the attack and sack of Dumbarton by the Viking 'Great Army' in the 860s has been confirmed by archaeology.

However, the nascent Scottish kingdom survived and continued its slow expansion. Strathclyde gradually fell into a relation of clientship, disappearing around the time of the battle of Carham in 1018. By the 10th century the threat of Wessex was very real and Constantine III led an army of all the peoples of the north to defeat at the battle of Brunanburh in 934 (commemorated in 'Egil's Saga').

Carham, however, confirmed the Scottish hold over Lothian, ample compensation for the loss of much of the original

Dalriadic heartland to the Vikings. Relations with the mighty Viking earldom of Orkney with its lands far south into Sutherland fluctuated wildly (Macbeth and Thorfinn the Mighty pilgrimaged together in Rome). The death of Macbeth's son, Lulach, in 1058 at the hands of Canmore is taken to mark the end of the old Celtic kingdom and the beginning of the mediaeval kingdom of Scots.

Christianity came to Scotland from Ireland at the hands of Columba in 563. Columba, of royal birth himself, was of immense political importance and is credited with the conversion of the Picts. The south of Scotland had already been converted by Ninian from 'Candida Casa' (Whithorn). Although the hold of Celtic Christianity began to wane after the Synod of Whitby in 664 it was not until the arrival of Canmore's wife, Margaret, that Roman Christianity completed its conquest of the north.

The northern world formed one cultural entity, as evinced by metalwork and such masterpieces as the Book of Kells, as well as the great High Crosses of Iona or Kildalton. The only exception to this lies in the strange Pictish symbol stones for which no fully convincing explanation has been given. These carry a series of symbols, individually or in groups, and are often 'christianised' with a cross often demonstrating Anglian interlace techniques to a high level. Since no written records exist from the Pictish kingdoms we have no internal evidence to adduce their purpose.

Linguistically, Scotland was divided between the P-Celtic (Welsh type) speakers—the Britons of Strathclyde and, possibly, the Picts, though there is argument over whether or not they spoke an Indo-European language; the Angles; and the Q-Celts (Irish). The Gaelic of the Q-Celts spread over most of Scotland with the Dalriadic advance and the other languages disappeared, apart from in Lothians and the Borders.

The period saw the change from a post Roman frontier society to a great cultural grouping around the Irish Sea towards an early medieval monarchy centralising in response to pressure from the south. Paradoxically, the existence of a strong Anglian kingdom of Northumbria proved essential to the maintenance of the Celtic world around the Irish Sea. The final collapse of Northumbria with the death of Eric Bloodaxe in 956 was perhaps the death knell to the fragile balance of power which had seen such a great efflorescence of art and culture.

H. Andrew

Deorsa Mac Iain Deorsa *see* **Hay, George Campbell**

Diaries. The appeal of diaries is as varied as the lives of those who have kept them. In one sense, they are the very essence of history, truthfully conveying the nature of everyday experience, with occasional excursions into the description of major events and upheavals in public life. They follow no uniform pattern, but instead may range at random over such subjects as the diarist's work, his family, acquaintances, eating habits, travels, or opinions. Some diaries are restricted in scope to minute and systematic note-keeping on, for example, financial affairs or the weather. From these, it is hard to gain more than an outline impression of the diarist's personality, yet they have their own value. Others in contrast are frankly confessional in character, revealing at least as much of the writer's inner nature as letters or other, more formal kinds of written communication. Many lively diaries combine with an otherwise straightforward record of events the expression of strong enthusiasms and prejudices.

Scotland has not given the world a Pepys or a Fanny Burney, but excellent Scottish diarists have not been lacking. Two of these were lawyers born and bred, James Boswell and Walter Scott. Boswell must rank among the most readable of all journal-writers, endlessly interesting not merely because of his candour in writing about his sex life—although this admittedly gives his work a bawdy flavour to match that of Pepys—but because he is genuinely interested himself in everything which happens to him. His London journal is a record of a proud, touchy, insecure Scot seeking to discover the great world and at the same time to establish his identity. The quality of the writing comes from a tension between his compulsive wish to note down what he observes among his fellow men and women—the lawyer's instinct as memorialist—and his introspective turn, which is compounded by bouts of melancholy. He reports conversations with the zest and care for detail of a born biographer.

The very different journal which Scott kept in his final, tragic years, stands as a heroic record of a great man's struggle against adversity. Unlike the young Boswell's, Scott's character was stable and completely formed when he embarked on the project with the words

> As I walked by myself
> I talked to my self
> And thus my self said to me.

But in Scott's case, too, the intimate journal form leads to remarkable writing at moments of self-discovery. Nothing in Boswell is more revealing than Scott's wry autobiographical jottings during his financial crisis in 1825:

> What a life mine has been. Half educated, almost wholly neglected or left to myself—stuffing my head with most nonsensical trash and undervalued in society for a time by most of my companions—getting forward and held a bold and clever fellow, contrary to the opinion of all who thought me a mere dreamer—Broken-hearted for two years—My heart handsomely pieced again—but the crack will remain till my dying day—Rich and poor four or five times—Once on the verge of ruin yet opend new sources of wealth almost over-flowing—now taken in the pitch of pride and nearly winged (unless the good news hold) because London chuses to be in an uproar and in the tumult of bulls and bears a poor inoffensive lion like myself is pushd to the wall—And what is to be the end of it? God knows and so ends the chatechism.

Scott's reference to the catechism here is playful, yet it points to a driving force behind Boswell's attempts to delineate experience satisfactorily and his own. Both were sons of Calvin in their prodigious verbal energy and severe self-scrutiny.

Lesser Scottish diaries abound. In the second rank must be grouped the troubled chronicle of James Melville, the sixteenth-century reformer, standing by the side of his uncle 'Mr Andro' (Andrew Melville) in his quarrel with James VI; Alexander 'Jupiter' Carlyle of Inveresk's autobiography, which spans the greater part of the eighteenth century; the 'Memoirs of A Highland Lady' of Elizabeth Grant; and the sad, spirited diary of Jane Welsh Carlyle. Each of these narratives has a distinctive style, and after reading any of them for a time we become familiar with the diarist's personal 'voice', so that it is almost as if we were hearing him or her speak, rather than reading cold print. Most remarkable of all in this respect, and indeed at times surpassing in interest both Boswell and Scott, is another lawyer, Henry Cockburn. Cockburn's *Memorials Of His Time*, written in the 1820s, and his later *Journal* and *Circuit Journeys*, convey with subtlety, penetration, and humour the changing quality of life in Scotland, and especially in Edinburgh, as he observed it between the time of the French Revolution and the railway age. Not only does he summarize shifts in attitude and behaviour succinctly, he has an eye for every kind of character and eccentricity, such as for instance those of 'a singular race of excellent Scotch old ladies' who helped to set the tone of society in his boyhood:

> They were a delightful set; strong headed, warm hearted, and high spirited, the fire of their tempers not always latent; merry even in solitude; very resolute; indifferent about the modes and habits of the modern world; and adhering to their own ways, so as to stand out, like primitive rocks, above ordinary society.

The group portrait is followed, in Cockburn, by individual character sketches of the most notable ladies to whom this passage refers, including Sophia 'or, as she was always called, Suphy' Johnston, a good carpenter and smith, who would declare to any man who ventured a foolish opinion in fashionable company—in the midst of which she sat in greatcoat, men's trousers, and heavy shoes—'That's surely great nonsense, sir'.

Just as the pace of modern living and the telephone have between them curtailed the art of letter-writing, so the full-scale diaries which many people kept as a matter of course last century have become increasingly rare. If it has always been true that many diaries have been little more than lists of appointments, interspersed with occasional comments, it is certainly the case today. Yet the impulse to record in detail the texture of daily life is not likely to yield completely to the laconic habit of the times or to new technology. Among twentieth-century Scottish diarists, mention should be made of the poet William Soutar, selections from whose work have been published under the title *Diaries Of A Dying Man*.

D. A. Low

Disruption, The, of the Church of Scotland in 1843 is rightly regarded as a crucial episode—if not *the* crucial episode—in its history since the Reformation. To that earlier cataclysmic event some of the basic issues at stake three centuries later bore striking similarity, foremost amongst which was the claim of the Church to exercise free, independent, spiritual jurisdiction, a jurisdiction nevertheless coordinate with the State and exercised in cooperation with the civil government. By the passing of the Patronage Act in 1712 the United Kingdom Parliament restored to patrons of ecclesiastical benefices rights of presentation which had had a varied history since the Reformation and which potentially could conflict with the freedom of congregations to secure through presbyteries qualified ministers of their own choice. It could also conflict with any desire on the part of the Church through its General Assemblies to erect unilaterally additional parish churches. In the eighteenth century a small number of secessions did take place as some members of parish congregations refused to accept presentees who were forced upon them by the courts of the Church acting in accordance with the law. In the next century relations between patrons and congregations and between the courts of the Church and the civil courts deteriorated when Evangelical, as opposed to Moderate views, began to be more widely held. To meet the needs of the day General Assemblies, in which the Evangelicals led by Thomas Chalmers were predominant, passed both the Chapel and the Veto Acts which they held to be binding upon the Church. Appeals against the operation of the Acts to the Court of Session led to a contrary decision. The Church was held to have exceeded its bounds, acted *ultra vires*, and encroached upon the statutory rights of patrons and heritors. Faced with the social and religious challenges of the day, the Church, in which those of an Evangelical persuasion were steadily increasing, particularly in the towns, believed that it had the inherent right, the freedom to act as it had done. Further, some believed that the State connection, epitomized in the upholding of the rights of patrons, was militating against the Church's obligation to meet the spiritual needs of the nation. Prepared to sacrifice the benefits of establishment, about one-third of the ministers demitted their charges, left their manses, and with the loyal support, often of the most active members of their congregations, broke away to form a Church of Scotland freed from the restricting Acts of Parliament, dependent solely upon the financial support of its members and yet with the determined objective of setting up a rival congregation in every parish, ministering to the needs of everyone—a Church both national and free.

The strength of evangelical fervour, the leadership of a number of prominent ministers and laymen, and the inability of the Parliament at Westminster (concerned also at that time with the affairs of the Church of England) to confront realistically the constitutional complexities of the Scottish ecclesiastical scene, despite several highly creditable efforts on the part of some members of both Houses, all contributed to the sundering of the Church. The movement may also have been furthered by the contemporary trend in the political field towards greater parliamentary democracy.

The Patronage Act was repealed by Parliament in 1874 and the claims of the Church to the exercise of a free spiritual jurisdiction recognized in 1921 by Parliament in 'Articles Declaratory of the Constitution of the Church of Scotland in matters spiritual' which became operative in 1926. Three years later a large majority in the separate Churches reunited. The Disruption of 1843 had a profound effect in the cultural life of Scotland at both national and local levels. Despite much bitterness and rivalry, considerable impetus was given to the development of congregational life, and in many other areas such as education and social welfare, the way was opened up for readjustment and improvement.

J. K. Cameron

Donn, Rob/Robert MacKay (1714–1778) was a native of Strathmore in Sutherland and, apart from a period of service with the Sutherland regiment from around 1759, he spent all his life in the north and northwest of Sutherland. He was, we are told, taken into the household of the local tacksman Iain Mac Eachainn (John Mackay) as a boy, in order that his poetic talents should be fostered. He worked in that household and in the service of Lord Reay as a cattleman and drover, with some hiatus caused, we are told, by his indulgence in hunting for deer and plain speaking in his poetry.

The life that is reflected in his poetry is that of the whole range of society in the north of Sutherland in his time. This was basically a traditional Gaelic society, with intrusions into it of new ideas and new *mores*. Both the traditional and the new are reflected in Rob Donn's poetry.

It is very clear, for example, that Rob Donn took his vocation as a poet very seriously; he is not slow to castigate bad verse and he is especially unhappy about people who put their gifts to bad use:

There are some bards
who think more of possessions than of their craft
some who cannot tell the truth
and some who tell it woundingly.
… How I detest the poet
who would praise me up as my state increased
or keep on praising my ancestors
though some of them in their day were thieves.
Where there is lightness of brain
though the faces were as sage as the rocks—
from that stock will not come an ounce
for which a pound's worth is not begged.

This seriousness reflects the status of the poet in traditional society, and his awareness that he had responsibilities as well as privileges. Rob Donn's poetic privileges were jealously guarded, but his responsibilities, as he saw them, ensured that he did not hesitate to put these privileges at risk. This is exemplified in his response to Lady Reay's marrying off a maid of hers made pregnant by a member of the 'gentry', and to her injunction to the poet not to comment on her actions in verse:

Into my head the gag was placed like a spike

With a sharp order and advice
concerning the mishap that has occurred,
less like love than like hunting …

But it will not do he says,

To give place to the wrongdoer
and to shut the accuser's mouth.

Quite apart from the fact that the stock will be spoiled, 'like folds spoiled by a bad bull,' it all stems from the sin of pride and the poem ends:

My opinion of you, pride,
that there is a dangerous companionship in your
considering the many similar shifts [nature
with which you seek to achieve your ends …

This poem also shows another side of Rob Donn's seriousness, in this case given its particular expression by the moral climate of his own time and place. This without doubt stemmed from the strong influence of evangelical forms of Christianity in Sutherland by the beginning of the eighteenth century, though he had access to other exotic experiences: for example, we are told that a local minister made him aware of the poetry of Alexander Pope. (He was also, incidentally, aware of contemporary developments in Gaelic poetry for his *Song to Winter* is conceived as an antithesis of Alexander MacDonald's *Song to Summer*). The language of this movement in its moral aspect speaks as surely through the poetry of social comment, of which the above is of course an example, as does the language of the tradition. Such poems as the one commenting on the attitudes of parish ministers make this clear:

We have got men as preachers
who are oppressive in their practices,
who seek ends no higher
than as much religion as will pass …

… like the shells of the strand
that are gathered in the summer,
you find twenty are empty
for every one that contains a pearl.

One of them says, on the sabbath,
that Christ is our Saviour,
and a week from that day
that only deeds are effectual.
He makes high flights
and he scuttles low:
and being neither bird nor mouse
he is an obscene bat.

Traditional Gaelic 'satire' tends very strongly towards invective. Rob Donn's has often an added component of pointed moral generalization which is, perhaps, his most distinctive contribution to the Gaelic verse tradition. It even comes in the acute observation of poems such as his elegy on William Millar, the tinker, with its graphic descriptions of William's low character and appearance:

Often have I seen your leap
to your most certain source of food
Your coat tails tucked under your arms
the hue of tobacco on your nose;
… an ill-cooked portion in your hand.

The poem, after a catalogue of those who would, for their own purposes, miss William, ends

… the gentry are a trifle sad,
since they have nobody in the Machair
who'll clean out a lavatory or a chamber pot.

Rob Donn made several more traditional elegies of some interest. One on the death of the Earl of Sutherland 1766 shows us again his feelings of responsibility as a poet. Though he is old he says he cannot leave the dead 'with not a word composed about him by a poet in his own country'. The elegy to Iain Mac Eachainn combines traditional praise and the language of panegyric with warmth of personal feeling. It ends typically by saying that although a 'mixture of flattery pours' through 'praising elegies' in his country

Though I were swearing
to the One who supports the elements for me
I praised nothing in this man
but a virtue I saw in him with my own eyes.

Rob Donn composed many different kinds of songs as well as these that we have mentioned, many robust and happy, some sad, all imbued with his exceptional wit. He was a considerable poet. His works were first edited in 1829 with later versions in 1870, and two in 1899, one of these by Gunn and MacFarlane containing some translations.

D. *MacAulay*

Donnachadh Ban Mac an t-Saoir *see* **MacIntyre, Duncan Ban**

Douglas, Gavin (1475?–1522), a son of the fifth Earl of Angus ('Archibald Bell-the-Cat'), was educated for the Church at St Andrews and studied later in Paris. He was a priest at Monymusk, Aberdeenshire, in 1496. By 1501, he was Provost of St Giles, Edinburgh, and in 1514 was named Abbot of Aberbrothock and Archbishop of St Andrews, though the pope could not be persuaded to agree to this appointment and Douglas had to be content with the bishopric of Dunkeld, given to him in 1515. Before he could take up that appointment, the Regent Albany, upholder of the French and nationalist parties and enemy of the Douglas house, returned to Scotland. Gavin Douglas found himself incarcerated in the castle of St Andrews for a year on the somewhat spurious grounds that he had obtained his appointment through the interference of the English king.

But Douglas made peace with Albany, and became sufficiently trusted to be sent to Rouen to complete negotiations for a Franco-Scottish treaty against England. Yet no sooner had Albany returned to France, than the poet and his nephew, the sixth Earl of Angus, tried to secure the return of the Douglas power. Though at first apparently successful, they failed to persuade Wolsey and Henry VIII to prevent Albany's return in 1521, upon which uncle and nephew had to flee to England. Stripped of his bishopric, deserted by his nephew and befriended mainly by Lord Dacre, Douglas spent his last year in exile. He died of the plague, and was buried in the Royal Chapel of the Savoy.

In spite of the political nature of his other interests, and his intrigues and misfortunes, Douglas found time to cultivate literature. 'King Hart' an allegory of the Heart of Man as king of a castle surrounded by courtiers like Strength, Wantonness, Green Lust and Disport, who attempt to influence his judgement—gives what was probably a fairly accurate impression of the ambience of the Stewart court. The poem is couched in deftly handled *ballat royal* stanza form. 'The Palice of Honour' is a dream-sequence 'pilgrimage' poem in which the narrator falls asleep (as in Dunbar's 'Golden Targe'), witnesses a debate amongst mythological personifications, and, after various adventures, finds himself in the Palace of Honour, staffed among others, by Constancy, Liberality and Dissention.

Without doubt, Douglas's greatest achievement is his rendering into Scots, in 10-syllabled metre, of Virgil's *Aeneid*, the first verse translation of merit to be made in Britain, and by far the largest work of verse of any quality ever produced in Scots. Douglas captures Virgil's pace with a rough power of his own, often achieving moving passages, as in the scene where Dido makes her final unsuccesful attempt to persuade Aeneas not to desert her and sail to Italy. Douglas provided each of Virgil's 12 books with prologues of his own, presenting us with facets of nature seen in realistic Scottish terms, thus achieving remarkable originality, and founding a tradition of realistic Scottish nature poetry. We all know days in which there are:
Sharp soppis of sleet, and of the snipand snow when:

The dowie ditches were all donk and wait,
The low valley flodderit all with spate,
The plain streetis and every hie way
Full of flushis, dubbis, mire and clay.

Douglas was the first poet to call his language 'Scottish' (as opposed to 'Inglis', the term previously in favour), and also the poet who reminded us, when faced with a 'difficult' work of art, to:

Consider it warely, read ofter than anis,
Weill, at ane blenk, slee poetry nocht ta'en is.

M. *Lindsay*

Drama. The Scottish contribution to world drama is second only to that of ancient Greece in terms of *dramatis personae*: Macbeth and Lady Macbeth, Mary Stuart, Lucia di Lammermoor, La Sylphide… . If it has been left to the dramatists, composers, choreographers, designers of other nations to put them on the stage, this is not from a lack in Scottish culture of a sense of the dramatic, but is due to circumstances which affected all forms of artistic expression in Scotland, benefiting some—bardic poetry, the ballad—but harmful to drama. Drama is relatively costly, with its complement of performers and supporting staff, costumes, settings, theatrical facilities; and for full development it has always required the economic base of court and city. Also, it is singled out for condemnation in one strain of Judaeo-Christian thought. The long minority of James VI, the unruliness of his nobles and the eventual removal of the court to London dealt a double blow to drama. Not only was it deprived of financial support, but also of its protectors against the Kirk. In Scotland no professional companies arose to continue the flourishing theatrical life common to all medieval Christendom, as they did elsewhere, the pertinent instance being England, where the patronage of Elizabeth and the nobility protected the companies from the Puritan civic authorities of London. In Scotland it was not until the eighteenth century that the theatre found an effective patron in an increasingly prosperous middle class. The furore over *Douglas* represented a last major attempt to rally opinion in the Kirk against drama.

The enthusiast for Scottish culture who cried out at the first night of *Douglas*, 'Whaur's yer Wullie Shakspere noo?' overlooked the facts that the cast was English and the play written with production by Garrick at Drury Lane in view. On no other art in Scotland has English influence been as dominant as on drama. The explanation is not simply the artistic pre-eminence of English drama: since the last quarter of the sixteenth century, London has been the centre of a major theatrical industry, with an export capacity and, in the case of Scotland, no trade or linguistic barriers. It was English companies on tour that brought the new professional drama to Scotland in the last decade of the century, once James had sufficient power to overrule the opposition of the Kirk. When James VII, as Duke of Albany, was at Holyrood, he brought in his train a company recruited in London. The pioneering Tony Aston was introduced to the 'Caledonians' by Allan Ramsay in a prologue of 1726. Ramsay built a new playhouse in 1736, only to have it closed the following year by Walpole's Licensing Act, theatrical activity in Scotland now being under the control of Westminster. His Lowland version of Italian pastoral, *The Gentle Shepherd*, waited over 30 years for a professional production, when the English company took 'the utmost care and application ... to learn the Scots dialect'. By 1741 the Licensing Act was being circumvented by the fiction that performances were 'concerts', a device which enabled managers to re-establish drama in Edinburgh and extend their seasons to take in the principal towns before the position was regularized by measures like the grant of Royal Patents to theatres in Edinburgh and Glasgow. By the early 1800s from Dumfries to Aberdeen, from Greenock to Leith there were theatres, several in the cities of Glasgow, Edinburgh and Dundee, all supplied by 'stock' companies resident in one theatre or covering several linked in a 'circuit'. London stars—Mrs Siddons, Kean—appeared, but as guest artists acting with regular mem-

bers of the company. Its residential character gave the theatre in Scotland some opportunity of becoming a Scottish theatre. Mackay gave life to character parts in the Waverley novels, delighting Scott. Painters of standing, Alexander Nasmyth and Sam Bough, furnished the scenery.

The underlying economic weakness was again revealed in the 1870s. The vast increase of the London theatre public brought into being the 'long run' system. The saving to be achieved by casting the single play which could now draw audiences for a great number of continuous performances, instead of engaging the larger permanent company required for a repertory of plays, was irresistibly attractive to unsubsidized, commercial managements. Moreover, with the new system the run could be extended by sending the company on tour: a current London success could even be exploited by sending out second and third companies. The extension of the new system outside of London would not have been possible without a new technology of transport, the railway. Faced with this competition, the stock companies could not survive. Scotland shared, however, in a theatrical boom which lasted up to the arrival of the cinema. The major theatres became part of the West End, except for the pantomime season, which was an occasion for local topicality. The talents of Barrie, Lauder, Mary Garden, Matheson Lang, Archer found rewarding employment in a British, even an international theatre. Scottish playgoers did not complain of a system which brought them a round of famous companies, including regular visits of Irving's from the Lyceum, the finest of the age.

A new course was set by the Glasgow Repertory Theatre, founded in 1909, and with one of its aims cannily phrased as 'the encouragement and development of purely Scottish drama by providing a stage and acting company which will be peculiarly adapted for the production of plays national in character, written by Scottish men and women of letters'. The initiative came from an English manager, Alfred Wareing, who three years before had arranged a visit to Scotland of the Irish Players. The Abbey was to remain the paragon for all who wanted to see 'a purely Scottish drama'. The Abbey, however, was part of a movement active from Moscow to New York, with aims given a different priority from theatre to theatre. Glasgow Repertory Theatre recruited a few Scottish actors and actresses who moved on to distinguished careers on the London stage. It produced a number of new plays by Scottish writers, none standing comparison with the work of the contemporary 'Manchester School'. Its first priority, however, was to present the new Ibsenite drama with, as far as could be, the best of the acting talent which had presented it for the Stage Society and for Barker and Vedrenne at the Court. No less than 10 plays by Shaw were produced, almost all new to Glasgow, including *Mrs Warren's Profession*, privately performed to evade the Lord Chamberlain's ban. Some work of contemporary Continental playwrights was shown, with *The Seagull* providing the first chance in the English-speaking world to see a Chekhov play.

Prominent among the aims of the movement in Britain, from which it took its name of 'Repertory Movement', was the provision of an alternative to the long run by the establishment of permanent companies presenting a repertory of plays, this to be made financially possible by subsidy from state, municipality or private benefactors. It was Archer and Granville Barker who produced the blueprint in *A National Theatre*, but their national theatre was not seen as reinforcing the monopoly of London, but on the contrary as providing a model for similar repertory theatres throughout the English-speaking world. Glasgow Repertory did not achieve true repertory: like all the other 'reps', while keeping the name, it had to settle for seasons of plays, each presented for a short run. It did succeed in bringing back a resident company to Scotland, and in attracting subsidy in the form of modest subscriptions from a considerable number of Glaswegians. Wareing boasted that it was a 'Citizens' Theatre', so providing a name for the later venture.

The Repertory Theatre, just when it had reached profitability, 'suspended active operations' on the outbreak of war in 1914. They were not to be resumed, and Scotland reverted to being part of the British commercial circuit. It was without a resident professional company until 1928, when the first of a succession of companies from the south began to supply Edinburgh and Glasgow with seasons mainly of West End successes. While professional theatre flourished in the cities, elsewhere it had been killed by the cinema, making way for an upsurge of the ancient tradition of amateur acting. It was left to a succession of amateur groups to continue the work of the Repertory Theatre. The Scottish National Players produced over a hundred new Scottish plays in the Abbey tradition of historical or rural setting, especially the Gaeltacht. Bridie wrote several plays for them, but he gave his more intellectually ambitious work to Barry Jackson and Anmer Hall, the English patron-directors who gave the artistic lead to the British theatre of the 1920s and 1930s. The Curtain Theatre produced the two best of McLellan's historical plays in Lallans. Glasgow Unity Theatre had an international repertoire, but in new writing followed the O'Casey tradition of the Abbey with plays set in the working life of the City.

In the late 1930s repertory theatres were started in Perth and Dundee, but a lasting measure of independence of London was not to be won, as the advocates of the repertory movement had foreseen, without subsidy, which became available with the creation of CEMA in 1940, with whose aid Glasgow Citizens' Theatre was founded in 1943. When CEMA was superseded by the Arts Council of Great Britain, with the Scottish Arts Council as a virtually independent committee, subsidy increased until drama has become as widespread in Scotland as in the days of stock companies and circuits—wider spread indeed with the start of a Gaelic touring company. The past has been far outstripped by the development of opera, ballet, modern dance, mime. Radio and television offer new outlets. For the first time Scotland has begun to export drama. Subsidy no longer simply provides an alternative to a prosperous theatre of private enterprise, which now hardly exists outside of the West End: it has become the main support of the whole theatrical structure.

The quality of Scottish theatre was first revealed to a wide public by Tyrone Guthrie's production of Lindsay's *Satire of the Three Estates* at the Edinburgh International Festival of 1948, with a cast drawn from the SNP, Curtain, Unity and Citizens'. This tradition, supported by the founding—by the Kirk—of the Edinburgh Gateway, was soon to be challenged, first by the influence of the new wave of English playwrights of the 1950s, but then much more seriously. In 1963 on the initiative of an American, Jim Haynes, the Traverse Theatre Club opened in Edinburgh, to be followed a few years later by the Close Theatre Club in Glasgow and the new regime at Citizens' of Giles Havergal. In the aftermath of the 1914–18 war the British theatre as a whole isolated itself from Europe and the new forms evolving in response to a social and cultural crisis: expressionism, political theatre, epic theatre, theatre of cruelty, of the absurd. Now in the 1960s at the Traverse, the Close and Citizens' half a century of evolution in the European theatre hit Scottish drama all at once. For the first time drama was allowed the same freedom of expression as literature when censorship, which the theatre clubs had been evading, was ended by the Theatres Act of 1968. The Scottish theatre was thrown into confusion. Citizens' Theatre alone, in a decade of astonishing creativity, assimilated the new influences to a style of its own, but under constant fire from rival camps. In 1981 a new major national company was formed, the touring Scottish Theatre Company. The outstanding success of its first season has signalled a new stage in the dialectic.

The power of drama, as a communal art, to express the culture of a community was evident in Lindsay's time. The awareness of Scotland, of Europe and of mankind which he shared with his 'famous auditors' is a huge cairn (albeit in need of rebuilding) compared with the scattered rickles of stone which is all that later history so often has to show. This survey has tried to explain why drama has less consistently than poetry been the force that explored and expanded Scottish culture; but to suggest, too, that it has been, and is, that force to an extent unrecognized in the accepted history of the arts in Scotland.

J. F. Arnott

Postscript. Developments in the last decade or so help confirm—though in some cases also qualify—J.F. Arnott's views. Recent events have certainly strengthened the place of European and indeed World Theatre on the Scottish stage. Through Robert David MacDonald's translations and adaptations, the Citizens company continued throughout the eighties their many astonishing forays into the European repertoire. Some of the very best of European theatre came to Glasgow in 1990, when it was European City of Culture, with visits throughout the year by a range of outstanding companies, some—such as the Maly Theatre of Leningrad—equipped with performance skills which virtually redefined for Scottish audiences the possibilities of the stage. Frank Dunlop's World Theatre Seasons at the Edinburgh Festival also helped over a longer period to ensure a particularly strong, continuing influence within Scotland of movements in staging, performance and theatrical imagination worldwide.

It would be wrong, however, to see the growing vitality in Scottish theatre in recent decades as the result only of imported ideas and energies, as J.F. Arnott half suggests. The inaugural production of Glasgow's Year of Culture, for example, Communicado's devised piece *Jock Tamson's Bairns*, combined some of the company's interest in Polish and other forms of experimental European theatre with the entirely Scottish words and ideas of Liz Lochhead. In her immensely successful translation of *Tartuffe* in 1986. Lochhead had already shown in another way, the power of Scottish setting and idiom as vehicles for European material—a lesson already suggested by Robert Kemp's translations of *Molière* in the forties, and more recently confirmed by, for example, Edwin Morgan's brilliant Scots adaptation of Rostand's *Cyrano de Bergerac* at the Edinburgh Fringe in 1992.

Such successes in translation share in a much wider recovery of Scots language for the stage consolidated in various ways by playwrights such as Donald Campbell, Hector MacMillan, Stewart Conn, Roddy McMillan, Bill Bryden, and John Byrne working at the Royal Lyceum and the Traverse in the seventies, a decade of solid new achievement in writing for the theatre. The immediacy created for the stage by these new playwrights' use of a language, more or less shared by the audience, was often extended by their direct reflection of the kind of life lived by this audience, or their ancestors. While Edwin Morgan rightly considered in 1967, that the theatre allowed 'huge areas of Scottish life [to] fly past uncommented on', this was very much less the case by the beginning of the eighties, especially given the development of a particularly Scottish stage interest—perhaps the legacy of Glasgow Unity's work, or Joe Corrie's, or ultimately of O'Casey and the Abbey—in ordinary urban existence and working life. The nature and problems of this everyday life have also continued to be powerfully addressed by a political theatre which has often found within the historical past significant homologies with the present. This kind of analysis was most successfully undertaken in the seventies by 7:84 (Scotland), especially in *The Cheviot, the Stag and the Black, Black Oil*. As this company experienced increasing difficulties in later years, John McGrath continued his work with Wildcat, using the extensive space of the Tramway in Glasgow as a setting, in *Border Warfare* and *John Brown's Body*, for broad, pageant-and-promenade forms of epic theatre which were among the best achievements of the eighties.

Originally Glasgow's old Transport Museum, first converted to house the only performances in Britain of Peter Brooke's magisterial production of the *Mahabarata* in 1988, the Tramway is only one of several new developments in Scottish theatre building. The opening of the Tron Theatre in Glasgow; the addition of two studio spaces to the Citizens, partly replacing the long-defunct Close; and the Traverse Theatre's move to a wholly new, larger building have all added to possibilities for smaller scale productions. Both the Citizens and the Royal Lyceum have been thoroughly refurbished, and there are new theatre buildings in Pitlochry, Dundee and elsewhere, as well as completely new premises for the Royal Scottish Academy

of Music and Drama, and a new Festival Theatre under construction in Edinburgh. Scotland is undoubtedly better provided with performance spaces than ever before, though ironically, in a time of recession and chronic underfunding of the arts, it is more difficult than ever to make good use of them. Despite genuine achievement and promise, funding crises forced the closure of the Scottish Theatre Company in 1987. Debate continues about whether it is worth following the direction its work suggested, towards a Scottish National Theatre, or whether the total of Scotland's extant theatrical activity already in some sense constitutes such a body.

At any rate, despite elements of difficulty and disillusion which have undermined some of the more confident vision of the seventies, new generations of playwrights directors and companies have continued to appear to build on the successes of that period, and to extend or reorient the work of some of the figures mentioned above. Their commitment to Scottish life, language, politics, histories and attitudes should guarantee a continuing power and particularity for Scottish drama, whether an actual National Theatre emerges or not. At the end of the twentieth century, with the nation almost released from the grey hand of the church, it seems likely that in one way or another the drama will sustain and further enlarge the significance it has acquired—largely in the last few decades—as a means through which, in J.F. Arnott's terms, Scottish culture and the nation's sense of itself can be 'explored and expanded'.

R. Stevenson

Dress, National. To a great many people throughout the world the mention of the word 'Scotland' evokes a highly romanticized picture of a splendid figure wearing a kilt. And yet the summer visitor will almost certainly see far more tartans being worn in Lowland cities than in the glens of the Highlands. But this does not mean that the origins of our national dress are either mythical or bogus. On the contrary they originate from very real and important events in the history of the country.

The national costume of Scotland has certain unique qualities which appeal strongly to the historian. Indeed the present day form of the dress embodies many aspects which are totally absent in other national costumes.

Although other European folk costumes may identify the wearers with a particular town or region, none identifies them with their own personal name or family. No other country has so many overseas societies throughout the world such as St Andrew and Caledonian Societies, displaying their national costume on appropriate occasions.

We are not concerned here with the obscure period before the seventeenth century. Indeed it was not until then that the costume emerged in a truly Scottish form. Previously the ancient Irish and Scottish Gaels were entangled in a variety of tunics, shirts and trunk hose. When they step out of this mist of antiquity we can regard their trunk hose as the ancestors of the Scottish trews, and their shirts as the ancestors of the Scottish kilt. Whereas their upper garments were of a more universal pattern, it was their leg coverings which later became identified as the most significant feature of their dress.

The history of the trews is uncomplicated, but it is when we examine the evolution from shirts to kilts that the story becomes much more complex and emotive. The study of the origin and antiquity of the kilt as it is worn today has generated a great deal of heat amongst modern writers.

The shirt-like flowing garment of the Irish Gael became displaced in seventeenth-century Scotland by what we call the 'belted plaid'. This new costume hardly justified the title of 'garment' because it was simply a rectangular piece of cloth roughly two yards wide and six yards long. The Gaelic description of the Highland belted plaid is *'féilidh-Mor'* or *'breacan an fhéilidh'*, whilst the Gaelic word *'plaide'* is used to describe a blanket.

The unique manner in which the belted plaid was put on is interesting. Firstly the wearer put a belt on the ground and then placed the tartan material on top of it, folding it lengthwise into pleats at right angles to the now hidden belt. He then lay down with his back parallel to the pleats and folded the two ends of the material apron-like over his front. Having fastened the belt he now stood up having a pleated skirt below the waist. Above the waist was a mass of material which he could fasten to one shoulder, drape over both shoulders, or drape over his head. At night he merely undid the belt, and rolled himself up in the plaid.

In the Scottish National Portrait Gallery there-is a splendid portrait of a Highland chief painted about 1660, by Michael Wright, a Scot who understood the mechanics of the belted plaid and illustrated it well.

Pictorial and documentary evidence of the belted plaid is abundant enough, although we would like to know more about the extent to which it was worn. A set of engravings by Van der Gucht, dated 1743, show very clearly the various ways in which it could be worn and its very simplicity would indicate that it was in pretty general use.

James Gordon, Parson of Rothiemay, writing in the 1640s, refers to the trews as winter wear. 'In the sharp Winter weather the Highland Men wore close trowzes, which cover the Thighs, Legs and Feet.' In fact trews were worn in the Highlands in summer and winter by all classes. Many eminent Highlanders and Lowlanders including the Duke of Perth, the Earl of Wemyss, the Chief of Macleod and Major Fraser of Castle Leather, were magnificently portrayed wearing their trews.

The famous Raeburn portrait of Sir John Sinclair in the uniform of the Rothesay and Caithness Fencibles is of particular interest to students of Highland dress. Born in the most northerly town in Britain in 1754, he raised his regiment of Fencibles 40 years later. Because of his firm conviction that the trews were of superior antiquity to the belted plaid in the history of Highland dress, he clothed his regiment accordingly and wrote the words of their regimental march proclaiming:

Let others boast of philibeg,

Of kilt and belted plaid,
Whilst we the ancient trews will wear,
In which our fathers bled.

Trews continued in use as part of the Highland dress but with one modification. Originally they were trunk hose but when Sir John Sinclair adopted them for himself and his Fencibles he cut off the feet and they became tartan trousers. Even today the tartan trousers worn by Scottish regiments are officially known as 'trews'.

The evolution of our national dress up to the early eighteenth century is fairly straightforward. Our bare-legged Scottish and Irish Gaelic ancestors wore shirts and mantles—men and women alike. Some of them also wore the trews which were possibly of even greater antiquity, and possibly more popular with the humbler folk. And then we have one of the first hints of a truly Scottish costume in a contemporary account of a Highland expedition to Ireland in 1594.

They are recognized among the Irish Soldiers by the distinction of their arms and clothing, their habits and language, for their exterior dress was mottled cloaks of many colours with a fringe to their shins and calves, their belts were over their loins outside their cloaks.

This could well be one of the earliest discriptions of the belted plaid. Evidence of its use during the next century is plentiful and the period is a peaceful hunting-ground for the costume historian. But with the birth of the eighteenth century the clouds gather and the storm breaks.

The origin of the kilt is one of the most hotly debated subjects in the history of costume. The mechanics of its birth are straightforward as the belted plaid was merely cut around the waist and the upper half discarded. The lower half was now a new and more practical garment—the kilt. The pleats were then stitched up, a flat apron introduced in front, and the result was the kilt as it is worn today.

But who actually invented the kilt? In March 1785, the *Edinburgh Magazine* published a letter dated 1768, written by a well educated Highland gentleman, Ivan Baillie of Aberiachen. The title of the letter was 'The Felie-Beg, no part of the Ancient Highland Dress'.

In this letter, Baillie claimed that about 50 years previously, one Thomas Rawlinson, an Englishman whom he knew personally, 'conducted an iron-work carried on in the countries of Glengarie and Lochaber ... and became very fond of the Highland dress, and wore it in the neatest form'. In order to make the dress handy and convenient for his workmen he abridged the belted plaid retaining only the lower half which 'was in the Gaelic termed *felie-beg* (*beg* in that tongue signifies *little*) and in our Scots termed *little kilt.*'

No evidence to the contrary being found, the invention of the kilt by an Englishman has provoked endless debate. Sir John Sinclair supported the argument whilst others denied it. Surely the place of Rawlinson's birth has little importance as far as the history of the kilt in concerned.

At present, the earliest paintings showing the little kilt are probably the portrait of Charles Campbell of Lochlane, painted about 1740, and now in the Scottish National Portrait Gallery, and another portrait of 'Young Glengarry' who died in 1761, and whose henchman appears to wear a little kilt.

The little kilt did not immediately replace the belted plaid, and in the mid-eighteenth century both were worn by the Highland regiments. For a while the military only wore the little kilt in undress order, but the days of the cumbersome old belted plaid were numbered and it was eventually replaced by the little kilt.

The evolution of Highland dress until the mid eighteenth century followed the normal environmental pattern, and then, because of a number of historical events, it took on certain aspects which make it quite unique in the history of costume. Within a century it changed from the ordinary functional dress of a small minority of Scots living in a remote part of the country, to a National Dress worn by Scottish Highlanders and Lowlanders throughout the world.

The first of these historical events to play a drastic part in the history of the Highland dress was the Jacobite Rising of 1745, when the House of Stuart attempted to overthrow the reigning House of Hanover. After their victory at Culloden, the Hanoverian government, as part of their policy to stamp out what they regarded as symbols of rebellion, passed an Act which decreed:

> That from and after the First Day of August, 1747, no Man or Boy, within that part of Great Britain called Scotland, other than such as shall be employed as Officers and Soldiers in His Majesty's Forces, shall, on any pretence whatsoever, wear or put on the Clothes commonly called Highland Clothes (that is to say) the Plaid, Philebeg, or Little Kilt, Trowse, Shoulder Belts, or any part whatsoever of what peculiarly belongs to the Highland Garb; and that no Tartan, or party-coloured Plaid or Stuff shall be used for Great Coats, or for Upper Coats ...

This proscription remained in force for 35 years until it was repealed by a Bill introduced by the Duke of Montrose. During that period the Highland dress only survived in a military form but it thereby acquired a glory which gave it world-wide renown. During the years between Culloden and Waterloo, over 100 battalions of the Line, Militia, Fencibles and Volunteers were raised in the Highlands.

When peace came, the Highland dress was not only proudly worn by the army, but also by civilians in a military style which has persisted to the present-day.

The next great historical event which set the seal of a national costume on the kilt was short in duration but permanent in effect. In 1822, His Majesty King George IV agreed to pay a State Visit to Scotland and thereupon the nation plunged into a tartan frenzy. The news spread that the king was to wear the kilt, and immediately Highlanders and Lowlanders alike besieged the tailors demanding 'The Garb of Old Gaul'. This it certainly was not. The elaborate costume worn at the levees, assemblies and balls was far removed from the ancient dress worn by the Highlanders in their native glens.

But the 1822 visit was the success it deserved to be. Visitors now flocked to see the Scotland of Sir Walter Scott's novels and its inhabitants in their 'picturesque' costume. Furthermore, the fact that a king, albeit a Hanoverian, had worn the costume, gave it Royal approval. The hundreds of Scots who now had clan tartans and kilts, paraded them with pride to which the Victorians added social status and a considerable degree of dignity.

J. Telfer Dunbar

Drummond, William (1585–1649) was descended from an old Scottish family, and through Annabella Drummond, Robert III's queen, related to the royal house. Educated at Edinburgh's High School and University he studied law on the Continent and in 1610 succeeded to the family estate of Hawthornden. For the rest of his life he devoted himself to poetry. His elegy for Prince Henry, *Tears on the death of Meliades*, appeared in 1613 and in 1616, *Poems, Amorous, Funereall, Divine, Pastorall*. The following year he published a poem, *Forthfeasting*, in honour of James VI & I's return visit to Scotland. In 1618 he was visited by Ben Jonson, who kept notes of the conversation that took place between them. Drummond's *Flowers of Sion* appeared in 1623. He may or may not be the author of a lively display of macaronics, *Polemo-Middinia inter Vitarvam et Nebernam*, that deals with a dispute over a right-of-way between the people of Tarvet and those of Newbarns, the dog-Latin of which survives through a 'reprint' of 1684.

In 1632 Drummond married Elizabeth Logan, the daughter of Sir Robert Logan of Restalrig, and from his retreat above the glen of the Esk watched the struggle of Charles I to assert his will over both his Scots and English subjects. He provided a piece, *The Entertainment*, for Charles's Scottish coronation in 1633. In his later years Drummond was saddened successively by the death of Charles I, the eclipse of Sir William Alexander and the still sadder death of his friend Montrose. One of his last sonnets reflects this mood of settled melancholy:

> Doth then the World go thus? Doth all thus move?
> Is this the Justice which on Earth we find?
> Is this that firm decree which all doth bind?
> Are these your influences, Powers above?

Drummond's poetry reflects the Italian and French poets of his day, many of whose books were to be found in the Hawthornden library of over 500 volumes.

As a prose writer, his *Cypress Grove* (1623), an eloquent meditation on death, provided a model for Sir Thomas Browne's *Religio Medici* (1642), and has an original tone. Drummond also wrote a *History of Scotland from 1423 to 1542*, and patented no fewer than 16 mechanical inventions. The castle of Hawthornden remained in the Drummond family until 1978. The Hawthornden Prize for imaginative writing was founded in 1919 to honour the poet's memory.

M. Lindsay

Dunbar, William (1460?–1520?). We do not know many details about his life. He is believed to have come from East Lothian, possibly descending from a branch of the Earls of Dunbar, and to have graduated Bachelor of Arts at St Andrews University in 1477 and Master two years later. He may then have become, for a period, a Franciscan novice, during which time, he tells us (in 'How Dunbar was Desyred to be Ane Frier'), he preached as far afield as Calais and Picardy. However, the vision of St Francis urging the poet to become a monk disappeared 'with stink of fiery smowk', giving place to a devil in friar's likeness; so Dunbar resolved instead to join the secular clergy, hopeful of securing a rich benefice.

He seems for a time to have been a civil servant, travelling to France in 1491 as Secretary to a Scottish Embassy. He was certainly a member of the Embassy that went to England in 1500 to discuss the proposed marriage of James IV and Margaret Tudor. Subsequently, he welcomed the princess's arrival in Scotland in 1503 as a bride with an aureate flourish:

> Now fair, fairest, of every fair,
> Princess most pleasant and preclare,
> The lustiest one alive that been,   *[most beautiful]*
> Welcome of Scotland to be Queen!

When he journeyed north in the queen's entourage in 1511, he addressed Aberdeen as 'thou berial of all tounis,/The lamp of beauty, bounty and blythness.'

He seems to have been something of a favourite of the queen's, as well as of her more cultured spouse. In the Lord High Treasurer's accounts, Dunbar is shown to have received a pension of £10 a year from the year 1500, rising to £20 in 1527 and £80 in 1570, although he never achieved the benefice (worth about £100) he so much desired. Between 1513 and 1515, a gap occurs in the records; when they resume, the poet's name no longer appears. He presumably died, therefore, sometime after Flodden, the latest possible date being 1520 (but this dating depends upon a nineteenth-century attribution to Dunbar of a poem, 'We Lordis hes chosen a chiftane mervellous' that may not be his).

Most of his work might well have disappeared, since only a few of his poems were printed by Chepman and Myllar in 1508. The bulk of his poetry survives almost by accident, through its appearance in the Bannatyne, Maitland, Asloan and Reidpeth manuscripts, hand-copied personal anthologies reflecting the tastes of the compilers. Indeed, the first collected edition of Dunbar's poems was not published until 1834.

Some difficulties of attribution therefore occur. The only important unsubstantiated poem (though included without attribution in the Chepman and Myllar collection immediately following two poems subscribed 'Quod Dunbar'), is the wittily energetic 'Ballad of Kynd Kyttock'. Anyone wishing to dispose of Dunbar's claim to the authorship of that particular miniature comic masterpiece has to persuade us that an otherwise unknown poet of equal technical skill, writing in Dunbar's manner, was operating in Scotland at the same time. 'Kynd Kyttock' shares, as well as stylistic similarity, the highly individual poetic energy that drives along 'The Dance of the Seven Deidly Sins', right to the sulphurous conclusion of its Lowlander's reel:

> Than cried Mahoun for a Heleand padyane: *[pageant]*
>
> Syne ran a feind to feche Makfadyane   *[fetch]*
> Far northwart in a nuke:
> Be he the correnoch had done schout,   *[lament]*
> Erschemen so gadderit him about,   *[Irishmen]*
> In Hell grit room they tuke.
> Thae tarmegants, with tag and tatter,
> Full loud in Ersche begowth to clatter,
> And rowp like revin and rook: *[raven]*
> The Devil sa devit wes with their yell,
> That in the deepest pot of hell
> He smorit thame with smuke.

Dunbar put much of himself into his poetry, recording frankly his moods and ailments, as in 'On His Heid-Ake', when he tells us that he suffered from what sounds like migraine. He also records his depression, caused by the cold winds, grey skies and stoney draughts of a medieval winter:

> Whone that the nicht dois lengthen hours,
> With wind, with hail and heavy schours,
> My dule spreit does lurk for schoir,
> My hairt for langour does forloir
>
> For laik of simmer with his flours,
> I walk, I turn, sleep may I nocht …

When he was frustrated, either by his own inability to get the king to grant the longed-for benefice, or by some lesser irritation, like the insolence of the Keeper of the Queen's Wardrobe, James Dog ('Madame, ye heff a dangerous Dog!', the poet complained), he would seem almost to sink beneath the weight of his own gloom. Yet in 'Ane His Awin Enemy', he concluded with an exhortation that is almost a secular grace:

> Now all this time lat us be mirry,
> And sey nocht by this warld a chirry,
> Now, whill thair is gude wine to sell,
> He that does on dry bread wirry,
> I gif him to the Devil of hell.

His most powerful personal poem, and indeed his best known piece, is his 'Lament for the Makaris', subtitled, 'When he Was Sek'. The liturgical use of the tolling refrain '*Timor mortis conturbat me*' is put to telling effect as Dunbar recounts the manner in which one by one death has removed the poets he most admired, concluding:

> Sen he hes all my brether tane
> He will nocht lat me lif alane;
> On forse I man his next prey be:
> *Timor mortis conturbat me.*

Whether reproving the merchants of Edinburgh, engaging in scurrilous formalized 'flyting' (abuse-hurling) with Walter Kennedy, sneering at the Highlanders in 'Epetaffe for Donald Owre', diverting us with the female conversation in 'The

Treatis of the Twa Maryit Wemen and the Wedo', in which frank views are exchanged on the sexual prowess of the ladies' respective menfolk, or rejoicing in the great celebratory organ-peals of 'Ane Ballat to Our Ladye' and 'Of The Resurrection of Christ', Dunbar is a supreme technician, handling a wide variety of metres and stanza-forms with absolute ease. In spite of the centuries between his time and ours, his personality comes through his verse with such evident force and his dark energy and humour seem so fundamentally Scottish, that he stands unquestionably with Burns and MacDiarmid as one of Scotland's three greatest poets.

M. Lindsay

Dundee. The earliest written reference to Dundee dates from 1054 AD. That there was earlier human settlement on the same site is clear. The name Dundee is in Gaelic Dun Deagh, meaning probably 'Fort of Daig(h)', but which fort is difficult to say, for there are two possibilities. One is the vitrified Iron Age fort on top of Dundee Law. The other is the fortified site on top of Castle Hill, which unlike the Law lay within the nuclear site of the medieval burgh. The Castle Hill was largely cleared away in the course of nineteenth-century street improvements. By a charter dated 1178 X 1182 King William gave his brother David the earldom of Lennox along with lands and towns including Dundee and Inverurie. These places were not at that time designated burghs but Dundee rapidly emerged as a royal burgh, having its rights confirmed by Robert I in 1327 and its feu-ferme charter from David II in 1360. In the later medieval period it was recognized as one of the four wealthiest towns of the realm. As such it was in Parliament from the earliest period of burghal representation in 1357–67. Despite rivalries with Perth, Dundee exploited its strategic site very successfully. An outcrop of volcanic rocks provided it with the last substantial dry site on the north side of the Tay estuary before the start of the marshes of the Carse of Gowrie, while its geographical situation was convenient for trade with the Netherlands, France and the Iberian peninsula, and the Baltic.

It was due to these extensive trading contracts that Dundee became affected at an early stage with Protestant ideas of a Lutheran kind which reached the burgh through its channels of trade with Central Europe, and which were expressed by the Wedderburn brothers of Dundee in their 'Gude and Godlie Ballats'. Judging by its contribution to the tax granted to James VI in 1585 for his marriage, Dundee was then the second wealthiest burgh in the kingdom after Edinburgh, followed by Perth and Aberdeen, and far ahead of Glasgow. The seventeenth century was a tragic one for Dundee. The burgh suffered terribly in the civil wars of that century, enjoying the melancholy distinction of being plundered by both royalist forces under the Marquis of Montrose, and Cromwellian troops under General Monck. The sack and massacre which followed the storming of the burgh by the latter's troops in 1651 marked the end of Dundee as the second wealthiest of Scottish burghs. Only with the development of the Scottish linen industry in the eighteenth century can Dundee be said to have recovered something of its former economic dynamism.

Eighteenth-century Dundee developed as both a commercial and banking centre for Tayside, and as the metropolitan centre of a coarse linen industry. The building of turnpike roads in the late eighteenth century and the opening of the precocious Dundee and Newtyle Railway in 1831 made it a regional capital. With the coming of steam-powered machinery from the late eighteenth century and of jute as the dominant coarse textile in the 1850s Dundee became a great but low-wage industrial centre, dependent on raw material imported from Bengal, and paying in the period between the two World Wars (1919–39) in staggeringly high unemployment for its excessive dependence on a single, vulnerable staple industry. Diversification of its industrial complex set in during the Second World War, leading to the introduction of new light industries, often American owned. The 1960s and 1970s saw a building boom which doubled the size of the burgh while its population remained roughly static. Like the building boom of the late nineteenth century, it conspicuously failed to add architectural distinction to a superb natural site.

Apart from the articles in the Old and New Statistical Accounts of Scotland, which are of great value, the best two secondary sources for the history of Dundee are the various publications of the Abertay Historical Society and the several Handbooks to Dundee and District produced by the British Association for the Advancement of Science to mark its periodic meetings in the burgh.

B. Lenman

E

Edinburgh began as a fortress on what is now the Castle Rock, the centre of the Celtic tribe known as Gododdin, called by them Dineidin, 'fortress of the hill-slope'. In 638 AD most of southern Scotland came under the dominion of the Northumbrians, and Edinburgh became a Northumbrian city with its name anglicized to Edinburgh. The MacAlpin kings captured Edinburgh in the mid tenth century and went on to establish Scotland's southern border at roughly where it is today. Malcolm III, who kept his court at Dunfermline, built a hunting lodge on the castle rock and his pious Queen Margaret had her husband build her a chapel there, which survives as the oldest building on the rock. Malcolm's son David 1 founded the Abbey of Holyrood in 1128 for Augustinian canons who gave the name Canongate to the road westward from the abbey to Edinburgh's eastern entrance, the Nether Bow: the Canongate remained a separate burgh until 1856. The

Church of St Giles, which became the High Kirk of Edinburgh, was founded about the same time as the abbey.

The protective presence of the 'fortress of the rock' encouraged the settlement around its base of merchants and craftsmen and the burgesses of Edinburgh made themselves felt from the early Middle Ages as a powerful force in the burgh. King Robert I granted Edinburgh a charter in 1329, confirming to the burgesses *burgum nostrum de Edenburgh, una cum Portu de Lethe* (Leith quarrelled with Edinburgh for centuries; in 1838 Leith was made a separate municipality and it was finally merged in Edinburgh by the Edinburgh Boundaries Extension Act of 1920). Claims by English kings, notably Edward I, to sovereignty over Scotland led to frequent raids on Edinburgh and the castle often changed hands. Bruce's nephew Thomas Randolph recovered it from the English in a brilliant manoeuvre in 1314.

The Stewart kings of the fifteenth century more and more looked on Edinburgh as Scotland's principal town and they made Edinburgh Castle their main residence. Meanwhile the life of Edinburgh went on in the narrow streets that went off at right-angles from the High Street, which ran along the ridge leading from the Castle to the Canongate and Holyrood. The herring-bone pattern, with narrow 'wynds' and 'closes' going off from the wide High Street, remained basically the shape of the city until the second half of the eighteenth century. After the disaster of Flodden in 1513 a protective city wall was hastily built. By this time the Cowgate, running east and west south of and parallel to the High Street, with the Grassmarket at its western end, was established as the fashionable quarter, and the Flodden Wall ran well to the south of it. This wall defined the Ancient Royalty or official burgh limits of Edinburgh for more than two centuries. During this period the city's population rose from an estimated 10,000 to over 30,000 while retaining its sixteenth-century area of under 140 acres. The expanding population had nowhere to go but up, and 'lands' of up to ten or eleven storeys high became a characteristic feature of the city. Sixteenth-century Edinburgh faced attacks from England and endured as well street fighting by rival families, visitations of the plague and violent behaviour by unruly apprentices. After the Reformation Parliament of 1560 Protestant pro-English and Catholic pro-French factions brought more disturbance and violence to the city; it also brought a new Puritan feeling in the Town Council, which from now on repeatedly banned popular festivities and street musicians. The Reformation also brought a new zeal for education and the building of a new High School. In 1582 James VI granted a charter for the foundation of the Town's College, which became Edinburgh University. James's permanent departure from Scotland in 1603 on becoming James I of England removed the Court from the city and left a much felt gap in cultural patronage. The attempt by his son Charles I to impose a pattern of Church government on Scotland identical with that of the Church of England produced controversy and riots in the city. The defiance of the Government by the Covenanters, and the turbulent state of national politics generally kept threatening Edinburgh with disturbance. With Cromwell's

subjugation of Scotland in 1651 Edinburgh settled down somewhat sullenly to a relatively minor role in the Commonwealth. The city welcomed the Restoration in 1660 with a surge of royalist celebration, but Charles II's Scottish policy did not please the citizens. Religious and political controversy again troubled Edinburgh life, until the 'Glorious Revolution' of 1689 produced a new mood. However, the indifference to Scottish feeling of William of Orange, the disaster of the Darien expedition (blamed on William and on the English) and seven years of awful summers and disastrous harvests beginning in 1689 brought more discontent to the city and more turbulent activity by its volatile mob. The mob was very much in evidence between 1702 and 1707 when the Scottish Parliament meeting in Edinburgh debated the Act of Union and finally passed it, to the anger of the citizens. Edinburgh was now no longer the capital of a separate kingdom and was uncertain of its status in Great Britain. The Porteous Riots of 1736, ostensibly against the reprieve of Captain Porteous for firing on the Edinburgh mob, was really an anti-Union and anti-English protest.

Gradually Edinburgh defined its new status, turning first to patriotic and antiquarian literary interests in a mood of nostalgia and then entering a confident phase of cultural self-assertion as a northern metropolis of Britain that could hold its own culturally among any in Europe. The 'Scottish Enlightenment' (q.v.), largely based in Edinburgh, combined paradoxically a pride in Scottish intellectual activities (a pride voiced especially by one of its leading lights, David Hume q.v.) with an uncertainty and even a sense of inferiority about the Scots language and traditional Scottish ways. The city burst its medieval bounds, spreading first south of the High Street in streets and squares built in a vernacular classical style and then, after the draining of the North Loch and the bridging of its valley, into what became known as the New Town, whose carefully patterned streets and elegantly designed houses in a more international Neoclassical style produced in the later years of the eighteenth century and the early years of the nineteenth one of the finest planned urban quarters in Europe, a visual rendering of the ideals of order, progress, harmony, proportion and rationality embodied in the Scottish Enlightenment. Late eighteenth and early nineteenth-century Edinburgh, the Edinburgh of Walter Scott (q.v.), the *Edinburgh Review, Blackwood's Magazine* and Lord Cockburn (q.v.), as well as of internationally famous philosophers and scientists, was in many respects the city's Golden Age. But its position as the capital of a country that was itself part of a larger political unit dominated by English influences remained undefined and Victorian Edinburgh lost the cultural confidence of the Golden Age and nourished itself on nostalgia combined with a progressive anglicizing of its speech and institutions. It was now, as an early nineteenth-century observer remarked, three cities: the Old Town, speaking of the picturesqueness, violence and squalor of the medieval period; the New Town, speaking of the order and elegance of the Scottish Enlightenment, and the spreading area south of the Meadows, where in Victorian times solid middle-class citizens established themselves in streets redolent of respectability. Edinburgh remained largely a professional city with the law predominant, and the New Town has remained the main residential area of its judges, advocates and solicitors. The Old Town became more and more of a slum as the nineteenth century developed, but was in considerable part restored and cleaned up in the second half of the twentieth. The destruction early in the second half of the twentieth century of much of the area between the High Street and the Meadows, representing a very Edinburgh kind of architecture before it turned to the more international style of the New Town, was a real loss to the city's character. But enough remains for its history to be visible in its streets and buildings to a quite conspicuous degree. In the twentieth century the city absorbed suburbs and neighbouring towns, so that today it has nearly half a million inhabitants extending from the Firth of Forth in the north to the Pentland Hills in the south. In 1975, in terms of the Local Government (Scotland) Act of 1973, Edinburgh ceased to be the 'County of the City of Edinburgh' and became that District of the Lothian Region known as the City of Edinburgh.

D. Daiches

Edinburgh International Festival and Fringe, The. From a meeting in 1944 between Harvey Wood, Scottish Director of the British Council, and Rudolph Bing, General Manager of the pre-war Glyndebourne Opera, came the Edinburgh International Festival. Bing was convinced that the great European festivals would take years to recover from the effects of the war still being fought and here was the opportunity for Edinburgh to point the way to reconciliation by mounting a festival of its own. With the end of the war in 1945, the Lord Provost of Edinburgh, Sir John Falconer, agreed the support of the civic authorities and a sum of £20,000 was voted for this purpose. Further contributions from business and private citizens made it possible to mount the first Festival in 1947.

From the start, the Festival provided a mix of music and drama from Scotland and abroad. In the three weeks of the first Festival 180,000 tickets were sold for the familiar—the BBC Scottish Orchestra, the Old Vic—and the less well-known—the Vienna Philharmonic, the Jouvet Company of Paris. Having provided the initial impetus, Bing was succeeded as Artistic Director by Ian Hunter (1950–55) who was responsible for the introduction of fine arts, programming exhibitions of Degas, Renoir, Cezanne and Gauguin. The next Director, Robert Ponsonby (1956–60) brought over La Scala Opera and the first Russian orchestra in 1960. Lord Harewood (1961–65) earned a reputation for adventurousness for events including an Epstein exhibition, a Shostakovich festival in the presence of the composer, and the foundation of a special chorus in 1965 which came to be known as the Edinburgh Festival Chorus. Peter Diamand (1966–78) made opera his speciality and his successor John Drummond (1979–83) was also strong on music. The charismatic Frank Dunlop (1984–91) shifted the emphasis towards theatre, was more populist (the programming of outrageous French circus troupe Archaos raised some

eyebrows) and introduced international themes, each year focusing on a different area of the world. Brian McMaster took over in 1992, initially cutting back on the international content and introducing seasons that concentrated on specific artists such as, in his first year, Tchaikovsky, C.P. Taylor and Harley Granville Barker.

From the International Festival's inception, small companies were attracted to the city with the intention of performing even though they had not been officially invited. Originally frowned upon by the authorities, the Fringe as it came to be known, flourished with a seemingly unstoppable energy and has come to make Edinburgh easily the largest arts festival in the world. Despite recessionary pressures and a level of competition that means companies must expect to make a loss, the Fringe has grown, to take over the whole city for up to four weeks in August and September. Even in the 1960s people were complaining that the Fringe had grown too big, yet by 1992, there were 550 companies performing 1196 shows, in over 110 venues.

The Fringe is now seen to be a kind of theatrical trade fair and *the* place to be seen, particularly for the rising young stand-up comedians who have proliferated in recent years. The most successful venues, notably the Assembly Rooms in George Street, command high rental fees and have encouraged a level of professionalism on the Fringe that many feel has reduced its spirit of spontaneity and surprise. In truth, the Fringe is now so big that there is bound to be something to suit all tastes, be that performance art in draughty church halls or exotic dance in made-to-measure theatres.

As if this wasn't enough activity for anyone, Edinburgh is also host to an International Jazz Festival, an International Film Festival, a biennial Book Festival, a Military Tattoo and an annual firework display that brings the city centre to a standstill on the last Thursday of the Festival.

R. Telfer and M. Fisher

Education. The late A. S. Neill, whose views on pedagogy have gone largely unheeded in his own land for many years, once observed that if education is learning, then Scotland may be considered a well educated country. However Neill had few illusions about his native land, regarding it as culturally barbarous and in educational matters decidedly backward. He described the Scots dominie as 'a dull devil fearful of compromising the little respectability he has and alarmed at anything that detracts from his petty dignity'.

Scottish education has changed since Neill wrote these words in the 1920s. Corporal punishment lingered on in the grim form of the tawse until the mid-1980s and was abolished only after the intervention of the European Court.

The disconcerting tendency to surround Scottish educational achievements with a smug mythology no longer persists to any great extent. Scots feel proud of their long educational tradition and are right to do so. This is not to say that everything is perfect. On the contrary, in the 1960s and 1970s Scottish education had to undergo some painful adjustments and with a rapidly falling birth-rate even more painful operations will have to be undertaken. Inevitably there will be drastic changes in institutions over the next two decades. However, as with those photographs of oneself taken in childhood, the person staring out of the picture is still the same person no matter how much one's personality has changed. Thus it is with Scottish education—the more it changes the more it stays the same. Those educationists and parents from other parts of the world who have never had first hand experience of the pettiness and penury, the might and majesty of Scottish education may be forgiven if, like Neill, they find it barbarous. The Scottish teacher, although he may be in some need of it, pays little attention to criticism. If he bothers to reflect at all on his chosen profession then his attitude is best summed up in the words 'I have a job to do and that is to knock some education into these thick heads'.

It is not too fanciful to claim that Scotland formed the basis of a national educational system as far back as 1560 when John Knox and his fellow Reformers produced the *First Book of Discipline*. Prior to this there were numerous Cathedral and Church schools. By the end of the fifteenth century every principal town in Scotland had a grammar school which taught at least the rudiments of Latin. An Act of 1496 stated that barons and freeholders of substance were to put their sons to school at the age of eight or nine.

> It is statute and ordanit throw all the realme, that all barronis and frehaldaris, that ar of substance put thair eldest sonnis and airis to the sculis, fra thai be aucht or nyne yeiris of age, and till remane at the grammar sculis, quhill thae be competentlie foundit and haue perfite latyne. And thereftir to remane thre yeris at the sculis of art and Jure, sua that thai may haue knawlege and vnderstanding of the lawis.

Some educationists have seen this Act, which had in fact very little effect, as being the first Education Act in Europe to attempt the introduction of some element of compulsory education. The truth is more prosaic. The Act is popularly attributed to Bishop Elphinstone who founded Aberdeen University and whose chief concern was that those who administered the law should be properly trained in a knowledge of its precepts.

The sections on education in the *First Book of Discipline* set out a scheme for a national system of education. There were to be elementary schools in every parish where five to eight-year-olds would be taught reading and Scripture by the minister; grammar schools were to be established in towns of 'any repute'—in these eight to twelve-year-olds would be required to study Latin grammar. In the larger towns, high schools were to be set up in which able and carefully selected pupils from the ages of 12 to 16 would study Latin, Greek, Rhetoric and Logic. At university, to which the more able scholars would proceed, Arts subjects would be studied for three years. Thereafter those who wished to proceed to medicine, law or divinity would study for another five years. This scheme was for rich and poor alike and was intended to be compulsory. Advancement from one stage to another depended on intellectual ability. This scheme failed to bear fruit but it has served as an ideal for Scottish education ever since. From the *First Book of Discipline* have come some of Scotland's greatest educational achievements; from it also have sprung many of the myths, misconceptions and misunderstandings which persist to the present day. In the *Book of Discipline* one thing is clearly defined and that is that the whole object of education is to see that men might be the better equipped to serve God, his Church and the Commonwealth.

Scotland's universities have always taken pride of place in her national education system. In the fifteenth century, Scotland with a population of less than a million could boast three universities, St Andrews founded in 1411, Glasgow in 1451 and Aberdeen (King's College) in 1494. These universities bore more resemblance to today's secondary schools than institutes of higher education, but their importance did not go unnoticed by the Reformers of 1560 who wanted them maintained and endowed to support the common good.

Edinburgh University was established in 1582 by Royal Charter. Unlike the earlier three establishments, it was not an independent institution since it was set up on the initiative of the Town Council which had a predominant voice in deciding the content of the curriculum and the appointment of the professoriat. It was not until the passing of the Universities (Scotland) Act of 1858, that Edinburgh received a constitution similar to the other three universities. Even today the links between Town and Gown in Edinburgh are much stronger than in other cities. Marischal College in Aberdeen was founded in 1593, which gave rise to the subsequent boast that Scotland had five university institutions when England had only two. Marischal and King's were united in 1860.

The development of the Scottish universities in the nineteenth century and the Acts of 1858 and 1889 led to long-overdue changes in their administration and curriculum. Some scholars, notably George Davie, in his wide-ranging *The Democratic Intellect—Scotland and her Universities in the 19th Century* (1961) have argued that Scottish universities underwent an irredeemable process of anglicization during this period and that they ceased to be truly democratic. More recently these views have been subject to re-scrutiny. The changes which occurred in the Scottish universities in the nineteenth century can be seen as part of the general reforms taking place in all educational institutions in Britain at the time. Certainly, Davie is correct in stating that Scottish education in general was reluctant to change. In the schools every effort was made to prevent premature specialization on the pattern of the English sixth form.

There has always been evidence available to show that there has been greater social accessibility to Scottish universities. The Robbins Report on Higher Education (1963) showed that 35 per cent of Scottish University students came from working-class homes compared with 29 per cent for the whole of the United Kingdom. However a difference of 6 per cent is hardly evidence of a *vast* gap between the two systems. Following from the Robbins proposals for expansion, Scotland today finds itself with eight universities—the four ancient ones,

Dundee, Heriot-Watt, Strathclyde, which all developed from existing institutions, and the foundation of Stirling. Non-university higher education is conducted in 14 Central Institutions (so called because 11 are responsible directly to the Scottish Education Department and 3 to the Department of Agriculture and Fisheries, Scotland) and two of the larger local authority colleges. It is a matter of bemusement to some observers that these establishments have been anxious to acquire all the imagined respectability of the ancient universities. Thus at one or two of these colleges titles such as Dean, Faculty and Professor are used, if not freely, then with considerable reverence.

Today there are 54 colleges of 'further education' undertaking a vast range of subjects and catering for a wide population of those in the 16–19 age group. Although these colleges have many students following general education courses, the majority of the classes held are at craft, operative or junior management level. Formerly they were known as technical colleges.

Technical education in Scotland had its origins in the Mechanics Institutes which are the forerunners of the present Central Institutions. Two of the most notable of them are now the University of Strathclyde and the Heriot-Watt University. The early Mechanics Institutes survived much longer in Scotland than their English counterparts. This may have been because, from their inception, they were markedly different in character from their English counterparts, placing much greater emphasis on scientific teaching. The first report of the Edinburgh School of Arts established in 1821 sets the tone of earnest self-improvement which characterized much of Scottish education in the nineteenth century.

> The great object of this institution is to supply at such an expense as a working tradesman can afford, instruction in the various branches of science which are of practical application to mechanics in their several trades, so that they may better comprehend the reason for each individual operation that passes through their hands, and have more certain rules to follow than mere initiation of what they have seen done by another ...
>
> the School of Arts has been established for the purpose of giving you real and substantial instruction, not to amuse a vacant hour and excite your wonder by exhibiting some curious and showy experiments; that it is in a word to enable you to carry away information that will be of solid advantage to you in the exercise of your trade.

The nineteenth century saw the most important developments in Scottish education. How these were arrived at is a matter of some conjecture. Scotland suffers from a dearth of first-rate historians of education. Country and parochial histories there are in plenty but there is still a great deal of valuable material to be sifted. As far as legislation is concerned the story is well documented but a chronology of the various Acts, although necessary, does not give us the full picture. As T. C. Smout has shown in his elegant book *A History of the Scottish People 1560–1830* (1969), education is much too important to be left to the amateur historian or the antiquarian. Equally the social historian ignores education at his peril.

By the middle of the eighteenth century it is evident that there was almost universal literacy in the Lowlands. At the same time the educational facilities available to the middle classes kept abreast with their demand for more and better education.

The Statistical Account for Scotland in 1826 stated:

> However humble their condition the peasantry in the southern districts can all read and are generally more or less skilful in writing and arithmetic, and under the disguise of their uncouth appearance they possess a laudable zeal for knowledge ... not generally found among the same class of men in other countries in Europe.

What must be borne in mind is that there were wide regional differences in the availability of schooling at this and earlier periods. The Gaelic-speaking areas of the Highlands and the city slums of the Industrial Revolution were alike in lacking much provision. By the 1830s it is clear that the national system of education was not functioning in the way its admirers claimed. In his book *Scotland a Half-Educated Nation* written in 1834, George Lewis, a Dundee minister, claimed that only one in 12 were enrolled in day schools and his figures are partially confirmed by government returns for the same year which showed that attendance at Scottish schools was 9.6 per cent whilst in England it was 9.0 per cent. According to Smout, by the 1820s the standards of literacy from region to region varied enormously. Thus we can make the claim that by the late 1850s a town like Edinburgh, which had become internationally famous for its educational facilities, had perhaps one third of its population more or less totally illiterate.

The 1872 Act established a truly national system of education and made education compulsory between the ages of 5 and 13. The parochial and burgh schools formed the basis of the new system and denominational schools could transfer voluntarily. Local management of schools was vested in school boards of which initially there were over 900. To oversee all this a central body, the Scotch Education Department, was set up.

Secondary education rapidly developed in the latter half of the nineteenth century with the establishment of many Higher Grade Schools or Departments set up under the Code of 1899. Eleven years earlier secondary education was given a specific goal with the start of the national leaving certificate at higher and lower grade.

The Education (Scotland) Act of 1918 is an important milestone in Scottish education because unlike the English Act of the same year it bestowed a special status on the denominational schools. The Act enabled the managers of these schools, the great majority of which were Roman Catholic, to transfer their schools on favourable terms to the management of the education authorities. The Church authorities had the right to approve teachers appointed to the schools as regards religious belief and character. The education authorities were responsible for maintaining the schools. This was to prove a distinctive and effective solution to a problem which took another 26 years to solve in England. Immediately prior to the Education Act of 1944, R. A. Butler constantly held up the Scottish model as an example of how the preservation of denominational interests could be reconciled within a national system.

Perhaps more importantly, the 1918 Act recognized that the size and resources of the parish Boards were too meagre for educational provision. The Act substituted 33 county and 5 city education authorities for the 1,000 which were then in existence. After 1975 there were 12 education authorities, nine regions and three all-purpose authorities in the western and northern islands, but the system was again under review in the early 1990s.

In Scotland, local authority schools in the past had no boards of governors and head teachers enjoyed a degree of control and authority unsurpassed in schools south of the border. Gradually this has changed and with the introduction of Schools Councils and the growth of parent-teacher associations and a more liberal atmosphere in the schools, the headmaster no longer retains the venerable aura of authority he once had. As one of the writers' daughters said recently of her headmaster: 'Poor wee man, nobody listens to him and he talks all the time'.

However, although a headteacher is still responsible for determining much of what goes on in his school, there is much greater central control of education in Scotland than in England; and the SED, through its inspectorate, has been able to wield some influence on school organization and the curriculum. On several occasions it has proved an innovatory body often shaping teacher opinion on such subjects as the curriculum and examinations. This is an important ingredient of Scottish education and to the anglocentric the administrative pattern of Scottish education still involves a high degree of central control. In this respect, Scotland is closer to the French educational system, than, for instance, England and Wales. In Scotland it is the SED which gives grants to students following courses of higher education. Similarly the SED have control over the colleges of education and the Central Institutions. In England, for the moment at least, the colleges of education, colleges of higher education, and the polytechnics are controlled by the local authority. The SED has no control, however, over the Scottish universities.

The General Teaching Council of Scotland which was established in 1966 has no counterpart in England. The Council is charged with the registration, admission and general conduct of teachers and exercises much the same powers as the General Medical Council. Similarly it can be argued that the teachers' unions, notably the largest, the Educational Institute of Scotland founded in 1846, have a far greater say in national educational circles than their confrères in the south.

If we attempt to isolate the chief characteristics of Scottish education then these might be as follows:

Education has always been considered as being important to the general well-being of the community.

Every child should have the right to education at any level, provided he can benefit from it.

Education should be provided as cheaply and as systematically as is possible.

There should be a strong practical streak in the training of teachers.

Teachers should eschew experiment and should bring their authority to bear on children.

If the term has any validity, education in Scotland has always been 'teacher-centred' rather than 'child-centred' although in the primary schools, at least, the last decade has seen greater emphasis on making the classroom a happy place in which to learn.

If we look to the major differences between the Scottish and English educational systems, we can single out several characteristics. The first is undoubtedly its greater antiquity as a *national* educational system, the second is its greater emphasis on 'academic education' and thirdly its lower degree of selectivity between pupils of differing abilities. Scots will claim that their educational system is 'more open', 'more democratic', and that access to university in Scotland has always been easier for the able pupil no matter what his social background. Here a note of caution must be sounded since these claims to greater equality are only partly true. The Duke of Argyll addressing the House of Lords in 1869 asserted:

> It is the universal custom all over Scotland that men in very different classes of society should be educated together in the parochial schools. You will have the children of the poorest labourer sitting beside the children of the farmer who employs him, the children of the clergyman of the parish, and even in some cases of the landed gentry, sitting on the same bench and learning from the same master the same branches of instruction.

Granted he was referring to the parish schools only. After the age of 12 many of the sons of the landed gentry and the nobility went south to English public schools or their Scottish counterparts which burgeoned in the second half of the nineteenth century.

Recent historical and sociological research has shown that some of the myths of Scottish education can be easily dismissed. In particular there are fewer working-class children going to university than 15 years ago.

The 1970s produced the spurs which were to change Scotland's schools. The raising of the leaving age to sixteen made urgent the need for an appropriate curriculum and certificate for the less academically able pupils. By the late 1980s, after delays caused by a damaging two-year industrial dispute with teachers, the Government had brought in Standard grade courses and examinations, and had imposed a hitherto-unprecedented level of control over secondary schools. By the early 1990s the 5–14 programme was establishing a similar national curriculum for all primaries and in the early years of secondary.

The traditional autonomy of the headteacher within his school and the teacher in the classroom was under attack from other quarters, too. Accountability and consumer rights were watchwords of the Conservative governments after 1979. Every establishment was given the opportunity to elect a parent-dominated school board. Controversial legislation allowed schools to vote themselves out of local authority control, although there was marked reluctance to use this new freedom. The effectiveness of all educational institutions from primary schools to universities was measured through Government-imposed performance indicators.

Dramatic changes in post-school education date from the 1960s, first with the doubling of the number of universities to eight and then in the 1990s another era of expansion saw four more colleges attaining university status. Further education colleges also developed rapidly, stimulated in the 1980s by Government concern at the level of youth unemployment. In 1993 the colleges were removed from local authority control and given a more entrepreneurial role in the growth area of vocational education. In a new guise an old characteristic of Scottish education has again appeared: much more than south of the border, school and university education had always been utilitarian and concerned with young people's future livelihoods.

H. Cowper and W. Pickard

Elliott, Kenneth (b. 1929), musicologist, studied music at the University of St Andrews with Cedric Thorpe Davie, and at the University of Cambridge with Robin Orr and Thurston Dart. At Cambridge he developed an interest in early music and, subsequently, in early Scottish music up to 1700 on which he is now the leading authority. Senior Lecturer in Music at the University of Glasgow, he is best known for his editions, arrangements and recordings of early Scottish music (for example *Music of Scotland 1500–1700*, Musica Britannica XV, *Early Scottish Keyboard Music* and two sets of arrangements of *Airs and Dances of Renaissance Scotland* for strings). He has appeared as soloist (mostly harpsichord) and continuo player with BBC Scottish Symphony Orchestra, Scottish Baroque Ensemble, John Currie Singers and at many international music festivals.

He has contributed articles to the New Grove Dictionary and has worked on editions of the complete works of Robert Johnson, Robert Carver, anthologies of sixteenth-eighteenth century Scottish songs and a history of Scottish music.

P. Hindmarsh

Engineering Industries. The 'Scotch engineer' became a stock character in the late Victorian period, when it was said that you could shout 'Hey, Mac' in the engine room of any steamship and be sure of a response. Certainly by that time Scotland's engineering industries excelled in many fields, and were unrivalled in their range of products. Men of Scottish origin had left their stamp on engineering wherever it was practised, and had exploited to the full the opportunities offered by expanding world trade—itself made possible by engineers.

Scottish expertise in engineering first [...] Georgian period. Prior to that time, engine[...] roughly into civil and military, and in both fiel[...] failed to distinguish themselves. The military roa[...] programmes of the middle decades of the eighteenth c[...] and the first major canal, the Forth & Clyde, were desig[...] and executed by Englishmen, as were most notable bridge[...]. By the end of the century, however, the situation had changed dramatically. Thomas Telford, a Borderer, had begun his domination of the civil engineering profession which he retained until the railway age, and within the next two decades John Rennie and Robert Stevenson had established themselves as outstanding engineers in their generation. Although Scotsmen never again held such commanding positions in the profession a steady stream of highly competent, sometimes brilliant, civil engineers succeeded them and designed the roads, railways, harbours, waterworks, drainage systems and the host of other constructions necessary for a civilization of growing sophistication. In their wake, Scottish civil engineering contractors developed erratic, but sometimes enviable reputations.

The later eighteenth century saw mechanical engineering beginning to split from civil engineering. Men like John Smeaton, the Yorkshireman, James Watt, and John Rennie could master both civil engineering in the modern sense, and mechanical engineering, but as machines became more numerous, and their variety increased, a degree of specialization was inevitable. At first the opportunities in England were greater, and James Watt, William Murdoch and John Rennie did most of their work there, but from about the turn of the century the rapid development of novel types of machines and of new ways of making machines gave another generation of engineers their chance.

At first mechanical engineering was a widely dispersed activity and before 1850 Dundee, Leith, Paisley, Greenock and Glasgow had all produced a range of products including marine, stationary and locomotive marine engines. By that time, however, the advantage of proximity to the coal mines and iron works of Lanarkshire was beginning to tell, and Glasgow, Paisley and Kilmarnock forged ahead during the next half century. The success of individual companies encouraged others to enter the industry, creating over-capacity in the regular depressions of the later nineteenth century. Growth was aided by the practice of sub-contracting some stages of manufacture, which allowed concerns with limited fixed capital to build up extensive businesses, phasing extension of capacity to returns.

Though the range of engineering products produced in Scotland was eventually immense, there were some clearly defined specialisms. Of these marine engineering was probably the most important. Though the first Clyde-built steamship, the Comet of 1812, was powered by a land engine, within ten years specialized engines were well developed, and by 1830 David Napier and his cousin Robert were emerging as leaders. These men trained the next generation of marine engineers, including Tod & MacGregor, J. & G. Thomson and Randolph & Elder. By 1850 the Clyde marine engineers had assumed a commanding lead over their British competitors which they strengthened by entering the iron shipbuilding trade. From 1850 until after the first World War the Clyde marine engineers either invented or rapidly absorbed all the important improvements in their speciality, producing the first successful compound, triple and quadruple expansion steam engines, and pioneering the use of the steam turbine and diesel motor.

Locomotive-building, widely dispersed in the early railway age, became concentrated, so far as main-line production was concerned, in Glasgow. Apart from the railway companies' works, the firm of Mitchell & Neilson (later Neilsons and Co.) was the most significant. The other two major concerns both sprang from this company, and when they all came together in 1903 to form the North British Locomotive Co. Ltd they formed the largest private locomotive-building complex in Europe, with a capacity of over 500 locomotives a year. Industrial locomotives were also made in large numbers in Kilmarnock and in the Airdrie district. Sugar machinery was another Scottish speciality, born out of the extensive West Indian trade with the Clyde. At first the machinery used was small in scale, and animal powered, but steam engines were introduced c. 1810, and from then until the 1920s the scale and complexity of equipment grew. Extension of sugar-cane cultivation into new areas as colonization spread brought new markets to the Glasgow sugar machinery industry, which towards the end of the nineteenth century produced 80 per cent of the world's output. The leading firms were The Mirrlees Watson Co. (and its predecessors), W. & A. McOnie, and A. & W. Smith & Co.; the last-named still flourishes.

Scottish companies also made their mark in structural engineering. The most famous concern was Sir William Arrol & Co. Ltd, builders of the second Tay railway bridge and of both Forth bridges, and specialists in steel-framed factory buildings. Other companies, such as P. & W. MacLellan, the Motherwell Bridge and Engineering Co. Ltd and the Aberdeen firm of John M. Henderson & Co. Ltd, exported bridges and piers to India and other developing countries. Motherwell Bridge were early specialists in bulk oil-storage tanks, a field in which they still lead.

Other important Scottish engineering products included shipbuilding and other heavy machine tools, rice machinery, jute, flax and carpet machinery, gas works and chemical plant.

The engineering industries suffered severely in the inter-war depression, when many of the smaller, and some larger companies ceased trading. Those that survived were able to take advantage of war-time and post-war demand, which remained at a high level until the end of the 1950s. Since then there has been a further shakeout of companies producing equipment for markets which have disappeared or drastically shrunk, notably locomotives, heavy machine tools, marine engines and textile machinery. Today Scottish engineering works still excel in a number of fields, including electronics, mining machinery, pumps, consumer goods, gas turbines (both land and aero) and boilers. Unfortunately, at least in some senses, control of many of these concerns lies south of the border or in the hands of multinational companies, and although Scotland still produces more than her share of engineers of all types, employment opportunities within the country have tended to decline.

J. R. Hume

Engineers and Inventors. Almost every history of the industrial revolution in Britain makes some reference to the relatively large number of Scots engineers and inventors who contributed to its success, but a comparative analysis shows Scotland in an even better light. Taking the numbers of eminent scientists and technologists *per million population* born in the various countries of Western Europe in each decade of the eighteenth and nineteenth centuries, Scotland begins to outstrip all the others from as early as 1725, reaching a peak in the middle of the nineteenth century, twice as great as the next most productive country, England.

Many of the Scottish men of science in the seventeenth and eighteenth centuries were also men of invention and industry, for example George Sinclair, Colin Maclaurin, James Stirling 'the Venetian', William Cullen, Joseph Black and others. George Sinclair (c.1625–1696) was appointed Professor of Philosophy at Glasgow University in 1654, and in the next year he took part in the search for a sunken Spanish galleon with a primitive form of diving bell he had invented. After moving to Edinburgh in 1666 he acted as consultant to several local mine-owners on geological problems and the drainage of their pits, and superintended the work of bringing piped water into the city from the Comiston Springs in 1676. Returning in 1689 to Glasgow, he was successively Professor of Philosophy and Mathematics until his death in 1696.

The latter half of the eighteenth century saw a remarkable flowering of engineering and inventive talent in Scotland. Andrew Meikle (1719–1811) was an East Lothian millwright who invented in 1750 the fantail which kept the sails of a windmill at the right angle to the wind, and in 1772 the 'spring' sail which counteracted the effect of gusts of wind. Robert Melville (1723–1809) was born in Fife and studied at the Universities of Glasgow and Edinburgh. He served in the Army and as a colonial governor in the West Indies, and on his return to Scotland he was asked by the Carron Company to advise them on the design of a more effective cannon. The result was a shorter, lighter gun first made in 1778, which became known as the carronade.

Often spoken of as the inventor of the steam engine, James Watt (1736–1819) himself made no such claim. Given a working model of a Newcomen engine to repair, he quickly saw how inefficient it was, and how that could be remedied by providing it with a separate condenser. That was one of the greatest single advances in the development of the steam engine, but he was also responsible for other improvements such as the air pump, steam-jacketted cylinders, double-acting engines, the sun and planet rotary mechanism (suggested by William Murdock), parallel motion and the governor for regulating an engine's speed. He was a rather diffident man who succeeded in business only through his partnership with Matthew Boulton—together they established the Soho Works in

Birmingham where they built more than 350 Boulton and Watt stationary beam engines from 1787 to 1801.

William Murdock (1754–1839) was born in Ayrshire and worked with his father, a millwright, then went south to Birmingham to work for Boulton and Watt. He erected engines for them in Cornwall, and at Redruth in 1784 he built a small high-pressure steam engine and installed it in a model road locomotive; Watt, however, did not approve of either high steam pressures or steam locomotion, and Murdock gave up his experiments. He succeeded in 1792 in illuminating his house in Redruth with coal gas, an invention which a few years later was taken up by Boulton and Watt, and eventually by the rest of the world.

Though he was not trained as an engineer, John Loudon McAdam (1756–1836) in his capacity as a road surveyor introduced improvements in road construction and maintenance that facilitated the greatly increased movement of people and goods, consequent upon the industrial revolution. The graded crushed stone he used in his roads remains today, with tar or bitumen binders, the material with which most roads are surfaced. An alternative system of road construction was developed by Thomas Telford (1757–1834), using large hand-placed stones in the road base and finer material on top. Telford and McAdam roads were equally satisfactory at the time, but the construction of 'macadam' roads could be mechanised, while Telford's could not. He was also an outstanding builder of bridges and canals; his 579-ft span wrought iron Menai Strait suspension bridge is still in use today, as is his Caledonian Canal (1803–23) through the Great Glen from Fort William to Inverness, and the Göta Canal in Sweden for which he was consulting engineer.

John Rennie (1761–1821) was born at East Linton and worked for a time as a millwright with Andrew Meikle. He also, unusually for an engineer at that time, studied at Edinburgh University for three years, from 1780 to 1783. After working for Boulton and Watt he moved to London in 1791 and quickly established a reputation as one of the foremost civil engineers in Britain, famous for his bridges, canals, docks and harbours. His elder son George (1791–1866) turned to mechanical and marine engineering, building the first screw vessel, the *Dwarf*, for the Royal Navy in 1840; his younger son John (1794–1874) was civil engineer to the Admiralty, and in 1831 completed London Bridge to his father's design.

Two of the earliest builders of steam ships were Scots. William Symington (1763–1831) completed the *Charlotte Dundas* in 1802 for use as a tug on the Forth and Clyde canal, but its wash was judged a danger to the banks and it was soon laid up and left to rot. Henry Bell (1767–1830) was more successful in that his *Comet* of 1812 plied regularly between Glasgow and Greenock, the first passenger-carrying steamboat in European waters.

It is worth remarking here that in the first half of the nineteenth century engineers were severely handicapped, not only by the limitations of their theoretical knowledge, but also by the lack of suitable materials and methods of fabrication and machining. Steel of reliable properties did not become generally available until about 1880; Nasmyth invented the steam hammer in 1839 (but did not build one until 1843); Whitworth had greatly improved the accuracy of machine tools by 1840; Rankine published the first edition of his celebrated treatise on the steam engine in 1859.

Throughout the nineteenth century, Scottish engineers and inventors remained in the forefront of the advances being made in many fields. James Baird (1802–1876), David Colville (1813–1898), David Mushet (1772–1847) and James Beaumont Neilson (1792–1865), all contributed to improvements in iron-founding, and Sir William Arrol (1839–1913) launched structural steel with a spectacular flourish when he completed the Forth Bridge in 1890. Notable locomotive engineers included Dugald Drummond (1840–1912), Patrick Stirling (1820–1895) of the 8-ft single, and Robert Fairlie (1831–1885) whose articulated locomotives ran on 52 railways in almost as many countries.

Civil engineering is represented by Sir Robert McAlpine (1847–1934), 'Concrete Bob' of Glenfinnan Viaduct fame; Sir James Brunlees (1816–1892) who built many railways in Britain and South America; Joseph Mitchell (1803–1883) who built most of the railways in the north of Scotland and wrote his rambling *Reminiscences* in two volumes, the second of which was not published at the time for fear of threatened lawsuits; William John MacQuorn Rankine (1820–1872), Edinburgh University graduate, Glasgow University Professor of Civil Engineering, writer of a series of text-books which expounded scientific principles in such a way that they could be understood and applied by practising engineers; John Scott Russell (1808–1882) who crossed swords with Isambard Kingdom Brunel over the building of the *Great Eastern*, and with the Institution of Civil Engineers, over his professional integrity; and the Stevenson family, beginning with Robert (1772–1850) who built the Bell Rock and more than twenty other Scottish lighthouses, and including six other lighthouse builders as well as Robert Louis (1850–1894) who studied engineering like the rest of the family at Edinburgh University, before turning to fiction rather than fact.

Two Scots stand out amongst the many early experimenters in electric telegraphy. James Bowman Lindsay (1799–1862) constructed a form of electric telegraph in 1832, suggested the possibility of electric welding in 1835, proposed a transatlantic submarine cable in 1843 (the first was successfully laid in 1866) and in 1853 he demonstrated wireless telegraphy through water. A Caithness man, Alexander Bain (1810–1877), patented in 1843 a system for the transmission of images by wire (foreshadowing today's fax machines) and a device for the automatic recording of telegraph messages. In spite of these and other bright ideas, like so many other inventors who were ahead of their time, he died a poor man.

To take just one field of engineering right up to the present day, electricity in all its forms seems to have had a special appeal for Scots engineers. Alexander Muirhead (1848–1920) was born in East Lothian but moved with his parents to London at an early age. His broad Scots accent was not understood there, and for some years he had to be educated privately, but later he graduated with honours from University College, London. In 1875 he patented a method of duplexing telegraph signals, and by about 1900 he was working with Sir Oliver Lodge on the development of wireless telegraphy. Henry Mavor (1858–1915) was born in Stranraer and in 1883 founded in Glasgow a firm which became within twenty years one of the country's leading manufacturers of electrical machinery. He was the father of Osborne Henry Mavor, better known as James Bridie.

Alan A Campbell Swinton (1863–1930) was born in Edinburgh, and later moved to London where in 1896 he was one of the first to explore the medical applications of X-rays, discovered only the year before by Röntgen. In a letter to the journal *Nature* in 1908 he described the principles of an electronic system of television, but although he worked on the idea for years and published further more detailed proposals for what is essentially the system in use today, he never carried out any experiments to see if his theories would work in practice. Sir Edward MacColl (1882–1951), born in Dumbarton, was an electrical power engineer who played a leading part in the development of the Falls of Clyde hydro-electric scheme in the 1920s, and became the Chief Executive of the newly-formed North of Scotland Hydro-Electric Board in 1943. John Logie Baird (1888–1946) of Helensburgh, studied electrical engineering at Glasgow University and overcame ill-health, poverty and lack of interest in the corridors of power to give the first public demonstration of television in London in 1926. His mechanical system of scanning allowed only a limited degree of refinement however, and finally in 1937, the BBC chose the rival Marconi electronic system for their TV transmissions.

Sir Donald Miller (b. 1927) graduated at Aberdeen University, was appointed Chief Engineer of the North of Scotland Hydro-Electric Board in 1966, moved to the South of Scotland Electricity Board in 1974 as Director of Engineering and General Manager, and has been Chairman of Scottish Power since 1982. He played a leading role in the modernization of electricity generation and distribution throughout Scotland in the past two decades. Alistair G.J. Macfarlane (b. 1931) was born in Edinburgh, graduated at Glasgow University and joined Metropolitan-Vickers in Manchester in 1953. Six years later he decided to concentrate on his research into feedback control systems, and moved to the University of London. Subsequently he held chairs of engineering in Manchester and Cambridge, and since 1989 has been Principal and Vice-Chancellor of the Heriot-Watt University, Edinburgh.

R. M. Birse

Episcopalianism. The Scottish reformers put regional organisation in the hands of individual overseers, whether called superintendents or bishops, though they did not believe in the transmission of an 'apostolic succession', and the overseers, who worked with synods and kirk sessions, were accountable to the general assembly. Opposition to individual overseers arose in the 1570s, when Andrew Melville advocated the parity

of ministers, and it was proposed that oversight be transferred to presbyteries. For over a century there was controversy between the supporters of the rival episcopalian and presbyterian principles. The government of the Church was modified many times, and the 'apostolic succession' was restored, but often what existed was a compromise in which bishops co-operated with presbyteries, sometimes under general assembly control. Thus one Church comprehended Presbyterians and Episcopalians.

In 1689, when James VII was deposed, parliament abolished episcopacy and in 1690 established presbytery. The Episcopalians, ejected from the Church, now had to form their own Communion. Many of them, who were prepared to accept William of Orange, Anne and the Hanoverians, qualified for toleration under a statute of 1712, but others, who were Jacobites (or 'non-jurors' who would not take oaths to the ruling line) were subjected to severe prosecution, especially after the Jacobite rebellions of 1715 and 1745. While the 'Qualified' congregations grew in strength, especially in Lowland towns, the non-jurors declined, but retained support in the northeast, parts of the West Highlands and—a little oddly—the Edinburgh area. When the non-jurors were at the lowest ebb of their fortunes, in 1784, they consecrated Samuel Seabury as the first bishop for the American colonies, which had just become independent and were not acceptable to the Church of England.

When the Episcopalians began their separate existence in 1690 their worship had differed little from that of the Presbyterians, but thereafter, while the 1712 statute tied the 'Qualified' to the English Prayer Book, the non-jurors turned to the Scottish Prayer Book of 1637, whose Communion Office they modified until by 1764 it had reached much the form which it retained until 1929.

The non-jurors prayed for the Young Pretender as 'Charles III', but when he died in 1788 they accepted King George, and in 1792 a statute extended toleration to them. It then became possible for them to merge with the erstwhile 'Qualified', and the two gradually merged to produce the modern Scottish Episcopal Church. During the eighteenth century the allocation of districts to bishops had been somewhat haphazard, but ultimately the fourteen old dioceses were allotted among seven bishops. The office of archbishop had lapsed early in the eighteenth century, and recourse was had to a 'Primus', for whose title there was precedent in the Dark Ages.

Nineteenth-century developments went far to make the Episcopal Church hardly recognisable as an heir of the Church established before 1689. Almost as a sequel to union between the non-jurors and the 'Qualified' (who always had strong English links), there were moves towards conformity with England. The English Thirty-Nine Articles were adopted; the use of the Prayer Book for Matins and Evensong, and the wearing of the surplice, became obligatory; kirk sessions were abandoned; for a time the English Communion Office was given precedence over the Scottish; and English terminology was adopted. In 1864, orders conferred by Scottish bishops received full recognition in England. Under the influence of the Oxford or Tractarian Movement, Scottish Episcopalians became more 'High Church' in their usage than the Church of England. Episcopalian worship had an appeal when Presbyterian services were still very austere, and the Church had a good record of 'mission' work in the slums. It reached its peak of membership about 1920.

In recent years Scottish Episcopalians have shared with other members of the Anglican Communion—and also with the Roman Catholic Church—far-reaching changes in practice, including something approaching abandonment of the Prayer Book and other usages, and also an emphasis on the character of the Church as an instrument of social policy rather than an agency of Christian worship.

G. Donaldson

Ettrick Shepherd, The, *see* **Hogg, James**

Exploration. The concept of geographical discovery reflects a form of arrogance known only to western men. The places discovered were in the first place never lost, never missing. The aborigines knew plenty about Australia before the white man arrived and gave it his name. Macchu Picchu had shyly withdrawn from view before Hiram Bingham 'discovered' it anew. The shores of Lake Ngami were populated before David Livingstone arrived. Everest was not discovered by Indian surveyors. Its presence was widely known. It was the fact that it was calculated to be the highest mountain in the world that constituted the discovery; science is discovery too.

We should therefore at the outset clarify what we mean by discovery. If we narrow the field to discovery by Scots, we might almost say that they never discovered anything; and that in this they were joined by most Europeans. They were simply too late. It was early man who made the discoveries when the world was still empty. Discovery in the arrogant western sense simply meant rediscovery and telling the folks back home about it. But there was also a genuine form, the sort that fits together discoveries like the pieces of a jig-saw puzzle; like the tracing of the Niger from source to mouth by Mungo Park. His was a first, a genuine synthesis of knowledge, and its collection involved no little hardship and, eventually, his death.

We like to see our explorers cast in a heroic mould, and the truth is they very often were. Men seldom seem to be better motivated than when searching for the missing link. But what sort of driving force pushes men and women far from home comfort, to engage in fantastic risks, and then to return to the arena again and again until the puzzle is solved? The North West Passage is a case in point. To the north of the Canadian mainland is a cold, barren wasteland of ice-floes and islands. Once mariners had learnt enough about the world to know that one could sail the Atlantic to Ungava Bay on the east, contiguous with the Atlantic, and sail north through the Bering Straits between Alaska and what is now the USSR, it became natural to speculate that there was a sea route linking them to lead to

the exotic spice islands of the east—spices so necessary to preserve food and to make it palatable. The Eskimo lived in those parts and travelled great distances, but not so far as to encompass the hundred degrees of longitude involved. In any case, their travel was a winter event. So one can assume that no one knew of the existence of a viable North West Passage for sailing ships. Frobisher, an Englishman, made the first foray as far back as 1576. But it was not until the tragic Franklin expedition of 1847, which simply disappeared into the void, that exploration of this area began in earnest. Thirty-nine expeditions set sail in the next 10 years to find the missing explorers. They were found eventually, dead, by the Kirkwall man, John Rae. The experience of these expeditions led to the gradual build-up of knowledge that allowed the Scotsman McLure to discover the key to the passage in the years 1850–53. Even so, the first entirely nautical journey was not effected till the Norwegian Amundsen made it in 1903–5.

It is often asked, especially by the English, whether Scotland's comparatively rich contribution to the synthesis of the world's maps came from the wildness of her nature or the poverty of her opportunities at home. But I would guess it came from neither. To know the mind of an explorer is to know someone who is neither exceptionally bold nor deprived. Usually he is intellectually obsessed with the question mark posed by the unknown. And if the Scots, proportional to their population, played a remarkably large part in world rediscovery by western man, it was probably due to economic circumstances which made for distant travel and an intellectual passion for knowledge. Moreover, there is undoubtedly something quite special about unknown territory that does not apply to cosmic physics or archaeology. It is that empty lands may be available for occupation by the discoverer. Moreover early explorers were often not too concerned about the rights of the indigenous population. Francisco Pizarro was not driven to conquer Peru by an obsession for knowing the unknown, but by a passion for gold and power. Nevertheless, one can only admire the fact that 108 men managed to conquer an entire kingdom.

There is little record of the Scots being quite so hard-hearted as Pizarro and his like, but then there is little record of equivalent material success. The expedition that sailed for Darien was undoubtedly materially motivated, and came to a bad end. Of the hard men, most were the agents of the Crown, by then the Crown in England, and laid claim to things that were not theirs in a name that was not theirs. Faithful servants, they were often faithfully rewarded with Governorships and trading rights. Perhaps they do not need a special place in the history of exploration for they have their own appropriate niche in the history of exploitation. We shall content ourselves with those who did explore, who synthesized the whole from the parts, and with another type of explorer—the one who actually trod virgin territory. To find this latter type one has to turn to the exploration of the vertical; mountaineering. This activity is arguably pointless. The summit of Mount Everest, or Chomolungma, as it was known before western arrogance butted in, is visible from many points and is considered to be of little use for raising crops or watching for flood waters. Its actual ascent is not really all that vital for the synthesis of geographical knowledge, especially now that we have aeroplanes. Yet because of its very pointlessness it is all the harder to point the finger at a would-be explorer and accuse him of mercantilism or territorial aggression. Climbing virgin mountains seems to be a true form of exploration, an activity carried out for its own sake, and one in which the Scots have taken a notable part.

But, let us return to earlier times. Exploration in Scotland never had its institutional base, as in England, where the Royal Geographical Society formed an important role as source of inspiration, a recipient of data and a supporting foundation. The Royal Scottish Geographical Society, try as it might, never quite managed the same role. That body, still alive and well today, is essentially a comfortable organization for armchair exploration. It reached its zenith in the period just before the First World War when it assisted in launching Bruce's two expeditions to the Antarctic. Both were called the Scottish National Antarctic Expeditions, and though warmly and positively supported by the people and businesses in Scotland, got the cold shoulder from the English fraternity, leading to some understandable bitterness. Bruce's expeditions were respectable scientific expeditions, which if they made no major contribution to geographical uncertainty, carried out some notable scientific work in the Antarctic.

On the whole it was well for an explorer in the older days to have some other objectives. Livingstone's medical and missionary work was a case in point, but he made many contributions to the map of Africa. He searched for, but never found for sure, the ultimate source of the Nile. It was, if anything, the discovery of Livingstone by the London newspaper reporter, Stanley, that made Livingstone's own name into a headline.

One of Scotland's greatest explorers on the North American scene was Alexander Mackenzie, who explored the river now named after him, which flows from the Great Slave Lake in the North West Territories into the Arctic Ocean. That discovery was in 1789. A quarter of a century later, John Ross, then a Rear Admiral in the Queen's Fleet, determined the position of the north magnetic pole which lies in the arctic islands to the north of Canada, and later went on to lead an Antarctic expedition. We do not know whether he suggested the idea himself, but today there is a Ross Island, a Ross ice shelf and a Ross Sea lying almost due south of New Zealand. These were bold voyages given the ships of the day. It was from the area that Scott (no connection) set out for the South Pole; an expedition, it seems, devoid of Scots, unless we include Nelson, who owned much land in the Shetlands and was the expedition's biologist.

But in the vertical plane Scots were early in the field, though not as early as the English. The first to gain a hold in the history pages was Alexander Nicolson, a sheriff, who, in the later part of the nineteenth century, made the first ascent of Skye's tallest peak, Sgurr Alaisdair. He shares a place with the

Sgianeatheach, John McKenzie, guide to numerous Victorian gentlemen, and a great breaker of new ground, with many Cuillin ascents to his credit. McKenzies have flitted through the pages of mountaineering history ever since. Then there was Harold Raeburn, the first man to show what fun it was to climb snow and ice, and that what could not be done in summer often was possible in winter. But the first to gain a more international reputation was Norman Collie, who climbed with such notable English climbers as Slingsby and Mummery. His 'via dei inglesi' on the north face of the Monte Disgrazia in the Italian Alps will undoubtedly be renamed as enlightenment spreads south.

We find, as the twentieth century opens, an accepted niche for the savant-climber, an eccentric niche. To suffer far from home in the mission field or tracing the origin of a river was laudatory, and scarcely a Scottish graveyard does not yield its evidence of the foot-loose character of the late nineteenth and early twentieth-century Scot. But respectability was still denied the mountaineer.

This role of eccentricity does not appear to have dampened recruitment, and the pursuit of the useless, as Lionel Terry described it, was a growing phenomenon. In the Alps, Euan McKenzie made several first ascents in the later 1880s and has his name on a roll of honour in the village of Breuil. McKenzies again! But the Alps were a singularly Victorian English domain for nearly all the golden years of discovery, and though there were kenspeckle climbers at large in Scotland, little was heard of them abroad, and their exploration was largely confined to homeland hills. Even here the name McKenzie again looms and looms again. The spirit of that period is captured beautifully in W. H. Murray's book, *Undiscovered Scotland*.

The post-Second World War period saw the first real interest by Scots mountaineers in going abroad to explore. Perhaps new, faster ways of travel had made it possible for people with little free time, and possibly increasing affluence had something to do with it. In any event, expeditions flourished, and some had a distinctly Scottish flavour. In 1958 a bunch of well tried mountaineers took flight to the northeast of Greenland and, in a tour de force, literally opened up one of the northern world's most fabulous climbing grounds, the Staunings Alps at latitude 72°N on King Oscar's Fjord. The area, known as the Arctic Riviera because of its wonderful anti-cyclonic climate, has since become a mecca for climbers, though there is nothing virgin left. But on that occasion the Scots knocked off seventeen virgin peaks. A few years earlier we had the first Scottish Himalayan expedition, whose tale made great reading—a small bunch of friends with meagre resources and no sponsorship, no government backing. At that time the unclimbed hills of Kumaon were numbered in scores. Their first outstanding achievement was to penetrate the Girthi gorge and make two fine first ascents, Uja Tirche (20,350 ft.) and Bethartoli Himal (20,840 ft).

It is perhaps fitting that this spate of genuine vertical exploration finally led to the highest mountain of them all, and that one of the pair who made the first and so far only ascent of the notorious southwest face of Everest was the Scot Dougal

Haston with the Englishman Doug Scott—at least he claims he's English!

M. Slesser

F

Famine, either local, or general, was a common event in sixteenth and early seventeenth-century Scotland, as well as in earlier periods. It became less frequent after 1650 and, for the Lowlands, disappeared in the eighteenth century. Sometimes it was caused by the devastation of war, more often by harvest failure. The main element in diet was grain and this was at the mercy of a short growing season. In the sixteenth century harvests were usually just adequate for a population which appears to have been growing, but the balance between production and consumption could easily be disturbed. There appears to have been general famine in the early 1550s, in 1562–63, 1571–73, 1585–87, as well as the general European food crisis of 1594–98. In the seventeenth century the most serious crisis was 1622–23, but there were Highland famines in 1604 and 1650, the Northern Isles suffered severely in 1634–36, and the war and English invasion of 1650–51 led to starvation in many areas. At the end of the century the general climatic deterioration which has been called the 'mini ice-age' led to a severe famine in the period 1696–1700—when, it is estimated, between 5 per cent and 15 per cent of the population died. This event has left vivid and moving contemporary descriptions and so gained exaggerated prominence.

There were also local famines, which in a primitive economy with poor communications could not be relieved. Crop yields on undrained soil were always low and between 20 per cent and 40 per cent of the crop would have to be kept for seed. In harvest failure this was impossible and so failures usually ran for two or three years.

The people who suffered most in harvest failure were the cottars, but those who worked in primitive industry, such as textiles, metal goods or brewing, were also liable to starve, lacking a market for their production. Death in famine was more often from disease rather than direct starvation. The spread of disease was encouraged by the existence of unburied corpses, and also by people crowding into the burghs in the hope of work. Typhus has been found, in many countries, to be the most common agent of death in famine conditions, but lack of diagnostic descriptions makes it impossible to be sure that this was the case in Scotland. There are also indications of dysentery epidemics.

The reduction of the frequency of Lowland famine in the later seventeenth century and its disappearance in the eighteenth, may have been a result of an improvement in the relationship between agricultural production and population. Certainly grain prices took a step downwards in the 1660s and corn was frequently exported in the early eighteenth century. Population growth before 1750 was slow. But structural changes in agriculture capable of producing a drastic rise in productivity did not occur until the 1770s, nor did the general use of the potato, the most important of the new crops. General economic growth did not start till the late 1740s, though improvements in communication came earlier. There were no general crop failures between 1700 and 1740 but in 1740 the harvest failed in Scotland as in the rest of Europe, and to this was added war dislocation. It also failed in 1757, 1765, the early 1770s, 1782 and 1799–1800. In some cases and areas these failures were followed by increased mortality, but there is no general connection between peaks in mortality and in food prices. Whereas in England and the Netherlands the disappearance of famine in the seventeenth century seems to have been caused by economic development, in Scotland it should be attributed to social organization. The Scottish Poor Law, though set up by statute in the sixteenth century, was not carried out until the mid seventeenth century and then only in places. But in the eighteenth century landowners and townsmen set out to organize relief both through the Poor Law and apart from it, and to bring in grain purchases to hold down local prices. Since the amount of food necessary to turn the threat of famine into a season of mere stringency was not great, this policy was successful in 1740 and later. In 1782 the London government also made available supplies to the north of Scotland.

In the Highlands where communications were much more difficult, the social ethos of the Lowland gentry not, for some time, established and the rate of population growth faster, famine continued to be a risk till the mid nineteenth century. It is clear that the seasons after the harvests of 1757, 1782, 1799 and 1800 were traumatic. 1836 saw a failure of the potato, relieved partly by aid from the south. When the potato failed again and totally in 1846 the government intervened successfully by placing two supply ships on the west coast and calling on landowners to purchase food from them for their tenantry.

Even when famine, in the sense of death directly or indirectly from starvation, had ceased to be a threat, harvest shortages caused long-term economic deterioration in the position of the people in the affected areas and in this sense, famine was not totally conquered.

R. Mitchison

Fashion and Design. When in 1838, two Glasgow tailors opened a tweed and tartan shop in Aldgate, later to move to fashionable Knightsbridge in London, the commercial success of Scottish textiles as pioneered by The Scotch House was assured. It is difficult to readily identify a name or distinctive design trend when considering what constitutes Scottish fashion. Yet immediately associated with the notion of Scottish fashion, are the varied and extensive ranges of high quality woollen yarns and cloth which are the mainstay of the international fashion industry in Paris, Milan, New York, and London.

The pre-war textile industry in Scotland manufactured and supplied some of the finest cotton shirtings and dress fabrics; Viyella yarns and fabrics were exclusively woven in Glasgow and the knitwear and hosiery industries were expanding from their traditional Border strongholds. Garment making, whether from the exclusive salons and workrooms of Murielle of Sauchiehall Street, or the fashionable department stores such as Jenners and Greensmith Downs in Edinburgh or McDonalds and Dalys in Glasgow to the large tailoring factories of Wallace and Weir and Charles Rattray all formed an important part of Scotland's pre-war economy. Original designs, created by the house designers, were generally based on what was directly dictated by Paris or in a modified adapted version to satisfy more realistic purchasing levels. These were some of the factors which were the basis of the vital ready-to-wear industry which would produce unisex jeans or separates for exclusive labels such as Daks and Jaeger in the mid-twentieth century.

After the Second World War, much of this fashion and textile industry was to change dramatically. The increasing number of emerging third world independent countries, now provided cheaper labour for the products which had previously been manufactured and imported from the mother country. The knitwear and textile industries initially did not reveal the serious situation that would accelerate in the 1960s with companies which would not or could not adapt to the new technologies.

Fresh design stimulus in the late 1950s was injected by young professionally trained designers, such as Bernat Klein, whose exotic palette of colours, derived from his own paintings, was translated into the world-renowned ribbon-velvet and wool-mohair tweeds (1963–64), which were much sought-after by the French couture houses during the 1960s. Roses, a wool-mohair tweed used by Chanel in 1962, could be considered as the design which established Bernat Klein internationally as a designer of exclusive fashion textiles, woven and printed, which drew much of their originality from the Scottish Borders landscape. Bernat Klein also turned his inimitable colour sense to the design of hand-knitted garments. These were produced by outworkers, an adaptive method of utilising professional skills, now made redundant due to the rapidly changing nature of the industry.

The knitwear industry, with its stable production base of fine lambswool to luxury cashmere would always have a captive world-wide market. But this too was challenged by both European and Far Eastern countries. Scottish knitwear had to face the same unpalatable facts as did the ready-to-wear and textile industries: modernise equipment, methods of production and standards of design as well as more aggressive marketing techniques or disappear.

This has been a traumatic and bitter experience for the fashion and textile industry in Scotland during the last thirty years to be further strained by the world-wide recession of the late 1980s and early 1990s.

The resurgence of craft production, especially that of the hand-knitted garment, during the 1970s, gave the knitwear industry the creative challenge that was needed to shake manufacturers out of a rather complacent 'the classic designs are all that is needed' attitude. Designer producers such as Bill Babar of 'Sheepish Looks', and Margaret Hyne seem to capture in their work something of that intrinsic Scottish quality as found in the traditional Fair Isle and Sanquhar knitting.

But can Scotland consider the prominent names associated with haute couture fashion as Scottish designers, despite their own acknowledgement of their 'Scottishness'? Ronald Paterson was a leading member of the Incorporated Society of London Fashion Designers during the 1950s. Jean Muir is probably one of the truly great British fashion designers and Bill Gibb is a Scot through and through, but all three trained and functioned as designers in London. Yet Gibb, possibly the only designer in this group expressed his 'Scottishness' in a number of his knitwear designs and introduced Kaffe Fassett to the potential glories of Scottish knitting yarns. Fassett's exuberant enthusiasm opened up many now accessible creative possibilities for the amateur hand-knitter. Pam Hogg is one of Scotland's youngest designers to achieve international status with her innovative creations, three of which are in the permanent collection of the Kelvingrove Art Gallery in Glasgow. She too is also based in London.

Apart from names such as Chris Clyne, Pod and Jois and Betty Davies, Scotland may not have many internationally recognised fashion designers based here, but as a nation, is as fashion-conscious albeit in a more limited way, with retail shops in Glasgow and Edinburgh, where Armani, Versace, Miyake, Lauren and Lacroix can now be bought. The Campus group, started in 1966, with shops in Glasgow and Edinburgh, gave the style-demanding Scot the opportunity to buy the exclusive 'named labels'.

As an arbiter of taste in men's fashion, John Taylor, born in Glasgow, established a unique position during the 1970s and 1980s as editor of the men's clothing trade magazine, *Superstyle* and editor of the influential *Tailor and Cutter*. Outdoor sportswear for activities inextricably associated with the Scottish countryside; hillwalking, shooting, fishing and golf are often marketed overseas under such evocative labels as 'Caber'.

Betty Davies founded the Campus Group in 1966, launched her award-winning label, The Academy Collection in Glasgow and Paris in 1987, and the Betty Davies Tartan in 1989. Her designs incorporating Harris tweed have been an important stimuli for this other 'unique' Scottish cloth. The new ceremonial robes for Edinburgh's Lord Provost, inaugurated in 1992 and those for the choirs of the High Kirk of St Giles and the Robin Chapel, are imaginative examples of this Edinburgh-based designer's work.

Chris Clyne although trained in England and originally based in London, moved to Scotland in 1980 where she had important links with a number of the Border textile companies. Her fashion company is very much associated with exclusive special occasion wear often using wool, cashmere and tartan for individual clients and retail outlets in Europe and the United States of America.

Marion Donaldson founded her Glasgow-based fashion firm in 1966 and initially identified with the young trendy, flower-people. Her clothes have weathered the worst effects of the recession and her work is now aimed at the upper middle market at home and overseas.

The four art colleges also provide a supply of imaginative young talent for the industry, as has been seen in the design work in printed textiles produced by groups of graduates from Glasgow (The Cloth) and Dundee (Design Bias). Edinburgh College of Art has a Fashion course which provides a comprehensive training in all aspects of garment design and production, and Gray's School of Art in Aberdeen has a pioneering design and knit course. The Scottish College of Textiles in Galashiels, its international importance indicative of the position textiles has had in Scotland despite the economic vicissitudes of the last few years pioneers and trains designers and technicians for the next century in addition to carrying out pure and applied research so vital for the continuing growth of the textile industry worldwide.

Tourism, regarded as one of Scotland's major industries, would be considerably affected, were it not for the close association with one of the immediately identifiable products which says 'Scotland'—tartan. Often ridiculed by the purists, yet regularly adopted by Paris as an expression of *le style ecossais* as used by Christian Lacroix for his 1991 Autumn Collection or in previous years by Yves Saint Laurent, Chanel and Ungaro. From its sixteenth-century use as trews for James V to Vivienne Westwood's unconventional and controversial handling of this unique Scottish textile form, it shows no sign of diminishing in popularity or innovative application.

Superbly designed cloth for the couture and ready-to-wear market has been, except to those not closely associated with the industry, a long-running success story. In addition to the work of Bernat Klein, Ebenezar Johnson of E. Y. Johnstone and Reid and Taylor have been names which are synonymous with quality and originality. The Scottish Colourists exhibition in 1988/9 demonstrated how Reid and Taylor used the vital characteristics of the paintings by Cadell, Hunter, Peploe and Fergusson to inspire the Autumn and Winter 1988–89 Collection by this company for luxury lightweights in merino wool cashmeres and twist worsted suitings. These are some of the names greatly respected and admired, designers and manufacturers, who acknowledged their stimulus and success to their Scottish heritage.

State and industry-funded agencies such as the Scottish Apparel Centre to merge in 1993 with the Scottish Textile Association and the Scottish Woollen Publicity Council further demonstrate that, despite the phasing out of the Multi-Fibre Arrangement, the international agreement which has provided protection from imports since 1960 from foreign competition, the Scottish fashion and textile industry and its designers are 'bonnie fechters'.

M. M. Campbell

Fergusson, Robert (1750–1774) was born in Edinburgh, the son of an Aberdeenshire clerk. Educated at the High School of Edinburgh and Dundee Grammar School, Fergusson started Divinity at St Andrews University. Financial difficulties following his father's death, however, ended his studies and forced him to walk to Edinburgh, where he became a writer or copyist in the office of the Commissary Clerk, a dull post he held down for the rest of his short life.

His earliest verse, including a conventional song for the castrato Tenducci to sing in an Edinburgh production of Arne's *Artaxerxes*, was in English, but he soon turned to Scots, perhaps after reading Ramsay's poems. 'The Daft Days', his first Scots poem, appeared in the January 1772 number of Walter Ruddiman's *Weekly Magazine* or *Edinburgh Amusement*. There followed in succeeding months 'Elegy on the Death of Scots Music', 'Caller Oysters', 'Braid Claith' and 'To the Tron-Kirk Bell', collectively establishing a new kind of Scots urban poetry and individually demonstrating that a more pointed Scots poet than Ramsay had arrived.

In October 1772 he was elected a member of the Cape Club as 'Sir Precenter', its roll of members then including the artist Alexander Runciman ('Sir Brimstone'), who made a realistic sketch of the poet on the back of his petition for entry, Alexander Nasmyth ('Sir Thumb'), the landscape artist and painter of the famous Burns portrait, and the folk-song collector David Herd ('Sir Scrape-Greystiel').

For just over a year, Fergusson joined in the Club's jollifications in a tavern in the piled-up Edinburgh Old Town—work had started on the New Town just four years earlier—until at one meeting Fergusson told the actor William Woods that he was on his way to denounce Lord Kames as 'one of the miscreants who had crucified our Saviour'. Religious mania set in, and a few months later, after a fall, he died in a madhouse.

But in what was to be his brief maturity, he added to the first handful of his 1772 poems his masterpiece, 'Auld Reekie', a racy survey of eighteenth-century town life in octosyllabic couplets. The poem traces the passing of an Edinburgh day from the moment when:

Morn, with bonny purpie-smiles,

Kisses the air-cock o' St Giles;
Rakin their een, the servant lasses
Early begin their lies and clashes ...

to:

Night, that's cunzied chief for fun,

Is wi' her usual rites begun;
Thro' ilka gate the torches blaze,
And globes send out their blinking rays.

His portraits include those who:

Near some lamp-post, wi dowy face,

Wi' heavy een, and sour grimace,
Stands she that beauty lang had kend
Whoredom her trade, and vice her end.

If, like Ramsay and Burns, Fergusson had lived even 12 years or so longer, he might have run in fruitful double-harness with the National Bard. As things are, he provided Burns with several models. In one instance at least—'The Farmer's Ingle', the model for Burns's 'The Cottar's Saturday Night'—many feel that the earlier poet was the more successful. Until the arrival of Sydney Goodsir Smith and Robert Garioch on the twentieth-century scene, no other poet quite captured the Edinburgh atmosphere as surely as Fergusson.

M. Lindsay

Ferrier, Susan Edmonstone (1782–1854) was the youngest of 10 children born to Burns's Edinburgh friend James Ferrier, WS, and his wife, a sister of John Wilson ('Christopher North'). Ferrier was one of the principal clerks to the Court of Session, in which office he was a colleague of Sir Walter Scott. Susan Ferrier's friendship with Scott lasted throughout his life, and she remained a comforting friend until his death.

She herself wrote three novels of manners, *Marriage* (1818), *The Inheritance* (1824) and *Destiny* (1831). She is in a sense the Scottish counterpart to Jane Austen in the way that Maria Edgeworth might be said to be the Irish counterpart. However, Susan Ferrier lacks the incision of the great English novelist. She deploys considerable ability in accurately depicting dour Scottish characters, and all her stories are illuminated with racy humour. Her tendency to religious moralizing reflecting her own views rather than those of her characters increases with each succeeding novel, so that the order in which they are written is also the order of their merit.

Susan's sister, Jane, who married General Samuel Graham, Deputy Governor of Stirling Castle, was a celebrated beauty known to Burns. With the artist Edward Blore she made drawings of the carvings in Stirling Palace, and published them under the title *Lacunar Strevelinense* (1817). Her brother, James Frederick, became a metaphysician whose *Institutes of Metaphysics* (1854) was highly regarded in its day.

Her niece, Helen Graham (1806–1896) kept for a short time a diary, published under the title *Parties and Pleasures: The Diaries of Helen Graham, 1823–26* (1957), which preserves some affectionate, if dryly observed, glimpses of her famous aunt.

M. Lindsay

Festivities and Customs, Seasonal. The efforts of the Scottish Reformers and their successors the Covenanters to suppress the numerous holy days of the medieval Church were so successful that only two major festivals have retained their importance throughout the country: Hallowe'en and Christmas or Yule, the latter generally shifted to the secular holiday of New Year. Though in recent years both have been celebrated in all parts of Scotland, they are really equivalents and either may be accompanied, for instance, by guising. Hallowe'en derives from the great winter feast of the pagan Celts, marking the beginning of the winter half of the year, and Yule from the pagan Nordic or Anglian feast of the winter solstice. Both were times when spirits walked abroad while mortals celebrated at home.

Hallowe'en is the Gaelic *Samhain*, the end of summer, and the Christian festival of All Saints was apparently moved from 1 May to 1 November in the ninth century when the Irish influence on the Continental Church was still strong, though All Souls on 2 November, corresponding more closely to the Celtic use of the day as a festival of the dead, was instituted rather later. In Gaelic usage as in Jewish the night belongs to the day following, and the main modern festivities have always been held on the night before 1 November, when the spirits were abroad. Bonfires were lit throughout the country on the hills 'to burn the witches' (though only rarely was an actual effigy burned) and sometimes as a ritual of purification boys jumped through the flames and torches were carried round the fields to protect them. Nowadays the bonfires are almost universally transferred to the burning of the Guy (exceptionally at Stromness in Orkney, the 'pop' or Pope) on 5 November, which has been introduced from England within the last century. Children today seem to think that the word 'guiser' comes from Guy Fawkes, for the request 'please to help the guisers' in the towns often comes from a couple of children with a scarecrow-like figure for the burning in a push-chair. In fact a guiser is someone in disguise, and the original adult guisers (mostly young men) covered their faces, wore strange and sometimes transvestite clothes, and disguised their voices usually with a Punch-like squeak, to ensure complete anonymity, almost certainly because in some sense the guisers actually represented the spirits of the community's dead who were about at Hallowe'en. In country districts where children still go guising properly, with 'false face' masks and turnip lanterns, knocking on each door and offering entertainment—'please to help the guisers and I'll sing ye a bonnie wee sang'—in exchange for apples, nuts or sweets, rather than money, it is a point of honour for the people of the house to pretend not to recognize a child however poorly disguised.

The 'mischief night' element (combined with the guisers' visit in the American threat of 'trick or treat') also seems to represent the activities of the spirits. Favourite pranks used to include moving carts and leaving them in ponds, stopping chimneys with a turf so that the house filled with smoke, and knocking on doors and windows with cabbage stalks: in parts of Orkney, for instance, boys are still likely to carry off movable objects such as gates and signs. More widely known now are the party games such as dooking for apples floating in a tub of water or catching a treacle-spread scone hung on a string from the ceiling, in both cases using the teeth only. Until recently, however, the main Hallowe'en diversion in all parts of Scotland was the attempt, mainly by girls, to divine whom one would marry. Most of the usual methods are mentioned in Burns's poem 'Halloween'. Some methods involved objects like a cabbage-stalk pulled at random in the dark, whose shape foretold the future spouse's form, the number of buds the number of children, and so on, or an egg-white dropped into a glass of water, which took a shape representing the husband's calling or the number of children. A pair of nuts, peas, orange pips or straws would be assigned to a couple and laid side by side in the embers to see if they burned quietly together or sprang apart. A blindfold girl dipped her hand in one of a row of saucers to see if she would get a fine young husband (clean water), a widower (dirty water) or none (empty). But the most feared rites were those where the future spouse was seen or heard by magical means: dropping a strand of blue wool into a kiln and asking 'wha hauds in my clew end?'; cutting an apple in front of a mirror in dim light and offering a piece on a fork over the shoulder which the wraith of the husband would take; measuring round ('fathoming') a corn-stack three times with outstretched arms until he came into them; sowing hempseed to see who came behind to pull the magically grown plants; or dipping the sleeve of a nightshirt in a burn where three lairds' lands met and leaving it to dry in front of the fire to see who came in to turn it over. Tales are told of coffins coming in to those who would die young and unmarried; and a few forms of divination, such as climbing backwards up a harrow set against a corn-stack, would tell how you would die rather than whom you would marry.

Yule or Christmas as such was only celebrated in the Episcopal northeast of Scotland, in Catholic parts of the Highlands, and in Shetland. Elsewhere the custom was so thoroughly displaced to New Year that the latter was called *Nollaig Bheag*, 'Little Christmas', or simply *Nollaig*, 'Christmas', in parts of the Highlands, and within living memory the newly imported custom of hanging up a stocking for presents took place not on Christmas Eve but on New Year's Eve in many parts of Scotland. Yule rites in mainland Scotland and the Western Isles might involve guising, football, shooting matches, lighting a special fire with a log or stump known as the 'Yule Carline' and burning a 'Yule candle', having the house clean and tidy and abstaining from work for several days—if the minister did not prevent it. Over a wider area north of the Forth it was an occasion for special meals of sowens or a great bannock in which rings, bachelors' buttons and so on were put to foretell the finders' future (the sowens were also usual at Hallowe'en), or in wealthier parts a 'Yule brose' made with beef. In the Lowlands and Borders the 'Goloshans' performed their play—a folk-play on the usual death-and-resurrection pattern—round the houses during a season ending about New Year but often starting on or before Christmas, though again in some places it was done at Hallowe'en instead.

The Shetland Yule season lasted for a full 24 nights, starting on Christmas Day Old Style, interpreted in different parishes as 5 or 6 January, and ending on 'Four-and-Twenty' or 'Up-Helly-Aa' (compare the old Scots name for Twelfth Night, Uphaliday). The modern Lerwick Up-Helly-Aa, fixed at the last Tuesday in January and with the traditional burning tar-barrel transformed into a Viking galley and the guisers decked in horned helmets, is more picturesque, but other parishes still hold their own Up-Helly-Aa. Even remote townships used to have their own cycle of dances and football games on Old Christmas Day, Old New Year and the twenty-fourth night if not more often. The bands were taken off spinning-wheels so that the fairies or trows who were about at this season did not use them—nor did the housewives!—and guisers or 'skeklers' in conical straw tunics and hats went round the houses through the season: they also appeared at weddings and at Hallowe'en. At the beginning of this century Christmas might still start before dawn with a candlelit breakfast including goose (or any other meat but pork) and a taste of whisky for everyone: the horses and cattle, as in the northeast, had a sheaf of corn each for their share, and a sheaf was even left out for the birds.

New Year, Gaelic *Calluinn* (from Kalends), and its eve *Hogmanay* (whose derivation is still disputed, but mostly likely is from the French: at any rate it was originally a cry raised on this night) took over most of these Christmas customs in different places, as well as those associated with Hallowe'en and other festivals, bonfires, divination and even tricks. Far the most important and general custom was guising or its modern derivative, first-footing. As at Hallowe'en this was done by men, especially younger men, and in this case the tradition has been carried on: perhaps women and children do less first-footing because of the association of the custom with drink, but it is also generally considered lucky for the real first foot, the first person to cross the threshold in the New Year, to be a man, preferably one with dark hair. First-footers nowadays bring a bottle, sometimes food and a lump of coal or something black: this seems to be new, but peats are mentioned among first-foot gifts in earlier times.

Traditional guising at New Year normally involved singing as well as collecting food for consumption on the spot or later. This might happen either on Hogmanay or New Year's Day, and in some places has survived apart from first-footing as a children's custom. A popular rhyme to chant was:

Rise up, guidwife, and shak yir feathers:

Dinna think that we are beggars:
We're only bairnies come to play:
Rise up and gie's oor Hogmanay.

Earlier versions had 'guid folks' instead of 'bairnies'. The usual 'God bless the master of this house' lines associated with carols and was sailing songs in England, or others, might be added to this. The Goloshans' play—also latterly often given by schoolchildren—ended with a similar song and a song with the refrain 'Be-soothan, be-soothan' (possibly Gaelic *Bi suthainn*, 'Be everlasting' or 'prosperous'?) was known in the northeast. The New Year Song used in Orkney and Shetland seems to belong to a Catholic festival, perhaps the Epiphany, with its refrain 'We are a' St Mary's men'—'Queen Mary's men' in some versions—and could extend to 50 verses of blessing and demand, with bits of a ballad about King Henry and Fair

Rosamund thrown in for good measure. Again, though it was used by adult guisers in many islands about 1900, the sole survival is among the children of Burray, Orkney, who add the 'Rise up guidwife' verse to it.

The Gaelic New Year Rhymes (*Duain Challuinn*) are much more varied: in many places several were known, ranging from ancient Ossianic lays to newly improvised farragos with satirical verses about local people and a good deal of pure nonsense. These were normally recited, not sung, though one or two convivial songs also have special associations with New Year. A *Duan* could be recited by a single first-footer; bands of young men also went round in Gaelic-speaking districts up to the beginning of this century using cowhides and sheepskin, apparently, to scare away any evil spirits. This was done both by beating the cowhide, which in earlier times at least was worn by the leader of the band, with shinty-sticks, fire-tongs or primitive whips, and by singeing a strip of skin from a sheep's breast (*caisean-uchd*) to make an evil smell around the houses, where it was held under the nose of each member of the household. A chant accompanied and referred to the beating of the hide. The shinty-sticks link this with the other Highland custom on New Year's Day itself, which was a game of shinty on a beach or some piece of flat open ground between two sides of no fixed number representing different villages, townships or estates, with little regard for rules or even necessarily fixed goals. The similar football games in Shetland were held several times in the Yule season; in Orkney however they were at New Year, or at least that is the occasion of the surviving Kirkwall Ball Game, played between 'Uppies' and 'Doonies' through a main street with well-barricaded shop windows, with one goal at the harbour and the other at the inland end of the town. Similar games of football or handball in mainland Scottish towns were usually played on Shrove Tuesday; the main survivor in Jedburgh is preceded by a 'Callants' Ba' ' at Candlemas.

Other New Year customs involve wearing something new or beginning a piece of work, for obvious reasons, notably among fishermen, who always liked to put to sea and catch something on that day. The first water drawn from a well after midnight, the 'flower' or 'cream' of the well, was sought after for luck in love, health or dairy work.

The rites once carried out at the opposite ends of the year echo those of the surviving festivals. So bonfires and rites of divination marked *Midsummer* or *Johnsmas* (24 June) and its eve throughout much of eastern Scotland from the borders to the Northern Isles, and at least at one place in the west, Tarbolton in Ayrshire. Bonfires on the heights, with a feast of milk gruel and the burying of 'Johnsmas flooers' (plantains) under stones to see if the torn-off petals grew again, are still just within living memory in parts of Shetland. Bonfires, divination and special bannocks marked *Beltane* (1 May) and its eve, the beginning of summer, opposite to Hallowe'en: witches were of course supposed to be abroad on Beltane Eve, the German Walpurgis-Nacht. The day's Gaelic name contains the word *teine*, fire, and it was probably the major fire festival of the Highlands. Originally two fires were lit by friction on wood

('need-fire') and cattle were passed between them to be sained or protected from evil before going to the summer sheilings. The beltane bannocks were rolled downhill like Easter eggs and the owner's future predicted from the way they fell. 'May dew' gathered before dawn had magical powers, including giving beauty to the face washed in it, and visiting Arthur's Seat in Edinburgh to gather it is the only Beltane custom still kept up by many.

Less still has survived of the two quarter days which came midway between the major Celtic festivals, *Lammas* (*Lùtnasdal*) on 1 August and *Candlemas* on 2 February, though they survive as season markers and the occasions of fairs and ball-games. In fact the official Scottish quarter days include these two, but the two major festivals are avoided, because of their sanctity perhaps (since the change seems to antedate the introduction of the Gregorian calendar and even the Reformation) and the other quarter days, the 'term days' on which rents were due and farm and domestic servants could seek new masters at 'hiring fairs', are later, on *Martinmas* (11 November) and *Whitsun* (15 May), a fixed feast borrowing the name of the movable Whitsunday. Candlemas (The Purification of the Virgin Mary) is another Christian feast substituted in the Lowlands for the pagan *Imbolc* on 1 February, which in the Highlands continued to be held on that day as the feast of St Bride or Brigit, though naturally the two tended to be confused. Candlemas was of course celebrated by lighting candles (sometimes extended to include torchlight processions or bonfires) and schoolmasters used to collect gifts of money, originally intended to buy a candle. In the Catholic Hebrides and earlier in other parts of the Highlands girls went guising on St Bride's Eve with a figure of the saint made from a sheaf of corn, which was later laid in a decorated 'bed' or basket prepared for it in a house.

Shrove Tuesday, soon after, was known in Scots as *Fastern's E'en*, in Gaelic as *Inid* (from *initium*, since Lent began that night). It was celebrated with ball-games, divination, and rich bannocks of oatmeal and eggs, usually more solid than pancakes; sometimes also with a sort of meat brose or porridge, so that in the northeast the festival was known as Bannock Night or Brose Day. In the Hebrides a hen was killed for the last meat before Lent. *Easter* was of course the season for eggs. Within living memory in many regions it was still customary for children to go round 'pace-egging' or thigging for eggs— yet another form of guising—and collect a gift of eggs at each house. The eggs were boiled and sometimes dyed at home, or cooked by the children themselves over a camp-fire for a private feast, and rolled down a hill to crack them: this also gave an opportunity for races and for divination by the way they ran. At one time people in the Highlands used to go to a high place to see the sun rise on Easter Sunday, when it was believed to dance for joy as it rose.

Few other saints' or holy days retained much importance except as the days of local fairs. *Michaelmas* (29 September) was celebrated in the Hebrides with a bareback horse-race (*Oda*) sometimes followed by a dance, and a cake known as *Strùan*, a bannock with an egg or treacle mixture on top, was baked for the occasion. *Handsel Monday*, the first after New Year, took over some customs from New Year or Twelfth Night, but was really the equivalent of English Boxing Day, when employees including public and farm servants were given food or money by their employers. *April Fool's Day* is celebrated on 1 April in Scotland as in England: the old name for the trickery was 'hunting the gowk' (or cuckoo). The following day is *Tailie Day*, known only in and around Kirkwall and Kirkcaldy, when children surreptitiously pin paper tails on the coats of passers-by.

We cannot here enumerate the many fairs, often with names like Lammas Fair or Marymass, still kept up or remembered in Scottish towns or open-air sites. One saint's day has even named a station, Georgemas Junction in Caithness. Many towns have a gala week in the summer, and where possible this is based on a local fair or gathering extended to fill a week or more. Highland Gatherings are one excuse in the north. *Common Ridings* are held throughout southern Scotland from June to August: the basic ceremony is one of beating the bounds of a burgh and its common lands in a horseback procession led by a 'Cornet' or 'Standard-Bearer' elected for that year. Many Common Ridings have been revived and reorganized, if not actually invented, during the past 40 or 50 years, and other burghs' marches have been ridden or walked for centuries at intervals of up to 21 years. Those which have been kept up annually for well over a century are Hawick, Lanark (Lanimer Day), Langholm, Linlithgow and Selkirk (all but Langholm in early June). Then there are gatherings organized by a single trade, notably the Whipmen's or Carters' 'Plays' (Biggar, Gilmerton, Irvine Marymass, the Penicuik Huntsmen, West Linton) and the 'Fishermen's Walks' at the end of the herring season of which the Eyemouth Herring Queen's Festival is now the sole, altered and extended relic. A few towns keep up the burning tar-barrels, torches or bonfires of New Year as a ceremony: apart from the well-known Lerwick Up-Helly-Aa and the Burning of the Clavie at Burghead, bonfires at Biggar and Wick, the Flambeaux Procession at Comrie and the Stonehaven Fireball Ceremony have continued. There remain two unique ceremonies: one is *Whuppity Stourie* at Lanark on 1 March, where children swing paper balls on strings round their heads (like the Stonehaven fireballs just mentioned) and chase each other round the church to the tolling of a bell. Originally this was done with bonnets and followed by a mock battle. The purpose is presumably to scare away evil spirits. The other remarkable occasion is the procession of the *Burry Man* round the bounds of South Queensferry. The Burry Man is covered all over (except eyes, hands and feet) in flannel on which a thick layer of large spiky burrs is stuck, a process taking several hours: he also wears a garland of roses and carries two flower-decked sticks. Though this resembles the English May ceremony of the Jack-in-the-Green, there is evidence that the Burry Man, who goes through the town the day before the Ferry Fair in early August, should be a fisherman, and similar ceremonies were performed at Buckie and Fraserburgh in the 1850s to bring better luck to the herring fishing: the burrs therefore seem to represent fish caught in the nets.

Finally, various customs were observed in the farmer's year. In the northeast the ploughman starting to plough and the sower starting to sow were handselled with bread, cheese and whisky: occasionally these were eaten off the plough beam or even stuffed in the coulter. In the Highlands the plough and the ground before sowing might be sprinkled with holy water, brine or urine to sain them. Any work of this sort had if possible to be begun when the moon was waxing and the tide flowing, to ensure increase, and never, of course, on a Friday. Sowers in Caithness wore only white, and in Shetland and Lewis at least it was customary to put an egg in the sowing-basket under the seed corn.

Many more customs went with the corn *harvest*. The last sheaf to be cut was called the Maiden (Gaelic *A' Mhaighdean, Gruagach*) or in the northeast the Clyack (apparently from Gaelic *caileag*, with the same meaning), in the south the Kirn and in parts of Galloway the Hare. This representative of the corn spirit was generally taken home and made into a 'Kirn-Dolly' or 'Kirn-Baby' in the south or stretched with the straws interlaced like a saltire on a wooden frame in the north, and hung in the farm kitchen until the New Year, when it was fed to the first horses to begin ploughing, to calving cows or to young calves. In some parts of the Highlands it was also called *A' Chailleach*, 'the old woman', but this is really the name for another sheaf, not quite the last cut, which was sometimes shaped and dressed like an old woman and taken to the field of another farmer or crofter who was later in finishing cutting his corn: in Skye it was called *A' Ghobhar Bhacach*, 'the lame goat', in the northeast the Carline, and in Orkney it was called the Bitch, and shaped like a dog. A third custom at the end of cutting was for each reaper to take his sickle or heuk by the point and throw it over his shoulder: the way it pointed when it fell predicted his fate, where he would next live or shear a harvest, but if the point fell in the ground he would die within the year.

When the corn was brought in nobody wanted to be the carter (or carrier in poorer districts) of the last load. Sometimes there was no more than that, or a vague threat that the Devil would be after him, but often this person would be hailed as 'Winter' ('Cauld Winter', 'Black Winter', 'Winter Peeack' or pip-squeak) on the mainland or 'Drilty' or 'Drittle-in-the-Slap' (slowcoach in the gateway) in the Northern Isles, and subjected to horseplay, even pelted with dirty water or rotten eggs, or blackened with soot. But in Aberdeenshire he might get a pair of mittens as compensation, and in the Northern Isles a bannock to be eaten on the spot. After this came the harvest-home celebration: *an deireadh bhuana*, 'the end of harvest' in Gaelic, elsewhere called after the last sheaf 'Kirn', 'Clyack Feast', or 'Maiden', in the northeast sometimes 'Meal-and-Ale' from a favourite dish, in Orkney 'The Muckle Supper', in Shetland the 'Aff-winnin'. Orkney farm servants got a preliminary 'Aff-shearing' or 'cutting-off butter', a dish of butter mixed with cheese, when all the corn was cut. The main dish at harvest homes was *stapag* (whipped cream mixed with oatmeal), Atholl brose or meal-and-ale (mixed with a little whisky), but some made do with mashed potatoes, and the usual rings and buttons for divination might be put in any of these. Any farmer who could afford it then had a dance in his barn or granary, and these occasions were long remembered— as well they might be by farm servants whose only other holiday was at New Year!

A. J. Bruford

Fiddle Tradition, The. Bowed string instruments were popular in Scotland long before the arrival of the violin from Italy, but, as in many other parts of Europe, the all-round superiority of the violin, particularly as an instrument for the dance, ensured that it would be readily taken up to vie with the pipes as Scotland's national instrument. During the seventeenth and early eighteenth centuries it was adopted among all levels of society. A scattering of references to earlier instruments (notably the rebec, crowd, fydil and viol) are to be found in the accounts of H.G. Farmer (1947), Francis Collinson (1966) and George S. Emmerson (1971). Among them are the historian Brantome's account of that probable first in 'fiddlers' rallies' when five or six hundred players of 'the vilest fiddles and little rebecs' serenaded Mary Queen of Scots in August 1561 during her stay at Holyrood Palace.

By 1700 there was sufficient interest south of the border in Scotland's lyrical song airs and lively dance measures for Henry Playford to issue a first *Collection of Original Scotch Tunes (Full of the Highland Humours) for the Violin* in which the flowing Scots Measure is seen to be a favourite dance genre. But as one surveys other publications (emanating at first from England but, after 1730, from Scotland itself) and a number of large manuscript collections (several of which were prepared by David Young, a professional music writer) one gets a clearer picture of the fiddle's Scottish repertory. There are numerous settings of what must have been popular dance songs, reels and jigs, (in 4/4, 6/8 and 9/8 time) and many airs have sets of variations attached, indicating the popularity of the violin as a recital instrument. Also included are hornpipes, both the older type in 3/2 time and the more modern kind in reel-time. In the Drummond Castle manuscript (*c.* 1740, one of Young's creations) a separate section headed 'the best Highland reels' includes numerous tunes later to be classed as strathspeys, but suggesting that the fiddle was popular elsewhere in Gaelic-speaking Scotland. We know from the Estate records of Dunvegan, which show payments in 1706 to MacLeod's 'violer' James Glass, and from occasional references in the poems of Gaelic bards of the time that this was indeed the case. There is too Martin Martin's account in 1703 of a visit to the Western Isles which mentioned that in the Isle of Lewis there were '18 men who play on the violin pretty well without being taught'. The repertory of men like Glass must surely have included sets of variations on Gaelic airs, perhaps like those found in the Angus Fraser manuscript (Eul. Ms. Gen. 614) though this purports to be a collection of harp airs.

Of the frequent balls given by professional dancing-masters in Edinburgh during the 1770s the Englishman, Capt. Topham, wrote: 'It is incredible the pleasure and satisfaction the inhabitants of this city take in this diversion.... I do not know any place in the world where dancing is made so necessary a part of polite Education' (Topham, 1776, pp.339, 344). This passion, particularly among the prospering middle classes of Edinburgh's new town, led to the creation of not only hundreds of new country dances but an enormous number of new tunes in reel and jig time and, after 1757 (the year of Robert Bremner's first *Collection*), there was a flood of publications. John Glen's two volumes of Scottish dance music (Edinburgh 1891 and 1895) give details of 59 collections that appeared between 1757 and 1800, 53 of them during the last two decades of the century.

This has been called the golden age of Scottish fiddling—the age of Niel Gow (1727–1807); of his sons, favourites of the Edinburgh Assemblies; of William Marshall, factor to the Duke of Gordon (1743–1833); and of Captain Simon Fraser of Knockie. All were famous not only for their published compositions but as players of taste and distinction. Yet these men and their literate musician colleagues, amateur and professional, who bought their music, must have been only the apex of a pyramid of fiddling activity, at the base of which must have been countless non-literate players who could 'turn a tune' for dancing in their own houses. This was certainly true of the northernmost isles—the Shetlands—where, according to the *Statistical Account* (1797–99) 'many of the common people play with skill upon the violin' and about whom Edmondston commented 'among the peasantry almost one in ten can play upon the violin'. The Gow family were aware of the liveliness of this essentially aural tradition when they noted that they never met 'two professional musicians who played the same notes of any tune'.

David Johnson (1972) has analysed the interaction between classical European styles and the Scottish idiom during the eighteenth century. Adam Craig, the first man to publish a fiddle-music collection in Scotland itself (*c.* 1730) was a competent violinist who played in the 'gentlemen's' orchestra in St Cecilia Hall. The elegant strains of William Marshall appear to combine the best of both traditions. Many of his finest airs, like some of Niel Gow's, are in strathspey style, but prescribed to be played 'slow' as recital pieces. This new genre, the Slow Strathspey, is still regarded as the ultimate challenge to those who would call themselves Scottish fiddlers.

If in the nineteenth century the passion for dancing ultimately waned, at least in the cities, there seems to have been no shortage of fine players elsewhere judging by George Emmerson's survey. Some of these were itinerant dancing-masters, like the Adamsons of Fife, whose teaching, repertory and itinerary are described by the Fletts (*Traditional Dancing in Scotland*, London, 1964). But all are overshadowed by the figure of James Scott Skinner (1843–1927), the self-styled 'Strathspey King'. Born the son of a Deeside dancing-master, his early training included six years with the Manchester-based juvenile orchestra known as 'Dr Mark's Little Men' and some training in classical violin from a member of the Halle orchestra. On his return to Scotland he continued the family profession but, as his fame grew, he became more of a concert performer, travelling throughout Britain and even visiting the USA. He combined a brilliant technique with the native professional's deep knowledge of the highly accented and sharply pointed fiddle style of the northeast, and his flamboyant manner survives in a number of recordings made between 1905 and 1922 (see Topic LP discs 12T280 and 12TS268, 1975).

Skinner enlarged the Scottish fiddle repertory by over 600 items and many are popular today amongst Scottish musicians. But, since World War I, an increasing range of musical instruments has been available. The accordion has taken over as the prime provider of Scottish dance music though some would consider that no Scottish Country Dance Band is complete without a fiddler. Fiddle playing, like bagpiping, has become a channel through which musical Scots may express their Scottishness. Most fiddlers join one of the many societies, some of which date from the nineteenth century; their programmes include concerts, competitive festivals and the popular 'fiddlers' rally' when players mass together for a public 'stramash'. Accordion and fiddle clubs have their own monthly magazine *Box and Fiddle* (circulation 1300–1500) and composition of new pieces continues unabated, their form and style being as highly conservative as ever. Many of the most highly regarded are the work of Shetlanders and most tunes still circulate aurally but by means of discs, radio and the ubiquitous cassette recorder. There is also, however, a lively market in printed collections including reprints of older volumes. The Edinburgh-based Hardie Press has recently set new standards in this field with their careful edited anthologies such as *The Beauties of the North* and *The Caledonian Companion* (see bibliography).

Of the outstanding players of the post-Skinner era, Hector MacAndrew of Aberdeen (1903–1980) was deservedly the best known. Other players of note, James F. Dickie of New Deer and William Hardie of Methlick, are also from the northeast while the fame of Shetland musicians like William Hunter, Arthur Robertson, Aly Bain and the late Tom Anderson, OBE (1910–1991), has spread far beyond their own islands. Aly Bain is one of the very few fiddlers who make their art their living, being one of the leading figures of the Scottish folk revival. Few instrumental groups in this lively musical subculture are without a fiddler, and it is here, in a less conservative milieu than that of the fiddle societies, that most experiments towards a modern Scottish musical idiom are taking place.

P.R. Cooke

Film. The relationship between Scotland and the dominant art-form of the twentieth century might be described as inequitable. As consumers of cinema we have been avid, but it has nearly always been someone else's cinema, usually America's. With few exceptions, Scots who have contributed to the development of the movies have done so abroad. The ideal of a self-sustaining feature-film industry in Scotland giving expression to our culture on the big screen is frustratingly unrealized,

and will probably remain so until, in John Grierson's words, 'the public authorities are persuaded'.

In fairness, the argument for a modest film industry has made progress in recent years and efforts to establish the necessary infrastructure to allow a continuity for indigenous feature film making have met with some success. The public funding of all aspects of film culture, from production to archiving has improved, but there is still a long way to go before Scotland can take its place with even the smallest film-making nations by producing, say, ten cinema films annually rather than the one or two (in a good year) at present.

It could, of course, have been different. Scots appear as significant players at all stages in the history of cinema. One even predates its invention. It was the French-born Scot William Kennedy Laurie Dickson (1860–1935), working with Edison in America, whose technical inventiveness brought about the Kinetoscope and other devices which gave birth to the medium of moving pictures in the early 1890s. Dickson has many crucial patents to his name but he can also be celebrated as the inventor of the 'close-up'.

Projected moving pictures were first shown to a paying public in Scotland on 13 April 1896 at the Empire Theatre in Edinburgh. Although technically it was not an auspicious debut (see the *Scotsman* of the following day), it marked the beginning of our fascination with the movies and the arrival of the exhibitors who have catered to our needs ever since.

Certain families became famous for their cinema chains, the Pooles in Edinburgh, (Cameo), the Singletons in Glasgow, (Cosmo), the Donalds in Aberdeen, and the Kemps in Ayrshire. The Greens built the biggest cinemas—two of the largest in Europe—and their Playhouse in Edinburgh remains testament to the scale of their success. They even invested direct in Hollywood with shares in United Artists. One of the most distinguished exhibitors was Sir Alexander B. King of Caledonian Associated Cinemas, but there were many local showmen, such as James Nairn in Inverness who supplied the enthusiasm and the enterprise that the trade needed to flourish.

From its high point immediately after the war, cinema exhibition declined steadily but even today there are probably about ten million admissions annually to Scottish cinemas. Patterns of exhibition have changed. In addition to the established chains, there are now multiplexes, and seven Scottish Film Council supported film theatres which provide public access to foreign-language and independent films. The film society movement, though now reduced to about thirty-five clubs, continues to meet a social and cultural need, especially in areas remote from other forms of cinema.

One particular society, the Edinburgh Film Guild (1930), may very well hold the distinction of being the oldest continuing society in the world. What is quite certain is that it gave birth to the world's longest running festival, the Edinburgh International Film Festival, founded in 1947, and still the premier British Film Festival.

Throughout most of cinema's hundred years, the images of Scotland on the screen have been put there by people and companies who were not Scots. Even genuine Scots such as

Alexander Mackendrick (b. 1912) (*Whisky Galore* 1949, *The Maggie* 1954) or John Grierson (1898–1972) (q.v.) (who produced *The Brave Don't Cry* in 1952), were working for non-Scottish companies with non-Scottish audiences very much in mind. Only in the last two decades have there been signs of a possible indigenous industry. Bill Forsyth (q.v.) with *That Sinking Feeling* (1980), *Gregory's Girl* (1981), *Local Hero* (1983), and *Comfort and Joy* (1984) and, in a very different genre, Bill Douglas (1934–1991) *My Childhood* (1971), *My Ain Folk* (1973) and *My Way Home* (1979), pioneered styles of popular and art films that hinted, tantalisingly, at the range of a possible Scottish Cinema.

In the early eighties, there were a number of productions usually associated with Channel Four Television, which suggested what could be achieved given the resources. Charles Gormley, (*Living Apart Together*), Mike Radford, (*Another Time, Another Place*), Bill Bryden (*Ill Fares the Land*), exemplify a new energy which has to some extent continued to date. In 1989 *Silent Scream* was directed by David Hayman and *Venus Peter* by Ian Sellar. Crucial to the continuing development of film in Scotland has been the contribution of home-based producers such as Paddy Higson and Christopher Young.

Internationally, Scotland's contribution to cinema has been spread across the spectrum of the medium and across the world. We may have produced only one world-class animator, Norman McLaren (1914–1987) whom Grierson took to Canada, but there have been plenty of Scots to be found in most of the disciplines. Screenwriters, mostly working for Hollywood, have included Neil Paterson (who won an Oscar for *Room at the Top*), Alan Sharp and Alan Scott. Scots, or at least Scots-born movie actors who made it to the 'household names' level, include Deborah Kerr, David Niven and Sean Connery (q.v.).

Perhaps only in one area of film making, so far, can we claim confidently that we have been with the best. As a form, the documentary was largely the invention of John Grierson and it is no coincidence that the first, and most significant example of his 'creative treatment of actuality' should be on a Scottish subject, *Drifters* (1929). Grierson's influence on Scottish film, mediated through the work of the Films of Scotland Committee, directed by Forsyth Hardy, was considerable. Through Hardy's work it led to the fostering of talents, several of whom have been referred to above, and to a genuine native representation of Scotland that ranged from industrial documentaries like the Oscar-winning *Seawards the Great Ships* (1960) or Laurence Henson's *The Big Mill* (1960) to the art films of Murray Grigor.

The challenge, now, is for the film-makers and the film institutions of Scotland (The Scottish Film Council, The Scottish Film Production Fund, Scottish Screen Locations and others including the television organizations) to win the argument for resources and encourage the talent to allow the Scots true expression through the medium of contemporary cinema.

D. Bruce

Fishing and Fisherfolk. There has probably been fishing in Scottish inshore waters as long as there has been coastal habi-
tation. Particularly in the sheltered waters of the lochs of the north and west coast and in the voes of Orkney and Shetland a simple apparatus of handline and baited hook and the smallest of boats were sufficient for making regular catches out of the abundant stocks of haddock, young saithe, codling, whiting. Long-lines, mounted with hundreds of hooks, might be used in offshore waters and the more erratic herring were caught with ground-or drift-nets. Such fishing to secure a supply for the home continued in combination with crofting in the islands and western Highlands till well into the nineteenth century.

It was along the east coast, apparently less well adapted for easy fishing because of its lack of natural shelter for bases, that we find the first communities composed entirely of specialized fishermen. They can be traced back at least to the sixteenth century but we know little of their way of life. By the eighteenth century, however, the picture is much clearer. Fishing villages, lying scattered almost the entire length of the east coast, would generally have not more than ten boats, or about 200 inhabitants, and most had a good deal less. They lived almost entirely by a long-line fishing for haddock and for cod and ling. Shell-fish bait, especially mussels, was in the main gathered by the womenfolk. The boats had to be kept small because often they had to be manhandled over open beaches and in them the crews might go forty miles over a stormy ocean to the cod-banks. Fishing communities kept very much to themselves and except in the way of trade scarcely mingled with the surrounding communities. The fish would be mostly cured, by drying or smoking, by the fishermen's families for sale either nearby or in more distant foreign markets.

These fishing villages, with some slight changes in the roll, continued as the main centres of Scottish fishing till the last quarter of the nineteenth century and, little changed in their customs and social structure, they formed the base for an immense expansion in scale of output and a dramatic development of method that was to take Scotland to the head of the fishing nations. The new dominant form of fishing was for herring and for this men trained in the older forms of line fishing rapidly developed a summer drift-net fishing, combined with line fishing at other seasons of the year. Herring were caught from the shoals that approached the east coast between July and September. Every morning the boats would land a catch to be gutted, packed and pickled in the curing yards for sale in a variety of home and foreign markets, of which the Baltic area came to be entirely dominant in a great expansion after 1850. Boats were increased in size and were ever better furnished with nets so that cost soared by nearly tenfold between 1800 and 1880. Yet the fishermen, traditionally the owners of the boats they worked, managed through small partnerships to retain full ownership, while employing outside labour in the season of high activity. The villages, greatly enlarged in population, continued to be very much communities apart, with little intermarriage with, or recruitment from, other groups. Yet they were in almost daily commercial interaction with a wide trading world.

In the 1840s, east-coast fishermen, aided by curers, in a

fresh expansion, had taken the search for herring to the west coast, later to Shetland and eventually to East Anglia; increasingly the year was taken up with herring fishing in the grounds around Britain and their power reached a peak in the 1880s with the adoption of large decked vessels, of up to 60 foot keel. The cure of herring, growing decade by decade, went increasingly to the Continental market, which reached through the Baltic ports, stretched southwards towards central Europe and eastwards into Russia. Only in the late 1880s was there any extended halt to this process of growth.

The increase in landings substantially accelerated between 1900 and 1914 as large numbers of fishermen adopted steamships (drifters) in place of the sailing vessels, which seemed to have reached the limit of their development in the 1880s. The new vessels had profound effects. Each crew with the new equipment, numbering nine men instead of seven, could rely on catching at least twice as much fish as the crew of a sailer. The historic maximum of landings of herring was reached between 1908 and 1913 with an annual cure of over two million barrels, mostly exported to the Continent. But, behind apparent prosperity, problems were growing. There was a high initial cost to be met on drifters and as a consequence landsmen, such as fish salesmen, were acquiring interests which might give them virtual ownership of boats. Yet some fishermen did manage to raise the money to take a large share, and some, in partnership with their fellows, were able to retain full ownership. But the success of the few tended to open a rift in the fishing community; owners of boats, or of shares in boats, now formed a group separate from those who, at the best, would have nets to put into the fishing venture. Nor were the profits as great as the increase in catch seemed to warrant, for steam drifters were burdened with very heavy fixed costs which might take almost the whole of a very considerable gross return.

After 1918 the problems began to bite hard. Much of the pre-war market was irretrievably lost and even a very restricted output could only be sold at moderate prices. Particularly after 1931, few of the drifters, which had virtually no other use than to catch herring, could be made to pay their way. Replacement and repair had to be neglected and by the mid 1930s a fleet that was now growing aged was year by year reduced by attrition. There was no obvious form of profitable replacement and no funds to acquire new boats; some fishermen, both owners and wage-earners, after years of struggle on the lowest of earnings, were driven from the industry. Yet some of the fishing communities held together and maintained their identities remarkably well and there were many families with an unbroken fishing tradition. For them solutions were found after 1945 with the development of the more flexible diesel craft, with new aids to fishing and with the growth of seine-net fishing for the varieties that could be sold at good prices in an expanding home market. There could be no revival of the herring fishing as it had been before 1914 but there were good incomes to be earned in other directions. Such was the resilience of the fishing communities that ownership of the most sophisticated and powerful apparatus was substantially retained in the hands of the fishermen.

Meanwhile, after 1880, a new form of fishing, based on a new type of fishing community, emerged as the virtual equal of the older types. This was trawling, in which a net is drawn along the sea-bed by a moving vessel. In Scotland it came to centre almost entirely on Aberdeen—and particularly on the rising district of Torry—and on Granton. From the outset steam vessels were used and, operating close inshore, they made high profits by short daily trips. The fleet grew swiftly, financed and owned by landsmen, notably fish salesmen; very few fishermen had any owning share in the vessels which they operated. The new fishing communities were composed partly of fishermen displaced from older types of line fishing but partly also of recruits from the general reserve of labour. The labour force in trawling was always much more restless, between one boat and another and between different forms of employment, than had been fishermen of an older type. The rise of trawling continued without interruption till 1914 but the fleet was forced, by the depletion of the nearer waters and by the closing to them of the Moray Firth, to resort to distant grounds around Scotland and the Northern Isles, to Faroe and, exceptionally, to Iceland. Larger vessels, more steaming time, and longer trips were necessary—in other words greater expense—but profits remained good till 1914. The inter-war years brought their problems, in spite of a good home market. The pre-war grounds still favoured by the Scottish vessels were failing, while costs, notably of coal, had risen disproportionately. Trawling, then, was only intermittently profitable. The fleet fluctuated in size although the long-run trend was not one of decline. It was poised for solid recovery and for comprehensive re-equipment in more favourable circumstances after 1945.

From the opening of the historical record, most of the full-time fishermen of Scotland have lived along the east coast. Elsewhere fishing has been usually combined with the holding of land, remaining secondary in a predominantly farming way of life. It is true that, particularly in the last quarter of the century, the men of the Outer Isles, and even more those of Shetland, made a strong bid for a place in the commercial herring fishing but the difficulties after 1931 killed their effort. Two groups only remain to rival the east-coast men in their power and success; they are centred on the villages of the eastern side of the Kintyre peninsula and the Shetland ports.

Now with the introduction of EC controls and quotas, fishing is entering another new phase in its existence.

M. Gray

Fleming, Sir Alexander (1881–1955) was born in Ayrshire and educated in Kilmarnock and London. He had worked on antiseptics early in his career as a doctor during the First World War but discovered penicillin in 1928, by chance, when a culture of staphylococci grew mould, subsequently found to have powerful antiseptic properties. He had to wait eleven years before the drug was produced in a usable form. In 1945 he shared the Nobel Prize for Physiology and medicine.

P. Ingalls

Fletcher, Andrew, of Saltoun (in East Lothian) (1655–1716), was the son of Sir Robert Fletcher of Saltoun and Innerpeffer who hired as tutor for his son Gilbert Burnet, the future Bishop of Salisbury and author of the *History of His Own time*. On Burnet's departure for Glasgow in 1669 Fletcher may have gone to Edinburgh University and he certainly completed his education by travelling abroad. On his return from his travels he was sent as a member for Haddingtonshire or East Lothian to the Convention of Estates that met in 1678.

Fletcher bitterly resented the activities of the Duke of Lauderdale, who ran Scotland for Charles II from 1667 until 1680. In particular he opposed the granting of taxation powers without prior guarantees of satisfactory government, and bitterly opposed the maintaining of a standing army by the Crown. From an early age he had developed a suspicion of royal government and of all hereditary power.

When Lauderdale was replaced as High Commissioner in Scotland by the Duke of York Fletcher's opposition to the government grew stronger and he aroused the Duke's enmity by his opposition in the Scottish parliament (to which he had been elected a member for Haddingtonshire in 1681). He violently opposed anything that smacked of arbitrary government in Church or state. He opposed the Test Act and other government measures and in 1683 he fled the country to join secretly with English opponents of the policies of Charles and his brother. He went abroad and eventually joined Monmouth in Holland and sailed with his force back to England in 1685. He was however prevented from taking part in Monmouth's rebellion by his hot-tempered shooting of the Mayor of Taunton in a quarrel and forced to flee abroad again. He eventually joined William of Orange in Holland, sailed with him to England in 1688, and then returned to Scotland.

Fletcher gradually became disillusioned with William as he saw that he had no concern for Scotland's interests, and he increasingly devoted himself to asserting the claims of Scotland against what he considered to be their sacrifice to English interests. His twin concern with the nature of royal power and with the economic plight of Scotland is seen in his earliest published writing, *A Discourse of Government with Relation to Militias* (1697) and *Two Discourses Concerning the Affairs of Scotland* (1698). In the former he argued fiercely against a standing mercenary army kept up (by the royal government) in time of peace and put forward a scheme for local militias; in the latter he discussed problems of Scottish trade and economics.

Fletcher was again a member for Haddingtonshire when Scotland's last parliament opened in 1703. By now Queen Anne was on the throne and the campaign for an 'incorporating union' between England and Scotland (seen by the government as the most effective way of closing the Scottish 'back door' to England by ensuring that Scotland would never be in a position to choose a different monarch from England's) was well under

way. Fletcher's part in the debates on the Union in Scotland's last Parliament (1703–1707) are his greatest claim to fame. His arguments against an incorporating union and in favour of federal union (and indeed for federal regional government throughout Britain) were based on his opposition to centralized power and to any kind of absolutism as well as on a sense of Scotland's nationhood. He fought in vain for his 'limitations', proposals to limit the power of the Crown in Scotland, to ensure Scotland's own say in its choice of monarch, and to secure the rights of the Scottish parliament and the freedom of the 'Religion, Liberty and Trade of the Nation from English or any foreign influence'. His disinterestedness and integrity were recognized by all: he asked nothing for himself and spoke as an independent patriot. When the Act of Union was finally approved by the Scottish parliament in January 1707 Fletcher turned from politics in despair and devoted the remainder of his life to farming and agricultural improvement in which he played a conspicuous part.

D. Daiches

Food. For as long as the world was believed to be flat (and for a good 200 years after), the merchant venturers of Europe and the Levant were accustomed to regard Scotland as a rugged tract of wilderness pinned to the furthermost margins of the map, a place inhabited by wolves and aurochs, wildcat and wild boar, and a stiff-necked and self-sufficient people who, with a very few gentlemanly exceptions, were more interested in feuds at home than foods from abroad. Which, in any case, they could not afford to pay for.

The new foods, new cooking techniques, and new eating habits that began to revolutionize and then refine the diet of so much of Europe after about 1200 AD passed Scotland by. Despite the French connection, despite the Scots nobility's undoubted familiarity with the rice and spices, almonds, sugar, fruits, and other delicacies so integral to the new cuisine, the great mass of Scotland's people continued, until after the Union of 1707, to eat much the same food, prepared in much the same way, as their ancestors had done a thousand years before. Or even earlier. Nowhere else in Europe—not even in Ireland—did a 'national' cuisine preserve its innocence for so long. Social and economic developments in the eighteenth and, more particularly, the nineteenth century were to play havoc with the traditional diet, but certain quite specific legacies remained, and still remain.

Here, it is possible only to summarize what was common to all—the nobleman, the merchant, the tacksman, the cottar. There were sharp regional, class, and occupational variations, of course; but before 1707, at least, the differences were as often differences of scale as of materials or methods. Where the clan chief's table held oatcakes *and* brose, mutton *and* venison, salmon *and* herring (and a good deal more besides), the peasant would sit down to the first and the last, and think himself fortunate.

Most of the genuinely traditional dishes of the Scots kitchen (which do not include such well-publicized specialities as clapshot, rumbledethumps, and stovies, all of them eighteenth-century introductions) *could* have been evolved soon after neolithic times. This does not mean that they are either poor or primitive; far from it. The late neolithic peoples who began to arrive in Scotland some time before 2,000 BC were very much more sophisticated than is generally realized. To a land that had hitherto supported only scattered hunting-fishing communities, they brought a food technology that had been developing for 6,000 years, an encyclopaedic knowledge of grain, milk, butter, cheese and ale; experience in the preservation processes of salting and drying; and, for good measure, the skill to make pots in which everything could be cooked.

They encountered problems at first, though less with their livestock than their bread grains. Sheep and goats settled well, and the newcomers soon began to domesticate the indigenous wild cattle, the aurochs. In the pig they were not interested. Not being a ruminant, it competed directly for human food. It could not be milked, and milk was by far the most important food product of the domesticated animal. And it had little stamina, an unsociable disposition, and a constitutional objection to being driven. To people on the move—to neolithic immigrants as, long centuries later, to Highland caterans and Border reivers—half a dozen pigs were more trouble than half a hundred cattle. Even today, the Scots remain markedly apathetic about the pig and most of its products.

Fortunately for the ale supply (and, from the fifteenth century on, the whisky supply), the newcomers found it possible to grow barley in Scotland. But wheat, in most areas, was consistently defeated by two kinds of weed—oats and rye. By about the sixth century AD, oats had become the main crop. Nutritionally, they were to prove valuable, for although they have a lower protein value than wheat or rye, they are higher in calcium and iron, and have anti-oxidant properties that delay deterioration in other foods. Modern research has suggested another benefit. It seems that a low-fat diet, supplemented by a pint of porridge every day for eight weeks, will—for anyone hardy enough to survive it—reduce blood cholesterol and diminish the risk of coronary disease. If this is indeed the case, the high, regular intake of oats in past times may have helped to protect against the reputed dangers of a regimen rich in dairy products.

Oatmeal and dairy products thus became the mainstay of the Scots diet. The fact would be apparent even if all other evidence were lacking, for it would scarcely be possible to think of a way of using oats, milk, butter, or whey that does not appear in the cook's repertoire. Oats, for example, could be made ready for eating within an hour or so of being reaped if the cook used the neolithic threshing method (still known in the nineteenth-century Highlands as *graddaning*) of setting fire to the chaff. This also toasted the grain and made it digestible. The meal subsequently produced by grinding in a rotary hand quern (a Roman development) could be mixed with water, milk, buttermilk, or whey, to make—depending on whether the liquid was hot or cold, scant or generous, and whether the cook was in a hurry or not—anything from an unbaked but edible dough (of the kind the ancient Greeks called *maza* and

the Romans *puls*), to oatcakes, bannocks, porridge, brose, gruel, *fuarag* or *stoorum*. The permutations were almost endless, though not quite. Oatmeal could not be used for pastry or for raised bread. Until the sixteenth century, however, this was no real deprivation, as neither was common in Europe before that time.

Medieval monks used the word *companaticum* ('what goes with the bread') as a portmanteau term for all the foods they regarded as a back-up to the basic food-grain. High on their own list would have been vegetables and fruit. But the Scots climate, outside the walled gardens of the monasteries, was unfavourable. It was not that medieval fruits and vegetables would not grow; it was just that, in most places, they demanded too much attention at a time when the great majority of peasants were engaged on more important matters, on cutting peats, or cultivating oats or barley, or caring for the beasts up in the shielings. Jedburgh might be famous for its pears. It might be possible to grow artichokes and asparagus, even to ripen figs (it was said) on the Black Isle in the seventeenth century. The Duke of Atholl might do wonders with rhubarb on eighteenth-century Tayside (though it was still considered a medicine, not a fruit). But throughout the period, vegetables meant onions, leeks and kail to Lowlanders and nettles to Highlanders; and fruit amounted to no more than a handful of brambles or wild raspberries.

What the Scots usually ate with their oatcakes or bannocks was butter, honey or cheese. The latter was made from skim milk, sometimes a mixture of sheeps', goats', and cows', and was often stored or transported in a goatskin bag—which may explain why customers in the Middle Ages were always complaining that Scots cheese was full of hairs. Not until the nineteenth century did Ayrshire begin to produce a commercial full-milk cheese (now known as Dunlop). The long dependence on cheese suggests why one Scots family in ten still eats it for breakfast, a taste shared with the dairy-farming Dutch.

The commonest alternative was fish, fresh in season, but more often salted or smoked. Although food had been preserved by salting or drying since neolithic times, success was at first problematical in the damp Scots climate. The salt extracted from sea water by fast boiling rather than natural evaporation contained minerals that adversely affected the curing process; not until the later Middle Ages was it possible to import salt that could be relied on for this purpose. Drying was equally hazardous, especially as many of the fish that swarmed in and around Scotland were oily; if wind-dried, their fats turned rancid before drying was complete. The process had to be speeded up over the fire, and if the smoke-cure had not been known since Roman times it would be tempting to argue that the Scots discovered it independently. In the peat-reeking, chimneyless Scots dwelling, fish (like people) may well have been smoked willy-nilly.

On the belt-and-braces principle, no doubt, fish were often salted *and* smoked. In the nineteenth century, salmon was even pickled in vinegar and exported to feed the London poor; a hundred years earlier, Scots farm servants had refused to eat it more than twice a week in any form, so common was it. Haddock, too, was salted and smoked, sometimes so lightly that, in the case of the Findon cure, the fish was said to be on the market 12 hours after it was caught and past its best in another 12. Herring, still small and lean enough when the shoals reached the north of Scotland at the beginning of the season to be plainly dried, became larger and oilier as they moved south. Then, they were either salted and smoked (i.e. kippered) or salted only. And in astonishing quantities. Loch Fyne was sometimes said to contain one part water to two parts fish, and as many as 14 million (20,000 barrels) were caught and cured there in a good year. Which makes it easy to understand why herring became, after oats and dairy products, the third staple of the Scots diet.

Meat was a rarity. With luck, a countryman—and in 1750 seven Scots out of eight still lived on the land—would find some game for the pot, but in the matter of domestic livestock he thriftily preferred the continuing benefits of milk and butter to the brief luxury of meat, and dined more often on eggs than on the hens that laid them. Such meat as there was usually came from a sickly beast, slaughtered in autumn because it would not survive the winter, though there might be an occasional summer bonus in the form of a lamb or sheep that had died of braxy, a bacteriological infection to which beasts that gorged themselves when newly weaned or when given sudden access to rich pasture were peculiarly susceptible.

Every bit of a carcase was turned to account. The blood went into meal cakes or black pudding (sometimes, in fact, the housewife would tap the vein of a living animal for this; it was a practice common among pastoral peoples). The hindquarters were made into hams; goat hams and mutton hams were much prized. The rest of the meat was salted for future stews, soups, and minced dishes; with only a cauldron and girdle in her *batterie de cuisine*, the Scots wife never became adept at roasting. And there were two special treats, boiled sheep's head—extolled in the nineteenth century, somewhat to their own surprise, by the English poets Coleridge and Southey—and, of course, haggis.

Music-hall jokes apart, the haggis probably had its origins in prehistoric times. Paleolithic hunters are believed to have cooked the more perishable parts of their kill (the heart, liver, brains, and the fat behind the eyeballs) in the animal's own paunch, hanging it in front of the campfire. The nomad Scythians were still doing it in the fifth century BC, and so were explorers in Africa in the eighteenth AD. 'A most delicious morsel', said one of them, 'even without pepper, salt, or any seasoning'. It would be a natural development, when crop-farming began, to spin the meat out with meal and a flavouring of wild garlic or onions. The pluck of one animal would then make several haggises, which could be stored in the anti-oxidant oatmeal kist.

The Scots diet did not begin to change decisively until the eighteenth century, with the introduction of potatoes, heavy-cropping and (until the blight of the 1840s) thought to be far more reliable than oats. For a few brief decades, there was a notable improvement in the condition of the peasant. By the end of the century, roughly 75 per cent of the Highland diet and somewhat less of the Lowland was supplied by potatoes, which offered not only vitamin C (then unrecognized) but welcome variety. Even so, Southey, who travelled more of the country than most of his contemporaries, still noted their affinity with herring. He had eaten these, he said, 'with proper constancy, at breakfast, at dinner, and at supper also, when we supt, wherever they were to be had, from Dundee to Inveraray', and had come to the conclusion not only that those from Cullen were the best, but that 'red herring and potatoes' were 'like bread and cheese, or pease and bacon, a noble illustration of pre-existent harmony and the fitness of things'.

Ironically, the potato was to bear much of the responsibility for the population explosion that took place in the Highlands around 1800, leading, with the Clearances and burgeoning industrialization, to a flood of immigration into the town and cities—so that the adequately nourished peasant became the undernourished factory worker, differing from his contemporaries south of the border only in that he ate porridge for breakfast, and spent any extra pennies on educating his children instead of on beer or bacon.

The early nineteenth century also saw the spread of tea-drinking, just at a time when sugar and wheat flour were becoming widely available. It was another example, perhaps, of Southey's 'pre-existent harmony', for wheaten pancakes and scones (which could be made on the girdle) were an admirable accompaniment to tea, especially when spread with butter and the newly familiar jams and treacle—which also, as it happened, went very well with oatcakes. Not until the late nineteenth century and the general introduction of the domestic oven did Scotswomen have the opportunity to turn their hand to cakes and pastries, and they were never to become dedicated breadmakers; there was no need, as commercial bakeries were by then becoming omnipresent.

According to received wisdom, this change in the everyday menu had far-reaching results. Two centuries ago, a diet of oatmeal, potatoes, dairy products, fish and occasional meat produced Scots fighting men, notably taller and sturdier than their contemporaries south of the Border. Now, however, the Scotsman is on average an inch shorter—and 40 per cent more likely to die of heart disease. Too many 'dangerous' foods and too few 'protective' ones? Superficially it's a tenable argument, though whether it ultimately proves to be a valid one is quite another matter. Dietary wisdom tends to come and go with the seasons.

Certainly, the Scots today are notorious for their addiction to sweet things, animal fats, salt, and alcohol, and there is a good deal to suggest that this is not only a response to climate—people in cool, damp countries always rely heavily on fats and carbohydrates—but a legacy from times past. A change in basic materials does not necessarily mean a change in accompaniments. The seasonings a cook was accustomed to use with oatmeal, she would later use with potatoes, and later still with wheat products. Oats need plenty of salt. They need assertive garnishes, sharp or sweet, to stand up to their own strong flavour. They need a sufficiency of butter to counteract their characteristic drying effect on the tongue. And dryness and saltiness encourage a high liquid intake—water, milk or buttermilk in early times, ale in later days, and tea now. Market research shows that many Scots now substitute biscuits for oatcakes; they buy 40 per cent more of them than Britain as a whole, including vastly more crispbread. They use more butter than anyone else, though still a mere 2.7 ounces per head per week (a fraction of an ounce more than in the darkest days of wartime rationing). Their bread, even the cotton wool kind, is two or three times as salty. They have a passion for jams, jellies, cakes, pastries and ice-cream. Although only marginally more Scots than English drink whisky at all, they drink far more of it. And they eat the equivalent of five bars of chocolate per head per week, compared with four south of the Border.

Fortunately, this fondness for 'comfort' foods and positive flavours, rarely blossoms into such gastronomic nightmares as the 'curry, haggis and chips' on offer in a few take aways; but a 1991 poll put sausage rolls and—separately—curry (which, nationwide, didn't rate a mention) at the top of the list of Scottish children's school meal favourites. For the apostles of salads and green vegetables, living in centrally heated houses and warmer, drier climes, it must all be very discouraging.

Although nearly twice as many Scots as southern English (32 per cent compared with 17 per cent) still shamelessly admit to being more interested in enjoying their food than in worrying about whether it is good for them, they have made some effort in the last ten years or so to mend their ways. Sixty per cent of cooks claim to have begun grilling in preference to frying. Meat consumption fell between 1980 and 1990 from 5.75 to 5 ounces per head per day, though it still remains higher than the national average. Fish consumption rose, from an admittedly low base, by 16 percent. Twenty one per cent of consumers were converted to wholemeal bread (compared with 40 per cent in south east England). Vegetable sales, which fell everywhere else, also went up, though interest in fresh greens remained well below the national average. And, still, the only fruit for which the Scots show real and increasing enthusiasm is the banana; sweetly and glutinously overripe, a favourite ever since it became widely available in the early years of the century.

It is a picture that shows old habits dying hard. Until quite recent times, even in the cities most Scotsmen contrived to live near their place of work and expected to take most of their meals at home. This not only inhibited the development of restaurants—with the notable exception of the ladies' tearoom pioneered by Miss Cranston in Glasgow in 1884—but ensured that Scots wives remained housewives for considerably longer than their contemporaries elsewhere, tied to a routine of full breakfast, two or three-course midday dinner, high tea consisting of 'kitchen' (something-and-chips or something-and-salad), plus a flanking array of breads, scones, biscuits and cakes, the remnants of which were scheduled to reappear, supplemented by sandwiches, at 9.30 pm for supper. It is hardly to be wondered that the Scotswoman, even today, remains faintly resistant to foods such as fish and green vege-

tables that cannot be well prepared and cooked ahead of time, to be kept warm or reheated on demand.

In terms of quantity, the Scots today are undoubtedly 'better' fed than they have ever been. But it is a sad comment on a changing world that where, once, they could not afford imported foods like rice and spices, what now puts a strain on their pockets are the finest of home produced foods—the wild salmon and venison, the lobster, kippers and Aberdeen Angus beef—that are the pride of Scotland and the envy of the world.

    R. Tannahill

Football. Football has managed a precarious existence in one form or another in Scotland for the best part of 600 years, encouraging varying degrees of hostility along the way. An anonymous poet in the fifteenth century wrote that the 'Bewties of the fute-ball' included 'Strife, discord, and waistis wanis' while in 1424 King James went one step further and ordered: 'It is statut and the king forbiddis that na man play at the fut ball under the payne of iiij d. (four pennies)... .'

The game as it is played today, however, did not begin to take shape until 1863 when the Football Association held its first meeting in London and published rules in the December of that year. Four years later Queen's Park FC were formed in Glasgow and another six years elapsed before Queen's Park, Clydesdale, Vale of Leven, Dumbreck, Third Lanark Volunteer Reserves, Eastern and Granville met in Dewar's Hotel, Bridge Street, Glasgow and agreed to form the Scottish Football Association.

If it is England that gave football to the world, it was in Scotland that game was first made great. Before the turn of the century Scotland beat England with gleeful regularity and the Scottish Football Association report for season 1878–79 was able to smirk: 'The international matches brought us, as we may say, the usual honours.' In 1887 another report indicated 'that the standard of Scotland still waved triumphantly over world football.' The 'wha's like us' attitude at least had its base in an understandable conceit.

In the present century, Scottish football took on many of the characteristics of the nation's weather forecasts. The outlook was mainly gloomy with occasional sunny spells which were all the more dazzling for their infrequent appearances.

On 31 March 1928 the following side danced their way into myth: Harkness, Nelson, Law, Gibson, Bradshaw, McMullan, Jackson, Dunn, Gallacher, James and Morton. In front of the Duke of York, King Amanullah of Afghanistan and countless Scots, that side of small, efficient, superbly talented footballers beat the 'Auld Enemy' 5–1 on their own territory. The side became known as the Wembley Wizards and that result started a cult which was to expand significantly over the next 50 years.

The bi-annual journey to Wembley assumed the trappings of a pilgrimage, a search for the true holy grail of Scottish football—cuffing the English. The only trouble was that after arriving on the Wembley stage to the flourish of 100,000 voices, often as not the Scots would fall flat on their faces. Indeed the victory of dreams in this fixture fell not to Scotland but to England in April 1961 when the white shirts annihilated Scotland 9–3 with Jimmy Greaves orchestrating the rout. Even this calamitous reverse failed to diminish Scottish appetites for the fixture and in the 1970s the tartan hordes made the trek in larger and larger numbers. But the behaviour of many of the fans in London was so poor that at the start of the 1980s a scheme had been devised to prevent Wembley tickets circulating in Scotland and the fixture faced an uncertain future.

Scotland's record in the World Cup, the major international football competition, was hardly distinguished even before the tragi-comic turn of events in Argentina. In 1954 Scotland set off for Switzerland with a manager Andy Beattie, but only 13 players ... and no track suits. The team trained in the green of Celtic, the blue of Dundee and the white of Preston, leaving Willie Fernie to observe that 'We looked like liquorice allsorts'. Scotland also played like them, losing 1–0 to Austria, 7–0 to Uruguay. In Sweden in 1958 Scotland lost to Paraguay but drew with Yugoslavia and France.

Scotland failed to qualify for the three tournaments held between 1962 and 1970, but in West Germany in 1974 made something of a hit. This was rather remarkable given what had gone before in the build-up to the finals. Jimmy Johnstone, a mercurial winger, had been involved in a midnight boating incident at Largs and Johnstone and Billy Bremner, the team captain, were severely reprimanded for an incident of 'high spirits' in Norway.

Still Scotland went on to defeat Zaire 2–0 (their first ever win in the competition) and were more than a shade unlucky to emerge from matches against Brazil and Yugoslavia with no more than draws. The team performed gallantly—but went out of the competition anyway, ironically without losing. And so to the wringing of hands in Argentine. Beaten by Peru, shamed in a draw with Iran, the Scots finally roared to a 3–2 win over Holland. It counted for little, however, other than to set minds thinking on what might have been. Much the same fate was to befall the National team in Spain in 1982, Mexico in 1986 and Italy in 1990. Even Scotland's only appearance at the finals of the European Championships in Sweden in 1992 was distinguished by glorious failure.

In club football, Scotland's proudest moment came in 1967, on 25 May of that year, when Jock Stein's Celtic—who had already won the Scottish Cup, the League Cup, the Glasgow Cup and the League Championship—defeated Inter Milan in the final of the European Cup in Lisbon. The defensive minded Italians took an early lead through a penalty kick and not until the 63rd minute of the match were Celtic on level terms. Tommy Gemmell, a virtuoso left-back, shot the equalizer, Stevie Chalmers grabbed the winner all Europe hailed a victory for attacking football. Stein's Celtic became the first British team to win the European Cup and the fact they did so with style and a home-grown side made Scottish satisfaction all the greater.

Since that triumph, Scottish football has been in decline. At club level the players are not there in significant numbers and it is only natural that that mediocrity should filter through from domestic to international level. The reorganization of Scottish football has made it more competitive but also more defensive

and that was a move away from traditional strength in attack. With each passing season fewer people pay to watch the game and the quality of the product is not what it was.

The exception to the rule on the domestic scene has been the re-emergence of a vibrant and powerful Rangers' side. The success enjoyed by provincial clubs such as Dundee United and Aberdeen in the 1980s led the Ibrox giant to get its act together in the 1990s.

Graeme Souness, the former Liverpool player, played a significant role in the Ibrox revolution as a volatile young manager who brought top players from England and abroad to Glasgow. His successor, Walter Smith, added stability and technical acumen to the formula. Behind the scenes, entrepreneur David Murray was a chairman who took Rangers into a different financial league from their rivals.

In 1993 Rangers began to enjoy success in Europe as well as at home. The problem for their rivals in Scotland at a time of economic recession, was how to keep up with the market leaders.

M. Aitken

Forsyth, Bill. (1946–) If one name was to be associated with the (cautious) development of a Scottish film industry in the 1980s, it would be that of writer-director Bill Forsyth. He entered the world of film-making immediately upon leaving school, working as apprentice to a documentary film-maker. There followed a brief stint at the (then) National Film School after which he returned to Glasgow and set up his own sponsored film company. His first two low-budget features *That Sinking Feeling* and *Gregory's Girl* heralded the arrival of a distinctive film-making voice, and one that would be attended to internationally. *Local Hero* brought Hollywood star Burt Lancaster to Scotland and perhaps, ultimately, took Forsyth to Hollywood where after two features he returned home unhappy at the experience. 1993 sees Forsyth at work in Scotland and abroad with an international star, Robin Williams, on a new film *Being Human* which, it is hoped, will reinforce the distinctive and idiosyncratic Forsythian vision.

D. Bruce

'Friend of the Highlanders' *see* **Caraid nan Gaidheal**

G

Gaelic, because of its ancient and continuous history of use in the country, is the Celtic language identified with Scotland, though it is only one such language closely connected with the country (*see* Celtic Languages). Literary and inscriptional evidence is, however, extremely scanty until many centuries after its introduction, and we have to rely heavily on evidence from Ireland. The language known as Old Irish (perhaps more accurately Old Gaelic) is as much the ancestor of Scottish Gaelic as of Irish Gaelic. It was a heavily inflected and complexly structured language, having five nominal cases and an adjectival declension only slightly less complex, three genders, an elaborate system of verbal forms (including archaic survivals such as a sigmatic future and preterite, a *t*-preterite etc.), a highly complex system of suffixes, especially in verbal forms, and a battery of infixed pronouns. It had three far-reaching developments that seem to have taken place largely in an insular context: (a) a system of initial mutations (shared to some extent with Brythonic languages e.g. Welsh), (b) a system of prepositional pronouns or conjugated prepositions (also shared to some extent with Brythonic), and (c) the opposition of velar and palatal (broad and slender) varieties of the consonants.

Scottish Gaelic has gradually shed much of the complexity of the declensional system, though still retaining the vocative, genitive and dative forms (the latter falling into atrophy in some dialects); it has two genders (having shed the neuter gender); it has a greatly simplified verbal conjugation, substituting for example analytical forms using personal pronouns (as in *cuiridh mi/ thu/ e*) rather than using a separate verbal form for each of 'I/you/he will put' (it still has irregular verbs, however, which retain old forms); the complex compound forms of words have been reduced by syncope and loss of syllables (as in Modern Irish also); the opposition of broad and slender consonants remains (although in a smaller number of consonants than in Irish); the system of prepositional pronouns survives also (as where we use *agam* 'at me', *agad* 'at you', *aige* 'at him', *aice* 'at her', and extend this to idiomatic usages e.g. *tha tasdan agam ort* 'there is a shilling at-me on-you'/'You owe me a shilling'); and the system of initial mutations survives too (e.g. *ceann* 'head', but *mo cheann* 'my head'; *athair* 'father' but *ar n-athair* 'our father'; some varieties of initial mutation are inadequately represented in the written form, as *an ceann* 'their head', where some such form as *ang heann* would be closer to what is said in some dialects).

Two considerable innovations within Scottish Gaelic are the preaspiration of originally voiceless medial and final stops, evidenced in the 1659 Psalms, and the loss of specific future forms in the verb, with the old present developing a future meaning (both usages appear in late seventeenth-century texts).

The earliest surviving snatches of continuous Gaelic in written form are the twelfth-century Gaelic notitiae in the ninth-century Book of Deer. These notes consist of (a) a legend regarding the naming of the monastery of Deer, and (b) several records of grants and privileges to the foundation. The language of these notes does not differ significantly from that of contemporary Gaelic writings in Ireland, and the explanation of this is presumably that within fairly loose limits the two

countries used the same literary language, which is called Classical Common Gaelic. A few usages appear in these notes, however, that may suggest the influence of Scottish forms on that literary standard, as practised in this remote part of Scotland (Buchan), e.g. the representation of the epenthetic vowel in *mareb* 'dead' and *Donnachac* 'Duncan', or the use of a Scottish-type nasalization. The evidence of the Book of Deer notitiae has been used to suggest that Scottish and Irish Gaelic had not moved apart significantly by the twelfth century. This is inherently improbable, since at least seven centuries had intervened since Gaelic arrived from Ireland, and three to four centuries later (when evidence becomes more plentiful) the two are seen to have moved significantly apart. But it has been shown by Professor K. H. Jackson that there was no significant rift before the tenth century. However, from a less academic point of view it is not of crucial importance to know when Gaelic began to move away from Irish, or Irish from Gaelic, since in due course each comes to be considered as a language in its own right, as may be said to have happened with English, Dutch and Frisian.

Modern Gaelic has a range of dialects, some of which show clear affinities with forms of Gaelic spoken in Ireland. The Gaelic dialects of Arran, Kintyre and Islay were particularly close to those of Rathlin (which is often reckoned as a Scottish rather than an Irish dialect), the Glens of Antrim and Donegal. There are many distinctions between the Gaelic of Perthshire (with its tendency to lose word-endings) and the Gaelic of e.g. East Sutherland or Lewis or Barra. The northern group of dialects (including the Outer Isles) break *e* in certain words, making a strong contrast, for example with Argyll (*bial/beul*). The Gaelic of Lewis has been strongly influenced, especially in its phonology, by Norse which must have been widely spoken there between the ninth and the thirteenth centuries, and yet it has conservative features also which link it to early Gaelic in Ireland. Despite these differences, none of the dialects can be said to be mutually unintelligible, and these differences are greatly exaggerated by native speakers. A good deal of work has been published on the dialects (*see* Bibliography).

Gaelic has had a literary standard for much of the historical period, earlier based on Classical Common Gaelic, and later on the Gaelic translation of the Bible (*see* Gaelic Literature). But it is somewhat deficient in modern official registers, and is used only exceptionally for scientific discussion. For such purposes it tends to borrow over-freely from English, though it has excellent potential for word-coinage from native roots, and some of this potential has been demonstrated. Further developments of this kind are dependent largely on extensions of official use of the language.

The main historical sources of loanwords have been Latin (for ecclesiastical, administrative and scholarly loans from the early period), Norse (especially technical loans for boats, rigging, fish, fishing etc.) and English, and the latter is now, naturally, the major source of both vernacular and literary loans.

Gaelic has for long had a settled orthography, with periodic revisions of the system as in the eighteenth century and at the present time (when a useful tidying-up operation was completed in 1978).

Change and development have continued. Gender and case usage continue to be eroded in speech. A Gaelic 'media-speak' has raised its voice more loudly, with calques, awkward translatorese and English plural suffixes becoming commoner. Yet at the same time there has been a strong input of new expressions and vocabulary. Two dictionaries in particular have codified some of this innovation: Derick Thomson's *The New English–Gaelic Dictionary* (1981, 1986 etc.) and Richard Cox's *Brìgh nam Facal* (1991). Cox's dictionary is the first Gaelic to Gaelic dictionary to be published. The use of Gaelic for a wider range of books since the 1960s has significantly influenced the positive developments.

D. S. Thomson

Gaelic Books Council, The. In September 1968 the Scottish Education Department (as was) awarded the University of Glasgow a grant of £5,000 a year, for three years, to be known as the Gaelic Books Grant and to be used to subsidise the publication of new and original works in Gaelic. The result of representations to the Scottish Office by Gaelic educationalists, the award was followed by the setting up of the Gaelic Books Council (Comhairle nan Leabhraichean) to advise on the administration of the grant from the Celtic department of the University.

The University continues to provide accommodation and services and the Professor of Celtic to act as Chairman of the Council, which has eight unpaid members from appropriate areas of interest and one assessor each from the University and the Scottish Arts Council. The ten meet four times a year to formulate policy. The Council's full-time staff consists of a Chief Executive who acts as administrator/editor, a secretary and, when resources permit, a Field Officer whose main work is in connection with the Council's mobile bookselling service and who travels throughout the country, although concentrating on the Highlands and Islands.

The Scottish Arts Council had provided a supplement to the Scottish Education Department's grant since the beginning, but from 1983–84 it became the main funding body (the allocation for the financial year 1992–93 being £87,500). Other assistance over the years has come from the Highlands and Islands Development Board (capital grants towards the purchase of mobile bookshops) and from Local Authorities such as Comhairle nan Eilean and Highland Regional Council (grants towards the running costs of the mobile bookselling service).

The setting up and funding of the Council arose from a recognition that for historical reasons, and in the absence of a reasonable commercial market, Gaelic publishing needed special stimulus and support; and the Council's most important contribution towards this has been the payment of direct publication grants to publishers. Grants are allocated to individual books submitted for scrutiny in typescript before publication, and they are paid immediately after a book is published (some 400 to date, with a value of around £280,000).

From the first the Council sponsored its own literary competitions and offered cash prizes to provide an incentive for the production of books in under-represented categories. In 1975 this was supplemented by the commissioning of authors to write books on a specific topic for an agreed fee, and this has now become the preferred method. The Council may approach an author, or vice-versa. The resulting books are placed with publishers, who are then able to apply for publication grants in the normal way.

The Council's comprehensive catalogue of Gaelic and Gaelic-related books in print, *Leabhraichean Gàidhlig*, was first published in 1975; the fifth edition appeared in 1993.

I. MacDonald

Gaelic Dictionary *see* **Scottish Gaelic, Historical Dictionary of**

Gaelic Folksong. The notion of 'Folk', created in Germanic Twilight and developed in the literate sections of industrialized societies, does not fit comfortably in a Gaelic context. At various points from the Middle Ages to the present day we can draw a distinction between oral and written poetry, for instance between the written poetry of classical Gaelic, which came to an end in the eighteenth century, and poetry in vernacular Gaelic, the great bulk of which was composed and transmitted orally. But this is not a contrast between 'folk' and 'official' or art literature: oral poetry does not belong to one social grade more than another and most of what has survived of it in the great collections of the past is addressed to leading members of society by authors of the same social standing or by poets whose calling conferred upon them the privileges of an influential caste.

It is true that the reduction of Gaelic society, virtually to a single class, means that contemporary oral poetry is more easily labelled 'folk' in contrast to the modern written tradition. But even here there are problems of classification and definition. To illustrate this we have only to point out that one of the oldest examples we possess of aristocratic vernacular praise-poetry was composed between 1593 and 1618 and recorded for the first time in 1954 from a crofter in South Uist. There is no essential difference between such a song and the poetry of the manuscript and printed sources of the past, those of the seventeenth and eighteenth centuries in particular. Yet scholarly opinion, basing itself on historical knowledge, properly rejects the idea that the latter should be classed as folksong.

The written record gives us a valuable check on textual transmission and variation over the last two centuries and more. We can thus point to a song which is still current (to take an example at the farthest extreme from the poem collected in 1954) and show that it combines part of Iain Lom's eulogy to MacDonald of Sleat in the 1660s with part of Niall

MacMhuirich's elegy to Alan MacDonald of Clanranald who was killed in 1715. The modern inheritance of traditional song displays different levels and categories, ranging in modes of transmission from a conservatism which clearly preserves a sense of the original text to an innovative approach which can produce a high degree of textual mutation. Much the same is true of anonymity and authorship. The view that folksong in general is anonymous can certainly not be applied to the Gaelic tradition without qualification Authors' names and circumstantial details of the composition of a song are still a conspicuous feature of the oral repertoire, in some cases taking us back nearly four centuries. In this connection we may note that when attribution of authorship or related information is lacking it is virtually impossible, on grounds of style alone, to distinguish between the work of an aristocrat and a peasant. Accidents of history, in which the Gaelic nation struggled for centuries to maintain an identity in Scotland, encouraged the development of panegyric addressed to the leaders and protectors of society. The aristocratic praise-poem has been something of an anachronism for over two hundred years, and is now very rare in singers' repertoires, but long before its primary function disappeared its rhetoric had become a pervasive style in Gaelic poetry. It is, indeed, traceable in the compositions of the present day and in the past it is the basis of that stylistic uniformity which binds the poetry of different social classes.

In common with folksong elsewhere, the Gaelic song tradition has been affected by written literature. From as early as the eighteenth century printed books were available and may have helped to stabilize texts. This is certainly true in the nineteenth and twentieth centuries: anthologies such as MacKenzie's *Sàr Obair* ('The Beauties of Gaelic Poetry') as well as editions of Rob Donn, Duncan Ban Macintyre (q.v.), and others, can all be shown to have had that effect. Much earlier, contact with classical Gaelic literature had brought new dimensions to oral poetry in subject-matter, imagery, rhythm and metrical form, all of which are discernible in the modern repertoire. One important inheritance from classical Gaelic is the corpus of Ossianic balladry. These ballads first took shape in the classical language but became immensely popular in demotic versions. Of the few that still circulate orally, one of the best known, *Duan na Ceardaich* (The Lay of the Smithy) can be dated to a classical original written around 1400. Another surviving heroic ballad, not of the Ossianic cycle, is *Laoidh Fhraoich* (The Lay of Fraoch). Its variants can be traced back to the fourteenth century by means of an ascription of authorship in the sixteenth-century manuscript Book of the Dean of Lismore. Other ballads again no doubt originate in the stream of popular tradition. Some Ossianic ballads survived into our own time by being used as Hogmanay rhymes. These were spoken or chanted by groups of young people who visited the houses of their township to celebrate the New Year. A small core of them are authentic Nativity carols (variants are connected with Easter); another central group exists with very slight variation as an announcement, opening with the words *I have come here to renew Hogmanay for you* and proceeding to

describe the ceremony; the remainder consists of miscellaneous rhymes, some of these being composed for the occasion by a local bard. Apart from the interesting survival of a handful of carols and charms, the most significant body of religious song derives from the Presbyterian Evangelical Movement which spans the last two centuries. These songs, which are generally of known authorship and use secular melodies, are still being composed.

One class of songs is almost entirely anonymous. They are the choral Waulking songs, which have survived as an accompaniment to fulling home-made cloth but earlier filled that role for a variety of communal tasks, especially women's work, although they are probably not all work-songs in origin. With few exceptions they are the compositions of women and have been transmitted almost exclusively in a female environment. Gaelic poetry can claim an unusual number of outstanding women poets, but it is these songs that enshrine their permanent contribution, intensely lyrical, intimate, passionate and vivid. In them we view the whole order of Gaelic society through women's eyes. They concentrate on elemental themes of love, jealousy, loyalty, betrayal and, frequently, death, for many are laments and some of the greatest of these, laments for men lost at sea. The poetry unfolds not in a smooth linear progression, but unevenly, with unpredictable and sometimes disconcerting changes of focus; indeed many of them are clusters of different themes. A small group is connected with Fairy beliefs: for instance, composed by fairy lovers or by humans who had been seized by the fairies. Others consist of borrowings from disparate traditions including Ossianic and similar heroic ballads, reshaped to the demands of their new role.

Women of all classes may at one time have participated in this choral tradition, and there is some slight internal evidence for that; but references to herding cattle, reaping, etc. as well as complaints by girls made pregnant or deserted by higher-born men, indicate the social placing. And the work-song function, which must always have been central, speaks for itself. All in all, this body of song, in which we can rarely use the concept of an 'original', comes closest to the notion of Folksong in Gaelic. Only in the twentieth century have they been extensively recorded, for the pioneer collectors evidently regarded them as being beneath their notice. They are found, almost exclusively now, in Skye and the Outer Hebrides but there are indications of a former distribution over a wider area.

Waulking song refrains consist mostly of meaningless vocables; true verbal refrains seem to be no older than the eighteenth century. The refrain has an important function in a large area of Gaelic song, associated with lyrical themes: the vocable elements that occur in certain song classes may have a genetic connection with waulking song choruses. Vocable refrains, not necessarily connected with these, are found in lullabies, which sometimes, predictably, use meaningless syllables.

The pastoral economy of the Gaels is reflected in a number of lullabies which contain references to cattle, e.g. 'Whose are the white backed cattle over yonder? They are mine, my love: they are yours, my dear.' Some songs, similar in content and used as lullabies are musically related to Pibroch, the classical music of the bagpipes. In content, however, Pibroch songs are at least as likely to be laments or to refer to battles and heroic deeds. A good example is *Pìobaireachd Dhomhnaill Duibh*, on which Sir Walter Scott based his 'Pibroch o' Donal Dhu'. It alludes to the Battle of Inverlochy of 1429 and is, apart from some demotic versions of ballads, the oldest dateable song still current among traditional singers. Pibroch songs are in Gaelic 'Great Tunes': *Puirt-Mhóra*; sg. *Port-Mór*. *Puirt-a-beul* ('Tunes from the mouth') use the melodies of dance tunes. They are usually light and humorous, frequently bawdy. Songs of humour have a wide range, from innocent merriment to satirical abuse. The satire is an ancient Gaelic form, originally one of the most powerful weapons of the poetic order and some of this aura still clings to it: according to tradition, as late as the eighteenth and nineteenth centuries, during the period of the Clearances, it was capable of dealing death to unpopular factors and oppressors of the poor. The verse debate has also a satirical edge to it. As with the Scots flyting, to which it is probably related, in the past well known poets took part, but the majority of Gaelic flytings are short extempore verses of repartee. These are spoken not sung, whereas in the waulking-song tradition there are several sustained flytings in which women protagonists eulogize their own clan and territory in contrast to those of their opponents.

An intense celebration of homeland is characteristic of Gaelic song: the fertility of the soil, abundance of wild-life, game-fowl and deer as well as flocks and herds. All of these songs involve the human community and the warmth and hospitality of its members: modern compositions are more limited in their allusion to place, social class and history than the songs which come from the 'heroic' past. A splendid exemplar of the latter is *Oran na Comhachaig* (The Song of the Owl), composed in Lochaber around 1600. In that district it was until recently recited in a very full and well preserved version of 66 quatrains which loses little by comparison with the oldest written variants in collections of the mid-eighteenth century. This recitation without melody is uncharacteristic: Gaelic oral poetry is almost invariably sung. On the other hand it is not uncommon to meet non-singers who have an excellent textual memory. In the present instance the melody was apparently lost in the course of the nineteenth century. But in the Outer Hebrides it survived and has been recorded with fragmentary versions of the text. The poem has roll-calls of great warriors and hunters and of the place-names round Ben Nevis. The difference between this and modern compositions is only one of scope. The celebratory act of uttering names, energizing a poetic map of ancestral territory and reinforcing a sense of identity, is an arresting feature of Gaelic song at every level. Songs of emigrants, from the Clearances onwards, and contemporary emigré songs, develop, according to their wistful and often bitter circumstances, from such origins. The temporary exile of sailors (relatively long in the days of the sailing ships) has produced a species of emigre poetry in which the poet thinks with yearning of his own community and the girl he left there. This is often true, too, of soldiers' songs of the British army, but their dominant emotions are pride in the Gaelic warrior tradition and discontent with army life. The first of these emotions is apparent as late as World War II. Until World War I, a pathetic sort of protest to the British establishment finds recurrent expression: 'Do not drive us off our ancestral lands to make way for sheep. Sheep will not die for you in the face of the enemy'.

Traditional singers have preserved examples of all the categories briefly discussed and much more. On the whole, lyrical poetry of one kind or another has survived better than the songs that express directly the traditional political and social values of Gaelic society, especially upper-class values. What is being composed now is not conspicuously lyrical, except, of course, in love-songs, which still show, at the level of the township bard of Highland and Island communities, a fascinating blend of native and borrowed elements. Among the latter there are traces of the influence of *amour courtois*. But the modern bard is also a spokesman who comments seriously, or in humorous and satirical modes, both on the events of village life and the events of the world brought to his notice by the media. More and more, these bards are literate in Gaelic and by that token are coming to occupy a position somewhat between the modern literary poets and the pop-song composers who are themselves involved in the modern Folksong Revival.

J. MacInnes

Gaelic Literature. Perhaps the earliest Gaelic production surviving in Scotland on which literary form has been imposed is the 'Duan Albanach', a metrical king-list dated *c*.1093, but it is likely that this was composed by an Irish author. The next such surviving piece of writing is the poem in praise of MacSween of Knapdale's fleet, probably to be dated 1310, and this has the appearance of being very secure in its literary tradition. For the next two centuries our Gaelic literary survivals are scanty, and consist mainly of bardic poems, though particular versions of sagas may eventually be shown to be rooted in this period also. There may be fragments of vernacular Gaelic verse or song as old as this also (e.g. the Harlaw incitement of 1411), but the lack of surviving MSS, and the unlikelihood of writers of MSS recording non-bardic material, gave only a minimal chance to vernacular survival. For the literary language was the learned, or semi-learned Classical Common Gaelic, shared by Ireland and Scotland, and this was what the literary patrons supported.

It is in the sixteenth century that we first achieve a view of a more diverse literary tradition than that just referred to. We glimpse this in the Book of the Dean of Lismore, for although this is the main source of our knowledge of bardic verse, we see here too that verse in syllabic metres was also being made by noble or chiefly amateurs, such as Duncan Campbell of Glenorchy and Isabel of Argyll, and that their work included courtly love poetry and satire and bawdry. We see too that heroic ballads were still being made, in more relaxed metres than those generally favoured for praise-poetry, and we can trace the history of these ballads, in popular circulation, through the eighteenth and nineteenth-century collections down to the oral tradition of the present day. But we also see in the sixteenth century the appearance (and more properly the surfacing) of poems in a language which can be called Scottish Gaelic, apparently by a different order or grade of poets referred to as *aos-dàna*. The poem *An Duanag Ullamh*, which is not later than the mid 1550s and may be 30 years earlier, is one such, and the type can be seen still in existence in the 1640s as practised by the Mackenzie bards of Achilty. It is sometimes referred to as 'semi-bardic' verse. Furthermore we find examples of different metres and fully vernacular language in songs which have survived and which can be dated to the second half of the sixteenth century ('Griogal Cridhe' *c*.1570, 'An Iorram Dharaich', *c*. 1585 are examples). The volume of such song, in an expanding range of metres and styles, grows steadily as the seventeenth century advances, and here one would hazard the guess that the song refrains and structures, and the melodies, point to a much more ancient history for this kind of composition. Over forty verse items, some fragmentary and some extensive, have been dated before 1600, mainly to the sixteenth century, but these illustrate such a wide range of metres, styles and conventions that one has to conclude that they form part of a tradition which goes back long before that century, and that some instances are probably rooted in traditions that go back some 500 to 700 years. The age and provenance of the older layer of verse in the body of material collected by Alexander Carmichael and published under the title *Carmina Gadelica* has still to be determined in detail, some useful preliminary work having been done by Hamish Robertson in a controversial study published in *Scottish Gaelic Studies* in 1976.

Although it was in the eighteenth century that the deepest inroads were made on the older forms of Gaelic society, the seventeenth century shows us the break with the literary tradition gradually taking place, with the consequent survivals and nuclei of change. Bards clearly not of the professional order, but having varying degrees of official status in the clan or in the chief's household, come into prominence, such as Iain Lom (q.v.), Màiri Nighean Alasdair Ruaidh (q.v.), Eachann Bacach who is one of the poets labelled *aos-dàna* or An Clàrsair Dall/Roderick Morison, who as bard and harper in the household of Iain Breac MacLeod had a professional niche but possibly owed it to personal factors. Iain Mac Ailein/John Maclean shows his connections with the learned bardic tradition which drew liberally on ancient Gaelic legend of a pseudo-historical kind, and shows a certain irreverence to such legend too. The professional bards had begun their swan-song, especially Cathal MacMhuirich (*see* 'Bardic Verse'), but their kind of poetry was to last until close to 1745. The semi-bardic poets were lamenting the decay of the old social system, whose traditional hospitality and liberality had been challenged by the Statutes of Iona (1609) and subsequent Privy Council enactments aimed at cutting Gaelic chiefs down to size. The styles we see surviving in popular folksong were a reminder of an old

submerged layer of verse-making, but would continue to be practised for a considerable time. Sìleas na Ceapaich, late in the seventeenth century, was showing the influence of her English religious reading on her Gaelic verse, and introducing novel metres, as that of the limerick. Duncan Macrae of Inverinate, compiler of the Fernaig anthology, was the centre, or at least the recorder, of a circle of political and ecclesiastical versifiers in Kintail and the surrounding areas. And in the last decade of the century Alasdair Mac Mhaighstir Alasdair (q.v.) was born, and for anyone who could read the omens that was a portentous event.

The emphasis on verse in this literary tradition is a very strong one. Prose has a somewhat narrower range until we come to relatively recent times, and before the eighteenth century is virtually restricted to (a) heroic and romantic story-telling (b) exposition, especially in the case of the medical treatises (c) religious or liturgical writings and (d) exceptionally, history, this being perhaps a natural extension of annal-keeping and genealogical record-keeping. It may be that the picture we have is distorted by the loss of manuscripts— that, for example, there was a more widespread use of Gaelic for other purposes such as legal documents (as in the surviving Islay charter of 1408, or the 1555 contract between the Earl of Argyll and O'Donnell of Tirconnell, or the MacLeod contract of fosterage of 1614)—but it is doubtful if this would seriously affect the overall balance. Sagas continued to be copied by scribes until the eighteenth century, Alasdair Mac Mhaighstir Alasdair providing a late instance, and then the stories went wholly into an oral tradition where they sometimes remained in a remarkably stable state until the mid twentieth century (as witness such stories as that of Conall Gulban, or a fragment of the *Táin*, or the Story of Deirdre, the former two collected as late as the 1950s). It is of interest that the hereditary succession which is a notable feature of the transmission of learned and artistic skills in the society, had relevance in the oral tradition also, the late Duncan MacDonald of South Uist, for instance, coming of a line of story-tellers who traced their descent to a line of bards which we know of in the early seventeenth century. Other hereditary lines were responsible for the medical manuscripts, e.g. the Beatons and the MacLachlans, and they along with the bardic MacMhuirichs (*see* 'Bardic verse') account for many of the older MSS which have survived. The MacMhuirichs are the main surviving examples of Gaelic historians (their history is in the Books of Clanranald), and the vivid nature of the more contemporary part of that history, especially of the Montrose Wars, would make us wish for more. All kinds of prose already referred to were committed to manuscript and stayed there until the late nineteenth century, except that religious and liturgical prose in Gaelic made a much earlier printing début. In fact, the first printed Gaelic book, either in Scotland or in Ireland, is of this kind, Bishop John Carswell's *Foirm na n-Urrnuidheadh*, a translation, with additions, of the Book of Common Order, which was itself a revision of the Geneva Book sometimes called John Knox's Liturgy. Carswell published this in 1567, including some additional matter such as an Epistle to the Reader, a

Poem addressed to the Book, and a form of Blessing for a Ship putting to sea. He turns aside in his Epistle to warn the reader against the dangers of paying too much heed to the lying stories about the Tuatha De Danann and Find mac Cumhaill, and this suggests that the attractions of the rival prose were strong. Carswell's prose, like that of the MacMhuirichs, Beatons, MacLachlans and indeed virtually all writers who wrote in surviving manuscripts before 1650, was a form of Classical Common Gaelic, literary Gaelic (common to Scotland and Ireland) rather than vernacular Gaelic.

Vernacular Gaelic prose is founded on the translation of the Bible (New Testament published 1767, Old Testament completed 1801). These translations were carried out by a group of Perthshire and Argyllshire ministers, and something of their stamp remains on most subsequent writing of Gaelic. The relatively early achievement of this canon gave Gaelic a signal advantage, for instance as compared to Lowland Scots, for it gave the language a secure and influential place in the Church, and consequently in education and writing generally. In the second half of the eighteenth century Gaelic sermons and other works of religion begin to appear in print in some volume. There is a fairly lengthy period of exploiting Gaelic prose in such modes before the range of uses begins to open out again in the nineteenth century.

Meantime poetry in the eighteenth century was adapting to the conditions of its time. Mac Mhaighstir Alasdair is a national, not a clan, figure in the poetry of the age, and he more than anyone led the tradition away from parochial preoccupations and standards. There is a wave of Jacobite verse (q.v.), but also the wit and pungent social criticism of Rob Donn (q.v.), the descriptive power and lyricism of Donnchadh Bàn MacIntyre (q.v.), the classical precision allied to the imaginative power of Dùghall Bochanan (q.v.), the romanticism and the realism of Uilleam Ros (q.v.), the wit and rhetoric of Iain Mac Codrum, and at the end of the century the dedication of Eóghan MacLachlainn/Ewen MacLachlan, who translated much of the *Iliad* into Gaelic and made poems on all the seasons. These are the best-known of the eighteenth-century poets, but verse was widely practised. Late in the century Gaelic poetry was transplanted to America, e.g. with Iain Mac Mhurchaidh the poet of Kintail and North Carolina, and early in the nineteenth century we have one of the most famous of Nova Scotian Gaelic poets, John Maclean who wrote traditional praise-poetry in Tiree in Scotland and later 'The Bard in Canada' (in the 1820s). There is an impressive innovation and originality in the verse of the eighteenth century, together with tremendous linguistic exuberance: a teeming vocabulary and a masterly deployment of sound effects. Poetry is seen as a natural medium for a wide range of themes: praise, elegy, incitement, social criticism, Biblical exegesis, political comment, natural description, love, satire, praise and dispraise of whisky or bagpipes, humorous accounts of local events. Poetry had retained its links with both the literary and the sub-literary worlds: it had survived the murderous attack on the civilization it grew out of.

That hard-won self-confidence blossomed in some ways in the nineteenth century, though it did not produce a volume of great literature. The language that had come so close to proscription became the language of education again, in the schools founded by the various Gaelic Schools Societies from early in the century. Gaelic periodicals were published (e.g. *An Teachdaire Gaelach* 1829–31, *Cuairtear nan Gleann* 1840–43, *Teachdaire nan Gaidheal* 1844–48, and *An Gaidheal* 1871–77). The volume of Gaelic book publication rose as the Gaelic Schools increased the literate public for such books. The majority of these books were religious or ecclesiastical in subject-matter: sermons, and other theological writings, hymns, Church polemics. A few were concerned with secular current affairs, and there was a little history, belles lettres and story-telling, the latter at first strongly influenced by the styles of the oral folk tales. Much of the publishing, and a significant part of the writing, was done by Gaels who had settled in Lowland Scotland, and who had founded a vigorous ghetto culture, especially in Glasgow and the Clydeside towns. This phase of Gaelic writing is especially associated with the period *c.* 1870 to 1914. It was then that many of the Highland territorial associations were founded in Glasgow, first as benevolent societies, but developing a cultural and linguistic role, though this in time often dwindled to a fairly rigid, if enjoyable, *céilidh* formula: songs and talk and tea. A second wave of periodical publication comes in this period also, with An Comunn Gaidhealach's *An Deò Gréine*, later re-named *An Gaidheal*, and the periodicals founded and run by Ruaraidh Erskine of Mar (e.g. *Guth na Bliadhna* 1904–25 and *An Sgeulaiche* 1909–11). Gaelic fiction is gradually and partially emancipated from the domination of the folktale (*see* Caraid nan Gaidheal), and there is some interesting journalism (especially in *Guth na Bliadhna*), and literary and other essays, for example those of Donald Mackechnie, Donald Mackinnon, and Donald Lamont.

The Land Troubles, and stirrings of Home Rule sentiment in the second half of the nineteenth century, stimulated much of the most vital poetry of the period (*see* Clearances, Verse of), and although John Smith and William Livingston are the most notable poets there is much of interest in the work of Mary Macpherson, Neil MacLeod and John MacFadyen.

The nineteenth-century confidence referred to earlier blossomed also in terms of scholarship, late in the century and early in the next, in the work of Donald Mackinnon, first holder of the Chair of Celtic at the University of Edinburgh, Alexander Cameron, Alexander MacBain, Alexander Carmichael, Ella Carmichael, and W. J. Watson. The period 1882–1916 saw the establishment of Celtic as a subject in three of the Universities, and of Gaelic as a full subject in Highland Secondary schools, and this period also saw the foundations laid in Gaelic studies generally. This took place against the background of, and partly in reaction to, the English-based educational policies introduced in 1872. A similar reaction can be sensed in the upsurge of Gaelic publication at the beginning of the twentieth century, including the relatively ambitious if unsatisfying attempt to write Gaelic novels (by John MacCormick and Angus Robertson). The improved status of

Gaelic in education produced in time a new generation of writers and a public for them, with such developments as the Gaelic newspaper column (John N. MacLeod in the *Stornoway Gazette* wrote in a relaxed, semi-popular style), short plays (John N. MacLeod, Hector MacDougall, Donald Sinclair), and, from the 1930s radio work (talks reviews, stories, features).

The final period is by no means the least exciting. The first signs of revolution in the form and voice of Gaelic poetry in this century can be detected in the work of First World War poets especially Iain Rothach/John Munro. Between the mid 1930s and the mid 1950s five poets brought a bicultural and bilingual sensibility to Gaelic poetry. These were Somhairle MacGhillEathain/Sorley Maclean, Deòrsa Caimbeul Hay/George Campbell Hay, Ruaraidh MacThómais/Derick Thomson, Iain Mac a' Ghobhainn/Iain Crichton Smith and Dòmhnall MacAmhlaigh/Donald MacAulay (qq.v.). This wave of new verse still continues, with many fresh developments in themes, poetic structures and metrical structures taking place, and with new poets, such as Aonghas MacNeacail, Maoilios Caimbeul, Màiri NicGumaraid, Meg Bateman and Anne Frater, joining the original band of innovators. The most striking result of this development is perhaps the replacement of a tradition of predetermined metrical structure and adornment by one of organically motivated structure and adornment. In consequence, there has been a revival of structural and rhythmical vitality in the verse, which goes hand in hand with the cultivation of a new range of themes and sensibilities.

The post-1945 period has also seen exciting work in fiction, the periodical spearhead this time being the quarterly *Gairm*, founded in 1951 and still appearing more than forty years later. The most prolific writer of fiction has been Iain Mac a' Ghobhainn/Iain Crichton Smith (q.v.), with collections of short stories and novels. One very interesting collection of short stories has come from Iain Moireach/John Murray: *An Aghaidh Choimheach* (1973). Donald John Maciver has published a large body of short stories and a detective novel, *Cò Rinn e?* (1993), and Iain MacLeòid has a comparable output including two novels, *Spuirean na h-Iolaire* (1989) and *An Sgàile Dhorcha* (1992). A succession of short stories has come from Colin Mackenzie over the years, and more recently from Dòmhnall Alasdair ('Seanchasan à Stobarrag' in *Gairm*), Màiri Montgomery among others. *Gairm* was also largely responsible for a broadening of the range of themes for Gaelic prose writers, and did much to encourage a greater range of expository, journalistic, humorous and literary styles to fit in with the expanding range of themes. This was accompanied by a good deal of work on the lexis and the orthographic presentation of Gaelic, so that the language has been made more usable and more supple. A valuable feature in this process has been translation from other literatures. The emphasis has been on verse, culminating in the anthology *European Verse in Gaelic* (1990), with some short stories, but there is need for an ambitious programme of translation. Drama promised something of a revival in the early 1960s, but this has not been sustained. Radio and television have played a useful part in

developing Gaelic journalism, but have been relatively weak in drama. Book publication has been greatly stimulated by the work of the Gaelic Books Council (q.v.). The growth of interest in Gaelic, in Scotland generally, exerts various pressures on the language and its literature. Writers who learned Gaelic in adolescence or adult life are now contributing to the literature, as Fearghas MacFhionnlaigh/Fergus MacKinlay in poetry and the novel, or Christopher Whyte in poetry, but this is not entirely new, for George Campbell Hay came to Gaelic in his later teens, and Ruaraidh Erskine of Mar made it his adopted language. There is both promise and challenge in this.

D. S. Thomson

Gaelic Psalms. The singing of the Psalms of David in metre, with Precenting, or 'Putting out the line' has now become an exclusively Gaelic custom, although it was at one time more widespread. It was initiated by the English Puritans who, after the Reformation, chose the Psalms of David sung unaccompanied in unison as that part of public worship in which the congregation would be truly involved. Many members of those congregations could not read however, and in 1643 the Westminster Assembly of Divines enacted that, 'for the present, where many of the congregations cannot read, it is convenient that the minister or some other fit person appointed by him and the other ruling officers, do read the psalm, line by line, before the singing thereof'.

The first translation of the Psalms into Gaelic was in 1659 when the Synod of Argyll published the first 50. Robert Kirke, minister of Balquhidder in Perthshire, published a translation of all the Psalms in 1648, and the Synod of Argyll published its completed version in 1694. The metre used was the ballad metre of the English metrical version, familiar to Lowland Scots from their folk songs but quite unfamiliar to Gaelic speakers. Any Gaelic poetry in ballad metre is a parody of the Psalms. But the singing of metrical Psalms with precenting became a well established tradition, in such a way that it is now regarded generally as the required way of singing for Gaelic-speaking congregations.

Upwards of 20 tunes are used, with names like New London, Martyrs, Bedford, Evan, Kilmarnock, French, Stornoway and so on. Some leader reads a portion of the Psalm, repeating the first two lines of the text at the end. Then the precentor starts to sing those lines, and the congregation joins in gradually once the tune has been identified. The first two lines are sung straight through, slowly, with varying degrees of ornamentation. The precentor then chants the third line and leads in to the congregation's part with them, incidentally giving them the first note of that phrase, then the fourth line, and so on until the portion to be sung is completed. Only the first two lines of the first stanza are sung straight through. The precentor usually bridges the gap between his line and the congregation's line with a short melodic embellishment at either end of it. The effect is a continuous sound, because although the lines are sung so slowly that the singers have to stop for breath at least once for each line, they never stop simultaneously.

This phenomenon of one continuous musical phrase, varying in length from about four minutes to about fourteen, depending on the number of stanzas sung (four stanzas is the normal upper limit) has puzzled the uninitiated for many years. Some very strange theories have been put forward to account for the *Long tunes* as they came to be called. They were supposed to have been learned in Germany by Scottish Covenanting soldiers; to be Swedish airs learned by soldiers in the army of Gustavus Adolphus; or to be Phoenician in origin, as the Gaelic language was supposed to be. Joseph Mainzer, a German musicologist who visited Scotland between 1842 and 1847 was given transcriptions of *Long* psalm tunes as sung in Ross-shire. Mainzer, who had not heard the tunes sung, added bar-lines and time-values at his own discretion. The result was slightly chaotic, with ornamental notes being given prominence and very inaccurate time-values. The tune French, as published by Mainzer in *The Gaelic Psalmtunes of Ross-shire and the neighbouring counties* (1844) is sung every year at the closing concert of the National Mod. People who know the tune within their own real Gaelic tradition are puzzled as to why the Mod version seems to bear no relation to theirs.

This way of singing is also used in family worship, led by a man of the household. Teachers of Psalmody were employed in Lewis last century, and many of the standard tunes became established in the Western Isles from that time. But the art of precenting is absorbed by anyone interested through exposure to its practice from early childhood, and is in general orally transmitted.

Singing in Gaelic with precenting is still a very strong part of the culture, wherever there is a sizeable number of Gaelic-speaking worshippers. There are at least five congregations in Glasgow where it takes place, three in Edinburgh, three in Inverness and many individual congregations throughout the north mainland of Scotland, as well as most congregations in the Western Isles. There are also Gaelic-speaking congregations in Canada that sing with precenting, putting out the line. It will only last, however, so long as Gaelic is preached, and many preachers are now choosing to conduct services in English.

M. MacLeod

Backfree Church, Lewis

Gaelic Short Story. The short story is at present the most popular literary form in Gaelic. This is in some measure due to the facilities provided over nearly 30 years by the quarterly *Gairm*, to the encouragement offered by Gaelic radio producers, and in a lesser degree to the establishment of literary competitions at the Mod.

The Gaelic short story is the product of a bilingual community and of a bicultural sensibility. It is, therefore, partly a borrowed form, more or less successfully grafted on Gaelic in proportion to the individual writer's creative powers. At the same time it is important to stress that some of the narrative techniques of traditional Gaelic storytelling have also contributed to its vigour. Beyond what is basic in these techniques or is implicit in the structure of the language itself, this, too,

varies greatly from one writer to another, according to ability and predilections. It has, indeed, been argued that in those areas where the traditional folktale has flourished most strongly the modern short story is correspondingly weak, which may suggest that the mere survival of folktales in a community is in itself an inhibitory factor. But this is not simple cause and effect. Modern Gaelic literature (although it owes much to Gaelic fraternities in Lowland cities, Glasgow in particular) has its origins in communities in which relatively high literacy has been combined with a tradition of radical, non-conformist and secular dissent. In these communities medieval romances and the like have not thrived. But there is still throughout the Gaelic area a flourishing tradition of naturalistic stories, serious and humorous, based on recent or contemporary events and characters. There is, besides, in the same background, a tradition of wit, repartee, bawdiness, and vivid impressionistic description. What is more remarkable than complementary distribution of folk-tellers and writers is that the bias of story-writing, especially in the past, has been towards dignity and formality at the expense of creative exuberance. Even when a writer retells a story which is full of zest in oral narration, instead of adding the subtleties of a new dimension, all too often he only succeeds in reducing the racy, colloquial style, particularly in dialogue, to a laboured dullness. The reasons are social and technical. Earlier writers, looking back at their native townships, frequently presented an image of correctness. But contemporary writers, even in their healthy desire to experiment and avoid parochialism, can also be inept in handling their medium. As a counterpoise, however, there are Gaelic short stories whose success depends entirely on brilliant experimental techniques. The technical reasons for stylistic lifelessness derive from the history of Gaelic prose. Beginning in homiletic writing, prose achieved a superb clarity in formal registers of the language. But it has tended to carry an expository and even didactic tone into creative writing. This is quite noticeable in the first phase of the short story, which extends from about 1880 to 1930.

Writers such as John MacFadyen and Neil MacLeod, and their immediate successors, to a great extent modelled their work on traditional tales, although a strong influence from contemporary music-hall is discernible in MacFadyen's humorous stories. An important figure of the early years of the twentieth century was the Hon. Ruaraidh Erskine of Mar, one of whose aims both as publisher and writer was to raise Gaelic literature to a metropolitan level. As part of this campaign he broke new ground with his series of detective stories. Between 1908 and 1911 John MacCormick published four collections; his adventure stories are still enjoyable. Unique because of its use of religious symbolism is Donald Sinclair's finely written story of the old fisherman and his godchild.

The second phase begins in 1944 with the publication of Portree High School's Gaelic magazine. Finlay J. Macdonald, Paul MacInnes, Winnie Young, among others, introduced as adolescents a vital, irreverent tone which has never deserted the genre. The tradition inaugurated in Portree has been extended by writers from a variety of backgrounds and brought to maturity in *Gairm* and through the BBC. There is some specialization, as in Eilidh Watt's collections of stories for young people and children, or D. J. MacIver's explorations of the paranormal; but the range is now very wide: 'humorous, sentimental, whimsical, psychological, atmospheric and off-beat,' as the editor of *Gairm* has reported; and the subject-matter is equally diverse. Besides those named below, collections have been published by Iain MacLeod and Mary Maclean. There are also a number of anthologies. The most prolific writers are I.C. Smith (q.v.) and the Rev. Colin MacKenzie, whose work grows out of native tradition and extends to detective stories, tales of mystery and science-fiction. In his writing there is a refreshing sense of experiment and a readiness to move out into the world in search of themes. MacKenzie's powers of invention are most marked in development of plot and creation of atmosphere. A writer who fulfils the demands of the bicultural situation of Gaelic is John Murray. Simultaneously traditional and avant-garde, Murray draws on the resources of his inheritance (as described at the beginning of this article) and combines these with various techniques of modern writing to produce short stories of great delicateness and perception. He is unmistakeably Gaelic not only because he uses the language: his parish is the world.

J. MacInnes

Gaelic Storytelling, Traditional. Despite occasional clear affinities with the traditions of Lowland Scotland, the Northern Isles and Scandinavia, and, of course, a considerable involvement in the widely shared common property of the International Popular Tale, Scottish Gaelic, in the field of storytelling as in so much else, exhibits a particularly close relationship with the Gaelic tradition of Ireland.

Gaelic society in both countries, for a variety of reasons, some of them historical and political, remained very much 'tradition-orientated' right up to modern times and has, in many ways, so remained to the present day. Indeed, while cultural ties remained very close, up to the seventeenth century, Scottish Gaels continued to be well aware of their Irish origins—and this was especially true of the literati of the Bardic schools whose usual vehicle of expression, in common with their counterparts in Ireland, was a classical and conservative form of Gaelic, based on Early Modern Irish literary usage.

The collapse of the old social order, in the seventeenth century in Ireland and the eighteenth century in Scotland, resulted also in the collapse of this hierarchy of professional poets, musicians, historians and storytellers which had depended on the patronage of the Gaelic-speaking nobility for its existence. The remnants and descendants of what had been a privileged, educated elite now merged with the general populace, bringing with them a considerable detritus of their learning and, indeed, some of their manuscript compendia of tales, historical tradition and poetry. There had, of course, been a constant process of mutual exchange going on between the oral and written literatures of Gaeldom for centuries—as, indeed, there had been in medieval societies elsewhere—but this reinforcement and enriching of popular oral tradition at a comparatively recent date appears to have been a crucial factor in the survival of numbers of tales that have reached our own times through several generations of oral transmission.

Leaving aside the Irish evidence, of which a considerable quantity exists: a striking case in point is provided by the Mac Mhuirichs, professional poets and historians to the Lords of the Isles and various MacDonald families in Scotland, though ultimately of Irish origin. The last of these professional scholars died in South Uist in the eighteenth century, but we have evidence that well into the nineteenth century a Mac Mhuirich manuscript was circulating in South Uist and that stories were being read and learned from it. We also have the testimony of Janet Currie in South Uist, herself a descendant of the Mac Mhuirichs, who in 1860 recited a tale to one of Campbell of Islay's collectors and gave a pedigree of oral transmission for it extending back over several generations to Niall Mac Mhuirich, one of the last of the trained poets and historians.

The problem of the mutual interrelation of oral and written versions of tales poses questions of considerable complexity. Some tales would seem to have had a mainly oral history of transmission, others to have been more popular in writing and still others to have moved equally easily in either medium. Many of these questions are admirably dealt with by Dr Alan Bruford in his book *Gaelic Folk Tales and Medieval Romances*. The book is concerned mainly with a remarkable group of Romantic Hero tales, composed for the most part in Ireland between the fourteenth and nineteenth centuries and having no real counterpart outside the Gaelic world, though they served much the same purpose and were designed for the same type of aristocratic audience as the European medieval Romances—tales of voyages and adventure and combat against odds, of wooings and of magic, such as *Conall Gulbann* (a tale of an Irish prince of that name); *Sgeulachd an Dìthreibhich* (*The Tale of the Hermit*) and *An Ceatharnach Caol Riabhach* (*The Lean Grizzled Champion*) to mention three that survived into the second half of the present century in Scottish Gaelic oral versions. Incidentally, the fact that such stories were conscious literary creations for an aristocratic audience and owed much of their transmission to manuscripts does not at all mean that versions of the same stories which have come down in oral tradition are necessarily inferior as literature to the written texts. Indeed there are demonstrable instances where the skills and sense of drama of generations of oral storytellers have improved the texture and impact of such tales.

These Romances, along with the earlier Hero Tales of the Cuchulainn and Fenian cycles, some of which have also survived in oral tradition as well as in manuscripts, and some of the great International Wonder Tales, or Märchen, comprised the most highly regarded aspects of the Gaelic storyteller's stock in trade both in Ireland and Gaelic Scotland. Examples of International Wonder Tales popular in both countries are: *The Dragon Slayer* (No.300 in the Aarne-Thompson Classification); *The Twins* (AT 303); *The Magic Flight* (AT 313, 314); *The Maiden who seeks her Brothers* (AT 451); *Cinderella* (AT 510); to mention only a few.

It was on these prestigious Hero Tales, Romances and Märchen, naturally enough, that the storytellers lavished their best efforts in terms of style and oral technique, for it was by their performance in such as these that reputations were established and developed. It is in tales of this kind that one is most likely to find the ornate, alliterative and archaistic 'runs' or decorative passages that were so much a feature of both the oral and the literary style in Gaelic story-telling. Runs were generally used as opening or closing formulae or for set-piece descriptions such as the arming of a hero, a ship putting to sea, crucial phases of a fight or battle, or the imposition of *geasa* ('spells' or 'taboos').

Such, indeed, was the concentration bestowed by the best reciters on tales of this kind that we have numerous accounts of astonishing feats of memory—some individuals having apparently been able to memorize long and complex tales at one hearing, especially if they themselves got an opportunity to tell them next day or very shortly afterwards. We also have instances of tellers being able to reproduce reasonably accurately, after generations of oral tradition, passages in Romances that conform pretty closely to manuscript versions of perhaps three centuries earlier. In some cases truly gifted practitioners like the late Duncan MacDonald of South Uist (d. 1956) could repeat some of the most prized stories virtually word for word at every telling. We have striking evidence for this in a number of recordings from Duncan, made at intervals of several years, of *Sgeulachd an Dìthreibhich*.

Incidentally, fidelity to their sources was a declared aim of both Irish and Scottish Gaelic storytellers, but this is one area where there is a certain amount of evidence for a divergence of the two traditions. In general, Irish tellers would seem to have allowed themselves rather more licence in their treatment of their texts and to have had a more innovative and creative attitude to their art. The best of the Scottish practitioners, on the other hand, would seem to have accorded to the tradition virtually the status of Holy Writ and to have tried to tell the most valued tales as nearly as possible exactly as they had first learned them.

Not all International Tale types enjoyed anything like the prestige accorded to the kinds of story mentioned above. For instance, storytellers of repute—almost always men—would not be expected to concern themselves with *Animal Tales*, such as the numerous Fox and Wolf Stories. These would be regarded as suitable only for children and would usually be confined to the family circle. Much the same would apply to *Formula Tales* such as *Am Bonnach Beag* (*The Fleeing Pancake*, AT 2025). Many stories listed under the rather misleading heading of *Jokes and Anecdotes* in Aarne-Thompson would not be considered worthy of notice, though others of this class might well form part of a good repertoire, for instance *The Master Thief* (AT 1525) or the *Whittington's Cat* type (AT 1651). Some *Religious Tales* such as *Christ and the Smith* (AT 753) and *The Devil's Contract* (AT 756B) would be regarded as quite acceptable as would some *Novellas* (Romantic Tales) such as *The Clever Peasant Girl* (AT 875) or *The King's Questions* (AT 922). Legends and memorates of ghosts, fairies and witchcraft, though widely known and told, would not normally figure prominently in a distinguished repertoire but it could well include historical legends of clan feuding and cattle-raiding, or the William Tell type of legend—attached in South Uist to the historical figure of Gillepàdruig Dubh, a famous local archer. Some onomastic legends and legends of supernatural creatures might also be considered worthy of a place, depending on their associations.

Incidentally, Campbell of Islay noted in 1860 that 'though each prefers his own subject, the best Highland storytellers know specimens of all kinds'. This tendency to have a wide repertoire but to prefer to specialize within it is still evident among the very best performers at the present time.

Just as their repertoires and the types of stories they prized most had much in common for both Irish and Scottish storytellers, so had their function in society. Tales seem to have been told on almost any occasion when people met together socially or for communal work. It could be a wake or a wedding, a funeral or a fair, or any number of other occasions, but by far the most important focus, certainly during the nineteenth century and well into the twentieth, was the céilidh house. Every township had at least one such house which was distinguished as a popular meeting-place and in these people gathered together to tell and listen to stories, to sing songs, to exchange local news and gossip, even occasionally to play cards or to dance. The normal evening work of the household such as spinning or carding or the twisting of heather-rope would often continue during much of the time, but when serious storytelling started close attention and strict silence were usually expected, apart from relevant exclamations aroused by some incident or, of course, critical or appreciative comment when a tale or a session was finished. There was a traditional formula, not always adhered to, that the first tale should be told by the man of the house and tales could then be told till dawn by the guests. In practice, however, it seems to have been unusual in recent times for such sessions to go on much after midnight. Such evenings of communal entertainment are well within the memory of people still living.

It was in such surroundings that the best storytellers developed their talents and found a ready-made and appreciative audience. However, already in the late 1850s when Campbell of Islay and his team began their great work of collection, the best of the storytelling tradition was already on the point of extinction in large areas of the mainland Highlands, though there were still plenty of shorter stories, legends and historical tradition to be got there. In the Outer Hebrides, on the other hand, especially in the Uists and Barra, the tradition was still in full vigour and still socially functional. People gathered in the long winter evenings to listen and to learn, and good performers were eagerly sought after and had a considerable standing in the community.

Indeed, despite hardships and disasters such as the potato famine, the Clearances, the collapse of the kelp industry, massive emigration, the occasional influence of some fundamentalist churchmen, and the much more damaging imposition of a totally English-based education system in the 1870s, storytelling continued to hold its ground pretty well even at the beginning of the present century. Lack of educational and economic opportunities still combined to keep many of the more intelligent people at home and a subsistence economy saw to it that competitive social pressures in the modern sense scarcely existed. The result was anything but a wealthy community, but it was a pretty well integrated one and one that provided suitable conditions for a flourishing oral tradition.

A gradually evolving situation was cataclysmically interrupted by the First World War. The Islands, like other areas, were stripped of their younger men-folk. Many died on active service. Many returning Servicemen settled in the cities and failed to return. Whole communities were saddened and the practice of ceilidhing never fully recovered. The gradual introduction of a cash economy, educational developments, mass media of communication, modern transport and new social and economic pressures all accelerated the decay of the old order. Well within living memory these Island communities still held numbers of men and women, often monoglot Gaelic speakers, and innocent of formal education, who could have achieved highly successful careers elsewhere had the opportunities existed.

Such people, staying at home, were the leavening influence on the rural life of the Highlands and Islands—as indeed elsewhere—and from their ranks were normally drawn the best of the bearers of oral tradition. Their social function was a natural consequence of the situation in which they found themselves. They supplied the needs that are now catered for by books, newspapers, films, radio and television. In these circumstances artistry in telling a story, a good memory and an extensive repertoire were obviously highly prized qualifications and they were assiduously cultivated.

As the demand for their skills declined, so did their numbers and their artistry. There are few left today who can tell any of the great tales and those with an extensive repertoire and a high degree of artistry are very few indeed. Most of those who know any of the major tales are passive tradition-bearers—people with good memories who can recall some of what they heard in their youth. It is very seldom that storytelling of the old sort has any real social function now, though in areas such as the Uists and Barra it continued to have some right up until the time of the Second World War—and even after in some cases among the older people.

This is not to say that no significant storytelling at all goes on nowadays. There are numbers of good stories still around—though usually of the shorter more anecdotal type. Most storytelling now goes on between interested individuals, or in the family circle, or for the benefit of collectors and students of oral tradition. Parents and grandparents do sometimes still tell fine tales to children and one can be pleasantly surprised by the discovery of unexpectedly talented and hitherto unknown practitioners. There is also some remarkable socially functional storytelling going on among Gaelic-speaking travelling folk, as there is among their non-Gaelic-speaking counterparts (*see* Scots Storytelling, traditional).

Indeed, though it is impossible not to regret the disappearance of the céilidh-house and of the near-professional reciters whose splendid talents were so eloquently and so recently deployed there, we should perhaps be thankful that so much does survive and that it is even now possible to observe at first hand the art of the storyteller in Gaelic Scotland. To experience even once the telling of a fine tale by a gifted performer is to be powerfully reminded that this is a dramatic art—no less a visual than an aural experience. The tape-recorder has greatly improved on the pen in the attempt to place something of a splendid heritage on record. It is also a matter for some satisfaction that, in recent years at least, some glimpses of a remarkable art have also been captured on film and videotape—but even more so that the art itself continues to be practised, even if not to flourish.

D. A. MacDonald

Gaelic Writing, Twentieth Century Renaissance of. It is often difficult to define or pin-point the interaction of a society's, or a people's, movements of thought and its literature. And the explanations of such interaction can be diverse, as is illustrated by the case of post-Union Scotland. Looking at the history of Gaelic revival over the last hundred years, it is difficult to resist the conclusion that there is a strong correlation between literary output and the assertion of identity in linguistic and other ways. The 1872 Education Act (Scotland) had the effect of replacing the old Gaelic schools with new buildings, better educational standards, but an English-based education. The decades of the 1870s and 80s were marked by purposeful and decisive action on the part of Highland tenants and smallholders, and this resulted in signal advances in status, the introduction of crofting legislation etc., together with a heightened political awareness. There are links between these developments and the growth of home-rule sentiment in the Highland area. Strong links persist between Gaelic writing and political nationalism. An Comunn Gaidhealach was founded in 1891. These developments are not presented in a causal sequence, but it is suggested that they represent a hardening of Gaelic identity in the period, and that this hardening is ultimately the basis of the twentieth-century Gaelic renaissance.

A factor of crucial importance, which was already showing in the later nineteenth century, was the build-up of Gaelic colonies in the cities, and the infiltration of Gaels into the professions in the Lowlands. Some important leadership in the Land Troubles came from this source, and it now began to contribute writers, scholars and entrepreneurs. A notable flow of Gaelic compilations and works of scholarship begins to appear: Sinclair's *An t-Oran-aiche*, Cameron's *Reliquiae Celticae*, Carmichael's *Carmina Gadelica*, and in the early years of the new century Sinton's *Poetry of Badenoch*, the *Songs of the Hebrides*, the *MacDonald Collection*, Maclean's *Typographia Scoto-Gadelica* and Mackinnon's *Catalogue of Gaelic Manuscripts*.

On the side of contemporary literature, Ruaraidh Erskine of Mar began his remarkable series of periodicals, *Am Bard, Guth na Bliadhna, An Sgeu-laiche* etc., which encouraged new work in prose, poetry and drama, and there were other periodicals, e.g. *MacTalla* and *An Deò-Gréine*. There was a more general burgeoning of prose-writing (essays by Donald Mackechnie and Donald Lamont, short stories by MacCormick and MacFadyen, and novels by MacCormick and Angus Robertson).

Meantime Gaelic was gradually fighting its way back into the schools, being introduced in a modest way into the examination system in 1905, and gaining ground thereafter as part of the Higher Leaving examination. The Gaelic Clause in the 1918 Education Act at least gave Gaels a lever for the placing of Gaelic in the curriculum, even if it was not used very effectively. Gaelic had earlier been introduced as a College and University subject (Free Church College, Glasgow, 1876, Edinburgh University, 1882, Glasgow University, 1900, Aberdeen University, 1916) and it was taught in the Teachers' Training Colleges in Glasgow and Aberdeen. In the 1910s, 1920s and 1930s, a series of strong Gaelic school departments was established, and an effective Gaelic Inspectorate. Some of that ground was lost in the following decades, but fresh developments took place, including the important Inverness-shire experiment in the 1950s and early 1960s, the Bilingual Education Project of the 1970s, the Gaelic nursery schools and Gaelic-medium schools of the last decade. The fight for adequate provision for Gaelic in education is a long-continuing one, and is at the root of the Gaelic renaissance. It continues still, at school, university and public levels: the activists change, the methods change, but the idealism remains constant.

An important build-up of structures has also gone on in this whole period. Various societies have been founded, e.g. the Gaelic Society of Inverness (1871) with its long series of Transactions, the Scottish Gaelic Texts Society (1937), Gaelic Choral Associations (late nineteenth and twentieth centuries) Comunn na h-Oigridh, the Gaelic Youth Movement (1930s), Gaelfonn Recording Co. (1950s), the Gaelic League (1940s), the Gaelic Books Council (1968), a Learners' Association (CLI) and a Gaelic pressure group (CNAG). Similarly new structures have come into being in the educational field, e.g. the EIS Gaelic Committee (1930s), the Bilingualism Committee of the Scottish Council for Research in Education (1956), the Gaelic Panel of the Examinations Board (1964), and the Gaelic College at Sabhal Mór Ostaig (1972). This College runs Gaelic courses for learners, a course in Business Studies, and is closely associated with Scottish Television in providing back-up for some Gaelic TV programmes. Both it and Lewis Castle College run training courses for Gaelic TV operators. Other important Gaelic organizations are the Historical Dictionary of Scottish Gaelic (q.v.), the Gaelic wing of the Scottish Linguistic Survey, and the School of Scottish Studies, which collects and analyses Gaelic folksongs, folktales, and other lore, has a large archive, and publishes (sparingly as yet) in articles and on discs. Much important collection of Gaelic oral literature has been carried out by other collectors also, e.g. John Lorne Campbell, Calum Maclean and K. C. Craig. The comprehensive *Companion to Gaelic Scotland*, encompassing language, literature, history, music, art etc., was published in 1983 (and 1987). (See Thomson in further reading).

The Gaelic Renaissance had an important standard-bearer in the Gaelic periodical *Gairm*, founded in 1951. Its first forty years were celebrated by a display in the National Library in late 1992. *Gairm* acted as a symbol of confidence and competence, encouraging the use of Gaelic for the discussion of a very wide range of topics, often giving a lead in public Gaelic issues, encouraging the work of successive generations of young writers, both in prose and verse, while at the same time retaining an interest in more traditional topics and literary modes, and contributing signally to the growth and sophistication of the short story in Gaelic. There is one well established learned journal which deals mainly with Gaelic matters, *Scottish Gaelic Studies*, and various Scottish periodicals include some Gaelic, especially verse, and review Gaelic books. The important contribution, in this respect, of William MacLellan's periodicals, especially in the 1940s, should be recalled, as also the interest of verse anthologists and literary historians. *The Stornoway Gazette* and the *West Highland Free Press* publish Gaelic every week. *Tocher* includes much Gaelic material, the *Scotsman* has regular Gaelic articles, and Church magazines have Gaelic sections.

Gairm magazine developed an important publishing wing, and eventually took over Alex. MacLaren, the main Gaelic publishing house to survive into the second half of the century. Gairm now publish dictionaries, handbooks, songs, poetry, fiction, plays and books on various topics. Acair, the Stornoway publishers, have produced a good list of children's and school books, and some general interest books. Gaelic publishing has been greatly helped by the work of the Gaelic Books Council (q.v.).

D. S. Thomson

Galt, John (1779–1839), businessman, travel writer, biographer, novelist and short-story writer, was born in Irvine, where he lived until in 1789 his parents removed to Greenock. In 1804 Galt settled in London, and most of his subsequent life was spent in England or abroad. In 1834 he returned as a sick man to Greenock, where he remained until his death. His work as a creative writer belongs mostly to the latter part of his life, and is shaped by a number of factors: the milieu and Covenanting traditions of his childhood; the agricultural and industrial revolutions as they affected the west of Scotland; his travels in Europe, the Levant and North America, especially Canada; the social, historical and psychological investigations which constituted an important part of the Scottish Enlightenment. He eventually developed an ethic, at once Calvinistic and Newtonian, of a providentially directed progress which makes use of human suffering and obsession in the fulfilment of its own impersonal, if generally benevolent, ends. Galt accepted the Calvinistic idea of a general providence, while rejecting that of one particular to the individual; the ironic and humorous effects in his novels often result from the mistaken belief on the part of a character (Micah Balwhidder or Leddy Grippie are good examples) that they themselves have witnessed, or participated in, acts of particular providence. A point of view closer to Galt's own is provided, characteristically, by the veteran midwife, Mrs Blithe, in a short story 'The Howdie': 'My experience has never taught me to discern in what way a come-to-pass in the life of the man was begotten of the uncos at the birth of the child'.

Biographies of individuals who substantially affected social and cultural history form a significant part of Galt's work; best known is *The Life of Lord Byron*(1830), but more relevant to the origins of his work as novelist are the studies of the 'ambitious, resolute, ostentatious' Cardinal Wolsey (*The Life and Administration of Cardinal Wolsey*, 1812), who rose to power from humble origins, and of the American painter, Benjamin West, a backwoodsman by birth, who nevertheless was President of the Royal Academy from 1792 until his death in 1809, and who introduced or at least popularized realistic modern costume in historical painting (*The Life and Studies of Benjamin West*, 1816; *The Life, Studies and Works of Benjamin West*, Part II, 1820). The last is almost an autobiography—'the whole materials of which it consists were derived from himself, and the work is in consequence, as nearly as it possibly can be, an autobiography'. From such investigations of the life and mind of an elder contemporary it was no enormous step to the fictitious biographies and autobiographies set in times of major social and cultural change, which make up Galt's distinctive contribution to the novel. The subject which gives power to his best imaginative work is the developing pattern of Scottish experience, at home and abroad, from the Reformation to the Reform Bill of 1832. In terms of historical chronology, he begins with *Ringan Gilhaize* (1823), an autobiographical account, spanning three generations, of Reformers and Covenanters; and continues with *The Entail* (1822), in some ways his most powerful book, a biographical study of the obsessed Walkinshaw family, again through three generations, from the Darien expedition to the Napoleonic Wars. Both are historical novels in the tradition established partly by Walter Scott, even more, perhaps, by Maria Edgeworth in her chronicle of four generations of an Irish family, *Castle Rackrent* (1800). More generally familiar are Galt's novels of modern history, the autobiographies, *Annals of the Parish* (1821), *The Provost* (1822), *The Member* (1832) and the biographies, *Sir Andrew Wylie* (1822), *The Last of the Lairds* (1826), and *Lawrie Todd* (1830). *The Ayrshire Legatees* (1821), which in a sense established the course of Galt's later work when it made a first successful appearance (1820–21) as a serial in *Blackwood's Magazine*, is an epistolary novel in the tradition of Smollett's *Humphry Clinker* (1721), and combines fiction with ironic reportage of current events, as do one or two other of Galt's works, for instance, *The Steamboat* (1822) and *The Gathering of the West* (1823). In the last decade of his life, Galt turned increasingly to the short story. Such little masterpieces as 'The Howdie' (1833) and 'A Rich Man' (1836) follow the same plan of ironic, sometimes riotously comic, observation of the providential process as it affected Scots and their communities.

Galt called *Annals of the Parish* and *The Provost* 'theoretical histories' and so drew attention to an important feature of all his best work. The phrase is misleading, however, in that it misses the imaginative delicacy and power by which he saw providence operating through, and often in despite of, human short-sightedness, cupidity, obsession and cruelty. During the nineteenth and early twentieth century full appreciation of his achievement was inhibited by the emphasis which he placed on these qualities, and by the frequent earthy vulgarity of his sense of humour. It is only recently that a proper assessment has become possible.

J. MacQueen

Gardens. The Scots have long been famed as gardeners, though perhaps most often as practitioners and plant collectors, rather than as innovators of design. Interest in gardening in Scotland seems to have reached its first peak of enthusiasm near the end of the seventeenth century. All at once, descriptions of gardens are found in private journals, topographical prints begin to show them, and the first specifically Scottish garden books are published.

Of the journals, two from the 1670s describe houses surrounded by numerous walled, hedged or moated enclosures, with summer houses, fishponds, fountains (some still designed to drench the unwary), statuary, knot gardens (the one at Pinkie was two hundred feet square, and seems not yet to have been called a parterre), orchards and kitchen gardens. Similar features are illustrated, though in a frustratingly perfunctory way, in contemporary prints. Some of the nicest of these are by Slezer and his associates, and show demesnes entirely in the European mode, with formal approaches to the house, of gravel walks and clipped lawns, flanked by orchards of regularly planted trees.

In real life, things may have been rather more haphazard. The first Scots gardening book, John Reid's *The Scots Gardiner* of 1683, is a delightful work, packed with sound advice. It was extremely successful, being reprinted well into the 1750s. The quickest glance suggests that even small gardens of the period were well, even delectably, planted. While he does give directions for laying out avenues and the rest, he seems to have most sympathy for quite modest establishments. For them he suggests that there should be no real distinction between kitchen and decorative garden; that within the formal plan, clipped holly should combine with fruit trees (apricots and peaches against a warm wall), roses (including musks, eglantines, yellow briars and the Frankfort), with herbs, vegetables and flowers. The walks might have been ornamented with pots of carnations and myrtle or, more grandly, lemons and oranges. He disapproved of these last two, thinking them too tender, 'wherefore I am not very curious of them, yet there is severals in this Countrey has them, and are at great pains in governing them.'

The remains of such gardens are fairly common, although it is mainly the architectural elements that survive. Walls, pavilions and fishponds can still be found, as well as something more uniquely Scottish. As many old houses were built on a sloping and defensible site, the only way to create a garden suitable for knots and parterres was in the use of terracing. By the end of the century, elaborate sequences of steps and terraces were common, and far more classical and Italianate than anything in England. The terraces at Aberdour were noted for their espaliered almond trees, and others will probably have had nectarines, figs and vines neatly nailed to the stone. A number still support splendid gardens, even if with a Victorian gloss as at Balcaskie, or partly grassed as at Culross. Many others lie in ruins.

Seventeenth-century gardeners traded widely. Leek and cucumber seeds were imported from France. Cauliflower seed was brought from Crete (probably its place of origin). Melon seed came in from North Africa and Spain (Reid thought melons more trouble than they were worth, which is still true). Lemon and orange trees were shipped to Leith from Genoa, and bulbs and rare seeds from Constantinople.

After John Reid's book, in the following year, appeared the grandly named '*Scotia Illustrata*' of Robert Sibbald. Though this gives a complete list of all plants grown in Scottish gardens (a list that could still be used to build a fine garden today, as well as showing how poor most modern 'restorations' are), it sadly fails to live up to its name. It illustrates no garden of its own day, let alone anything earlier. However, a painting by John Vosterman, of the late 1670s, does show a rather simplified version of the most astonishing and dramatic of all early Scottish garden remains; the knot garden at Stirling Castle. By the time of the painting it was already more than 150 years old, and apart from the spectacular ground-works, all that remained were some statues and a few hedges (now themselves vanished). The Stirling 'knot' is entirely regal in scale, being far larger than a similar, if earlier, survival at Kenilworth. The mind's eye must clothe the grassy banks at Stirling with elaborate hedges of box, holly, rue and hyssop, with trellis arbours shaded with jasmine, honeysuckle and vine, and no doubt with many bushes of the fine white rose later to be called the 'Jacobite', but in fact a garden plant since well before the Roman empire.

Of medieval gardens, almost nothing remains. Monastic institutions gave their names to many fruit trees and a few flowers, all of which were probably bred within their walls. Many of these plants were valued well into the nineteenth century, though all but a beautiful pink seem to have vanished from commerce. Castles must have been victualled and their inhabitants cured of disease. All must have had, therefore, orchards, vegetable 'yards' and herb 'yards'. It was common practice to surround these only with barriers of wattle, which has left no trace. A few ancient fruit trees, planted in regular 'quincunx' were often to be seen about such habitations well into the eighteenth century.

Even while *The Scots Gardiner* was still being read, with its delight in both plants and formalism, the landscape garden movement began to achieve its first victories in England, and to seep steadily North. By the 1740s, Lord Kames started to advocate the new style (and to practise it at Blair Drummond). Soon, other lawyer-landowners followed suit. Fortunately, there seems to have been a strong affection up here for the late developments of the formal style (perhaps because of its association with Stuart rather than Hanover). Many formal layouts, still in young growth in the 1730s and 1740s, survived the onslaught of the new garden image, and are still to be seen. The magnificent *allés* and *patte d'oie* at Tyninghame survived with their original trees until the 1940s, and are now perfectly replanted, if not yet very atmospheric. Much formal planting remains at Hopetoun and Hamilton, and the remarkable series of ramps and terraces, described in the making by Defoe, at Drumlanrig still remain, if bereft of their decoration. However, the most complete survival of all, and a charmer, with canals, formal ponds, alleys, and splendid bastioned outworks, is at Newliston. It dates from the 1720s, and survived even the demolition of the old house and the building of one entirely to Georgian taste.

When the landscape movement began to elevate gardening to an art, the kitchen garden, once a place for as much pleasure as profit, came to be seen as an increasingly distinct department. Scots energy seems to have become channelled in two directions. Enthusiasm, imagination, and money were poured into kitchen gardens, so that they became increasingly efficient, productive and beautiful. The same three qualities were also put into forestry, and so although the landscape itself slowly changed as millions of new trees grew, 'landscape gardening' itself fell rather in the middle. Scotland produced no major designers. The best worked in Russia, a number of landed gentlemen moved a tree or two, and the painter Alexander Nasmyth (q.v.) made some modestly elegant gardens, many of which survive. Of the three major English exponents of the style, Kent and Brown had no Scottish commissions, and Repton only one, in Fife and now derelict.

The result was that, by the late eighteenth century, the kitchen gardens of Scotland were the envy of England, and even of Europe, and their design offered employment to a number of as yet unsung 'engineers'. Of many fine gardens, the largest supplied the tables of Dalkeith Palace. It produced melons, cucumbers and cherries the year round, had two vine houses 50 feet long producing many varieties of grape, a pineapple house of 40 feet (which would have produced several hundred fruit a year), and 400 square feet of melon frames. Much further down the social scale, even minor lairds, were they interested in gardening, would have dined off asparagus and artichokes, as well as many vegetables now no longer in use. If they had only four horses, their gardener could have produced early peas and beans, and a pineapple a week.

Because Scots gardners were well educated and well trained, they were much in demand south of the Border. By the mid eighteenth century, the ancient Scots gardeners' lodges had thriving branches in London, and the head gardeners of most notable estates were Scottish. In the forestry department, English foresters bought huge quantities of Scottish seed (collecting tree seeds was a profitable occupation), and millions of seedlings were shipped south from Leith. However, the latter trade fell away about 1800, when it was realized that greedy Scots nursery-men tried to grow too many plants per tray, and many weak saplings died.

Scotland also began to produce more Scottish garden

writers. James Justice wrote a splendid work called '*The Scots Gardener's Director*' in 1754, spent all his money on gardening, and died in penury. Walter Nicol, amongst a number of interesting books, wrote the first gardening book designed especially for the middle classes: '*The Villa Garden Directory*'. Undoubtedly, the most influential was John Claudius Loudon. He moved to London at an early stage, was amazingly productive, and both chronicled and directed changes in garden design. His '*Encyclopaedia of Gardening*' of 1822 is an immense and fascinating work. Like Justice and Nicol, he died impoverished.

By the time of Loudon's major work, the landscape movement was beginning to fall apart. Scots began to see their own architecture and culture as Picturesque; they stopped building rather good copies of English classical houses, and started putting up rather bad ones of their own vernacular towers and manors. Rather little Scots landscape had been suited to the 'home counties' idyll of Lancelot Brown, but a great deal of it turned out to be perfectly suited to the next mode of gardening, and one which developed a distinctly Scottish style.

New plants had been trickling into British gardens throughout the sixteenth and seventeenth century. By the middle of the eighteenth century, the trickle had become a small river, and by the end of it, a flood. A few forest gardens, or arboreta, had been established in Scotland by that date (fine ones can be seen at Dawyck and Scone), and they seem to have given the lead for a new sort of Scots garden. With much of the gardening fraternity of Scottish extraction, it is not in the least surprising that most of the eminent plant collectors of the nineteenth century were of the same nationality. Douglas, perhaps the most famous, and the rest sent back to Kew, Edinburgh, and private gardens, huge quantities of new material, including many conifers, many herbaceous species, and above all, hundreds of rhododendrons.

The flood of new species coincided with an upsurge in the creation of wealth. New rich Scotsmen (and English), bought cheap Scots land, built themselves sad baronial halls, and surrounded them with what might be called 'magnates' gardens'. Typically, these consisted of a parterre near the house, but filled with new bedding plants, not the charming miscellany liked by John Reid. The beds were liberally garnished with topiary and historical stonework (often good old sundials from better gardens). However, beyond all this spurious antiquity (Drummond Castle has a very large example), real new beauties were being created. Rhododendrons, azaleas, and the rest, from three continents, flourished in the damp and dappled shade, and the acid soil, beneath our own pines or exotic conifers sent from the Americas by Scots collectors. Beyond the fine new plantings (Benmore and Dundock Wood are good examples), rose the wild landscape that terrified eighteenth-century travellers, vastly impressed Marshall when he tried to landscape part of it in the 1790s and had now come fully into its own as substance or setting for Victorian gardens.

This new sort of gardening soon diversified. In some gardens, the masonry adornments to the parterre multiplied alarmingly, producing so many terraces, bridges, obelisks and vases that an almost funerary garden resulted (a rather attractive example can be seen at Keir). In others, the owner's collecting instinct triumphed, and some gardens, especially in the mild parts of the western seaboard, became botanical treasure houses (Inverewe and Logan).

In the early years of this century, the nostalgia for earlier garden style took a more scholarly turn, and there were some interesting 're-creations'. Rather good parterres and pavilions appeared at Pollok House near Glasgow; arbours, sundials and oldfashioned flowers were combined to make a charming garden at Kellie Castle; impressive landscape parks appeared at Mellerstain and, with a rather too narrow lake, at Manderston. The same house also boasts an astonishingly opulent kitchen garden of the same date, complete with blue and gold ironwork gates (quite inappropriate) and a perfect dairy.

Today, there are good modern gardens scattered all over Scotland. Many are small, many are private, and each one is something of an oasis. There are surely still too many front gardens with tightly pollarded trees, and a square of grass or bright pink gravel ringed unadventurously with hybrid tea roses or tuberous begonias. Perhaps, though, things are getting better. More and more gardens are opening to the public, and garden visiting is on the increase; something which always serves to illumine the gardens for miles around. Certainly, some of the best 'Open' gardens are equal to the finest of any country, and many (including Tyninghame, Balbithan, and Branklyn), should make the owner of any garden plot, however small, view his land with a new awareness of the possibilities of a Scots garden.

    D. C. Stuart

Geddes, Patrick, is one of the most obscured, though at the same time one of the most influential, of thinkers. He is often called a pioneer of town-planning, but his planning abilities were just one expression of a polymathic genius which comprehended biology, ecology, sociology, the arts, and adult education. His refusal to be pigeonholed and specialised, far from being a maverick intellectual attribute, is in fact directly related the generalist tradition of thought in Scotland which has this century been explored under the title of 'democratic intellectualism'.

Geddes was born in Ballater in Aberdeenshire in 1854 and died at the Scots College he had founded in Montpellier in the south of France in 1932. The many points of interest in his life include studying evolution with T. H. Huxley in London, helping to found the Sociological Society, and being appointed Professor of Botany in Dundee (1888). As a town planner he carried out studies on the conservation and regeneration of urban environments in, among other places, Edinburgh, Dunfermline and Dublin, as well as developing an evolutionary analysis of the growth and decline of cities. Major studies were also carried out in India and it was there that in 1919 he was appointed the first professor of Civics and Sociology at the University of Bombay. As an educational reformer Geddes initiated student-run university residences in Edinburgh in which he revitalised the medieval tradition of universities as at least in part democratic, student-run bodies. He also pioneered Summer Meetings in Edinburgh, early examples of the Summer Schools that are now taken for granted world-wide. One can say all this without even mentioning what is perhaps his best known achievement, the Outlook Tower.

The Outlook Tower is located at a key point within the psychogeography of the city of Edinburgh between the symbol of State power, the castle, and the then symbol of rejection of the authority of that State in matters spiritual, the Free Church College (now New College of the University of Edinburgh). Furthermore it is on a ridge of rock coextensive with the remains of an extinct volcano which we now call Arthur's Seat. Truly an outlook with which to begin thinking about the evolution of cities, regions and cultures. Through it one could learn, not just through words and images but from direct experience, about a multiplicity of aspects of Edinburgh, Scotland, Europe, and the world, all of which had a bearing on how people made their lives through their work in a particular place, and here Geddes emphasised the categories (adapted from Le Play) of Place, Work and Folk as essential to any analysis. But Geddes not only drew attention to the necessity of exploring any environment in terms of its natural characteristics and the way in which those characteristics relate to the folk who live there and the work done, but also by specifying the psychological attitude necessary for any such analysis, that is to say an emotional, intellectual and co-operative engagement with that place, those folk and their work; he expressed this latter notion in his 'three S's', – Sympathy, Synthesis and Synergy.

The Tower was described in its heyday as the world's first sociological laboratory and Geddes' follower Lewis Mumford, identified it as the point of origin of the Regional Survey Movement. It was an assertion of the importance of all areas of knowledge, all arts, all sciences, all religions, within the context of a real place, explored in terms of the unity of the local and the international (and that unity of local and international is the key to Geddes' emphasis on the Region). The view from the terrace or the camera obscura was directly related to the information in the rooms beneath. Knowledge was not split off from perception. Geddes summed up this idea in his educational motto 'Vivendo Discimus' (By Living We Learn). A companion motto was 'Creando Pensamus' (By Creating We Think). In the light of these mottos it is no surprise that Geddes was a powerful advocate for the unity of the creative, the intellectual and the practical found in the arts, both in drama— his dramatisations of history, presented as educational pageants, ranged from the earliest times to the present—and in the visual arts, in particular the work of Celtic Revival painters such as John Duncan and Phoebe Traquair. His own significance as a visual thinker (part of a culture of visual thinking in Scotland which includes James Clerk Maxwell and D'Arcy Thompson) is evident in his diagrams in particular the *Arbor Saeculorum*, the *Valley Section*, and the *Notation of Life*.

Throughout his life Geddes resisted the fragmentation of knowledge consequent on misguided notions of specialisation in education, that took as their model the production-line rather than the person. This was not, of course, a denial of the value of specialisation; rather it was an assertion that specialisation without the recognition of the importance of the context within which that specialisation takes place, was a social disaster. Geddes advocated breadth of vision at a time when specialisation was getting into its mechanical stride with the consequences of restriction of thought and environmental depredation, with which we are all now familiar. But Geddes saw these educational and ecological problems with clarity when most were blind to them.

M. Macdonald

Gibbon, Lewis Grassic/James Leslie Mitchell (1901–1935)

had a hectically brief career in which he established himself as the most important Scottish writer of fiction of his time, writing at a distance from his beloved yet hated countryside in a manner oddly reminiscent of Stevenson in Samoa. Both men found much to irk them in their native country, though the later writer settled in Welwyn not for reasons of health but from free choice. There, several hundred miles off, he could see the Mearns of Kincardineshire with a new clarity. Guided by his memories and the plangent nostalgia which obviously warred with recollected distaste for the rigours of crofting life, a bookish and lonely child in an uncaring community, he wrote rapidly and with growing mastery a series of semi-autobiographical sketches which culminated in the triumphant *Scots Quair—Sunset Song*, *Cloud Howe* and *Grey Granite*. Television serialisation has made them well known throughout Britain and widely in North America; while *Sunset Song* is the most popular, the books follow from and depend on one another, and should be read together.

Gibbon evolved a style of literary Scots modelled on the pattern of a Scot speaking English: the rhythms are Scottish, the vocabulary just sufficiently so to make it distinctive while leaving it intelligible. The style stamps the books with originality, and evokes with considerable success the sounds and the atmosphere of the communities lived in by the heroine whose adventures and successive marriages link the plots. Chris Guthrie, crofter's daughter in Kinraddie, marries a farmer in *Sunset Song* only to see their way of life, like her husband, destroyed by the Great War. The symbolic interpretation is quite clear, and can be applied to *Cloud Howe*, where she turns to the Church in marrying a minister, moving with him to a small town hit by the early Depression. The first marriage has fruit in a son, the second is only to produce a still-born child: again the meaning is plain. In *Grey Granite*, Chris moves to the city, to depression and relative poverty, and to a loveless and childless marriage with a displaced agricultural worker seeking work in the depressed city. *Grey Granite* is in many ways a cheerless book yet it faces, as few twentieth-century novels from Scotland have done, the city life, its challenges and realities. The Aberdeen of the novel, thinly disguised, is the breeding-ground for the internationalist and communist ideals of Ewan, Chris's son—as it was for the young reporter James Leslie Mitchell who had worked there. No nationalist, the novelist and his fictive character Ewan work not for a revival of the old Scotland, but for a newly created, juster and more free new Scotland. Chris, at the end of the trilogy, significantly returns to her native Scottish countryside, and Ewan marches off to London.

A prolific writer, Gibbon crammed into his short creative life a mass of miscellaneous work, intriguing science fiction, an excellent historical novel *Spartacus*, archaeological writing (he was a well informed amateur), polemics (including a devastating and witty survey, *Scottish Scene*, co-authored with Hugh MacDiarmid). Fame came slowly but steadily, and when he died with tragic suddenness in 1935, he seemed to have found his subject matter, and an important voice in which to give it shape.

Like his predecessor George Douglas Brown, Gibbon presents an enigma: where would he have gone on from his early successes? The fragments and unfinished projects make it difficult to speculate. His success in creating, above all in *Sunset Song*, a concentrated and vividly credible realistic picture of Scottish country life is astonishing. Style, characterisation, narrative technique fusing the most intimate personal observation with sardonic objective aside blend to form a picture of Chris—so intimate and so personal that she is never in danger of being only Chris 'Caledonia', a vehicle for the author's views on Scotland. A vehicle she has to be, and the technique works unsteadily, but by the end we are more moved by her personal bereavement than by the desolation of Kinraddie in 1918, at the sunset of a way of life killed by war. The novel describes both, and our consciousness of both endures.

Gibbon's work suffered years of general neglect, scarcity of publication, critical silence. From late in the 1970s there have been distinct signs of a long-overdue 'revival'—widespread teaching in schools, repeated republication (fittingly in the "Classics" series of the Canongate Press, as well as in the national and international vehicle of a Penguin Classic), and a steady move to republish his other work. His native village now houses a Grassic Gibbon Centre, his country now acknowledges him as a major author of the modern period. Criticism has at last tackled his style, his narrative innovation, his analysis of a country in change. He is, indeed, a classic. Had he lived, he would have found a voice large and flexible enough for the many-sided life of a modern Scotland. As it is, he did much more than celebrate the sunset of the old Scotland: he showed it was possible to write critically about life after the kailyard.

I. Campbell

Glasgow emerges into history in the early twelfth century with the appointment of Bishop John Achaius as bishop to the see of Glasgow and the building by him of Glasgow Cathedral. A charter granted later in the century by William the Lion to Bishop John's successor Jocelin shows that Glasgow was already a bishop's burgh and market town, and as such it flourished in a small way throughout the Middle Ages. The medieval picture is one of ecclesiastical overlords and active

merchants and craftsmen. Early in the fifteenth century the old wooden bridge across the Clyde was replaced by an eight-arched stone bridge, while in mid-century Pope Nicholas V was persuaded to issue a Bull founding the University of Glasgow. In January 1492 Pope Innocent VIII promoted the see of Glasgow to archiepiscopal rank.

Medieval Glasgow was dominated by the cathedral on high ground on the west bank of the Molendinar burn where St Kentigern or Mungo was traditionally supposed to have built his original wooden church. South from the cathedral towards the Clyde ran the High Street, which was crossed just below the Cathedral by Rotten Row coming in from the west and Drygate from the east. The cross formed the first centre of Glasgow. The second centre, which proved more permanent, was Glasgow Cross, where the north-south line of the High Street and its continuation Saltmarket was crossed by the Trongate and Gallowgate.

In 1656 Thomas Tucker, an Englishman sent by Cromwell to advise on Scottish excise and customs matters, reported that Glasgow 'seated in a pleasant and fruitful soil, consisting of four streets handsomely built in form of a cross, is one of the most considerable burghs of Scotland, as well for the structure as trade of it. The inhabitants, all but the students of the college, which is here, are traders and dealers.' In 1726 Daniel Defoe found Glasgow 'a very fine city' with its four principal streets 'the fairest for breadth, and the finest built that I have ever seen in one city together'. He praised the stone houses and admired their uniformity of height and front. He found Glasgow 'a city of business; here is the face of trade, as well foreign as home trade; ... The Union has answer'd its end to them more than to any other part of Scotland, for their trade is new form'd by it.' The Union of 1707 opened the American and West Indian colonies to Glasgow traders, and a spectacular increase in the tobacco trade resulted. Trading for tobacco in Virginia under what became known as the 'Glasgow store system' (which involved buying the crop outright from the planters before shipping it to the Clyde and also setting up their own stores in the tobacco colonies, furnished with goods brought in on their west-bound ships, where tobacco growers could buy on credit) brought great wealth and influence to the Glasgow 'tobacco lords' in the eighteenth century, who built themselves mansions to the west, thus encouraging the westward expansion of the city, which went on apace throughout the century. Sugar from the West Indies, with its by-product molasses, and rum made from molasses, was another source of Glasgow's eighteenth-century wealth. The American war posed a serious threat to Glasgow's tobacco trade, and after the war Glasgow merchants turned increasingly to cotton importing. The development first of the fine linen industry and then of the cotton industry brought a surge of new population into Glasgow both from the surrounding districts and from the West Highlands. In 1708 the population of the city was calculated as 12,766. In 1801 it was 83,769.

In the late eighteenth and early nineteenth centuries Glasgow became the centre of a cotton spinning region, with mills established by the sides of streams within a twenty-five-mile radius of the city. But the advent of the steam power-loom removed the need of water power and enabled the cotton workers to be herded into the city. The related industries of bleaching, dyeing and fabric printing developed rapidly in and around the city. In the same period Clyde shipping increased enormously, and produced attempts to improve the navigability of the river at Glasgow, and massive dredging and excavating, much of which took place in the fourth and fifth decades of the nineteenth century, eventually produced a channel 20 feet deep at low tide.

The coming of the steamship gave an enormous boost to Clyde shipbuilding, encouraged by the development of iron production and the expansion of the Lanarkshire coalfields. Shipbuilding and marine engineering both benefited from the proximity of supplies of iron and steel and expanded rapidly throughout the second half of the nineteenth century. This in turn further promoted the growth of the city's population, which rose to over half a million in 1891. By this time Glasgow had become part of the Clydeside conurbation, an area heavily dependent on shipbuilding and engineering. It was this dependence that made Glasgow so vulnerable to depression: in the 1930s a severe drop of the level of employment in the heavy industries of the Clyde Valley affected the consumer-goods industries and service trades of the city, so that the whole region became a 'depressed area'. This in turn encouraged the development of left-wing politics which ever since the successes of the Independent Labour Party in Glasgow in 1922 had made 'Red Clydeside' a by-word.

The rapid growth of Glasgow's population in the nineteenth century had serious social consequences: the emergence of slums, the stigmatizing of Glasgow in the Chadwick Report of 1842 as 'possibly the filthiest and unhealthiest of all the British towns of this period', represented the debit side of a picture of which the credit side was the undoubted wealth of the city and the building of some splendid Victorian architecture. Victorian Glasgow, the 'second city' of the Empire, was a city of pride and prosperity as well as of slums and squalor. The problem of Glasgow slums proved unusually intractable; the clearance of slum areas and the construction of massive high-rise buildings to take the displaced population in the mid-twentieth century, together with the decanting of certain sections of the population into specially designed peripheral estates and new towns, created as many new problems as those that were solved.

During the 1970s, the continuing clearance of the most neglected tenements and the destruction of some of the older parts of the city to make way for new road systems changed the face of much of Glasgow. At the same time, however, there was a growing appreciation of the intrinsic distinction of the city—in its architecture, its urban quality, and its rich culture. It was recognised as the finest surviving example of a great Victorian city, extensive parts were designated as conservation areas, and surviving tenemental quarters were improved and rehabilitated.

This change in the perception of Glasgow prepared the way for the well-publicised campaign of the mid-1980s, aimed to attract business investment and thereby reverse the decline of the economy of the city. National and international events—notably the Garden Festival (on reclaimed dockland) of 1988 and the European City of Culture of 1990—were designed not only for the entertainment of its citizens, but also to establish Glasgow on the European scene in the late twentieth-century post-industrial age. There is evidence of some success in this campaign: a recent (1992) survey of business attitudes has moved Glasgow well up the league of the European cities as a place to locate new enterprises.

The most obvious manifestations of this revival of Glasgow's fortunes are to be found in developments in the city centre: in the glazed-over shopping precincts of St Enoch Centre and Princes Square, in the curtain-walled offices and hotels around Blythswood Hill, and in the post-modern middle-class housing of the Merchant City. But there has also been massive public investment in less-privileged areas of the city. The Glasgow Eastern Area Renewal (GEAR) project (1976–1987), which reversed hitherto established policies of overspill and new town settlement, sought to improve the quality of life in one of the parts of the city most devastated by the earlier clearances; and, currently, the peripheral estates, to which many of the former inhabitants of the inner-city were transported in the 1950s, are undergoing extensive reconstruction.

The economic recession of the 1990s has, however, limited Glasgow's ability to further its ambitious programme of renewal. The population continues to decline (by 10 per cent in the 1980s), unemployment remains uncomfortably above the Scottish average, and there are still tracts of dereliction around the city centre. The seeds of regeneration will need nourishing for Glasgow once again to flourish.

D. Daiches and P. Reed

Glasgow School, The. Between 1882 and 1895 (approximately) a group of painters re-established the integrity of the art of painting in Scotland and brought a new vitality to it. There had been finer Scottish painters than any single one of the Glasgow School, or the Glasgow Boys as they preferred to call themselves, and William McTaggart, far more adventurous and committed, was developing his own kind of impressionism at that period which took him close to the mainstream of the new European masters, and yet the Glasgow Boys with a rather simple conviction of what was required, made a significant contribution to Scottish painting, a contribution which pointed a way forward. They shifted the emphasis from the dominant glossy, punctilious academicism, and from the enfeebling genre of 'every picture tells a story' school to an indissoluble respect for the object-in-paint. Their fundamental doctrine was that every picture was made of paint, and from the first brush-stroke the spectator was not to be allowed to forget this, and every subject was to be given its own value. This may appear so obvious that it is difficult to understand the excitement that the Boys created in the many paintings they exhibited in the Munich exhibitions from 1890. But they themselves came together spontaneously in a common cause against what they referred to as 'the glue-pot school', and the freshness and vigour of their paintings, especially when seen together as they may be in the Glasgow Art Galleries' collection, within the period of their first decade, is markedly felt. They began more from a resistance to what did not ring true, than from an articulated theory; and this may account for their dislike of being regarded as a School, and their preference for the term Boys, which suggests the robust zest in many of their paintings, and hints at the friendships which created their community. It also suggests how they could accept Bastien Lepage, who retained some degree of the sentimental in his paintings, particularly in the much admired *Le Mendiant* and *Pas Mech*, the portrait of a ragged but sweet-faced boy (*National Gallery of Scotland*), though there is also realism in the portrayal. The term Boys does not take account of the aesthetics implied in two remarkable works, *The Vegetable Stall* by W.Y. Macgregor and *Galloway Landscape* by George Henry, and there were others. It may explain how rapidly their force as a group was dissipated.

In a letter to Dr T. J. Honeyman (9 January, 1941) R. Macaulay Stevenson stated that there were 23 Glasgow Boys. One cannot be certain of the membership of those on the periphery, for there was no such thing as card-carrying. In any case it could be stated that just over half that number truly belonged to the group, others claimed for it by William Buchanan in his admirable catalogue for his exhibition, *The Glasgow Boys*, at the Glasgow Art Gallery and Museum (September 1968), such as Sir D.Y. Cameron and Sir George Pirie simply show its influence. The character and strength of the School was determined by a few artists. At the centre were two painters and two locations.

In 1883 James Guthrie (1859–1930), with E.A. Walton (1860–1922), discovered the village of Cockburnspath in Berwickshire. The landscape in which the village is set is undramatic. The absence of Highland characteristics with inevitable romantic associations, demanded a reappraisal of its aesthetic possibilities. The exquisite landscapes of Walton witness to a linear interest in the gentle unfolding of pastoral vistas and to the dappling of light by the scattered trees. These provided for Walton's sensitive 'poetic' painting. On the other hand the fields under cultivation with people at work called for the recognition of substance, and this is acknowledged particularly in Guthrie's landscapes. Guthrie had already painted his large, rather weighty, *Highland funeral*, (1882—Glasgow Art Gallery and Museum), It was, however, his *To Pastures New* (1882–83—Aberdeen Art Gallery) with the sensation of *en plein air* about it and the ample figure of the girl with geese, which pointed the way to the more interesting realization of *A Hind's Daughter*, in which the girl stands stolid in the field of cabbages and brussels sprouts, these alive with flecks of light, as if, despite the failure of any member of the Glasgow School to admit the full impact of impressionism, its presence is felt.

Cockburnspath provided parameters which, while encompassing a range of interests, gave a sense of relatedness to the paintings of Guthrie and his friends, Walton, Crawhall (1861–

1913), Henry (1858–1943), Whitelaw Hamilton (1860–1932), and T. Corsan Morton (1859–1928). The controlling factor was not, of course, the place, but like the Barbizon, it suited the growing understanding of the objectives of the School. Implicitly and explicitly the lively, witty portrait of *Crawhall* (1884—Scottish National Portrait Gallery) by Walton indicates the middle ground on which the School stood. Crawhall is depicted, pipe in hand with mud on his boots, standing at ease in front of the back of a large canvas a chance moment caught. Top right of the canvas are the words—partly obliterated: 'Joe Crawhall the Impressionist by E.A. Walton the Realist'. Informality, spontaneity and implied comment gave life to the portraits of the Boys throughout the 1880s. Realism and impressionism combine in *The Fur Boa* (1892—Glasgow Art Gallery) by William Kennedy (1859–1918). There were other more specific influences—those of Whistler and Bastien Lepage, who advised Lavery (1856–1941): 'Always carry a sketch book. Select a person—watch him—then put down as much as you remember. At first you will find very little, but continue and you will soon get the complete action.' Lavery's responsive brush to movement and to social style is seen at work in *The Tennis Party* 1885—Aberdeen Art Gallery) and the grand style of life is registered with immediacy in his portrait of *R.B. Cunninghame Graham* (1893—Glasgow Art Gallery and Museum) but Lavery's society interests were to betray his skills. Making evident the properties of the medium was not confined to painters as may be gathered from the *Maquette for the Burns Statue* (1895—Aberdeen Art Gallery) by Pittendrigh Macgillivray, the one sculptor of the School. It announces the handling of the plastic material throughout. This is no more than an honest professionalism, but allied to a sensitiveness to what was to be perceived, it gave that freedom in painting which refreshed the art of painting in Scotland.

Almost any of the paintings of bird or beast by Crawhall testify to this, none more so than his gouache, *The Pigeon* (c. 1890—*Glasgow Art Gallery and Museum*) or there are the glowing water-colours of Arthur Melville (1855–1904), though here atmosphere is everything. *The Vegetable Stall* by W.Y. Macgregor requires different terms of reference for comment, which brings us to the consideration of the second major influence and location of the group.

By about 1881 W.Y. Macgregor (1855–1923) was holding life classes in his studio at 134 Bath Street, Glasgow to which came James Paterson (1854–1952), Corsan Morton, Alexander Roche (1861–1921), Lavery, Hornel (1864–1933) and Millie Dow (1848–1919). Henry, Walton and Crawhall also attended. Discussion and criticism were free, but, it would appear the voice of Macgregor, the son of a Glasgow shipbuilder was dominant. 'Hack the subject out as you would were you using an axe' said the painter generally regarded as the 'father of the school', 'and try to realize it; get its bigness. Don't follow any school, there are no schools in art.'

The advice was not always heeded. The exuberance, richness of colour and decorative effects of Hornel, after *A Galloway Idyll* (1890) and *The Dance of Spring* (1890–1893—Glasgow Art Gallery and Museum)—both of which paintings acknowledge the linear rhythm of the Galloway landscape—lose touch with a basic reality. Regrettably a feature of the work of the Boys, just when it suggested it was achieving a focus which might lead to an independent vision, was simply dissipation. When Stuart Park wrote of flower-painting that it should have 'adequate carrying power', and having by this time painted his *Roses* (1889—Glasgow Art Gallery and Museum) with its formal strength in the petals, one felt that he had listened to Macgregor and looked with understanding at Cezanne, but his development was a glossy prettiness.

Macgregor was different. In 1884 he painted *The Vegetable Stall*. Oskar Kokoschka, in front of this picture in the National Gallery of Scotland said to Stanley Cursiter, then Director of the Gallery: 'To think that picture was painted before I was born—and I never knew!' In its truth to the colour and substance of the vegetables the painting has the directness of a new realism. It has 'carrying power'. It is as if the rhubarb, leeks, potatoes and turnips, strewn on the stall had created their own aesthetic. In this respect the painting has similarities to Henry's *A Galloway Landscape* (1889—Glasgow Art Gallery and Museum). The landscape in the area of Galloway which gave rise to the painting is distinctly odd. The rhythms of the sloping fields are broken up with bushes and protuberances. This counter to fluency gives an energy to the scene that suggests the presence of natural forces. Henry has summed up the condition in his painting. The strong rhythm of the stream allies itself to that of the small hills as if to contain a latent force. This is no decorative effect. Macgregor's *Vegetable Stall* and Henry's *A Galloway Landscape* are the only supreme achievements of the Glasgow School.

G. Bruce

Golf. From the outset Scotland played a major part in the shaping of the modern game of golf, indeed Scotland remains prominent in what has become an extremely popular pastime throughout the developed world. Scotland can with justification claim to be the 'home of modern golf', insofar as it was here, primarily on east-coast links terrain between 1730 and 1900, that the format of the modern game evolved.

Dr Robert Price in *Scotland's Golf Courses* writes of four distinct phases in the development process. The origins pre-1735; the early Scottish Golfing Societies or Clubs 1735–1849; expansion, the organisation of the sport and the development of equipment 1850–1899 and the Modern era since 1900. A selective but comprehensive piecing together of evidence relating to the origins is to be found in *A Swing through Time, Golf in Scotland 1457–1743*, compiled by Olive Geddes. The book uses the earliest written records to shed light on golf's birth, the techniques and equipment used and the social standing of the game.

The earliest known written reference to golf in Scotland dates from 1457, when Parliament decreed that, 'ye fit bawe and ye golf be uterly cryt done and not usyt'. Instead the people were to practise their archery. The 1457 Act does not specify where golf was being played, but if it was in enclosed spaces such as churchyards and streets, as many golfing historians have surmised, the potential hazards can easily be imagined. The links, as areas of open, common land along a coastal strip, provided a better location for golf, although they also accommodated common grazing, military training and a range of recreations. They were in effect the people's playground. That it was necessary to repeat the ban of 1457 in 1471 and 1491, suggests that even the combined efforts of Parliament, the Town Councils, the Kirk Sessions, and the Guilds, were not entirely successful.

There is little certainty about the origin of the word 'golf', other than its possible derivation from Dutch 'kolf' or 'colf', meaning 'club', suggesting an indeterminate connection with club-and-ball games in the Low Countries. All attempts to prove that golf originated in Holland or anywhere else than Scotland have failed. One of the most distinctive features of golf is the difference in the number of clubs the player uses. Only one other game, 'Jeu de mail', is known to have reached even the two-club stage of evolution. But golf was probably past that stage in James IV's time; well past it by 1629, when the Earl of Montrose sent a lad to St Andrews to collect 'sax new clubs' and 'sum auld clubs'.

Olive Geddes' writings take us to 1743, and the eve of the founding of the earliest societies or golf clubs as they became. The oldest, the Honourable Company of Edinburgh golfers dates back from 1744, when the City of Edinburgh had a silver club made for annual competition on Leith Links. Those who agreed to play in the first contest drew up a code of rules, which was also adopted by the Society of Golfers formed at St Andrews in 1754. This, now the famous Royal and Ancient is the governing body for the game world-wide. By the end of the century there were ten clubs, and twenty by 1848, when the traditional leather ball was generally replaced by the 'gutty', which, being much cheaper and more durable, led to an enormous increase in the number of golfers, and to the substitution of irons for most of the woods. There were only some 17 courses in Scotland in 1848. After modest growth until the late 1870s, course numbers increased dramatically between 1890 and 1910, followed by a more gradual growth until the boom of the 1980s in Scotland and abroad.

In 1993 there are approximately 700 clubs in Scotland, 450 course-owning. In addition there are some 50 public-courses and a small number of proprietorial or commercial developments, generally linked to hotels or estates. The game was originally and for many years, the preserve of wealthier male adults but junior (boy) memberships, and more recently the growth of opportunities for lady and girl golfers have followed. Many clubs continue with Associate, rather than full membership, rights for women golfers. Yet many restrictions are disappearing as opportunities increase for men, women and children to learn, to play and to enjoy the game.

Golf is also a competitive sport, and the Open Championship (the first professional strokeplay competition, instituted in 1860) has played a prominent part in popularising the game. Rising playing standards, the organisational expertise of the R and A, media and commercial interests, ensure that the Open

Championship is a major annual event in the golf and sporting calendar across the world.

The game is currently played in over 60 countries and there are professional tours (major series of competitions for full-time tournament golfers), covering Europe, North America, Asia, Australasia and Africa. The game remains prominent within Scotland's sporting fabric; golf clubs are a focal point within most Scottish communities. Consistent with the fact that it has been from Scotland that many of the leading players, teachers, course designers and administrators have come and spread their influence on golf throughout the world.

A. Chainey

Gow, family (18th c–19th c). The Gow family—father and sons and uncle—are still revered as the leading composers, music publishers and, above all, fiddlers in a tradition which still flourishes today. The father Niel (1727–1807) was employed by the Duke of Atholl, but played regularly at society dances as well as local ceilidhs, his brother providing a bass part on cello. Niel's energetic bowing style in strathspeys was legendary, but he was a distinguished composer of slow airs such as the *Lament for the Death of his Second Wife*, and his dance tunes for reels, strathspeys, jigs and hornpipes are among the most characteristic and stylish ever written. His son Nathaniel started life as a Scottish state trumpeter, but is remembered as a violinist, composer and publisher—chiefly of his father's compositions. Niel's other sons, William, Andrew and John, also played and composed for fiddle.

J. Purser

Grahame, Kenneth (1859–1932) was the son of an Edinburgh advocate and great grand-nephew of the minor poet James Grahame (1765–1811) whose poem 'The Sabbath' is still sometimes quoted in anthologies. Kenneth Grahame's mother died when he was young, so he was brought up by his grandmother in Berkshire and educated at St Edward's School, Oxford. He joined the Bank of England, and eventually became its Secretary from 1898 to 1907.

His children's classic *The Wind in the Willows*, written to amuse his son Alastair (who died in his twenty-first year) was published in 1908, and has been constantly in print ever since, the adventures of Rattie, Mole and Toad of Toad Hall (under which title A.A. Milne later dramatized the story) offering fresh appeal to each succeeding generation. Grahame's other books included *The Golden Age* (1895) and *Dream Days* (1898).

M. Lindsay

Gray, Sir Alexander (1882–1968) was an Angus man, educated at Dundee High School and the Universities of Edinburgh, Gottingen and Paris. His academic record was a brilliant one. After service with various governmental departments he became Jaffray Professor of Political Economy at Aberdeen University in 1921 and Professor of Political Economy and Mercantile Law at Edinburgh University in 1935, where he remained until his retirement in 1956. He was a member or the chairman of several government commissions. In 1939 he was made a CBE and in 1949 KT. Both Aberdeen and St Andrews Universities conferred on him their LLD degree.

He wrote much on his own academic subjects, but is more generally remembered by a handful of poems, some of them from originals by Heine or European balladry, which he successfully 're-created' into Scots, notably 'The Deil O'Bogie' and 'The Fine Fechtin' Moose'. These 're-creations' and the best of his original work are to be found in his *Selected Poems* (1948), to which he later added *Sir Halewyn* (1949) and *Four and Forty* (1954).

M. Lindsay

Grierson, John, popularly known as the 'father of the documentary film', was born in Stirlingshire in 1898. He studied film in the US from 1924 to 27 and on his return to the UK established a documentary film unit which brought together many of the brightest talent of the day to pursue Grierson's social purposes. These purposes could be defined as 'citizenship education' and in films such as *Drifters*, *Night Mail* and *Coal Face*, Grierson presented to the public at large aspects of the Nation at work. These films became models for documentary activity around the world and Grierson himself participated in the establishment of the National Film Board of Canada where, as the Board's Director, he moved beyond national concern to global ones. He died in 1972.

D. Bruce

Grieve, Christopher Murray *see* **MacDiarmid, Hugh**

Gunn, Neil Miller (1891–1974) born at Dunbeath, Caithness, was the son of a fishing-boat skipper and the seventh of nine children who survived. Gunn was educated at the village school and, less formally, as he himself put it, in solitude as 'the prehistoric boy in a modern strath ... the nut-cracking young savage on his river stone'. In 1906 Gunn became a civil servant, working first in London then in Edinburgh, and from 1934 as a Customs and Excise Officer in Inverness. In 1937, to the consternation of his colleagues, among them the Irish novelist Maurice Walsh, he abandoned his pension rights by leaving the service to devote himself entirely to literature. Thereafter, he made his home in various parts of the Highlands, for a time near Cannich and finally at North Kessock.

His first novel, *The Grey Coast* (1926), attracted Scottish attention, but he won a European reputation with *Morning Tide* (1931), ostensibly about a boy bred for the sea, and his reaction to the skill and bravery of his brother and father in a storm, but concerned about the economic disintegration of the old way of Highland life, forcing Alan, Hugh's brother, to emigrate.

Sun Circle (1933) probes back to the impact of the Vikings on the Picts, and the fusing of the two peoples. *Butcher's Broom*

(1934) again deals with the tearing up of human roots under the pressures of the Clearances. *Highland River* (1931) is about another boy with the 'swallow of life in his hand', and the story also symbolizes the river of life. It was awarded the Tait Black Memorial Prize. *The Silver Darlings* (1941), considered by many to be Gunn's finest achievement, is a splendid sweep of a story, dealing with a social situation resulting from the enforced movement of the Highland people from their cleared straths to the coast, and the resulting development of the fishing industry.

The middle-period Gunn novels leave behind them the trappings of Highland history and explore the landscape of the Highland mind. In *The Green Isle of the Great Deep* (1944), Young Art and Old Hector (themselves the title of a subsequent novel) seek out the hazelnuts of knowledge. In *The Serpent* (1943) and *The Drinking Well* (1946) the placing of the symbolism is inherent in the title. In both books young people leave the Highlands to go to cities, Glasgow in the one case, Edinburgh in the other, eventually returning to their native places to find the sources of true wisdom.

As a novelist, Gunn never quite came to terms with the problems of urban society, and in his later years retreated behind a cover of Zen Buddhism. His final novels, *The Key of the Chest* (1945), *The Shadow* (1948) and *Bloodhunt* (1952) all reflect his attempts to deal with the problem of violence in society.

An outline of Gunn's philosophy is contained in his autobiographical volume, *The Atom of Delight* (1952).

Much to his embarrassment, Gunn's work became popular in Nazi Germany, and most of his 1930s novels were translated into German. The English-reading public that had taken him up so enthusiastically before the war were much less enthusiastic in their support for his later novels, and he published no novels at all during the last 21 years of his life. But the strong survival qualities of his style, his unravelling of the Highland character and his understanding of the interweavings of Highland history, together make him by far the most important novelist to come out of northern Scotland, a fact now being recognized by the republication of most of his early and middle-period works.

M. Lindsay

H

Hallowe'en *see* **Festivities and Customs, Seasonal**

Handwriting. Few specimens of Scottish handwriting survive from before the twelfth century. They are mostly religious manu-

scripts, such as the ninth-century volume associated with the Celtic monastery of Deer, which is written in the Insular script practised by Irish and Anglo-Saxon scribes. Hands based on Insular forms were used for Scottish Gaelic texts until *c.* 1750.

The Latin texts, most of them religious or legal in character, that were produced from the twelfth to the fifteenth century were written with a quill on parchment and (from the fourteenth century) paper. Writing was at first a rare accomplishment, restricted to churchmen and scribes trained for the needs of the church who were subsequently employed in royal government. Eventually clerks were trained within the secular administrative departments and by the late thirteenth century were joined by another group of professional penmen, notaries public.

The scripts practised by these writers fall into three categories: book hand, used for liturgical and 'literary' texts; charter hand, used for the most formal of legal documents; and court, or business, hand, used for legal and administrative purposes. For most of the Middle Ages forms of book hand (called Gothic or Text) were upright and angular, with accentuation of light and heavy strokes of the quill and, in some cases, the addition of serifs. Charter hand was an adaptation of book hand with lengthened stems and tails. Court hand had many forms, representing stages of evolution towards cursiveness and hence speed. Their writers made extensive use of abbreviation, by contracting and suspending words, to ensure an economic use of space and regularity in margins and lines.

From roughly 1450 to 1550 there were signs of growing literacy in the noble, landed and mercantile classes: documents were often signed as well as sealed, for example. The invention of printing had rendered book hand largely obsolete, but court hand was practised in increasingly free forms, until in the 1520s there emerged in Scotland as in England an all-purpose script, Secretary Hand, distinguished by its epsilon-e, the descending leftward curve of the h, the circular k, the two-stemmed r, and the long approach strokes to certain letters. Originally an upright script, it later acquired a slope when executed at speed. Alongside it appeared Italic, created by the scholars of Humanism and imported for private and official use by Scots who had studied under them.

In the next 150 years penmanship again became an art— Esther Inglis (d. 1624) was a noted calligrapher. The subject was now widely taught by writing-masters, who set up schools and published copy-books: David Brown, for example, taught writing in the grammar school of Edinburgh, and his *Calligraphia* was printed at St Andrews in 1622. The scripts they taught included forms of Secretary and Italic (later called Roman) and hybrids of the two, whence sprang, late in the seventeenth century, Round Hand.

During the eighteenth century Round Hand predominated, acquiring a slope and looped stems and tails. During the nineteenth century the use of fine steel pens enabled up-and-downstrokes to be thinned and thickened, and elaborate ornamentation added. A report on parochial schools in 1854 advocated 'a fair, round, symmetrical hand' and bitterly criticized fashionable decoration. In the course of the twentieth century, Scotland has shared in the Italic Revival: her leading exponent of the script is Tom Gourdie.

C. A. McLaren

Hay, George Campbell/Deòrsa Mac Iain Deòrsa (1915– 1984) was born in Argyll, the son of J. MacDougall Hay the Scottish novelist, author of *Gillespie*. A graduate of Oxford University and a keen student of languages he worked as a translator in Edinburgh in the years before his death in 1984. George Campbell Hay has published translations from many European languages into Gaelic and this has been a useful service to his fellow Gaels, but it is as an original poet of stature in Gaelic (and indeed in Scots) that he has made his most important contribution.

Hay's earlier work such as we find in some of the poems in *Fuaran Sléibh* (1947) is concerned, among other preoccupations, with exploring the potential of traditional Gaelic metres for expressing both traditional themes with contemporary implications and these new to Gaelic poetry. His technical ability is clearly evidenced in this early work and it lays a secure foundation for his later poetry where the craftsmanship is always of a high order. This early verse also served to reintroduce into Gaelic verse some of the features and effects of classical verse, which had by then been to some degree lost, in a guise in which they were acceptable to modern readers, and, indeed, exciting to those interested in the craft of verse-making.

Of importance also, for example, is Hay's interest in natural description and his ability to express that interest in simple language and complex verse. This is well exemplified in a poem like 'Do Bheithe Bóidheach' ('To a Bonny Birch Tree'). The structure of this poem reveals characteristic features of his style and method. The first stanza establishes the visual dimensions of space and height:

A cloud sailing in the sky
foliage between it and my eye.

Then we have a stanza where the tree is an image of a musical instrument played on by the wind

harp of the wind your stringed top,
the tendrils of the branches play tunes.

The third stanza sees the tree as a magical object, a 'jewel', 'a fairy land' for the birds. The final stanza asserts that better than all these attributes is simply to see the tree itself

gently nodding,
slender, entwined, fresh, with interlacing top,
and dew in beads on each bough.

The poem, which on the face of it seems simple, is in fact constructed with great care, with elaborate systems of rhyme, assonance and alliteration. But the elaboration and care are unobtrusive and subsumed in the artistic whole. Other poems of Hay's dealing with natural phenomena show the same exceptional gifts for seeing and expressing.

The early preoccupation with this kind of verse develops in Hay at a later period to a poetry which looks at man with compassion and insight. The change in preoccupation appears to coincide, to a considerable degree, with Hay's experiences of the Second World War. Europe, for example,

the ancient sanctuary of art
the tender heart of humanity

he sees as reduced to 'a promontory of Asia' with all her finest features destroyed.

The war becomes more central still in the poem which describes the town of Bizerta burning during the night watch. He sees the fire as an evil creature clapping its wings, so powerful that it 'dims the stars'. It interferes with the structure of the universe, and yet it is silent. This silence suggests to him the part anonymity plays in the tolerating of war:

What is their name tonight
the poor streets ...?
And who tonight are ...
shouting in frenzy for help and are not heard?

Related to such experiences and no doubt pointing up resemblances with crofters in Argyll is the poem 'Atman'. Atman had 'thieved from necessity' and is whipped and jailed; his basic crime was poverty, and Hay very clearly aligns himself with him against a justice that is blinded by 'scrutinizing its account books'. Atman's eye could still 'derive pleasure from the shape of the world', and he was worth knowing.

His experiences in the Middle East seem also to have reawakened in Hay an aspect of his early work seen in poems such as the one to 'Kintyre' in *Fuaran Slèibh*. This is reflected now in nationalistic and inspirational verse such as 'The Duty of the Heights' which exhorts the youth of Scotland to aim for the high places for that is the only way to avoid 'destruction ... as a landslide'. It is also seen in, for example, the poem 'Meftah Bâbkum es-Babar' ('Patience is the Key to our Door') which takes this Arabic saying as a text and denies its application:

Seek in our new handiwork
sore rough rejoicing life

Otherwise we will be 'a thing demeaned hidden in a corner'.

These same preoccupations are to be seen in Hay's later work. Among his publications are *Fuaran Sléibh* (1947); *Wind on Loch Fyne* (1948); *O na Ceithir Airdean* (1952); *Mochtàr is Dùghall* (1982); contributions to *Four Points of a Saltire* (1970) and to *Nua-Bhàrdachd Ghàaidhlig* (1976); and many poems in occasional publications. A complete collection of his verse is being prepared for publication.

D. MacAulay

Henryson, Robert (*c*.1420–*c*.1490). Almost every aspect of Henryson's life and work raises problems. The only reasonably certain biographical facts are that in 1462 he was incorporated in the recently founded University of Glasgow, that he was then a Licentiate in Arts and Bachelor in Decreits, and was described as *vir venerabilis;* that three times in 1478 he witnessed deeds in Dunfermline, and was styled notary public; and that he was dead by 1508, the year in which Dunbar's 'Quhen he was seik' was printed by Chepman and Myllar. It seems likely that he was a graduate of a Continental university, and as his poetry contains social criticism which can more easily be read in terms of the reign of James III (1460–1488) than of that of James IV (1488–1513), it seems likely that he had given up poetry, perhaps was dead, by about 1488. No one under the age of 35 is likely to have been described as *venerabilis;* it therefore seems likely that Henryson was born before 1427. He is first described as 'Schoolmaster in Dunfermline' in 1571, some 80 years after his death, and if there is any truth in the description, he probably moved from Glasgow to Dunfermline in or about 1468, when the abbot of Dunfermline provided a house for the town schoolmaster together with lands and rents worth 11 merks yearly for the maintenance of poor scholars to be taught there gratuitously.

There are also many uncertainties about the poetry. The collection known as *The Morall Fabillis of Esope the Phrygian* is, as it stands, probably an editorial creation of the second half of the sixteenth century. There is no independent manuscript evidence that Henryson himself grouped the poems as they appear in the Charteris and Bassandyne prints of 1570 and 1571 respectively, and good evidence that he did not. The separate existence, for example, of a three-part beast epic, *The Tod*, is proved by internal textual evidence, and by the introductory sentence in the Bannatyne manuscript (1568). *The Tod*, like *The Wolf that gat the Nekhering throw the wrinkis of the Foxe that begylit the Cadgear*, and *The Wolf and the Lamb*, contains no reference to Aesop, while the references in *The Preiching of the Swallow* and *The Lyoun and the Mous* differ from the simple introductory phrases in the majority of fables. It seems likely, in fact, that the collection juxtaposes at least four items; the 'translatioun' of Aesop to which Henryson refers in his *Prolog;* the more elaborate and independent *The Preiching of the Swallow*, linked by a second *Prolog* to its sequel, *The Lyoun and the Mous; The Tod*, and a group of separate tales. The generally accepted text contains many verbal corruptions, some the result of Protestant censorship after the Reformation. No satisfactory edition at present (1980) exists.

Two other long poems have survived. *The Testament of Cresseid* forms a supplement and correction to Chaucer's *Troilus and Criseyde. New Orpheus (Orpheus and Eurydice)* is an elaborate account of the journey to Hell made by Orpheus in an attempt to bring his wife, Eurydice, back from the dead. It is followed by a long *moralitas*, and the poem as a whole represents Henryson's most extended attempt at the fable form. His most important shorter poems are 'Robene and Makyne', 'The Garmont of Gud Ladeis', 'The Bluidy Serk', 'The Prais of Aige' and 'The Annunciation'. It seems likely that some poems have been lost; it is, indeed, a minor miracle that anything at all has survived the vicissitudes of the sixteenth and seventeenth centuries.

Henryson has the broadest sweep of all the early Scottish poets. His felicity, as well as his virtuosity, with language and metre is less ostentatious than Dunbar's, and so to some extent has passed unnoticed. His greatness is most plainly to be seen in the range of general principles and ideas which informs his poetry, allowing it to encompass equally tragedy, satire, complaint, comedy and lyric. His tragedy is of a philosophic, even Platonic, kind in terms of which calamity results from neglect of the contemplative life, regarded by Henryson as both the summit of human existence, and the way of transcending that existence, otherwise necessarily confined to the deceitful world of material things. It is her own negligence which makes Cresseid the victim of the seven planets, from whose prison she escapes only when she accepts responsibility for her own past actions. Orpheus, the rational soul, brings his music to almost perfect accord with the Platonic Soul of the World, but a moment's forgetfulness prevents the redemption from Hell of the lower appetitive soul, his wife Eurydice, and both are lost. *The Preiching of the Swallow* and *The Paddok and the Mous* follow the same pattern, and stop short of the tragic only because the actors are presented in animal rather than human form. Pythagorean and Platonic numerology plays a part in all these poems.

Complaint is most obviously to be seen in the *moralitates* of *The Scheip and the Doig* and *The Wolf and the Lamb*. In most of the remaining fables satire is mixed with a comedy that can sometimes be astringent. *The Uponlandis Mous and the Burges Mous, The Foxe that begylit the Wolf in the schadow of the Mone, The Wolf and the Wedder* and 'Robene and Makyne' are pure comedy which sometimes approaches farce. Henryson's lyric gift found its finest expression in the elaborate *Complaints* of *The Testament of Criseyde* and *New Orpheus*, the bell-like modulations of 'The Annunciation', and most unusually perhaps in the joyfulness of 'The Prais of Aige'—'The more of age, the nerar hevynnis blisse'—a joyfulness directly resulting from the otherworldliness, which, despite the profusion of realistic and even ugly detail, is the keynote of Henryson's poetry.

J. MacQueen

Heraldry. Students of ceremonial and proto-heraldry should read Professor A.M. Hocart's *Kingship* (OUP, 1927) and his *Kings and Councillors* (Cairo, 1936). Through Hermes and Agni, he demonstrates the original equation of inviolable heralds with both the Ancient Greek *kerux* and the Vedic *brahman*. Both originate alike in duly invested mouthpieces of the divine king: separated over the aeons into those who speak for the king, and those who speak for the divinity. When ritually invested in an archaic form of the royal garments, the highest herald becomes himself a substitute king: remotely akin to the *archon basileus* of Athens' golden age or the *rex sacrorum* of republican Rome. In Scotland today, it's sufficient in this very ancient context to note that, when the Lord Lyon King of Arms is dressed in the royal tabard which is the Queen's most sacrosanct personal coat, he is inviolable and the voice of his proclamation is the Voice of the Sovereign. Put more dramatically, Lyon, the highest herald of all, with armorial jurisdiction throughout the whole realm of Scotland, is not only a law lord: he is a King, with a crown of his own. In a sense, he is the custodian of that Spirit of Caledonia which is allegorically incarnate in the Queen.

Glimpses of a still pagan Dark Age world nearer to the dawn of heraldry survive in romantic symbolism that became Christianized in the armorial art of the Age of Chivalry. The boat of Freya doubtless became the Black Galley that appears in the Arms of the group of west Highland families related to Olaf, King of Mann and the Isles (1103–1153), descended from Norse sea-kings whose pagan Ynglingar forebears had incarnated the god-spirit Frey. Again, an interesting Scottish study might supplement Sir Anthony Wagner's 'The Swan Badge and the Swan Knight' (*Archaeologia*, xcvii, 1959) and explain how such great Scottish medieval houses as Kennedy and Wemyss, Stirling and Lindsay and the Thanes of Cawdor came to bear the coveted swan badge. For their contemporaries, Cleves and Gonzaga and Hohenzollern, Bohun and Henry V and Warwick the Kingmaker, all had female line descents from the House of Lorraine who claimed descent from the legendary Guarin of Lorraine or Lotharingian Garin—Lohengrin the Swan Knight.

Certainly Scotland formed part of the world and ethos of armorial Heraldry from the very beginning. The dawn of systematic Armory as we know it, in the sense of hereditary as opposed to merely personal coats of arms—whether displayed also on shield or banner—took place throughout Western Christendom during the second quarter of the twelfth century. This period not only coincided with the reign of Olaf of Mann and the Isles, common ancestor of the Galley coats mentioned above, but then still subject to Norwegian paramountcy. It also coincided on the Scottish mainland precisely with the reign of our most chivalric king, David the Saint (1124–1153), whose friends when he was Earl of Huntingdon, and whose principal companions and courtiers after his accession to the throne, were at the heart of the rapidly evolving new fashion.

Dr J.H. Round's analyses of the English groups of families bearing Arms based on the coats before 1150 of the comital houses of Mandeville and Clare, relate to a number of nobles who must have been personally well known to King David. But Geoffrey H. White's more recent work on 'the Warenne group of checkered shields' (G.E.C. vol. xii, pt i, 1953) based on the gold-&-blue checkers of Count Ralph of Vermandois at the same period, may be considered conclusive for Scotland too. For Count Ralph's niece Ada de Warenne married in 1139 our King David's son and heir Henry, then Earl of Huntingdon and in 1152 styled *Rex Designatus* shortly before he predeceased his father. This lady, who belonged so conspicuously to one of the groups of families most closely identified with the dawn of heraldry, was the mother of our kings Malcolm the Maiden and William the Lyon.

Indeed, our later Stewart dynasty's Anglo-Breton progenitor Walter fitz Alan, created first Great Steward of Scotland and granted the vast fief of Renfrew by King David I, was of an age to have arrived in Scotland among the relations or family connections of Ada de Warenne in 1139; and it seems likely that the famous Stewart checkers—blue-and-silver across a golden field—also belong to the 'Warenne group of checkered shields'. Another famous Scottish coat traceable to the actual dawn of heraldry is that of the twelfth-century Hay lords of Erroll, who already bore on their earliest seals the same three (red) escutcheons (on silver) as the sires de La Haye Hue in the Cotentin peninsula of Normandy whence they sprang.

So Scotland has belonged to the general stream of Western European heraldry from the very beginning. Within this mainstream, Scotland falls into the West Frankish as opposed to the East Frankish branch. Among the East Franks, predominantly the Germans of the Holy Roman Empire, *whole families* rather than individuals had rank and Arms: so that *all* the members of a comital family such as Stolberg were Counts and all tended to bear the same Arms. Among the West Franks, especially the French and their allies, *individuals* had personal rank and Arms: so that only one member of a comital family such as Hay was Earl of Erroll and bore the plain Arms at any one time, and each other member of his family wore instead a 'differenced' and separate personal version of the basic family 'three escutcheons' coat. One Hay cadet might add a blue border, another Hay cadet might charge an ox-yoke above the three escutcheons: but their Chief alone wore the original coat. Scotland, with her close links with France even before the Auld Alliance, belonged from the first to this latter and more systematic school of heraldry, and is still the country which adheres most closely to it in all its original purity.

We learn from a French herald of the fourteenth century that every Christian realm should have 13 heraldic royal officers-of-arms for ceremonial purposes: as did therefore both Scotland and England. *The English of course still do*. But a Whitehall economy drive in 1867 reduced Scotland's number to seven: the Lord Lyon, three Heralds and three Pursuivants, instead of our true establishment's six heralds and six pursuivants. The heralds are paid £25 a year each, and the pursuivants get £16—no nonsense about expenses—so the drastic cutting of our Scottish establishment in half, which has caused immense inconvenience ever since, saves the United Kingdom the paltry sum of £123 a year. The seven survivors are, however, of course still members of the Scottish Royal Household. For particular occasions, usually when an ordinary royal officer is not available, the Lord Lyon occasionally appoints an *ad hoc* unpaid Pursuivant-Extraordinary named after one of two royal palaces, Falkland or Linlithgow. And in accordance with medieval practice, for very special occasions, when everybody is needed to make up for our 1867 loss, Lyon borrows one or more of the three surviving private pursuivants of our medieval earldoms: Slains Pursuivant, officer of the Lord High Constable (the Earl of Erroll), Endure Pursuivant of the Earl of Crawford, and Garioch Pursuivant of the Countess of Mar.

A coat of Arms is regarded as property like a piece of land, that is to say it's what is legally known as incorporeal heritage. And the Scottish attitude to such property has always been sensible and practical. Once upon a time, a man might sell his farm to several different people, give them all charters, and then abscond. To prevent this, the Sasine Register was set up by statute in 1617 to record such charters as were *prima facie* valid, and then a prescriptive period of some years was allowed during which aggrieved challengers could come forward to disprove their validity: after which the registered charter title was good, and every landholder knew where he stood.

Similarly, it was reasonably thought that while nobody was obliged to have a coat of arms, nobody ought to be so ridiculous as to want a bogus one, let alone be allowed to usurp somebody else's. So in 1672 a similar statute set up Lyon Register, in which anybody (or his heirs after him) who could prove a pre-1672 right to arms, could record it—subject to a similar prescriptive period to allow for challenge—and it was thereafter illegal to use an unregistered coat.

The administration of Lyon Register was entrusted to the Lord Lyon, assisted in the daily work of Lyon Office by the then Lyon Clerk. They are royal officers on fixed salaries, assisted by secretaries who are civil servants. *All* the fees payable for granting or recording Arms in Lyon Register go direct to HM Exchequer as a form of revenue-raising taxation: apart from paying the particular painter who has to do the actual painting of the entry and extract. Lyon Court would not have it otherwise, lest it be thought they had a pecuniary interest in its decisions. There is also a Procurator-Fiscal of Lyon Court to prosecute those who use unregistered Arms without authority and thereby deprive the Inland Revenue of its rightful dues.

Cadets are entitled by right to a duly 'differenced' version of the basic coat of the Chief of their Name; so they are armigerous by birth (including bastards). But they may not use Arms until their genealogy is proved before the law-lord Lyon in his *judicial* capacity, and their particular mark of 'difference' has then been agreed with his lordship and duly 'matriculated' in Lyon Register. In his *ministerial* capacity, Lyon the King-substitute will also grant and record new Arms to suitable people of good character who have not got any already.

It may be thought that with so wide an eligibility to be 'ranked among the noblesse of Scotland' by bearing Arms, we would soon reach the Gilbertian state 'When every one is somebody, Then no one's anybody'. But the Scots have never equated pride of ancestry with class distinction: a Campbell may be a duke or a dustman, yet both share in the traditions and insignia of Clan Diarmaid. Every Scot is somebody: there's a vertical though not a horizontal difference of status between a Campbell and a Macdonald that saves them both from the drab uniformity of Gilbert's epigram.

So, in the case of a new grantee belonging to an historic Name, such as Lindsay or Campbell, Lyon will either treat the petitioner as an 'indeterminate cadet' or at least in more remote cases indicate by some allusion to the Chief's Arms that the petitioner has, as it were, been 'naturalized' into that Name. For our Highland Clans and Lowland Names were in a sense little nations of their own, and—unlike Ireland and many Continental nations such as Hungary where an alien aristocracy lorded it over conquered peoples, or even the English who were conquered by their king in 1066—Scotland was essentially an unconquered free federation whose Sovereign was the head of the national family as Chief of Chiefs.

Legal disputes about the ownership of Arms are initially settled in Lyon Court, from which there can be appeals to the Court of Session and thence to the House of Lords. Sometimes these Arms carry famous designations with them, as in the case of Maclean of Ardgour. Again, a Peer of Scotland may establish his right of succession by rematriculating in Lyon Register, since only he is entitled to certain heraldic 'additaments of honour'. But perhaps the most important and sometimes difficult cases that the Lord Lyon has to decide are those of disputed Chiefships, whether Highland or Lowland. For the only piece of legal property to which a Chief *as such* has an undoubted and justiciable right is the plain 'undifferenced' Arms of the Name; and the successful claimant is the one who after due proof is allowed to rematriculate these Arms in Lyon Register. And, with the growth of clan societies and the general mobility of world-wide Scots brought about by the aeroplane, the emotional role of the Chief has suddenly become more important than at any time since the first half of the eighteenth century. Simultaneously, there has been such a growing desire to record Arms in Lyon Register that, while only 16 volumes sufficed for all the entries in the 231 years from 1672 to 1903, the Register has now reached 57 volumes, 41 of them therefore recording the twentieth-century renascence of Scots Heraldry.

Indeed, Heraldry, with its sister science Genealogy, is probably more happily entrenched in Scotland, or rather among the widespread Scots, than among any other peoples. This is because of the inherent clannishness of the Scots, both Highland and Lowland, and their firm attachment to their ancestral roots. As Lord Basil Hamilton was to remark in the seventeenth century, 'There is some strange thing in blood, I believe most in Scotch of any nation, none knowing that of clanship so much'. The Hamiltons were not Highlanders; yet many an historic Lowland Name like Douglas or Kennedy that would never have called itself a 'clan', nevertheless understood what it meant to act collectively and to feel 'clannish'.

These sentiments are perhaps felt more strongly by overseas Scots, than by those who have remained at home and tend either to take them for granted or even to feel vaguely embarrassed by the tourist trade's overdone 'tartan tosh'. Although tartan originated in the Highlands, there is a longer history of the Lowland use of tartan as a general affirmation of Scottishness than is perhaps always realized, even before its official banning by statute from 1746 to 1782 gave it the spicy prestige of national defiance. And of course few modern Highland clan tartans are much, if any, older than Lowland family ones. Those approved by their Chiefs are recorded in the official Register of Tartans at Lyon Office.

In the early days of struggle to build a new life from scratch, folk have little time for anything beyond the purely utilitarian. And so it was with the sturdy Scots settlers who peopled the New World and the Antipodes during the Scottish population explosion at the turn of the eighteenth and nineteenth century. However, once a new base of prosperity had been established, they began to look back to our homeland for their roots rather in the manner so popularized by Alec Haley's book *Roots*.

But there is a marked difference: Mr Haley most particularly does *not* tell us that his negro Mandingo forefathers once ran the principal black slave-trading empire in West Africa. But a MacLeod living in Toronto would be delighted to recall the banquet at Dunvegan where some unsuspecting but doomed Campbell spies had bowls of blood set in front of them before being suddenly dirked. This romanticization of ancestral 'warts and all', turning nasty, bitter feuds into what modern social anthropologists call a 'joking relationship', is perhaps the greatest service that Sir Walter Scott rendered to us Scots apart from also putting us back on the Map of Europe.

But Mr MacLeod in Toronto, or in any other vast conurbation where mobile individuals seek to maintain some valued identity other than that of mere useful cogs in the essential industrial machine, has more, besides the tartan and traditions of an historic Name that in most countries would be limited to a narrow aristocracy. He has also more especially certain *heraldic* rights of his own through our system of crest-badges.

Thus what distinguishes Scots heraldry today from that of most other countries, is its *modern* use of all the varied heraldic contrivances that elsewhere were at their zenith only in the late Middle Ages. We stick to the principle of a 'differenced', and therefore different, legally protected coat of arms for each individual who chooses to record one. These personal coats are of course inheritable by their own heirs. But our system caters more fully than elsewhere for those clannish instincts that inspire the members and supporters, 'the tail', of those great groups of families with their allied namesakes that make up our historic highland Clans and lowland Names.

This is achieved through the fundamental record, the basic matriculation of the Chief of each Clan or Name. First, this sets out the Chief's own Arms, which forms the basic *coat* to be 'differenced' individually by each rematriculating cadet and to be 'alluded to' in new Arms granted to other bearers of the Name. Flown in rectangular form as a flag, these basic Arms form the *banner* that marks the Chief's presence in person, i.e. a flag of the 'coat' he still wears in heraldic theory and would have worn in a tournament. Secondly, there is his headquarters flag or *standard*, several yards long, which is of the liveries and displays the heraldic *badges* that his kindred and followers may wear. Thirdly, there is the *pinsel*, a triangular flag embroidered with the Chief's name and his *crest-badge*, displayed to mark his homely patriarchate on clannish occasions, which is formed by surrounding his crest with a strap-and-buckle inscribed with his motto and which may be used by the whole following of the Clan or Name. In the fly, the pinsel often has the slogan— the gathering or war cry—and the *plant-badge* which they may all use as well.

Since the original forefathers of our chiefs were grand, indeed often royal, as the Blood and Name spreads outwards it carries with it a tradition that ultimately mingles and reconciles democracy with aristocracy, and aristocracy with royalty. Mr MacLeod in Toronto belongs to the clan who are the Children of Leod, and Leod was a thirteenth-century Hebridean prince of immemorial Norse royal ancestry; Mr MacLeod has an ancestral stronghold for pilgrimage at Dunvegan; he has a tartan and plant-badge to link him with MacLeod history; and even if he does not choose to record a personal version of the MacLeod Arms in Lyon Register, he nevertheless has a legal right to wear and use as heraldic insignia the *crest-badge* of a beflagged black bull's head within the motto Hold Fast. And the world population of such as the MacLeods and Campbells is to be numbered by the million, as anybody who has scanned transatlantic telephone directories will know. What is unique today in Scots Heraldry is the legal entitlement of innumerable superbly proud Scots to the use of armorial crest-badges and other heraldic insignia to acknowledge, mark and satisfy harmless but noble feelings of clannish sentiment which, in the oft-quoted words of the late Dame Flora MacLeod of MacLeod, is 'beyond and outside and above divisions between nations, countries and continents ... it takes no note of age or sex, rank or wealth, success or failure. The spiritual link of clanship embraces them all.' But above all, our Heraldry should not be pompous, it should be fun.

Sir Iain Moncreiffe of that Ilk, Bart., CVO, QC Albany Herald

Highland Games. To a great many people throughout the world the mention of Highland Games tends to evoke a particular image. An image which is closely associated with the traditional organised Highland Gatherings of the nineteenth century such as Braemar (1817), Lonach (1823), Glenisla (1856), Ballater (1866), Aboyne (1867), Argyllshire (1871) and Cowal (1871) to name but a few. An image which is closely associated with kilted athletes and dancers, the skirl of the pipes, local and in some cases royal patronage, the distinct sub-culture of the heavies, the sense of bonhomie and the smell of wintergreen as the athletes prepare for the hill-race.

Yet just as important are the many less formal Highland Gatherings or Games, such as those at Glenelg, where the skirl of the pipes, mass commercialisation and tartanry are noticeable only by their absence. The North Uist Highland Gathering dates back to the early 1900s and yet traditional events such as caber tossing and hill running are highly improbable since North Uist has few trees to cut down and the island hardly rises above sea level. The atmosphere of these less formal events is more in keeping with the informal ceilidh than the more formal, rationalised, commercialised professional Highland Games Circuit of the 1990s. Both of these images of games are equally modern and equally Celtic and yet one is continually marginalised while the other is readily visible and kept alive in the consciousness of the tourist and the Scottish public at large.

Many of the folk origins of the Highland Games of today have a popular history which pre-dates the more organised formalisation of the Games. Describing his childhood on Islay in the 1820s and 1830s, the land reformer John Murdoch talks of shinty, cock-fighting, athletic events and feats of strength as being those traditional Highland sports (*John Murdoch, unpublished autobiography, Vol 1*, Mitchell Library, Glasgow). One of the points of origin of 'Tossing the Caber' lies with the raising of the couples of the traditional Highland houses. The hairst kirn or gathering after the harvest had been collected was another seasonal celebration at which dancing, throwing the putting stone and hurling the hammer all contributed to a joyous celebration of communal loyalty and friendly rivalry. Writing in the 1820s one writer describes such a harvest-kirn celebration at which 'a party of Celts amused themselves by their extraordinary feats in putting the stane, hopping leaping and running' (Percy Yorke, *Three Nights in Perthshire*, 1821). Many other illustrative examples could be given to establish the point that the folk origins of today's Highland Gatherings contributed to a way of life and pattern of social development which pre-dates by far the more organised Highland Games which became so popular during the late Victorian period.

Queen Victoria's attachment to Balmoral and the Braemar Royal Highland Gathering is often mistakingly quoted as the single factor which contributed to the popularity of the Games between about 1860 and 1900. As the traditional role of the monarchy declined during the 19th and early 20th centuries royal games became increasingly important in regulating a particular definition of Britishness. Such events as the Braemar Royal Highland Society Gathering, the Argyllshire Gathering and Oban Ball, contributed to a growing nucleus of activities which helped to define a British, Scottish and Highland sporting calendar which also included the Derby (Epsom), Ascot racing week (Gold Cup) and various shooting seasons in the Highlands.

The royal attachment is but one explanation for the past and continuing popularity of the Highland Games. If Highland Games contributed to the social calendar of high society they also attracted visitors to many communities. They provided a sense of fun and social cohesion for some people and a sense of rivalry and competitiveness between neighbouring communities. The professional Highland Games circuit has helped to support certain local economies, and the material wealth of certain individual athletes who perform feats of physical and athletic strength at local, national and international levels. Highland Games have been vehicles for patronage, certain forms of tradition, commercialism, recreation, and a focus for group and community identity.

Writing during the 1930s, Neil Gunn continually questioned the commercialization of the Scottish Highland Games (*Scots Magazine* 1931, No XV(6)). Commenting upon one particular event Gunn recalls an occasion when the dancers were called together and the prize piper, who had carried off all the money that day, appeared not in Highland dress but in blue suit and bowler hat. The judge, obviously astonished, called the piper over and asked him to explain what the rig-out meant. Not recognising the importance of the blue ribbon tradition of the best piper having the honour of playing for the dancers at the last event, the piper explained that he had wanted to catch an early train and therefore had jettisoned his borrowed kilt so that he "could beat it" at the earliest moment. What the writer was in fact being critical of, was the in-roads being made by an urban commercialised culture which took little cognisance of tradition, local people and local customs.

The Aboyne Highland Games were established in 1867. Like all Highland Games they provide a sense of fun, enjoyment, a day away from work, an attraction for the tourist and an opportunity for local people and from afar, to catch up with one another. Yet a nominal degree of unity sometimes conceals the fact that at the same event different seating arrangements, different styles of dress, different accents as well as flags serve to both unite and segregate different groups of people. At Aboyne, the ceremonial display of flags serves not just as display of colour for the tourist but also an indicator of who is present at the Games. The raising of the flags during the day follows a distinct order. At the opening of the Games the National Cross of St Andrews is raised on the central flagstaff; this is closely followed by the flag of the Marquess of Huntly or Chief to the Games; this in turn is followed by the banners of local lairds and other patrons to the Games, marking their arrival at the ground, while a special flagstaff is erected to hold the banner of any of the offices of State in Scotland should they arrive.

In the 1990s Highland Games present themselves in different forms and sizes. The reasons for the rise and fall of certain Highland Games are as different as they are similar. Many of the folk origins of earlier Highland Games and pastimes contribute to todays Highland Games. Such Highland Games continue to contribute to the local economy of both the Highlands and Lowlands. They exist for both the "reel" and real Highland Society although the reasons for attending such events may be drastically different. A different sense of community, place and function of Highland Games may exist in Halkirk, North Uist, Braemar, Lonach, Airth, Aberdeen, Glenelg, Cowal and Aboyne but all provide insights into Scottish history and contemporary culture.

G. Jarvie

Highlands, The, since 1745. The Highlands traditionally formed a region quite distinct in culture and society from the rest of Scotland. In outward appearance, agricultural practices and living standards the scattered rural settlements in which most Highlanders lived could be paralleled elsewhere in the country, but in no other part did kinship, real or fictitious, form the basis of the social and political structure at so late a period as in this clan-dominated region. The Highlands of the seventeenth and early eighteenth century were still, in some senses, 'a state within a state', where chiefs had virtually absolute power over their people and a private army of kinsmen and followers at their backs.

This social and political system had its cultural counterpart in a distinctive language, Scottish Gaelic, and a rich body of poetry, music, tales and traditional lore which was cultivated and transmitted mainly, but not exclusively, by families of hereditary bards, musicians and historians called 'seanchaidhs' whom the chief maintained. The chief and his ancestors were the focus of much of this tradition, and poets and bards eulogized their liberality and heroic virtues. But all ranks of society—chief, tacksmen (the clan gentry) and commoners—shared a common language and culture.

The beginnings of change go back to the seventeenth century, but it was the Jacobite Risings, especially that of 1745, which many clans supported, that gave the government the opportunity and will to destroy the independence of the Highland chiefs. Immediately after Culloden in 1746 the authority of the State was asserted as never before, by stern reprisals, by forfeiture of estates and the abolition of ward-holding and independent jurisdictions. The ban on the possession of weapons destroyed the real basis of the chiefs' power. The proscription of the wearing of tartan and Highland dress struck mainly at the Highlanders' pride and sense of identity, but for reasons of policy it did not apply to the new Highland regiments. Some 30, starting with the Black Watch, were formed between 1740 and 1815 and won fame wherever they served. In a master-stroke of policy the government gave military commissions to chiefs and their relatives and so ensured that clansmen would enlist. Clan loyalties, potentially so disruptive to the State, were thus converted into a support of the Hanoverian establishment.

These measures prepared the way for more pacific but far-reaching changes which were intended to 'civilize' and domesticate the wild Highlanders, to teach them habits of order and industry and finally abolish their culture. These aims were promoted in a variety of ways. On the estates of forfeited chiefs government Commissioners established schools, with English as the medium of instruction. There were innovations in agriculture and land-tenure. Both on these estates and more widely through the Highlands linen manufacture and other new industries and skills were promoted and villages created. (The settlements established for war-veterans on forfeited estates in the 1760s foreshadowed the later crofting townships). The government's economic and educational schemes were reinforced in every part of the Highlands by those of private lairds, the SPCK and other charitable bodies.

Now that the chiefs had been deprived of their status as leaders of clan armies, they tended, as Dr Johnson observed, to look for compensations in the pursuit of wealth and a grander life-style. By the late eighteenth century they had become as devoted to 'improvement' as lairds in the Lowlands. They expressed their new tastes in elegant mansions, landscaped gardens and other delights, and to support these and other innovations turned to their estates to yield a better revenue by applying a more scientific agriculture and by exploiting fishings, woods, quarries and minerals.

Better lairds like the fifth Duke of Argyll aimed, at the same time, to raise the tenants' standard of living, give them greater security of tenure and provide more diversified employment for cottars. The introduction of new crops, especially the potato, was to have far-reaching effects. The handsome towns and villages which appeared in the Highlands from Bowmore to Beauly from *c.* 1750 to 1825 were planned by lairds or government as centres for the development of trade and industry and the civic virtues. The success of these optimistic schemes was essential to the Highlands, now fully exposed to a fully-fledged market economy which threatened native industries and employment and the stability of tenants. These problems were compounded by a new phenomenon, a steady rise in the population.

It was in these critical decades in the late eighteenth century that many lairds and their families began to settle in the centres of fashion and power. They were, to quote the 23rd chief of Macleod, 'sucked into the vortex of the nation and allured to its capitals'. The vivid memoirs of Elizabeth Grant of Rothiemurchus depict such families living uneasily between two worlds, still much attached to the Highlands but tending sooner or later to be weaned away by their new interests. They accumulated debts and often became bankrupt. Survival came to depend on obtaining more revenue from the agents and factors who, in their absence, managed their estates. It was revenue lost to improving schemes.

Already by the 1770s old tenant families, including kinsmen of the chiefs, were being squeezed from their land by soaring rents. Sheep were the most profitable line and in the following century the spread of vast sheep-farms to all parts of the Highlands (though not to all estates) was attended by large-scale clearance of tenants. Few clearances received the publicity of those carried out on the Sutherland estate between 1807 and 1819. Most provoked no resistance but they left deep wounds that have still not healed and the Gaelic poets recorded the perpetrators in bitter and powerful verse.

Emigration to the American colonies and eastern Canada began to flow strongly after *c.* 1770 and in the nineteenth century extended its range to many parts of the North American continent and to Australia and New Zealand. The emigrants included tacksmen as well as small tenants. Many were victims of clearances, but other factors contributed which cannot be laid at the lairds' door: crop failures, especially those caused by potato blight in 1837 and the late 1840s, the rapid growth of population, the generally poor success of the schemes of economic development and the collapse of the kelp market after the boom of the Napoleonic years.

Ironically, as Highlanders emigrated or were absorbed into the anonymity of the Lowland towns, writers, artists and people of fashion came to admire the land of Ossian. Under the influence of the new romantic movement, the Highlands no longer appeared dismal and threatening, as they had to earlier travellers, but as a grand and timeless setting for caterans and Fingalian heroes. There was a vogue for highly romantic antiquarianism. Societies arose devoted to Highland dress, weapons, games and dancing, and Highland pageanty, stage-managed by Sir Walter Scott, added colour and panache to the celebration of the visit of George IV to Edinburgh in 1822. The Highlanders had ceased to be a threat; they could now be admired as a spectacle.

This romantic image, widely influential in the nineteenth century, was remote from the reality of life in the Highlands. In spite of emigration the population still numbered over 250,000 in the late nineteenth century and was heavily concentrated in coastal areas, often in crofting townships established when the interior passed under sheep or during the kelp boom. The new class of crofters, created from the ranks of the former tenants and cottars, supplemented the produce of their holdings by labouring, fishing and migratory work.

A new class of lairds, too, was arising, at the expense of the old landed families, many of whom had been ruined. Deriving their wealth from the professions, trade and manufactures, they might be popular as individuals but had not the claim on tenants' loyalty that the more responsible traditional lairds still enjoyed. Clanship was declining as a binding force in Highland society; religion and politics were of growing concern, and ministers and Land League leaders were the new arbiters of opinion. Probably a majority of Highlanders supported the League in the struggle which finally won security and fair rents for crofters in 1886, and many subsequently took part in agitation for the extension of the crofting area. They saw themselves not as revolutionaries but as traditionalists, restoring rights to land which had been enjoyed by their ancestors under former chiefs and unjustly taken away by modernizing landlords.

The crofters and cottars were indeed a conservative force in Highland life and fell heir to much of its tradition. Representatives of the old chiefly families, notably the folktale collector, John Francis Campbell, preserved much that was invaluable, but it was the ordinary Highlanders who, after the 'men of the arts' lost the customary patronage of chiefs in the eighteenth century, gave encouragement and boundless respect to the bards, musicians and *seanchaidhs* in their midst, so that the tradition not only survived into the twentieth century but remained creative. If the songs of the bards became popular, reflecting the everyday concerns of small rural communities, it was a sign of vitality and growth.

The power of the state to produce uniformity had, however, grown immeasurably since 1746. With the introduction in 1872 of compulsory, universal education, based on English, successive generations of young Highlanders were to learn the skills and values of western urban civilization and experience 'the allurements of the capitals'. The Gaelic language and culture, and the distinctive society that had sustained them, were to be in greater jeopardy than in the aftermath of Culloden.

E.R. Cregeen

Hislop, Joseph (b.1884, Edinburgh d.1977) became one of the world's leading tenors, especially appreciated in the Argentine and the USA for his leading roles in Puccini opera. He appeared with Gigli, Galli-Curci, Melba, Tetrazzini and Chaliapin, who said of him 'tonight I sang with a real tenor, not a painted doll!'. He finally returned to Sweden (where his vocal talents had first been recognised while serving an apprenticeship in engraving). Nilsson and Bjorling were among his pupils.

J. Purser

Historiography. For Scottish history in the Dark Ages we are largely dependent on writings originating in England, Ireland or Scandinavia, because Scotland itself produced little save scanty annals, somewhat cryptic lists of kings, and hagiographical writings, notably Adamnan's work on Columba (c.700). Among medieval chronicles easily the most important was the

Chronicle of Melrose, which borrowed from a variety of sources for events from the early eighth century until about 1170 and was then continued, as a contemporary record, for almost another 100 years.

In the fourteenth century works appeared in which the annalistic structure was superseded. John Barbour's poem *The Brus* was an attempt to furnish Scotland with a 'Romance' to match those of other medieval literatures. It contains some demonstrable historical errors, but, written by a near-contemporary, it does represent history as well as literature. By the time Barbour died in 1395 two other important works had been at least partly written. Andrew Wyntoun, who like Barbour wrote in Scots verse, lived from about 1350 to about 1424. His *Orygynale Cronykil of Scotland* is 'original' in the sense that it started with the Creation. His rhyming couplets are often perfunctory rather then inspired, but at their best they provide eminently quotable references to events in the writer's own day as well as in previous centuries. The Latin *Scotichronicon* was the work of John of Fordun (d. c. 1384) and his continuator Walter Bower (d. 1449), both of whom evidently had access, as Wyntoun had, to earlier material now lost. Yet Wyntoun and Fordun alike went far beyond any conceivable evidence when they produced picturesque mythology about the origins of the 'Scots', their wanderings from the Mediterranean to Ireland and Scotland and the succession of their kings. The *Scotichronicon* is an outstanding source and the reputation it enjoyed is indicated by the number of MS copies which still survive.

Histories in something more like the modern sense have their origin in the sixteenth century, when a succession of historical scholars began which has never since failed. John Major (1467–1550), who had a propagandist motive in so far as he was an enthusiast for Anglo-Scottish union, recounted events in both England and Scotland down to the end of the fifteenth century in his *Historia Majoris Britanniae* (1521)—a punning title, which could be read as either 'History of Greater Britain' or 'Major's History of Britain'. Major was critical of the old mythology, but attempted to explain why it had arisen, and his work, in its maturity, conforms to a pattern which prevailed until fairly recently.

Some of Major's successors were less judicious. Hector Boece (?1465–1536), in his *Historia Gentis Scotorum* (1527), reiterated and elaborated the old fables and added inventions of his own. Yet the vernacular translations of his work have a liveliness which ensured the survival of his stories: his account of Macbeth and the witches, for example, accords closely with what a Scot still learns at his mother's knee. The charge of undue credulity can be levelled also at Robert Lindsay of Pitscottie (? 1532–c. 1580), whose *Historie and Cronicles of Scotland*, designed as a continuation of Boece, is a source of many a picturesque and dramatic tale of the later fifteenth and early sixteenth centuries.

Contemporary with Pitscottie was George Buchanan (1506–1582), whose *Rerum Scoticarum Historia* was published in the year of his death. Like Major, Buchanan was a pamphleteer, for he was writing to support a thesis about Scottish constitutional law which he expounded in his *De Jure Regni apud Scotos*, and his prejudices, especially against Mary, Queen of Scots, led him to distort what he must have known to have been the truth. Buchanan's ambitions were primarily literary and this led him to disregard accuracy even when he had no propagandist motive for doing so. He wrote for effect, and his chief significance lies in his presentation of a version of Scottish history in superb Latin prose. Partly owing to his fame as a scholar and a Latinist, his *Historia* remained a standard comprehensive history of the country until the nineteenth century and created what was regarded as an authorized interpretation, a lot of which is even now sometimes accepted.

Another contemporary of Buchanan was John Knox (?1513–1572), who was again a pamphleteer, this time on behalf of Protestantism. But Knox was something of a pioneer in a practice which would probably never have entered Buchanan's head but which had a great future, for the texts of documents make up something like a quarter or a third of his *History of the Reformation of Religion in Scotland*. Knox was also, unlike his predecessors, an autobiographer: a later writer would probably have entitled the work a *History of His Own Times*. Knox's vivid narrative, from a man who did not number humility among his virtues, has given him a pre-eminence among Scottish reformers which he may not deserve.

Within 30 years or so of Knox's death two more important autobiographies had been composed. Sir James Melville of Halhill (1535–1617) tells extraordinarily well the tale of his experiences as soldier, courtier and diplomat, and like Pitscottie he has such an eye for the picturesque that it is hard to refrain from quoting him even when his narrative is so obviously coloured by his self-importance as to be untrustworthy. Another James Melville (1556–1614), minister of Anstruther and nephew of the presbyterian leader, Andrew Melville, wrote as an avowed partisan of the presbyterian party and his narrative is coloured not in this instance by personal vanity but by admiration for Uncle Andrew. Like Knox, Melville presented a lot of documents, but he also gives, without self-consciousness, much personal detail about his education, his adventures when a fugitive from a hostile Scottish government and his encounter with shipwrecked Spaniards from the Armada.

The practice of reproducing documents was carried further by David Calderwood (1575–1651), whose *History of the Church of Scotland* contains more documents and extracts than narrative, and he preserved material from general-assembly records which are no longer extant. Belonging to the same school is the less well-known Alexander Petrie, minister of the Scots Church at Rotterdam and author of *A History of the Catholic Church*, published in Holland in 1662. Petrie may have been a conscious imitator of Thomas Fuller, whose *Church History of Britain* had appeared in 1655. Petrie, not content with Britain, surveyed the whole of Christian history, and like Fuller he is most useful when he comes near his own day and reproduces documents. There was, however, another Scottish parallel to Fuller, in John Spottiswoode, whose *History of the Church of Scotland*, published (like Fuller's work) in 1655, goes back to early times. Spottiswoode does produce documents, but his work is in the main a more literary kind of history than Calderwood's or even Petrie's, from a writer with a notion that history is something that can be read.

The fashion of collecting documents is again exemplified in the work of Sir James Balfour of Denmilne and Kinnaird (*c.* 1598–1657), whose passion for MSS led him to collect and copy state documents, registers of religious houses and charters. He appears to have been free from propagandist intention, so that in him we have, perhaps for the first time, the love of source material of any period, for its own sake. The bulk of what remained of Balfour's collections was acquired in 1699 for the Advocates' Library and was thus available for the publishing clubs in the nineteenth century, who were much in Balfour's debt. He too had an English parallel, in the work of Sir William Dugdale, to whose *Monasticon* Balfour contributed, and in that of Sir William Segar, who as Garter King of Arms held the English office equivalent to that of Lyon held by Balfour. Indeed, in historiography as in other forms of literature it is not difficult to discern a court-centred Anglo-Scottish culture in Jacobean and Caroline times.

After the dislocation caused by the Covenanting wars and the Cromwellian occupation, cultural progress was resumed, again under royal patronage. The office of historiographer royal is first heard of in 1663, but the man who did the most valuable historical work was the versatile Sir Robert Sibbald, who held the offices of king's physician and geographer royal. With Charles II's encouragement Sibbald launched a scheme for a series of county histories and descriptions, but only a few were completed.

Robert Wodrow (1679–1734) was in the Knox and Calderwood tradition rather than the Balfour tradition, for his interest was in almost contemporary history and he was avowedly propagandist. His work's emotive title *The Sufferings of the Church of Scotland* (1721) must not obscure the immense importance of the documents which he so industriously transcribed, although most of them have since been printed elsewhere. Wodrow, a Whig and Hanoverian, reflects the triumphant presbyterianism of the post-Revolution period, with which the future lay, but he had active contemporaries in the Jacobite and Episcopalian camp. Possibly those conservatives were uncomfortably aware that the future was not likely to lie with them, and consequently had to convince themselves that the past, at least, was on their side. Similar stimulus was given to historical studies by the debates preceding the Union of 1707, which turned to arguments about the past relations between Scotland and England and about the antiquity and independence of the Scottish monarchy.

However, the work produced in the early eighteenth century was not all polemical. For one thing, there was much printing of works which had been composed earlier but had not previously been published—classics like Hope's *Minor Practicks* (1726), Craig's *Jus Feudale* (1732), Home of Godscroft's *History of the House of Douglas and Angus* (1734) and Balfour of Pittendreich's *Practicks* (1754)—and there were new editions of Knox and Buchanan. Besides, the way in which an initial propagandist purpose could lead to disinterested scholarship is demonstrated in one outstanding contribution to historical scholarship—the book commonly called Anderson's *Diplomata* (1739). James Anderson (1662–1728) had examined Scottish history in connection with opposition to the Union and he had gained an acquaintance with medieval charters and similar early material. In some ways a successor to Sir James Balfour, but far more of a scholar, he conceived the idea of publishing facsimiles and transcripts of a range of Scottish charters, concentrating on the twelfth to fourteenth centuries. His handsome and impressive volume also contains engravings of the seals of Scottish sovereigns and of coins, facsimiles of medieval forms of letters and of abbreviations used by medieval scribes, making the work in effect a manual of palaeography and a Scottish parallel to Jean Mabillon's *De re diplomataria* (Paris, 1681).

None of Anderson's contemporaries had quite his breadth of interest, but some of them were like him working on original documents and records. It was the age of Thomas Rymer's *Foedera*, that massive collection of English state papers, and no one in Scotland tried to emulate its bulk, but Thomas Ruddiman (who saw Anderson's *Diplomata* through the press) produced two modest volumes of *Epistolae Regum Scotorum* (1722)—letters of James IV, James V and Mary.

Meantime, despite the work done during a century and more on comparatively recent history, the old fables had held sway for earlier periods. But Thomas Innes, in his *critical Essay on the ancient Inhabitants of Scotland* (1729), followed in the pioneering steps of an Irish writer, Thomas O'Flaherty, who in 1685 had entered the campaign against the ancient legends—to the indignation of patriotic Scots. Innes not only cited early sources, but reproduced some of them, such as king-lists, and coolly eliminated the 40 imaginary kings who had been inserted between 'Fergus I' in 330 BC and the historical Fergus, son of Erc, with whom the royal line really began about 500 AD.

Walter Goodall (*c.* 1706–1766), an assistant to Ruddiman in the Advocates' Library and like him a Jacobite and Episcopalian, followed in the footsteps of James Anderson, who had produced four volumes of *Collections* on Mary, Queen of Scots. Goodall's *Examination of the Casket Letters* (1754), where he printed a mass of documents, largely from English archives, has been a mainstay of every writer on Mary's reign from that time to the present. Goodall also prepared an edition of the *Scotichronicon* (1759) which is only now being superseded by a series of nine volumes, comprising text, translation and notes, edited by Professor Donald Watt and others.

Bishop Robert Keith (1681–1756), the chief ornament of the Episcopalian school, links the scholars of the older tradition with the writers who set the pattern of more modern historiography. He produced, with Goodall's help, a *Catalogue of Scottish Bishops*, but his main work was his *History of the Affairs of Church and State in Scotland* (1734), dealing almost entirely with the reign of Mary. Keith wrote a consecutive narrative, but he was essentially a collector of source material. To that extent he was in the Calderwood and Wodrow tradition, but

he outdid them by trying to devote equal attention to secular and ecclesiastical affairs and by making extensive searches, especially in the national archives of Scotland, which then lay neglected and in disarray in the Laigh Parliament House. Keith did not deal with near-contemporary history, like Calderwood and Wodrow, nor did he work over several centuries, like Balfour and Anderson. He concentrated on a specially interesting and significant period.

It is therefore clear that long before the so-called 'Enlightenment' of the eighteenth century there had developed and persisted a healthy tradition of devoted and valuable historical scholarship, with stronger emphasis on the presentation of original material than on literary appeal, though the latter had not been lacking. That oracle Dr Johnson was never more wide of the mark than when he said in 1773, 'It was but of late that historians bestowed pains and attention in consulting records, to attain to accuracy'. How little he knew about earlier Scottish work. The contrast between the old tradition and the characteristics of the 'Enlightenment' is at once apparent if we compare Keith with William Robertson (1721–1793), who concentrated on the same period as Keith. True, he extended his account of 1603, but two-thirds of it is devoted to Mary's reign and his narrative becomes distinctly thinner after he could no longer rely on Keith. Robertson, unlike Keith, used mainly printed sources because he had no taste for what he called 'the unpleasant task' of searching for MS material and was far too much of a gentleman to enjoy grubbing about in the Laigh Parliament House. On the other hand, Robertson has more study of causation, more analysis, more characterization, and he was both more judicious and less partisan than most of those who preceded and many who followed him.

In the very last years of the eighteenth century other scholars were at work, particularly William Tytler and Malcolm Laing, who took opposite sides in the Marian controversy, and John Pinkerton (1758–1826), commonly regarded as something of an eccentric because he spurned the Celtic heritage, but author of a *History of Scotland from the Accession of the House of Stewart to that of Mary* (1792), in which he used state papers to good effect.

In the nineteenth century we move into the greatest period of publication of historical source material, largely by private—or collective—enterprise in the form of clubs. Clubs for every conceivable purpose had proliferated in the eighteenth century. There was an Antiquarian Club as early as 1703, and the Society of Antiquaries of Scotland was established in 1781. But the publishing club was a novelty. Their enormous output continued the pre-Enlightenment practice of individual collectors and editors. The real innovation came with official publication, as part of a new regime for the Scottish national archives which dates from the appointment of Thomas Thomson as deputy clerk register in 1806. He inherited the results of generations of neglect and there was a vast amount of repair, binding, arranging and indexing. But Thomson aimed at making records widely accessible through publication, and he began the great series of record publications which continued until very recently. In addition to his official work, Thomson was the leading light in the Bannatyne Club, the first of the great publishing clubs, founded in 1823. Among Thomson's friends and associates were Sir Walter Scott (admitted advocate in the same year as Thomson), who became first president of the Bannatyne, and Patrick Fraser Tytler (1791–1849), who strongly supported the publication policy and at Scott's suggestion undertook his *History of Scotland* in nine volumes (1828–1843), which is still useful because of the author's industry in examining records. Within a few years the Bannatyne had several imitators—the Maitland, Abbotsford, Spalding, Wodrow and Spottiswoode clubs or societies—and others followed later, the Scottish History Society in 1887.

The association of Thomson and Scott was in some ways a curious one, because, while scholarship is by no means absent from Scott's work and he had a genuine interest in original source material, he is more representative of the dissemination of romantic images which have bedevilled Scottish history ever since. Rubbish about clans and tartans still does a good deal to bring Scottish history into disrepute.

The vigorous activity launched in the Thomson era was maintained. Cosmo Innes (1798–1874), professor of constitutional law at Edinburgh, completed the publication of the *Acts of Parliament* which Thomson had started, edited many volumes for the societies and brought together a lot of his essays in three volumes which still offer the *locus classicus* on a number of topics. He did not attempt a general history, but his son-in-law, John Hill Burton (1809–1881), who was less of a record scholar than Innes but a prolific writer, produced a *History of Scotland* in eight volumes, covering a much longer period than Tytler and long remaining a standard work. William Forbes Skene (1809–1892) studied the earlier history as no one had done before, and his three volumes on *Celtic Scotland*, though now known to have many flaws, have not yet been superseded. Sir William Fraser (1816–1898), deputy keeper of the records, produced over forty volumes in which histories of Scottish noble and landed families were written, with copious selections from their muniments.

A bequest from Fraser established the first Chair of Scottish History, at Edinburgh in 1901. Peter Hume Brown was the first holder, and he followed in the steps of Tytler and Hill Burton, with a three-volume *History* which successfully survived the competition of the more journalistic Andrew Lang and remained the standard work for more than half a century. Hume Brown was an editor of record volumes as well, and he and David Masson, Edinburgh's professor of rhetoric and English literature, were the chief editors of the Register of the Privy Council. A second Chair, at Glasgow, followed in 1911, with Robert Rait as its first holder. The *Scottish Historical Review* had been founded in 1904. Yet it was evident that Scottish history was not competing successfully, as a serious academic subject at any rate, with 'British' (which meant English) constitutional history. When the British Empire was at its zenith, the assumption was that the Westminster model of parliamentary government was destined to prevail throughout the world, and institutions other than those of England were regarded as inferior, backward and even barbarous. Even Scottish historians were apologetic in the modest claims they made for their subject.

Thus the recession which overtook Scottish history after the First World War may not have been due entirely to the loss of young lives in the struggle. There seemed to be neither men, money nor enthusiasm: record publications almost dried up, the Record Office was grossly understaffed, societies reduced or suspended their publications, few monographs and no significant general histories were produced, and in 1928 the publication of the *Scottish Historical Review* was suspended. One positive step was the foundation in 1934 of the Stair Society, devoted to the history of Scots law.

Very soon after the Second World War there was a spectacular turn for the better. The *Scottish Historical Review* resumed publication in 1947, the Scottish History Departments began to turn out young scholars with both the equipment and the enthusiasm, the Record Office staff was expanded out of all knowing and the work of the record authority greatly extended. Official publication was for a time resumed on a modest scale, existing societies increased their membership and new societies were found. A substitute for Hume Brown's three volumes was at last provided in the four-volume *Edinburgh History of Scotland* (1965–1975). A few years later there came *The New History of Scotland* in eight slim volumes, with an emphasis largely on interpretation. A rough count shows that in the last thirty years over 500 monographs on a wide range of topics have appeared, and at present over a dozen one-volume Histories of Scotland are in the bookshops. The greatest contribution to record scholarship has been the *Regesta Regum Scotorum* (Four vols. published since 1960, four more to come).

G. Donaldson

Hogg, James (1770–1835) has suffered more than many from an apt nickname which has become more widely disseminated than has actual knowledge of the man or his work. The 'Ettrick Shepherd' certainly justified his nickname, growing up poor and semi-illiterate in a border country incredibly rich with history and oral tradition. His mother was an important source for Scott when he was gathering the *Border Minstrelsy*, and her son listened closely and well. Long novels (many of them worthy of much more attention than they have received, perhaps eclipsed by the brilliance of *The Confessions of a Justified Sinner*), short stories, sketches, poems, articles, reviews, parodies—Hogg was a versatile writer driven by his intense energy, and his slender means, to produce more than was good for his reputation, yet far too much for the neglect which has overtaken most of his work.

Once he found his place in literary society, Hogg rapidly began to enjoy playing the 'Shepherd'. Gentlemanly, pleasant, boisterous, genial, he enjoyed the same *éclat* that Burns had known in Edinburgh, but he enjoyed it for many more years, and learned to adapt to London too. He could amuse, and he could charm with the gentlemanliness of his manners. The public mind preferred to remember the shepherd, not the gentleman, and when the *Noctes Ambrosianae* made immortal the 'Shepherd' of uncouth jokes and ill-regulated enthusiasms, Hogg's image was set fast in this form. Wilson and Lockhart, though friends of Hogg's, satirized him frequently and sometimes viciously. Their private joke became a public misconception, and it has endured.

The work which has done most to rescue him is the recently revived *Confessions*. Basically, this is the supposed diary, with editorial comments, of a debased Calvinist, a religious pervert who believes himself exempt from all moral law because 'justified' to eventual admission to Heaven. This character, Robert Wringhim, is preyed on by a Hawthorn-like mysterious stranger, and easily persuaded (using his own perverted religious arguments) to acts of increasing ferocity and impiety, including murder and rape. The reader recognizes the stranger as the devil, but the proud Sinner does not. The form of the book, cleverly telling and re-telling the same events from different viewpoints, with deliberate discrepancies which both discredit the actors and cast an artistically excellent uncertainty over the devil's appearances, carefully confuses the issue to the point which renders the r eader incapable of sharp-edged judgements. Confused as Wringhim himself, yet terribly fascinated by the exploration of the psychology of perversion, the reader is left to make his own mind up on several parts of the action, and this in part is what gives the novel its enduring appeal.

Yet *Basil Lee, The Brownie of Bodsbeck*, many of the poems, and a large number of periodical contributions, require revival and republication, and the work of reassessing the career of the Ettrick Shepherd will require decades. Behind the facade he wore so cleverly, there was obviously a shrewd observing intelligence very akin to Burns's own, as shown in the shrewd letters home to Ayrshire from the salons of Edinburgh. His talents were many-sided, but in no form did he excel more than in religious satire, in the extraordinary, vivid and generically subtle form of the *Confessions*. For many years critics denied the work (which was published anonymously) could be Hogg's, on the odd ground that it was too good for him. A rudimentary acquaintance with the wider work of the Shepherd suggests that nothing could be further from the truth.

I. Campbell

Home, John (1722–1808) was born at Leith, the son of the town clerk. He was educated in his birthplace and at Edinburgh University, numbering William Robertson, the historian and a future Principal, and Adam Fergusson among his friends. He fought on the Hanoverian side in the Rising of 1745. He was taken prisoner and lodged in Doune Castle after the battle of Falkirk, but contrived to escape. He filled the charge of Athelstaneford, East Lothian, until his Church career was brought to an end by the Church Court as a result of production of his play *Douglas*, brought out with considerable success in Edinburgh in 1756 and in London the following year. So great was its popularity that on the first night, an enthusiastic voice

from the gallery is reputed to have called out 'Whaur's yer Wullie Shakespeare noo?' On leaving the Church Home became private secretary to the Earl of Bute and thereafter tutor to the Prince of Wales, who, on his succession to the throne as George III, granted Home a pension of £300 per annum.

None of his later plays—*The Siege of Aquileia* (1760), *The Fatal Discovery* (1769), *Alonzo* (1773) and *Alfred* (1778)—had the success of his first venture. His *History of the Rebellion of 1745* (1801) is interesting in so far as it relates to his personal experiences. He spent his final years in the midst of Edinburgh's brilliant circle of talkers, Principal Robertson at the centre of these 'New Athenians'. Today, he is remembered most readily for the amusing lines he produced when the London government imposed heavy duty on claret:

> Bold and erect the Caledonian stood,
> Old was his mutton and his claret good;
> Let him drink port, the English statesman cried—
> He drank the poison, and his spirit died.

M. Lindsay

Housing. Scottish towns appear uniform and dull, dominated as they are by tenements, stone villas, bungalows and council houses whose occupants refrain from demonstrating any external individuality. The Scottish identity, unlike the English, has never been associated with a house, for the Scottish housing tradition has been renting property and never owning it. Thus the tenant, moving from the turf and stone rural hovel of the eighteenth century, through the made-down house in the medieval cores of towns in the early nineteenth century, into the one- and two-roomed tenement of the second half of that century, and finally being swept along in slum clearance schemes and compulsorily rehoused in some remote council estate, in a house chosen and located by some anonymous housing official, had never developed much pride in the external appearance of his house.

The pattern of housing began to be remade in the eighteenth century. Social stratification of the medieval burgh was vertical, with merchants living on the ground floor, the well-to-do on the first floor and descending upwards to the poorest in the attic. In Edinburgh in 1776 the use of horizontal distance to create social distance began with the move of some of the well-to-do George Square. Henceforth, the one-class dormitory suburb was to dominate the thinking of the newly emergent middle class. The immediate success of this development led to the creation of the New Town of Edinburgh which, regardless of its name, was simply a residential district. The idea was taken up in Glasgow, Aberdeen and Perth in the following generation.

The nineteenth century was the age of towns: cities burst forth to become metropolitan in size, older burghs were encased in new suburbs, and new towns sprang up from empty fields especially in the coalfield areas of the Central Lowlands. The very speed of the change created housing problems which are still with us a century and a half later. Reports, committees and royal commissions brought their collective attention to the appalling housing conditions suffered by the labouring class. The problem had many facets: the condition of buildings was often poor in the extreme; overcrowding was the rule rather than the exception; water was obtained from a well in the street; sanitation was non-existent. The stress did not end there, for the houses were often near evil-smelling, dirty and noisy industry. It was not until the 1861 census was taken that the harsh truth was established: 34 per cent of families in Scotland lived in one room and 37 per cent in two rooms. One per cent even lived in single rooms without a window. One observer concluded, 'the single-room system appears to be an institution co-existent with urban life among the working classes in Scotland'. This then formed the inheritance of Scots from the magnificence of the Victorian Imperial Age. Cholera, typhoid, tuberculosis, rickets, influenza were often the prize in this urban lottery and drink was used to block out the all-pervading misery.

During the nineteenth century the principle of state interference in housing, which usually left rights of property intact, was insinuated into the statute books. Several Acts of Parliament were passed giving local authorities the power to deal with the housing problem. The Dwelling Houses (Scotland) Act 1855 gave power for associations of persons acting in the public interest to acquire dilapidated property at a price fixed by the sheriff; this was the forerunner of compulsory purchase. The Nuisances Removal Act 1855 empowered and obliged local authorities to provide adequate privies, maintain premises in a safe and habitable condition, clean and whitewash insanitary houses, and close any house where a nuisance was 'such as to render the house unfit for human habitation'. Housing legislation proceeded slowly and often the Acts were but a dead letter. The turning point came in 1875 when Sir Richard Cross introduced a new principle in his Artisans' and Labourers' Dwelling Act: instead of singling out individual owners he identified whole areas where houses were so ruinous and congested that nothing short of demolition would solve the problem. Thus in an age of unfettered capitalism parliament found the wisdom to authorize the state to undertake comprehensive urban renewal, plan the cleared areas and build houses for the working classes. A passion for sanitary purity rather than ideological salvation set Scotland upon the path to a council-house society.

Yet government policy up to the beginning of World War I had remained unambiguous: 'Private enterprise has always been and so far as can be foreseen, will continue to be the main source of the provision of houses ... and building by local authorities will not be required except where private enterprise has failed to provide such houses.' Investment in tenements for private renting was a common form of savings in the latter years of the nineteenth century, but a severe loss of confidence in the first decade of the new century shut off funds. By 1914 private enterprise had almost entirely ceased to provide capital to build houses for letting.

Pressure for an inquiry into housing in Scotland led the Secretary of State to establish in 1912 a Royal Commission on Housing which reported in 1917. The Commissioners found the existing housing legislation a complicated muddle. When they went on to look at housing generally, they found a situation far worse than the existing statutory provisions admitted to: overcrowded tenements, inadequate sanitation, one-roomed houses, miners' housing, rural housing, the housing of navvies and much more were all in desperate need of attention. The expressed position of the majority of the Commissioners was that 'the State must at once take steps to make good the housing shortage and to improve housing conditions, and that this can only be done by or through the machinery of the public authorities.' These findings led directly to the Housing and Town Planning (Scotland) Act of 1919, the most significant piece of legislation in the development of today's urban Scotland. One new and important feature of the Act was the introduction of state subsidies for housing. Local authorities were to contribute towards the annual loss on council houses the product of a nominal rate of four-fifths of a penny (in England a penny rate), the remainder of the annual loss being paid by central government. Thus the liability of local authorities under this scheme was limited, whilst that of the government was unlimited. This revolutionary form of subsidy was considered essential in order to persuade many councils to act, and on these terms most authorities went ahead with schemes. The result was an uncontrolled increase in local authority housing costs, the average per house rising from £225 pre-war to £959 in 1921, with four-apartment houses exceeding £1,000. In August 1921 the government decided that no new tenders for houses would be entertained and that house building under the 1919 programme should cease after completion of houses already tendered for. Henceforth governments ensured that they exercised close control over housing expenditure and never again entertained an open-ended commitment to build working-class houses.

Central government became embroiled in house construction even earlier than the 1919 Act. A new naval dockyard was started on the shores of the River Forth near Dunfermline and housing was required for a sudden influx of 1,200 workers who could not find sufficient homes in the existing housing stock of Dunfermline or Inverkeithing. A planning wrangle arose between the burgh of Dunfermline, the Admiralty, the Local Government Board and even the local tramway company. Work on the dockyard progressed, but nothing was done about the housing. Research conducted by the Garden Cities and Town Planning Association revealed that the English dockyard workers who were to make up the bulk of the labour force would not entertain the thought of living in a tenement, so a new garden-city town was planned. The Housing (Rosyth Dockyard) Act was passed in 1915 and the government set up the Scottish National Housing Company Ltd which became the forerunner of the Scottish Special Housing Association. The results of this activity marked a radical change in Scotland's traditional building industry—out went stone and in came brick, out went the tenement and in came the cottage, out went burgal congestion and in came the garden city. In short Scotland developed an urban schizophrenia which has caused many of today's problems and shows little sign of recovery.

The period after 1924 was a time of disillusionment in the provision of local authority housing, and economy, not quality, was the criterion. Subsidies were reduced in 1928, but restored to their former levels in July 1929. Clearly, government was desperately trying to find the right level of financial support to keep the housing programme going at a controlled rate, but the trickle of houses failed to alleviate urban congestion. In 1930 an Act was passed to clear some of the worst slums, but the result was to create some of Scotland's most notorious housing estates. The policy followed was of strict economy and the housing estates were set on the outskirts of towns where land was cheap. The tenement was revived but set in a garden suburb setting. The result was the creation of a place like Blackhill which should shame any society into taking more responsibility for its housing policy; neither the landlords, Glasgow Corporation (now District Council), nor the tenants have anything to be proud about.

By 1939 municipal estates had become important elements in Scotland's settlement pattern. War brought house building to a halt, but not the formation of plans for a brighter post-war world. Up to the war the approach to town planning had been through the development of existing communities, but part of the post-war housing needs were to be met with completely new towns. The New Towns Act 1946 was one of the first major bills passed by the newly elected Labour Government. The new era started in Scotland with the designation of East Kilbride in 1948. Its target population was 50,000 at a maximum density of 36 houses to the hectare, mainly terraced houses grouped together in residential areas. The same characteristics were envisaged for Glenrothes in Fife, and together they became Scotland's Mark I new towns. Cumbernauld was started in 1956, Livingston in 1962 and Irvine in 1968. Together they now house 214,200 Scots. The sad brief saga of Stonehouse new town in which the first keys were handed over to tenants on 10 May 1976 and the whole project was cancelled two days later, is a clear indication that the new town movement is dead. The five towns that arose in the post-war years will be a memorial to the visions of politicians and planners for a brave new world based on the utopian environment of the garden city.

The seeds of high-rise living can be traced back to the early post-war housing schemes in Glasgow which incorporated some ten-storey blocks. In 1947 several councillors and the city architect visited Marseilles to inspect multi-storey housing and the sight of Le Corbusier's *L'Unité d'Habitation* won converts. However it was not until 1951, with the reduction of multi-storey construction costs, that the Corporation decided to rebuild the Gorbals in this fashion. Thus began a progress which made Glasgow the foremost exponent of high-rise living in Europe. Other Scottish towns followed Glasgow's lead and there is hardly a large burgh without its multi-storey block on the outskirts. One house in every five built since the end of the war has been in a block of six storeys or more, and in the early 1970s this figure rose to one in every three.

The role of council houses extends deeply into the fabric of Scottish society. At its height about 58 per cent of the population, in towns like Airdrie, Kilsyth and Coatbridge lived under this form of tenure compared to only 29 per cent in England. By the late 1970s housing tenure in Scotland seemed fossilized in this mode. Looking back on 25 years of post-war housing the Green Paper of 1977 on Scottish Housing could assume that the major physical task of house-building had been accomplished, and that an era of improvement could begin. In many ways this was true. The revival of the tenemental inner-city was to bring back gleaming sandstone tenements to Edinburgh and Glasgow, renewing civic pride that made mockery of the English 'inner-city problem'.

Scottish housing was on the brink of a revolution with the election of the Thatcher Conservative government in 1979. Underlying the stated agenda, there was the Government's strong ideological dislike of public sector housing and their desire to see choice expressed through market mechanisms. The first goal was to increase the number of people living in owner occupation which stood at 36.4 per cent in 1981. Within a decade more than half of Scotland's households, 52.8 per cent to be precise, had purchased their home. At the same time, those living in public sector rented accommodation fell from 52.1 per cent in 1981 to 38.4 per cent in 1991. The number of new homes being built in the public sector was a mere 1,546 in 1991, less than the number of homes demolished in that year. The remaining 8.8 per cent of households live in housing associations and the few remaining privately-rented houses. The end of the Thatcher decade saw a decline of more than 250,000 homes to rent in Scotland.

After 1979, investment in social housing virtually ceased. The need for this form of housing continued to grow, often in unforeseen directions and in conditions exacerbated by several years of general economic recession creating in Scotland consistently high unemployment in spite of being a major oil producer. Another new problem became that of affordability, so that about half of new households could not afford to buy the cheapest available home in their area. Homelessness appeared like a spectre from the Victorian Age. Since the passing of the Homeless Persons Act of 1977, the number of homeless in Scotland rose from 16,034 in 1978-9, to 30,859 in 1986-7 according to Shelter (Scotland). The character of homelessness changed at the same time from the traditional alcoholic down-and-out, to young people denied state assistance, the mentally ill as their hospitals were closed and dispossessed householders who suffered mortgage repossessions: each new group the casualties of some innovative legislation. Added to these demands, are those generated by changing demographic pressures of household formation such as the growing number of single-parent families and divorced households. Potentially, but barely catered for, are those demands for shelter generated by the Care in the Community Act which is throwing a new burden on local authorities, when they are struggling to survive a decade of attrition from central government.

Finally, the part of the housing stock which is below tolerable habitation, a figure estimated to be around 105,000 homes, the majority of which are the public housing stock of the 1960s. In short the solution has become the problem. The regeneration of peripheral housing estates—Castlemilk in Glasgow, Ferguslie Park in Paisley, Wester Hailes in Edinburgh and Whitfield in Dundee—present the most important, complex and difficult tasks for the future. About every problem conceivable are found in these areas: widespread heating and ventilating faults with consequent condensation, make life unbearable for many tenants. Tower-blocks and deck-access schemes show that their declared promise was a mirage. Frequent lift breakdowns, vandalism and cramped design accompanied by a wide variety of social problems have left them a reputation of being 'human filing cabinets'. The geographical and social isolation has created a view that it is better to tear down 'difficult-to-let' schemes and start again, like Niddrie in Edinburgh. Scottish housing in the 1990s presents a stark dichotomy, on the one hand half the population now owns their own house and seems satisfied, the other half live in a housing stock which is relatively new but of poor quality and the tenants are not happy, and there is relatively little chance of this situation changing. Maybe this is one issue in which a Scottish problem should have a Scottish answer.

I.H. Adams

Humanism, associated with the Renaissance, that 'New Learning' in which there was emphasis on man's significance, and on return to the classical sources of European culture, began in Italy. The presence of a copy of Petrarch's *Vita Solitaria* in Glasgow Cathedral library in 1433 suggests that Italian humanism may have touched Scotland at a fairly early date. In the same year William Turnbull, future founder of Glasgow University, returned from Rome to Scotland as a papal nuncio. He was in Italy again, not long afterwards, as royal agent at the humanist-thronged papal court, and as an advanced student in the university of Pavia, which numbered among its teachers about that time such notable humanists as Lorenzo Valla, Francesco Fidelfo, Theodore of Gaza and Maffeo Vegio. Turnbull was only one of a number of influential Scots with extensive personal experience of Rome, Florence, and other centres of humanist learning in Italy, France and Germany in the fifteenth and the early sixteenth centuries.

If by humanism we understand revival of interest in the classics of Greek and Latin literature, and an effort to emulate the style of Cicero and other ancient writers, there is clear evidence of humanist influence at the court of James III (1460–88). His secretary, Archibald Whitelaw, read and annotated classical texts, studied a commentary on the speeches of Cicero, could write in a polished Ciceronian style, and had at least some acquaintance with Greek. Interest in Greek could be picked up in Italy by a churchman like Turnbull; and there was at James I's court, for several years, at least one person who might have encouraged such an interest, the king's Greek doctor from Venice, Master Serapion.

James IV's secretary, Patrick Panter or Paniter, was like Whitelaw an accomplished Ciceronian, and before the end of James's reign humanism was clearly growing in Scotland. The education Act of 1496, which directed the nobility to send their eldest sons to school until they were proficient in Latin, is one sign of this. Two of James's own sons were sent to Italy to advance their education and had no less a person than Erasmus to teach them Greek and rhetoric. Erasmus had friends in the small academic world of Scotland, especially in the humanist circle associated with the new university of Aberdeen whose first principal, Hector Boece (c. 1465–1536), corresponded with him, and emulated Livy's style in a history of Scotland which was published in Paris in 1527. In James's reign there were Scots in Paris attending lectures on Greek, including the famous John Mair or Major (1479–1550) who is mentioned as a personal friend, in 1512, by Girolamo Aleandro who gave the lectures.

Aberdeen had its own recognized specialist in 'humanity' in John Vaus, master of the grammar school and from 1516–1538 professor in the university, author of *Rudimenta Artis Grammaticae*, first published in Paris in 1522, with second and third editions in 1531 and 1553. His library, judged by the volumes which have survived, held a representative collection of humanist texts, ancient and modern, including Boccaccio's *Genealogiae Deorum* (Paris, 1511). There is evidence to suggest that before the middle of the century there were humanist teachers in other grammar schools, for example, at Perth, Edinburgh, Montrose and Elgin.

Elgin was within the sphere of influence of the Cistercian abbey at Kinloss which engaged the services of the Italian humanist Giovanni Ferrerio in 1531 to teach young monks. By residence or by correspondence Ferrerio influenced humanist friends in Scotland for nearly 50 years. His friends included bishops Robert Reid of Orkney, Henry Sinclair of Ross, and James Beaton, archbishop of Glasgow. Ferrerio illustrates the international network constituted by humanist scholars, which included a number of Scots who made distinguished careers on the Continent but remained in touch with home, among them Florence Wilson (c. 1504–1551) from Elgin, and Henry Scrimgeour (1509–1572) from Dundee.

Wilson's treatise *De Tranquillitate Animae* (Lyons, 1543) is a good example of humanist writing. In his earlier published work (1532) he showed some knowledge of Hebrew and at one time he possessed a copy of the standard Hebrew dictionary by Sebastian Munster, which he presented to the most accomplished of Scotland's humanist writers, George Buchanan (1506–1582) poet, dramatist, historian and polemicist of the Scottish Reformation party. Buchanan, who studied and taught in France and Portugal, was regarded in his time as one of Europe's greatest poets. Latin poetry flourished for a period in Scotland, winning recognition among humanists elsewhere and culminating in the anthology *Delitiae Musarum Scoticarum* edited by the poet Arthur Johnston (1587–1661) from Aberdeenshire, and first published in 1637. Latin prose of good quality continued in the work of John Lesley, Bishop of Ross (1526–1596) of whom C. S. Lewis wrote 'His builded periods are those of a judicious classicist'. With his *De Origine, Moribus et Rebus Scotorum* (Rome, 1579) Lesley joined Boece and Buchanan among the historians.

Critical principles characteristic of humanism are found among Scots who were learned in law, notably Henry Scrimgeour whose critical edition of Justinian was published in 1558. As librarian to the great industrial and banking family of the Fugger he collected classical manuscripts (his collection is now the core of the Vatican Library's Palatine collection) and corresponded widely with other scholars, crossing religious boundaries in his scholarship. Scrimgeour had taught Greek at Bourges as early as 1543. James VI's tutor Sir Peter Young, and the great Protestant churchman and reformer of Scottish universities, Andrew Melville (q.v.), were his nephews. Among his friends was Edward Henryson, who was employed as Greek tutor to one of the Fuggers in 1547, and who lectured on Greek and on Law in Edinburgh in 1556 under the patronage of Robert Reid, Bishop of Orkney, Abbot of Kinloss, Prior of Beauly, and Chancellor of Scotland.

Another of Edward Henryson's patrons was Bishop Henry Sinclair, President of the College of Justice, whose own library witnesses to his humanist culture in the 120 or so volumes which survive. It is rich in Greek texts and shows interest in Homer and other classical poets, philosophy, natural history, biblical studies, theology, and Scottish and foreign history. Sinclair belonged to the family of Roslin, in which humanism found influential patrons. Gavin Douglas (c. 1475–1522), Bishop of Dunkeld, is a witness to this in his rendering of Vergil's *Aeneid* into Scots, partly for the benefit of Latin pupils. A lost version of Ovid's *Remedium Amoris* and, later, John Bellenden's translations of Livy (1533) and of Boece's *Historia Gentis Scotorum* (1536) suggest the existence of a reading public with fashionable classical interests which required support in the vernacular.

The rich vernacular poetry of Robert Henryson, William Dunbar and Gavin Douglas illustrates how currents of late medieval culture and the new learning were mingling in Scotland. Humanism had already affected the growth of Italian and French vernacular literature. The Scottish poets combined high technical accomplishment with linguistic inventiveness and introduced words characteristic of humanism; for example 'elegance' in Henryson. Henryson, schoolmaster in Dunfermline in the last quarter of the fifteenth century, who almost certainly had studied abroad as well as at Glasgow University, is not purely medieval but, rather, a transitional figure. It is tempting to see his fine poem *The Testament of Cresseid* as humanist, in the light of Cresseid's conclusion.

Nane but myself as now I will accuse (l. 574)

no longer attributing her leprosy to an arbitrary turn of Fortune or a whim of the gods but to her own way of life, of which it was a consequence in terms of contemporary medical theory. (Lechery leading to excess of the hot humour leads to leprosy.)

The reign of James VI produced William Fowler's *The Triumphe of the most famous Poet, Mr Frances Petrarke* (1587) and Stewart of Baldynneis's version of Ariosto's *Orlando Furioso*, as well as the far better poetry of Alexander Montgomerie, occasional recipient of royal patronage. As patron, and in his own academic accomplishment, James might claim a place in the history of humanism in Scotland, but much more as an example of the ruthless political pragmatism of Renaissance leaders, that man-centered approach to life frequently, though not always correctly, associated with humanists. In Scotland that approach was challenged by the Kirk. Protestant leaders, notably Andrew Melville, ensured the continuation of Greek and Hebrew studies in the universities; but as the seventeenth century went on Petrarch and Boccaccio, even Henryson, Douglas and Dunbar retired into obscurity. There was some not very distinguished Latin verse published from time to time such as Ninian Paterson's Latin epigrams in 1678. Archibald Pitcairne (1652–1713) wrote more praiseworthy Latin poems, published posthumously in 1717. Latin grammar and the Shorter Catechism dominated the schools and humanism was in eclipse, until the emergence of a rather different version in the eighteenth-century Enlightenment.

A. Ross

Hume, Alexander or Home (1560–1609), a son of the fifth Lord Polwarth, was educated at St Andrews and on the Continent. Originally intended for the law, he devoted himself instead to the Church and was minister of Logie, Stirlingshire, from 1598 until his death. His *Hymnes or Sacred Songs where the richt use of Poetry may be Espied* (1599) is a narrow performance reflecting his religious views, but he is best remembered for his one fine poem, 'Of the day Estivall', the celebration of a high summer's day.

M. Lindsay

Hume, David (1711–1776) is by any reckoning to be counted amongst the greatest of the world's philosophers. In addition he achieved eminence as a historian, an economist, and a political theorist. He was also one of the most lovable of men.

He was born in Edinburgh (though the family estate was at Ninewells in Berwickshire) on 26 April 1711, and died in the same city on 25 August 1776. He was educated at the University of Edinburgh and made some study of the law but then abandoned it for philosophy. He spent three years, 1734–37, in France, where he wrote his *Treatise of Human Nature*, the most comprehensive and, in the opinion of a majority of scholars, the most important of his philosophical works. It was published in 1739–40, when Hume was back in Britain. In 1744–45 he was a candidate for the Chair of Moral Philosophy at Edinburgh but was passed over in favour of a hack because his Treatise was thought to be hostile to religion. Much the same thing happened again with the Chair of Logic at Glasgow in 1751–52. from 1752 to 1757 Hume was Keeper of the Advocates' Library in Edinburgh, a post which gave him excellent facilities for writing his *History of England*. At a later period in his life he had a diplomatic career, first as personal secretary to the British Ambassador in Paris, 1763–65, then as Official Secretary to the Embassy, 1765, and finally as Under-Secretary of State in London, 1767–68.

In epistemology Hume is best known as an empiricist and a sceptic, but his distinctive positive philosophy lies in his naturalism. Empiricism is the theory that all genuine knowledge depends upon experience (of the senses and feeling). Hume carried this view further than his predecessors, Locke and Berkeley, applying it to our knowledge of the self as well as of material things. Hume's 'mitigated' scepticism was directed against rationalism, the theory that necessary truths about the real world are known by reason. In contrast to this, Hume's naturalism explained our beliefs about the world as being the result of tendencies in human nature, notably the association of ideas by the imagination. The imagination fills gaps in our experience and then builds up notions of completed wholes, whether of things or of persons. The most striking aspect of Hume's theory of knowledge is his critique of causation, with the accompanying problem of justifying inductive reasoning. He pointed out that we do not observe the necessary connection which is an essential part of our idea of causation, and he explained it as a projection upon the world of the subjective feeling of being compelled to expect that a sequence which has occurred regularly in the past will continue to be repeated.

This notion of projecting feelings upon the world is perhaps the basic idea of Hume's naturalism. He derived it from the ethics of Francis Hutcheson (q.v.), which formed the starting-point of Hume's own ethical theory. Moral goodness for Hutcheson is benevolence approved; the feeling of approval by spectators is projected upon its object, benevolence, and viewed as a quality of that object. Hume applied the same idea to causation in his theory of knowledge, but he also extended it in his theory of ethics. He distinguished between natural and artificial virtue. Natural virtue is more or less what Hutcheson had described, except that Hume explained the approval of the 'moral sense' as an effect of sympathy with the happiness produced by benevolence. But there are also other (artificial) virtues, notably justice, which do not always produce happiness. Hume explained our approval of them as the effect of association of ideas; the general aim of the rules of justice is utility (general happiness), and our sympathy with that aim is carried over by association to instances which do not maximize utility.

Hume made a signal contribution to the philosophy of religion, especially in his *Dialogues concerning Natural Religion*. Most thinkers of the Enlightenment were sceptical of the claims of revealed religion but thought that an enlightened reason could accept deism, religion based on the evidence of nature, and particularly the evidence of design for a benevolent purpose. Hume showed that they were not sceptical or rational enough. When we know from experience that a particular object was made by a person, we can reasonably infer of a similar object that it, too, was probably made by a person. But since we have no experience of the maker of any object like the universe, we have no adequate foundation for drawing the required analogy in this instance. Although regularity in the universe suggests some faint analogy with the products of human intelligence, it does not justify us in inferring benevolent purpose or any other moral qualities.

Hume's history is now outdated but it enjoyed great success in its own day and continued to be popular for a long time. It broke new ground in going beyond political to cultural history and was vastly more readable than its predecessors. In economics and politics Hume wrote no large-scale treatise but some of his essays express views which are both original and important. His chief contribution to economics is in monetary theory. Criticizing the mercantilists, he developed what economists now call the quantity-theory specie-flow doctrine. (Needless to say, Hume himself used no such barbarous language.) Within a country, the amount of money is irrelevant to real wealth, for an increase or decrease of money is soon reflected in a corresponding increase or decrease of prices. But this relationship has the effect, in international trade, of making the amount of money in each country tend towards an equilibrium at which exports equal imports. The virtue of Hume's political theory is its realism. He pointed out that the idea of a social contract is unnecessary for the justification of political obligation; the utility of government is quite enough. The notion of consent is essential, but not in order to legitimate political power; the truth is that such power depends on consent or 'opinion' as a matter of fact.

D. D. Raphael

Hutcheson, Francis (1694–1746) is the chief proponent of the moral-sense theory of ethics and one of the originators of utilitarianism. He had a considerable influence on the Scottish Enlightenment, especially through Hume and Adam Smith (who was one of his students).

He was born at Drumalig, in County Down, Ulster, on 8 August 1694, and died in Dublin on his fifty-second birthday, 8 August 1746. He was educated at the University of Glasgow and, after a short period as a minister in Ulster, conducted a new Academy for Dissenters in Dublin from about 1721 to 1730, when he was appointed Professor of Moral Philosophy at the University of Glasgow. He remained in that office until his death. Hutcheson wrote his most distinctive philosophical works, *Inquiry into our Ideas of Beauty and Virtue and Essay on the Passions and Affections; with Illustrations on the Moral Sense*, during his Dublin period. His later works, *System of Moral Philosophy* and some short (though better organized) textbooks, are a valuable indication of his teaching at Glasgow but are less original than the two early books. Hutcheson made a great impression as a teacher at Glasgow, where he introduced the practice of lecturing in English instead of Latin, revived the study of Greek literature, and was renowned for his eloquence and generosity alike.

Hutcheson obtained the first idea of the moral-sense theory from Lord Shaftesbury (Anthony Ashley Cooper, third Earl of Shaftesbury), but in Shaftesbury it is little more than a name, while Hutcheson turned it into a genuine theory. It is the view that we have a natural tendency to feel approval of benevolent motives. Virtue or moral goodness is the quality which we attribute to such motives, but that quality is really a projection of our feeling of approval. The theory turns into utilitarianism because the object of approval, benevolence, seeks to promote the happiness of others; a wide benevolence is more approved than a narrow, and so 'that action is best, which procures the greatest happiness for the greatest numbers'.

Hutcheson's method was empiricist, since he derived ethical qualities from human experience, the natural tendency to feel approval or disapproval, which he called the moral sense. However, although he effectively criticized rationalist philosophers, such as Samuel Clarke and William Wollaston, who believed that ethical qualities are objective facts known by reason, he was initially less concerned to attack rationalism than to refute egoistic accounts of ethics. The important thing for Hutcheson was that virtue (the motive of benevolence) is disinterested and that our judgement of it (approval by the moral sense) is also disinterested. In order to support this view he showed that egoistic theories neglect vital conceptual distinctions, which he illustrated perceptively with a variety of examples.

The *Inquiry*, Hutcheson's first book, compared virtue with beauty, the moral sense with an aesthetic sense. According to Hutcheson, the feeling of moral approval is aroused by benevolence, while the feeling of aesthetic appreciation is aroused by unity in variety. His later work in ethics is eclectic, drawing upon some of the characteristic beliefs of the ancient Stoics and the view of his contemporary, Bishop Joseph Butler, that conscience has a unique authority. Acceptance of the latter doctrine really undermines the original theory of a moral sense analogous to the sense of beauty.

Hutcheson's later work is more significant, however, for what it does outside ethics proper. In his lectures at Glasgow he followed the tradition of his predecessors in taking moral philosophy to include jurisprudence as well as ethics. The term 'jurisprudence' covered the general principles of law and government. Hutcheson's account of law related it to his theory of ethics so as to give what would now be called a 'rule-utilitarian' account of legal rights. In treating of government he dealt with a number of topics in economics and thereby kindled the interest of Adam Smith in that branch of learning. Like Smith, Hutcheson gave prime place to the division of labour, distinguished use value from exchange value, and advocated economic freedom. The extent of his influence can be seen especially in Smith's *Lectures on Jurisprudence*. His influence on Hume was equally profound, since his moral-sense theory, implying that the quality of virtue is a projection of the feelings of spectators, seems to have given Hume the key idea for his naturalistic philosophy as a whole.

D. D. Raphael

I

Iain Lom *see* **MacDonald, John**

Iain Mac a' Ghobhainn *see* **Smith, Iain Crichton**

Industrialisation transformed radically the pattern of life in Scotland. Ways of earning a living totally different from the tradition of hard and not always successful efforts to wrest bare subsistence from the land raised the standards of all to heights undreamed of by even the more affluent of past generations. Concentration of the population in the central Lowlands brought new hazards and opportunities in urban living, which gave rise to cultural changes that left much of Scottish society little different from that in other urban, industrial areas of the United Kingdom.

The dating of the origin of such sweeping and protracted changes can never be exact. Legislative attempts to encourage industrial growth pre-date the parliamentary union of 1707; the Board of Trustees for Fisheries and Manufactures was a semi-official agency set up in 1727 to provide further encouragement; the foundation of Carron Company in 1759 gave Scotland one of its most famous industrial enterprises. However important individually, such examples were only portents of the cumulative industrial and social changes which came in the wake of the growth of the cotton and other textile industries later in the eighteenth century, and of the heavy industries in the nineteenth.

The most evident cause of the industrial transformation was the adoption of new technical processes—mechanical means of spinning and weaving in textiles, the hot-blast at the furnaces—but alone such new technologies are inadequate explanations of a complicated process, and their economic consequences—even of Watt's steam engine—were minimized by adaptations and improvements in the old methods which preceded them. The cultural influence of any new technology was not then necessarily sweeping or dramatic. Much depended on how far it could be incorporated into traditional methods, particularly in the early days into the domestically organized production which was often an adjunct to predominantly agricultural activities. But a break—even if not a dramatic one—had to be made from traditional methods to gain the advantages of the division of labour and so to improve the low standards of most Scottish industrial production of the early eighteenth century. The most significant break came from the adoption of new means of power, of water and later of steam. Some of the earliest technical improvements in the manufacture of textiles needed no ancillary power and were incorporated into domestic production, but the need for additional power both removed established industrial processes from the inefficiencies and restraints imposed by domestic production, as when the scutching of flax came to be carried out in some 250 specialist mills in the 50 years before 1770, and gave birth to new enterprises, as when the water frame and the mule of the later eighteenth century enabled the Scottish cotton industry to emerge gradually from the old linen industry, the first by providing yarn suitable for cheap calicoes, the second yarn suitable for fine muslins.

The application of power had an immediate and obvious cultural effect through its influence on the location of new industrial enterprises. The initial move was to water-supplies. In 1787 water-power drove 19 cotton mills; 39 a decade later. The economic attraction of water remained for those plants which had an adequate supply, but the use of steam gave a new technical freedom of industrial location and construction moved nearer the source of raw materials, be it the coal for power or the imported raw material for the cotton industry. The new textile mills of the early nineteenth century were more concentrated in Glasgow (chiefly in Bridgeton and Govan) and in Dundee than in their surrounding countrysides. The physical concentration of industry was beginning. But the large, isolated new mills built in the late eighteenth century to exploit the potential of water-power—Blantyre, Catrine, Deanston, New Lanark, Stanley—have frequently been depicted as representative, even though few in number, of the new industrial order. Physically they were, and—where they survive—are, impressive, and their planned communities were attempts to combat the problems of a sudden influx of migrant labour—Highland, Irish, pauper—to a new area. It was otherwise in the small mills, especially those on the east coast, which were tied to the less rapidly expanding linen industry, or in the numerous makeshift adaptations from other uses which appeared throughout Scotland. But social or evironmental provision, even on the scale of New Lanark, perhaps especially when based on the ideology of Robert Owen, was inadequate compensation in the minds of many for the changed way of life which it involved.

Life in the mills was a new and contrasting experience, but not because the unwholesome physical environment, so vividly revealed by parliamentary investigations of the mid-nineteenth century, was compared with arcadian rural surroundings. Those who entered the mills were not used to idyllic conditions before they did so, but in the industrial society of the mills they saw a threat to their traditional skills and way of life. At the other end of the social scale, the landed interest also saw the industrial society as a threat to their traditional power, though one neither formulated nor perceived clearly. The losses, though often intangible, were immediate and were not offset by any material benefits which later generations were to reap from industrialization in the enjoyment of a higher standard of living. To some, however, the loss was very tangible: the loss of individual freedom to determine the speed of work by the collective need for discipline and regimentation in any mechanized establish-

ment, perhaps most of all in a well regulated model mill such as New Lanark; the irrelevance of rural skills in an urban community; more specific, but perhaps most memorable of all, the uselessness of the technical skills of the handloom weavers as the tide of their prosperity receded from the high-water mark reached when spinning alone was mechanized to the ebb of despair and degradation when power was applied to weaving. The plight of the handloom weavers remained the classic instance of a skill no longer required in an increasingly industrialized society.

The heavy industrial growth of the nineteenth century permeated Scottish life more extensively still, being sometimes a dominating, even a creative force, as in mining communities. Increasing exploitation of coal in the eighteenth century led finally to the impossibility of perpetuating the old Scottish system of colliers' serfdom as the difficulties of recruitment to which it gave rise impeded the expansion of output. Still more extensive exploitation of coal in the nineteenth century, and of the blackband and other iron ores, needed both canals and railways, especially those such as the Monkland Canal and the Glasgow and Garnkirk railway, which stretched into the geologically rich but landlocked parts of north Lanarkshire. Ironworking expanded especially in the mid nineteenth century. Twenty-seven blast furnaces producing 37,500 tons of pig iron in 1830 increased to over 100 with an output of nearly 400,000 tons in 1844. Coal and iron ore mining grew commensurately. Much of the pig iron was not processed further in Scotland. In the mid-nineteenth century roughly two-thirds of the annual production was shipped out of the country, half to England and Wales and half overseas. When the demand from the ironworks became less buoyant in the later nineteenth century coalmining continued to forge ahead independently on the same path to send from Scotland 38 per cent of its record production of 42,600,000 tons in 1913. Both coalmining and ironworking exploited the geological resources quickly and—as in the open-topped blazing blast furnaces—wastefully and conspicuously.

When the various processes of manufacturing cheap steel became available in the later nineteenth century, the geological conditions were less favourable. Scottish ore resources were depleted, and did not include the non-phosphoric ores initially required. If raw material supplies were less favourable, demand was not. Steelmaking was grafted into an older Scottish tradition of skilled heavy engineering, which gave the Clyde its reputation in shipbuilding, from the *Comet* of 1812 through various adaptations to the triple expansion engines and Scotch boilers of the 1860s, a reputation well established even before new methods of construction confirmed it. Most of the early steamships were of iron and in the 1880s, pioneered by Denny's of Dumbarton, steel replaced iron. Shipbuilding was only the best example of a distinguished and widespread heavy engineering tradition on which Scottish industry continued to flourish until 1914.

The availability of power was a major determinant of the location of the early cotton mills. The availability of the raw materials determined the location of the heavy industries.

There was no choice over the location of a coal or ironstone pit, and little over the ironworks which used the bulky raw materials, and as the heavy industries spread from their geological base in the Monklands parishes in the lower ward of Lanarkshire they transformed much of Scottish society. Demographic change reflected the pattern of industrial opportunities. Glasgow's population increased by one-third between 1831 and 1841; by mid-century it was the only part of Scotland which received a net movement from all other parts of the country. At the same time a rising stream of Irish migrants spread from its traditional areas of often only semi-permanent settlement in the agricultural southwest to live permanently in the developing areas of the central belt, bringing cultural and religious tensions which persisted long after the migration. Few penetrated further, except, slightly later, to the textile industries of Dundee and the east. The trend towards the concentration of the population continued as the rate of population growth slackened later in the nineteenth century. Glasgow and Clydeside recorded the greatest increases, even when the crofting counties and the southwest began to register absolute losses. The typical Scot became an urban dweller and encountered a crop of new problems, or old problems in a new guise. Most who could afford to do so preferred to escape to more salubrious quarters, where the evidence of industrialization was less obtrusive, but the harshness of life in the new industrial society was there to be seen by those who wished. In Glasgow in 1832 there was a spirit dealer to every 14 families. In 1841 the Scots drank 23 pints of spirits annually per head of population; the Irish, 13; the English four. Life was not only harsh in the urban communities; it was short. In spite of some medical advances, as in the successful attack on smallpox by vaccination, the death rate probably increased in the early nineteenth century as the toll of young life in the towns was taken by the three great urban diseases of typhus, tuberculosis and cholera. Though most horrific, the last, unlike the two others, was epidemic and not endemic, and not the greatest killer statistically.

The continued expansion of Scottish industry in the nineteenth century seemed so secure, and bred such individual and social confidence, especially among the more influential, that such vast social problems could be regarded without dismay as temporary blots on society to be removed by using the material benefits of industrialization in socially responsible ways. Much effort was directed in the industrial areas to inculcating such ways: the temperance movement was the antidote to alcoholism. But the comforting confidence in continued successful industrialization was itself misplaced. Industrial prosperity rested on assumptions which had to be realized for its continuation, and for the welfare of the society to which it had given birth. It was firmly linked to meeting the needs of an expanding international economy, whether for the raw materials of coal or pig iron or for the work of the highly skilled who made the ships and the steam locomotives. Scottish industrial society was just as firmly linked—though less consciously—to the maintenance of a steady flow of imports of cheap food to improve the standard of living, more directly and probably more effectively than by the efforts of trade unionists, politicians or social reformers. By the early twentieth century there were signs that, while Scotland still needed to import such necessities, exporting was becoming more difficult. Industrialization in other countries, and rising tariff barriers, deprived the Scots of markets. More seriously still, the exports—even the skilled engineering products— were geared to meeting the international needs of the nineteenth and not of the twentieth century. The Scots were not producing the consumers' durables the wealthier parts of the world were increasingly seeking, nor were they producing them even for their own domestic market. Singers came from the United States, and a number of early Scottish ventures in car production bore little fruit. The weight of the Scottish tradition was against light engineering. The warning signs were present in the early twentieth century but were not recognized in the high-noon of Edwardian confidence in the future of Scottish industry; when they became patently obvious in the aftermath of the First world War the hollowness of the pre-war confidence was revealed, but a shock was then administered to the confidence of Scottish industry, from which it is doubtful if there has been a complete recovery. The experience was as demoralizing as that of the handloom weavers a century earlier, only it was on a wider scale. Between the wars much Scottish industry had to recognize that the world wanted its products no longer. That lesson could not easily be learned; it seemed reasonable to wait and see if the world would not change its mind, or if an increasingly omnicompetent state would act as surrogate.

Before the industrial collapse, even in the nineteenth century, some of the undesirable legacies of early industrialization in the urban communities were tackled. The movement to improve public health was helped more effectively by fear of infection among the better-off following the cholera outbreaks of 1832, 1848 and 1854 than by appeals to their better nature. In 1855 a Glasgow Act paved the way for an effective remedy there by providing for the Loch Katrine water supply. But bad housing does not spread like cholera, and it remained the most intractable problem of the environment. In 1871, 32.5 per cent of Scotland's houses had only one room; in 1911, 12.8 per cent, and of those 56 per cent had more than two persons in each room. If a measure of overcrowding of more than two persons per room is applied, 45.1 per cent of Scotland's population was overcrowded in 1918. Overcrowding was a rural as well as an urban problem, but density was at its worst in the urban industrial areas, helped especially by the prevalence of the tenement as their common form of housing. Glasgow had 60 persons per acre in 1911, almost twice that of Dundee and Edinburgh.

Such a society with a major social legacy of industrialization still unsolved had to accommodate the large-scale and long-term unemployment and destitution of the inter-war years. Increasingly, remedies were sought in public action, whether for the direct problems of industry or the indirect problems of its social consequences, past or present. The need to improve housing led the public authorities to build two-thirds of the new houses in Scotland between the wars against only one-quarter in England and Wales. By the early 1970s council housing was over 80 per cent of the total in the old heartland of the heavy industries in Airdrie and Coatbridge. As a steady stream of basic industries were nationalized after 1945—coal, steel, shipbuilding—a large part of Scottish industry came under public ownership, while many of the newer industries which then came to Scotland were offshoots of other enterprises, frequently from overseas, encouraged and helped to come to Scotland by government subventions. What was least successful were efforts by Scots, or even by government, to change radically the outdated structure of much of Scottish industry.

Prospects looked bright for two decades after 1945. Immediately after the war strange names, often from the United States, became such a familiar part of the Scottish industrial scene that they employed about 100,000 by the latter 1970s. From the late 1950s, when the problems of the established industries became increasingly apparent, dramatic government initiative tried to promote the modernization of the industrial structure which was so sorely lacking, by bringing a steel strip mill to Ravenscraig and vehicle production to Bathgate and to Linwood. The high optimism of the early 1960s was soon lost. By the later 1970s foreign firms were beginning to curtail their operations; by the later 1980s the new industrial order, which it was hoped would replace the old, was as moribund. The closure of Ravenscraig in 1992 was merely a belated recognition that it was an inappropriate location for a strip mill, which some had suggested from the start. Too often the desire, and the policy, was to support the jobs, the firms, the industries where they were. To do otherwise involved drastic occupational and geographical change, and that was always unacceptable in such a conservative society as industrial Scotland. Self-satisfied confidence in Scottish industry, engendered by successes based largely on fortuitous endowments of coal and iron ore in the nineteenth century, was not easily eradicated.

R. H. Campbell

Industrialists. Industrial activity in Scotland has been of the profoundest importance both internally and externally as Scottish products were over long periods extremely influential in world trading; a few still enjoy that status.

Going back to the 18th century the Hopes of Hopetoun were the most notable mining family, developing Leadhills and trading in lead ore and products with Holland. In 1749 the Englishman, Samuel Garbett, and John Roebuck established the first large-scale sulphuric acid works in the world at Prestonpans, also for the Dutch market. Garbett and Roebuck diversified into ironworking, joining with William Cadell to found Carron Company in 1759. Carron was uniquely innovative both in the scale and variety of its products, and remained without parallel in Scotland. It nurtured for a while the talent of James Watt who, however, is best considered an English industrialist.

Towards the end of the 18th century the scale of industrialisation grew and of the men who exploited the growing opportunities for trade, David Dale stands out. Linen trader turned cotton manufacturer and much else besides, Dale was controller of much of the Scottish cotton industry by 1800. His commercial acumen and technical perspicacity was emulated by Kirkman Finlay of James Finlay & Co. who combined ownership of cotton mills on a large scale, and by the Graham family, whose connection with the Larcefield cotton works was eventually much less important than their involvement with Port wine.

By 1820 the dynamism of cotton was slackening and the new field for investment was engineering. David and Robert Napier, marine engineers, pioneered steam navigation between 1812 and the mid-1840s, and Robert made a very big business out of it. A succession of men trained in, or linked with Robert's business took Clyde shipbuilding to world leadership in quality ship construction. Tod & McGregor, J & G. Thomson and John Elder were all among the biggest and most successful marine engineers and later shipbuilders of their period, and the technical advances they made did much to encourage increasing volumes of world trade.

While marine technology was maturing, James Beaumont Neilson's hot blast process revolutionised the Scottish iron smelting industry. Neilson's own family took advantage of this, founding the Summerlee and Mossend Ironworks, and pioneering the large-scale manufacture of locomotives. The giants of the iron industry were, however, the Bairds. James Baird was the richest of them, and the family business still survives. The Tyneside Dixons, the Houldsworths, also from south of the border, and James Merry were also notable. The same firms also mined coal on a very large scale.

At about the same time the Scottish chemical industry was prospering on the basis of demand from the textile industry. Charles Tennant was the most commercially successful of the pioneers, but Charles Mackintosh (inventor of the waterproof) was more innovative, though like Watt, he moved south to reach his fulfilment.

In the second half of the 19th century industry became much more complex, and it is hence more difficult to select significant men. In textiles, the Clarks and Coats made Paisley thread dominant in world markets, James Templeton did much the same for carpets, and the Crombies of Aberdeen and the Ballan of Peeblesshire and Patons of Alloa established notable reputations in wool textiles. The new technology of steel brought to the fore William Beardmore who became for a time Scotland's greatest industrialist and John Colville, whose family laid the foundations for Scotland's greatest steel empire.

In shipbuilding, William Pearce, and English emigre, Lord Aberconway of English steelmakers, and John Brown & Co. came to dominate the Clyde for prestige shipbuilding but Russell and William Lithgow built up a remarkable tramp ship business on the lower Clyde. Lithgow's sons James and Henry, became all-purpose entrepreneurs during and after the First World War.

Of other industries, whisky should be highlighted, where

the Usher, Dewar, Buchanan and Walker families all achieved outstanding success. The unsung hero was William Ross who made the Distillers Company the leading force in the industry. Sir William Arrol put steel, bridges and buildings and Sir Robert McAlpine put railway contracting into the big business league and at a more refined level of technology the managers of the Singer sewing machine factory at Clydebank, and more briefly George Johnstone and Alexander Govan of the Scottish motor industry made notable contributions. In locomotive building the Reid and Barclay families were particularly notable.

These industrialists take us to the 20th century when the development of multi-national companies has made the purely Scottish large-scale business an anachronism. Among the Scots who have operated on the larger stage with success are Sir Charles Tennant and Sir Harry McGowan, the latter founder of Imperial Chemical Industries. The first Viscount Weir, operating from a Cathcart base, was architect of the National Grid and of the Air Force of the Battle of Britain period, but as a policymaker rather than as an industrialist.

The generally depressed condition of Scotland in the inter-war years saw the Lithgow brothers assume great importance in heavy industry, but comparatively few other major industrialists were operating on the Scottish stage. Nor has there been a great deal since 1945, with governments preferring to encourage inward investment rather than native talent. The heros of Scottish industry during the post-war period have been the survivors: Sir Eric Yarrow and Sir Robert Easton of Yarrow Shipbuilders; Sir William Lithgow and Sir Ross Belch on the lower Clyde, Whyte and Mackay and Invergordon distillers in whisky. There have been successes in new industries, like Prestwick Circuits and, more ephemerally, in contracting. But it becomes invidious to name names when one is dealing with the living or very recently dead. Modern industry in its international mode is too reticent about its decision makers. Frequently one becomes aware of powerful figures in the multi-national companies who are Scottish by birth or immediate ancestry but their roles are shadowy. For something like 150 years however Scottish industrialists were among the leading Scots of their day and could rank among the most accomplished of their generation.

J. R. Hume

Inverness. Two excavations in Inverness in 1979 uncovered traces of early settlement; a line of charcoal showed the occupation of Castle Street from about 4000 BC, as did a large accumulation of oyster shells at Muirton. When the Raigmore Clava-type Stone Circle was excavated in front of the new A9, postholes of unknown antiquity were found below the cobbled paving of the 3000 BC site.

Controlling the northern crossing of the Ness, of the Great Glen itself, with valleys, river and sea meeting here, Inverness must always have been important. Written evidence begins towards the end of the seventh century with Adamnan's *Life* of St Columba. When Columba came to visit King Brude about

565–80, he found him in his royal fortress, ruling Pictland from Shetland to Perthshire and Argyll, if not further south.

In 1040, Macbeth, then Mormaer of Moray, the vast province reaching from coast to coast, revolted against King Duncan I and left Inverness for a power-base further south.

The Royal Burgh's charter from King David I may date from before 1153, reaffirming the trading monopolies and privileges of the town, which needed defending against the encroachments of 'clannit men and strangeris nocht beand Merchandis' for several centuries thereafter. Not only did Inverness export wool, pelts, hides, timber, herring and salmon, it imported hemp from the Baltic, made it into ropes and exported them all over the world, probably in Inverness-built ships. In 1249, the Count of St Pol had a 'navem mirabilem' built here, and as late as the 1940s the Thornbush Quay was adapted to repair up to three 'Landing Ships, Tank' at once. There were, and are, maltsters and distillers, but the 12 brewers of ale have gone.

In 1296, Edward I of England reached Elgin and at Easter 1297 his Constable at Inverness was Sir Reginald Le Chen. Soon after, Andrew de Moray and Alexander Pilches, burgess of Inverness, his lieutenant, liberated the north and swept down to share the victory of Stirling Bridge with Wallace in September 1297. When the English king invaded again in 1303, Inverness made no resistance, unlike the garrison of Urquhart Castle.

In 1411, Donald of the Isles found the gates closed against him and burned the Bridge, 'the famousest and finest of Oak in Britain'. In 1654 its successor fell 'by the inadvertancy of a carpenter', but although 200 people were around it, only four had broken 'leggs and thighs', 16 were bruised and no one was killed. In 1685 a stone bridge was built, which fell in 1849 and was followed in 1852 by the well remembered Suspension Bridge. This was demolished and the present handsome bridge was built in 1963.

Queen Mary was refused access to her own castle in 1562 and stayed briefly in a house on the north side of Bridge Street. It was demolished in 1968 and the medieval stone cellars rebuilt in the entrance to the HIDB building.

The oldest surviving building is the lower part of the tower of the Old High Church. All that is left of the Dominican Friary is a broken pillar, but from the Friars' school came the old Grammar School and today's Royal Academy.

In the Civil Wars of Charles 1, Montrose, leading the Royalists, tried to take the castle in April 1646, but Huntly did not support him, and he failed. In 1649, after the king's execution, the Mackenzies crossed Kessock Ferry on 22 February and took both the town and the castle without fighting on that day. In May, Middleton retook them for the Covenanters. This was followed by the building of the Citadel, which was largely demolished at the Restoration.

In 1715, the Mackintoshes captured the castle, but two months later, in September, Rose of Kilravock took Inverness for the Hanoverians. During the 'Year of the Prince' 1745–6, both town and castle remained in Hanoverian hands. In 1773, Johnson and Boswell stayed in Bridge Street.

But big changes began with the Caledonian Canal in 1803. Inverness, not waiting to be joined by railways from the outside world, built a double line to Nairn in 1855, and built locomotives, too. Not until 1898 was the line through Carrbridge opened. In 1933, Highland Airways Ltd was founded by E.E. Fresson and on 29 May 1934, he inaugurated the first regular British internal airmail, from the Longman Airfield to Kirkwall, carrying 2,000 letters. In 1977, the *Inverness Courier* celebrated its 160th anniversary, and by then oil had been discovered.

There are but two Freemen of the old Royal Burgh, Her Majesty Queen Elizabeth the Queen Mother, and Rear Admiral Sir Anthony Miers, VC.

The Inverness Field Club's Centenary Volume, *The Hub of the Highlands; the Book of Inverness and District* and their *Old Inverness in Pictures* will put flesh on this bare skeleton.

L. Maclean of Dochgarroch

Irish in Scotland, The. 'Scotland is the name of what you call Ireland' Stevenson's Catriona told her David Balfour. 'But the old ancient true name of this place that we have our foot-soles on, and that our bones are made of, will be Alban.' It added only a new strand to the complex web his Lowland upbringing was encountering in discovering the Highland mind, but it does testify to the antiquity of the Irish-Scottish connection. The modern name of Scotland does derive from an ancient name from Ireland, and testifies to Irish invasion and displacement of the ancient Picts in pre-Christian times.

The history of both countries is intimately connected in the first millennium AD. The forms of Gaelic in use in both countries' not only belong to the same branch of Celtic (*q*-Celtic) but to modern times have remained so strikingly similar that the Scots-Gaelic of the Western Isles should present few problems to the native speaker of Donegal (though not of Connacht or Munster) Irish. Pre-Christian mythology testifies to close links: part of the action in the stories of Cuchulainn and of Deirdre takes place in Scotland, and as was shown by the antiquary Macpherson (only to be denounced with gross exaggeration as a forger) the Fenian cycle has a major place in Scottish as well as Irish oral tradition. St Patrick's origins (not to speak of existence) are matters of intense controversy, but a strong tradition links him with Romanized southwest Scotland, and St Columba was but one of many Irish missionaries to essay the reconquest of Scotland, this time for the Christian faith. He was also doubtless one of a large number of Irishmen to take refuge in Scotland having made their native land too hot to hold them.

The Iona monastic settlement associated with Columba became the North British focal point of inspiration for the Celtic Church, which opposed the modernizing campaign from Rome and held to its own forms of tonsure, dating of Easter, and tradition of apostolic succession from St John rather than St Peter. Its advance was halted and turned back at the Synod of Whitby (663 AD) where Northumbria elected to accept the ruling of St Wilfrid, speaking for Rome, in preference to that of St Colman of Iona. Southern Ireland had already capitulated, but Scotland, Wales and Cornwall fought a rearguard action for many decades. Modern attempts to link the Norman influence brought to the court of Malcolm III by his wife, St Margaret, with the final extirpation of the Celtic Church are anachronistic.

Links between Antrim and southwest Scotland were naturally strongest. The ancient kingdom of Dal Riada spanned the North Channel. The Antrim sept of MacDonnell maintained close connections with Scottish Macdonalds. Bruce on the run took refuge in Rathlin Island off Antrim, the home of the fabled spider. Scottish mercenaries played an important part in Irish resistance to the Normans and internecine warfare, with numerous instances of comparable Irish incursions in Scotland. Alasdair MacDonnell proved Montrose's most formidable ally in the civil wars, partly arising from native Irish resistance to the Scots and Border Protestant settlers in Ulster.

The collapse of the Stuart cause in Ireland in 1691 led to the emigration of many Irish soldiers to service in Europe, to be known as the 'Wild Geese', a few of whom appeared in the service of Prince Charles Edward in the insurrection of 1745 (in which Ireland itself played no part). They made themselves greatly unpopular with the Scots, and many of Charles's blunders were ascribed to their bad advice.

The mobility of Irish labour within Ireland itself led to seasonal migration to Britain in the late eighteenth century which intensified in the early nineteenth. The digging of Scottish canals in the period 1775–1825 attracted many Irish labourers, largely Catholic and probably primarily Gaelic speakers, in that Gaelic survival became increasingly restricted to the mountainous Irish west coast where agriculture was poorest. They collided with Highland migrant labour, and ethnic hostility flared frequently, both on the Caledonian canal, where the Highland work force had particular patriotic reason to resent the Irish invasion, and later on the Union canal, where both groups were resented by all classes among their hosts in Edinburgh and West Lothian. The hideous working conditions and understandable Ishmael complexes of the navvies both on canals and on their successors, the railways, increased their isolation from the community.

Although on specific operations the navvies remained signed on for the duration of the digging, seasonal migration remained a strong feature especially in Glasgow, Kilmarnock and the West. Even today Donegal continues to supply construction workers during the winter who return for the summer months until harvest. But gradually the ranks of the Irish in Scotland swelled as more and more labourers took up permanent residence. Outside the West, Dundee proved the area on which Irish made the most significant numerical impact.

Ironically, Edinburgh, with far less visibility of the Irish in the social and economic life of the city, produced some of the most famous Irish figures in nineteenth-century Scotland. William Burke and William Hare, two former navvies on the Union canal, took advantage of the intense demand for anatomical specimens among competing Edinburgh lecturers in medicine to undercut the flourishing resurrectionist business by murdering and selling 16 persons in 1828 to Dr Robert Knox, among the victims being several fellow-Catholics from Ireland. Despite the common belief, it seems certain they never robbed graves, having no use for the middleman. Eventually they were arrested, but since their smothering technique made the detection of murder almost impossible, the Lord Advocate persuaded Hare and his wife to turn King's evidence on which Burke was convicted, hanged and dissected, crowds of over 20,000 viewing the hanging and subsequently the corpse on the dissecting-table. Hare was protected by Lord Advocate Rae from further proceedings, fled to England and disappeared. Despite the excitement of the Catholic emancipation crisis at the same time, no anti-Irish riots took place, although Edinburgh was the scene of many anti-Catholic demonstrations over the preceding half-century and the subsequent century.

Much of Irish labour in Edinburgh was casual, including hawking, scavenging, carting, and refuse work, being domiciled in the streets below the broad thoroughfares and—in common with Irish Catholic patterns elsewhere in Scotland and the North Atlantic—crowding around Catholic churches. The ghetto around St Patrick's in the Cowgate produced James Connolly in 1868 from a family of carters. Connolly, in common with many Irish labourers, took service in the army, but returned to Edinburgh by the 1890s where he played a significant part in the tiny Socialist working-class movement. After experience as an organizer, speaker and journalist in the Socialist cause, he went to Ireland in 1896 and commenced a 20-year career in Ireland and America which won him the foremost place among original Socialist theoreticians produced by the British Isles in the past century. He retained ideological and familial links with Scotland, lectured and wrote for Scottish audiences and sought unsuccessfully in 1913 to win total support for the Dublin locked-out workers from the entire British working class on lines influenced by the American IWW of which he was a member. After the outbreak of war, his attempt to evangelize the Irish in Ireland, Scotland and North America by building a Socialist dimension to Irish nationalism recoiled on him, and, despairing of working-class solidarity in a war in which the workers were slaughtering one another, he opted for participation in the Easter Week Rising of 1916. It was almost certainly a counsel of despair undertaken in an effort to win a credential for Socialism in the event of ultimate Irish revolutionary nationalist success, but after his execution he was simply drafted as a nationalist into the new Ireland's pantheon. However, his anarchosyndicalist ideas continued to inspire a small following in Scotland, by no means limited to the Irish, his most notable disciple being John MacLean: the magazine *Forward* for which he had regularly written continued to reflect something of his ideas, and it is possible to see them reflected in the independent labour movement in Scotland during the 1920s and 1930s.

The third notable Irish contribution to nineteenth-century Edinburgh was of a very different kind. The huge Irish working-class emigration from the mid-century great famine onward has tended to dwarf the significant literary emigration which had been note-worthy since the Reformation. Irish journalists took the road to London with significant results throughout the nineteenth century, among them the Doyle family, of whom John Doyle ('HB') and his son Richard ('Dicky') were famed as cartoonists; a less successful son Charles again reflected a characteristic Irish tendency in seeking less strenuously competitive fields in Edinburgh where he became the father of Arthur Conan Doyle. Although the future creator of Sherlock Holmes has left few stories of Scotland ('The Man from Archangel', *The Mystery of Cloomber*) and fewer still of Ireland ('The Green Flag'), it seems clear that his Edinburgh medical training and urban experience played a much broader part in the making of his Holmes stories than has hitherto been recognized. Much of Holmes's London bears striking resemblances to Doyle's Edinburgh, and the arrogance and scientific dedication of the Edinburgh medical faculty is reflected both in Holmes and in Doyle's other famous creation, Professor Challenger. Like other Scottish literary emigrants, Doyle could present England to the English with a concealed detachment which induced sharper and more memorable contours than most native English versions, and his Irish Catholic antecedents took that detachment to a farther level.

Conan Doyle was, however, very unusual in being a Scottish Catholic (albeit fairly rapidly ex-Catholic) middle-class writer of Irish antecedents: middle-class Scottish Catholic writers are seldom of Irish extraction, Scottish Catholic writers of Irish extraction are seldom middle-class. Of the latter, the most notable are Patrick MacGill at the beginning of the twentieth century, and in our own time William McIlvanney, Jimmy Boyle and Larry Winters. MacGill's harsh and vivid evocations of the horrors of navvy life, *Children of the Dead End* (1914), and of the social origins and apparent inevitability of Irish prostitution, *The Rat-Pit* (1915), have been largely forgotten, but they remain invaluable to the social historian of the Scotland of his day and, with all their flaws, possess power and intensity. McIlvanney has done his most outstanding work in the novel *Docherty* (1975), a brilliant portrait of life among Irish Catholics in twentieth-century Kilmarnock, showing the mix of social pressures, ethnic isolation, clerical control, political stimulation, sexual innocence, generation conflict, ancestral loyalties and sibling rivalry. A saga is hoped for. Boyle and Winters were both convicted murderers whose books *A Sense of Freedom* (1977) and *The Silent Scream* (1979) respectively conveyed the horrors of socio-psychological catastrophe in their lives. Boyle, both in his book and in dramatic work he inspired, posed the crisis of the individual driven into violence by a society where he finds no place; yet there is in his work an evangelism whose transmission of his message testifies against the total despair his work portrays. Winters committed suicide, and the posthumous volume of his writings embodies tragic efforts to battle against that despair and come to some self-identification which, in the end, failed. Although neither of them exhibit a particularly Irish preoccupation in the senses that, say, McGill and McIlvanney do, they remain a testament to that part of the Irish experience in Scotland which has never escaped from the nadir, where the ghetto becomes a whirlpool of self-destruction.

Much of the history of the Irish in Scotland is an essay in self-betterment along classic immigrant lines. The proximity to Ireland and the distance from English centres of power made that process both more painful and slower than is evident among the Irish in much of England and North America. Irish political organization was fairly firmly established and Catholic newspapers in Scotland before 1922 reflected domestic Irish interest first and Scottish concerns a long way behind. The Irish were expected to supply vigorous support for Daniel O'Connell's movement for Repeal of the Union in the early 1840s, and were firmly mobilized into the Parnell movement of the 1880s. Under the influence of John Ferguson, a publisher (Cameron & Ferguson) of Protestant origin and Fenian affiliation, the left-wing of Scottish Parnellism sought to make common cause with the agrarian protest movement among the crofters in the Highlands and Islands, itself influenced by the success of the land war in Ireland. But the split caused by Parnell's complicity in the O'Shea divorce (1890) proved as disastrous in Scotland as elsewhere, lines of battle being in part though by no means exclusively dictated by clericalism *versus* radicalism. Further splits in the Irish movement reflected themselves among the Irish in Scotland, remoteness from both Ireland and London adding invective to the exchanges usually in inverse proportion to awareness of the realities. The turn towards violence in Ireland in 1916 and in 1919–21 increased the isolation of the Irish from Scottish politics and led their critics, including a sub-committee of the General Assembly of the Church of Scotland (1923), to charge them with being aliens primarily responsive to Irish rather than Scottish interests. The charge had some justice, although the racism with which its makers imbued it had not. In any event the ironic sequel was that the hostility of the Labour party to Lloyd George's campaign of repression in Ireland led to a firm Irish turn towards Labour. Already the signs of this were present in the Irish movement to positions of consequence in the Scottish trade union movement. As with much Irish participation in trade unionism elsewhere, it has been a search for larger slices of the capitalist cake rather than any revolutionism of the Connolly type. This has even applied to the Irish presence in Scottish Communism as exhibited by such figures as Mick McGahey, the miners' leader; the appearance of revolutionary goals implied by rhetoric and by hostile criticism seems less significant than the immediate gains to be obtained by the norms of bargaining and industrial action. On the other hand the Irish in Scotland, however conservative in social attitudes, show few signs of defecting from Labour to the Tories as is evident among the Irish bourgeoisie in England. Irish support for the Liberals in Scotland was always secondary to Irish domestic political considerations—all the more so because the most famous Liberal in pre-1922 Scotland was the Earl of Rosebery, no friend to Irish issues—and there seems no sign of revival of that old flirtation today. The Scottish National Party does attract some support among Scottish intellectuals of Irish origin, but little among the Irish working-class in the west of Scotland although it may be making gains in Dundee.

A legacy of dependence on alcohol—which, as Sir Walter Scott remarked of the Irish immigrants of his day, gave them heat, food and drink at one go—has apparently softened the harshness of ghetto life and the tensions induced by confrontation with a popular Protestant faith, although it has taken its toll in social disorder, violence, depression and poverty. Ironically it has proved a form of assimilation: Scotland is less hostile to heavy drinking than are many other cultures in which Irish immigrants became conspicuous by their alcohol consumption. Violence and alcohol have followed Irish enthusiasm for the Scottish cult of association football, another instance of an assimilation eliciting fresh assertions of ethnic identity. The Glasgow Celtic football team grew out of clerical attempts to foster manly sports and undoubtedly it has attracted a following far beyond the Irish and Catholic communities. Even the identification of Celtic with Papal and Irish loyalties by zealous friends and enemies often leads non-Catholic supporters to hail a win with cheers for the pope, presumably as a team mascot. Although Celtic is less obviously an ethnic team today, the firmly Orange identification of its great rival, Glasgow Rangers, to say nothing of the more sanguinary hostilities in neighbouring Northern Ireland, gives a heavy incentive to greater violence during the clashes of supporters. Despite this there is little sign of the rival ethnic communities bringing the civil war in Northern Ireland to Glasgow; whether the savage football rowdyism actually contains any such sentiment, or is likely to prove the match to some future conflagration, is as yet unknown. It remains an irony that during the many decades of the twentieth century when support for Celtic was the most considerable mark of Irish Catholic ethnic identification in Scotland, nationalist athletic policy in Ireland would have banned all such supporters as votaries of a 'foreign game' as opposed to the Gaelic football proclaimed as the true symbol of Irish patriotism. It is an indication of the ultimate divergence of the Irish in Scotland from the homeland of their ancestors, however surprising such a conclusion might be to Celtic (and Rangers) fans. Other formerly Irish-centred football teams, such as the Edinburgh Hibernians, have assimilated more quietly.

The phenomenon of Glasgow Rangers reminds us that for all of the heavy Lowland and Borders Protestant Scottish immigration to Ulster in the seventeenth and nineteenth centuries, there has been considerable traffic in the reverse direction. Orange lodges made their mark in the central belt of Scotland, often winning support in response to the competition and clannishness of the Irish Catholic work force. They retained considerable strength during the xenophobic 1930s, and their working-class Toryism remained a minor headache to the Labour party up to very recent times. So notable a figure in British politics as Andrew Bonar Law, with his Glasgow antecedents and Ulster priorities, was a reminder of the strength of Scottish-Ulster Unionist links. Since World War II such Orangeism as has remained has from time to time shown itself rather more intransigent than its Ulster counterpart, as when in the late 1950s some of its emissaries took up the cudgels (sometimes literally) for the Rev. Dr Ian Paisley, a highly unpopular figure at all times with the official Ulster Unionist establishment. At the same time that establishment could count on friends among the more moderate traditionalists in Scottish Toryism. These factors no doubt played their part in retarding any mass conversion among the Irish Catholic bourgeoisie in Scotland to Toryism, and Labour organizers have been free with unjustified allegations as to the Orange links of the Scottish National Party, with similar results. Orange marches may dwindle, but Rangers' supporters are still a reminder of the intensity of popular Orange sentiment.

The position of the Roman Catholic clergy is a somewhat uncertain one. Administered by Vicars-General since the Reformation the Roman Catholic community in Scotland finally had its hierarchy of Archbishops and Bishops restored by the Vatican in 1878, over a quarter-century behind the equally unpromising English. The chief cause of the delay lay in the ambitions of the Irish clergy in general, and of Paul Cardinal Cullen in particular, to make Scotland an Irish ecclesiastical fief in all but name as they had so successfully done for Catholic dioceses elsewhere in the English-speaking world. In general the hierarchy have been successful in keeping their numbers restricted to clerics of Scottish birth, and while certain Irish priests in Scotland have made themselves disagreeably conspicuous for bombarding their ethnically mixed congregations with Hibernolatry at all times, the tendency has decisively weakened. It has nevertheless been a hard struggle for Scottish Catholics of Italian, Polish, English and native Scottish descent to assert their identities against the Irish powers for organization and administration; and the fact that the contribution of the Irish in Scotland to Scottish Catholic intellectual life is far below their proportion within the Catholic community, tells its own story. Church-building, largely of an unimaginatively architectural conservatism; diocesan and parish administration, accompanied by little enthusiasm for lay initiatives out of the norm; maintenance of rigid *apartheid* in education, coupled with heavy episcopal homilies: all can be underlined as representative of the Irish achievement in Scottish Catholicism. There have been certain signs that Scotland is not immune to that emergence of a liberal—even a radical—Irish Catholicism which has become manifest in the United States, England and Ireland itself. Candour nevertheless obliges this Irish Catholic writer in Scotland to remark that liberalism among the Scottish Catholic clergy, and indeed laity, is primarily to be found among the non-Irish Catholics, particularly the native Scots. The fact that with a few exceptions ecumenism is not conspicuous in the ranks of the established (Presbyterian) Church of Scotland, to put it mildly, may offer an additional explanation, but not an excuse.

The history of the Irish in Scotland has not been a particularly pleasant one, either for themselves, or for those who encountered them. For all that, it has been a significant one. Numerically, the Irish in Scotland in modern times have transformed the demography of Glasgow, Greenock, Paisley, Dundee, Kilmarnock and many other urban centres. If both the Irish and their hosts have collaborated in building the ghetto walls high, the Irish can claim to have posed the problem of a culturally pluralistic society anew in a Scotland whose Lowland establishment was preparing itself to assert its final triumph—almost its final solution—over the assertion of pluralism formulated by the Highlands. It might seem incredible to the warring bands of Irish and Highland navvies, yet the Irish invasion of the nineteenth century gave new heart to the cause of preserving the Highland and Island identities. Faced with the Irish challenge to the proclamation of a cultural monolith, the Lowland establishment was forced to rekindle the concept of many Scotlands even if this did involve paying its respects to the Highland Beelzebub against the Irish Satan. And if the Irish preoccupation with political mechanics was depressing, at least it gave stability to that challenge to the monolith. It still has to deal with its own monolithicism.

O. Dudley Edwards

Iron and Steel. In 1814, Sir John Sinclair classed the iron industry among 'the secondary or less important Manufactures of Scotland'. Before the establishment of the Carron Works in 1759—an event with which the foundation of the modern iron industry is usually identified—charcoal iron had been made in Scotland, often with English capital and enterprise, but with a dispiriting lack of economic success. Carron was the first concern in Scotland to smelt with coke. Its example was not quickly followed. Two or three decades passed before the productive capacity of the Scottish iron industry was boosted by the laying down of works at Wilsontown (1779), Clyde (1786), Muirkirk (1789), Omoa (1789), Glenbuck and Devon in 1792 and Calder, Shotts and Markinch in the closing years of the eighteenth century. It has been estimated that some 23,000 tons of pig iron was produced in Scotland in 1806, about 9 per cent of the British make. Thereafter, the industry stagnated, the victim of high costs and inadequate local demand. No major new works were erected for a quarter of a century and although the industry's annual output crept erratically upwards, Scotland's share in British production had slipped to but half of the 1806 figure by 1825, a proportion that might have been even smaller had the Scottish iron industry not been protected from Welsh competition by distance and high transport costs.

Yet within a few years pig iron production in Scotland was to enjoy an unprecedented expansion. In 1830, 27 furnaces had produced 37,500 tons; by 1860 there were 133 furnaces in blast producing a total make of roughly one million tons. This transformation was a consequence of the invention of the hot-blast by J.B. Neilson in 1828. This not only permitted the exploitation of Scotland's unique 'black band' ironstone but so reduced fuel costs that by the late 1830s Scotland had become the lowest-cost iron-producing region in Britain. Scottish pig was able to compete in all the major domestic and foreign markets. High profits accrued to the ironmasters whose total costs were further reduced by the economies of scale. Further investment followed and a number of family firms, among them the Bairds of Gartsherrie, William Dixon, and Merry and Cunninghame, established princely fortunes.

The product of this massive endeavour could not be absorbed by the Scottish economy. By the late 1840s over two-thirds of Scotland's pig iron was exported; 20 years later, despite the belated development of malleable iron production, over half the total output was still being despatched to markets outside Scotland. Few of the great ironmasters built puddling furnaces. Instead, they integrated backwards, increasing their firms' incomes by investment in coal. The consequence was that the pig iron and forge sections of the iron industry possessed but tenuous ownership and locational linkages. This structural weakness was exacerbated with the coming of cheap steel. The earliest attempts to employ the Bessemer process in Scotland were unsuccessful. If William Dixon, who made the most elaborate trials at the Govan Works, had failed, who could hope to succeed? The ironmasters, affluent from sales of pig and coal, drew back. The fiercely competitive malleable ironmasters in Coatbridge had no similar cushion. More ductile and potentially cheaper than malleable iron, steel would, the more far-sighted of them believed, supersede their product. The example of the Steel Company of Scotland, established in 1871 by Charles Tennant and a group of steel users, who adopted the Siemens open-hearth process for the production of acid steel from imported haematite ores, pig iron and scrap, could not be ignored. In the late 1870s, several progressive malleable iron makers went in for steel. By 1885 Scottish steel production was roughly 20 per cent of the total British make and the economic wellbeing of the Steel Company and the new steel producers, among them William Beardmore & Co. and David Colville & Sons, had become inextricably bound up with the fortunes of the shipbuilding industry, the source of their major demand. Meanwhile, the majority of the ironmasters concentrated on improving their blast furnace practice and increasing their efficiency by the installation of by-product recovery plant. They continued to be heavily involved in coal mining. Thus, in the period preceding the First World War, the Scottish iron and steel industry remained unintegrated and locationally dispersed; hot metal working was impossible.

The events of the First World War aggravated this situation. Not only did there take place a massive increase in steel-making capacity without a commensurate expansion in smelting, but the deleterious effects of this imbalance were worsened by changes in the ownership of the steel plants immediately following the war, when almost the entire steel-making capacity of Scotland fell into the hands of shipbuilders anxious to secure their necessary sources in what was believed would be a sustained reconstruction boom.

These expectations were dashed by the collapse of the boom in mid-1920. There followed nearly 20 years of depressed demand during which heroic attempts were made to eradicate the fundamental weakness of the industry. Under the leadership of Sir John Craig, Colvilles came to dominate Scottish iron and steel. By 1937 this firm had brought the bulk of Scotland's steel making and heavy rolling capacity under its control and

technical rationalization was at last made possible. Interrupted by the Second World War, Colvilles' modernization and integration programme was resumed in 1944. Criticized for its refusal to embark on a more radical scheme involving the construction of a tidewater plant on the Upper Clyde, Colvilles persevered with more modest, socially responsible and practical schemes which culminated in the creation of the Ravenscraig complex in the late 1950s.

There was at this time a growing demand for a modern plant in Scotland to produce thin plate. Only thus, it was argued, could the dependence of the Scottish iron and steel industry on the notoriously fluctuating and ultimately declining shipbuilding industry be overcome and the continuing diversification of the Scottish economy be sustained, but all the plans to meet this need foundered on Scotland's chronic shortage of coking coal. Without adequate coal supplies, the building and commissioning of additional blast furnace plant was prohibited and the consequent scarcity of pig iron retarded the expansion of ingot output and semi-finished metal products. It was at this point that economic considerations were subordinated to political considerations. Colvilles succumbed to intense Government pressure and reluctantly agreed to erect a strip mill at Ravenscraig.

The Ravenscraig strip mill, commissioned in 1963, was the last major capital development scheme undertaken by private enterprise in Scotland. A technical masterpiece, it was a financial disaster. With nationalization in 1967 the British Steel Corporation inherited in Scotland an industry which by national standards was technically in good shape, well managed and, its financial indebtedness notwithstanding, confident of its future direction. Indeed, in 1968 the Scottish and Northwest Group announced its proposals for a £300 m fully integrated iron and steel works at Hunterston on the Firth of Clyde. Only later, when British steel production failed to maintain the upward trend of the late 1960s, was the economic unreality of the plan fully exposed. At the time, it seemed to the infant BSC to smack of a pre-emptive bid calculated to enlist the vociferous support of all facets of Scottish opinion and harness the powerful political pressures which had contributed to the success of the campaign for a Scottish strip mill. Sorely embarrassed, the Corporation sought to kill this example of regional exuberance by implementing its intention of reorganizing its activities on a product basis. The multi-product groups and their constituent companies were dissolved; the names Colvilles, Bairds and Scottish Steel disappeared.

Nevertheless, despite frighteningly escalating costs, the steel industry in Scotland has continued to be modernized. The old open-hearth furnaces at Clyde Iron Clydebridge, Lanarkshire, Dalzell, Glengarnock and Ravenscraig have either been closed or are scheduled for closure, but it was intended that investment in plant at Ravenscraig, Clydesdale tube works and Dalzell was to continue and the electric arc furnaces at Hallside were to be supported by a direct reduction plant at Hunterston. The unfavourable demand conditions which the industry is currently experiencing has accelerated closures and retarded development plans. The future for iron and steel in

Scotland is uncertain. Once established the industry has always shown a stubborn reluctance to relocation. Technical developments and a secular improvement in demand may one day permit a glorious resurrection of the steel industry in Scotland, but only the most optimistic would make such a prediction.

   P. L. Payne

J

Jacob, Violet (1863–1946), the daughter of W.H. Kennedy-Erskine of Duns, married Major A.O. Jacob. She made her name as a poet with *Songs of Angus* (1915), *More Songs of Angus* (1922) and *Bonnie Joann* (1922), the best of which were later collected under the title *Scottish Poems* (1944). Though her poems are set firmly in the nineteenth-century song tradition, using traditional stanza forms and rhythms, she manages to infuse such songs as 'The Neep-Fields by the Sea' and 'Tam i' the Kirk' with a clear bright imagery, reflecting her native Angus, and a note of genuine pathos. She recorded the history of her ancestors in *The Lairds of Dun* (1931).

   M. Lindsay

Jacobites was a term used to describe supporters of the senior and exiled branch of the royal House of Stuart after the Glorious Revolution of 1688 when James VII of Scotland and II of England was ousted from his thrones by his own eldest daughter Mary and her husband the Dutch prince William of Orange. James fled to France, and after participating in a brief Irish campaign, he settled down there under the protection of Louis XIV at the palace of St Germains, not too far from Paris. The word Jacobite is derived from 'Jacobus' the Latin for James, but in the mouths of the Whigs who supported the Glorious Revolution it was certainly meant to carry an implication of fraudulence. The word was meant to recall the biblical story related in Genesis chapter 27, verses 1–45, of how Jacob tricked his father Isaac into giving him the blessing intended for his brother Esau. The reason for this insinuation was, of course, the quite bogus Whig story that James Francis Stuart, the son and heir of James VII and II, was not the legitimate son of his father and his queen Mary of Modena, but a 'supposititious child' smuggled into the palace in a warming-pan.

   In Scotland there was no spontaneous revolution in 1688. A revolution occurred as the result of the dramatic course of events in England following the invasion of that country by an army led by William of Orange. Indeed the Convention of Estates which met in Edinburgh to try to control an unstable and dangerous situation in Scotland seems to have been swung decisively in favour of William mainly by the arrogance and ineptitude of the message it received from James. Major-General John Graham of Claverhouse, Viscount Dundee, then left the Convention and emerged as the leader of the first Jacobite rising in Scotland. With a mainly Highland army he routed the Whig or Williamite forces commanded by General Hugh Mackay at Killiecrankie in Perthshire in July 1689, but was himself killed in the action. Fought to a standstill by a Cameronian regiment at Dunkeld, his army was eventually disgracefully routed by Mackay's cavalry at the Haughs of Cromdale. What is remarkable about this first Jacobite rising is how few men of consequence joined it. Staunch former supporters of King James like the Earl of Strathmore and the Marquis of Atholl refused to commit themselves. Claverhouse had only some 2,500 men, drawn from smaller clans like the MacGregors, the Camerons, and the various branches of the MacDonalds. Scottish Jacobitism could only grow when the memory of the high-handed autocracy of James VII faded.

   Fade it did, and Jacobite sentiment undoubtedly grew in Scotland, fostered by the preaching of hundreds of Episcopal clergymen who refused to accept the Presbyterian settlement of the Kirk by Law Established which followed the Revolution. Other resentments played their part. William was an unsuccessful and uninterested king of Scotland. The 1690s saw severe dearth in the land. Above all, the passing of the Act of Union of 1707 under the reign of William's successor, Queen Anne, handed the leadership of Scottish national sentiment to the Jacobites. James VII had died in September 1701. His son James Francis Stuart (later known as 'the Old Pretender') was recognized by Louis XIV of France as king of England, Ireland and Scotland. By 1708 England and France were locked in a great war over the Spanish succession and there is every reason to think that when James Francis reached the Scottish coast in the Spring of 1708, his 'ancient kingdom' (as the exiled Stuarts always called Scotland) was ready to fall into his hands. The English government later admitted that there could have been no serious resistance north of Berwick, but the French admiral aboard whose fleet James Edward was carried, refused to land him or the embarked troops, and fled northwards at the sight of English ships.

   Scottish Jacobitism reached its peak in the 1715 rising, which owed nothing to the exiled court (now evicted from France after the Peace of Utrecht of 1713). Rather was it an expression of deep-rooted discontent sparked to explosion by the opportunist leadership of 'bobbing John' Erskine, Earl of Mar, who so mismanaged his career that after the accession of the new Hanoverian dynasty to the throne of Britain in 1714, he found he had no political future short of rebellion. The Duke of Argyll, the High Chief of the Whig Clan Campbell, who commanded the government forces in Scotland during the 1715 was emphatic that benorth Tay nine people out of ten were in favour of the rebellion. There is no reason to doubt the accuracy of his estimate, and it must be said that there was a great deal of potential sympathy for the rising south of the Tay. There was a small rising on the Scottish side of the Borders, and a significant rising in the northeast of England.

Tory resentment at the exclusive nature of the new Whig regime set up after the accession of George I meant that the Jacobites could count on support all over England if success attended their arms. In Scotland the disappointing economic consequences of the Union plus the systematic violation of its terms, and discrimination against the Scots nobility by the Westminster Parliament created something like a national rising which was frustrated mainly by the paralytic incompetence of Mar. By the time he fought the confused battle of Sheriffmuir in November 1715, the opportunity for quick success was gone. The landing of the Old Pretender shortly afterwards had no effect and he and Mar fled from advancing government forces by taking ship for France from Montrose early in 1716.

Though the Scottish courts successfully obstructed the penalization of the rebels, the fiasco of the '15 gravely wounded the Scottish Jacobite cause. Nor was it helped by the next rising which was a small one in 1719, rapidly crushed by General Wightman in a battle in Glenshiel in the northwest Highlands. The Scottish rising was a mere diversion in an abortive plan sponsored by Cardinal Alberoni, the first minister of Spain, for an invasion of England. Both its failure and foreign sponsorship (several hundred Spanish infantrymen fought at Glenshiel) discredited the rising. By the 1740s economic prosperity was marked enough in Scotland to buttress the Union. Why there ever was a '45 is a problem. Only a tiny minority of Scots supported it.

Without Prince Charles Edward Stuart, the son and heir of the 'Old Pretender', it could not have happened. His daring and egotism were essential. However, his landing in Scotland would have been impossible without the concealed sponsorship of the French government. Thereafter, the '45 is best seen as a demonstration of the gross inefficiency of the British government. Having conquered Scotland almost bloodlessly Prince Charles confirmed his conquest by a victory at Prestonpans outside Edinburgh. Lord George Murray, the best Jacobite general, led a remarkable march to Derby where Charles was with difficulty persuaded to retreat. A further victory at Falkirk for the Jacobites was followed by total defeat at Culloden near Inverness in April 1746 and by a policy of punishment and confiscation which destroyed any basis for future rebellion. Charles's brother Henry showed that he considered the family cause hopeless by accepting a cardinal's hat in 1747. Futile plotting went on for a number of years, but when Charles finally drank himself to death in 1788 even the remnant of Scottish Episcopalians who had continued to uphold the divine right of the exiled Roman Catholic Stuarts recognized that Jacobitism was dead.

B. Lenman

Jacobite Gaelic Poetry. James VII's departure from his throne came just too late to be of interest to the Gaelic professional poets, whose last extant works, in the classical language and syllabic verse, date from the early 18th century. The last of them, Niall MacMhuirich, died in 1726, and when he composed

poetry relevant to Jacobite politics he did so mainly in the vernacular and in the stressed metres which are the norm for Jacobite poetry.

Jacobitism comes across in extant Gaelic poetry as in some measure an extension of the political feeling engendered by the conflict over Charles I in 1644 and after. For one thing, the conflict over Charles and the conflict over James after 1688 both gave rise to an overwhelming preponderance of pro-Stuart poetry over anti-Stuart, despite the prominent anti-Stuart stance of various clans, especially the Campbells, in both cases.

The 'First Phase' of the Jacobite Movement, covering events from 1688 till 1719, corresponds roughly with the period of transition in Gaelic poetry from what is typical of the seventeenth century to what is typical of the eighteenth. In broad terms, extant seventeenth-century vernacular poetry has very little of the lyrical: it is mainly encomiastic poetry, with many close similarities to the classical poetry which it was in the process of replacing, and the poet is therefore following established patterns of praise of heroes and political partisanship. As Donald MacAulay (q.v.) puts it (*Nua-Bhàrdachd Ghàidhlig*, p. 46): 'The verse had to make an immediate impact, and skill in versification and verbal wit culminating in the well wrought, memorable phrase was therefore the basic requirement.' This is the type of verse mainly composed by Iain Lom (q.v.) (John MacDonald, *c.*1624-*post* 1707), whose work also exemplifies the close relationship between poetry of the Montrose period and that of the early Jacobite period.

The poetry of the transition period, like that of the seventeenth century, had to make an 'immediate impact' because the tradition was essentially a non-literate one (whether or not individual poets could write): its normal vehicle of transmission was the oral tradition. Practically all the Jacobite poems extant from before 1730 were songs, and have survived only through the work of collectors who, after the '45 had dealt what appeared to be a death-blow to all things Gaelic, set about noting down all the Gaelic poetry they could from oral recitation: their manuscripts and (from 1776) published collections are our main source for the poetry of the First Phase. Since oral tradition undoubtedly introduced textual changes over a century or more, we can rarely be sure of having the exact text originally composed, and the texts we have therefore depend very much on their various editors.

The poetry of the eighteenth century is best known from works composed about the middle of the century and later, when lyric poetry came into its own. The most famous poet of this time is Alasdair Mac Mhaighstir Alasdair (q.v.) (Alexander MacDonald), whose poetry is in some ways closer to that of the present day than to that of Iain Lom.

The transition period between 'seventeenth-century' and 'eighteenth-century' poetry, covering roughly the years 1690–1730 and most of the Jacobite First Phase, contains a mixture of both types of poetry: more of the personal element than before, but with the heroic ideal still intact.

In the Last Phase, covering the '45, we are on somewhat firmer ground as regards text, for Mac Mhaighstir Alasdair, usually considered the greatest of the Jacobite poets, was literate (to say the least) and published a collection of poems in 1751. But he is not the only poet of the Last Phase: for most of the others we have to rely again on the later collectors, though in this case, of course, the gap between composition and earliest extant written version is often quite small. But even printed originals have to be edited and annotated, so that in general reliable texts of, and information on, Jacobite poetry may be found only in a fairly small number of recent editions, and a few good critical works which draw on poems not yet fully edited. Mac Mhaighstir Alasdair's work has not yet been edited satisfactorily or comprehensively (his Jacobite work is an exception to this), and many other poets of the Jacobite period still await a good editor and translator.

The most easily accessible examples of the poetry of the First Phase may be found in the publications of the Scottish Gaelic Texts Society. The works of Iain Lom were published in 1964 by Annie M. Mackenzie (*Orain Iain Luim*, vol. 8), and include poems on the Killiecrankie period, the massacre of Glencoe, the right of William and Mary to rule, and the Treaty of Union. Another Jacobite poem from 1689 appears in William Matheson's edition (SGTS vol. 12; *The Blind Harper*, 1970) of the works of Roderick Morison (*c*.1656– *c*.1714).

For the Rising of 1715 the best-known name is Sìleas na Ceapaich (ed. C. Ó Baoill, SGTS vol. 13; *Bàrdachd Shìlis na Ceapaich*, 1972); a daughter of the chief of the MacDonalds of Keppoch, she married a Gordon about 1685 and perhaps died about 1729. Her name seems to have attracted the ascription of several poems on Sheriffmuir which are not, in fact, her work. Gaelic poetry, as we have it, seems to ignore the 1719 Glenshiel affair almost entirely.

This constitutes only part of the extant poetry of the First Phase and there is room for an anthology of Jacobite poetry of the First Phase which would include further poems, mostly from minor poets, especially on Killiecrankie and Sheriffmuir. Such an anthology, fortunately, already exists for the Last Phase in John Lorne Campbell's *Highland Songs of the Forty-five* (Edinburgh: John Grant, 1933), where the Introduction points out the importance of this poetry as evidence for the motives and beliefs of the Highlanders who supported the Stuarts.

C. Ó Baoill

James I, King of Scotland 1406–1437. As the strong and effective king who ended the intolerable disorder which had existed under the weak early Stewart government since 1371, James I's reputation stands high. The first four years of his rule after his return from English captivity in 1424 produced a deluge of legislation, on a quite new scale. He left nothing untouched. Administrative reforms, the idea of a new supreme civil court—the Session—and legal aid in the form of the 'poor man's advocate', licensing laws, the attempt to bring shire representatives to parliament on the English model, the act against heresy, again on English lines: all these, and his expedition to Inverness in 1428, where he executed three Highland chiefs and imprisoned some 50 others, amply demonstrated his immense drive and energy.

Yet this whirlwind activity is not satisfactorily explained in terms of inherited chaos; the intermittent regional disorder under the early Stewarts is not evidence of general anarchy. Probably more relevant is the complex personality of the king himself. He was a highly accomplished poet and devoted family man, but at the same time vindictive and avaricious; intelligence and energy led him to embroil himself in everything, but were not enough to enable him to think through his ideas adequately, so that the last nine years of the reign deteriorated into muddle. His savage Highland expedition, for example, created rebellion where it had not existed before; his attempt to regain Roxburgh from the English in 1435 was ill-conceived, ill-supported, and ended in fiasco. More generally, his undoubted interest in justice was effective in that he understood very well the importance of local justice and tried to strengthen it by reinforcing the traditional role of the kin and the principle of compensation for the wronged. But apart from that, much of what he said was only the pious propaganda expected of kings, never translated into practice; and there is no evidence that his great innovation, the Session, actually functioned.

In later years, greed became his dominant characteristic, undoubtedly clouding his judgement. Relations with his parliaments were soured when he spent the taxes levied for his English ransom on what has rightly been called 'a reckless spending spree'; this created effective opposition to further financial demands. Vindictiveness was added to avarice in his treatment of his own kindred, beginning with the extermination of the Albany family in 1425, which got rid of his nearest relatives who had held power before his return, while greatly enriching the crown. Politically, the crushing of the Stewarts had much to commend it; it ended the imbalance of Stewart power, created in the 1370s because of the vast size of the first Stewart king's family. But it led to the drama of February 1437, when a few members of his family, relying on the general hostility James had raised against himself, killed him. They miscalculated in hoping for support for their action. Kings could be hated with impunity in fifteenth-century Scotland, but not murdered; and the murderers were savagely executed. Yet many must have breathed more easily when they heard that James I was dead.

J. Wormald

James I (1394–1437). During a time of truce, James I was captured at sea by the English on 22 March 1406, while on his way to France. He was handed over to the English king, Henry IV, and kept prisoner first in London, then under Henry V in Windsor. While in captivity James became familiar with the work of Chaucer, and fell in love (and eventually married) an English noblewoman, Lady Joan Beaufort. These various circumstances are reflected in his love poem 'The Kingis Quair' (The King's Book).

The poem was found by William Tytler in the Bodleian Library, Oxford, in 1783, in a manuscript copied in two different fifteenth-century hands, neither of them that of the king. On the opposite page to that on which the poem begins, author and title are stated. At the end of the work a colophon in Latin in the second hand ascribes the poem to 'James the First, the illustrious King of Scots'. While no original known to be in James's hand exists, the circumstantial evidence in favour of his authorship is thus strong. It seems probable that 'The Kingis Quair' was begun in 1423, and finished a year or so later, after James's return to Scotland.

The main influences on the poet are the *De Consolatione Philosophiae* of Boethius, which inspired the poet's reflections on the comforts of philosophy, and the *Somnium Scipionis* of Macrobius, which inspired the structural idea of the dream-sequence in the poem. Literary influences are Chaucer's 'Knight's Tale' and 'Troylus and Criseyde', and Lydgate's 'Temple of Glass'.

Couched in the *rime royal* stanza, the language, the tone, the curious mixture of Scots and Chaucerian English and the freshness of the imagery add up to a poem of great charm through which runs a note of sincerity outwith the traditions of courtly poetry.

> Unworthy, lo! bot only of her grace,
>   In lufis yoke, that easy is and sure,
> In guerdoun of all my lufis space
>   She hath me tak, her humble creature.
>   And thus befell my blissful aventure
> In youth of lufe, that now, from day to day,
> Flourish ay new, and yet further, I say.

It seems possible that two very different, but equally germinal, poems of rustic love life, 'Christis Kirk on the Green' and 'Peblis to the Play', may also be by James, presumably written much later. The historian Major makes royal attribution of 'Peblis to the Play' in his Latin *History of Great Britain* (1521), an attribution also subscribed to by Bannatyne. Only the inaccurate Thomas Dempster advanced (in 1627) the improbable claim of James V.

M. Lindsay

James II, King of Scotland 1437–1460. In one significant respect, this reign has much in common with that of James I; it witnessed the second great onslaught on an aristocratic power-bloc, in this case the family of Douglas. The rise of this family, since the days when Robert I rewarded the good Sir James, had been consistent and on occasion spectacular, it reached its greatest heights during the minority of James II, when three Douglas brothers held earldoms, dominating the southwest and the north. Yet the idea that they used their power to menace the crown was not put forward until the sixteenth century. The one contemporary chronicle makes it clear that the king took the initiative against the Douglases, using William Earl of Douglas's absence in Rome in 1450–51 to seize some of his lands. And it is far from certain that the sensational murder of Earl William in 1452 was committed simply because James lost his temper with a magnate who would not break a

treasonable bond with two other nobles. Such bonds were commonplace amongst the late medieval aristocracy and gentry; and there is at least a hint in the contemporary chronicle that the murder was not wholly unpremeditated. A better clue to what happened is found in the fact that some of those with the king came from Douglas's area of influence in the southwest. It was not what the Douglases did; it was what they were that created resentment. Too many people were kept out of high places because of the utter dominance of this family. The king got support, despite doubts about his methods, because he was the king, and because of the patronage at his disposal. The Douglas collapse, complete by 1455, opened the way to the much greater social and political balance of power among several leading families, and therefore between king and magnates, which was never again seriously upset until the seventeenth century.

The creation of this balance of power, and generally good relations between the king and his greatest subjects, the men who controlled the localities, do much to explain James II's success as king; they far outweighed the occasional unscrupulous action, as when the crown used its superior power to fight off rival claimants to the earldoms of Mar and Moray. A further explanation can be found in his own high estimate of his prestige and power. He was, for example, the first king since the thirteenth century to look beyond the British Isles for a bride; he treated the Danish king, and to some extent the English king, as inferiors, and the French king as an equal who would do well to listen to the king of Scots' advice. This had its effect, in a century which witnessed the fostering of national pride by historical writers, beginning with Barbour in the late fourteenth century, and going on to Fordun, Wyntoun and, in James's own time, Bower.

The strength of, and respect for the crown is demonstrated by the parliamentary tribute to James in 1458, a tribute to his success in maintaining order in his kingdom. That success was cut off abruptly when his interest in that great status-symbol, artillery, proved fatal at the siege of Roxburgh in 1460, where he was killed by an exploding cannon. Comparison with his English contemporary, the morally far more admirable but politically inept Henry VI, highlights what was wanted of a fifteenth-century king: toughness, efficiency and the ability to maintain political equilibrium. These things this king provided in full measure.

J. Wormald

James III, King of Scotland 1460–1488. Of the 28 years of James's reign, 20 were years of personal rule, more than any other king save James IV and James VI. Yet only two events are well known: the hanging of his low-born favourites at Lauder Bridge in 1482, and his death in battle against his subjects in 1488. The contraction of the reign into two crisis-points made it possible to regard James as the king who failed because he relied not on his natural counsellors, the magnates, but on tailors, musicians, and most famous of all, the nobody of genius Cochrane, the architect who built the magnificent

Great Hall at Stirling, became Earl of Mar and, by the eighteenth century, could be described as James's 'Prime Minister'. A cultured king thus stirred up the mass hatred of his uncultured aristocracy, who destroyed his favourites and ultimately destroyed him.

Recent seminal research has shown that this will not do. The favourites emerge as the villains of the piece only in the late sixteenth century, although they have held the stage ever since, despite such contrary indications as doubt about who they were, and the demonstrable fact that the Great Hall was built in the reign of James IV. They became prominent because later writers came to explain James III's failure in terms traditionally used for kings who failed: that they were badly advised, by the wrong people. The reality was much more complex. James, like the other Stewart kings, had an exalted idea of his position. Unlike them, he tried to take it too far, proposing three grandiose campaigns to annex territory in France and the Low Countries, schemes frustrated by the prosaic reaction of parliament, who told him that fame as a ruler would come from success at home rather than risky gallivanting abroad. He was not a success at home. Throughout his reign, parliaments criticized his failure to take an interest in justice, that fundamental responsibility of any king. He failed also to establish good relations with his greatest subjects, because of whimsical and arbitrary behaviour; he gave and took away offices, even title and lands, and he never understood the need to reward adequately for particular services. Even his one far-sighted policy, friendship with England, which began with the first firm treaty, as opposed to temporary truces, in 1474, brought him little credit; England was too firmly the traditional enemy, and an unpopular king could not change a social attitude reflected, in the very decade of the treaty, by Blind Harry's epic poem 'The Wallace'.

The crises of 1482 and 1488 were therefore attacks on the king, not his favourites. Yet the significant fact is that only a minority of his subjects ever rose against him. The rebel army of Sauchieburn in 1488 contained only two earls and a handful of lords; and the fact that, as was said at the time, the king 'happinit to be slane' was almost certainly an embarrassment rather than an intention.

J. Wormald

James IV, King of Scotland 1488–1513. James IV was an immensely popular king. Greater wealth of evidence, peace at home, the flowering of the arts, and even its tragic end, have given this reign its appeal to historians, and in older histories at least, have encouraged the idea of 1488 as the great divide between the medieval past and the Renaissance present. That idea is of course too simple; the reign of James III was far from barren in learning and the arts. But in contrast to James III, James IV was a man of strong personal charisma; the contemporary Spanish ambassador, Pedro de Ayala, who most unusually found Scotland more congenial than England, described him as handsome, highly educated and intelligent, active and effective. The complaint of his great court poet,

William Dunbar, about the king's niggardly patronage and failure to appreciate the supreme importance of his poets at court is no more than a standard grievance; and while credit for the developments in education—the foundation of Aberdeen University and the 'Education Act' of 1496 which instructed eldest sons of landowners to learn 'perfyte Latyne' and then study law—must be shared at least with William Elphinstone, bishop of Aberdeen, certainly the king was the focal point of this brilliant era. His court, following the fashion established in late fifteenth-century Burgundy, was a place of dignity, ceremonial and pageantry. In his reign, that most revolutionary development, the printing press, was introduced into Scotland, benefiting from and giving further impetus to the growth of lay literacy. These, along with his building up of a navy, his interest in artillery, his scientific experiments, show that James also had a lofty belief in his position. But in his case, unlike his father's, this was seen in the increase of pride and prestige at home, and ferocious energy in governing his country, overseeing local and central justice, mounting an onslaught on the Highlands and suppressing the Lordship of the Isles, and making himself known to his subjects in his extensive travels, whether on pilgrimages, justice-ayres, or visits to the mistress he installed at Darnaway on the Moray Firth.

Yet his vision of his place in Europe brought ultimate disaster. His continuation of the policy of friendship with England, sealed by the 'Treaty of Perpetual Peace' in 1502 and marriage to Margaret Tudor in 1503, resulted in intolerable tension when the new ally and the old, France, were at war. His belief in Christendom encouraged him to make repeated demands for a European crusade against the Turks, led by himself; this solution to internal European power struggles only bored and irritated the great powers, including the 'Warrior Pope' Julius II. After four years of turmoil and shifting alliances, James committed his kingdom to the folly of invasion of England in the interests of France. His popularity ensured considerable support; an immense army went south to meet a second-division English force in September 1513. There in the mud of Flodden, dreams and visions became reality: total defeat, the death of the king, many who had been key figures in his government, and great numbers of his soldiers. All that was left of this reign of splendid achievement was an eighteen-month old baby to succeed, and a crisis for the kingdom.

J. Wormald

James V, King of Scotland 1513–1542. James V was in many ways the most ruthless and efficient of an efficient line of kings. His internal policy differed somewhat from normal Stewart policy. He departed from the idea of reliance on the Earls of Argyll to control the west, allowing lesser families, resentful of steadily growing Campbell power, to undermine Argyll's authority. His hanging of Johnnie Armstrong, immortalized in ballad, was only the most famous of a series of attacks on border magnates and chiefs. More generally, he made less use of his nobility than other kings, something for which he was criticized by his grandson James VI. Maintenance of law and order certainly interested him; money interested him more. Forfeitures, high compositions extorted for landgrants, were a feature of the reign. They had a significant effect on his income. Few kings have ever been known to lend money as opposed to borrowing it; James V was one of the few.

More sensational was his extortion of money from the Church. The problem of James's own religious convictions, or how far he had any, is beyond solution. His attack on the bishops, after the performance of David Lindsay's brilliant and biting 'Satyre of the Three Estates', suggests that he was aware of the need for reform. But he had a heavy responsibility for dubious appointments in the Church; his bastard children were beneficed at a young age by a compliant papacy, too fearful of pressure from Henry VIII on his nephew James to resist James's blatant appeals on behalf of infants described as showing remarkable and precocious piety. His foundation of the College of Justice was a device to wring further sums from the Church, taxed heavily to fund a paid judicial bench. But the money was not used for the judges, who threatened strike action after James's death; and it is the palaces of Falkland and Stirling, not the College of Justice, which stand as the true monument to James V. Whatever his beliefs, an avaricious king looked at the great wealth of the Church—ten times that of the Crown—with a covetous eye; and the Church of the 1530s could not stand out against him.

He had considerable success in foreign relations. The new element of religious struggle added to the old world of politics gave him a unique advantage. Where his father had been caught between England and France, James could play off one against the other, keeping the papacy in a state of agonized interest. The Scottish monarchy's belief in its own importance had real meaning; James could and did look very high for brides, marrying first the daughter of the French king, and second Mary of Guise, beating no less a ruler than Henry VIII in the race for the hand of this member of the most powerful family in France.

To some extent, the legend of James as the poor man's king derives from the fact that his fortune was made by taking money from those who could best afford it: France, the Church, and some of the landed aristocracy. But collapse came swiftly when James tried to force an unwilling nobility to invade England in 1542. Memories of Flodden were too close; even closer were memories of James's treatment of them. Dazzling and impressive as his reign was, it ended in despair by the time he was 30.

J. Wormald

James VI, King of Scotland 1567–1625. James VI has an almost unique claim to fame; he was the first king in Britain since Alfred to write his own account of kingship. His first work, *Trew Law of Free Monarchies*, was written in response to the threat posed by the extreme Presbyterians, who asserted the doctrine of the two kingdoms, temporal and spiritual, which in practice gave them the right to interfere in matters temporal while denying to the king any such right in matters spiritual. The academic and theoretic *Trew Law* countered this with the claim of kingship by Divine Right, introduced into Scottish political thought for the first time. *Basilikon Doron*, the textbook written for his son Henry, is a much more personal and practical statement of the realities of kingship. What emerges is not the vain pedant (a view which seriously misrepresents James) but a man of learning, wit and humanity; what also emerges is the shrewdness and political skill of the king, his moderation and flexibility, as well as his ambitions and limitations, the most striking of which was his contempt for the Highlands.

James lived in a fast-changing world. Tensions and insecurity brought into society by the Reformation inevitably affected political life. The king's government had seen great developments; laymen, drawn mainly from the lairds, had taken over from the clergy as professional lawyers and administrators, a process detectable at the beginning of the sixteenth century, and complete by the end. Bureaucracy, 'red-tape', centralization, were now marked features of government. Yet Scotland was still an intensely localized society; and at the centre of all that was new was a king whose approach was very traditional and personal. He understood the importance of relations with those whose power in the localities made them the crucial link between ruler and ruled. And at council, parliament and the general assembly of the Kirk, he was a regular attender, cutting through formalities to use his skill in debate and manipulation, of both people and government or Church business, to get what he wanted.

This undoubtedly successful style of kingship explains why James VI in Scotland was much more effective than James I in England. When, in 1596, Andrew Melville (q.v.) plucked the king's sleeve and called him 'God's silly vassal' in the course of heated debate, he was reflecting not the lack of respect with which Scotsmen are thought to have treated their kings, but the shared enjoyment of passionate argument between an academic king and his greatest academic opponent. In England, the monarch was far more cut off from the centres of political and ecclesiastical debate; only rarely, as at the Hampton Court Conference, could James manage, with some success, to deal with problems and dissensions by personal intervention. Moreover, although he returned to Scotland only once— against considerable opposition in England—his persistent interest in Scotland, shown in his strenuous attempts to bring about union of the kingdoms, or if not that, at least a better deal for Scottish merchants, horrified and antagonized his English subjects. In the end, he suffered in both countries. His concern for his northern kingdom was finally expressed in a determined effort to impose ecclesiastical reforms, the Five Articles of Perth, between 1614 and 1621; distance had inevitably lessened his sureness of touch with his Scottish subjects. Yet given the intolerable difficulties under which he laboured, his rule of Scotland from England was remarkably effective; its success is thrown into sharp relief by comparison with the follies and ultimate disaster of his son Charles I.

J. Wormald

James VI of Scotland, I of England. James VI (1566–1625), born in Edinburgh, the son of Mary Queen of Scots and Lord Darnley, had an extensive education, his tutors including the Scots Latinist George Buchanan. James's earliest publications were his *Essays of apprentice in the divine art of poesi* (1584) and *Poetic exercises at vacant hours* (1591). He is best known, however, for his *Demonologie* (1599) a treatise on withcraft, and the *Basilikon Doron*, written the same year for the instruction of his son, Prince Henry, in the duties of kingship. His antipathy to tobacco is reflected in his *Counterblast against Tobacco* (1604).

James gathered around him a group of poets, the most gifted of whom were Alexander Montgomerie and Sir Robert Ayton (qq.v.), known as the Castalians. Other members of the group included Sir William Alexander and Robert Kerr, Earl of Ancrum.

In some ways James was more important as an influence than as an author. Yet nothing he wrote is quite without interest. His views on rhyme, the use of words and the virtues of alliteration, together with the necessity for variety and the importance of music, retain a much greater liveliness, however, than his views on the virtues of pursuing old women as witches. His verse never quite overcomes a certain gawkiness, and does so most nearly in the sincerely-felt sonnet he wrote upon the death of Montgomerie. Few doctors in the late twentieth century would disagree with his objections to tobacco:

> Have you not reason then to be ashamed and to forbeare this filthy noveltie, so basely grounded, so foolishly received, and so grossely mistaken in the right use thereof; in your abuse thereof sinning against God, harming your selves both in persons and goods, and raking also thereby the markes and notes of vanitie upon you; by the custome thereof making your selves to be wondered at by all forreine civill nations, and by all strangers that come among you, to be scorned and contemned? A custome loathsome to the eye, hatefull to the nose, harmefull to the braine, dangerous to the lungs, and in the black stinking, fume thereof, neerst resembling the horrible Stigion smoake of the pit that is bottomlesse.

M. Lindsay

Jenkins, Robin (b.1912) was born at Cambuslang and educated at Hamilton Academy and Glasgow University. For a time he taught English in Glasgow and at Dunoon, Argyll. In 1956 he went to Afghanistan to teach, from where he went to Spain and then to British North Borneo (now part of Malaysia). He returned to Dunoon, where he has since made his home.

From his first novel, *So Gaily Sings the Lark* (1951) Jenkins established his terrain; that of daily Scottish ordinariness. He himself has stated that as we have been a long time 'acquiring

our peculiarities ... it is the duty of the Scottish novelist to portray them'.

His succeeding Scottish novels were *Happy for the Child* (1953) a sensitive evocation of Scottish childhood; *The Cone-Gatherers* (1955), in which the vulnerability and hollowness of privilege are probed from different angles; *Guests of War* (1952) dealing with the class confrontation when deprived city children were evacuated into more affluent surroundings because of the war; and the best of them, *The Changeling* (1950) which examines the relative influences of heritage and environment on a child, bringing together the lives of a progressive teacher and a slum family child. *Fergus Lamont* (1954) explores the destructive elements of Scottish society, with which we are all familiar.

In 1960, Jenkins moved his fictional scene abroad with *Some Kind of Grace*, followed by *Dust on the Paw* (1961) set in Afghanistan, called in the book Nurania, its hero Manchester-educated Abdul Wahab, who attempts to reconcile his idealism with the advantage to be gained by following the main chance. The characterization is penetrating and as shrewdly observed as are the 'liberated' foreigners of Graham Greene.

After a book of short stories, Jenkins returned to Scotland for his thematic material. *Poverty Castle* (1991) is a charming, if somewhat improbable, tale about a novelist writing in the midst of his domestic circumstances. Apart from George Blake, Jenkins is the only outstanding novelist of the Scottish Renaissance (with which he has never publicly associated himself) to write of urban dilemmas, sometimes low-key (as with the English Beryl Bainbridge), but to deal with them on a securely-sustained plane of outstanding literary achievement.

M. Lindsay

Johnson, James (*c*.1772–1811), music publisher and engraver. Born Ettrick Valley; in business in Edinburgh from *c*.1772 ; died Edinburgh, 26 February.

Johnson was Edinburgh's leading music engraver for much of his life: between 1772 and 1790 he prepared plates for over half the music published in Scotland. Soon after starting business he changed from copper engraving to a cheaper pewter process which he was supposed, erroneously, to have invented.

Most of Johnson's engraving was done for other publishers; but his own publication, the song-book *The Scots Musical Museum* (6 volumes, 1787–1803) is noteworthy. After the first volume the editorship was taken over by Robert Burns, and the subsequent volumes contain the bulk of Burns's collecting and re-writing work on Scots folksong. The collection has been reprinted three times for its scholarly value, in 1839, 1853 and 1962.

D. Johnson

Jones, John Paul (1747–92) is known popularly as the father of the American Navy. Born John Paul in Galloway he was apprenticed as a sailor and made several trips to America. During the American War of Independence he fought on the American side and distinguished himself against the British. In 1788 he joined the Russian fleet and fought in the Russo-Turkish war. He is buried in the US.

P. Ingalls

K

'Kailyard' can mean different things to different people. To many today it sums up a sentimentalized attitude to Scotland, an escapist view probably set in the past, probably in the country, probably avoiding scrupulously the contentious issues of an urbanized modern Scotland. To the literary historian, the term is associated with the exceedingly successful novelists of the late nineteenth century, Crockett, Maclaren and Barrie (q.v.) who (with all the tremendous differences between them) are lumped together in this frequently derogatory definition.

Kailyard fiction is not easy to analyse. Certain features recur: a tendency to operate in a rural agricultural community usually one or two generations in the past (a point used subtly in Barrie's *Window in Thrums* with its flashbacks); a restricted cast featuring one or more ministers (for Church schisms were a staple for such collections as Barrie's *Auld Licht Idylls*): worthy dominies of village schools who in Maclaren's novels seem capable of producing endless child prodigies who collect Firsts and university Chairs at an early age; for the rest, hard-working ordinary people drawn from a very narrow section of the population, tenant farmers or above, to the exclusion of the very rich and the very poor. Another group excluded, the reader notices after a while, is women, for their role in the kailyard is frequently a very subordinate one. They support, they rear families, but the central role is given to the men.

Narrow, too, are the range of plots and the permissible range of emotion. Situations recur. Death is a frequent visitor, and family feuds and rifts predominate also. Children run away from home to 'the city', that fearful off-stage Hell, and return to be reconciled to dying parents. Incomers and petty tyrants are put down. Overall is the unspoken consensus of 'the Glen', the menfolk who discuss affairs freely in marketplace and churchyard, uttering pronouncements of decent humanity and unquestioned authority. This, with wide variations, is the Kailyard.

Two points have to be made at once. One is straightway to underline the variety of the kailyard even in the hands of its most famous three practitioners, for there is a world of detailed difference between Crockett's Galloway, Maclaren's Drumtochty and Barrie's Thrums—as there is between any of these and Barrie's later self-critical *Sentimental Tommy* and *Tommy and Grizzel*. Along with this goes the admission that there is much in the kailyard of considerable literary quality, for all three were capable of excellent writing in the course of their uneven output. Like the lesser writers of their time they could plumb terrible depths, but they could write in general very well, and sensing a market, they wrote for it copiously.

The kailyard satisfied, in some measure, the desire in Scotland for a literature which recreated a bygone age more specifically Scottish than an increasingly urbanized, industrialized British modernity. If Cockburn was right in his *Memorials* to see 1805 as the last 'purely Scotch' age, then the kailyard looks back to the middle of the nineteenth century to a Scottishness which predates the normalizing of railways and industrialization. Theirs is Dalmailing before the new road, Barbie before the railway. Railways enter their world, if at all, as a branch line, to take the farmers to market and back again. Beyond that the lines run into another world, unknown, unheeded. The cities and scars of a modern Scotland exist elsewhere, and while Thrums has its mills and even its hard times, the major Scottish conurbations could as well be on the surface of the moon. And this was the literature which pleased a world-wide market—and curiously and significantly, pleased the Scottish market too. Perhaps many Scots overseas preferred to read about a Scotland they remembered. Perhaps the Scots at home preferred the same—explaining the curiously static quality of much recent Scottish entertainment in song and sketch, cartoon and film, as if the country were seen through a time-machine. The kailyarders recognized a taste for this partial vision, and wrote for it with ability.

At times, they reached bathos, vicious bad taste, patronizing typecasting for the amusement of a Scottish or English superior reader. The boundaries of offence are difficult to draw just because Scottish readers seem also to have enjoyed the joke. But certain aspects have worn badly, most notably the sentimental. *Bleak House* and *Middlemarch* have their sentimentality too, but it is always in good balance; the kailyarders lacked this balancing virtue, they often sank into the predictable Bible reading or Psalm, the reunion of families seconds before a death, the last-minute change of heart by wicked father or tyrannical landlord. A market existed, and a taste for this fiction, whose genealogy is not easy to see.

The enormous success of the Burns tradition doubtless encouraged an uncritical Scottishness, easily perverted into the values we associate with kailyard. Local '*Whistlebinkie*' poetry also contributes to a developed market with pre-formed tastes. But perhaps more important is a line of enquiry on which much remains to be done. The Scotch Philosophy of an Enlightened eighteenth century encouraged a carefully-defined 'sentimentalism' designed to elicit strong emotional responses from a readership interested in those responses, and keen to see in them a guide to a deeper understanding of their own characters. To such an audience Mackenzie's (q.v.) *The Man of Feeling* (1771) was a distinct success, for philosophical as well as literary reasons; its enormous popularity in Britain and Europe extended its readership far beyond those whose tastes and reading would encourage Mackenzie's intentions. Also its popularity prolonged its reading beyond the limits of the Scotch Philosophers, encouraged by the imitations of John Wilson whose *Lights and Shadows of Scottish Life* and *Trials of Margaret Lindsay* picked up and amplified the sentimental motifs to create a self-indulgent 'sentimentalism' far removed from the tough-minded Mackenzie. Even Galt (q.v.), whose successful output is far too good for the accusations of kailyard sometimes raised against it, used sentimental scenes frequently at a time when their application would be ambiguous to large numbers of his readership. From his success to the weaker scenes of Margaret Oliphant and George MacDonald (qq.v.), was perpetuated and developed a set of tastes, and a scenario of scenes and characters which the alert kailyard novelists were able to recognize and exploit. Must we not take account of this genealogy of the kailyard, alongside the obvious explanations from Victorian sentimentalism? Much remains to be done in this field.

But always, generalizing on the kailyard, we come back to the talent of the major practitioners, and the very diverse appearance and critical quality of the genre. Even the novel most credited with the destruction of the kailyard, Brown's (q.v.) *The House with the Green Shutters*, satirizes by a triumphant imitation of the kailyard form, destroying the credibility of the characters and situations only after capturing the audience's attention by an apparently innocuous opening promising another kailyard Scottish village. To that extent, his novel is not so much anti-kailyard, but an illustration of the extreme flexibility of a genre which is not dead, but which survived in the latter half of the twentieth century in a surprising variety of forms.

Curiously, the groundwork for the evaluation of this most successful phenomenon remains to be done. Yet its popularity has been too universal, and too long-lasting, to ignore.

    I. Campbell

Kelly, Thomas Alexander Erskine, sixth Earl of (1732–1781), composer. Born Kellie Castle, Fife, 1 September; studied at Mannheim with Johann Stamitz, c.1752–6; returned to Edinburgh, 1756; died Brussels, during health-cure visit to Belgium, 9 October.

Kelly was Scotland's greatest symphonist during the classical period. Born into an artistic, eccentric family (his maternal grandfather, Dr Archibald Pitcairne, and his brother, the Hon. Andrew Erskine, were both noted poets), Kelly's education was interrupted by the 1745 Rebellion; he was, however, able to do a European 'Grand Tour' in the early 1750s and to study composition with Johann Stamitz, then the leading exponent of the new Mannheim orchestral style.

Kelly returned to Scotland in 1756 a master of this avantgarde musical idiom which was soon to sweep Europe. He became vice-president of the influential Edinburgh Musical Society and took an important part in its administration: it was probably thanks to him that the Society built St Cecilia's Hall for its concerts in 1762. Bremner published 10 of Kelly's symphonies between 1761 and 1770. These were frequently played by the Society, and during the 1760s and 1770s became a local attraction for cultured visitors to Edinburgh.

Kelly wrote several further syphonies which were not published, and are now lost. His other surviving compositions include six trio-sonatas (1769), and about 25 minuets dedicated to female friends and relations.

    D. Johnson

Kelvin, William Thomson, (1st Baron Kelvin of Largs) (1824–1907) was born in Belfast, son of a Professor of Mathematics. The family moved to Glasgow when he was eight. At the age of ten he entered Glasgow University and went to Cambridge at sixteen. At twenty-two he was appointed Professor of Mathematics and Natural Philosophy. His contribution to physics was discovering the second law of thermodynamics and introducing the absolute (Kelvin) temperature scale. He was also a prolific inventor and, after patenting some of his inventions, became a wealthy man. He was buried in Westminster Abbey, alongside Sir Isaac Newton.

    P. Ingalls

Kilt *see* **Dress, National**

King, Jessie Marion (1875–1949) was a designer and illustrator born in Glasgow. She studied at Glasgow School of Art from 1895 to 1899, where the principal Fra Newbery noticed her talent, and went on to study in Italy and Germany. She became internationally renowned for her designs, working on silver, pottery and book illustration and exhibited along with C.R. Macintosh in Turin where she won a gold medal. Her work was delicate and refined, taking as its themes legends and fairy stories. At the beginning of the First World War she moved back to Scotland, to Kirkcudbright, and lived there until her death.

    P. Ingalls

Kingship, Fifteenth and Sixteenth-Century. The monarchy of this period appears to have much in common with the post-war British economy: the stop-go pattern. The paradox of the subject is that it presents us both with the spectacle of a line of kings of impressive ability, and with the spectre of repeated minorities on a scale unparalleled in Europe. Every ruler, from James I to James VI, came to the throne as a minor; three succeeded as infants of under two years, while James IV at 15 was unusually old. After James V's death in 1542, an already bad situation worsened; apart from the problematic six-year interval of Mary's rule, there was no adult king for some 40 years, the years of Reformation and fundamental change in foreign policy. This central fact about the monarchy had a profound effect on foreign contemporaries and later historians. Kings personally gave motivating force to government, called parliaments and councils, were responsible for justice, made war and peace. If, for reasons of youth or inability, they could not do so, political equilibrium in the state was so seriously distorted as to cause almost intolerable problems for all save the few concerned only with self-interest. Repeated interruptions of personal royal rule made it impossible for Scottish kingship to develop along the increasingly autocratic lines of the English and French monarchies. Institutions of government remained comparatively undeveloped, while the social and political power of the aristocracy survived to an unusual extent, producing critical comment by late sixteenth-century English observers. This formed the basis of a historiographical tradition, going back to the seventeenth century, in which, consciously or not, the Scottish situation was measured against the uniquely sophisticated English government and its degree of control over the nobility, and found sadly wanting. Sympathy went to a well intentioned monarchy, blame to an overmighty aristocracy. Kings always got the benefit of the doubt; magnates never did.

It is, however, possible to take a different view. The problems faced by Scottish kings throw into sharp relief their remarkable success. In the fifteenth century, there was never any dynastic challenge to the crown, apart from the unsuccessful usurpation attempt by James III's brother, Alexander Duke of Albany, in 1482. This contrasts strikingly with the unstable English situation, where there were six successful usurpations between 1399 and 1485. Moreover, the two occasions when kings died violent deaths, James I in 1437 and James III in 1488, are not evidence of a weak monarchy, but were the extreme reactions of a few people to an immensely strong one. James I, vindictive and avaricious, was murdered by a few of his kinsmen who had suffered from 13 years of bullying and greed. James III survived for 20 years of arbitrary and whimsical rule before being killed — accidentally—in battle against a small minority of the aristocracy. Between them came James II, who pitted his strength against the mightiest of magnate families, the Earls of Douglas, and obliterated them. This is not the whole story of the fifteenth-century monarchy. But it does demonstrate its power; and the absence of any general magnate challenge to the crown, even when one of their numbers was murdered by a king, makes it hard to sustain the idea of overmighty nobles and weak kings.

The self-confidence of these kings is further reflected in their complete indifference to monarchs' usual practice of surrounding themselves with a mystique based on a mythical line of ancestors, the recipients of saintly or divine favour, or on special powers. The ancient line of Scottish kings was certainly known about, but it was fostered not by the monarchy, but by historians and political theorists; and James VI's horrified scepticism, when he found that as James I he was expected to touch the scrofulous for the King's Evil, did not endear him to his English subjects. Scottish kings positively underlined the fact that their origins were far from mythical or divine; they used the name 'Jacobus Seneschallus'—James the Steward—and gave it dignity by transforming the idea of the officer who looked after the household into the king who looked after the realm.

This gives us a clue to the particular nature of Scottish kingship and the source of its strength. To an unusual degree, it remained *laissez-faire* kingship. The crown made little attempt to centralize control, but instead continued to devolve it to the great men of the localities, 'the armes and executers of (the king's) laws', as James VI wrote. This was not simply a negative policy made inevitable by recurring minorities; it was positive and effective. One crucial reason was that for most of the late Middle Ages Scotland was not at war; when she was, it was mainly defensive warfare. Unlike its English counterpart, the monarchy did not have to sell ambitious policies of foreign conquest, for which money was required. Repeated demands for taxation significantly affected the relationship between centre and locality, producing a high level of political involvement and criticism; it also had a profound effect on the development of a highly vocal lower house, of gentry and burgesses, in the English parliament. By contrast, the almost complete absence of taxation in Scotland greatly reduced the possibility of tension between centre and locality. Until the Reformation created a new world of ideological politics, therefore, the lairds had no particular incentive to demand their own voice; that voice could be, and was, expressed by the natural leaders of local society, the magnates. The monarchy, although steadily enriching itself by building up its lands, usually at the expense of unfortunate individuals, and by exploiting the wealth of the Church, was not seen to bear down heavily on society generally. Scottish kings were certainly conspicuous spenders; they were as concerned as any of their European counterparts to maintain their prestige by patronage of the arts, and by living in visible splendour. In a poor and remote country, that was a particular matter of pride, for themselves and their subjects, untarnished by any general hostility created by their methods of raising money.

Secondly, the problems created by the geography of Scotland made reliance on men of local power essential. It is arguable, although there are many detailed reservations, that the alienation of Highland and Lowland society became a reality only in the seventeenth century, when the government had become far more centralized and therefore remote. Crown reliance on Campbell and Gordon power in the west and north did not ensure total success; but by persuading these two great families that their interests could be identified with the crown's, the monarchy did maintain a measure of control and unity within its kingdom. There is no strong evidence, until James VI's dream of union between England and Scotland made Highland language and custom an embarrassment, that the monarchy was hostile to Gaelic society; the suppression of the Lordship of the Isles, for example, by James IV—who knew Gaelic—had political, not social motivation.

As the focal point, the overseer, of a very disparate society, the crown had a position of remarkable strength. Institutional weakness did not mean political weakness; indeed, institutional sophistication may blind us to the fact that there is a distinction between government intention and achievement, and the Scottish monarchy, whose strength was so strongly personal, is a valuable reminder of that fact. The king alone could offer political stability; thus, however harsh his methods,—and there is no doubt that many resented individual actions of every king—he would always find support. The crushing of the Stewarts by James I and the Douglases by James II was made possible because these families, by their very existence, created an imbalance of power within the state, which the crown could, and should, correct. Lacking a private army and a host of paid officials, the crown was bound to rely on cooperation from its greatest subjects; that is only to say that, like any government, it had to have consent. How much it got is nowhere better illustrated than in the fact— much more prosaic, but much more revealing than the occasional magnate rebellion—that after every minority the king could issue an act of revocation, revoking all grants made in his name; that is an extraordinary testimony to the fact that the magnates were prepared to accept that the crown's rights overrode their own material gains.

The structure of political power was beginning to change by the reign of James VI, not primarily because of royal policy, but because the growth of lay literacy, from the fifteenth century, produced a group of lay lawyer administrators, firmly entrenched in law and government by the late sixteenth century. Lawyers are far better than kings at devising rules, tightening up procedures; these people had an undoubted impact on professionalizing a hitherto casual and informal bureaucracy. That, and the introduction of regular taxation, was to open up a gulf between centre and locality. At the same time, the authority of an already powerful parliament was enhanced. Whereas in England, Henry VIII's use of the Reformation parliament strengthened the authority of king-in-parliament, in Scotland, parliament acted in defiance of the crown in bringing down the old Church in 1560, and that made it potentially very dangerous indeed. In such a situation, a long tradition of managing men, not through formal channels but directly, stood that traditionally-minded monarch James VI in good stead. It was the wrong tradition, as he was to find, for ruling England; it was undoubtedly right for ruling Scotland.

J. Wormald

Kinship and Lordship. A general historiographical problem is the relationship between kinship and lordship, and the extent to which they conflicted with one another; for example, one of the greatest medievalists of this century, Marc Bloch, argued that feudal lordship developed because of the weaknesses of kinship, and directly at the expense of it. Medieval Scotland offers us a great deal of evidence which suggests that the opposite could be equally true, and that kinship and lordship were complementary, each strengthening the other; it provides a model for medieval societies which did not have highly developed central governments, and where the localities remained relatively untouched by the centre.

In the early Middle Ages, the picture is too incomplete to substantiate this argument in any detail. The obligations of kinship, fundamental to society, were unwritten; by contrast,

lordship was recorded, mainly because it involved a tangible commodity, land. In the later Middle Ages, however, the increasing tendency to document a far greater range of matters, from the important to the trivial, included documentation of the personal nature of lordship; and this makes it clear that lordship was understood in terms of kinship. There survives a remarkable collection of agreements between lords and their men, and lords with other lords, known as bonds of manrent and maintenance (promises of service and protection) and bonds of friendship. These are personal agreements. They were almost always made by men who were not kinsmen, but who promised to act as though they were: 'in affeccione and obedience as he (the lord) war my fader naturell and I his sone naturell', as one bond expressed it.

Several factors explain the unusually strong survival of kinship in fifteenth and sixteenth-century Scotland, in the Lowlands as well as the Highlands. It was agnatic; the kin-group consisted of the males of the family, descended from a real or mythical ancestor. The use of the surname, by now common in the Lowlands, provided an easy means of identification, 'name' or 'surname' being synonymous with 'kin'; and the agnatic nature of kinship is further reflected in the fact that a wife retained her own family name, and did not take that of her husband. There were, therefore, fewer problems of divided loyalties, such as weakened cognatic kindreds, where obligations were owed to relations by marriage. Yet kinship remained strong not only because of such definition, but also because of its flexibility. Men of the same surname living at different ends of the country did not recognize kin-loyalty; geographic cohesion was as important as the blood-tie, so that, for example, the Gordons in the northeast formed a separate kin-group from those in the south. Moreover, the linking of kinship and lordship meant that men looked beyond their kinsmen for help and support; the obligations of kinship spilled over into lordship, and further into relations with neighbours for whom mutual support offered mutual advantage. Thus lordship and good neighbourliness derived their *raison d'etre* from the older obligations of kinship, but were in practice equally important. These obligations were all crucial in a society where royal government was largely *laissez-faire* government, and where for most people the local head of kin or lord was more immediately relevant than the king. In the absence of state control, of police force and insurance company, security for life and possessions was found through personal contact, personal alliances. Such alliances were used for war and feud as well as for peace. But the attention which has been focused on the violence within society should not obscure the extent to which kinship and lordship were undoubted forces for stability in the localities.

J. Wormald

Knox, John (*c.* 1514–1572). That one man in his time plays many parts is particularly true of Scotland's best-known ecclesiastic.

Roman priest and Protestant convert; companion of George Wishart, the future martyr, and chaplain to the men who avenged Wishart's death by assassinating Cardinal Beaton; slave for nineteen months in the French galleys; radical preacher in Edward VI's England; pastor to refugee congregations in Dieppe, Frankfurt and Calvin's Geneva; inspirer and organiser of Scotland's hard-pressed 'privy kirks'; passionate supporter (after his return home in May 1559) of the 'Lords of the Congregation' in their rebellion against the Queen-Regent's Francophile regime; minister of the High Kirk of Edinburgh (St Giles) from July 1559 until his death; chief architect of the Protestant order introduced by the Reformation Parliament of 1560; arch-enemy of Mary Queen of Scots throughout her personal rule; exultant celebrator of Protestantism's consolidation in 1567, and disillusioned chronicler of the strife and degeneracy that followed: merely to outline Knox's career is to realise how controversial a figure he was (and is)—and how difficult to categorise.

To call him Protestant, Calvinist, Puritan may do justice to his essential attitudes, but hardly conveys the singularity of the man. He is not an immediately congenial character today, being too sure of the rightness of his cause, too convinced that the Church of Rome was an idolatrous 'synagogue of Satan', too ready to interpret the Bible (his supreme authority) with uncompromising literalism, too much at home among the theocratic savageries of the Old Testament. We are repelled by the rancour with which he pursued his enemies, and the draconian rigour of the disciplinary system that he helped to establish.

Yet he was a deeply compassionate pastor and an incomparably eloquent preacher. His democratic sympathies, and his long advocacy of the right to rebel against unjust and 'ungodly' rulers, culminated in memorable encounters with Mary at Holyrood and elsewhere. He had courage and a rare disinterestedness. Though partisan, his *History of the Reformation* has been praised for its 'depth of insight, brilliance of presentation and animation of style'. And his compatriots incline to regard him—despite his European sojourns and his orientation towards England in language and policy—as almost the archetypal Scot: bleakly austere, sardonically humorous, fiercely independent.

Perhaps our final verdict depends on how we view the great manifestos of 1560 which owed more to him than anyone else. The *Confession* gave the newly-reformed Kirk a concise and vigorous statement of its faith, and exercized a determinative influence upon its subsequent thinking. The *Book of Common Order*, 'Knox's Liturgy', revolutionized worship—providing services in the vernacular, centring everything on the reading and preaching of the Word, restoring the communion cup to the people, and enriching praise with their singing of the metrical psalms. The *Book of Discipline* sketched the outlines of a truly Christian commonwealth, with a national system of education for all, careful provision for the poor, the sick and the old, and cooperation between Church and State in the service of God and humanity. Together, they may well be the most interesting and important memorials we have of Scotland's past.

A.C. Cheyne

L

Labour Party, The. Labour's present position as electorally the most successful party in Scotland came relatively late in its history and has never reached the 50.1 per cent of the total vote here nor by the Scottish Conservative and Unionist Party in the 1955 General Election, let alone the 58 per cent taken by the Liberals in their great 1906 victory. Yet Labour's strength in Scotland in the Thatcher years as England swung to the right, has seemed to its critics simply to underline its impotence on the issue of Home Rule and the reluctance of its leadership to challenge the legitimacy of a Conservative regime with no Scottish mandate.

Pressure groups like Scottish Labour Action who want an autonomous Scottish Labour Party pledged to Home Rule invoke our tradition of independent radical politics dating back to the Highland Land Leagues and the original Scottish Labour Party formed by James Keir Hardie, among others, in 1888. The latter body agreed to its incorporation within the Independent Labour Party founded at Bradford five years later, but when the ILP joined with the Trade Union Congress in forming the Labour Representation Committee in 1900 Scotland's position in fact remained a distinctive one. The 1903 electoral pact between the new LRC and the Liberals did not apply here and for all practical purposes a second Scottish Labour Party existed until 1909, that year really being the origin of the Scottish Labour's current organisational relationship to the party in England.

Electoral success was slow to come for Labour in Scotland, partly because of the 1903 pact not being operative in Scotland and also because of our Liberal tradition being a tenacious one with support amongst all classes. Labour's breakthrough came in the 1922 General Election when it won 29 of the Scottish seats at Westminster and 32.2 per cent of the total votes cast. This vote held solid until the National Government's landslide victory in 1931. Within this period, for many Scots, the ILP *was* the Labour Party because of its crusading zeal for socialism and the magnetism of some of its members, like James Maxton, MP for Bridgeton from 1922 until his death in 1946. In 1925, over one third of the ILP's United Kingdom branches were in Scotland and MacDonald the Labour leader kept his individual membership after close colleagues like Snowden had resigned theirs.

The powerful position of the ILP could make for tension

between it and the new divisional or constituency based parties created under Labour's 1918 constitution, especially over the financing and running of election contests.

Relations between it and Labour were further strained by the extent to which ILP activists like Maxton and John Wheatley, MP for Shettleston 1922–1930, became bitter critics of MacDonald's leadership and used the Glasgow Federation of the ILP as a base from which to attack him. The ILP's Scottish leadership however took a different view, distrusting the confrontational tactics of Maxton and Wheatley and opposing the party's disaffiliation from Labour in 1932.

This deprived Labour of the rhetorical skills of Maxton, who supported the ILP's breakaway, while Wheatley, the most able minister in either of Labour's two minority governments had died in 1930. The next decade was one in which the Labour Party had to rebuild support and organisation in a Scotland devastated by unemployment and drained of population by emigration. Scottish Labours' recovery began with the 1935 General Election and the party gained in prestige from Churchill's decision in 1941 to bring into his Cabinet, Tom Johnston as Secretary of State for Scotland.

Johnston represented Clackmannan and West Stirling in Parliament from 1922 to 1924 and again from 1935 to 1945 after an interlude as member for Dundee from December 1924 to 1929, but was best known as a co-founder and editor of the independent socialist weekly *Forward*. His good working relationship with Churchill facilitated important wartime legislation for Scotland like that creating the North of Scotland Hydro-Electric Board. This set the pattern for a period after 1945 of enlightened Labour corporatism under which some managerial power in nationalised industry and the National Health Service was devolved to Scotland, but the post-war Labour government gave no priority to Home Rule legislation.

This had still been Scottish Labour policy in the 1945 General Election in which the party's candidates performed less well in Scotland than in England—winning 39 seats and 47.6 per cent of the vote, but the level of support achieved was still enough for Labour to build upon in subsequent elections even as it retreated from its historic commitment to Home Rule.

Scottish Labour finally turned its back on this at its 1958 conference, a decision which had to be re-assessed within a decade in response to the resurgence of a nationalist movement capable of overturning a huge Labour majority in the 1967 Hamilton by-election.

The Party's Scottish Executive and annual conference however needed the pressure of an anxious leadership in London before it came out for devolution in 1974, which more articulate voices had long supported like that of John P. Mackintosh, MP for Berwick and East Lothian from 1966 until the February 1974 election, and then again from October 1974 until his death in 1978.

Not all Scottish Labour MPs were converted and some, like Tam Dalyell, exercised the right to oppose Labour's devolution policy in the 1979 referendum. Its failure to provide the required 'yes' vote from a minimum of 40 per cent of the

Scottish electorate brought down the Callaghan government and Mrs Thatcher and the Conservatives gained office in the resulting election.

The years since have seen Labour in Scotland consolidate its support in many regional and district councils, where it has fought hard to defend essential services against Conservative rate-capping and privatisation.

The introduction of the poll-tax in 1988 was the target of a major Labour campaign in Scotland, though the party's leadership decided against non-payment, a tactic favoured by the Militant Tendency and some leading figures in the Scottish National Party.

At least Labour in Scotland can claim to have achieved a damage limitation exercise in the Thatcher years, but its long domination of some local authorities in the central belt has exposed it to controversy.

A current case in point concerns the Monklands District Council in Lanarkshire which covers the constituencies of both the party leader and his 'shadow' Secretary of State for Scotland. Critics of the local authority's recruitment and investment policies point out that all the Labour Councillors are Catholics and the suggestion has been made that the predominantly Protestant town of Airdrie has been the loser as a result. Whether or not this is so, the issue is a reminder of how important to Labour here is the Catholic electorate of Irish descent. This in fact has been so since the Representation of the People Act of 1918 and of Labour's decision in that same year to support the principle of separate Catholic schools within the existing local authority system.

Monklands does typify the heartlands of Labour support in west central Scotland. An effective challenge to Labour by the Scottish National Party depends upon success in such areas, so Labour's leadership has sought to avert such an outcome by reaffirming the movement's Home Rule commitment. Labour has supported the 1988 Claim of Right for Scotland, joined the Scottish Constitutional Convention in 1989 and many of its activists, though not the party's Scottish leaders, took part on 12 December 1992 in a demonstration for Scottish Democracy which brought 25,000 people on to the streets of Edinburgh.

I.S. Wood

Laing, R.D. (1927–89) was born in Glasgow. He studied medicine at the university there, graduating in 1951. He practised as a psychiatrist in the city for three years before moving to London to the Tavistock clinic. In 1960 he published the groundbreaking study *The Divided Self*, which criticised conventional psychiatry for its depersonalisation of patients and for its reliance on the term 'mental illness'. His other publications, *The Politics of Experience* (1967), *Knots* (1970), *The Politics of the Family* (1976) and *The Voice of Experience* (1982) combined philosophy with psychiatry.

P. Ingalls

Lang, Andrew (1844–1912) was born in Selkirk, the son of the county sheriff clerk. Educated at Edinburgh Academy and the Universities of St Andrews, Glasgow and Balliol College, Oxford, he eventually became a Fellow of Merton.

But from 1875, when he married and settled in London, he earned his living as a general man of letters, turning out elegant journalism, essays (*Letters of Dead Authors* and *Books and Bookmen*, both 1886), studies in mythology, notably *Myth, Ritual and Religion* (1887) and *The Making of Religion* (1896). His considerable scholarship is reflected in his translation of Theocritus (1880) and the *Homeric Hymns* (1899), as well as in the translation of the *Iliad* (undertaken with Myers) and several other books studying Homeric themes.

His *History of Scotland* (1900–7), though to some extent now superseded, still makes elegant reading while his series of *Fairy Books* designated by different colours, delights successive generations of children.

Most, though not quite all, of his vast quantity of verse eventually appeared as *Collected Poems* (1923) edited by his widow. Most of it is too occasional to have retained its substance. However, his 'Almae Matres', contrasting the atmosphere of St Andrews with that of Oxford, is still much anthologized, while 'Cleveden Church' and 'Twilight in Tweed', both concerned with the vanished possibilities of youth, also rise to the level of poetry. It would be true to say, however, that Lang—to Stevenson 'Dear Andrew with the brindled hair'—never quite realized his full potential as a poet.

He is commemorated at St Andrews University through the Andrew Lang Lectureship, founded in 1926 by a bequest of Sir Peter Redford Scott Lang, Regius Professor of Mathematics, 1879–1921. The Lecturer is appointed by the University Court for one year and delivers at least one lecture on Andrew Lang and his work, or on one of the subjects on which he wrote. Many of these lectures are subsequently published.

M. Lindsay

Language *see* **British; Celtic; Pictish; Scottish Language**

Law. Much of the law administered by Scottish Courts derives from statutes of the United Kingdom Parliament imposing uniform social or economic policies on the kingdom as a whole. Welfare law and industrial law are of great practical importance yet contribute little to the science of jurisprudence. Legislation, whether by way of statute or as subordinate legislation formulated by government departments or organs of the EEC is usually pragmatic and concerned with results rather than with the application of principles. Though such legislation may become the law in Scotland, 'Scots law', for present purposes must be more narrowly defined as the legal system which has been evolved from received principles by judges and legislators as an aspect of Scottish culture and in response to Scottish needs. Scots law in this sense is a 'mixed

jurisdiction'—that is, it has been influenced in its development by both the great legal traditions of the Western world, the Roman or Civil law tradition, and the Anglo-American Common law tradition. Unlike most modern Civil law systems Scots law has not been codified and—except for statute law particularly framed for application to Scotland—has been largely developed by judicial decisions based on received principles stated in institutional treatises which draw on comparative sources. For an account of the evolution, *see* Law, History of.

Sources. The formal sources of Scots law comprise Legislation (including some unrepealed statutes of the pre-Union Scottish Parliament) Authoritative Writings, Judicial Precedent, Custom and Equity. When about the middle of the nineteenth century the Scottish courts came to recognize in modified form a doctrine of the single binding judicial precedent in cases where the law had been laid down by a bench of judges in the Court of Session or High Court of Justiciary, the courts also came to attach like weight to the opinions of a limited class of authors expressed in certain legal treatises. These are referred to as 'the institutional writers' and include Lord Stair (Father of Scots Law), Mackenzie, Bankton, Kames, Erskine, Bell and Hume. 'Custom' originally was virtually synonymous with the common law of Scotland, as declared by the courts and expounded by writers of authority, but latterly through English influence has also acquired the meaning of usage or local custom. By contrast with the dichotomy of Law and Equity in English jurisprudence, in Scots law 'equity' is not a separate branch of the law but implies a judicial discretion which, in the interests of justice, may modify or amend fundamental rules of the common law.

Administration of justice. The final appellate court for civil matters is the House of Lords in which, when acting in a judicial capacity, only those who have been appointed 'Lords of Appeal in Ordinary' or who have held high judicial office sit. By convention at least two of these Lords of Appeal are Scots lawyers. Normally five judges hear an appeal. The High Court of Justiciary (which is the final court for criminal matters) and the Court of Session, the supreme court in Scotland for civil matters, are staffed by the same 25 judges. Judges of the High Court of Justiciary go on circuit throughout Scotland and normally sit singly to conduct jury trials—appeals being heard in Edinburgh by a Bench of judges. The head of the Court is the Lord Justice General who also holds the office of Lord President of the Court of Session, while the Lord Justice-Clerk who ranks second in seniority, carries special responsibility for criminal work. Though the Court of Session remains in theory a collegiate body—and to decide matters of great difficulty may sit as such—for the discharge of normal business it is divided into an Inner House and an Outer House. The Inner House exercises mainly appellate functions and sits in two Divisions each of four judges—the First Division in which the Lord President presides and the Second Division in which the Lord Justice-Clerk presides. In the Outer House judges sit singly as 'Lords

Ordinary'. Scotland is divided into Sheriffdoms and the bulk of legal business is conducted in the Sheriff Courts established in the principal towns of Scotland—the Sheriff exercising a considerable jurisdiction in both civil and criminal matters. There are moreover many specialist courts and tribunals from which appeal usually lies to the Court of Session. The practising profession is divided into two branches—advocates belonging to the Faculty of Advocates (the Scottish Bar) and solicitors to the Law Society of Scotland, though solicitors may also belong to one of the ancient legal bodies such as the Society of Writers to Her Majesty's Signet, Society of Solicitors in the Supreme Court, Royal Faculty of Procurators of Glasgow or Society of Advocates in Aberdeen (who—somewhat confusingly—are solicitors and not members of the Scottish Bar). Until recently advocates enjoyed an exclusive right of audience before the supreme courts, but it is now possible for individual solicitors to be licensed to appear. The elected Dean of the Faculty of Advocates, an office of considerable prestige, is head of the Scottish Bar, while the Law Officers of the Crown (Lord Advocate and Solicitor-General for Scotland) are selected by government from the Faculty.

The Scottish Law Commission. In 1965 the Scottish Law Commission was established by statute to take and keep under review all the law of Scotland with a view to its systematic development and reform including codification—eliminating anomalies while simplifying and modernizing the law. The Commission is appointed by and reports to the Lord Advocate, but is independent of government control. It comprises a Chairman (a High Court judge) four other Commissioners and a small supporting staff. It is the body which should ensure that Scots law will meet the challenges of changed circumstances without losing coherence as a system or rejecting its heritage. Implementation of law reform is, however, inhibited by the division of administrative responsibility for Scottish legislation—there being no equivalent in Scotland to a Department of Justice, while Whitehall departments as well as Scottish departments may claim responsibility for different aspects of essentially Scots law such as bankruptcy. The prospect, held out in the Scotland Act 1978, of a legislature specifically concerned with enacting laws for Scotland has receded for the moment. Though codification was envisaged as one of the means by which the Scottish Law Commission would develop the law systematically, law making process, parliamentary procedure in particular, is at present ill adapted for the enactment of codes on the Continental model.

Branches of the law: *(1) Constitutional law*. The basic skeletal constitution is contained in the Articles of Agreement set forth in the Treaty of Union of 1707 which were separately enacted by the former Scottish and English Parliaments and have constituent force. When on 1 May 1707 the Treaty took effect, the former states of Scotland and England and their respective parliaments ceased to exist and were replaced by the new state of the United Kingdom of Great Britain and the new parliament of that state—a situation not always fully recognized by English lawyers. Certain aspects of nationhood have survived the incorporation of Scotland and England in a unitary state. The Articles of Union prescribe certain things which parliament may not lawfully do and provide fundamental safeguards for the Scottish legal system. They do not, however, as do later eighteenth-century constitutions, provide for inalienable individual rights or liberties. Though the Scottish Commissioners who negotiated the Union Agreement wished a federal union, this constitutional solution was—and is—rejected by the English—whose enthusiasm for federalism, as Dicey noted, stops at the Channel. Much of the constitutional law of the United Kingdom concerning central government is of English derivation and on matters concerning the country as a whole English law is often—and frequently unjustifiably—assumed to be the law of the entire state. However, there is substantial devolution of administrative powers in relation to Scottish affairs. Control of administrative action and judicial protection of individual liberty do not depend on prerogative remedies—such as *habeas corpus* as in England—but on specific statutory provision or general remedies afforded by the law and on the '*nobile officium*', a reserve of equitable power entrusted to the supreme civil and criminal courts to deal with exceptional situations. One prominent feature of recent years has been the rise of judicial review of administrative action.

(2) Criminal law. Unlike the law of many other countries where criminal law is set forth in statute form or codified, the substantive criminal law of Scotland is not so regulated, at least so far as serious crime is concerned. Drawing on Civil (i.e. Romanistic) and Canon law for basic principles and influenced by doctrines shared with English law, it is set forth in certain authoritative treatises and in the reported decisions of the High Court of Justiciary. These have developed accepted principles with robust common sense as much as by metaphysical analysis. There are also many statutory offences. Criminal law is primarily concerned with wrongs inflicted on the community as a whole rather than on the individual—though, of course, both public and private interests may be affected. The Lord Advocate is ultimately responsible for prosecution in the public interest, and it is only in most unusual circumstances that a private citizen may prosecute. Prosecution in practice is by Advocates-Depute in the High Court and by procurators fiscal in the Sheriff Courts—which deal with the greater part of criminal business throughout the country and have comprehensive jurisdiction but restricted sentencing powers. Trial may be by solemn procedure in the High Court or Sheriff Court before a judge and jury of 15 or, in the Sheriff Court (or District Court for lesser offences) by summary procedure before a judge. With few exceptions, an accused cannot be convicted in Scots law on evidence which is not corroborated in the essentials. The jury's verdict may be by simple majority and three verdicts are competent—guilty, not guilty and not proven. This last is regarded by many as anomalous. It is popularly interpreted as indicating that the jury suspected the accused to be guilty but did not find the matter proved beyond reasonable doubt. Disposal of juvenile offenders is normally

determined by a 'Children's Hearing'—an inelegant statutory designation—the members of which are laymen specially trained for the office. Scots law had from medieval times provided for the defence of accused persons; in modern times there is statutory provision for legal aid, although whether this is framed in wide enough terms is open to doubt. Criminal procedure, unlike substantive criminal law, is largely regulated by statutory provisions which seek to ensure fair trial having regard both to the public interest and the interest of the accused.

(3) Persons, family law and succession. Among legal systems which resemble each other generally, the most substantial divergencies will usually be found in family law—and its extension beyond death in the law of succession. In all modern systems these chapters of the law are in a state of turbulence. The long-accepted pattern of ascendancy of husband and father, preferment in matters of succession to land of males according to rules of primogeniture, cohesion of the nuclear family, discrimination against illegitimate relations and life-long endurance except for rare exceptions—of the marriage bond is now disrupted. Scots law now in domestic relations substantially recognizes equality of the sexes, has abolished the privileged position of the heir at the law, typically the eldest son, in relation to land, has removed most disabilities suffered by those born out of wedlock, and since 1976 grants divorce for irretrievable breakdown of marriage. The age old distinction which divided those below the age of majority (once 21, latterly 18) into pupils (males under 14, females under 12) and minors was largely replaced in 1991 by statutory prescription of 16 as the age of legal capacity. Sixteen has also been for some time the minimum age for marriage, though the age of 18 would be more in accord with the practice of modern western countries. The disadvantages of early marriage are reflected in the present high Scottish divorce rate. Marriage is regarded as an essentially personal matter, no parental or other consents being required. Regular marriage may be before a minister of religion, an authorized registrar or other celebrant as specified in the Marriage (Scotland) Act 1977. Irregular marriage—an important social factor until July 1940 since Scotland alone in Europe maintained the pre-Tridentine law—is now only recognized in the limited category of marriage by cohabitation with habit and repute i.e. living together as husband and wife for a substantial period and being accepted as such by friends or relatives. The consequences of intestate succession are regulated by the Succession (Scotland) Act 1964 as amended. This act grants 'prior rights' in respect of a dwelling house and plenishings to a surviving spouse in addition to the 'legal rights' of surviving spouse and children, which were and are recognized at common law over either half or two-thirds of a deceased's moveable estate—depending on whether he or she is survived by spouse and children (or remoter descendants) or by one class only. Though a testator may defeat a claim to 'prior rights' by will, he cannot so defeat 'legal rights'. Thus Scots law does not accept a doctrine of entire freedom of testation.

(4) Property. The two main influences in the development of the law of property in Scotland have been feudal in the case of land law and Roman in the case of moveables. Technically rights in land are referred to as 'heritable'. Formerly land was inherited by the 'heir at law' determined by primogeniture and priority of males. Since the Succession (Scotland) Act 1964 these rules no longer apply and the only truly heritable rights concern the law of arms. Feudal theory facilitated the imposition in perpetuity of conditions on the use of land and the perpetual rendering of feudal services in modern times by the payment of feu duty. Subinfeudation was not prohibited in Scotland as it was in England by the Statute *Quia Emptores* 1289–90. The system came to pivot upon the public registration of deeds affecting land—as contrasted with registration of title. Over the past thirty years there has been widespread public interest in the reform and modernizing of Scottish land law, while town planning by public authorities has overlaid the town planning schemes of feudal conveyancers and feudal conditions may now be set aside judicially. Though feudal tenure is not actually abolished, creation of future feu duties has been prohibited since 1974 and provision is made for redemption of existing duties. In 1970 certain feudal reforms were enacted and the law of security over land recast. Legislative provision for progressive registration of title to land—such title to be guaranteed by the state—was made in 1979. The process of reform and replacement of feudal land law and conveyancing continues—the policy being one, not of revolutionary change, but of discarding what is obsolete while preserving what remains serviceable.

The common law of Scotland in relation to corporeal moveables is comparable in matters of classification, terminology and theory to the laws of other legal systems throughout the world which have inherited the legacy of the Civil law. Thus original ownership can be acquired by occupation or specification (i.e. creation of new things) or prescription. Importance attaches to possession in good faith and a clear distinction is made between property rights and contractual rights. The Civil law approach contrasts strikingly with that of Anglo-American systems where the law of 'personal' (i.e. moveable) property has been a haphazard development within the interstices of other branches of the law such as contract, tort and criminal law. English law imposes liability for 'conversion', a 'property tort' or civil wrong, upon those who acquire or otherwise deal, however innocently, with another's moveable property without authority. In Scots law no such liability is incurred by a possessor or former possessor in good faith—whose duty is merely to restore the property to the owner, or, if possession has ceased, to account for any profit made. It is a basic rule in Scots law as in Roman law that transfer of ownership or a security right should be effected by *traditio* (delivery) or by public registration. Possession is regarded as the badge of ownership. This rule is difficult to reconcile with the realities of modern economic life when the owner may wish to raise a loan on property which he needs to use, or when the owner is prepared to allow another to possess or enjoy property on hire-purchase or conditional sale. In a commercial context the Civilian common law of Scotland has been overlaid by legislation primarily intended for English use such as the Sale of Goods Acts 1893 and 1979—which supersede the Scottish common law requirement of delivery in sales of corporeal moveables—and the Consumer Credit Act 1974—a bureaucratic measure of exceptional technicality. Incorporeal property rights, such as rights to debts, claims arising from contract or delict, shares in companies, goodwill and patents, cannot be transferred by physical delivery, but are transferred by assignation and intimation—and in some cases registration is also required to complete the right of an acquirer.

(5) *Trusts.* The law of trusts in Scotland was formerly regarded either as an aspect of contract law or as a consequence of holding an office of trust. Modern trust law is, however, regarded as a separate legal category. Trust implies the separation between control which ownership gives and actual enjoyment of the trust property. The trustee or trustees own property which they administer for the beneficiary as required by a declaration of trust by the truster. Scots law recognized trusts before English law influenced the system and does not accept the English concepts of legal and equitable ownership. The beneficiary in a Scottish trust has a personal claim to property or its income rather than a property right. In commercial matters and arrangements of family property and other aspects of modern life the influence of English chamber practice is considerable. Revenue law, applicable throughout the United Kingdom, views issues in terms of English law almost without exception.

(6) *Obligations.* The Scottish law of Obligations both in theory and terminology owes much to the Roman or Civil law which was developed as the *ius commune* of Europe before the era of modern codification. Obligations may be classified according to whether they arise (a) by force of law; (b) from a wrongful act or omission (Delict); or (c) from agreement or binding unilateral promise.

Obligations imposed by the law irrespective of fault or acceptance by the person obliged may result from moral duties which the law reinforces, such as the duty of parents to maintain their children, or from the duties imposed on those who would otherwise be unjustly enriched at another's expense. Thus an obligation of restitution or repetition is imposed on those who come into unauthorized possession of another's property or money to restore it to the owner; an obligation of recompense is imposed on those who gain unjustifiably as a direct result of another's loss—'salvage' is governed by similar principles—and duties are imposed on those who have spontaneously assumed the management of another's affairs during his absence or incapacity. Other obligations imposed by law under this head are similar to liability to make reparation for loss caused by fault (delictual liability) except that for reasons of policy liability is imposed irrespective of fault. Such liability may be imposed, for example, on employers whose employees sustain injury at a workplace if they can show breach of a statutory duty.

Delictual liability is imposed on a person who causes loss or injury to another through his fault—whether deliberate or negligent. There may be 'negligence' without moral fault.

Deliberate wrongdoing seldom concerns the civil courts in Scotland today, especially as a statutory scheme of compensation is available to victims of injury inflicted by persons dealt with in the criminal courts. The leading House of Lords case of *Donoghue* v *Stevenson*, decided in 1932 ('the case of the snail in the bottle') has been widely influential in Anglo-American jurisprudence as well. In it the court laid the foundation for future development of liability for negligence in Scotland and England based on the test whether a reasonable man should have foreseen that his act or omission might cause harm to another. This branch of the law is still developing, and it is uncertain how far liability will be extended to cover cases where foreseeable economic loss is caused to another without involving damage to his person or property.

Scots law goes further than other legal systems in imposing liability on a party who undertakes an obligation unilaterally—without requiring acceptance as in the case of contract. However, the value of this doctrine is limited by specialties of proof unless the promise is linked with another transaction such as a promise to keep open a contractual offer for a specified time or a promise incorporated in a contract with another to benefit a third party. Most obligations voluntarily assumed result from contracts. The basic principle of the Scots law of contract is that promises seriously undertaken will be enforced—and not, as in English law, that promises have been 'bought' by some consideration. The parties may regulate their contractual relationship in detail by specific terms and conditions which the law will interpret to give effect to the parties' apparent intention. There are, however, various 'type contracts' such as deposit and hire (and formerly sale) into which the common law itself will import terms once the parties have agreed the essentials. Especially in commercial matters the common law of contract is largely overlaid by statutory contractual regimes—such as the Sale of Goods Act 1979—which were drafted primarily as English legislation. Moreover, the freely negotiated contract is in modern times largely replaced in consumer transactions by the printed standard form contract imposed on the weaker party. During the earlier 1970s parliament enacted detailed legislation for the protection of consumers. In commercial contracts each party may put forward his printed terms for incorporation in the contract—resulting in 'a battle of forms' The courts or an arbiter must then determine whether and to what extent agreement has been reached. The reform of various antiquated rules governing the constitution and proof of certain contracts, notably those concerning the sale of land, is currently (1993) under consideration.

T.B. Smith and W.D.H. Sellar

Law, History of. Scots law is not, like Roman law or English law, an essentially original creation—a byproduct of some juristic *Volksgeist*. In its classical form it was a highly successful manifestation in a national context of Western Europe's shared legacy of Roman, Canon, feudal and customary law which English law eventually rejected. English Common law in its infancy, however, played an important part in the development of Scots law. Since the early nineteenth century the shared European *ius commune* has to some extent been fragmented by national codifications. Scottish private law might also have been codified at that time on the foundations laid by the Scottish institutional writers. However, the delayed consequences of the Union of 1707 precluded that development and fostered increasing influence of English law on the law of Scotland. When that influence has been accepted after careful and comparative evaluation it has been beneficial. When it has been imposed imperiously from without or accepted uncritically with parochial subservience or lack of confidence it has too often proved detrimental. The Scottish legal genius at its best has been selective and synthetic, adopting and adapting by comparative techniques solutions first developed in other systems. The quality of justice in any country may fairly be tested by reference to its administration not only in the higher courts but also in the lower courts which handle most legal business. However, the quality of a country's laws, as an aspect of culture—the intellectual side of civilization, refinement of mind, tastes and manners—must be evaluated by reference to their development and exposition in the highest courts, in literature and in legal education. Scots law was creatively restated as a coherent system in the late seventeenth century and reached its classical period in the eighteenth century. Scots and English law continued to diverge even after the Union with England in 1707.

Early developments. Before the Wars of Independence Scoto-Norman law borrowed extensively but selectively from England many of the institutions, techniques, forms and customs which had proved successful there, and wove these into a system drawing also on other sources—Celtic, Civil (Romanistic) and Canon law. The twelfth and thirteenth centuries saw the gradual development of a distinctively Scottish common law—common, that is, throughout the kingdom of the Scots. After the struggle for independence this foundation continued to be built on, although Scots law remained open to the influence of the *ius commune*. The most important treatise of medieval Scots law, *Regiam Majestatem*, probably compiled shortly after 1318, drew much on the earlier Anglo-Norman work known as 'Glanvill', but also contained Romano-Canonical material.

Much of the country's law business was conducted by churchmen, either in the Church courts, which had considerable powers of jurisdiction, especially in matters testamentary and matrimonial, or in lay courts where the baron or lord was an ecclesiastical institution, or in the king's Council or Parliament. Many churchmen in Scotland had been educated in Civil and Canon law at the leading Continental universities and naturally they applied in practice the theory in which they had been trained. The establishment of the pre-Reformation Scottish universities also contemplated the training of clerics—who were to become the 'civil service' of their day—in these disciplines. In the lay courts the hereditary principle was dominant on the bench, both in the ordinary royal courts such as that of the sheriff and also,

by definition, in the baron courts and courts of lords of regality. Bishop Elphinstone, founder of King's College, Aberdeen, inspired the statute of 1496 requiring barons and freeholders to send their sons to be educated in law at the universities, so as to improve the quality of local justice—a hope that was blighted on Flodden Field 1513. It is remarkable that even during the troubled times of the fifteenth century a number of enlightened statutes were enacted, for example, for the protection of small tenants and to establish prescriptive periods. *Regiam Majestatem* and other old treatises came in the fifteenth century to be venerated as the 'Auld Lawis' harking back reputedly to a golden age of justice before the Wars of Independence.

A firm foundation for scientific jurisprudential advance was provided when in 1532 the Lords of Council and Session who had administered centralized royal justice were reorganized on a permanent basis as a College of Justice—the Court of Session. Until the Reformation the Lord President and one half of the Court of fourteen other Senators were churchmen. The establishment of a permanent professional judiciary and the emergence around the same time of a secular legal profession made possible a more consistent development of a law of Scotland. Procedure followed the Romano-Canonical patterns widely used in Continental Europe. Unlike the position in England proceedings were initiated by a single form of summons; remedies depended on rights—not conversely—and there were few procedural barriers to litigation. No dichotomy between law and equity was recognized, the Court of Session inheriting both the equitable jurisdiction of the Council and the common law jurisdiction of the ordinary courts. To supplement and systematize the provisions of feudal, customary and statute law, judges and practitioners drew freely upon the developed Civil law which was—with national variants—accepted as the *ius commune* of Western Europe apart from England. Legal education in the Scottish universities did not flourish after the Reformation. Indeed leading Reformers were hostile to its development in Edinburgh. Consequently many of those who intended to practise as Advocates before the Court of Session—some of whom would later assume judicial office—pursued their legal studies in the leading law schools of France and later of the Netherlands. A high standard of general and legal education was expected of Advocates, who were on the whole of aristocratic or landed families, while judges enjoyed considerable social distinction. The Court's decisions were collected in unofficial collections or 'practicks' but until the end of the seventeenth century there was no systematic comprehensive formulation of law of Scotland which could be regarded as an important aspect of Scottish culture. The nearest approximation was Craig's *Jus Feudale*, an institutional treatise published in 1655 (although written some 50 years before), which placed the development of Scotland's feudal land law in its historical and comparative European context.

The classical age. Scottish private law became a coherent and rational system largely as a result of a creative and authoritative restatement in one treatise, The *Institutions of the*

Law of Scotland by James Dalrymple, Viscount Stair, Lord President of the Court of Session, first published in 1681. He is Father of Scots law in the same sense as Grotius, by whom he was much influenced, is Father of Roman-Dutch law. Stair, a philosopher by training, marshalled the judicial decisions and statutes, feudal and customary law in force in Scotland in his day—but systematized the whole by reference to natural law and to the developed Civil law. His contemporary, Sir George Mackenzie, a distinguished scholar and practitioner, Dean of the Faculty of Advocates and founder of the Advocates Library, published his smaller *Institutes* in 1684 and his *Laws and Customs of Scotland in Matters Criminal* in 1678. These works presented Scots law within the mainstream of the European tradition (from which English law had largely excluded itself)—national laws being local variants of the shared tradition. Individual national solutions might be valued, but the outlook was cosmopolitan—rather than parochial. In due course other authoritative writers, who are accorded 'institutional' status, have built upon the foundations laid by Stair and Mackenzie—Bankton, Kames, Erskine and Hume in the eighteenth century, and Bell in the early nineteenth century. Their status is probably now unique—since the writings of their counterparts in other European systems have been superseded by national codifications. Madame H. David has aptly described the authority of these authors in a legal context by analogy with that of the Fathers of the Church in relation to the Canonical Scriptures.

The classical period of Scots law—when it had achieved maturity and confidence—falls within the second half of the eighteenth century. Stair had provided a compendium of the law and had demonstrated its coherence as a whole. Though Scotland and England had entered an incorporating union in which central government was controlled overwhelmingly by English influence, the attitude of government—in reaction against Stuart policies generally—was opposed to intervention, and interference with local organs of government. Once the dominant English politicians had secured the suppression of a Scottish Parliament which might otherwise have determined succession to the Crown on a person or line unacceptable to English interests—Scottish legal institutions were left free to develop without much legislative interference from London. The main foreign influences on legal thinking were the law teachers of Leiden, Utrecht and Groeningen and the compendious civilian treatises of Dutch scholars. Stair's approach to natural law differed, however, from that of Grotius in that Stair derived law primarily from divine will, of which reason was but a subsidiary instrument. Erskine, who in his *Institute*, published posthumously in 1773, followed in the tradition of Stair but with less concern for theory, recognized that sociological factors as well as reason determine a country's laws. So too did Lord Kames (1696–1782) who also favoured a more historical approach to the law. There was, for Kames, a close connection between law and the social and economic circumstances of society. He was a prolific author on the history of law and also an advocate of law reform—an apparent paradox. However, he had grasped that only one who has a deep understanding of the historical background to a rule of law and its original social and economic context can see when it is no longer required and can be safely discarded. Parliament House, the home of the Court of Session, was the pivot of the political, social and intellectual life of Scotland during the Age of Enlightenment in the eighteenth century. The Faculty of Advocates was a social as well as an intellecutal élite. Though judges like Kames and practising advocates were much concerned with the law as a science, scholars who were not all professional lawyers—philosophers of the Scottish enlightenment such as Adam Smith, David Hume (qq.v.) and John Millar—were the first group of thinkers about law to challenge both natural-law ideas accepted on the Continent and also Hobbesian positivism. They regarded law as a means of social control which could only be properly studied as a developing social institution. These philosophers both in Edinburgh and Glasgow, as Adam Smith observed, acknowledged the judge, Lord Kames, as their master. As the eighteenth century progressed, Scottish law faculties grew in competence and confidence in the fields of Scots, Civil and Public law. Erskine, Baron David Hume (nephew of the philosopher) and G. J. Bell were professors of conspicuous ability in Edinburgh as was John Millar in Glasgow. Their classes attracted students of promise from Britain as a whole.

Though there were undoubtedly placemen in the Scottish judiciary who contributed little to the law in its classical period, the collegiate court in which no fewer than nine judges sat to consider any matter of importance did not lack men of vision and talent. Eventually, procedure became unduly protracted and cumbrous, and the laconic reported decisions based on the opinions of so many judges too often failed to give the practising profession clear guidance in principle. At the Union the House of Lords, in which no Scots lawyers sat, had acquired appellate jurisdiction in civil matters. This jurisdiction was increasingly invoked thereafter by litigants whose prospects might prosper in an alien forum schooled—so far as the decision makers were lawyers—in a different system of jurisprudence from that of the judges who had given judgment in Edinburgh. The House of Lords from time to time imposed solutions of English law. However there was little voluntarily received influence of English law except in the field of mercantile law—which English lawyers under Lord Mansfield's leadership had grafted onto the common law—and in criminal law, English doctrines having to some extent influenced Hume in his institutional *Commentaries on the Law of Scotland Regarding Crime*. In general, before the abolition of the forms of action, the technicalities of English private law made reported cases incomprehensible except to initiates. The publication of Blackstone's *Commentaries on the Laws of England* (1765) presented English law in a form which could be more readily understood, however perplexing it might seem to a mind trained in the Civil law.

Defects in procedure rather than of substantive law justified criticisms of the system in the late eighteenth century. The classical age of Scots law may be taken to have ended in about

1830 by which time civil jury trial on the English model had been introduced and the Court of Session had been reorganized. The motives of the Scottish Whigs and Tories had diverged, but each faction had contributed to securing these objects. To the Whigs integration with or reception of English institutions seemed to be associated with attaining wider political liberties. After they had succeeded, Parliament House, which had been the focus, became 'little more than the rump of the Enlightenment'. Moreover, parliament at Westminster, which had rarely legislated on purely Scottish matters—except on measures suggested and formulated by the Scottish interests concerned—increasingly cast off that restraint after the legislative reorganization of the Scottish courts. Among the indirect consequences of the triumph of the Scottish Whigs in a general political context was the reduction of Scotland to provincial status and the subordination of her cosmopolitan and culturally superior legal system to an English ascendancy.

Nineteenth and twentieth centuries. At the end of the eighteenth century, due to the Napoleonic Wars and the new era of codification on the Continent, the already declining custom for Scottish students to study the civil law in the universities of France and the Netherlands virtually ceased. The consequences appeared a generation later. Citation of Civilian and European authorities declined, and English law became the main external source of Scots law—especially after the abolition of the forms of action in England resulted in easier comprehension by Scots lawyers of English reports. (Even so, the hazard for Scots lawyers of misconstruing reports of English decisions continues.) Since England had a much larger population than Scotland, it followed that there would be made more judicial decisions on fact situations in England, and that these would become persuasive precedents for citation in the Scottish courts. English legal literature analysing these decisions and statute law applicable throughout Britain also came to be relied on by Scottish practitioners. Whereas formerly a series of decisions might establish a *usus fori*, the Scottish courts came to recognize a doctrine of the single binding precedent (*stare decisis*), although in a more flexible form than in England because of the collegiate nature of the Court of Session. This development was assisted by improved reporting of decisions after reorganization of the Court of Session (*see* Law) and by the influence of English practice. As a side effect of recognition of *stare decisis*, a special authority was attached to the opinions of the institutional writers. The House of Lords in the exercise of its appellate jurisdiction in civil causes tended to assimilate Scots law to English solutions, and indeed until 1876 no statutory provision was made for any Scottish judge to sit in the ultimate court. The commercial community, impatient of differences in law between Scotland and England, constantly urged assimilation of commercial law in Britain—which in effect meant anglicization—despite the fact that, as a Royal Commission recognized in 1854, there was little evidence as to inconveniences actually experienced as a result of differences

between Scots and English commercial law. These pressures were greatly increased as company mergers and nationalization concentrated control of commerce and industry in London or southern England. The large Whitehall departments concerned with trade, industry, consumer protection and social welfare likewise have sought uniform solutions based on English legal forms and theories for Britain or the United Kingdom. They have serviced governments increasingly concerned to intervene by statute in all aspects of social and economic activity or decline. Scottish criminal law on the whole was left to independent and successful judicial development. No criminal appeals lay to the House of Lords. Though Scottish criminal procedure eventually became statutory, it remained essentially Scottish in preparation and formulation.

Scottish legal education stagnated for long periods, instruction in the Civil law tended to follow antiquarian patterns of little relevance to the law in practice, and too often Scots law, especially criminal law, was taught inadequately. After the First World War few major contributions were made to Scottish legal literature for many years, and no work has been canonized with institutional status. The smallness of the market for Scottish legal treatises discouraged all but the most dedicated of authors to write comprehensively on aspects of Scots law. After Hitler's War there was a resurgence of interest in Scots law as an aspect of Scottish culture—a movement associated with Lord President Cooper and law teachers influenced by him. Despite strong pressures for assimilation with English law and periods of limited creativity, Scots law has nevertheless proved remarkably resilient, and the last 25 years have witnessed something of a renaissance in legal scholarship and writing. Scots private law depends more on generalized rights than does its English counterpart. Remedy depends on right rather than conversely, and Scots law still maintains the tradition of arguing deductively from principles to particular cases. Though the Scottish judiciary is reluctant to assume the praetorian role of Lord Denning in England, they, like their predecessors, are capable of developing the principles of the law which they administer to respond to changing social and economic conditions. Were constitutional reforms conferred on Scotland substantial legislative powers over the whole field of Scots law and Scottish affairs generally, the challenge would meet with an appropriate response from those who still cherish their legal tradition as an aspect of their national culture. Confidence, Lord Clark concludes, is the clue to civilization. Law is an aspect of civilization. Imbued with a new confidence born of opportunity and responsibility, Scots law and Scottish lawyers could yet make a major contribution to contemporary Scottish culture within a European framework and in the best of philosophical and comparative tradition of the classical era. Since the United Kingdom acceded to the Treaties setting up the European Communities, common law and statute law in both Scotland and England have been in effect subject to Community law—described by the Court of Justice of the Communities as 'a separate legal order'. This law will inevitably increase in scope and complexity and affect the coherence of national legal systems.

T.B. Smith and W.D.H. Sellar

Lexicography. The origins of the lexicography of Scots lie in the practice by seventeenth-century editors of Scottish poems of adorning their margins with glosses of vernacular Scots words into English for the benefit of English and, it may be, anglicized Scottish readers. Early in the eighteenth century comes the separate glossary in alphabetical order, familiar to every reader of Scots literature, such as Allan Ramsay's (q.v.) Glossary to his 1721 Poems or Robert Burns's to his *Poems* of 1786 and 1787.

As it happened, the first in time of these alphabetically ordered glossaries remained for many decades the most ambitious and the most important for the history of the Scottish dictionary. This was a glossary by Thomas Ruddiman, librarian, grammarian and, later, printer, to the first modern edition (1710) of Gavin Douglas's (q.v.) 1513 translation of Vergil's *Aeneid* into Scots. The compilers of this volume claimed on the title-page that this 'large Glossary', which runs to some 88 folio pages in double columns, 'may serve for a Dictionary to the Old Scottish Language.' Other remarkable features of this glossary include the near exhaustiveness of its word-list, its copious allusions to contemporary Scots usage, especially northeastern Scots usage (Ruddiman came from Boyndie in Banffshire), and the fact that it provides one or more text-references for most of its entries in the manner of later 'historical dictionaries'.

Another of the early foundations of Scottish lexicography was Sir John Skene's remarkable dictionary of ancient Scottish legal terms, *De Verborum Significatione, The Exposition of the Termes and Difficill Wordes, conteined in the foure buikes of Regiam Majestatem* (1597).

These two works served as principal sources for the first fully comprehensive piece of Scottish lexicography, *An Etymological Dictionary of the Scottish Language*, by John Jamieson, DD, published by subscription in two volumes of over 300 pages each in 1808. Jamieson was a Secession Church minister who had begun the collections towards his *Dictionary* 20 years earlier, stimulated by a conversation on the origins and vocabulary of Scots with the Icelandic philologist Grim Thorkelin, then visiting Forfar. Jamieson's was the first completed dictionary published in these islands to substantiate its definitions with dated and referenced quotations from original texts set out in (more or less) chronological order; it was thus the earliest British historical dictionary. Encouraged by the widespread approval given to his *Dictionary* and aided by contributions sent in by a number of enthusiastic helpers, who included James Hogg and Sir Walter Scott, in 1825 Jamieson issued a *Supplement* to the original work in two further large volumes. In one or other of its various abridgements or reissues, conflating the original Dictionary and the Supplement, Jamieson's *Dictionary* dominated Scottish lexicography down to the 1950s, really long after it had been superseded.

The work which superseded it was the 12-volume *New English Dictionary on historical Principles* (1884–1928), subsequently re-named *The Oxford English Dictionary* (OED). The accomplishment of this magnificent dictionary owes most of all to the unflagging energy, great lexicographical skill and vast erudition of James A.H. Murray, a Scot from Denholm in Roxburghshire, who can lay some claim to having been the greatest lexicographer ever. As well as treating English over its history, this dictionary also more than doubles the information on Scots to be found in Jamieson. On Modern Scots still more information is incorporated in the six-volume *English Dialect Dictionary* (EDD) (1898–1905), compiled by Joseph Wright, then Professor of Comparative Philology in Oxford.

The moving spirit behind the further progress of Scottish lexicography in the twentieth century was William Craigie, native of Dundee and from 1901 co-editor, with Murray and Henry Bradley, of the OED. In 1907 a suggestion by Craigie in a lecture he gave in Dundee engaged William Grant, Lecturer in Phonetics at Aberdeen Training Centre, in preparations for a new dictionary of Modern Scots. Then in 1919 in an address to the Philological Society in London, entitled 'New Dictionary Schemes', Craigie set forth his plan for a series of major new historical dictionaries, one for each main period in the history of English and Scots. These, he hoped, would greatly supplement and to some extent supersede OED.

Two of the dictionaries which resulted from this proposal were Craigie's own *Dictionary of the Older Scottish Tongue*, of Older Scots down to 1700 (DOST), which in 1991 under Craigie's successors, A.J. Aitken, J.A.C. Stevenson, H.D. Watson and Margaret G. Dareau, had published in seven volumes and one further fascile as far as letter S, and Grant's dictionary of Modern Scots, *The Scottish National Dictionary* (SND), largely edited by Grant's successor David Murison and completed in 10 volumes in 1976. Both of these are 'historical dictionaries' on the OED plan, supporting each definition with copious arrays of quotation-examples and backed by huge collections (over 1½ millions for DOST) of quotation 'slips', as well as, in DOST's case, computer-generated concordances of Older Scots.

Besides the large works, a tradition of smaller-scale dictionaries date from 1818, when John Jamieson produced an abridgement of his 1808 folio dictionary in one octavo volume, omitting the quotations, and the poet and schoolmaster Ebenezer Picken issued anonymously and quite independently his small *A Dictionary of the Scottish Language*. Much the most comprehensive work of this kind before 1985 was A. Warrack's *Scots Dialect Dictionary* (first published by W. and R. Chambers in 1911 and still in print as *Chambers Scots Dictionary*.

All previous one-volume dictionaries have been eclipsed by the Scottish National Dictionary Association's *The Concise Scots Dictionary* (CSD) (1985), Editor-in-chief Mairi Robinson, abridged from SND and DOST and, in part, OED. This remarkably comprehensive work encompasses the whole of the history of Scots in 815 pages of word-list along with a highly informative introduction and back-matter. It is unusual among concise dictionaries of any language in showing the time span and dialect distribution of every meaning, derivative and phrasal use. Lucidly and succinctly defined, it also provides etymologies and the pronunciations of the principal variants of every word in Modern and also, following philological reconstruction, Old Scots. In 1988 the SNDA produced an abridged and simplified version of CSD, *The Pocket Scots Dictionary* and in 1990 *The Scots Thesaurus*, ed. Iseabail Macleod, which presents 20,000 of CSD's words, with definitions, arranged in semantic fields and with an English into Scots index.

In response to an aspiration towards a 'revival' of Scots, several small dictionaries of English into Scots have appeared since 1947, most notably William Graham's *The Scots Word Book* (1977, 1980). At the time of writing SNDA's editors are at work on a more complete and detailed English into Scots dictionary, partly based on Graham's unpublished collections.

Glossaries and dictionaries of more localised varieties of Scots and of the usage of professions, trades and other activities have been produced since the early nineteenth century: such as William Aiton's and William Leslie's glossaries of the agricultural vocabularies of Ayrshire and of Nairn and Moray respectively (both 1811), James Barrowman's *Glossary of Scots Mining Terms* (1886), the local dictionaries of Thomas Edmonston (Shetland and Orkney, 1866) and Walter Gregor (Banffshire, 1866), and many recent works of these and other specialist kinds, including a number of semi-jocular or jocular collections.

Another branch of Scottish lexicography, which flourished from the mid-eighteenth century down to the twentieth, are the numerous published lists, usually alphabetical, of characteristic Scottish expressions, produced to enable Scottish speakers and writers to learn to eschew them, such as James Beattie's famous 'Scoticisms' of 1787 'designed to correct Improprieties of Speech and Writing'. Scotsmen have also played important parts in the development of general English lexicography, notably in the persons of John Ogilvie, compiler of the *Imperial Dictionary* (1850), the first modern dictionary of English with pictorial illustrations, Charles Annandale, responsible for its four-volume 1885 revision, and a succession of able editors of Chambers and Collins dictionaries. However, the outstanding contribution is without doubt that of Scottish editors of and assistants to OED, its *Supplements* and its associated dictionaries, especially *The Shorter OED*, most of all James Murray and William Craigie. Thanks to these people and others, quite large numbers of Scotticisms are recorded in all general dictionaries of English. There are nevertheless many other Scotticisms which, though used daily by middle-class English-speaking Scots, remain at the time of writing unrecorded outside the pages of SND and CSD.

A.J. Aitken

Leyden, John (1775–1811), antiquarian, poet, linguist, medical doctor, folk-song collector, editor and orientalist. Born Denholm, Roxburghshire, 8 September; studied and worked in Edinburgh, 1790–1802; left Scotland for India, 1803; died Batavia (now Jakarta), Indonesia, 28 August.

It seems only accidental that posterity has denied Leyden the fame of his contemporary Samuel Taylor Coleridge; as an intellectual all-rounder, Leyden was Coleridge's equal. Leyden's formal training was in surgery: he was a diplomate of the Edinburgh Royal College of Surgeons, took an external MD degree at St Andrews, and spent his last eight years as an army surgeon in the Far East. But he also, between 1800 and 1802, helped Walter Scott to collect ballads for the *Minstrelsy of the Scottish Border*; toured the Highlands and Hebrides in 1800 to research Ossianic legends; published, in 1801, the first modern edition of the mid-sixteenth-century tract *The Complaynt of Scotland*, adding to it a pioneer glossary of sixteenth-century Scots words; and edited the *Scots Magazine* for six months during 1802.

Between about 1795 and 1802 he also found time to write many substantial poems, mostly on Border themes. These now seem faded; but their craftsmanship is assured, and Scott's slightly later poetry owes them a considerable debt. Collected editions of Leyden's poems were published in 1819 and 1858.

Leyden's contribution to Scottish musical scholarship is no less impressive, especially considering that he made it before the age of 27. His *Preliminary Dissertation to the Complaynt of Scotland* contains indispensible material about Border folk-music in his own day. He collected, and thereby preserved, two valuable seventeenth-century Scottish musical MSS; the 'Leyden vocal MS' (National Library of Scotland Adv. MS 5.2.14), which he acquired at the age of 13 from the effects of the minister of Ancrum; and the 'Leyden lyra-viol MS', now in Newcastle University Library. He was probably also an owner of National Library of Scotland MS 3346, a delightful record of fiddle music in Edinburgh between 1765 and 1790.

D. Johnson

Libraries. It was Sydney Smith's opinion that early nineteenth-century Edinburgh was for a literary man 'the most eligible situation in the island', and its first justification for that title in his view was its 'good libraries liberally managed'. In this respect Edinburgh was typical of Scotland as a whole. When in 1850 the first Public Libraries Bill was being debated at Westminster a Scottish MP successfully insisted that Scotland should be excluded from the provisions of the Act because of the 'excellent libraries' established in almost every burgh. The Scot's traditional regard for book-learning is thus corroborated.

The National Library of Scotland was established under that name only in 1925, but its new title simply recognized that the Advocates' Library, whose collections of books and manuscripts the National Library inherited, had been almost from its foundation in the late seventeenth century a national library in everything but name. In 1709 the Advocates' Library had been given the privilege of legal deposit, a right confirmed by later copyright legislation and continued to the present day. It is the only Scottish library entitled to receive a copy of every book, periodical and newspaper published in the United Kingdom.

During its formative years in the eighteenth century the library had as keepers such scholars and men of letters as Thomas Ruddiman and David Hume, and in the nineteenth century it was claimed to be 'the most accessible of all the great libraries in the United Kingdom'. Carlyle declared that essentially the library belonged to Scotland.

The library's main building, on George IV Bridge in Edinburgh, was begun in the late 1930s and opened in 1956. There the visitor will find many of the library's treasures on permanent or changing display in the exhibition rooms, and the reader and research worker has ready access to the rich collections of books and manuscripts. Naturally the particular strength of the libraries lies in its Scottish material, manuscripts of Scottish interest and of Scottish authors, new and old, and books printed in or relating to Scotland. But the library is well provided with foreign literature, particularly from Europe and in the humanities.

Since 1974 the National Library has been responsible also for interlibrary loans in Scotland.

The libraries in Scotland's four older universities have long served not only the staff and students in their academic communities, but 'all respectable persons, properly introduced', to quote a Parliamentary Return of 1849. The university libraries in Glasgow and Aberdeen were founded with the universities in 1451 and 1495 respectively; Edinburgh university library dates from 1580; and the present library in Scotland's oldest university, St Andrews (1411), was founded in 1611, although the idea of a university library was under consideration as early as 1415 and there are links with the original Priory Library founded there in 1144. Glasgow and St Andrews university libraries are now accommodated in modern buildings opened in 1968 and 1976, and Edinburgh university library's new building, also opened in 1968, is the largest of its kind in Europe.

Three of the four newer universities, in Glasgow (Strathclyde), Edinburgh (Heriot-Watt) and Dundee, emerged from earlier educational foundations and their libraries are much older than their status as universities. The Andersonian Library in the University of Strathclyde, for example, was founded in 1796. Scotland's only completely new university for nearly four centuries was established at Stirling in 1967, and its library too is a new foundation.

In Edinburgh and Glasgow a number of 'learned libraries' survive from an earlier age: the libraries of the Royal Colleges of Surgeons (1505) and of Physicians (1681) of Edinburgh and of Physicians and Surgeons of Glasgow (1698), the Signet Library (1722) and the library of the Royal Society of Edinburgh (1783).

In these towns again and throughout Scotland there are many educational libraries in schools and colleges of all kinds and in training hospitals. There are industrial libraries, libraries in government departments, newspaper libraries and the libraries of various societies and institutions. These, and libraries of all types to a total of 373, are listed in a guide published by the Scottish Library Association, *Library Resources in Scotland* (3rd ed. 1976).

In cities and towns and even villages throughout Scotland there have been public libraries of one kind or another since at least the late seventeenth century, and occasionally a present-day library is able to trace a link, however tenuous, with some such predecessor. A few of the early libraries still exist, though no longer active. Innerpeffray Library near Crieff dates from 1680 and is accommodated in the building erected for it in 1750-1. Robert Leighton (1611–84), the principal of Edinburgh university who became bishop of Dunblane and later archbishop of Glasgow, bequeathed his books for the use of the clergy of the diocese of Dunblane, and the Leightonian Library is still housed in the seventeenth-century crow-stepped building that his nephew erected for it near the cathedral.

But the public library service that is to be found throughout Scotland today is a creation of the later nineteenth century and the early twentieth, and its development was very largely the story of Andrew Carnegie's benefactions and the continuing interest in libraries of the United Kingdom Trust he founded. The first Carnegie library was opened in 1883 in the donor's native town of Dunfermline.

Over the next 50 years or so the whole country was covered by a network of burgh and county libraries administered by some 80 library authorities. (With the reorganization of local government in 1975 their number has been reduced to 40.)

The public library service has been described as a national service locally administered. There may therefore be a marked difference in the standard of service provided by even neighbouring authorities, but the best services in Scotland are comparable with the best anywhere. Size is sometimes but not always a relevant factor: the larger and richer the authority, the greater the chance of a comprehensive and efficient service. There are excellent library systems in the larger cities, Glasgow, Edinburgh, Aberdeen and Dundee, but the more sparsely populated parts of the country, even if they are less wealthy, may have opportunities for excellence in particular ways, and the mobile library brings books to the most isolated reader.

A public library can be no better than its community wants it to be. At its best it will be the centre of the intellectual life of the area it serves.

W. R. Aitken

Lindsay, Maurice (b.1918). The publication of Maurice Lindsay's *Collected Poems 1940–1990* confirmed his distinctive voice, his vision and his imagination. His range of subject, form and language is wide, reaching from the barbed fables of the Scots *Bairnsangs* in the 1940s to the astringent satires on the abuse of power of his later work; from lyrical studies of children and childhood to that rare achievement, the poetry of ideas in the autobiographical *A Net To Catch The Winds*; from the boisterous and bawdy comedies in light verse to the finely-controlled moral passion in the sequence, 'On Trial'.

His sequence, 'Fifty Years On', shows his love of the sonnet, the characteristic form in his later work, and shows too an imagination open to new experience without ever being possessed by experience. 'Fifty Years On', along with *A Net To Catch The Winds* and the prose autobiography, *Thank You for Having Me*, give the chronological facts of Lindsay's life.

He was born in Glasgow in 1918 and educated at Glasgow Academy and the Royal Scottish Academy of Music, but a musical career was frustrated by an injured wrist and war service from 1939 to 1945. After the war he was a music critic and literary journalist for the Glasgow *Bulletin* and the BBC in Scotland until 1961, when he was appointed Programme Controller of Border Television. In 1967 he returned to Scotland as Director of the Scottish Civic Trust, and since retiring from the Trust he has served on Europa Nostra, the Council of Europe's advisory body on conservation.

What that chronology partly conceals is Lindsay's promotion of Scottish literature. He edited *Poetry Scotland*, *Scottish Poetry*, succeeding editions of *A Book Of Scottish Verse* and *Modern Scottish Poetry* and the journal *The Scottish Review* with the late Alexander Scott. He is the author of *The Burns Encyclopedia*, of critical biographies of Burns and Francis George Scott, and of the *History Of Scottish Literature*.

J. Aitchison

Lindsay of Pitscottie, Robert (1520?–1565?) like his kinsman Sir David Lyndsay of the Mount, was a Fife man. It seems probable that Robert Lindsay's father may have been a tenant farmer near Cupar. We know that the historian's own son, Christopher, got married in 1591, when he was described as 'lawful heir to the late Robert Lyndsay of Pitscottie', but little else of a biographical nature.

However, Lindsay's *Historie and Cronicles of Scotland* was not only the most important work of its kind to be written, but is one of the small handful of sixteenth-century Scots prose works that may still be read with pleasure.

Lindsay regarded his work as a continuation of Boece's *Historie*, already translated by John Bellenden, an overlap being provided between Boece's eighteenth book and Lindsay's opening chapter. Lindsay had a vivid eye for detail, and diligently sought out information not only from his kinsman Sir David, but from Sir Andrew Wood (the grandson of the famous Scots admiral of that name), Lord Lindsay of the Byres, the historian John Major, Sir William Scott of Balwearie and Sir William Bruce of Earlshall. He was therefore well informed with regard to his own times. When he draws upon older authors his chronology is apt to be vague and his facts erroneous. His style is always delightful, and to him we owe the story of the apparition that appeared before James IV in St Michael's, Linlithgow, unsuccessfully attempting to dissuade the kings from embarking on the expedition at Flodden, and the colourful account of the death of James V. Lindsay's *Historie* was first published in 1778.

M. Lindsay

Linklater, Eric (1899–1974). Born at Dounby, Orkney, he was educated at Aberdeen Grammar School and Aberdeen University, where he began by studying medicine but ended up with an English degree. In the 1914–18 war he was an officer in the Black Watch, leaving the army as a major. He was severely wounded in the head at Passchendaele.

After the war he was for a time Assistant Editor of the *Times of India*. In 1927 he came back to his *alma mater* as an Assistant Lecturer in English, and wrote his elegantly amusing study, *Ben Jonson and King James* (1931). His first novel, *White Man's Saga* (1952) deals with the Orcadian custom of establishing pre-marital proof of fertility, and proclaimed a writer who was both an elegant stylist and a wit in the picaresque tradition of Smollett.

From 1928 to 1930 he travelled America on a Commonwealth Fellowship, the outcome of which was the uproariously funny *Juan in America*, preceded the year before by the novel that established his wider reputation, *Poet's Pub* (1930). His affection for Orkney and his pride in his Norse descent were reflected in *The Men of Ness* (1932), and towards the end of his life, in the topographical survey *Orkney and Shetland* (1965).

Magnus Merriman (1934) was another new departure, its humorous satire on Edinburgh characters, including the Scottish Nationalists (with whom Linklater was then associating), punctuated by bawdy verse.

Adoption of an Aristophanes theme provided the idea for *The Impregnable Women* (1938), localized fantasy for *Laxdale Hall* (1951), subsequently made into a successful film. *Private Angelo* (1946) in some ways the finest and funniest of all his novels, gives plain enough evidence of Linklater's hatred of war, a fact that may surprise those who undervalue this author, assuming his interest in soldiers of all ranks to imply an imperialist attitude.

His other outstanding novels include *Ripeness is All* (1935) and *Juan in China* (1937). During the 1939–46 war, Linklater was for a time commander of the Orkney Fortress Royal Engineers before taking up an appointment on the staff of the Director of Public Relations in the War Office, a position he held for four years.

After this, his second war, he turned to drama with *Love in Albania* (1948) and *Breakespear in Gascony* (1958), though a tendency to wordiness of dialogue made his wit less effective on the stage than on the printed page. From 1945 to 1948 he was Lord Rector of Aberdeen University.

He moved from his Dounby home, first to Rossshire, then to Aberdeenshire, but never deserted the north. In every sense a rounded man of letters, he produced a volume of autobiography, *The Man on my Back* (1941) and a travel book, *A Year of Space* (1953). His factual re-telling of Scottish history in his final books was the only aspect of the writer's craft in which he was not notably successful. Those who knew him remember the wit that flashed out in a booming voice, from the domed, bespectacled features. Happily, shortly before he died the Scottish Arts Council made an archive film, *Eric Linklater*, in which he talks about his attitudes to life and the craft of writing which he served so enthusiastically.

M. Lindsay

Literature: Early Poetry. Early Scottish poetry follows, or seems to follow, two main patterns. There is some overlap, but broadly speaking it is fair to say that one dominates the fourteenth and fifteenth centuries, the other the sixteenth. Appearances plainly are to some extent deceptive; the accident of manuscript survival necessarily governs any attempt at a literary history, and the names of poets, otherwise unknown or scarcely known, which are listed in Dunbar's 'Quhen he was seik' ('Lament for the Makaris') and Sir David Lindsay's *Testament of the Papyngo* indicate how far twentieth-century estimates may be from the actualities of the fifteenth and sixteenth centuries. It does nevertheless appear that the early period was dominated by long poems, original or in translation, initially for the most part narrative, for individual manuscripts of which there was a modest but steady public demand. In the sixteenth century many achieved the dignity of print; a *Wallace*, of which fragments survive, appeared in or about 1508 (Edinburgh, ?Chepman and Myllar), a *Bruce* in 1571 (Edinburgh, Lekpreuik), and it is well known that the tracts printed by Chepman and Myllar in the Southgait of Edinburgh in or about 1508 include medium-length poems by Robert Henryson (*c.*1420–*c.*1490), William Dunbar (*c.*1460–1513) and others. Sixteenth-century poets sometimes made their appearance directly in print; thus manuscript material is of relatively little importance for the poetry of Sir David Lindsay (?1486–1555). The tradition of early Scottish poetry however is primarily one of manuscripts.

First among the long poems is the *Bruce*(*c.*1375) of John Barbour (*c.* 1320–1395), archdeacon of Aberdeen, traveller, scholar and administrator. The appeal and power of his poem results from the way in which he transmutes a carefully factual account of the second war of Scottish independence with the qualities of twelfth and thirteenth-century French courtly and heroic romance, of which he had a considerable knowledge, and scholastic philosophy and psychology. The exemplary careers of Bruce and Douglas, counterpointed against that, for instance, of Bruce's headstrong brother Edward, make the poem something of a manual of kingship, directly relevant to the state of Scotland in the third and fourth quarters of the fourteenth century. And of course Barbour was an excellent storyteller. The *Bruce* is preserved in two late-fifteenth-century manuscripts, St John's College, Cambridge MS, G.23 and the more important National Library of Scotland, Advocates' MS, 19.2.2.

Barbour wrote two other substantial historical poems, now lost, *The Brut* and *The Stewartis Orygenalle*, the first a retelling of the legendary history of Britain from the time of Brutus, first settler in the island, the second a history of the house of Stewart, which in 1371 and in the person of Robert II (1371–1390) became the royal line of Scotland.

For more than half a century Barbour's narrative poetry in octosyllabic couplets seems to have remained the prime model for Scottish poets and translators. His chief disciple was Andrew of Wyntoun (*c.*1355–1422), prior of St Serf's Isle in Loch Leven, whose 'cornykkillis callit Originall' aimed to set the legendary and factual history of Scotland within the framework of the Christian world-picture, and by doing so to demonstrate the links joining the Scottish monarchy and people to the overall providential scheme. His first intention was to complete the work in seven books, corresponding to the seven ages of the world; later he found his formal purpose better suited by nine books corresponding to the nine orders of angels.

Barbour was also in some sense the model for the translators who produced the voluminous *Legends of the Saints* and a *Troy Book* of which fragments survive (both are preserved in fifteenth-century manuscripts, the *Legends* in Cambridge University Library MS, Gg.II.6., the fragment in CUL MS, Kk.V.30. and Bodleian MS, Douce 148.), and *The Buik of the Most Noble and Valiant Conquerour Alexander the Grit*, completed in 1438, preserved in a unique copy printed by Alexander Arbuthnet (1537–1585) at Edinburgh in 1580, and derived from parts of the second and third branches of the *Roman d'Alixandre*.

The *Wallace* (?1478) of Blind Harry (?1440–*c.*1495) moves away from Barbour's versification and concern for historical fact, while at the same time it complements and outdoes the *Bruce* in its presentation of the popular hero of the first war of Scottish independence as warrior, lover, outlaw and martyr. It is preserved in the Advocates' manuscript which also contains the *Bruce*, but, as has been noted, reached print at an early date.

In the sixteenth century the main examples of the long poem are the *Eneados* (1513), the fine translation of Virgil's *Aeneid* by Gavin Douglas (1474–1522), bishop of Dunkeld, and the *Monarche* (1554), a survey of world history from Creation to Judgement in terms of Nebuchadnezzar's dream as recorded in the *Book of Daniel*, and told from a Protestant point of view by Sir David Lindsay.

The most popular among these poems would seem to have been Wyntoun's *Chronicle*, which survives in nine manuscripts, the *Wallace* and the *Monarche*, both of which remained continuously in print from the sixteenth to the late eighteenth century. The *Bruce* also retained some popularity into the eighteenth century, and the *Eneados* received at least a conventional respect, exemplified by Thomas Ruddiman's great, but scholarly rather than popular, edition of 1710.

Some shorter narrative and near-narrative poems attained a status almost equivalent to that of the most celebrated of the poems already mentioned. Examples include the *New Orpheus* (*Orpheus and Eurydice*) of Robert Henryson, Douglas's *Palice of Honour* (1501), Dunbar's *Goldyn Targe* and *Tua Mariit Wemen and the Wedo*. All four were printed early in the sixteenth century, Henryson and Dunbar by Chepman and Myllar, Douglas by Thomas Davidson *c.*1530–1540, and it is probably significant that in early references all four are given the dignified title of 'treatise'; 'the traitie of Orpheus kyng and how he yeid to hewyn and to hel to seik his quene' (Chepman); 'ane

Treatise callit the Palice of Honour' (John Ross, 1579); 'ane litil tretie intitulit the goldyn targe' (Chepman); 'the tretis of the tua mariit wemen and the wedo' (Maitland Folio Manuscript, 1570–1585). The use of the word probably stems from the encyclopedic element present in all the poems, and the allegory conspicuous in the first three. In the *Tua Mariit Wemen and the Wedo* the use is also ironic.

The poems of medium length all owe something to the literary programme instituted by James I (1394–1437), who in his *Kingis Quair* (Bodleian Library MS Arch. Selden B24, *c.* 1505, a British rather than a Scottish anthology, compiled for Henry, third Lord Sinclair, who died at Flodden) became the first Scottish poet to follow the Chaucerian fashion of combining narrative with allegory and dream vision, and to use a verse form of greater range and subtlety than the octosyllabic couplet. The tradition thus instituted had a long history; the last poem of substance which belongs to it is *The Cherrie and the Slae* (first printed 1597 by Waldegrave, Edinburgh, but at least in part much earlier) by Alexander Montgomerie (*c.*1545–1597), a poem which in popularity seems to have surpassed even the *Wallace* and the *Monarche* by remaining in print until the mid nineteenth century.

The poetry in the Asloan Manuscript (*c.*1515), the first of the large sixteenth-century anthologies, now in the National Library of Scotland, may be taken as marking the transition between the older and the newer styles in Scottish poetry. Unlike most later anthologies, the collection includes both verse and prose. In its present mutilated state, it has lost much of the verse component, but it is clear that Asloan's preference was for longer pieces. In the part of the manuscript which has survived, the two longest are the anonymous *Buke of the Sevyne Sages* (a translation of a collection of moral tales), and a devotional poem, *The Contemplacioun of Synnaris*, by the Franciscan friar William of Touris (?*c.*1455–*c.*1505). The first has 2,782 lines, the second 1,560. *The Buke of the Howlat* (1,000 lines), a rhyming alliterative poem by Sir Richard Holland (? 1420–?1485), Henryson's *Wyplandis Mous and Borrowstounis* and *New Orpheus*, together with fragments of the anonymous *Talis of the Fyve Bestis* and *The Buke of the Thre Prestis of Peblis* also survive, while the list of contents shows that the manuscript once contained texts of *The Goldyn Targe*, of *The Paddok and the Mous*, the linked *Preching of the Swallow* and *The Lyoun and the Mous*, the three parts of *The Tod and The Testament of Cresseid*, all by Henryson, the fantastic and popular *Colkelbie's Sow*, and finally two short ryhming alliterative romances, *Rauf Coilyear* and *Golagras and Gawain*. With the exception of *The Goldyn Targe*, these are all fifteenth-century works. Among the remainder, four Marian hymns, two anonymous, one by Walter Kennedy (*c.* 1460–1508) and one by Dunbar, together with Dunbar's 'The Fenyeit Freir of Tungland', survive and are entitled 'ballatis', the word normally used to categorize the short poems which became dominant in the sixteenth century. Twelve more are included in the contents list, and it is perhaps worth noting that Henryson himself, perhaps in mock modesty, calls *The Testament of Cresseid* 'this ballet schort' (line 610). Had Asloan been the only early poetic manuscript to survive,

we should have known a good deal about Henryson and his approximate contemporaries, but our knowledge of Dunbar would have been limited to, at most, ten poems.

A smaller, more directly devotional collection of poetry and prose is preserved in British Museum MS. Arundel 285 (*c.*1540). Most of the verse pieces are short, but like Asloan and British Museum MS. Harleian 6919 (*c.*1550), it includes William of Touris' *The Contemplacioun of Synnaris*. This is preceded in Arundel by the unique copy of Walter Kennedy's longest (1,715 lines) poem, *The Passioun of Crist*.

Not much on the development of literary taste is to be deduced from the two other minor pre-Reformation collections of Scottish verse, the Makculloch MS (1477) in Edinburgh University Library (Laing MS, No. 149) and the Gray MS (*c.*1500) in the National Library of Scotland (Advocates' MS, 34.7.3). The poetic contents of both are additions, made on blank leaves and fly-leaves, in one case to a lecture notebook, in the other to a miscellany of Latin documents.

Sixteenth-century ballatis are by contrast with most of what has gone before shorter, more private (though never entirely so; many were obviously written for court performance), and often occasional. Knowledge of them depends substantially on three great post-Reformation manuscript anthologies, which reflect the tastes of three very different compilers, who seem nevertheless to have shared one common intention, that of counteracting the cultural ravages deliberately and inadvertently inflicted by the Reformers. The most important is National Library of Scotland, Advocates' MS 1.1.6., the Bannatyne Manuscript, which includes an overlapping preparatory Draft Manuscript. The completion of this occupied the leisure of George Bannatyne (1545–1605), an Edinburgh burgess, during the months of plague which afflicted the city in 1568. The manuscript contains about 400 items, which are framed by three poems of Bannatyne's great namesake and distant kinsman, John Bellenden (*c.*1490–*c.*1548), archdeacon of Moray and precentor of Glasgow, translator of Boece and Livy. (Bannatyne and Bellenden are variant spellings of the same name.) The first, 'The Benner of Peetie', deals in traditional fashion with the debate of the Four Daughters of God and the Incarnation, and forms a fitting introduction both to the collection as a whole, and its first section, 'Ballatis of Theoligie'. It is followed, rather less appropriately, by 'The proheme of the croniculs', the prologue written by Bellenden for his translation of Boece. The last poem in the manuscript, as Bannatyne left it, is 'the secound prolloge or proheme of the Histery of the Croniclis of Scotland'—Bellenden's epilogue, in fact, to his translation. Bannatyne, it is fairly obvious, wished to claim, quite properly, that for Scottish vernacular literature his anthology had an importance at least comparable to that of Bellenden's translations, a claim doubly emphasized by the choice of the third poem to be included, Gavin Douglas's 'Prologue' to the tenth book of his epoch-making translation of Virgil. The translators had attempted to enrich the vernacular; Bannatyne set out to show the riches which it already possessed.

The anthology is divided into five main sections, some of which are themselves subdivided. The first (poems no. 2–49; I employ Arabic numerals for the main collection rather than the clumsy roman of Tod Ritchie's edition), 'ballatis of theoligie', has four subdivisions, (a), nos. 2–28, is general, with particular emphasis falling on first and last things and the Old Testament. It ends with 'The song of the virgin Mary', a paraphrase and expansion of the *Magnificat*, which offers the perfect transition to (b), nos. 29–38, 'Ballatis of the nativitie of chryste', (c), nos. 39–41, 'Finis de passione et sequitur de resurrectione', and (d), nos. 42–49, 'Exortationis of chryst to all synnaris to repent thame of the same'. The second section (poems no. 50–159) 'verry singular ballatis full of wisdome and moralitie', again opens (nos. 50–67) with a general subdivision, followed (nos. 67–159) by 'certane ballattis agane the vyce in sessioun, Court, and all estaitis'. The third section (poems no. 161–233), 'ballettis mirry and Vther solatius consaittis', is undivided. Bannatyne's rubric for the fourth section (poems no. 238–380) includes his own subdivisions: 'ballattis of luve, Devydit in four pairtis. The first (nos. 240–320) Ar songis of luve. The secound (nos. 321–359) ar Contemptis of luve And evill wemen. The thrid (nos. 360–368) ar contempis of evill fals vicius men. And the fourt (nos. 369–380) Ar ballattis detesting of luve and lichery'. The fifth section (poems no. 381–402), 'the fabillis of Esop with diuers vthir fabillis and poetical workis maid and Compyld be diuers lernit men', is undivided, consists mainly of fifteenth-century poems of medium length, and may have been an afterthought on Bannatyne's part.

Most of the poets represented belong to the sixteenth century; they include Dunbar, Douglas and Lindsay (the latter pair mainly in extracts), who are well represented elsewhere, but for many others Bannatyne is the only, or by far the most important, source. Alexander Scott (*c.* 1515–1582), for instance, would scarcely be even a name but for Bannatyne, nor should we have known of the 1552 Cupar performance of Lindsay's play, *Ane Satyre of the Thrie Estaitis*, and the existence of the Cupar Banns, the brief farce which served as a kind of 'trailer' for the play. Bannatyne, as has already been noted, is also an important authority for several fifteenth-century poems, for Henryson's *Fabillis* especially, and for much comic narrative verse. He gives better texts than Maitland for many poems by Dunbar. It is probable that, had conditions in the late 1560s and the 1570s been less hostile, he would have had his anthology printed. But at least it survived.

During the period mentioned, the Reformers had a considerable quantity of devotional and satiric verse printed in such collections as *The Gude and Godlie Ballatis* (*Ane Compendious buik of godlie psalmes*, Edinburgh, ?J. Scot, 1567). The manuscript tradition continued, however, in many ways as the voice of the opposition.

Sir Richard Maitland of Lethington (1496–1586), a lawyer and politician, who in 1561 became an ordinary Lord of Session, and in 1562 Keeper of the Great Seal, was responsible for the compilation of the Maitland Folio Manuscript (Magdalene College, Cambridge, Pepysian MS 2553). As he was himself blind, the manuscript is the work of several hands between 1570 and 1585. The collection seems to have begun with Maitland's own poems, composed from the late 1550s onwards, and notable both for their support of the Queen Regent, Mary of Guise, and her daughter Queen Mary, and for their hostility to the general course of events from 1560 onwards. Forty-one are included among the 182 items which make up the book. Poems by other authors seem to have been added at least substantially because they fitted Maitland's own taste, which inclined to the sententious, the political, and the satiric. He gave particular prominence to Dunbar, no fewer than 59 of whose extant 83 poems are included. Modern regard for Dunbar's poetry owes not a little to the prominence which Maitland gave him. The remainder of the anthology includes an extract from Wyntoun, four short poems by Henryson, four by Walter Kennedy, two often attributed to Douglas, one by Alexander Scott and two by the compiler's eldest son, Sir John Maitland (1543–1595). If one leaves Maitland's own work out of account, only a tiny fraction of the anthology belongs to the second half of the sixteenth century. Maitland in his prolonged old age looked back to the days of his youth, and beyond.

The handsome Maitland Quarto Manuscript, also in the Pepysian Library, and compiled in 1586 by Maitland's daughter Marie, stands in marked contrast. Poets of the fifteenth and early sixteenth century are excluded. She includes 43 of her father's poems; the majority of the remaining 52 items are anonymous, but named authors include the first post-Reformation principal of King's College, Aberdeen, Alexander Arbuthnot (1538–1583), Alexander Montgomerie, James VI (1566–1625), and Thomas and Robert Hudson, two of four probably English musicians with an identical surname who were attached to James's household as early as 1567. The anthology, in other words, is primarily a collection of later sixteenth-century non-devotional pieces, the majority of which, apart from Maitland's own poems, are not to be found in the Folio Manuscript or in Bannatyne. Many are elaborate love lyrics, often designed for musical accompaniment. Obviously there is some relationship to the work of James VI's Castalian Band of poets—the king himself, Montgomerie, Stewart of Baldynneis (?1545–?1605), the Hudsons, and, more distantly, William Fowler (1560–1612)—whose works, for the most part, survive only in manuscript. A sign that the ballat tradition was drawing to an end is the inclusion in the manuscript of a number of sonnets, the new literary form introduced into Scotland by, or under the influence of, the young king. The Quarto Manuscript marks at once the end of several traditions of the older Scottish poetry, and the beginning of some new ones.

Editions of the poets, several of the prints, and all the manuscript anthologies mentioned have been produced by the Scottish Text Society. See also the bibliography and separate articles on individual poets included in this volume.

J. *MacQueen*

Literature: Early Prose. Pre-Reformation Scottish prose is preserved for the most part in manuscript. Relatively little achieved the dignity of print, and much was written for a particular patron or for limited circulation. A single fine manuscript (Abbotsford Library Z.1.) preserves Gilbert Haye's translations, made in 1456 for William Sinclair, Earl of Orkney and Caithness, Chancellor of Scotland, and another (NLS Advocates MS 18.2.8.) preserves *The Meroure of Wysdome*, written in 1490 by John of Ireland (*c.* 1440–*c.*1496) for the instruction of the young James IV.

Two manuscripts, Cambridge University Library Kk. 1. 5., No. 6 (second half of the fifteenth century) and the more important Asloan MS (*c.*1515), each contain what may be called a prose anthology of relatively short compositions. Any piece which appears in such a collection presumably possessed some general appeal, devotional, educational or even political. Kk. 1. 5., No.6 contains (a) *The Craft of Deying*, a translation and abridgement, probably made early in the fifteenth century, of the anonymous Latin *Ars Moriendi*, (b) *Dicta Salamonis*, a paraphrase of the Old Testament *Ecclesiastes*, and (c) *The Vertewis of the Mess*, a brief treatise on the benefits of attendance at Mass. The Asloan collection is more extensive and more secular. Only one primarily devotional work is included, *Of Penance and Confession*, a substantial treatise, occupying 40 folios, composed by the author of *The Meroure of Wysdome*, John of Ireland. *The Porteous of Noblenes* and *The Spectacle of Luf* are both moral treatises intended for lay audiences. The first, a translation by Maistir Androw Cadiou of the *Bréviaire des nobles* by Alain Chartier (*c.*1390–*c.*1440), deals with the 12 virtues necessary if a nobleman is to deserve the name. Asloan may have taken the text from a version printed by Chepman and Myllar in 1508, of which a fragment survives. *The Spectacle of Luf* is allegedly a translation from an unidentified Latin original, made in 1492 at St Andrews by Maistir G. Myll, 'ane clerk quhilk had bene In to venus court mair than the space of xx yeris'. It is a disincitement to love in eight parts, particularly interesting in that it contains a reference to Henryson's (q.v.) *Testament of Cresseid*, or alternatively to the 'uthir quair' which Henryson claimed as his source.

Ane Extract of the bibill of the sex werkdays according to the sex agis, quhilkis restit in the sevynt is a compendium of universal history and geography, based primarily on allegorical exegesis of the Old and New Testament, but making use of such encyclopaedic sources as Boccaccio's *De Genealogia Deorum. The divisioun of all the warld callit the cart* is a Scots adaptation of various chapters of Trevisa's translation of Higden's *Polychronicon*.

All the remaining works in Asloan are concerned with Scottish history or pseudo-history. The most important is the mutilated *Ane schort memoriale of the scottis corniklis for addicoun*, but the manuscript also contains (a) *The Scottis originale*, (b) *Ane tractact of a Part of the ynglis cronikle schawand of thar kingis part of thar ewill and cursit governance*, and (c) *Ane tractat drawin owt of the scottis cronikle begynnand in the thrid age of the warld*.

The scale of the prose works of Gilbert Haye (*c.*1400–?*c.*1499) and John of Ireland is markedly greater. Haye, who lived in France for almost a quarter of a century, and became chamberlain to Charles VII, is a translator, and all his productions, whether in verse (the Taymouth *Alexander*) or in prose, are based on French originals. His longest prose work, which in his manuscript occupies 85 folios, is *The Buke of the Law of Armys*, a translation of the *Arbre des Batailles* of Honoré Bonet (*c.*1340–*c.*1400). It is divided into four parts, (a) 'the tribulacioun of the kirk before the nativitee of Criste', (b) 'the tribulaciouns and destructioun of the four principale realmes grettest of the warld' (i.e. Babylon, Carthage, Macedonia and Rome—the main emphasis falls on Rome.), (c) 'bataillis in generale', (d) 'bataillis in specialitee'. *The Buke of the Order of Knychthood*, which follows, occupies more than 18 folios, and contains eight chapters. It is a translation of *Le livre de l'ordre de chevalerie*, which itself is an anonymous fourteenth-century French translation of the Catalan *Libre qui és de l'Orde de Cavalleria*, written by the celebrated Ramon Lull (1232–1316). *The Buke of the Governaunce of Princis* occupies the last 26 folios of the manuscript, and contains a prologue and 40 chapters. It is a translation of a French version of *Liber de Regimine Principum or Liber de Secretis Secretorum*, a work which throughout the Middle Ages was accepted as the manual of kingship sent by Aristotle to his pupil, Alexander the Great.

John of Ireland is only incidentally a translator, and *The Meroure of Wysdome*, his most sustained surviving opus, is in a sense original, and is certainly designed on a massive scale. To date, only five of its seven books have been published. Ireland is primarily an academic, Bachelor, Master and Doctor of Theology in the Sorbonne, where he lived and taught for almost 30 years. His book is another manual of kingship; his method is scholastic, but adapted to the needs and capacities of a king still in his teens. Wisdom is a gift of the Holy Spirit; worldly wisdom 'js oftymes na wisdome bot foly'; to establish a proper foundation for Wisdom in the young man, the first three books are expositions of Christian fundamentals, Pater, Ave and Creed. Book IV demonstrates that 'the faith of ihesu contenit in the creid, and the articlis of it, ar richt proffitable to trow and ressonable'. Book V is concerned with free will, Book VI with the sacraments. Only in Book VII with 'law, police, iurisdiccioun and dominacioun' do we reach anything resembling a conventional manual of kingship. The book is remarkable for its range and balance, and uncommonly well adapted to its purpose.

The Scottish Renaissance and Reformation continued the earlier dependence on translation, while at the same time widening its scope. The Scottish Renaissance was more inclined to find models in the ancient historians than among orators and philosophers—in Livy rather than in Cicero. John Bellenden (*c.*1495–*c.*1548), another Sorbonne Doctor in Theology, who in 1533 became archdeacon of Moray, a post which in 1538 he exchanged for the precentorship of Glasgow, was commissioned by James V to translate the first five books of Livy. He had already (1531) completed a translation of Boece's *Scotorum Historiae* (Paris, 1527). The translation of Livy survives only in manuscript, but that of Boece was printed in Edinburgh, at latest by 1540. The vivid, if unreliable, continuation and expansion of the translation of Boece 'from the

Slaughter of King James the First To the Ane thousande fyve hundreith thrie scoir fyftein zeir' by Robert Lindsay of Pitscottie (q.v.) (*c*.1532–1580) was not printed until 1728, but survives in many manuscript copies. It was obviously popular.

The next major example of Renaissance prose, *The Complaynt of Scotland* (Paris, *c*.1550) has a more complicated background. Structurally, it is a very free rendering and adaptation of *Le quadrilogue invectif*, written in 1422 by the Alain Chartier already mentioned. Chartier, in the *personae* of Dame France and her sons, the three French Estates, criticizes the policies which led to the sweeping English victory at Agincourt (1415); correspondingly in chapters vii–xx the Scottish author, who may have been Robert Wedderburn (*c*.1510–*c*.1553) or the shadowy Sir James Inglis, in the *personae* of Dame Scotia and her sons, the three Scottish Estaitis, criticizes the policies which led to the sweeping English victory at Pinkie (1547). Chartier was an orator and poet who in style anticipated the French Renaissance; the Scottish work successfully captures this quality, and indeed develops it, especially in chapter vi, 'Ane monolog of the actor', an encyclopedic pastoral interlude which occupies the pause between the five introductory chapters and the main body of the work.

Some later pieces of Renaissance prose deserve mention. The first, by George Buchanan (q.v.) (1506–1582), is *Chamaeleon*, a characteristically witty but ungenerous satire directed against the unstable and unfortunate William Maitland of Lethington (1525–1573). Buchanan's satire was written *c*.1570, but not printed until 1710.

In early youth James VI (q.v.) (1566–1625) produced *Ane Schort Treatise Conteining Some Reulis and Cautelis to be observit and eschewit in Scottis Poesie* (1584), the first critical treatise on Scottish poetry. *Daemonologie* (1597) is characteristic of one unpleasant aspect of Renaissance and Reformation thought. The last manual of kingship to be mentioned in this article is James's *Basilicon Doron*, which was written in Scots (British Museum MS Royal 18.B.xv.), privately printed in English (Edinburgh, 1599); a revised edition in English was finally made generally available (Edinburgh, 1603).

Any account of the prose literature of the Reformation must include some reference to a basically pre-Reformation (Lollard) document, the transcription (*c*.1520) into Scots by an Ayrshire man, Murdoch Nisbet, of the revised English New Testament, completed in 1388 by John Purvey (*c*.1353–*c*.1428), on the basis of the slightly earlier work of John Wycliffe (*c*.1329–1384) and Nicholas of Hereford (*ob*.*c*.1420). The first notably Lutheran document is *The Richt Vay to the Kingdome of Hevine* (Malmo, 1533), a translation by John Gau (*c*.1495–1533) of *Den rette vey till Hiemmeriges Rige* (Antwerp, 1531) by Christiern Pedersen. *The Confession of Faith*, a treatise on Justification by Henry Balnaves (?1502–1570), was written in prison at Rouen after Cardinal Beaton's murder in 1546, and eventually printed at Edinburgh in 1584. The influence of Calvin and Geneva, operating primarily through John Knox (*c*.1505–1572), appears in *The First Book of Discipline* (1560–61. Circulated in MS until printed with *Second Book* in 1621),

and in *The Second Book of Discipline* (1578). The use of *The Book of Common Order* (Geneva, 1561 and many subsequent editions), originally the service book of Knox's English congregation at Geneva, became standard after 1560. English, in fact, became the characteristic written language of the Reformers, and is especially conspicuous in John Knox's masterpiece, *The History of the Reformation in Scotland*, part of which was published posthumously and anonymously in 1587, and immediately suppressed. It was published in full, but still anonymously, in 1644. Knox wrote a number of treatises, the most famous of which is *The First Blast of the Trumpet against the Monstrous Regiment of Women* (Geneva, 1558), aimed at the Queen Regent, Mary of Guise. Doctrinally, however, the most important, as well as the lengthiest, is *An Answer to the Cavillations of an Adversary respecting the Doctrine of Predestination* (London, 1591).

Catholic prose, devotional, doctrinal and controversial, survives in some quantity. Devotional material in British Museum MS Arundel 285 (*c*.1540) includes *Ane Dewoit Exercicioun in the Honour of the Croun of Thorne* and *The Thre Rois Garlandis of the Glorius virgin Mary*. The most important statement of doctrine not primarily intended for controversial purposes is the *Catechism* (St Andrews, 1552), usually attributed to Archbishop Hamilton (1512–1571). The most accomplished controversialists are Quintin Kennedy (1520–1564), Commendator of Crossraguel in Ayrshire, who wrote *Ane Compendius Tractive, conforme to the Scripturis of Almychtie God, Ressoun and Authoritie* (St Andrews or Edinburgh, 1558), and Ninian Winzet (*c*.1518–1592), schoolmaster of Linlithgow and post-Reformation abbot of Ratisbon, who is best known for *Certane Tractatis for Reformatioun of Doctryne and Maneris* (Edinburgh, 1562) and *The Buke of Four Scoir Thre Questions, tueching Doctrine, Ordour, and Maneris* (Antwerp, 1563). In the latter part of the century Catholic tractates continued to appear from continental presses, as witness the fascinating prison *Disputation* (Paris, 1581) between Nicol Burne, 'Professor of philosophie in S. Leonardis college, in the Citie of Sanctandrois ... brocht up in the perversit sect of the Calvinistis, and nou ... ane membre of the halie and Catholik kirk' and 'the praetendit Ministeris of the deformed Kirk in Scotland'.

Finally, a brief reference must be made to the *Memoirs of his own Life* by Sir James Melville of Halhill (1535–1617), and the *Autobiography and Diary* of James Melville (1556–1613) (qq.v.). Edition of most works mentioned have been produced by the Scottish Text Society.

J. MacQueen

Literature in the Twentieth Century. The Great War, rather than the coming of a new century or the death of Queen Victoria, could be said to mark the beginning of modern Scottish literature. In the early part of the century, nineteenth-century traditions continued to be strong. The novels and stories of John Buchan (1875–1940) (q.v.) and Neil Munro (1864–1930) staked out their own areas of interest within the romance territory where Robert Louis Stevenson (q.v.) had worked at greater depth before them. When novels of real force appeared, such as *The House with the Green Shutters* (1901) by George Douglas Brown (1869–1902) (q.v.) and *Gillespie* (1914) by John MacDougall Hay (1881–1919), they still dealt with the small, tightly-knit rural communities the Kailyard (q.v.) writers had made so much of; their savage inversion of Kailyard values, their vision of the small community as a nest of ingrown and distorted passions, with greed, egoism, callousness, brutality, and domineering ambition high on the list, seemed almost too neat, as if Kailyard and anti-Kailyard were a servomechanism, a closed system from which too much of normal life, and particularly life as lived in industrial and urban society, had been excluded; but the demonic power of the two books remains. When Frederick Niven (1878–1944) used the urban setting of Glasgow for novels like *Justice of the Peace* (1914) and *A Tale that is Told* (1920), his modest realism (much scorned by Hugh MacDiarmid) could perhaps have done with some of the robustness of Brown and Hay; yet he has been unduly neglected. Also neglected, partly because his stories tend to be lightly fictionalized sketches rather than fully imaginative creations, is R.B. Cunninghame Graham (1852–1936) (q.v.); his *Scottish Stories* (1914) have style and perception. In drama, the plays of J.M. Barrie (1860–1937) (q.v.) are clearly important, but belong to his later, London years and have little connection with Scotland or the Scottish theatre. In poetry, good traditional verse in Scots came from Violet Jacob (1863–1946) (q.v.), Marion Angus (1866–1946) (q.v.), Charles Murray (1864–1941) (q.v.), and Pittendrigh Macgillivray (1856–1938), with some experiments in reviving a more archaic, medieval Scots by Lewis Spence (1874–1953). John Davidson (1857–1909), writing in English, and showing an interest in city life and scientific ideas, had a greater influence, both outside and inside Scotland, T.S. Eliot and Hugh MacDiarmid (q.v.) in particular acknowledging his impact.

The general revival of Scottish writing which began after the First World War, and which is usually referred to as the Scottish Renaissance, is associated especially with the name of Hugh MacDiarmid (1892–1978). The term 'Scottish Renaissance' may be interpreted both narrowly, as a movement in poetry which aimed to explore and extend the potential of the Scottish vernacular for serious work, and more broadly, as the emergence of a number of interesting poets, novelists, and playwrights, not linked by any one programme but evincing overall a renewed vigour in Scottish culture: Edwin Muir, William Soutar, Neil Gunn, Lewis Grassic Gibbon, (qq.v.) Naomi Mitchison, Fionn MacColla, James Bridie (q.v.) and many others. Hugh MacDiarmid himself, though primarily a poet, was also a tireless publicist for the wider issues, with his eye on (to use his own words) 'a big Scottish Renaissance movement and the re-establishment of an independent Scottish nation', and his *Contemporary Scottish Studies* of 1926 included chapters on politics, education, and historiography as well as on literature, music, and art. In other prose books, such as *Albyn* (1927) and *At the Sign of the Thistle* (1934), MacDiarmid continued to illustrate his belief that the artist should concern himself with the struggles of his nation

to establish and define its identity and its values, within an unparochial awareness of what writers in other countries were contributing to the fund of cultural ideas. All this would have meant less if he had not given ample evidence of his own creative powers, and of his own ability to change the course of Scottish poetry, whether in the strange lyrics of *Sangschaw* (1925), the multi-faceted meditation of *A Drunk Man Looks at the Thistle* (1926), the imaginative adventurousness of *Stony Limits* (1934), or the 'poetry of knowledge' in *In Memoriam James Joyce* (1955).

Edwin Muir (1887–1959) made his name first as a critic and as a translator, less immediately as a poet. He was in many ways the natural complement of MacDiarmid, reserved where MacDiarmid was boisterous, persistent rather than provocative, suspicious of progress and science and (eventually) politics, where MacDiarmid embraced all three. Although MacDiarmid in his *Contemporary Scottish Studies* gave Muir high praise as a critic, Muir's later pessimism (as expressed in *Scott and Scotland*, 1936) about the use of Scots and about the future of Scotland as a nation seemed like a betrayal. Here, by a curious reversal of roles, it was Muir who was too dogmatic, and MacDiarmid who kept options open, and in the succeeding half-century neither writing in Scots nor the idea of Scottish nationalism disappeared. Muir's own poetry made its way gradually but steadily into critical esteem. In the volumes from *The Narrow Place* (1943) to *One Foot in Eden* (1956) he developed a distinctive poetry of spiritual exploration, using dream, memory, history, and myth, adumbrating Christian ideas through pagan subjects, drawing on the deep images of an Orkney boyhood, glancing at the dark fable of contemporary European politics, imagining wars to come.

The prolific Lewis Grassic Gibbon (1901–1935) published in his short life many books of fiction, as well as archaeological studies, but by general consent his masterpiece was the trilogy of novels called *A Scots Quair* (*Sunset Song*, 1932; *Cloud Howe*, 1933; *Grey Granite*, 1934) and in particular the first part of it. Written with great lyrical and dramatic energy, the trilogy gained by being much more than a chronicle or evocation of changing patterns of life in the northeast of Scotland during the first quarter of the century: the tensions in Gibbon himself between loving and hating a way of life bound to the land, and also the fascination he found in archaeological theories of a pre-civilized golden age, combined to produce a unique resonance, far from simple nostalgia, if not always from melodrama.

The life of crofters and fishermen in the north of Scotland was the staple of the fiction of Neil Gunn (1891–1973), but with shimmerings and underpinnings from Celtic mythology, Zen Buddhism, and the genre of parable. He is at his best in *Morning Tide* (1931) and *Highland River* (1937), where he shows a subtle insight into boyhood and adolescence, or in the more realistic and outgoing fishing saga *The Silver Darlings* (1941); less successful when he ventures into more overt political allegory in *The Green Isle of the Great Deep* (1944). There was a stark, almost crude power in his first novel, *The Grey Coast* (1926), which is impressive still.

The more fragmentary *oeuvre* of the obsessed and intense Fionn MacColla (1906–1975) has a strength, tang, and precision of its own. The pressures that have always threatened to shatter Highland culture are the theme of the rather rhetorical *The Albannach* (1932), the more vivid and steely *And the Cock Crew* (1945), and the broad satire of *The Ministers* (1979).

Other novelists of the inter-war years include Naomi Mitchison (b. 1897), with a series of excellent historical novels ranging from ancient Sparta (*The Corn King and the Spring Queen*, 1931) and the ancient Celts (*The Conquered*, 1923) to the Jacobites (*The Bull Calves*, 1947); Eric Linklater (1899–1974) (q.v.), an entertainer but a good one, with the picaresque ebullience of *Juan in America* (1931), the more native satire of *Magnus Merriman* (1934), the sly ironies of *Private Angelo* (1946); Compton Mackenzie (1883–1972) with his ambitious but too indulgent *The Four Winds of Love* (1937–1945); and George Blake (1893–1961) (q.v.) with the flawed but lively West of Scotland realism of *The Shipbuilders* (1935), *David and Joanna* (1936), and *The Westering Sun* (1946). Individual novels stand out which are hard to classify but demand to be registered: Norman Douglas's witty and outrageous *South Wind* (1917), David Lindsay's exercise in metaphysical science-fiction, *A Voyage to Arcturus* (1920), Nancy Brysson Morrison's touching love-story, *The Gowk Storm* (1933).

After the Second World War, despite a renewed wave of nationalist feeling in Scotland, novelists seemed to find their sense of identity even more problematical. Many of the best talents—Muriel Spark (b.1918), Alexander Trocchi (1925–1984), James Kennaway (1928–1968), Alan Sharp (b.1934), Gordon Williams (b.1934)—left Scotland, and it would be too glib to claim from this any measurable detriment or betterment in their art, but so much expatriation does make it harder to define what a 'Scottish' novelist is. In so far as there is a Scottish tradition, it could only be enriched and expanded by Trocchi's *Cain's Book* (1960), Spark's *The Prime of Miss Jean Brodie* (1961), Kennaway's *Household Ghosts* (1961), Sharp's *A Green Tree in Gedde* (1965), and Williams' *From Scenes Like These* (1968). These pungent novels of the guilts and pressures and hopes and frustrations of a Scottish background—and to them must be added the work of non-expatriates, such as *Mr Alfred MA* by George Friel (1910–1976), *The Changeling* by Robin Jenkins (b.1912)(q.v.), *The Dear Green Place* by Archie Hind (b.1928), *Docherty* by William McIlvanney (b.1936)—testify to the reality of the talent available. Nor need Scottish subject-matter loom large, as was shown in quite different but convincing ways by Allan Massie (b.1938) and Iain Banks (b.1954). A new dimension of originality and force was added with the highly imaginative novels of Alasdair Gray (b.1934) (especially *Lanark* and *1982, Janine*) and the skilful probing of alienation in James Kelman (b.1946) (*The Busconductor Hines* and *A Disaffection*). The short story and novella produced impressive practitioners in Fred Urquhart (b.1912)(q.v.), George Mackay Brown (b.1921)(q.v.), Iain Crichton Smith (b.1928)(q.v.), John Herdman (b.1941), Alan Spence (b.1947), Elspeth Davie (b.1919), and Janice Galloway (b.1956).

In poetry, the example of Hugh MacDiarmid gave a new lease of life to the Scottish language. The sardonic 'whigmaleeries' of William Soutar (1898–1943); the wry humour and social mockery of Robert Garioch (1909–1981); the lyrical impetus of Sydney Goodsir Smith (1915–1975)(q.v.); the genre portraits of Tom Scott (b.1918); the sharp satire of Alexander Scott (1920–1989)(q.v.); the intellectual exploring of the canon of Scots by Alastair Mackie (b.1925); the less literary approach of Duncan Glen (b.1931) and Donald Campbell (b.1940); the use of urban patois by Tom Leonard (b.1944); the Dundonian eclecticism of W. N. Herbert (b.1961)—all relate to a very Scottish concern with language, even when they disagree about MacDiarmid's specific programme for an enriched *omnium-gatherum* Scots. What could still be achieved by the use of a Scots that on the face of it might seem literary and artificial was shown by Goodsir Smith's exuberant, many-toned sequence of love elegies, *Under the Eildon Tree* (1948). If Scots-language poetry has proved durable through being flexible, English-language poetry in Scotland came into its own in the twentieth century by losing self-consciousness and forgetting past shortcomings. After Edwin Muir, George Bruce (b.1909)(q.v.) and Norman MacCaig (b.1910)(q.v.) continued in different ways to confirm the natural availability of English: Bruce with an honest, hewn-out depicting of family and community, MacCaig with a fascinated, questioning awareness of the strangeness of man's existence in a world of nature. W. S. Graham (1918–1986) and Burns Singer (1928–1964) explored communication itself; Maurice Lindsay (b. 1918)(q.v.) and Stewart Conn (b.1936) explored the world of everyday experience; Edwin Morgan (b.1920) explored language, the city, and the sense of the present; Iain Crichton Smith and George Mackay Brown used highland and island settings to explore wider social and religious realities; Robin Fulton (b.1937), explored topologies of image and time; Alan Jackson (b.1938) and David Black (b.1941) used the bizarre and the grotesque to explore political and psychological states; Douglas Dunn (b.1942) used a verse of measure and restraint to explore both personal and socio-historical themes; Liz Lochhead (b.1947) explored the resources of voice and tone through dramatic character and story-telling. Succeeding talents who have produced striking work include Valerie Gillies, Ron Butlin, Andrew Greig, Frank Kuppner, John Burnside, Robert Crawford, Graham Fulton, Jackie Kay, and Kathleen Jamie.

Scotland's thin and broken dramatic tradition showed some encouraging if precarious signs of recovery during this century. The engaging, witty, provocative morality-plays of James Bridie (1888–1951) enlivened the 1930s and 1940s, and about the same time an attempt to revive vernacular drama was made by Robert McLellan (1907–1985), Alexander Reid (1914–1982), Robert Kemp (1908–1967), and Alexander Scott. The Scots plays include some highly effective theatre scenes, but the movement as a whole relied too much on lightweight historical material and lacked depth and intensity. Later, despite interesting plays on the theme of the creative artist by Tom Gallacher (b.1934), the very personal tough-delicate plays of Joan Ure (1919–1978), and the varied approaches, both historical and contemporary, of Stewart Conn, the main thrust was in the direction of a vigorous social realism, particularly in urban settings, in the work of Roddy McMillan, Hector MacMillan, Bill Bryden, Donald Campbell, and John Byrne; a mixture of realism and fantasy in Tom McGrath also made its mark. Byrne's *The Slab Boys* (1978), Campbell's *The Jesuit* (1976), and McGrath's *Animal* (1979) showed both force and inventiveness. For much of the recent period, the popular success of very 'physical' theatre companies like 7:84, Wildcat, and Communicado, who used much music, song, and movement, tended to overshadow individual playwrights, unless the playwright found this a congenial vehicle, as Liz Lochhead did with Communicado's production of *Mary Queen of Scots Got her Head Chopped Off* (1987). Excellent but frustratingly sporadic work has come from Chris Hannan, Peter Arnott, John Clifford, Marcella Evaristi, and Iain Heggie. Recurring discussions on whether a National Theatre in Scotland would help or hinder the process of focussing these undoubted but scattered talents—discussions without consensus—indicated the mixture of vibrant hope and uncompleted business that tended to characterize Scottish theatre.

   E. Morgan

Literature in the Nineteenth Century. The novel has been called the 'dominant form' in modern western literature. In Scotland, its rise to dominance was not gradual but sudden, and followed as a direct result of the success of *Waverley* in 1814. Not only did Scott (q.v.) publish all of the best novels, with their astonishingly varied action, language, and characters, in the 10 years from 1814 to 1824; the same period saw the emergence as novelists of Susan Ferrier, John Galt, and James Hogg (qq.v.). Each of these writers went his own way in fiction, but all owed a common debt to the spirit of inquiry about man in society which stemmed from the Scottish Enlightenment (q.v.).

   The rise of the Scottish novel can be seen as a response to the end of war, the expression of a specifically Scottish cultural identity, and of Scottish anxiety, after Britain's involvement in the long struggle against Napoleonic France (compare Hugh MacDiarmid's assertion of a Scottish viewpoint in poetry 100 years later). Scott's example was crucial in two ways. He created interest in Scottish themes on the part of the reading public and hence of publishers; and he introduced Scots dialogue as an intrinsic element in Scottish fiction. To some extent, too, his handling of character and of history provided models for the other novelists: but Susan Ferrier's interest in contemporary 'manners' is distinctive, and Galt differs markedly from Scott both in point of view and in linguistic texture, as does Hogg. Hogg's masterpiece, *The Private Memoirs and Confessions of A Justified Sinner* (1824), points forward to the psychological novel of the twentieth century.

   The early nineteenth century was also marked by varied accomplishment in publishing (q.v.) and in periodicals (q.v.). From 1802 onwards Francis Jeffrey and his fellow contributors made the *Edinburgh Review* a formidable journal of politics and of literary criticism. The *Edinburgh* was joined in 1809 by the *Quarterly*, which was inspired by Scott although published in London. Then in 1817 *Blackwood's Edinburgh Magazine* was started, and was soon enlivened by regular contributions from Galt, Hogg, and from its unofficial editors, Scott's son-in-law J. G. Lockhart (q.v.) and 'Christopher North' or John Wilson. The latter was author of *Noctes Ambrosianae*, a long-running series partly in dialect.

   Unfortunately, the brilliance of this period did not last. Already in the 1820s there were signs in *Blackwood's Magazine* of the growth of an inferior, largely nostalgic prose literature. John Wilson's *Lights and Shadows of Scottish Life* (1822) and D. M. Moir's *The Life of Mansie Wauch* (1828) exploit a vein of Scottish sentiment without really coming to grips with anything of living cultural significance. Their work is rather like Galt watered down. This kind of approach, often accompanied by 'pawky' humour or drollery, became very common as the century wore on, leading in the later Victorian period to the heyday of the so-called Kailyard (q.v.)—which was also foreshadowed over many decades by seemingly endless feeble verse imitations of Burns.

   The narrative and lyrical vigour of Scott and Hogg apart, it was not a good century for Scottish poets. Song flourished, but strong originality was lacking. It would be wrong to suggest, however, that Scottish fiction in the mid and later nineteenth century lacks all distinction. In their different ways, such writers as George MacDonald, Margaret Oliphant, and George Douglas Brown (qq.v.), all reveal a continuing pulse of life in the novel. George Douglas Brown's uncompromisingly bleak work *The House With The Green Shutters* marks the rejection of Kailyard values while drawing on the strengths of nineteenth-century Scottish fictional tradition.

   Something which had been apparent from the beginning of the century was the fact that Scotland could not offer adequate professional stimulus or outlets to all of her able writers. A pattern was established whereby gifted young Scots, often with thoughts of journalism, drifted south, either to be forgotten or to make their names in London. The outstanding example is Carlyle (q.v.), whose thunderous tracts and historical disquisitions awoke the conscience of early Victorian Britain. Carlyle was known as 'the sage of Chelsea'; but he remained recognizably Scottish in inspiration, and his participation in London literary life influenced many young Scottish writers of ambition. A tragic instance of a young poet in the south cut off from his cultural roots is that of John Davidson.

   The outstanding writer of the latter part of the century is Robert Louis Stevenson (q.v.). With hindsight, it is possible to see him both as a successful 'English' writer and as a key transitional figure in the Scottish literary tradition. His family background (generations of Stevensons had been Scottish lighthouse engineers) and upbringing in Edinburgh helped to give him a finely tuned sense for the nation's heritage, while adversity and far-flung travel in search of health matured his genius. Alone among Scottish writers after Scott, he made a commanding vernacular contribution both in verse and prose. His interest in adventurous travel and in diabolism links him with earlier Scottish authors, while the subtle psychology of a number of his novels establishes his outlook as attractively modern. His last novel *Weir Of Hermiston* (1896) remains in its unfinished state the most tantalizing of all his many books.

D. A. Low

Literature in the Seventeenth and Eighteenth Centuries.

The change in cultural climate which brought the age of the Makars to an end can already be seen in George Bannatyne's five-volume 'Ballat Buik' of 1568, which both faces backwards to the poetry of the Makars and the courtly tradition of the past and at the same time shows the influence of the Reformation (officially effected in Scotland by the Reformation Parliament of 1560) by its exclusion of certain kinds of devotional poetry (such as hymns to the Virgin) and inclusion of some 'ballatis detesting of luve and lichery'. It shows no interest in folk poetry, though a folk tradition already existed side by side with the tradition of court poetry in the sixteenth century. Some popular songs (as well as courtly songs) were parodied into expressions of Protestant religious feeling in the early 1640s by the brothers Wedderburn in the collection generally known as the *Gude and Godlie Ballatis*. Other poems and songs of popular revelry and celebration were circulated in broadsides or handed down orally, and there were also ballads, rediscovered, imitated, collected and 'improved' with vigour in the eighteenth and early nineteenth centuries. But, although the Reformation brought about significant changes in the literary climate—suspicion of traditional folk festivities and their musical and poetic accompaniments being the most important—the most sudden and dramatic change was the result of the removal of the Court from Scotland in 1603 when James VI left to become James I of England. Court patronage of the arts, especially poetry and music, was of the highest importance in a country too poor to afford 'Great House' patronage on any considerable scale, and its disappearance, together with the disappearance of the sophisticated tradition of court poetry and music (closely associated with each other) radically altered the nature of Scottish literature.

The situation was changing, too, with respect to language. James's court poets who accompanied him to England turned to the English language and an English audience to operate in a medium that was in a sense foreign. The seventeenth-century poets in Scotland lacked a cultural centre and a focus. Drummond of Hawthornden (q.v.) wrote in English with his eye on Elizabethan precedent. The prestige of the English versions of the Bible, first the Geneva Bible and then the Authorized Version, in regular use by Scottish Protestantism, led to a slightly antiquated standard English becoming the language of the pulpit and of formal moral utterance while Scots remained the normal spoken language. Knox's *History of the Reformation in Scotland* had been written in a deliberately anglicized Scots so as to reach an English readership. So the Reformation as well as the Union of the Crowns helped to establish English as the formal written language of educated Scots. Scots itself steadily deteriorated from being a literary language with its roots in spoken speech but capable of almost any degree of elaboration, sophistication and 'aureation' in literary usage into a series of regional dialects. Poets now came to use Scots in a nostalgic or patronizing or deliberately rustic mood. Robert Semple of Beltrees (*c*.1595–*c*.1668) produced in his 'Life and Death of the Piper of Kilbarchan', otherwise known as the 'Epitaph of Habbie Simson', a mock elegy celebrating the tunes and festive activities lost with the death of the piper, a half-humorous, half-patronizing, half-nostalgic picture of Scottish folk festivities which set the tone for innumerable imitations. The stanza form (6 lines with the first three and the fifth rhyming and the fourth and sixth shorter lines also rhyming) was later called by Allan Ramsay (q.v.) 'standart Habby' because it became so popular in Scottish verse: it was a favourite with Burns. This was a development of an old tradition of celebration of popular festivities, such as 'Peblis to the Play' and 'Chrystis Kirk on the Green', but the sense of loss rather than participation in Semple's poem marks a significant change.

The lack of a courtly tradition in Scottish poetry after 1603 explains the lack of a Scottish Cavalier poetry in the seventeenth century. The sole representative of such a poetry is the handful of poems written by James Graham, Marquis of Montrose (1612–50), whose poems had to be written in English because of the disappearance of the appropriate Scottish tradition but who, significantly, in the eight-line poem written on the eve of his execution, in spite of himself used one Scots word—'airth', direction—in the powerful opening line. But it is worth noting that the only lively poet on the Covenanting side, William Cleland (1661–1689), also wrote in English, but in a breathless racy style that is far from courtly.

The Union of 1707, after the effects of the Reformation and of the Union of 1603, further increased the prestige of English as the literary language of Scotland. But it also had many other effects. One was to send politically frustrated Scots national pride in search of a national poetic tradition that could provide comfort. The resulting movement—towards anthologies, collections and imitations of older Scottish poetry, editorial and antiquarian activities and in general a desire to record the more picturesque and distinctively national aspects of Scotland's past—can be said to have begun with James Watson's (q.v.) *Choice Collection of Comic and Serious Scots Poems* (1706–11). Watson's prefatory note boasted that this was the first anthology of poems 'which has been publish'd in our own Native *Scots Dialect*'. There were other varieties of what has been called 'patriotic publishing' in the early eighteenth century. Thomas Ruddiman (1674–1757) came to Edinburgh from Aberdeen at the turn of the century imbued with that combination of Jacobitism, Scottish Episcopalianism and passion for the Latin classics characteristic of Aberdeen and the northeast. He was all for re-establishing Scotland's national cultural prestige by reviving a Scoto-Latin culture, and to this end he both edited the complete works of George Buchanan (q.v.) and provided a glossary for the edition of Gavin Douglas's (q.v.) translation of the *Aeneid* published by his associate Robert Freebairn. But it was altogether too late in the day for Ruddiman's brand of what might be called vernacular humanism to take root in Scotland, even though Latin poetry continued to be written in Scotland in the early eighteenth century, notably by Dr Archibald Pitcairne (1652–1713), who first encouraged Ruddiman to leave Aberdeen and pursue a scholarly and publishing career in Edinburgh.

Allan Ramsay came to Edinburgh from his native Leadhills at the turn of the century to further his twin ambitions of cultivating himself as a gentleman and founding a literary circle. He both modelled himself on the Queen Anne wits and tried to project a strong, often nostalgic, Scottish identity, thus illustrating a cultural confusion that dogged him all his days. A collector of older Scottish poetry who worked in the Watson tradition, a writer of vernacular poems of low life in urban Scots and of a gentle pastoral in which Scots is domiciled naturally in a rural Lothian setting, an 'improver' of old folk songs who dressed them up in impossibly genteel language, Jacobite and anti-Union but only obliquely and in verses he attributed to older poets, Ramsay strikingly illustrates the cultural cross-currents of immediately post-Union Scotland. Robert Fergusson (q.v.), better educated and more assured, was more confident in his choice of Scots for his poems celebrating his native Edinburgh, even though he was also attracted by the eighteenth-century English mock-heroic style and by the style of Shenstone's elegies, both of which he frequently indulged in. Fergusson's Scots has a *gravitas* lacking in Ramsay's, even though it is lively and sometimes colloquial: there are overtones of Ruddiman's vernacular humanism in his feeling for language. Burns (q.v.) was more clearly torn between a genteel tradition that had been steadily emerging in Scotland and especially in Scottish education and a desire to evoke the life he knew in the language of the people. Educated not, like Fergusson, in the Latin classics but in English poetry from Shakespeare to his own day and trained to write a clear and formal neo-classic English, he discovered for himself both the Scots folk tradition and (through anthologies and fragmented and inadequate versions) something at least of the great 'art' literature of an older Scotland. It was his discovery of Fergusson that gave him confidence to go on writing Scots poetry, though often his language is an English tipped with Scots or a Scots tipped with English. He could be sentimental and rhetorical in the English vein of the time, and he could handle rhetorical verse with skill. His encounter with two editors of Scottish songs with music set him off collecting, restoring and recreating a great body of Scottish folk song of which only fragments remained. Many of these fragments had already been made available by earlier collectors, notably by David Herd, whose two volumes of *Scots Songs* (words only) published in 1776 are one of the more important of the many eighteenth-century collections. In traditional Scots animal poems and verse letters, in ecclesiastical and social satires, in one notable narrative poem, in innumerable 'occasional' poems descriptive, celebratory or confessional, and in a great body of songs written to existing airs in which he evoked moods of love, hate, conviviality, work and play against a background of the seasons as experienced by a working farmer, Burns displayed the range of his genius.

The reaction to the Union begun by Watson's *Choice Collection* took various forms as the century progressed; on the antiquarian collecting side it can be said to have culminated in Scott's *Minstrelsy of the Scottish Border.* A reaction of a very different kind set in later in the century. This was not nostalgic and antiquarian, but progressive and purposive. Those who illustrate it were not anxious to perpetuate the use of Scots (which they regarded, in David Hume's words, as 'a very corrupt dialect' of English); though proud of being Scottish they accepted that Scotland was now North Britain and wished it to represent Britain proudly before the world. They wished to be among the *avant garde* of European thought, both scientific, philosophic and critical. They believed in reason, progress, 'improvement'. They believed in investigating human motives and emotions, as Lord Kames did with his fluent pen and inquiring mind. In David Hume (q.v.) this movement produced Scotland's greatest philosopher; in William Robertson, the pioneer historian in Europe of the period; in Hugh Blair its finest literary critic; in Henry Mackenzie (q.v.) its best periodical essayist and influential sentimental novelist; in Adam Smith (q.v.) its first and greatest political economist; in Adam Fergusson its pioneer sociologist; to say nothing of chemists, mathematicians and medical men. This was the 'Scottish Enlightenment' (q.v.), whose causes are hard to define precisely but which was certainly in some degree a belated response to the Union of 1707. Craig's original plan for Edinburgh's New Town was the visual embodiment of the ideals of the Scottish Enlightenment: its elegantly ordered patterns of streets and squares represented harmony and reason and progress.

Walter Scott (q.v.) bestrode both movements, the antiquarian and the enlightened. Fascinated from childhood with the romance of the past, with anecdotes of Border warfare and all kinds of picturesque violence, influenced as a young man by emergent German romanticism, he was a great lover of the 'crowded hour of glorious life'. At the same time he was seriously interested in history as an 'enlightened' study of the past, especially in the recent history of his own country, which helped to explain the Union of 1707, the Jacobite rising of 1745 and the present state of Scotland and its relations with England. He believed in progress, commercial prosperity, peaceful forward movement in union with England, while wishing at the same time to retain for Scotland as much as possible of its traditions, institutions and customs. He was especially interested in historical change, in those periods of history when a traditional code ceased to be viable and new ways had to be found. The heroes of his heart may have been the picturesque defenders of a lost way of life, but the heroes of his head were the bridge-builders, those who could find a way not only of surviving but also of modulating the past into the present while appreciating the best elements of each. This is the true theme of all his best novels. 1560, 1603 and 1707 between them produced traumatic changes in Scottish identity. It is no wonder that eighteenth-century Scotland was obsessed with history, that it became, as Hume said, the historical people in a historical age, and that the century ended on the brink of the emergence of the historical novel.

D. Daiches

Lockhart, John Gibson (1794–1854) was born at Cambusnethan, Lanarkshire, where his father was minister, and educated at the universities of Glasgow and Oxford. He studied law at Edinburgh, and was called to the Bar in 1816. However, the attractions of a career in literature proved stronger than those of law. After translating Schlegel's *Lectures on the History* with John Wilson ('Christopher North'), he became one of the leading contributor's to *Blackwood's Magazine* from 1817.

Peter's Letters to His Kinsfolk (1819), a delightful series of sketches of Scottish society written in the form of letters, has been reprinted many times. Lockhart followed this work with four novels, *Valerius* (1821), *Adam Blair* (1822), *Reginald Dalton* (1824) and *Matthew Wald* (1824).

Valerius is the story of a Roman Briton who falls in love with a Roman girl, whom he then discovers to be a Christian. Threatened with martyrdom, she is rescued by her lover and brought to Britain. Though the novel has interesting studies of character, Lockhart quite fails to evoke period atmosphere, so that his characters exist in a kind of literary vacuum.

Reginald Dalton, a sketch of undergraduate life and manners in early nineteenth-century Oxford, contains a portrait of Lockhart's father, but its charms do not compensate for its obvious exaggerations.

Matthew Wald blends religious fanaticism with melodramatic crime, and in the double character of the hero of the title, hints at the theme Stevenson was to use successfully in *Dr Jekyll and Mr Hyde*. But Lockhart's story is flawed by unacceptable improbabilities.

Only his second novel, *Adam Blair*, still has serious claims to our attention. Based on a true story from that chronicle of ministers of the Church of Scotland, *Fasti Ecclesiae Scoticanae*, it is a tale of guilty love; the story of a man who 'moves from a comfortable state of single 'sinless' existence into the realms of experience and reality' as T.C. Richardson puts it. It is an interesting excursion into those dark religious-inspired ills that for so long affected the Scottish psyche.

For a second edition, Lockhart made important revisions that greatly strengthen the probability of certain of the actions of his major characters. It is therefore a pity that the Edinburgh University Press edition of 1963, the most recent, reverted to the first-edition text for purely pedantic reasons. Though *Adam Blair* may not be a masterpiece of the first order, it goes a long way towards discrediting Saintsbury's quip that 'Lockhart had every faculty for writing novels except the faculty of novel-writing'.

Lockhart has been most remembered, however, for his two biographies of Burns and of Scott. His *Life of Robert Burns* appeared in 1828, and has been almost continuously in print. Elegantly written, it is, however, unreliable in many details, and is nowadays of little practical value. The tendency to gloss over unpleasant facts and to romanticize is also apparent in his greatest work, his *Memoirs of the Life of Sir Walter Scott* (1837–38). Lockhart had married Scott's daughter Sophia in 1820, and his knowledge of, and affection for, his great father-in-law is apparent in every page. Points of detail, like the famous death scene with its 'Be a good man' quotation, have been questioned by later scholars, but the strength of Lockhart's character-drawing and the impressively broad sweep of his accomplishment keep this biography, along with Boswell's *Life of Johnson*, in its pre-eminent position as one of the two finest in Scottish literature.

As a poet, Lockhart was less successful. *Napoleon* (1821) has little to it but once-fashionable smoothness; nor is the Byronic *Mad Banker of Amsterdam* any more convincing. His *Ancient Spanish Ballads* (1823) do not get beyond the level of accomplished versifying. He is remembered today in anthologies for his vivid sketch of a well known Glasgow character, Captain Paton, and for the moving stanzas he wrote on the death of Sophia, 'When youthful faith has fled'.

Much of Lockhart's energies necessarily went into ephemeral journalism. Apart from his Blackwood connection, from 1824 until 1853 he was editor of the *Quarterly Review*. His 'Hidalgo' look and cold and reserved manner made him many enemies, but those who penetrated his reserve had warm regard for him. He is buried at Scott's feet in Dryburgh Abbey. It is through him that Sir Walter's line of descent runs.

M. Lindsay

Lordship of the Isles, The, was made up of a group of semi-independent clans, some related by blood to the leading family of Clan Donald and others holding their lands from it, accepting its authority, and contributing to its power. Descended from Somerled, king of the Isles in the time of Norse supremacy, the MacDonald dynasty became a minor monarchy, and after the Western Isles were ceded to Scotland in 1266 its head acknowledged the King of Scots as his master when forced to do so. He issued feudal charters in medieval Latin (only one Gaelic charter, a grant of lands in Islay in 1408, has survived); in some the consent of his council is expressly mentioned, and a judge and 'archpoet' appear as witnesses along with island chiefs like Maclean and MacLeod and others of the 'royal blood of Clan Donald'.

John, son of Angus *og* MacDonald who supported Robert Bruce, was the first of four generations to style themselves *Dominus Insularum*. He inherited the family's lands in Islay, and others in Lochaber and Morvern forfeited by the MacDougalls, adding Knoydart and Moidart, Barra, Uist and Harris by marriage; in 1354 he obtained MacDougall acceptance of his rights to Mull and parts of Tiree and Jura, and King Robert II (whose daughter Margaret was his second wife) secured him in possession of Kintyre and Knapdale. His son Donald fought a royal army at Harlaw near Aberdeen in 1411 to assert a right through his wife to the earldom of Ross, and their son and successor Alexander was recognized as earl by the crown and died at Dingwall in 1449. John, the fourth and last lord, supported the

Yorkists in England and made a treaty with Edward IV, which led to his forfeiture by the Scottish Parliament in 1475; the earldom of Ross was annexed to the crown, but he remained Lord of the Isles until his island and seaboard possessions were taken from him in 1493 as penalty for a rebellion raised by his nephew Alexander of Lochalsh, and John died 10 years later a pensioner of the king.

Attempts by various members of Clan Donald to re-establish the lordship during the decades of unrest which followed all failed, and the old regime came to be thought of as a golden age. Lord of the Isles is now one of the royal titles borne by the heir to the British throne.

R.W. and J.M. Munro

Lorimer, Sir Robert (1864–1929). To describe him as the Lutyens of Scotland is not as careless a comparison as it may seem. Both men had the same respect for the Arts and Crafts tradition and both later felt the same fascination with classicism. Both displayed lifelong reverence for the architectural traditions of their respective countries and both enjoyed the privileges of the rich and enlightened patronage of the Edwardian age.

Robert Lorimer was born in Edinburgh in 1864, the son of a distinguished lawyer, Professor James Lorimer. Robert was educated at the Edinburgh Academy and spent three years at Edinburgh University, although he left without a degree. In 1885 he became an articled pupil of Hew Wardrop, an architect whose office contained many of the most talented young architects of the period. In 1889 he moved to London, working in the offices of G.F. Bodley and James MacLaren.

Lorimer set up in practice back in Edinburgh in 1892. Although his practice was launched with work on large country houses such as Earlshall, Fife (1892) and Minto House, Roxburghshire (1894), he was responsible in the 1890s for a remarkable colony of some 20 cottages in the Colinton area of Edinburgh. Here he was to develop a distinctly Scottish approach to Arts and Crafts ideals. His detailed planning was thoughtful; his handling of materials showed a love of traditional detail and sound construction.

Lorimer's opportunity to prove that he could translate the lessons of the Colinton cottages to the larger scale of the country house came in a series of commissions between 1900 and 1916. One of the first was Rowallan, Ayrshire (1902–6). The style is Scots Baronial but not that soaring theatrical kind favoured by David Bryce. It is more sober, it relies on good rubble stonework and crisp vernacular details and eschews fanciful skylines. The interiors are more chaste than their Victorian counterparts, and the evidence of good revived craftsmanship is visible everywhere. Ardkinglas, Argyll followed in 1906–8, the more modest essay in granite Rhu-na-haven, Aberdeenshire in 1911–12, and the remodelled Balmanno, Perthshire in 1916–21, where Lorimer designed a graceful new formal garden.

One of his most impressive houses is in the classical style: Marchmont in Berwickshire (1914–19). Lorimer recast the eighteenth-century house by Thomas Gibson to the point where it amounts to an original work. His handling of the 'classical language' is confident and his interiors with their fine plaster ceilings are unrivalled in Scotland at this period.

The Scottish National War Memorial (1923–28) and the Thistle Chapel, St Giles (1909–11) are clear evidence of Lorimer's ability to handle academic Gothic at a time when it was not a fashionable style.

The extravagant patronage and formality of Edwardian life now seem so remote that it is difficult to perceive within this dazzling world the solid and humble contribution that Lorimer made to bringing to life a Scottish tradition that had lain dormant since the seventeenth century.

M. Higgs

Lyndsay of the Mount, Sir David (1486?–1555). The poet and satirist was the son of David Lyndsay of The Mount, a house that stood about three miles from Cupar, overlooking the Eden. Lyndsay was born either here or at Garmylton, near Haddington, and educated at St Andrews. He served at the Court of James IV, and may have staged the 'apparition' in St Michael's Church, Linlithgow, designed, unsuccessfully, to warn the king against embarking on the campaign that ended with the disaster of Flodden. Lyndsay found himself charged with the task of amusing the future James V, carrying that prince on his back. In 1522 he married Janet Douglas, the king's seamstress, and seven years later was knighted and appointed Lyon King at Arms. He was at Falkland when James V died after the rout of Solway Moss, leaving the baby Mary as Queen of Scots.

Lyndsay undertook various diplomatic missions to Denmark, France and England, urged Knox to become a preacher, favoured the Reformers, yet died a Catholic. He did not, however, survive long enough to experience the excesses of the Reformation. His principal literary achievements are 'The Dreme' (1528), 'The Complaynt to the King' (1529), 'The Testament and Complaynt of our Sovereign Lord's Papyngo' (1530), 'The History of Squyer Meldrum', and the morality play on which his fame now rests. *Ane Pleasant Satyre of the Thrie Estatis* (1540).

Most of his work is social verse, whether couched in *rime royal* (as in 'The Dreme') or octosyllabic couplets (as in 'Squyer Meldrum'), urging the reform of the Catholic clergy and the virtues of good government. Only very occasionally did Lyndsay rise to the aureate manner of the 'high style' of his time.

On the other hand, his witty and satirical directness and his handling of colloquial speech in *The Thrie Estatis* set the tone that the eighteenth-century Revival was to develop. Among the many metres and forms used in his morality successfully modernized by Robert Kemp and several times staged at the Edinburgh International Festival with unqualified success was the stanza form, derived from one used by the Troubadours, later dubbed 'Standard Habbie' and popularized by Burns.

The dialogue of *The Thrie Estatis* is realistic and lively, as typified by the scene between Sir Robert Rome-Raker, 'ane perfect public Pardoner', and a poor man, from Kemp's acting version:

Pardoner:	Ane thousand year I lay upon thy heid, With *totiens quotiens*; now mak nae mair plead. Thou has receivit thy pardon now already.
Poor Man:	But I can see naething, sir, by our Lady!
Pardoner:	What craves the carle? Methinks thou art not wise!
Poor Man:	I crave my groat, or else my merchandise.
Pardoner:	I gave thee pardon for a thousand year!
Poor Man:	How sall I get that pardon? Let me hear!
Pardoner:	Stand still, and I sall tell thee the haill story! When thou art deid and gaes to Purgatory, Being condemned to pain a thousand year, Then sall thy pardon thee relieve but weir!
Poor Man:	Sall I get nothing for my groat till then?
Pardoner:	Thou sall not! I mak it to you plain!

So expert, indeed, is Lyndsay's handling of dialogue that one is tempted to believe his own claim that *The Thrie Estatis* was not his first play, and assume that the others have been lost.

   M. Lindsay

M

Mac Amhlaigh, Dòmhnall *see* **MacAulay, Donald**

MacAulay Donald/Dòmhnall MacAmhlaigh (b. 1930) has been publishing Gaelic poetry since 1956, though only one substantial collection has appeared: *Seòbhrach as a' Chlaich/Primrose from the Stone* (1967). He has also published an influential bilingual anthology of the new Gaelic Verse: *Nua-Bhàrdachd Ghàidhlig* (1976). His most pervasive themes are connected with his native island community (Bernera, Lewis), that community's structure, *mores*, language, history, and the relation in which he finds himself to these, both in terms of memory and as a returning exile. There is both celebration and criticism. Some of this is expressed in a relatively straightforward way, but by far the preferred mode is an oblique one making use of imagery and symbol. Sometimes a deliberate ambiguity is imposed and the community is addressed as a woman, an object of love, and whole poems can be clothed in this ambiguity (as in some Gaelic islands a girl at a betrothal meeting could be described in terms of a boat). This obliquity goes naturally with MacAulay's subtlety of mind which normally shuns any form of simple, obvious statement, or dogmatism of viewpoint though there are occasional exceptions, as in a poem on rearmament and one on NATO.

Some of the poems about Lewis are also concerned with questions of art: the place of poetry in the society, the artist's relationship to society. Others are love poems, and some fit into more than one system. The love poems almost seem to intrude on other topics, and we get an authentic impression of autobiography: of the welter and muddle of living being deliberately recreated, instead of being distorted into order.

There is an interesting group of five poems with a Turkish background (written during a short stay as a serviceman in Turkey) which provide valuable perspective. In 'Amasra, 1957' he gets a fresh view of Lewis religious self-righteousness, and in 'Latha Feille'/'Holiday' he constructs with deft descriptions an impression of the geographical and social layering of the Turkish society, ending with a lyrical affirmation of the lowest layer's virtues:

> … under black shawls
> stirred by the wind of history
> a living eye waiting
> though burdened and disparaged;
> teeth white as lime about
> a tuneful tongue, and cheeks
> like the pomegranate.

And in addition to the Turkish layers we sense others: the poet as politically conscious serviceman, as radical Lewisman etc.

More recently MacAulay has been writing poems about the Northern Irish dilemma, and also introspective poems about the individual's series of relationships with different aspects of society and experience.

Another impressive series of poems consists of elegies, or near elegies for persons or places: *Am Foghar*, 1958/For J. S.', *An t-Sean-bhean*/'The Old Woman', 'Ceartaigh' and an elegy for his grandfather with its particularly fine orchestration of emotion. These contain some of his most lyrical poetry.

MacAulay's characteristic form is free verse, using paragraphing, line length, rhythm, rhyme and assonance in the structural build-up of the poem. His rhythms are varied and subtle, with a strong correlation with the rhythms of speech, and he can use rhyme and off-rhyme freely, both at the ends of lines and internally. An interesting twist can be given by expressing what are essentially rhyming quatrains in free verse form, as in 'Crìonadh'/'Withering'. The use of organic imagery is also characteristic of his work. Often the imagery is either coextensive with the poem (so that it is arguable whether 'Briseadh'/'Breaking' is a love poem or a poem about Gaelic activism/scholarship/poetry) or dominates it as in 'Do Fhearsgrìobhaidh ainmeil'/'To a well-known writer', with its image of the fisherman looking for bait but becoming diverted by the challenge of walking over slippery rocks and keeping his balance. A characteristic variant of MacAulay's is to bring the imagery into play in the latter half of the poem (as in 'A' Cheiste'/'The Question' or 'Comharra-stiùiridh'/'Landmark') and allow it to reverberate. The poem 'Landmark' might well be taken as one of this writer's most characteristic poems, in terms of theme, structure, metre and resonance.

He has produced English versions of a good number of the poems, in the two books already referred to.

D.S. Thomson

Macaulay, Thomas Babington (1800–1859) first Baron Macaulay, the son of a West Indian merchant, Zachary Macaulay, was born at Rothley Temple, Leicestershire, and educated privately and at Trinity College, Cambridge, where he became a Fellow in 1824. He gained distinction as a classical scholar and a debater, though was weak in mathematics. About the time he left university his father's firm failed. He therefore decided to read law, and was called to the Bar in 1826.

He had already contributed to *Knight's Quarterly Magazine*, and in 1825 formed his long connection with the *Edinburgh Review*, for which many of his finest historical essays were written. His first contribution, on Milton, established his fame, and opened to him much of London society, where his remarkable powers of conversation made him popular. Literature and public life were henceforth to be his chosen paths.

He entered the House of Commons representing Calne in 1830, and after the passing of the Reform Bill sat as a member for Leeds, holding office as Secretary to the Board of Control, which dealt with the running of India. From this position he was appointed a member of the Supreme Council of India, to which country he went in 1834. His codification of Indian criminal law was a major and successful undertaking.

He returned to England in 1838, and set to work upon his major opus, *The History of England*. Politics and journalism, however, were to delay its completion. He was elected to parliament as member for Edinburgh, a seat he retained until 1847, and from 1839 to 1841 was Secretary for War. In 1846 until he lost his seat, he was Paymaster General in the Government of Lord John Russell.

The Lays of Ancient Rome, his most famous verse collection, appeared in 1842, 'Ivory' and 'The Armada' being added to the second edition. Although 'Horatius' survives in school anthologies, Macaulay's Scott-like movement of verse rarely gets beyond the successful depiction of physical action.

In 1843 he collected his Edinburgh Review articles under the title of *Critical and Historical Essays*. These include his studies of Pitt and Warren Hastings, and a shrewd estimate of Byron in the form of a review of *Moore's Life of Byron*.

Having been turned out by Edinburgh in 1847, Macaulay devoted himself to finishing his *History*, the first and second volumes of which were published in 1848, the third and fourth being delayed until 1855. No other work of its kind had met with such a successful reception, both in Britain and America, and it was translated into many foreign tongues. Although given to Whig bias, Macaulay's *History* has a vivid literary quality of interest particularly to Scottish readers through his description of the campaigns of Monmouth, the massacre of Glencoe and the circumstances surrounding the disaster at Darien.

Edinburgh again returned him to Parliament in 1852, but later that year his health begain to fail and he did not seek any office. His political *Speeches* appeared in 1854. In 1857 he was created Baron Macaulay of Rothley. He died unmarried in December 1859, and was buried in Westminster Abbey.

Macaulay, though of distant Scottish descent, is not, of course, in the true sense a Scottish author; but his long literary and public connections with Edinburgh, and the fact that several of the finest passages in his *History* relate to Scottish affairs justifies his inclusion here.

M. Lindsay

Macbeth. The best-known name among early Scottish kings is surely that of Macbeth (reigned 1040–57), but the man himself is a figure of controversy, of mystery and indeed of myth. Historical fact about him, itself limited, has been almost effaced by writers of fiction among whom William Shakespeare was neither the first nor the last. Myth has long exerted its influence, *The Latin History of Scotland* by Hector Boece (1527) narrates the encounter of Macbeth and Banquho with the witches, the ambition of Macbeth's wife spurring her husband to crime, the murder of Duncan, the murder of Banquho (from whom the Stewarts descended), and the final scene at Birnam and Dunsinane. The spirited Scots vernacular of Boece's translator, *Bellenden* (1536) gives the narrative in substance and often in the very words in which it has been retold down at any rate to my own childhood. Such an exciting tale was seized on by other narrators, through whose pages it came to the attention of Shakespeare, whose powerful drama gave permanence to the fictional Macbeth.

Fact, by contrast, turns on the state of the succession to the Scottish throne. Malcolm II, who died in 1034, left no sons. One of his daughters, Bethoc, married Crinan of Dunkeld and was the mother of Duncan, who became king (but in his thirties and not the old man of legend). Another daughter of Malcolm had married Sigurd, Earl of Orkney, and had a son Thorfinn, who probably contested Duncan's right to the throne. A third claimant was Macbeth, mormaer of Moray, whose mother was presumably the daughter of a previous king. (Macbeth's wife, Gruoch, was also in the royal line, but his marriage did not give him a good claim.) It seems that Thorfinn and Macbeth allied against Duncan, and, after defeating him in battle and killing him, divided the spoils—the kingship going to Macbeth and nine earldoms to Thorfinn. Dorothy Dunnett, in her novel *King Hereafter*, ingeniously identifies Thorfinn with Macbeth. Macbeth, like his ally or *alter ego* Thorfinn, was generous to the Church and they both went on pilgrimage to Rome. He remained king (though not without challenge) until 1057, when he was defeated and killed (nowhere near Dunsinane but at Lumphanan in Aberdeenshire) by Malcolm, elder son of Duncan, who had found a refuge and support in England.

G. Donaldson

MacCaig, Norman (b. 1910), an Edinburgh man, was educated at Edinburgh's Royal High School and Edinburgh University. From 1934 to 1967 he was a school teacher and from 1969 to 1970 a headmaster. He spent two years from 1967 as Fellow in Creative Writing at Edinburgh University. From 1970 for a further two years he was Lecturer in English Studies at Stirling University, and from 1972 until his retirement, Reader. His awards include two from the Scottish Arts Council, two from the Society of Authors and the Heinemann Award made in 1967. He is a Fellow of the Royal Society of Literature and in 1971 was awarded the OBE.

After beginning under the banner of the New Apocalypse movement with *Far Cry* (1943) and *The Inward Eye* (1946), MacCaig 'found' himself with *Riding Lights* (1956). He had by now applied disciplined techniques and immersed himself in metaphysics, throwing at first the shadow of Donne; but by *The Sinai Sort* (1957) and *A Common Grace* (1960) he was clearly his own man. MacCaig's themes are drawn from his native Edinburgh, and from the West Highlands of his ancestors, where he spends much of his time in summer. In his middle— some might say his best—period, MacCaig's metaphysics are allied to an intellectual toughness and colourful imagery.

In the 1960s and 70s MacCaig began to experiment with free verse, journeys to Italy and America widening the scope of his subject matter. A *Collected Poems* appeared in 1990. Though some of his later work features a kind of metaphysical sleight-of-hand, turning words cleverly when the poet has little of consequence to say, his achievement is a rich and considerable one; an original way of looking at Scotland and its attitudes, often provocatively, but always richly and visually sensuous. He has never really received the kind of British critical recognition that seems his due, though most Scots would now see in him their finest living poet.

M. Lindsay

MacCrimmon (17th–19th centuries) This famous family of Highland bagpipers held lands from the MacLeods for whom they produced several generations of outstanding pipers to whom the composition of many piobaireachd is attributed. A lack of secure evidence has led to a reassessment of their importance in the oral and written traditions, but there can be no doubting that they were figures of importance at a time when the form of piobaireachd was probably at its most fertile.

J. Purser

MacCunn, Hamish (b. 1868, Greenock; d. 1916, London) won a scholarship to the Royal College of Music, London at the age of 15. For three years he studied composition, under the formative influence of Parry and Stanford, piano and viola. His first important composition, an overture *Cior Mhor* (1885), produced by Manns at the Crystal Palace, was followed by three further Scottish overtures, also featured by Manns: *The Land of the Mountain and the Flood* (1887), *Ship o' the Fiend* (1888) and *The Dowie Dens o' Yarrow* (1888). The first, a

remarkable achievement for one so young, is as popular as ever—Mendelssohn and Dvorak with a Scottish accent.

MacCunn's reputation was enhanced by a subsequent series of Scottish cantatas and ballads, among them *The Lay of the Last Minstrel* (1888, Glasgow Choral Union), *Bonny Kilmeny* (1888, Paterson Concerts, Edinburgh) and *The Cameronian's Dream* (1890, Paterson Concerts, Edinburgh). The production in Edinburgh (1894) by the Carl Rosa Company of the Opera *Jeannie Deans*, the first opera by a Scotsman on a Scottish subject to be premiered there, marked a change of direction towards the theatre. *Diarmid* (1897) followed, but did not equal the success of his first opera. By 1900 MacCunn was firmly established. He was musical director of the Carl Rosa Company, and later also conducted for the Moody Manners Company, and at various London theatres. During the early years of this century Scottish subjects took second place: the opera *The Golden Girl* (1905), the ballad *The Wreck of the Hesperus* (1905) for example. However, towards the end of his career he renewed his creative nationalism in four ballads for chorus and orchestra. Other works include over 100 songs, half to settings of Scottish poets, part songs and short instrumental and orchestral works.

P. Hindmarsh

MacDiarmid, Hugh (pseud. of Christopher Murray Grieve, 1892–1978) poet, publicist, and politician, born in Langholm near the English border, he owed much to the radicalism and republicanism of his postman father and to the encouragement of his teacher at Langholm Academy, the composer F. G. Scott (q.v.). He gave up teacher-training in 1911 for journalism and politics, working for the ILP and the Fabian Research Department until his war service with the RAMC (1915–19). The 1920s saw him in Montrose, where he worked for the *Review*, one of the two local papers, in addition to being a Labour Councillor, a Justice of the Peace, and, from his Angus base, the founder of the 'Scottish Renaissance' movement. After a brief period as a journalist in London and Liverpool (1929 and the early 1930s) he lived in poverty on a Shetland croft (1933–41), then took up factory work in Glasgow as a fitter before becoming first engineer on a Clyde estuarial vessel. He was awarded a Civil List pension (1950) and moved to Biggar, Lanarkshire, in 1951. He helped to found the National Party of Scotland (1928), supported the Social Credit movement of financial reform, joined the Communist Party in 1934 (expelled 1938; rejoined 1957). In recent years he has often travelled to Russia, Eastern Europe and China.

In *Caledonia*, Anthony Powell wrote of the Scots:

> Such Mediocrity was ne'er on view,
> Bolster'd by tireless Scottish Ballyhoo—
> Nay! In two Qualities they stand supreme;
> Their Self-advertisement and Self-esteem.

It was this mediocrity in the provincial Scotland of the 1920s and 1930s that MacDiarmid attacked in his polemical journalism, unmasking 'the whole gang of high mucky-mucks, famous fatheads ... and all the touts and toadies and lickspittles of the English ascendancy' (*Lucky Poet*, 1943). Unable, however, to overcome the national inferiority-complex within himself, he deliberately used his own form of self-advertisement as part of a literary and political strategy which became increasingly tedious from the 1950s onwards.

All the turns and twists of MacDiarmid's development are best seen as responses to the central predicament of the modernist writer: how to coax art out of the fragments of a culture that seemed to be dissolving, and shore them against the ruins of the time. Objectively, he was a factor in the movement to revive the Scottish nation; subjectively, Scotland was a weapon in his personal struggle to write good poems. In the early 1920s he saw in the resources of the Scots language as revealed by Jamieson's dictionary an enormous creative potential and an implied metaphysic: insights explored at the miniature level in the volumes *Sangschaw* (1925) and *Penny Wheep* (1926), where lyrics which at first sight seem pure poetry yet make cosmological statements of great intensity. Linguistically, the 2,600-line *A Drunk Man Looks at the Thistle* (1926) belongs with Joyce's *Ulysses* and *Finnegan's Wake* to the experimental phase of early modernism. In content and form it is a verse anatomy of the condition of Scotland whose strategy expands the 'I-thou' relationship of the lyric (poet seeing and addressing thistle, as Burns saw and addressed the mouse) into a meditative monologue and a dance of interweaving themes. MacDiarmid here manages to present concepts at the very moment when they first appear in the mind, and makes poetry out of the to-ings and fro-ings of one kind of thinking. *To Circumjack Concrastus* (1930), employing thinner Scots, moves outwards to the external world, using symbols as exploratory tools. It is arguable that the poems in *Scots Unbound* (1932), *Stony Limits* (1934) and the *First* (1931) and *Second Hymn to Lenin* (1935), together with others from the later 1930s, some in attenuated Scots, some in English, form the summit of MacDiarmid's achievement. The best British political poetry of the decade is found alongside poems from a wide variety of other genres—meditations on private themes ('At my Father's Grave'), satire ('Prayer for a Second Flood'), compressed lyrics ('Milk-wort and Bog Cotton') and the extended contemplations 'On a Raised Beach' and 'Lament for the Great Music'. It might not be too fanciful to compare these last two with the austere, bleak yet convoluted Sibelius of the later symphonies and tone-poems. Just as in *Tapiola* Sibelius tries to render the essential forest, the strangeness of trees as individuals and in the mass, so in 'On a Raised Beach' there is, amongst many levels of meditation, an inscaping both of single stones as things in themselves and of the beach as a collectivity, as well as an attempt to realize the very quality of 'stonyness'.

In his work since the 1930s MacDiarmid responded to the problems of the modernist artist not so much through the realization of the Scottish essence (though this never ceased to be a subsidiary aim) as through a heroic reaching out after both fact and reason. Facts, scientific data, ideas, whole ideologies—these were now his raw materials. Sometimes he grouped them in patterns whose purpose was aesthetic rather than illuminatory, sometimes he strove to break down the barriers between the poem and the reality outside it, including the writings of others, so that huge chunks of other people's prose are often incorporated into the main body of his text. Excerpts from the long poems he was working on were published in his autobiography *Lucky Poet* (1943), *In Memoriam James Joyce* (1955), *The Kind of Poetry I Want* (1961), *Collected Poems* (1962, rev. 1967; completely new enterprise, 1978). The governing tension of this later poetry is that between science on the one hand and meditative experience on the other. At the centre we are always aware of MacDiarmid himself, immersed in his strong solution of books, contemplating information, compiling vast lists, rummaging in scrap-books for newspaper cuttings and in dictionaries for specialist terms and recherché words. These activities, too, are nothing if not national. They are an expression of the Great Scottish Dream of universal knowledge, of the world subjected to the same spirit of Enlightenment that inspired the eighteenth century and the Athens of the North.

T. Crawford

MacDonald, Alexander *see* **Alasdair Mac Mhaigstir Alasdair**

MacDonald, George (1824–1905), the son of a farmer, was born at Huntly, Aberdeenshire, claimed to be descended from one of the 120 MacDonalds who escaped the Massacre of Glencoe. Educated at Aberdeen University and Highbury Theological College, he became a Congregationalist minister at Arundel, Sussex in 1850. Three years later, partly for reasons of health and partly because his heterodox views, relating to German theology and to the possibility of heavenly provision being arranged for the heathen, did not find favour with his flock, he resigned his charge. Thereafter he earned his living from literature, augmented by occasional professorships and lecturing tours. During an American lecture tour he turned down the offer of a church in Fifth Avenue, New York, with a stipend of $20,000 a year.

This vein of unworldliness was reflected in his dramatic poem, *Within and Without* (1856) and in his *Poems* (1857). All of them are flawed by a vein of sentimental religiosity which is often used in place of poetic resolution.

It is perhaps doubtful if MacDonald was really a poet at all, though he was to employ poetic fantasy to good effect in prose in his most successful novel, *Lilith* (1895), in which he recreates a world where myth can produce wisdom unattached to symbolism (though, even here, he relaxes into a somewhat feeble transformation-through-redemption resolution to end the book) and *Phantastes* (1858), an excursion into the world of fancy much influenced by German Romanticism in general and by Novalis in particular. *Lilith* influenced David Lindsay's remarkable *Voyage to Arcturus* and explores terrain even more thoroughly charted in our own times by Tolkien in his *Lord of* the Rings. *Phantastes* caused C.S. Lewis to feel that in reading it he had crossed 'a great frontier'.

Of his novels of Scottish manners—in all, his output included 25 'three-decker' novels—*Robert Falconer* (1868) shows him at his best in creating Scots character and in handling its dialogue. Other works include *David Elginbrod* (1862); *Alec Forbes* (1865); *The Marquis of Lossie* (1877) and *Sir Gibbie* (1879), which, after *Robert Falconer*, is perhaps his best.

His reputation survives, however, through *Lilith* and *Phantastes*, both reprinted in our time, and through the best of his children's books, also several times reprinted, *The Princess and the Goblin* (1877) and the *Princess and Curdie* (1887). C.S. Lewis edited *George MacDonald: An Anthology* (1946) which shows MacDonald in some aspects of his best, but also at his less than best, the editorial viewpoint being in part a religious rather than a purely literary one.

M. Lindsay

Macdonald John/Iain Lom (*c.*1624–*c.*1710). The work of Iain Lom or Iain MacDhòmhnaill (John MacDonald) has survived in sufficient bulk (some 3,000 lines) to give a fair impression of his range. He had close connections with the Chiefs of the Keppoch MacDonalds, and having played some part in the Civil War (especially the Battle of Inverlochy) continued to take a close interest in Highland and Scottish affairs throughout the century. He has a series of poems on the Keppoch Murder of 1663, attempting to stir other MacDonald leaders to take vengeance; he has a poem addressed to Cameron of Lochiel, probably when he visited Charles's court in 1685, poems on the Battle of Killiecrankie, the Massacre of Glencoe, William and Mary, and the Union of the Parliaments in 1707. Others of his poems are addresses to or elegies for Highland chiefs, and in many of these there is a wealth of fact and opinion bearing on the events and personalities of the time. This is mainly public poetry, partly the work of a MacDonald clan poet (and by converse, a Campbell satirist), but to an important degree also, the work of an observer of the nation's business.

There are many facets of Iain Lom's verse that have a close affinity with the best of the localized poetry of comment, satire and humour which we later refer to as 'village verse'. The verbal wit is to some extent common to both, as is the exuberance of rhythm and the freedom of expression. But in Iain Lom we see these applied to a wide range of topics, and woven into lengthy sequences, sometimes forming part of a close, sinuous argument about political and current affairs, or the murder of a chief (which to Iain Lom is as heinous as regicide).

His eulogy can be unusually incisive, almost clinical at times, and it is perhaps the same temper of mind that shows in his vivid imagery, as in the poem on the restoration of Charles II, where he seems to be referring to the killers of the Marquis of Huntly:

> *Leam is éibhinn mar thachair,*
> *Mar dh'eirich do'n bhraich ud,*

> *Bha gach ceann dith 'na bachlagan bàna.*

> (what happened to that fermented grain
> pleases me—each individual grain had
> white sprouts coming from it.)

Many of his figurative references are similarly cryptic and oblique. He makes frequent use of biblical story, and indeed his figurative style has something in common with that of the evangelical preacher. Many of his poems have a strong rhythmic surge, which makes the statement persuasive, as in 'Tom a' Phubaill'. There are many political and social assessments, as this of the Marquis of Argyll:

> The sharp stroke of short pens protects
> Argyll, he who is as talkative as a parrot;

in a stroke, the contrast is made between the old and the new systems.

His use of language is creative; he borrows English words easily, for items of military or legal technology; he makes free use of metaphor; his tolerance of cliché is low.

D. S. Thomson

McEwen, John Blackwood (b. 1868, Hawick; d. 1948, London) spent his formative years in Glasgow, graduating in 1888 from the University. In 1893, two years after moving to London, he entered the Royal Academy of Music to study composition with Frederick Corder and piano with Tobias Matthay. He returned to Scotland in 1895, to take up an organist post in a Greenock church. A year later he was appointed teacher of piano and composition at the Glasgow Athenaeum School of Music. In 1899 he accepted a similar position at the Royal Academy in London. From 1924 until his retirement in 1936 he served as its Principal, in succession to Mackenzie. He received the honorary degree of Mus. D. from Oxford and LL D from Glasgow and was knighted in 1931.

McEwen, like his fellow Scottish exile William Wallace, was devoted to the cause of British composers, being a founder member and honorary Secretary (1905–18) of the Society of British Composers. Ever conscious of the frustrations of limited recognition, he endeavoured to provide some means of encouragement and recognition for future generations. To this end he bequeathed the residue of his estate to the University of Glasgow, as the nucleus of a fund to promote the composition and performance of chamber music by composers of Scottish race or descent. The annual McEwen commissions (begun in 1955) and the triennial McEwen series of concerts, inaugurated in 1956, are the tangible results of his beneficence and a memorial to his devoted service to Scottish music.

Although his music was hardly innovatory, McEwen's musical outlook was more liberal than many of his British contemporaries: for example, he actively encouraged his pupils to study the music of Debussy and Ravel—influences apparent at times in his own well ordered, but predominantly Germanic style. His output includes five symphonies, the

Solway (1922) being the most familiar, three Border Ballads for orchestra, *Coronach* (1904), *The Demon Lover* (1906), *Grey Galloway* (1909), a number of choral works and songs. However, he is best remembered for his chamber music: in particular four of the 16 string quartets, No.4 in C minor (1904), No.8 *Threnody*, No. 11 in C minor (1911) and No. 13 *Biscay* (1913); the fifth of the six violin sonatas, *Sonata-Fantasia* (1921); the Piano Trio in A minor (1937). Unpublished settings of 14 poems by Margaret Forbes for inflected voice and piano (1943) mark a belated response, within his own musical idiom, to the device of *Sprechgesang*, introduced by Schoenberg over 30 years previously.

P. Hindmarsh

McGibbon, William (*c*. 1695–1756) violinist and composer. Born in Edinburgh, studied in London with William Corbett; had returned to Edinburgh by 1726; died Edinburgh, 3 October.

McGibbon was Scotland's leading native composer during the first half of the eighteenth century. His surviving work comprises 24 trio sonatas (four sets of six, *c*. 1727, 1729, 1734 and *c*. 1745), 6 sonatas for flute or violin and continuo (1740), 6 sonatas for two flutes (1748), a set of *La Follia* variations (*c*. 1735), and a number of minuets. He was also leading violinist for much of this period to the influential Edinburgh Musical Society.

Up to 1740 McGibbon's career seems to have been modelled on that of the Italian master Archangelo Corelli (1653–1713). Like Corelli, he was as well known for his playing as for his compositions, and had cautiously published first trio sonatas and then solo sonatas. But after 1740 his energies were diverted into Scots fiddle music. He published 128 folk-tune settings (in three sets, 1742, 1746 and 1755) which demonstrated conclusively that Scots-folk and Italian-baroque idioms could be combined without losing the flavour of either. His folk-tunes remained in print almost continuously till 1810, and it was as a folk-composer that later generations remembered him.

McGibbon's family were musical, for his father Malcolm (d. 1722) was a professional oboist, and the obscure composer Duncan McGibbon probably a near relation. The fact that he left his estate to Edinburgh Royal Infirmary suggests, however, that he was the last of his line.

D. Johnson

Macintyre, Duncan Ban/Donnchadh Bàn Mac an t-Saoir (1724–1812) is probably the best known and loved of the eighteenth-century Gaelic poets. His image of an outdoor, company-loving extrovert may not be exact, but it has both truth and appeal. He was gamekeeper and City Guardsman and Breadalbane Fencible, made songs of praise to Campbell chiefs and gentlemen, drinking songs, satires and a few lovesongs, and his most memorable work is in a small number of poems which describe and celebrate the countryside he loved (the

Argyll-Perthshire borders), the deer that he hunted there, and his own reactions to the social and economic revolution that affected that countryside in the second half of the eighteenth century. The chiefs and gentry were close to the final phase of their role as leaders of a Gaelic society, and sheep were already replacing men on the hills and in the valleys. How sharp his perception was of the finality of these changes is difficult to determine. He is not very outspoken about those who introduced the changes, though he wishes long life to the fox cubs, hoping they will keep down the sheep. His bardic praise of the Campbell gentry is in part an automatic continuation of the tradition though in his lament for Colin of Glenure (victim of the Appin Murder) personal warmth and admiration are evident.

It is certain that Macintyre was influenced by Mac Mhaighstir Alasdair, who published a collection of his poems in 1751. It is likely that this influence was mediated through friends and patrons such as the Rev. James Stewart and John Campbell, both of Killin, for Macintyre could not read. Both in the use of metre and structure, and in the choice of themes and sub-themes, he was indebted to the older poet (e.g. to the metre and structure of 'Moladh Mòraig' and the themes of Mac Mhaighstir Alasdair's seasonal and topographical poems). His main achievement was to blend all these influences, and add his own very close observation and his lyricism, especially in the long poem 'Moladh Beinn Dòbhrain'/'Praise of Ben Doran' which probably dates from the 1750s. This is an elaborate praise-poem (though I think the irony of its subject being a mountain was unconscious), carefully structured both metrically and thematically, and having the stags and hinds as its *dramatis personae*, moving fluidly against a backcloth filled with varied detail. The shaping and control of this masterpiece are not matched in the great bulk of Macintyre's work, though his lyricism and linguistic skill are evident even in as late a poem as 'Cead deireannach nam beann'/'The Last Farewell to the Hills', dated 1802. It has been suggested that he may have benefited from the advice of literary friends, especially in the decade before his poems were published in 1768. Some of his poems were dictated to the Rev. Donald MacNicol of Lismore, and edited by John Stuart, son of the Killin minister.

Good translations (by Hugh MacDiarmid and Iain Crichton Smith) are available of the 'Praise of Ben Doran'.

D.S. Thomson

MacKay, Robert *see* **Donn, Rob**

Mackay Brown, George (b.1921) was born in Stromness, Orkney, where he now makes his home. He was educated at Stromness Academy, Newbattle Abbey College and Edinburgh University. Through his novels, short stories, plays and poems he has expressed the ethos of the Orkney Islands, reflecting the Orcadians' communal concerns and culture and their individual characters more effectively than any other writer; reflecting, too, the past (an awareness of which in Orkney is more alive than in most places), through the present, always with a sense of realism, especially in his earlier work. Since his conversion to Roman Catholicism in 1961, a mystical incantatory note has gradually appeared, particularly in his verse, tending to distance him a little from those who do not share his religious premises.

He himself has said that his themes are 'birth, love, death, resurrection, ceremonies of fishing and agriculture' and through these primeval concerns he has captured the 'feel' of his compatriots' way of life and the continuity of their customs.

His first book of poems published outside Orkney, *Loaves and Fishes* (1959), established the individual tone of his poet's voice, the deliberate homespun rural texture of his verse. This was consolidated by *The Year of the Whale* (1965). Signs of his mystical preoccupation tilting the balance with reality in favour of ritual first showed in *Fisherman and Ploughs* (1971), a kind of versified history of Orkney. A good selection of his best work is to be found in his *Selected Poems, 1954–1983* (1991).

His novels include *Greenvoe* (1972) dealing with the communal life of a local community in which they struggle against the forces of history, and the retelling of the story of Orkney's patron saint, *Magnus* (1973), *Time in a Red Coat* (1984) and *Vinland* (1992).

His short stories, the best of which are character studies in prose glimpsed with the intensity of poetry, are to be found in *A Calendar of Love* (1967), and *A Time to Keep* (1969). Of his plays the most successful has been *A Spell for Green Corn* (1967), although several of his stories have been successfully realized dramatically on television. *An Orkney Tapestry* (1969) is his tribute to the topographical and other features and values which he enjoys in Orkney.

He has won several literary prizes, and in 1974 was awarded the OBE. Since the formation of the Orkney Festival, he has collaborated with the composer Peter Maxwell Davies, providing texts for several of his compositions.

M. Lindsay

Mackenzie, Alexander Campbell (b. 1847, Edinburgh; d. 1935, London) is generally regarded as the father of the Scottish musical revival. Educated in Germany (1857–62) and subsequently at the Royal Academy of Music, London, he settled in Edinburgh (1865) as music teacher, choral conductor and violinist. A period of composition in Florence followed, and at 41 he was appointed Principal of the Royal Academy of Music, London. During his tenure, younger Scottish composers Wallace, MacCunn, Drysdale, McEwen studied or taught there. He was knighted in 1895 and made a KCVO in 1922, two years before his retirement. His influence and reputation in England at the turn of the century were surpassed only by Parry and Stanford at the Royal College of Music.

He was a prolific composer in all traditional forms—operas, oratorios and cantatas, three concertos (two violin and one piano), countless orchestral, chamber and instrumental pieces and songs. An early Piano Quartet in E-flat major (Op. II) and a short *Benedictus* for violin and piano or orchestra still receive occasional performances. His 'Scottish' compositions are most characteristic achievements; among them, two *Rhapsodie Ecosaisses* (1880, 1881) for orchestra, choral setting for Burns's *The Cottar's Saturday Night* (1888), Suite *Pibroch* (1889, Leeds Festival with Sarasate as soloist) and *Highland Ballad* (1893) for violin and orchestra, the *Scottish Piano Concerto* (1897, Royal Philharmonic Society with Paderewski) and his latest major work the Scottish Rhapsody *Tam o'Shanter* (1911).

P. Hindmarsh

Mackenzie, Henry (1745–1831) was the son of an Edinburgh doctor. He was educated at Edinburgh High School and University, where he studied law. He became Comptroller of Taxes for Scotland in 1799, a post he held until his death. He was editor of two short-lived periodicals, *The Mirror* (1779/80) and the *Lounger* (1785/7), both modelled on *The Spectator*, as a result of which he was sometimes called 'the Northern Addison'. He practised the cult of sentimentalism, and both in this respect and in the matter of style and punctuation, owed much to Sterne. In his most famous novel *The Man of Feeling* (1771), the hero's unceasing tearful pity, braced neither with the force of detached indignation nor the political desire (or ability), to nurture practical reform, becomes wearisome. *The Man of the World* (1773), intended as a balancing study, has its sentimentality somewhat tempered, but the literary contrivance is no less obvious. *Julia de Roubigne* (1777) couched in the by then somewhat old-fashioned form of letters, deals with a heroine who believes that her unofficially betrothed young man has married another abroad, and so weds a rich nobleman out of gratitude to her father. But the former lover returns from the West Indies to claim her hand, having made his fortune. The husband misinterprets an innocent if damp-eyed farewell between his wife and her former lover, and instead of making a few elementary inquiries, poisons his wife. On discovering his mistake, he then poisons himself, with no great loss to the gallery of literary characters.

Mackenzie's social perceptions were keener than those of many of his contemporaries, leading him to disapprove of the British conquest of India, the slave trade, press ganging, land monopoly and political favouritism. His enthusiastic if somewhat misguided essay hailing Burns in the *Lounger* as a 'heaven-taught ploughman' and his still warmer welcome to the author of *Waverley* greatly encouraged both Burns and Scott. He advised Burns over the disposition of his copyright for the Edinburgh editions of his poems to William Creech, and was in fact the dedicatee of *Waverley*. Mackenzie helped found the Royal Society of Edinburgh in 1783, and the Highland and Agricultural Society in 1784. Mackenzie's extensive notes for an autobiography were published under the title *Anecdotes and Egoisms* in 1927, edited by Harold William Thompson.

M. Lindsay

Mackintosh, Charles Rennie (1868–1928) was born at no. 70 Parson Street, Glasgow. His father, a superintendent of police, was respected for his honest dealing with everyone, a characteristic which was inherited by his son, Charles. After the family moved to no. 2 Firpark Terrace, Dennistoun, the father, William Mackintosh, was the better able to practise his hobby of gardening—especially the cultivation of flowers, a love for which grew early in Charles. It would appear Charles never wished for a career other than being an architect, so that after attending Allan Glen's School he was apprenticed to the firm of John Hutcheson in 1884, in which year he began attending evening classes at Glasgow School of Art. The following year Francis H. Newbery was appointed headmaster of the School, a man in sympathy with the work of the Glasgow Boys and readily appreciative of the inventive talent and skills of his student Charles Rennie Mackintosh. The conditions in Glasgow were propitious for new developments, though, as might be expected, when Mackintosh joined the established firm of Honeyman and Keppie in 1889, he did not immediately have the opportunity of showing his individuality in architecture. Yet by his mid-twenties Mackintosh had shown evidence of developments in two directions, apparently widely divergent, which later he was to bring together in those masterpieces by which he came to be acknowledged as Scotland's most original architectural genius.

On the one hand Mackintosh's design for the Diploma awarded by the Glasgow School of Art Club (1893) has the style of the modern 'Art Nouveau' (though with a reference to Celtic art) sensitive, divorced from common life, and on the other hand he gave two lectures to the Glasgow Architectural Association (1891 and 1893), which revealed a committed concern about the true function of architecture and its appropriate function in Scotland. He wrote:

All great and living architecture has been the direct expression of the needs and beliefs of man at the time of its creation, and now if we would have great architecture created, this should still be so.... It is absurd to think it is the duty of the modern architect to make believe he is living four, five, six hundred or even one thousand years—

The last of the historic claim of this architecture to which I will call your attention is that it is the national architecture of our own country and of our forefathers. All I mean to urge is the simple fact that, by whatever members of our family of nations it was shared, it was nevertheless the architecture of our own country, just as much Scotch as we are ourselves—as indigenous to our country as our wild flowers, our family name, our customs or our political constitution.

Original examples are at our own doors, the very houses in which some of us live: the monuments of our own forefathers, ...

Mackintosh's greatest achievement, his directive to his contemporaries throughout Europe, the *Glasgow School of Art* witnesses to what he drew from his national heritage, and to the use he made of *avant garde* styles, both elements wholly incorporated in the building. The drama of the massive wall of the east facade—reminder of the solid geometry of the Scotch castle, the reaching for height, with the fascinating fenestration of the west face, the confrontation of the glass of the large windows of the north facade, boldly interrupted by the decorative flourishes of large iron brackets which sweep upwards from below the first floor windows, and inside the strong anouncements of timbers of their functional purpose, the generous spaciousness of the studios, the wholly different effect of the library where light filters from the astragalled windows amongst wooden verticals of pine wood, with not a hint of the willowy curves of art nouveau until one enters the Board Room (now the Mackintosh Room) or Director's Room, where the curves are restrained, and the effect is of that white purity of vision, characteristic of even the most decorative of Mackintosh's furnishing—all this in the building which won the competition for Honeyman and Keppie in 1896 is the summation of Mackintosh's genius. Mackintosh's originality arose more out of a modern, and therefore appropriate, application of traditional Scottish practice, than out of a seeking for novelty. *Scotland Street School* (1906) is an example of this, and the distinction of Makintosh's houses, though here the furnishing, with its ready reference in curves, decoration, and design to new developments puts the emphasis on an individual imagination, is in the adaptation and development of tradition. Among these *Windyhill* (1900) at Kilmacolm, and *Hill House* (1902–3), Helensburgh, are outstanding. Pevsner wrote of them:

they are in their general outline descendants of the Scottish manorhouse but their composition of windows, of chimneystacks, of oriels is of a subtle irregularity, at first appearing arbitrary, but then revealing itself as most sensitively placed and scaled—very much what Le Corbusier did in his late works, only without their brutality.

To the owner of *Hill House*, Walter Blackie, Mackintosh said: 'Here is the house, It is not an Italian Villa, an English mansion house, or a Scotch castle. It is a dwelling house.' He might well have said something similar to Miss Cranstoun on his completing *The Willow Tea Rooms*, or any of the other tea rooms in Glasgow commissioned by her, ending with the words: 'It is a tea room.' In this relaxed and gossipy atmosphere, there was room for the free expression of Mackintosh—and for the influence of his wife, Margaret Macdonald—in elegant, fluent, inventive design, especially in his use of the shapes and visual rhythms of flowers. It was in the area of domestic design, furnishing and decoration that Mackintosh made his first impact on Europe at the Vienna Secessionist Exhibition of 1900, but his influence on modern architecture was more widely and strongly felt in the Haus Eines Kunstfreundes competition of 1901. From this there spread on the Continent an awareness that the true father of modern architecture had arrived.

Unfortunately after 1909, when the west wing of the Glasgow School of Art was completed, there were no major architectural commissions for Mackintosh, and his influence waned in Britain. He took to painting more seriously, turning from his delicate rendering of flower studies to watercolours in which he introduced the architecture of rock formations and a drama of light and dark on stone with such power as to suggest he had extended the range of that medium.

Still this was a sad ending to the most individual genius in Scottish architecture and the greatest architectural influence in Europe of his day.

G. Bruce

Maclean, Sorley/Somhairle MacGill-Eain (b.1911) was born in Raasay. A graduate of Edinburgh, he was a schoolmaster in Edinburgh and Plockton, Ross-shire. After retirement he was Writer in Residence at Edinburgh University and at Sabhal Mor Ostaig in Skye. He now lives in Skye.

His collection of poems *Dàin do Eimhir agus Dàin Eile* (1943) was the first published collection of Gaelic verse in the modern idiom. As such it has had tremendous influence; indeed it can be said that its publication altered the whole face of Gaelic poetry. This was not so much because it used new verse structures—new metres and *vers libre* were not one of its striking features—but because it spoke with a new voice. This voice was contemporary (whilst maintaining clear traditional virtues such as eloquence) and it spoke of contemporary things. It was imbued with a passion and used a dialectic which belonged to the modern world, especially the world of the 1930s. It reintroduced intellectual force into Gaelic verse at a time when the voice of the literate end of the tradition was at a low ebb—though the 'village bards' continued to compose with their own splendid invention and wit. At the time, Sorley Maclean's verse seemed startlingly innovative, and indeed for its time it was; perhaps in the future it will be seen as the essential bridge between the old verse and the new.

Much of Maclean's verse was written during a comparatively short period of time in the late 1930s. The poetry of this period centred largely on an intense and indeed shattering experience of love, which highlighted a set of conflicts and contradictions in life, experience and language, triggered off a veritable explosion of poetic energy, and fused the contradictions into marvellous poetry.

Of this experience Maclean says,

> Were it not for you the Cuillin would be
> a serrated blue rampart
> girding with its boundary wall
> all that is in my barbarous heart ...
> ... but you imposed an order on them
> beyond my own pain ...
> ... and there blossomed the Tree of Strings
> in its leafy branches your face ...

This poem contains three of the prime symbolic images of the sequence, the 'Cuillin' a multifaceted symbol, here referring to his native experiences; the 'Tree of Strings', representing the art of poetry, and 'the face' a symbol of haunting beauty

(cf. the poem 'The Haunting' for example), that recurs again and again in these poems.

Maclean was strongly influenced by socialist theory and the socialist programmes of the 1930s, and some of the conflicts relate to consequent interpretations of duty, for example in a poem called 'The Cry of Europe' he asks,

> Would white body and sunshine forehead take
> ... from me ... the spite of the bourgeois and
>   the poison of their creed.

And when he contemplates the loss of his love he rationalizes

> I did not choose a death on a cross
> when Spain was in dire extremity
> and how then could I hope for
> the unique gift of fate ...

Not all of Maclean's poetry from this period was obsessed with the love theme. We have poetry dealing with intellectual questions. His Marxist dialectic was reinforced by exposure in his university studies to the English metaphysical poets (as the last-quoted poem reflects) and it would be wrong to forget that the Gaelic tradition had its own kind of intellectual inventiveness. These elements come together in poems like 'The Heron' and in 'The Knife' (which does deal with love) and are reflected in poems such as 'Calvary' and 'The Black Tree'.

To the pre-1945 period belong the war poems such as 'Heroes', 'Death Valley' and 'An Autumn Day', which reflect his experiences in the Western Desert. A rather different kind of poem from this period is 'The Woods of Raasay' where the wood is used as a fertile theme for the exploration of experience. It begins as a kaleidoscopic celebration of the variety and resources of the wood: 'You gave me helmets ... ecstatic helmets ... proud helmets, sparkling helmets, red-brown helmets ... green helmets ... the helmet of poignancy and the helmet of serenity ... ' And it ends by questioning its symbolic coherence—perhaps even the coherence of symbolism itself (which was a basic stylistic influence on Maclean).

From the post-1945 period we have poems of interest also such as 'A Girl and Old Songs', 'Palach' and 'At the Grave of W. B. Yeats' (an important source of influence). There are two fine elegies, 'A Memory of Alexander Nicolson, one of my Uncles', a short and powerful evocation of the man and his place, and 'Elegy for Calum I. Maclean' a long elegy on his brother (the notable scholar of Gaelic folk culture) which exploits the conventions of Gaelic traditional panegyric to define the meaning of Calum's life in the context of the Gaelic world.

The best poem from this period and one of Maclean's finest achievements is the poem 'Hallaig'. Elegaic in tone it uses the imagery of trees and a land of the dead (Hallaig is the site of the graveyard) to explore the desolation of Gaelic culture and the problematic nature of its renewal.

Maclean's poems are published in *Dain do Eimhir agus Dain Eile* (1943) and *Reothairt is Contraigh: Spring tide and Neap tide. Selected Poems 1932–72* (1977). *O Choille gu Bearradh* (1989). He contributed to *Four Points of a Saltire* (1970) and *Nua-Bhàrdachd*

Ghàidhlig: Modern Gaelic Poems (1976). Translations appear in all these and also in *Lines Review* 34 (1979) and in *Poems to Eimhir* translated by I. C. Smith (1971) and his verse has appeared in many other anthologies. There has been a collection of his non-poetical writings *Ris a' Bhruthaich* (1985) and a collection of essays on his work *Sorley MacLean: Critical Essays* (1986) edited by R.J. Ross and J. Henry, and his verse has attracted much critical attention in periodical literature.

D. MacAulay

MacLeod, Baron George Fielden, of Fuinary (1895–1991), son of Sir John MacLeod, a Glasgow MP, was educated at Winchester and Oxford. After a distinguished career in World War I (he was awarded the MC and the Croix de Guerre) he studied theology at Edinburgh University and became a minister in the Church of Scotland, serving notably in Govan, Glasgow. He is best known as the founder of the Iona Community which restored the historic abbey to its present condition. He was also a writer and broadcaster and was Moderator of the Church of Scotland in 1957–8. He became a life peer in 1967.

P. Ingalls

MacLeod, Mary / Mairi Nighean Alasdair Ruaidh (c.1615–c.1707), daughter of an aristocratic family of the MacLeods of Harris and Skye, was born in Harris, probably in Rodel, where she is buried.

Mairi was a maker of praise-poems, which she addressed to the great men of her time, most of them members of her clan. Within the panegyric framework her poetry reflects the fluctuations of her patrons' attitudes and those of her own career in relation to them. In contrast to written, classical Gaelic poetry Mairi's poems were composed and transmitted orally in demotic Gaelic, first appearing in print in 1776. Collector-editors have preserved over 1,000 lines of her verse; of the 16 poems in the standard edition one has been wrongly ascribed and three others are doubtful but one complete song and a short rhyme, both still current orally, and one extempore verse can be added to the canon, while two anonymous poems in printed sources may also be her work. Mairi's poems were designed to be sung: a few of the melodies of her songs, recovered originally from oral tradition, are still to be heard.

Mairi Nighean Alasdair Ruaidh's work is not only a vital link between these two traditions of poetry but also proves that classical Gaelic was not necessarily unintelligible to an oral poet whose medium was the vernacular. Her songs are a paradigm of the code of rhetoric which between her time and ours became a pervasive style in Scots Gaelic poetry.

J. MacInnes

MacLeod, Rev. Norman *see* **Caraid nan Gaidheal**

Macpherson and Ossian. There is probably no Scottish literary event in our history that created so great a stir at home and abroad as the publication of James Macpherson's alleged translations of the poems of Ossian in 1760, 1761–62 and 1763. Apart from the immediate interest and controversy, which continued with varying degrees of intensity for 50 years, translations of his work continue to be published to the present day, and its influence can be traced in many works of literature, and in other art forms, over the last 200 years.

The sequence of events that brought Macpherson to literary fame may be summarized quite briefly. He was born near Kingussie in 1736, was a student at both of Aberdeen's Universities, King's College and Marischal College, and at Edinburgh University, and by 1756 was back in his home country, in charge of the charity school at Ruthven, close to the army barracks which had been built there in 1718, after the '15 Rising. By 1758 he was employed as a tutor in Edinburgh, and in that year published the turgid epic called *The Highlander* which foreshadows the plot of Macpherson's *Fingal*. In October, 1759 he went to Moffat with a pupil of his, and there he met the dramatist John Home. When the conversation turned (or was turned) to Highland poetry Macpherson claimed to have in his possession several pieces of ancient poetry, and in the following days unwillingly yielded to pressure to show translations of the poems to Home who in due course showed them to Dr Hugh Blair (in 1760 to become Professor of Rhetoric and Belles Lettres at Edinburgh) and other friends in Edinburgh while later in 1759 Home showed them to friends in London 'where they were equally admired'.

Macpherson's introduction to Blair led to a period of friendship and collaboration, and to the publication early in 1760 of a small book of 'translations', *Fragments of Ancient Poetry collected in the Highlands*. This met with a remarkable reception. The *Scots Magazine* for June and July devoted much space to the publication. Thomas Gray wrote to Walpole and to Thomas Warton about the fragments, saying to Warton 'this man is the very Demon of Poetry, or he has lighted on a treasure hid for ages'. Hugh Blair arranged a dinner, attended by 'many of the first persons of rank and taste in Edinburgh', and funds were raised to enable Macpherson to go to the Highlands and gather the material for further publications, and in particular for the epic poem at whose existence he had already hinted in the Preface to the *Fragments*.

Macpherson set out on a six-week trip in August 1760, and undertook a second one between late October 1760 and early January 1761. He visited Perthshire, Argyllshire, and Inverness-shire, including the islands of Skye, North and South Uist, Benbecula and Mull. We know a good deal about the contacts he made, and his methods of working both in the field and in Edinburgh where he returned with his manuscripts. Some of the manuscripts he collected can be reasonably identified, and many specific ballads are named, with their source, or variant sources. With help from various hands Macpherson interpreted, collated, arranged, translated and supplemented these Gaelic materials, in Edinburgh, and by early December 1761 the first edition of *Fingal*, an epic, had been published both in London and in Edinburgh. It was discussed in depth and detail, in Scottish and English magazines, and by January 1762 went into a second edition. There then began that flow of dissertations, accusations (including the passage-of-arms with Johnson) parodies, translations and illustrations, with by-products such as dramas, operas and other musical works, which has continued since, with such early items as Cesarotti's Italian verse translation of 1763 and such latter-day items as the Japanese translation of 1971 and the Russian one currently in preparation.

The relationship between Macpherson's 'translations' and the Gaelic ballads he collected has often been misunderstood and misrepresented. In his time translation often meant something akin to adaptation or interpretation. Thus, for instance, a translation by Jerome Stone of the ballad of Fraoch, which appeared in the *Scots Magazine* in 1756, and which no doubt influenced Macpherson, was very free, but could be paired with the original. One has to look harder for the pairings in Macpherson, but they are there. Sometimes he has quite close translations of short passages, but at other times merely takes hints and suggestions (of plot, episode, names and turns of phrase) from the ballads. In *Fingal* he used two main ballads, those of 'Garbh mac Stàirn' and of 'Mànus', to give him the main outlines of his plot. He used another three, 'Fingal's Visit to Norway', 'The Lay of the Maiden' and 'Ossian's Courtship' for the main episodes, and he used several other ballads in a more restricted way. But in his second epic 'translation', *Temora* (1763), he makes far less use of the ballads, and the work suffers a loss of clarity and specificity.

To this groundwork of plot and episode Macpherson added a considerable superstructure. He filled out the plot with romantic episodes, emphasizing the love interest and the interest of wild nature; he constructed an elaborate system of pseudo-history (drawing on the work, also, of Irish and Scottish pseudo-historians), and antiquarianism, with 'learned' footnotes and dissertations, and he imposed stylistic criteria, derived from his reading of the Classics and of the Authorized Version, on the works. His experiments in prosody have led some critics into regarding him as an early founding father of *vers libre*. His influence on writers as diverse as Goethe and Yeats is a matter of, at least, historical interest, and a few of his purple passages still retain some attraction in their sentiments and their cadences.

D.S. Thomson

Marriage. A consideration of marriage in Scotland must cover several different aspects—the legal aspects, the relevance of marriage to the position of men and women in society and the ritual associated with marriage.

Legal aspects. Until the Reformation, marriage in Scotland, as in most of Europe, was a sacrament and came under the charge of the Catholic Church. It was both a legal and religious bond indissoluble in life. But with the Reformation, marriage became a legal contract, one of the utmost importance, but essentially an agreement between the two people involved. There were two results. Divorce became possible

and, although a church marriage was still the regular form, a number of other irregular forms of marriage became legally acceptable. The first was marriage by habit and repute, that is co-habitation which was accepted as a marital union. The second was marriage by declaration *de praesenti*, that is by declaration before witnesses. The third was marriage by promise *subsequenti copula*. The so-called 'Gretna Green' marriages, the second type, continued to be popular over many years, especially with couples from other countries with more stringent laws of marriage. In 1939, however, a law was enacted which made marriage by declaration or by promise no longer valid forms. Occasionally petitions are still brought to the Court of Session in Edinburgh to legitimate long-standing marriages by habit and repute. Marriage under Scots law is monogamous, that is neither spouse should be married to another at the time of the wedding nor may either contract another union during the current one. Choice of spouse must be freely made by both, although formerly the parents' consent was necessary, especially in the case of the girl.

Relevance of marriage to the position of men and women. In traditional times and in many cases today, the role of a woman was intimately bound up with her sex role as a wife and mother. Whether or not she had any paid employment, her place in society was determined by the men in her life—her father and then her husband. While a man's role was essentially a public one played out on the political, economic and religious stages, a woman's major role was domestic, played out in the privacy of the home. For a man, entry to full adult status was achieved when he took up the work at which he would be employed for the rest of his life, but for a woman her full adult status was achieved when she married. Her whole premarital life was a preparation for this and we can see this symbolized in the custom of the 'bottom drawer'.

The way in which men and women are designated indicated their position very clearly. A man's name and title reflects his age and employment but gives no indication of marital status. Personal names indicate subordination or intimacy. Males who are not working, e.g. boys, are called by their personal name. Those who are very subordinate socially are also called by their first name, as are those with whom one is intimate. Otherwise, a man is given his full designation, Mr So-and-so.

But, up to the present time, with women a very different picture emerges. As with men, intimacy or great social disparity permits the use of personal names but otherwise a woman's marital status is clearly indicated by her name and title. Before marriage a woman bears the designation Miss; after marriage Mrs. Her traditionally subordinate legal position is indicated by the use of her father's surname before marriage and her husband's surname after marriage.

It is a sad fact that this way of naming is of comparatively recent innovation and very different from earlier Scottish customs of naming women. The designations, Miss and Mrs were used, but in another fashion more analogous to the distinction between Master and Mr. Miss was the title of a young woman. With age, gravity and respect, a woman—whether married or not—became known as Mistress

So-and-so. On marriage a woman kept her own family name. This custom can still be seen in legal documents where names are set out as Mary Smith (her maiden name) or Brown or Jones, depending on how many husbands she has had. It may also still be seen in the way that names are set out in the death columns of newspapers.

Marriage Ritual. In Scotland generally there was or is little formal wooing ritual although the practice of bundling might be included under this heading. In the long dark cold nights of the north a young man would come to court his girl and they would lie in the same bed but the girl would be wrapped up like a package to protect her virginity.

The engagement is a ritual which marks the promise of each to marry the other. Formerly, in the north and west, there were friendly ceremonies at which the bridegroom would ask the girl's family for her hand in marriage. Now, there may be a party and in some country districts friends of the couple may bring along small gifts towards the setting up of a home. Traditionally the engagement period was one of preparation. Ideally the marriage should take place only when the young couple could establish a complete and independent household. This is no longer such a requirement although it is still important to some engaged couples. The most important ritual aspect of the engagement is the ring. It is made of precious substances and this indicates to the young girl the significance of the step which she is taking.

There is no legal liability on the wife's parents to give a dowry with their daughter but it was an old Scottish custom that a tocher (from the Gaelic *tochar*) or portion should be brought by a wife at her marriage. We can understand this if we look at the social system of which it is a part. Descent is the way in which a society arranges the transfer of property and titles from one generation to another. The Scottish system was a cognatic one, that is, there was no proscription on goods or offices descending through females although male rights tended to be dominant over those of females. We can see survivals of this in the fact that the most ancient Scottish titles may descend to a woman although those granted since the union of England and Scotland may not. Although, generally, a son had priority over a daughter in the matter of inheritance, the woman had a right to her share of the family fortunes, large or small, and this was signified by the tocher. As marriage in Scotland is virilocal, that is, a woman must leave her home and live with her husband on marriage, it was at marriage that a woman received her portion of the inheritance.

All changes in the status of an individual in society are marked by ritual ceremonies. There are various functions accomplished by the rites. Firstly they publish the changes to the rest of society and ensure that all the people who are in contact with those changing status know of the alterations and will therefore know of the new behaviour which they will have to adopt *vis-a-vis* the status-changers. Secondly, the rites encapsulate for those actively concerned with new rights and obligations which they are assuming. Thirdly, the rites emphasize the significance of the status changes.

If we look at a wedding we can see these aspects. The Scottish wedding itself is based on the Christian ritual and is not peculiarly Scots. Many weddings are now held at Registry Offices but the ritual remains amazingly constant. Traditionally weddings were held of Friday or Saturday, days which allowed the festivities to culminate in the kirking of the couple on Sunday. When the date is set invitations are sent out to all those kith and kin to whom the change in status is particularly relevant. Formerly this was even more important as marriages were not merely the joining together of two individuals but were looked on as alliances between two potentially hostile kin groups. This may be one factor in the traditional constraint between affines which reveals itself in the 'mother-in-law' jokes. Presents are sent by those who are invited and these might be thought to symbolize the involvement of the kin group in the union. There is still a custom, although it is declining in popularity, of a formal display of presents.

The first function of the ritual is to focus on the prior role. Before the actual ceremony of marriage the young pair are members of an unmarried category. The rites and horse-play which take place the day before the wedding emphasize the fact that the young man and woman are leaving the state of irresponsible celibacy.

On the day of the wedding the bride should not see the groom before the ceremony. They are preparing for a ritual transition and have been removed from their erstwhile category. But they have not yet been admitted to their new status. Such intermediate states are always ritually dangerous and they must both be protected.

The church ceremony emphasizes the significance of the event by the special clothes worn, by the audience who witness the status change and by the ritual which explicates the requirements of the new status. The groom wears his best formal clothes. The bride usually wears white, symbol of virginity and chastity.

The actual marriage ceremonies always occur at the girl's home-place. This may be because wife-givers are generally considered superior to wife-receivers. The latter come as supplicants for the hand of the bride.

At the ceremony the bride is accompanied by bridesmaids, unmarried girls from the group she is leaving. The groom has his best man to assist him, together with other young men, the ushers, who help generally. The seating reflects the ancient group aspect of marriage. In most societies the right hand is seen as the dominant side: the left as subordinate. Male dominance is shown by the fact that the groom's kith and kin sit on the right hand side of the aisle, the bride's group on the left. In almost all ceremonial the superior arrives last. Wife-givers are dominant over wife-receivers. Therefore the groom and his best man arrive before the bride who, with her father, comes last. The bride is veiled to symbolize her withdrawal from her old role in society and her transitional state. The father, representing his kin group, 'gives' the bride to the kin group of the groom, indicative of marriage as an alliance. During the ceremony the bride and groom are instructed in the rights and duties of their new status—care of each other and the procreation of children. The bride is given a gold wedding ring. It is both a symbol and a sign. Its shape and substance are symbolic of the eternal bond. Its wearing signifies to others her marital status.

After the service the bride and groom process slowly through the ranks of the participants. The bride is unveiled as her new social self. Customarily, at the church door the two are deluged with rice or confetti. The rice symbolizes fertility. Paper confetti has taken the place of the traditional petals which symbolized sweetness and love. Less frequently now there is 'poor-oot' when coins are tossed or poured out on to the group of children normally attracted to the ceremony. It is yet another way in which the new condition of bride and groom can be emphasized and published and it also reiterates the theme of their involvement in the community.

After the wedding there is usually a reception or party where the wedding cake is cut and distributed. The cake symbolizes fertility and prosperity and its cutting is the first joint act performed publicly by the married couple. It is an affirmation of the identity of the new married unit. Thereafter speeches are made and toasts are drunk. They are the modern form of traditional invocations and libations to the forces of good to ensure the future well-being of the couple.

The honeymoon is a relatively recent innovation when bride and groom go away for a period to become accustomed to their new status. More ancient is the custom of the bride and groom going straight to their new home where the groom carries the wife across the threshold. All thresholds, whether of place, time or status, are ritually dangerous. The house threshold symbolizes the transition from individuality to duality: from virginity to conjugality: from childhood to adulthood. The bride therefore must be protected for if she trips the augury for the married future is black indeed.

M. Noble

Mary, Queen of Scots 1542–1567. Between ourselves and the historical Mary stand two legendary figures. One is the romantic, ill-fated Catholic martyr, the other the woman so ruled by her passions as to end in political disaster and personal vilification. These legends began in her own lifetime, the first assiduously fostered by herself when nothing else was left to her in her last years, the second by the great scholar George Buchanan, used by her opponents to justify her enforced abdication in 1567, with political theory and gutter-press attack on her personal life. Since her death in 1587, these legends have been the subject of thousands of books, sometimes scrutinized by serious scholars, occasionally producing works of great literature, but far more often perpetuated in fictional drivel.

Neither image is convincing. Mary's Catholicism does not explain her downfall. She did nothing to help Scottish Catholicism; she took action against Catholic priests, and in the crisis after the Darnley murder, sought political support by recognizing the reformed Church which had been brought into being by parliament in 1560 acting without the authority of the crown. The papacy and European Catholic powers had hoped for much from a queen who came to Scotland when the new Church was in its infancy and a Catholic revival not inconceivable in this great age of the counter-Reformation in Europe; they were justified in washing their hands of her. Nor were romance and passion the driving force of her life. Her marriages were both political. In the inept Darnley she wrongly saw the chance to free herself from the political dominance of her half-brother James Earl of Moray, and she married Bothwell not because he was the masterful lover so familiar in romantic novels, but because her political blundering after the Darnley murder left her with no other ally.

It is therefore as a politician that she should be assessed. She faced two considerable problems. Her 19-year minority was the period of religious reformation and diplomatic upheaval, when the Auld Alliance with France gave way to the new with England, creating pressures not resolved even by her much more intelligent mother Mary of Guise, regent in the 1550s. Moreover she was a woman, and thus handicapped in an age when successful monarchy could demand military as well as political skill. The speeches of both Elizabeth and Mary, lamenting the disadvantages of their sex, the murderous matrimonial career of Henry VIII in the desperate attempt to get a male heir, testify to the very real problem of female rule. Yet neither of these problems was insurmountable. The sixteenth century produced a number of remarkable women rulers, whose achievements leave only Mary Tudor and Mary Stuart sadly wanting. Moreover, the way ahead was clearer during her personal rule than it had been during her minority, when basic issues were still utterly unresolved. There was a period of comparative calm between 1561 and 1565, the period when, significantly, Mary appears as little more than a figurehead in a government managed by two brilliant politicians, Moray and Maitland of Lethington. Only with the Darnley marriage when she attempted to seize control of events did things go badly wrong; 1565–67 were years of political upheaval, with little sign of coherent policy. She both created and failed to deal with crises. The Darnley murder, the most sensational crisis, was not in itself of overriding significance; her involvement—which seems highly likely—merely adds her to the long list of those who had a part in the attempt to eradicate her previous mistake. Far more important were her unerring ability to choose the wrong man, and her inept inactivity after the murder which enabled her opponents to single her out for particular opprobrium. Her own part in the resultant civil war produced her most disastrous political misjudgement, when she fled to England leaving her supporters with nothing to support; thereafter, all that remained was a long anti-climax, mercifully ended when a series of ill-conceived plots forced an agonized Elizabeth to execute her.

Yet if she was less than impressive in life, the dramas she created, from the Rizzio murder to her execution, offer plenty of reason for her abiding appeal after death. In one thing her judgement was absolutely right: her motto 'In my end is my beginning'.

J. Wormald

Matthew, Sir Robert H. (1906–1975). Although he was

personally responsible for a number of distinguished buildings, it is more for his world-wide influence on the organization of architectural practice and the search for high standards of design in government of offices that he is remembered.

He was the eldest son of John Matthew, the partner of Sir Robert Lorimer. He attended Melville College and studied architecture alongside Basil Spence at the Edinburgh College of Art. On leaving the College he was drawn, like many of his generation, into government service, joining the Department of Health for Scotland, becoming first a deputy architect and later their Chief Architect and Planning Officer.

His special skills in organizing a large government office were recognized when he was invited to become Chief Architect to the London County Council in 1945. Although the architect's department had had a long and worthy history, Matthew built upon this to establish an organization that was held in high esteem throughout the world. His courage was shown with the successful completion of the first major public building of the post-war period, the Royal Festival Hall (1951); the centrepiece of the Festival of Britain South Bank Exhibition. His steadfast belief in delegating authority allowed many of the brightest talents of the younger generation to blossom under his leadership. Some of the best housing of the post-war period emerged from his department.

In 1953 he returned to Edinburgh, originally intending to devote himself to education after his appointment as Professor of Architecture in the University, but he soon found that his skills as an architect were in demand. In the early years of private practice he took particular pride in the designs for Turnhouse Airport (completed 1956) and New Zealand House in London (1957–63). However, the quantity of work that soon flowed his way forced him to establish a partnership and organize his many offices on the model of his successful LCC department.

During these years of busy practice he became firmly established as a public figure in his campaign for the development of good modern architecture. His voice was persuasive, and as President of the Royal Institute of British Architects (1962–64), President of the International Union of Architects (1961–65) and as founder and first President of the Commonwealth Association of Architects (1965–69), his views were made known throughout the world.

Matthew was acutely aware of changing tastes in architecture, and added his powerful voice to the conservation movement in Scotland in the 1960s. Nevertheless, he firmly held that conservation should never be allowed to inhibit the challenge of creating an environment which reflected the best aspects of the modern world.

M. Higgs

Mavor, Osborne Henry/'James Bridie' (1888–1951) was born in Glasgow, the son of an engineer. He was educated at Glasgow Academy and, as was the practice of the comparatively well-to-do of the time, spent nine years at Glasgow University, ostensibly taking a medical degree but writing and

otherwise enjoying himself. He eventually qualified in 1913, and with his friend the future politician Walter Elliot, joined the Royal Army Medical Corps, serving in Flanders, Mesopotamia and Russia. Twenty years or so later he was to return to the RAMC, briefly serving in Norway.

After 1918, he settled as a practitioner in Glasgow, became a consulting physician at the Victoria Infirmary, and was for a time a Professor of Medicine at the Andersonian College.

In 1929, however, Glasgow audiences saw his first play, *The Sunlight Sonata*, which introduced Beelzebub, seven lively Deadly Sins and three wan redeeming Graces; not characters until that time frequently seen on a Scottish stage. In all, some 40 plays came from Bridie's pen. *The Anatomist* (1931) had Henry Ainley in the leading part, achieved London production, and is the earliest of his plays still regularly revived. It deals with Dr Knox and Burke and Hare, the rascally suppliers of bodies for the Doctor's dissection. *A Sleeping Clergyman* (1933) set out to prove most amusingly that 'to make for righteousness is a biological necessity'

For the remaining 18 years of his life Bridie dominated the Scottish stage with a series of quasi-Shavian conversation pieces, often dealing with the problems of individualists in a conformist society. These included *Tobias and the Angel* (1930), *Susannah and the Elders* (1937), *Mr Bolfrey* (1943), *The Forrigan Reel* (1944) and *The Baikie Charivari* (1952). Many of his plays also scored London West End successes.

Whereas Shaw always offers us witty dogmatism, Bridie, like Brecht in this one respect, is usually content to tease out the questions, examine the ambiguities of alienation, and leave the audience to provide its own answers. Thus in *Daphne Laureola* (1949), one of Bridie's last plays, Lady Catherine Pitts is condemned to live her life in a world of her own imagining because of her inability to face up to reality. The examination of character that Bridie carries out to justify this disorientation is in marked contrast to the kind of light social dramas that formed the repertory fare of the Branden Thomas and Wilson Barratt companies in Scotland during the between-the-wars period. Bridie is concerned with the degradation of civilization, whether at the hands of men like *Dr Angelus* (1941), who have gone off on a moral holiday, or Dr Knox, the anatomist, who carried zeal for his profession too far.

In *John Knox* (1947), and in what many consider to be his best play, *The Queen's Comedy* (1950), Bridie did attempt to provide answers; in the former case through a dialogue on the steps of heaven between Knox and his earthly protagonist Mary, Queen of Scots, and in the other (an up-dated version of the Trojan War) through an explanation by Jupiter. Both endings are ineffectual, if not embarrassing.

For all his sophistication, Bridie, the Lowland Scot, was constantly perplexed by the antithetical conundrums of good versus evil, sin against righteousness, dignity contrasted with ludicrousness. His purpose was to point out the edges of such contrasts, not implying reforming solution, and to remind us that through all our perplexities there runs a certain strain of continuing human adaptability.

Those who apply Victorian class terminology to the truths

of art sometimes dub Bridie's plays 'middle class'. Such pretentiousness is defused by Bridie's half-mocking attitude to his own achievement, reflected in his autobiography *One Way of Living* (1939) and in his collection of random reflections and aphorisms, *Tedious and Brief* (1944) and *Mr Bridie's Alphabet for Little Glasgow Highbrows* (1934). He was the principal founder of Glasgow Citizen's Theatre in 1943, and was made a CBE in 1946. A painting by Sir Stanley Cursiter in the Kelvingrove Galleries, Glasgow, shows Bridie in the company of Gunn, Muir and Linklater.

M. Lindsay

Maxwell, James Clerk (1831–79) was a physicist, born in Edinburgh. He studied at Edinburgh University and at Cambridge. In 1856 he was appointed Professor of Natural Philosophy at the University of Aberdeen and worked in King's College, London, from 1860 until 1865 when he returned to Scotland to continue his research. In 1871 he became the first Cavendish Professor of Experimental Physics at Cambridge. His *Treatise on Electricity and Magnetism* (1873) was hugely influential.

P. Ingalls

Medicine, History of. Scotland enjoys the unusual distinction of having had a royal personage as its first notable physician, for James IV (1473–1513) took a special interest in medical affairs and did not disdain to treat the sick and even to practice dentistry. He seems also to have had an interest in research for it is said that in 1493 he put two young children in charge of a dumb woman alone on the isle of Inchkeith to find what language they would learn to use. According to his historian, 'some say they spake good hebrew but as myself I know not.'

James IV is also believed, with greater credibility, to have induced the Town Council of Edinburgh to grant (in 1505) a 'Seal of Cause' to the barbers and surgeons, which led subsequently to the establishment of the Edinburgh College of Surgeons.

A successor, James VI, made an even greater contribution to the conduct of medical practice by his Charter of 1599 which enabled Peter Lowe and his associates to found the Faculty of Physicians and Surgeons (now the Royal College of Physicians and Surgeons) in Glasgow. The charter conferred extensive powers to license medical practitioners over the greater part of the southwest of Scotland. It authorized the Faculty to examine all surgeons and discharge them if unworthy, to supervise the sale of drugs and poisons, and to give free advice to poor diseased folk. It was a miniature Health Service three and a half centuries before its time.

These two Colleges, and the College of Physicians of Edinburgh which was founded in 1681, were mainly concerned with the conduct of practice, and doubtless with the status and rewards of practitioners.

Medical Schools. Formal medical teaching only began with the development of medical schools.

The Edinburgh Medical School. Although Edinburgh started last it soon outstripped the others. Archibald Pitcairn (1652–1713) may justly be regarded as the founder and he with Robert Sibbald and James Halket were the first three Professors of Medicine to be appointed by the town's College, the forerunner of Edinburgh University. Under Alexander Monro (1697–1767), who taught Anatomy for 40 years, the school attracted students from every part of the known world. In succeeding years other famous figures were James Gregory (1753–1821), who's 'Gregory's Mixture' was a popular remedy for stomach disorders, Charles Bell (1774–1842) anatomist famous for his observations on the nervous system, James Syme (1799–1870) now remembered as the originator of 'Syme's amputation', and the general practitioner Dr John Brown (1810–1882) who will enjoy more lasting fame as the author of 'Rab and his Friends'.

During the latter part of the nineteenth century two men gained world renown, James Young Simpson (1811–1870) who introduced chloroform as an anaesthetic, and Joseph Lister (1827–1912) who came to Edinburgh from University College in London to study under Syme, later succeeded him in the Chair of Surgery and remained in Edinburgh until his return to London in 1877.

The Glasgow Medical School. Although a Chair of Medicine had been established in 1714 the founding of the medical school can properly be attributed to William Cullen and Joseph Black thirty years later. Cullen (1712–1799) came from his practice in Hamilton in 1744, established himself as a teacher in a wide range of subjects and was appointed as Professor of Medicine in 1751. Four years later he moved to Edinburgh to occupy the Chair of Chemistry and transferred to the Chair of Medicine in 1766. Joseph Black (1728–1799), more famous as a chemist than a physician (he identified 'fixed air' now known as carbon dioxide, and introduced the concept of latent heat) started as Cullen's assistant, succeeded him in the Chair of Medicine in Glasgow in 1757, and followed him to Edinburgh in 1766.

Thereafter, the Glasgow School attracted few great figures for many years. William Hunter (1718–1783), who had studied in Glasgow University for four years, was not attracted to stay but went south in 1740 to attain fame as obstetrician and physician in London, whither he was followed by his brother John (1728–1793) who attained even greater renown as anatomist and surgeon.

In 1860 Joseph Lister was appointed to the Chair of Surgery and during the nine years before he returned to Edinburgh he brought fame to the Glasgow School by his recognition of the bacterial origin of wound sepsis and its prevention by antiseptics. His pupil and successor, William Macewen (1848–1924), exploiting the new freedom to which Lister's antisepsis had given the key, established himself as a surgeon of world renown.

Also worthy of mention are Robert Watt (1774–1819), who published the mammoth *Bibliotheca Britannica* which is still in use, and John Macintyre (1857–1928) who within six months of Roentgen's first paper had established an X-ray department in Glasgow Royal Infirmary.

The Aberdeen Medical School. Although there had been 'mediciners' at King's College since before 1522 and Professors of Medicine at Marischal College since 1700 the medical school in its modern sense may be said to date from 1860, when the two Colleges were fused as constituent members of the University of Aberdeen.

Before that time Alexander Gordon (1752–1799) had been the first to recognize the contagious character of puerperal fever and the special role of doctors and nurses in transmitting it. In the related field of surgical infections Alexander Ogston (1844–1929) described the *staphylococcus pyogenes* and recognized it as the major cause of acute suppuration. In the field of literature Francis Adams (1796–1861) had gained fame as the translator of Hippocrates.

The Medical School of St Andrews. Although St Andrews was the first University to be founded in Scotland (1411) and had had a Chair of Medicine since 1722, its medical school, in the modern sense, only dates from 1897, when University College, Dundee was affiliated with the University. In the event the School proved short-lived and came to an end when the affiliation was discontinued in 1967. Since then Dundee has had a complete medical school while St Andrews teaches only premedical subjects.

Medical exports. Since the eighteenth century Scotland's largest medical schools have nurtured medical graduates far in excess of the country's needs and the consequent *vis a tergo* combined with innate adventurousness led to large-scale emigration.

The stream started with Tobias Smollett (1721–1771) and James Lind (1716–1794) who went south to join the navy as surgeons and gained fame respectively in literature and in researches on scurvy. The stream flowed more copiously in the nineteenth century, when in some parts of industrial England most of the general practitioners were Scottish graduates. In the United States each of the four founders of the first medical school (Philadelphia, 1765) had studied, albeit briefly, in Edinburgh. In Australia and New Zealand Scots took prominent parts in founding the medical schools. Conversely, many doctors from these dominions came to Scotland (especially Edinburgh) for postgraduate study, a traffic which continued until the middle of the twentieth century.

As explorers, David Livingstone (1813–1873) gained fame in Africa, John Richardson (1787–1865) and John Rae (1813–1893) in the Arctic. In the armed forces, John Pringle (1707–1782) was an authority on the diseases to which armies were subject, James McGrigor (1771–1858) became Director-General of the Army Medical Service and one of Wellington's most trusted advisers, William Burnett (1779–1861) was the first Medical Director-General of the Navy.

In the field of tropical diseases, Patrick Manson (1844–1922) was an authority on filariasis and was the founder of the London School of Tropical Medicine, David Bruce (1855–1931) demonstrated the cause of Malta fever and identified the trypanosome responsible for Tsetse-fly disease, William Leishman (1865–1926) discovered the causal organism of kala-azar.

The Highlands and Islands Medical Scheme. The Dewar Report of 1912 conceived a revolutionary scheme to provide a medical service for the scattered and impoverished people of the crofter counties of northwest Scotland. The scheme subsidized doctors, expanded the nursing service, appointed consultant specialists and made many improvements in the few hospitals in the area. It gained wide esteem, not least by reason of the good relationship between the local people and the centralized administration in Edinburgh. In 1948 it became incorporated in the National Health Service.

The National Health Service. The inauguration of the National Health Service in 1948 was a milestone in Scotland's medical history. Originally the Service was tripartite. In the part relating to environmental health it was based on the sure foundation of the Public Health departments of the local authorities so its effect was mainly to unify, extend and amplify them. But in the other two parts, relating to primary medical care and to hospital treatment, its effects were revolutionary and emphatic.

Primary health care. Despite the improvements wrought by the Industrial Insurance Act of 1911 the most needy sections of the population had no organized medical care, the resources available to general practitioners were deficient in respect of accommodation, equipment and access to diagnostic facilities, there was no organized basis for collaboration between doctors and auxiliary workers. Practitioners worked singlehanded and many of them were grossly overworked.

The new service gradually remedied many of these defects. An increasing number of practitioners have combined in teams based on Health Centres in which they are supported by nurses, secretaries and other auxiliaries. They have access to the diagnostic facilities offered by hospital X-ray and scientific departments. In their training they follow specific curricula and later they have opportunities for study leave and attendance at refresher courses. Their patients receive free advice and treatment, and medicines are provided at a reduced charge or, for pensioners and others in special need, free of charge.

Although some complain that efficiency has been gained at the cost of diminished personal attention there is general acknowledgement that the scheme has been a success.

Hospital service. Before 1948 the great majority of hospitals in Scotland were voluntary hospitals, that is to say they were dependent on voluntary contributions and were staffed by doctors who gave their services without remuneration. But since the financial depression of 1929 they had become increasingly impoverished and unable to support the increasingly expensive requirements of modern hospital care.

Under the National Health Service five Regional Boards were set up, respectively based on Inverness, Aberdeen, Dundee, Glasgow and Edinburgh, to control and administer all the hospitals in their areas. The material deficiencies of accommodation and equipment were remedied by massive injections of funds, and in the course of years as building restrictions were lifted a programme of hospital building got under way. Medical members of hospital staffs were appointed on a salaried basis, most of the younger doctors electing to go full-time, and the establishment of doctors, nurses and auxiliary workers was greatly increased.

Beyond these material considerations, the Hospital Service provided a basis for collaboration between hospitals, and made it possible to set up units on a regional basis for such specialties as neurosurgery, cardiac surgery and plastic surgery.

In Scotland the universities were given special responsibilities. As a consequence the teaching of students and graduates was extended to hospitals formerly designated 'non-teaching' and university research units and even whole university departments were installed within the hospital curtilage. In consequence, university attitudes towards teaching and research were enabled to permeate the whole hospital organism.

The state of the nation's health. Since medical records began Scotland has made a poor showing on all such health criteria as maternal mortality, infantile mortality, expectation of life, nutritional standards and the incidence of squalor-related diseases such as tuberculosis. In recent years improved child welfare services, new drugs, new techniques of immunization and, even more effective, environmental improvements such as improved nutrition, better housing and the abolition of smog have brought about vast improvements in the general health. At the present time apart from the disabilities of old age, most diseases are man-made, the results of alcoholism, cigarette smoking, indolence and over-eating.

Sir Charles Illingworth

Melville, Andrew (1542–1622) left his mark on Scotland's culture as an outstanding academic reformer and an intrepid, forceful defender of reformed ecclesiastical principles. His early education in the Humanities was received at the Burgh school of Montrose, from which he entered St Andrews University in 1559 as a student in St Mary's College. His home and early background were Protestant, but this fact did not deter him from furthering his studies in Classical and Biblical languages at Paris, and in Law at Poitiers under some of the foremost international teachers of the day before moving to Geneva there to lay the foundations of his reformed theology and ecclesiology at the feet of Calvin's successor Theodore Beza, the distinguished Humanist and Biblical scholar. On arrival at Geneva his academic attainments and talents were speedily recognized by his appointment as a teacher in Humanity in the lower division of the Academy. He had also at this time the opportunity of meeting some of the outstanding scholar refugees who flocked into Geneva, such as Scaliger and Hotman, and his fellow Scotsman, Henry Scrimgeour.

The reorganization of the three medieval universities had from the outset of the reformation in 1560 been recognized by the reformers as essential, but for a variety of reasons, among them academic conservatism and the unsettled political climate, nothing had been accomplished. On his return to Scotland in 1574, Melville took up this stupendous challenge by accepting appointment as Principal of the well-nigh decayed

Glasgow University. Within two years that university had been completely transformed. A new era had opened not only for Glasgow but for Scotland's other universities. Melville proved himself 'a man of unusual talent and of unaccustomed learning in Scotland' by completely transforming the curriculum in accordance with his forceful avowal of the Ramist critique of Aristotle, and by replacing the outmoded system whereby every regent took his class through the entire course with specialist teachers each one of whom was responsible for his own particular part of the educational programme. In 1577 Melville's reforms at Glasgow were at the hands of the Regent Morton, embodied in a charter of new foundation—the *nova erectio*—which also sought to put the university finances on a securer basis than had hitherto existed. This charter remained the basis of university education there for the next 300 years. Success at Glasgow made Melville the obvious choice for carrying through the much discussed but long delayed refoundation of the St Andrews Colleges, finally enacted by the Scottish Parliament in 1579. This scheme owed much to earlier plans, especially those of the *First Book of Discipline*, whereby one of the Colleges was to become exclusively a College of Theology. Melville was undoubtedly behind this reorganization. As head of the 'new' St Mary's College, he exerted profound influence on the university and throughout the Church for the following 25 tempestuous years.

His emphasis upon the study of the Biblical languages and the common heads of theology must have had a profound effect on academic studies, but Melville was no scholar-recluse. He regarded his work as inextricably related to the life of the Church and the nation. His repeated assertion and defence of the claim that the Church was a kingdom, of which King James was but a member, brought him continually into conflict with the crown, led to several visitations of the University by the King himself or other royal commissioners, to the exclusion of academic teachers from taking part in the courts of the Church, and finally to a summons to London, followed by imprisonment in the Tower, from which he was released only to spend the last decade of his life at the Protestant Academy at Sedan. As an educational reformer he brought the Scottish universities into closer contact with the latest continental trends and his abilities lay basically in the vigour with which he applied to the Scottish situation the new techniques in education, which he had learned in France and Switzerland. Unfortunately, his active life seems to have prevented him from leaving behind any significant theological work. He did, however, practise to a very high degree of accomplishment the contemporary obsession with neo-Latin verse, much of which survives in publications and in manuscript form.

J.K. Cameron

Melville, James (1556–1613), born in Montrose, was the son of the laird of Baldovie, Forfarshire, and nephew of the reformer, Andrew Melville. The uncle, when principal of Glasgow University, appointed his nephew a regent or professor there. James Melville later became principal of St Mary's

College, St Andrews, where he also acted as professor of Hebrew and Oriental Languages. Towards the end of his life he was banished to England for his attitudes in Church politics, and was on his way back to his native land when he died at Berwick-on-Tweed.

His *Autobiography and Diary*, published in 1829, includes a powerful description of the last days of John Knox. Much of the book is taken up with Church disputations long since forgotten, though the gossipy garrulousness of the style preserves a certain animation.

M. Lindsay

Melville of Halhill, Sir James (1535–1617), the son of Sir John Melville of Raith, Fife, became a page at the age of 14 to Mary, Queen of Scots at the French court, and later a member of her Privy Council and a Gentleman of the Bedchamber. He acted as her envoy to the Elector of Palatine and also to Queen Elizabeth.

On one celebrated occasion the English monarch tried to force Sir James to declare some of her own qualities and abilities higher than those of his employer. Towards the end of the interview with Elizabeth, the Queen wanted to know what kind of exercise Mary practised. Wrote Melville: 'I said, that the Queen was bot new com bak from the Highland hunting; and when she had leaser fra the affairs of hir country, she read upon gude bukis, the histories of divers countries and sometimes wald play upon lute and virginelis. She speirit gin she played well. I said, raisonably for a Queen.'

The story comes from Melville's lively *Memoirs of my own Life*, the manuscript of which lay hidden in Edinburgh Castle until its discovery in 1660 and publication three years later. The Bannatyne Club brought out an edition in 1827, and in our own day the Folio Society has produced a modern edition.

M. Lindsay

Migration. Before the mid-eighteenth century the virtual absence of statistical data renders generalization about migration an extremely hazardous exercise. It is reasonably clear, however, from the fragmentary detail available, that the movement of people both within and out of the country took place only on a relatively small scale. This is not to imply that migration and emigration were always peripheral activities. The expansion of burghal units, a process which seems to have accelerated in the later seventeenth century, indicates a consistent trickle of people from the countryside to urban areas too unhealthy to produce much growth from their own demographic resources. In addition, emigration was already established as a safety valve for excessive population growth in the early modern period. Students, traders and mercenary soldiers from Scotland had long had intimate contacts with Europe while the movement of Scottish 'beggars' to England is sketchily documented in contemporary sources. During the seventeenth century, ease of access, religious pressures and harvest failure made Ulster a favourite area for Scotsmen especially during the 'lean years' of the 1690s.

These movements, however, pale into relative insignificance in comparison with the trend of migration in the eighteenth and nineteenth centuries. Between 1750 and 1900 the population distribution of Scotland was transformed in consequence of the twin processes of industrialization and urbanization. In the mid eighteenth century, some 51 per cent of Scots lived north of the Tay and only 37 per cent in the central lowlands. The typical Scot was a countryman and most urban communities of any size tended to be found in the eastern Lowlands. By 1871 this pattern had fundamentally altered. In the later nineteenth century 61 per cent of a vastly increased population lived in the central region; two-thirds of all Scots resided in urban communities and the west-central district, centred on Glasgow and the Clyde, had become the most dynamic area of demographic growth in the country, containing in 1871, about 37 per cent of Scotland's total population.

These momentous developments came about because of the interaction of a series of influences of which structural change in the national economy was by far the most significant. The textile revolution, between 1780 and 1830, and metallurgical developments later in the nineteenth century drew population from rural areas both within and outside Scotland. Contrary to popular belief, however, the 'cleared' crofting communities of the Highlands were not simply decanted into the burgeoning cotton towns and mining villages of the south. The 'Clearances' certainly upset the balance of traditional population distribution in the north but this in itself did not always lead directly to permanent exodus to the Lowlands. Temporary migration allowed a permanent move to be postponed and cultural and linguistic differences between Highlander and Lowlander may have further impeded easy movement from north to south. Highland depopulation eventually did take place but it was more fundamentally related to a chronic imbalance between a steeply rising population and scarcity of employment opportunities in the crofting regions.

The vast majority of the new urban dwellers were short-distance migrants from surrounding rural areas, in the Lowlands, and from Ireland. In the late eighteenth and early nineteenth century agrarian change did not cause depopulation because 'improved' farming in most areas required more hands per acre than the old system. Nonetheless, in time, higher wage levels in industrial areas, the attraction of the 'bright lights' of the city and the rigours of farm work did encourage a rising tide of migration from the countryside. The movement of the Irish was also sporadic before the 1830s but the 'Great Famine' of the 1840s was a decisive watershed. It caused a major acceleration in migration and new Irish communities (both Catholic and Protestant) became established mainly in the west-central region and to a lesser extent in and around Edinburgh and Dundee.

The 'in-migration' of the Irish was paralleled by the 'out-migration' of native Scots. By the later eighteenth century Europe had ceased to be a common area of settlement and had been replaced by Canada and the United States. Even Ulster became but a staging-post for America. Evicted Highlanders, depressed handloom weavers and unemployed farm servants were the most common emigrants for much of the nineteenth century but after *c.*1880, when transatlantic emigration became very significant in numerical terms, members of most occupational groups were involved. The boom in overseas investment, economic developments in the dominions and dramatic advances in sea communication combined to attract more Scots than ever before to America, Canada and Australia. In precise terms, there was a net loss of 483,000 persons from Scotland between 1871 and 1901, a figure equivalent to about a quarter of the total natural increase for that period.

This flow was sustained well into the twentieth century and the magnitude of emigration provides a telling indicator of the structural weaknesses of the Scottish economy after the Great War. Between 1901 and 1961, 1,388,000 Scots left their native land, equivalent to about two-thirds of the natural increase in population. Domestic migration trends, however, were more complicated. By the mid twentieth century Irish migration was no longer of any significance. The main immigrant group indeed were skilled workers from England who were recruited to assist in the development of the new 'science-based' industries established after the Second World War. In the same period urban growth began to slacken and diversify. While industrial towns did continue to expand, if only because of the natural excess of births over deaths, migration from country to town declined to minute proportions. Much more significant was movement within the urban sector itself due to the development of middle-class suburbs, the creation of new towns such as East Kilbride, Cumbernauld, Livingston and Irvine, and the redevelopment of many urban centres resulting in the creation of large council housing schemes. Even more important, perhaps, for the future was the resurgence of the economy of the east of Scotland based on oil-related development. It remains to be seen whether this will be ultimately reflected in a new geographical transfer of population from the decaying conurbation around Glasgow to the more vigorous areas of the north and east.

T.M. Devine

Miller, Hugh (1802–1856) vividly personified the tensions of contemporary Victorian Scotland in his life and writings. He became a folk-hero, mourned by shocked thousands when conveyed to a suicide's grave in Edinburgh. In death he was sanctified by his literary widow and his biographer, Peter Bayne, and their plaster saint did not sustain the interest of the public. Something of the man's disturbing personality was revealed in Colin Maclean's libretto to Barrett-Ayre's opera *Hugh Miller* (1974) and readers have been reintroduced to the force and beauty of Miller's writing by such works as George Rosie's perceptive selection *Hugh Miller, Outrage and Order* (1981).

When Miller was born in Cromarty, landless Highlanders were employed there by resident Lowlanders. The tension

which he felt between the Lowland culture of his shipmaster father and the Highland stock of his mother is evident in his autobiographical work *My Schools and Schoolmasters*. After his father was drowned, when Hugh was five, the family was supported by his mother's needle. She was descended from the Sutherland seer Donald Ross whose shadow may have cast a dark morbidity over Miller's mind and disposed him to believe in ghosts and fairies. As an itinerant stonemason he experienced the miseries of bothie life and, in Edinburgh, saw the power of organised labour. Silicosis ended his labouring years, but he had gained insights and opinions which rang true for many when expressed in his later editorials.

In 1834 he was appointed accountant in the Commercial Bank in Cromarty, which allowed him to develop his interest as a writer and better fitted him as the husband of his gentle wife Lydia Fraser. His book of poems of 1829 was not a success, but his 'Letters on the Herring Fishery' in the *Inverness Courier* were well received. Since 1829 he had collected folk legends conscious that 'if I myself do not preserve them, they must perish'. Published as *Scenes and Legends of the North of Scotland* in 1835 they were well reviewed.

A religious man, Miller was interested in church politics and his sympathies blazed out for the congregation of Auchterarder whose wishes had been overruled by Lord Brougham in the latest patronage case. His 'Letter from one of the Scottish People … ' was printed by Robert Paul, manager of his bank in Edinburgh. This, together with 'The Whiggism of the Old School' (1838), marked him out as a force in the cause of the Evangelical Party and, in the following year, Miller was appointed editor of their new newspaper *The Witness*. As such he became a leading figure in the disruption of the Church of Scotland in 1843. His independent line in *The Witness* led to differences with the Free Church leadership, and in 1845 the paper became the property of Miller and his partner Robert Fairly.

Miller was a skilled geologist and used his editorials to serialise *The Old Red Sandstone*, published as a book in 1841. Readers were fascinated by the challenges which this new science brought to Christian Orthodoxy and admired Miller's examination of the issues in many subsequent articles. It is characteristic of his search for truth that theology and geology should be argued together. Miller's exploration of the interface between science and religion in his later books *The Testimony of the Rocks* and *Footprints of the Creator* identified fields on which battle would be joined when *The Origin of the Species* was published by Darwin three years after his death and from which the smoke has not yet cleared.

C.D. Waterston

Mitchell, J.L. *see* **Gibbon, Lewis Grassic**

Model Villages or 'planned villages' is the term usually applied in Scotland to the new rural settlements created in the century *c.* 1750–1850. They were not the first planned settlements: various burghs from the Middle Ages to the seventeenth century were no less the deliberate creations of their lords, such as Newburgh in Aberdeenshire (medieval), Stornoway and Campbeltown in the Highlands (seventeenth century), and Kilmaurs in Ayrshire (sixteenth century). What distinguished the model villages, however, was, firstly, the regular grid plan on which most were built, secondly, their explicit economic and social purpose as an integral part of the improving movement and, thirdly, their great number. No one has made a full count of how many there were, but Dr Lockhart combed the counties of Aberdeenshire, Moray, Banff, Kincardine, Angus and the eastern part of Perthshire and found 97. The total in the whole of Scotland must lie between 200 and 300. Some were total failures, quickly abandoned, like Strelitz and Benniebeg in Perthshire; others have outgrown their origins and become sizable country towns like Oban, Callander or Moffat; but many remain physically much as they were, monuments to the hopes and tastes of the lairds who created them.

Not all the purposes of the model villages were the same. A few were created by replanning existing settlements for aesthetic considerations, for example in association with reconstructing a great house. Inveraray in Argyll is a splendid example of this, its theatrical setting on the side of Loch Fyne owing something to the design of no less a figure than William Adam. A few were intended to be settlements of old Hanoverian soldiers after the '45, rather on the model of the Roman *colonia* where the legions were settled in barbaric provinces to civilize and hold down the natives. Kinloch Rannoch had such an origin, and one of the early veterans settled there was so appalled by the conditions that he asked to be reappointed 'as a soldier in any of the Garrisons of North Britain, or to any other Charity your Honours shall think proper'. The overwhelming majority, however, were intended as centres of industry, crafts and services where a population displaced by agricultural reorganization (or simply growing faster than employment opportunity on the farms) could be found employment without evictions from the estate, and where the food requirements of the villagers settlers could themselves act as a market to the improving farmers.

This pattern was set in the earliest days, when John Cockburn of Ormiston from 1738 began to rebuild the village of Ormiston in East Lothian with accommodation for 40 linen weavers and their attendant spinners, as well as blacksmiths, shoemakers, candlemakers, bakers and maltsters. His village was so busy that one neighbouring landowner noted approvingly 'there is not a boy or a girl of seven years old but has something to do, so that you will not see one in the town except in an hour of play'. Ormiston was influential; so was the example of Ireland where many similar villages were being constructed to encourage country textile trades—Sir Richard Cox, *A Letter … shewing from Experience a Sure Method to establish the Linen Manufacture* (1749) described his experience in building Dunmanway in Co. Cork, and circulated extensively among the Scottish improving elite, especially in the northeast.

Different kinds of villages tended to be built in different phases of the period. From the 1750s to the 1780s the characteristic settlement was inland, on a rigid rectilinear plan, involving the rural linen trade and developing local market status. Lord Deskford's New Keith, the Duke of Gordon's Huntley and James Urquhart's Newbyth, all in Aberdeenshire, are good examples: this county, for so extensive a lowland area, had been under-provided with market settlements in the past, and was catching up with areas like Fife and Lothians that had long been better provided.

The successors to these were in many respects the factory villages of the Central Belt built in rural locations by industrialists or their landed allies who needed a fast-flowing stream to turn their water wheels combined with a plentiful local labour force willing to work at the mill. New Lanark, with its associations with David Dale and Robert Owen, is the best preserved and best known of these, but they ranged from Catrine and Eaglesham in Ayrshire to Deanston and Stanley in Perthshire, and even Spinningdale on the Dornoch Firth.

The development of the planned coastal fishing village belongs to the next phase from the 1790s to the end of the Napoleonic Wars in 1815, and was characteristic of the Highlands and the shores of the Moray Firth. One of the first was the creation by a philanthropic joint-stock company, the British Fisheries Society, which in 1788 began to lay out a new town at Ullapool in Wester Ross in order to employ idle Highlanders and develop the economic potential of the sealochs. Ullapool was the forerunner of a number of other, similar but privately financed settlements, not all so ambitious, down as far south as Lochgilphead in Argyll and Bowmore in Islay; and this group was paralleled in the east by the British Fisheries Society creation of Pultneytown (Wick) in 1809, and numerous privately organized Banffshire fisher towns. The temporary collapse of the fishing industry at the end of the Napoleonic Wars brought their foundation to an end.

The last and final phase of the movement occurred in East Perthshire, Angus and Kincardineshire in the second quarter of the nineteenth century, when the coarse handloom linen weaving industry began to seep from Dundee back into the villages of Strathmore where labour was more abundant and prepared to accept lower wages providing they were given a small holding to go with the loom. This was the origin of a series of very late settlements, like New Alyth and Friockheim built in the 1830s and 1840s. It was, however, a swan song, for almost immediately further technological advances made the handloom redundant even here, and these villages too were left high and dry without any clear economic function.

The main value of most of them today is scenic: when the traveller relaxes in the elegance of Grantown-on-Spey, rents a holiday cottage at Plockton or admires the village green at Kenmore by Loch Tay, he is enjoying, though he may not know it, the fruit of a Georgian taste that believed that economic improvements and well laid-out settlements were two aspects of the same thing. They did better than most have done since.

T.C. Smout

Montgomerie, Alexander (1540?–1611?), the last of the Scots Makars (or 'Scottish Chaucerians') was the younger son of Hugh Montgomerie of Hesilhead, Ayrshire, and a relation of the Earls of Eglinton. Through his mother, Lady Margaret Fraser, Montgomerie enjoyed kinship with James VI. He seems to have been a soldier, a 'Captain', who, while in Spain, turned from Calvinism to Catholicism and became involved in the Counter-Reformation, including participation in a ludicrous plot to capture Ailsa Craig, in the Clyde, as a stronghold to support a Spanish invasion. Summoned before the Privy Council to explain this treason, he failed to appear, was 'put to horn', and died, possibly in 1597, 1602 or, at the latest, 1611. James VI wrote a sonnet in Montgomerie's memory ('What drowsy sleep doth seal your eyes, allace!').

In between these events, Montgomerie managed to be a prolific poet, patronized by Esmé Stuart, Sire d'Aubigny, the King's Catholic cousin, and leading member of the 'Castalian band' who surrounded James. He was a prolific and skilful writer of sonnets. His allegory 'The Cherrie and the Slae', on which he seems to have worked over a prolonged period, revising it to make it carry religious and political overtones once his reckless actions had led to the suspension of his royal pension, is ostensibly an examination of whether to reach out for the cherry on the cliff, or be satisfied with the more easily accessible sloe. Courage and Hope spur him on, Dread, Danger and Despair try to discourage him. In the end, Reason claims that the cherry can be reached, and Wit shows the poet how to get it.

One stanza of the complicated form chosen (with a bob-wheel in the final quatrain, used later by Burns) shows the fresh colours Montgomerie employs.

> The dew as diamonds did hing
> Upon the tender twistis ying
> Owre-twinkling all the trees;
> And ay where flours did flourish fair,
> There suddenly I saw repair
> Ane swarm of sounding bees.
> Some sweetly has the honey socht,
> Whill they were cloggit sore;
> Some willingly the wax has wrocht,
> To keep it up in store.
> So heaping, with keeping,
> Into their hives they hide it,
> Precisely and wisely
> For winter they provide it.

Like most of the Castalian poets, Montgomerie wrote many of his verses to be sung to 'musick fyne' (composed music, as opposed to folk-song or Church music) a beautiful example—for which happily the melody survives—being the 'Adieu to His Mistress', included in *Music of Scotland from 1500–1700* (1957). His flyting with Polmont is a racy example of the then traditional poetic practice of abuse-slinging, a diluted prose form of which is still regularly to be met with in the correspondence columns of the *Scotsman* newspaper.

M. Lindsay

Morgan, Edwin (b. 1920) is one of Scotland's most popular contemporary poets and one of its most distinguished. He lectured in English Literature at the University of Glasgow from 1947 until 1980, becoming Professor in 1975. Morgan established himself as a major poet with the publication of *The Second Life* (1968) followed by the *Instamatic Poems* (1972) which 'fixed' events forever lost in newspapers or on television. *From Glasgow to Saturn* (1973) revealed his enthusiasm for science-fiction and space exploration. Morgan's war experiences are dealt with in *The New Divan* (1977). *Poems of Thirty Years* (1982) runs to over four hundred pages and collects poems from pamphlets and anthologies as well as from his books. *Sonnets from Scotland* (1984) continues the playfulness of Morgan's science-fiction poetry. A *Selected Poems* appeared in 1985. Subsequent publications include *From the Video Box* (1986) *Themes on a Variation* (1988) and *Collected Poems* (1990). Morgan's verse is taught extensively in schools. (Almost every school pupil in Scotland will have studied 'King Billy' and 'In the snack-bar' at some point.) He has also translated widely, from German, Italian, Spanish and Russian, writers such as Pasternak, Mayakovsky and Lorca.

P. Ingalls

Muir, Edwin (1887–1959) defies easy encapsulation. A poet who wrote verses of beguilingly simple form, he presents formidable challenges of interpretation and full comprehension. A lucid and wide-ranging critic, fully informed on British, continental and more esoteric literatures, he wrote with apparent simplicity and presented complex but cogent answers. A translator, with his wife Willa, of prolific output, he is responsible for much of British familiarity with Kafka's work. He spent many years in Europe, in Prague, Dresden and Rome. Above all, he left a compelling *Autobiography* to chart his life and spiritual times, a refreshing and fascinating account which explains so much, yet fails completely to penetrate to the shy, enormous intelligence behind it. Muir did not betray his thoughts comfortably or easily. He remains much of an enigma.

His early years in Orkney remained in his poems and prose the 'Eden' of a happy and protected childhood, the strong constants of family value, strong Christian framework and powerful island community spirit sustaining him in childhood years remembered as stable, comforting, unchanging. Removal to the mainland brought disease and ruin to the family, and spiritual shock and near nervous breakdown to the adolescent Edwin to whom the squalor of Glasgow in the Depression, and the horror of work in a bone-processing factory at Fairport, were almost beyond endurance. The dark years of this nightmare, the struggle in London to make a living by teaching and writing while submitting to rigorous psychoanalysis, the strength and comfort of his marriage, are catalogued with honesty in the *Autobiography*. Europe he found attractive, but war and revolution barred him from the Prague he had known, and the Dresden he had loved before its obliteration.

Eden seemed far off. Muir's evolving poetry was of stress and conflict, the labyrinth of life populated by dreadful stirrings of savage beasts, each nightmare image fearfully potent. Escape came not in a return to Eden, but in the adjustment which made possible a partial return. *One Foot in Eden*, his beautiful final collection of poems, indicates how far he had come. Powerfully moved by the open, unembarrassed Christianity of Catholic Italy, Muir evolved a personal peace which could take account of the war, the world, his private nightmares, and weave them all into a composite picture of life as tremulous, yet as secure, as the Angel and the Virgin in the painting of the Annunciation which so powerfully moved him in the Via degli Artisti in Rome. The late poems are intense explorations of states of mind: the over-exposed and much-discussed poems on horses should not undermine the lucidity and clarity of their statements about Muir's belief. In the later poem the horses come, complete with the foals which give hope for a better future, to re-establish contact with surviving man in a broken post-war world. They do not transport man back to Eden, they stay to work, and they make possible the re-establishment of some kind of partial Eden in this world, an Eden which takes account of the bleak realities. In this way,

> Strange blessings never in Paradise
> Fall from these beclouded skies,

and in this knowledge Muir lived, one foot in his native Scotland to which he returned for most of his later years, and the other in his memories. The labyrinth's walls are broached, for poetry had given him—not escape—but 'birdwings' to fly free. He could live with his world.

Critic, translator, autobiographer, poet, Edwin Muir takes a place in our literary history which can stand comparison with Eliot's. He made important and controversial critical statements while shrinking from publicity and controversy: *Scott and Scotland*, attacking much of the 'Renaissance' of the 1930s, was a bombshell. Shunning open political commitment for much of his life, he acted as a focus for intelligent thought quite free of narrowness. Perhaps most importantly, he was a Scot and a British writer quite at home in a local context, and yet at home in a European and a world-wide context, blessed with great abilities to communicate. He is steadily taking his place in anthologies not only of modern Scottish verse, but of modern verse, and he has earned his place in both.

I. Campbell

Murray, Charles (1864–1941) was born at Alford, Aberdeenshire, and educated at Gallowhill School. He served his apprenticeship with Walker and Beattie, a firm of civil engineers in Aberdeen, and after a year in the surveyor's department of another Aberdeen firm emigrated to South Africa in 1888. The following year he became a partner in a

Johannesburg firm of architects and engineers, and in 1899 manager of York Gold Mining Company. During the Boer War he served as a lieutenant in the Railway Pioneering Regiment, and in 1901 became Deputy Inspector of Mines, Transvaal.

His professional progress thereafter was rapid. In 1902 he was Registrar of Crown Titles, in 1905 Under Secretary of Public Works, Transvaal, and two years later Chief Engineer and Secretary. In 1910 he was appointed Secretary for Public Works for the Union of South Africa. During World War I he served as a lieutenant colonel in the South Africa Defence Corps from 1917. Aberdeen University made him a Doctor of Law in 1920 and he was made a CMG in 1922, two years before he retired. His last years were spent at Banchory, in Kincardinshire.

In 1926 Murray was presented by John Buchan with a portrait of himself by Fiddes Watt RSA and a bust by H.S. Gamley RSA. The Charles Murray Memorial Trust was founded in 1942.

Murray's first privately published volume, *A Handful of Heather* (1893) was later withdrawn by the poet. *Hamewith* (1901), first published in Aberdeen, has gone through many editions, the most recent—*Hamewith: The Complete Poems* (1979)—including also the contents of *A Sough o' War* (1917), *In Country Places* (1920) and the posthumously published *The Last Poems* (1949).

Murray claimed to have first written his verses to please his father. The Vale of Alford and its characters supplied him with his themes, his imagery and his language. Nan Shepherd has called his work 'a poetry of externals', and this is both its strength and its weakness. Too often it depends for its effects upon pithily expressed descriptions that have a purely local and surface significance. Murray's great fame and following has always remained fairly centred on his native northeast.

Occasionally, the traditional manner and conventional forms which he usually adopted were given a jolt, and he anticipated the Scottish Renaissance. This is particularly true of 'Gin I was God', with its hint of a manner to be developed more fully by MacDiarmid, and of what is perhaps his finest achievement, 'Dockens Afore His Peers (Exemption Tribunal)', which vividly portrays in operation a countryman's self-interest and insensitive cunning. His most popular poem 'The Whistle' is a vivacious portrait of a boy whose home-made whistle led to conflict with his schoolmaster. However, even when his verse is at its most sentimental and parochial, his Aberdeenshire Scots always rings true.

M. Lindsay

Museums and Art Galleries. When the eleventh Earl of Buchan conceived the idea in 1780 of founding what he called a 'Temple of Caledonian Virtue', he not only brought together some objects and pictures that are still part of the national collections but also set in train the long process of acquisition and display that has by now produced a Scotland singularly well endowed with public repositories of all sorts. Lord Buchan's objectives were in part nationalistic for he—like Sir Walter

Scott—saw historical pride as a factor in national self-identification, and it is with perfect justice that the best of our public collections today, national or local, should concern themselves with things Scottish.

The natural inheritor of Lord Buchan's vision is the National Museum in Queen Street, Edinburgh. Growing indeed from the Society of Antiquaries of Scotland which he founded, the National Museum provides the definitive collection of objects of archaeological importance and historic interest in terms of Scotland's past. Working in sections that study pre-medieval Scotland, Scotland in historic times and Scottish country life, the Museum possesses such remarkable pieces as the Traprain Law Treasure, the silver from St Ninian's Isle, the Monymusk Reliquary and the Fetternear Banner, but of as great importance are the growing representations of—for example—Scottish seventeenth and eighteenth century silver, Scottish costume, or the incunabula of golf. For almost all its life this great collection has been inhibited by an inadequate building. Constructed in the 1880s to serve as a Portrait Gallery and shared immediately by the Museum, the Queen Street building stands as a monument to non-functional design and misguided philanthropy. From both professional and public points of view removal to another site can neither come too soon nor hold out greater promise for the display of superb collections in a wholly appropriate manner.

One exciting direction in which the National Museum's enterprise has been able to move is in the foundation of a new Agricultural Museum situated appropriately at the showground of the Royal Highland and Agricultural Society at Ingliston. Sponsored by the Scottish Country Life Museum Trust this new building obviously serves its market, evidenced not only by the numbers who come to see it—48,000 in its first season after full completion—but also in the nature of its audience. This shows a very high proportion of people actively involved in the countryside, and here is public interchange at its best. Not only do the visitors appreciate the history of their agriculture shown before them but they feed back to the museum staff comment and information vital to the growing record.

Edinburgh, for reasons of its capital status, accommodates the two great national museum-gallery institutions of Scotland. The Royal Museum on Chambers Street is of course the largest and has a function that to a great extent combines those of the Science Museum, the Natural History Museum, the British Museum and the Victoria and Albert Museum in London. In other words it is not only international in its content but interdisciplinary in its interests. Departments of Art and Ethnography, Natural History, Geology and Technology together make this the most comprehensive museum display in Britain under one roof. Inevitably this implies the same problems of accommodation from which the Queen Street museum suffers, but a high degree of selectivity in display and the reconstruction of large sections of the building have made overcrowding less apparent. Some items, of course, like aircraft can never enter the building and are housed in East Lothian, but it is a matter of no small wonder that the colossal

City Mills waterwheel from Aberdeen was successfully re-erected in one of the technology halls.

The Royal Museum has pointed the way to a new advance in display-interpretation—the conveyance of information at appropriate levels to the vastly disparate categories of the general public that visit here each year. The section that concerns itself with 'Evolution' has most ingeniously succeeded in offering multi-level explanations so that it is possible for the uncommitted to skim off a general message of instruction while, it has been said, a more leisurely and total absorption of information offered can bring the visitor to first-year university standard!

A prime function of museums and galleries must be to facilitate changing exhibitions drawn from beyond their own collections; sadly not all buildings can afford the space for a permanent exhibition hall. It was an act of courage therefore that provided the Royal Museum with such a facility and a long list of exhibitions of a nature appropriate to the Museum has wholly justified the step. Proceeding apace are plans for the new Museum of Scotland to be housed in a special building next to the Royal Museum in Chambers Street. This exciting project will bring together objects, and some paintings illustrating the history of Scotland's decorative arts as well as its prehistory.

The National Galleries organization of Scotland now embraces three distinct buildings together with a specialized Department of Prints and Drawings. Parent to these diverse children, the National Gallery on the Mound is the original foundation and in the public eye the most important of the family. It has also the curious claim, surely totally unchallenged, to be the only national art collection in the world to be built directly over a railway tunnel! Recent extensions of the accommodation downwards have considerably narrowed the gap between the stability of great art and the transience of commuter man! Despite the accession of space which it thus received, the National Gallery of Scotland remains one of the most manageable of the world's great art collections. Its modest presentation of public rooms offers comprehensibility without fatigue and ensures by its very discipline of spatial constraint that the paintings regularly exhibited are well considered and well chosen. The Gallery however represents for Scotland a synthesis of the functions of the National Gallery and the Tate in London, and one could be aware of some tension between the need to exhibit the masterpieces of European schools and the claims for wall-space of the Scottish painters. The compromise has been a happy one: Rembrandt's *Hendrijke Stoffels*, Raphael's *Bridgewater Madonna*, Constable's *Dedham Vale*, the Van der Goes *Trinity Panels* all grandly displayed—these still leave room and dignity for the grandest Raeburns, for Runciman's *King Lear* or Hamilton's *Achilles*.

The Scottish School is—for various historical reasons—best represented by its portrait painters but it is logical, and refreshing, that National Gallery policy 'dropped off' not a few non-portrait pictures by Scottish hands to be shown in the Scottish National Portrait Gallery in Queen Street. Here again imagination and a sense of drama has produced modifications in display which not only excite and interest the visitor but also detract from the sensation one used to have of viewing great art in a hospital ward—the fault, one hastens to add, not of this century's curators but of last century's architect! A national portrait collection is at the best of times a hard thing to come to grips with. In part it represents a 'national Valhalla', a testimonial to Scottish fame, but it also most surely encompasses the work of Scotland's (and England's) best painters and there is always the problem of combining in one display personal merit with artistic greatness. With paintings like Gainsborough's *Duke of Argyll* or Dobson's *Charles II* or Raeburn's *Alexander Adam*, definitive portraiture and artistic accomplishment go hand in hand, but it is not difficult to find tedium for the eye in the nineteenth-century rooms.

The Scottish National Gallery of Modern Art is the youngest member of the National Galleries family. It is now permanently housed in a finely classical former school in the Belford district of Edinburgh, and offers the most exciting opportunities to see contemporary art both in the permanent collection and in important temporary exhibitions.

On the horizon is the possibility of a National Gallery of Scottish Art, but its scope and indeed its location - Edinburgh, Glasgow or wherever - are still to be decided.

Museum sponsorship beyond the Government institutions of Edinburgh is rich and varied. It extends from the quasi-national provision of Glasgow where the city's museums and museum-services are as comprehensive as those just described, to the delightful and little Old Ironmongery Museum in Selkirk, hidden in Halliwell's Close and representing the affection and modest enterprise of one committed man. All are linked together by the Scottish Museum Council which from its base in Edinburgh works by grant and technical advice to raise standards of display and conservation wherever encouragement is needed. At the time of going to press, the St Mungo Museum of Religion Life and Art opens in Glasgow.

How to survey this plenitude of provision? Broadly speaking museums are divisible into two categories—those that deal generally with the history or natural environment of their area, and those that have some sort of special theme. Local history museums of course are the commonest. Their appeal is instantaneous—whether to the nostalgia of the local resident or the curiosity of the visitor. Some—like Dumfries—serve the history of a vast area, others—like the museum in the Signal Tower at Arbroath—admirably tell the story of a neighbourhood and its industry. Certain town museums are fully inspired by a sort of textbook clarity of arrangement, as is that at Elgin, others are equally delightful—and one thinks of Inverkeithing—for the wholly unexpected discoveries that can be made among the relics of local displenishment sales and the personalia of local great citizens (in the case just quoted, the founder of the Russian navy!). As the urban scale increases, and so the funding available, so the excellence of the local history display improves. Glasgow's People's Palace and its Hagg's Castle, or Edinburgh's Huntly House are comprehensive records of a city's social life and craft-accomplishment and the same holds true of smaller cities

like Dundee and Kirkcaldy, each with its first-class local history display.

From local history in general, two museum developments follow—the museum that concentrates on one man's life and work, and the museum of folk-history. One-man museums can be dreary in the extreme. With the greatest ease they can turn themselves into mausolea into which even the greatest enthusiasm of the curators can scarcely inject life. They scatter the country, from Hugh Miller's cottage at Cromarty down by way of Barrie at Kirriemuir to Burns in Ayrshire or Jim Clark at Duns. Their purpose is, one must suppose, to show the environment however lowly from which great worth came and if they could concentrate more on this and less upon the icon-value of the man, more interest might be generated. On the other hand the appeal of the folk-life museum is real and immediate. It is the appeal of one's own roots, and who can visit the village-shop displays at Gladstone Court Museum, Biggar, to take just one example, without being intensely moved by atavistic memory? At Glamis the Angus Folk Museum gives a more rural picture of cottage life, as indeed does the Ceres Museum in Fife, but the father and mother of this entire family must surely be the Highland Folk Museum at Kingussie, the most comprehensive record one could wish for of a virtually extinguished way of life.

More specialized interests follow. A Museum of Scottish Tartans has been established in the weaving village of Comrie and has made some notable acquisitions—not least with reference to Queen Victoria's John Brown! On the coast of Fife, at Anstruther, a situation of equal appropriateness was found for the Scottish Fisheries Museum in 1969 and here the historic paraphernalia of the fishing industry is displayed within a courtyard of old harbourhead buildings. Transport museums and museums of industrial history have been the great development of the last twenty years and here again the variety is wide. Glasgow's Transport Museum is—as one might expect—among the finest in Britain with coverage extending from horse-vehicles through tramcars and early steamships to the city's first underground railway, but more modest and more specialized are the motor museums at Doune and Myreton, both privately founded. On-site industrial museums stand out for their achievements. This is particularly the case with New Lanark, an award-winning 'exhibition' set in restored mill buildings and with highly imaginative systems of display. In the east of Scotland, at Newtongrange and Prestongrange is the embryo of a larger Scottish coal-mining museum, while — on a smaller scale indeed, but highly to be commended — is the Lead-Mining Museum at Wanlockhead, complete with hard-hat experience into a mine.

Battle-sites are difficult and probably lend themselves best to dramatized audio-visual interpretation, as at Bannockburn and Culloden, rather than to museum treatment, but regimental museums less so. Certainly Scotland has no scarcity of pride in this respect and whether at Stirling, with the Argyll and Sutherlands, or at Perth, with the Black Watch or the old 'HLI' at Glasgow Scottish courage at home and abroad is well illustrated. For, if one may say so, the more academic study of military history the Scottish United Services Museum in Edinburgh Castle is the principal resource and has now for many years been a department of the Royal Museum.

Finally to turn again to art galleries, beyond Edinburgh all the larger towns and cities have their collections. At Glasgow the Kelvingrove collection (with its world-renowned Giorgione) and the Burrell Collection, now in a splendid new building, have resulted in an endowment which many a European city must envy. Aberdeen's collection has a strong emphasis on contemporary art, those at Dundee and Kirkcaldy are more concerned with the nineteenth century. An off-beat delight for the inveterate picture-hunter must be the Orchar Collection at Dundee, an enormously curious representation of nineteenth-century industrialist's taste. But curiosity is the great motivation of museum and gallery visitors everywhere and it would be the greatest shame if all our display-collections were so polite and well-ordered as to defy the description 'curious'!

B. Skinner

Music Hall and Variety Theatre. The music hall tradition in Scotland began at the turn of the century when custom-built theatres opened in the cities and towns to serve as venues for the leading London music hall stars of the day, but as appetite for this entertainment grew so did the local talent. Almost every seaside town had its own theatre creating a touring circuit. The summer season began when the large theatres in the cities closed for the summer months. Theatres on the Clyde and Ayrshire coasts were particularly popular.

Early stars. The man most often associated with Scottish music hall is Harry Lauder. Born in Portobello in 1870 he began his career in London singing Scots songs. He successfully exported his singing and brand of pawky humour overseas, especially to America, and was knighted for his services to the theatre in 1919. He died in 1950. Dave Willis (1895–1973) began his career at the early age of thirteen when he appeared in pantomime. His often unscripted comic sketches and songs were original and topical. At the same time, Harry Gordon (1893–1957) from Aberdeen was delighting audiences in numerous shows and in pantomime. His comedy was built on brilliant observations of speech, mannerisms and character. Of a later generation, Lex MacLean (1908–1975) stands out. He began his solo career as a comedian in 1947 after serving an apprenticeship in John Brown's shipyards. Other comic stars of the period included Alec Finlay (1906–1984) often partnered by Will Fyffe (1885–1947), who made famous the song 'I Belong to Glasgow', Tommy Lorne (1890–1935) and Tommy Morgan (1898–1958).

The Shows. Typically, the shows consisted of individual and ensemble song, dance or comedy acts with some speciality acts — acrobats mainly. During the summer season there were often two shows a day and programmes changed regularly. Howard and Wyndham's *Half Past Eight* (and later *Five Past Eight*) shows are considered by many to be the apogee of the genre. They began as an experiment to have a summer season

in Glasgow along the lines of seaside entertainment. The first performance opened in 1933 and the shows continued until well into the 1960s. Many present-day performers made their name in these shows and were later to transfer to radio and television: Chic Murray, Stanley Baxter, Rikki Fulton, Dorothy Paul, Johnny Beattie, Jack Milroy, Jimmy Logan, Kenneth McKellar and Calum Kennedy.

Pantomime. The music hall tradition has all but disappeared in its variety form although there are occasional shows in seaside towns during the summer months. The pantomime however has had an enduring success in Scotland and it is in this form that the turns of the old music hall survive. Some of its stars too come from the variety theatre: Una McLean, Walter Carr and Stanley Baxter (who first appeared in panto in 1952) appearing alongside newer faces such as Gerard Kelly, Andy Gray, and Alan Stewart.

C. Arnold

Musgrave, Thea (b. 1928) received her initial technical grounding at the University of Edinburgh under Sidney Newman and Hans Gal. A postgraduate scholarship enabled her to study with Nadia Boulanger, in Paris. She was the first British composer to win the Lili Boulanger Prize (1952). Her first works were made known by the Saltire Singers, whom she later joined for two years as an accompanist and coach. She has taught at London University (Extra-Mural Department) and at the University of California, Santa Barbara and has served on several important committees—Central Music Advisory Panel (BBC), Music Panel of the Arts Council, Executive Committee of the Composers' Guild. In 1973 she was made an Honorary Fellow of New Hall, Cambridge and subsequently received an Honorary Doctorate from the Open University. Married to the conductor and violist Peter Mark, she is now resident in the USA.

She has written in large and small-scale forms with clarity and economy, an acute sense of colour and proportion and originality of concept and procedure. Her early works are tonal, neo-classical and largely vocal, relying on the internal logic of regular patterns and ostinati: Five Songs for baritone (1950), *Suite o' Bairnsangs* (1953, Scottish Festival, Braemar), Four Madrigals (1953), Ballet *A Tale for Thieves* (1953). After the *Cantata for a Summer's Day* (1954, Saltire Singers), her first major success, her style became increasingly chromatic and angular: for example, the one-act opera *The Abbot of Drimock* (1955), Five Love Songs (1955) for soprano and guitar and Divertimento (1957) for strings. The exploration of freely chromatic and serial techniques in *Obliques* (1957, BBC Scottish Symphony Orchestra) and String Quartet (1958, McEwen Commission) found release in a series of fully serial works: *A Song for Christmas* (1958), *Triptych* (1959, Saltire Society) for tenor and orchestra, *Trio* (1960) for flute, oboe and piano, *Colloquy* (1960) for violin and piano, Chamber Concerto No. I (1962, McEwen Commission) and *Sinfonia* (1963, Cheltenham Festival).

In *Serenade* (1961) and *Scottish Dance Suite* (1959) Musgrave had begun to reconcile her own free-ranging imagination with the technical discipline essential within an atonal context. In three subsequent major works, *The Phoenix and the Turtle* (1962, BBC) and *The Five Ages of Man* (1963, Norwich Festival) for chorus and orchestra and the three-act opera *The Decision* (1964–65) she reverted to a less fragmented, lyrical style, (though still chromatic), more compatible with large-scale thought.

The kind of musical dialogue tentatively explored in *Chamber Concerto 1* and *Colloquy*, was expanded, during the late 1960s, into a musical argument which is inseparable from the deployment, actions and reactions of the participants—the *dramatis personae*. In redefining her musical language, through a greater improvisatory freedom of melody, harmony, colour and rhythm within a single accumulative structure, Musgrave has evolved what she calls 'dramatic-abstract' forms: dramatic in presentation, involving flexible systems of cues and aleatoric devices, interaction between concertante 'thematic' groups, and at times, the actual physical movement of players within the ensemble; but abstract in intent, containing no programme. The series of chamber and orchestral works written within this framework lay great emphasis upon virtuosic display: Chamber Concertos 2 and 3 (1966), Impromptus 1 and 2 (1967 and 1970), *Space Play*: Concerto for Nine Instruments (1974, Koussevitsky Foundation); concertos for orchestra (1967, Feeney Trust), clarinet (1968, Royal Philharmonic Society), horn (1971, Dartmouth Congregation for the Arts, USA), viola (1973, BBC); *Night Music* (1969, BBC) and *Momento Vitae*, (1970, BBC Scotland) for orchestra; *From one to another* (1970), viola and tape and *Orfeo I* (1975), flute and tape. The logical extension of this concept is evident in her recent works for the stage, where characters underpin the musical discourse: the two-act ballet *Beauty and the Beast* (1969, Gulbenkian Foundation for Scottish Ballet), the operas *The Voice of Ariadne* (1973, Royal Opera House), *Mary, Queen of Scots* (1977, Scottish Opera) and *A Christmas Carol* (1979).

Among native Scottish composers, Musgrave enjoys an international reputation; the joint commission of *Harriet, the Woman called Moses* (1984) by the Royal Opera House, Covent Garden, and the Virginia Opera can be seen as confirmation of this reputation on both sides of the Atlantic.

P. Hindmarsh

Music of Church and Court, 1500–1700. This short survey of Scottish music before 1700 deals in very general terms with the extant repertory—sacred and secular, vocal and instrumental—composed in the great traditions of European polyphony. Any account, however, must necessarily remain fragmentary, as so much music has been lost or destroyed through political expediency, religious fervour or sheer neglect. What has managed to survive represents a remarkable and individual body of music that today continues to gain in currency and prestige as more music is brought to light, published and performed.

Sacred polyphony is hardly documented at all before the sixteenth century. It certainly existed, as there are numerous accounts from the thirteenth to the fifteenth centuries of the foundation of ecclesiastical buildings and the provision of singing men and boys to furnish music for them. Only one early source survives from this period—the thirteenth-century manuscript 'Wolfenbüttel 677': traditionally associated with St Andrews, it contains some of the French Notre Dame repertory of sacred polyphony and also some unidentifiable pieces that may be of local origin.

One of the most important of these religious foundations was the Chapel Royal and one of the most important sources of sixteenth-century Scottish music the Carver Choirbook. This manuscript seems to have been related to the large-scale reorganization of the Chapel Royal at Stirling under James IV in 1501. It contains Flemish and English music, as well as the extant works of the distinguished Scottish composer Robert Carver (c. 1490–after 1546). Carver's surviving five Masses and two motets owe something to the late medieval decorative and rhythmically animated chordal styles of contemporary English composers such as Lambe and Wylkynson, and to the more truly Renaissance imitative style of Flemish composers such as Josquin and Isaac. All these features are to be found in, for example, the Mass *L'Homme armé* for four voices and the motet *O bone Jesu* for 19 voices, both probably dating from the 1520s. (For these and many other compositions mentioned in this article see *Musica Britannica* XV.) The first is remarkable for its technical virtuosity and the fact that it is the only British Mass based on the famous popular song that was a favourite *cantus firmus* for Mass composition with continental composers in the fifteenth and sixteenth centuries; and the second for its spectacular handling of the marvellously rich tapestry of 19 voices (perhaps simply reflecting the number of singers available to Carver at the time). Carver's music is conceived on an impressive scale and shows a truly creative musical talent. The principle of 'structural imitation through harmony'—the hallmark of music of the High Renaissance—gradually spread from the Continent to Britain and became fully established during the second quarter of the sixteenth century. In Scotland the music of David Peebles (c. 1510–1579) shows the process of adopting this style in the motet *Si quis diligit me* of about 1530, as does the roughly contemporary music for the Roman rite of Robert Johnson (c. 1500–c. 1560)—though all of it is extant only in English sources. Johnson was accused of Lutheran heresy and fled to England, where he turned to the composition of music for the newly established Reformed Anglican Liturgy.

One of the principles of the Reformers in Germany, Switzerland, France and England was that sacred music should be sung in the vernacular and simplified for its more immediate comprehension and even participation by the congregation. And so, when the Reformation reached Scotland in 1560 in a particularly virulent form—unsympathetic to polyphonic music—simple psalm-tunes drawn from the international repertory and set in a strictly chordal style became the official form of Church music. However, imitative settings and even anthems in a more ambitious though note-against-note poly-phonic style were allowed in more privileged places such as Chapel Royal or song-school. Composers who had been trained in the old religious houses were invited to contribute to the new forms: David Peebles (reluctantly) composed set-tings of 106 Proper tunes (i.e. tunes associated with one particular metrical version of a psalm), smoothly wrought in melody and harmony; John Angus (fl. 1543–95) set the canti-cles (metrical versions of e.g. *The Lord's prayer*); Andrew Blackhall (1536–1609) composed anthems (e.g. *Judge and re-venge my cause*), psalms in reports (i.e. imitative settings after the style of the French composer Goudimel) as well as psalm-settings and canticles; and Andrew Kemp (fl. 1560–70) wrote canticles, anthems and 44 psalm settings in a somewhat rugged harmonic style, as well as original psalm tunes. The first printed Scottish psalter appeared in 1564, but only the tunes were included.

The tragedy was that the new form of service made no proper provision for music, and so standards of performance and composition inevitably declined. Two attempts to im-prove matters had some measure of success: the song-schools were reorganized by Act of Parliament in 1579 and made the responsibility of the burghs; and after 1603 valiant but sporadic efforts were made to keep the Chapel Royal going. These resulted in the publication of several printed psalters with part-music (all-purpose 'Common Tunes', that could be sung to any psalm in common metre), culminating in Andrew Hart's fine *The Psalmes of David* (Edinburgh, 1635) that contains (besides Common tunes and psalms in reports) many earlier settings of proper tunes by Peebles and his contemporaries. But James VI's and then Charles I's persistent Episcopal poli-cies eventually produced a violent reaction in Scotland. A narrow Presbyterianism triumphed, admitting into public worship only a dozen Common tunes (fine though they were) such as *French* or *Martyrs*—a situation that was to prevail for the rest of the seventeenth century and indeed far beyond.

The earliest secular vocal music that survives in Scotland dates from the late fifteenth century. *My heartly service*, an extended ceremonial piece celebrating the rural festival of Plough Monday, is set for two voices and instrumental ground. Such a combination of solo voices and instrument is in fact very close to the classic texture of the later medieval European song-forms and must have already been used in Scotland. A distinctive Scottish literature had begun to emerge as early as the thirteenth century, and one of the most distinguished lyric poets of the fifteenth century—the monarch James I himself—is known to have been a composer as well, at least during the time of his captivity in England (1406–24). *My heartly service* could lend itself well to dramatic presentation in the manner of some fifteenth-century English carols. It is recorded along with two other similar pieces which together are described as 'medleys', and all are patently akin to the early sixteenth-cen-tury French vocal form, the *fricassée*.

In the early sixteenth century rival English and French factions operated at the Scottish court, the French eventually prevailing during the later reign of James V (1513–42), when the king twice brought a French queen back to Scotland in 1537 and 1538 and French culture flooded into the country. One of the most influential musical forms of the sixteenth century, the French chanson, had recently been developed by Claudin de Sermisy as a strophic form in chordal or mildly imitative style for four voices, and was successfully adapted in Scottish set-tings of texts by Steill, Scott, Fethy and others. Part-songs like *Richt soir opprest and Departe, departe* may even be the work of John Fethy (fl. 1539–48) and Alexander Scott themselves, for we know that one was a composer and the other 'musician and organist'. Further links with the French song-repertory were fashioned by matching existing French music with a new Scott-ish text (e.g. *D'où vient cela / For love of one*), or a Scottish translation of a French lyric with new music (e.g. *Secourez-moi madame / Support your servand*).

During the regency of Marie de Guise (1554–60) and the reign of her daughter Mary Queen of Scots (1560–67) French ties were maintained; and even from the reign of James VI (1567–1603) there survives a group of part-songs dating from the 1580s that still owe a great deal to the Franco-Scottish tradition of song-writing. Several were inspired by the lyrics of Alexander Montgomerie, influential leader of the self-styled 'Castalian Band' of poets and musicians with King James as figurehead. As examples of these, the deeply felt *Adeu, O desie of delyt*, one of many poems in the 'Helicon' stanza, is matched with an internationally current tune and set in an expressive chordal style by Andrew Blackhall; and the playful *In throu the windoes of myn ees*, though set in a more varied contrapuntal texture, yet remains remarkably true to the older song forms of pre-Reformation Scotland.

In spite of the departure of the court in 1603 and the subsequent fragmentation of court culture, the Scottish song tradition managed to survive for a time among the musical amateurs of the northern castles and in the more important song-schools such as Aberdeen and Glasgow. It was during the seventeenth century that that other tradition of Scottish music—folksong—began to be written down for the first time, though to be sure it must have existed for centuries before. Curiously, it was set down in instrumental versions for lute, lyra-viol, cittern, harpsichord or violin, with only rare instances of texts being recorded. Obviously in a living tradi-tion such as this, new melodies in the true folk idiom were always being composed and added to the basic stock, but occasionally an older courtly melody seems to have been transformed into a folksong (e.g. *Then wilt thou goe*) or a new song composed that has features of both styles (e.g. *Celia I lov'd thee*).

Proof of the lasting popularity of the courtly repertory can be seen in the inclusion of some items in Forbes's *Songs and Fancies* (Aberdeen, three editions: 1662, 1666, 1682), the first publication of secular music ever to appear in Scotland. But the tenacity of that tradition had been weakened by a century of bitter civil and religious strife, and it had all but faded by the end of the century. It was the folk-songs that were to reappear in overwhelming numbers in the eighteenth-century printed collections and become exclusively associated for over

250 years with the idea of 'Scottish song'—and indeed of 'Scottish music'.

In the field of instrumental music it is again to the beginning of the sixteenth century that we must turn for the earliest examples of consort music. *Ane exempill of tripla* dates from about 1520 and sets what looks like a French popular song in the traditional manner as a *cantus firmus* in the tenor part. It comes from a later Scottish treatise of the 1570s, possibly linked with the reorganization of the teaching of music in the song-schools in 1579. A slightly later and more substantial piece from the same source, *Salve, rex gloriae*, is another *cantus firmus* setting of the Helicon tune, this time highly imitative and on grounds of style perhaps the work of David Peebles. After the Reformation the same form was cultivated by John Black (fl. 1546–87) in a number of very fine *Lessons* on the psalms, using the proper psalm-tunes as tenors, alongside pieces in the characteristic late Renaissance form of the freely composed polyphonic fantasia.

That other popular late Renaissance instrumental genre—dance-music—was also prominent at the Scottish court. A group of dances, possibly the work of a member of the Hudson family of musicians from York who became part of the young King James VI's household and represented the English Protestant element there, includes a setting of another internationally current tune, here entitled *Prince Edward's Paven*; and the splendid *My Lord of Marche Paven* is the work of Scottish composer James Lauder (fl. 1547–93), devoted Catholic servitor to Mary during her imprisonment in England, and possibly composer of some of the part-song settings of lyrics by his fellow Catholic Montgomerie.

Music for keyboard has come down to us by William Kinloch (fl. 1582), also associated with Catholic intrigue, and by Duncan Burnett (fl. *c.*1615–1652), scion of a noble Scottish family and Master of the Glasgow song-school. Their music exploits in an individual way the idioms, figuration patterns and variation technique of contemporary English virginalist music. These features recur in the idiosyncratic seventeenth-century instrumental arrangements of folk-music already mentioned, notably in the settings for violin of folk-tunes with variations of the end of the century which were to prove enormously influential in the fiddle collections of the eighteenth century.

K. Elliott

Music in the Scottish Lowlands, 1700–1800. Music in eighteenth-century Scotland was vastly superior in quality, quantity and modernity to that of the century before. As far as one can tell from surviving records, the seventeenth century consisted largely of uneventful ticking over of institutions and compositional forms inherited from the sixteenth: thinly scattered highlights are Duncan Burnett's harpsichord pieces, written in Glasgow in the 1620s, two manuscripts of folk-tune settings for plucked-string instruments (John Skene of Hallyards' mandora-book of *c.*1627 and the Balcarres lute-book of *c.*1695), one belated madrigalian publication in

Aberdeen (John Forbes's *Cantus, Songs and Fancies*, three editions, 1662, 1666 and 1682), and the continued singing of sixteenth-century madrigals and court-songs at burgh music-schools and in country houses.

Certainly, this was how the eighteenth century viewed the seventeenth; as something dim and old-fashioned, whose very records were hardly worth preserving. For the eighteenth century was a period of burgeoning growth, during which Scotland did its utmost to catch up with 100 years of European music on which it felt it had missed out. Musical societies were formed in the larger towns; public concerts began (probably in Edinburgh in 1693); the aristocracy brought dancing back into fashion in defiance of the Church of Scotland, and created an enormous demand for new dance music; folk music was published for the first time; from 1722, organs were reintroduced into Episcopal churches; many parish church choirs were formed after 1755. Scotland's up-to-date musical taste by the mid-century can be shown by the contents of the Aberdeen Musical Society's library in 1760, two-thirds of which had been published during the previous 15 years.

After 1770 glee and catch singing also caught on in Scotland. By this time the indigenous court-song traditions represented in Forbes's *Cantus* had sunk without trace; the few Scottish glees that were written (e.g. R.A. Smith's *Marjory Miller*, composed *c.*1805 in Paisley to a lyric by Tannahill) are unmistakably descended from the alien English madrigal.

The acid test of a country's music is the quality of its original compositions. Scottish classical music in the eighteenth century stands up to this test better than is generally believed: between 1725 and 1780 several of Edinburgh's composers produced first-class work, even though Edinburgh reserved its greatest enthusiasm for Corelli, Handel, Hasse, Johann Stamitz, Arne, Geminiani, and Haydn. During the 1760s and 1770s the musical time-lag between the leading continental centres and Edinburgh was only 10 years—a record with which present-day Scotland cannot compete, despite gramophone records, radio, and air travel. Though not at the forefront of European musical developments, Scotland was definitely contributing to them, not passively spectating as she had done the century before.

Some concrete examples will perhaps show best where Scotland stood in relation to other countries. Edinburgh's first symphonies were written twenty years ahead of St Petersburg's. Francesco Barsanti's op. 3 concertos, published in Edinburgh in 1742, are the only known *concerti grossi* with solo kettledrum parts; their horn parts are as imaginative and technically difficult as anything J.S. Bach wrote for the instrument. The Earl of Kelly's *Six Overtures op. I* (1761) were the first Mannheim-style orchestral works to be printed in Britain. Kelly's lyrical clarinet writing in his E-flat overture of 1767 anticipates Mozart's by ten years. William McGibbon's *La Follia* variations for violin and continuo, written about 1735, are a fine example of a distinguished seventeenth-century Italian tradition, but also include many original touches. J.G.C. Schetky, who was born at Darmstadt in 1737 and settled in Edinburgh in 1772, was unable to get any of his compositions published until he moved to Scotland; after this he achieved a publication a year for the next 20 years. His E-flat cello sonata (op. 4 no. 4, 1776) is one of the finest ever written for the instrument.

Other composers, less well equipped technically than the aforementioned, also made vigorous, tasteful contributions to the musical scene: noteworthy are the 2nd, 9th and 10th sonatas for violin or flute (1737) of Charles McLean, a music teacher in Montrose and Aberdeen; the 1st and 6th violin sonatas of David Foulis, a Fellow of the Royal College of Physicians of Edinburgh; and the superb flute sonata in G major (no. 4, 2nd set, 1762) by John Reid, who was an army general. All this took place despite a certain distrust of local musical enterprise, which is still in evidence in Scotland.

Eighteenth-century Scottish classical music did not, in the long run, prove very exportable. Kelly's, Reid's and Schetky's compositions were published in London and so promoted in England; only Kelly's appear to have reached the Continent. (The evidence for this is an entry in James Boswell's journal for 1764, reporting that he had heard one of Kelly's symphonies played at the theatre in Kassel.)

From 1780 Edinburgh lost what degree of musical autonomy it had gained during the previous 80 years. Turnpike roads cut the journey time from London from ten days to three or four, making whistle-stop tours possible for travelling virtuosi. Previously, star singers and players had tended to reside in provincial towns for months at a time, taking on pupils as well as giving concerts, fruitfully exchanging ideas with the local professionals. (Schetky's move to Edinburgh in 1772 was originally intended to be for one year; in the event, he died there in 1824.) Thus improved communications meant, paradoxically, that less of value was communicated. Music in York, Newcastle, Norwich, Bath and Bristol suffered at this time, as well as that of Edinburgh and Aberdeen. Railway developments in the 1840s made matters even worse; and it was not until university music departments and symphony orchestras were founded in Scotland, in the late nineteenth century, that new motives appeared for foreign musicians to settle, and for Scottish musicians not to emigrate.

Folk music should not be separated from classical music too rigidly. It differed in its self-consciously nationalistic idiom and in some of its performance aspects, but many eighteenth-century players, singers and patrons were equally at home in both. Many connections between the two can be found. William McGibbon was the outstanding classical composer of his generation, but was even better known for his folk-tune settings. James Oswald's 96 sonatas for flute or violin and continuo entitled *Airs for the Four Seasons* (two sets, 1755 and *c.* 1765) successfully inserted Scottish elements into the Italian tradition of Vivaldi's *Quattro Stagioni* concertos. Barsanti's op. 4 overtures (*c.* 1743) contain two movements with Caledonian flavourings: the Paesana ('country dance') finale of no. 2, which is based on the violin style now known as Shetland fiddling, and the second movement of no. 9, which introduces the *jig Babbity Bowster* as a fugue subject. Folk composers also knew their way around classical music. Niel Gow, Scotland's

most sought-after band-leader from 1770 to 1800, used to play Corelli's sonatas at home for fun. The famous and still current jig *Hamilton House* was written about 1783 by Joseph Reinagle junior, at that time leader of the Theatre Royal orchestra in Edinburgh. There are ample indications that oral ballads were still being sung in landowning families up to 1780. Very many folk-fiddlers could read and write musical notation, to judge from the hundreds of their surviving manuscripts.

Scottish folk music of the seventeenth century, when authentically performed, tends to disappoint present-day audiences: it sounds less Scottish, more like English and European Renaissance music, than they expect. Occasionally rationalizations for this are sought (surviving MSS give emasculated, upper-class versions; the true tradition was going on unrecorded among illiterate peasants, etc.); but the truth is that present-day Scots fiddle style was very largely a creation of a later period, 1720–50.

The main cause of this was the importation of the Italian baroque violin into Scotland. During the late seventeenth century the newly redesigned violin became Europe's dominant instrument. When it reached Scotland it took over folk as well as classical music: other hitherto viable folk instruments (recorder, gamba, lute, mandora, Border bagpipe, oboe) were pushed into the background. It also made inroads into the Highlands during the years 1747–82, when the great Highland bagpipe was proscribed as an instrument of war. A curious consequence of this is that Scots fiddle technique, owing to its conservativeness, is now the most authentic survival of Baroque violin playing left anywhere in Europe.

During the 1720s and 1730s experiments were made in incorporating Baroque style into sets of variations on popular tunes: such variations were apparently a traditional type of recital piece, often improvised during performance. The pioneers included Adam Craig, David Young, Charles McLean, James Oswald, and William Forbes of Disblair; but it was McGibbon whose work in this direction (*A Collection of Scots Tunes, Some with Variations*, 3 vols., Edinburgh, 1742, 1746 and 1755) was regarded as definitive. McGibbon solved the problem of modernizing folk music without losing its essence; and his variation sets circulated all over Scotland and became models for the next two generations of composers. Variations continued to develop after McGibbon's death; there are good later examples in Robert Bremner's *Scots Tunes for the Violin* (Edinburgh, 1759) and in James Gillespie's fiddle-book (Perth, 1768; now National Library of Scotland MS.808).

Around 1770 folk music entered a new professional era. The Gow family of Inver, Perthshire, set up a series of dancebands which—with encouragement from the Duke of Atholl—were able to make a full-time living from playing at aristocratic functions all over the country. Previously fiddling at dances had been part-time, strictly local, and often unpaid. The fiddler/composer William Marshall achieved similar renown through the patronage of the Duke of Gordon, and other fiddlers (Alexander McGlashan, Robert Mackintosh, Daniel Dow) attempted to follow their lead. A simple way of attracting patrons' attention to one's talents was to compose new dance-tunes with dedications (e.g. 'Lord Carron's Strathspey'). By the end of the century such short, slick pieces had become indispensible tools for professional success, and had replaced the long variation sets as folk music's major genre.

Scottish church music during the period followed a separate pattern, and was influenced by folk and classical music only indirectly. It was strongly centred around the Metrical Psalter, regarded at the time as a holy book of almost equal importance to the Bible.

As a result of the Reformation, the main parish churches in the Lowlands had been provided with professional choirs. These choirs were supplied by local publicly-run music schools; in 1635—as is shown by the collection *The Psalmes of David* published in Edinburgh that year—their repertory consisted of some 200 unaccompanied psalm-settings, many of them in intricate contrapuntal arrangements. After 1635, however, church music declined rapidly. In 1650 a new psalter was printed giving all the psalms in standard common metre, so that a wide variety of tunes was no longer necessary; many burgh music schools closed; due to the lack of trained musicians, precentors were appointed whose musical talents were minimal. The Church's repertory shrank to a mere 12 tunes, all in common metre; and by 1700 most parishes were singing psalms unharmonized, with complex folk-type decorations, in completely uncoordinated rhythm, so that (as Bremner wrote in 1762) 'the People in one Seat had sung out the Line, before another had half done'. This 'heterophonic' style of singing became established throughout Scotland, and acquired religious associations for participants.

From 1722, however, the Episcopal Church adopted English church-music models and began to install organs and re-form choirs; and during the 1750s a piece of enterprise by an Aberdeenshire landowner, Sir Archibald Grant of Monymusk, had far-reaching consequences.

Grant disliked heterophonic singing and decided to stamp it out on his estate. In 1753 he had an English private, Thomas Channon, discharged from the army to become Scotland's first full-time choir-trainer in the Monymusk parish. Channon's success was so spectacular that on 2 January 1755 he was invited to bring his combined Monymusk choirs, totalling 70 members, to Aberdeen to give a public demonstration. Following this, Aberdeen Town Council appointed Channon to a new post of burgh choir-master; Glasgow created a parallel post the same year and appointed Thomas Moore from Manchester; Edinburgh followed suit in 1756 with Cornforth Gilson from Durham. Soon parish-church choirs had become a new fashion; in consequence, the Church of Scotland introduced modern English hymn-tunes into its services.

By 1800 heterophonic singing had been thoroughly discredited. It continued for some time, however, as part of family prayers in private houses (see the description of psalms as 'wild warbling measures' in Burns's 'Cotter's Saturday Night') and was still current in the Highlands in the nineteenth century. Even nowadays, it may still occasionally be heard in the Outer Hebrides.

D. Johnson

Music in the Nineteenth and Twentieth Centuries. A summary account of any period of history such as this is inevitably selective and mainly concerned with trends which in the retrospective view are seen to have been influential. Pride of achievement in the Scottish scene is no less a feature of the national character than elsewhere but an unacceptable degree of special pleading would be necessary to claim lasting importance for Scottish musical activity in the first eight decades of the nineteenth century. This was a barren period and no work composed, nor any organization primarily concerned with the performance of music, has endured. Dominating the circumstances of life was the shift from agriculture to industry with the accompanying concentration of population in the cities, most notably in Glasgow and surrounding areas. The pursuit of material prosperity did not at the same time accommodate nor encourage musical composition as an expression of the national spirit. There were no worthy successors to McGibbon and Erskine, whose contributions seemed to hold so much promise in the eighteenth century. Only the national song, as instanced by such publications as George Thomson's *Select Collection of Original Scottish Airs* (1793–1841), prevailed against the too ready acceptance of foreign importations. No facilities existed to encourage native composers. The Scottish Church was adamantly opposed to music as an enrichment of its services and unlike the Episcopalian, Roman Catholic and Congregational minorities, resisted the use of the organ until as late as 1873. Nor was any formal training in music available: although General John Reid made possible the founding of the Reid Chair of Music in 1839 internal wranglings delayed the establishment of degree courses at Edinburgh for 50 years. About the same time the Glasgow Athenaeum School of Music (eventually to become the Royal Scottish Academy of Music and Drama) was founded.

Despite lack of encouragement a few composers continued to assert themselves and notably among them the short-lived John Thomson (1803–41) first of the Edinburgh Reid Professors. Resistance to academic recognition of music did not inhibit the organizing of annual memorial concerts as stipulated in General Reid's will. The first of these, in 1841, presented a long and in our eyes amorphous collection of large and small-scale instrumental and vocal works by 20 composers, among them Thomson himself who contributed an overture and a chorus. In a less restrictive environment his influence could perhaps have been more lasting: the overture to his opera *Hermann or The Broken Spear* dated 1834 (Reid Library) shows ability in writing an extended piece, responsive to the example of late eighteenth and early nineteenth-century European composers.

The last two decades of the nineteenth century provide more of interest. At this time Alexander Campbell Mackenzie (1847–1935) came into prominence as one of the three leading figures in the British musical renaissance. Mackenzie's contribution was not confined to Scotland and in his lifetime his influence approached in importance that of both the Irishman Charles Villiers Stanford (1852–1924) and the Englishman Hubert Parry (1848–1918). It is significant that Mackenzie's major appointment was that of Principal of the Royal Academy of Music in London: no equivalent post existed in Scotland. Of Mackenzie's vast corpus of compositions, at one time widely performed throughout Britain, only the Scottish Piano Concerto (1897) and one or two other works are still given occasional performances. The *Second Scotch Rhapsody* op. 24 for example indicates a national awareness absent from the compositions of John Thomson.

A more lasting reminder of Mackenzie's influence is seen in the work of William Wallace, Learmont Drysdale, Hamish MacCunn and John Blackwood McEwen, all born in the 1860s. They followed Mackenzie's lead in acknowledging the importance of their Scottish heritage. Wallace (1860–1940), proficient both in medicine and music was an engaging character who after 1918 confined his attention to music. He settled in London and like Mackenzie joined the teaching staff of the Royal Academy of Music. As an author he is worth reading for very personal views expressed in *The Threshold of Music* (1908) and *The Musical Faculty* (1914). In composition his main importance lies in six symphonic poems: the last of these, *François Villon*, is an accomplished and rewarding example of original creative thought deserving of more attention than the occasional performance it now receives. Learmont Drysdale (1866–1909) was also committed to two disciplines and at the age of 21 deserted architecture for music. In the later years of his short life he chose to leave London for a professional career of teaching and composing in his native land. His Overture *Tam o'Shanter* was awarded the Glasgow Society of Musicians prize in 1890: 30 years later the score was published by the Carnegie United Kingdom Trust: neither this nor any other work remains in the orchestral repertory. Hamish MacCunn (1868–1916) has fared a little better. His concert Overture *The Land of the Mountain and the Flood*, written at the early age of 19, has in recent years become widely known through regular broadcasts by the BBC Scottish Symphony Orchestra, a recording by the Scottish National Orchestra and the use of its main themes in a BBC television series. MacCunn's stature as a composer was enhanced when the Carl Rosa Opera Company commissioned the opera *Jeannie Deans*—the libretto based on Scott's *The Heart of Midlothian*. The first performance in Edinburgh (1894) was a tangible acknowledgement of the changing circumstances of Scottish musical life. Even so, the fourth of the composers of this transitional period, John Blackwood McEwen (1868–1948) spent most of his life in London. He followed Mackenzie as Principal of the Royal Academy of Music. In composition he remained active throughout his life. The large-scale symphonies and choral works have not survived but the chamber music, notably some of the 16 string quartets, is still heard in recital programmes. McEwen deserves respect for an adventurous attitude to composition at a time when there was little response in Britain to radical departures on the European mainland. At the age of 75 he showed remarkable resilience in setting 14 poems by Margaret Forbes for inflected voice and piano. It is fitting that he should be remembered in the regular series of McEwen Memorial Concerts of Scottish Chamber Music which his

generous bequest to the University of Glasgow has made possible.

Two other notable personalities were influential between the world wars, Donald Francis Tovey and William Gillies Whittaker respectively Professors of Music at Edinburgh and Glasgow Universities. Tovey, through his scholarly writings and teaching opened up new horizons to his students and brought a wider perspective to the study and performance of the classical and romantic repertory. Whittaker's personality was equally stimulating in the role of teacher and accompanying this was a dedicated commitment to the music of J.S. Bach; his editions, perceptive commentaries and the performances he directed were fundamental to a new appraisal of the church cantatas. Both were active as composers, Tovey being remembered for the cello concerto he wrote for Casals and the opera *The Bride of Dionysus* and Whittaker mainly for many choral settings of his native Northumbrian folk-music.

Of the three composers who resolutely advanced the cause of Scottish music in the later decades of McEwen's life only Francis George Scott (1880–1958) has maintained some contact with British audiences. Both Ian Whyte (1901–60) and Erik Chisholm (1904–65) are now very rarely performed: they are, however, still remembered for their lasting influence in other matters. Whyte was BBC Scotland's long-serving and indefatigable first Director of Music and Conductor (and founder) of the BBC's Scottish Orchestra. Chisholm was zealous in promoting performances of little-known masterpieces of the past and a wide range of contemporary European music. Neither was able to come to terms with acceptable and enduring twentieth-century attitudes to composition. In the case of Whyte instinct and intuition were not matched by equally sound intellectual processes; his compositional thought was basically improvisatory. Chisholm's creative force was also inhibited: he never arrived at a truly viable and consistent idiom, which could accommodate a fluent inventive capacity. Scott attempted less than his two younger compatriots and in the outcome his concentration on song has been more rewarding. Within the limits of his imaginative and expressive resource he makes a profound impression in many settings of Scottish poetry of the sixteenth to twentieth centuries. Reference is made elsewhere in this volume to the extensive lists of compositions of these and other composers mentioned (qq.v.).

A further potent development in most aspects of the Scottish cultural scene began around the year 1950. It was now possible to be more outward-looking and to assert with a measure of confidence that artistic events in Scotland, both creative and promotional, could attract attention in Great Britain and beyond. Central to this post-war initiative was the remarkable vision and enterprise of the founders of the Edinburgh International Festival, the courageous if belated decision to establish the Scottish National Orchestra on a full-time basis and the increasing repute of the BBC's Scottish Symphony Orchestra. In the decade before 1960 these three organizations together stimulated awareness that the experience of music could also embrace rich and rewarding international resources. Supplementing their efforts were those of the many chamber music societies, music clubs and competition festivals throughout the country. The training of musicians was also given greater impetus in the expansion of Departments of Music in the universities of Edinburgh, Glasgow, Aberdeen and St Andrews and on the more practical side, in the Royal Scottish Academy of Music. Essential preparation for entry to these establishments was provided by courses of music instruction in the primary and secondary schools leading to Ordinary and Higher certificates of proficiency.

Not unexpectedly composers in Scotland began to respond to these changing circumstances although not until the next decade did this become very evident. An innovation which Sir John Blackwood McEwen's generous bequest made possible and of which he would certainly have approved was the scheme of annual and triennial McEwen Commissions and Memorial Concerts of Scottish Chamber Music first promoted by the University of Glasgow in 1954. At a time when commissions to composers were rarely given anywhere in Britain this scheme was unique in fostering creative activity on a continuing basis. The cultural impetus of the post-war years was given further shape and purpose by the founding of Scottish Opera in 1962. This remarkable act of faith and enterprise has proved to be the most influential artistic innovation in Scotland of recent years. It is certain that neither Alexander Gibson the prime mover, nor those associated with him could have foreseen that this venture would so quickly achieve international status and acclaim.

About this time an appointment significant for the welfare of Scottish music was that of Watson Forbes as BBC Head of Music, Scotland. His extensive experience in chamber music and the practicalities of the London music scene enabled him to generate extensive interest in contemporary music with a special regard for that of Scottish composers. In the encouragement given to a younger generation of composers, among them Thomas Wilson, David Gwilt, Sebastian Forbes, David Dorward and Martin Dalby, he added extra impetus to what was being achieved through the McEwen bequest. The Edinburgh Festival also gave support in this direction with the promotion of such works as William Wordsworth's Fourth Symphony (1953) a festival commission and Iain Hamilton's Sinfonia for Two Orchestras jointly commissioned by the Festival and the Burns' Federation. Equally active in commissioning Scottish composers was the Scottish National Orchestra but of even greater consequence was their Musica Viva performance of Stockhausen's Gruppen for three orchestras in St Andrews Hall, Glasgow (soon to be destroyed by fire and a disastrous and continuing restriction on large-scale orchestral enterprises). The performance of Gruppen—the British première—marked consolidation of post-war attitudes and was evidence that the overall perspective of Scottish music differed only in scale from that of London and other centres in England.

Much had happened therefore since 1950. Facilities in Scotland for the performance of new music and the encouragement given to native composers became the envy of those less fortunately placed in other parts of Great Britain. Musica Nova was established in 1971 by the Scottish National Orchestra (now the Royal Scottish National Orchestra) (q.v.) and Glasgow University to promote interest in new music, national and international and during that decade performances were given of major works by numerous leading composers, many of them commissions. Earlier in 1968 the Scottish Music Archive (now called the Scottish Music Information Centre) was brought into being by Glasgow University with the support of many organizations and institutions throughout the country, its object, similar to that of Donemus of Holland, to provide for the documentation, study and where not otherwise available, performance material of Scottish music of all periods. A flood of commissions benefited the growing corpus of composers native to or resident in Scotland. Few of these would have been possible nor would the granting agencies have continued to flourish without the financial support of the Scottish Arts Council, an organization with major responsibility, through the very large sums at its disposal, for sustaining vital aspects of the cultural scene. Additional support, on a lesser scale, was given by other public bodies: for example, to the Edinburgh Festival, Scottish National Orchestra and Scottish Opera by major cities, districts and regions. A later and welcome extension was the support of commerce and industry, usually tied to large-scale opera productions and works of the orchestral repertory requiring augmented resources. At the time of going to press, an independent review of the music provision in Scotland is under way: this will determine, amongst other things, the future shape of two of Scotlands' orchestras, the BBC Scottish Symphony Orchestra and the Scottish Opera Orchestra.

Smaller organizations also played an important role in the decade that followed. Pride of place went to the Scottish Philharmonic Society with its tripartite responsibility for the Scottish Baroque Ensemble, Scottish Chamber Orchestra and Scottish Philharmonia. Later, smaller in size but no less active in their specialized commitments were the Haddo House Choral Society, the New Music Group of Scotland, the Edinburgh Quartet, the John Currie Singers, Cantilena, the National Youth String Orchestra of Scotland, the National Youth Orchestra of Scotland, the Scottish Early Music Consort, the Paragon Ensemble, Capella Nova, Scottish Ensemble, Hebrides Ensemble, The Sinfonia of Scotland, and numerous festivals, societies, clubs and individual artists. In the educational field provision was made for the training of exceptionally talented young musicians in St Mary's Music School, Edinburgh.

A high degree of musical activity cannot be regarded as entirely satisfactory unless the art of composition is a contributory factor. At the present time composers in Scotland would appear to be favourably placed and yet they suffer, as do their fellows in other countries, from very limited appreciation by audiences in the opera house, concert hall and recital room. Nevertheless a tangible reminder of the stimulating natural environment enjoyed by composers living in Scotland was given by the decision of Peter Maxwell Davies to settle in Orkney.

Since the beginning of the twentieth century the practice of composition in Scotland has come a long way and has become increasingly responsive to influences from abroad. Scottish composers have been keen to make up lost ground in utilizing the expensive resources of electronic music available in studios in Glasgow and Edinburgh.

Even so, the list of works in the Scottish Music Information Centre's latest catalogue of Printed and Manuscript Music (1993) provides evidence of wide-ranging creative commitment: in the opera and symphonic sphere Hamilton, Musgrave, Orr, Wilson and Harper have contributed major works of impressive range and extent. Other leading composers, notably Wordsworth, Leighton, Stevenson, Dorward, Dalby, Forbes, McGuire, McLeod and Geddes have written for orchestral and choral forces of varying sizes with equal success. All mentioned have also been engaged in the field of chamber (and solo instrumental) music, together with Crawford, Spedding, Purser, Paterson, Hearne, Weir and Sweeney. Composers of a younger generation are also energetic: Macmillan, Dillon, Lunn and MacQueen. They will be helped however by the realization that the climate in which they are working differs vastly from that of the early pioneers of twentieth-century development.

F. Rimmer

Music, Shetland

General. Selections from the many traditional Shetland fiddle tunes are often heard today on the radio, although traditional songs number a meagre dozen. A post-war renaissance, with composing and recording almost commonplace and new music often reaching publication, has put Shetland music on the map.

To clarify the picture we must first look into the remote past, contrasting Shetland's little legacy with the rich inheritance of two island groups, environmentally similar, also under Norse domination for centuries.

Any claim to a distinct culture in song implies distinct language or dialect. With Scottish infiltration well before the 1469 separation from Norway, Old Norn was declining by 1500. Except in the remoter islands Shetlanders were mostly bilingual by 1600. 'By 1700 Scots was universal, with Norn lingering on till about 1750.'

In Foula, 1774, Low wrote down the Hildina folk-ballad, 35 four-line verses, significantly 'the most entire' surviving. Old Norn was dying.

In Faroe, 1770, Svabo began writing down the traditional folk-ballads. Later over 200 were published, 44,000 stanzas, all this during the harsh operation of the Danish trading monopoly. Faroe emerged bilingual.

Elsewhere the bagpipe, 'Instrument of War' proscribed since 1746, skirled defiance. The Gaelic, having five centuries earlier survived Norse occupation, was again surviving. By 1921 Mrs Kennedy-Frazer's three volumes had merely scratched the surface of 'Songs of the Hebrides'.

Shetland, without a language, found literary expression slowly. Ellis, in 1889, thought Shetland speech too new 'to be a true dialect'. Linguistic insecurity was coupled with oppres-

sive insecurity in crofting life. But the Crofters' Act was at last curbing Shetland's worst tyranny for three centuries. Perhaps as a consequence of this, the next decade saw publications on Shetland folklore, history, antiquities; two collections contained superb long poems, 'Scranna' hilarious yet philosophic, 'Mansie's Crü' lyrically contemplative. The Shetland dialect was alive.

Shetland had not been without music. Ar. Edmonston had earlier praised various musical accomplishments including composition. A touring minister 'everywhere praised the compass and sweetness of the voices'. But the poet who addressed his hard-toiled mother: 'a' da sang du ever sang/Wis 'Hushy Ba' ta me' probably spoke, as poets do, for many others.

In 1944 music-teacher Jean Boyd organized Shetland's First Music Festival, and a Folk Music Concert, an 'outstanding success'. Next year the Folk Society was formed, prime inspiration Neil Matherson's, to promote conservation and creativity. Earlier collecting had ranged from, say, the Smith/Sutherland Unst fiddle tunes to any scrap of doubtful sol-fa which would yet start a trail.

In June 1946 *Country Magazine* featured the BBC's first live Shetland fiddling and folk-songs. In 1947 clear choice from various 'firsts' is the Shetland Folk Book, the main repository since for folklore and music. Adjudicating at that year's festival, Kenneth Roberton could announce 'something like a musical revolution in these islands.'

After revolution, the slow consolidation was to bring other remarkable 'firsts': the now indispensible Fiddlers' Society, their founder-leader Tom Anderson, active throughout since his de-mob.; his county scheme of instruction in traditional playing; repatriate Mrs Robertson's unique collaboration with her poet husband in compiling our treasured song-book. Who better than they to 'put on some detail' as we forecast the future with assurance?

J.R.S. Clark

Fiddle Music. The violin, generally referred to as the fiddle, is the traditional instrument of Shetland. It seems to have come to Shetland either from Scotland or from the Continent of Europe about 1700.

Shetland fiddle music may be divided broadly into three categories: listening tunes, ritual tunes (weddings etc.) and dance music. The older Shetland fiddle music was very Norse in character, and some of the old tunes like 'The Muckle Reel of Finnigarth', 'The Silver Bow', 'The Day Dawn' have their roots in the Hardanger fiddle music of Norway.

The wedding tunes also have their counterparts in Norway, and such melodies as 'The West Side Bride's March' are similar in construction to Hardanger fiddle music used for the same purpose.

Music for dancing was mainly reels, and 6/8 traditional melodies are in the minority. The reel probably came in from Scotland early in the eighteenth century, and the earliest Shetland reel composition we have found is dated 1759. Little or nothing of the music was written down previous to 1800 and transmission was oral.

Tunes were exchanged by fiddlers travelling from district to district in the course of their various trades, and at weddings where fiddlers from different places would play together and listen to each other.

The technique of playing the Shetland fiddle is quite distinctive, and follows more the style of the Hardanger fiddle than either Scottish or Irish, although there are some similarities with the latter. The playing of two or more strings at one time with open strings ringing, combined with bowing techniques of one note down and three up gives the music a special sound. In some melodies the fiddle tuning is scordatura, the G string raised to A, and the D string raised to E as in the tuning of the Hardanger fiddle.

The technique of Scottish strathspey playing was not known by most Shetland fiddlers until the first quarter of this century, and strathspeys brought to Shetland were played in reel time for the dance 'The Shetland Reel', and in many cases retitled with local names.

Several collections of tunes have been made during the last 50 years and with the coming of the tape-recorder many of the older fiddlers have been recorded. The Shetland Folk Society and the Shetland Fiddlers Society play the music regularly, and traditional fiddle music is now being taught in many schools in Shetland.

Fiddle music is being composed by many Shetland musicians at the present time, and several books of tunes have been published. The Shetland Folk Society have published a good cross-section of traditional melodies, and the present writer is compiling a book for teaching purposes. Several gramophone records are now available of traditional players, and in recent years a number of overseas students have travelled to Shetland for tuition by the present writer.

An interesting change in the popularity of the fiddle today is that it now has become more of a listening instrument rather than for dancing, and this has led to the composition of many slow airs.

T. Anderson

Songs, *Traditional*. The Unst Boat Song is the only surviving example of a traditional tune with Old Norn words. (A dialect phrase occurs where the original Norn has been lost.) The opening line, 'Starka Virna Vestilie', has been translated as 'A strong wind is blowing from the west'.

Not surprisingly, traditional dialect songs include lullabies. These were often sung to the rhythm of the spinning-wheel. The lullaby 'Baloo-Balilli', known also as 'The Bressay Lullaby' is familiar to audiences throughout Scotland.

'Minnie o Shirva's Cradle Sang', a lullaby in slow, rocking rhythm, recalls for the drowsy child some of the events, sights and sounds common to the daily round of crofting life.

Work at the spinning wheel has often been accompanied by song. 'Da Delting Spinning Sang' is a well-known example, with lively words and music. Another spinning song is 'Da Norrawa Wheel', with thoughts which follow dreamily the progress of 'da treed' (the thread) until 'da sweerie' (the box holding the pirns) 'foo' (full) 'is gotten aa'.

Of other traditional songs, probably the best known are 'Boannie Tammie Scolla', 'In a Moarneen o Mey, O', and 'Da Shaalds o Foula'.

These songs are all included in 'Da Sangs at A'll Sing ta Dee', edited by T.A. Robertson and published by the Shetland Folk Society shortly before his death in 1973.

Words have sometimes been added to traditional tunes. 'The Galley Song', which is sung at the Norse festival Up-Helly-Aa, has a traditional Norwegian tune, with words by John Nicolson.

Modern. The song book referred to contains nearly 50 dialect songs written during the last 100 years. Eight of these songs have words by Vagaland, set to music by six different composers. 'Da Sang o da Papa Men' and 'Da Rabbit's Lullaby' are well known. The latter was made familiar, when she was only six years old, by Shirley Peterson, whose singing endeared her to TV and radio audiences. The tune of 'Stoorbra Hill' (another popular song) was composed by Tom Georgeson, the words being added by Vagaland.

Since the publication of the collected poems of Vagaland in 1975 further local talent has provided music for more of his lyrics. There are now some 18 songs in all, enough to make a collection.

The work of other Shetland poets has produced such spirited songs as 'Gyaain ta da Far Haaf', 'Da Twinin o't' and 'Farewell to Yell', and, by contrast, lullabies like 'Shetland Lullaby', 'Isles Asleep' and 'Baain da Bairn'.

Song writers who composed both words and music are Sinclair Shewan and John Barclay. The former wrote 'The Fetlar Lullaby', which has a permanent place in Shetland song. The latter's most popular compositions are 'Da Isles o Gletness' and the humorous 'Whaur da Green Girse Growes'.

Love poems like 'Dee and Me' (G.P.S. Peterson) and 'Simmer Sang' (Vagaland) used the dialect so effectively that they were 'songs' in their own right even before music was added, and, if it is accepted that in song-writing the lyric has equal importance with the music, the requirement seems to be met in most of these Shetland songs.

M. Robertson

N

Nairne, Lady Baroness Carolina (1766–1845) was born Carolina Oliphant at Gask, Perthsire, where she grew up to become known as 'The Flower of Strathearn'. She married Major Nairne, her second cousin, in 1806. After the reversal of attainder, he became the fifth Lord Nairne. On his death, she travelled widely on the Continent, finally settling in the new house of Gask ('the auld hoose' of her song, in the meantime, having been pulled down).

Of her 87 songs, many first appeared in *The Scottish Minstrel*, an important collection edited in Paisley by R.A. Smith (1790–1829).

Lady Nairne's songs possess neither Burns's depth of perception nor his passion, but her devotion to the lost cause of Jacobitism inspired her to touch a heartfelt tone in that most moving of all non-Gaelic laments for that which has gone, and gone for ever, 'Will ye no come back again?' Indeed, her cry for the return of the Prince over the Water in some strange way articulates the overtones of modern Scotland's restless search for her lost identity whenever the song is sung communally. Her other successes include 'The Rowan Tree', 'The Auld Hoose', 'The Land o' the Leal', 'Caller Herrin', 'The Hundred Pipers' and 'The Laird o' Cockpen', making her, after Burns, by far Scotland's most enduringly popular songwriter.

M. Lindsay

Nasmyth, Alexander (1758–1840) was primarily a Scottish landscape painter, he also executed portraits and stage scenery and occasionally practised as an architect and engineer. His landscapes hold a position midway between the eighteenth-century Picturesque tradition and the Romantic approach of the nineteenth century. He lived mostly in Scotland. His father was a master builder in Edinburgh who sent him to the Royal High School. He afterwards attended the drawing school of the Board of Trustees. From 1774–78 he was in London as assistant to the Scottish painter Allan Ramsay. On returning to Edinburgh Nasmyth specialized in cabinet-size portraits and family conversation pieces in both indoor and outdoor settings. Amongst his early patrons was Patrick Miller of Dalswinton for whom he painted a family group and made mechanical drawings in connection with Miller's interest in steam navigation. Miller financed a visit to Italy in 1782. Whilst in Rome Nasmyth copied a landscape by Claude; his determination to specialize in landscape dates from this period. By 1785 Nasmyth was back in Edinburgh. Failing to get the Mastership of the Trustees' Academy, he resumed portraiture which increasingly gave way to pure landscape.

By 1786 he had met Robert Burns, they visited Roslin Castle together and in the following year Nasmyth painted the poet's portrait. In 1788 they were amongst the passengers on the first voyage of Miller's steamboat on Dalswinton Loch.

Nasmyth married Barbara Foulis of Woodhall in 1786. Their first son Patrick, the landscape painter, was born the following year, the eldest of four sons and six surviving daughters. All the girls practised landscape painting taught by their father. James, the youngest child, was the inventor of the steam hammer and a competent amateur artist. Nasmyth built himself a house at 47, York Place, Edinburgh and opened a successful drawing school where he taught, assisted by his daughters.

Nasmyth's outdoor sketches reveal his fresh approach to nature, but he also used miniature models of trees and buildings to aid composition in the studio. His fine views of Edinburgh and the surrounding countryside are surpassed by his landscapes in the West of Scotland and Perthshire, where lochs, wooded shores and distant mountains lent themselves best to his Claudian methods of composing. Nasmyth was prepared to paint landscapes in the studio working from sketches made on the spot, either by himself or members of his family. This accounts for the continuing appearance of Italian scenes amongst his exhibited works. However he also painted with close reference to nature. Four views on Kintyre show his sensitivity to local weather and light conditions, revealing his Romantic tendencies. From about 1810 open vistas tend to give way to more enclosed scenes of steep-sided glens, often with waterfalls, influenced by Dutch seventeenth-century landscapes.

Nasmyth breathed new life into the painting of views of Scottish country seats. He also had a hand in the picturesque layout of the grounds of some of his wealthier patrons, including Lord Bredalbane at Taymouth and the Duke of Argyll at Inverary. His best known structure however is a circular classical temple, known as St Bernard's Well, set beside the Water of Leith, Edinburgh.

Nasmyth provided illustrations for Sir Walter Scott's *Border Antiquities and Provincial Antiquities*. A few sketches for his stage designs survive, including six sets for *The Heart of Midlothian* at the Edinburgh Theatre. His famous act-scene for the Theatre Royal, Glasgow, was of a view down the Clyde towards Dumbarton Castle. He exhibited regularly in Edinburgh and occasionally in London at the Royal Academy and the British Institution.

F. Irwin

National Mod, The, is the facet of the Gaelic movement that is most widely known about. This moveable festival of Gaelic music and literature (with ancillary exhibitions of crafts, recitals of pipe-music, fiddlers' rallies etc.) is run by An Comunn Gaidhealach/The Highland Association, a pressure-group for the Gaelic language founded in 1891, and now having its headquarters at Abertarff House, Inverness, offices in Glasgow, Oban and Stornoway, and branches throughout Scotland, with some English outliers also. The first National Mod was held in Oban in 1892, with 10 competitions, 50 competitors, and a running time of three hours. Now it is liable to last a week, with a very large number of competitors. The competitions are literary (short stories, poetry, essays, playlets), oral (speeches, recitations, conversations) and musical (solos, duets, quartettes, choral competitions, clarsach, piano, violin, recorder playing, piping). The character of the festival is mainly musical, with standards that can be quite high particularly for choral and top solo events. The Mod Medallists (one of each sex) make annual news, and some go on to fruitful singing careers. The earliest famous medallist was Roderick MacLeod in 1894. Between 1930 and 1961 the top place in the major choral event was taken by one of three choirs: Campbeltown, Greenock and Glasgow Gaelic Musical Association, but there are numerous choirs, large and small, competing. The first crowned bard was James Thomson in 1923. A network of Provincial Mods supplements the work of the National Mod.

An Comunn Gaidhealach is deeply involved in other activities of an educational and propagandist kind, but its Mod is likely to continue to capture headlines. It could with profit streamline its range of competitions, and give more emphasis to quality recitals and the sponsorship of new musical work, both vocal and instrumental.

D.S. Thomson

Newspapers. The first newspaper to be published in Scotland is believed to have been an Edinburgh reprint of the London *Diurnal Occurrances, Touching the dailie proceedings in Parliament from the 27 of December to the third of Januarie, 1642.* The Parliamentary proceedings referred to concerned the struggle then taking place between Charles I and Parliament.

No newspaper is known to have survived the next turbulent years of civil strife in Scotland until the *Mercurius Scoticus* appeared in Leith in July, 1651 just weeks before the defeat of the Scots army at Worcester. This defeat forced Charles II to flee into exile and placed Scotland under the government of Cromwell. The weekly *Mercurius Scoticus* was suppressed by the English commissioners and the next newspapers issued from Leith were reprints of London papers, such as the *Diurnall of Some Passages and Affairs*; the *Mercurius Politicus*; the *Faithfull Intelligencer from the Parliament's Army in Scotland* of 1659 which advocated General Monk's policy of restoring Charles II.

The Restoration took place in 1660 and in January 1661 the appearance of the *Mercurius Caledonius*, edited by a Scotsman, Thomas Sydserf, and published by some Edinburgh booksellers, marks the real beginning of the Scottish newspaper press. But it was short-lived and control was again imposed by the Government through the Scottish Privy Council, a body which was abolished in 1708. *The Kingdoms Intelligencer of the affairs now in agitation in Scotland, England and Ireland, together with foreign intelligence*, also founded in 1661, survived until possibly 1668. 1680 saw the first issue of the *Edinburgh Gazette*. It was not issued again until 1699, after the Revolution and, although undergoing many variations in title, survives to this day in altered form. The first *Edinburgh Courant* appeared in 1705. The relaxation of censorship with the abolition of the Privy Council in 1708 allowed more liberal ideas to prevail which slowly encouraged the free expression of opinion. The *Edinburgh Evening Courant* appeared in 1718, the *Caledonian Mercury* in 1720; both were leading Edinburgh newspapers and flourished until 1859 and 1886 respectively.

The embryo newspaper had other difficulties with which to contend from the reign of Queen Anne. Paper was heavily taxed so newspapers were small, usually four pages; newspapers themselves were subject to a stamp tax and, in 1712, a tax was levied on newspapers which carried advertisements.

The news purveyed in these early papers comprised 'meagre tidings of what had happened long before, or never happened at all'. The seat of government had passed to London, 12 days' journey by stage-coach which, until 1754, ran once a month. The postboy on horseback took 10 days but the hazards to letters were considerable. The Edinburgh papers copied news of Parliament from the London papers; local news was scarcely touched on and nearly half the space was devoted to advertisements. Circulation was small: a weekly newspaper cost 2d. at a time when a schoolmaster earned £8 per annum. Nevertheless, newspapers circulated beyond their original subscribers, round the clients of the Edinburgh taverns or from house to house in an entire parish in country districts.

Although Edinburgh was no longer the seat of government after 1707, it was still the seat of the Law and the Church and it had a university, all factors in the great blossoming of Scottish intellectual life which centred on Edinburgh in the eighteenth century and which gave it a central place in the growth of newspaper journalism. But, in the beginning, the literary periodical flourished rather than the newspaper though often the line of demarcation was blurred. The *Scots Magazine* (1739) still included 'news' whilst the *Edinburgh Chronicle* (1759–1760) and the *Edinburgh Advertiser* (1764–1859) contained literary material.

The eighteenth century saw the beginning of the 'provincial' Scottish press. The *Dumfries Mercury* produced at least 18 issues in 1721, but no other paper followed until the *Dumfries Weekly Journal* in 1777, discontinued in 1835. Aberdeen, again a university city, produced the *Aberdeen's Journal* in 1747, which still continues as the *Press & Journal* (Aberdeen). This became the most important paper in the north. A *Dundee Weekly Intelligencer* is believed to have appeared in 1755.

Until roads and bridges could be built or improved, it was impossible to be reliably informed of events in different parts of the country. Until 1749, Glasgow had no regular communication by stage-coach with Edinburgh and not until 1788 with London. The commercial prosperity of Glasgow did not dawn until the middle of the century. There was a short-lived *Glasgow Courant* in 1715–16 and another from 1745–60. Of the five other eighteenth-century Glasgow newspapers, only two did not outlast the century. The *Glasgow Advertiser* (1783) became the *Glasgow Herald* in 1805 and so continues; the *Glasgow Journal* ran from 1741–1846 and the *Glasgow Courier* from 1791–1866.

As the century advanced, reporting of local news gradually increased and correspondence was included. The growing demand for electoral reform and some relaxation of the laws against Catholics were reflected, although only tentatively, in the 10 newspapers then extant. Impetus for expansion was given by the French Revolution. For example, the *Kelso Chronicle* (1783–1803) seems to have had radical leanings and the *Kelso Mail* (1797; amalgamated with the *Chronicle* of 1832 in 1949) was founded in opposition. Newspapers appeared in Greenock (1802), Ayr (1803), Inverness (1807), Perth (1809) and Montrose (1811).

The excesses of the French Revolution led radicalism or mere criticism of the Government to be regarded as sedition but after 1815 the danger of war passed and domestic matters came to the forefront again. *The Scotsman* was founded in 1817 in opposition to the existing Tory papers in Edinburgh. It carried as an innovation a leading article which influenced the development of other papers. Newspapers were founded in other centres: the *Stirling Journal* (1820–1970); the *Stirling Observer* (1836) is still extant; in Cupar, the *Fife Herald* began in 1822; the *Paisley Advertiser* (1824–1850) and the *Elgin Courier* (1827–1834).

The Scottish newspapers still copied from the London papers but now they began to copy from each other. Advertisements still occupied a great part of the space but matters of Scottish interest were now being discussed, and there was the beginning of an interest in matters concerning progress in science, philosophy and the arts.

By mid-century the daily newspaper had made its appearance. The *North British Daily Mail* began in Glasgow in April 1847 and ran until amalgamated with the still current *Daily Record* in 1901. The electric telegraph came into operation in 1845 and railways from 1848 made communications throughout the country easier. Newspapers now employed agents in different parts of the country to send back news. But it was not until the abolition of Stamp Duty in 1855 that the newspaper was able to expand beyond the usual four pages. Two years earlier, the duty on papers carrying advertisements had been abolished and in 1861, the last shackle, the duty on paper, was removed. The number of papers increased, both in the main centres and in the smaller places where now newspapers appeared for the first time. By the end of the century, technical improvements had brought about a reduction in the cost of newsprint and the Education Act of 1872 an expansion of the reading public.

A phenomenon of the last two decades has been the proliferation of the 'free' newspaper, delivered to every house in the neighbourhood. These papers carry mainly advertisements although most contain informative local news.

The growth in recent years of social history studies, including family history, has led to the newspaper of the past being regarded as an essential source for researchers. Unfortunately, the cheap newsprint of the last hundred years, made of wood pulp, was not made to last. With age it turns brown and brittle and disintegrates. Scottish libraries were in the van in the conservation field when, in 1956, the Scottish Central Library (now part of the National Library of Scotland) produced a list of titles held in Scottish libraries and encouraged them to acquire microfilm copies of their local titles not in stock. The list was updated in 1984 and included publishers' holdings and Scottish titles held in the British Library Newspaper Library at Colindale, south of the Border. An appeal was started by the National Library to raise money to allow it to set up a microfilm unit to microfilm to archival standards those files most at risk. The problem is not unique to Scotland and the British Library has now instituted its 'Newsplan' programme to preserve all British local newspapers. Indeed, for a variety of reasons, the British Library has a more comprehensive collection of Scottish titles than any source in Scotland. The Newsplan project for Scotland is being administered by the Scottish Library and Information Council.

In 1981 there were 162 Scottish newspapers. In 1993 there are now 150, including the 'free' papers. Publishers number 32—of that figure most publish from 2 to 6 titles; the largest group is Scottish & Universal Ltd of Irvine with 32. Control of *The Scotsman* has passed to the international Thomson Corporation, the *Daily Record* and the *Sunday Mail* to the Mirror Group Newspapers.

J.P.S. Ferguson

Northern Isles, The, form two distinct island groups: the Orkneys, lying a few miles north of the Scottish mainland, and Shetland, lying 50 miles beyond the northernmost of the Orkney group. Although always associated, the two archipelagos differ in many ways, but both have throughout their history been sought as valuable settlement and trading places. This is as true in the 1970s with the exploitation of North Sea oil resources as it was in the third millenium BC. The visible results of their desirable position can be seen in the prehistoric monuments which cover these islands: more per square mile it is said than in any other part of Britain.

One of the best preserved of man's earliest settled community dwelling-sites can be seen in Orkney, where the prehistoric religious and cultural monuments are still impressive enough to awe the modern visitor. The finest Iron Age broch in Scotland lies on a small Shetland isle and the famous St Ninian's hoard of silver vessels and brooches comes from another. The Pictish peoples had a flourishing and cultured society here, to which carved symbol stones bear witness. But it is the Viking association with the islands which gives them a character quite different from any other part of Scotland. Those superlative seamen from Norway found them a most convenient refuge from which to launch their seasonal raids all over Europe from ninth to the eleventh centuries AD, and from where to control the trade routes of the northern seas. The Norsemen quickly imposed their rule and settled on the rich grain lands of Orkney and up the sheltered 'voes' of Shetland. A powerful family of earls emerged during the tenth century who were so famous in the north that they had a saga devoted entirely to their deeds. This work of semi-historical literature was first written down late in the twelfth century (probably in Iceland) but still gives a vivid picture of the life of the ruling caste in Orkney and their internecine struggles for power. The other monument to the fame of the Norse earls is the twelfth-century cathedral of St Magnus in Kirkwall, built by the earldom family to honour one of its members who was slain *c.*1115 by a rival claimant to the earldom.

With the decline of Norway in the late Middle Ages the 'Golden Age' of the Northern Isles came to an end, and the expansionist Stewart kings determined to control this independent earldom off their northern coast. Both James II and James III worked hard to get possession of the islands, which was achieved finally by a marriage alliance with the king of Denmark-Norway in 1468 although Orkney, and in 1469, Shetland, were only pledged as part-payment of the dowry. Theoretically this pledge could be redeemed today. The Northern Isles have continued to be a vital outlying part of Britain in times of war. The wrecks of the German and British fleet in Scapa Flow are as much a reminder of the importance of these islands' geographical position as the monuments of an earlier age.

B.E. Crawford

O

Oliphant, Mrs Margaret (1828–1897) was born at Mussel-burgh as Margaret Wilson, the daughter of James Wilson, and married her cousin, Francis Wilson Oliphant, a stained-glass artist. In 1859 she found herself a widow with three young children to maintain, as well as brothers and a nephew. All her sons showed signs of brilliance, but died while still dependent on her, and her nephew died almost immediately after she had finished paying for his education. She therefore became, at the beginning of her writing career, an indefatigable pen-pusher. Inevitably, some (though not all) of her work suffers from the hasty effects of over-production. 'It has been my fate in a long life of production', she complained in the preface to *The Heir Presumptive and the Heir Apparent* (1892), 'to be credited chiefly with the equivocal virtue of industry, a quality so excellent in morals, so little satisfactory in art.'

She was one of the most talented as well as one of the most loyal members of the Blackwood group, and most of her fiction, as well as much of her biographical writing and her reviewing, first appeared within the pages of *Blackwood's Magazine*.

Her fiction can be broadly divided into two categories: the novels based on Scotland and Scottish manners, and those with an English setting, of which the most famous were those forming *The Chronicles of Carlingford* (1861–66). *Miss Marjoribanks*, the first of them and a minor masterpiece, filling a gap in English fiction by women novelists between Jane Austen and George Eliot (on whose *Middlemarch* Mrs Oliphant seems to have exerted some influence), is her only novel available in a modern edition, edited by Q.D. Leavis. Its central male character, Dr Marjoribanks, is a Scottish medico happily settled in England, while his daughter has 'large Scotch bones' and 'moral solidity', standing in the way of her appreciation of English humour. The novel is in part thus a study of the impact of Scottishness on English rural life.

Mrs Oliphant's Scottish novels—among the best are *Mrs Margaret Maitland* (1849), *A Son of the Soil* (1866) and *Kirsteen*

(1890)—make use of her girlhood memories of her native country, memories she updated and stimulated by frequent return visits long after she had settled in the south, and cater for the interest in Scotland and the Scottish way of life created by Queen Victoria.

Mrs Oliphant was a shrewd observer of character, and many of the *mores* of Victorian society as it existed in Scotland are reflected in her fictional relationships. The middle-class attitude to the advantages of marriage and its worldly prospects are nowhere more tellingly portrayed than in the relationship with mother-approved men experienced by the heroine of *Effie Ogilvie* (1886).

In addition to her many novels and short stories, she produced several biographies, of which by far the finest is her *Life of Edward Irving* (1862), a penetrating study of the secessionist preacher, a gifted and inspired man ultimately betrayed by his own idealism.

Her *Annals of a Publishing House* (1897), the history of Blackwood's, is essential reading for anyone interested in the Scottish literary scene during the nineteenth century, its portraits of Lockhart and Wilson (both of whom she knew) being especially sharp. Her *Autobiography and Letters* have been republished with a modern preface by Q.D. Leavis. They make up a document of compelling human interest, the quality of human goodness they reveal making one think of Southey's letters or Scott's *Journal*, though without reaching the high peaks of public interest reflected in the private musings of the author of *Waverley*.

M. Lindsay

Organs and Organ-building. Throughout recorded musical history and until the late eighteenth century the organ exercised a profound influence. Introduced into the early Christian Church it became the mainstay of musical accompaniment: not until the twelfth century, however, did Scotland figure in this when monastic churches with solemn Catholic ritual became established. First mention of an organ is June 1250 at Dunfermline Abbey. Though the friars turned their attention to organ-building, the earliest known lay organ-builder in Britain—Hugo le Organer—was resident at Dunfermline in AD1303.

During *c.* 1400–1560 the organ exerted special influence on developing musical composition—polyphony and counterpoint. From the time of James I (r. 1406–37) the 'amiable' organ was heard everywhere and instruments of improved design were provided. The first choral foundation, established in 1468 at the Chapel Royal in Stirling Castle, drew foreign musicians. At 1505 there were three pairs of organs in the chapel, maintained by one Gilliam, maker 'Kingis organis'. Further pairs were provided.

At the Scottish Reformation (1560) instrumental music was proscribed and organs removed. After the purging of the Stirling chapel (1571) James VI (r.1566–1625) re-established the Chapel Royal within the palace of Holyroodhouse. In 1617 Thomas Dallam of London installed an organ: this was found derelict in 1643, the General Assembly of the Church having forbidden the use of all musical instruments in worship five years earlier.

At the Revolutionary Settlement of 1689 the Presbyterian Church of Scotland (the 'Kirk') was 'established' by William III. The continued ban on instruments did not, however, apply to the now-disestablished Episcopal Church where the best traditions of music were sustained with ever-increasing demands for organs. As there were no reputable organ-builders in Scotland at this period and until the second decade of the nineteenth century, new instruments were installed by English artisans: the most notable of these was John Snetzler of London. Two of his organs are still intact and in use.

The nineteenth century heralded progressive development in instrumental design: organs continued in demand, especially chamber instruments for concert halls and domestic usage. Several were built by English-trained Scottish craftsmen. Hamiltons of Edinburgh (c.1820–1939) supplied a wealth of instruments: the inventive genius of David Hamilton junior provided the first pneumatic-lever mechanism ever for tracker organs in his 1835 instrument at St John the Evangelist, Edinburgh, adding to it seven years later the first pedal organ in Scotland. Organ-building on a massive scale began with the lifting of the instrumental ban (in 1867) in the Kirk. Thanks to a devotee of organ music—Dunfermline-born Andrew Carnegie—Scotland enjoyed good measure of his generosity from the seven million dollars he gave for some 8,000 organs in Britain and North America.

By 1901 the work of master-builders of the British Romantic Organ school was in evidence in Scotland—William Hill, 'Father' Henry Willis, Thomas Lewis and Arthur Harrison, to mention a few. The twentieth century saw further instruments, much rebuilding to classical/baroque tonal specifications and general restoration, as also the advent of the electronic organ—a debatable poor relation of the 'king of instruments'.

G. Burgess-Winn

Ossian *see* Macpherson and Ossian

Oswald, James (c. 1711–1769) composer and publisher. Born probably in the Stirling area; taught in Dunfermline, 1734–5; resided in Edinburgh, 1736–41; moved to London, 1741; appointed Composer-in-Ordinary to George III, 1761; died Knebworth, Herts.

Oswald's mercurial talent expressed itself in many musical directions. He was, in turn, a dancing-master, composer, editor and publisher, and may also (from one remark in Allan Ramsay's *Epistle to James Oswald*, published in the *Scots Magazine*, October 1741) have been a professional singer.

Proper assessment of Oswald as a composer has yet to be made; many of his compositions were published anonymously or under pseudonyms. He wrote fluently in both the Scottish and Italian styles and at times combined them, successfully and

indeed seminally. His folk-tune variations, some published before he left Scotland in 1741, others included in his 15-volume collection *The Caledonian Pocket Companion* (London, 1745–c.1770), employ Italianate violin techniques that were taken up by local fiddlers all over Scotland; his classical compositions introduce 'Scotch snap' rhythms which were to become widely fashionable in London during the period 1760–90.

Other composers, notably William McGibbon, combined Scots and Italian idioms in their work; but Oswald developed this compound style more radically and daringly than McGibbon, particularly in his later works *Airs for the Four Seasons*, 1755; John Reid's second set of sonatas, 1762—which Oswald helped to compose; and an extraordinary recreation of Gaelic folksong in drawing-room terms, *The Maid of Selma*, written about 1765 to texts from Macpherson's Ossian).

Edinburgh's cultural élite never forgave Oswald for shaking the Scottish capital's dust from his feet after only five years, then successfully promoting Scottish music in London. McGibbon, who remained in Edinburgh all his working life, became a legendary figure; Oswald's name was derided 50 years after his death, in one of Wandering Willie's speeches in Walter Scott's *Redgauntlet*. But Oswald is arguably the greater composer of the two.

D. Johnson

P

Painting, 1700–1900. The Baroque art of Catholic Europe found no favour in Scotland. When at the Restoration it became the established style in England, Scotland remained aloof and instead retained her links with the art of Holland. In 1694, when the Flemish portrait painter John Medina (c. 1659–1711) arrived in Edinburgh, he found little opportunity to display his mastery of a style derived from Rubens. What was most typically required of him was the modest half-length rather than the baroque extravagance of the full-length portrait. Also, even if there had been no objection to the Baroque on religious grounds, any significant possibility of the kind of aristocratic patronage on which it depended was effectively removed together with the institutions of political power in 1707. The ceiling painted for the Catholic Duke of Gordon in Gordon Castle by John Alexander c.1690–c.1757) in 1720 (now destroyed) was a late and exceptional example of Baroque painting and of aristocratic patronage in the European manner.

Medina's painting is however comparable to that of Kneller

in the south. His successor, William Aikman (1682–1732) continued to practise the style, and from about 1723 till his death in 1732 he worked successfully in London. The landscape painting of James Norie (1684–1757), the leading decorative painter in Scotland, is comparable to that of his southern contemporary George Lambert. By 1730, too, English painting had moved away from the European international style and with contacts of this kind continuing the English and Scottish traditions might have been expected to merge. Instead, however, inherent intellectual and social differences, and the absence of great patronage kept a distinct character for Scottish art. Its social basis after the Union is clearly revealed in the document that records the foundation in Edinburgh in 1729 of the country's first art institution, the Academy of St Luke. With the exception of two law lords there was no noble patron and the signatories, though of more or less standing, seem to have been all tradesmen. As well as John Alexander and James Norie, the artists included Roderick Chalmers, house painter and herald painter, and Richard Cooper, engraver, father of the Richard Cooper who succeeded Alexander Cozens as drawing master at Eton. Prominent among the lay members were William Adam and Allan Ramsay, the poet (q.v.). Allan Ramsay junior also signed though he was only 14. The institution was short-lived but it was significant. Allan Ramsay's efforts on behalf of Scottish literature are well known. St Luke's Academy shows that he was one of a group and that their sense of responsibility extended to the visual arts. Their efforts were not in vain. Robert Adam and the younger Ramsay were both brought up in this circle. One went on to become the outstanding portrait painter, the other the outstanding architect of their generation, and, excepting only Gavin Hamilton and David Allan, there is an unbroken chain from master to pupil that begins with the founders of St Luke's Academy and includes virtually every major artist in Scotland till well into the nineteenth century.

The achievement of Allan Ramsay (q.v.) (1713–1784) as a painter has to be seen against this background to be properly understood. He was certainly indebted to Hogarth, to lesser English painters, and to French art, but his continuing loyalty to the intellectual life of Edinburgh shaped his art more fully than is apparent if it is only seen in an English context. Compare, for example, his portrait of *Lord Drummore* (Private Collection) to Hogarth's *Captain Coram* (Foundling Hospital, London) which probably inspired it. Hogarth portrays Coram himself with brilliant naturalism, but has placed him incongruously among the paraphernalia of the late baroque grand portrait. Both painter and sitter are ill at ease. By contrast Drummore's achievement is written only in his face and pose. The brilliant light endorses the clear intelligence of his face. Nothing else is necessary. The picture is wholly natural and individual.

Ramsay elevated portraiture to the level of a humane science. His marvellous portrait of *David Hume* (SNPG) reflects not just the close knowledge of a friend, but the penetration of an equal and kindred intelligence. The values on which his art was based persisted in Scotland to flower again in the painting of Raeburn (q.v.). Significantly however his style was superseded in England within his lifetime by that of Reynolds based on the revival of the conventions of seventeenth-century aristocratic portraiture.

Ramsay's most important contemporary was Gavin Hamilton (1723–1798) for whom, too, art was a mental, not simply mechanical pursuit. He spent most of his life in Rome and as doyen of the painters there helped make the city a centre for Scottish artists. His most important work was his *Iliad* cycle of six pictures begun in 1759. When engraved they were intended to form an epic narrative series. He explored the idea of a primitive Homer pioneered by Thomas Blackwell in Aberdeen and developed by Robert Wood. He also based his idea of an epic style in painting on the interpretation of the role of Homer as an inspiration to the visual art of ancient Greece put forward by George Turnbull, also from Aberdeen and a follower of Blackwell in *A Treatise on Ancient Art* (1740). Hamilton began an alliance between painting and Scottish literary thought which was central to the distinctive development of Scottish painting in the later eighteenth century. The two artists closest to him in Rome who continued this development in the next generation were Alexander Runciman (1736–1785) and David Allan (1744–1796).

Alexander Runciman was trained in the Norie firm and so was a member in the younger generation of the Edinburgh circle that had produced Ramsay and Adam. Its continuing vitality is affirmed by the extraordinary precocity of the work of his younger brother John. His *King Lear* (SNG) of 1767 focuses for the first time in painting the view of the relationship of man and nature that was to preoccupy Romantic art for two generations. Alexander's most important work was the Ossian cycle, known as the *Hall of Ossian*, painted in 1772 in Penicuik House (now destroyed). He continued Hamilton's idea of epic painting, but for the first time he also sought to emulate the primitive vigour that was believed to characterize bardic poetry. By his use of landscape he also identified the poetic spirit with the natural world; but the landscape, like the poetry is explicitly Scottish and so natural and national are seen as related qualities. This parallels exactly the implicit justification of the use of the vernacular by his friend Robert Fergusson in the poem 'Hame Content' written in the following year. Though Runciman's interpretation of Ossian was obviously influenced by Hugh Blair and by Macpherson himself, its express nationalism is therefore closer to the inspiration of the revival of vernacular poetry.

The idea of a national landscape that had its root in this conjunction of poetic and antiquarian ideas remained central to Scottish painting for more than a century. It was developed first by Runciman's pupils, Jacob More (1740–1793), Alexander Nasmyth (1758–1840) (q.v.), and George Walker. More abandoned the style in favour of a conservative Claudianism on moving to Rome *c.*1774, and Walker's work is fairly prosaic, but Nasmyth's blend of history and nature at its best transcends topography to create a kind of poetic landscape of association.

Though he did not succeed Runciman in the Trustees Academy (founded in 1760 and Scotland's first permanent art institution) Nasmyth was also important as a teacher. A distinguished group of painters in the next generation was indebted to him. His kind of landscape was adapted to form the basis of the Greek scenes of Hugh William Williams (1773–1829) that earned him his sobriquet 'Grecian', and of the Spanish and Middle Eastern landscapes of David Roberts (1796–1864). The amateur painter, the Rev. John Thomson of Duddingston (1778–1840), encouraged by Scott, developed it into a more expressive style to describe the wilder and more rugged aspects of the Scottish landscape. Thomson in turn provided an important model for Horatio MacCulloch (1805–1867), the outstanding interpreter of Highland scenery. MacCulloch's painting certainly reflects the inspiration of Scott and the developing fashion for the Highlands, but it is not a pictorial derivative of a literary fashion. His painting belongs in the tradition founded by Runciman. Scott's exploitation of the triple conjunction of landscape, poetry, and history as aspects of national identity was so successful that the prior and independent exploration of these ideas by the painters has been overlooked.

The exchange of ideas between literature and art that took place in the development of literary subject and landscape painting, took place even more directly in the development of genre. The vernacular poets were led by their choice of language to look for their subject matter in common life. David Allan, following their example, abandoning his aspirations to be a conventional history painter, put himself forward instead as a painter of common life. In the dedication to Gavin Hamilton of his illustrations to Allan Ramsay's *Gentle Shepherd*, published in 1788, he suggested, though modestly, the equality of humble social description to more exalted forms of art. His pictures of the manners and customs of the unspoilt country people, he claimed, reflect true nature. Some of his most successful designs were illustrations to Scots songs collected by Burns. Thus the identification of painting and poetry was made directly and was extended to include the traditions of popular song. With his *Penny Wedding* (SNG) Allan also introduced to Scottish art the representation of popular music making which became one of its recurrent themes at a time when it was virtually absent from the rest of European art. It indicates a desire to identify directly with popular culture whose consequence was the revival of a kind of direct and self-sufficient social imagery that had not been seen since the seventeenth century in Holland. Though Allan's own talent was too weak to take this very far, in the hands of Wilkie (1785–1841) in the next generation it was the most significant contribution made to the European tradition by Scottish painting. Between David Allan and Wilkie however stood Raeburn (1756–1823).

Raeburn's art is diverse. He could match the flash and dazzle of Lawrence, but his most distinctive work is very different and belongs in the tradition of direct portraiture that derived from Ramsay through David Martin (1737–1797), his pupil. In his best work, such as the double portrait of *General and Mrs Francis Dundas* (Private Collection), or even in an early painting like the astonishing portrait of *James Hutton*, the geologist

(Private Collection), Raeburn shares with Ramsay a sense that individuality is something utterly concrete and independent of all social considerations. Unlike Ramsay however, and perhaps influenced by Runciman, he worked without preliminary drawing. Instead he drew with the brush. The resulting spontaneity adds vivid immediacy to Ramsay's directness.

The links with older artists are not the only basis on which Raeburn's distinctive qualities may be seen to be Scottish. In one of his most outstanding pictures, the portrait of the fiddler *Niel Gow* (SNPG) of *c.*1793, he took up independently the key theme of Scottish genre painting and, far surpassing anything that Allan could achieve, he identified the strength and simplicity of his own painting with the qualities of the nation's music in which Gow was preeminent. Thus it is possible on the one hand to align Raeburn's sense of the individual with that of Burns, and on the other to explain the force of his example to Wilkie.

Wilkie was one of a group of genre artists that included Alexander Carse, William Lizars, John Burnet, and a little later Walter Geikie (1795–1837) who were all pupils at the Trustees Academy of John Graham (1754–1817). Graham was, it seems, himself a pupil of Runciman and, though an indifferent painter, he was a very important teacher. He taught in the Academy from 1797 to his death in 1817. In this time he set it up as an effective art school and inspired several generations of painters with a respect for natural truth.

In 1805 Wilkie left Edinburgh to settle in London. The style of Scottish genre that he took with him proved an immediate success, but also proved difficult to transplant. He was both applauded and not taken seriously enough. *Distraining for Rent* (SNG) was consciously undertaken as his masterpiece and was an attempt to vindicate his claim to be a serious painter, but it misfired. His picture of social distress in agrarian Scotland in 1814 was regarded as close to sedition, yet, outside of portraiture he was the first artist in the modern tradition to treat the dignity of the individual as natural, needing no gloss of style, and wholly independent of class or occupation. This was in the tradition of Burns, but his sense of the interdependence of natural justice and the dignity of man was not appreciated by an English audience.

Curiously the small and seemingly quite inoffensive portrait of Scott and his family at Abbotsford in 1818 (SNPG), though perfectly understood in Scotland as a private picture, also provoked hostility in England as a 'vulgar group' unworthy of 'an elegant poet'. Wilkie's Scottish art and his English public were clearly at odds with each other. Hazlitt, comparing him unfavourably with Hogarth, identified the reason and at the same time dismissed the quality on which Wilkie's European reputation was based: 'Hogarth never looks at any object but to find a moral or ludicrous effect. Wilkie never looks at any object but to see that it is there.' The conflict of taste eventually produced a nervous breakdown in 1825. On his recovery Wilkie seemed wholly committed to an academic style in the Reynolds tradition, yet he could still produce a masterpiece when he returned to his original inspiration. *The Cottar's Saturday Night* (Glasgow City Art Gallery) of 1838 illustrates

Burns, but also, reflecting his own upbringing and citing Rembrandt for support, it asserts the central principle of the Reformed religion. It shows a household at peace with itself because its members are free to answer for their own consciences.

Wilkie's naturalism had a wide reputation, but in Scotland his influence also had another side to it. After Runciman there was little serious history painting till Wilkie sought actively to promote a Scottish historical style. He did this through works of his own like the never finished *John Knox preaching* (Tate Gallery), but also by encouraging others, especially William Allan (1782–1850). In this way a style of narrative history painting was established, much influenced too by Walter Scott, that was practised by artists like Allan, James Drummond (1816–1877), and Thomas Duncan (1807–1845) throughout the middle decades of the century.

Pursuit of the higher branches of art, as they were still held to be, was also encouraged by the formation of the Scottish Academy in 1826, to become the Royal Scottish Academy in 1836. Amongst the early academicians David Scott (1806–1840) devoted his life to the idea of high art, but, though his seriousness of purpose and single-mindedness sometimes give an awkward strength to his grand designs, his talents were ill-matched to his aspirations. Like his friend Haydon in the south, he died disappointed by the world's reluctance to recognize a doubtful genius.

Scott's exact contemporary, William Dyce (1806–1864), shared similar ambitions but was a man of subtler perceptions. He was one of several Scots to have a strong admiration for the art of the German Nazarenes and, established in London as one of the leading figures in British art, he was an important intermediary between German and British painting. His most original achievement however was the creation of a kind of moral landscape. In pictures like *The Man of Sorrows* (SNG), or *Pegwell Bay* (Tate Gallery), both of 1859, thought and feeling are focused in an intense naturalism. He may have been influenced both by photography and the younger Pre-Raphaelites in this, but his achievement is distinct and independent.

The most characteristic achievements of Scottish painting remained throughout most of the century ultimately dependent on Wilkie's social naturalism. Amongst his immediate heirs the outstanding artist was Walter Geikie. His drawings and etchings of scenes in the streets and closes of Edinburgh are often humorous, but they include some of the most direct and unsentimental images produced anywhere in his time. He accords the dignity of art to all classes of men, including the drunk and the simple-minded. He was deaf and dumb and in 1889 the otherwise admirable Robert Brydall dismissed him cruelly: 'As so often happens in the case of mutes, he failed to develop any of the higher qualities that are necessary to constitute an artist.' He was however not a naive. His refusal to judge was part of a conscious artistic attitude. Echoes in his art of the urban imagery of the poetry of Robert Fergusson seem to be conscious too and suggest that he identified himself, not just with the tradition of Wilkie, but with the wider Scots tradition of which he was part.

Geikie died in 1837. The Disruption six years after his death has been seen as a collision between the values of the old Scots tradition and those of an anglicizing establishment. If this is so, then Brydall's dismissal of Geikie in very much the same terms as Hazlitt had dismissed Wilkie and his failure ever to establish a reputation as a serious artist, suggest that art reflected this same conflict. Significantly, too, the ideals of the seceders found striking artistic expression in the calotypes made by D.O. Hill (1802–1870) and Robert Adamson of the members of the Disruption Assembly in preparation for Hill's massive painting recording the event (Free Church of Scotland). Though he did not complete the picture for more than 20 years and it was scarcely an artistic success, the fact that it appears to acknowledge the influence of David's revolutionary *Oath of the Tennis Court*, of 1790 is some indication of the spirit in which it was undertaken. There is no doubt about the artistic success of the calotypes however. Their strength and simplicity is in the tradition of the direct portraiture of Ramsay and Raeburn. The contemporary series of the fisherfolk of Newhaven are likewise in continuity with the art of Geikie. Hill's pioneer use of photography does not merely reflect his ingenuity. It identifies the Scots visual tradition with the fundamental point of the seceders, the right of a congregation to choose its minister freely and according to the merits of the individual.

The Disruption, or at least the 1840s, seem to represent a watershed in the history of art in Scotland. The radical imagery of Geikie and Hill was not developed. Nevertheless there was no break in continuity. The portraits of Sir John Watson Gordon (1788–1864) and Sir Daniel MacNee (1806–1882) show that public taste for the directness of Raeburn did not fade. The painterly naturalism of the genre paintings of John Philip (1817–1867) clearly begins in that of Wilkie, and the Faed brothers, John (1819–1902) and Tom (1826–1900), in their scenes of Scottish rural life not only continue the tradition of Wilkie's subject matter, but also, in spite of sentimentality, preserve respect for a visual language based on observed fact.

Under the teaching of Robert Scott Lauder (1803–1869) in the Trustees Academy in the 1850s, and encouraged by the example of the Pre-Raphaelites in the south, a group of younger artists brought new energy to this tradition. Amongst Scottish painters Sir Joseph Noel Paton (1821–1901), Sir William Fettes Douglas (1822–1891), and William Bell Scott (1811–1890), brother of David, all felt the influence of Pre-Raphaelitism. Scott was in fact very close to the Pre-Raphaelite group, but compared to them the pupils of Scott Lauder belonged much more consciously in the Scottish tradition. Compared to older genre painters on the other hand, like the Faed brothers for example, Erskine Nicol (1825–1904), or Sir George Harvey (1806–1876), the work of these younger painters is quiet and simply constructed.

W.Q. Orchardson (1832–1907), John Pettie (1839–1893), and Tom Graham (1840–1906) took the style south and in the 1860s and 1870s developed it into a sophisticated but essentially naturalistic narrative style that made a distinctive contribution to English painting in the later part of the century. George Paul Chalmers (1833–1878), Hugh Cameron

(1835–1918) and William McTaggart remained in Scotland and continued to use Scottish rural subject matter. Among them McTaggart (1835–1910) was the outstanding painter. There are almost always figures in his pictures, but from the mid 1860s onwards they are increasingly overwhelmed by the landscape. He became a pure landscape painter, but even in the absence of figures his landscapes remain related to human presence and human feeling by the manifest involvement of the artist. This distinguishes him from his contemporaries Peter Graham (1836–1921), Joseph Farquharson, and John MacWhirter who carried on the tradition of MacCulloch's Highland landscapes. He clearly felt the influence of Pre-Raphaelitism, and especially of Millais, in his early career, but, by combining Pre-Raphaelite open-air painting and colour with the informal tradition of Scottish genre, he created a personal and highly expressive style. His free brushwork conveys his own subjective state in the face of the landscape that it describes. This is exclusively the landscape of Scotland. Though his general theme is man and nature it is explored in particular terms. As at the beginning of the development of Scottish landscape painting, nature and nation are identified.

Although for McTaggart links with continental painting were unimportant, its influence in Scotland was already apparent in the 1870s in the work of Sir George Reid (1841–1913) and Robert MacGregor. The activities of dealers and of collectors like John Forbes White brought the native tradition increasingly into contact with allied traditions in Holland and in France. The effect, especially of French painting, was to encourage a greatly simplified way of painting and freedom from narrative and associative subject matter. Under this impulse some superb pictures were produced. W.Y. MacGregor's *Vegetable Stall* of 1884 (SNG) is supremely successful in making one his sense of the concreteness of things and of paint. The same can be said of Guthrie's *A Hind's Daughter* of the previous year (also SNG) and under the leadership of these two men a brilliant group of painters flourished in Glasgow in the 1880s and 1890s including Lavery, Walton, Hornel, Henry, Crawhall and a considerable number of others. The general level of achievement of this group is remarkable, but by the mid-1890s the influence of Whistler, of Japanese art, and of the decorative concerns of the Arts and Crafts movement that flourished in both Edinburgh and Glasgow tended to push these painters away from the forthright painting of the 1880s towards more artful arrangements of composition and of brushwork. In spite of this decline however, contact with *avant-garde* French painting continued to be a significant factor for art in Scotland. George Henry's *Galloway Landscape* of 1889 is a masterpiece of European Post-Impressionism. The continuing influence of French Symbolism is apparent also in Edinburgh in some of the work of Charles Mackie, J.H. Lorimer and William Yule and in the intellectual and literary preoccupations of the circle of Patrick Geddes and the *Evergreen Review* during the 1890s. In the younger generation this relationship persisted down to the First World War in the painting of Peploe, Fergusson, Hunter and Cadell, but, though it produced much first-class painting it meant that creative leadership for Scotland in the visual arts was no longer to be found within Scotland. There was no longer that essential imaginative drive on which great art depends. There is much individuality of manner in the painting but no sense anywhere of a particular individual pursuing a compelling personal vision that dictates its own forms. In his generation there is no equivalent in painting to Charles Rennie Mackintosh (q.v.). Perhaps it is significant that Mackintosh, like R.L. Stevenson, used his sense of a native Scots tradition as the frame of reference for his response to more exotic influences. James Caw in 1908, in the book that has remained for most of the twentieth century the definitive history of Scottish painting, sought to identify its essential character in terms of the purely neutral qualities of colour and handling rather than the committed sense of reality that characterized its greatest achievements. It seems that by the end of the century painters had lost sight of the real character of their own tradition. *See also* Painting in the Twentieth Century; the Glasgow School; Nasmyth; Raeburn; Ramsay, Allan, the Younger.

D. Macmillan

Painting in the Twentieth Century. There are several different ways in which modern Scottish art can be approached: as an autonomous school with its own leaders, followers and trends, as an aspect of the larger subject of European art, or as a gloss on the nature and problems of Scottish society. In favouring the first approach, criticism of Scottish art has neglected the fact that Scotland shows in a small compass and extreme form the problems of European art in establishing for itself a social context. The interconnection of the forms of modern art with deep social, political, philosophical and psychological change has been widely discussed in relation to western art as a whole. This debate has hardly been applied to Scottish art, but surely not because Scotland lacks the discontents, the wearing-out of existing social, political and religious forms. Scottish art has not been open to analysis in this way because it has not found its own language of change in a specific Scottish modern art. Nevertheless, this should not relieve criticism from the need to assess the social context of Scottish art or permit it to claim for that art an autonomy it does not really possess.

In this article, which has no pretensions to deep analysis, the aim has been to provide a mild corrective by emphasizing aspects of the situation which may be sufficiently obvious, but are usually overlooked in writings on the Scottish School. Before looking at the salient groups and individuals of the recognized history of Scottish art in this century it would be interesting to glance at the continuous backcloth to their activities provided by the exhibiting societies in Edinburgh and Glasgow. One might write a history of Scottish art solely by reference to them. Few artists in Scotland have not used them, and one, the Royal Scottish Academy, is the organ by which the world of artists takes its place in the social framework. The societies provide the only true account of grass-roots art in Scotland. Their exhibitions were until recently extensively reviewed, not only in the Scottish press. They are said to be parochial; the RSA despite its national claims was said to be an Edinburgh society. This is not entirely true. It was most true in the early years of the century (in 1900, over half of the exhibitors came from Edinburgh and only 13 per cent from Glasgow, but a quarter came from elsewhere in Scotland). The Royal Glasgow Institute was more cosmopolitan, with more exhibitors from England and abroad who were no doubt attracted by the possibility of sales in that great commercial city. As almost the only outlet for artists, the Societies promised limited rewards. Until the late 1950s, the vast majority of works were priced at £25 or less. Even in 1959, only seven works at the RSA would have cost a purchaser more than £250. These low-priced works included many by Academicians and Associates. Evidently election to the Academy did not bring with it the power to command high prices. By way of contrast, the painter James Pryde, himself a Scot but operating outside Scotland and the Scottish system, received £3,000 about 1921 from the Cowdray family for a mural at Dunecht Castle.

Exhibitors between the wars were more evenly divided between Glasgow, Edinburgh and the rest of Scotland with English artists coming in increasing numbers in the 1930s. Prices remained for long consistently low, just as the subject-matter of the works exhibited showed an astonishing consistency throughout the whole period, with landscapes by far the largest group in 1979 as in 1900. The typical Scottish artist, now as then, is a landscapist, as likely as not in watercolour, living in Edinburgh or Glasgow or in the country (not in Aberdeen or Dundee) and with such modest financial pretensions that he cannot be earning his living by his sales. Present statistics do not provide material for an analysis of the *buyers* at these exhibitions. Observation suggests that their conservatism, hesitancy and parsimony are now so great that the level of professional achievement in the exhibitions is reaping no real reward at all. If that is true, the principle of supply and demand has broken down throughout the entire system. This very breakdown has, of course, been the greatest problem of the arts for decades, and has been, not solved, but kept at bay by a system of state support that has grown, in the 1960s and 1970s, to be of overwhelming importance to the status quo.

The Scottish exhibiting societies are proportionately more important in Scotland than anywhere else in Britain. Their relative accessibility to artists and public and their valued independence from the state support system might have encouraged widespread small patronage and democratic support. If that is increasingly not so, it sharpens still further the stark problem of maintaining the arts (as presently defined) in Scotland with its demographical imbalance and its clearly drawn class structure. Yet patronage in Scotland has always been dangerous to artists. Our period opened with the industrial wealth of the west of Scotland still almost at its height but, because it could not tolerate nonconformism, this wealthy patronage had already blighted the promise of the Glasgow School (q.v.). The marriage between wealth and artistic *avant-gardism*, which fuelled the whole development of modern art in Europe and later in America, was never celebrated in Scot-

land. Here, private patronage remained an artistic liability almost as great as neglect was an economic one. The movements and changes of Scottish artists in this century could be plotted in terms of their reactions to both hazards. The desire to escape which has motivated many Scots artists is not only caused by the negative aspects but by the actual nature of the success that they could aspire to have. We should be glad of the fact that Scotland does reward its leading artists, in a less devious and uncertain fashion, perhaps, than other parts of Britain. But we can also hope that the artists will not always be made to sacrifice to a relentless bourgeois gentility to enjoy success. Only a liberalization of Scottish society can make any impression on this problem.

The 'Four Scottish Colourists' who mark the proper beginning of modern Scottish art were all aware of these hazards and evaded them in their own fashion. Taking their starting point in the Glasgow Boys, they renewed their fires by travel to France and enthusiastic study of Manet, Impressionism and Post-Impressionism, whereas the Glasgow Boys looked to French, Belgian and Dutch *plein-air* painting and sentimental realism as exemplified by Bastien-Lepage. The Colourists were not all equally open to the more radical example, but all had taken from it, by 1914, the high colour key that gave them (much later) their name. Not all could follow the implications of high colour which, in the hands of the *fauves* who were their contemporaries, served to unite the whole canvas as a light-giving source, diminishing the role of colour as description or as a gauge of distance. Can one wonder? As late as 1939, a critic of the great exhibition of Scottish art at the Royal Academy fixed grudgingly on this very point, remarking that with the Colourists, everything was flat on the picture plane—if, he said, that was the desideratum they certainly had it. It was S.J. Peploe (1871–1935) who best understood the unitary nature of modern painting and his so-called 'cubist' period during the first war was really an attempt to reinforce colour with form in order to assert this unity over the representation of objects.

The best work of the Colourists had probably been done by 1918, except in the case of Leslie Hunter (1871–1931), whose accomplished landscapes of the 1920s have absorbed some of the lessons of the *fauves*. Peploe returned to colour as a purely descriptive medium and settled down to produce the long series of charming flower pieces, interspersed with landscapes and still life, that seduced collectors in the difficult inter-war years (even though a reviewer in 1931 still called them 'harsh'). F.C.B. Cadell (1883–1937) who had always been a chic painter with much *bravura*, subdued his brushwork into hard-edged areas of flat colour in an elegant 'art deco' style in the 1920s, only to lapse into some banality in the 1930s. Cadell was 'well connected' and admired the gentlemanly self-amusement he professed to see in the paintings of Gainsborough and Whistler. The longest-lived of the Colourists, J.D. Fergusson (1874–1961) was the most radical temperament among the four, was a mordant draughtsman in early days, and understood the abrasive vitalism of the modern movement. Fergusson delayed his final return to Scotland until the Second World War, but preferred a sun-baked existence in the south of France to keeping up with painting in Paris. After his fauve-expressionist period before 1914, he developed and stuck to a hedonistic manner in which 'southern' colours were conflated with a kind of idealistic objectivity and neo-classicism. Fergusson's return to wartime Glasgow in 1939 must have been painful but he and his wife Margaret Morris attracted a small group of artists on whom some of the southern warmth rubbed off, the 'New Scottish Group' which included one unbreakable Scots talent in the Glasgow painter Donald Bain (1904–1979) as well as giving comfort to the influential refugees Jankel Adler and Josef Herman.

Scotland naturally shared in the depression in art that affected the whole United Kingdom after the first war, and had no such commanding figures as Wyndham Lewis or Jacob Epstein, impressive even while rejecting their earlier radicalism. The scene between the wars seemed to belong to the old and the comfortably established. The contraction of Scotland's heavy industrial base and the shrinkage of wealthy patronage, social unrest and fear of red revolution could only strengthen the tendency of the middle class to keep to what they knew. In relation to this uniformity two figures stand out retrospectively: William Johnstone (1897–1981) and James Cowie (1886–1956). Johnstone, a rebellious radical, followed a predestined path out of Scotland and rejoined the Scottish scene only in the last decade of his life. Cowie, a more introverted man, met the Scottish scene more with disdain for its sloppiness than with contempt for its conventionality. A meticulous draughtsman with a brooding eye for the strange within the ordinary, he developed a small exclusive brand of native surrealism. Cowie remained in Scotland as a school teacher and finally as warden of Hospitalfield House where Joan Eardley among other painters encountered his abrasive personality. Johnstone had a quasi-surrealist phase but found his longer-term language in a form of abstract expressionism. As principal of two London art schools he gave aid and comfort to several young emigré Scots who went on to become prominent on the London scene.

Johnstone's sole exhibition in Edinburgh in the 1930s was a disaster; Cowie scarcely fared better. Neither was part of the new image of Scottish art as it began to appear at the end of the inter-war period. That period, in England, was marked by the emergence of intellectualist and formalist concerns in art, backed by the skilful writing and presentation which began the process of winning an intellectual and social consensus for modern art. These concerns were not echoed in Scotland, where 'pure' painting still ruled. The formation of the 1922 Group, founded by graduates of the Edinburgh College of Art in that year, including W.G. Gillies (1898–1973) and William McTaggart (1903–1981), marked the beginning of the ascendancy of Edinburgh painting in Scotland, which was such a feature of the years after 1945. These artists were joined by Anne Redpath (1895–1965) and John Maxwell (1905–1962) to form the core of the Edinburgh School. All of them arguably did their best work during and shortly after the war, but extraneous historical reasons gave them an opportunity to shine during the late 1940s and 1950s. The revaluation of

Edinburgh as a beautiful and undamaged city and the drawing power of its Festival brought critics and connoisseurs to it and put a premium on the contemporary art that could be most easily seen there. These artists were apt to the opportunity. They were highly attractive painters whose concerns were intriguingly different from those of London and less troubled by theoretic modernism, colourful and transmitting pleasing echos of the French masters to whom most of them were devoted. It is not surprising that they became the face that Scottish art presented to those beyond its borders. The influence of the Edinburgh School was exerted through the RSA and by the actual involvement of its members in teaching at the Edinburgh College of Art. A large number of younger artists were affected by their methods and ideas though these were never formulated outside the College.

The Edinburgh painters, like the Colourists, were empiricists, uninterested in any theoretical development of art or extension of its boundaries, or in provoking critical discussion. This has been counted to them as virtue, but it prevented the emergence of the dialogue that has always accompanied change. The Edinburgh School stood for a gentle personal development within the conventions, asserting colour once again as more evocative than descriptive, placing expressiveness over representation, respecting the unity of the picture plane. The other feature of the school which was owing particularly to John Maxwell was the introduction of a Chagall-like fantasy, something quite unknown to the Colourists. Younger adherents brought other elements into play, with Robin Philipson (b. 1916) in particular enlarging the physical bounds with expressionist brushwork and ambitious size. These developments together, which were widely influential, began to give the Edinburgh exhibitions a definable flavour. This painting had little realist aspect—it was warm, sensuous and decorative, and tended to treat all subject-matter on the level of fantasy or dream. Thus the School could embrace poetic naturalism and, in due course, the approach to abstraction through synthesizing colourful elements of landscape or still life.

The Edinburgh ascendancy must have resulted in unfairness to individuals but there was no powerful opposition from elsewhere. Painters centred on the art colleges in Aberdeen and Dundee mostly fitted in quite happily with the Edinburgh scene. There were certainly individuals in Glasgow just as capable of carrying the flag of Scottish painting, such as William Crosbie (b. 1915) or David Donaldson (b. 1916), who are both Academicians. But the general difference between Edinburgh (or east of Scotland) and Glasgow (or west of Scotland) painting, always a factor in Scottish art, is hard to define. The Glasgow taste was for more dialogue with the subject, originally based on a sound pictorial analysis but often expressed in a meaty manner of painting which, for all its bravura, sticks closer to the definition of appearances than its Edinburgh equivalent. Joan Eardley (1921–1963) was a great modern Scottish painter who bridged the gap between these tendencies and easily transcended both. Her devotion to the personal encounter with reality and her respect for the integrity of a canvas made much contemporary painting look trivial and anodyne, or trivial and meretricious according to the context. Eardley's concern with aspects of social reality was exceptionally rare in Scotland, and although she accepted membership of the Academy she was incompatible with its rituals. In her affair with the sea she recalled the elder McTaggart to many people, but equally in her paintings of Glasgow children she can be seen to revive a facet of the Glasgow Boys' work, as for example in Sir James Guthrie. A deep shyness led Eardley to attack the human predicament in Glasgow only through its soon-to-be-blighted children, effectively but not without a touch of her predecessors' sentimentality.

Eardley's work was beginning to be known and to sell in London at the time of her premature death in 1963. The relationship of Scottish painters to London is almost a separate subject of enquiry. Their separation, at least partly voluntary, from the great post-war art debate kept them out of the mainstream galleries and dealers. Resentment was caused by the neglect of Scotland by national agencies, especially the British Council. However, the brilliantly successful policy of the British Council was to promote strong British teams in the *international* art debate, and some spectacular successes were scored. As Scottish artists had scarcely participated nationally, they could hardly expect to participate internationally. Individually, some Scottish artists had considerable followings in London. Official exhibitions were more tentative and peripheral affairs. Scottish painters of the generation of Gillies and Maxwell could be afflicted by *mauvaise honte* in the face of the more critical attitude in a capital where visual art was being seriously debated. Their defensiveness had its obverse in the break made by other artists with Scotland.

The role of 'emigré' Scots in London was judged outside the scope of the original edition of this article. It was a decision that now seems unfair, but it is equally unfair to the major artists concerned to cram their names into a couple of paragraphs. This is nevertheless all that can be done in the space available. Needless to say the drift of Scottish painters to London is as old as Scottish painting. We can perhaps best consider those who left their imprint behind, or continued to influence the scene from a distance. All the Colourists, for example, spent much time out of Scotland, but their integral role in the Scottish school was not compromised Scots who adopted modernism in the twenties and thirties, however, like William Johnstone, Wilhelmina Barns-Graham (b.1912), William Gear (b.1915) and Margaret Mellis, had to wait many years before they were re-established and, although highly regarded, have had no substantial sequel among younger artists. On leaving Scotland they took with them their nationality, certainly, but not an approach to painting that was at all recognizably Scottish.

In the post-war years it was more possible for a young Scottish artist to leave Scotland and yet be a hero to his peers at home. Alan Davie (b.1920), who retained something from his conditioning at Edinburgh College of Art, was admired for his freedom of expression and technique and, eventually, his conspicuous success. William Crozier (b.1930) was maybe less

conspicuous but has remained greatly influential as a teacher. He also can be seen, with his trenchant abstracts developing in time into 'landscapes of the mind', as having taken what he learned in Scotland to a higher pitch of development. John Bellany (b.1942) took the issue more directly with the assumptions of the Edinburgh College, which he thought not Scottish enough. He was not so much a seeker or explorer in the south, but a cultural refugee from his own country. It gave him in time a special status with his younger compatriots. Sir Eduardo Paolozzi's fame (b.1924), his exceptionally wide cultural terms of reference and appetite for the contemporary, have given him immense prestige in the country of his birth. But it has not swung the general tendency away from painting towards his own kind of constructive sculpture.

What I noted 13 years ago about 'advanced' artists not having to leave Scotland, has its obverse now in the fact that those artists who do leave need no longer be seen as separate. That is an immense gain to the health of Scottish art. The harsh fact remains that the tiny market in Scotland cannot sustain the many fine artists we produce, and artists are obliged to follow their market and cannot avoid being influenced by it.

The generation born in the 1930s was the last who were likely to subscribe to the older conventions of the Edinburgh or any other School. This was the generation that, in England, produced the pop-art wave which transformed the scene almost overnight. No such big-scale, irreverent figurative paintings, or such dazzling hard-edged abstracts, were produced in Scotland. A different movement in opposition to Edinburgh conventions arose with the realist group including John Bellany (b. 1942) who diagnosed correctly that the problems of Scottish art and artists were due to social inanition but differed widely in their treatment of it. A less socially focused movement towards representational clarity grew in force during the 1960s. Robert Callender (b. 1932) and Archie Brennan (b. 1931) were the closest to pop, the former with large paintings spilling out into three dimensional extensions, the latter using his medium of tapestry to simulate items from the pop vocabulary such as car tyres. The presence of John Johnstone (b. 1937) and David Evans (b. 1942) at the Edinburgh College of Art has encouraged a gentle poetic realism, not without ambiguous content, but still having much in common with the decorative semi-figuration of much east-of-Scotland painting, and stopping far short of the mordant super-realism seen in America.

The confusion and uncertainty of aim, the search for new language and matter to satisfy the young artists' longing to do something significant, has characterized Scottish art in the 1970s just as it has elsewhere. The accumulated conventions of the Schools have been fragmented without a new coherent pattern emerging. It has been the time for exceptions and oddballs. There have always been those, but they have left Scotland. Recently some have stayed within the country and even within the framework. The most conspicuous 'exception' since the early 1960s has been Ian Hamilton Finlay (b. 1925) who has been immovably based in the Scottish countryside while maintaining a network of international contacts through his correspondence and printed work. The most creative mind among all the artists, he has placed himself in bitter opposition to all art institutions in Scotland. Working from an early position within concrete poetry and still naming himself a poet, Finlay has engaged a number of diverse typographers and craftsmen in giving visible form to the cultural metaphors that his wide reading and analogizing intelligence give rise to. The narrowness and lack of cultural absorbency of a small country have certainly shaped the careers of the mavericks. But the most hopeful development is the existence of artists who have evaded the Scottish *mauvaise honte* in the face of England and abroad or the corresponding rejection of their own country and who have been able to assume the international freedom of the *avant-garde* artist while content to go on living in the Scottish framework, provided they can find some work here. They would include Glen Onwin (b. 1945), whose work combines conceptual, assemblage and painting elements, and Kenneth Dingwall (b. 1938) and Alan Johnston (b. 1945) who belong to a more platonic tradition in modern art, with reductive techniques that do not, however, exclude the expression of personal feeling. Parallel to this development of a small resident *avant-garde* has been the growth of small art associations, notably the print workshops which have utilized the print explosion to the benefit of Scottish artists and of improved contacts with England and abroad.

If Scottish art institutions become more responsive to the existence of an *avant-garde* group within the Scottish framework and if some of the entrenched positions in the Colleges of Art are thereby challenged, it will make a considerable dent in Scottish isolationism and make Scotland a more desirable place for artists to live in. But it will come at a time when not only the nature of public support for art, but the whole idea of an *avant-garde*, ranging far outside the concerns or the sense of relevance of the whole community, is being increasingly challenged under the pressure of intractable social problems. *Avant-garde* artists, critics and historians are of course aware of this and it has swung a significant number of individual artists in the western world into directly political activity. The dream of the Russian artists in 1917, of an alliance between the *avant-garde* and the people, remains enticing today. However, the anti-bourgeois credentials of those artists did not ensure their survival; today, the *avant-garde* and the grassroots community art movement remain far apart. Meanwhile, there has been little or no overtly political *avant-garde* in Scotland although there is now at least one gallery interested in showing this work. So Scotland is only now becoming aware of the problem. The lines are drawn in Scotland with exceptional clarity: a well organized bourgeois art world with a large amateur component and a progressive fringe, and a tiny number of independent artists of *avant-garde* tendency, confront a working class that has hardly begun to be aware of the possibility of expression through art. The question remains open whether Scotland can ever create in its visual art, as it has occasionally done in literature or in its institutions, the expression of an intellectual democracy facing its own problems.

Postscript (1993). What has changed in the 1980s and 90s is the perceived status of Scottish painting as much as its content. As well as new artists and new attitudes, there have been new galleries, new opportunities for publicity and exhibition. There have been two serious studies of recent Scottish art in the context of the history of the school as a whole. They are the new edition of William Hardie's *Scottish Painting: 1837 to the Present*, and Duncan Macmillan's *Scottish Art: 1460–1990*, both published in 1990.

In the eighties, status was conferred by social reclâme and commercial success as much as by recognition by 'authority' (which however usually followed). The process was documented in detail in the catalogue of the exhibition 'The Vigorous Imagination' at the National Gallery of Modern Art in 1987, an exhibition which was itself a recognition of a group of artists more punchy, and more in the public eye, than could easily have been assembled before. But it must be remembered that not many of the artists represented in that exhibition had then, or have now, an assured future based on sales or commissions. Private and public hesitancy and parsimony still blight the Scottish scene. However, the success of a few conferred status on the work of many more.

When I wrote the 1980 text, the advance of Scottish art in Scotland seemed to be marked by our ability to keep some of our *avant-garde* artists, who might earlier have gone to London or abroad, in the country. The *avant-gardism* then lay in an international current of platonic minimalism, conceptualism and the many strands of non-mimetic art by which artists expressed their involvement with the material aspects of life, nature and the environment. The most outdated statement in the earlier text was that there was 'little or no overtly political *avant-garde* in Scotland'. Within three or four years just such a movement was to appear. It had a predecessor in John Bellany whose powerful social realism of the 1960s had seemed almost lost to Scotland, but has now been fully reclaimed. His realism was always tempered by symbolism which became more private and more turbulent with the years, but Bellany was inspiring not so much for his themes as for his deep involvement with life and the boldness and generosity of his means.

Bellany is an east of Scotland man. Strangely, the boiling social pot of Glasgow had never produced a conspicuous visual art of social realism. But the claims of Glasgow School of Art to have been the seed-bed and the spearhead of the new realism of the 1980s seem to be well founded (see 'The Vigorous Imagination', op.cit). Four artists in particular are associated with the movement: Steven Campbell (b.1953), Peter Howson (b.1958), Adrian Wiszniewski (b.1958) and Ken Currie (b.1960). Of these, only Currie has a Political (with a P) dimension. What really unites them is that they are figurative painters on a generous scale, and their work can be read, puzzled over, interpreted and enjoyed in the same manner as paintings always have been. The same might be said of a majority of the 17 artists in that exhibition. The youngest, Stephen Conroy (b.1964), painter of enigmatic figures in an Edwardian gloom, achieved a prodigious *succès d'estime* and proved to be a superb portraitist.

The fact that all these were painters, and figurative painters at that, made the task of promoting them to the public easier at a time of dissatisfaction and disillusion with the endless obscurities of the *avant-garde*. It helped that they were Scottish, and had no ready parallels in England, and for a time it was possible to believe that Scotland had spearheaded a permanent move towards greater accessibility of modern art to ordinary experience. This had some truth, in so far as the desire of Scottish artists to communicate, even enigmatically, remains strong. But there was great exaggeration in the idea that painting itself had somehow triumphed. Even in the exhibition cited, the impressive fabric work of Samantha Ainsley and installation of David Mach were evidence to the contrary, and it is no surprise that Mach's reputation, especially outside Scotland, has proved at least as durable as any of the painters'. If Glasgow is still leading in the internationalisation of Scottish art, what is coming out of it now is more likely to be an installation dealing with, say, some socio-economic issue, rather than an expressionist or realist painting. The problem of how to make the public understand the language which the youthful *avant-garde* so doggedly persists in speaking, of course remains.

The influence of the artists and grouping mentioned was great, but of course they were not the whole. 'The Vigorous Imagination' did not represent the whole spectrum of innovative painting, omitting for example those that were associated with the 369 Gallery in Edinburgh, such as Fionna Carlisle, Caroline McNairn and Andrew Williams, and the continuing tradition of platonic abstraction. Nor did it recognise the notable contribution to sculpture made by the nature school, those working in the open with natural materials, both durable and ephemeral. If Andy Goldsworthy is the most prominent name associated with this sort of work, there are several native Scots such as Valerie Pragnell who have devoted themselves to it with great success.

These are the only groups and names it is possible to mention in this brief appendix, and they will have to serve just to represent an art scene of astonishing variety for a small and not conspicuously art-conscious country. The background remains as I described it in 1980, with a large number of practitioners of no particular allegiance, whose work seldom meets with a purchaser but who are as dogged in their devotion to their art as any *avant-gardist*. There is a change even in the annual exposures of the exhibiting societies which is not perhaps for the better, with far more artists, both amateur and professional, exhibiting and unfocused *angst* which they have not the skill to transmute into gold. But that is another cultural problem. The economic problem is that public and private support for art is at its lowest ebb for thirty years. This, more than yet another change of fashion, has deflated the hopes of the sanguine and publicity-conscious eighties. All the same, the ground gained has not been lost. Never again will Scottish artists have to take automatic second place to their English and foreign contemporaries.

D. Hall

Paisley Shawl. The pattern by which the whole world now

knows the name of Paisley, actually originated in the ancient Babylonian civilization. There, it represented the growing shoot of the date palm and was considered to be symbolic of the renewal of life. It was preserved throughout the centuries as a motif in Indian art and during the seventeenth century was adopted as the favourite decorative device of the Kashmiri shawl weavers. These shawls, which were very highly regarded by the princes of Kashmir, began to be exported to Europe in the mid eighteenth century by the British East India Company. They were very quickly adopted by fashionable ladies in London, but only reached a limited market because of their extremely high cost—around £300 each! British manufacturers, particularly in Edinburgh and Norwich, soon realized the potential for a shawl woven 'in imitation of the Indian'. (Minutes of Board of Trustees for Manufacturers in Scotland, 4 July, 1781.)

The weaving of these shawls was not introduced into Paisley until about 1805. Then, an Edinburgh manufacturer with too many orders on his books for his own weavers, knowing that there were skilled weavers unemployed in Paisley because of a depression in the town's silk industry, sent orders for them to weave. The Paisley manufacturers, known locally as 'bigcorks', quickly saw the possibilities of this new line of weaving, and very soon the town was producing its own imitation Indian shawls. Throughout the first half of the nineteenth century Paisley built up its shawl-weaving industry, at first by 'pirating' designs from Edinburgh and Norwich (before 1842 designs could not be patented), thereby undercutting their prices. In later years Paisley concentrated on mass-production, and the Paisley product became relatively so numerous that the shawls (and the pattern) came to be named after the town.

The Kashmir shawl had quickly become an indispensible part of the fashionable lady's wardrobe, complimenting, as it did so well, the draped lines of early nineteenth-century fashions. Despite a failure by the manufacturers to imitate the feel of the genuine wool of the wild Himalayan cashmere goat, the new imitations were enthusiastically welcomed by the less wealthy. British designers developed the original concept, and through continuing technical improvements were enabled to increase the amount of pattern on the garment. With the accession of Queen Victoria in 1837 there was a sudden change in popularity for the shawl (a square garment), since the young Queen made it clear that she preferred the plaid (rectangular). Thereafter plaids were all the rage. In fact the large size of the plaid made it the perfect outdoor wear over the ever-widening crinoline skirts of the 1850s and 1860s. 1870 however saw the introduction of the bustle-skirt with all the detail at the back where it would be hidden by a plaid. The era of the 'Paisley' came to an abrupt end.

After 1870 the decline of the industry was rapid. The younger weavers turned to other trades, but the older men who could not or would not change were kept at their looms with whatever handloom work the manufacturers could find for them. Products of the period included bedspreads, butchers' aprons, ponchos for South America, and a blanket-like shawl popular in Southern Ireland. The last true Paisley plaid was woven as part of a special order in 1903, but the last handloom weaving shop survived until its closure at the beginning of the Second World War, when one of its last two remaining Jacquard looms was handed over to Paisley Museum.

The Paisley weavers were a rare breed of men. Their relatively quiet occupation, and the four or six men in each loom shop, allowed plenty of opportunity for reflection and discussion. There built up a tradition of the weaving population as being Radical in politics, and secessionist in religion. They were all poets at heart and their leisure time was spent in such pursuits as rambling around the local countryside, fishing, bird-watching and gardening. The only sport that claimed their attention was curling. However the status of the weavers as master craftsmen declined with the introduction of division of labour into the industry and with the increasing mass-production. As a result Paisley lost more than an industry in the 1870s, it also lost a part of its character.

V. England

Periodicals, Literary. Scotland was later in starting to publish periodicals than England, having no titles worthy of note until the first *Scots Magazine* was launched, in the wake of the English *Gentleman's Magazine*, in 1739, followed in 1755 by the first, short-lived *Edinburgh Review*. However, despite the lack of such early eighteenth-century editor-writers as Defoe, Addison, and Steele, the Scottish achievement in periodical publishing has been varied and distinctive.

Some of the constraints and opportunities in this area of publishing have been common to Edinburgh and London, even if they have produced different results. In Scotland, as in England, the fate of periodicals has been determined partly by methods of editing and printing, partly by the transport system of the day, which for a long period made distribution difficult (a point vividly illustrated by the opening pages of *The Heart of Midlothian*), partly by the presence or absence of libraries, and partly by unpredictable fluctuations in public demand. North of the border, as south of it, the spread of formal education in the nineteenth century created a new market for enterprising publishers of periodicals, while by contrast in our own time radio and television have added to the individual reader's range of cultural choice, and so to the challenge confronting periodicals.

It is also part of the common pattern that specifically or exclusively 'literary' periodicals are relative newcomers on the scene, the product not only of strong literary interests on the part of editors and of their readers, but also of the increasing diversification and specialization which has taken place in publishing since the late nineteenth century. *Akros* and *Lines* are literary periodicals in the strict sense, 'little magazines' like *Agenda* or *Gambit*. The tradition, or rather precedent, to which they look is that created by C.M. Grieve in *The Scottish Chapbook* and elsewhere from 1922.

Literary periodicals have played a vital role in the modern Scottish 'Renaissance', both by publishing original poetry and prose in Gaelic, Lowland Scots, and English, and by supplying a forum for the expression of ideas. *The Scottish Chapbook* had, as one of its chief aims, a wish 'to insist upon truer evaluations of the work of Scottish writers than are usually given in the present over-anglicized condition of British literary journalism'. In criticism, it sought to 'elucidate, apply and develop the distinctively Scottish range of values'. As a practising journalist, Grieve used every available means to keep his various causes in the public eye. The charge can be brought against some of the periodicals of the Scottish Renaissance that they have at times been coterie publications, with the weaknesses of the genre—backbiting, insularity, and the habit of taking in each other's washing—but they and the small printer-publishers who have kept them going, sometimes with help from the Scottish Arts Council, are in a real sense the lifeblood of modern Scottish literature. It should be added that in spite of his distaste for the 'over-anglicized' state of the literary Press in Britain, C.M. Grieve contributed to a wide range of non-Scottish periodicals, from Orage's *New Age* (which also published early work by Edwin Muir) and Eliot's *Criterion* to the mass-circulation *Radio Times*.

It does not follow that because twentieth-century Scotland has produced literary periodicals in the strict or pure sense, it has lacked general periodicals of literary interest; nor that these were absent earlier. In fact, the main Scottish tradition in periodicals remains, as it has always been, general or miscellaneous. Admittedly, it is now difficult to find sufficient public support for a serious Scottish monthly or quarterly. This was vividly illustrated when *Scottish International* (1968–74), which had been heavily subsidized by the Scottish Arts Council, went to the wall. But there were at the end of the 1970s *Brunton's Miscellany*, *New Edinburgh Review*, and other journals of similar scope, just as in the late 1950s *Saltire Review* and then *New Saltire* aimed to supply a different kind of stimulus from the perennially popular *Scots Magazine*; and if *Blackwood's Magazine* was not the focus of literary experiment and political satire of its early years (1817–1830), when contributors included J.G. Lockhart, John Wilson or 'Christopher North', and James Hogg, 'Maga' continued to appear until 1980. Similarly, while there is not a Scottish weekly of the same type as *The Listener*, *New Statesman*, or *Spectator*, the *Scotsman*'s weekend supplement continues the earlier *Weekly Scotsman*'s practice of publishing poetry and short stories as well as criticism of the arts. *The Times Educational Supplement Scotland*, edited in Edinburgh, carries regular reviews, as does the older *Scottish Educational Journal*, which was C.M. Grieve's choice for his series 'Contemporary Scottish Studies' in the 1920s. An attempt to found an independent Scottish fortnightly in 1975 aroused considerable interest, but *Question* or *Q* lasted for only two years.

The ghost which haunts Scottish periodical publishing is that of the *Edinburgh Review* founded in 1802 by a group of young Whigs, mostly lawyers, who included Sydney Smith, an Englishman, and the Scots Francis Jeffrey and Henry Brougham. This was the third Review to bear the name of the capital. That of 1755–6 had been of high intellectual quality—one of the contributors was Adam Smith—but the public was divided over its frankly critical tone, which was unlike anything they had come across before in periodicals; and Gilbert Stuart's *Edinburgh Magazine and Review* (1773–6) gave offence through the editor's occasional indiscretions. The thinking behind the 1802 publication, while partly inspired by the example of 1755, was even more daring. Instead of supplying a little information about a large number of new books, in the style of eighteenth-century magazines—and of the useful current quarterly *Books in Scotland*—Jeffrey and his colleagues decided to be much more selective in their approach.

They wrote at length about what they judged to be the most significant publications, ignoring the rest; and sometimes deliberately chose a book for review merely as a peg on which to hang a long essay devoted to a topic of pressing interest in politics or economics. These latter concerns were very much in the forefront of the *Edinburgh's* strategy for national reform; the blue and buff colours of the journal were those of the Whig party. Poetry and fiction were reviewed regularly, and by a strict, even a severe standard, but as Jeffrey told Walter Scott, an early contributor, 'the right leg of the Review is politics'. The *Edinburgh Review*, published by Archibald Constable, quickly established itself as the most searching and original, as well as the best-paid journal in Britain: it prided itself on making and breaking reputations. Its heyday continued into the Victorian period—the *Review* itself lingered on until 1929—and this despite the fact that from 1809 there was a Tory rival to it, in the *Quarterly Review*. The *Quarterly* was published in London, but the publisher was a Scot, John Murray, and behind it was a disagreement among Scots. The initiative which led to its being started came largely from Walter Scott, who objected to what he judged to be the *Edinburgh's* unpatriotic politics, and also to an unflattering review of *Marmion* in its pages. Thus it can be claimed that Scotland was responsible for two outstanding nineteenth-century quarterlies, each with a European reputation. As William Chambers's three-halfpenny weekly *Chambers's Edinburgh Journal*, begun in 1832, was the first cheap periodical of an educational nature in a publishing boom at the other end of the market, the Scottish taste for learning in this period thoroughly justified itself.

These periodicals all sought to maintain the wide-ranging intellectual tradition of the Scottish Enlightenment, prizing informed versatility above a narrow specialization. True to that tradition, they were sometimes more like encyclopaedias issued in parts than periodicals in the usual sense. The *Edinburgh Review* was wordy, but beside it much modern literary journalism looks thin. Its refusal to compromise was, in the end, a weakness; yet in its own way it remains a vital example for the future.

D.A. Low

Photography, Early. It is at first sight surprising, yet the immediate stimulus to the development of photography in Scotland was provided by the Disruption of the Church of Scotland on 18 May 1843. A new body, the Free Church, split from the old, in defence of the democratic right of congregations to appoint their ministers, a right guaranteed by the Acts of Union of 1707 but removed by Westminster four years after those Acts were signed. Those who made up the new Church were thus united by the fact that they had taken a stand on principle. It is important to understand this for many of these people, far from being religious fundamentalists, were numbered among the outstanding thinkers of their time and it is because of this that their role in the development of photography makes sense. Among them were the scientist Sir David Brewster and the artist David Octavius Hill.

Within a few days of the Disruption, Hill had decided to paint a major group portrait of those involved (a project which eventually came to fruition in *The Signing of the Deed of Demission* completed some 20 years later). The difficulty which confronted him was how to record all the features of the 450 or so people who had to be portrayed. They had come to Edinburgh from all parts of Scotland and were about to return to face the problems of securing the rights of the new Church in their home parishes. A solution was offered to Hill by Sir David Brewster who suggested that he use the very new process of photography. To this end he introduced Hill to Robert Adamson, who was just in the process of setting up a photographic studio in Edinburgh. Robert's brother, Dr John Adamson, had succeeded the previous year in making the first calotype in Scotland, an achievement based directly on Brewster's correspondence with the English inventor of the process, William Henry Fox Talbot, whose pioneering work is the origin of most of the photography that we take for granted today.

After some initial doubts Hill went into partnership with Adamson, and by July they had begun to produce some of the outstanding works of the early years of photography. So much so that Brewster felt able to write to Talbot in the following terms: 'I think you will find that we have, in Scotland, found out the value of your invention not before yourself, but before those to whom you have given the privilege of using it.' It is clear that for Brewster the making of an image, however beautiful in itself, was not enough. What he is saying to Talbot here is that in the work of Hill and Adamson, photography has, for the first time, a social significance. In this sense, the work of Hill and Adamson is a direct successor to the moral reflections of David Wilkie in paintings such as *Distraining for Rent*. More widely Hill and Adamson's work should be seen as part of a tradition of visual thinking in both arts and sciences which includes not only Wilkie and Brewster, but architects like Adam and Playfair, engineers like Telford, the Stevensons and Watt, engravers like William Miller, philosophers like Hume and Hamilton, and, later, physicists such as James Clerk Maxwell, polymaths such as Patrick Geddes and biologists such as D'Arcy Thompson. So photography may have been a new invention, but there was a culture of visual thinking in Scotland ready to assimilate it.

What must be emphasized is that at the time Brewster wrote to Talbot, Hill and Adamson were already treating their photographs as works in their own right, not just as aids to Hill's painting. Soon they were engaged on their great Newhaven project which is the first major use of photography as a record of the folk of a particular place.

The contribution of Scottish photographers in the latter half of the nineteenth century was thus firmly rooted. Names such as George Moir, Thomas Annan, Thomas Keith, Clementina Lady Hawarden, John Muir Wood, William Donaldson Clark, Robert MacPherson and George Washington Wilson come to mind immediately. Further afield, in Russia in the 1860s one finds William Carrick helping to establish photography there. And then at the turn of the century, and marking the end of this great early period, is James Craig Annan, whose pictorialist work and experiments with photogravure provide a direct link between the Scottish nineteenth-century tradition and the early twentieth-century work of Alfred Stieglitz and the Photosecessionists of New York.

M. Macdonald

Pibroch, a loanword current in Lowland Scots since early in the eighteenth century, must presumably have been derived from Sc.G. *pìobaireachd*, 'piping, pipe-music (in general)', but strictly denotes only the same kind of Scots Highland bagpipe-music or pipe-tune as Sc.G. *ceòl-mór*, *port-mór*, 'great music', 'great tune, piece of *ceòl-mór*'.

Ceòl-Mór. Two quite different kinds of Scots Highland bagpipe-music exist: *ceòl-mór*, which comprises *c*.250 ancient traditional laments, salutes, gatherings, marches, etc., all (with few exceptions) first written down, printed, and published as pipe-tunes between 1790 and 1840, but some first briefly quoted by Joseph MacDonald (1761/2); and *ceòl-beag*, 'small music', which comprises various slow airs (sometimes intermediately classified as *ceòl meadhonach*, 'middle music'), quicksteps, reels, etc., mostly of recent origin. *Ceòl-mór* possesses its own unique musical forms and phrase-patterns; and, though distinctly clannish, the exultant spirit which it most-often expresses is also essentially heroic. It is said to have been developed mainly by the hereditary pipers maintained by some Highland chiefs throughout the period of incessant clan warfare, civil war, and rebellion which began in the late sixteenth century and finally ended with the abolition of the hereditary jurisdictions in 1748; and most of its special characteristics may be ascribed to the fact that it was composed solely for oral transmission in an exceptionally martial and aristocratic pre-literate society.

Tonality. The modes most often employed in *ceòl-mór* include: (*a*) three overlapping pentatonic modes, namely the G-Mode (G′ A′ B′ — D″ E″), the A-Mode (—A′ B′ C#″—E″ F#″), and the D-Mode (—A′ B′—D″ E″ F#″); (*b*) several hexatonic modes (incl. G′ A′ B′—D′ E″ F#″); and (*c*) an extended heptatonic mode (G♭′ A′ B′ C#″ D″ E″ F# G♮″ A″). But, probably because true semitones were not much liked, C#″ and F#″ are both somewhat flatter, and G♮″ perceptibly sharper, than in the natural scale; and each of the three pentatonic modes already mentioned has its own relationship with the drones which are invariably tuned in unison with A. It would probably be true to say that, although approx. 46 per cent of all extant pibrochs are pentatonic, and 38 per cent hexatonic, only 8 per cent are heptatonic, and only another 8 per cent are composed in any other mode.

Motifs. In *ceòl-mór*, each whole phrase is normally composed of two tonally contrasted half-phrases, each composed of two strictly conventional *motifs*. Since most of these *motifs* are regularly employed in the same or similar metrical contexts for the same musical purposes (e.g., especially, as phrase-beginnings or endings), they may be compared with the verbal *formulae* used in composing all such traditional epic poems as the *Iliad* and the *Odyssey*; and in the light so widely diffused by modern Homeric studies we may safely surmise that they were evolved in the course of oral transmission.

Composition. Another common characteristic possessed by all traditional pibrochs is that each consists of a ground (*ùrlar*, 'floor'), followed by one or more variations (*lùtha*, cp. perhaps Lowland Sc. *liths*, 'sections'). In his 'Account of the Rules & method by which the Pipe Composition & Time were regulated', Joseph MacDonald not only insists that in all regular pibrochs the ground 'commonly consisted of 4 [equal] Quarters of two, four, or eight bars each, and that such was 'The Antient Rule for regulating Time & Composition', but also implies that he obtained both these pieces of information from his best traditional sources. Now, in terms of his 'Antient Rule' all regular phrase-patterns employed in *ceòl-mór* may, for present purposes, be classified as either (*a*) Symmetrical, or (*B*) Unsymmetrical; and in all such regular phrase-patterns the ground is not only composed of four equal quarters of two, four, or eight bars each, but thus also comprises two equal half-measures of four, eight, or sixteen bars each. Whatever their phrase-patterns, all regular pibrochs consequently possess the same general metrical form.

Symmetrical Phrase-Patterns. These may broadly be classified as either Twofold or Fourfold Symmetrical Patterns; and the latter may further be subdivided into Primary and Secondary Fourfold Symmetrical Patterns. In all Twofold Symmetrical Pibrochs, the ground is composed of Phrs. A and B, two tonally contrasted whole phrases of two bars each, and its distinctive phrase-pattern may best be schematized:

A B, A B*,   [Cp. esp. *The Old*
B A, B A*   *Men of the Shells*]

—where Phr. B* is essentially a much-altered repeat of Phr. B, and Phr. A* similarly a much-altered repeat of Phr. A. Phrs. A and B have here been paired in two possible ways (AB, BA). In all Primary Fourfold Symmetrical Pibrochs, the ground is likewise composed of Phrs. A and B, two whole phrases of two bars each, but (except in so far as either of them undergoes any further development) the order in which these two phrases are arranged may best be schematized:

A A, B A,   [Cp. esp. *The Blue*
B B, A B.   *Ribbon* etc.]

Phrs. A and B have now been combined in all four possible ways (AA, BA, BB, AB). But in all Secondary Fourfold Symmetrical Pibrochs, the ground is composed of phrs. *a* and *b* two tonally contrasted half-phrases of one or two bars each, and of Phrs. A and B, two tonally correlative whole phrases of two or four bars each, and (*exceptis excipiendis*) the order in which these four phrases are arranged may best be schematized:

a b A, B A,   [Cp. esp. *Black*
b a B, A B.   *Donald's March*, etc.]

Thus, despite all differences already noted, each of these three phrase-patterns is perfectly symmetrical; and one common characteristic which they all possess is briefly that the second of the two equal half-measures of which the ground is composed is essentially an altered repeat of the first, in which two whole phrases (or two half-phrases and two whole phrases) are interchanged. All three Symmetrical Phrase-Patterns employed in *ceòl-mór* thus comply with precisely the same fundamental commutative law. Only 30 years after Joseph MacDonald's death, when the first few pibrochs were being written down, his 'Antient Rule' had at last, however, suffered the iniquity of oblivion; and, not only in Colin Campbell's *canntaireachd* (1797), Angus Mackay's MSS. (1826–40), and Angus Mackay's *Collection of Ancient Piobaireachd* (1838), but also in all other printed collections of *ceòl-mór* except Donald MacDonald's *Ancient Martial Music of Caledonia* (1822) and Gesto's *canntaireachd* (1828), all such strictly Symmetrical Pibrochs have hitherto been visually misrepresented as examples of either the '4:6:4:2 (or 1) Metre' or the equally chimerical '6:6:4 Metre', [for both which see especially Thomason (Intro.), pp. viii–ix; P.S., 3.94, 6.167; and Kilberry (Intro.), pp. 13–15: but cp. Lorimer (1962, 1975–78]. Some such confusion is often imported in transgressing the invisible interface between oral and literary transmission.

Unsymmetrical Phrase-Patterns. In all regular Unsymmetrical Pibrochs (often nowadays called 'Four-Lined Airs'), the second of the four quarters of the ground is always an unaltered (or scarcely altered) repeat of the first, but each of the last two differs substantially from all others. All that need here be said about their diverse phrase-patterns is briefly (a) that, although much less stereotyped than those employed in Symmetrical Pibrochs, most of them are almost equally repetitive, and (b) that in all such elaborate examples as *The Lament for Patrick Og*, *The Lament for Viscount Dundee*, *The Old Woman's Lullaby*, and especially *The Lament for the Children*, exactly the same underlying commutative tendencies may easily be discerned.

Variations. All variations are normally based on the same 'theme-notes', and consequently possess the same governing phrase pattern, as the ground from which they are derived. Sometimes the ground is immediately followed by a 'thumb variation (*siubhal òrdaig*)' in which A, the 'thumb-note', is regularly substituted for the top note of each successive phrase, or by one or more introductory variations of purely melodic or lyrical type: but most pibrochs end with a series of strictly conventional variations in which the theme-notes are first isolated and then successively combined with various increasingly complicated sets of embellishments respectively called

leumlùth, taorlùth, and *crùnlùth*. Any such variations may be omitted: but, if played, *leumlùth* must be followed by *taorlùth*, *taorlùth* by *crùnlùth*. The ground is often repeated after the last variation, and until towards the end of the nineteenth century may also, in many tunes, have been repeated between *taorlùth* and *crùnlùth*. With their energetic internal rhythms, the embellishments introduced in the closing variations strike the ear with, in one of Joseph MacDonald's most appropriate phrases, 'an agreeable Surprise'. But, in most pibrochs, the ground is uncommonly slow and stately; and the repetitive and analytical procedure pursued in the closing variations whets the relish inherent in the unique combination of tonal contrasts which he so aptly calls its 'taste'.

Oral Transmission. Especially when combined with commutation, the repetitive patterns employed in all regular pibrochs may often have facilitated spontaneous composition; and by tending to restrict deliberate composition to a few well-worn regular forms which could be learnt mainly by means of such *unconscious* assimilation as that described, e.g., by Lord (1965, pp. 33–4), by guiding pibroch-players into a well-trodden way of holiness such that the wayfaring men, though fools, should not err therein, they must also have helped to ensure that so many regular pibrochs survived in oral transmission.

Canntaireachd. Pibrochs were often learnt mainly by hearing them sung by older men (and women), not necessarily pipers, in *canntaireachd*, a traditional vocal notation in which melody-notes are systematically represented by vowels, gracenotes mainly by consonants; and Calum Johnston (1890–1972) recalled that in boyhood he could already sing several complete pibrochs in *canntaireachd* before he first began learning to finger his chanter.

Functions and Functional Types. A great many extant pibrochs seem to have belonged to two main functional types, namely (a) Panegyric Pibroch, including both the Heroic Lament (*Cumha*) and the Salute (*Fàilte*), and (b) Martial Pibroch, including the March (*Caismeachd, Spaidsearachd*), the Gathering (*Cruinneachadh*), and the Battle-Tune (*Blàr, Làtha*); and, no matter how tenderly personal the feelings expressed in *ceòl-mór* may often have been, its predominant functions were not only to promote a spirit of ardent loyalty to the pibroch-composer's own clan, but also to glorify its past and present chiefs, and thus incidentally to foster much the same heroic virtues as those commemorated (though not always commended) in the *Iliad*. Though Joseph MacDonald says (1761/62) that it was also used to 'Solemnise rural Diversions in Fields', it has now become much less popular than *ceòl-beag*; and even in battle it cannot often, since Waterloo, have been used to 'Animate a Sett of Men approaching an Enemy'. Yet no other distinctively Scottish art-form seems so truly expressive of the *ingenium praefervidum Scotorum*; and in the 'Lament for the Great Music' in which he proclaims that 'This Scotland is not Scotland', Grieve/MacDiarmid amply vindicates its relevance to modern Scottish, European, and international culture.

R.L.C. Lorimer

Pictish Language, The. It is likely that an offshoot from the Continental Celts settled in northern Scotland some centuries BC. Whether these were a simple extension of the British occupiers of Britain up to the Forth and Clyde (*see* British Language), or whether a rather more separate Celtic nation, is uncertain, but perhaps the second; Bede treats their language as different from that of the Britons, and there is some linguistic evidence which supports this, though whether it was more than a matter of dialect is not really clear. They perhaps called themselves Priteni, 'The People of the Designs', referring to their having tattooed themselves, possibly with the famous 'Pictish symbols'; certainly the Romans called them Picti, 'The Painted People'.

There are no texts in their language extant, because when they learned to write, from the Church, they wrote in Latin, and we have only some scanty personal names and place-names to guide us. Most are unquestionably Celtic, and moreover what is called 'P-Celtic', that is, sprung from the Continental Celtic milieu from which the Britons also came, and not from the 'Q-Celtic' whch was the source of Irish and Scottish Gaelic. A remarkable piece of evidence for this is the place-names, numerous all through Pictland, beginning with Pictish *pett*, meaning something like a farming community or a manorial unit. This gives *Pit-* in hundreds of names like Pitlochry; it is related to the Gaulish source of French *pièce* (cf. 'parcel of land'), and is clearly P-Celtic, i.e. not Gaelic. For personal names, Calgacus 'The Swords-man', a war-leader, and Argentocoxos 'Silver-Leg', a chief, are examples of undoubted Celtic names during the Roman period; and a post-Roman instance is the eighth century king Unuist son of Wurguist, 'One Choice son of Super-Choice' (Oengus son of Forcus in early Gaelic).

There is reason to think these Celtic Priteni were only part, though the ruling part, of the population of Pictland. Mingled among them there seem to have been descendants of a more ancient race, not Celtic at all. We know this not only from non-Celtic personal names in early sources, and from a few apparently non-Celtic place-names, but more strikingly from over 30 inscriptions carved on stone in the Ogam alphabet learned from the Gaels of Dál Riada. These are in an unintelligible language, not Celtic and not even Indo-European (with weird names like Nanammovvez). Compare the parallel way in which Basque, a non-Indo-European language, has survived to the present in overwhelmingly Spanish and French cultural contexts; though this language in Pictland was not Basque. Thus the 'Picts' would represent a mixed people, of both Celtic and pre-Celtic antecedents.

K. Jackson

Pipe Band, The. Although some may agree with seventeenth century English diarist Samuel Pepys that the skirl of the bagpipes is 'at its best, simply barbarous music', to the Celt, and to many other people as well, there is no sound quite so wonderful. Most people associate bagpipes with Scotland for the Scots have raised the instrument to the status of a national symbol, and the piper describes for them all the triumphs and misfortunes of the nation's history.

Most of the Highland piper's music dates from after the sixteenth century. Before then, strolling players improvised their music or played variations on folksongs. At the end of this century the bagpipe seems suddenly to have jumped into general favour and we find it established as a regular institution in every town in Scotland and included in the statistical accounts of these towns there are records of payments being made annually to the Town Piper or Pipers. Amongst Town, or burgh, Pipers perhaps the most widely known was the family of Hasties in the Border town of Jedburgh. They were the hereditary Pipers of that town for more than 300 years, up to the end of the nineteenth century. There was, in many of these same towns, a Town Drummer, or Drummers and so it is that we find in records, references to Bands of Pipers (minstrels), and Bands of Drummers—the forerunners of the Pipe Bands?

After the abortive risings of 1715 and 1745 in Scotland, the Government of the day decreed the proscribing of Highland dress and the playing of the bagpipes. So deep was the fervour of the Scot for the instrument that this ban, which existed for around 36 years, failed to silence its strident notes. At the Falkirk Tryst of 1783 the Highland Society promoted a competition for bagpipe playing and many of the participants were pupils of the celebrated MacCrimmon School of piping in Skye and the schools of the MacArthurs and others who provided tuition in the art. As the Government set up their regiments to control the Highlands after the risings, they were, one would say, obliged to make provision for pipers to be an integral part of each regiment and it was not so very long after this introduction that the drummers, who were very much 'part and parcel' of the army and accustomed to playing alongside the Fifes, began to line themselves up with the pipers and here we had a further extension of the banding together of pipers and drummers.

The pipes and drums as the musical combination which we recognize today emerged around 1881 when the Government decided upon the reorganization of the Territorial and County regiments of the British army. Then all Scottish regiments, whether Highland or Lowland, were provided with pipe bands. It is generally accepted that the onset of the First World War was responsible for our pipe-band enthusiasm. Records show that there were only seven battalions with pipe bands landing in France in 1914 but by 1918 there were over 100 pipe bands and the reason for this great increase in numbers was due to the fact that prior to the War there were only two battalions and a depot battalion to each regiment, and then, as a result of tremendous recruitment campaigns we had, for instance, around 18 or 20 battalions of The Highland Light Infantry and many battalions of The Black Watch; The Gordon Highlanders; The Royal Scots; The Royal Scots Fusiliers; The Seaforths; The Cameron Highlanders; The Cameronians; The Argyll & Sutherland Highlanders and many of the Lowland Regiments such as The King's Own Scottish Borderers, and every battalion had its own pipe band.

On the cessation of hostilities the pipers and drummers who had survived the Great War returned to civilian life and of course carried their pipe band enthusiasm with them. The post-war years of the 1920s witnessed a great expansion of pipe bands as towns, villages, clubs and societies, industrial complexes and Territorial Army units set up their very own bands. In 1930, in response to a crying need for a governing body to lay down rules and regulations for the control and efficient running of the pipe band contests which were by then becoming a very important facet of Highland gatherings, the bands throughout the land banded themselves together. A new harmony now emerged and with it, The Scottish Pipe Band Association prospered and bands were equally alert to the fact that membership was definitely to their advantage. Bands were graded, in the early days of the Association, into three grades and this system persists to the present day when there are now six grades, in accordance with ability, and each year a review and reassessment of bands in the various grades takes place. The Association, being ever mindful of the propagation of the music, established the Pipe Band College in Glasgow, the only college of its kind in the world, and it is materially contained in the Association's Headquarters in Glasgow and the curricula are designed so that certification in all aspects of pipe band music is available at elementary, intermediate and advanced levels. This sphere of operations is universal and has, since the inception of this college, established the pipe band as a musical ensemble of striking character, embodying the finest traditions of our national heritage.

Healthy competition, provided at the various gatherings throughout the land during the summer months, has been a great factor in the advancement of piping and drumming skills and these contests, allied to the splendid instruction being disseminated throughout the bands by dedicated leaders will thus improve globally the standards of musicianship.

R.J. Black

Place-Names. The study of Scottish place-names, compared with that of England, Wales or Ireland is extremely complex. We are dealing with names which have evolved from not one, but at least five distinct languages—English, Cumbric, Pictish, Gaelic and Norse—and the consequent variety of cultural background which these involve. Hence, the fabric of Scottish names is intricately bound up with the various interrelations between these racial groups.

In the words of W.F.H. Nicolaisen (*Scottish Place-Names*, 1976, p.47), 'The naming process is a continuum which has never been interrupted since it first began. In fact, naming is so intimately linked with the history of the human race, and its mastery over the world that surrounds it, that ultimately the history of naming may be the same as the history of the human spirit.' This is a clear statement of the importance of place-names indeed of personal names, in any society, and Scotland is no exception. Place-names, in particular, reflect the history of the country, its language, landscape, climate, agriculture, industry and culture.

As in England, the earliest names which survive in current use are the names of major rivers. These demonstrate the importance of rivers and streams in the early economics, as means of transport, barriers to communications, sources of food and cultivable land in the river valleys. There is the added significance, also, of rivers being awarded the status of deities, especially in the early Celtic times, or even in a pre-Celtic Britain. This is particularly true of early forms of river names which end in *-ona*, e.g. Deuona (Don), Dubona (Devon), Abona (Avon), Nektona (Nethan) and Lemona (Leven). Other major rivers, like Clyde, Tay, Dee and Adder are certainly in this early category, though not necessarily associated with river-deities.

The majority of Scottish settlement names, however, date from the period 700–1100. This was when the major movements of population took place, and when the political upheavals which characterized the post-Roman period were being replaced by more stable societies. During this time, the Anglo-Saxon peoples of the kingdoms of Bernicia and Deira had established themselves in southeast Scotland; the Gaelic speakers of Dalriada had expanded into Pictland and the Central Lowlands; the Cumbric peoples of the south were coming under increasing pressure from the competitors which surrounded them; and the Norse had, by the mid ninth century, effectively overrun the Northern Isles, northern Scotland and practically the entire chain of the Western Isles. By the year 1000, then, a kind of stability had been achieved, if only of a temporary nature. The language and culture of the Picts had now been all but overshadowed by Gaelic, and the increasing influence of English, spreading north from the Forth. It is in this context that we must view the place-name situation.

Pictish place-names are limited in number and confined to the northeast of Scotland, Fife and Angus. The most numerous group involves the element *pit-*, 'share', 'portion', in such names as Pitlochry (Perthshire), Pitreavie (Fife), Pitmedden (Aberdeenshire) and Petty (Inverness-shire). Some 300 names in *pit-* have survived, although many have Gaelic second elements, probably due to the existence of a bilingual period in the ninth and tenth centuries. Other distinctive Pictish names include *aber* 'confluence' (still widely used in Wales) in names like Aberdeen, Abernethy (Perthshire), Aberlady, (East Lothian); *pert* 'wood', 'copse' (Perth) and *pren* 'tree', as in Primrose (Fife), and Primside (Roxburghshire). Several of these elements are found in the area of British (Cumbric) speakers south of the Forth–Clyde line, including *pren, aber* and *pert*. In this area, the use of *cair* 'fort', 'manor house', is widespread, e.g. Cramond (Midlothian), Caerlanrig (Roxburghshire), and Carfrae (Berwickshire). Another term, *tref*, 'dwelling', 'village' is found, like *caer*, only in Cumbric Scotland, when it occurs as a first element, as in names like Traprain (East Lothian), Traquair (Peebles), and Terregles (Kirkcudbright).

Although at no time in its history was Gaelic the language of the whole of Scotland, no single county has entirely escaped its influence. Gaelic names form the most numerous group in Scotland, although in the Anglo-Saxon area they are relatively few in number. The element *baile* 'village', 'farm', 'hamlet' is the most important numerically of Gaelic names which indicate permanent settlement by Gaelic speakers. *Baile* is most common in the central belt, Fife, the northeast and the Moray Firth basin, as well as in Ayrshire and Galloway. Names like Balintore (Rossshire), Balerno (Midlothian), Balfour (Angus), Baldon (Wigtownshire) and Balblair (Nairnshire) are typical examples. Other common settlement elements include *achadh* 'field', as in Acharn (Perthshire), Achgarve (Ross-shire), Auchattie (Kincardinshire), Auchenbowie (Stirlingshire), Auchinleck (Ayrshire) and Auchans (Renfrewshire); *cill*, 'cell', 'church' as in Kilbowie (Ayrshire), Kilblain (Dumfriesshire), Kilbucho (Peeblesshire), Kilchalman (South Uist) and Killearn (Ross-shire). The majority of topographical names, especially north of the Forth–Clyde line, are Gaelic. This includes names for almost all mountain and hill features, lochs and minor streams. In the more fertile parts of the northeast and Fife, however, a sizeable proportion of these names are Scots or English.

The Anglo-Saxon (or Anglic) contribution to the place-names of Scotland begins with the settlement names coined by the seventh-century settlers in the southeast, in particular those containing the elements *-ingham* as in Whittingham (East Lothian) and Coldingham (Berwickshire); *-ington* as in Edrington (Berwickshire), Carrington (Midlothian); and *-tún* as in Yetholm (Roxburghshire) and Morton (East Lothian). The latter is a term which continued to be used in place-name coinage in Scotland until the late medieval period, e.g. Ingliston (West Lothian), Newton (frequent) and Johnston (Renfrewshire). The Middle Ages was marked by a spread of *-ton* names throughout southern Scotland and up the east coast, as well as by other English place-names mostly connected wih agriculture, e.g. *-field*, *-lea*, *mill*, *moor* and *rig* (OE *hrycg*). Later, Scots became the dominant element in place-names throughout all non-Gaelic Scotland.

While the Pictish kingdom was under pressure from Dalriada, the Viking raids which began in the eighth century began to take the form of a migration of mainly Norwegian settlers into Northern Scotland from about 790 onwards. The sparsely peopled Northern Isles and Hebrides were, in particular, intensively settled by these incomers, with a consequent establishment of Norse settlement and topographic names in great depth and detail, so that almost all the settlement names of the Northern Isles and the majority of those of the Outer Hebrides are of Norse origin. In the Hebrides, the northwards expansion of Gaelic clearly came into conflict with Norse, which assumed dominance, quite possibly in a bilingual situation by the end of the ninth century. However, the number of Norse topographical names on the western mainland testify to strong Norse influence all down the west coast as far south as Kintyre. In Galloway, an influx of Scandinavian speakers from Ireland, or from northwest England is suggested by a significant number of Scandinavian names.

The major Norse settlement elements include *bolstadr* 'farmstead', as in Norbister (Shetland), Grimbist (Orkney), Lybster (Caithness), Habost (Lewis), Cornabus (Islay) and Ullapool (Ross-shire); *stathr* 'dwelling', 'farm', as in Gunnista (Shetland), Grimeston (Orkney), Tolsta (Lewis) and Hosta (North Uist); and *setr*, 'dwelling' as in Voxter (Shetland), Inkster (Orkney), Wester (Caithness), and Earshader (North Uist). The element *dalr* 'valley' is present in both groups of islands and common on the western mainland where it suggests seasonal rather than permanent settlement, such as in Helmsdale (Sutherland), Bracadale (Skye), Slathadale (Rossshire) and Laudale (Argyll). In addition a considerable proportion of topographical features, especially islands and coastal features, have Norse names or contain Norse elements borrowed by Gaelic.

I.A. Fraser

Popular Music. Although rock'n'roll, the pop music hybrid which attained global acceptance in the decades following the Second World War, is essentially an Afro-American form, its 'white' components have increasingly been seen as owing much to Scots and Irish culture. As in the broader scenario of immigration, Americans frequently do not distinguish between these closely-related Celtic peoples.

Lonnie Donegan (b. 1931, Glasgow), the first Scots-born artiste to get a hit record in America, was billed as 'the Irish hillbilly' in the 1950s US press and similar confusion greeted the Proclaimers when the Fife duo—who sing pop songs in broad Scots—toured the States in the 1980s.

Scottish (and Irish) pop music has historically been characterised by the commercial domination of London and the United States and by a dualistic artistic approach which either attempts to incorporate traditional Celtic styles into more contemporary American forms or identifies completely with black American music. Whereas in the English-language and instrumental areas (Van Morrison, Moving Hearts) the Irish have been the more successful fusionists, the Scots have arguably achieved more in the Gaelic language (Runrig, Capercaillie). When it comes to black music, the Scots are in a league of their own.

Both English and Irish musicians have made meaningful connections with rhythm and blues and its rock offshoots (Rolling Stones, Eric Clapton, U2) but Scots—and particularly Lowland, urban Scots—have identified with American soul music over decades and generations in a way which other cultures have not. Notwithstanding the shared experience of Presbyterian church and city, the reasons for this are not absolutely clear, save, perhaps, in Glasgow and Dundee where early, influential groups the Alex Harvey Big Soul Band and the Poor Souls respectively, made contact with American soul groups in the German club scene of the early 1960s and brought back the best of their repertoire.

Scottish soul music reached its apogee in the 1970s with the Average White Band, a mix of Dundee and Glasgow soul musicians who came together in London and failed to find commercial success until a fortuitous meeting with legendary US soul producer Jerry Wexler, took them to the prestigious Atlantic record label and a simultaneous number one album and single in both the black and white American charts—the only white group ever to achieve this.

Other Glaswegian soul singers such as Frankie Miller (b. 1950) and Maggie Bell (b. 1945) have achieved cult status both in the UK and America and Scottish identification with soul music has carried on into the 1990s: it is evident in the work of some of the more recent groups to achieve commercial success—Hue and Cry and Wet Wet Wet (both from the Glasgow area), Danny Wilson (Dundee) and Deacon Blue (Glasgow and Dundee). Simple Minds (Glasgow), the Blue Nile (Glasgow) and the Shamen (Aberdeen) have also enjoyed considerable success but in differing, electronic styles which are perhaps less easy to categorise in a Scottish context.

Scots have actually always enjoyed commercial success across the broad range of pop music but in statistically small numbers. Both Lulu (b. 1948, Glasgow) and Donovan (b. 1946, Glasgow) topped the US charts in the 1960s. Jack Bruce (b. 1943, Glasgow) was a member of the influential Cream group; and in the 1980s, Annie Lennox (b. 1954, Aberdeen) was consistently voted one of the world's leading pop stars. There have also been major 'teenybop' phenomena: the Bay City Rollers (Edinburgh) in the 1970s and Wet Wet Wet in the 1980s and 90s. The decision by the Clydebank group to consolidate both musically and commercially in Scotland says much about the maturing managerial awareness of today's musicians and the changing economic climate of the record industry.

The indigenous live music scene in post-war Scotland depended heavily on Lowland mining communities and on Highland villages and small towns whose network of halls enabled groups to play regularly and undertake tours. Indeed, the first Beatles tour *anywhere* took in both of these areas (e.g. Alloa and Elgin). The Highland circuit still exists but discotheques have replaced many small town venues and larger-scale live events tend nowadays to take place in and around the conurbations. Recording remains something of a cottage industry.

Musically, indigenous success has come from the country dance circuit (Jimmy Shand, Andy Stewart) and from the vibrant Scottish folk scene whose practitioners frequently move into the pop mode. Graham Lyle (b. 1944, Largs), Gerry Rafferty (b. 1947, Paisley) and Barbara Dickson (b. 1947, Dunfermline) all worked in this area before achieving pop success.

Over the last fifteen years or so, more meaningful musical fusion has been undertaken by Michael Marra (b. 1952, Dundee), the Proclaimers and, most notably, the Gaelic groups Runrig (Skye) and Capercaillie (Argyll). That they have all achieved a degree of artistic and commercial success suggests important roles for the rich Scots and Gaelic musical traditions in the future development of Scottish pop music.

J. Wilkie

Printed Book, The, Until the End of the Eighteenth Century.

The reign of James IV (1488–1513) is often described

as a Golden Age, an oasis of comparative peace and cultural prosperity in Scotland's turbulent history. The king was a man of wide interests not only anxious to enhance national prestige but keen also to introduce the benefits of contemporary technological advancement to his kingdom. One of the major achievements of his reign is the Royal Patent of 1507, in favour of Walter Chepman and Androw Myllar of Edinburgh, establishing the first printing press in Scotland. The art of printing was late in coming here as it was more than 50 years since Gutenberg had printed his great bible at Mainz in Germany and more than 30 since Caxton set up his press at Westminster. This late development has meant that there are no Scottish incunables but towards the end of the fifteenth century there is some evidence that Scots abroad were becoming involved in the new invention of the printing press. Jacobus Ledelh was the first Scot whose books were published in his own lifetime, two of his works being printed in Paris *c.* 1495 by Jean Higman and Wolfgang Hopyl, and in the following year the name of another Scot 'David Lauxius Edinburgensis' appears in a Parisian colophon as press-corrector to the same printers, the earliest mention of a Scot in the history of the printing trade.

The first Edinburgh printer, Androw Myllar, was not, however, trained in Paris but in Rouen where in 1505 and 1506 he had two books printed for him. As an Edinburgh bookseller he was already known to the King. The Royal Patent of 1507 relates how Myllar in partnership with a wealthy Edinburgh merchant, Walter Chepman, undertook to 'bring hame ane prent with al stuf belangand tharto and expert men to use the samyne'. The 'expert men' and the gothic type that Myllar brought home were both French, thereby bestowing upon the earliest products of the Scottish press a very different character from that of England whose first printer, William Caxton, had acquired his training in Germany and the Low Countries. Despite the marriage in 1503 of Margaret Tudor to James IV closer Anglo-Scottish relations did not immediately materialize and this is reflected in early Scottish printing types and design which, as in architecture and much else, reflect the refining influences of the 'Auld Alliance'. It is all the more regrettable, therefore, that so little survives from our first national press which flourished in the Cowgate of Edinburgh between 1508 and 1510. Of the pioneering work of Chepman and Myllar all that now remains are a few tracts of poetry, fragments of a folio edition of *The Wallace* and the renowned Aberdeen Breviary. For two decades after Flodden there is almost complete silence. The only printer known to have worked in Scotland during this dark period is John Story who printed the *Compassio beate Marie* in Edinburgh not later than 1520 employing types similar to those used in Chepman's Aberdeen Breviary. Not until the emergence of Thomas Davidson in Edinburgh between 1532 and 1542 and John Scot who operated in both St Andrews and the capital in the 1550s is there the beginning of a reasonably continuous record of printing in Scotland. It cannot be denied that the known output of the pre-Reformation press is pitifully small, barely more than a score of books. One can only speculate about what may have perished during the English invasions of the 1540s and the religious revolution of 1559–60, but there can be little doubt that much has failed to survive for on economic grounds alone it would have been unwise for any printer, then as now, to undertake the great expense of setting up a press merely in order to print a handful of books!

After the Reformation records and surviving examples of Scottish printing are more numerous. The most prolific printer at this time seems to have been Robert Lekpreuik (1561–82) who printed Acts of Parliament, proclamations and religious tracts in Edinburgh, Stirling and St Andrews. In general the break with France is reflected in the use of type imported from London, although this had become evident much earlier in the books of Thomas Davidson. Until the end of the seventeenth century London was to remain the predominant influence on Scottish printers who for the most part obtained their types directly from England and not from Europe. There were some notable exceptions—Thomas Bassandyne's use of French 'civilité' type in, for example, Robert Henryson's *Morall fabillis* (Edinburgh, 1571) and the Dutch textura which John Ross used for *The Actis of the parliament* (Edinburgh, 1575). However, the norm was to print in roman, as did both Bassandyne and Alexander Arbuthnet when they undertook the great task of printing Scotland's first bible (1576, 79). The main body of the text is set in a roman which continued in popular usage on both sides of the border for the next 100 years. Towards the end of the sixteenth century Anglo-Scottish printing practices grew much closer when two London printers, Thomas Vautrollier and Robert Waldegrave, moved to Edinburgh. Waldegrave gained the favour of James VI who appointed him King's Printer, much to the annoyance of Queen Elizabeth who had ordered the destruction of Waldegrave's English press for printing puritanical tracts. While in Edinburgh he printed the King's *Daemonologie* (1597) and his 'Basilikon Doron' (1599) and when Elizabeth died in 1603 Waldegrave returned to London with King James.

After the union of the crowns opportunities for printers within Scotland to enjoy court patronage were inevitably reduced but they flourished in other directions. Although Edinburgh retained its preeminence, printing began to spread beyond the confines of the capital, to Aberdeen in 1622, Glasgow in 1638 and Leith in 1651. In the previous century there had been brief periods of activity at St Andrews and Stirling but apart from Glasgow and Aberdeen provincial printing made no great advances in Scotland until the middle of the eighteenth century. The best workmanship continued to be done in Edinburgh, much of it in the early decades of the seventeenth century by printers such as Andro Hart, Thomas Finlason, Robert Young and John Wreittoun. Admittedly their work cannot equal the finest European standards but it has a certain robust and distinctive charm tempered by conservatism and is unmistakably Scottish.

Unhappily the traditions of good craftsmanship did not long survive the adverse effects of the Civil Wars and the Interregnum of the mid seventeenth century. The opposing factions were fully aware of the power of the press in the war of propaganda, the result being a great increase in the quantity of material printed and a corresponding decline not merely in literary content but also in standards of typography and design. A flood of proclamations, tracts, news sheets and sermons poured forth. Slipshod press work, slovenly design and poor legibility are the hallmarks of this period. The nadir was reached in the productions of Andrew Anderson and his successors, who unfortunately monopolized much of the market in Edinburgh for the latter half of the century. Anderson is severely criticized by James Watson in his preface to the *History of the Art of Printing* (Edinburgh, 1713), the first attempt in Scotland at a history of printing. Some of the work done by Anderson's contemporary in Glasgow, Robert Sanders, is little better.

About 1680 there are signs of improvement as an upsurge of interest in science, medicine, law and antiquities is accompanied by a return to higher standards of typography. A partnership between an Edinburgh merchant, David Lindsay, and two Dutchmen, Joshua van Solingen and Jan Colmar, produced two of the most impressive books to come out of late seventeenth-century Scotland—Murray of Glendook's *Laws and Acts* (1681) and Sir Robert Sibbald's *Scotia Illustrata* (1684)—both printed in handsome roman and italic which, in the opinion of A.F. Johnson (*Selected Essays on Books* and *Printing*, 1970), were the first Dutch types used in Scotland. Neither of these types is found in contemporary English printing but the italic was later used as a model by William Caslon. Dutch influences remained for some time and are most evident in the Edinburgh printing of James Watson senior (1685–87) and again in the work done by his more famous son, the author and printer (1695–1722), who did much to remind his contemporaries of the obligations of good design. Both Watsons and David Lindsay enjoyed the benefits of royal patronage. A significant aspect of this period was the importance of royal favour and protection exercised on behalf of those who were known or suspected to be Roman Catholics, thereby arousing fierce political and religious antagonism. Another foreigner and Catholic who benefited in this way was Peter Bruce, possibly German by birth, who in addition to establishing a paper mill at Restalrig acquired the press of the elder Watson in 1687 and was appointed royal printer in the same year. His printing career was, however, short-lived. A mob wrecked his press in Holyrood Palace at the time of the Revolution in December 1688.

In the more settled conditions of the eighteenth century English influence on Scottish printing is once more paramount, no doubt assisted by the much closer mercantile links which followed from the parliamentary union of 1707. The influence of William Caslon's type-faces is apparent in many Scottish books at this time, for example William Maitland's *History of Edinburgh* printed by Hamilton, Balfour and Neill (Edinburgh, 1753). This was truly an age of elegance, a time of rapidly rising standards in the visual and literary arts, all duly reflected in the printed book. The rich creativity of this period extended beyond the printed page to the binding which encased it. Two distinctively Scottish styles of binding developed and remained popular for much of the century—the 'wheel-pattern' and the quaintly named 'herring-bone' both styles being quite different from contemporary work in England and abroad. Edinburgh was the centre of book-binding, the finest work being done in that city later in the century by James Scott and William Scott, who brought the art in Scotland to its highest level. In the art of book-illustration the century produced a major artist, the outstanding and versatile David Allan, but apart from his work Scotland cannot boast of a strong tradition in this field. The eighteenth century was also the age of the scholarly printer, of men like James Watson and Thomas Ruddiman, rekindling interest in older Scottish literature. In the two major cities of Edinburgh and Glasgow good though not outstanding standards of typography were being attained but the real turning-point came in the middle of the century with the close and fruitful association of the brothers Robert and Andrew Foulis of Glasgow with the first Scottish type founder, Andrew Wilson. Wilson's type faces show the influence of both Caslon and John Baskerville of Birmingham but he also proved to be an important original designer and a potent influence on later generations of printers. The happy combination of Wilson's talents with the printing, publishing and bookselling activities of the Foulis brothers raised Glasgow to fame as a major printing centre and gave Scotland its first press to enjoy a European reputation. Foulis excelled in producing accurate texts of classical authors, notably the Horace of 1744 and the Homer of 1756–58, the latter printed in their famous Double Pica Greek type. For the remainder of the century the name of Foulis outshone all its rivals in Scotland, although excellent work was being done elsewhere in Glasgow by Robert Urie and in Edinburgh by William Smellie and the Ruddimans.

Outside the two major cities provincial printing had made little progress in Scotland before the advent of greater political stability and economic prosperity in the second half of the eighteenth century. Aberdeen is exceptional in that it can boast of a long tradition, beginning in 1622, of local printers producing almanacs, periodicals and contemporary European literature, but in the eighteenth century the leading provincial press was undoubtedly that of the Morisons of Perth who continued to print their elegant literary texts and schoolbooks well into the nineteenth century. Like Foulis the Morisons were remarkable for the diversity of their business enterprises as booksellers, printers, publishers, binders and stationers. In the field of book illustration they were pioneers and gave employment to many leading engravers and artists. However, perhaps the best known of all Scottish local printers is John Wilson of Kilmarnock, printer of the first edition of Burns (1786), an elegant volume which in typography and design is not unworthy of its great author. It may be no exaggeration to claim that the success and fame of the Kilmarnock Burns contributed largely to the rapid development of good local printing in the Scotland of the late eighteenth and early nineteenth centuries. The precedent set by Burns and Wilson was followed by the young Walter Scott, when in 1799 he chose to entrust the publication of his early poems to James Ballan-

tyne of Kelso, the beginnings of one of the most famous and fateful partnerships in the history of the printed book.

T.A. Cherry

Prohibition. In the nineteenth century the fame of Scotland's national drink was matched by the notoriety of her drinking habits. The old social controls and conventions that had governed alcohol consumption in rural Scotland crumbled as new drinking patterns emerged among the growing industrial work force. Drunkenness and the violence it occasioned became commonplace in the streets of industrial towns and Glasgow, the epicentre of industrialization, was described as the 'Modern Methopolis'.

In Scotland, as in other countries which experienced severe alcohol problems, there was a vigorous and extreme counter-reaction. A temperance movement sprang into existence, seeking at first to reform individuals by propaganda and persuasion, but when this failed, resorting to legislative compulsion. From the 1850s into the present century, successive campaigns were mounted for two main forms of legislative control over drinking, stricter licensing laws and what was known as permissive prohibition.

Permissive prohibition (better known by the euphemisms, local option or local veto) worked by empowering the electorate of designated areas to hold referenda to decide whether alcohol should be sold within these areas. It was a democratic concept which appealed to men of radical outlook, including some well-known former Chartists. Such men disliked licensing laws because they were operated by an undemocratic magistracy and discriminated against working men who were the main users of the pub.

While licensing laws implicitly recognized the legitimacy of the trade in drink and had the limited objective of controlling sales, permissive prohibition was intended to abolish the social use of alcohol entirely and was regarded by many of its advocates as a means to wider social objectives. Permissive prohibition was eminently compatible with the philosophy of radical liberalism. Working men, slaves to drink through physical addiction or social custom, would, it was believed, use their power at the polls to remove the evil which oppressed them. Once the opiate of the masses had been removed by the masses themselves, a more self-reliant and politically effective working class would emerge.

The temperance reformers in Scotland advocated separate Scottish legislation on the drink question. The drink problem in Scotland, they argued, was different in nature and greater in dimension than in other parts of the United Kingdom. There was some truth in this, but also an element of opportunism in this national particularism.

The Scottish temperance movement was more politically effective than its English counterpart. Prohibitionists, who were usually radical liberals, adopted the technique of pressurizing MPs to support the measure in parliament. In Liberal-dominated Scotland there was soon a majority of MPs pledged to vote for it and the cry went up, why should the

English hold us back? By the turn of the century conditions were favourable for the success of the prohibitionist campaign. Sixty years of temperance propaganda had had some effect on Scottish society's attitude to alcohol. Assertions about the evils of drink that had once been ridiculed had become the conventional wisdom. Temperance ideas had successfully penetrated the churches so that both major Presbyterian denominations were prepared to support permissive prohibition. The Liberal MPs from Scotland, almost without exception, were pledged to vote for it. Anti-drink sentiments were also strong in the Labour movement, particularly in the growing ILP. Public opinion in Scotland, at least as far as it was represented by major religious and political institutions, was in favour of permissive prohibition. The Liberal election victory of 1906 established favourable conditions at Westminster and permissive prohibition finally became law under the Temperance (Scotland) Act of 1913, a law which was and remained unique to Scotland. As a means of prohibiting the use of drink, permissive prohibition had obvious limitations. It forbad the sale but not the manufacture of alcohol and it was at best local in its effects, creating problems and anomalies at the border of 'wet' and 'dry' areas. Dissatisfaction with these limitations and awareness of developments in the USA led to the formation in 1901 of the Scottish Prohibition Party with a platform of complete national prohibition of the manufacture and sale of alcohol. The founder of the party was Edwin Scrymgeour of Dundee, a man of deep if eccentric religious beliefs and general political convictions which aligned him approximately with the socialism of the ILP. Little would have been heard of Scrymgeour but for his election as Prohibitionist MP for Dundee in 1922, defeating Winston Churchill. It is doubtful that this indicated overwhelming support for national prohibition in Dundee. Scrymgeour's socialist leanings, the local reputation he had made during the war and, it is said in Dundee, the women's vote, got him elected. The old established anti-drink movement in Scotland regarded national prohibition as politically impracticable and Scrymgeour's bill got little support in Parliament. The fact that the Clydeside group of Labour MPs voted with him perhaps indicates that the old Scottish connection between radicalism and hatred of drink was not yet completely dead. Scrymgeour's career as the only Prohibitionist ever to represent a British constituency ended with his defeat at the 1931 election.

While complete national prohibition in the American style was never a serious proposition in Britain, the 1920s saw at last the implementation of the 1913 Act. The results of the first wave of veto polls in 1920 showed that the long-proclaimed popular demand for the abolition of the liquor traffic by the votes of the people, if it had ever existed, was no longer there. Fourteen parishes, 15 burghs with populations under 25,000 and 12 wards of burghs, including four in Glasgow, voted themselves dry. All licensed premises within these areas were closed without compensation. Success for prohibition was greatest in the fishing ports of the Northern Isles and the northeast coast, where temperance sentiment was traditionally strong. More surprisingly, two mining towns, Kilsyth and

Kirkintilloch, went dry. Permissive prohibition came too late to have any hope of being widely adopted. Over 60 years had passed between its initial inception and its implementation. It came into operation at a time when temperance sentiment and the temperance movement were in rapid decline, when drink consumption had fallen far below nineteenth-century levels and when new social problems like mass unemployment seemed more urgent than the old demon drink.

The intention of the old radical temperance movement was that, in permissive prohibition, they had a weapon against drink that could be put directly into the hands of the Scottish people. It is a weapon they have largely declined to use. 1920 proved to be the high point of prohibitionist success and since then further polls have gradually repealed most of the 'dry' resolutions. By 1972 there remained only eight parishes, one burgh and eight wards of burghs without public houses. Considering the many years of bitter controversy and hectic campaigning that went into obtaining permissive prohibition for Scotland it has proved quite ineffective as a means of combatting the damaging effects of alcohol consumption. Its significance lies in the feelings and ideas that it embodied rather than in practical achievement. Permissive prohibition remained on the statute book until it was repealed by the Licensing (Scotland) Act of 1976. By then it was no more than a spectre from a former era, a reminder of the depth of feeling that had once existed against drink in Scotland, an experiment in direct democracy that was out of place among the planners and experts of the modern administrative state.

D.C. Paton

Publishing in the Eighteenth, Nineteenth and Mid-Twentieth Centuries. In the second half of the eighteenth century, the state of Scottish publishing was uneven but lively. On the one hand, the prevailing pattern was still that of publisher-booksellers rather than of publishers as such; a full specialization of function lay in the future. On the other hand, in at least one instance publishing expressed in as practical a form as the architecture of Robert Adam the highest ideals of the Enlightenment. The Foulis Press in Glasgow set a standard of editorial and typographical excellence which would not readily be surpassed in the production of works of learning anywhere in Europe.

In Edinburgh, where much of the country's publishing was based, William Smellie edited and printed in parts in 1768 the original *Encyclopaedia Britannica*. Smellie lacked the aesthetic sense of the brothers Foulis, but his, too, was an extraordinary initiative. He was a friend of William Creech (1745–1815), whose printing-house and bookshop in the High Street were on the site formerly occupied by Allan Ramsay's bookshop. Creech was a successful, tight-fisted businessman, who by 1799 was said to be worth £30,000 through having cared for nothing but profit throughout his career. He published Henry Mackenzie's periodicals the *Lounger* and *Mirror*, and the works of several of the literati, including Hugh Blair, Dugald Stewart, and Adam Ferguson; and his shop became, in the words of

Henry Cockburn, 'the natural resort of lawyers, authors, and all sorts of literary idlers, who were always buzzing about the convenient hive'. Creech brought out the second and third editions of Burns's *Poems, Chiefly In The Scottish Dialect* in 1787 and 1793 respectively. At first, the poet liked and trusted him, but later he wrote

His solid sense by inches you must tell,
But mete his subtle cunning by the ell

for with Burns, as with others who had less to offer, Creech drove a hard bargain. He showed sound commercial judgement, however, when making arrangements with London booksellers to handle his books. Not for Creech the kind of financial connection with agents in London which was to spell ruin for more than one of his successors.

In the generation after William Creech had created and then enjoyed his position of power, Scottish publishing entered a period of expansion. New firms were set up; periodicals from Scottish presses attracted a great deal of notice; large-scale publishing projects were confidently begun and in many cases carried through to completion. For a time it looked as though the Scottish capital was in process of displacing London as the natural main centre of publishing in Britain. Among the factors which contributed to this publishing boom in Scotland were the availability of credit on apparently secure terms to individuals who were prepared to seek it out both in Edinburgh and in London; the presence in Scotland of ambitious young men who had behind them a broad-based school or university education, but who saw few prospects of lucrative or congenial employment; belief in the printed word as an instrument of education and progress in society; and the driving force of two very different men of genius, Archibald Constable and Walter Scott.

Constable (1774–1827) was a native of Fife who began his career as a bookseller's apprentice in Edinburgh. He started to publish sermons and pamphlets on his own account in 1798, and three years later took over the *Scots Magazine*, having recognized that ownership of periodicals might be made a source not only of solid profit but of useful contacts with writers and hence of patronage. The following year he took a further and bolder step in this direction by accepting responsibility as first publisher of the newly founded *Edinburgh Review*. The stimulating and often iconoclastic approach of Francis Jeffrey and his fellow reviewers meant that the *Edinburgh Review* got talked about, not only in Edinburgh but throughout Britain. As a result, many fresh possibilities opened up for Constable. An example of his enlightened publishing practice was his purchase in 1812 of the *Encyclopaedia Britannica*. This was, he said, his 'greatest speculation', for it was by no means certain that, even with his vigorous backing in Edinburgh and London, sales would be on a scale to justify the investment. With shrewd intelligence, however, Constable employed as the editor of a Supplement to the third edition of the *Encyclopaedia* a versatile man with exactly the right qualifications, Macvey Napier. As a result of this decision, and his policy of paying well for contributions, the *Encyclopaedia* was greatly improved by the time Constable came to sell it in 1826 to A. & C. Black.

If Constable made Edinburgh famous as a literary mart, Scott's was the creative literary energy which kept the city before the minds of the reading public. The association between the two men, a brilliant and ultimately tragic one, began in the early years of the *Edinburgh Review*. Constable paid Scott £1,000 for *Marmion*, and with characteristic largesse marked the success of the poem with the gift of a hogshead of claret, so that many of Scott's guests were invited to share a bottle of 'Marmion'. In later years there would be other, more splendid presents from publisher to author. Constable's hope was that Scott would allow him to publish all his original work. Partly with this in view, he commissioned from Scott several scholarly publications, including many-volumed editions of Dryden and Swift. Scott responded eagerly to Constable's enterprising spirit, liking especially the fact that the publisher was based in Edinburgh rather than London. But soon both men were faced with difficulties. Scott found Hunter, Constable's partner at this time, rude and overbearing. Moreover, he came to detest the political views expressed in the *Edinburgh Review* in the critical period 1808 to 1809 when, as he saw it, no patriotic Briton should think of making peace with Napoleon, as the *Review* advocated. For his part, Constable felt increasingly uneasy with the condition Scott made that the printing of his own books and also of some other works should be carried out by an old Kelso school-friend James Ballantyne, in whose firm Scott had a financial interest.

In 1809 Scott played a leading part in helping John Murray, a Scots publisher in London, to launch a Tory review, the *Quarterly* which came to rival the *Edinburgh*; and he also felt confident enough to help set up James and John Ballantyne as publishers, with himself as an unpublicized partner. These moves, and especially the first, caused a breach with Constable. For several years relations between Scott and Constable were cool, but then in 1813 the publishing business which had been established in the name of Ballantyne faced a severe financial crisis. Scott turned to the experienced Constable for advice and assistance. These were readily supplied, although the situation was so grave that it was also necessary for Scott to receive a bank guarantee for £4,000 from his kinsman, the Duke of Buccleuch. It was in this way that Constable became the natural choice to publish *Waverley* in 1814.

The renewed publishing relationship between Constable and Scott was to bring extraordinary success to both in the next ten years. For the most part it worked smoothly, although at one stage Scott caused Constable to feel acutely resentful by entrusting to a rival Edinburgh publisher, William Blackwood, his 'Tales of My Landlord'. Unlike the other novels, these were not published as 'by the Author of *Waverley*'.

Once again, Scott had stipulated to Constable that the Ballantynes should be involved at the printing stage. The publisher accepted this arrangement, knowing that while John Ballantyne often acted foolishly, James was a thoroughly professional printer, and both were devoted to Scott. Constable's own special flair was for the kind of energetic promotion and distribution required by a best-selling novelist in Regency times. Six thousand copies of *Waverley* were sold in the first six months, and two thousand copies of *Guy Mannering* the day after it was published. While it is possible to argue that any publisher fortunate enough to have had the Waverley novels on his list might have done equally well, the evidence suggests that Constable and his new partner Cadell made the most of their opportunities.

Cadell was cautious and prudent, rather in the manner of Creech, whereas Constable—who was his father-in-law—lived as he worked, in considerable style. Scott himself was always open-handed, spending freely. In particular, he spent large sums of money adding to his estate at Abbotsford. He knew it was risky to sign 'bills of accommodation' for profits calculated on literary work which still had to be completed or indeed begun, but his earning power as a writer made this practice seem reasonable enough.

All would have been well but for a financial panic which swept through Britain in 1825. The causes of this included large-scale speculation in stock-jobbing companies, and especially in South American ventures. Publishing was affected in common with many other forms of business. Constable's London agents, Hurst and Robinson, went down in the general collapse, and although Constable, now an ailing man, tried to do all he could to protect his interest, the combined resources on which he could call proved to be insufficient. His own firm, and James Ballantyne's printing business, were both involved and so also inevitably was Scott, who courageously decided to sign a trust deed and pay off all he could of the combined Constable debt of over £100,000 by writing as many books as possible in the years remaining to him.

Ironically, when disaster overtook him Constable was on the point of making one of the most significant publishing breakthroughs of the nineteenth century. Earlier than anyone else, he had seen that there was a large potential market for 'cheap literature'. Shortly before the crash in 1825, he told Scott that he planned to sell novels and other works to a wider public than had ever been reached before, by charging only a few shillings instead of guineas. Scott greeted the idea with enthusiasm, saying that Constable would become 'the grand Napoleon of the realms of print', and it was at once agreed that Scott would write a life of 'the other Napoleon' for inclusion in the new series. *Constable's Miscellany* was launched in 1827, and included a number of excellent books, among them Lockhart's *Life of Burns*; but later in the same year Constable died, and it was left to other publishers to exploit his exciting idea.

Of the other Scottish publishers who set up business in the first 30 years of the nineteenth century, the most important from a literary point of view was William Blackwood (1776–1834). He had begun, like Constable, as a bookseller's apprentice, and after periods in Glasgow and London he opened as a bookseller and publisher in Edinburgh in 1804. From the beginning, according to Mrs Oliphant in her *Annals of a Publishing House*, he sought 'to make his place of business a centre of literary society, a sort of literary club where men of letters might find a meeting-place'. It took some years for him to make headway against his rival, Constable, but he published successful works of travel and biographies, profited by being the Scottish agent of John Murray, and developed a strong special line in books of Scottish interest. Helpful (if sometimes adverse) publicity came as a result of the magazine he launched in 1817—after he had got rid of the original editors, and employed John Wilson and John Gibson Lockhart as principal contributors under himself. The writers whose books he published in the next 10 years—James Hogg, John Galt and Lockhart among them—were in many cases regular contributors to *Blackwood's Magazine* (popularly known as 'Maga'), taking part in its festive social life and assured of a welcome in Blackwood's bookshop at all times. As Blackwood also published Susan Ferrier's *Marriage* and *The Inheritance*, his achievement as publisher of Scottish novels by contemporaries of Scott was a substantial one. But for his active interest and encouragement, several of the finest books of the period would not have been written. His practice of publishing serially in his magazine excellent (as well as nondescript) fiction anticipated that of English periodicals of the Victorian age. Given this imaginative precedent, it is hardly surprising that *Blackwood's* was later to attract such contributors as George Eliot and Joseph Conrad.

Mention has been made of Constable's sale of the *Encyclopaedia Britannica* to A. & C. Black in 1826. Adam Black was a native of Edinburgh and graduate of Edinburgh University who, after working in London, became in 1807 a publisher in his native city, where he took his nephew Charles into partnership. In time, Adam Black served as MP for Edinburgh and was twice Lord Provost. The purchase of the *Encyclopaedia* led to a period of intensive work in the preparation of its seventh and eighth editions. Then in 1851 the Blacks bought from Cadell (who had climbed back to prosperity after the Constable crash) the copyrights and stock of all Scott's works. Scott remained a money-spinner for the owner of copyrights, and the Blacks saw to it that the firm expanded and diversified. In 1890 A. & C. Black moved from Edinburgh to London. Many changes have taken place since the firm was based in Scotland, but their specialization today in reference publications such as *Who's Who* and the *Writers' and Artists' Yearbook* shows continuity as well as development.

Other names to reckon with from the period before 1850 are those of Thomas Nelson, William and Robert Chambers, and William Collins, all publishers who began with a strong religious or educational commitment characteristic of their age and Scottish background.

Nelson was a native of Stirlingshire who as a young man gained useful bookselling experience in London. In 1798 he started a bookshop in Edinburgh, from which in due course he began to publish popular religious works in cheap monthly parts. His missionary and commercial zeal led him to travel to other places in Scotland where he sold his books, and it was a logical step to employ one of the first travelling representatives in Scottish publishing. His son continued the firm's tradition by using the country's railway network to get his books sold all over Britain. The Nelson list gained a best-seller in the early twentieth century in John Buchan, but its bias remained broadly educational.

For sheer determination, it would be hard to match the story told by William Chambers in his *Memoir of Robert Chambers With Autobiographic Reminiscences* (1872). William, the elder brother, who like Adam Black eventually became a Lord Provost of Edinburgh, started as a bookseller's assistant in the city, with scarcely a penny to his name. One way in which he earned his daily bread—in the shape of a hot roll—was to read to a baker from 5 a.m. till 7.30 a.m. each day. In 1819, with his apprenticeship over, he had scraped together enough money to begin selling books on his own account. He gradually built up trade, partly through the expedient of handling cut-price 'remainders of editions which hung on the hands of publishers'. His brother Robert, after undergoing his own hardships, joined William in a bookselling and publishing business which, as the years passed, went from strength to strength. *Chambers's Journal*, begun in 1832, pioneered a new form of serious but inexpensive periodical publishing; and Robert wrote many successful books, including *Traditions of Old Edinburgh* and *Vestiges of Creation*, a forerunner of Darwin's *Origin of Species*. One of Chambers's most notable achievements was their *Encyclopaedia*.

Whereas all of the publishers described above were originally established in Edinburgh, the house of Collins, arguably the most successful of all British publishers, has always been associated with the west of Scotland. William Collins, born in 1789, was running a school when he decided in 1819 to become a publisher instead. His motives were evangelistic; and his special ambition was to promote the books and ideas of his friend Thomas Chalmers, a leading Scottish churchman. For seven years he was in partnership with Chalmers's brother Charles. This did not work out, and in 1826 Collins broke away from Charles Chalmers, although his determination to publish religious books remained.

His son, William Collins II, who joined him as a partner in 1843, became Queen's Printer for Scotland in 1862, and provided paper mills for the growing business, which he converted into a limited company. He served as a Lord Provost of Glasgow, and was knighted in 1881. In the next generation the interests of the firm expanded overseas, and the process of growth and diversification went on steadily in the first half of the twentieth century. Publishing flair does not always pass from father to son in a family business, but this quality was very much in evidence in the Collins empire, which include thriving paperback divisions and such best-selling authors as Agatha Christie, Alastair Maclean, and—in keeping with the religious tradition, which has always been marked—the theologian William Barclay.

The main distinguishing characteristic of Scottish publishing has been its emphasis on books which promote learning. Blackie, a Glasgow firm, for more than a century specialized in publishing school-books. In Edinburgh, John Bartholomew, founded in 1826, was one of the world's most experienced cartographic publishers, their work ranging from the map included in Stevenson's *Treasure Island* to the *Times Atlas*. While the Scottish universities cannot boast a continuous publishing tradition to rival those of Oxford and Cambridge, the printing firm of McLehose served Glasgow University well from the mid-nineteenth century, and the design and illustrations in books published by Edinburgh University Press in the mid-twentieth century were of a high standard.

It is obviously impossible in a brief survey of this kind to do justice to regionally-based presses in Scotland, let alone to the remarkable achievements of Scottish printers since the eighteenth century. Mention should certainly be made, however, of the prolific output of the Drummond Tract Press in Stirling, of T.N. Foulis early in the present century, and of such distinctive local publishing concerns as the Tullis Press in Cupar last century. Edinburgh was particularly strong in printing at most periods, with firms of the calibre of T. and A. Constable and R. and R. Clark.

D.A. Low

Publishing in the Late Twentieth Century. By the mid-century, indigenous and independent Scottish publishing seemed in partial decline, as well-established firms maintained their strength by moving south or throwing in their lot with larger groupings. Their search for access to greater resources and economies of scale by publishing for the wider British and international markets had consequences for the Scottish publishing scene and the nature of the lists. (Before the war, the Porpoise Press, publisher of Neil Gunn, had lost its distinctive identity within Faber.)

By the 1960s, Thomas Nelson was on its way to becoming a Surrey-based specialist imprint of International Thomson; Edinburgh University Press under Archie Turnbull produced a small but beautiful annual list, often designed by George Mackie; small publishers such as Callum Macdonald had maintained distinctively literary outlets, while larger independents such as Chambers and Blackie found their niches in the reference and educational markets; Collins, still a family firm, was a major international force. In the 1970s companies such as Canongate (Stephanie Wolfe Murray) and Mainstream (Bill Campbell and Peter MacKenzie) were founded against a background of rising Scottish cultural and political consciousness, publishing fiction and general non-fiction aimed at a market not confined to Scotland, but with a distinctively local flavour to the lists of authors and subjects. In such cases the more ambitious literary or art publishing, which attracts subsidy and wins prizes and plaudits, was often underpinned by titles of tourist or sporting interest.

The 1970s and 1980s saw the successful re-establishment of a Scottish general publishing industry, bringing to the fore new literary writers (Alasdair Gray, James Kelman—the major names of the urban west), and re-exploring Scottish art, music, history, in attractively-produced and well-illustrated books, reflecting increasing professional competence in editing, design, and marketing. Throughout the period, small companies came and went, and even the best-known independents had to adapt to changing times. Richard Drew, who had a list of modern literary classics and popular reference works, joined Chambers, which had itself become part of the French Groupe de la Cité; Canongate, having sought to expand as part of the Musterlin Group, was a victim of their subsequent receivership and had to buy back its independence. By the early 1990s, the recession which was affecting almost the whole British general publishing industry was causing list-pruning and retrenchment, as the small-firm problems of marketing and under-capitalisation produced strains. Collins, meanwhile, had passed from family hands in the 1970s and from independence to the control of Rupert Murdoch in the 1980s: as HarperCollins it was essentially a London and New York-based house, looking to the world market but retaining in Glasgow its reference publishing, its manufacturing capacity as one of the last major publisher-printers, and its warehouse.

Blackie, founded in 1809, survived as the largest independent, with a turnover of £3m, until it was broken up in 1991, with the children's, academic/scientific, and educational lists going in different directions, the last, ironically, to the southern-based Nelson. Longman, itself part of the huge Pearson group, had already transferred the operations of the long-established Oliver and Boyd imprint to its Essex headquarters, but retained in Edinburgh its medical imprint, Churchill Livingstone, publishing from Scotland for an international market. Academic publishing had responded to the growth in Scottish intellectual life and the national debate: John Donald had an extensive list of historical monographs; Scottish Academic Press (founded 1969) had associations with several institutions and published both books and learned journals, until it went into receivership in 1991. Aberdeen University Press, part of Robert Maxwell's complex empire, was in 1992 dragged under following his death. In the late 1980s, Edinburgh University Press adopted, under the tragically brief leadership of Martin Spencer, a policy of increasing output, notably of Scottish literary and historical titles, while taking under its wing the former student imprint Polygon (founded 1969), which by the early 90s had a significant reputation in social history, poetry, European literature in translation, and especially new paperback fiction at moderate prices. (In 1993 Polygon won the *Sunday Times* Small Publisher of the Year and received a special award from the Scottish Arts Council for its literary publishing.)

By the beginning of the 1990s, the 70-plus members of the Scottish Publishers Association, of whom about one third had existed for over five years, collectively represented a degree of maturity and expertise. The SPA itself, the Scottish Book Marketing Group (a joint publisher-bookseller venture), the Edinburgh Book Festival (Europe's largest public book event), Book Trust Scotland—all based at the Scottish Book Centre in Edinburgh—and other organisations helped to extend the market for Scottish books and writers through publicity, author events, and the dissemination of information. Crucial to the support of many organisations, authors, and print-based activities, including the magazines which underpin cultural debate, has been the funding of the Literature Department of the Scottish Arts Council, which by the 1990s was spending over £700,000 annually, subsidising many individual publications of literary or cultural merit and easing the risk-taking, on which healthy and adventurous Scottish publishing will continue to depend.

I. *McGowan*

Pubs. RLS once remarked that 'a Scot of poetic temperament, and without religious exaltation, drops as if by nature into the public house'. This statement is certainly true, but it must be added that the Scot whose only poetry is the racing page and the Scot who is seemingly as high as a kite on the Bible are both likely to be discovered in it with fair frequency.

There is a copious literature documenting the place of alcohol in Scottish life, past and present. A leader in *The Scotsman* on 22 May 1850 approached the subject without pussyfooting:

> That Scotland is, pretty near at least, the most drunken nation on the face of the earth is a fact never quite capable of denial. It may seem strange that Edinburgh, the headquarters of the various sections of a clergy more powerful than any other save that of Ireland, should, in respect of drunkenness, exhibit scenes and habits unparalleled in any other metropolis, and that Glasgow, where the clergy swarm, should be notoriously the most guilty and offensive city in Christendom... .

The tone here is already distinctly 'Victorian'; a hundred years previously, in the convivial howffs of Auld Reekie, poets, professors, philosophers, anti-quaries, judges and court officials were drinking cheek by jowl with soutars, slaters, joiners and candlestick makers, and Boswell could expostulate, 'I did not get drunk; I was however intoxicate'. Robert Burns collected bawdy songs ('The Merry Muses of Caledonia') for the delectation of the Crochallan Fencibles, a drinking club which foregathered at Dawney Douglas's tavern in Anchor Close, almost opposite St Giles; at Dawney's too (we may be quite sure) he raised his glass to the memory of Robert Fergusson, his 'elder brother in the muse', who had composed drinking songs for the Cape Club 20 years earlier, and who had sung, like no poet before or since, the hamely luxury of an Edinburgh tavern:

> Whan big as burns the gutters rin,
> Gin ye hae catcht a droukit skin,
> To *Luckie Middlemist's* loup in,
>   And sit fu snug
> Oe'r oysters and a dram o' gin,
>   Or haddock lug ...

In the twentieth century, it took a long time for us to disengage from the uncouth hug of hypocritical Victorian sabbatarianism. To visitors from the south Scotland was the

> land o' Grundy,
> Burns, and back-street pubs, and Sunday.

Scottish pubs seemed bare joyless drinking-dens compared to cheery jovial English hostelries. It took a writer of the genius of Hugh MacDiarmid to turn a squalid vice into a virtue in his pantagruelian essay 'The Dour Drinkers of Glasgow', first published in 1952:

You stand at the counter with your toes in that narrow sawdust-filled trough which serves as a comprehensive combined ash-tray, litter-bin, and cuspidor... . The majority of Glasgow pubs are for connoisseurs of the morose, for those who relish the element of degradation in all boozing and do not wish to have it eliminated by the introduction of music, modernistic fitments, arty effects, or other extraneous devices whatsoever. It is the old story of those who prefer hard-centre chocolates to soft, storm to sunshine, sour to sweet. True Scots always prefer the former of these opposites. That is one of our principal differences from the English. We do not like the confiding, the intimate, the ingratiating, the hail-fellow-well-met, but prefer the unapproachable, the hard-bitten, the recalcitrant, the sinister, the malignant, the sarcastic, the saturnine, the cross-grained and the cankered, and the howling wilderness to the amenities of civilization, the irascible to the affable, the prickly to the smooth. We have no damned fellow-feeling at all, and look at ourselves and others with the eye of a Toulouse Lautrec appraising an obscene old toe-rag doing the double-split. In short, we are all poets (all true Scots—that is, all Scots not encased in a carapace of conventionality a mile thick) of *l'humour noir*, and, as William Blake said, 'All poets are of the devil's party'.

As the old privately owned pubs (like The Meadow in Buccleuch Street) came under the suzerainty of the big brewers, and began to get tarted up with all manner of plastic abominations, many must have felt that MacDiarmid's 'dour drinkers' had got it right after all. Better the sawdust-filled trough than a mess of muzak! The sad thing is that in all too many Scottish pubs—there's no use blinking it—one still finds the worst of both worlds: the unspeakable kitsch-and-keich interior, and the aboriginal neanderthal drinking habits. In *The Galliard* of Autumn 1949 Robin Cockburn faced the latter head-on:

We Scots have got to learn how to enjoy drinking. Not by any stretch of the imagination could the average Scots reveller be called 'happy'. Generally he's a sodden mass of inert misery, a kind of walking foregone conclusion.

And his whole approach to the business is wrong, by reason of its pendulum consistency. Like this:

Nip-pint, Nip-pint-
Mustn't-get-drunk, musn't-get-drunk.
Nip-pint, Nip-pint-
Tae pot wi' it a', tae pot wi' it a'.
(Continue ad inf.)

This is an incubus which will be on our backs for a long time yet. Luckily, there are quite a few pubs (like Sandy Bell's in Forest Road, Edinburgh) where we can discern the future through a glass gladly. Sandy's has been the principal howff of the modern folk revival, and is probably the nearest thing to the Crochallan Fencibles' rendezvous that Auld Reekie can offer. Jeannie Robertson sang there! The folk musicians were already beginning to tune up in it when there were still NO SINGING notices in some of the High Street dives. *Verboten* has no place in a Scottish pub! 'Freedom and Whisky gang thegither'.

H. Henderson

R

Raeburn, Sir Henry (1756–1823) was a major Scottish portrait painter resident in Edinburgh, who left an unrivalled pictorial record of Scotland's professional elite during a period when the 'Athens of the North' was noted for its intellectual supremacy. Portraits of members of the legal and medical professions, University professors, men of letters, and ministers of the Kirk, outnumber those of his aristocratic clientele. As neither sitters' books nor account books survive, it is difficult to establish a precise chronology for his stylistic development, especially his early career before he began to exhibit.

Raeburn was the second son of the proprietor of a textile mill at Stockbridge. He was educated at George Heriot's Hospital, Edinburgh. In 1772 he was apprenticed to James Gilliland, an Edinburgh goldsmith and remained with him until at least 1778. During his apprenticeship he began to paint miniature portraits. His first full-scale oil portrait can be dated 1776. It is generally accepted that at this stage he received advice from David Martin, an established portrait painter. About 1780 he married Ann Leslie (née Edgar), a widow of means. In 1784 he left for Italy, spending two months in London on the way, where he apparently gained experience in the studio of Sir Joshua Reynolds.

Nothing is known of his stay in Rome apart from a record of his having painted a miniature whilst there. This commission was negotiated by James Byres of Tonly, the resident Scottish antiquary and dealer, whose advice 'never to copy any object from memory, but from the principal figure to the minutest accessory to have it placed before him', Raeburn took as a guiding principle for his future career.

In 1786 he returned to Edinburgh. It seems probably that he had made a slow start as a painter and that the joint impact of Reynolds and Rome was responsible for his remarkably quickened progress over the next decade. At first Reynolds's influence is apparent, but Raeburn's personal style had evolved by the early 1790s. The first portraits painted after his return vary between bust-lengths, like enlarged miniatures in pattern, and three-quarter-length seated poses. A series of more ambitious open-air portraits show his increasing preoccupation with effects of lighting, culminating in a double portrait of Sir John and Lady Clerk of Penicuik. This was his first painting to be exhibited in London in 1792, where it was acclaimed by the critics for the 'bold touch and strength of effect'. However the strength of his chiaroscuro was more often unfavourably criticized and he was later to modify it.

In 1798 Raeburn moved into his new studio and gallery at 32, York Place, Edinburgh. He played an active part in the artistic life of the city, lending his gallery for exhibitions.

Raeburn was unusual in dispensing with preliminary drawings. Having arranged the sitter in a chair on a platform with his easel beside it, he walked slowly backwards, palette and brushes in hand, gazing at his subject. He then strode briskly forward and attacked the canvas. Raeburn said that 'nothing ought to divert the eye from the principle object: the face', and accordingly always began with the features. He used brushes a yard long, no maulstick and a relatively restricted palette. His sweeping descriptive strokes are often left unmodified, which caused less discerning contemporaries to condemn Raeburn for his 'lack of finish'. Arms and hands were often treated in too summary a manner to please his clients.

Raeburn's particular genius lay in his ability to 'plunge at once through all the constraint and embarrassment of the sitter and present the face, clear, open and intelligent as at the most disengaged moments' (R.L. Stevenson). Edinburgh society did not demand a fashionable image and Raeburn painted without flattery or idealization. For this reason he was most successful with mature subjects and with children, whose frank, open faces were exactly suited to his methods. The refusal to idealize meant that Raeburn could fail when painting official portraits on a grand scale. Nor was he always successful wih young women, whose faces, if not naturally pretty, were too immature to stand up to the painter's literal approach. Raeburn's full-length portraits of the Chiefs of Clans and Highland lairds in full dress, are a unique contribution to British Romantic painting. He captured the assurance and dignity of his subjects and the magnificent costume provided the necessary overtones of grandeur.

In 1810, hoping to take over the practice of the recently deceased John Hoppner, Raeburn visited London, but returned to settle permanently in Edinburgh. He continued to send portraits to the Royal Academy and was elected ARA in 1812 and a full Academician three years later.

At the height of his career he suffered financial difficulties due to the failure of his son's business in 1808. This helps to account for the unusual number of copies he was prepared to undertake. His prices rose steadily: in 1798 he charged 75 guineas for a full-length figure in a landscape. In 1817 he quoted 150 guineas for a full-length portrait of the Earl of Hopetoun with a horse. But this was well below London prices; Sir Thomas Lawrence's estimate for this same commission was £500.

Amongst Raeburn's last portraits was a bust-length of Sir Walter Scott. A mutual liking and respect which had failed to be established at their earlier meeting in 1808, when Raeburn had painted Scott's portrait for the publisher Constable, was the happy result of this late encounter.

Raeburn's career was crowned in 1822 when George IV conferred a knighthood on him during the royal visit to Edinburgh. The following year he was appointed King's Limner and Painter for Scotland, but died in 1823 before he could paint the portrait of George IV in Highland dress.

F. Irwin

Railways in Scotland were affected, inevitably, by the geography of the country; Highlands made construction expensive and difficult, Lowlands encouraged concentrations of population which in their turn encouraged the building of a tight network of lines. Railways sprang up wherever the centres of settlement ensured a return for the high capital investment, and even (as in Fort Augustus) where the low population could never hope to repay the enormous cost. Some centres (such as Strathpeffer) were by-passed through local politics and intransigence of landowners: some (like Elgin) were served by a proliferation of lines, the result of seemingly reckless commercial competition between the various companies which built and exploited the early lines, and established the pattern of Scottish railways which survives to the present.

The earliest lines were associated with mine workings, 'tramways' of stone, timber or metal designed to ease the passage of heavily laden trucks to a loading point, usually on a waterway. The motive power could be human, animal, gravity or eventually steam. The limitations of all other forms of traction were clear in the tiny loads and short distances possible for such lines as the 'Innocents' Railway from Edinburgh to Dalkeith. Inter-city services surmounting sharp gradients, and carrying profitable loads of passengers and freight, required the development of steam traction in the 1830s. All its power was to be required in a railway geography which presented difficulties in open country (the Slochd, Beattock) as in the city (Cowlairs bank in Glasgow from Queen Street station). In the big cities suburban trains were to hustle commuters to work and shape the pattern of leisure activities, while in the country the lines were to have a profound effect on market patterns, location of industry, tourism. It is small wonder that Scotland's kailyard eschews the main-line railway and dwells with satisfaction on the branch line. Both were to play an important part in economic development, the former in a national context, the latter in the comfortable establishment of local market centres.

The 1830s and 1840s were characterized by the establishment of local lines of an experimental nature (such as the Glasgow to Ayr route) and by the controversies which gave birth to the five major operating companies which built many lines, and absorbed those of their smaller competitors. The North British and Caledonian were the giants, the former being created in 1844 and the latter a year later, pushing construction rapidly ahead to link the main lines from the south to Edinburgh and Glasgow respectively. The North British lines eventually controlled the 'East Coast Main Line' to Berwick and thus to London-King's Cross and the workings north from Edinburgh, while in general the Caledonian operated the main line from Glasgow over Beattock to Carlisle, whence it was carried over Shap towards London-Euston. Other lines, often parallelling those of their commercial opponents, grew to a dense net in central Scotland.

Three other main companies grew from the chaos of smaller attempts. The Glasgow and South Western, as its name implies, operated between Glasgow and Carlisle over the territory west of the Caledonian main line. The Great North of Scotland operated north-wards from Aberdeen towards Inverness, while the Highland Railway thrust imaginative and fiercely-graded lines from Perth to Inverness and beyond. The Highlands were traversed by lines to Kyle of Lochalsh and Wick, to Mallaig and Oban—lines which are feats of engineering still to be respected, while their light passenger and freight loadings make them continuously open to threat of closure. Two conspicuous feats of engineering opened out the 'East Coast' line from Edinburgh to Aberdeen—the bridging of the Tay and Forth estuaries. Sir Thomas Bouch's bridge from Wormit to Dundee was blown down in a disastrous storm accident in 1879 but the impetus of development was such that its replacement was ready in 1887 and the Forth bridge, larger and even more impressive in its engineering, in 1890. In effect, the speed of construction was such that from the hectic promotions of the mid 1840s to the completion of the Lowland network as it remains substantially today took only 30 years. The Highland lines took longer, naturally.

The companies rejoiced in their achievements and their identities. The proud Caledonian operated prestige trains to immaculate standards of cleanliness, particularly in respect of the legendary 'Caledonian Blue' of its richly decorated locomotives. The North British, keenly aware of the commercial value of operating speed, did all in its power to popularize its rapid services to the south, while the low constructional specification of its main lines through Fife precluded (as it still does) sustained high speed north of Edinburgh. Occasionally the competitors joined forces, whether to operate a branch line jointly (such as that from Montrose to Bervie), grudgingly splitting the receipts, or whether sharing tracks from Kinnaber Junction (just north of Montrose) to Aberdeen, trains from as far away as Euston and King's Cross finishing their journey of over 500 miles on a mutual stretch of line along a difficult terrain. Public attention focused on this feature markedly in 1895 with the famous 'Railway Races' in which both companies vied to bring their overnight services from London to Aberdeen at the higher speed—not to Aberdeen, but to Kinnaber Junction, where the first arrival inevitably reached Aberdeen ahead of the other. The entertaining reading of the feats of locomotive firing and driving are exciting even today, though the risks are very plain in the reckless disregard of speed limits. The railways could only gain from popularity, and they did.

In the twentieth century railways in Scotland continued to expand, with the filling of gaps and the building of small branches. Yet a pattern was established after the First World War which was to prove significant. Wartime neglect, and increasing competition from other forms of transport, helped dictate the amalgamation of the operating companies into major groupings extended from the English giants in 1923. Thus the London, Midland and Scottish took over the Caledonian and GSW, along with the Highland lines, while in general the London and North Eastern took over the old North British and GNSR. Old loyalties among railwaymen persisted, rolling stock changed little except in colour, and for a long time the same locomotives (albeit in dingy and uninspired liveries compared with their early splendour) seemed to work on the same routes. Yet rationalization was inevitable, and slowly standard locomotive types and rolling stock penetrated all parts of the country, reducing maintenance costs and improving efficiency, at the expense of local tradition. Remorselessly road transport eroded the profitability of the smaller branches, while bus, car and tram eroded the profitability of most city suburban lines (witness their total extinction in Aberdeen, and near-total disappearance in Edinburgh). The Second World War merely accelerated the process. Branch lines were temporarily restored to popularity, but wartime neglect was prolonged and serious, and traffic rapidly fell off after the return to peacetime conditions. The railway companies again were rationalized, this time to 'British Railways' in 1948. Again little seemed to change for a time, then a gradual standardization took place, the local giving way to the centrally designed in locomotives, rolling stock, station design, operating procedures. Nothing, however, could arrest the steady growth of road transport in Scotland as in the whole of the British Isles. Railways since nationalization have continued to shrink in mileage (particularly after the Beeching proposals of the 1950s), in rolling stock and in passenger traffic.

It would be unfair to end on this note. Inter-city main lines were steadily upgraded since the war to conditions which in some cases far outshone pre-war prestige company standards. Displaced steam engines from England revolutionized working from Aberdeen to Glasgow, while later still high-speed trains made schedules from Aberdeen to London possible which would have been suicidal even to the enginemen of the great races of the 1890s. Certain lines (notably Edinburgh to Glasgow) generate consistently high traffic, while suburban workings in Glasgow have been extensively electrified, in part making good the damage of the ill-considered abandonment of the tramways in 1962. Certain areas of goods traffic—bulk transport of coal, specialized carriage of motor-car components or finished vehicles—are highly adaptable to rail transport and as such form a profitable feature of railways in Scotland. Government subsidy has long reprieved certain lines with no commercial basis for success, notably those to Mallaig and Kyle of Lochalsh. Within very tight monetary restrictions, a programme of steady modernization and even restitution (on the line from Perth to Inverness) has been pursued throughout the 1960s and 1970s. Scottish railways arose despite natural obstacles to fulfil a clearly defined need in the mid nineteenth century. In the later decades of the twentieth the need has changed, and an enormously expensive investment like a railway system has to change with its traffic demands. Some change is necessary curtailment, some is necessary modernization which, however necessary, is sometimes too expensive to be politically expedient. In some areas of passenger and freight working the future of the railways seems secure within present limits of available resources, in others the only justification for retention would be a social need, particularly where alternative transport (in winter particularly) is unsatisfactory. Certain losses sustained (including the 'Waverley Route' from Edinburgh to Carlisle via Hawick) cannot be made good, while others (the Penmanshiel tunnel collapse which severed the east coast main line in 1979) must be repaired even at enormous cost, for Scottish railways, as well as being a picturesque part of Scotland's heritage, are a prime social asset. As such, their future is a complicated one, but their survival in some form seems assured.

I. Campbell

Ramsay, Allan (1686–1758) was born in Leadhills, Dumfriesshire, the son of the overseer to the Hopes of Hopetoun. Ramsay claimed kinship with the Ramsays of Dalhousie. After schooling in Crawford, Ramsay became apprenticed to an Edinburgh wigmaker. In 1719 he set up as a bookseller, and in 1728 opened the first circulating library in Scotland. But for the opposition of the Church, he would also have established a regular theatre in Carruber's Close.

Soon after his arrival in the capital he began to establish himself in Edinburgh society, becoming a member of the Easy Club, of which Pitcairn and the grammarian Thomas Ruddiman were fellow members. The Club published Ramsay's poems as he threw them off. In 1716 he published an additional canto to *Christis Kirk on the Green* (attributed to James I). In 1720 a collection of his own poems appeared, subscribed to by Pope, Steel, Arbuthnot and Gay. *Fables and Tales* came out in 1722. In 1724 the first volume of his anthology of old and new Scots songs, *The Tea-Table Miscellany*, was published, being completed with three additional volumes in 1725, 1727 and 1732. Ramsay only indicated tune-titles in his anthology, leaving Alexander Stuart to produce in 1726 his *Music for Allan Ramsay's Collection of Scots Songs*.

Alongside this work as a writer of songs and a cobbler of folk fragments, Ramsay also set about resuscitating the neglected Scots Makars of the fifteenth and sixteenth centuries in his anthology *The Evergreen* (1724). Considerable liberties, however, were taken with some of the texts.

Ramsay's wider popularity was assured in 1725 by his pastoral drama with music, *The Gentle Shepherd*, which established the ballad-opera tradition three years before Gay's *The Beggars' Opera* was staged.

No one would claim *The Gentle Shepherd* to be a major masterpiece, but the verse used in this tale of rustic love at the time of the Restoration has many pleasing touches, and presents a convincing picture of rural manners. The rustic characters speak Scots, but the restored laird, Sir William Worthy, uses Augustan couplets girdered with impeccable moral sentiment.

After the success of this pastoral, Ramsay retired, his son, Allan Ramsay the portrait painter, building him a home on the Castle hill, the grey oriel of which still gazes across Princes Street as part of Ramsay Gardens, its windows looking over the fine statue of the poet at the foot of The Mound.

Ramsay's best original work developed the colloquial tone pioneered in Scots by Lyndsay's *Thrie Estatis*, and applied it to Edinburgh characters like Lucky Spence, the brothel-keeper, or the 'Wretched Miser', whose last advice Ramsay amusingly noted. Using the 'Standard Habbie' stanza form—probably learned from Semple's mock-elegy for 'Habbie Simson, the Piper of Kilbarchan' through Watson's anthology *A Choice Collection of Comic and Serious Scots Poems* (1706, 1709, 1711), a book that provided a cornerstone to the eighteenth-century Scots Revival Ramsay's pawky wit and gentle satire found rewarding targets. He made his dying miser thus address his gold:

> My life! my god! my spirit yearns,
> Not in my kindred, wife or bairns—
> Sic are but very laigh concerns
>   Compar'd with thee;
> When now this mortal rottle warns
>   Me I maun dee.

a foretaste of the tone of Burns's 'Holy Willie's Prayer'. Ramsay also achieved real success with the best of his conversational Epistles, another form to be developed later by Burns. As a song-writer, Ramsay lacked Burns's taste and sure ear for the integrity of Scots. 'My Patie is a young thing', however, has a charm of its own.

Because he provided a leg-up to Fergusson and to Burns, both better poets, Ramsay has been somewhat unjustly neglected. Carefully selected Ramsay's best work can still provide a rewarding experience in its own right.

M. Lindsay

Ramsay, Allan, the Younger (1713–1784), the greatest Scottish portrait painter of the eighteenth century, was born in Edinburgh on 13 October 1713 (New Style), being the son of the poet of the same name. He was educated in Edinburgh at the Royal High School, and received some instruction in drawing at the short-lived Academy of St Luke before continuing his studies in London under Hans Hysing. After a short period back in Edinburgh, Ramsay proceeded in 1736 to Rome to work under Francesco Imperiale. In Rome he drew at the French Academy, coming also under the influence of Pompeo Batoni. In 1737 he studied in Naples under Francesco Solimena, whose impact, together with that of Batoni, is apparent in the sophisticated polish of his early portraiture.

In the autumn of 1738 Ramsay established himself as a portraitist in London, and soon enjoyed immense success, receiving commissions from such great Scottish families as the Argylls, the Haddingtons and the Buccleuchs, and also attracting many important English patrons, including the Earl of Hardwicke, the Earl of Coventry and Earl Stanhope. Together with Hogarth, he played the leading part in creating the new British school of portraiture which was now to meet an increasing demand for lively characterization and unaffected naturalness. He frequently visited Edinburgh, but most of his portraits of Scottish sitters were executed in his busy London studio: among these, the full-lengths of Norman, twenty-second Chief of MacLeod (1747) (Private Collection) and of Archibald, third Duke of Argyll (Glasgow) are representative of the power of his early manner. No less important are the imposing full-lengths of Dr Richard Mead (1747), presented by the artist to the Foundling Hospital in London, and of Philip Yorke, first Earl of Hardwicke, the great Lord Chancellor (engraved 1749). In such pictures the 'grand manner' of European Baroque, reinterpreted with a tasteful restraint, is introduced into British portraiture.

During the 1750s Ramsay's style underwent a radical change: under the influence of contemporary French painting, Italianate dignity gives way to an essentially *rococo* elegance, in which delicate drawing combines with subtle modulations of often pastel-like colour. The quiet informality of such pictures as the three-quarter-lengths of John Sargent the Elder and Thomas Lamb of Rye (both 1753) introduced a new element into fashionable portraiture and influenced the art of Gainsborough. These qualities were to be developed further in a series of portraits painted in 1754 during a protracted visit to Edinburgh, where Ramsay founded the debating club known as the Select Society, whose members included his friends David Hume and James Adam, William Robertson, Adam Smith, Alexander Wedderburn, William Wilkie, Lord Monboddo and Lord Kames: the three-quarter-length of Lord Drummore and the half-length of Mary Adam (Yale) are supreme examples of the 'natural portrait' in British painting. Also from this year are the charming pair of half-lengths of Lady Walpole Wemyss and Lady Helen Dalrymple, which are among the first of Ramsay's portraits to show the now decisive influence of the French crayon-painter Quentin de La Tour, whose naturalness of style Ramsay commended in his essay *On Taste*. Ramsay's development from the masculine vigour of the 1740s to the almost feminine grace of the 1750s and 1760s is reflected no less clearly in his many surviving chalk studies—studies of attitudes, costumes, heads and, not least, hands—which witness to a devotion to drawing quite exceptional among portraitists of the period.

In the summer of 1754 Ramsay returned to Italy, living mainly in Rome and drawing again at the French Academy, besides making a number of chalk studies in Rome and Florence after such exponents of gracefulness as Raphael, Andrea del Sarto and Domenichino. In Rome he became a member of the circle of Robert Adam, and several watercolours of the ancient ruins, made in Adam's company, reveal something of the classical and archaeological bent of Ramsay's cultured mind. At the same time his defence of Greek architecture in

his essay *On Taste* made a minor contribution to the Roman-Greek controversy in which Piranesi and Winckelmann became the leading figures.

On his return to London in 1757, Ramsay was commissioned by Lord Bute, who was to become Prime Minister after the accession of George III, to paint a full-length of the future King, then Prince of Wales (1757); and the success of this sympathetic portrait must have been partly responsible for Ramsay's appointment in 1767—in effect from 1761—as George III's Principal Painter. Ramsay's State Portrait of George III in coronation robes (1761), the group of Queen Charlotte and her two eldest children (1764) (Buckingham Palace) and a profile portrait of the Queen holding a fan (*c.* 1762) are of similar quality. Ramsay now chiefly confined himself to sitters who had connections at court. The masterpieces of his maturity include full-lengths of Charles, fifth Earl of Elgin (*c.* 1758–60), Richard, second Earl Temple (1762) (Melbourne) and Lady Mary Coke (1762). The three-quarter-lengths of Elizabeth Montagu (1762) and William Guise (1764?) and the famous half-length of the artist's second wife Margaret Lindsay (*c.* 1760) (Edinburgh) combine intimate portraiture with a refined delicacy which is comparable to that of Nattier, and which Reynolds now sought to imitate—the rivalry of the two artists in the 1760s being epitomized by the important commissions given to Reynolds and Ramsay by Baroness Holland for her gallery at Holland House. On the scale of the half-length, Ramsay's powers as an interpreter of character are seen at their best in his portraits of William Pulteney, first Earl of Bath (*c.*1762), the Hon. Philip Yorke (*c.* 1762) and Jean-Jacques Rousseau (1766) (Edinburgh).

In the early 1770s Ramsay retired from painting, which became difficult after an accident to his right arm in 1773. He devoted his later years to literary pursuits, writing chiefly upon political affairs, and became an intimate of the Johnson circle. He made two further visits to Italy, in 1775–77 and in 1782–84, spending much of his time writing a learned essay on Horace's Sabine farm (never published). Returning home from his last Italian visit, he died at Dover on 10 August 1784. Ramsay was twice married—first to Anne Bayne (d. 1743), the daughter of Alexander Bayne, professor of Scots Law at Edinburgh University, and secondly, in 1752, to Margaret Lindsay, the daughter of Sir Alexander Lindsay, Bart., of Evelick. His pupils included David Martin (1737–1797) and Alexander Nasmyth (1758–1840), and for many years his principal assistant was Philip Reinagle (1749–1833), who was largely responsible for the numerous copies of Ramsay's State Portraits of the King and Queen ordered from his studio. (*See also* Painting, 1700 to 1900.)

A. Smart

Reith, John Charles Walsham (1889–1971), first Baron Reith of Stonehaven, was the first Director-General of the BBC. A man of commanding presence and autocratic temper, he exercised a powerful influence on the development of broadcasting both in Britain and overseas.

The son of a minister of the Free Church, he was educated at Glasgow Academy and Gresham's School, Holt and served an apprenticeship in locomotive engineering in Glasgow. In the First World War he was an officer in the Cameronians and the Royal Engineers and was badly scarred by a sniper's bullet.

He became general manager of the infant British Broadcasting Company in 1922, when it had a staff of four. He quickly saw possibilities in the new medium for moral betterment and social improvement and exerted himself to free it from commercial control and have it established under royal charter as a public corporation.

He was knighted in 1927, and remained in masterful control of his creation until 1938. He insisted on the highest standards and on the importance of leading rather than following public taste. A doer rather than a thinker, he always maintained that he did no more in his public life than apply the lessons he had imbibed as a child in the manse of the old College Church.

Reith was a man of restless energy and boundless ambition, constantly scanning the horizon for new challenges and brooding over the opportunities which he felt had been denied him. He left the BBC before he was 50, and although he lived into his eighties he felt that he was never again offered work which fully extended him.

He became Chairman of Imperial Airways and quickly turned it into a public corporation on the BBC model. He joined Chamberlain's government as Minister of Information and subsequently served under Churchill as Minister of Transport and Minister of Public Building and Works. He did not possess the suppleness necessary to a politician, however, and lacked all instinct to compromise. There was also a profound incompatibility between him and Churchill, and when the latter felt obliged to carry out a reshuffle in 1942 he found no room in his new administration for the man he referred to as 'Wuthering Heights'.

Reith then did important work as a Captain RNVR in preparing for the allied invasion of Europe. After the war he chaired the Commonwealth Telecommunications Board, the Hemel Hempstead New Town Corporation and the National Film Finance Corporation. He was also for nine years, a vigorous Chairman of the Colonial Development Corporation. He was elected Rector of Glasgow University and twice served as Lord High Commissioner to the Church of Scotland.

He found happiness only fitfully in his private life, and in spite of his Knighthood of the Thistle and many other honours, regarded himself as a failure. In later years, he thought and spoke a great deal about returning to Scotland, but he did so only in the last year of his life when he was granted a grace and favour residence by the Queen. He died in Edinburgh and his ashes are buried at Rothiemurchus.

I. McIntyre

Religious Fiction. An easy target for those who would account for the absence of Scottish theatre, or the imperfect development of parts of Scottish literature, the Church in Scotland is not easy to write about critically. Above all, when presented in fiction, it attracts equivocal judgements and attitudes. In the first place, the Church affects the writing of fiction. James Carlyle in eighteenth-century Ecclefechan would not read a novel, his son Thomas was to record, for he had been brought up to regard fiction, along with most imaginative literature, as idle and sinful. In *Rob Roy* Scott was to reflect a similar situation in the exaggerated exchanges between Francis Osbaldistone and his father. Religious disapproval of types of literature, including fiction, undeniably existed, and must be taken account of.

At the same time, the religious communities of Scotland since the Reformation have encouraged a curious blend of private experience and public morality which may not seem encouraging to the novelist who pursues social observation. The fiercely personal and private self-discipline encouraged by the Scottish Presbyterian Church combined frequently (and oddly) with a local congregational public discipline which, for good motives, regarded all life and conduct as open to inspection and censure by the Session, and in the long term by an omnipresent and omniscient God. Fiction, its automatic assumptions including a neutral observer and the existence of areas of privacy, has had to take account of this in Scotland.

Finally, one must admit the diversity of religious life and experience in a country where oversimplified dismissive treatments often attempt sweeping and unjustified generalization. Every country can point to religious debate and disagreement, but to write successfully about the Covenanters, or about the post-Disruption divisions in a Scotland of Auld Kirk and Free Kirk requires a tact which the weaker kailyard authors did not always possess. Scott, Galt and Hogg (qq.v.) had their successes with the earlier theme, but they were uneven ones, for the theme itself shows diversities of belief and interpretation not easy to generalize on. Private areas of religious experience, too, could yield delicate diversities when sympathetically handled by novelists of George MacDonald's calibre—for a religious system which left so much to the individual conscience produced a society where the unexpected awaited any novelist who had the tact to explore the possibilities of the subject.

One area of obvious success had come from attempts of Scottish fiction to approach the subject satirically. Far from suppressing Scottish literature, the Church in Scotland could be argued quite seriously to have made possible some magnificent literature of protest, including Burns's 'Holy Willie', and Hogg's cast of malignant perverted Calvinists in the *Confessions of a Justified Sinner*. It is worth stating the obvious, that both Holy Willie and the Wringhim family are perverts, and not orthodox Calvinist Christians held up to ridicule. As arrogant would-be dictators, profiting from a convenient religious system to dictate to their fellow-Christians, they are rightly ridiculed, in the context of their religious communities. The tensions between strong characters and their communities have been explored often and successfully, whether in the form of John Guthrie in Lewis Grassic Gibbon's (q.v.) *Sunset Song*, veering to abnormality of character and perversion of sexual lust and using his religious belief as an excuse for disgusting acts, or in the other dominating figures like Galt's Provost Pawkie, or George Douglas Brown's Gourlay who (like Hay's Gillespie) domineer in their communities without imposing their private *mores*. Even the short list cited varies from the case of Barbie, with weaklings for its two ministers, where Gourlay's dominance is quite distinct from the Church, to the case of Guthrie where it is inextricable from early twentieth-century Established Church teaching. The important point is that the examination is made by the novelist not in terms of a isolated Christian individual, but in the tension between that individual and his community. In the context of a Scottish Presbyterian community, a family like the Gourlays or the Wringhims can have enormous influence on those surrounding them. Lengthy weekly public worship and private family prayer, the stress on private morality and public accountability, all played their part. Faced with an eccentric or arrogant private misinterpretation of Christianity, the disproportionate effect achieved by an individual in his community is the ideal basis for satire. As much in Scotland as in New England, it produces masterpieces of educative fiction and (in Hogg's hands) disturbing ambiguity.

The mention of Hogg suggests another area in which religious fiction in Scotland can be credited with a considerable positive achievement. Satire arose from an unsympathetic religious community perhaps, but satire could be modified into a fictitious portrait of that community which permitted constructive criticism in a way which orthodox morality might be unprepared to admit. Millions of people found acceptable ways of reconciling the demands of the Scottish Church with an application in ordinary everyday life, a family and community involvement which permitted harmonious self-development. Such people are to be found everywhere in Galt's fiction, in Mrs Oliphant, in MacDonald's Glamerton, in Scott's working-class families which constitute the back-ground (and sometimes the foreground) of so many of his novels. Such people are a credible ground against which the more exaggerated moral struggles at the heart of the plot can be depicted.

Such people, necessary to the rounded portrait of Scottish religious life, can be brought more or less into the central arena of the plot, thereby permitting an examination of the 'ordinary' people whose religious life is sound and harmonious in most circumstances. Their certainties do not always stand up to stress, and obliquely the novelist questions the basis of their certainties: sometimes they triumph, sometimes they fail, and the blame for the failures is sometimes human imperfection, sometimes misapplied religious belief.

A celebrated case is Douce Davie Deans, at the centre of Scott's masterpiece *The Heart of Midlothian*. Scott plainly sees much to admire in Davie's lifestyle and belief, notwithstanding Davie's prolonging in peacetime a set of rigorous and inflexible religious ideals forged in a time of religious persecution, and little adapted for his present circumstances, or those of Jeanie and Effie who are brought up unquestioningly to accept them. Davie is a man of honour and Scott honours him for that. Yet his attitude to Davie at the time of Effie's trial shows distinct ambiguity, for David's own rigid code makes him dishonour

Effie rather than deviate by the slightest degree from his principles even to save her life. He would rather deny her existence. Had Stevenson lived to complete *Weir of Hermiston*, he would have had to write something very similar for the condemnation of Archie by his own father, to uphold public standards of morality.

Yet while Scott rightly focuses interest and attention on the head of the family, his ambiguity is shown in his treatment of Jeanie, who rightly supplants her father in the reader's attention and interest as the novel proceeds. Her religious values are those of peace-time, her standards less rigid, her attitude to minor peccadillos more humane. Yet at heart she shares her father's rigidity when applying absolute standards to life, and rather than perjure herself to save Effie, she condemns Effie by her silence in court—*and then* embarks on the journey to London, to save her sister's life by an act of benevolent intervention, practical Christianity which would never have crossed her father's mind. Unattractive though her dogmatism can be at times, the future plainly lies with Jeanie; the ambiguity her author shows is clear in his admiration for what she does, and his distaste for her inherited religious dogma. Like Boswell, Scott had reason to know the system well and to dislike its rigidities, and like Boswell he took refuge in ambiguities with which to criticize it, to hasten its change without resorting to open satire which might alienate his goodly audience, and so undo its effect in advance. His treatment of the Deans family is a tribute to their Christianity, but an implicit criticism of its application. It is not typical—but then that was hardly its intention.

Both the openly satirical, and the implicitly questioning, modes of religious fiction operate in curiously similar ways. Neither, at their best, resorts to oversimplified typecasting, nor to crude mockery. Both allow their fanatics to be human beings (Wringhim is human enough when he discovers himself doomed to a Hell he had imagined the exclusive preserve of others) to elicit our tragic pity) caught in a society where attitudes clamour for change and readjustment faster than human nature will permit. Wringhim's conservatism is the other side of the coin from the conservatism displayed by Galt's Balwhidder—yet both are together in examining the problems of relating private faith to public observance of the peculiarities of the Scottish Presbyterian Church. Perhaps the greatest success that religious fiction has achieved has been in the very tentative and ambiguous nature of its picture of this process, and its avoidance of open mockery of a painful and difficult problem at the heart of Scottish experience.

I. Campbell

Robert I, the Bruce (1274–1329), son of Robert Bruce, Lord of Annandale (in right of his wife, Earl of Carrick), and grandson of Robert Bruce, competitor for the Scots throne in 1291, was King of Scots, 1306–1329, and is regarded as one of the two founders of the independent kingdom of Scotland, the other being William Wallace (q.v.). (*See also* Scotland 1100–1488.) The real achievement of Bruce was to restore the

Scottish realm as it had been under Alexander III (d. 1286), independent and governed by its own laws and institutions. The Bruce family, originating at Brix near Cherbourg, had been settled in Annandale since *c.* 1120, Bruce himself being head of the seventh generation of the family in Scotland. At the death of Alexander III Bruce's grandfather asserted his claim to the throne despite national acceptance of the King's grand-daughter the 'Maid of Norway', and when the Maid died in 1290 he proved readier than most Scots to acknowledge the pretended overlordship of Edward I of England if it would gain him the Scottish throne. When the Court of Claims preferred John Balliol as king, the Bruces gave only nominal loyalty to the new dynasty. The Competitor died in 1295, and when King John resisted Edward I in 1296 the Earl of Carrick and his son, the future King, took the English side, although after he had deposed Balliol Edward I contemptuously refused Carrick the vacant throne.

Wallace's rising against English rule in 1297 marked a turning-point in Bruce's career. Defying his father, he led an abortive anti-English revolt and in 1298, following Wallace's defeat at Falkirk, was made joint Guardian of Scotland with John Comyn the younger of Badenoch, who represented the Balliol interest. Until 1302 Bruce was a prominent leader of the patriotic movement, probably helping to put John de Soules into the Guardianship in 1301. In 1302, however, fearing the consequences of a restoration of Balliol as king of Scotland, with French help, Bruce submitted to Edward I. He served the English King for four years, but was not trusted enough to be given a position of prominence in the administration of Scotland. Along with the bishop of Glasgow, Bruce advised the English parliament of 1305 (the year of Wallace's capture and execution) on the future government of what Edward I now called the *land* (no longer the *realm*) of Scotland. Conscious of his hereditary claim to the Scottish throne and influenced by the leaders of the Scottish Church, Bruce de-cided to defy Edward I in the winter of 1305–6 and put himself at the head of a revived national independence movement. The public enthronement of Bruce at Scone in March 1306 was precipitated by the murder of Comyn of Badenoch, whom Bruce may have tried to win over to his cause. Both events roused the ageing Edward I to vigorous and vindictive activity in which Bruce was put to flight and his supporters savagely punished. Returning in 1307, Bruce slowly but surely wore down his enemies, English and Scots, and established a new pattern of brilliant guerilla tactics and 'scorched earth'. The recovery of many English-held castles and the Isle of Man (1307–14) left only Stirling and Berwick in enemy hands, and the great battle of Bannockburn (23–24 June 1314) was occa-sioned by Edward II's attempt to relieve Stirling Castle. Here Bruce proved his military mastery in a pitched battle, as he had already done in guerilla warfare, by decisively overwhelming the large English army of mixed cavalry and foot with his own much smaller infantry force; but it went hard for the Scots that Edward II himself escaped from the field.

From 1314 to 1329 Bruce was occupied with three main objectives, restoring royal government within his realm,

winning recognition of his title and his kingdom's indepen-dence from the papacy and Christendom at large, and persuading the English monarchy and government to make peace. In his rule of Scotland Bruce modelled himself on Alexander III and governed with a strong sense of justice and a desire for reconciliation. In particular, his old foes of the Balliol and Comyn factions were largely won over, and Low-lands and Highlands treated on an equal footing. Recognition abroad came fairly soon from Scandinavia, the Low Countries and Hanse cities, and France; from the papacy only in 1324, after the Pope had been sent a letter from the Scots barons in 1320 (the 'Declaration of Arbroath') offering a classic state-ment of the case for Scottish independence. Peace with England proved by far the hardest goal to attain, despite the recovery of Berwick (1318), long years of raiding south of the Border, a prolonged campaign in Ireland (mainly under the King's brother Edward Bruce), and military encounters at Byland (1322) and Stanhope (1327) in which Edward II and Edward III respectively were nearly captured. Edward III at last made the Treaty of Edinburgh with Bruce in March, 1328, ratifying it at his parliament of Northampton later in the year. The treaty acknowledged Bruce's title and Scotland's indepen-dence of England with territorial limits which included Berwick and the Isle of Man. To cement a future alliance between the countries, Bruce's five-year-old son David (by his second wife, Elizabeth de Burgh) married Edward III's sister Joan, but since the marriage produced no children, the royal succession passed (1371) to Bruce's grandson Robert Stewart, son of Bruce's eldest child, Marjorie, the daughter of his first wife Isabel of Mar.

G. W. S. Barrow

Roman Scotland. The inclusion of an article on Roman Scotland in a volume devoted to Scottish culture requires some justifi-cation. Despite the scale of the impact which the Roman invasion made on contemporary communities, the overall pe-riod of Roman occupation was as comparatively brief as the physical extent of their context was limited: barely two de-cades in the first century AD, a quarter of a century in the second, and a handful of years in the early third; field-armies may have penetrated to the shores of the Moray Firth, and seaborne reconnaissance embraced the Northern Isles, but an enduring Roman presence was rarely experienced north of the Tay.

The reason for considering these fleeting episodes in a cultural context are nevertheless convincing. Scotland pro-vides an appropriate stage on which to view the labours of an early imperial power operating at the limits of its dominion, the evidence for which includes a range of ancient military installations better preserved, considering the impermanent materials of their fabric, and more thoroughly studied, than in most other provinces of the former Empire. Secondly, by reason of the above, the content and study of Roman Scotland, like the dark matter of outer space, acts as a lens to bring obscurer topics into sharper focus. The study of Roman

Scotland thus serves, on the one hand, to crystallise perceptions about contemporary native society, offering an alternative framework inside which to study the Iron Age peoples of Scotland; on the other, it provides an analogy for approaches to archaeological evidence for periods far distant in time, but closely mirroring the Roman experience—the Wars of Independence, the campaigns of Montrose, the '45, even Neolithic expansion, are all apt instances! Finally, and culturally most important, attitudes to Roman Scotland, as evinced by people in Scotland, provide informative reflection of changing perceptions of national identity.

The archaeological content and historical outline of the occupation may briefly be conveyed. Roman troops advanced north of Cheviot and Solway *c.* AD 79 under the command of Julius Agricola, governor of Britannia from 77 to 83; almost all of Scotland south of the Forth-Clyde isthmus was overrun and held until about the end of the century, but *c.* AD 86/7 the northernmost conquests, which extended at least as far as Strathmore, were abandoned, probably because part of the British garrison was withdrawn for service on the Danube.

In the first 40 years of the second century, the northern frontier of Britannia rested on the Tyne-Solway isthmus, eventually developing into the Hadrian's Wall line, whose outpost forts once more established a marginal Roman presence in Scotland. About AD 140, a second large-scale advance was mounted, a new frontier-barrier of turf, the Antonine Wall being constructed from Forth to Clyde, with an occupied zone extending to the north as far as the Tay. After various vicissitudes, this frontier, too, was given up *c.* AD 163 and Hadrian's Wall brought back into operation.

The closing decades of the second century saw an increase of hostile pressure, with the northern tribesmen penetrating south of the Wall and requiring to be either rebuffed in battle or diverted by a Caledonian danegeld. Eventually, the only solution was for an Imperial expedition, and *c.* AD 208 Septimius Severus and his sons took the field, advancing at least as far north as the Mearns and, after a series of attritional campaigns, leaving behind short-lived garrison-posts on the east coast at Carpow and Cramond. Thereafter, although the northern tribes (then emerging as the Pictish nation), may have called forth occasional punitive expeditions, all attempts at permanent occupation by the Romans were at an end.

Those structural remains of Roman conquest, which are of a scale or character to be assessed as jewels in the heritage crown of any nation, fall into four main categories: temporary works constructed by armies in the field; the road-network; major permanent bases and garrison-posts; and linear defence-systems or frontiers.

The first group consists largely of marching-camps, the defended resting-places of Roman armies on campaign, erected at the end of each day's march. Most of these ephemeral structures, which are particularly well-represented in Scotland, compared with other provinces, have been discovered as a result of aerial reconnaissance, but a few rare examples survive as upstanding earthworks, notably at Ardoch in Strathallan. Extensive stretches of Roman roads also survive, mostly in upland areas—in Lauderdale, in southern Roxburgh, or between Annandale and Clydesdale, where the skill of the Roman road-engineer working in difficult conditions is marvellously displayed. There are many types of permanent garrison-posts, ranging from watch-towers to the headquarters of legions, and all categories are represented by the Scottish material. The most important is the first-century base, possibly of the Twentieth Legion, at Inchtuthil on the Tay, a little to the east of the Dunkeld gap. Over fifty acres in size, and accommodating almost six thousand troops, it formed the strong-point at the centre of a chain of briefly-held frontier garrisons deployed along the Highland Edge. Of similar importance is the 12-acre composite legionary and auxiliary base at Newstead, on the Tweed near Melrose. Newstead's history is more complicated, embracing at least four periods of occupation, divided equally between the first and second centuries. In each of them, it appears to have represented the command-centre for Roman control of southern Scotland. Both sites have been extensively excavated.

Scotland can also boast examples illustrating various stages of development in Roman frontier-policy: the early attempts to divide Caesar's land from *barbaricum*, by increasing the density of roadside garrisons and surveillance-posts, are well exemplified by the Forth-Tay system, first recognised in the sector known as the Gask Ridge, to the south-west of Perth; the developed form of frontier, whose physical manifestation was a running barrier heavily defended by resident garrisons, is represented in Scotland by the Antonine Wall. This imposing frontier extended for nearly forty Roman wall-miles, from Bridgeness on the Forth to Old Kilpatrick on the Clyde. Completed in *c.* AD 142, the barrier itself was built of turf, although two of its eighteen defending forts were stone-walled. Behind its protective screen, the Romans doubtless intended that a pacified southern Scotland would grow gradually into a stable province, instilling a Romanised way of life in what had previously been an arena for tribal rivalry. The brevity of the Antonine occupation precluded such development, however.

In view of that historical failure, it is all the more remarkable that Scotland's Roman past should have occupied such a prominent position, albeit intermittently, in the nation's consciousness. That prominence was not achieved until after the Renaissance, the Scottish people's previous awareness of the Roman invasion being mainly indirect, mediated by the epitomic accounts of writers like Gildas, Nennius and Bede, or more allusively through the medium of place-names—for example, Graham's Dyke for the Antonine Wall, Dere Street for the main arterial route between Tyne and Forth, Arthur's Oon (Oven) for the monumental structure near Camelon. However, once the literary evidence became generally available, and archaeological material—coins, altars, inscriptions—began to accumulate, the competing claims of the scholar and the patriot also made their appearance. Crudely put, antiquarian satisfaction that the grandeur of Rome could be recognised on Scottish soil was tempered by national pride that the might of the legions had ultimately yielded to Caledonian resistance.

Those sentiments apart, until the middle of the nineteenth

century, the antiquarian study of Scotland's ancient past was largely monopolised by the students of her Roman history. The researches of Robert Sibbald (1641–1722) and Alexander Gordon (1692–1750), which found expression in published form (respectively, *Historical Inquiries* in 1707 and *Itinerarium Septentrionale* in 1726), partly depended on work carried out in the field, and study by a galaxy of eminent predecessors (for example, Buchanan, Irvine, Pont, Adair and Edward), who combined an interest in ancient history with pioneering work in one or several of the developing applied sciences—medicine, architecture, cartography. Such involvement in the practical side of investigation transmuted an historical pursuit into archaeology, although still archaeology of a decidedly antiquarian cast. The gradual introduction of an academic discipline into these studies was accompanied by a movement towards more systematic approaches, towards more rigorous analysis and synthesis, and eventually a widening of archaeological curiosity to embrace the non-Roman past. These were essentially the fruits of the enlightenment. Paradoxically, the process which led, *via* Maitland and Chalmers, to the great synthetic and popularising work of Robert Stuart, whose *Caledonia Romana* was published in 1845, led also to the birth of prehistoric studies and, in relative terms, to a temporary decline in scholarly interest in the traces of Rome.

Before that point was reached, however, Major-General William Roy (1726–1790) had demonstrated, during the Military Survey of Scotland, how great were the potential benefits of combining field-survey and experience of military matters, with an interest in the Roman past. Inspired by Robert Melville's identification of four Roman marching-camps in Strathmore, Roy conducted his own field-research into the campaigns of Agricola, publishing the results in his epochal *Military Antiquities of the Romans in North Britain* (1793). Archaeology and maps were to be inextricably intertwined ever after.

The next high tide in the study of Roman Scotland, was engendered by the programme of site-excavation mounted by the Society of Antiquaries of Scotland between 1895 and 1905, followed immediately by James Curle's excavation at Newstead (1905–10). From the earlier projects grew the controlled practice of site-examination by excavation, though still with much to be learned; from Newstead came the lesson that the study of individual sites in Scotland had necessarily to be integrated with the comparison of structural, and especially artefactual, evidence from Roman sites elsewhere in the Empire.

The years between the two World Wars witnessed the extension of scientific excavation to other sites, notably on the Antonine Wall, and in 1934 the publication of the monograph *The Roman Wall in Scotland*, by the numismatist and scholar Sir George Macdonald, not only drew together the results of such work, but also established a benchmark for the presentation of Roman archaeology.

Developments in the past five decades have been characterised by an accelerating process of specialisation: detailed examinations of individual sites, such as Castledykes, Inchtuthil, Birrens, Elginhaugh and Newstead; intensive appraisal of specific areas of artefactual evidence—coins,

pottery, inscriptions and sculpture; the enormous enhancement of the database through the application of aerial survey, which has contributed more to the study of Roman Scotland than almost any other province in the Roman Empire; the application of ever more sophisticated techniques to the examination of the natural and man-made environment of Roman sites; and, not least, to the reappraisal of the native context of Roman occupation. In all of these, as in the recurrent re-interpretation of the derived historical evidence, the archaeology of Roman Scotland is being reshaped with a vigour which reflects, perhaps surprisingly, that of the current cultural context.

G. Maxwell

Royal Scottish National Orchestra. The history of the Royal Scottish National Orchestra dates back over a hundred years to 1981, when the Scottish Orchestra was formed, although its antecendents had been in existence since 1844. It became the Scottish National Orchestra, a full-time body serving the whole of Scotland, in 1950, since when it has achieved remarkable international prestige—under Karl Rankl, Hans Swarowsky, Sir Alexander Gibson (now Honorary President), Walter Susskind, Neeme Jarvi (now Conductor Laureate), the late Bryden Thomson and most recently Walter Weller who took up his appointment as Music Director in January 1992.

The Orchestra's international status was acknowledged in 1978 with the grant of patronage by Her Majesty The Queen, and in January 1991, in recognition of the SNO's Centenary she conferred the title 'Royal' on the orchestra.

In addition to making around 130 appearences each year in Scotland, the Royal Scottish National Orchestra appears regularly at many of the major British festivals, including the Henry Wood Proms and the Edinburgh International Festival.

In recent years the RSNO has received outstanding critical acclaim and built up a considerable reputation as an award-winning recording orchestra. Its recording of *Prokofiev Symphony No. 6* won the Gramophone Award for best orchestral recording in 1985 and *Symphony No. 7* was runner-up in 1986; both are part of a highly successful complete cycle of *Prokofiev Symphonies*. In 1990 the orchestra won the Gramophone Award for best concerto recording with Neeme Jarvi and Lydia Mordkovitch.

The Royal Scottish National Orchestra has given many World and British premieres and its commitment to contemporary music includes the IBM Composers' Competition and Music Nova. It also played a major role under Sir Alexander Gibson in the first twenty years of Scottish Opera and is committed to a wide range of educational projects designed to encourage participation and appreciation amongst young people.

F. Ferguson

Ruaraidh MacThòmais *see* **Thomson, Derick**

Rugby Union. Recreational pastimes formed part of the lives of the populace of early Scotland. It is known that Roman soldiers in Britain found relaxation in *harpastum*—a hard-ball game which, it is claimed in some quarters, led eventually to the Border Ba' games. Although conjecture, a strong case can be made for this belief when it is recognised that the main Roman route into Scotland was across the Cheviots, past Jedburgh and Ancrum, and on to Newstead near Melrose. The Romans were encamped there for more than a century and it is almost inevitable that local communities acquired and developed some of their customs.

Evolving Border ba' games formed the basis of football in Scotland. Local people divided themselves into two sides—no maximum number being specified. There were few rules and no playing fields: the games were played in the streets. The divisions were usually along local geographical criteria—e.g., the 'Uppies' against the 'Doonies'. The object of the game was to carry the ba', mostly by sheer brute force, to touch some agreed target at the far end of the opposition's area. It would seem that kicking was not an option: the mass of bodies ruled that out—and such folly of action would probably have resulted in the would-be kicker injuring himself. The ba' in these games was quite small, about the size of a modern tennis ball and, being made from leather, it was quite hard. Examples of Border ba's can be seen in the Scottish Rugby Union's Museum at Murrayfield. An annual symbolic game is still played in some areas.

In the early 19th century such games were no longer considered to be a popular pastime. Following six long hard working days each week, the working classes had little time or energy for play. Football, as a nationally-enjoyed game went into decline. It was saved from total extinction by being taken up in some schools, and in universities, as an acceptable recreation.

These educational institutions developed kicking and/or handling games along lines, and with rules, to suit their own needs. There is evidence of a handling game having been played at the High School in Edinburgh in 1810. Eventually, when they became former pupils and students, these gentlemen formed clubs and teams and organised and governed the game in its formative years.

Several new schools were formed in Scotland during the first half of the 19th century, among them Edinburgh Academy (1824), Loretto (1827), Merchiston (1833), Glasgow Academy (1845) and Trinity College, Glenalmond (1847). It is known that simple and crude forms of football were played at all of these schools, but it was in Edinburgh that the handling game first took root and spread to other areas of the country.

Two young men, Francis and Alexander Crombie, came from Durham School to Edinburgh in 1854. Francis joined the Academy as a pupil but Alexander had already left school. Apparently, neither brother had played football at Durham but they took with them a knowledge of the rules of football as played at Rugby School and this they passed on. Francis is recorded as having been the first school football captain and Alexander became actively involved in the formation of the Edinburgh Academical Football Club. He qualified for membership under a rule which allowed relatives of school pupils to become members. In 1858 he became the first captain of the Football Club—a position he held for eight years.

During the same period, a boy named Hamilton came to the High School in Edinburgh (in 1856) from an English public school and brought with him the 'Rules of Rugby Football' as he had known them in the south. This document was instrumental in the High Schools' adapting their existing game to this new form.

The first-ever inter-school match recorded in Scotland was the High School *versus* Merchiston, played on 13 February 1858. However, the game suffered from lack of uniformity of both rule and ball. In the High School, in the early 1860s, football was played with '... monstrous inflated globes of vast circumference and ponderosity ...'. H.H. Almond, a master at both Loretto and Merchiston and a founding father of the game in Scotland, describing an incident in a Loretto *versus* Merchiston match, wrote: '... but so little did any of us, masters or boys, then know about it, that I remember how, when Lyall ran with the ball behind the Merchiston goal the resulting try was appealed against on the ground that no player may cross the line whilst holding the ball. The previous rule at Merchiston had been that he must let go of the ball and kick it over before he touched it down. It must be said in excuse for this and other similar sins of ignorance, that the only available rules were those printed for the use of Rugby School. They were very incomplete and presupposed a practical knowledge of the game'.

Gradually, over several years, the game approached that then being played at Rugby. There were local variations which, inevitably, resulted in disputes. Almond again: '... well into the 1870s the only schools able to play each other on even terms were the Edinburgh Academy, Merchiston and the High School'.

From the mid 1860s senior (former pupils) clubs started to appear in both the Glasgow and Edinburgh areas and these clubs, making good use of the then new railways, began to play each other. In those early club matches play was often halted whilst captains and umpires tried to settle some point of difference. Such disputes and mix-ups were frequent.

Such a state of affairs could not continue indefinitely and a group of men from the Edinburgh Academical Football Club convened a series of meetings and, in 1868, with the agreement of the other schools and clubs, set out and had printed rules for the game in Scotland. The resulting booklet *Laws of Football as played by the Principal Clubs in Scotland* became known as *The Green Book*. Alas, no copy survives but it is worthy of note that neither the clubs nor *The Green Book* felt it necessary to include the word 'Rugby' in their title. Indeed, the Scottish Football Union, formed in 1873, did not alter its name to become the Scottish Rugby Union until 1924—the year prior to the opening of Murrayfield.

In December 1870, following a series of Scotland v. England eleven-a-side football matches played in London, (all of which were won by England), a group of Scots players issued a letter of challenge in the *Scotsman* and in *Bell's Life in London*, to play an England twenty at the carrying game. The English could hardly ignore such a challenge and this led to the first-ever rugby international match being played at Raeburn Place, Edinburgh, on Monday, 27 March 1871. The Scots won the encounter by a goal and a try to a try (a points scoring system had not then been devised).

The development of the game saw the foundation of the Scottish Football Union in 1873, a change to fifteen-a-side (from twenty-a-side) in 1877, the formation of the International Rugby Football Board in 1886, and the instigation of a points scoring system in 1889. Changes to the laws of the game have been made at various times and this process still continues today.

In 1897 land was purchased at Inverleith, Edinburgh. Thus the SFU became the first of the Home unions to own its ground. The first visitors were Ireland, on 18 February, 1899 (Scotland—3 Ireland—9).

International rugby was played at Inverleith until 1925. The SFU had purchased land, belonging to the Edinburgh Polo Club, at Murrayfield, in 1922. There they built the first Murrayfield stadium which was opened on 21 March 1925. England were the visitors and a more fitting climax to the international rugby season could not have been scripted: it was pure *Boys' Own* stuff!

Scotland already had victories over France at Inverleith (25–4), Wales in Swansea (24–14) and Ireland in Dublin (14–8). England, the Grand Slam champions of the two previous seasons, already had a win over Wales (12–6) and a drawn game (6–6) with Ireland—both played at Twickenham; they were to go on to defeat France in Paris by 13–11, in April. The 70,000 spectators at Murrayfield were treated to a stupendously exciting match in which the lead changed hands several times before Scotland secured the 14–11 victory which gave them their first-ever Grand Slam.

The Calcutta Cup. The Calcutta Cup was gifted to the Rugby Football Union in 1878 by the members of the short-lived Calcutta Rugby Club. The members had decided to disband: the Cup was crafted from melted-down silver rupees which became available when the Club's funds were withdrawn from the bank. The Cup is unique in that it is competed for annually by only England and Scotland. The first Calcutta Cup match was played in 1879 and, since that time, 99 matches have been played. England have won the Cup on 49 occasions to Scotland's 36. There have been 14 drawn matches.

The mythical 'Triple Crown'. There is no trophy for winning a 'Triple Crown'. This is achieved by one of the 'Home' countries defeating the other three in any one season. Scotland first achieved the feat in 1891 and have won the accolade on 10 occasions since then.

The equally-mythical 'Grand Slam'. As with the 'Triple Crown', there is no trophy for the 'Grand Slam'. To gain this distinction a country must defeat France as well as the other three 'Home' countries. To date, Scotland have achieved this success on only three occasions: 1925, 1984 and 1990.

The 'highs' of 1925, 1984 and 1990 were interspersed with many 'lows'. By far the most humiliating defeat (0–44) was that at the hands of South Africa at Murrayfield in 1951. That match was the third in a sequence of 17 consecutive defeats beginning with the match versus Ireland on 24 February 1951. Scotland were not to taste victory again until 5 February 1955 when they defeated Wales 14–8 at Murrayfield.

Up to season 1972–73 Scotland's rugby clubs participated in what was known as an 'unofficial championship'. It provided very unbalanced competition: some clubs played more fixtures than others and some fixture lists provided stiffer opposition than others. The resulting league table at the end of each season gave a very unbalanced and difficult-to-comprehend set of results.

Starting in season 1973–74, the Scottish Rugby Union organised the full member clubs into seven leagues. This suited some of the 'open' clubs but many of the older former pupils clubs found it difficult to compete successfully and were forced into going 'open' themselves to try to recruit some of the better players. In the first 14 seasons of league rugby the Division I championship was won by Hawick on ten occasions.

J.McI. Davidson

S

Saints, Early. Little genuine historical or biographical information has survived about early Scottish saints. Frequently no more than a place-name (Kil*marnock*, 'cell of my Ernóc', Kil*lumpha*, 'cell of Iomchadh') has survived to indicate that a cult once existed. The saints so commemorated are often Irish, sometimes Welsh or Cornish, whose legends, if they have been preserved, may sometimes contain references to journeys made by the saint to places in Scotland. Examples are Boethius, the Irish patron of Kirk*buddo* in Angus, and Cadoc, the Welsh patron of Cambuslang near Glasgow. In general, the extant legends (the word is used in its primary sense, 'matter to be read aloud' on commemorations of the saint) are charter myths, explaining and validating in pre-scientific terms the institutions, customs and beliefs prevailing at a particular time in a particular area of ecclesiastical influence. They are thus aetiological, providing sacred origins in addition for such material things as buildings, artefacts, unusual rock-markings, notable trees, medicinal springs. Legends are generally written in Latin with some pretence to style; even if no Latin original is known, vernacular legends are usually to be regarded as translations or adaptations of a Latin original. The medium used is usually prose, but sometimes verse.

A complete legend usually includes an account of the two most significant events in a saint's life, his birth in the flesh, and his birth into the full life of the spirit on the day of his death, together with an account of the miracles performed by him during his life and posthumously at his tomb. Each miracle normally has some charter significance. The influence of New Testament miracle stories is strong. Not infrequently the literary form parodies elements in the secular hero tale (Lord Raglan, *The Hero*, London, 1936; J. de Vries, *Betrachtungen zum Märchen*, Helsinki, 1954). As a whole, or in individual episodes, the legend may embody international tale-types (A. Aarne, S. Thompson, *The Types of the Folktale*, 2nd revision, Helsinki, 1961), and almost invariably international motifs (S. Thompson, *Motif-Index of Folk-Literature*, 6 vols., Bloomington and Helsinki, 1932). The legend thus combines features characteristic of traditional folk-literature with others derived ultimately from the Bible and the panegyric oratory of the later Roman Empire, as mediated by the pattern works of Christian hagiography, Athanasius' *Life of Antony* (before 373) and Sulpicius Severus' *Life of Martin* (c.400). Some legends have stronger elements of biography than others, but their primary importance is as myth, to be interpreted in terms of intellectual, cultural and social history.

Christian hagiography parallels closely that of other cultures and religions—the stories, for instance, of Moslem and Buddhist saints, and the hero-cults of the ancient Greek city-states.

Legendary material was utilized by early Scottish historians, for instance, Fordun (c.1320–c.1384), Bower (c.1385–1449), and Boece (c.1465–1536). The *Aberdeen Breviary* (1510) has preserved fragments or condensed versions of a number of Scottish legends, one of which, that of Machar of Aberdeen, has also survived in the form of an extended fifteenth-century verse rendering in Scots. A Norse version of the Orkney legend of St Magnus (*ob*.?1117) has been preserved in the thirteenth-century *Orkneyinga Saga*.

Independent, fully developed Latin legends have survived for three early bishops, Ninian (Nynia), Servanus (Serf), and Kentigern (Mungo), and for one abbot, Columba (Colm, Columcille). For the most part, these last explain the origin and validate the authority of the organized Church in one of the more or less independent kingdoms of sub-Roman Scotland. Historically, the earliest is a bishop, Ninian, whose *floruit* is the turn of the fourth and fifth centuries—the very end, that is to say, of the Roman period in Britain. It is probably significant that his area of episcopal authority, the modern Wigtownshire, perhaps also the rest of Galloway and the Isle of Man, lay close to Carlisle, one of the most northern urban centres of the Christian Roman Empire. There are some hints that the sphere of Ninian's influence extended from Wigtownshire northwards to the Scottish midlands and westwards to Ireland. The earliest complete version of his legend is a late eighth-century Latin poem, the *Miracula Nynie Episcopi*, composed by an Anglian monk of his principal church at Whithorn, and preserved in an eleventh-century MS. Bede (*ob*.735) was familiar with the material in some form; the original legend certainly predated Anglian settlement in Galloway, and cannot be later than the middle seventh century.

The prose *Life* of Ninian by Ailred of Rievaux (1109–1167) is not directly based on the *Miracula*, but derives by way of an Anglo-Saxon intermediary from the same early source.

Servanus, whose dates are uncertain, seems to have been the bishop who established organized Christianity in Manaw, the partly British, partly Pictish territory on both sides of the upper Forth estuary, which included Clack*mannan* and Sla*mannan* within its borders. His main church was at Culross in west Fife. His legend is mentioned in a document of the second half of the twelfth century, and is preserved in a thirteenth-century MS, probably of Glasgow origin. The first and second parts contrast strikingly with each other. The first tells of the saint's miraculous birth to royal parents in Canaan, and his distinguished early career in Alexandria, Jerusalem, Constantinople and eventually Rome, where he was Pope for seven years. The second tells of his humbler achievements when under angelic guidance he abandoned the papacy to carry out his mission in Manaw. For the original audience, the myth gained much of its power from the combination of the domestic with the exotic.

Kentigern and Columba were contemporaries. Columba died in 597 and the most probable date of Kentigern's death is 612. An apocryphal story exists of a meeting between the two. Their legends, however, are very different. Kentigern's main church was Glasgow, the centre of episcopal authority in the British Kingdom of Strathclyde, which extended beyond the Clyde valley into Nithsdale, Annandale and upper Tweeddale, perhaps also into Lothian, Cumberland and Westmorland. The legend preserves material of significance for all these areas. It is preserved in two main forms, the earlier and more interesting of which, composed between 1147 and 1164, survives only in substantial fragments, dealing with the birth-story of the saint (a variant of Aarne Thompson 934C, Man will Die if he ever Sees his Daughter's Son), his boyhood deeds, and his relationship with the mad prophet Lailoken or Merlin. The other, composed between 1175 and 1199 by Jocelyn of Furness, is complete, but the material, where it can be compared with the earlier version, has suffered a good deal of ecclesiastical bowdlerization. Some parts of the legend have a close and curious relationship to secular Arthurian romance.

The legends of Servanus and Kentigern incorporate some material of Gaelic origin and provenance, but like the legend of Ninian, they belong primarily to a people whose language was Cumbric, the P-Celtic tongue of southern Scotland and northern England, closely akin to Welsh. Columba is the earliest saint of the Q-Celtic Scottish Gaelic community, and insofar as he is the saint of Scottish Dalriada, with its spiritual centre at Iona, his legend bears some functional resemblance to that of Ninian, Servanus or Kentigern. At most however this resemblance is partial. The authority of Columba's signs and miracles is made to extend over Ireland, Pictavia, Strathclyde and Northumbria; his legend forms the charter myth of the Columban Church as it existed in the lifetime of the compiler of the extant form of the legend, Adomnan (c.625–704), ninth successor of Columba as abbot of Iona, and himself also a saint. The charter element is clear. Adomnan ignores biographical sequence and concentrates on the systematic presentation of the attributes through which Columba bequeathed authority to his Church—prophetic revelation (Book I), miracles of power (Book II) and angelic apparitions (Book III). Incidentally, much fascinating, and even touching, domestic detail is provided (the story, for instance, in I.48. of the pilgrim crane which was storm-blown to Iona from Ireland), but the final emphasis is on power, exercised with restraint and humanity, over a wide and politically disparate geographical area.

Partly as a result of the history of the Pictish Church, subjected as it was to alternate domination by Iona and Northumbria, a non-Pictish origin in Irish or Roman territory is assigned to most of the saints whose churches are in territory historically Pictish. Servanus may serve as a geographically peripheral example of the latter. More central is Bonifatius, founder of Restennet near Forfar, who is described in the *Aberdeen Breviary* as an Israelite, descended from the sister of the apostles Peter and Andrew, who had been Pope, like Servanus, before he set out to evangelize Pictavia, or perhaps originally only Circinn (Angus and the Mearns), one of the seven kingdoms of the Picts. By contrast, Drostan of Deer in Buchan, who has a Pictish name, and for whom a short Gaelic legend is provided in the twelfth-century *Book of Deer*, and Machar of Aberdeen are both made associates of Columba. A later saint, whose influence seems to have been extensive, and for whose existence good historical evidence has survived, is Maelrubha of Applecross in Wester Ross. He was an Irishman, born in 642, who became a monk of Bangor in Co. Down, withdrew to Scotland in 671 and in 673 founded Applecross, over which he presided until his death in 722. The *Aberdeen Breviary* preserves fragments of a meagre legend. One saint native to Pictavia may be bishop Duthac of Tain in Easter Ross, but if he is correctly identified with the chief confessor of Ireland and Scotland who, according to the *Annals of Ulster*, died in 1065, he belongs to a period much later than the end of a separate Pictavia. The identification is not certain. A legend is preserved in the *Aberdeen Breviary*.

The total contribution of the Picts to Scottish hagiography is unimpressive. Yet a church in Pictish territory eventually outstripped Whithorn, Culross, Glasgow and Iona to become the central shrine of medieval Scotland. The primacy of St Andrews substantially depends on its claim to an indirect apostolic origin by way of the Greek monk Regulus or Rule, who is said in a legend, the oldest extant form of which is preserved in a twelfth-century MS, to have brought the relics of St Andrew from Constantinople to Pictavia after the apostle in a vision had granted the King of the Picts victory by the sign of the cross over a numerically superior enemy. The story resembles that told of Constantine, the first Christian Roman emperor, and his victory in 312 over his pagan rival Maxentius at the Milvian Bridge. The mythical content of the legend is small, but the charter force of the apostolic name seems to have been so great that even after the disappearance of the Picts as a separate nation, the Culdee communities, which claimed descent from Regulus and his monks, retained and enlarged their prestige until Andrew became the Scottish patron saint

and St Andrews eventually the site of the first archbishopric in Scotland.

The names of a number of other interesting early Scottish saints must simply be listed: Baldred of Tyninghame, East Lothian, and the Bass Rock; Blane of Kingarth, Bute and Dun*blane*, Perthshire; Boisil of St *Boswell's*, Roxburghshire; Cainera of Kir*kinner*, Wigtownshire; Colman of Portma*homack*, Easter Ross; Constantine of Govan, Glasgow, and Kirk*constantine*, Ayrshire; Donnan, martyred in Eigg, patron of the many Kil*donans*; Medana of the two Kirk*maidens*, Wigtownshire; Molaise of La*mlash* and Holy Island, Arran; Moluag of Lismore, Argyll and the many Kil*moluags*; Munnu of Kil*mun* on Holy Loch, Argyll; Triduana of Rescobie, Angus, and Restalrig, Edinburgh. The reign of Malcolm III (1058–1093) saw the introduction of a concept of sanctity new to Scotland, and best illustrated by the legend of Margaret (*c.*1046–1093), Malcolm's English queen, which was composed by her confessor Turgot (*ob.*1115). it is little more than a pious and discreet short biography, wholly lacking the element of charter myth.

J. MacQueen

Salmon Fishing and Poaching. The right to fish for salmon in Scottish waters, both sea and river, derives originally from the crown: the practice of poaching is probably as ancient. Over the centuries grants of this right have been made to corporate bodies and to individuals, in various forms in different places; intending game fishers must therefore secure written permission to fish for salmon from those on whom the right has been locally devolved.

The 1862 Salmon Fisheries Act appointed Commissioners with powers to make by-laws for the regional regulation of fisheries. The Commissioners prescribe close seasons for both net and rod fishing, fix mesh sizes for nets, and pronounce on the legality of fishing gear and techniques. They employ water bailiffs armed with powers to search, seize catches and equipment, and arrest. Fishery patrol vessels, naval helicopters, and river-board launches collaborate to prevent drift-netting off the east coast, banned in 1962 to preserve stocks though still allowed under licence in English waters, to the particular annoyance of River Tweed fishermen.

There are today only three legal methods of catching salmon—by fixed engines around the coasts, by moveable engines in tidal estuaries (both commercial fishery methods), and by rod and line. The most common type of fixed engine is the stake net. As the name implies, the nets are strung vertically across stakes driven into the sea bed in lines or 'leaders' which guide migrating fish into chambers or bag nets where they are trapped. Other traditional fixed engines include rise nets, which are staked bag nets opening and closing with the tidal flow and ebb—mentioned in Scott's *Redgauntlet*—and dip nets operated from fixed scaffolds. In tidal estuaries draught seines, led out by boat in an arc from the river bank and hauled back by winch and hand, are widely used. On the River Nith the traditional haaf-net, a portable bag net strung across a rectangular frame, is still used by a few licensed fishermen. Stationed chest-deep in tidal channels, they wait for a fish to enter the net, quickly lift it to the surface, and there despatch it with the 'priest', a jocular name for the club which administers the last rite.

In earlier times salmon were taken with the leister, a four-pronged spear, or with the gird, a long-handled dip net suspended from a circular frame, often by 'burning the water', i.e. using torches at night to attract fish. Salmon poachers have used these and many other devices ranging from nets to wire rabbit snares, dynamite, and cyanide. Attitudes to poaching are ambivalent: lairds have sometimes turned a blind eye when a local poacher takes a fish in hard times, but strangers and ruthless methods are universally condemned. For game fishers, the efficacy of modern spinning gear and artificial lures is unquestionable; but the built cane or older greenheart rod and salmon fly demand greater skill and give the finest sport. The word 'salmon' was taboo in older folk speech, 'the red fish', 'the gentleman', 'the beastie' being used as by-names.

S.F. Sanderson

Science. The lament is one of the most highly developed Scottish art forms. By the 1830s and 1840s laments were regularly sounded on the apparently paradoxical theme of the decline of Scottish science. Paradoxical because, in the first place, we are not generally accustomed to thinking of science ever being in decline; ineluctable forward march is one of the most pervasive popular images of science. And, in the second place, we are not used to conceiving of science as anything but a universal enterprise, transcending all national boundaries. Scottish painting, yes; Scottish poetry, certainly. But Scottish *science*?

Yet such laments were a regular feature of commentary on Scottish science by the middle third of the nineteenth century. In order to understand what might be meant by Scottish science we are bound to start by looking at these laments. What did the Scots themselves think was distinctive about their science? What did they believe had brought about its decline? What sustained a Scottish science, and why did many, but not all, Scots value it?

Two leading themes appear in the nineteenth-century lamentational literature. First, it was said that the whole of Scottish intellectual life, of which science was just one part, was being sucked into the all-absorbing whirlpool of English culture. Scottish identity was perceived to be under threat from English forms, and in this respect, attitudes towards Scottish science were little different from attitudes towards Scottish education, the use of Scottish literary forms, and the reform of Scottish political institutions along English lines. Under attack, Scots defended themselves. Asserting Scottish distinctiveness in scientific culture, and trying to preserve it against what seemed overwhelming odds, were aspects of nineteenth-century cultural nationalism.

The other lamentational *motiv* specified what it was about the general form of Scottish science which was both valued and threatened. It was widely said that Scottish science had de-

clined in scope, in its metaphysical framework, and in general philosophical import. Where once, in its Enlightenment vigour during the eighteenth century, Scottish men of science had produced grand cosmological schemata and inquired into the foundations of scientific knowledge, now, it was claimed, science was in danger of becoming a 'mere mechanical knack'. As Carlyle said of algebra in the 1820s, it was little 'else than a cunningly constructed arithmetical mill'; one simply turned a crank and ground out an answer. Naturalists unfavourably contrasted the zoology and botany of the 1830s and 1840s with the breadth of James Hutton's geology and natural philosophy, Joseph Black's chemistry, and William Cullen's medical theory; all that Scotland produced now, it was claimed, was a 'small philosophy of mosses'.

Thus, in saying that Scottish science was in decline, nineteenth-century commentators were not claiming that there was quantitatively less science than there used to be; there was indisputably more. What they meant was that a distinctively Scottish 'philosophical' character of science was being eroded, and that the new science, lacking this dimension, was indistinguishable from science in, for example, England. The two major lamentational themes were therefore closely related. In the eyes of the commentators the loss of Scottish cultural identity referred to a perceived decline in a distinctive philosophical framework for science under the onslaught of English modes.

The nineteenth-century Scots were not the only observers to note the distinctiveness of their scientific culture. Nor were Scottish evaluations always shared by the English. During 1857–61 the English historian Henry Thomas Buckle produced his three-volume *Civilisation in England*, the third volume of which was an extended characterization and condemnation of *Scottish* culture, society, philosophy and science. Buckle claimed that Scottish intellectual productions traditionally had a 'deductive' bias; that is, they proceeded from agreed first principles to facts, instead of following the 'correct' (and traditionally English) inductive method of going from the accumulation of facts to their connecting principles. This, Buckle said, was wrong-headed and pernicious; it ultimately derived from the domination of Scottish culture by the deductively-minded Presbyterian clergy. Buckle warned against the penetration of English science by Scottish philosophy; Scottish tendencies were to be guarded against, and, where found, combatted.

The identification of the distinctive qualities of Scottish science continues to occupy historians. In 1961 Dr George Davie's *The Democratic Intellect* characterized eighteenth and early nineteenth-century Scottish science as having a metaphysical and 'humanistic' bias. He attributed the decline in that distinctiveness to 'anglicizing' tendencies within Scottish society, and he passionately defended the lost tradition.

What was the metaphysical bias of Scottish science? In large part it manifested itself in pervasive concern for the foundations and uses of scientific knowledge. Science was not simply a set of techniques one learned; it was not merely something one did. It was an intellectual pursuit the unique certainty of which one endeavoured to comprehend, and the social implications of which one discussed as an integral part of the exercise. Nowhere are these biases better seen than in Scottish mathematics. Dr Davie and other historians have remarked upon the Scots' preference for geometry over algebra and their particular justifications for this preference. Since the Scots regarded mathematics as the foundation of all scientific knowledge, understanding how they thought about mathematics is the key to explaining the distinctiveness of Scottish science in general.

The Scots, from Robert Simson in the 1720s on, thought of geometrical propositions as being at once statements about the real world of objects and also as being mental abstractions from that world. They were not just the one or the other. Thus, doing geometry was not simply manipulating formal symbols and sets of axioms; neither was it merely a distilled form of physics. Conceived in this way geometry had a cohesive function in scientific culture; it 'glued together' the study of the natural world and an exercise of pure reasoning. It could act, therefore, to maintain a kind of cultural solidarity.

The question why the Scots should have thought of mathematics in terms of cultural integration is best addressed in the pedagogical context, particularly that of the eighteenth and early nineteenth-century university. The Scots disdained, even dreaded, educational specialization. What was wanted as the product of their educational institutions was a liberally educated man, able to reflect on the basis of knowlege and to agree communally with other men on its foundations. What was not wanted was a mere intellectual 'mechanic', able only to perform unthinking intellectual tricks. When the Scots defended geometry they frequently did so in pedagogical terms. Geometry was good for training the mind; following Euclid's demonstrations accustomed the mind to extended chains of rational inference; geometrical methods displayed fundamental points of reasoning which could be applied to a wide variety of other intellectual exercises. This was contrasted with algebraic techniques. When the Scottish universities were under attack in the 1820s and 1830s for their neglect of algebra, the metaphysician William Hamilton replied that 'the feeblest reasoner feels no inferiority to the strongest calculator'; algebra, Hamilton said, 'is like running a rail-road through a tunnelled mountain'; geometry is 'like crossing the mountain on foot'. The Scottish universities taught mathematics 'philosophically'; geometry, the philosophy of knowledge, and moral philosophy were seen as integrated enterprises. A consequence of this educational preference was that the Scots clung to their geometrical, 'synthetic' methods long after the French and the English at Cambridge had developed algebraic, 'analytic' methods and fruitfully applied them to physical problems. A polemical war between Cambridge and the Scottish universities over the respective virtues of their curricula in the 1820s and 1830s was largely expressed in terms of the pedagogical and scientific values of algebra versus geometry.

The moral force of Scottish perspectives on mathematics is evident in the connection between geometrical preferences and the philosophy of Common Sense. This distinctively Scottish philosophy was developed from the middle of the eighteenth century as a concerted moral response to the scepticism of David Hume in Edinburgh and the deterministic materialism of Joseph Priestley in the north of England. In defending Newtonian natural theology, the Scottish Common Sense philosophy also justified the Scots' abstractionist view of geometry. God, they said, created both the real world of natural objects and men's minds; the latter were divinely constituted so that we could apprehend the primary properties of God's nature. Just as the Newtonian God was a geometer, so we, in geometrizing, could at the same time perform an intellectual and a religious exercise. Thus, Scottish Common Sense moral philosophy and Scottish views of geometry reinforced each other. And the key to both is an overarching concern for moral and cultural solidarity.

Scottish philosophical biases naturally spilled over into physics. When John Leslie died in 1832, the succession to his Edinburgh University chair of natural philosophy was contested by David Brewster, who defended the value of the Scottish mathematical tradition, and the Cambridge-orientated James David Forbes, who thought that algebra-deficient Scottish education severely handicapped the teaching of modern physics. Brewster, supported by his ally William Hamilton, argued that a non-esoteric, mathematically-undemanding physics was in keeping with Scottish pedagogical goals. He wanted a physics which stressed the experimental and practical aspects of the science and not the rarified algebraic techniques of 'cloistered' Cambridge. Science should be taught and practised, Brewster said, in such a way as to relate it to the practical and humanistic concerns of the nation, and not to divorce it therefrom. Physics, in George Davie's phrase, should serve in training 'the democratic intellect'. In the event, Brewster lost his contest with Forbes, and in 1838 Philip Kelland, a Cambridge algebraicist, supported by Forbes, was elected to the Edinburgh chair of mathematics. The 'reform' of Scottish university education was the main agent in the erosion of a distinctively Scottish scientific tradition.

Scottish concern for solidarity, and the use of scientific culture and concepts to further social integration, are also evident in non-mathematical branches of natural knowledge. One of the most visible instances of this is the development of a distinctively Scottish physiological theory in the middle of the eighteenth century. When the Edinburgh Medical School was established in the 1720s, its original professors taught the physiological doctrines of the Dutch 'iatromechanic' Hermann Boerhaave whose writings treated the body as a complex hydraulic machine animated by a 'Cartesian' soul. Christopher Lawrence has shown that when the first generation of Leyden-trained Edinburgh medical professors were replaced in the 1740s and 1750s, the new teachers began to produce a different model of how the human body worked. Robert Whytt and William Cullen, followed by Alexander Monro, *secundus*, and John Gregory, emphasized the importance of the nervous system as the means of effecting the overall integration of bodily functions. The nerves were, they said, imbued with a 'sentient principle' ('sensibility') which allowed them to bridge the Cartesian gulf between mind and body. Since, in this theory, the nerves also responded to and were shaped by man's environmental circumstances, one's 'feelings' were a function of how one lived. Moreover, the nervous system communicated feeling between one organ of the body and another by an act of 'sympathy'. Thus, this mid eighteenth-century Scottish theory accounted for and stressed organic physiological integration; it explained the relations between man's moral qualities and his conditions of existence; and it constructed a telling analogy between bodily and social solidarity. Again, aspects of Scottish science were marked by the same obsession with cohesiveness and integration which was the leading theme of Scottish moral and social philosophy. Interestingly, this Scottish physiological theory was actually put to use by Scottish social theorists to justify the role of 'men of feeling' as the natural leaders of civilized society. The theory was an important resource in arguing that Lowland intellectual élites were best placed by their environment and mode of life to acquire true sensibility and to direct the progressive 'improvement' of Scottish society. Hume, Adam Smith, Adam Ferguson, and Lord Kames all used aspects of this physiological theory in their social philosophies.

The question remains *why* Scottish science displayed this preoccupation with cultural and social solidarity. Nicholas Phillipson and John Christie have sought an answer in the historical relations between politics and culture following the Treaty of Union with England in 1707. While Union left Scotland with an autonomous law, Church and educational system, it stripped the nation of its primary political arena, the Scottish Parliament. What has been called the 'national trauma' of Scotland's loss of independence provided the impetus for the development of the social and intellectual forms of the Scottish Enlightenment.

The major tasks taken up by Enlightenment culture and the institutions which produced it were two-fold: first, to develop a programme for the material and cultural 'improvement' of the country, and, second, to create social forms which could unite Scottish intelligentsia and landed classes in achieving those ends. By the 1740s and 1750s institutions like the Society of Agricultural Improvers, the Philosophical Society of Edinburgh, and the Select Society had succeeded in creating a solidarity of interest amongst literati and aristocracy in the cause of 'improvement'. In the middle of the eighteenth century a unique situation had been brought about wherein Scottish cultural activity took on the functions elsewhere performed by direct political behaviour. Scottish culture, of which science was an important component, was thus strongly loaded with political significance.

Some consequences of the political load carried by Scottish culture have already been shown in the solidarity-maintaining function of many of its key scientific concepts. Other consequences are visible in the areas of science most vigorously pursued in Scotland and in the social organization of Scottish scientific activity.

Agricultural improvement was agreed to be an enterprise in which landed classes and men of science could unite and make common cause. From the 1720s on, Scottish men of science were taking up problems of practical concern to agriculturists and offering their expert advice in the solution of problems in soil analysis, manuring, horticulture, and the like. Indeed, many eighteenth-century men of science owned small estates, especially in the Lothians, and were themselves active improvers. By the last third of the eighteenth century it was not unusual to find professors like the chemist Joseph Black and the natural historian John Walker spending much of their time working on matters of practical import to landed interests. A concrete manifestation of this link was the appointment of Andrew Coventry in 1790 to an Edinburgh chair of agriculture, the first such professorial chair in a British university.

By no means all Scottish scientific studies bore such a direct relationship to agricultural concerns. But some branches of the natural sciences could be more easily justified to landed patrons in these terms than others. When the Royal Society of Edinburgh was founded in 1783, it was designed to cater for all aspects of 'physical and literary' knowledge. Soon, however, the natural sciences began to predominate over non-scientific topics, and, within the sciences, geology, mineralogy, and meteorology were by far the most popular. By the first decade of the nineteenth century, through the efforts of James Hutton, Sir James Hall, Thomas Charles Hope, Robert Jameson, and an host of lesser figures, the Royal Society of Edinburgh had become in effect an organization for research and discussion in the sciences relating to the earth. A large proportion of Fellows were landowners who patronized earth sciences and who often themselves participated in these branches of scientific activity. The work of the famous Scottish school of geology may not have had direct practical impact, but it was enabled to flourish through the social and cultural links between Scottish men of science and the landed classes.

Another implication of the historical connections between Scottish science and the landed classes is apparent in the ways in which scientific organizations were constituted. In other national settings the period from 1750 to 1830 witnessed an increasing tendency to separate scientific studies from other areas of culture, to segregate the organizations catering for science from those devoted to literary subjects, and to divorce the scientific professional from the amateur. In Scotland this tendency was strenuously resisted and even, in some respects, reversed. The Philosophical Society of Edinburgh (founded in 1737) stipulated that one-third of its members should be 'Gentlemen' who were not professionally engaged in science or medicine. The Royal Society of Edinburgh was, as we have seen, intended to be a general cultural organization; 60 per cent of its original Fellows were not, by any definition, men of science. As late as the 1860s, by which time English metropolitan science was increasingly conducted in specialized, 'disciplinary' societies, the Scots were still energetically defending the socially inclusive, exoteric nature of their chief scientific forums. Physicists like David Brewster and James David Forbes positively dreaded the isolation of what they called 'a learned class' of scientists from the company and patronage of amateur gentlemen. The social bond between

Scottish men of science and aristocrats was regarded 'as a compliment on either side'. Retarded specialization and professionalization were the price many Scottish men of science were eager to pay for maintaining their social and cultural integration with the country's landed power elites.

What finally eroded the Scottish scientific tradition? Dr Davie has eloquently contended that its downfall by the middle of the nineteenth century was the handiwork of 'anglicizing' groups. It is true that there were groups chipping away at distinctively Scottish educational patterns in science and asserting the superiority of English models. But it still needs to be asked *why* they adopted this stance and what were the conditions making for their success. Ultimately, the answer has to be sought, not in English scientific imperialism, but in changes within Scottish society itself.

Just as a distinctive Scottish science rose through its links with landed élites, so it declined when Scotland developed alternative social power bases which challenged both the political domination of traditional élites and the version of science which had been elaborated in concert with them. The very industrializing and differentiating tendencies described by Adam Smith and deplored by Common Sense philosophers became the agents through which the old Scottish science of solidarity was attacked and defeated. This conflict is most apparent in the early nineteenth-century Edinburgh conflict between iconoclastic and largely bourgeois phrenologists and their enemies, the mental philosophers of the university Common Sense tradition. In the eyes of Edinburgh's and Glasgow's rising Whig and Radical mercantile groups, the old Scottish science was the science of the 'Old Corruption'. They advocated the reform of Scotland's universities to make their curricula more responsive to the requirements of modernizing, specializing, urban economic life. It was not treason, but a new vision of what Scotland was, that brought down the old scientific culture.

The nineteenth-century laments on the decline of Scottish science were thus one part in a chorale of defiant lamentation on the decline of an old order in Scottish society. The nationalistic vision of solidarity was, after all, a particular vision, historically developed and maintained to serve particular social interests. As Scottish society became more like that of England, so authentically Scottish voices were raised to bring scientific knowledge into line with the new social realities. What, if anything, remains of the old Scottish scientific tradition is unclear. Science in Scotland flourishes, but of the Enlightenment science of solidarity there is scarcely a trace.

S. Shapin

School of Scottish Studies was founded by the University of Edinburgh in 1951, as an interdisciplinary research centre for Scottish subjects. Modelled on similar institutes in Scandinavian countries and in Ireland, it has systematically built up over the years extensive Archives of field recordings of traditional and changing forms of Scottish music, song, tales, folklore, and ethnology in general. The Archives rank with national archives elsewhere and are international in importance.

The School is also a centre for research into the languages and place-names of Scotland: it houses the Place-Name Survey of Scotland, the Linguistic Survey of Scotland, and the Institute for Historical Dialectology.

It has two regular publications: *Tocher*, which appears twice a year and presents material from the Archives, with English translations from Gaelic where needed, and the annual academic journal, *Scottish Studies*, in which appear the results of recent research into appropriate Scottish subjects.

From the 1970s, the School has increasingly become a teaching department within the Arts complex of the University, teaching Scottish Ethnology up to Honours level. With the setting up of an established Chair in Scottish Ethnology in 1990, the holder of which is also Director of the School, Edinburgh University became the first British university to offer a full degree course in the subject, with elements that include custom and belief, material culture both rural and urban, linguistic geography and onomastics, and traditional music, narrative, song and society. Research and teaching in Scottish ethnology is conducted within the framework of Europe and beyond, to keep perspectives wide.

A. Fenton

Scotland, 1100–1488. Three themes dominate the history of Scotland between the death of Malcolm III Canmore and Saint Margaret in 1093 and the accession of James IV (q.v.) in 1488. First among them must be placed the achievement of unity and identity by the Scottish kingdom under the leadership of a remarkable dynasty, descendants of Malcolm and Margaret in the first, third, fourth and fifth generations (1097–1286). Second comes the prolonged and dour struggle, at times wavering, at times heroic, to preserve the separate identity and independence of Scotland against the powerful onslaught of the first three English Edwards (1296–1357). Finally, in the context of a Scotland thoroughly integrated within western Christendom of the later Middle Ages, we have to reckon with the Scots' failure fully to reconcile the two principal strands of their own historical make-up. The older of these strands consisted of the conservative, paternalistic society and culture of Dark Age and earlier medieval Scotland, kindred-based and Celtic-speaking, which, as the harsh simplicities of the Norman era yielded place to the Auld Alliance with France and to the age of chivalry and of the Makars, became increasingly identified with the Highlands and the Western Isles, and was increasingly impelled to look to Ireland for inspiration and support. The younger strand was provided by the eastward- and southward-oriented English-speaking society of the North Sea littoral and the country south of Clyde and Forth—what came to be thought of and called the 'Lowlands'. If we are to understand the course and character of Scottish history, it is of the utmost importance to realize that a consciously 'Scottish' identity was adopted, indeed somewhat aggressively sought and prized, by this English-speaking society. The bitter struggle against the ambitions of the English crown was not in the least weakened or deflected by the external influences so powerfully at work within this society over many generations, whether English, Anglo-Norman or Continental (i.e. Scandinavian, German, Dutch, Flemish and—especially strong during the fourteenth and fifteenth centuries—French).

The long-drawn-out struggle against England might thus appear as a paradox, for a progressively anglicized and europeanized Scotland ought surely to have been easily absorbed within the grand imperialisms of an Edward I (who conquered Wales) or an Edward III (who conquered France). But to argue in this way is to miss the essential quality of Scottish development, to ignore the facts of geography, to be unaware of the extent to which Celtic and external elements were intermingled, and to underrate the force exerted by the idea and practice of kingship. It is above all with kingship, the Celto-feudal monarchy of the twelfth and thirteenth centuries, that the achievement of Scottish identity and unity is bound up. In contrast with Ireland and Wales there was in Scotland, on the eve of the Norman era, only one single effective kingship, stemming directly from the merger of the Scottish and Pictish dynasties in the ninth century, capable without too much difficulty of suppressing particularist kingships such as those of Cumbria, Galloway or Argyll. In contrast with England, this single Scottish kingship survived the coming of the Normans and could proudly boast a legitimacy and antiquity never quite within the grasp of the Norman or Angevin kings of England, powerful as they might be. This ancient kingship was marked by an immemorial inauguration rite beside the River Tay at Scone, an ancestry solemnly traced back through Fergus son of Erc to the first Scotsman, 'Iber Scot', and a conservative relationship with the provincial earls who formed a partly official, partly territorial nobility.

There is little to suggest that the canonization of Queen Margaret (d. 1093), which occupied Scottish Church leaders in the closing years of Alexander II's reign and was solemnized in 1250, had much more than a religious significance. True, it could not have gone ahead without royal support, and perhaps it was prompted by the decision of Henry III in the 1240s to rebuild Westminster Abbey and to associate this great shrine and its cult of St Edward the Confessor with his own not very popular dynasty and historical English nationalism; but the Scots kings did not need the sanctity of their ancestor Margaret to buttress their position within the Scottish nation.

To begin with, however, the sons of Malcolm and Margaret offered dangerously many hostages to fortune. Eager to learn and adopt Norman and feudal ways, they might easily have opened the door to a real Norman conquest of Scotland in which their own monarchy would have been engulfed. Fearful of hostility from upholders of the Celtic order and from rival claimants to the throne, the three brothers Edgar (1097–1107), Alexander I (1107–24) and David I (1124–53) were each in turn too dependent on the powerful Norman kings of England, William II Rufus and his brother Henry I. But on Henry's death in 1135 David I abandoned any lingering clientage still existing between the Scottish and English monarchies and until his death nearly 20 years later pursued a policy clearly based on the concept of an independent kingdom of Scotland,

striking his own coins, shaping his own foreign relations and (vainly) seeking metropolitan status for his chief church at St Andrews. David has been called one of the most attractive figures of twelfth-century Europe. He was undoubtedly a complex and interesting character, embodying on the one hand the traditions of the native Scottish dynasty and on the other the innovative ideas which he had absorbed from his youth upwards at the court of Henry I, especially ideas of military feudalism and centralized royal government. The influence of his mother is shown in David's lifelong religious devotion and in his rather old-fashioned view of church reform, according to which a disciplined clergy leading holy lives would enjoy full royal protection in their management of the spiritual sphere but should make no attempt to dominate the King in the secular sphere. In carrying out his policy of careful, firm and ultimately irreversible innovation, David was at first greatly helped by his possession (through his wife Maud de Senlis, daughter of Earl Waltheof and Judith, William the Conqueror's niece) of the vast 'Honour of Huntingdon', a complex of estates stretching across ten or eleven shires of east midland England. This not only gave him experience of governing a feudal lordship to be used as a model for feudalizing Scotland, but also provided a recruiting ground whence he could draw men who would become his barons north of the Border.

Under David I feudalization went ahead fast in southern Scotland (except Galloway) and even in Moray after the failure of Earl Angus's revolt in 1130. The process was intensified under David's grandsons Malcolm IV (1153–65) and William I 'the Lion' (1165–1214), and spread much more widely across the country. New families flocked to Scotland from several regions of England (notably Somerset, Yorkshire and the northwest), and also from French Flanders, Normandy and intervening districts. Thus, before 1214, the Bruce family had settled in Annandale, a branch of the Balliol family had come to Angus and Galloway, and the Breton Walter, son of Alan, David I's Steward, had been given Renfrewshire and founded the family which won the Scottish throne in 1371. By the time the process had begun to falter in Alexander II's reign much of the habitable land of Scotland had been divided into baronies and knights' 'fees' or 'feus'. Some scores if not hundreds of castles had been built as the physical basis of the military service which became the normal tenure whereby the new estates were held.

Hand in hand with feudalization went the setting up of many burghs, i.e. market towns whose in-dwellers ('burgesses') were given explicit privileges as traders and craftsmen, among them Berwick upon Tweed, Roxburgh, Edinburgh, Ayr, Stirling, Perth, Aberdeen and Inverness (all king's burghs) and Glasgow, Dunfermline, Dundee and St Andrews (fostered by local ecclesiastical or secular lords). An equal impetus was given by David I and his successors to the process whereby the Church in Scotland was brought into line with its counterparts in England and France, e.g. in the establishment of a diocesan and parochial system and in generous encouragement of the various monastic orders—Cistercians, Cluniacs, Augustinians and many more—characteristic of western Christendom in that period.

All this internal consolidation and bringing up-to-date was accompanied by territorial definition. Although by 1157 the Scots kings had effectively failed in their ambition to rule the country which now forms the northernmost region of England, Malcolm IV and William I subdued Galloway, mainland Argyll and much of the north as far as Caithness. Alexander II followed this with a campaign to wrest the Hebrides from their *de jure* Norwegian suzerainty and *de facto* local independence, but died near Oban in 1249 just as success was possibly within his grasp. The struggle was resumed by his son Alexander III as soon as he came of age, culminating in the defeat of the Norwegian forces at Largs and death of their king, Hakon (1263) and in the making of the treaty of Perth (1266). By 1286 the kingdom of Scotland stretched from the Isle of Lewis and Caithness in the north to the Tweed-Solway line and the Isle of Man in the south.

The conflict with England had both long-term and immediate causes. Since the twelfth century the development of both countries had been characterized by a steady process of definition, of territorial boundaries, of concepts of kingship and suzerainty, of national identity. The Angevin ('Plantagenet') kings of England, especially Henry II and John, had revived the old claim to overlordship of Scotland, while the Scottish kings, conscious of their success in subduing or annexing outlying territories and strengthening their power, were less and less willing to concede even a nominal English claim. William the Lion, captured by Henry II in 1174, had suffered 15 years of outright feudal subjection but bought his freedom back in 1189. Neither Alexander II nor his son was prepared to rule other than as an independent king. While Henry III was king of England the issue was allowed to lie dormant, but his more overbearing son Edward I revived English claims in 1278. He allowed the death of Alexander III in 1286 to pass without a showdown, all the more surprisingly since the heir to the Scottish throne was the sickly child Margaret, granddaughter of Alexander III and daughter of Eric King of Norway. Edward I was content to negotiate with the Scots leaders (on terms largely drafted by the latter) a marriage between the Maid of Norway and his own son and heir Edward of Caernarvon (1290), but the scheme, which might in time have led to a form of union between England and Scotland, was at once frustrated by the Maid's death while on her way to Scotland.

The Scottish parliament had not determined who should succeed to the throne if Margaret of Norway died childless. Edward I was invited to preside over a court to choose a successor. He insisted on doing so as overlord, obtaining recognition from the claimants and, indirectly, from the leading prelates and nobles. The court's choice fell on John Balliol Lord of Galloway, but after his accession Edward I deliberately emphasized Balliol's feudal subjection, demanding his attendance at the English court and military service overseas. The Scots magnates' answer to this was to force Balliol to make a treaty with the French King in 1295, inviting a war in 1296 which was as inevitable as it was easy to win for Edward I, who

deposed Balliol and set up an occupation regime. William Wallace (q.v.), a young Renfrewshire free-holder, led a dramatic uprising in the spring of 1297 which culminated on 11 September in a brilliant victory over an English army at Stirling bridge, and in Wallace's being made Guardian of the realm for the absent King John. Next summer Edward I inflicted a crushing defeat upon Wallace at Falkirk but failed to exploit his success. Resistance grew and took on a truly national quality, led by the bishops, Lamberton of St Andrews and Wishart of Glasgow, and by leading barons such as John de Soules, John Comyn of Badenoch and Robert Bruce, grandson of Balliol's chief rival for the crown in 1291. When French and papal support melted away in 1304 Edward I reasserted his power over Scotland, had Wallace brutally executed in 1305 and later the same year promulgated an ordinance which envisaged indefinite English government for Scotland.

The centuries-old kingdom of Scotland seemed at an end when in February 1306 Robert Bruce slew John Comyn at Dumfries and immediately claimed the throne, undergoing an inauguration ceremony at Scone (25 March). Although temporarily put to flight by the outraged Edward I, Bruce held on until the succession of Edward II in 1307 gave breathing space and the opportunity to crush Bruce's powerful foes within Scotland, especially the Comyns in the north and the Macdougall lords of Lorn in the west. By 1309 Bruce was clearly 'King Robert' in fact as well as in title, and five years later he won the crucial battle of the Scottish Middle Ages, overwhelming the army which Edward II brought to annihilate him at Bannockburn, just south of Stirling (23–24 June 1314). In 1320 an eloquent declaration justifying the Scottish struggle for independence was embodied in a collective letter addressed by the nobles of the realm to Pope John XXII.

The fourteenth century thus began with heroic conflict and one memorable triumph, but for the most part it was a time of frustration, might-have-beens and near disaster. England, no less fiercely nationalistic than Scotland and much more militaristic, refused to accept the verdict either of Bannockburn or of Robert I's patient rebuilding of the kingdom of Alexander III during an arduous 23-year reign. What the first two Edwards failed to accomplish was attempted, with what for a time seemed much greater success, by the bellicose Edward III, who wiped out a major Scottish army near Berwick in 1333 and (after Robert I's youthful heir David II had returned from temporary refuge in France) enjoyed the outstanding triumph of destroying the French feudal host at Crécy and having the king of Scots captured at Durham all within the autumn of 1346. Despite heavy ransom payments and frequent devastation of much of their land the Scots would not submit, and by 1357 a more chastened England, laid low by the Black Death and at last facing serious setbacks in France, made the treaty of Berwick whereby David II was restored to his throne free from the humiliating conditions of revived English overlordship which Edward III had originally demanded. After a valiant effort to restore royal authority, David died childless in 1371, the last of the ancient line of Scottish kings and their Balliol and Bruce offshoots descended from the two elder daughters of

Earl David of Huntingdon. The crown passed to King David's nephew Robert, sixth hereditary Stewart of Scotland in succession to Walter son of Alan, appointed by David I.

Robert II came to the throne at the relatively advanced age of 55, and he and his son John (who symbolically changed his name to Robert when he succeeded his father in 1390) seem to have been reluctant to assume the full *persona* of royalty. Unnecessarily conscious of being great baronial magnates among equals, they ruled rather as Guardians, and significantly died at the Stewart (not royal) castles of Dundonald and Rothesay respectively. English aggressiveness had revived with the accession in 1399 of the usurping house of Lancaster. At the moment of Robert III's death in 1406 his only surviving son James was captured by the English off the Yorkshire coast while being taken to France for safety. The new King was kept prisoner for 18 years while first Henry IV and then his son Henry V applied military and diplomatic pressure in a vain effort to reduce Scotland to feudal subjection. The government of Scotland was in the hands of Robert III's younger brother Robert Stewart Earl of Fife (from 1398, Duke of Albany) who, though stopping short of outright treason or an attempt on the throne, and claiming no more than the title of 'Governor', was notably reluctant to press for his nephew's return from captivity. He may have hoped for James's death and Scotland's acceptance of his son Duke Murdoch as king. Instead, the death of Albany (1420) and Henry V (1422) opened the way for James's restoration (March, 1424) and it was Murdoch who paid the penalty. Allowed to perform, as Earl of Fife, the traditional duty of setting a new king upon the throne at Scone (the last occasion on which this ancient ceremony took place there), Murdoch was executed for treason, with several close kinsmen, in 1425.

James I's reign in Scotland, beginning with such dramatic harshness, may be seen as marking the start of a new era for Scotland in many respects. Despite the advent of gunpowder and artillery, an important technological advantage in the long run to the much wealthier England, there would in future be no serious threat of an English conquest of Scotland, and no such conquest was attempted before the time of Oliver Cromwell in 1650. Scots military prowess was now deployed more prominently in France than at home. The Auld Alliance with France, whether dating from 1295 or the twelfth century, was at its most effective between 1415 and the 1480s, when numbers of Scots nobles and gentry fought in the armies of Charles VI, Charles VII and Louis XI and won lands and titles in France. But the French enjoyed no monopoly of Scots attention. Relations with England were not uniformly hostile, and James I's marriage to Joan Beaufort helped to encourage literary contacts between post-Chaucerian England and a Scotland whose own king was now a poet. Trade with Scandinavia flourished, as well as with the Hanse cities of the Baltic and North Sea and with the Low Countries. Against this background it was almost inevitable that James III, finding a Danish bride in King Christian's daughter Margaret (1469), should seize the opportunity to take the northern isles of Orkney and Shetland, into which there had already been considerable Scottish penetration,

in pledge for his wife's unpaid dowry and should also annex the earldom of Orkney (1472).

In the hands of James I and his son James II the Scottish monarchy shed the reputation for being weak and ineffectual which it had acquired between 1371 and 1424. The threat of 'overmighty subjects' may have been exaggerated, but the crown undoubtedly needed to 'manage' the nobility. If James I asserted royal authority too cruelly and vindictively, provoking his own murder in 1437 (the first time for three and a half centuries that a king of Scots had been deliberately slain), his son pursued a more politic approach and was careful never to allow any powerful coalition of noble families to be arrayed against him. Instead, he succeeded in gaining wide support in his conflict with the senior line of the house of Douglas ('Black Douglases'), even though the sixth earl had been judicially murdered during the King's minority and James himself killed the eighth earl while supposedly protected by a royal safe-conduct (1452). James III, in some ways the most interesting man among the early Stewart kings, proved less skilful than his father, though he too survived a perilous minority, and deserves credit for annexing the Northern Isles and for his courage in pursuing reconciliation with England when this policy, however essential, was bound to be intensely unpopular. Although the earliest royal Stewarts, being themselves Highland lords, had understood the Gaelic west, the first three Jameses saw the Highlands only as a problem which they could not solve. It was to be left to the more sympathetic James IV not only to suppress the Lordship of the Isles but also to put in its place a royal leadership which the Highlanders could largely accept.

G.W.S. Barrow

Scotland, 1488–1688. Rebellions against the misuse of royal authority punctuate the years between 1488 and 1688, a period which opens with the murder of James III (q.v.) and ends with the deposition of James VII (q.v.). If the significance of the King's death can be overestimated, it nevertheless initiated a new relationship between the Scots and their sovereigns for though monarchy continued to be respected as an institution, an increasing concern, as illustrated by the writings of George Buchanan, can be detected that kings and queens ought to be accountable for their actions.

In other ways too the end of the fifteenth century instituted a new era. In the literary field William Dunbar and Robert Henryson were joined by Gavin Douglas who, in the spirit of the times, produced an effective Scottish translation of the *Aeneid*. The Renaissance also found expression in an Education Act of 1496 and the advent of the printing press. Yet in his love of pilgrimage, zeal for crusade and sense of chivalry, James IV (q.v.) retained an essentially medieval outlook. His love of buildings, on the other hand, is indicative of the growing importance of secular architecture. The royal palaces at Holyrood, Linlithgow and Stirling on which James lavished attention were enlarged by his son who combined with his love of architecture a cunning and ruthless personality. The foundation of the College of Justice with paid judges in 1541 was nevertheless significant in the development of civil law, but James V's (q.v.) political sagacity did not always match his ambitions and led to defeat by the English at Solway Moss in 1542. Artistic patronage lapsed during the ensuing crisis and intellectual activity centred increasingly on reform of the Church.

The late medieval Church was by no means beyond redemption. Religious houses were facing a secularization of their revenues as commendators were appointed to their headship, but with the exception of the border monasteries razed by the English in 1544–45, monks and canons in scarcely diminished numbers carried out their observances. So too with the friars who, if unmindful of the poor, found support for their services among the urban middle class. Religious devotion also found expression in pilgrimage and the foundation of collegiate churches. Faults are more discernible among the secular clergy and satire and statutes alike testify to rapacious and illiterate priests. Nevertheless, there is little sign of popular reaction to such charges. Society itself, however, was changing and new standards were being demanded by an educated and articulate minority. A Protestant solution was possible, but a sizeable proportion of the Church's critics looked for reform from within. That this proved to be unattainable was not from lack of endeavour, but because vested interests of both prelates and crown were unwilling from financial gain either to follow the example of England and establish a national Church or to implement reforming statutes. Protestantism thrived on this failure, but its appeal can be overestimated. With the exception of Kyle in Ayrshire, the movement drew its support from east-coast lairds whose rise in status by obtaining Church lands in feu is a feature of this period. With limited support, the movement which followed initially the teachings of Luther, but latterly of Calvin, could not be assured of success and it was fortunate for their cause that Catholicism became identified with a French attempt to gain control over Scottish affairs.

Although an alliance with France had existed for several centuries, it was revitalized in the early sixteenth century as friendly relations with England, consummated in 1503 in the marriage of James IV and Margaret Tudor, deteriorated. This was partly a matter of royal temperament exacerbated by the accession of Henry VIII, but also contrived by a conscious French policy designed to keep Scotland within her orbit. The fatal culmination of this policy came at Flodden in 1513, but the very magnitude of the defeat provided support for the Franco-Scottish alliance which following the Treaty of Rouen (1517) was further strengthened by the marriage of James V and Madelaine de Valois in 1537, and after her premature death by that to Mary of Guise. After the King's death in the wake of defeat at Solway Moss, the principal aim of French foreign policy was to perpetuate the alliance by marrying the dauphin, Francis to Mary, Queen of Scots. In this they were abetted by the queen-mother who became regent in 1554 after a struggle with the earl of Arran, who as governor had initially promoted the idea of an English marriage and whose forced

retraction had led to the 'rough wooing', and Scottish defeat at Pinkie in 1547. The French marriage in fact precipitated a crisis, for not only were the Scots magnates alarmed at the political consequences, but a revival of Protestant persecution led to an alliance of the two interests. John Knox provided rebellious subjects with a godly justification and in turn gave the Protestants powerful political support.

This alliance culminated in the Reformation which not only broke the links with France, but also abrogated papal authority and outlawed the mass. The appeal of Protestantism in 1560 can be overestimated, but its triumph thereafter is indisputable. With its standards defined in the Confession of Faith and its discipline reinforced by emergent Kirk Sessions, the Church established an influence over the nation which it retained for centuries. The effect on certain aspects of culture, such as music and literature, may have been deadening, but on the credit side lies the concern, as expressed in the First Book of Discipline, for the poor and the promotion of schools and universities. As an institution, however, the Kirk was to loom largest in its claim that the jurisdictions of Church and state were separate entities. This doctrine inherent in the writings of Knox and clarified by Andrew Melville and the Second Book of Discipline created tension which reverberated throughout the sixteenth and seventeenth centuries as a struggle between kings and General Assemblies respectively promoting government of the Church by bishops or presbyteries.

If debates continued on how the Church should be governed, no such uncertainties existed about worship. Only practices based upon scriptural authority were acceptable, and in consequence all holy days including Christmas and Easter were 'utterlie to be abolischet'. On the same grounds the sacraments were reduced to two—baptism and communion—and to be valid were to be conjoined with public preaching. For this reason private baptism and communion were forbidden; communion was to be given in both kinds to communicants sitting, as to kneel was to recognize the real presence. These attitudes had a marked effect on the life of the nation and also terminated the processions and festivities which had been a feature of the pre-Reformation period.

The political consequences of the Reformation may not have been so far-reaching, but the implications of rebellion against royal authority had to be faced when, following the death of her husband, Mary returned to her native kingdom in 1561. From the outset she faced a difficult, but not impossible, task as the first four years of her personal reign demonstrated. While refusing to renounce Catholicism, her actions gave little comfort to her co-religionists and the margin of support accorded to the reformed Church allowed it slowly to confirm its dominant position. Mary's policies stemmed from the belief that as Scotland was only a stepping-stone to her ultimate destiny as Queen of England, the governance of her northern kingdom could be left in other hands. However, with the ending of that dream, her determination to be at least queen in her own kingdom proved to be her undoing, as such authority could only be asserted with the support of a husband, and Mary failed to choose wisely. Both Darnley and Bothwell proved unacceptable and her personal reign ended as it had begun, with a political revolution.

The ensuing civil war was ended through English intervention which in turn strengthened the improvement in Anglo-Scottish relations heralded by the Reformation. No formal alliance was constituted, but successive Scottish governments found it politic to remain on friendly terms with Elizabeth. In other respects the relationship between the two countries was not so good; the border remained unruly and the common bond of Protestantism was a fragile link as the views of Scottish Presbyterians were anathema in an England already threatened by religious schism. Trade helped to preserve the balance and Scottish exports to England especially of fish and salt were a welcome adjunct to the economies of both countries.

The deposition of Mary brought the Reformed Church the official recognition previously denied to it, but while Protestantism was thus secured, the difficulties of the Church were not at an end. Its claims to order its own affairs were unacceptable to the state and led to recurrent battles. In the early stages of the conflict the Church relied upon fears of a Catholic revival to further its cause while the crown was forced to rely on its increasing political strength. Despite setbacks such as the Black Acts of 1584, the Church had the better of the initial struggle and victory was apparently secured in the Golden Act of 1592. However, as the Catholic threat diminished and royal power increased in virtue of the expected succession to the English throne, the scales tipped in the King's favour.

If the union of 1603 reduced problems such as border lawlessness, it also created new tensions between kingdoms whose only organic unity lay in joint kingship. The adoption of a union flag and the assumption by James of the title King of Great Britain were designed to mask the problem, but attempts to create a closer union met with little success. In consequence of a contrived legal decision, Scots were no longer regarded as aliens in England, but the claim that Scots and English drew closer as a result of union is questionable. The difficulty in framing policies acceptable to both countries led in Scotland to an increasingly authoritarian regime in both Church and state, for although General Assemblies met until 1618, the pattern of ecclesiastical government had been dictated by the crown before that date. Bishops who were politically and ecclesiastically important to the crown, controlled the Church which nevertheless was allowed to retain a conciliar structure with synods, presbyteries and kirk sessions all playing their part in discipline and organization. If James had let matters rest, he might have left a Church at peace, but hostility to the Five Articles of Perth in 1618 resulted not only in opposition to the liturgical changes which they proposed but also to the bishops who controlled the Kirk. These difficulties were compounded by increasing financial and economic problems and by the end of his reign in 1625 King James's peace rested on very flimsy foundations.

These problems constituted an unwelcome legacy for his son Charles I, who, faced with a crisis in royal finances, adopted measures which his father had evaded. Some reallocation of ecclesiastical revenue was necessary both for the welfare of crown and Church alike but Charles's attempts by means of a general Act of Revocation were tactless. Opposition from those who possessed teinds was inevitable, but might have been contained had Charles not embarked upon a series of fiscal and ecclesiastical policies which united the nation against him. The final crisis precipitated in 1637 by the foisting of a prayer book upon the Scottish Church by royal authority was not only an act of folly, but gave his opponents a base from which they could initiate a revolution in both Church and state.

This opposition found expression in the National Covenant which not only protested against past abuses in Church and state, but also called for future assurances. If its tone was constitutional the intention of its promoters stood in marked contrast. The Glasgow Assembly of 1638 condemned the office of bishop and reasserted its own authority over the Kirk, while parliamentary-appointed committees controlled by the magnates, but containing lairds and burgesses, ruled the state. However, the security of the revolution was not assured and this as much as a desire to presbyterianize England led to the Solemn League and Covenant of 1643 by which English parliamentarians seeking military assistance promised to impose a uniformity of doctrine, worship and government in the Churches of Scotland, England and Ireland. This design did not command universal support, and the rising of Montrose, which was only crushed in 1645 by withdrawing the main Scottish army from England, heralded the end of covenanting unity. Thereafter, further schism appeared with the Engagement of 1647 after which the magnates, who had realigned with the King in order to safeguard their political supremacy, were forced after their defeat at Preston in 1648 to bow to a new challenge. In consequence Scotland was ruled by an oligarchy of lairds and ministers until they in turn compromised their principles to secure enforcement of the Covenant through negotiations with Charles II and were routed by Cromwellian forces at Dunbar in 1650. Although a combination of Engagers and supporters of Montrose momentarily regained power and condemned their opponents in a series of resolutions—hence their new name of Resolutioners, their triumph was short-lived. Having crushed their rivals—now known as Remonstrants from the Remonstrance in which they condemned those guilty of 'backslydinge breache of covenant', the Resolutioners were themselves defeated at Worcester in 1651 as Scotland fell to the Cromwellian forces.

The subsequent military occupation brought an unwelcome respite to a Scotland torn by faction, but nevertheless allowed a period of reconstruction. This was most fruitful in its economic aspects for if war-weary Scotland was not able to take full advantage of the equal trading concessions offered by the Cromwellian union with England, the west-coast merchants were already forging links with the New World. In the political and ecclesiastical fields the effects were less significant, but even here the eclipse of the magnates' dominance, as illustrated in the abolition of heritable jurisdictions in 1652, conferred upon the lairds some of the power to which they had earlier aspired. Ecclesiastically the occupation witnessed a declining support for the heirs of the Remonstrants, now known as Protesters; less emphasis being laid upon the Covenants and more on the Resolutioner policy of protecting the established Church from state interference. Adherence to the presbyterian cause was widespread and constituted a major problem at the restoration of kingship in 1660.

Autocracy was to be the hallmark of the Restoration monarchy. Politically this produced little opposition and even this disappeared after 1681 when subscription to the Test and Succession acts became the ultimate test of loyalty. Royal authority was more severely tested in the ecclesiastical sphere as a settlement based upon expediency brought inevitable opposition. If there was no return to the liturgical innovations of the pre-Covenant period, the suppression of the General Assembly and the foisting of bishops and constant moderators upon synods and presbyteries demonstrably subordinated the Church to the state. In consequence many adherents, including a sizeable proportion of lairds, preferred to worship at conventicles. Attempts to solve this problem varied, but compromise met with little success and repression led to two armed risings which, although defeated at Rullion Green in 1666 and Bothwell Bridge in 1679, delivered a deathblow to hopes of a peacefully accepted episcopal Church.

If the ecclesiastical issues were longstanding, changes were taking place in other fields. Legal studies were advanced with Stair's *Institutions of the law of Scotland* and the foundation of the Advocates Library while scientific studies flourished in cartography, mathematics and natural science. The latter found practical expression in the foundation of the Physic Garden in Edinburgh in 1676 while the foundation of the Royal College of Physicians in 1681 led to the expansion of medical science in the following century. Society, however, remained essentially rural and primary exports such as wool and fish remained as they had been for centuries the mainstay of the economy. The development of coal-mining from the sixteenth century onwards constituted a welcome addition to the small list of exportable commodities and provided, alongside an expanding production of salt, one of the brighter features of an ailing economy which required a greater proportion of manufactured goods. Attempts to expand in that direction met with only minimal success and although poor-quality woollen cloth found a market, other ventures in cloth-manufacturing enjoyed only transitory success and could not withstand English and foreign competition. Nevertheless, some industries such as sugar-refining in Glasgow were viable and on the west coast in general a new, if illicit, trade with the American colonies held out promises for the future. New markets were essential as the traditional east-coast trade with Holland and France declined in the face of war and the English Navigation Acts. These weaknesses in the economy increasingly led the Scots to believe that only a renegotiation of the terms of the personal union which bound them to England could alleviate their plight.

For the time being, however, religious issues predominated and although James VII inherited in 1685 a seemingly impregnable authority which allowed the almost total eradication of nonconformity, unity in the established Church was more apparent than real. When James in endeavouring to aid his fellow Catholics passed two Acts of Indulgence in 1687, Presbyterians quickly took the opportunity to establish their own ecclesiastical structure, and were thus poised to seize the initiative when similar policies in England led to the Glorious Revolution and deposition of the King in 1688. If coercion had militated against similar action in Scotland, the Scots, untrammelled by elaborate theories of kingship, simply declared that James by his misdeeds had forfeited the crown. Pressure to replace episcopacy with presbyterianism became irresistible although complete freedom from the state was not to be achieved. Parliament likewise was not entirely freed from royal control but the abolition of the committee of the Articles nevertheless precipitated within two decades a constitutional crisis which would lead to an incorporating union between England and Scotland. No one could have foreseen such an event in 1688, but the conclusion of this further rebellion against royal authority clearly indicated that the Revolution marked yet another significant turning point in the political and ecclesiastical affairs of the nation.

I.B. Cowan

Scotland Since 1688. The Glorious Revolution, as the English called the events of 1688–89, led the Scots into an inglorious period of confusion, division and disaster. It is probable that the majority of Scots were uncomfortable under the newly dominant combination of political Whiggery and Presbyterianism, particularly since Presbyterian Church dominance was exercised with such intransigence that over two-thirds of the ministry were forced out of their parish cures, either at once or within a few years. For religious, territorial or political reasons many Scots either were Jacobite (q.v.) or retained a sympathy for Jacobitism, a willingness to regard the political settlement as still reversible. The settlement had been forced on Scotland by her southern neighbour who was prepared, if necessary, to fight the issue out on Scottish soil. In the event the military issue was decided, marginally, in the summer of 1689 in favour of the new régime, when the Jacobite Highlanders lost their general at Killiecrankie and subsequently failed to force their way through to the Lowlands. But a large part of the southwest Highlands was not truly reconciled even after the application of a policy of forgiveness backed by the threat of terrorism. The northeast contained many dissatisfied adherents of the Episcopal Church and the policy of intruding unwelcome Presbyterian ministers caused disorder well into the eighteenth century. To these political dissensions was added economic failure, in the closing up of export markets, the collapse of attempts to find new ones, the famine of the 1690s and an unfavourable balance of trade.

In spite of political discontent and instability the Scottish Parliament entered into a creative period. In many areas of the life of the country formative statutes date from the short period before the Act of Union (q.v.), when the Scottish Parliament was free from the restraints of royal control. The richer lairds, the 'baronage of Scotland', liberally represented in it, were asserting themselves politically. This assertion, also in cultural terms, continued after the Act of Union, and is one of the streams that met in the great flood of the Scottish Enlightenment (q.v.) in the second half of the eighteenth century. The administrative system of Scotland, once the Privy Council had been abolished in 1708, was assimilated to that of England. It was a system of almost complete local autonomy in the hands of crudely selected local groups. The royal burghs managed their own affairs with increasing inefficiency and corruption, and county society controlled itself loosely through Justices of the Peace, Commissioners of Supply and occasional county meetings of landowners, with the functions of all such bodies ill-defined. At the parish level, however, social discipline was maintained by the active intervention of the lowest court of the Presbyterian Church, the kirk session, on which landowners usually sat, and jurisdiction was also maintained by baron courts. This all meant that nobody 'controlled' the landowners so long as their actions were within the law, but that they themselves had considerable disciplinary power over the peasantry. Patronage gave them also a considerable say in Church affairs. The law itself was an organ of landowning, for the judges and most of the advocates came from this class. The law added a professional expertise and *esprit de corps* to a group already tightly held together by kinship ties, common interests and assumptions. Such a structure of society could have been simply a means of perpetuating conservatism, and indeed for some 30 years or so this seems to have been the case. The country was economically backward, dependent, and socially conservative for most of the first half of the eighteenth century. However, and there almost always is room for a 'however' in generalized statements in Scottish history, there were elements working for change. An appreciation of the arts flourished in the better-off social groups, a strong sense of patriotism helped to give rise to a number of societies and clubs founded for purposes of blends of social responsibility and intellectual indulgence, the position of the basic industries of the country improved and the Glasgow merchants financed and expanded the tobacco trade with America by a skilful use of every possible penny. Political stability, even if imposed by association with England rather than independently achieved, had a considerable effect in terms of business confidence in spite of the Jacobite rebellions of 1715 and 1745.

Scotland also began to receive at last an economic and social return from her seventeenth-century investment in education. The normal literacy of her peasantry, and its acquisition in long hours of school work, made for a disciplined work force strongly imbued with the ethic of work, and on the whole inclined to social conformism. The link between schools and universities led a small stream of ambitious youths from the farm to the ministry; more significantly it both fed back to the parishes the failures in this process as educated schoolmasters and kept a group of lively intellects employed in the universities as professors. One of the long-standing achievements of Scotland since 1600 has been the creation and training of professional groups, equipped technically and psychologically

for specific tasks. The seventeenth century had seen the establishment of the ministry as such a group and the creation of a corps of school teachers, later the self-assertion and homogeneity of the lawyers. To these were added now bankers, doctors and university professors. A considerable number of the doctors were to seek careers outwith Scotland, particularly from the opportunities given them by Union. But within Scotland these groups, centred particularly in Edinburgh, formed another stream in the Enlightenment.

A sudden intellectual renaissance is not easily to be explained. The eighteenth-century Scottish Enlightenment (q.v.) can be seen as a secular achievement, opposed either to the Church as a whole or to its more evangelical wing. The intellectual adventure of the movement concentrated on the study of man in society, which contrasted sharply with the emphasis of evangelical theology seeing man solely in his relationship with God. It can be related to the clubs and professional groupings in the cities, to the exploratory work carried out by members of the universities in efforts to expand the appeal of education and to enlarge its market, to the deliberate policy of investment by the city of Edinburgh in its university as a magnet to bring people and their spending power to the city. It can be related, and was by those who participated in it, to the sudden spurt in economic growth of the third quarter of the eighteenth century which allowed Scotland to share in England's industrial revolution. The intellectual adventurousness of Enlightenment thought stopped short of criticism of either the social or the political structure of the country, so powerful interests were not brought to oppose it.

If these crude relationships are all that can be offered in a short outline for ideas about the causation of the Enlightenment, one is on firmer ground about its effects. Coupled with the economic successes of the day it gave upper-class Scots an enormous and not entirely justified sense of superiority while securing their loyalty for the political structure which made it possible. But by the early nineteenth century Scottish self-confidence also drew from a totally opposing current which had been maintained throughout the eighteenth century, that of popular evangelical thought and dogma. This element had included, if ineffectually, the major part of the ministry in the eighteenth century. In the period of revulsion from the secular and radical thinking that had followed the first French Revolution it had come to the fore as a pre-eminent Scottish feature. Linked with the new evangelical movement from England it was eventually to run the Church on the rock of schism and break her in two in the Disruption (q.v.) of 1843. Coupled with the intellectual achievements of the eighteenth century and the continued large part that Scottish writers and thinkers were playing in the intellectual life of Britain in the early decades of the nineteenth, it gave the Scots a sense of righteous leadership. Scotland was the country which had discovered the accepted explanation of how the material world was conducted in political economy, pioneered the study of man as a social creature and opened the door to new sciences, but it was also the country which had defied attempts of the state to control religious matters and where a considerable party in the Church claimed the reciprocal right to tell the civil law what rights it was to acknowledge. It was a country which had moved rapidly in agricultural and industrial development, so that its farming was now conspicuous for good order and productivity. The incomes of the farm population had risen strikingly in the eighteenth century and this as well as the opportunities for indoctrination provided by Church and school may account for its docility in the drastic reorganization that had taken place. Scots were filling the posts that Empire provided, as administrators, diplomats and traders, and were stretching the tentacles of Scottish banking over the Empire. They were also the medical men who promoted public health in the towns throughout Britain and in the armed forces, and the writers who manned the leading literary, scientific and political journals of the day. In specialized areas of science—geology is perhaps the most conspicuous—Scots had given ideas to the whole world.

Some of this self-esteem and confidence was shown to be misplaced even by the middle of the nineteenth century. Scotland was seen also to be a country of cavernous class divides, of urban poverty, deprivation and crime, and of an atmosphere stifling to artists and creative writers. Her industrial success was achieved and maintained, it seemed, by a series of flukes in timing, so that a new sector opened unexpectedly just as an old one closed. As the cotton industry of the industrial revolution stagnated and showed signs of incipient decline her heavy industry was created by the discovery of how to use the blackband ironstone of the west. As this became worked out, engineering skills and the need to create a new, steam-powered merchant marine gave rise to the enormous success of ship-building at the end of the century. But the economy, perhaps inevitably in a small country, was unbalanced, and in the great area of the Highlands and Islands there was a total divorce between the possibilities of economic development and the social needs of the population. It was not clear in the nineteenth century, and it is still not clear today, how much Scottish industry relied on relatively low wages, with consequent discomfort to the workforce. It seems clearer that the Scottish economic, religious and social systems relied on a social conformity in many ranks. With the increase of influences entering both from overseas and from England this could not be expected to last indefinitely.

In the late nineteenth century Scotland's unsolved problems seem conspicuous and her self-confidence abated. The country was also suffering from political and governmental neglect. After 1885 the separate institutions of government, grudgingly created, were bound together in the Scottish Office to give something of coherence, but Westminster and the main parties found it difficult to give time or attention to specifically Scottish needs. Basic legislation was often delayed for English expedience—this had been particularly conspicuous over the efforts to refound the school system. There was a need for a coherent structure of local government. The Liberal party relied on Scottish seats whenever it was in power, but took the support of Scottish voters for granted. The Labour party was

to do the same in the twentieth century. Yet Scottish class gulfs made the Scottish electorate unwilling to abandon Liberalism and support the Conservative party, associated in many people's minds with a class of privileged landowners. Within Liberalism the Scots tended to hold to the right, or to get deflected on to clichés of liberal thought rather than to create a programme suited to their own needs. Scotland had, through political association, become in many ways assimilated to England, a situation which seemed a fine thing when England was very much the richer and Scotland the more creative partner, but which now had disadvantages.

Even those aspects of Scottish life which seemed unmistakably successful just before the First World War had inescapable disadvantages. Heavy industry accentuated the swings of the business cycle and did not provide much in the way of jobs for women and boys. Lowland farming relied on a vast gulf in income and life-style between farmer and labourer. The past successes of Scottish writers in England had encouraged a strain of sentiment and quaintness which was a denial of real literature. The genuine literary culture of the Highlands was cut off by language from the mass of the nation and under constant repression from religious extremism. The reunification of the Church was accompanied by a series of intransigent splinter groups taking their inspiration from the seventeenth century. There was a variety of left-wing movements in the Clyde area which were powered by the rigours of industrial life, but which lacked an adequate and relevant theoretical base of their own.

The First World War was a shock to Scotland as to all European countries, damaging confidence in the benevolence of God and the progress of mankind, and straining the economy. Some particular localities also suffered exceptional losses in men. The long-term effect was to bring to an abrupt end the boom in her industries. The elements of weakness already present but not conspicuous came to the fore. Their impact was enhanced by the failure of the economy to find a new and expanding sector. It is the nature of heavy industry to make it difficult for a successor to be bred. In the inter-war period Scotland suffered excessively severe and prolonged depression. Emigration, marked even in the relatively prosperous nineteenth century, continued to make its vote of no confidence in the economy. The benefit that it had given, of building close personal links for many with people in the British Commonwealth and the United States, was only small compensation.

It is therefore not surprising that self-conscious nationalism, almost non-existent in the late eighteenth and early nineteenth century, began to be expressed between the wars. There had been nationalists and national issues since the 1870s, but these had been of a crankish sort, fusses about points of pedantry such as heraldry, assertions of unproved Celtic history, ecclesiastical one-up-manship, the display of pedigrees or tartan. In the inter-war period there was a more serious demand for a bigger say in the future of Scotland, which led to the creation of the Scottish National Party. In the 1960s renewed economic discomforts, though not on the inter-war scale, and the unfortunate combination of over-government with a lack of time for legislation led to more and more vocal nationalism, linked to a new literary movement. By then the Empire could no longer supply jobs to enterprising Scots, so the ambitions of the country were forced onto the British scene. By the 1970s there was considerable pressure for separation or devolution. In the 1980s the combination of a strong and steady Labour preponderance in Scotland with a Conservative majority in Parliament, carrying through a policy of centralisation, reinforced this.

Before that development, the most significant political movement in Scotland since Jacobitism, the various left-wing groups of the First World War and the 1920s, often collectively given the name of the 'Red Clyde', had run into the ground. Their diversity had made cooperation difficult but their failure is more reasonably seen as part of the general failure of British political groups to provide for the two main needs of the inter-war period, economic recovery and international peace. For a time the men of the Red Clyde had had a disproportionate effect in British Labour life, during the war with the Shop Stewards' Movement and, in the 1920s, more solidly supported in the Independent Labour Party, which had held within the Labour Party of the 1920s the position of the Scots in the Britain of the early 1800s, the source of ideas. Neither movement had been sustained and much of the talk of both had been in clichés—the Scots are a great nation of verbalizers with the advantages and disadvantages that this brings. To native verbiage Marxism had added its own special phraseology. The attempt to regain the Scottish lead in politics in a different political and ethical system ended in mistaken political judgements and ineffectuality.

The Second World War brought a renewed sense of immediate purpose to Scotland, even more than it did to other countries, for during it there was a specific effort made to work the system of government to benefit the country. The impetus of this, and attempts at economic diversification, carried on well into the post-war period, and the country did not return to the doldrums. The literary revival showed that the country contained a disproportionate number of poets, both in Scots and in Gaelic. There was a considerable contribution to science, though it did not match the efflorescence of the nineteenth century, and a new sensibility to the arts, unfortunately not particularly manifest in the inescapable art of architecture. But the modern problems are not ones solved simply in cultural terms. There are still fundamental economic difficulties. The discovery, in the 1960s, of oil in waters which could reasonably be claimed as Scottish rather than British, has given Scottish self-assertion a claim for special attention but has not swiftly invigorated the older sectors of the economy. Much of the oil revenue has been used as short-term government aid, rather than as a means of reinvigorating the Scottish economy. It is still the case that the country has to manufacture some commodity of sufficient value to the rest of the world to outweigh the inconvenience of obtaining it from a source distant and off the main routes of communication, and there has been little recognition of the country's need for better transport links with the south and with Europe. Nature has

provided a scenery on which tourism can be based as well as the oil. Neither of these alone is likely to be enough to supply the rising expectations of a population of over five million. There are also fundamental problems facing many twentieth-century states of the balance between government control over the aspects of the whole economy which have international or general monetary effects and the need to allow for individual or local initiatives. These are bound to be particularly severe in a country which possesses a strong sense of national identity and yet has undergone two centuries of cultural, institutional and economic assimilation to another. In the eighteenth century legislation was a rare event and such Acts of Parliament as affected Scotland were usually the result of considerable pressure by various bodies considered, both by themselves and by others, to be representative of public opinion within Scotland. In the nineteenth century social problems common to the whole of Britain led to legislation initiated by governments, by members of parliament and by theoretical reformers. It was unlikely that a common parliament would devise basically different solutions for the two kingdoms, and it was also easy for Members of Parliament to draw up Bills suitable only for that part of the joint country they knew best, which was more often England than Scotland. In the twentieth century economic problems have forced frequent interventions which, though intended to have a general effect, have usually in practice reserved the benefits for the southeast of England and the disadvantages to all the more remote areas. There is a general need for decentralization of government and perhaps of industrial and commercial structures too, which has not been adequately supplied even by governments doing their best to promote economic growth in the more remote areas, because such efforts have taken their leadership from London. Inspired by either national or regional sentiment, many parts of the United Kingdom had been moving towards greater local autonomy, reversing the trend of two centuries, but in the 1980s this was reversed and the government showed hostility to the idea of any power base other than Whitehall. The result of this was to enhance Scottish national consciousness and to raise stronger claims either for separation or for a Scottish legislature. There are in many big nation states similar demands which involve new thinking in constitutional, legal and institutional areas, and raise the possibility of a new Europe of smaller or federal states and regions. For any of these to occur there needs to be a willingness to dump a great deal of what has been reckoned as the achievement of the past, and for legislatures to stay their legislative hand. The paradox of modern Scotland is an extreme form of one found in many other countries too.

R. Mitchison

Scots Abroad. The Scot on the move has been a constant and disturbing feature of Scottish history almost as far back as can be traced. Into and out of the boundaries of the political entity now known as Scotland, men and women from the Lowlands, Highlands and Islands have moved in a complicated and often

bewildering pattern of interaction since at least the sixth century when the original Scots from Ireland colonized Argyll.
That this is a folk-movement of considerable consequence for
national and international history is clear; but, because migration statistics with any degree of reliability are not available for
the British Isles until the middle of the nineteenth century and
after, the interpretation of the importance of the emigration
of Scots, both for their native land and for the foreign countries
in which they settled, is not always easy. The difficulty is
increased by the recognition of the fact that much of this
migration has been into England. As Robert Louis Stevenson
pointed out in his essay, 'The Foreigner at Home': 'It is not
only when we cross the seas that we go abroad.'

The crossing of the seas, however, is the outstanding feature
of the Scots abroad: first the North Sea and the Irish Sea, and
later the seas further afield, especially the Atlantic Ocean. But
the Atlantic migration, particularly of the eighteenth and nineteenth centuries, can be overemphasized by the student of
Scots overseas. When John Hill Burton produced in 1864 the
first book on this subject, *The Scot Abroad*, the significant
Scottish contribution to North and South America was clear;
and yet Burton devoted the greater part of his work to the Scots
in Europe, especially in the period of the Auld Alliance with
France, 1296–1560. His emphasis was not misleading. The
patterns of enterprise and settlement which distinguish Scottish migration in medieval, Renaissance and Reformation
Europe were carried over into the New World and beyond.

At this time the process began whereby, in the larger cities
of the Continent, especially in France, the Low Countries, the
German states, Sweden and Denmark, Scottish communities
were established. None of them was as substantial as the
community of Scots at Rotterdam which grew to about a
thousand strong at the beginning of the eighteenth century.
Sometimes these Scots in medieval and early modern Europe
kept their own identity; but frequently they merged with the
local people, spreading names of Scottish origin all over the
Continent and into Russia. Smaller but distinctive groups of
Scots gathered around the universities and monasteries of
Europe. Until Scotland's own universities were founded in the
fifteenth century, Scots in search of higher education were
often obliged to seek it on the Continent. The wandering
Scottish divine was a recognized feature of medieval and Renaissance Europe. The Abbey of St James at Ratisbon, for
example: although it had eleventh-century Irish origins, by the
beginning of the seventeenth century a purely Scottish community had been established there, at which such notable
Scottish Catholics as St John Ogilvie received some of their
education. An epoch of Scottish scholarship on the Continent
may be said to have opened with John Duns Scotus, the subtle
Franciscan philosopher who studied and taught at Paris and
died in 1308 while lecturing at Cologne, and to have closed
with George Buchanan, the eminent Scottish scholar (1506–
1582) who studied and taught in France, Portugal and Italy.
With other very different Scots, often anonymous, such as the
wandering pedlars and the soldiers of fortune, a Scottish mark
was made on medieval Europe that was not entirely obliterated

when the Renaissance and Reformation stimulated the growth
of the European nation states of today.

By this time, Scotland's own sense of national feeling was
in the ascendent; and, as with the other states of Europe, it was
accompanied by an urge to found colonies overseas. Indeed,
before Columbus and Vasco da Gama at the end of the fifteenth
century opened the eyes of Europe to the prospects of settlement and trade far afield, Scottish colonizers were at work
closer to home. Settlers from the Lowlands were colonizing
Orkney and Shetland, dependencies of Norway and Denmark
which were handed over to Scottish rule in 1468. And
Scotland's frontier overseas was extended in another colonizing venture close to home throughout the seventeenth century
as a result of the Plantation of Ulster by James I. By the
beginning of the eighteenth century, there were some 80,000
to 100,000 mainly Protestant settlers of Scottish descent in the
north of Ireland. Essentially frontier folk, many of them moved
on to the new frontiers of North America. In the 50 years
before the American Revolution broke out in 1776, substantial
numbers of Ulster Scots emigrated to America, stimulating the
spirit of independence in the emerging new Republic. They
brought to the United States and, later, to the Canadian West
a unique mixture of independence and intolerance.

The original Ulster Scots, however, operated largely within
the framework of the English empire. But other Scots had
ambitions for independent Scottish colonies in the New
World. From 1621, when Sir William Alexander of Stirling's
short-lived experiment of Nova Scotia was started, to 1695,
when the abortive Company of Scotland Trading to Africa and
the Indies was established to create a Caledonian emporium on
the isthmus of Darien near Panama, Scottish colonial schemes
for Cape Breton, Virginia, East New Jersey and South Carolina
as well as for Nova Scotia and the Panama area were projected.
They were soon swallowed up into the English, French and
Spanish empires. The disastrous failure of the Darien scheme
by 1700 put paid to the dreams of an independent Scottish
colonial empire; and, for many ambitious Scots, it seemed that
the road to an overseas empire lay through parliamentary union
with England.

The achievement of this in 1707 opened a new epoch of two
and a half centuries in which Scots, utilizing the framework of
early English overseas ventures in colonization and commerce,
played a major part in the creation of the British Empire.
Where opportunities were lacking in the British Empire, enterprising Scots sought chances for social mobility and social
service in the empires of other European Powers, especially in
the French colonies and in Spanish America. But it was to the
British Empire that they turned first.

On the eve of the Union of 1707, the British Empire was
expanding in three main directions: across the Atlantic to
North America and the Caribbean sugar-producing islands;
and through the Mediterranean or round by the Cape of Good
Hope to India and southeast Asia. Although the lack of an
adequate fleet had been one of the reasons for the failure to
create an independent Scottish overseas empire, Scottish sailors were not slow to take advantage of the opportunities which

the British Navy and merchant fleet afforded them. Indeed, when steam in the second half of the nineteenth century took the place of sail in extending the frontiers of empire, the Scottish ship's engineer came into his own, as Rudyard Kipling's 'McAndrew's Hymn' illustrates. Scottish sailors were added to the types of wandering Scots. And, as the Scots both before and after the era of the American Revolution pushed the boundaries of the British Empire east as well as west, new types were added, born of the Scottish Enlightenment, the Industrial Revolution in Scotland, and the growth of evangelical zeal in the Scottish Churches in the nineteenth century: the doctor; the educator; the scientist; the technician; the manual labourer; the skilled industrial worker; and the typically Scottish missionary who often combined all of these roles in his or her work amongst the non-Christians of the world far beyond Scotland.

As settlers, the Scots, whether from the Protestant Lowlands or the Catholic and Episcopalian Highlands, were already well established in North America before the American War of Independence. Those who remained after the break with Britain, often through their correspondence with relations at home, encouraged other Scots to cross the Atlantic, achieving ultimately the outstanding Scottish success story abroad: Andrew Carnegie in the United States (1848–1919). Those who could not stomach the new Republic, such as Flora MacDonald and her soldier husband, joined the Loyalists and went on to Canada, the West Indies or all the way back home.

In the growth of Canada, Scots other than the Loyalists have played an important part, not only in the Maritime Provinces and Ontario but also in the west. For example, the first white man to reside in British Columbia was a young ship's surgeon, John Mackay, who lived with the Nootka Indians between July 1786 and September 1787. Perhaps even more Scottish names are scattered across the map of Canada than anywhere else in the world. And in the making of Canadian Confederation, it is significant that its first two Prime Ministers, from 1867 to 1891, were Scots, John A. Macdonald and Alexander Mackenzie, the stone-mason from Dunkeld. Furthermore, Highland migrants, such as the Pictou settlers in Nova Scotia in 1773 and the Gaels who went to Prince Edward Island and the Red River Colony under the aegis of the Earl of Selkirk from 1803 to 1819, have ensured that, next to Scotland, parts of Canada are the main Gaelic-speaking areas of the world.

In the other regions of substantial British white settlement overseas, Scots have been notable. In Australia, Scots were amongst the first settlers, involuntary as well as voluntary, in the late eighteenth century; and when in 1900 the federal Commonwealth of Australia was founded, it seemed almost inevitable that its first Governor-General should be a Scot, the Marquis of Linlithgow. New Zealand, in spite of its great distance from home, attracted Scottish emigrants as early as 1820; and, when the Disruption of 1843 occurred, settlers from the Free Church of Scotland established what was intended to be a distinctly Scottish city, Dunedin, in the antipodes. In New Zealand, as elsewhere in the British Empire, Scottish emigrants have contributed to the growth of democracy:

for example, when Peter Fraser, an emigrant from Easter Ross in 1910, helped to form the New Zealand Labour Party and went on to become Prime Minister from 1940 to 1949.

Although the Scottish mark on South Africa should not be underestimated, especially in such educational institutions as Lovedale, Scots settlers, because the Cape Colony did not pass into British hands at the end of the Napoleonic Wars, were not amongst the original white pioneers. Because, however, the first pioneers, the Dutch, had also been products of the Calvinist Reformation, several Scots settlers were assimilated into the Dutch-derived, Afrikaner way of life. But some Scots, such as those who went out to the Cape in 1820, became part of their own frontier process in South Africa; and one of them, Thomas Pringle, may be considered the founder of South African poetry and prose in English.

In those parts of the British Empire where white settlement was not to prove dominant, Scots have been no less conspicuous. Throughout India and southeast Asia, within the vast orbit of the East India Company which reached out to China, Scottish soldiers, speculators, traders, teachers, missionaries, doctors and administrators were part of a complex process of conquest and modernization. It was a process which made many Scots wealthy, especially during the time of Henry Dundas's membership of the Board of Control for India between 1784 and 1801 when he used his position to put his countrymen into lucrative positions in India. Before the Indian Mutiny of 1857, Scottish centralizers in India such as the Marquis of Dalhousie when he was Governor-General from 1784 to 1801 often pushed the pace of modernization too rapidly, leaving their successors in the Indian Civil Service to cope with rising Indian nationalist resentment. One of them, indeed, Allan Octavian Hume, was a founder of the Indian National Congress in 1885. Modernization meant the extension of commerce; and the great Scottish trading houses in India extended their power throughout southeast Asia, bringing out from home into their service generations of Scots. It was a period which closed with the independence of India, Pakistan, Ceylon and Burma in 1947; and the last Scot to be at the centre of power was the second Marquis of Linlithgow, who was the Viceroy of India from 1936 to 1943.

Next to India, the Scottish presence in the nonwhite world has perhaps been felt most in tropical Africa. In the exploration of Africa, Scots were to the fore, notably James Bruce of Kinnaird in Ethiopia and the Sudan from 1768 to 1774, Mungo Park of Foulshiels in the Gambia and Niger regions between 1795 and 1805, David Livingstone of Blantyre in southern, central and eastern Africa from 1853 to 1873, and the Edinburgh-trained geologist, Joseph Thompson, who conducted expeditions in east, west and north Africa between 1878 and 1891. David Livingstone, indeed, more than any other person in the nineteenth century, drew the attention of the developed world to the possibilities of tropical Africa with his typically Scottish vision of Christianity and commerce triumphant over slavery in the interior. He had a dream, too, of the settlement of central Africa by the honest poor of Scotland such as his own family. It was not to materialize; but it touched off missionary and trading ventures in what are now the African states of Malawi and Kenya. John and Fred Moir from Edinburgh set up the Africian Lakes Company which worked closely in the 1870s and 1880s with the Scottish Presbyterian missions at Blantyre and Livingstonia, centres of evangelical and educational activity which took their names from the heritage of David Livingstone. Similarly, Sir William Mackinnon's Imperial British East Africa Company combined Christianity and commerce in the founding of the East African Scottish Mission in 1891. And, on the other side of the continent, the career of Mary Slessor, the Dundee mill-girl who went out to the United Presbyterian Church mission in Calabar in what is now Nigeria, symbolizes the courage and competence of the individual Scot in West Africa. Apart from small groups of Scottish settlers in the central, eastern and southern regions, the Scottish contribution to Africa has been largely individual.

The same may be said of the Scots in the Pacific Ocean area. Although Scottish communities certainly made a mark on Australia and New Zealand, even in these it is often the individual Scottish wanderer who first claims attention. The determination of John McDouall Stuart from Dysart, Fife, who first crossed the Australian continent from south to north and back again in 1861–62, is typical of several Scots explorers in these regions. And it is probably not accidental that the prototype of Defoe's castaway, Robinson Crusoe, was a Scot: Alexander Selkirk from Largo who was put ashore on the uninhabited island of Juan Fernandez in the South Pacific for five years in 1704. The many scattered islands of the Pacific Ocean, no doubt, encouraged Scottish individual rather than communal enterprise; and Scottish connections of British seamen, as the Empire began slowly to expand in these remote regions in the late eighteenth century, made sure that the presence of Scotland was not forgotten. New Caledonia in the western Pacific and the New Hebrides in the southwest whose Scottish names can be traced to 1774 and Captain James Cook, who had a Scottish father, are the outstanding examples of Scottish nomenclature in these regions. As in Africa, individual Scottish missionaries were not lacking in the spread of the Gospel; and some were martyred for their faith, notably the Congregationalist James Chalmers in New Guinea in 1901. Men of Scottish descent, particularly Sir Arthur Gordon, Governor of Fiji from 1875 to 1880, as in other parts of the growing British Empire, entered the colonial administrative services; and missionaries and administrators often strove to uphold native customs and to abolish the infamous labour traffic to Australia. Of all the Scots in the Pacific islands, however, whether impelled by duty, trade, adventure, escape from the constraints of civilization or other motives, it is always to Robert Louis Stevenson, with his six years of wanderings in the South Seas and his death at 'Vailima' in Samoa in 1894, that one turns as a supreme example of the Scot abroad.

From the great explorer of Canada, Alexander Mackenzie of Stornoway who found in 1789 a new river route, which came to bear his name, to the Arctic ocean, to William Speirs

Bruce, discoverer in 1903 of Coats Land which he called after the Paisley family that provided the funds for his Antarctic expedition, Scots have spanned the extremities of the earth. There can be few places around the world where their names and influences are not to be found. Now that the British Empire which gave such scope to their migratory genius has gone, and the United States of America on which they made a special mark began its policy of limiting immigration in 1921, the opportunities for Scots abroad have narrowed. Only the future can show whether the pressures which led and which lead them to seek such opportunities can be satisfied within a new international order or through fundamental changes in the structure of society at home.

G. Shepperson

Scots Storytelling, Traditional. In Scotland as in England 'popular narrative has had a tendency to take the form of the ballad' (Stith Thompson, *The Folktale* p. 19). Tales of enchantment, romantic tragedy and family feud alike are often best known as ballads, and favourite chapbook subjects such as *The Turkey Factor* or John Burness's *Thrummy Cap* are folktales retold in English or Scots verse in the eighteenth century. Prose storytelling in English tends to include few Märchen (international wonder-tales, often misleadingly called 'fairy tales') and concentrate more on jokes and anecdotes, legends about local historical events and figures, or migratory legends and circumstantial 'memorates' reflecting belief in the supernatural—ghosts, witches and real, dangerous fairies. According to Walter Gregor evening entertainments in the farm kitchens of the northeast 150 years ago regularly included both ballads and legends 'for the most of the supernatural', changelings, water-kelpies, witch hares, the devil, but also 'of the wars between England and Scotland'. A few supernatural legends were collected by Gregor himself, by Scott's follower Thomas Wilkie in the Borders, and by various hands in Galloway, Orkney and Shetland. Tales concerning historical figures and great families more often survive as the basis of romantic literary stories in several chapters, first published in periodical form: the most successful example was Wilson's *Tales of the Borders*. Many more tales of murders, hauntings, wicked lairds and persecuted Covenanters are summarized in local histories, travelogues and guidebooks, though they may feature in current oral tradition as subjects of conversation rather than as entertainment.

Outside the family circle, where old comic anecdotes and little moral tales have often been kept up, storytelling to larger, adult audiences such as existed in eighteenth-century Lowland Scotland and more recently in the Highlands continued in situations such as farm bothies, at slack times aboard fishing boats, at social working parties such as cardings, and generally in crofting areas where there were social evenings equivalent to Gaelic ceilidhing. Notably in Shetland visiting 'in aboot da nyht' was normal recently enough for it still to be possible today to hear legends of trows (fairies), seal-people, witchcraft, wicked lairds, escapes from the Press Gang or excisemen, and heroic feats of seamanship, similar to those recorded over the past century by many collectors such as Jessie Saxby, John Nicolson and Andrew Cluness in Shetland and Walter Traill Dennison, W.R. Mackintosh and Ernest Marwick in Orkney. As told today, these stories combine the resources of an expressive dialect, often dramatic delivery, the immediacy of narrative concerning local families and places, and a striking mixture of natural and supernatural happenings both told as fact—as are the many tall tales of seamen and others.

Until recently it was thought that Märchen or 'fairy tales' in Scots as against Gaelic had vanished almost without trace: as early as 1827 Peter Buchan the ballad collector could write 'They are now wearing obsolete, being discarded from the farmer's ingle cheek.' The sixteenth-century *Complaynt of Scotland* names several folktales then current, along with romances of a more literary sort. They include 'The Red Etin', 'The Black Bull of Norroway', and 'The Well [MS Volf] at the World's End', all of which turn up among the 16 'Fireside Nursery stories' included by Buchan's contemporary Robert Chambers in his *Popular Rhymes of Scotland*, perhaps not in the tellers' actual words but at least in good broad Scots reconstructions. 'The Red Etin' is in fact taken from a collection of 14 tales gathered by Buchan himself, presumably not far from Peterhead, which otherwise only survive in a very stilted English form. Apart from a few scattered tales picked up in the Northern Isles and the northeast over the next century the only international wonder-tales from Lowland Scotland were in these collections, until in the 1950s Hamish Henderson and Maurice Fleming recorded some fine stories from members of the Stewart family of Blairgowrie, from Jeannie Robertson the great ballad-singer and other travelling people (tinkers). The travellers have continued to tell Scots tales of magic and enchantment long forgotten by the settled population, both within the family huddled for warmth in a tent at night and between families sharing a campfire, and they became a treasured part of their family and racial heritage, only now being reluctantly revealed to outsiders in its true wealth. In the 1950s the 30 known Scots Märchen were doubled: in the 1970s newly found storytellers look likely to increase the number tenfold or more. Their Scots is not very broad, but the style can be engagingly racy, the body language we are now starting to film can tell almost as much as the words, the imaginative detail can be as fantastic as in any language, and old descriptive phrases like the 'runs' of Gaelic storytellers have been remembered which must be part of an ancient Scottish stock—'He's hey tae the road and ho tae the road, through sheep's parks and bullocks' parks and all the high and the low mountains of Yarrow: and there was no rest for poor Jack, till the birds were making nests in his heid and the stones were making holes in his feet.' There has been influence from chapbooks of 'George Buchanan the King's Fool' and Jack the Giant-Killer, so that Jeannie Robertson's giant roars 'Vee vye vum, I feel the smell of an Englishman' where Chambers's, Red Etin said 'Snouk but and snouk ben, I find the smell of an earthly man'—but it matters more that we are lucky enough to have living exponents of an art whose roots are firmly in old Scotland. *See also* Gaelic storytelling, traditional.

A. Bruford

Scott, Alexander (1920–1989), an Aberdonian, was educated at Aberdeen Academy and University, where his studies were interrupted by army service, during which he won the Military Cross (1945). In 1947 he was appointed Assistant Lecturer at Edinburgh University. The following year he moved to Glasgow University as Lecturer in the Department of Scottish Literature, then newly founded, and which, as Reader, he latterly headed. His was the first academic appointment to be made solely in Scottish literature. He was thus largely responsible for training the majority of teachers who first disseminated the subject in Scottish schools.

As a poet he used both Scots and English, and vigorously carried the banner on behalf of the Scots tradition. From *The Latest of Elegies* (1949) to his *Selected Poems* (1975) it might be thought that Scots was his language for satire and wit-writing, English that for poems of feeling. However, in later years his poetic aphorisms, widely circulated, were couched as often in English as in Scots.

His Scots has about it a lean, muscular toughness, deriving from the fact that it was his first tongue. There is none of that sense of artificiality and strain too often apparent when those with somewhat lesser gifts than MacDiarmid attempt to revive archaic words. Scott's Scots could well be taken as a prototype of the language at its best at a moment when to many it appeared to be under direct siege from the influence of the media.

Scott's wit, whether in his verse or in his plays—mostly written in the 1950s and of which *Right Royal* (1954) starring Duncan Macrae, was the most successful—has a sardonic cutting edge powered by the passion of total conviction.

As a critic, whether reviewing or in such work as *The MacDiarmid Makars* (1972) he made it clear that he knew exactly what he liked. Indeed, he was sometimes accused of recognizing only black or white, with no in-between shades of grey. *Still Life* (1958), his study of the life and work of William Soutar—whose *Diaries of a Dying Man* (1959) he edited—is a minor biographical masterpiece.

His editorial work included *Contemporary Scottish Verse* (1970) with Norman MacCaig; the *Hugh MacDiarmid Anthology* (1972) with Michael Grieve; and *Modern Scots Verse* (1978). He co-edited, with the present writer *The Comic Poems of William Tennant*. He received the Festival of Britain Award for Scots Poetry and verse drama in 1951, a Scottish Community Drama Association Award in 1954 and a Scottish Arts Council Award in 1969. He died in 1989 leaving behind an unpublished verse collection to be included in his *Collected Poems* edited by David Robb, at the moment of writing, awaiting publication.

M. Lindsay

Scott, Alexander (*c.*1515–1583). There is speculation both about Scott's background, and about the year of his birth. It seems likely that he was a law student in Paris when about fifteen, since he is named as appearing there in a *tableau vivant*. In 1548 he was 'musician and organist' with the position of Canon at the Augustine Priory of Inchmahome, and later 'parson of Balmaclellan', in the Stewartry of Kirkcudbright. These positions were doubtless procured as a result of his friendship with the Erskine family, two of whom were Commendators of Inchmahome. Scott appears to have been deserted by his wife, and later to have had two 'natural' sons legitimatized in 1549, by which time their father was Prebendary of the Chapel Royal, Stirling. He lived to enjoy a pension from the Augustinian house of Inchaffray, acquire lands in Fife and Perthshire, and see his son, Alexander, well set up.

Scott, the musician, was a master of the love-song, drawing his own melancholy tone from the short-lined tight rhyming stanzas of his English contemporary Wyatt. 'Lo! what it is to lufe' reflects sadly on the experiences of betrayal that were probably highly personal.

> Lo! what it is to lufe
> Learn ye, that list to prufe
> Be me, I say, that no way may
> The grund of grief remufe,
> Bot still decay, both nich and day:
> Lo! what it is to lufe

For consolation he reflected:

> Als guid luve comes as goes,
> Or rather better.

One of Scott's finest lyrics is that beginning 'Adieu, my awin sweit thing', from 'The Lament of the Maister of Erskine', said to have been in love with the queen-dowager, Mary of Lorraine, and killed at the battle of Pinkiecleugh in 1547. 'Up halesome hairt' celebrates consummated love in spirited fashion.

Scott also produced two longer poems; a 'New Year Gift to the Queen Mary', full of unspeakable alliteration and by that time old-fashioned aureate terms, and an equally old-fashioned flyting, the 'Justing and Debait ... betwix William Adamsone and John Sym'.

M. Lindsay

Scott, Francis George (1880–1958), the son of a mill-furbisher, was born in Hawick and educated there and at Edinburgh University and Moray House Training College. He left the university without taking a degree but qualified as an English teacher and taught at Falkirk, Langholm, Dunoon and Glasgow. At Langholm, one of his pupils was C.M. Grieve, the future poet 'Hugh MacDiarmid', many of whose lyrics Scott was later to set.

After taking the degree of Mus. Bac. at Durham University, Scott became lecturer in music at Jordan-hill Training College in 1925, a post he occupied until his retirement.

He also studied composition briefly under Roger-Ducasse,

but the need to provide for a growing family prevented him from achieving his wish to devote himself entirely to composition. Nor had he the opportunity to work with an orchestra. With the exception of his short overture 'Renaissance', his orchestral scoring tends to be somewhat ineffective.

It is as a writer of songs that he is now best remembered. There being no continuing Scottish musical tradition, Scott had to fashion a substitute of his own, mainly from the stuff of Scottish literary tradition, with which he was thoroughly familiar. His earliest mature songs in the first of his six books of *Scottish Lyrics* are mostly settings of Burns and his associates, and derive from the folksong they transcend. His strong lyrical vein drew its power from the same source throughout his musical life. The rest of his songs are to be found in *Seven Songs for Baritone Voice* (1946), and *Thirty-Five Scottish Lyrics* (1949).

After a reunion with his old pupil Grieve, by then 'Hugh MacDiarmid', in the early 1920s, at a time when Scott had become interested in the harmonic theories of the New Viennese school, he set a number of the young poet's lyrics, in some of them using such devices as bi-tonality and achieving remarkable and daring originality. The partnership between the two men continued, though not at this forward-looking level, and resulted in many other fine if less original MacDiarmid settings. By about 1930 the poet had abandoned lyricism for his collage-like later extended 'poetry of ideas', of no use to Scott, the composer, and which, as it happened, Scott, the critic, disliked. He had suggested to MacDiarmid the idea of 'A Drunk Man Looks at the Thistle', helped the poet construct the poem out of its component parts, and supplied the two final lines.

Scott then turned to the verses of the Perthshire poet William Soutar, though the composer thought much of Soutar's work lifelessly encased in the needless straitjacket of the ballad stanza, and to the English and Scots work of the Gaelic poet, George Campbell Hay. Hay's conflict with authority before and during his war service silenced him as a poet, and for the rest of Scott's life he sought unsuccessfully his 'ideal' poet-collaborator among the medieval Scottish Makars and their modern successors.

Scott was awarded an Honorary Doctorate of Music by Glasgow University the year before his death. He is buried in Hawick.

His lecture-essay on Pibroch, on which he was an authority, is included as an appendix in Maurice Lindsay's biographical study *Francis George Scott and the Scottish Renaissance* (1980) published, along with a centenary edition of his selected songs and a gramophone record, to mark the centenary on 25 January (Burns Night) of the composer's birth; an event also marked by an audiovisual exhibition in the Scottish National Library, Edinburgh. There is now a Francis George Scott archive in the Mitchell Library, Glasgow, made up of bound photostat volumes—the originals are available by special arrangement—containing all his manuscripts, scores and work-sheets.

M. Lindsay

Scott, Sir Walter (1771–1832). Ballad collector, editor, poet, novelist, biographer, critic and historian. The son of a calvinistic Writer to the Signet and of the daughter of a Professor of Medicine, Scott early imbibed the historicism and the antiquarian tastes of the Scottish Enlightenment, first at the High School and University of Edinburgh, then later from the history-oriented legal profession when he was an advocate in the capital (1793–1806), Sheriff of Selkirkshire (1799–1832) and Principal Clerk to the Court of Session (1806–1830). After his marriage in 1797 to Charlotte Carpenter (1770–1826), his life was largely one of work and business, the instruments of what later became his ruling passion—the role of landed proprietor at mock-feudal Abbotsford (bought 1811). The last heroic years, when everything was subordinated to clearing his debts, are finely presented in his moving *Journal* (ed. W.A.K. Anderson, 1972). He was made a baronet in 1820, and in 1822 stage-managed the pageantry of George IV's state visit to Scotland. It was then that the Highland Laddie of Jacobite tradition became a Hanoverian's pet, and then, too, that Scott most showed himself 'a sham bard of a sham nation' (Edwin Muir).

As a poet, Scott evolved from ballad editor (*The Minstrelsy of the Scottish Border*, 1802–3, ed. T.F. Henderson, 1902) to ballad imitator ('The Eve of St John' and 'Glenfinlas', printed in the *Minstrelsy*) to a writer of extended narrative poems drawing sometimes on ballad techniques and sometimes on ballad themes (*The Lay of the Last Minstrel*, 1805; *Marmion*, 1808; *The Lady of the Lake*, 1810, set in the Highlands and more of a romance than a ballad-epic). *Rokeby* (1813), set in Yorkshire during the English Civil War, is a poem striving to become a historical novel, and its 'villain', Bertram, is a semi-Byronic hero, a bare year after that type (so influential in Europe) had made his official *début*. Scott's longer poems, those schoolroom warhorses of 50 years ago, are rising in critical repute. They are currently valued for the pace of their action, brilliant contrasts of light and colour, fusion of landscape description with national feeling, narrative framing devices and multiple time-effects (in *The Lay of the Last Minstrel* no less than 12 layers of time can be seen) and their robust and sometimes realistically imagined battle scenes (Flodden in *Marmion*, Bannockburn in *The Lord of the Isles*, 1815). *The Bridal of Triermain* (1813) pioneers the nineteenth-century vogue for Arthurian romance-imitation, while such shorter pieces as 'Proud Maisie' and 'Jock of Hazledean' are among the best lyrics between Burns (q.v.) and MacDiarmid (q.v.).

If Scott had written nothing else, he would still be remembered as a major editor and biographer. His editions of Dryden (18 vols. 1808) and Swift (19 vols. 1814) remained standard until well into the nineteenth century, and their prefatory volumes are outstanding examples both of the 'life and times' school of literary criticism and of the biographical art, in which such Scots as Boswell, Carlyle, Lockhart and John Buchan (qq.v.) have excelled. His articles for the *Edinburgh* and *Quarterly* reviews, particularly on antiquarian subjects; *The Lives of the Novelists* (1821–4); *The Life of Napoleon Buonaparte* (1827); the well-structured, robustly written child's history of Scotland, *Tales of a Grandfather* (1828–30); and the *Letters on Demonology and Witchcraft* (1830)—all testify to the almost Renaissance breadth of his interests. When the younger Byron captured the market for longer poems, Scott responded by developing the historical novel, a genre for which he possessed unrivalled gifts.

The best of the first Waverley novels, on Scottish subjects (*Waverley*, 4 edns. 1814; *Guy Mannering*, 1815; *The Antiquary, Old Mortality*, 1816; *Rob Roy, The Heart of Midlothian*, 1818; *The Bride of Lammermoor*, 1819), together with the later *Redgauntlet* (1824), are by common consent superior to the medieval and Tudor-Stuart romances (*Ivanhoe*, 1819; *The Monastery, The Abbot*, 1820; *Kenilworth*, 1821; *The Pirate, The Fortunes of Nigel, Peveril of the Peak*, 1822; *Quentin Durward*, 1823; *The Betrothed, The Talisman*, 1825; *Woodstock*, 1826), or the hybrids *St Ronan's Well* (1824), which is both contemporary and Scottish, and *The Fair Maid of Perth* (1828), both medieval and Scottish. In both these kinds Scott developed a unique blend of novel and romance later extended in different ways by Hogg and Stevenson (qq.v.), as well as the characteristic strategy of a young but insipid outsider suddenly involved with historic personages and events, a middle-of-the-road hero whose vacillations and wanderings between contrasting cultures and warring factions help Scott in his main aim of bringing the past to life. His masterpiece, *The Heart of Midlothian*, does not conform to this general pattern. The heroine, Jeanie Deans, is at once a strongly drawn individual and a type who stands for the nation itself, as her successor Chris Guthrie does in *A Scots Quair*, by Lewis Grassic Gibbon (q.v.), and the agonizing moral choice on which the action turns is brilliantly set against the political and cultural tensions of the time. Although the poets and novelists of the Scottish Renaissance reacted strongly against Scott's novels, such critics as the historically minded George Lukács and David Daiches, as well as others whose approach is 'archetypal' and 'mythic', like Northrop Frye, have done much to enhance his reputation as a serious and even epic novelist. Abroad, he fathered a new type of romantic historiography, and his influence on Fenimore Cooper, Manzoni, Balzac and the classical Russian novelists is well known. In Scotland, his handling of language and characters drawn from common life was developed in different ways by Lockhart and Galt (qq.v.), and in England by the Brontës, Mrs Gaskell, Dickens and Hardy, while the negative side of his work has proliferated into that tourist tartanry and North British *kitsch* which has proved so hard to overcome in the present century.

T. Crawford

Scottish Arts Council is central government's main vehicle for supporting the arts in Scotland. From 1947 for twenty years it was the Scottish Committee of the Arts Council of Great Britain. In 1967 it became the Scottish Arts Council with a separate Council and very considerable autonomy over its policies and the way it allocates its funds. It remains part of the Arts Council of Great Britain and shares its Royal Charter objectives to develop and improve the knowledge, understanding and practice of the arts; to increase the accessibility of the arts to the public throughout Great Britain; to advise and cooperate with government departments, local authorities and other bodies on any matters concerned directly or indirectly with these objects. But its policies and funding role has developed to respond to the specific and different needs of Scotland.

The Arts Council of Great Britain and hence, the Scottish Arts Council, function under what is known as the arm's length principle whereby government approves the overall policy of ACGB but does not involve itself directly in the work of the Council or in its funding decisions.

The Scottish Arts Council currently has 21 members appointed by the Arts Council of Great Britain with the approval of the Secretary of State for Scotland. They are appointed for a term of three years renewable for a further 2 years only. In addition the Chair is appointed, usually for a four year period, by the Secretary of State for National Heritage again with the approval of the Secretary of State for Scotland. The Chair also sits on the Council of the Arts Council of Great Britain.

All members are appointed for their personal knowledge and expertise and are not representative of any group, organisation or interest.

The Council is advised by, and delegates some decision making powers to, specialist committees for art, combined arts, dance, drama, literature and music. All Council members, with the exception of the Chair, Deputy Chair and the three members of the Planning and Resources Committee, sit on artform committees. Membership of these committees is approved by Council each for a term of three years renewable for a further two. Here too, people are appointed for their personal expertise and are not representative of other interests.

Every year suggestions for Committee membership are canvassed widely through public advertising. Final decisions about membership are based on a number of factors including the need to ensure a balance of artform and other experience and expertise, a suitable spread of geographic base and background, and to take into account equal opportunity considerations.

Currently the Scottish Arts Council receives 10.45 per cent of the Government allocation to the Arts Council of Great Britain. In 1992–93, the total budget was over £22 million. Of that total, only 8 per cent is spent on administration and overheads with the balance being used to support artists and arts organisations throughout Scotland.

With its available funds, the SAC provides ongoing revenue grants to about 60 major organizations—theatres like the Citizens Theatre in Glasgow, the Traverse in Edinburgh and the Byre in St Andrews; art galleries and workshops like the network of Printmaker Workshops in Inverness, Dundee, Aberdeen, Glasgow and Edinburgh; musical ensembles and promoters like Cappella Nova and Assembly Direct; literary organisations like the Scottish Poetry Library and Book Trust; arts centres like the Centre for Contemporary Arts in Glasgow and the MacRobert in Stirling; and the major festivals like the Edinburgh International Festival and Mayfest. It funds the four national companies, Scottish Opera, Scottish Ballet, The Royal Scottish National Orchestra and the Scottish Chamber Orchestra and also provides project funds, touring grants, bursaries and awards to individual artists, new initiatives and small companies.

In 1967, the Arts Council gave 100 grants—almost every application was successful and received funding. By 1992, the number of grants given had increased to over 800 but more importantly the number of applications regularly exceeded the funds available with the ratio of unsuccessful to successful applications in some areas rising to 4:1.

The four national companies alone account for 46 per cent of the arts budget. Over 80 per cent of the budget is dedicated to ongoing revenue support for the 60 major organisations mentioned above. Still, the limited balance for 1991–92 managed to support over 120 bursaries, awards and travel grants to musicians, writers, artists, dancers and playwrights; to support 86 music clubs and arts guilds to organise 500 professional performances; to help to commission over 22 new plays and 22 new music scores; to support 18 writing fellowships, 17 visual artists and 3 dance artists in residence; to assist the publication of 107 books and magazines and to meet the costs of 1,850 visits of writers to schools.

But the Scottish Arts Council is not alone in supporting the arts in Scotland. Local authorities played a growing role until by the beginning of the 1990s, they were estimated to be the country's major arts funders contributing up to £1 million per year. Economic development agencies such as the Scottish Tourist Board, Highlands and Islands Enterprise, Scottish Enterprise and the network of Local Enterprise Companies were also persuaded of the benefits of the arts to Scotland's economy and started to invest.

Increasingly the Scottish Arts Council sees its role not only as funder of the arts but also as their advocate, trying to create a climate in which arts can flourish and in which funding is drawn from a wide range of sources. It has worked with local authorities to develop and implement arts plans; it has persuaded local enterprise companies of the importance of the arts and cultural industries to the regeneration of urban and rural areas. It has helped to develop agencies to encourage business sponsorship and support in kind. It has improved the information services available to artists and arts organisations. It has helped to develop an arts management training agency in Scotland. It has worked with local education authorities to advocate the importance of arts and education. It has worked with the Scottish Tourist Board on arts and tourism initiative and it has been active in support for the development of Gaelic culture.

Above all it has worked collaboratively with other agencies, the most recent example being *The Charter for the Arts in Scotland*, published in early 1993. The *Charter* was the result of the most extensive consultation ever undertaken in the arts in Scotland and its production was overseen by a Steering Group led by the Arts Council and comprising representatives of the Scottish Museums Council, Scottish Film Council and the

Convention of Scottish Local Authorities. The Charter is both inspiration and aspiration. It is not a statement from the funding bodies but rather a reflection of the views and hopes of all those who contributed to the process. As such it provides a shared vision for the future development of the arts, a framework in which all the bodies concerned can develop their own detailed plans.

S. Reid

'Scottish Enlightenment' is a fairly new term in the historians' vocabulary (I have even heard two distinguished living historians claim to have invented it). As such, it denotes an area of scholarly interest rather than a clearly defined episode in Scottish history. For most people, the phrase suggests such questions as these: Why did Scottish society generate so vigorous an intellectual life during the eighteenth and early nineteenth centuries? Is there a peculiarly Scottish component in the philosophical, historical and scientific enquiries of Scottish intellectuals? What is the nature and significance of the eighteenth-century literary revival and Scottish writers' concern with the rival claims of Scots and English as vehicles for serious literature? It is not easy to handle, let alone resolve such questions because, although the subject is attracting serious attention, general discussions of its historical significance are sadly lacking. In this rather fluid state of scholarship any discussion of the subject is bound to be personal and this one is no exception.

The Scottish Enlightenment may be defined as a period bounded by the Glorious Revolution of 1688 and the death of Sir Walter Scott in 1832. Its period of greatest activity and achievement lay between the 1750s and the 1780s. Thus the early years of the eighteenth century appear as a prologue and the early years of the nineteenth century, the age of Francis Jeffrey and Walter Scott, a particularly glorious epilogue to what we may call the high period of the Scottish Enlightenment. Any discussion of the social history of the Scottish Enlightenment is bound to focus on the history of Edinburgh, Glasgow and Aberdeen, the three principal centres of intellectual activity. Of these, Edinburgh was pre-eminent. While the other two cities were important centres of learning for only a few decades in the middle of the century, Edinburgh remained intellectually active throughout the whole period and was regarded as the cultural capital of Scotland by contemporaries at home and abroad. Its university, and its aristocratic and intellectual salons were attractions which no other city could rival and no provincial intellectual could ignore. Many Scottish intellectuals removed to Edinburgh to work or to retire; all were in the habit of visiting the city when circumstances allowed. Indeed Glasgow and Aberdeen may be regarded as cultural provinces whose role was to fertilize and, perhaps, transform the cultural life of metropolitan Edinburgh.

All discussions of the social history of the Scottish Enlightenment must then begin with Edinburgh and consider why that city was so peculiarly well adapted to support a complex and creative intellectual society. Historians have always agreed that the question can only be answered properly if it is set against the background of the consequences of the Union on Edinburgh's social life. Until recently, it was assumed that the Union placed Scotland under direct rule from London, depriving the city of its metropolitan institutions, encouraging the landed classes to migrate to London, leaving social leadership in the hands of a professional bourgeoisie of lawyers, ministers, professors, doctors and merchants. It was from this population, it is argued, that Edinburgh's literati was drawn and it was in their attempt to keep alive what J.G. Lockhart called 'the threatened spirit of national independence' that the ideological motive power of Scottish intellectual life seemed to reside.

But this classic view rests on a serious misapprehension. If the Union deprived Edinburgh of her political institutions, it did not deprive her of her social elite. For while it is true that the greatest nobility took the high road to London, the lesser nobility and gentry did not. Notwithstanding the increasingly popular habit of making short visits to London in the summer months, for much of the eighteenth century men of rank and property continued to regard Edinburgh as the focal point of their social and political world. This aristocratic society dominated the professional life of the city and the country at large, controlling the patronage of the Church and the membership of the Faculty of Advocates. The University was reconstructed in order to provide their sons with the polite education appropriate to their rank. It was not until the last quarter of the century that the aristocratic foundations of Edinburgh society began to crumble as men of rank and property began to abandon Edinburgh in favour of London, leaving social leadership in the hands of a now bourgeois professional society. In other words, during the high period of the Scottish Enlightenment, Edinburgh was an aristocratic, not a bourgeois city. But the Edinburgh of Sir Walter Scott was a city which had undergone a social revolution of the first magnitude.

While it is undoubtedly true that most of Edinburgh's literati were professional men, it would be wrong to think of the College, the law courts or the General Assembly as the institutional focal points of the city's intellectual life. Throughout the eighteenth century an astonishing number of intellectual clubs and societies sprang up which were to perform that function. Some were large, formal and aristocratic; others were small, informal to the point of unruliness and composed of men of humbler origins. Yet all had the same function, to draw together men with literary and philosophical tastes from all walks of life so that members could test their ideas against the common opinion of their companions. They were institutions which were designed to make learning and letters useful to society generally, and particularly useful to Scotland.

When these developments are seen in an international perspective none of them seem to be in the least surprising. Edinburgh was a provincial capital which had developed socially, politically and culturally in much the same way as Dublin, Philadelphia, Boston or Charlestown, Bordeaux, Toulouse or Dijon. For these cities were all centres of provincial government, society and culture whose life revolved around provincial elites upon whom the good government, prosperity and happiness of the province depended. In this world, Edinburgh appears as *primus inter pares*, a provincial capital which generated an intellectual life of incomparable richness.

Why should it have done so? There can be no certain answer. Nevertheless it is hard not to be struck by the remarkably high social status which intellectuals enjoyed in Edinburgh and the civic importance which was attached to the pursuit of the polite arts and sciences. What is interesting is that high status seems to have been connected with the changes which had been brought about by the Union. That at least is the conclusion to which the history of the two most aristocratic and formal clubs in Edinburgh points. *The Honourable the Society for Improvement in the Knowledge of Agriculture* (1723–?45) and the *Select Society* (1754–?63) were highly aristocratic societies. The first grew out of its members' interest in agricultural improvement. In time it acquired a more general interest in economic improvement at large and began to take up many of the projects for encouraging economic growth that the old Scots parliament had pursued before the Union. The Select Society had its origins in its founder-members' desire to discuss moral and political questions and to encourage the improvement of the manners of Scottish society at large. Its founders, which included men like David Hume, Allan Ramsay, Alexander Carlyle and Adam Smith, had intended that it should be a small society of men of letters. But within a matter of months it had become as aristocratic a society as the Honourable Society had once been and had inherited its interest in economic improvement. The social and ideological links these two societies have with the old Scots parliaments allow us to think of them as para-parliaments, designed to demonstrate that political leadership still lay in the hands of a traditional governing class. For all that, the primary purpose of the Select Society continued to be literacy and philosophical debate. It suggests that polite learning had come to acquire a political, not to say patriotic significance in mid eighteenth-century Scotland. And it could be argued that Scotland's traditional aristocratic élite had come to regard the intellectuals as a *corps d'elite* which provided their class with the sort of leadership it was unable to provide for itself. Certainly contemporaries frequently commented on the high status of men of letters in an aristocratic society and it was generally understood that the city's reputation rested on the achievements of her philosophers and men of letters. By the 1760s contemporaries looked on Edinburgh as a true republic of letters whose identity rested on cultural, not political foundations. And they described it, variously as a Modern Athens, the Athens of Britain, an Athens of the North.

If the intellectual life of mid eighteenth-century Scotland is discussed in terms of twentieth-century disciplines, it seems bewilderingly various and it has become commonplace for historians of the natural, medical and social sciences to study the contribution of Scottish intellectuals to the evolution of their particular disciplines. An intellectual historian on the other hand is obliged to search for contemporary points of reference for their philosophy. Throughout the eighteenth and early nineteenth century, the overriding preoccupation of Scottish writers was with what they called manners and we should call the study of human behaviour. Moreover it was directed towards what contemporaries called improvement and we should call the problem of adapting values and behaviour patterns to suit the demands of modernization. At a superficial but nonetheless significant level it took the form of a preoccupation with clothes, equipage, accent, prose style and the minutiae of social deportment. In the intellectual world, however, these concerns were simply a function of a more serious preoccupation with what David Hume called the Science of Man and it is this concern, patronized by a largely aristocratic, politically minded élite which forms the intellectual backbone of the Scottish Enlightenment.

The Scottish philosophers believed that man was a sociable animal who relied on society to provide him with security, sustenance and a sense of identity. A properly conceived Science of Man involved studying the process of socialisation. It meant examining our appetites and intellectual endowments. It meant considering how we became aware of the opinions of others and learned to respect and manipulate social rules and conventions. It meant enquiring into the origins of our possessive attitudes to private property and our curious willingness to submit to established political authority. It meant studying the role of religion and economic activity in stimulating and corrupting human progress and the studying of the culture of the modern world comparatively, contrasting it with the more primitive form of human civilization that had preceded it. The philosophers saw that this secularly-minded, materialist, approach to the study of human nature was of the greatest practical importance. It would teach men and women to understand their capabilities and to realise that their personalities were shaped by psychological and historical forces which were often beyond their control. It would teach them to be adaptable and to realise that by being so they would be useful to themselves and to the public generally.

This programme for a Science of Man was brought to maturity in the 1750s and 1760s by philosophers like David Hume, Adam Smith, Lord Kames, Adam Ferguson, William Robertson, and John Millar, but its roots lie in earlier intellectual developments in intellectual circles in Glasgow and Edinburgh. Some of them are to be found in the moral philosophy classroom of Glasgow University and in the jurisprudence that was being taught by the first professor of moral philosophy, Gersholm Carmichael and his celebrated pupil and successor, Francis Hutcheson. Some of them lie in the salons of Edinburgh where the literati discussed the essays on manners and morals that had been written by two great London moralists, Richard Steele and Joseph Addison. By the 1720s these Scots were laying the metaphysical foundations of the Science of Man. At the same time, the poet Allan Ramsay was developing a new form of Anglo-Scottish literature which was designed to show how Scottish literature could be refined by an understanding of modern manners. In his *Gentle Shepherd* (1725) he drew an imaginary picture of an essentially Scottish rustic community, drawn together by a common culture which was animated by Addisonian sentiments. Interestingly and significantly, it was a representation which contemporaries found true to life and led them to think of the work as 'The National Pastorale'.

David Hume, however, provided the true foundations for this Scottish Science of Man. His attempt to banish unnecessary metaphysical speculation from philosophy, and religion from the discussion of moral and social conduct; his extraordinary analysis of the role of belief in shaping our ideas and values; his discussion of the sympathetic mechanisms which govern our relationships with other men and women, made it possible, for the first time, for philosophers to think of men living in a society, drawn together by cultural as well as political bonds. At the same time, Hume and his friends began to turn from the study of man to the study of history and the evolution of society itself. They considered the economic, social and cultural foundations of societies in different stages of evolution, the causes and effects of their progress from rudeness to refinement, the principles which underlay their laws and political systems and governed their modes of political behaviour. Simultaneously medical professors, like William Cullen, Robert Whytt and John Gregory set out to locate the physiological sources of the sympathetic mechanisms on which social life depended. Practical theologians like Hugh Blair, whose *Sermons* (which began to be published in 1777) were to be one of the most influential manuals of devotion in the Anglo-Saxon world, set out to show exactly how private religious devotions could help to relieve the anxieties of men living in an essentially secular, changeable world.

The Science of Man Hume had founded was developed by his close friend Adam Smith at Glasgow. Hume and his friends understood the general nature of those principles which governed the life of man in society and caused society itself to progress from rudeness to refinement but not their particular operations. It was left to Smith, in his extraordinary *Theory of Moral Sentiments* (1759)—as a remarkable a contribution to eighteenth-century psychology as Freud's *Interpretation of Dreams* was to be to a later generation—and in his *Wealth of Nations* (1776), to elucidate the exact nature of the psychological and historical process by which human interaction and historical change took place.

Neither Hume or Smith were determinists. Nevertheless there is a determinist streak running through their concept of the Science of Man. It was legitimate for contemporaries to wonder whether morality had become no more than a matter of adapting one's behaviour to suit the spirit of the age. The future happiness and prosperity of society seemed to have more to do with the operations of an invisible hand than with good government and the responsible exercise of power by a virtuous governing elite. Religion, instead of being the cornerstone of public morality and private virtue, seemed simply to have become a source of private consolation to the anxious. Perhaps it was better for Scotsmen to resign themselves to the inevitability of change and a closer union with England and salve their patriotic consciences by remembering the glories of

a bygone age. That, at least, seemed to be the teaching of Ossian, the great Celtic bard, whose supposed poems, largely manufactured by James Mcpherson (q.v.) and given historical significance by Hugh Blair, began to appear in 1762. Ossian was portrayed as a Chieftain and Bard, the last of a line of Celtic heroes whose civilization had become historically redundant and was on the point of extinction. Ossian (at least as Blair portrayed him) was the spokesman for a new, sentimental style of stoicism, which taught men to resign themselves to the inexorable forces of history, to celebrate the passing of a civilization which had been virtuous in its way, in long, rhetorical lamentations.

Charming though this literary fatalism might be, its moral and political implications were, nevertheless, capable of disturbing thoughtful and virtuously minded men. Adam Ferguson, in his *History of Civil Society* (1767) and John Millar in his *Historical View of the English Government* (1787) re-examined some of the central historical and sociological premisses on which the Science of Man had been founded in the belief that it must surely prove possible to discover an independent and creative role for the virtuous politician to play in this modern world. In Aberdeen, Thomas Reid and James Beattie and their circle turned from the moral to the metaphysical foundations of the Science of Man in order to re-examine Hume's theory of belief and discover whether it was possible to release religion and morality from the deterministic and agnostic bondage in which its authors seem to have placed it. The principles of their Common Sense philosophy are discussed elsewhere but they were of crucial importance to Scottish cultural history. As they were developed by Reid's greatest pupil, Dugald Stewart, professor of moral philosophy at Edinburgh from 1785-1829, the critique of Hume's philosophy was mistakenly felt to be compelling and decisive. By the 1790s it was being taught in every Scottish university and was rapidly gaining favour in America and France. At the same time Stewart, a prolific writer, revisited every corner of the Science of Man, re-evaluating its central principles against the principles of Common Sense philosophy in order to construct a new version which was more cautious intellectually, more closely geared to the task of legitimizing and reinforcing deeply seated and traditional religious, political and cultural values. It was designed, quite explicitly, to provide a value system which would provide young men destined for public life a self-confident if self-critical frame of mind.

The first three decades of the nineteenth century mark the final phase of the Scottish Enlightenment. The intellectual life of Glasgow and Aberdeen had lost its power. Edinburgh had become a bourgeois city whose society was dominated by a legal elite, whose cultural life was framed by a sentimental, Ossianic nostalgia for what Henry Cockburn called 'The last purely Scotch age'. Men of letters analysed the social changes which had taken place in the city, noted the passing of the distinctive manners of a bygone age and feared that Scotland would soon become, in Walter Scott's words, 'an inferior species of Northumberland'. Nevertheless this bourgeois society brought forth a new variant of the Science of Man, a new approach to the problem of teaching modern men and women how to adapt to the pressures of change in a modern and increasingly turbulent age. *The Edinburgh Review* (1802-1929) founded by a young lawyer, Francis Jeffrey, represents a distillation of the moral principles of Dugald Stewart, sharpened by a ferocious, and often disconcertingly iconoclastic temper. It was to become violently partisan in its radical-whig politics and soon inspired tory rivals—notably the London-based *Quarterly Review* (1809-1967) and *Blackwood's Edinburgh Magazine* (1817–present). These Reviews represented a revolution in a style of moral journalism which had been invented by Addison and Steele and was to be of almost equal importance in shaping the values of bourgeois society in the early decades of the nineteenth century. For these journals encouraged their readers to adopt a style of political and literary criticism which was rooted, not in eternal principles sanctioned by reason, time and the authority of great men, but in the experience of ordinary literate and responsible men living in a modern age. It was a style of criticism directed towards determining the capacity of political and literary ideas to contribute to the ease and understanding of men living in a modern age.

The moral world of the reviewers was complemented by that of Walter Scott. As a poet and novelist, Scott presented himself to his contemporaries as a storyteller whose task was to amuse and instruct his vast audience with stories about men and women from different walks of life in different ages, whose lives had been caught up in social and historical events which lay beyond their control. Scott's heroes and heroines belong to the world of Hume's Science of Man. They are benevolent, sociable and honourable in their way, motivated by a desire to live at ease with themselves and society at large, yet often perplexed by the rival claims of the past, present and future. Some take refuge in the strange but beguiling world of ideology—only Hume saw the power and dangers of ideology as clearly as Scott. But Scott believed that all ranks of men in all ages had the capacity to adapt themselves to change in their own ways and it is with them, he believed, that the future of civilization rested. But it is Scott's Scottish novels, which trace the history of the Scottish people from the later seventeenth century to his own age, which give Scott his heroic stature as a moralist and man of letters. For they show a nation learning to adapt its ancient but underdeveloped civilization to the changing demands of a more stable, commercially orientated and humane age. It was a process, in which, he seemed to imply, the Scottish nation at large had won its identity.

Scott's death in 1832 is generally taken to mark the end of the Scottish Enlightenment as a distinctive phase in Scottish history. But it was not an isolated event. Francis Jeffrey had resigned as editor of the *Edinburgh Review* in 1829. A Royal Commission which began work in 1825 had exposed the most serious structural weaknesses in the Scottish university system which had once been the envy of the civilized world. The bank crisis of December 1825, which had destroyed Scott's fortune, destroyed the foundations of Scotland's remarkable publishing industry. Perhaps the most significant event of all was the

departure of Thomas Carlyle for London. Unable to adapt himself to what he felt to be the oppressive social and cultural pressures of Edinburgh life, he left for London in 1829. Carlyle was the only man who was capable of developing the Science of Man in an age which was increasingly preoccupied with the moral and political problems of industrialization and with the explanatory powers of German literature and philosophy. Had he been able to adapt himself to Edinburgh life, it is just possible that the distinctive culture of the Scottish Enlightenment could have continued to develop for another generation.

N.T. Phillipson

Scottish Language, The. Modern Scotland has three languages, English, the official speech of the country, taught to all and spoken in one form or another by all; Gaelic, the Celtic tongue brought from Ireland by fifth-century immigrants, spoken now alongside English in the western seaboard and the Hebrides; and Scots, the historical speech of the Lowlands, which derives from 'Inglis', the English of Northern England. The history of these tongues goes hand in hand with the political history of Scotland.

In Roman times Britain spoke an early form of p-Celtic, which survives as Welsh, as opposed to the q-Celtic of Ireland, but with the departure of the Romans, the Angles and Saxons invaded southern Britain and by the early seventh century the Angles had crossed the Humber and Tweed and established their *hams* and *tuns* in southeast Scotland reaching beyond Din Eidyn, which they captured and renamed Edinburgh. Christianized by the Celts from Iona about 635, their Northumbrian church spread as far west as Wigtownshire and the inscription on the cross in Ruthwell Kirk near Dumfries of a few verses from *The Dream of the Rood* provides the earliest monument in Scotland of the Scots tongue (*c.*730). Linguistic records are thereafter very scanty but point to a slow and steady penetration of Inglis through southern Scotland to the gradual extinction of the British language except for place-names, which are mainly Welsh, with a Gaelic superstratum in the tenth century when Strathclyde and later Lothian came under the control of Alba, Scotland north of Forth and Clyde. This enlarged kingdom, in effect the Scotland of today, became bilingual in Gaelic and Anglo-Saxon. Over the centuries some Gaelic words have been taken over into Scots, like *bog*, *cairn*, *glen*, *strath*, *loch*, *airt* (direction), a few law terms now obsolete, some medieval borrowings, as *capercailie*, *caber* (rafter), *partan* (crab), *sonsie* (lucky, plump), *slogan*, *usquebae* (whisky), and, with renewed contacts in the Jacobite period, *claymore*, *pibroch*, *sporran*, *filibeg* (kilt). And by far the majority of northern Scottish place-names are of Gaelic derivation.

Meanwhile the Scandinavian invasions in the north of England in the ninth century had driven a wedge between the Angles of Lothian and their countrymen south of the Humber and imposed their kindred Norse tongue on the Inglis. Many of the phonological features of Norse were taken over, such as the unpalatalized *k* and *g* before front vowels, *sk-* for *sh-*, *au* for

$\bar{e}a$, *ei* for $\bar{a}$, reflected in words like *kirk, kist, breeks, sic, steek, brig, rig*, where English has *ch* and *dge* forms; in *get, gi(v)e*, for obsolete English *yet, yeve, garth* for *yard, lowp* for *leap*, and *ain* for earlier *awn*, English *own*; and there was a considerable accretion to the vocabulary of words still in common use, e.g. *brae*(slope), *ettle*(aim), *frae*(from), *gar*(compel), *ferlie* (marvel), *gate*(road), *graith*(equipment), *hoast*(cough), *low*(flame), *neive*(fist), *rowan*(mountain ash), *lug*(ear), *strae*(straw), *til*(to), *tike*(dog), *tyne*(lose). In Scotland the full effect of this was not felt till after the Norman Conquest of England when new settlers came as servants and retainers of the French-speaking barons and churchmen who spilt over from England into Scotland and whose influence on the Celtic court led to their acquisition of large domains and the establishment of the feudal system in the northern kingdom also in the eleventh and twelfth centuries.

French influence on the language can be divided into three stages, Norman French till about 1200; and Central or Parisian French thereafter, both of which came to Scotland via England and account for the large French vocabulary they have in common. Some words, lost to English, have survived in Scots, as *leal*(faithful), *ashet*(plate), *aumrie*(cupboard), *cowp* (capsize), *douce*, *jigot*(leg of mutton), *mavis*(thrush), *houlet*(owl), *tassie*(cup); others have followed different phonological rules in Scots, as *failyie*(fail), *spulyie*(spoil), *cunye*(coin), *fenyie*(feign), *bouls*(bowls), *succar*(sugar), *creish*(grease). The third source, the Franco-Scottish Alliance (1296-1560), bypassed England and added further words, as *Vaig*(roam), *effeir* (appearance), *disjune*(breakfast), *spairge*(spatter, *fash* (bother), *visie*(aim), *vivers*(rations), *caddie*, *gardyloo* (call to dodge a splash), *hogmanay*(new year's eve).

These social and political changes spread this Anglo-Norse-French fusion speech far beyond the confines of southern Scotland over the eastern Lowlands as far as Moray and into Caithness, and the Gaelic-speaking area shrank correspondingly. Another consequence was the rise of the burghs and industries and the immigration of craftsmen, especially from the Low Countries, a connection which lasted until the eighteenth century and added to the Scots vocabulary many Dutch words still current, as *crune*(sing softly), *bucht*(sheep-pen), *redd*(tidy up), *dowp*(buttocks), *dub*(pool), *kyte*(belly), *loun*(boy), *mutch*(woman's cap), *pinkie*(little finger),*golf*, *scone*.

New distinctions developed over the next four hundred years between the speech of the north and southern English. The long back vowels $\bar{a}$ and $\bar{o}$ began to move forward in the north towards an $\bar{e}$ and *ü* position, but upwards in the south to $\bar{o}$ and $\bar{u}$, as in *gae, go, sune*, soon. The shift of the other vowels in consequence produced a further difference in $\bar{u}$ becoming a diphthong in the south but remaining a monophthong in the north, as in *house, down, cow*, Scots /hus/,/dun/,/ku/; the long front vowels developed along similar lines in both dialects, $\bar{i}$ becoming diphthongized as in *fire, mine*; $\bar{e}$ had an open and a close form which ran together in the sound /i/ in the fifteenth century, 200 years earlier in Scotland than the corresponding change in England, which was not so thoroughgoing

and frequently prevented by other phonological factors, hence such distinctions as between English *bread, deaf, red*, and Scots *breist, deif, reid*. The Middle English diphthongs are variously developed in Scots and tend to remain in final position, as *hey*, hay, *wey*, way, *Mey*, May, *pey*, pay, *gey*, gay, very; but conversely, *dee, lee, flee*, for English die, lie (falsehood), *fly*. When non-final however the diphthong *ai* fused with $\bar{a}$ as the sound /e/ and the spellings became interchangeable, so *sare, sair*, for English sore, *rade, raid*, English rode and also road; *i* then came to function as a sign of vowel length and a new series of spellings resulted, as *heir*, hear, here, *noit*, note, *buit*, boot. The consonant 3 before other consonants and in final position has tended to retain the fricative sound, spelt *ch* (as in *loch*), in *nicht, lauch, teuch, laich*(low), *heich*(high); a final *l* after a short back vowel was lip-rounded to *w*, producing again new diphthongs as in *baw, waw* (the words becoming monophthongs later), *know*, knoll, *how*, hole, *row*, roll, *fu*(*w*), *pu*(*w*), etc.; *wh* retains the sound of both elements, not *w* only; and in Scotland in any position the *r* is still trilled.

Grammatical features include the survival of old plurals in *kye*, cows, *een*, eyes, and in certain adjectives, *saidis, presentis*, and the relative pronoun (the) *quhilkis*; present tenses of verbs take *-s* in the plural when the subject is a pronoun not immediately preceding or a noun, the present participle ends in *-and*, the gerund in *-ing*, all these distinctions being now obsolescent; the conjugation of verbs differs somewhat from English, some strong verbs becoming weak and weak strong. Word usage also varies in prepositions, adverbs, and in the definite article; conjunctions include *gif* or *gin* for *if*, *nor* for *than*, *sin* for *since*. The indefinite article *ane* appears before consonants as a written, but not spoken, convention from the sixteenth century to the eighteenth.

By the end of the fourteenth century this speech had become adequate for the needs of legislation, administration, and the keeping of records, and was already the vehicle of literature, notably Barbour's romance, *The Brus* (1375). By the end of the fifteenth, the accumulation of these and other differentiae, the disappearance of Northern English as a literary medium, the growth of a native poetry of high quality, and above all the political independence of Scotland combined to make the Scots aware also of their linguistic distinctness from the metropolitan speech of England, and to give the national name of Scottis to what they had previously called Inglis, though the old name lingered on alongside the new for more than a century. In 1513 Gavin Douglas explicitly discusses the problem of using 'Scottis' in his translation of Virgil's *Aeneid*, and his policy of borrowing to extend its vocabulary; a similar line is taken in the anonymous *Complaynt of Scotland* (1548), itself a translation of a French work.

Meanwhile the Scottish poets had been experimenting with considerable virtuosity in styles, a courtly, 'aureate', highly Latinized style, derived from Chaucer, Lydgate and the French romances, a more prosaic plain style, as in Henryson's *Fables* or Dunbar's various addresses, or in Lyndsay's *Satyre*, and the colloquial vernacular style of popular and humorous pieces, like *Christis Kirk, Peblis to the Play, The Wyf of Auchtermuchty*,

Colkelbie's Sow, which are valuable indicators of how the commons actually spoke.

But just when the Scots language was coming into fullness of resource, the first of three great reverses overtook it. The Reformation caught Scotland without a vernacular translation of the Bible and the only available one was the Geneva English version of 1560. The Scots were introduced to Southern English with the authority of the Word of God and a linguistic dichotomy sprang up which associated English with the solemn, formal and intellectual, and Scots with the homely, sentimental and humorous aspects of life. To this new spiritual prestige of English was added the social prestige after the King of Scots came to the English throne in 1603 and the Scottish courtiers and litterateurs adapted their speech to their new milieu. Finally with the Parliamentary Union of 1707 the language of the south achieved political status over the whole country; all formal and official writing now uses English, with the occasional Scotticism persisting until the late eighteenth century, and some legal idioms surviving to the present day as the expression of the independence of Scots law.

While Scots prose had given way to English in the seventeenth century, Scots poetry, especially of the popular type, survived through the seventeenth in ballads and folk-song. In the eighteenth much of this was anthologized and formed the basis for the revival of a literature in theme and language of the sentimental and vernacular sort. This popular tradition reached its climax through Ramsay and Fergusson in Burns and his success inspired not only poetic imitators but also prose writers like Scott and Galt, who used Scots in a limited role as a realistic vehicle for the speech of their humbler characters, and they too have had many successors. But with the breakdown of a metropolitan standard spoken Scots began to disintegrate into regional dialects of which there are now four main varieties, distinguishable chiefly by their vowel systems, and the growing intrusion of English has led to confusion in its phonemic and grammatical structure and to the constant attrition of its vocabulary. Socially too it has become déclassé though it is still widely understood and spoken in various degrees of fusion with English in vocabulary and pronunciation according to the context of the situation and the speaker's own background and feeling.

In the 1920s Hugh MacDiarmid, in demanding a new infusion of intellect as opposed to sentiment into Scottish poetry and with it a redevelopment of the resources of Scots by restoring archaic words, borrowing from other tongues or by new creation under the slogan 'Back to Dunbar', was in effect resuming the policy of Douglas and following similar language revivals in other countries. Support for these ideas led to the Lallans (Lowland Scots) movement, now the Scots Language Society, which is active in promoting the extended use of Scots, both in speech and writing. Once again the fate of the language is becoming linked with political events and no doubt the growth of Scottish Nationalism in the past half century will continue to influence the future of Scots.

D. Murison

Scottish Music Information Centre, The, was founded in 1968 by Professor Frederick Rimmer as the Scottish Music Archive. Its object was to form a reference library of music, both manuscript and printed, by Scottish composers, and of associated materials. The initial priority was to promote contemporary music and to assist living composers to win a hearing. But importance was also attached to music of earlier periods, resulting in a growing collection of antiquarian publications and microfilm, and a comprehensive listing of manuscript sources of material held elsewhere. Substantial bequests included unpublished and published work by J. B. McEwen, W. G. Whitaker, Ian Whyte and Cedric Thorpe Davie. The Archive was housed within Glasgow University premises but responsibility for its policy and organization was also shared by representatives from the Universities of St Andrews, Aberdeen and Edinburgh, the Royal Scottish Academy of Music and Drama, the Scottish Arts Council and the BBC.

The first published catalogue (1970) listed some 1,500 items. By the time of the second edition (1979) this had grown to some 5,000. Since many of the works were unpublished, a photocopying service was essential in making them available for purchase (at cost price) and in producing performance materials for a number of (mainly orchestral) works, of which over fifty could be hired from the Archive.

In 1985 the Archive was relaunched as a Music Information Centre, one of over thirty worldwide, which expanded the scope of its activities to cover both classical and traditional music, from all periods. Among the new projects initiated by John Purser (manager 1985–88) was the creation of a publishing division, Scottish Music Publishing, which has produced twenty-six contemporary works for solo instruments, an edition of six violin sonatas by the eighteenth-century composer David Foulis, and a popular book of bagpipe tunes by Robert Wallace. The Centre took over the publication of the quarterly magazine *Stretto*, replaced in 1988 by a monthly newsletter *Music Current*, listing contemporary music events in Scotland and performances of Scottish work abroad.

The collection of manuscripts was substantially enlarged in 1987 by the presentation by Peter Maxwell Davies of material relating to most of his output since 1970 (when he came to live in Scotland).

The Scottish Music Information Centre is subsidized by the Scottish Arts Council and acknowledges financial assistance from Scottish universities, media organizations, trust funds, and Scottish Regional, District and Island Councils.

A. McKay

Scottish National Party, The. The National Party of Scotland was formed in 1928 in response to the failure of other strategies to deliver constitutional change. A cross-party Scottish Home Rule Association had existed since 1886. The Liberal Party and the Labour Movement had supported the establishment of a domestic Scottish Parliament for many years. Yet despite this, nothing had been achieved. The failure to implement the Scottish Home Rule bill of 1913 and the lack of support for the bills in 1924 and 1926, signalled clearly that Labour and Liberal leaders could not be relied on. John McCormick, one of the founders of the National Party, said of Scottish politicians, ' ... as positions of power and influence open up to them, they gradually forget their Scottish sentiment'.

The late 1920s was also a period which had seen the emergence of a Scottish cultural revival and many leading literary figures were actively involved in the National Party's formation and its early years. Compton MacKenzie, Hugh MacDiarmid, Neil Gunn, Cunninghame Graham, Eric Linklater were political nationalists.

Delegates from several pressure groups—the Scots National League, the Scottish National Movement, the Scottish Home Rule Association, the Glasgow University Nationalist Association—came together to form the National Party with the aim 'to secure self-government for Scotland with independent national status within the British group of nations'.

A few months after its formation a vigorous Glasgow University rectorial campaign for Cunningham Graham successfully projected the nationalist cause into public consciousness. The two principal popular newspapers in Scotland, the *Express* and the *Record*, competed in the following few years to stress their Scottishness through support for the home rule cause.

In 1932 the Cathcart Unionists Association broke away from its parent body and declared its support for a sovereign Scottish Parliament with joint U.K. machinery for defence and foreign affairs. They formed the Scottish Party with the support of the Duke of Montrose, Eric Linklater and many leading personalities in local government, legal and church circles. Its political complexion was more centre-right than the National Party. In 1934 these two parties merged to become the Scottish National Party. They had achieved substantial publicity for the nationalist cause but little serious electoral support.

The late thirties was not a fruitful time for nationalism in Scotland. The unpopularity of fascist nationalism in Europe and the growing threat of war shifted the emphasis towards Britishness, an emphasis further strengthened by the outbreak of war.

The war produced schism in the SNP. Conscription was the issue which divided the party. Should Nationalists accept conscription by a British state whose authority they did not recognise? Douglas Young, the classicist and poet, led the anti-conscription faction and was elected as party chairman in 1942. This prompted the resignation of a number of senior members including John McCormick. There were strategic differences between the factions on other issues. Should the SNP operate as a party or through a broad alliance with other parties and civic groups? McCormick supported the latter strategy and established the Scottish Convention out of which came the Covenant movement. The SNP won their first seat in Motherwell in 1945 but lost it in the General Election a few months later.

The principal nationalist activity in the late 1940s took place around the Covenant not the SNP. The Covenant, demanding a Scottish Parliament, gained two million signatures and widespread institutional support. Its demand was ignored by the Labour Government and the Conservative Government which followed it. Apart from a few symbolic acts like stealing the Stone of Destiny, nationalism was completely marginalised until the early 1960s.

In by-elections in 1961 and 1962, the SNP performed comparatively well. In the 1966 General Election it put up 23 candidates and averaged 15 per cent of the vote in these seats. Winifred Ewing's success in the Hamilton by-election in 1967 made the SNP and the constitutional question a central issue in Scottish politics. It was to continue as such over the following 25 years. Although they gained only 12 per cent of the vote and one seat in the 1970 election, by October 1974, helped by the discovery of oil in Scottish waters, they won over 30 per cent of the vote and 11 seats. The SNP of the sixties and seventies was characterised more by the skilled working class and the lower middle class than by the intellectuals who had played a central role in its formation.

The success of the SNP pressurised the Labour Government to promote legislation for a Scottish Assembly. In the 1979 referendum, the Assembly proposal was supported by 52 per cent of Scots voters but did not achieve 40 per cent of the total electorate and was not implemented.

The 1980s was a period of growing support for a Scottish Parliament but not all of this was expressed in support for the SNP. The unpopularity of the Conservative Government in Scotland greatly strengthened support for constitutional change in most sectors of Scottish society apart from the Conservative Party and some sections of the business community. The eighties also saw a growth in cultural nationalism, particularly in popular music. The SNP continued to support full independence but emphasised the European dimension and its support for participation in the EC. It gained 21 per cent of the vote in the 1992 election but only three seats and failed to make a major breakthrough.

I. Lindsay

Scottish Opera. The rise of Scottish Opera from a humble beginning in 1962 to an International Company in 1978 is a story of which all Scotland can be proud. It began with the appointment of Alexander Gibson as Musical Director of the Scottish National Orchestra. Gibson, born in Motherwell in 1926, had begun his musical education in Scotland and after military service continued his studies at the Royal College of Music in London. In 1952 he joined the music staff of Sadler's Wells Opera and within a few weeks made his debut as an operatic conductor. In 1957 he became Musical Director at the early age of 32—a record in an important European Opera House.

In Glasgow it was soon apparent that the fine National Orchestra would be free in the summer months to take part in some weeks of opera. At the same time valuable experience would be provided for the increasing number of students training at the Royal Scottish Academy of Music. As a pilot for a more ambitious scheme in following years, in June 1962, Gibson, with the help of interested friends, organized six performances at the King's Theatre, Glasgow. His long-term view of the whole project was that only the best available singers be engaged and that the works be performed in the original language. with these aims in mind Gibson assembled a splendid cast for Puccini's *Madame Butterfly* sung in Italian. French singers sang Debussy's *Pelléas et Melisande* in this year, 1962, the centenary of the composer's birth and the sixtieth anniversary of the première of this work at the Paris Opéra-Comique. Music critics from London and elsewhere were attracted by the courage of a new and untried company's tackling the formidable French work in the original and columns of critical acclaim were an assurance that the new venture had a future.

As in all artistic endeavour, finance had to be found and it is to the credit of Scottish Television that along with a cash grant of £1,000 they provided, by means of special programmes, advertising favourable to Scottish Opera. The inevitable deficit was met by grants from the then Scottish Committee of the Arts Council and other sources. One of the founders of the company was guarantor for a substantial bank overdraft.

For a second season, 1963, extended to include Edinburgh, a young man came from Sadler's Wells as part-time manager. In this way Scottish Opera gained the services of Peter Hemmings who became full-time Administrator in 1966. The team of Gibson and Hemmings was augmented by Peter Ebert, who as Director of Productions brought a wealth of experience acquired in Europe and America. A steady expansion of the company was the result of the enthusiasm and foresight of these gentlemen. Aberdeen was added to the list of venues in 1964 and a major breakthrough was the invitation to appear at the Edinburgh festival of 1967 where, with the exception of one year, it has appeared annually ever since.

In Scotland performances with principals, chorus and orchestra, have been given at Ayr, Dundee, Dunfermline, Elgin, Greenock, Inverness, Kelso, Kirkcaldy, Lochgelly, Oban, Perth, St Andrews and Stirling in addition to the many appearances in Glasgow, Edinburgh and Aberdeen. The major English cities have regular visits and Scottish Opera has appeared in Germany, France, Switzerland, Italy, Portugal, Poland and Iceland.

The acquisition of the Glasgow Theatre Royal in 1975 as the artistic base of the company was of paramount importance. In this theatre productions are planned, rehearsed, mounted and put into the repertoire.

As well as encouraging Scottish singers, operas have been commissioned from Scottish composers such as Iain Hamilton's *Catiline Conspiracy*, Robin Orr's *Full Circle* and *Weir of Hermiston*, Thomas Wilson's *Confessions of a Justified Sinner* and Thea Musgrave's *Mary, Queen of Scots* in the 1970s. In the mid 1980s, Richard Mantle was appointed Managing Director, followed by the appointment of American conductor, John Mauceri, to the post of Music Director. Sir Alexander Gibson

then became the company's first conductor Laureate. Under this new leadership Scottish Opera continued its artistic excellence with acclaimed productions of *Das Rheingold*, *La Forza del Destino*, *Salome* and *Oedipus Rex*. In 1991 Richard Jarman succeeded Richard Mantle as Managing Director and 1992 saw the 30th anniversary of Scottish Opera.

Credit must be given to the Arts Council, Scottish Local Authorities and large business organizations who have given so much of the money to maintain the company.

R. Telfer and E. Navickas

Sculpture, Early Medieval. Sculpture provides the best evidence we have for cultural life in Scotland in the period AD 600–900. A large number of monuments, many of high artistic quality, have survived. Examples occur in all four cultural areas of early medieval Scotland. Each area has its own characteristic sculptural form and style, but they also have features in common, and the degree of contact and estrangement imposed by political circumstances seems to have provided the right kind of inspirational balance conducive to lively artistic production.

Pictish sculpture falls into a number of distinct phases. The earliest brilliant series of symbolic designs incised on smooth-faced free-standing boulders shows a native talent for draughtsmanship, composition and the art of incision. The designs, which are found repeated in essentially the same form all over the Pictish area, consist of stylized objects, geometric shapes, and animals. The animal art is particularly fine. It shows a hunter's knowledge of animal anatomy but the designs are deliberately stylized at certain points and are confined to a full profile viewpoint in response to the symbolic rather than descriptive nature of the art. The meaning of the symbolism is not known. Among the many theories some of the more tenable are that the symbols stand for social and occupational classes of persons, that they represent individual lineages, or that they define land tenure.

The symbol stones were probably erected in the seventh century, the time when boulders bearing an incised symbol of the cross were being set up over the graves of the first Pictish Christians, converts of the monks of Iona. In the eighth century Pictish sculptors produced more ambitious slab-shaped monuments which displayed both the native symbolism and the Christian cross. These monuments were properly quarried and dressed and the sculpture is now in shallow relief. This technical advance was probably due to the influence of Anglian sculptors and architects from the north of England who were called in by a Pictish king to teach the Picts how to build in stone. This period also saw a great extension of the ornamental repertoire based largely on decorative manuscript art.

Pictish artists reacted to these new influences creatively. The splendid symbol-bearing slab at Aberlemno churchyard, Angus, uses animal ornament extracted from one of the decorated pages of the *Lindisfarne Gospels*, but its interlace-covered cross employs a uniquely complex pattern and the three-tier battle scene on the reverse of the slab is a purely

Pictish solution to the problem of filling the space available on the characteristic slab monument. The profile riders, usually part of hunting scenes, which figure prominently on Pictish slabs, may preserve a theme popular in a lost tapestry tradition.

As the century progressed Pictish sculptors produced work in very high relief and some had the confidence to present figure sculpture in full face. The most intricate manuscript and metalwork designs were carved on a number of different levels of relief: interlaces and key-patterns, and above all swirling compositions of spirals, rivalled only in the pages of the *Book of Kells*. The great monuments at Meigle, Perthshire, Nigg and Hilton of Cadboll, Easter Ross, and the tomb-shrine is the high point. Its serenely classical rendering of David slaying the Lion in a pastoral setting has rightly been described as among the finest examples of Dark Age art in Europe.

It is at this period that the links with the other cultural areas are clearest. A fine group of free-standing crosses in the west of Scotland is centred on Iona. These are the work of sculptors commissioned by the Scots of Dalriada. The best known are the crosses of St Martin and St John on Iona itself. These crosses show the same technical skills as the Pictish slabs. Culturally speaking the Pictish cross slab at Nigg and the St Martin's cross are identical. The central Christian symbol is embodied in a massive stone monument and enhanced from a common stock of ornament. Only the presence of the Pictish symbols on the Nigg stone disturbs this view. Whatever the meaning of the symbolism it was of no use intellectually to anyone other than Picts, even in this overwhelmingly Christian context. The Pictish symbols remain a deeply rooted cultural phenomenon not explicable in terms of Christian art.

The shape of the heads of the Iona crosses suggests an awareness of Northumbrian cross types. The most celebrated of these crosses happens now to be located in modern Scotland at Ruthwell, Dumfriesshire. Other important examples of sculpture produced by the English who lived south of the Forth are found at Jedburgh and Aberlady. The decoration of the Ruthwell cross speaks eloquently of the Mediterranean and East Christian world opened up to the Northumbrians and their neighbours by the efforts of the abbots of Bede's monastery at Jarrow and Wearmouth who stocked their libraries and adorned their buildings with books, pictures and other art objects brought from France and Italy. The figure sculpture on the Ruthwell cross attempts a spiritual commentary in visual terms based on biblical and hagiographical exegesis of a kind which can be paralleled only in the much later high crosses of Ireland. The interest of the Picts in scenes connected with David and the Psalter shows that they also shared the growing interest in the illustration of the biblical text as opposed to its mere decoration, and the portrayal of the Virgin and Child on the St Martin's Cross is part of the same development.

The art of the Britons who occupied southern Scotland has not survived in the same way as that of the Picts, Scots and Angles. This is a pity for here there may have been a measure of continuity in stone carving from Romano-British times on. There was at least one important British artistic centre at Govan on the lower Clyde. Here a large collection of slabs and sarcophagi are decorated in late Pictish and English styles but also have some individual features which require further study.

In the ninth and tenth centuries when the Picts and Scots had merged politically sculptural standards declined although some ambitious free-standing crosses were erected in central Scotland. In Ireland the political upheaval of the Viking invasions led to the direction of all artistic endeavour towards the least vulnerable medium—stone sculpture. In comparison Scoto-Pictish sculpture failed to flourish. This must be attributed to some extent at least to the downgrading of Pictish culture and the consequent end to the uniquely motivating force of the enigmatic symbolism.

I. Henderson

Sculpture, Late Medieval to Present. In the eighteenth and nineteenth centuries, sculpture played a secondary role to painting in the visual arts in Scotland. In consequence, it is sometimes said that the country does not have a strong sculptural tradition; but some of the grandest prehistoric monuments in the country, like Callanish for instance, are truly sculptural. The carved stones of the Picts and the early Scots, too, are by far the most impressive evidence for the civilisation that those peoples shared. They are characterised by complex and delicate, carved interlace and zoomorphic shapes and also by the vivid representation of animals and humans. Examples of Pictish carved stones are found all over eastern Scotland, important examples are at St Andrews, Meigle and Aberlemno, for instance, and they link up with Celtic carvings in the west, like the major group of crosses at Iona, and Northumbria in the south, like the Bewcastle cross. Work like that on the doorway of Dalmeny church indicates that this tradition continued into the Romanesque period in the Lowlands, and there are grave stones in Argyll that bear witness to its continuation in Highland culture well into the Renaissance period.

The surviving evidence from the medieval period is fragmentary as so much of what did once exist was ecclesiastical and so was destroyed in the Reformation. Nevertheless, it is clear that sculpture was important both inside and outside churches. In the later part of the period some of the great churches like Melrose were clearly richly decorated with carving. The outstanding survivor is Roslyn Chapel from the early fifteenth century, which combines architectural form and sculptural detail in a way that is unique in the British Isles and is in many ways closer to Iberian models.

By the late fifteenth century, it is possible to match documentary records to the richness of some of the relics of sculpture that survive, for instance in the tomb of Bishop Kennedy in St Salvators Chapel, St Andrews. These indicate that sculptural work was often bought overseas and that artists too were imported. James IV for instance employed an 'Almeyn', who was probably a Fleming, on his father's richly sculptured tomb at Cambuskenneth. Such artists may have helped to establish a native tradition too however. Carvings from the late fifteenth century on the Trinity College Apse, Edinburgh and on the sacrament house in Fowlis Easter church, Angus, have a quality similar to some of the remarkable wood-carvings that survive from the following century. The Beaton panels made for Arbroath Abbey, the choirstalls and the heads carved in wooden roundels for Stirling Castle are amongst the finest examples of this, though it survives in some quantity and is still in situ in King's College, Aberdeen and Dunblane Cathedral. It is best described as a kind of blunt vigour. It relates to contemporary Flemish work, but it seems to be distinctively Scottish. It is also seen in the exterior stonework of Stirling Castle, and the spectacular fountain at Linlithgow (c. 1538.). These examples suggest that there was a workshop established connected with the court.

Demand for this kind of work diminished with the Reformation, but the tradition survived in secular carving like the carved stone panels in the garden of Edzell Castle (c. 1600), the carving done for Edinburgh and Glasgow Universities seventeenth-century buildings (demolished) and in the many fine sundials of the seventeenth century, like those at Newbattle. Tombstones in churchyards throughout the country from the 1580s onwards, are often amazingly richly carved and carved decoration on ordinary houses is common in period. There is also fine heraldic carving, for example in the magnificent royal arms at Holyrood Palace, designed by the painter Jacob de Wet in 1677.

During the seventeenth century, the tombs of the great became occasions for quite spectacular sculptural displays. These seem mostly to have been imported, as in the early example of the tomb of the Earl of Dunbar in Dunbar church (c. 1611) by Maximilian Colt, from England; but the tradition continued and there is no reason to attribute all the remarkable tombs of the time, like that of Archbishop Sharp in St Andrews, (1679) for instance, to foreign artists.

The greater formality of architecture from the late seventeenth century onwards limited the scope for sculptural invention, but the quality of work, for instance in carved overmantels, indicates that the tradition of the mason-carver did not fade and it was from this background that the first artist-sculptors emerged. They worked mostly in the field of portrait sculpture and some among them, such as William Gowans, who may have been a pupil of Rysbrack (fl. c 1770) and Robert Burn (fl. c. 1790–1816), were distinguished. At least one sculptor, William Jeans, was studying in Rome in 1771, but he is only known by the figures of ancient Britons on the portico of Penicuik House. The most remarkable artist in the field of portrait sculpture was perhaps James Tassie (1735–99), who specialised in small-scale profile portraits using vitreous paste. John Henning (1771–1851) also worked in miniature. He began making portrait sculpture, but after moving to London, he made his name with his miniature copies of the Elgin Marbles.

By the early nineteenth century, sculpture was established as a distinct profession. Leading practitioners were Laurence MacDonald (1799–1878) and Thomas Campbell (1790–1858), both spent long periods in Rome and worked in an elegant neo-classical manner derived from Canova. Samuel Josephs (1791–1850) was an English artist who settled in Edinburgh. He had a very successful career as a portrait sculptor and by the mid-century there were a number of others working in this field, as the numerous portrait busts in the collections of the older Scottish institutions bear witness. It was, however, with Alexander Handyside Ritchie (1804–1870), a pupil of Thorwaldson, and Sir John Steell (1804–1891), that the sculptor's profession could be said, finally, to have been established. Steell was prolific and he established his reputation with the group *Alexander Taming Bucephalus* (1833), but his most ambitious work was the Albert Memorial in Charlotte Square, Edinburgh (1876) which earned him his knighthood.

James Pittendreigh Magillivray (1856–1938) was, however, the first Scottish sculptor to try to move towards a more modern freedom of expression and away from the formal constraints of the portrait bust and the monument. Nevertheless, as a pupil of William Brodie (1815–1881), who was himself a pupil of Laurence MacDonald, and although he was influenced by Rodin, Macgillivray belonged firmly in the tradition of Scottish sculptors. Although he produced competent monuments like his bronze of *John Knox* in St Giles, Edinburgh, he was at his best on a small scale and when he was being more informal.

In spite of Macgillivray, the relationship of sculpture to architecture remained vital well into the twentieth century. This was endorsed by the work of the architect Sir Robert Lorimer, who encouraged sculptors to work with him. For the first time, extensively in the Thistle Chapel (1909–11)—where the remarkable woodcarvers Alexander Clow (1861–1946) and his brother William (dates not known) did the most important work—and then on the Scottish National War Memorial, one of the most ambitious artistic enterprises of its time where there are outstanding works by Pilkington Jackson (1887–1973), Alice Meredith Williams (c. 1870–1934), Alexander Carrick (1882–1966), Phyllis Bone (1894–1972) and others.

Between 1920 and 1960, sculpture was dominated by artists associated with Lorimer, though his own son, Hew Lorimer (b. 1907), a pupil of Eric Gill and sculptor of *Seven Liberal Arts* on the National Library of Scotland, Elizabeth Dempster (1909–1987), Tom Whalen (1903–1975), George Innes (1913–1970) and others were more consciously modernist though direct carving was still their preferred technique. Some of the most remarkable early modern sculpture by Scots was the work of C.R. Mackintosh (1868–1928) and J.D. Fergusson (1874–1961); artists not generally seen as sculptors; for example Mackintosh's plaster reliefs for the Willow Tea Rooms (1904) and Fergusson's *Eastra, Hymn to the Sun* (1924).

Innovation has been a feature of sculpture since the war. Although architects like Robert Fairlie were still employing sculptors in the 1950s, the modernist style of architecture generally had no place for sculpture and so broke the traditional relationship of these two arts. This breach also coincided with the increasing irrelevance of the technical characteristics that traditionally distinguished sculpture from painting. A painter like William Johnstone (1897–1981) could move from two dimensions to the three dimensions of sculpture with no change of aesthetic. Younger artists, like Will Maclean (b. 1941) have also moved quite naturally from working as painters to working in three dimensions. Nevertheless, some of the most distinguished artists to come from Scotland in the post-war era, such as Sir Eduardo Paolozzi (b. 1924) and William Turnbull (b. 1922), have worked as sculptors in the traditional sense. There have also been a number of successful monumental works, such as Paolozzi's *Monte Cassino* in Edinburgh (1991) and Jake Harvey's (b. 1948) *Hugh MacDiarmid Memorial* at Langholm (1983), as well as public sculptures like Gavin Scobie's (b. 1940) *Eden* at Eden Court, Inverness (1977). New found freedom has meant difficulties both of an aesthetic and a financial kind, however, and these have not been entirely resolved by the provision of public funding through the Scottish Arts Council. Nevertheless, some of the most ambitious and successful younger artists, like David Mach (b. 1956), are sculptors.

D. *MacMillan*

Sectarianism, in the context of modern Scottish society, is generally a reference to religious tensions between Protestants and Catholics. More specifically, it might be defined as unfavourable regard for other people on account of their religious beliefs or religious designation. Until recently the subject has been relatively neglected by scholars; the work of J.E. Handley on the Irish immigrant experience in Scotland (*The Irish in Modern Scotland*, 1947) offered the only substantial commentary, from one point of view, until the publication of important books by the sociologist Steve Bruce (*No Pope of Rome*, 1985), and the political and social historian Tom Gallagher (*Glasgow: The Uneasy Peace*, 1987).

The subject is bound up with the impact of Irish immigration into Scotland from the early nineteenth century. The strong stain of anti-Catholicism among many Scots found expression in hostility towards the bulk of the newcomers on account of their Roman Catholic religion. Protestant Irish immigration, on the other hand, led to the rise of the Orange Order in the west of Scotland, an organisation whose robust populist character appealed to those Scots fearful of Irish Catholic cultural and political expansion. Such fears could also be compounded by perceptions of the Irish Catholics as an economic threat regarding competition for jobs in the heavy industry heartlands of west-central Scotland. Affrays between Protestants and Catholics took place regularly in the poorer districts of Glasgow, and in the Lanarkshire and Ayrshire coalfields during the nineteenth century. The Orange Order developed an overwhelmingly proletarian social profile as a result. On the Catholic side there existed similarly exclusivist populist organisations, such as the Ancient Order of Hibernians.

By the twentieth century a subculture of religious sectarian conflict could be said to have emerged, and in the decades to come it expressed itself vividly through such phenomena as the Rangers-Celtic football rivalry. Politically, after World War One, the lines were less clearly drawn, with the Labour Party able to command working-class support across religious lines; however, the Conservatives (Unionists) continued to draw significantly on an 'Orange' working-class vote until the 1960s. Echoes of Irish problems were often heard: Catholics complained of discrimination in certain occupational sectors; Protestants complained about state-subsidised Catholic schools. In the inter-war era the Scottish Presbyterian Churches, as well as the Orange Order, campaigned against Irish Catholic immigration and suspected the Catholic Church of building up a political power base in Scotland.

Gradually, relations between the Churches improved. In addition, the Catholic community in the post World War Two era enjoyed significant social mobility and largely ceased to be regarded as 'alien'. Tensions surrounding employment lessened, and housing was never to be the explosive issue it became in Northern Ireland. Moreover, Scotland in the twentieth century underwent a degree of secularisation unknown in Northern Ireland, and such factors, combined with the absence of a Scottish national question which divided on religious lines, kept conflict manageable.

As the twentieth century draws to a close the subject's most dispassionate and thorough investigators (Bruce and Gallagher) consider sectarianism as essentially a left-over from the past. They question just how much meaning the term 'sectarianism' has in a society where there is now widespread social and cultural interaction across religious lines, and much intermarriage. However, the amount of media attention given to the issue in recent years suggests that there is still some life left in the Orange–Green subculture in Lowland Scotland; football, some say, remains a vital lightning conductor. Recent controversies in education and local government suggest that the capacity of religious-based or religion-related issues to cause social and cultural divisions has not been exhausted.

G. *Walker*

Sheep, Breeds of. Few countries have such a wide variety of sheep breeds as Scotland. The unimproved Soay, which lives feral on St Kilda, is the oldest breed in Europe. The Soay is a relic from prehistoric times of the first domestic type. This is shown by the similarity of Neolithic sheep bones with those of the Soay, and the finding of the same fleece type as the Soay in Bronze Age textiles. The primitive features shared with the wild ancestor are a short tail and a brown coat with a natural spring moult. Selective breeding by man over thousands of years has given modern sheep a long tail (which is frequently docked) and white wool which grows continuously. The Soay has woolly as well as hairy fleeces, but the latter are already much less hairy than in the undomesticated wild sheep.

A stage intermediate between prehistoric and modern sheep is seen in the Orkney and Shetland type. This has a short tail, and a tendency to moult, so that in the past these breeds were 'rooed' (plucked) instead of being shorn. Orkney and Shetland sheep have the same hairy and woolly fleeces as the Soay, but there is a range of colours: black, white and grey in addition to the brown of the Soay, which is known in these breeds as 'moorit' (moor-red). These natural colours have been exploited by the Shetland knitwear industry, but the full range is seen today in only the Orkney breed which remains on North Ronaldsay, where it has survived because of a wall excluding the sheep from the better land and restricting them to the sea-shore, where they are unique in living on sea weed.

The Orkney-Shetland type represents the dominant sheep of Europe from the Iron Age until after the Middle Ages. In Scotland it was known as the Dunface or Old Scottish Shortwool. Another variety that persisted was the Hebridean, and relic breeds of this type are the black, four-horned St Kilda (Hebridean) and the piebald, four-horned Jacob. A brown, four-horned breed is the Loghtan of the Isle of Man. The well known, white-faced Cheviot breed which developed on the Border Hills probably originated from the Dunface. This has a short fleece used in tweeds.

The more widespread black-faced and horned Scottish Blackface, now the most numerous breed in Britain, reached Scotland from the north of England only in the eighteenth century, and was the main breed taken to the Highlands, following the clearances. The fleece of the Blackface is long and hairy, and mainly used in carpets. An early type of Blackface persisted in the Hebrides, and this type survives in the feral stock left by the St Kildans on Boreray when they were evacuated in 1930.

The Scottish husbandry system is one of stratification in which Blackface and Cheviot ewes are kept on the hills until they have produced five crops of lambs. They are then drafted to lower ground and crossed with a Border Leicester ram. This is a modern 'synthetic' breed developed from a cross between the Cheviot and English Leicester. The Blackface-Border Leicester cross is known as the Greyface, and the Cheviot-Border Leicester cross as the Halfbred. The ewes of both these crosses are kept on grassland and mated with a ram from a Down breed to produce fat lamb. Common Down rams used are the black-faced, polled Oxford and Suffolk.

M. L. Ryder

Shetland Music *see* Music, Shetland

Shinty or Camanachd (Gaelic) is the name of the team game indigenous to specific parts of the Highlands of Scotland, and played, mainly by Highlanders, in various population centres throughout the country. It is played with ball and curved club (caman) between two opposing teams of twelve players each, the winner scoring the greater number of goals (hails).

Shinty was introduced into the western Highlands of Scotland as a result of the sixth-century invasion of Christianity—and Gaelic—through Columba. Records of ball and club games can be traced far further into the past, however. An ancient Greek bas-relief dating from the 5th century BC depicts athletes equipped with curved clubs engaged in just such a kind of game. Whether the Athenians obtained this sport from wandering Celtic peoples, or conversely, the Celts from the Greeks, the fact is that it is among the Celtic peoples that such ball and club games have flourished and developed Shinty being one of the highly successful survivors.

Shinty (the anglicised name probably derived from Gaelic 'sinteag': a 'bouncing motion', or 'long strides'), is first recorded in Ireland in the *Book of Leinster* in the twelfth century (the game in question having taken place in 1272 BC!), and it survived in that country up till the end of the nineteenth century. It was supplanted there by Hurling, a close relative, played with a larger ball and shorter, flatter club. Hurling was the summer game, and Camanachd the winter. Camanachd declined in Ireland, though it survived till the turn of the nineteenth and twentieth centuries. Hurling was established as the official ball and club game in Ireland in 1884 by the Gaelic Athletic Association in Dublin. Meanwhile Camanachd thrived under many different names (e.g. shinny; cammon; cammock; camag; cluidh; bhall; iomain) throughout most of Scotland, as well as in parts of Wales and in Cumbria, with one form of it being recorded, in the seventeenth century, as being played on ice. In Fife, one version of the game had players with club and ball competing to get the ball into a hole in the ground—a precursor of golf. Throughout Scotland—including the islands to the west, the game was played between neighbouring communities on religious feast days (including Christmas and New Year), before any codification of rules existed. Different rules applied everywhere, with local tradition dictating—as did the design of club and ball—the latter being usually small, of wood or tightly bound hair, or of birch fungus wrapped in heather.

Shinty never received the political imprimatur in Scotland that Hurling did in Ireland, (this can account, partly, for the fact that the game today is barely mentioned in newspapers or radio/TV outside the Highlands) and ebbed and flowed according to many influences: Clearances and sabbatarianism playing their parts in either dispersing it to other lands (especially Canada, where it developed into Ice Hockey) or causing it virtually to disappear for spells. The watershed between it being a game of mass community involvement and the team game that we would recognise today was the challenge matches between Strathglass and Glenurquhart at the Bught Park in Inverness in 1887 and 1888. The immense interest, throughout the Highlands, in these matches proved the game's attraction as a spectator sport. The first of these matches had twenty-two players in each team and the second, twenty three. The game was now flourishing, but different organisations played under different rules. A national organisation was essential, and the Camanachd Association was formed in 1893 at a meeting in Kingussie. Codification of the rules and the organisation of the game into leagues followed, and the modern game had arrived.

However, this rationalisation had its negative side to it, as evidenced by the disappearance of the game in some of the more distant parts of the Highlands and Islands—particularly in the Uists. It was perceived to be impossible for these places to take part in national competitions due to travel difficulties.

Today, the game in the Highlands is mainly played in the former counties of Inverness-shire (including Skye), Ross-shire and Argyll. Elsewhere in Scotland it is played in Glasgow, and in the ancient universities. There is even the London Camanachd Club for Highland exiles.

B. Denoon

Shipbuilding. At the end of the Napoleonic Wars shipbuilding, in Scotland, was an insignificant small-scale craft. Numerous tiny yards, rarely employing more than 20 or 30 men, produced small wooden vessels for local traders and fishermen. More than three-quarters of all construction came from east-coast yards. The Clyde was unimportant. Sixty years later shipbuilding was a complex large-scale heavy engineering industry. Scottish yards built vessels for the world market; 'Clyde built' was a by-word for good construction, and the Clyde was already the single most important shipbuilding river in the world. Few industries were so completely and so swiftly transformed by the technology of the new age of industry.

The twin revolutions in shipbuilding in the nineteenth century were the replacement of wind power by steam power, and the substitution of iron for wood. Scottish engineers were leading inventors in marine engine and boiler technology, and leading innovators in the early adoption of iron for hulls. Steam navigation developed on the foundation of three major technical events. In 1812 Henry Bell launched his *Comet* on the Clyde, demonstrating the commercial potential and technical feasibility of steam navigation. In 1836, in London, Thomas Smith and John Ericson introduced, independently, versions of a screw propeller. By 1845 Smith's version was being widely substituted for paddles. The third innovation was in 1853 when Glasgow engineers Charles Randolph and John Elder introduced a successful marine compound expansion engine, promising fuel economies of up to 40 per cent over existing engines. When linked to improved boilers, notably James Napier's haystack tubular boiler in 1830, and most potently to James Howden's cylindrical tank, or 'Scotch Boiler' of 1862, these advances captured river traffic in the 1820s, Atlantic routes in the 1840s and 1850s, and with compound expansion, world long-haul routes fell to steamers in the 1870s.

The combination of more powerful engines and the rapidly revolving screw propeller in the 1840s finally exposed the unsuitability of wood for steam vessels. The Mersey and Thames builders were prominent in constructing the small iron tonnage of the 1830s, but after 1845 Clyde builders dominated construction in both the new power and the new material. Between 1850–70, Clyde yards built and launched 70 per cent of all iron tonnage in Britain, and two-thirds of all steam tonnage.

This leadership was maintained up to the First World War by a continuous innovation in refining the marine steam engine, notably with A. C. Kirk of Fairfield's triple expansion version in 1874, and the quadruple expansion engine by Walter Brock of Denny's in 1885. Scottish builders also led in the switch to steel hulls, entirely replacing iron in construction in the decade to 1889. Between 1870 and 1914, Clyde yards regularly built over one third of British tonnage.

By 1914 Scottish Shipbuilding was internationally renowned. Its prestige rested on the enterprise and inventiveness of its engineers and naval architects who had brought the reciprocating marine steam engine to its ultimate form, and were sustaining this by heavy investment in the new steam turbine, building both the Parsons and the Curtis models. The skill and experience of the local workforce supported this position. For a century Scotland had been in the forefront of innovation and change, boldly anticipating and influencing the needs of British ship-owners and prospering with the dominance of world trade and trade routes by the British mercantile marine.

Few could have guessed that this juggernaut would not continue its relentless upward progress, but by the end of the First World War events were beginning to turn against Scottish builders. The British mercantile marine came under growing challenge from foreign flags who steadily placed orders with domestic yards rather than with British builders. Foreign shipbuilding, boosted in war, consequently captured an increasing share of a slow-growing market. Alternative technologies in diesel engines and welding, even though adopted readily in Scotland, placed foreign builders at least on an equal footing.

These were great challenges and given the excellence of Scottish production, and the history of innovation, one might have expected a vigorous adjustment. But the stagnation of world trade combined with a huge surplus of shipping to burden Scottish yards with heavy unused capacity. For the Scottish industry the inter-war years, at best, represented a stationary economy in which the main initiative was rationalization. One third of Scottish capacity was closed; great yards like Beardmore's were liquidated, and survival replaced growth as the main strategy of the remaining yards.

The Second World War briefly reversed this stationary state and re-endowed the industry with vigour. Post 1945, for more than a decade, the Scottish yards enjoyed full order books in a seller's market as expanding world trade and shipping outgrew the threat of competition from slowly reviving European and Japanese yards. But by 1960 orders began to bypass Scottish yards attracted to foreign builders by lower, and frequently fixed, prices, better credit arrangements and, critically, early and reliable delivery dates. In the last analysis delivery was the most important factor, and foreign advantages rested on modern flow-line production in modern yards enjoying high productivity. No Scottish yard was entirely redesigned till after 1969 when Scott-Lithgow began to lay down the new facilities for building very large cargo vessels. This was a bold step, but in most of the industry the legacy of the depression had been an encouragement of short-term attitudes to orders, investment, technology and labour. Most companies rode the tide of post-war prosperity on *ad hoc* investments and fringe reorganization, neglecting longer-term objectives. Consequently in the renewed competition of the 1960s, Scottish yards mainly gained orders at prices that could not pay and slender reserves were soon exhausted. Not even government-encouraged regrouping into Upper and Lower Clyde divisions following on the Geddes report in 1966 halted the deterioration, and a series of liquidations led finally to public ownership in 1977.

Nationalisation in retrospect merely delayed the final demise of the industry. British Shipbuilders initially comprised thirty-two shipyards, six marine engine works and six general engineering shops. This represented 97 per cent of merchant shipbuilding and all naval construction capacity, and employed 87,000 men. Within five years 25,000 jobs had gone and half the yards were closed. By 1988, after receiving in excess of £2 billion in all forms of support, the government refused further public funds and adopted a policy of privatisation. This was in a context of a persistently weak market for new tonnage, and in a world industry still increasing capacity as new centres like Korea, Manchuria and Brazil brought in new yards.

Under privatisation profitable naval yards like Yarrow on the Clyde were returned to private ownership, while the truncated merchant yards were left to struggle. Against British Shipbuilders' wishes the Govan Shipbuilders yard was sold to the Norwegian shipping group, Kvaerner. By 1990 it was the only large merchant yard in operation in Scotland. Today, even if the long predicted, but still elusive, market upturn occurs, there is no merchant industry of any consequence left in Scotland to respond. Moreover, with the collapse of the Soviet Union and the re-evaluation of defence expenditure, even the future of the surviving naval yard, Yarrows, is uncertain beyond 1995. It is unlikely that the bicentenary of the *Comet* in 2012 will be supported by any shipbuilding activity of any note in Scotland, and the rise and fall of Scottish shipbuilding will have taken less than 200 years, the final dissolution orchestrated in a decade of public ownership.

A. Slaven

Silver and Gold Work. Little precious metal work has survived from the medieval period. Most important is the small group of university maces or verges, and the canon-law mace at St Andrews at least could well be Scottish. Like the others, of gothic tabernacle form, it is mentioned in a document of about 1461 but is probably earlier. The gothic form reflects the Continental education of university teachers; but if the canon-law mace is Scottish it points to the existence of skilful craftsmanship, and it is not surprising that in 1540 James V was able to commission an Edinburgh goldsmith, John Mosman, to fashion the royal crown, which is now the oldest crown in the British regalia. The gold of which it is made is probably Scottish. Later in the same century Edinburgh and its then independent neighbour burgh of the Canongate were producing sophisticated silverware which included such masterpieces in the Renaissance style as the Tulloch, Craigievar, Fergusson and Galloway standing mazer bowls, and also several of the

earliest communion cups, exquisitely designed. The Reformation of 1560, so often decried for its effect on the arts, in fact gave rise to some beautiful silver vessels.

Before the end of the sixteenth century goldsmiths were an organized craft and belonged to the guilds of Hammermen. Hallmarking began in Edinburgh by mid century, silverware being required to carry the punches of the maker, the town and the deacon of the craft. A date-letter was added in 1681, in Edinburgh and Glasgow. Other burghs had their guilds also and had right of assay until the nineteenth century.

Much Scottish silver followed English styles, but some pieces are peculiar to Scotland. The quaich is one: a shallow drinking vessel with two or more opposed handles. Originally of wood, usually stave-built, quaichs in the later seventeenth century were mounted in silver and then made entirely of silver, often engraved with lines perpetuating the old stave construction. Another Scottish piece is the 'thistle' cup, shaped like a teacup based in a calyx of applied lobes. In the eighteenth century came a big output of domestic silver, which included the celebrated 'bullet' teapot. Two made of solid gold have survived, both by James Ker of Edinburgh, and race-cups were also made in gold. Tea and coffee urns were in demand in Edinburgh, some with strange snake handles, and an article like an outsize toast-rack was made to take toasted bannocks. Provincial silverware (that is, made in towns other than Edinburgh or Glasgow) is usually simple in design, but is now much prized. Aberdeen produced some of the finest from the early seventeenth century onwards.

I. Finlay

Simpson, Archibald (1790–1847) of Aberdeen was the leading architect during the rapid expansion of the city between 1800 and 1840. He was born in 1790, the son of a local clothier, educated at Aberdeen Grammar School, and then spent a brief period at Marischal College. His architectural training started in the office of a local builder, James Massie, but in 1810 he entered the office in London of Robert Lugar. After a visit to Italy, the details of which are unknown, he returned to Aberdeen and set up in practice in 1813.

In the next 30 years, Simpson designed many of the principal public buildings in the city, making skilful use of the local Rubislaw granite and evolving a powerful and chaste Greek style.

On Union Street, the principal thoroughfare of the planned improvements which followed from the Aberdeen New Streets Act of 1800, he was responsible for a number of designs including Union Buildings (1819–22) and the County Assembly Rooms (1822) with their noble Ionic portico and fine sequence of Greek interiors.

The view down Union Street from the Castlegate is framed by two of Simpson's grandest classical designs. To the left, the Athenaeum (1822–23) with its lofty Ionic order framing the windows to the former reading room on the first floor, and to the right the elegant façade of the Clydesdale Bank, formerly the North of Scotland Bank (1839–42), turning the corner into King Street with its giant Corinthian order.

Typical of early nineteenth-century practice, Simpson could turn his hand to designing in the Gothic style. He used a simplified Perpendicular style for St Andrews Cathedral, King Street (1816–17) and he graced the Triple Kirks (1843–44) with a soaring octagonal spire in brick based on one of the spires of St Elizabeth, Marburg, in North Germany.

His finest church, however, is St Giles in Elgin (1827–8), where he employed his favourite Greek style. It is a masterly design with a grand hexastyle Doric portico and a spire ingeniously adapted from the Athenian Monument of Lysicrates.

Simpson's most elegant contribution to civic architecture was the bold layout of housing which included Bon Accord Square and Crescent (1823–26). The almost undecorated surface of the great sweep of Bon Accord Crescent is one of the most striking essays in picturesque town planning in Scotland.

Although Simpson was said to have been a man of 'strong and indeed eccentric character', his buildings are never marred by this eccentricity. It is their chaste and powerful simplicity which still makes them stand aloof from the modern townscape of Aberdeen.

M. Higgs

Skara Brae, Orkney. Orkney turns a bleak cliff-face to the Atlantic waves, but half-way down that west coast is the sheltered Bay of Skaill. Five thousand years ago the bay was smaller and the waves less violent; the climate was slightly warmer than today and there were fewer storms. The prehistoric houses of Skara Brae lie on the very edge of the shore now, but they were built in grassland well back from the sea before the bay was scoured out to its present extent. Long after they were abandoned, the houses were gradually buried by windblown sand, ensuring the remarkable state of preservation that survives today.

The buildings were first exposed by coastal erosion in the mid 19th century and have been excavated on several occasions since then. The major campaign was led by Professor Gordon V. Childe in the late 1920s, when most of the houses were uncovered, but excavations in the 1970s by Dr David V. Clarke of the National Museums of Scotland, provided scientific information about dating and economy. Radiocarbon analysis has shown that the settlement flourished between about 3100 BC and 2500 BC, at a time when farming was well-established throughout Scotland. The people of Skara Brae cultivated wheat and barley, bred cattle, sheep and a few pigs, hunted deer and made full use of the resources of the sea. The size and species of fishbones found in their middens show that they fished not only from the shore but also with lines from boats well out to sea. They gathered shellfish, particularly limpets which may have been used as fishbait rather than food, and utilized the carcasses of seals and whales washed up on the shore.

Skara Brae is extraordinarily evocative of prehistoric life. The later houses are so well preserved that the walls stand to roof level and the winding passages linking them together are still roofed in places. But it is the furniture that almost brings them alive. The quality of the local sandstone is such that it was used to build bed-units and dressers, cupboards, shelves and tanks let into the floor. There seems to have been an accepted blueprint for the design of these dwellings: a square room some 6m across with rounded corners and a single entrance, a central rectangular hearth, the dresser against the wall opposite the entrance and a bed against the walls to left and right. Earlier houses were similar except that the beds were set back into the thickness of the walls (as they were in 19th century farmhouses in Orkney). Houses were built, modified, demolished and rebuilt over some 600 years, and perhaps only six or so dwellings were in use at any one time.

Skara Brae is one of three sites in Orkney where houses of this type have been found, but it is far better preserved than the other two at Barnhouse in the centre of the mainland and at Rinyo on the island of Rousay.

A. Ritchie

Smith, Adam (1723–1790) was a product of Scotland's Age of Enlightenment, and a unique contributor to that time when it seemed intellectual effort could sharply reduce human misery. His achievement was to synthesize political economy as it emerged from moral philosophy, and to argue powerfully that if natural liberty was enjoyed in the economic as well as political sphere, human drives would lead to the creation of wealth of benefit to all. He did warn that the chief instrument for producing wealth, division of labour, could cause 'mental mutilation' of the workmen involved, and his antidote of universal education revealed a national bias.

Born a sickly child sometime before 5 June 1723 when he was baptized, he was raised by a remarkable mother, Margaret Douglas, daughter of a substantial Fife laird. His Aberdeenshire father, also Adam, who died the previous January, had legal training, was secretary to a Campbell magnate, and in 1714 became Comptroller of Customs in Kirkcaldy, where his son grew up. Smith attended the burgh school there, and would get an additional education from observing the port's trade, local industries (coal mining, salt-panning, and nail-making), and farming on nearby estates. At 14 he went to Glasgow University, where he displayed a bent for mathematics and physics, but found particular stimulation in the teaching of Francis Hutcheson, then at the height of his reputation as a moral philosopher. Hutcheson took a positive view of human nature, stressed the need to seek the greatest happiness of the greatest number, and asserted the value of natural liberty, all themes that appear in Smith's own work. In 1740, Smith went to Balliol College on a Snell Exhibition retained until 1746, but he was not enthusiastic about the education then provided at Oxford. On his own he read widely in modern languages, and apparently was punished for reading David Hume's *Treatise of Human Nature.* When he returned to Scotland he made use of his studies by giving lectures in Edinburgh (1748–51) on composition, taste, and jurisprudence.

Their success resulted in his election as Professor of Logic then of Moral Philosophy at Glasgow, where he remained for the 13 years he described as the happiest of his life. We have reports of the lectures he gave on the subjects formerly tackled in Edinburgh, and his Glasgow course also covered natural theology, ethics, and political economy. Through the 1750s he became fast friends with Hume, and maintained links with the Edinburgh literati such as Blair, Ferguson, Kames, and Robertson. In addition, he had the benefit of the company of Glasgow merchants, who shared their practical knowledge with him. At the end of the decade, publication of his ethics lectures in the form of *The Theory of Moral Sentiments* (1759) brought him fame as a philosopher and a man of letters.

Though not a landmark in moral theory, the book is a sophisticated extension of the arguments of Hutcheson and Hume to the effect that moral distinctions are based on feelings, and it presents an ingenious account of the role of sympathy. The point of the 'theory' is to show how a selfish creature like man is led by natural means to limit his passions, and aspire to happiness measured by moral quality. The later *Wealth of Nations* is not in conflict with this teaching, and deals with the complementary problem of aspiration to happiness of a material nature.

Smith left Glasgow in 1764 to tutor the third Duke of Buccleuch during two years spent in France and Geneva, in the course of which he met Voltaire and enjoyed contacts with the *philosophes* and physiocrats. It is very likely that Quesnay and Turgot helped him to gain new perspectives on economic issues such as the circulation of capital, and the balance between productive and unproductive sectors in the economy. On his return home, he devoted 10 more years to research and writing before the appearance of the *Wealth of Nations* (1776). Its publication may have been delayed to catch the attention of MPs, then preoccupied with the conflict between Britain and the American colonies, whose economic origins in the enforcement of the Navigation Acts are examined in the book.

Smith's thesis is that, provided government does not intrude into the marketplace at the behest of sectional interests, the drive to better one's condition (the 'Scotsman in every man', according to Bagehot), coupled with the 'propensity to truck, barter, and exchange', will produce economic prosperity. His friends feared that the abstruse nature of the supporting economic analysis would impede understanding of the book, and hence the programme of institutional reform it advocated. They need not have worried. The 'curious Facts' attracted attention, and the 'very violent attack' on government restrictions and economic privilege appealed to the rising capitalist classes. Successive movements for fiscal reform, free trade, and popular education all owed something to the book's thrust.

From a modern standpoint, however, the more durable part of the book is the analytic one, which largely defined the scope of 'classical' economics until the revisions of Jevons and Marshall in the later nineteenth century: the theory of price, and of wages, rent, and profit (Bk I); the discussion of macro-economic issues in relation to 'circular flow' (II); the comprehensive picture of the economic history of Europe from the fall of the Roman empire (III); the critique of mercantilism

and physiocracy (IV); and the review of the state's role in allocating resources for defence, justice, and public works and institutions (V).

In 1778 Smith was made a Commissioner of Customs in Scotland and settled in Edinburgh, where his Sunday suppers in Panmure House drew together the literati and visitors of note. His closest friends were the medical scientist Joseph Black and the geologist James Hutton, who acted as his literary executors. At his request they burned many of his papers, but rescued and published as *Essays on Philosophical Subjects* (1795) fragments of the great works he contemplated on aesthetics and the history of philosophy and science. Of these the 'History of Astronomy' is invaluable for giving Smith's account of the motives and principles underlying intellectual systems. Before he died, on 17 July 1790, he received 'with very great satisfaction' copies of the much-expanded sixth edition of *The Theory of Moral Sentiments*, which includes a new part dealing with the practical and political application of moral theory. His grave, marked by a simple inscription, is in the Canongate kirkyard.

He is credited with an optimistic faith in individualism and the benefits of an expanding economy, a faith which he may certainly have inspired in others by the tenor of the *Wealth of Nations*, not always with good results, for example, in the case of attempts to develop the Highlands. His true legacy to Scotland and the world, however, is that of a tireless inquirer into social phenomena who counselled frugal use of resources, who was penetrating in analysis, and who systematized his findings in an original and fruitful way.

Fully annotated texts of Smith's writings are available in the *Glasgow Edition of the Works and Correspondence of Adam Smith* (Oxford U.P., 1976–). A *Life* will complete this edition.

Smith's library survives, principally divided between Edinburgh University Library and that of the Faculty of Economics, Tokyo University: see James Bonar's *Catalogue*, 2nd edn. (London, 1932) and Hiroshi Mizuta's *Supplement* (Cambridge U.P., 1967). The Baker Library, Harvard, contains an extensive collection of Smithiana. The leading modern exponents of Smithian economics are the members of the Chicago School, e.g. Milton Friedman and George Styler.

I. Ross

Smith, Iain Crichton/Iain Mac a' Ghobhainn (b. 1928). His Gaelic/English bilingualism provides one of the many dualities that give rise to tension in the writing of Iain Crichton Smith. He has used both languages consistently over a long period, writing poetry, short stories and novels in both, one-act plays in Gaelic, and radio drama in both. It is unusual to find a writer doing this over a long period. Smith may be said to make both good and bad use of his facility. Probably a bad use, on the whole, is his practice of taking two bites at the same cherry: producing two variants of the same story—'An Dubh is an Gorm' and 'The Black and the Red', 'An t-Aonaran' and 'The Existence of The Hermit' but it is noticeable that his greater success even in such cases lies sometimes in the one language, sometimes in the other. Where the intention is not to reduplicate a story, more interesting connections can emerge, as in his English poem 'At the Reservoir' (*The Law and the Grace*), and the fourth song in his 'Ochd òrain airson Céilidh ùr' (*Bìobuill is Sanasan-reice*). Quite separate from these reduplications, of course, is his translation into English of his Gaelic poems, collected in *The Permanent Island*.

The duality of his experience and thought is illustrated in his book titles: *The Law and the Grace, Bùrn is Aran* (Bread and Water), *Thistles and Roses, An Dubh is an Gorm* (The Black and the Blue), *Bìobuill is Sanasan-Reice* (Bibles and Advertisements), *Maighstirean is Ministearan* (Masters and Ministers). There are tensions in his work between belief and agnosticism, religion and secularism, between theology and psychoanalysis, between the individual and society, the old and the new, emotion and intellect, life and death, or as he puts it in *The Law and the Grace*:

> the struggle's what we live by, not the whole unknown completion

His first Gaelic book was a collection of short stories, with a short section of poems, called *Bùrn is Aran*. The stories are the most distinguished part of the book, making it a minor classic. Here he is mainly concerned with a Gaelic background, and especially with misfits, including returned exiles, in a Gaelic society. Several of the stories have a bare, haunting simplicity of line and fine evocation of atmosphere, unobtrusively built up e.g. 'An Coigreach', 'An Fhidheall', 'An Duine Dubh' and 'An Bùrn'. Other stories are slightly flawed by linguistic and conceptual mannerisms which betray some failure of observation (whether of dialogue or of psychology), but the overall impression is of a sector of experience memorably caught and transmitted. His second collection of Gaelic stories, *An Dubh is an Gorm*, is still concerned with misfits, individuals, tensions, Freudian analysis, but ranges more widely, making use of the confrontation of Gael with Lowlander (at University, after Culloden) and taking subjects from farther afield (Napoleon, the Jews in Germany, Rhodesia). *Na Speuclairean Dubha* (1989) is a psychological detective novel, and his most recent collection of short stories, *Na Guthan* (1991) continues to show wide range and much subtlety. Probably his most enduring Gaelic fiction to date is *An t-Aonaran* (1976). It is once again on the theme of the individualist and the misfit (most of the characters showing different facets of these), but more fundamentally it is concerned with problems of art and communication. Despite surface melodrama the book is rich in symbolism. The observation and the style are very assured, and the book has the bonus of controlled humour.

His Gaelic poetry, even more than his prose, is closely attached to the Gaelic area, though *Bìobuill is Sanasan-reice* (1965) explores the world of advertisement and make-believe, and sometimes uses free verse rather than stanzaic structures. *Eadar Fealla-dhà is Glaschu* (1974) is more concerned with fleeting glimpses of the worlds of cinema and television. *Na h-Eilthirich* (1983) explores the theme of exile (personal and

general) and *An t-Eilean agus an Cànan* (1987) brings his strange blend of satire and compassion to bear on the disintegrating Gaelic society of his island home. The characteristics of the poetry in general are imagery and wit, an intelligent ordering of ideas and words and what Robin Fulton has called 'the ellipsis in the thought, the unexpected associations'. The sensuousness is visual rather than auditory. He brings to his writing of Gaelic poetry a wide reading and knowledge of poetry generally, and has made many translations from modern European poetry into Gaelic.

Although the volume of his English work is now much greater than that of his Gaelic, and shows, in general, greater range and depth, especially in his poetry, his Gaelic writings are still central to his achievement, as his Gaelic sub-conscious is a dominant factor in his psyche.

D. S. Thomson

Smith, Sydney Goodsir (1915–1975). The son of a forensic expert who as Professor (later Sir) Sydney Smith occupied the chair of forensic medicine at Edinburgh University, Sydney Goodsir Smith was born at Wellington, New Zealand, and spent his earliest years in that country. Educated at the Universities of Edinburgh and Oxford, he taught English to the Polish army during part of the war and in 1945 joined the British Council for a short time. For most of his life he was a freelance writer, journalist and broadcaster.

He dedicated almost his total creative effort to writing verse in Scots, and is generally regarded as, after MacDiarmid, the second finest poet to use the language regularly. His early books *Skail Wind* (1941) and *The Wanderer* (1943) show him grappling awkwardly with the muscles of a tongue that was his by right of birth but not by early wont and usage. Some of the lyrics in *The Deevil's Waltz* (1946), *So Late into the Night* (1951) and *Figs and Thistles* (1959) were once much admired, and a few still retain their power. Smith, however, often displayed a faulty ear when writing in strict metrical forms. He eschewed the use of imagery almost entirely, relying on the force of the words and of his own passion to carry forward the lyric impulse.

His masterpiece—and indeed, almost all his finest pieces—are looser in metrical style, but are braced with a pungent wit and a Poundian use of quotation and irony. *Under the Eildon Tree*, a set of 23 variations dealing with the relationship of some of the world's, and mythology's, greatest lovers, relating them to the poet's own experience of love, has a power far beyond anything else the poet wrote. 'The Grace of God and The Meth drinker' (1959) shows the width of Goodsir Smith's sympathies, and is in the same personal vein, a highly original genre that also takes in *Kynd Kittock's Land* (1965).

Smith's patriotic excursion into drama, *The Wallace*, though performed in the Assembly Hall at the Edinburgh International Festival, does not often reach far beyond rhetoric. His Joycean prose-fantasy *Carotid Cornucopius* (1947), though a *jeu d'esprit*, does not arouse associated echos of meaning in the manner of Joyce's *Ulysses*, though much of Smith's book is very funny.

A lovable man who carried his learning lightly, he was responsible for bringing back into modern general circulation Burn's *Merry Muses of Caledonia*. Unfortunately the *Collected Poems* (1975), in the preparation of which he himself had no hand, includes pieces specifically rejected by the poet, excludes a comic masterpiece 'the Riggins o' Chelsea', and abounds in textual and other errors.

M. Lindsay

Soldiers and Soldiering. In addition to the powerful nations in arms whose conquests dominated the pages of history, certain ethnic groups, on their own account or in the service of others, gained high reputations as soldiers. Not least among those were the Scots. Prior to the creation of permanent national armies forces were raised and disbanded according to the needs of the moment and battles were factional contests which were seldom the result of truly international conflict. The armies assembled to resolve princely quarrels, or to support a cause, were little more than armed rabbles incapable of carrying out any but the simplest military manoeuvre and dependent almost entirely on weight of numbers. Bands of untrained levees under warrior nobles were not soldiers in the accepted sense, this title only being applicable to a specialist minority. These were the mercenaries who, under Captains versed in the Art of War, gave their disciplined services to whoever wished to employ them. After permanent regular armies had been established in the seventeenth century, certain major powers continued to use foreign soldiers of proven quality. These were no longer independent mercenary companies but regular regiments constituting an integral element of the Army whose uniform they wore. Scotsmen served foreign monarchs in both categories, notably in France where their martial prowess was well known, and in 1422 a troop of Gendarmes Ecossais formed part of the royal entourage. Companies of Scots Foot Guards and Archers were raised in 1425 and when the Maison du Roi, the Royal Household Guard, was formally founded in 1445 these Scots continued as the King's close bodyguard.

Louis XIV was the creator of an army which was to become a model for the rest of Europe and in the course of its organization he established the form and functions of the Maison du Roi, including the permanent status of the mounted and foot companies of Scots, a feature to continue as long as the French monarchy survived. The Gendarmes and Gardes Ecossais fought against Marlborough and in the campaigns at which the Maison du Roi was present and although contrary to popular legend they were not the entire Royal Guard but only a small part of it, they were an élite within an élite, the Scots Gendarmes being one of the four companies known as Grande Gendarmerie.

In addition to the Scottish units in the Household the arrival in France of many Scots during the eighteenth century caused an increase in the foreign establishment. Six regiments of Infantry of the Line were recruited from Scots with Jacobite sympathies, of which Royal Ecossais raised in 1744, fought at Fontenoy in 1745 and in 1746 was part of the French contin-gent at Culloden where they opposed the British Royal Scots, themselves originally a French regiment. Raised in 1633 under a warrant issued by Charles II, they served in the French Army during the Thirty Years War and the Franco-Spanish War as the Regiment d'Hebron. Their Colonel, Sir John Heburn, was created a Marshal of France and many officers remained in French service after the return of the regiment to Britain in 1661 to begin its long history as the senior corps of British infantry.

The Swedes and Dutch also made considerable use of Scottish fighting men and it was experience in these countries which qualified a number to become senior officers in forces raised later in the United Kingdom. During the reign of Gustavus Adolphus the Scottish connection with Sweden was strong as he had a Scottish bodyguard and corps of his army entirely composed of Scots. The Scots Brigade was the spearhead of the Swedish Army at Leipzig and after this battle many towns and castles in Germany had Scottish governors.

When the English Civil War broke out with its subsequent effects on Scotland, many officers and men came back to Britain bringing with them experience gained in foreign service. Among these was Alexander Earl of Leven and David Leslie, Leven holding the rank of Marshal in the Swedish Army.

Scots were involved in the Wars of Dutch Independence and bands of mercenaries were active in 1568. In 1572 companies were raised in Scotland for Netherlands service developing into a brigade which was to be in almost continuous action until 1592. This formation, having been recruited in Scotland, was recalled for a time but returned to Holland to resume its role as a Dutch corps. Britain and Holland were at war in 1664 and the officers and men of the Scots Brigade had to take an oath of allegiance to the States General. Those who refused were released to return home, but the majority, who had families in the country they had made their own, decided to remain.

During the War of Austrian Succession Scots continued to fight in the uniforms of France, Holland and Britain, still confirming Daniel Defoe's comment in 1707 that they were the best soldiers in Europe and should all be in the service of the United Kingdom 'instead of cutting each other's throats in the service of foreign princes'.

The last substantial field force to remain in the army of a foreign power was the Dutch Scots Brigade which was finally disbanded in 1782. On their return to Britain the members asked to be absorbed into the British Army and in 1793 a little-known Scottish regiment was formed with the title of the Scotch Brigade. This corps received the British designation of 94th Foot but had a direct lineage to the Scottish regiments which had worn Dutch uniform for over a hundred years and which were themselves descended from seventeenth-century mercenaries. As part of the British Army the 94th served during the Napoleonic Wars with considerable distinction but disappeared from the Army List in 1818.

Scottish soldiers served all over the world and in addition to the three main armies which used their talents, they were to be found in Poland and Germany and in fact they would go to any region in need of reliable fighting men. It was however as members of the British Army that they became most renowned, the regiments of Scotland having a special place in its long history. In 1660 Charles II ordered the Earl of Newburgh to raise a troop of Life Guards in Edinburgh. This and other Royal Guards formed a British version of the Maison du Roi which developed into the Household Cavalry and Foot Guards of the present day. The Scots Troop of Life Guards held their first parade on Leith Links, but with the Scots Troop of Horse Grenadiers, raised in 1702, were absorbed into the regiment of Life Guards at the Union in 1707.

Several other mounted formations had Scottish origins but the most famous was the regiment of dragoons formed in 1681 from independent troops created three years earlier. This became the Royal Scots Greys which enjoyed a continuous existence until 1971, since when its traditions have been carried on in a new amalgamated regiment called the Royal Scots Dragoon Guards. The 17th (Edinburgh) Light Dragoons existed between 1759 and 1763 and a number of Fencible Cavalry regiments were raised between 1795 and 1802, the Yeomanry, created during the Napoleonic Wars, continuing to constitute an effective cavalry contribution from north of the border until the outbreak of the First World War.

It is the infantry however which has had the greatest impact in terms of Scottish national identity, caused by a combination of genuine and well earned military reputation, the picturesque appearance of Highland regiments and not least because of the completely bogus tartan image imposed on Lowland units by the Victorians.

During the Civil Wars of the seventeenth century a regiment of Scots Guards was raised which fought at Dunbar and shared the general disaster of Worcester. They were reformed at the Restoration to become the 3rd Foot Guards which now serves as the Scots Guards. The Royal Scots Fusiliers raised in 1678 by the Earl of Mar were next in seniority to the Royal Scots, and in 1689 William III commissioned the Earl of Leven to recruit a regiment in Edinburgh later to become 25th of the Line. In the same year the 26th Foot (Cameronians) was formed which, on amalgamation with the 90th Perthshire Light Infantry in 1881, completed the quartet of surviving old infantry corps which, in addition to the Guards, had served the United Kingdom since before the Union of Parliaments of 1707.

In 1725 companies of soldiers were recruited in the Highlands to act as a police force and in 1739 a decision was made which was to have an increasing influence on the character and image of the Scottish soldier. The Highland Independent Companies were formed into a regiment of British infantry known as the Royal Highland Regiment, establishing the standards for all units subsequently raised in the Highlands. The infantry uniform was modified to accommodate the native garb, the unique dress thus created developing into a national costume.

Between 1739 and 1800 24 regiments were raised in the northern areas of Scotland, the majority having a relatively short existence, being formed and disbanded during the Seven Years War and the War of American Independence. Although

Highland troops were recognized as formidable opponents at this period, it was during the Napoleonic Wars that their unusual dress and soldierly qualities began to be firmly associated in the minds of friend and foe alike. Numbers such as 42nd, 71st, 72nd and 79th acquired the significance which was to be almost mystical in years to come and home-defence units appeared in large numbers. Forty Fencible regiments were formed in Scotland on a full-time basis and between 1794 and 1815 about 50,000 men served in the part-time Volunteers or Local Militia. The contribution by Scots to Britain's auxiliary forces was always substantial and support for the Rifle Volunteers created in 1859 was no exception. By 1862 84,240 had enrolled and in 1871 the percentage of volunteers to population was twice that of England or Wales, a factor to continue when the force was affiliated to the regular army in 1881.

In 1908 all volunteer units, including infantry battalions, became Territorials who, wearing the badges of famous regular regiments, fought in two world wars as an integral part of the army. The story had gone full circle, causes, loyalties and weapons had changed over the centuries, but wherever Scottish soldiers went their like had been there before.

W. A. Thorburn

Somhairle MacGill-Eain see Maclean, Sorley

Soutar, William (1898–1943), the son of a Perth joiner and contractor, was educated at Perth Academy and, eventually, at Edinburgh University. In 1916 he left school to join the navy, served in American waters and with the Grand Fleet, an experience which took him onto a Q boat, a light cruiser, a battleship and a tramp steamer. He entered the university on demobilization in 1919 and published his first book of verse anonymously in 1923, the year he graduated.

He had already begun to feel the effects of the disease that was to cripple and eventually kill him, a form of spondalitis for which there was then no known cure. Unable to hold down a job because of his growing ill health, he soon became a bedridden invalid in his father's house. Several volumes of verse appeared at intervals, including *Seeds in the Wind* (1933) Scots poems for children, *The Solitary Way* (1934), *Poems in Scots* (1935), *In the time of Tyrants* (1939) and *But the Earth Abideth* (1943).

His adoption of a simple but somewhat monotonous hymn-like stanza in the belief that it carried the memorability of the ballad severely constricted his powers of expression in all but a handful of his English poems. It is therefore mainly through his Scots poems, Whigmaleeries, lyrics and riddles, that his carrying voice developed.

A so-called *Collected Poems* (1948), edited by Hugh MacDiarmid, omitted most of Soutar's best work. His *Selected Poems* (1961), edited by W.R. Aitken, contains much of the finest of his work, and has been twice reprinted.

There is an excellent biographical and critical study, *Still*

Life (1958) by Alexander Scott, who also edited Soutar's remarkable *Diaries of a Dying Man* (1959).

   M. Lindsay

Spence, Sir Basil (1907–1976). Although Basil Spence's architecture is clearly international in outlook, his early training and practice in Edinburgh were to leave their mark on his later work throughout Britain. The strong artistic personality that he brought to his work was to raise it above the general mass of post-war modern buildings. His use of traditional materials gave his designs a permanence and monumentality rare for the period.

   Basil Spence was born in Bombay of Scottish parents, but attended George Watson's College in Edinburgh. He trained as an architect at the Edinburgh College of Art, but between the third and fourth years of his course worked in London for the celebrated architect, Sir Edwin Lutyens. Upon leaving the College of Art in 1932, he joined William Kinninmonth in practice. The two young architects, who had met as students, then became sole partners in Rowand Anderson, Paul and Partners. This partnership was to produce some of the first experiments in the unabashed modern style of the period in Scotland. Lishmor, Easter Belmont Road, Edinburgh (1932) was their first essay in this style. However, much of the work followed the traditional mould established by Lutyens and Lorimer. Some were Georgian in character, others such as Broughton Place, Peeblesshire (1937–38) were skilful modern versions of seventeenth century Scottish baronial architecture. The most stylish is Gribloch, Stirlingshire (1938–39), a sleek horizontal modernist composition in traditional materials.

   In 1938 Spence won the competition for the ICI Pavilion at the Empire Exhibition in Glasgow, and this was to establish him as something of a specialist in the field of exhibition design and help him survive the lean years after the Second World War. His first London design was the Sea and Ships Pavilion for the Festival of Britain in 1951, but in the same year he achieved instant fame by winning the prestigious Coventry Cathedral competition.

   From then on his reputation was assured and although some notable buildings by Spence were built in Scotland, the most sensitive of which is his housing at Dunbar (1953), his major works are to be found in England and abroad.

   Sussex University (1960), where he was inspired by the post-war architecture of Le Corbusier, is perhaps his most individual and graceful design, although his finest work is surely the British Embassy in Rome (1961–68), a serene and stately composition which stands as a worthy neighbour to Michaelangelo's brilliantly mannered Porta Pia.

   M. Higgs

Spottiswoode, John, Archbishop (1565–1639), son of the minister of Mid Calder, was educated for the Church at Glasgow University. He gained the ear of James VI and became closely associated with the sovereign's attempts to restore Episcopalian Church government in Scotland. Spottiswoode was Archbishop of Glasgow and then of St Andrews, and in 1635 was made Lord Chancellor of Scotland. Following the rising caused by the introduction of the service book with the preparation of which he had been associated, he had to flee from Scotland and was excommunicated by the General Assembly of 1638. He was commissioned by the King to write his *History of the Church of Scotland*, published posthumously in 1655, and instructed to 'speak the truth, man, and spare not'. He commands a cool narrative style, and is neither pugnacious nor vindictive, though his viewpoint is naturally that of an Episcopalian.

   M. Lindsay

Stenhouse, William (1773–1827) antiquarian and writer on Scottish folksong. Born Roxburghshire; died Edinburgh, 10 November.

   Stenhouse's fame rests on one work: the *Illustrations of the Lyric Poetry and Music of Scotland*, designed as a series of notes to each of the 600 songs in *The Scots Musical Museum* (published by James Johnson, largely edited by Robert Burns, Edinburgh, 6 vols., 1787–1803). The *Illustrations* were commissioned by Blackwood about 1815, were completed by 1820, but were not published until 1839. Described by David Laing as 'a mass of curious matter regarding the poetry and music of the last century', they include reminiscences by and about Burns, Stephen Clarke, George Thomson, and others engaged in folksong research in the 1790s, as well as Stenhouse's own childhood recollections of folksong in Roxburghshire.

   Stenhouse's work has characteristic defects: he tended to copy inaccurate facts out of earlier studies, and to supply dates and Scottish origins to tunes too dogmatically; nevertheless, it remains indispensible to present-day research.

   D. Johnson

Stevenson, Robert Louis (1850–1894) was born in the New Town of Edinburgh, son of a well-to-do lighthouse engineer and a minister's daughter. As a child he was delicate and frequently ill, and it was while playing in bed with toy soldiers and the characters of a toy theatre that his sense of dramatic incident and commitment to story-telling precociously evolved. In his more active periods he got to know his native city in a very intimate way, savouring the differences between the New Town and the Old Town, between the richer and the poorer areas, between the sights and sounds of then still rural Colinton where he often stayed at his maternal grandfather's manse and the more urban areas, and, in his teens, between the Pentland village of Swanston where the family took a country cottage, with the freedom of the Pentland Hills all around, and the smoking city visible below. By the time he entered Edinburgh University in 1867 Stevenson had not only stored his memory with sights and sounds of Edinburgh and of other parts of Scotland he had visited but had also begun to associate particular scenes with appropriate fictional activities.

Stevenson's father wanted him to follow the family profession of lighthouse engineer, but he resisted, and they compromised on law, though Stevenson never had any intention of seriously following law as a profession: to be a writer was his one consuming ambition. As a student he led a somewhat self-consciously bohemian life with friends who shared his increasingly rebellious attitude to what they regarded as the stuffy hypocrisy of the Edinburgh bourgeoisie. In January 1873 a dramatic confrontation with his father (whom he loved and admired in spite of differences of belief) on the question of religion provoked a prolonged crisis between himself and his parents. Stevenson relieved his feelings in correspondence with Mrs Frances Sitwell, a much older woman of beauty and intelligence who much later became the wife of Sidney Colvin, and with his lifelong friend Charles Baxter. All the time he was 'playing the sedulous ape' to older writers, producing essays which show him seeking to embody in craftsmanlike prose his often somewhat turbulent feelings about life. Some of these early essays are merely exercises, others show him wrestling with the expression of disturbing moral problems, others again show his ability to evoke people and places. His health remained uncertain and he was subject to violent bronchial infections. In 1873 he was sent to Menton for his health. In 1876 a canoe trip on the Continent with his friend Sir Walter Simpson produced his first book, *An Inland Voyage* (1878), a somewhat precious account of his adventures. In 1875 he met in Edinburgh the critic, journalist and poet W.E. Henley, who became a close friend until their later quarrel, and in the same year he was in France with his lively cousin R.A.B. Stevenson. There he met Mrs Fanny Van de Grift Osbourne, a considerably older lady separated from her husband. Mrs Osbourne returned to America in August 1878 and Stevenson felt himself committed to her. A tour with a donkey in the Cévennes in autumn 1878 produced his second travel book, *Travels with a Donkey* (1879). In August 1879 he left for America and crossed the continent under very difficult conditions (described in essays later published as *Across the Plains* (1892) and *The Amateur Emigrant* (1895). He reached California and Fanny in an exhausted state, married her (now divorced) after a severe illness in May 1880, and in August returned with her to Scotland and a reconciliation with his parents. In Braemar in the autumn of 1881 he began *Treasure Island*, published in 1883, which established his reputation as a writer of boys' adventure stories. In search of health Stevenson with his wife tried various parts of southern France and elsewhere, then settled in Bournemouth in 1885, the year of the publication of his verses evoking his childhood in Edinburgh, *A Child's Garden of Verses*. The following year he achieved soaring fame with the publication of *Dr Jekyll and Mr Hyde*. This tensely dramatic story of the conflicting elements within a character reflects Stevenson's lifelong interest in the coexistence of good and evil. He himself was both heir to a Calvinistic tradition and a conscious bohemian, and the conflict between his religious and his hedonistic impulses, between his sense of tradition and his need for revolt, between *pietas* and rebellion, represented something very deep in his character that is reflected in one way or another in all his novels and stories. 1886 also saw the publication of *Kidnapped*, a story of Scotland after the '45 which cunningly relates psychology, history and topography. In this novel he fitted action to place in a way he had wanted to do from childhood.

In August 1887 the Stevensons left Britain for America, still in search of health, which Stevenson finally appeared to find voyaging in the South Seas. It was in America that he began *The Master of Ballantrae* (1889), a novel that deals with dull virtue and attractive villainy with a characteristic sense of moral ambiguities. In 1889 the Stevensons settled in Samoa, where Stevenson bought an estate and established himself in patriarchal fashion as a significant figure in Samoan life and politics. By this time he was already an international legend. He died suddenly in Samoa in December 1894, not of the dreaded consumption which had been diagnosed as continuously threatening him and which modern medical opinion thinks may have been bronchiecstasis, but of a cerebral haemorrhage. He left unfinished his masterpiece *Weir of Hermiston* (published posthumously in 1896) in which his imagination returned to Edinburgh and its surrounding hills; in his picture of the stern Lord Hermiston and his humane and sensitive son, set against appropriate local backgrounds, he explored with a new depth the moral ambiguities involved in the relation between father and son which was a theme that had haunted him since his rebellious youth.

In the years after Stevenson's death a reaction set in against the adulation of the 'heroic invalid' and he was seen as a poseur and at best a good children's writer. Critical re-estimation from the late 1940s has increasingly seen him as a significant figure in English and more especially Scottish literature. His friendship with Henry James, who greatly admired his work, is now seen as indication of a commitment to serious literary art as deep and genuine as that of the American master.

D. Daiches

Stevenson, Ronald (b. 1928, Blackburn) studied at the Royal Manchester College of Music and the Accademia di Santa Cecilia, Rome. Between 1963 and 1965 he was Senior Lecturer in music at the University of Capetown. Of both Scottish and Welsh descent, he chose, on his return, to live in the Scottish Borders, pursuing a career as composer, pianist and lecturer. He has performed extensively and broadcast in Britain, South Africa, Germany, Italy and the USSR.

Stevenson's output is wide-ranging and includes piano and cello concertos, instrumental sonatas, several song and choral cycles, the longest single movement in the piano repertoire and well over 200 songs. Within an idiom predominantly tonal in orientation, three main strands of development are evident: first, his profound admiration for the music and philosophies of Busoni has formed the backbone of his aesthetic. *The Prelude, Fantasy and Fugue* (1949–60) on themes from Busoni's 'Dr Fantasy', which he later reworked as the first Piano Concerto, a didactic *Twentieth Century Music Diary* and various piano transcriptions are among the practical results of this early preoccupation. Second, the concept of a 'World Music', a more recent interest, has resulted in the 80 minute *Passacaglia on DSCH* for piano (1960–62), and the second Piano Concerto *The Continents* (1972, BBC Commission). Both are epic, polyglot works, absorbing elements from Eastern, African and Western cultures. Third, Stevenson has also absorbed much of the music and spirit of the Scottish national heritage, particularly in instrumental and vocal works, which include settings of MacDiarmid, including the song cycles *The Infernal City* (1971) and *Border Boyhood* (1970), John Davidson (*Songs of Quest*, 1974) and other Scottish poets. His major work *The Keening Song for a Makar* and recent vocal work *In Memoriam Robert Carver* evoke beauty and continue the motif centring on Scottish heritage.

P. Hindmarsh

Stuart, Charles Edward (Bonnie Prince Charlie) (1720–1788) was born and died in Rome. He was the elder son of the unhappy marriage between James Francis Edward Stuart (James III, or the 'Old Pretender') and Maria Clementina Sobieska, daughter of the Polish Prince James Sobieski. A second son, Henry Benedict, was born in 1725. As grandson of the exiled James VII and III, Charles was the Jacobite titular Prince of Wales, and last hope of a cause which, by 1725, was at a low ebb due to the failure of the 1715 and 1719 risings, and the collapse of Jacobite plotting in England in the 1720s.

Brought up in Bologna and Rome, Charles had a wide if shallow education. He was fluent, but not entirely at home in English, Italian, and French. He was also musical, and a good cellist, but more horseman and hunter than scholar. His nominal participation in the Spanish siege of the Neapolitan fortress of Gaeta in 1734 was followed by a successful propaganda tour of northern Italy in 1737.

The approach of war between France and Great Britain in 1743 brought Charles to the heart of the diplomatic chessboard. The death of Cardinal Fleury, a minister who had sustained an Anglo-French understanding, was followed by the conversion of Louis XV's government to the idea of a Stuart restoration. From November 1743, a surprise French landing near London was being planned. Charles reached Gravelines early in 1744 to act as its political figurehead, but loss of surprise and storm damage to transports led to cancellation in March 1744.

Charles resolved to raise a rebellion in Scotland to force the French to reconsider invasion. Though Scottish Jacobites had demanded significant French prior commitment, Charles sailed in July 1745 with only two ships. One, a leased French battleship, was intercepted and forced back. Rebuffed in the Hebrides, Charles reached the west Highland mainland at Arisaig where a combination of charm, promises of committed French and English Jacobite support and stress on the weakness of government forces in Scotland enabled him to raise an army.

After the unexpected collapse of Hanoverian resistance in Scotland, Charles pushed his reluctant advisory council into a narrow decision to invade England. Though tactically brilliant, the invasion collapsed politically at Derby in December 1745 when his council, already alienated by his equivocation on the need to repeal the Union of 1707, bearded him with his lies about the French and the English Jacobites and insisted on retreat. By the time of the final defeat at Culloden in April 1746, Charles was hardly speaking to his best general, Lord George Murray.

After six months as a fugitive, Charles benefited from a tacit conspiracy between Scots Whigs and Jacobites to send him safely back to France. He sentimentalised about Scotland in a lengthy decline marked by unsuccessful love affairs, a disastrous barren marriage in 1772 to Louise of Stolberg, and rampant alcoholism.

B.P. Lenman

Supernatural Beliefs. In Scotland, as elsewhere in Europe, most people in the country and many in the towns still believe to some extent in supernatural or paranormal phenomena not generally sanctioned by official Christianity. Though such 'superstition' is often scoffed at today and may be mentioned merely in mocking anecdotes about the credulity of the last generation, most people are uneasy about spilling salt or walking under ladders, and beliefs which were certainly widespread a century ago may still flourish in particular communities or occupational groups. The notoriously dangerous and chancy business of fishing, for instance, is still hedged about with superstition: fishermen who may be devout Baptists on shore may still be terrified of mentioning creatures such as pigs, rabbits, cats or salmon at sea, still more of seeing one in the boat or on the way there. Elaborate circumlocutions may be used to avoid talking about a minister or even one's wife, and few fishermen like to have a minister or even a woman aboard their boats. It is unlucky to count fish or boats at sea, lucky perhaps to spit in the mouth of the first fish you catch, unlucky to whistle (which may raise a wind) and so on. Above all there are one or two people in every fishing village the sight of whom is enough to make any fisherman on his way to the harbour turn back and refuse to go to sea that day. Such a person is generally spoken of in Scots as having 'an ill fit' or a bad foot: the Gaelic term is *droch-chòmhdhalaiche*, meaning a bad person to meet—on your way to the market or any important business as well as to the sea. On the other hand some people, especially children, might be said to have a 'guid fit' and be asked to walk a short distance with the person setting out.

There is no space here to treat properly of the numerous minor beliefs about good and bad luck, about the unnatural behaviour of natural objects and creatures, the small customs connected with buying and selling, birth, death and marriage, or the secret societies of which only the Freemasons expanded outside their original professional boundaries. But the fraternity of the Horseman's Word flourished in country areas until recently, despite its associations with the devil. It may be better to concentrate on two more prominent aspects of belief, in supernatural beings and in the supernatural powers of humans.

Supernatural Powers. The belief in witchcraft (q.v.) lasted long past the last of the witch trials but popular belief had little time for the compacts and meetings with the devil which feature so prominently in the trials. The belief that one could give oneself up to the devil did survive, and a tradition in the Northern Isles states that the method involved lying on the shore between high and low tide-mark with one hand on top of the head and one on the soles of the feet and promising all between these hands. More widespread were tales that the devil held a school for enchanters in Italy, and the first Lord Reay among other Highland chiefs was credited with having studied there and lost his shadow when the devil 'took the hindmost' to leave his last lecture as payment, but was deceived into taking the shadow for the man. This legend is widespread in Europe, and typical in that the devil gets the worst of the bargain. Another widespread tradition is that of the Black Book of magic which can only be sold for a smaller price than it was bought for and cannot be thrown away or burned, and sends out imps which keep demanding more work until the inexperienced user sets them an impossible task like twisting ropes of sand. Apart from 'Tam o' Shanter', the witches' Sabbath appears mostly in rather light-hearted legends where an intruder, for instance, sinks witches sailing in sieves at their meeting by uttering the name of God, or succeeds in turning the tables on the witch who rode him in the shape of a horse to the meeting, and has her shod as a mare.

Popular as against official belief has always concentrated on the Evil Eye (*an droch-shùil* in Gaelic, or *cronachadh*, 'causing harm'). There is some confusion as to whether this is an involuntary power or a deliberately acquired one: there may be a collision between Celtic and Germanic ideas here, though both types can be paralleled for instance in Africa. Involuntary Evil Eye according to Highland belief is a hereditary ability, normally motivated by envy and activated by viewing (and often praising) the object of envy. The belief was most often used to account for ailments of children and domestic animals, especially cattle, but where it has survived it can now explain, say, the failure of a car's or boat's engine. As in many parts of the world anyone praising a baby or animal too highly, or seeming too eager to buy an animal which the owner would not sell, might be suspected of 'overlooking' or casting the Evil Eye on it, or at least of drawing the attention of one who had the power. The remedy may involve spitting and uttering a short charm (in Shetland *Tweetin say dee*, 'Shame be to you'), countering praise with dispraise, or alternatively with even higher praise, or when the symptoms began, pursuing the overlooker and taxing him openly with his crime. Individuals and families known to have the Evil Eye would be avoided or cautiously approached to avoid offending them, though they might be so unable to control the power that a man could cause the death of his own best cow or a mother harm her own baby just by seeing them.

Ways in which a witch could deliberately vent her ill-will included causing sickness and death (again especially among children and animals), delaying childbirth, as in the ballad 'Willie's Lady,' (Child 6,) or raising storms and wrecking ships, often by sympathetic magic, agitating water in a tub until a floating wooden bowl (caup) or eggshell representing the ship sank. A similar use of images caused death: rather than wax dolls Highland witches used a *corp créadha*, 'clay body' of unfired clay which could be left in a stream, where as the water carried off its substance the victim slowly wasted away. But the most frequent accusations concerned the lesser offence of invisibly stealing the goodness from foodstuffs, taking their 'profit' or 'fruit' (Gaelic *toradh*). The seventeenth-century confession of Isobel Gowdie of Auldearn gives methods for taking the profit of various things, including inedible ones like dunghills and dye-vats. Recent accounts describe the taking of the profit of a field of standing corn or a fishing-boat's catch, for instance, by cutting some of the crop in a specified place, way or time, or borrowing something from the boat or farm, with varying results—sometimes a poor quality of crop or catch, sometimes none. With far the most usual accusation, taking the profit of milk, the results vary similarly. The methods include gathering the dew of the field where the victim's cows pastured with a hair rope before dawn on May Day; sucking the cow's milk in animal form; borrowing a peat from the victim's hearth as she churned; or again borrowing or stealing some of the cows' food and water. The cows' milk might become thin and watery, or even though it looked normal might be too weak to churn into butter—and as there are many natural reasons why cream, or still more the whole milk used for churning in Shetland and elsewhere, may not make butter, there were many occasions to suspect witchcraft. On the other hand specific witches are often said to have had the milk of the whole district's cows literally on tap through a spigot driven into the wall, or to have milked them through the pot-chain over the witch's own hearth—with the result that the cows ran dry, which can also happen naturally.

The taking of profit could be prevented by the use of charms such as served to ward off many sorts of harm, whether caused by witches, fairies or less defined powers: leaves from the Bible, an old knife, horseshoe or other form of 'cold iron', or rowan twigs kept in the cow's stall—the same things might be kept under the pillow of a baby or a woman in childbirth to prevent them being taken by the fairies. A sixpence or a sprig of pearlwort in the churn might save the butter. Various charms or phrases for 'saining' those at risk are also remembered, or cattle might be sained by waving a glowing peat around them. In stories a man hearing the dew-gathering witch cry 'Aa to me!' might cry 'Some to me!' and his wife's churn fill to the brim with butter; in fact in Shetland less than 50 years ago a would-be witch gathering grass and water from a neighbour's land to take their profit had them emptied about her ears. However, the witch could not usually be caught red-handed and the victim's aim was to identify her and force her to restore what she had taken. The most effective method was said to be to cork some of the affected cow's urine tightly in a bottle and leave it by the fire until a corresponding burning and blockage in the witch forced her to come and beg for relief.

Other Highland cures for all manifestations of the Evil Eye involved the use of *uisge far airgid*, water in which silver coins had lain, or a *snaithle*, a thread usually of red wool on which a known healer tied knots, saying secret charms: this might be tied round the wrist of a sick baby or the tail of a sick cow. In Shetland cows smitten with unaccountable ailments might have their backs combed with a wool card or the claws of a live cat, or 'pooderie straes', firecrackers made of straws filled with gunpowder, might be set off round them to scare away fairies or witches.

Certain skilled men and women were thought to have healing powers, and charms and other secrets were often handed down in families, from man to woman and from woman to man in successive generations, sometimes to this day. The powers of the seventh son of a seventh son included healing scrofula or eczema by a touch, as well as clairvoyance. More than natural power also resided in certain plants such as rowan, *mothan* (pearlwort) and St John's wort, which were antidotes to magic. Numerous holy wells reputed to heal different ailments, or all kinds, were resorted to long after they ceased to be sites of pilgrimages in honour of the saints after whom many were named. Lunatics were brought to St Maolrubha's Isle in Loch Maree to be towed behind boats; in the eighteenth century needfires were kindled and even cattle sacrificed in them to an unnamed god to check a murrain; and at least one Hebridean boulder still has nails driven into it by people hoping to cure their toothache—but folk medicine is a study on its own.

Not all supernatural harm need be witchcraft—a woman evicted from her home who curses the evicting landlord or factor is simply calling down the vengeance of God in the manner of the early Celtic saints, and one who caused several deaths and injuries with such a curse quite recently was said to be a respected and God-fearing person. Traditionally the curse was more effective if uttered fasting and with the hair combed loose. A special fate is attributed to some hated factors, including Patrick Sellar: they were eaten alive by worms.

The less harmful activities of witches are also reported: making love charms (in the form often of an ordinary-looking bannock with unmentionable ingredients), flying (in Scotland with the help of a magic cap more often than a broomstick) and shape-shifting. Cats and hares were the forms usually taken, and the story of the hare wounded with a silver bullet and followed by the trail of blood to the house where the witch lay bleeding from a wound in the spot where the hare had been hit is the most widespread and enduring witch legend in the British Isles. Many stories are told too of the feats of male enchanters or warlocks, from Michael Scot in the thirteenth century to 'Iain Dubh' (Black John) MacLeod within living memory, including illusions such as making the cockerel crow in the pot, contests of magic with witches, journeys on the devil's back to Rome, splitting hills and forming sandbanks with the Black Book and its servants, or merely forcing the farmer's wife who had refused them a drink to dance and sing along with all the harvest workers on the farm until they all collapsed.

Close to the warlocks stand the prophets, beginning with Merlin and Thomas the Rhymer and continuing with more local figures of whom the best-known, Coinneach Odhar (Dun Kenneth), later called 'the Brahan Seer', is first mentioned as the leader of a band of witches in Easter Ross in the sixteenth century. Almost every island had its prophet, some in clan times, others only a hundred years ago, who predicted the coming of such things as aeroplanes: Coinneach Odhar predicted the railways, the Highland Clearances, and the extinction of the Earls of Seaforth. Whatever one may think of such prophecies without being sure when they were manufactured, it is much harder to doubt that there is some basis for the various forms of clairvoyance claimed for hundreds of adults and children. This ability goes under the general name of second sight (in Gaelic *an dà shealladh*, literally 'the two sights'). Strictly speaking second sight, like the Evil Eye, is an innate, sometimes hereditary, involuntary power. According to Robert Kirk's seventeenth-century treatise *The Secret Commonwealth*, it can be deliberately acquired, and as more recent accounts confirm someone disturbed by constant visions of future death and disaster can also get rid of the power by exorcism or other means. A particular vision can be shared by a second person if the seer puts his hand on the other's head and his foot on the other's foot, and he looks over the seer's shoulder.

Second sight is generally concerned with death—a person is seen near his home when he is known to be, say, in Australia, or out of doors when he is lying sick in bed, and is known to have died or be about to die: later news confirms that he died about that time. The Highland seer (*taibhsear*) may see the funeral procession or other details of the burial, and have to deduce from those taking part whose funeral it is. Seers may also be able to predict where the body of a drowned person will come ashore, or whether or not a boat missing for a long time will come safely home. They might also see the future wife of a man sitting beside him. It is also still known for a person to be seen in a place years before he comes to that place and is at once recognized—a sort of *déjà vu*. This is called *manadh a' bheò*, the portent of the living, and there is an overlap in Gaelic belief between *manaidhean*, portents which may be seen by anyone, and the visions of those gifted with the second sight. (In practice it is widely accepted that many people may have such a gift to some extent.) *Manaidhean* are more obscure, but still tend to portend death or disaster: typical examples are sounds of crying, or of sawing in a joiner's shop where coffins are made, a crushing weight on a bed where a coffin will be laid, pictures falling off the wall for no reason, or the appearance of mysterious lights or birds. Convincing instances of such portents and more specific visions coming true are still often told of, not only in the Gaelic-speaking parts of Scotland—where the belief has been updated to include phantom cars seen where an accident later happens—but for instance in Shetland where the Scots terms *foregang* (or *ganfer*) and *feyness* are still used for them, and though less openly discussed, probably throughout Scotland. Related beliefs include prophetic dreams, and deliberate divination, now by reading teacups and palms, formerly by trance as described by Kirk, by spending the night wrapped in a cow's hide as described by Martin Martin, by *slinneanachd*, examining a sheep's shoulder-blade, by looking through a stone with a hole in it such as Coinneach Odhar was said to have, and so on (see also Hallowe'en divination under *Seasonal Customs*).

Supernatural Beings. Ghosts play relatively little part in Highland belief, just because there are so many more stories of people being seen before or at the time of their deaths. There is no exact Gaelic equivalent to 'ghost': the usual translations are *bòcan* meaning any bogey or frightening spirit, and *taibhs(e)*, a vision of the dying quite as often as of the dead. If the spirits of the dead haunt a place, it is normally because they have something to do or tell about. A mother's ghost cares for her child, debtors and wrongdoers return to see that things are put right. If a gravestone is misused the occupant of the grave comes to see that it is put back. Nearly always the haunting ceases when someone is bold enough to speak to the ghost and find out what must be done. The ghost of an unbaptized child can be laid by giving it a name, even a nickname.

Lowland apparitions may be identified as, say, the ghost of a laird's discarded mistress, but throughout Scotland it is as likely that whatever is said to haunt a particular spot is a wholly supernatural bogey as the spirit of a departed person. Such beings are not necessarily insubstantial, and may attack and wrestle with travellers who disturb them. They range from the white ladies and black dogs which turn up throughout Western Europe and America to such mysterious figures as the Headless Body (*Colunn gun Cheann*) or the great Grey Man of Ben Macdhui. Poltergeist phenomena, often involving clods of turf or peats being thrown around houses by no human hand, have been reported since the seventeenth century, but again, these are not ghosts.

Most supernatural beings in Scotland seem to have some kinship with the fairies. The 'sociable' or 'trooping' fairies, small people who live underground, are given particularly to music, dancing and theft, are similarly described throughout the British Isles, and indeed have parallels in the beliefs of almost every human tribe or race. Officially the fairies had a kinship in their turn with the devil: associating with them was a frequent charge in witch trials, and according to legend they had fallen from heaven with Lucifer, but being less guilty stayed on the surface of the earth. The ballad of Tamlane (Child 39) mentions the tradition that they paid a periodic tax or teind to hell which involved the devil taking some of their number. They were also associated with the dead, or at least the likenesses of dead people were seen among them—either famous people like Thomas the Rhymer and James IV who were expected to rise again in Scotland's hour of need, or in recent legends common people, especially women who had died in childbirth. Their Gaelic names such as *daoine sìdhe* make it clear that they are the same as the *aes side*, 'otherworld people', of early Irish tradition, officially represented by Christian historians as the *Tuatha Dé Danann*, former inhabitants of Ireland driven literally underground by the invading Gaels. Recent theorists have echoed this, seeing the fairies as a folk memory of, for instance, the Picts: but in fact the leaders of the *aes side* can clearly be identified by their names with pagan Celtic gods, and the fairies are best seen as representing a survival of the pagan pantheon and all the attendant minor spirits of the wild corresponding to ancient Greek nymphs and satyrs.

Sometimes they are benign deities, like the *fata* or personal genius from whom the name fairy comes (via French *feé*) along with the fairy godmothers of Continental folktales. They teach their art to pipers or blacksmiths, or help with harvest work. Just as often, however, a mortal gets a fairy cup by stealing it or learns a tune by overhearing it as he passes a fairy hill. The ancient Gaelic figure of the *leannan sidhe* or fairy lover (female or male) appears in tales, often with a sad song attached, for the mortal lover usually either deserts the fairy or is killed rather than allowed to go into the fairy hill, though sometimes he gets some good advice before the parting. A wish for fairy help is not always wise: in a legend with international parallels the ploughman who wishes for some buttermilk from the churn he hears working in the fairy hill and then refuses it when it is offered, is cursed and dies, though his companion who did not wish but accepts the drink is blessed—though usually to taste fairy food or drink puts one in their power. The young men in the story best known from Scott's 'Glenfinlas', told of sites all over the Highlands with the name *Airigh na h-Aon-Oidhche* (Single Night Sheiling), wish for their sweethearts to be in the lonely bothy with them, and fairies (?) in the semblance of the girls come to them, and cut their throats. In most parts of Orkney and Shetland, though a few islands preserve an older distinction, the *trows* (compare Norse *troll*) are equivalent to the fairies. Certainly they are nothing like the butterfly-winged miniatures of Victorian illustrators, derived from Elizabethan writers' fantasies: in Scotland, and indeed throughout the British Isles, the fairies of tradition are either as big as humans or no smaller than a child of five, and their main characteristic is that they are dangerous.

Derived from gods who had much to do with fertility, they live underground, in fairy hills which may be the remains of prehistoric chamber tombs or natural mounds, even mountains like Schiehallion, whose name seems to mean 'the fairy hill of the Caledonians'. Mortals may annoy them by digging drains or planting tether-pegs through their roofs. Their underground world has its own laws of nature and occasionally its doors are open: the most wide-spread of all fairy legends in the Highlands and Northern Isles tells of a man who went into the local fairy hill when it was open at Yule or Hallowe'en and spent a year dancing there with a keg of whisky on his back, though when rescued he thought he had hardly finished one reel. Sometimes they are 'good neighbours' who borrow a housewife's pot or sieve, milk or oatmeal, and repay the loan. Their alien, semi-divine nature appears more clearly when they are in a crowd, the *sluagh* or fairy host, occasionally a formal cavalcade like that which passes the crossroads at midnight in 'Tamlane', more often a band of airborne mischief-makers like the 'Wild Hunt' of other countries, sometimes seen as an eddy of dust on a still day which may drop a stolen woman if you throw your bonnet at it, sometimes visiting a house at night and carrying off a paralysed man to a field half a mile away—in the more impressive accounts—or taking a man to America and back overnight—by his own unconfirmed account. Local people thought to be dead may be seen among the *sluagh*, but can very rarely be saved from them. The fairies of different areas gather for shinty matches and take mortals to help them, or shoot people or cattle with *elfshots*, identified as prehistoric flint arrowheads, and formerly blamed as the cause of any inexplicable illness. Especially in the mainland Highlands men out alone in the hills are liable to be chased by fairies who might tear them to pieces if not escaped by crossing running water, drawing a circle with an iron knife, or hearing the cock crow.

Fairies and other supernatural beings, as well as serving to express the awe and reverence felt for wild nature, had several functions which are shown in such stories: to act as a nemesis on rash wishes; to serve as bogeys to frighten children away from dangerous places or wandering after dark and discourage anyone from going too far into the hills alone; and above all to act as scapegoats for anything which inexplicably went wrong, especially illness. A cow suddenly taken ill was elfshot; a woman who died in childbed had really been taken by the fairies to nurse their children (but in cases where a real woman is named the husband may hear how he could get her back but never dares to do it); a fretful, stunted or mentally deficient child is a changeling—the fairies have taken the real child and left an old fairy to benefit from the mother's milk. Fortunately stories require the changeling to reveal himself by speaking or playing the pipes before being thrown on the fire or over a waterfall to get back the real baby, and reputed changelings who were not too ill might survive in fact into old age. Fairies stole cattle as well as people (no doubt those which went missing in the hills) and took the profit of milk and corn like witches.

The numerous solitary fairies and spirits similarly combine the functions of helpers, bogeys and occasionally scapegoats: only the more important can be mentioned by name. Domestic spirits like the Brownie or the Belly Blind of the ballads might give help with chores, or advice, but they hated to be seen, and as all over Europe they could be given nothing but food or drink: leave them clothes or a pair of shoes and they would vanish and work no more. Another sort of Brownie, usually called *Gruagach* in Gaelic, was the tutelary spirit of the cattle, and milk was poured into a hollow stone as an offering to him in places well into the last century. Both sorts of Brownie overlap with the female *Glaistig* of the Central Highlands, who according to J. G. Campbell was the spirit of a human farmer's wife so attached to her land that she 'had a Fairy nature given to her'. But though sometimes she cares for cattle or households other accounts of the Glaistig make her equivalent to the supernatural *Cailleach* (meaning simply old woman) associated with different mountains, notably Beinn Bhreac (a name which recurs in many parts of the Highlands), who is the nearest thing in Gaelic belief to a full-blown, terrifying nature goddess. She herds the wild deer, can leap from mountain peak to peak in a flash, perhaps even controls the weather: in a widespread story

also told of mortal witches she tries to kill a hunter sheltering in a mountain bothy but is driven off by his dogs. This *cailleach*, physically immensely powerful and sometimes huge, is akin to the giants' mother, more dangerous than the giants themselves, who appears in folktales. (Giants are mere storytellers' lay figures, ogres to be killed or colossi to have dropped islands or standing-stones, and play no part in stories which were believed.) Various other spirits of the wild such as the malignant Brown Man o' the Muirs and the mischievous satyr-like *Uruisg* who haunted Highland streams are also mentioned from time to time by tradition.

The *Glaistig* also occasionally filled another role, that of the Irish banshee, heard crying just before any death in a particular family; another equivalent was the *Caointeach* or *Caoineag* ('Keening-Woman'). But the spirit most often seen before a death was the *Bean-Nighe* ('Washing-Woman') who was seen or heard by a stream, washing the shrouds of those about to die, especially before a battle. In fact the best-known 'banshee' of the Highlands is the headless ghost of Eoghan a' Chinn Bhig ('Hugh of the Little Head'), which appears on horseback before the death of any MacLean of his own house of Lochbuie. He met the *Bean-Nighe* before a battle against his own father, seized her from behind by the breast in the required fashion, asked his fate, and was told that he would die unless his wife gave him butter without being asked for it. She did not, and he was duly beheaded and carried off by his runaway horse to his new duties.

Finally there are the water-spirits. Some were believed to be grey seals in the sea but could take human shape on land, but accounts vary as to whether these were the same as the inhabitants of an actual kingdom under the sea, or at the other end of the scale the shape-shifting Lapps or 'Norway Finns' of Shetland belief, from whom the seal-people are sometimes wrongly called 'Finn-men'. Seal-people are best known from the story of the man who stole a seal-woman's skin and lived with her until she found the skin and went back to the sea, known throughout the Highlands and Northern Isles and said to be the origin of the MacCodrum family of North Uist. On the east coast the story is told of a mermaid; otherwise mermaids are vague figures, seen before storms like the Blue Men of the Minch. The sea-people also have cattle which at times have been captured and bred with land-cattle to give an excellent strain, recognizable by their short notched ears.

Finally there is the water-horse in its various forms: the Highland *Each Uisge*, which normally haunts lochs, the Lowland Kelpie in rivers, the Orcadian Tangie in the sea and the Shetland Nyuggle, found in rivers or lochs or coiled round the vertical water-wheel of a Shetland mill to stop it turning. All of them tempt people to ride them and then dash with them under the water, where a heart and lungs floating to the surface may tell of their fate; most of them can be captured with care or a magic bridle and used to plough or carry stones for a building; the first two can also take human form, and the *Each Uisge* may appear as a handsome young man and seduce maidens. The Loch Ness Monster used to be called Each Uisge and is sometimes said to have a horse-like head, and though these creatures, and the *Tarbh Uisge* or water-bull, may be associated with small lochs as well as very deep ones, it may be worth adding one point which has a bearing on this borderline of the natural and supernatural: the flying, fiery dragon of general European tradition is rare in Gaelic stories, and monsters are nearly always depicted as coming from the sea or a loch, swimming, and not venturing far on to the shore.

A. Bruford

T

Tannahill, Robert (1774–1810), the son of a Paisley weaver, followed his father's trade, first at Lochwinnoch, on leaving school at the age of 13, then in Bolton, Lancashire, and finally in his own town, where in 1805 he helped found a library for working men. His lyrics appeared in Glasgow periodicals and in 1807, to popular local acclaim, in book form. Many of his verses were composed for R.A. Smith (1780–1829), the editor of *The Scottish Minstrel*, which, after *The Scots Musical Museum* of which Burns was virtually the editor, is a valuable collection. Tannahill became depressed, allegedly over difficulties in the organizing of a second edition of his poems, and drowned himself in the Paisley canal.

A slightly sentimental follower of Burns as regards both choice of theme and form, he exhibits the growth of Romanticism in that his love-lyrics are apt to lose sight of the lady amidst his description of the scenery surrounding her. 'The midges dance aboon the burn' is a perceptive lyric, though his two songs best remembered locally are 'Jessie, the Flower o' Dunblane' and 'Thou bonnie Wood o' Craigielea'. The Paisley cottage where he lived and worked has been conserved as a museum by the Paisley Burns Club.

M. Lindsay

Tartan has its roots in the past, but the idea of distinct patterns belonging to each clan and of the Highland garb being the national dress of Scotland are relatively modern.

From early times the Highlanders are said to have favoured brightly coloured clothes of striped or checked material. James V, father of Mary Queen of Scots, wore hose of 'Heland tartane', and many writers tell of the distinctive dress of the Highlanders, although they are not always clear about its exact form.

Tartan as now produced consists of cloth woven in stripes of various colours crossing at right angles and arranged in the same sequence in both directions (warp and weft). The weave used is the 'twill', in which the threads cross first over two,

then under two, producing the effect of a diagonal rib on the web. Some seventeenth-century portraits show less regularity, and personal whim and the dyes available probably dictated the weaver's and wearer's choice of design, which can sometimes be identified with districts rather than families. Worn in the form of a single garment belted at the waist (later divided into kilt and shoulder-plaid), it was so much a part of the Highlanders' military tradition by the time of the Jacobite risings that the Government prohibited the wearing of any part of the Highland garb in 1747, by an act which was not repealed until 1782. During this period of proscription it could legally be worn only by regular troops, and the Highland regiments introduced a formal dress and stylized patterns, which were reflected in civilian wear once the ban was lifted. Uncertainty about the 'correct' pattern led to some genuine inquiry and a lot of commercial improvisation and invention, culminating in the 'tartan frenzy' of George IV's visit to Edinburgh in 1822. Within a few years most of the modern designs had been adopted and published, and the concept of 'clan tartans' was accepted and adapted to modern fashions. Some informality of dress has returned with the growing popularity of outdoor pursuits, and the harsh effect of chemical dyes has been modified by a revival of the mellower (so-called 'ancient') colourings.

J.M. and R.W. Munro

Tartanry. Long recognised as an icon of Scottishness, familiar throughout the world in illustration, in packaging, in dress, tartan has a long and disputed history. The colours and intricate patterns of tartans have a relatively short life, and most of the well-known tartans of today are a modern development. Today tartans are profusely, sometimes incredibly diverse and an integral part of the tourist industry: the term signifies rampant pseudo-Scottishness directed at a visiting market rather than at an informed historical consciousness.

Like the kailyard (q.v.) the widespread and indiscriminate use of tartan arose from a generalised picture of Scotland unmodified by any close information. Film and literature showed little discrimination in depicting national costume and national taste, and the search for rapid icons by which to identify countries soon fixed on tartan as the instantly recognisable symbol of Scotland. Packaging for food and drink, symbolism on posters and notices, décor, formal and informal dress were the obvious applications for tartan in this mode, alongside the growth of an entertainment industry where song, dance and costume were rapidly and often unhistorically created for general impression rather than for detail. Like the kailyard, this form of Scottishness achieved a wide currency, which it still enjoys. Unlike, say, a national flag, the stars and stripes, tartan is not a national symbol with associated subtext, but a decorative item. Only a more informed knowledge of its history and its application will separate the purely decorative users of tartan from an effort to restore tartan to a proper context, restrained by a historical consciousness of the originals.

I. Campbell

Tennant, William (1784–1848), the son of a merchant and farmer, was born at Anstruther, Fife. He was crippled from birth. After a local education he became a clerk in his brother's corn merchant's business, using his leisure to study languages and literature. In 1813 he became schoolmaster at Lasswade Parish School, Midlothian. From there he moved to Dollar Academy as classics master. Still dependent on crutches, he accepted an offer of the chair of Oriental Languages at St Andrews University in 1835.

In 1812 he published a mock-heroic poem in ottava rima, *Anster Fair*, an elaborate and amusing variant on the old Scots theme of public celebration. Not only are the local people and their customs amusingly described in such set pieces as the bagpipe contest, but there are also gently satirical sketches of the boatloads of the polite and erudite who sailed across from Auld Reekie:

> They come, the cream and flower of all the Scots,
> > The children of politness, science, wit,
> Exulting in their bench'd and gawdy boats,
> > Wherein some joking and some puking sit ...

Anster Fair was widely and favourably reviewed. It seems highly probable that Byron may have read a review with copious quotation which appeared in the *Quarterly Review*. It is thus possible that Tennant's up-dated eighteenth-century tone and witty handling of the stanza form may have provided a model for *Beppo* and *Don Juan*.

Occasional good things are to be found in Tennant's Shakespearean-style plays, notably *Cardinal Beaton* (1825) and *Papistry Storm'd* (1827). He wrote in addition two other plays, *John Baliol* (1825) and *The Thane of Fife* (1822), as well as a *Syriac and Chaldee Grammar*, regarded in its day as outstanding.

M. Lindsay

Textile Industries. The making of textiles is a basic economic activity in most societies, and given our climate it is hardly surprising that since earliest times there has been a manufacture of cloth from natural fibres for clothing and furnishings in Scotland. Dispersed throughout much of the country, much of the output for long was low in quality and intended only for very local markets. But gradually during the seventeenth century the focus of the textile sector—particularly in the Lowland towns—began to shift away from mere subsistence manufacturing towards the production of yarn and cloth for more distant customers. Traditionally, the main Scottish staples were wool and flax (domestic supplies being augmented by imports in both cases); in the later eighteenth century these were joined by cotton, the leading component of the Industrial Revolution in Scotland, a supernova manufacture which was to flower gloriously and decay sadly within less than a hundred years. In the mid-nineteenth century came jute, a fibre imported from Bengal, the processing of which became a speciality of the Angus area, notably in 'juteopolis' Dundee itself. In terms of employment, the high-water mark of the Scottish textile sector came in the 1830s. Thereafter the steady adoption of labour-saving machinery in all stages of production from the dressing of the fibres to the finishing of the cloth reduced employment, although the aggregate volume and value of output continued to rise. The industry was never just concerned with cloth, important though that side was; amongst important ancillary activities were the manufactures of thread, carpets and linoleum. Of recent years, competition from elsewhere in the UK and abroad has led to some contraction in almost every branch of the natural fibre industry, with only a limited amount of diversification into synthetics to offset the decline.

It is hard to generalize about the development of textiles in Scotland as the experience of the component industries whether wool, flax, cotton, silk or jute, was far from uniform. For much of the eighteenth century, growth was concentrated on linen, the first Scottish textile manufacture to achieve an international reputation. Its increasing penetration of markets outside Scotland, in the face of fierce competition from the established producers of Ireland and Germany, was underpinned by a judicious government subsidy on exports to America and the West Indies for the coarser linen, such as Osnaburg in which the Scots excelled; its development was also assisted by the work of a public body, the Board of Trustees for Fisheries and Manufactures set up in 1727, and greatly stimulated by the British Linen Company, the very large-scale private undertaking chartered in 1746. Substantial though the growth of this industry was, with cloth output doubling every 20 years or so, before 1780 expansion induced relatively little change in the traditional domestic structure of the industry. Entrepreneurs did extend the giving-out system into more distant areas; spinning in particular became widely diffused from the Orkneys to the Borders, with local agents for Lowland manufacturers issuing dressed flax for spinning-up by the domestic workforce either on the spindle or more commonly the wheel, collecting the yarn when ready, and paying the women either in cash or kind. Essentially, output was raised by the recruitment of more labour, not through mechanization, save for a limited application of water-power to the scutching of flax. Equally, fixed capital investment was minimal, except in the finishing sector, in the many bleach- and print-fields set up throughout Scotland.

Nevertheless, there were some signs by the 1770s that the linen industry was being held back by shortages of yarn, caused in part by English demand for its use in the mixed linen-cotton fabrics of northwestern England. Paradoxically, therefore, the immediate impact of the advent of cotton with its new technology able to spin both warp and weft cotton yarn, was to permit linen to resume its growth in the east of Scotland, although cotton quickly supplanted the older industry in the west, drawing off labour, capital and management skills alike (as in the case of David Dale). The first cotton-spinning mills were scattered wherever there were adequate supplies of water, some being established by partnerships of Scottish and English entrepreneurs, in a sweep from Sutherland to Gatehouse-of-Fleet. But with the switch to larger, steam-powered mills c. 1800, yarn production became increasingly concentrated in west-central Scotland, with, however, important outposts at Aberdeen and Perth. The other textile industries were to follow the lead of cotton in the mechanization of spinning; it took time to develop satisfactory techniques for machine-spinning flax and wool. But slowly and surely, mill-spun yarn ousted the hand supplies first in flax, then in wool, and by the 1830s household spinning was an occupation in its last throes. This had serious social consequences for the many older or single women who had relied on hand-spinning to support themselves; for them the disappearance of this admittedly long and monotonous type of work was an economic disaster. Some of the younger women were able to stave off the evil day by switching into the much harder work of hand-loom weaving, but, as they were to find, that trade was only working out its notice.

Page after page of the first *Statistical Account* attests the prosperity of the handloom weavers—whether of linen, cotton or wool—in the 1790s; as one contemporary put it: 'there is a remarkable change ... their buildings, their expence (sic) of living and their dress, are almost totally changed'. Demand for textiles was booming, and ample supplies of yarn, mill or handspun, were assured; small wonder that these were the golden years of the craft. Things began to alter for the worse during the Napoleonic wars, however, and set firmly on a downwards path after 1815. From then on earnings (despite longer working hours) fell steadily in every branch of the weaving; from 21s.6d. per week in 1814 to a mere 6s. in 1830 in the case of the coarse linen weavers of Forfar. The basic problem was that the handloom weaver became caught between the hammer of mechanization, as viable power-looms were developed first in cotton, then in linen and finally in wool, and the anvil of oversupply of labour. Not only did women join the workforce but there was an increasing influx of Irish, something that the Scottish weavers were powerless to prevent. By the early 1830s there were over 85,000 weavers in Scotland (two-thirds in cotton) as against perhaps half that number 30 years previously. With the reduction in economic standing came also a loss of independence; more and more the weaver became tied to a particular manufacturer who decided whether or not there was work for him. In many towns and villages there was an increasing tendency for the weavers to be gathered together in workshops or weaving factories under supervision, instead of working individually at home, something that most detested. By the 1850s, the power-loom was in the ascendant, and handloom weaving became confined mostly to older men who could not learn new ways (the 'Auld Lichts of Thrums'); only in some branches of the woollen and specialist table-linen manufactures was resistance prolonged. With the handloom weaver went his culture; many had been avid amateur theologians, naturalists or political radicals, and of the weaver-poets William McGonagall is the most famous, if not the most able. The withering of weaving left a vacuum in many agricultural districts. The village weavers of Kincardineshire, Angus and Fife had long been an important source of seasonal labour for the harvest; they for their part,

with their wives and children, had often been glad of a break in the fields away from their damp, earthern-floored cottages.

By mid century, the factory not the home had become the centre of most textile production, and machine not human power the basis. First to be mechanized had been the spinning, then the ancillary processes like heckling—the strikes of the 'drouthy hecklers' of Dundee only hastened the end—and then, bit by bit, the weaving. One serious consequence was the reduction in male employment. In the 1880s there were still over 100,000 employed in Scottish textiles, but two-thirds of these were women; manual dexterity and low wages were the chief considerations, not physical strength. Initially, there was considerable resistance to work in the mills; many resented the impersonal discipline of the machine and the clock. The hated factory bell of one thread business at Huntly found its way into the nearby river Deveron, to the general satisfaction of the workforce. Conditions in mills and factories varied immensely. Perhaps the worst kind of work was in the wet-spinning flax mills of eastern Scotland, where to the long hours (progressively reduced) common to all factories was added the discomfort of often working in soaking clothing. In Dundee, the conditions of life were as bad outside the factories as within them, with the housing of the textile workforce a particular offence, despite the very large profits made in jute during the Victorian era. If jute dominated Dundee, the economies of other Scottish towns were equally dependent on textile staples, wool in Hawick, cotton thread in Paisley and so on; such dependence could be precarious. Competition from elsewhere in the UK or abroad began to intensify, not that that appears to have been the only factor in the decline of cotton which set in by the 1870s; low labour productivity and lethargic management played their part. Not all was gloom, however, even in cotton. There was some compensation for the total collapse of the Paisley shawl industry in the 1870s in the continuing growth of the cotton-thread sector; but generally the story in textiles was one of growing difficulty and stagnation, even in the hitherto expanding sectors of tweed and jute. The First World War offered some temporary relief, but the inter-war years saw many spinning mills of flax and cotton closed, with redundancies or short-time working widely experienced in other branches. Today the textile sector is not as large as it once was, however, with the reduction or demise of many traditional industries it still plays, in its alliance with the clothing industry, a major part in the economic life of the country. The traditional areas of high quality woollen and animal fibre knitwear and woven goods are still strong. The newer technologies based on synthetic materials hold their own and there are still companies, operating in niche market areas such as heart valves and breathable outerwear, who continue to find new end uses for textile products made in Scotland.

A.J. Durie and D. McKenna

Thomson, Alexander (1817–75). Although known as 'Greek' Thomson, it is not for his academic use of Greek motifs that

Alexander Thomson is revered. It was his powerful sense of architectural geometry, and his ability to use a wide variety of historical elements and fuse them into a dramatic and original personal style, that established his reputation.

Thomson was born in Balfron, Stirlingshire in 1817, the seventeenth of 20 children. After the death of his father in 1824, the family settled in Glasgow. The young Alexander worked first in a lawyer's office but his talent for sketching attracted the attention of an architect Robert Foote, who employed him as an apprentice in 1834. When Foote retired in 1836, Thomson became an assistant of John Baird I and in 1849 he finally established his own practice in partnership with John Baird II (no relation).

In the early years of his practice, his talent blossomed in the designs for a number of villas. One of the first was Craig Ailey, Kilcreggan (1850), an Italianate design with deep overhanging roofs, a design made more imposing by the use of a rustic rock plinth. A similar composition is used in the Knowe, Pollockshields (1852–53) and in the ingenious Double Villa at Langside (1856). The finest of this group is Holmwood in Cathcart (1857–58), a powerful arrangement of bold forms capped by his characteristic shallow roofs. The villa is decorated both inside and out with incised Greek ornament of the greatest refinement.

In his churches, although he used the Greek portico to great effect by poising it well above eye level, the towers of both Caledonia Road (1856) and St Vincent Street (1859) are compositions of remarkable originality. There are references to the Romanesque, to Assyrian, Egyptian and Indian architecture, but the dramatic effect overrides any consideration of sources.

In his designs for terrace housing, he was to achieve the same geometric clarity. Walmer Crescent (1857), Moray Place (1858–59) and Great Western Terrace (1867) all show the powerful hand of Thomson but have an individuality well suited to their sites.

Thomson's commercial buildings show no dilution of his architectural principles and confirm his will to experiment. For the Buck's Head Building in Argyle Street (1863), he designed one of the most elegant iron-fronted facades in the city. In the Egyptian Halls, Union Street (1871–73) his ability to maintain an intensity of architectural expression over a long facade is masterly.

By strict adherence to his principles, Thomson lost many commissions, but his single-mindedness gave his work a clarity and consistency which is rare in Victorian architecture. He both enjoyed and suffered the role of an isolated genius.

M. Higgs

Thomson, Derick S./Ruaraidh MacThómais (b. 1921) was born in Lewis and has for long been Professor of Celtic at Glasgow University. He is something of a phenomenon—or a node of many phenomena—and the worlds that meet in his poetry are multifarious. Although the synthesis is not yet complete, one can see that one day it will be; and at times one is bold enough to hope that his 'broken image' (dealbh briste)

will, with some future generation, be made whole again. He is a professor who is not an academic; someone who must be reckoned one of the Glasgow Establishment who is yet a Scottish Nationalist; a writer, now, of *vers libre* who is yet a master of the old forms and puts them to use and echoes them … one could go on. It is a confounding error to say in a facile way 'from the sheiling to Solzhenitsyn' and smile and pass on, for then you would miss things like:

Chunnaic mi ròs a' fàs air stalla na h-eachdraidh.

Some of his early lyrics are traditional masterpieces, but in 'Gaol is Gràdh' (*Saorsa agus an Iolaire*) he is where speech and sound meet.

Gaelic? The Lewisman saves the scholar from becoming a formalist. It is not only a *modus vivendi*, because, first and foremost, there is the poet coining and transmuting language:

leis a' chaile-chridhe-bianain,
leis a' mharcan-seachran-sìne,
leis an earball-saillte-sàile …
    (*An Rathad Cian*)

There are Lewis turns in plenty in his language—bothtaichean dubha … pruganan fraoich … tha mi dol a-steach gha mo gharadh—but one must always remember that he is a leading Celtic scholar.

It is obvious that he and Somhairle MacLean must have influenced one another, and in *An Rathad Cian*:

air cho fialaidh's gum bi briathran
aig a' cheann mu dheireadh
ruigidh sinn inbhe nam beathaichean snàgach …

he seems to echo Sorley with a deep resonance, and in *An Dealbh Briste* he sees the Coolin from the west in a way reminiscent of Sorley looking to it from the east.

To consider technique, a crucial aspect of all poetry today, we can take a hint from the fact that his first published poem is entitled 'Seann Orain' and that in *Saorsa agus an Iolaire* there are two renderings of prose poems by Alexander Solzhenitsyn.

leis a' chruas, leis a' chràdh,
leis a' chuimhne, leis a' chridhe …
    (*An Rathad Cian*)

is picked up again in *Saorsa agus an Iolaire* by 'an gràdh/ ag ràdh/ cràdh' and there is nothing weird in thinking of cynghanedd and 'D; aaanfhocail' and the experimental poem in his latest book, *Saorsa agus an Iolaire*, as interrelated. 'Smuaintean An Coire Cheathaich' (*An Dealbh Briste*) is, in form, a conventional Gaelic literary poem and 'Tràigh North Berwick'(*ibid.*) is a very beautiful folksong which begins:

An oidhch' ud air an tràigh dhuinn
cha b'ann fo mhulad bhà sinn… .

In *An Rathad Cian*:

leis a fheirg,
leis a' mheirg air mo bhilean …

aichill coincides with full English rhyme and there is alliteration, and there is double assonance in:

milsead ùr an fheòir is ...
air an ùr-dhòrtadh... .

There is hardly a line of Ruaraidh MacThómais's poetry in which the same complex technique is not to be observed.

His early lyrics have all the lyric magic, and it has persisted. 'Fàs is taise' (*An Rathad Cian*) opens wonderfully—Ceò mhìn 'na laigh' air na buailtean—but towards the end there is, almost brutally, —is thàinig an dolla á Hong Kong. 'Nuair thig an dorch' is lyric magic throughout. Almost all of Derick Thomson's work is very complex and allusive in many ways, form, content and other things. In 'An Odhrag' (*An Rathad Cian*) he says:

tha mi saor anns an apeur
's mi tuiteam.

Is it the lark, Màiri Mhór Nan Oran's lark in 'Nuair Bhà Mi Og', or the leap 'dans le néant' or both? —while 'saor' and 'speur' are consonant rhyme, being an instance of what I like to call the 'r sonore'.

Ann am meadhon Ghlaschu,
ann am meadhon mo bheatha,
ann am meadhon Alba,
'na mo shuidh air prugan ...
(*An Rathad Cian*)

What are his worlds? Lewis, Glasgow, Scotland, Europe, mankind in general. Viewed from Scotland, from Britain, from the British Isles, from Europe and from the world at large Ruaraidh MacThómais's nationalism is of prime importance. Two of his heroes are John MacLean and Douglas Young ('Armann', *An Rathad Cian*; 'Faoisgneadh', *An Dealbh Briste*) and Scotland haunts the first and latest of his books. In *An Dealbh Briste* we find:

Bratach na h-Albann a' mire ri'm chrìdh... .
sgal na pìob-móire, sgal-dòchais na h-Albann... .
sgal-dòchais na h-Albann, nach tuig thu, Mhicmeanmain.

and in *Saorsa agus an Iolaire* we meet with 'Fóghnan na h-Alba' and 'Na Ròmanaich an Albainn' and the courageous declamation about Seoc an Aonaidh (the Union Jack).

Derick Thomson is a very complex and vital poet, committed, a technician and a deep thinker with colloquial instants, a man of insight, a scholar who is glad to have fire in his belly and the man who has done more for Scottish Gaelic than any other man living.

Publications include: Collected Poems *Creachadh na Clàrsaich/Plundering the Harp*, published 1982, a section of 23 new poems and a large number of new English versions of the poems in general; *Bàrdachd na Roinn-Eòrpa/European Poetry in Gaelic*, published 1990, ed. Derick Thomson and *Smeur an Dòchais/Bramble of Hope*, published 1992 (50 poems, some of them extended sequences).

G.C. Hay

Thomson, George (1757–1851)

Thomson, George (1757–1851) Scottish song-book editor. Born Limekilns, Fife, 4 March; lived in Edinburgh from about 1774; died Leith, 18 February.

Thomson was an amateur musical enthusiast who devoted much of his life—and not a little of his money—to editing and publishing *A Select Collection of Original Scotish Airs* in six volumes (Edinburgh, 1793–1841). Thomson's editing method was to take already popular tunes and commission new lyrics for them from prominent living Scottish poets, coupling these with new musical arrangements (mostly for solo voice with violin, cello and piano) from prominent European composers. His poets included Burns, Scott, Hogg, Joanna Baillie, David MacBeth Moir, and David Vedder; his composers Pleyel, Kozeluch, Haydn, Beethoven, and Henry Bishop. Much of Thomson's correspondence with his contributors has been preserved.

Two main motives inspired the collection: Thomson's love of Viennese classical music, and his desire to 'clean up' traditional bawdy lyrics. In both, Thomson was a man of his age. Unfortunately, these aims had the effect of removing almost everything authentically Scottish from the collection, and it has remained a curiosity instead of becoming the standard classic which Thomson intended.

In 1847, aged nearly 90, Thomson contributed a lively account of the eighteenth-century Edinburgh Musical Society to Robert Chambers's *Traditions of Edinburgh*. It is also noteworthy that his granddaughter married Charles Dickens in 1836.

D. Johnson

Thomson, James/'BV' (1834–1882)

Thomson, James/'BV' (1834–1882), the son of a sea captain, was born at Port Glasgow. His mother, Sarah Kennedy, was a Galloway woman and a follower of the secessionist Edward Irving. When the boy was six, his father contracted paralysis. Two years later, the family moved to London, where the father lapsed into religious mania and hopeless invalidism. When the future poet was eight his mother died, and he was put into the Royal Caledonian Asylum to be educated.

Leaving there he became an army schoolmaster, and while stationed at Cork, fell in love with Matilda Weller, the daughter of a sergeant. Her death three years later distressed Thomson to the point of unbalance. He tried his hand at journalism and in business as a secretary to a mining company, then served as a war correspondent with the Carlist army in Spain. He failed in all three activities, and returned to London, where he was befriended by Kingsley and Meredith, but sank steadily into alcoholism.

Apart from some neatly finished verse trifles, and the rather sickly 'To Our Ladies of Death', Thomson's achievement is in the smoothly fashioned stanzas of *The City of Dreadful Night*, in which his total pessimism is deeper even than that of Leopardi (whose 'Dialogues' he translated). Basically, Thomson lamented:

The sense that every struggle brings defeat
Because Fate holds no prize to crown success;

That all the oracles are dumb or cheat
Because they have no secret to express …

His belief that 'all is vanity and nothingness' and his passionate declaration of the non-existence of the God of his Victorian contemporaries anticipate the 'flyped' Calvinism later propounded by his fellow-Clydesider John Davidson.

Thomson's admiration for Shelley and Novalis is reflected in his pseudonym, 'Bysshe Vanolis', the second word of which is an anagram of the German poet's name.

M. Lindsay

Thomson, James (1700–1748) was the son of the minister of Ednam, Roxburghshire who was soon called to nearby Southdean. The poet was educated at the village school, in Jedburgh and at Edinburgh University. However, his Divinity professor thought the style of one of Thomson's sermons 'too flowery', so Thomson left for London, taking with him part of what later became his poem 'Winter'. He was appointed tutor to the Earl of Haddington's son, Lord Binning, and was soon introduced to Pope, Arbuthnot and Gray. 'Winter' appeared in 1726 (the year of Ramsay's 'Gentle Shepherd'), followed by 'Summer'(1727), 'Spring' (1728), and 'Autumn' (1730), when the four sections were brought together as *The Seasons*.

Thomson had by this time also attempted writing for the stage with the tragedy of *Sophonisba*, which, though at first successful, contains one of the worst lines of English verse, 'Oh! Sophonisba, Sophonisba, oh!' parodied from the gallery as 'Oh! Jemmy Thomson, Jemmy Thomson, oh!'

In 1731, acting as tutor again, Thomson accompanied to the continent Charles Talbot, the son of the Lord Chancellor. On their return, Thomson received the sinecure of the Secretaryship of Briefs, a source of support he lost by failing to apply for its continuance from Talbot's successor.

Thomson returned to the stage with *Agamemnon* in 1738, and *Edward and Eleanora* in 1739, in which year the Prince of Wales granted him a pension of £100 per annum and he was made Surveyor-General of the Leeward Isles, a post which, after he had paid for a deputy to do the actual work, left him with a further £300 a year.

He retired to his villa at Richmond. With David Malloch (or Mallet) he wrote the *Masque of Alfred*, for which Arne provided music, and which included Thomson's 'Rule, Britannia'. Two more plays followed: *Tancred and Sigismundo* in 1745 and *Coriolanus* in 1748, the year in which Thomson published the two cantos of his allegorical poem in the Spenserian stanza, *The Castle of Indolence*. In August of that year he caught a chill, developed a fever and died in his forty-eighth year. He seems to have been a much liked easy-going man who did not marry, it is said, because he discovered that his love for Elizabeth Young was not returned.

There are evocative descriptions of nature in *The Seasons*, couched in melodious blank verse. Terms such as 'the finny race' for 'fish' may jar the modern reader, but they are simply the eighteenth century's equivalent to the 'aureate termis' of the Scots Makars 'high style'. An extract from 'Winter' gives a taste of Thomsonian flavour:

As yet the trembling year is unconfirmed,
And Winter oft at eve resumes the breeze,
Chills to pale morn, and bids his driving sleets
Deform the day delightless; so that scarce
The bittern knows his time with bill engulfed
To shake the sounding marsh; or from the shore
The plovers when to scatter o'er the heath,
And sing their wild notes to the listening waste.

Unlike his poem 'Liberty', which Dr Johnson gave up attempting to read, 'The Castle of Indolence' achieves a sensuousness that foreshadows Tennyson's 'The Lotus Eaters'. The first canto describes the haunt of Indolence, where there

Was nought around but images of rest:
Sleep-soothing groves, and quiet lawns between;
And flowery beds that slumberous influence kest,
From poppies breathed; and beds of pleasant
Where never yet was creeping creature seen. [green,

Thomson heired the nature-painting tradition of the Scots Makars. The sensibility he passed on, however, might be said to have affected the whole future course of poetry in English.

M. Lindsay

Tinkers, The. In Scotland and Ireland, as well as in parts of Scandinavia, there are still to be found nomadic or quasi-nomadic groups whose way of life resembles that of the gypsies, although they have little or no gypsy blood in them. It is impossible to speak with certainty of their origin, but it seems likely that they are the descendants of a very ancient caste of itinerant metal-workers whose status in tribal society was probably high. One of the trades associated with them from early times was that of tin-smith, and it is clear that to primitive man the ability to use metals seemed very close to magic; consequently, both 'black' and 'white' smiths for long enjoyed immense prestige, not only as craftsmen but as wielders of secret powers.

When the gypsies arrived in western and northern Europe in the fifteenth and sixteenth centuries, there was no doubt a certain amount of biological and sociocultural mixing between them and the aboriginal itinerants whom they encountered (and in some areas appear to have displaced). In certain regions a measure of fusion took place between the two groups, and a mixed 'tinkler-gypsy' race came into being, but at the present day the gypsies and tinkers view each other as quite distinct groupings, and there is not much love lost between them.

The ranks of the Scots tinkers have been augmented at various periods as a result of events in the country's troubled history. Some of the tinker groupings make up a kind of 'underground' clan system of their own, and individuals are intensely conscious of kinship and family ties. They want nothing to do with tramps and other solitaries, feeling themselves as distinct from this type of itinerant as they are from the Romany gypsies. A very intelligent tinker youth once put the distinction in a nutshell when, referring to an Irish tramp who used to wander around Scotland, he declared: 'That sort of lad just lives from day to day, but we (tinkers) live entirely in the past.' (It should be stressed that the term 'tinker' itself is disliked by the fraternity because of its frequent use in a derogatory context; tinkers call themselves 'travellers'.)

Unlike the true gypsies, whose language is (or used to be) Romany, the tinkers use a cover-language known as 'cant'. The cant of the tinkler-gypsies of Galloway and southeast Scotland has quite a strong admixture of Romany in it, but north of the Forth-Clyde line the amount of recognizable Romany in the cover-tongue is hardly more than 15 per cent. The tinkers of the north and west, whose native language is Gaelic (or was, until very recently), have a cover-tongue of their own which resembles one of the secret languages of Ireland. Their name for it is 'Beurlacheard', or 'lingo of the cairds' (the tinkers). That this is a very ancient cover-tongue is shown by the fact that some of the vocabulary which it reflects and deforms is archaic Gaelic.

Like the gypsies, tinkers sometimes make money by telling fortunes. Quite a number are believed (by themselves and others) to possess the gift of 'second sight'. Belief in the existence of fairies is still very widespread among them. There are in the archives of the School of Scottish Studies a large number of supernatural tales recorded from tinker informants; these include stories about brownies, elves, changelings, water-kelpies, fairy funerals, fairy music heard by mortals, and—last but not least—'a wee green man' seen in the Sma' Glen. Ghosts are feared, though there are but few tales of them harming living persons. Belief in witches and the black art is also common.

One rather curious item of tinker folklore deserves mention. A sort of mystical aura surrounds the name of the MacPhees, one of the Scots tinker clans. The MacPhees are regarded by some as the 'original' tinkers, the 'first on the road', but even so an undoubted 'hoodoo' seems to lie over their very name: it is bad luck to hear or speak the name MacPhee, and a substitute name such as MacFud, MacaFud or MacaTuttie is supposed to be used in place of it.

Although the 'flattie' (non-tinker) population for long feared that the tinkers were child-stealers (witness the lullaby 'Hush ye! Hush ye! Dinna fret ye! The black Tinkler winna get ye!), the folklore of the tinkers shows clearly and even poignantly that they lived in much greater fear of the ordinary population than the 'flatties' did of them. This persecution complex found, and still finds, expression in gruesome folklore about 'burkers' (body-snatchers) who were supposed to be continually on the wait to waylay and murder travelling folk, and sell their bodies to the anatomy schools. Paraded by an accomplished storyteller at the camp-fire, the ghoulish trappings of the burker stories conjure up a phantasmagoric *grand guignol* world reminiscent of Dylan Thomas's 'The Doctor and the Devils'. Lum-hatted black-frockcoated 'noddies' (medical students) drive the 'burker's coach' into the country-

side to try and find isolated tinker encampments; the coach is long and black-draped, looking like a hearse; blood-hounds lope silently beside it; the horse's harness is swathed in cloth to prevent it chinking; the horse's hooves have rubber pads on them. In some of the stories the tinker victim gets his throat cut, and his relatives discover too late that he is missing; in others, there are hair's-breadth escapes from the villainous doctors and 'noddies.'

Although we can well believe that defenceless ragged nomads were occasionally the victims of murderous body-snatchers, we must probably look further back in history in order to understand the deeper-lying reasons for this persecution complex. In the seventeenth century it was a capital crime in Scotland merely to be an 'Egyptian'—Egyptian, for the courts, meaning not merely a gypsy, but any sort of wanderer, vagabond minstrel or travelling tinsmith of no fixed abode. If it could be proved that a travelling man of uncertain occupation was 'halden and repute to be an Egyptian', he was as good as dead. Among the victims of this law was the famous fiddler James MacPherson, who was hanged at Banff in 1700; his name is immortalized in the folksong 'MacPherson's Rant', which survives on the lips of present-day tinker singers.

H. Henderson

Todd, Ruthven (1914–78), the son of an Edinburgh architect, was schooled at Fettes, from which he embarked on a literary career. For a short time he edited from Edinburgh the periodical *The Scottish Bookman*. After his first marriage, which produced a son but ended in divorce, he took a job as a copywriter with a London advertising agency. During the war he worked for a time in civil defence, and then in a Charing Cross Road bookshop. In 1944 he moved to Tilty Mill House, near Dunmow, Essex. At one stage he lent the house to the painters Colquhoun and McBryde and a Scottish poet (called by Todd 'Bothy Scots') who sold off some of his most prized possessions and otherwise indulged in vandalism, in return for his generosity, a betrayal and a loss that distressed him for the rest of his life. He left for America in 1947 and in 1959 became an American citizen. His remaining years were spent in Martha's Vinyard, in Mallorca (in a cottage lent to him by Robert Graves) and finally in Greenwich Village, New York.

Todd was one of those gifted people who never quite achieve what is expected of them. His vein of Kafkaesque prose fantasy, first revealed in *Over the Mountain* (1939), was succeeded by *The Lost Traveller*, published in 1944 but actually written 1935. Although *The Lost Traveller* had a considerable success in America among younger readers when it reappeared in 1968, Todd did not follow this line through. He became an expert on Blake, and was twice awarded Guggenheim Fellowships, though in neither case did the expected book result.

His best poetry is mostly his earliest, contained in *Until Now* (1941) and *The Acreage of the Heart* (1944). In it he reflects on his Scottish ancestry and upbringing, or on the contrast between human frailness and the relentless destruction of wartime London, through colloquially mannered verse with freshly observed imagery:

I was born in this city of grey stone and bitter
Of tenements sooted up with lying history;   [wind,
This place where dry minds grow crusts of hate, as
Grow lichen ...   [rocks

His collected poems appeared in London under the title *Garland for a Winter Solstice* (1961). His splendid studies of Blake, Fuseli and John Martin, *Traces in the Snow* (1946), though never republished, is in some ways his finest prose achievement, has been much quoted from and is worthy of re-issue. Although none of his autobiographical writing has appeared outside America, of particular interest to us in Scotland should be *In the House of my Father*, a book about growing up in Scotland.

M. Lindsay

Tovey, Donald Francis (b. 1875, Eton; d. 1940, Edinburgh), son of an Eton schoolmaster, graduated with a first class honours degree in music from Balliol College, Oxford in 1898. He began his early professional career as a pianist, composer and concert organizer in London. Apart from his own concerts, he regularly appeared in recitals given by the Classical Concerts Society. In 1913 he achieved a notable success as the soloist in the premiere of his own Piano Concerto, in the Queen's Hall, under the baton of Sir Henry Wood.

When, in 1914, he was appointed Reid Professor of Music at the University of Edinburgh, his scholarly abilities came to the fore. Until his retirement in 1939 he remained the tireless conductor of the Reid Orchestra. As a writer, lecturer and composition teacher his influence was widespread. His analytical programme notes, collected in the famed *Essays in Musical Analysis* (1935–39), still remain unchallenged in the field of narrative musical analysis and criticism. He is also remembered for his work on Beethoven and for his edition and completion of Bach's *Art of Fugue*—perhaps his greatest single scholarly achievement.

His music, notable for its Brahmsian seriousness of purpose and extended musical argument, includes an opera, *The Bride of Dionysus* (1907–18), Symphony (1913), Cello Concerto (1935), beloved of Pablo Casals, for whom it was written, *Sonata Eroica* for solo violin and many other large-scale chamber and instrumental works.

P. Hindmarsh

Townscape belongs to everybody. But it is only seen through one's own pair of eyes, and there is nothing like the first excitement of seeing places for oneself. Since I began my own discovery of Scottish towns nearly 30 years ago, many of them have changed for better or worse. Drab towns (of which we have plenty, especially if one just drives through them) have become drabber; the suburbs of my native London, although so different, gave me a taste for this particular quality. Many

good things have simply disappeared, like the exciting narrowness of Dundee's Wellgate, and the majority of the handsome shop-fronts that gave extra distinction to the streets of Cupar. Overdone or ill-judged restoration, which can sever the vital connection between a place and its function, is not unknown. But this is not about conservation, still less a lament for past glories. Townscape is a matter of the present time.

First then for the discoverer of Scottish towns (as to me in the early 1950s) there is Edinburgh. Arrival at Waverley station puts you right in the middle of it, in the cleft between Old and New Towns. To the south is the castle rock, like the parent of the big smoke-weathered stones of which the city is built; and its long tail down which the Royal Mile finds its way to the turreted palace of Holyroodhouse, presenting to the inside the two faces of a stone corridor, to the outside a craggy silhouette that is man-made (mainly by historically conscious Victorians), and yet seems natural in its freakish permanence. At the east and west ends of this clear cut line stand respectively Edinburgh's acropolis (the Calton Hill, with its glorious failure of a Parthenon) and a mysterious cluster of spires, Gothic and Venetian. To the north of it the New Town extends. Princes Street, in the forefront, denies its Georgian origin since its regimented blocks, under the castle's command, are filled with monuments of Victorian commerce. Across the valley between Old and New Towns lie William Playfair's calm Grecian galleries.

This extraordinary panorama, in which to specify a single landmark is to omit several others, is Scotland's supreme collaboration of nature, history and architecture. But like all good townscapes it contains an invitation—indeed a hundred invitations—to explore further. Here are some examples at random. In the the Royal Mile I would pick the odd experience of finding Advocates' Close, one of the many small openings in the flat masonry frontage, and looking through its arched pend down stone steps into space, with the giant Gothic spire of the Scott Monument appearing a blackened miniature far below. In the New Town there is the moment when James Craig's central vista, splendid in its plan but thus far hesitant and fragmented in its architecture, opens out into the mature unity of Robert Adam's Charlotte Square. Then there are the later New Towns (each one was given this name at the time of its planning), stretching out into the whole northern half of the compass. Thus the downhill, apparently unstoppable vista which changes its name three times (Frederick, Howe and St Vincent Streets), lined with big tenements stepped precariously down the slope, is suddenly confronted by the tower and huge doorway of St Stephen's Church and must swerve to the left towards the little centre of Stockbridge, which was the only sensible direction it could take anyway. Here Ann Street, beyond the river crossing, plays at being a grand urban terrace behind its pretty front gardens. And what about the outer spread of the city? Here we see the villas and the remorselessly bay-windowed lines of tenements, all of the finest stone; and further, the twentieth-century housing which is for the most part grandiose on the map, yet miserable in execution, lacking the diversity which should be the essence of a living-space shared by many people.

A glance at a street map can give the first clue to any townscape and the way it has evolved. Glasgow's plan is vastly different from that of Edinburgh, and the distinction between 'organic' medieval development and formal Georgian expansion, though equally obvious, is far less dramatic and clear-cut. Of the old city only the landmarks remain; the blackened but splendid cathedral of St Mungo, one priceless but isolated house, and the three widowed steeples of the Tolbooth, the Tron and the former hall of the bold seventeenth-century merchants who defied Charles II's Navigation Laws. Otherwise we now have little but the names of the streets, since the pride of Jacobean Glasgow has been swept away by Victorian progress, and the latter has declined into chaos or desolation. Rottenrow (the cathedral canons' walk) is probably luckiest, for it has a new if bewildering townscape of academic buildings; they belong to Strathclyde University, those of the older university having migrated westwards in the 1860s to make way for a railway goods yard, now defunct.

Georgian Glasgow, unlike Georgian Edinburgh, leaves you in no doubt that it has taken over the function of town centre from its medieval predecessor. Its gridiron plan, in which the street names tell the story of commercial success (beginning with Virginia), spread steadily to the west and culminated in Blythswood Square. This, on its hilltop, is more or less intact, and likewise the great Georgian monuments of the Royal Exchange (now Stirling's Library) and St George's Church have survived, each closing a vista and hemmed in, Glasgow fashion, by a square. Adam's Trades House still stands in Glassford Street, and here and there a Georgian house or town mansion can still be found; most evocative of late Georgian prosperity is the intimate, half-deserted space of Virginia Court. Much of the remainder has been swept away by the mighty tide of Victorian redevelopment. And lest anyone should be turned away by that fact, it should be remembered that Glasgow was a place where Victorian confidence was fully matched by architectural excellence. So this compact centre is a place of continual astonishment, each regular street-corner being turned to reveal the works of great architects on their mettle; Greek Thomson, the Burnets and many others, till we come to Mackintosh's decisive rejection of historical style at the famous Art School. Further west beyond Sauchiehall Street appears the strange silhouette of Charles Wilson's Trinity College, a cluster of *campanili* on Woodside Hill. And yet further, the long palatial terraces of Great Western Road. As to the Gorbals, and other tracts of sub-standard housing that should have earned equal notoriety, it is for other writers to say whether their present state is better or worse than their past. If you go for a walk in any of these places you will see fragments of new housing surrounded by huge deserts of flattened rubble—the townscape of moral indignation and unfulfilled plans.

These two great cities, less than 50 miles apart, form the urban axis of Scotland. What about the rest? A townscape gazetteer would overflow this volume, so I can only attempt some generalizations to guide an imaginary visitor who shares my tastes.

The fabric of Scottish towns is mainly Georgian and Victorian, even where earlier layouts and landmarks (such as churches) have survived. Many places still have the odd town residence of a landed family from the seventeenth century or even before, but for a whole townscape of that date one must go to the little town of Culross on the north side of the Forth estuary. Famous for coal, salt and blacksmith-work, it was made a Royal Burgh by James VI and then slowly declined, the railway adding insult to injury by taking away not only its trade but its harbour. Thanks to restoration by the National Trust for Scotland it is still there today, with some 50 houses of the period (the earliest dated 1577) along the former waterfront or huddled along the steep causeways which come together at the mercat cross. Their walls are all of harled rubble except at the edges, with here and there a carved lintel or shop-sign; the windows small, irregular and suspicious-looking. What can a Dutch merchant from a rich, showy seaport like Veere or Hoorn have thought of this poky, smoky little place and the oddly small crowsteps on the house gables? Only the wrought stone of the old abbey up the hill, the proud monuments in the kirkyard and the new mansion nearby with its terraced gardens will have impressed him.

The medieval plan of St Andrews, at the furthest tip of Fife, is based on three streets converging on the cathedral. This was essentially a place of pilgrimage, only made into a Royal Burgh in 1620. Most towns, beginning with the 14 that are known to have been planted by David I, have their origins in trade and therefore in transport. A river-crossing as near as possible to the sea was a favourite site; both Ayr and Dumfries still have their medieval bridges. The position of Edinburgh and Stirling was obviously decided by defence, but otherwise the main streets correspond with the main routes, widening out in the middle for market use and lined with burgess houses. Montrose still has one of the most impressive of these multi-purpose streets, and although its town hall is Georgian and the beautiful church spire very nearly Victorian, there remain a few of the narrow gable-end frontages for which the town was well known; and behind the continuous building-line some nice examples of rig development. The building-over of rigs, or back gardens, is not of course an exclusively Scottish habit, but nowhere else was it such a systematic and intensive process as when Scottish towns were required to expand within themselves. Thus through an arched pend one leaves the big public space of the high street or *hie gait* to enter a narrow close, lined on each side with dwellings and often terminated by a grander house at the bottom of the old garden. Edinburgh's tenemented closes are the most famous, but those of Elgin are particularly worth exploring, and few of Scotland's older towns have completely lost them; some of the best are naturally the most neglected. Only St Andrews retains a number of old rigs in their original use, along with others built over in this way.

Towns that are ribbon-developed along important routes are specially vulnerable to the sort of change that exploits a much-frequented site and, in the end, to the pressure of traffic which can grow to the point where it actually obstructs the access to buildings and prevents their proper use. Linlithgow now has an efficient by-pass which enables people to live once again in the upper storeys of its long high street, but the main routes through many towns like Falkirk and Kirkcaldy are the scene of a straight fight between traffic and shopping. Minor 'road improvements' to ease the flow of vehicles at one place often have the effect of moving the pressure somewhere else. Widened sightlines, one-way systems, the junk of lights, arrows, notices and barriers, all are self-defeating and all are the enemies of townscape.

From about the middle of the eighteenth century, when Scotland was seeing its way to becoming a rich country instead of a poor one, there is a sudden increase in every kind of town building. Kirks and town halls and handsome town mansions appear, at first rather pompous but increasingly graceful as the century goes on. So do the rows of plain cottages built for or by manual workers (particularly weavers, like James Barrie's father at Kirriemuir), and that most Scottish type of urban dwelling—the big plain tenement with a gabled chimney-stalk midway along the front wall. There is a veritable procession of these along Nicolson Street in Edinburgh, and among many others the tenement built in their high street by the shoemakers of Banff can be mentioned, because this is one of the best places to see the Georgianizing of an already distinctive old town.

Most towns also had a formally planned Georgian extension. An enterprising landlord with a well sited field would commission from an architect a layout which the advertisement would call 'regular', and designs for terraces (or latterly villas) that were almost always 'elegant'. They were built by owner-occupiers or by speculative builders for re-sale, but both would have to stick to the drawings and other conditions, and pay an annual duty to the original landlord as feudal superior. The system of feudal control is now on the way out; its successor is planning control which can be just as strict, especially if the buildings are officially listed or in a conservation area. Perth, an unusual town in its original compact layout, also has the most distinctive of all Georgian expansions. Masterminded by Thomas Hay Marshall the Provost, it consists not of a closed pattern of streets but a ring of outward-looking terraces which greet you as you approach from the north or south over the green, well planted 'Inches'.

Even more striking is the appearance on the Georgian map of Scotland of some 200 totally new towns and villages. They started at the beginning of the eighteenth century with re-founded villages like Kinross or Gifford, the old settlement having been displaced by the building or improvement of a great country seat. Inveraray, with its long arcaded frontispiece facing Loch Fyne, is the grandest and one of the latest of these transplanted towns. Then there were the towns and villages set up to serve as marketing and even manufacturing centres for improved agricultural land—some of the earliest in East Lothian (Saltoun and Ormiston) and the most numerous and successful in Aberdeenshire, including Keith and Huntly. Fishertowns, sometimes government backed, sprang up even

on the remotest parts of the coast. their habit is to point their gables to the sea, each cottage or terrace standing in the lee of the next. Most specialized of all are the water-powered mill-towns like New Lanark on the Clyde and the lesser-known Stanley on the Tay, or Deanston on the river Teith, whose industrial buildings have luckily found a new use as a distillery.

If the industrial townscape was a mere adjunct to the Georgian age, it was an essential part of the Victorian way of life. Heavy engineering paid for the sumptuous houses of Glasgow's Park circus. Workers from the crowded tenements of Hilltown operated the grand mills of Dundee (many of them still standing) to the greater glory of the Jute Kings in their giant suburban palaces which are now practically a thing of the past. It is too easy to moralize about Victorian society and Victorian taste; and at the same time to forget that high quality was a hallmark of most Victorian building. As to their housing, its chief defect today is not so much in poor space-standards and amenities (these after all can be improved), but in recent neglect and bad management for which the Victorians can hardly be blamed. At least there is no moral excuse for condemning the splendid inheritance that has survived.

The main Victorian contribution to the Scottish scene is a whole range of new or revived building types which took their places excellently in the established towns; the banks that acknowledge the classical ancestry of the neighbouring Georgian houses, the churches punctuating the long vista, the baronial town halls and well built, airy board-schools. Few town centres have a dominant Victorian character; Inverness, which can still claim this, is in danger of losing it. but no town of any importance lacks some reminder of the age when Scotland, with excellent craftsmen and scholarly, imaginative architects, was able at last to exploit one of its greatest natural resources—its universal wealth of good stone.

Stone gives every Scottish town its characteristic colour, and, because diversity is part of the essence of towns, its chances for interesting deviation. Thus Edinburgh, with miles of hard yellow sandstone from the Craigleith and Hailes quarries, was shocked (but in the long term enhanced) by the red sandstone imported from Dumfriesshire for the Venetian gothic Portrait Gallery at the far end of Queen Street's dignified Georgian parade. Glasgow, whose own sandstone from Giffnock does not weather so well or so beautifully, welcomed the invasion and particularly enjoyed using red stone for tall and narrow redevelopments about the turn of the century. Most spectacular is the Clydesdale Bank in Buchanan Street, striped red and cream like a layer cake, which used to be one of Miss Cranston's tea-rooms. In Dumfries itself there are very few contrasts; it is almost entirely (painted Georgian fronts being the only departure) a deep, beefy red. And since this stone is easily carved when fresh from the quarry, the Victorian masons set on it with glee. Their rich, half-vernacular carving makes Dumfries the one major exception to the rule of discipline and scholarship in Victorian Scotland. Further to the southwest there is Creetown granite, and granite of much the same pale grey colour is of course the staple material in Aberdeen. Hardest of all building stones to work (except for the tough whinstone of many parts of Scotland which can only be squared to random sizes) it is seen first in the rough, at the cathedral and chanonry of Old Aberdeen; then mechanically sawn and dressed in the austere Georgian terraces of Aberdeen itself. Archibald Simpson was the architect who devised an architectural language for this intractable stone. But it was also he who designed the tall red brick spire of the combined Free Churches, a pointed gesture of defiance in the midst of his own granite city. Brick, indeed, tends to crop up in any town that could produce it and wherever absolute uniformity was not required.

These and many other local variations survive in the historic townscape, but are seldom seen in today's buildings—still less in today's towns—for architects tend to select their materials out of a list of nationally available products. In the maintenance and repair of old buildings it is important that traditional and local materials shall be insisted upon, and the the necessary skills shall be kept profitably at work. But architecture is only one of the elements of townscape. The main one is use. Usefulness is what makes a town, and its guardian (though never its originator) is the town planner with his armoury of controls. Diversity of use is essential to the public sections of a town, just as single use is vital to the more private ones. If most people would sooner live in the carefully tended diversity of Haddington than in one of the segregated compartments of Cumbernauld, it is not just because Haddington is older, more deeply rooted in time and place. It is because it works.

C. McWilliam

Trade Unionism. Evidence of organizations of craft workers in eighteenth-century Scotland abounds. In some cases these associations of journeymen were essentially friendly societies, collecting funds for widows, orphans and the sick, but they could, on occasion, become the focus for industrial action against employers. This tended to happen more often when the traditional pattern of the fixing of wages by local justices of the peace began to fall into disuse. Groups of workers sought to maintain fixing of 'fair prices' by local magistrates, when the alternative was the downward pressure on wages of unregulated competition; but JPs proved less and less willing to interfere in relations between employers and employed. When the Lanarkshire weavers' union in 1812 sought to get a fair rate fixed by the magistrates, they found that although their right to do so was accepted, employers were able to defy the rulings with impunity. Indeed the leaders of the weavers' union found themselves imprisoned for the offence of combining in a union—the first time the action of simple combination had been regarded as an offence in Scotland.

In spite of the dangers of legal action, unions grew and spread in early nineteenth-century Scotland. In almost all cases they were organizations of craftsmen such as printers, tailors and shoemakers, whose aims were largely defensive. Their aim was to maintain the customary craft relationships and rates of wages, in the face of an industrializing society, which was bringing new employers and new workers into the trades and where division of labour allowed a variety of half-skilled workers to undertake tasks formerly confined to skilled, time-served men. Even the new factory workers, like the cotton spinners, organized from about 1810 in the powerful Glasgow Association of Operative Cotton Spinners, tended to follow the pattern of the older craft unions, by seeking to keep 'incomers' out of the union and, therefore, out of a job.

The continuing development of industrial techniques, together with the pressure of population in growing cities, made it more and more difficult to restrict entry and there were occasional outbreaks of violence against non-unionists. The extent to which violence was an integral part of early Scottish unionism has tended to be exaggerated, and the severe sentences of seven years' transportation imposed upon the leaders of the Associated Cotton Spinners' Union in 1838 were largely a response by the authorities to the rapid growth of trade unions which came about amid expanding trade in the early 1830s. Some of these unions were attracted by ideas of cooperative production being spread by such Owenites as Alexander Campbell, but, on the whole, the Scottish unions seem to have seen such schemes as a useful way of keeping unemployed workers out of the labour market. Few felt that they were a viable alternative to the capitalist system.

All the early unions were vulnerable to economic fluctuations and a defeat in a major strike was likely to mean the collapse of the union. Yet, generally, organizations quickly revived. Scottish unions tended to remain locally based, but from the late 1840s there were amongst the trades attempts to link local unions in national organization. In almost all cases, these national unions were federal in structure, with power and funds kept firmly in local hands, and there was little of the trend towards centralization which distinguished much of English unionism in the mid nineteenth century. One of the most significant federal unions to emerge was the United Coal and Iron Miners' Association of Scotland in 1855, largely the work of Alexander McDonald who persuaded county miners' unions to cooperate. This, in turn, stimulated a British-wide organization.

Another important mid-century development was the growth of trades councils consisting of representatives of local unions. The aim of these was to provide a forum for a variety of issues that affected the working class, but could not readily be discussed by individual unions. There had been earlier attempts at united action to deal with specific crises affecting unions, but it was only with the formation of an Edinburgh Council of Trades' Delegates in the mid 1850s and of the Glasgow United Trades Council in 1858 that permanent organizations were established. The Dundee and the Aberdeen Trades Councils followed in 1867 and 1868. Because of the lack of powerful national organizations in Scotland, trades councils attained a great importance within the Scottish trade-union movement.

Although all trades had union organization of some kind by the last quarter of the century, the striking feature of Scottish trade unionism was its weakness. The majority of workers were not organized (less than 4 per cent of the population in

1892): unions were generally unable to resist wage reductions or to maintain any kind of control over employment, with the result that Scottish earnings tended to be below English levels. Scottish employers were, on the whole, slow to accept the value of trade unions within an industrial relations system. Few of the Scottish unions developed a comprehensive range of friendly benefits, which could give unions stability, and there were frequent fluctuations in membership. It was the weakness of craft unionism that partly explains the readiness of Scottish skilled men to encourage the organization of unskilled workers and there was a remarkable spread of unionism among formerly unorganized groups of workers from the 1880s onwards.

Trades councils continued to play a central role and, in the late nineteenth century, they became a forum for the often heated political discussion which the spread of socialist ideas stimulated. In Glasgow and other cities trades councils gave backing to independent working-men candidates in both local and general elections and campaigned for issues such as municipal housing and municipal ownership of public utilities. It was on the initiative of trades councils that a Scottish Trades Union Congress was formed in 1897 to deal with specifically Scottish issues. At the first Congress in Glasgow some 55 organizations with over 40,000 members were represented, out of a Scottish trade-union movement of around 150,000.

From the 1890s, many of the English-based unions began recruiting north of the border. These stronger and generally more efficient unions had more to offer members than had the smaller and weaker Scottish ones and UK-wide unions were a logical response to UK-wide firms. Some purely Scottish unions remained, but amalgamations became increasingly common: for example, the Scottish Railways Servants went into the Amalgamated Society of Railways Servants in 1893, the Scottish Associated Carpenters into the Amalgamated Carpenters in 1911.

On the political side, the Scottish trade-union movement showed a particular dynamism, and it was largely as a result of political activities that the west of Scotland labour movement began to acquire the reputation of 'red Clydeside', a reputation that was in marked contrast to that of earlier decades. Politically active socialists came forward during the years of the First World War to give leadership at shop-floor level as shop stewards to the skilled workers. They appeared particularly among the engineering workers in Glasgow's large munitions industry, who were faced with the problems of dilution of labour when the work-force expanded rapidly to meet the insatiable need for shells on the western front. Strikes and the anti-war speeches of a few like John MacLean confirmed Clydeside's reputation for militancy. Yet, what militancy there was was limited and sporadic and the 40-hours strike among engineering workers on the Clyde in January 1919 proved to be not, as some hoped and others feared, the beginning of the revolution, but rather the end of a brief period of militant unrest.

Since a high proportion of the Scottish work force was in those older staple industries most affected by the inter-war

slump, Scotland suffered particularly badly during these years. The unions could offer little response and the process of absorption of purely Scottish unions continued. From time to time, Communist Party groups sought to instil some fervour into the membership and the Minority Movement was particularly active in the 1920s among Fife and Lanarkshire miners. On the whole, however, unemployment levels which rose as high as 16 per cent of the working population, discouraged any kind of forward policy.

In a survey of unions taken by the Scottish Trades Union Congress in 1924 there were estimated to be some 536,000 trade unionists in Scotland, 11 per cent of the population, which was a considerably lower proportion than for the United Kingdom as a whole. In 1947, when a further survey was made after a war in which trade-union organization had been officially encouraged, the Scottish trade-union movement had risen to around 900,000 members, 17.7 per cent of the population and only slightly less then the UK proportion. In 1944, as in 1924, there was a marked concentration of trade unionism in those industries which predominated in west central Scotland. Since 1947, however, the growth of new industries outside this area, together with the growth of unionism in formerly poorly organized sectors, particularly in white-collar jobs, has meant a more even spread of unionism. Membership of the STUC reached a peak of 1.09 million members in the 1970s, but since then has declined. Under the double onslaught of changing economic and industrial conditions and government hostility, membership of unions has fallen back to the levels of the 1950s and 1960s. Once powerful areas such as the National Union of Miners have lost more than 80 per cent of their membership in a decade and a similar picture is to be found across the manufacturing industry. In contrast, professional, white-collar unions such as the EIS have been relatively successful at holding its 45,000 strong membership and NALGO membership has increased substantially. Scotland, however, remains a relatively heavily unionised area compared with most other regions of the UK, and the STUC has been remarkably successful in making its voice heard on a range of issues.

W. H. Fraser

Tramways played a major part in the urban geography of developing Scotland, in the industrialized west, in the major conurbations of the east coast. Smaller systems plied in centres such as Stirling and Perth, Kirkcaldy and Dunfermline before the motor-car made them redundant in the 1930s; holiday systems at Rothesay or Ayr suffered extinction at much the same time. Oddities like the short line from station to hotel in Cruden Bay succumbed for much the same reasons—competition from motor traffic, and mounting costs which rendered short or lightly trafficked lines impossible to justify against the cheaper and rapidly more reliable bus and motor-car.

In the cities things were quite different. Some systems were never modernized, but carefully and economically maintained till sheer obsolescence caught up with them—notably Dundee, where in the mid-1950s almost everything fell due for replacement at once, and the cheaper and easier alternative of scrapping was chosen. Aberdeen, too, kept its old material running well, but there tracks and equipment were considerably more modern, including superlative bogie trams a mere nine years old when they were scrapped. Edinburgh had a staid and old-fashioned hard-working medium city system, an efficient mover of crowds, ideally adapted to its hilly contours and tight corners. Maintenance was at all times meticulous and new cars were built up till 1950; here too a strange and indecent haste to abandon brought about total extinction in six years. By 1958 (when Aberdeen's last cars ran) only one system remained.

Glasgow's trams were legendary for their number, their quality, their route colours, their exotic termini such as 'Auchenshuggle', their exploits in war and peace in shifting crowds, their 'Green Goddess' modern cars second-hand from Liverpool, their own 'Coronation' and 'Cunarder' modern cars (some dating from 1954) which represented the peak of modern British practice. Glasgow's was a big-city system with substantial sections of reserved tracks, and ideal rush-hour conditions for the tram to operate in its best environment, the fast and safe shifting of crowds in a dense city pattern. Not even here could the tram survive, and by 1962 Glasgow's legendary trams were a memory. There electric suburban railways and modernized underground lines have partially replaced them. Otherwise the diesel bus is the universal mode of transport.

In the energy debate of the 1970s and later the decision to abandon a highly efficient electric mode of transport, free of pollution and running on locally generated energy, may well seem to have been hasty and short-sighted. Local politics played a large part, and the financial arguments were often superficially carried through. Certainly costs for installing modern tramways ('light rapid transit') are very high, yet justified in conurbations such as Glasgow and, to a more marginal extent, Edinburgh. In efficiency and social value these costs may well be justified, as they are very widely in Europe and the rest of the world, particularly in modernizing existing systems. In Scotland, where the assets of existing tramways are all gone, they are unlikely to reappear. Only the legend remains.

I. Campbell

Travellers. If we except the Romans, Vikings, and other notable precursors, the earliest written records of visitors to Scotland date from the thirteenth century. During the next 500 years a succession of travellers, including representatives of several European nations and many suspicious, observant Englishmen, noted down their varied impressions in letters and diaries. Until the eighteenth century, however, the Highlands remained virtually unknown, and elsewhere in Scotland poor roads and unreliable inns were a deterrent to all but the most determined wayfarers.

Then the road-building of Wade and others, and later the new roads and canals of Telford, helped to open up the north. This period of improvement in communications coincided with a revolution in taste which made mountain scenery, previously spurned, suddenly fashionable. Inspired by the works of Sir Walter Scott, people flocked to Scotland, and especially to the Trossachs and Highland Perthshire. Queen Victoria's love of the Highlands—itself a product of this phase of culture—added further to the popularity of Scotland with tourists. The nineteenth-century railway network was very extensive, ensuring that while certain parts of Scotland remained inaccessible to all save walkers and climbers, less active travellers also had a chance to get to know different regions.

The contribution of the twentieth century has been the partial destruction of an excellent railway and steamer network, the motor-car and all that goes with it, and the systematic development of a tourist industry in both Highland and Lowland Scotland. Travellers today come from all over the world, and to judge from the registration plates on cars touring the Hebrides in the summer months, Scots are quite often outnumbered by overseas visitors.

The early literature of travel in Scotland contains many references to the poverty and backwardness of the country. Froissart, for instance, writing in the fourteenth century, remarked that 'nothing is to be had in that country without great difficulty'. Both iron to shoe horses, and leather to make harness, saddles, and bridles, had to be brought over from Flanders by sea. Prolonged warfare and economic insecurity had robbed the nation of her nobility and produced a peculiarly grudging outlook:

> In Scotland you will never find a man of worth: they are like savages, who wish not to be acquainted with any one, and are too envious of the good fortune of others, and suspicious of losing anything themselves, for their country is very poor.

All he could find to say in favour of the Scots was that they were 'bold, hardy, and much inured to war'.

More than a century later, Don Pedro de Ayala came to Scotland as the ambassador of Ferdinand and Isabella of Spain, and formed a more detailed impression. In a long letter to his employers, he described both the Scottish King and his country. His shrewd assessment of James IV centres on the impetuous and proud nature which would one day be responsible for the fatal journey south to Flodden ('He is not a good captain, because he begins to fight before he gives orders'). But Don Pedro also drew attention to the King's well earned popularity:

> he does not think it right to begin any warlike undertaking without himself being the first in danger. His deeds are as good as his words. For this reason, and because he is a very humane prince, he is much loved. He is active, and works hard.

Part of the interest of Don Pedro de Ayala's account is that, despite having spent six months or longer in Scotland, he had only a very hazy notion of the size of the country, and its shape:

> Judging by what I have read in books and seen on maps, and also by my own experience, I should think that both

kingdoms are of equal extent. In the same proportion that England is longer than Scotland, Scotland is wider than England; thus the quantity of land is the same.

It was not until after 1595, when Mercator's atlas was published, that an approximate idea of the geographical outline of Scotland began to be disseminated, and for a long time after that Scottish topography was little understood by the average traveller.

The English tradition of somewhat patronizing or disdainful reference to Scotland—which reaches its complex, maddening, yet humane climax in Dr Johnson—goes back a long way. There are several examples from the seventeenth century, including the Cheshire puritan Sir William Brereton, who noted about Edinburgh in 1636:

> this city is placed in a dainty, healthful pure air, and doubtless were a most healthful place to live in, were not the inhabitants most sluttish, nasty, and slothful people.

Brereton may well have had good cause to complain, but a better-natured if less succinct English commentator was the angler Richard Franck, who delighted in Scottish salmon, and who seems to have heard tell—in 1656—of the Loch Ness monster. At any rate, he wrote in a travel narrative cast in the form of a dialogue:

> What new inviting object have we now discovered? The famous Lough-Ness, so much discour'd for the supposed floating island; for here it is, if any where in Scotland.

A few years later, a more scientific English investigator of the life of Scottish waters, if a less entertaining one, was the pioneering naturalist John Ray, who was possessed by a classifying zeal, rather than by prejudice or by rumour. Already, travellers were of many distinct types.

Someone who worked as an accountant under General Wade in the north of Scotland was a young English officer called Edward Burt. He sent home a series of letters, subsequently published, which gave his often unfavourable comments on the land and people into whose midst he had come. At this date, 1725, the stock response to Highland landscape was still one of distaste; Burt noted:

> gloomy spaces, different rocks, heath, and high and low. To cast one's eye from an eminence toward a group of them, they appear still one above another, fainter and fainter, according to the aerial perspective, and the whole of a dismal gloomy brown, drawing upon a dirty purple; and most of all disagreeable when the heath is in bloom.... But of all views, I think the most horrid is, to look at the hills from east to west, or vice versa; for then the eye penetrates far among them, and sees more particularly their stupendous bulk, frightful irregularity, and horrid gloom, made yet more *sombrous* by the shades and faint reflections they communicate one to another.

Fifty years later, this kind of verdict was going out of fashion and it has not returned since. It was displaced by an enthusiastic

and positive appreciation of the 'sublime' or awful feature of mountain scenery. Cliffs and waterfalls especially held appeal, and in the nineteenth century countless visitors to the Highlands sketched or rhapsodized about romantic Scottish waterfalls and mountains. Several factors contributed to bring about this change in outlook, but the single most potent influence behind the new enthusiasm was undoubtedly Scott, whose narrative poem *The Lady of the Lake* (1810) served throughout the nineteenth century as a vivid and remarkably accurate guidebook to the beauties of the Trossachs. He drew in his wake Turner, who further romanticized the Scottish scene. Thus the way was prepared for Landseer, whose 'Monarch of the Glen' summed up afresh the grandeur which so many had learned to recognize in the Highlands. Many visitors to Scotland came on business, in the Victorian period as later, but Queen Victoria's Scottish journeys and love for Balmoral conferred royal authority on the idea of Scotland as a country to visit primarily for enjoyment.

D.A. Low

U

Union. Once the monarchies of England and Scotland were united in the person of James VI there were advantages to the monarch in closer ties between the countries. James VI put forward plans for a union in law, religion and economic regulation. He did not, however, propose to join the two parliaments. His suggestions failed in the English parliament and all that happened was that he was able to persuade the lawyers to treat people born since his accession to the English throne as citizens of both countries.

In this insistence by the joint kingdoms of their separation in law and other institutions, Scotland and England were acting parts similar to those acted by other 'united' states in Europe—most notably the different kingdoms which had come together to create Spain. In several of these cases dynastic union led eventually to war. In Britain, after a period of mutual interference, antagonism and war in the mid seventeenth century, it led to a closer junction, which suggests either monarchs of unusual political talents or predisposing forces. The latter seems the more likely explanation. The forces in question were probably the island nature of the joint territory and considerable similarities in religion and language. But it was some time before the various elements involved, the monarchy and the parliaments of the two countries came to see real advantage in a closer relationship.

For the monarchy the realization was relatively swift. After the period of mutual intervention in the Great Rebellion and the shotgun union under Cromwell, Charles II made considerable efforts to keep the affairs of the two countries apart. Yet as king he could have only one foreign policy, and as this came more and more to embody trading and colonial policy, more and more it created hostility in the partner with less significant trade and no colonies, Scotland. It was the Scottish attempt to break into the closed shop of colonial powers, at the expense of William III's foreign policy, in the Darien scheme of 1695 which finally converted the monarchy to the policy of closer union.

There had already been projects for a parliamentary incorporating union between the two countries in 1670 and 1689 and an attempt at economic union in 1668. The 1668 and 1689 attempts appear to have failed from lack of enthusiasm in the English parliament, that of 1670 in the Scottish, though it has also been alleged that the King was not really behind this attempt. But Charles II had certainly tried to persuade the English parliament to modify its tariff on Scottish goods in the 1660s. All these attempts occurred when the memory of the enforced union under Cromwell, from 1653–60, was still fresh.

In spite of predisposing forces towards closer relations, both countries in the seventeenth century experienced developments that pushed them apart. The outcome of the Great Rebellion was to bring to England limitations on the power of the crown and an increase in that of parliament. There were also increases of wealth in England, the expansion of her colonies, and the creation of re-export trade which had no parallel in Scotland. Meanwhile in Scotland it became harder after 1661 to hold the country within a system of episcopal Church government similar to that of England and in 1690 the attempt was abandoned for Presbyterianism. The proliferation of Stuart descendants of James I and VI made it, however, unlikely that the two countries would come to be inherited by different people unless the rules of succession were altered by one or other parliament. By the end of the seventeenth century parliamentary sovereignty had become sufficiently established for this to be possible and so the issue of parliamentary union was necessarily combined with the issue of the Hanoverian succession.

This junction is one of the reasons why the topic became more urgent after the Revolution of 1688–89. Union was raised as a topic in 1689 by William III and might have been part of the reconstruction of the constitution that took place in both countries then, but there was an absence of enthusiasm for it anywhere. The much more independent position adopted by the Scottish parliament after 1690, and the instability of political groupings in Scotland made the country difficult to manage. In the reigns of William and of Anne there developed a system by which the Scottish ministers were, in practice, the nominees of the English ministry and expected to obey English orders, but the difficulty of managing the Scottish parliament placed a limitation on this control. Scottish ministers were, for instance, unable to prevent the launching of the Darien scheme. What made the issue of parliamentary union urgent was the death of Anne's son the Duke of Gloucester in 1700.

The English parliament in the Act of Settlement of 1701 placed the succession in the Hanoverian line of Sophia, youngest daughter of James VI's daughter Elizabeth, as the only Protestant line descending from the joint monarchy. Any different Stuart succeeding to Scotland would have a claim to the English throne and war would be inevitable. This political problem did much, but took some time in the doing, to persuade the English parliament that Union would be worth the sharing of economic advantages. There was an additional political argument once the war of the Spanish Succession had broken out in 1702 (again a war for trading and colonial advantages in which the Scots did not share): the possibility of Scotland being used for a French invasion of England. There were, though of less importance, economic arguments on the English side for Union, for Scotland made possible breaches in the system of prohibition of the export of English raw wool, and was also a constant source of smuggled goods.

For the Scottish parliament to accept the idea of Union took longer. It was evident that the sacrifice of independence and of institutions would be greater for the weaker and smaller country, and there were considerable fears of a repetition of the policy of Charles I's attempt to assimilate the two Churches. There were more people in Scotland either open Jacobites or at least prepared to consider the return of the older Stuart line as practicable than in England. There was also an outbreak of intense hostility to England both in parliament and outside it when the disasters of the Darien expedition became known. These were attributed to English hostility rather than to the fatuities of the whole plan.

There was an attempt at Union in 1703 which found the English ministers still unconverted, and even very resolute pressure by Queen Anne could not take the English commissioners, who were appointed, far. In any case the Act setting up the Scottish commission was of doubtful validity.

The failure of 1703 was followed by a period of intense hostility to England in the new parliament of Scotland which first met in May 1703. Scottish suspicion of England was shown in two Acts which went to the heart of the political problems involved, the Act of Security and Settlement which stipulated that without guarantees for the sovereignty of the kingdom the successor to Queen Anne, who would be of the royal house and Protestant religion, would not be the same as the monarch of England, and the Act anent Peace and War which asserted the right of the Scottish parliament to make decisions on such matters for Scotland. The Act of Security had to be accepted by the Scottish ministers in 1704 or the parliament would not have voted supply.

The response of the English parliament to these Acts was an ultimatum, the Alien Act. Unless the Scottish appointed commissioners to discuss Union or accepted the Hanoverian succession by Christmas 1705, Scottish exports to England would be prohibited and Scots in England treated as foreigners. This Act was a drastic threat to the Scottish economy for the exports concerned, particularly linen and cattle, were probably the biggest trading items Scotland had, and certainly the trades most rapidly expanding. Over the century since the

Union of Crowns Scotland had suffered interruption of her trade with other European countries because of English war policies, while her trade with England, always of great importance whenever the countries were at peace, had prospered. The Scots showed their popular anger in the judicial murder of some of the crew of an English ship accused, on totally inadequate evidence, of piracy against ships involved in the Darien venture, but in parliament they toed the line and appointed commissioners for Union.

Given the long tendency of Scots not to knuckle down when threatened by England, and the evidence for violent anti-English feeling from 1703–5, there are puzzles in explaining why the Scottish parliament agreed to negotiate. It has been suggested that the hostility to England was feigned or that bribery either by money or by honours did the trick. Certainly 'influence' was brought to bear on politicians—it would be surprising if it had not been. It should be remembered English policies had moved in the direction of stability and that the 'whig' ministry of the period was much more consistent and coherent in policy than earlier groupings. Scottish politics in the period after 1689 show other sudden reversals of aim by political groups and this lack of settled policy may be involved here. There was also certainly the influence of a new political party, the Squadrone, small but of influential membership, a breakaway in 1704 from the country or nationalist opposition party. This new party made the core of a ministry and its existence weakened the opposition, even though Queen Ann dismissed it in 1705. It was with, first of all, the second Duke of Argyll and subsequently the Duke of Queensberry in power that the last negotiations for Union were undertaken.

The recent hostility of the Scots and the recent difficulty in finding a Scottish ministry able to control the Scottish parliament were of importance in making the English ready to make concessions provided the Scottish commissioners agreed on the basis of an incorporating and not a federal union. Examples of successful federalism were not easy to find, and since the English feared the Jacobite impulses of Scotland and wished to be able to drown Scottish political opinion, incorporation was the only practical possibility. The Scots were given a small number of seats in both houses of the English parliament and a low financial contribution. In return the English not only agreed to freedom of trade within the system of the Navigation Laws, but also to financial compensation—the 'Equivalent'—for the obligation on the Scots to help service the English National Debt. (The Scottish government's debts were ignored and made for ill feeling later.) Two vital institutions were left independent in Scotland, the Presbyterian Church, which was apparently protected by special Acts, and Scottish law.

The Union passed in Scotland in spite of considerable protest, from ministers of religion and from the burghs, though it seems to have been supported by landed society. In the next few years there were considerable grounds for annoyance in both countries at behaviour in the other—the main aspects of this were English annoyance at Scottish smuggling, and Scottish indignation over interference with the independence of the Church by the reintroduction of ecclesiastical patronage. It was a generation before the economic concessions enabled Scots to enrich their country. Probably important elements in the success of Union in the later eighteenth century were the pattern of very little government control of home affairs accepted in both countries and the creation, eventually, of institutions by which the opinion of the political élite in Scotland could be formed and sounded about proposed legislation. This meant that the Scots could develop their own law to suit their own society, and that legislative needs could be met. However, in the nineteenth century there is reason to think that Scotland was neglected both by parliament and by the major parties at least until the creation of the Scottish secretary in 1885. The continuation of the Scottish legal system meant that Edinburgh in a very real sense remained a capital, and became, in the later eighteenth century the centre of the Scottish Enlightenment (q.v.).

In the mid twentieth century there has developed a somewhat sour attitude to Union. The blessings of the large nation state have seemed less conspicuous with the passing of Empire, and many regions in Europe have experienced movements aiming at modification or dissolution of their connections with larger communities. In Westminister the overloading of the parliamentary timetable has made it difficult for the Scots to obtain legislation. The economic discomforts of the decline of Britain from world economic leadership have been more conspicuous in peripheral areas than in the southeast. There have developed movements both for a return to national independence and for some sort of home rule. The existence of these is not a valid historical comment on the decision of 1707 which indubitably brought advantages to each country. Scotland would have achieved political stability without it, eventually. It is possible that she would also have achieved economic growth in the eighteenth century but this would have been slow. It is difficult to think of it happening at all under threats of war from the neighbouring country.

R. Mitchison

Urquhart, Fred (b. 1912) was born in Edinburgh but brought up in Fife. His collected short stories in two volumes, *The Dying Stallion* (1967) and *The Ploughing Match* (1968), reflect the earthy vigour of the farming folk belonging to the grandchildren's generation of Grassic Gibbon's character, Chris Guthrie. Urquhart's understanding of the social forces that bind together agricultural communities, however, never had to contend with any of the implied 'isms' that ultimately blunted Gibbon's social perception. Later collections include *A Diver in China Seas* (1980), *Seven Ghosts in Search* (1983) and *Full Score* (1989).

Urquhart's range of characters is wide, his realisation of them at its most vivid when the localities in which they exist also take on a more general significance. Rightly, Stevie Smith once referred to Urquhart's 'diamond style'. Urban life—the pathetic and sometimes tawdry existence of the semi-articulate—has also attracted his skill, and is effectively deployed in his early novel sensitively depicting an Edinburgh adolescence, *Time Will Knit* (1938—revised 1988). *The Palace of Green Days* (1979) deals with a brother and sister returning to the evocation of the joys and tragedies of childhood. He is working on a sequel dealing with the pair in later life.

Urquhart's work has been translated into several European languages. A non-fictional account of his own childhood is to be found in *As I Remember*, edited by the present writer. Urquhart lived for forty-seven years in London and Sussex, but returned to Musselburgh, a few miles from his birthplace, at the age of seventy-nine.

M. Lindsay

Urquhart, Sir Thomas (1611–1660) was the son of a similarly named laird of Cromarty. The younger Sir Thomas was educated at King's College, Aberdeen, prior to extensive European travel. He fought against the Covenanters at Turiff in 1639 and had to flee to England, where he entered the service of Charles I, who knighted him in 1641. Urquhart was a strange combination of originality, learning and eccentricity, bordering perhaps on insanity. He is said to have died from a fit of immoderate laughter on hearing the news of the Restoration.

His original works include *Trissotetras* (1645) and *The Jewel*, which he wrote in the Tower of London after being incarcerated there for taking part in a Royalist rising in 1649. This book was followed in 1652 by *Ekskubalauron*, a denunciation of Scottish Presbyterianism, and, in the following year, his treatise on a universal language, *Logopandecteision*. His most important achievement, however, was his translation into euphuistic Scots of the first three books of Rabelais, in which undertaking he was assisted by Peter Anthony Motteux, a Frenchman who had settled in England, and who completed the translation after Urquhart's death.

M. Lindsay

Vernacular Movement, The. Arguments favourable to the revival of literature in Scots arose out of the sixteenth-century Ancient versus Modern controversy. Two propositions, especially, distinguished Modern thinking from Ancient, and persisted in different forms for several centuries to come: namely, that national languages are the proper expression of each nation's unique genius; and, second, that the language of poetry is natural and unpolished, the spoken tongue of the uneducated.

English linguists and antiquaries were soon to apply these ideas of the critics to Scotland. This was done in conjunction with the revival of Old English in the 1620s, under the aegis of Henry Spelman and William L'Isle. Later in the century *Christ's Kirk On The Green* was edited with *Polemo Middinia* by the Anglo-Saxon scholar Bishop Edmund Gibson, who first deemed this unaureate, folk-derived poetry classic. In his day Scottish songs and ballads too enjoyed a vogue in England, chiefly through the plays and song collections of Mrs Behn, Tom D'Urfey, and Playford. Long before Ramsay, these song collectors and composers invented the myth of a pastoral Scotland, full of unlettered Jockys and Moggys, who spoke a pure poetic tongue.

In Scotland the two theories of national and poetic language appeared quite early. James VI is generally recognized as the father of historical criticism in Britain though, before him, Gavin Douglas had proposed giving Scottis the status of the heroic languages ('Proloug', *Aeneis*). In 'Ane Schort Treatise' (1584) King James vindicates his writing a work on this well-worn subject on the grounds of a unique Scottish language and poetry. Moreover, in the 'Treatise' he condemns imitation of foreign models and makes a place, however patronizingly, for a lively rural poetry, using 'vplandis words'. Dryden's friend, Sir George Mackenzie of Rosehaugh, carried the torch for Scots in the seventeenth century, proclaiming its superiority over English and French (*Pleadings, In some remarkable Cases*, 1673). He draws the distinction between English, a courtly, 'invented' language, weak in character and Scots, a 'natural', 'firy' and 'bold' tongue, spoken by the 'commons' and by 'learned men and men of Businesse'. After Mackenzie of Rosehaugh these arguments were taken up by the founding fathers of the revival: James Watson, editor of Mackenzie's *Works* (1716–22); and Thomas Ruddiman, Mackenzie's successor as Keeper of the Advocate's Library.

The eighteenth-century antiquaries and poets inherited the legacy of the Moderns while subtly tailoring their assumptions to suit literary and philosophical trends. Ruddiman is the obvious case in point. In 1710 he and his colleagues sagaciously produced an edition of Gavin Douglas's *Aeneis* and revived the age-old contentions of the Scottish historical school. In the editorial notes, Ruddiman maintains, bearing the English antiquaries in mind, that Middle Scots literature is classic, on a par with Chaucer and Gower, and its language equal to Greek and Latin. With Mackenzie he contrasts the 'force' of Scots with the weak, diffuse quality of English. Ruddiman deviates little from what came before him, but with one noteworthy exception. He is among the first to suggest that the living speech of the 'vulgar' is in great part Old Scots; a necessary ingredient for the literary prestige of the colloquial Scots of Ramsay and his successors. For sound practical and philosophical reasons Ruddiman intentionally blurred the difference between the aureate diction of Douglas and the makars and the Middle Scots of *Christ's Kirk On The Green* and the folk-based works. Sir John Clerk of Penicuik was another Scottish antiquary who built upon the old Ancient versus Modern controversy. His 'An Enquiry into the Ancient Languages of Great Britain' (1790), intended for the Edinburgh Philosophical Society in 1742, is an apology for vernacular Scots, citing historical precedents for different languages in the same nation and affirming that the low Scots tongue is actually the 'genuine Saxon' in its purest form. Judiciously Clerk weaves the watch-words of two centuries into his defence: 'polish', 'beauty and energy' (poetic language); 'sound and gratification', 'custom' (national genius). The opinions of Dr Alexander Geddes, vernacular poet and antiquary, were known decades before his valuable contributions to the Society of Antiquaries of Scotland in 1792. He carries the inferences of his predecessors even further, and to their logical conclusions, moving from an affirmation of the 'richness, energy, and harmony' of Scoto-Saxon to the 'confessed superiority' of the poetry it produced. In the second premise of his syllogistic defence, he avers that despite the loss of Scots among the learned, it yet lives on in its 'native purity' in the dialects of the common folk. We are prepared for the final deduction that a modern Scots poet could use vernacular words with greater effect than would be induced 'by their English equivalents' and that a conflation of dialects might be used to good purpose.

Another group in Scotland, the literati, supported, at least as much as they opposed, the Vernacular Revival. Literary historians have rightly noticed Beattie's list of Scotticisms to be avoided; the conscientious polishing of English prose by the eminent writers of the Scottish Enlightenment; Sheridan's Edinburgh lectures on elocution; Boswell's embarrassment at hearing spoken Scots; Hume's characterization of the vernacular as a 'very corrupt Dialect' of English (Letter to Gilbert Elliot of Minto, 2 July 1757). This was one side of the coin. The two seminal ideas of the Moderns had reached the literati in a different guise, with the growth in Europe of primitivist and genetic, or culturally relativist, theories of history. These theories assimilated by the literati fostered the national 'folk' literature. Such central figures as Adam Smith, James Beattie, William and Alexander Fraser Tytler, Boswell, and Lord Hailes lent direct patronage to several vernacular poets; had a hand in some of their publications; or made contributions themselves to the movement. In their writings Smith, Boswell, and Monboddo agreed with the antiquaries about Scots language. Their contentions were familiar enough to the reading public for Smollett to have amusingly recast them in *Humphry Clinker* ('To Sir Watkin Phillips-Morpeth, July 13'). The use of Scots for pastoral poetry especially pleased the literati. Henry Mackenzie calls the *Gentle Shepherd* the finest modern pastoral; remarks on its 'Simplicity' and 'Force'; and laments the passing of its language: presently 'one of its Beauties' (*Letters To Elizabeth Rose of Kilravock*, Nos.30,73). This was orthodox critical opinion, endorsed by the foremost Enlightenment critic, Hugh Blair ('Pastoral Poetry—Lyric Poetry', *Lectures On Rhetoric And Belles Lettres*).

The arguments of those who openly shunned the vernacular movement reveal the same curiously mixed feelings. Dr William Robertson, who spent a lifetime excising Scotticisms from his prose, was no friend to the Revival. Yet in his *History of Scotland* (1759) he takes exception to the arbitrary English linguistic standard imposed upon Scots after 1603. At that time, it was, in his estimation, not inferior in 'elegance' or 'purity' to English; nor was it so at the 1707 Union. Furthermore, he speculates somewhat longingly upon a glorious and continuous tradition of Scots letters that might have been. There were others, like Sir John Sinclair (*Observations On The Scottish Dialect*, 1782) and James Elphinston (*Propriety Ascertained In Her Picture*, 1787), whose pleas against Scots were less convincing and more emotionally confused. What logic was there to their setting out to dismiss the dialect as a thing of the past, and then ending up in a recapitulation of the antiquarians' defence of the language?

So much had the Modern argument won the day. Several ideas branched from the two seminal ones of the sixteenth century. Scots, with Old English, literature was accepted as classic. Scottis was taken to be the purest Saxon and assumed a place beside ancient Greek and Latin. As a forceful, northern tongue it was thought to surpass English in strength and economy. Custom was its source and philosophical justification, its validity residing in its suitability for the people who spoke it. Its literary possibilities were only limited by the genius of the artist.

If the theories that promoted vernacular language were centuries old they were at the same time quite modern. The Revival is a matter of new forces buttressing old ones: it both continues from the past and moves forward with the times.

The eighteenth century saw the rise of a peculiar type of primitivism which supervened from the modern's discontent with urban life. Men like Rousseau, who had a striking impact in Scotland, were repelled by the modern city; instinctively they withdrew, in imagination, to the country, where time seemed to have stood still. Effectively, what Rousseau did in Switzerland, and Hutcheson, Kames, Smith, Reid, and the others did in Scotland, was to superimpose an ideally conceived rural past upon the rural present; quite simply, to make the modern rustic a primitive, untainted and vigorous. This had important linguistic repercussions. In *On The Origin Of Language* and *Emile*, Rousseau made claims for folk speech, consistent with the antiquaries' own, which lent additional weight to their assertions, and which chimed sympathetic chords among the literati. For the Revivalists, who had adopted a literary 'folk self' and who wrote in the language of Scots peasants, European philosophy furnished necessary props for their movement.

In England different manifestations of primitivism were conducive to the Scots Revival. The first literary historians, Thomas Warton, Percy, and Gray, accorded special attention to Douglas, Dunbar and Lyndsay, and to Scots song and balladry, and urged the Scots to write a history of their own poetry. More generally, English primitivist beliefs about untaught poets, and the Arcadian status given to Scots peasants, as in Collins's 'Ode on the Popular Superstitions of the Highlands of Scotland', reflected upon the Revival. Collins went so far as to compose a poem in Scots which was circulated in Scotland among the literati. Furthermore, to the Englishman, Scots was better suited for the rationalist pastoral than were his own provincial dialects; it was classed as a 'Doric', Theocritean language. By 1772 John Aikin could speak of the unmistakable 'advantage' Ramsay had gained in using it ('Essay on Ballads and Pastoral Songs').

Historicism was the other beneficial Enlightenment force. The celebrated Montesquieu based his thesis of the 'general spirit' of a people upon variations of climate, soil, and topography; and attributed to the variations a nation's 'natural genius' (*The Spirit of Laws*). Likewise, in Voltaire's scheme of things, each nation possessed a unique '*génie*', expressed in its customs, manners, and language. Expounding this theory in *The Temple Of Taste*, Voltaire's Cardinal de Polignac says,

> Nature, which is fertile, ingenious, and wise, speaks to all mankind; but with different accents; thus every people has its distinct Language, as well as Genius... .

It followed that each country had a distinct literary expression to complement its language. Literature was by definition national and local. In Europe these notions bred a strong reaction, mainly to a culturally predominant France, as vernacular revivals sprang up in the Scandinavian countries, marking obvious parallels with the two—the Scots and Gaelic—revivals in Scotland.

In England and Scotland historical-mindedness led to the formation of a school of British Historicist Criticism. At the end of the seventeenth century the seeds of it existed in Sir William Temple's concept of national 'humour'. By the time of Edward Young's *Conjectures On Original Composition* they had reached full fruition. In the *Conjectures* Young protests that a genuine poet must stay at home, compose in his own tongue, and rely upon his innate knowledge. Goldsmith similarly enunciated a system of historicist criticism in *An Enquiry Into The Present State Of Polite Learning In Europe*, also written in 1759. Great poetry, he says, requires a flourishing vernacular honed and strengthened by a national system of criticism, whose rules accommodate 'the genius and temper' of the nation. In Scotland the Aberdeen professor, Thomas Blackwell, published the popular, *An Enquiry Into The Life And Writings Of Homer* (1735). In it he begins with climate and national genius, and advances the argument 'that a Poet describes nothing so happily, as what he has seen; nor talks masterly, but in his native Language, and proper Idiom.' Like his fellow primitivists, he thinks a polished tongue unfit for a poet. Blackwell's theories belong to a context of Scottish apologetics of which he was well aware, and are an implicit vindication of Scots. The effect of the historicist critics is apparent in pastoral theory and poetry from the Pope-Philips controversy onwards, after which a more native practice began to evolve.

In the application of primitivist and historicist theories the Scots vernacular poets acted with the antiquaries; they were a segment of the antiquarian movement. One detects this in their insinuating themselves into what had become the classic tradition of Middle Scots literature. They deliberately equated the 'ancient' doric with 'our provincial dialects'; with the language of their poetry. It followed that Revivalist poets should present themselves to an accepting literary world as neo-ancients, in direct succession from Douglas, Dunbar and Lyndsay.

Philosophically, it behoved them to follow Rousseau. We find this in the poet's dedications, which usually transform modern rustics into their forefathers of a lost golden past. The Scots poets made it clear that theirs was an untutored, north-country language of poetry, as in William Wilkie's 'Fable XVI', where he would have us believe that Scots peasants unconsciously speak natural poetry. It was in keeping with this that vernacular poets assumed unlettered, rural personae, who only copied from nature. This was primitivism with practical ends in mind.

If they were historicists for the same reasons, they cannot be accused of limited awareness and narrow nationalism. Unquestionably, David Herd, for example, had digested his Voltaire before prefacing his *Ancient And Modern Scottish Songs* (1776) with comments on 'the joint influence of climate and government; character and situation' in forming the 'distinct national styles' of song. Ramsay too was acutely aware of the literary forces of the moment when he stated in the preface to his poetry (1721), 'Pursue your own natural Manner, and be an Original', and quoted Dr Young on the title page of his second anthology (1728) to the same purpose. The imposition of English language or French and Italian song threatened to stifle the Scottish genius. This was the lesson of historicist philosophy.

There was, then, a European-mindedness among these Revivalists, due primarily to educational ties and Continental associations. Dr Archibald Pitcairne, author of *The Assembly* and *Babell*, Clerk of Penicuik, Hamilton of Bangour, and Dr Alexander Geddes were men who had either studied or taught at the finest universities of Europe, or both; who had resided there for long periods and had undertaken the Grand Tour. They were sophisticated men, renowned for learning. For the others, the printers, antiquaries, and poets, virtually all of whom were university educated, the Scottish universities, imbued with Continental philosophy, introduced them to the works of Montesquieu, Voltaire, and Rousseau. Then there were self-educators like Ramsay, founder of Britain's first circulating library, and owner of a book shop that was the rendezvous of the Edinburgh wits. David Herd, a not untypical figure of the Revival, possessed a full Enlightenment library; his friends and publishers, Martin and Witherspoon, had projected a publication of Voltaire's *Works*. Robert Fergusson's friendships included his editor, Arthur Masson, who carried recommendatory certificates from Diderot and d'Alembert; and the poet Thomas Mercer, whose *The Sentimental Sailor* (1772) was dedicated 'To John James Rousseau'. Some years earlier, in 1767, the Ruddimans had published *The Poetical Works Of ... William Meston*, minor vernacular poet, with a dedication 'To Mess. Courayer and Voltaire'.

There is another explanation for the Revivalists' susceptibility to contemporary philosophical and literary notions. Though this was never defined, and was certainly no cause of internal dissension, two outlooks coexisted within the vernacular movement. One of these, held by Ramsay and his successors, was more modern and consciously primitivist: one thinks of the romantic Jacobite or the pre-Romantic pastoralist; and the other, the main impetus behind the early Revival, and the more continuous outlook, was that of the traditional Scots humanist, in the Renaissance classical sense and in the Augustan humanist sense, as Paul Fussell defines it. From Douglas through Geddes the Scots humanists belonged to an older Scottish culture than that of the ascendant one after the Reformation, the Glorious Revolution, and the 1707 Union. Almost to a man Episcopalians and Catholics, with a few Presbyterian but Royalist exceptions, they kept alive a different Scots *Weltanschauung*. Their construct of the universe was hierarchical and counterpoised: God, the angels, the Stewart king, the bishops, and so on, each serving in his ordained place, right down to the vermin of the earth. This model, balancing order with diversity, poised a universal human nature against the more varied idea of accumulated national wisdom, or national genius. From this was derived their emphasis upon historical continuity and a steadfast reverence for the past against sudden innovations: overall, a cultural conservatism. Thus the eighteenth-century humanists in Scotland wished to preserve the Scots classicist and vernacular culture of Douglas. Their tradition, resurrected by Freebairn, Watson, the Ruddimans, and others of the Episcopalian enclave in Edinburgh, which centred in Old St Paul's, can be traced through William Meston, Alexander Nicol, Claudero (James Wilson), Fergusson (its culminating figure who, like Douglas, had planned his own translation of Virgil—a translation of the *Georgics*—into Scots); Reverend John Skinner, Dr Alexander Geddes, and Fergusson's friend Dr Andrew Duncan, whose *Carminum Rariorum Macaronicorum Delectus* (1813), though in no way as influential a work, was a latter-day counterpart of Watson's *Choice Collection*, being a Latin and Scots vernacular compilation. Most of them were Latinists; all of them, if not practising Latinists, shared the values of a Scots humanist culture. At the Reformation the humanist reacted to sudden religious innovations, but equally to the Presbyterians 'quha not onlie knappis suddrone in your negatiue cofession, bot also hes causit it be imprentit at London in contempt of our native langage' (John Hamilton *Ane Catholik And Facile Traictise*, 1581). From the dark seventeenth century up to the Revival it was the Royalists who kept the vernacular tradition in literature alive. And it was the diehard humanists who led the Vernacular Revival, looking backward to Bishop Douglas, and forward to Montesquieu and Rousseau, whose notions fitted so neatly into their scheme of things.

F. W. Freeman

Verse of the Clearances *see* **Clearances, Verse of**

Wallace, William (d. 1305) has been best described in the statement of an anonymous contemporary that he was 'for many years captain of the Scottish people against King Edward I of England'. Had there been no succession dispute over the Scots throne in 1290–92 and no subsequent war between John Balliol and Edward I it is probable that Wallace would have lived and died unrecorded by history or legend. A fierce hatred of foreign occupation and oppression and an utterly fearless spirit turned Wallace in 1297, almost overnight, into a national leader. For the next eight years he fought the English with extraordinarily single-minded dedication until by the date of his capture and execution (August, 1305) he had become famous throughout western Europe. Without question Wallace was the greatest of the heroic warrior leaders of popular nationalism in the later Middle Ages. His deeds passed into legend among both Scots and English even in his own lifetime; they inspired lost works referred to by the chronicler Wyntoun and also the fiercely nationalistic epic poem *The Wallace* by the poet usually called Blind Harry, who adapted the Wallace saga to fit the situation facing Scotland in the 1470s when James III's pro-English policies seemed to threaten his country's independence.

Wallace was a younger son of a Renfrewshire family whose ancestors had come to Scotland from the Welsh borderland in the mid-twelfth century in the train of the first Stewart, Walter son of Alan. No members of this family are found in the very full lists of Stewart freeholder vassals whose homage to Edward I was recorded in August 1296 to underline the English conquest. As a result the Wallaces seem to have been outlawed. In May 1297 William, doubtless aided by brothers and friends, killed the English sheriff of Lanark, and soon afterwards, in the company of William, lord of Douglas (father of Bruce's 'Good Sir James'), attacked the English justiciar at Perth who narrowly escaped capture or death. Wallace expelled all the English clergy in Scotland, while the occupying forces fled to strong castles or to England. Joining forces with young Andrew Murray whose revolt in the north had run parallel to his own, Wallace, now 'general of the army of Scotland', prepared for battle on the north side of the River Forth at the bridge of Stirling. His opponents, John de Warenne Earl of Surrey and Hugh Cressingham, the hated chief of the occupation regime, were no match for the Scots who (11 September 1297) inflicted a devastating defeat. Despite Murray's death from wounds, Wallace rallied the Scottish kingdom, of which he was appointed 'Guardian', led a massive raid into English Northumbria and established links with the powerful trading cities of Hamburg and Lubeck. In the spring of 1298 Edward I returned from Flanders to lead a full-scale campaign intended to wipe out Wallace and conquer Scotland for good. So seriously did he view the situation that he transferred the English government to York. He defeated Wallace's army at Falkirk (22 July 1298) but only after a day-long encounter in which the Scots infantry, forming a truly national army, gave a good account of themselves. Before the battle Wallace, with grim humour, told his men: 'I have brought you to the ring: now dance if you can'. Despite heavy Scottish casualties, Edward I was unable to exploit his victory. Although Wallace gave up the office of Guardian (which passed to an uneasy collective leadership of great nobles) he remained active in the national cause. In 1299 or 1300 he went to France (possibly by way of Norway) to plead for a renewal of the treaty made between Philip IV and the Scots in 1295. The original letter in which King Philip commended to Pope Boniface VIII his 'beloved William le Waloys, knight, of Scotland' is still preserved in the English Public Record Office. While Wallace laboured at the French and papal courts, his followers spied on English military activity in Gascony and his compatriots under Sir John de Soules fought a valiant defensive campaign in southern Scotland. But in 1303 withdrawal of both French and papal support for the Scots allowed Edward I to overrun Scotland as in 1296, and early in 1304 most of the national leaders submitted to him on terms which, though not dishonourable, would have put an end to the independence of Scotland. At this lowest point in the national fortunes Wallace, Soules, Simon Fraser and William Olifard (Oliphant) were the only Scotsmen of note to hold out firmly against English domination. After some desultory skirmishing both south and north of Forth, Wallace was driven into hiding, only to be betrayed in Glasgow by one of his own men and handed over to Sir John Menteith, governor of Dumbarton castle, who sent him to Edward I. Without being seen by the English king Wallace was tried in Westminster Hall by a special commission of five judges 'according to the law and usage of (England)' and convicted of treason, waging war against the English king and various crimes of violence. Wallace, who had never been Edward I's liege man, denied the charge of treason, but he was convicted merely on notoriety and dragged through the London streets for execution at the Smithfield elms by hanging, disembowelling and beheading (23 August 1305). Within six months Bruce had killed his rival John Comyn and re-established the ancient Scottish kingship for whose preservation and liberty Wallace had contended throughout his career. *See also* Scotland 1100–1488.

G.W.S. Barrow

Wallace, William (b. 1860, Greenock; d. Malmesbury, Wilts, 1940) was educated at Fettes College, Edinburgh and studied medicine in Glasgow, Vienna and Paris. He did not pursue a musical career until 1889, when, abandoning his ophthalmic

work, he entered the Royal Academy of Music, London, first as a student, then, after being elected ARAM and FRAM, as a member of the professorial staff.

He was a versatile, energetic musician. In addition to his composing, he was, for many years, Chairman and a Trustee of the Royal Philharmonic Society and an entertaining, contentious writer on musical subjects: *The Threshold of Music* (1908) and *The Musical Faculty* (1912) make stimulating reading. A notable Wagnerian, he wrote *A Study of Wagner* in 1925, and, like so many of his Academy colleagues, responded fervently to the influence of Wagner, Liszt and Strauss. He is perhaps best remembered for six Symphonic Poems. The first, *The Passing of Beatrice*, after Dante (Crystal Palace, 1892), bears the distinction of being the first British work to be styled Symphonic Poem, while the last, *Villon* (New Symphony Orchestra, London 1909) is generally considered to be his finest achievement. In *A Scots Fantasy, In Praise of Scottish Poesie* (1894), Symphonic Poem No. 5 *Sir William Wallace* (1905) and the Cantata *The Massacre of the Macphersons* he took account of Scottish subjects. He also composed a large scale Choral Symphony and many songs and choral pieces.

P. Hindmarsh

Watson, James (d. 1722), Scottish printer. Son of James Watson (known as the Popish Printer) and originally a native of Aberdeen, Watson spent all his professional life in Edinburgh, printing first at Warriston's Close (1695–97) and then at Craig's Close (1697–1722). In 1709 he opened a shop 'next door to the Red Lyon, opposite the Luckenbooths'. Much of his professional life was spent in a legal battle to establish his claim to be one of the King's Printers in Scotland after the expiry of the Anderson printing monopoly in 1712. (*See also* The Printed Book until the End of the Eighteenth Century.) A decision in his favour was finally given in the House of Lords in 1718. In 1700 he was imprisoned in the Edinburgh Tolbooth for printing seditious pamphlets on the Darien disaster, but was released from it by the Edinburgh mob. He died in Edinburgh on 25 September 1722.

His two most notable productions were a translation of La Caille's *History of Printing* (1713), in his introduction to which he gives a graphic and valuable account of the history of Scottish printing, and his *Choice Collection of Comic and Serious Scots Poems* (3 parts, 1706–11). This was probably initially inspired by the nationalist fervour which preceded the 1707 Union. It epitomizes what was known of earlier Scottish poetry at the beginning of the eighteenth century and represents a conscious attempt to resuscitate the independent native poetic tradition which had been declining since the removal of the Scottish court to London in 1603. The collection appears to have been thrown together without any attempt at method or chronology, and though it includes several poems which are not Scottish it omits much of the finest early Scottish poetry; Dunbar, Henryson, Douglas and Lyndsay are completely ignored, and Watson unfortunately did not have access to the Bannatyne MS on which Ramsay later drew extensively. He did, however, present a fairly representative selection of sixteenth and seventeenth-century Scottish poetry, including such important early works as 'Christ's Kirk on the Green' and Montgomerie's 'The Cherrie and the Slae.' The seventeenth-century popular tradition is represented by the poems of the Sempills of Beltrees and anonymous pieces such as 'The Mare of Collingtoun'; and the courtly English language tradition by the poems of Ayton, Montrose and Sir George Mackenzie. It is rarely possible to establish where Watson found his material, but many poems appear to have derived from printed copies (especially broad-sides), sometimes of very doubtful authority. Others may have been contributed from private manuscript collections in response to Watson's advertisement for material (*Edinburgh Courant*, 12–14 August 1706). The evidence suggests that he transcribed the texts he used faithfully, without alteration.

The chief importance of the *Collection* lies in its contribution to the eighteenth-century vernacular revival and to the work of Ramsay, Fergusson and Burns who found in it many of the metres and genres which they adapted in their own work.

Harriet Harvey Wood

Whisky. Important as icon and intoxicant, whisky was one of the few cultural artefacts to retain the appellation 'Scotch' long after that term had acquired pejorative connotations for English speakers.

Scotch whisky is strong liquor whose consumption has been an integral part of the lives of the Scottish people for some hundreds of years. The origins of whisky distilling are unknown, the earliest historical reference being an entry in the Scots Exchequer Roll of 1494. Whisky was used mainly by the lower classes until the 19th century, when it rose in social status to become acceptable to most male drinkers (and some female, including Queen Victoria) in the United Kingdom.

Typically, Scotch whisky is made from barley, water, yeast and (usually) peatsmoke. The barley is malted by soaking until it germinates, a process which causes the formation of an enzyme which facilitates the conversion of the starches in the barley into sugars. The germination is halted by drying the malt over a fire, usually containing some peat. The peat smoke, adhering to the malt, contributes to the aroma and taste of the mature whisky. The dried malt is ground and mixed with water and yeast. The yeast works upon the sugars and converts them into alcohol, producing an ale. The ale is distilled in a copper pot-still (an onion-shaped vessel) to yield a clear spirit, mostly ethyl alcohol, but containing minute traces of a very large number of very complex organic compounds. It is a discontinuous process which even today shows its cottage-industry origins. The new spirit is put into oak casks, where it matures for at least three years.

The spirit thus described is pot-still malt whisky. It is to this image that all Scotch whisky refers, even though spirits may lawfully be called Scotch whisky which have been made in a different type of still from grains, most of which are not barley.

This, patent-still grain whisky, results from a typically industrial mode of production whereas malt whisky uses the technology of a pre-industrial society.

Most Scotch whisky, like much Scotch culture, makes an obeisance to a historical ideal but does not choose to emulate it. However, to say that current practice differs from traditional image is not to imply that the modern methods have no roots. From an early date, whisky was made from a variety of grains other than barley. A modicum of barley is essential, since the barley alone can produce the enzyme necessary for starch conversion. But from at least the 17th century and probably from much earlier, whisky was commonly being distilled from an ale made from any starchy cereal available. Probably little distinction was made between malt and grain whisky. Most whisky was drunk immature anyway.

Nowadays Scotch whisky is deemed fit for consumption only after maturation in an oak cask. The period varies: some grain whiskies are put into blends after as few as three years but malts are usually matured for at least eight years before being bottled. Most malts are at their best after ten or twelve years in cask.

All whisky was pot-still whisky until the early 19th century, when various patent stills were invented with a view to rendering alcohol production more profitable by eliminating the batch production which pot stills entail. Improvements in profitability were desirable given the increasing size of the distilleries and the greater amounts of capital at risk if they failed. In the 18th century, failure by distillers was commonly the result of arbitrary changes in the Excise duty imposed by a callous and incompetent Government. The situation improved following the 1824 Act, which produced an economic climate more favourable to orderly trade and less favourable to illicit distilling, which until then had been extensively practised. The 1824 Act virtually brought to an end whisky distilling as a domestic occupation.

Both malt and grain whiskies were produced throughout the 19th century, the latter thanks to a patent still invented by Aeneas Coffee, an Irish exciseman. Because of its inexpensive raw materials and economies in production permitted by continuous operation of the patent still, grain whiskies could be sold much cheaper than malt whiskies. Malt whisky was generally acknowledged to be much the better spirit, but despite its endorsement by George IV when he visited Edinburgh, little malt was drunk beyond the Scottish Border until the 1970s.

The great rise in Scotch whisky production occurred in the latter half of the 19th century. Various factors combined to make blended whisky the standard drink of the British upper classes and, through the political and economic hegemony of the British Empire, of a large part of the world. Blended whisky was a mixture, in varying proportions, of malt and grain whiskies. As a rule, the higher the proportion of malt, the more expensive the blend. Blended whisky was drunk from open-topped glasses, mixed with ice and soda water. Its popularity owed at least as much to mass advertising and values of social conformity as it did to any qualities of nose or taste. Indeed it is remarkable how few of the advertisements of a century ago make any mention of the taste of Scotch whisky: how many portray it as a drink for gentlemen.

Five generations of Scots were unaware of the existence of their national drink in any form other than blended whisky. Acquiescence in this must stand as an indictment of the Scottish establishment and of the radicals who opposed it; there are few parallels in European history. By the 1950s, malt drinkers were to be found only in small pockets: the Edinburgh literati in Milne's bar; Stewart's Bar in Drummond Street (who until 1990 bottled casks of Glenlivet in their cellar); the officers' messes of a few Highland regiments. But for the great majority of the population, their national drink in its most characterful form, a liquor which for quality of nose and taste is equal to the finest cognac, was unobtainable.

The exhumation of malt whiskies has been the most culturally significant development in the whisky industry in the 20th century. The revival can be attributed to social movements such as the recovery of Scottish national self-confidence in the 1960s, the emergence of gastronomy (or at least interest in food) in the 1970s and the effort of a few patriotic intellectuals, of whom the leader was indoubtedly David Daiches, who championed their national drink as well as the authentic elements of their national culture. It is noticeable that neither the big battalions of the Scotch whisky industry nor the kilt-wearing anglicised establishment had much to do with it.

It is possible that the superlative qualities of single malts may help to maintain the prosperity of the Scotch whisky industry as one of the few remaining elements of Scottish industry which are significant in international markets. It is also possible that the resurgence of malts may speed the disappearance of the pejorative use of the term 'Scotch'. Neither, alas, is certain.

P. Hills

Whyte, Ian (b. 1901, Dunfermline; d. 1960) studied piano and composition, under Stanford and Vaughan Williams, at the Royal College of Music, London. He became music director to Lord Glentanor in 1923 and, in 1931, BBC Scotland's first Director of Music. In 1935 he founded the BBC's Scottish Symphony Orchestra. Ten years later he resigned as Director to concentrate on conducting and composition. Onerous though duties with the BBC Scottish Orchestra were, his interest in composition was compulsive and the list of original compositions is impressive; including an opera, two operettas, ballets (*Donald of the Burthens*—produced Covent Garden, 1951—is notable for the inclusion of bagpipes in its finale), two symphonies, two symphonic poems, three concertos, three string quartets (No. 3 the first McEwen Commission, 1954) and numerous piano, vocal and chamber works.

He was an intuitive rather than intellectual composer, whose fluency, aural sensitivity and genius at keyboard improvisation were much admired. His extensive research into the sources of traditional Scottish music provided the material for over 200 arrangements (orchestral, chamber and choral),

songs and incidental works for broadcasting in an extensive series 'Music from Scotland's past' (broadcast 1935–39). He was awarded the OBE and a Doctorate of Music, Edinburgh University, for his devoted service to Scottish music.

P. Hindmarsh

Witchcraft became a civil crime in Scotland in 1563 when a statute forbade 'ony maner of witchcraftis, sorsaries or necromancie under pane of deid' for both the witch and his or her client. It is clear that parliament was thinking in terms of 'white witchcraft' (divining for lost objects, telling fortunes and the like), of which there were sundry cases before 1563 and a few dozen between then and 1590, the year in which James VI returned from his wedding festivities at the court of Denmark. James clearly absorbed there the current continental ideas concerning 'black witchcraft' (that witches' supernatural powers derived from a compact with the Devil, reinforced by communal orgies with Satan in person as well as other witches, known as Sabbats), for no sooner had the king returned to Scotland than he personally directed the trial of several persons accused of conspiring with the Devil in sabbats at North Berwick to sink the ship bearing him back from Denmark. In 1597 he published a slim volume entitled *Daemonologie* to justify to his subjects the recent spate of persecutions and to instruct them in the wickedness of the demonic pact. Between 1590 and 1736 (when the statute of 1563 was repealed) at least 2,000 persons, more than 80 per cent of them women, were accused of witchcraft before the central courts in Edinburgh and a minimum of 600 were executed, mostly by strangulation followed by burning. More people still were dealt with on suspicion of witchcraft by local courts, especially the ecclesiastical ones, and this involvement of the Kirk is reflected in the high proportion of witchcraft cases which came from areas in which 'godly discipline' was most firmly established: Clydeside, the eastern Borders, the Lothians, Fife, the northeast and the Northern Isles.

The pattern of persecution was uneven chronologically as well as geographically. After the spate of trials between 1590 and 1597 there was a lull until 1628–30, then another hiatus in the 1630s. There was considerable activity against witches throughout the Covenanting period, with a peak in 1649, but the largest 'witchcraze' came in 1658–62 with over 500 cases. After that, prosecutions began to decline until the 1770s, after which there was only the isolated case. The last execution for witchcraft took place in Dornoch in 1727. This chronological pattern of persecution matches that of other west European countries, where a 'witchcraze' occurred between about 1580 and about 1660. Such outbreaks were often associated with the end of a period of conflict between the different Christian creeds: the victory of one denomination seems to have been celebrated with an offensive against all unbelievers. In Scotland it was the triumphant Calvinists who organized the chastisement of the 'enemies of God', whether they happened to be servants of the Pope or of the Devil.

G. Parker

Woollen and Knitwear Industries. Scotland is justly renowned for woollen products of high quality: top-grade hand-knitting wools, fine-spun yarns, tweed cloth, fancy knitted garments, carpet-making and some underwear products. Historically ubiquitous, the manufacture of wool products today is largely centred on the hand-woven Harris tweed of the Hebrides, the factory-produced tweed of the Borders and the knitting industries of the west of Scotland and the Borders.

The commercial importance of Scotch tweed dates from the 1820s when the traditional black and white checked plaiding of the Galashiels district was adopted by Glasgow and London merchants in response to both the popularization of Scottish history and culture by the writings of Sir Walter Scott, causing tartans to be in vogue, and a change in fashion away from breeches and hose to trousers and half-hose. The accidental coining of the term 'tweed' by a London invoice clerk from a mis-reading of the word 'tweel' (twill) presented the industry with an unsurpassable brand name. Tweed manufacture was adopted in the Hillfoot region by the 1850s as the tartan shawl trade there declined, while Aberdeen, for long a centre of stocking and cloth production, gave the name 'Crombie' to the overcoatings trade. Highland woollen firms helped to popularize the 'District' checks such as 'Glenurquhart' and 'Glenfeshie', themselves modifications of the Border 'Shepherd' check, which were designed for use on the many large Scottish hunting estates as camouflage uniforms. Together with mixture designs like 'Lovat' and 'Heather', which were clear attempts to reproduce colourings in the Scottish landscape in cloth, these fabrics laid the basis of men's informal outerwear, their designs being still commonly found in sports jackets today. From the 1880s the hand-woven cloths of the Hebrides began to be widely marketed under the stimulus of commercially minded local lairds taking advantage of improved communications to and within the mainland. By this time, however, the tweed industry was already being threatened by cheap Yorkshire tweeds and by a switch in public taste towards lighter, less durable products giving rise eventually to wool substitutes in suitings and a tendency towards the wearing of knitted garments. Thus the prosperity of the tweed industry in the nineteenth century has not been matched in the twentieth.

The origins of knitting in Scotland are obscure. Knitting hosiery on 'wires' (needles) by men and women while tending livestock was well enough established by the eighteenth century for the export of worsted stockings to become an important element in the economy of Aberdeen until *c.* 1800. The future of knitting, however, lay with the hand stocking-frame first introduced into Scotland at Haddington in the 1680s. Frame-knitting only became commercially significant, however, after the frame had been introduced to Hawick in 1771 whence stems the burgh's prestigious knitwear industry of today. The nineteenth century witnessed a great expansion of production there based at first on lambswool hosiery; then on a wide variety of woollen underwear products made on the wide hand-frame and on steam-driven flat frames from mid-

century; to be followed in the present century by a concentration on ladies' and mens' outerwear in the form of sweaters and cardigans. In the west of Scotland the knitwear industry, centred in and around Kilmarnock, originated in the making of fisherman's bonnets, and now specializes in medium quality outerwear.

The differences between the Border and the west of Scotland knitting industries lie mainly in the selection and treatment of the raw material. Hawick goods are almost invariably high-grade, 'fully-fashioned' garments using virgin wools and formed to fit the contours of the body to provide maximum elasticity and comfort. Much of the production of the west of Scotland trade is also fashioned but the garments are generally lower-quality, 'cut and sew' products, often made from synthetic fibres. Purity of raw material has been a traditional feature of the Border woollen industry since the use of improved Cheviot wool in the late eighteenth century. Imported fine wools soon replaced Cheviot, and Hawick knitwear now makes great use of cashmere and other fine yarns from wool dyed in delicate pastel shades prior to the spinning and knitting processes. The garment is then carefully trimmed and finished, resulting in an artistic creation pleasurable to see and to handle. The respective markets for the typical products of the two regions tend to reflect these differences in manufacture. Hawick exports a large proportion of its output, mainly to the high-income areas of Europe, Scandinavia and North America, whereas the bulk of the output of the west of Scotland industry is aimed at the mass market at home.

The distinctive aesthetic features of the high-quality woollen products of Scotland therefore result from skilled pattern designing and styling based upon the sensitive dyeing and finishing of top-grade raw materials.

C. Gulvin

Y

Young, Douglas Cuthbert Colquhoun (1913–1973) humanist, who disliked his second name, and would much rather have been called Claverhouse, was born at Tayport, but spent part of his childhood in Bengal. Urdu, not Scots, was the language he learnt 'at nourris knee'. He received a classical education (privately combined with many other studies) at Merchiston, St Andrews (where his fellow-students accused him of omniscience and nick-named him the Deity, or more familiarly, God), and Oxford, and then taught Greek at King's College, Aberdeen, from 1938 to 1941. In his late teens he began writing learned poetry in Greek, Latin, Scots, and English, and may deliberately have emulated such celebrated Scottish humanists as the Admirable Crichton, Henry Scrymgeour, and Arthur Johnston. By 1933 he had already become an active supporter of the SNP, which he finally joined in 1938. But his nationalism was always irradiated with internationalism; and in 1935 he had also joined the Labour Party. He was very tall; and even in company with his mentors Sir Darcy Wentworth Thompson and W. L. Lorimer his then unfashionable black beard gave him an exceptionally distinguished appearance. Despite the misgivings with which the Anglo-Scottish academic establishment contemplated his political aberrations, his urbane affability disarmed, flattered, and fascinated many distinguished listeners who might otherwise have been antagonized by the *brio* with which he buttonholed them; and, not only in academic and literary circles, but also amongst the Scottish landed gentry, he acquired a great many lifelong friends.

During the Second World War he courageously refused to be conscripted, twice failed to persuade any Scottish judge of the relevancy of his contention that the statutes under which he was accordingly convicted both contravened the Anglo-Scottish Union of 1707, and spent altogether one year in prison, which, with such agreeable cellmates as Homer, Aeschylus, and Theognis, he found 'by no means boring'. He was meanwhile, however, elected chairman of the SNP, and in the by-election held at Kirkcaldy towards the end of the war was placed second, with 40 per cent of all votes cast. In 1948, when the SNP prohibited membership of any other party, he remained a member of the Labour Party, and finally left the SNP.

After the war he taught humanity (Latin) at University College, Dundee, from 1947 to 1953, and then for 15 years taught Greek at St Andrews. No vacant Scottish professorial chair for which he applied was ever bestowed on him: but he was appointed Professor of Classics at MacMaster University in 1968, and only two years later became Professor of Greek at the University of North Carolina. The pace at which he read, wrote, taught, and peregrinated had never slackened; and in 1973 he died suddenly at Chapel Hill, with his Homer open in front of him.

Though well received, Young's Teubnerian *Theognis* (1961) was considered somewhat conservative. *Auntran Blads* (1943) and *A Braird o Thristles* (1947) both contain some excellent Scots poems, epigrams, and translations (e.g., especially, to name only three, 'Fife Equinox', 'Luve', and 'Hektor's Twynan frae Andromacha'); and but for one startling solecism, which he could easily have corrected, the Greek elegiacs which he composed on I September 1939 might fitly have been introduced into the Palatine Anthology. His prose includes *Chasing an Ancient Greek* (1950) and *St Andrews* (1969), both minor classics of modern Scottish literature; and his 'Miltonic Light on … Homeric Theory' must be one of the most sustained and funniest *reductiones ad absurdum* ever contributed to any learned periodical. All recollection of his invigorating and informative conversation will perish with his contemporaries, but his life and works will be remembered because they demonstrated his commitment to the beliefs that without Hellenism there can be no Europeanism, and that it is possible to be both Scottish and civilized.

R.L.C. Lorimer

Further Reading

The books and articles listed below are in no way intended to be a comprehensive guide to the many aspects of Scottish culture covered in this *Companion*. Inclusion has been at the suggestion of the contributors; and exclusion implies no criticism. The material mentioned here in many cases should be seen as supplementary to the texts and other books mentioned in the articles themselves, where fuller information can usually be found. Some of the titles will be out of print and available only from libraries.

The alphabetical ordering of the entries in the main body of the *Companion* is not repeated here. Instead, this Bibliography is arranged under the thematic headings listed below. Some titles mentioned in the introductory General section recur later.

General	*Textiles*	*Eighteenth Century*	**Philosophy**
Architecture	**Institutions**	*Nineteenth Century*	**Politics**
Archaeology	*Education*	*Twentieth Century*	**Printing, Publishing,**
Customs and Folklore	*Law*	*Gaelic*	**and Libraries**
Diaries and Memoirs	*Religion*	*Celtic*	**Regional Studies**
Food and Drink	**Land and Land-Use**	**Medicine**	**Science**
Industry	**Language**	**Music**	**Scots Abroad**
Coal	**Literature**	*Discography*	**Sport**
Engineering	*General*	**Newspapers**	**Travellers and**
Fishing	*Ballads*	**Painting and Sculpture**	**Transport**
Iron and Steel	*Medieval and Renaissance*	**Performing Arts**	

General

Donaldson, Gordon and Morpeth, Robert S.: *A Dictionary of Scottish History*, Edinburgh, 1977, repr. 1988
———: *Who's Who in Scottish History*, Oxford, 1973

Mitchison, Rosalind: *A History of Scotland*, 2nd ed., London, 1982

Menzies, Gordon, ed.: *Who are the Scots?*, London, 1971
Chadwick, H. M.: *Early Scotland*, Cambridge, 1942
Feachem, R.: *A Guide to Prehistoric Scotland*, 2nd ed., London, 1977
Henderson, Isobel: *The Picts*, London, 1967
Piggott, S., ed.: *The Prehistoric Peoples of Scotland*, London, 1962
Wainwright, F. T., ed.: *The Problem of the Picts*, Edinburgh, 1954

Dickinson, W. C.: *Scotland from the Earliest Times to 1603*, Edinburgh, 1961
Ritchie, R. L. G.: *The Normans in Scotland*, Edinburgh, 1954
Barrow, G. W. S.: *Kingship and Unity: Scotland 1000–1306, The New History of Scotland*, NHS II, London, 1981, repr. Edinburgh, 1989
———: *Robert Bruce and The Community of The Realm of Scotland*, 3rd ed., Edinburgh 1992
Checkland, Sydney and Olive: *Industry and Ethos: Scotland 1832–1914, NHS* VII, 2nd ed., Edinburgh, 1989
Duncan, A. A.: *Scotland: The Making of the Kingdom*, Edinburgh, 1975

Grant, A.: *Independence and Nationhood: Scotland 1306–1469, NHS* III, London, 1982–1984, repr. Edinburgh, 1991
Harvie, Christopher: *No Gods and Precious Few Heroes: Scotland 1914–1980, NHS* VIII, London, 1981, repr. Edinburgh, 1993
Lenman, Bruce: *Integration, Enlightenment, and Industrialization: Scotland 1746–1832, NHS* VI, London, 1981
Mitchison, Rosalind: *Lordship to Patronage: Scotland 1603–1745, NHS* V, London, 1983, repr. Edinburgh, 1990
Nicholson, R. G.: *Scotland: the Later Middle Ages*, Edinburgh, 1973
Donaldson, Gordon: *Scotland: James V to James VII*, Edinburgh, 1965, rev. ed. 1971
Smout, T. C.: *A History of the Scottish People 1560–1830*, London, 1969, repr. 1987
Smyth, Alfred P.: *War-Lords and Holy Men: Scotland 500–1000, NHS* I, London, 1984, repr. Edinburgh, 1989
Wormald, Jenny: *Court, Kirk, and Community: Scotland 1470–1625, NHS* IV, London, 1981, repr. Edinburgh, 1991
Campbell, R. H.: *Scotland since 1707*, Oxford, 1965, 2nd ed., Edinburgh, 1985
Lenman, Bruce: *An Economic History of Modern Scotland*, London, 1977

Burleigh, J. A. S.: *A Church History of Scotland*, Oxford, 1960
Donaldson, Gordon: *Scotland: Church and Nation through Sixteen Centuries*, London, 1969
O'Dell, A. and Walton, K.: *The Highlands and Islands of Scotland*, London and Edinburgh, 1962
Thompson, F.: *The Highlands and Islands*, London, 1974

Wainwright, F. T., ed.: *The Northern Isles*, Edinburgh, 1962

Craig, David: *Scottish Literature and the Scottish People*, London, 1961
Daiches, David: *The Paradox of Scottish Culture*, London, 1964
Hart, Francis: *The Scottish Novel: A Critical Survey*, London, 1978
Henderson, T. F.: *Scottish Vernacular Literature, A History*, London, 1900
Kinsley, James, ed.: *Scottish Poetry: A Critical Survey*, London, 1955
Lindsay, Maurice: *History of Scottish Literature*, London, 1977, rev. ed. London, 1992
Millar, J. H.: *A Literary History of Scotland*, London, 1903
Speirs, John: *The Scots Literary Tradition*, London, 1962
Wittig, Kurt: *The Scottish Tradition in Literature*, Edinburgh, 1958

Campbell, J. F.: *Popular Tales of the West Highlands*, 4 vols., 2nd ed., London, 1890, repr. Edinburgh, 1993
Maclean, Magnus: *The Literature of the Highlands*, 2nd ed., London, 1925
Thomson, D. S.: *An Introduction to Gaelic Poetry*, London, 1974
Williams, J. E. C.: *Literature in Celtic Countries*, Cardiff, 1971

Cursiter, Stanley: *Scottish Art*, London, 1949
Dunbar, J. G.: *The Historic Architecture of Scotland*, 2nd rev. ed., London, 1978
Fenton, Alexander and Walker, Bruce: *The Rural Architecture of Scotland*, Edinburgh, 1981
Finlay, Ian: *Art in Scotland*, London, 1948
———: *Scottish Crafts*, London, 1948

Collinson, Francis: *The Traditional and National Music of Scotland*, London, 1966
Farmer, H. G.: *A History of Music in Scotland*, London, 1948
Flett, J. M. and T. M.: *Traditional Dancing in Scotland*, London, 1964
Shire, Helene M.: *Song, Dance and Poetry at the Court of Scotland under James VI*, Cambridge, 1969 [Of much wider significance, for an understanding of the courtly tradition in Scottish culture than the title suggests.]

Dunbar, J. T.: *History of Highland Dress*, Edinburgh, 1962, repr. London, 1979
Grange, R. M. D.: *A Short History of Scottish Dress*, London, 1966
Clement, A. G. and Robertson, R. H. S.: *Scotland's Scientific Heritage*, Edinburgh, 1961

Symm, J. A.: *Scottish Farming Past and Present*, Edinburgh, 1959
———: *Chambers Scottish Biographical Dictionary*, Edinburgh, 1992
Barrow, G. W. S.: *The Anglo-Norman Era in Scottish History*, Oxford, 1980
———: *Robert the Bruce and the Scottish Identity*, Edinburgh, 1984

Beveridge, Craig and Turnbull, Ronald: *The Eclipse of Scottish Culture: Inferiorism and the Intellectuals*, Edinburgh, 1989
Craig, David: *On the Crofter's Trail: In Search of the Clearance Highlanders*, London, 1990
Donaldson, Gordon: *All the Queen's Men: Power and Politics in Mary Stewart's Scotland*, London, 1983
———: *Scotland: the Shaping of a Nation*, Newton Abbot, 1974, rev. 2nd ed. 1980
Donnachie, Ian and Hewitt, George: *A Companion to Scottish History: From the Reformation to the Present*, London, 1989
Donnachie, Ian and Whatley, Christopher: *The Manufacture of Scottish History*, Edinburgh, 1992
Fry, Michael: *The Dundas Despotism*, Edinburgh, 1993
Hanley, Clifford: *The Scots*, London, 1982
Lindsay, Joyce and Maurice: *The Scottish Quotation Book: A Literary Companion*, London, 1991
Linklater, M. and Denniston, Robin, ed.: *Anatomy of Scotland*, Edinburgh, 1992
Lynch, Michael: *Scotland: A New History*, London, 1991
Mason, Roger and MacDougall, Norman, ed.: *People and Power in Scotland: Essays in Honour of T. C. Smout*, Edinburgh, 1993
Nairn, Tom: *The Break-Up of Britain: Crisis and Neo-Nationalism*, rev. ed., London, 1981
Pittock, Murray G. H.: *The Invention of Scotland: The Stuart Myth and the Scottish Identity, 1638 to the Present*, London, 1991
Scott, Ronald McNair: *Robert the Bruce, King of Scots*, London, 1982
Small, Alan, ed.: *The Picts: A New Look at Old Problems*, Dundee, 1987
Steel, Tom: *Scotland's Story*, London, 1985 [published in conjunction with the Channel 4 television series]
Bold, Alan: *Bonnie Prince Charlie*, Andover, 1992
Daiches, David: *Charles Edward Stuart: The Life and Times of Bonnie Prince Charlie*, London, 1973
Kybett, Susan Maclean: *Bonnie Prince Charlie: A Biography*, London, 1988
Maclean, Fitzroy: *Bonnie Prince Charlie*, Edinburgh, 1988
McLynn, Frank: *Charles Edward Stuart: A Tragedy in Many Acts*, London, 1988
Barclay, William: *Ethics in a Permissive Society*, London, 1971
Crosfield, Philip: *What is the Scottish Episcopal Church?*, Edinburgh, 1991
Donaldson, Gordon: *The Scottish Dimension: The Story of Christianity in Scotland*, Edinburgh, 1985
Goldie, F.: *A Short History of the Episcopal Church in Scotland: From the Restoration to the Present Time*, 2nd ed., Edinburgh, 1976
Mullan, David George: *Episcopacy in Scotland: The History of an Idea, 1560–1638*, Edinburgh, 1986
Kaplan, Wendy, ed.: *Scotland Creates: 5000 Years of Art and Design*, Glasgow, 1990
Rockett 88, Glasgow, 1986- [fashion and design magazine]
Scott-Moncrieff, George: *Living Traditions of Scotland*, Edinburgh, 1957

Meller, Helen: *Patrick Geddes: Social Evolutionist and City Planner*, London, 1990

Donaldson, Gordon: *Knox the Man*, Edinburgh, 1980

———: *John Knox*, London, 1983

Lamont, Stewart: *The Swordbearer: John Knox and the European Reformation*, London, 1991

MacDiarmid, Hugh: *John Knox*, Edinburgh, 1976

Muir, Edwin: *John Knox: Portrait of a Calvinist*, London, 1930

Ridley, Jasper Godwin: *John Knox*, Oxford, 1968

Shaw, Duncan, ed.: *John Knox: A Quarter-centenary Reappraisal*, Edinburgh, 1975

———: *John Knox and Mary Queen of Scots*, Edinburgh, 1980

Walt, Hugh: *John Knox in Controversy*, London, 1980

Rosie, George: *Hugh Millar: Outrage and Order: A Biography and Selected Writings*, with an introduction by Neal Ascherson, Edinburgh, 1981

Dougan, R. O.: *The Scottish Tradition in Photography*, Edinburgh, 1949

Hannavy, John: *A Moment in Time: Scotland's Contributions to Photography, 1840–1920*, Glasgow, 1983

Stevenson, Sara and Morrison-Low, A. D., ed.: *Scottish Photography: A Bibliography, 1839–1989*, Edinburgh, 1990

Stevenson, Sara: *Thomas Annan, 1829–1887*, Edinburgh, 1990

Stevenson, Sara and Morrison-Low, A. D.: *Scottish Photography: A Bibliography: 1839–1989*, Salvia Books, 1990

Stevenson, Sara: *Hill and Adamson's The Fishermen and Women of the Firth of Forth*, Edinburgh, 1991

Hannavy, John: *A Moment in Time: Scottish Contributions to Photography 1840–1920*, Glasgow, 1983

Buchanan, William: *The Art of the Photographer J. Craig Annan*, Edinburgh, 1992

Craig, Cairns: 'Visitors from the Stars: Scottish Film Culture', *Cencrastus* II, New Year 1983, pp 6–11

Hardy, Forsyth: *Scotland in Film*, Edinburgh, 1990

Scottish Central Film Library: *Social Subjects on 16mm Film and Video*, Glasgow, 1985

———: *The Arts and Design on 16mm Film and Video*, Glasgow, 1985

———: *Science Subjects on 16mm Film and Video*, Glasgow, 1985

Architecture

Cruden, Stewart: *The Scottish Castle*, London, 1960, 3rd ed., 1981

Howarth, Thomas: *Charles Rennie Mackintosh and the Modern Movement*, London, 1952

Lindsay, Ian G.: *The Scottish Parish Kirk*, Edinburgh, 1960

McWilliam, Colin: *Scottish Townscape*, London, 1975

Morton, R. S.: *Traditional Farm Architecture in Scotland*, Edinburgh, 1976

Tranter, Nigel: *The Fortified House in Scotland*, 5 vols., Edinburgh, 1962–66

Youngson, A. J.: *The Making of Classical Edinburgh*, Edinburgh, 1966, repr. 1993

Birrell, George: *Edinburgh, Princes St and the New Town*, Edinburgh, 1986

Cruden, Stewart: *Scottish Medieval Churches*, Edinburgh, 1986

Dean, Marcus: *Scotland's Endangered Houses*, London, 1990

Dunbar, John G.: *The Architecture of Scotland*, 2nd ed., London, 1978 (previous ed. published as *The Historic Architecture of Scotland*, London, 1966)

Fenton, Alexander and Walker, Bruce: *The Rural Architecture of Scotland*, Edinburgh, 1981

Gifford, John; McWilliam, Colin; and Walter, David: *Edinburgh*, Harmondsworth, 1984

Gifford, John: *Highland and Islands*, part of 'The Buildings of Scotland' series by Penguin, London, 1992

Gomme, Andor and Walker, David: *The Architecture of Glasgow*, 2nd ed., London, 1987

Hannah, Ian C.: *The Story of Scotland in Stone*, Stevenage, 1988

Howard, Deborah, ed.: *Scottish Architects Abroad*, Edinburgh, 1991

Kenna, Rudolph: *Scotland in the Thirties*, Glasgow, 1987

Kersting, Anthony F. and Lindsay, Maurice: *The Buildings of Edinburgh*, London, 1987

Lindsay, Maurice: *The Castles of Scotland*, London, 1986

Macaulay, James: *The Classical House in Scotland 1660–1800*, London, 1987

McKean, Charles: *The Scottish Thirties: An Architectural Introduction*, Edinburgh, 1987

McKean, Charles: *Architectural Contributions to Scottish Society Since 1840*, Edinburgh, 1990

McKean, Charles and Walker, David: *Edinburgh: An Illustrated Architectural Guide*, new ed., Edinburgh, 1992

McKean, Charles; Walker, David; and Walker, Frank: *Central Glasgow: An Illustrated Architectural Guide*, Edinburgh, 1989

McKinstry, Sam: *Rowand Anderson: the Premier Architect of Scotland*, Edinburgh, 1991

Naismith, Robert J.: *Buildings of the Scottish Countryside*, London, 1989

Royal Incorporation of Architects in Scotland: *The Architecture of the Scottish Renaissance*, Edinburgh, 1990

———: *Scottish Architecture in the Nineteen Eighties*, Edinburgh, 1987

Scottish Development Department: *Scotland's Listed Buildings: A Guide to Their Protection*, rev. ed., Edinburgh, 1981

Sinclair, Fiona: *Scotstyle: 150 Years of Scottish Architecture*, Edinburgh, 1984

West, T. W.: *Discovering Scottish Architecture*, 2nd ed., Princes Risborough Shire, 1985 (previous ed. published as *A History of Architecture in Scotland*, London, 1967)

Williamson, Elizabeth; Riches, Anne; and Higgs, Malcolm: *Glasgow*, part of 'The Buildings of Scotland' series by Penguin, London, 1990

Worsdall, Frank: *Victorian City*, Glasgow, 1982

Archaeology

Hanson, William S. and Slater E. A., ed.: *Scottish Archaeology: New Perceptions*, Aberdeen, 1991

Inverness Field Club: *The Dark Ages in the Highlands: Ancient Peoples, Local History*, Inverness, 1971

Nicholson, Ranald: *Scotland: The Later Middle Ages*, vol. 2, *The Edinburgh History of Scotland*, Edinburgh, 1974

Ross, Stewart: *Ancient Scotland*, Moffat, 1991

Breeze, David J.: *The Northern Frontiers of Roman Britain*, London, 1982

———: *Roman Scotland: A Guide to the Visible Remains*, Newcastle, 1979

Crawford, O. G. S.: *Topography of Roman Scotland, North of the Antonine Wall*, Cambridge, 1949

Keppie, L. J. F.: *Scotland's Roman Remains: An Introduction and Handbook*, Edinburgh, 1986

MacDonald, Sir George: *The Roman Wall in Scotland*, 2nd ed., Oxford, 1934

Ritchie, Anna: *Invaders of Scotland: An Introduction to the Archaeology of the Romans*, Edinburgh, 1991

Feachem, R. W.: *Guide to Prehistoric Scotland*, 2nd ed., London, 1977

Renfrew, Colin, ed.: *The Prehistory of Orkney: BC4000–1000AD*, Edinburgh, 1985, repr. 1990 [with postscript by Colin Richards]

Ritchie, Anna: *Scotland B.C.: An Introduction to the Prehistoric Houses, Tombs, Ceremonial Monuments and Fortifications in the Care of the Secretary of State for Scotland*, Edinburgh, 1988

Childe, V. Gordon: *Skara Brae*, rev. ed. the late V. G. Childe and D. V. Clarke, Edinburgh, 1983

Clarke, David and Maguire, Patrick: *Skara Brae: Northern Europe's Best Preserved Prehistoric Village*, Edinburgh, 1989

Customs and Folklore

Cowan, Edward J., ed.: *The People's Past*, Edinburgh, 1980, repr. 1993

Grant, I. F.: *Highland Folk Ways*, London, 1961 (repr. pbk ed., London, 1975)

Innes of Learney, Sir Thomas: *Scottish Heraldry*, Edinburgh, 1978

Larner, Christina: *A Sourcebook of Scottish Witchcraft*, Glasgow, 1977

McNeill, F. Marian: *The Silver Bough*, 4 vols., Glasgow, 1957–68

Ross, Anne: *Folklore of the Scottish Highlands*, London, 1976

Scarlett, J. D.: *The Tartans of the Scottish Clans*, Glasgow, 1975

Anderson, Janice and Swinglehurst, Edmund: *Scottish Walks and Legends in Western Scotland and the Highlands*, London, 1982

Bennett, Margaret: *Scottish Customs from the Cradle to the Grave*, Edinburgh, 1993

———: *The Cannibal Family of Sawney Bean and Stories of South-West Scotland*, illustrated by John Mackay, Glasgow, 1991

Carmichael, Alexander: *Charms of the Gaels: Hymns and Incantations*, Edinburgh, 1992

Gunn, Robert P.: *Tales From Braemore: A Collection of Caithness Folklore and History*, Caithness, 1991

Hendry, Ian D. and Stephen, Graham, ed.: *Scotscape: Lore, Legend and Customs*, Edinburgh, 1978

Larner, Christina: *Enemies of God: The Witch-Hunt in Scotland*, London, 1981

Lochhead, Marion: *Edinburgh Lore and Legend*, London, 1986

Penman, Alastair: *Some Customs, Folklore and Superstitions of Galloway*, Castle Douglas, 1992

Steel, David and Judy: *Mary Stuart's Scotland: the Landscapes, Life and Legends of Mary Queen of Scots*, London, 1987

Diaries and Memoirs

Fyfe, J. G., ed.: *Scottish Diaries and Memoirs 1550–1746*, Stirling, 1927

———: ed.: *Scottish Diaries and Memoirs 1746–1843*, Stirling, 1942

Ponsonby, A. ed.: *Scottish and Irish Diaries from the Sixteenth to the Nineteenth Century*, London, 1927

Food and Drink

Burnett, John: *Plenty and Want*, London, 1966, rev. ed. 1978

McNeil, F. Marian: *The Scots Kitchen*, Glasgow 1929, repr. 1971

———: *Recipes from Scotland*, Edinburgh, 1978

Pattullo, Diane: *Scottish Cooking in Colour*, Edinburgh, 1977

Tannahill, Reay: *Food in History*, St Albans, 1975

Wilson, C. Anne: *Food and Drink in Britain*, London, 1973

Daiches, D.: *Scotch Whisky, its Past and Present*, London, 1969, 3rd ed., 1978

McDowall, R. J. S.: *The Whiskies of Scotland*, 3rd ed., London, 1975, 4th ed., 1986

Brander, Michael: *The Essential Guide to Scotch Whisky*, Edinburgh, 1990, rev. edn., 1992

Cooper, Derek: *Introduction to A Buyer's Guide to Food and Drink in the Highlands and Islands of Scotland*, Inverness, 1989

Daiches, David: *A Wee Dram: Drinking Scenes from Scottish Literature*, London, 1990

Devine, T. M.: *The Great Highland Famine Hunger: Emigration and the Scottish Highlands in the Nineteenth Century*, Edinburgh, 1988

Fenton, Alexander and Myrdal, Janken, ed.: *Food and Drink and Travelling Accessories*, Edinburgh, 1988

Hazell, Katriana: *Not Just Haggis: Food and Drink in Scotland*, Edinburgh, 1986

Hope, Annette: *A Caledonian Feast*, Edinburgh, 1987

———: *A Caledonian Feast*, London, 1989

Hope, Annette and Barfoot, Michael: *A Remarkable Improvement: Historical Aspects of Food, Drink and Health in Scotland*, Edinburgh, 1990

Kinchin, Perilla: *Tea and Taste: The Glasgow tea rooms 1875–1975*, Wendlebury, 1991

Lockhart, G. W.: *The Scot and his Oats*, Barr, 1983

McDowall, R. J. S.: *The Whiskies of Scotland*, 3rd ed., London, 1975

McNeill, Marian, F.: *The Scots Cellar*, various eds, 1956 →

Moss, Michael: *Scotch Whisky*, Edinburgh, 1991

Sprenger, Richard A.: *The Food Hygiene Handbook for Scotland*, Doncaster, 1991

Tannahill, Reay: *Food in History*, London, 1973, rev. edn., 1988

Industry

Coal

Duckham, Baron F.: *A History of the Scottish Coal Industry 1700–1815*, Newton Abbot, 1970

Galloway, R. L.: *Annals of Coal Mining and the Coal Trade*, 2 vols., 1898–1904, repr. Newton Abbot, 1971 with bibliography by Baron F. Duckham

Halliday, Robert: *The Disappearing Scottish Colliery: A Personal View of Some Aspects of Scotland's Coal Industry since Nationalization*, Edinburgh, 1990

Hyde, E. D.: *Coal Mining in Scotland*, Newtongrange, 1987

Thomson, Marion: *Class Consciousness: A Comparative Study of the Twenties and Eighties in Two Scottish Mining Communities*, Toronto, 1992

Engineering

Birse, Ronald M.: *Science at Edinburgh University*, Edinburgh, 1993

——: *Engineering at Edinburgh University: a Short history, 1673–1983*, Edinburgh, 1983

Moss, Michael S. and Hume, John R.: *Workshop of the British Empire: Engineering and Shipbuilding in the West of Scotland*, London, 1977

Fishing

Anson, Peter F.: *Fishing-Boats and Fisher Folk on the East Coast of Scotland*, London, 1971

Coull, James R.: 'Fisheries in the northeast of Scotland before 1800', *Scottish Studies* 13, 1969

Gray, Malcolm: *The Fishing Industries of Scotland, 1790–1914*, Oxford, 1978

March, Edward J.: *Sailing Drifters*, London, 1952

Iron and Steel

Birch, Alan: *The Economic History of the British Iron and Steel Industry, 1784–1879*, London, 1967

Butt, John: 'Capital and enterprise in the Scottish iron industry, 1780–1840', in Butt, John and Ward, J. T., ed.: *Scottish Themes: Essays in Honour of Professor S. G. E. Lythe*, Edinburgh, 1976

——: 'The Scottish iron and steel industry before the hot-blast', *Journal of the West of Scotland Iron and Steel Institute* 73, 1965–66

Byres, T. J.: 'Entrepreneurship in the Scottish heavy industries, 1870–1900', in Payne, P. L., ed.: *Studies in Scottish Business History*, London, 1967

Campbell, R. H.: *Carron Company*, Edinburgh, 1961

——: 'Early malleable iron production in Scotland', *Business History* IV, 1961–62

——: *The Rise and Fall of Scottish Industry, 1707–1939*, Edinburgh, 1980

Gibson, I. F.: 'The establishment of the Scottish steel industry', *Scottish Journal of Political Economy* V, 1958

Heal, David W.: *The Steel Industry in Post-War Britain*, Newton Abbot, 1974

Hume, J. R. and Moss, Michael S.: *History of William Beardmore & Co., 1837–1977*, London, 1979

Hyde, Charles K.: *Technological Change and the British Iron Industry, 1700–1870*, Princeton, NJ, 1977

Miller, Andrew: *The Rise and Progress of Coatbridge*, Glasgow, 1874

Payne, P. L.: *Colvilles and the Scottish Steel Industry*, Oxford, 1979

Kelman, James: *Fighting For Survival: The Steel Industry in Scotland*, Glasgow, 1990

Textiles

Gulvin, C.: *The Tweedmakers: A History of the Scottish Fancy Woollen Industry, 1600–1914*, Newton Abbot, 1973

Durie, A. J.: *The Linen Industry in the Eighteenth Century*, Edinburgh, 1978

Lenman, B.: *From Esk to Tweed*, Glasgow and London, 1975

Institutions

Education

Craigie, James: *Bibliography of Scottish Education before 1872*, London, 1970

——: *Bibliography of Scottish Education from 1872–1972*, London, 1974

Davie, G. E.: *The Democratic Intellect: Scotland and her Universities in the Nineteenth Century*, Edinburgh, 1961

Hunter, S. Leslie: *The Scottish Educational System*, 2nd ed., Oxford, 1972

Scotland, James: *A History of Scottish Education*, vols. I and II, London, 1970

Donaldson, Gordon, ed.: *Four Centuries: Edinburgh University Life 1583–1983*, Edinburgh, 1983

Kirkwood, Colin: *Vulgar Eloquence: Essays in Education, Community and Politics*, Edinburgh, 1990

Humes, Walter M.: *The Leadership Class in Scottish Education*, Edinburgh, 1986

Law

Gloag, W. M. and Henderson, R. C.: *Introduction to the Law of Scotland*, 9th ed., Edinburgh, 1987

Smith, T. B.: *A Short Commentary on the Law of Scotland*, Edinburgh, 1962

Walker, D. M.: *Principles of Scottish Private Law*, 2nd ed., Oxford, 1975 (4th ed, 1988)

Wilson, W. A.: *Introductory Essays on Scots Law*, Edinburgh, 1978

Walker, David M.: *A History of the School of Law, the University of Glasgow*, Glasgow, 1990

——: *The Law of Contracts and Related Obligations in Scotland*, 2nd ed., London, 1985

——: *Legal History of Scotland*, Edinburgh, 1988

——: *The Scottish Legal System: An Introduction to the Study of Scots Law*, 6th ed., Edinburgh, 1992

Styles, Scott Crichton, ed.: *The Scottish Legal Tradition*, Foreword by Lord Mackay and Afterword by Lord Dervaird, new enlarged ed., Edinburgh, 1991

Religion

Cowan, Ian B. and Easson, David E.: *Medieval Religious Houses in Scotland*, 2nd ed., London, 1976

Croft Dickinson, W., ed.: *John Knox's History of the Reformation in Scotland*, 2 vols., London and Edinburgh, 1949

Drummond, Andrew L. and Bulloch, James: *The Scottish Church, 1688–1843: The Age of the Moderates*, Edinburgh, 1943

——: *The Church in Victorian Scotland, 1843–1874*, Edinburgh, 1975

——: *The Church in Late Victorian Scotland, 1874–1900*, Edinburgh, 1978

Goldie, Frederick: *A Short History of the Episcopal Church in Scotland*, 2nd ed., Edinburgh, 1976

Herron, Andrew: *A Guide to the General Assembly of the Church of Scotland*, Edinburgh, 1976, new ed. 1986

McRoberts, D., ed.: *Modern Scottish Catholicism, 1878–1978*, Glasgow, 1979

Boyd, Kenneth M.: *Scottish Church Attitudes to Sex, Marriage and the Family 1850–1914*, Edinburgh, 1980

Cowan, Ian B.: *The Scottish Reformation Church and Society in Sixteenth Century Scotland*, London, 1982

Pagan, Anne: *God's Scotland? The Story of Scottish Christian Religion*, Edinburgh, 1988

Land and Land-Use

Bryden, J. and Houston, G. B. F.: *Agricultural Change in the Scottish Highlands*, London, 1976

Caird, J. B.: 'Changes in the highlands and islands of Scotland, 1951–71', *Geoforum* 12172, 1972

Coppock, J. T.: *An Agricultural Atlas of Scotland*, Edinburgh, 1976

Crofters Commission: *Guide to the Crofting Acts*, Edinburgh, 1976, repr. 1986

Fenton, A.; *Scottish Country Life*, Edinburgh, 1976, repr 1989

——: *The Northern Isles, Orkney and Shetland*, Edinburgh, 1978

Franklin, T. B.: *A History of Scottish Farming*, London and Edinburgh, 1952

Handley, J. E.: *Scottish Farming in the Eighteenth Century*, London, 1953

——: *The Agricultural Revolution in Scotland*, Glasgow, 1963

Houston, J. M.: 'Village planning in Scotland, 1745–1845', *The Advancement of Science* V, 1948

Hunter, James: *The Making of the Crofting Community*, Edinburgh, 1976

Ryder, N. L.: 'The evolution of Scottish breeds of sheep', *Scottish Studies*, 12, 1968

——: *Sheep and Man*, London, 1982

Smout, T. C.: 'The landowner and the planned village in Scotland, 1730–1830', in Phillipson, N. T. and Mitchison, Rosalind, ed.: *Scotland in the Age of Improvement*, Edinburgh, 1970

——: 'Famine and famine relief in Scotland', in Cullen, L. and Smout, T. C., *Comparative Aspects of Scottish and Irish Economic and Social Development 1600–1900*, Edinburgh, 1977

Symon, J. A.: *Scottish Farming Past and Present*, Edinburgh and London, 1959

Tait, A. A.: *The Landscape Garden in Scotland 1735–1835*, Edinburgh, 1980

Watson, S. J.: 'Agriculture', in Meikle, H. W., ed. *Scotland: A Description of Scotland and Scottish Life*, London and Edinburgh, 1947

Fenton, Alexander: *Country Life in Scotland and our Rural Past*, Edinburgh, 1987

——: *North East Farming Life*, Banff and Buchan, 1987

Society, Religion and Technology Project: *While the Earth Endures: A Report on the Theological and Ethical Considerations of Responsible Land-Use in Scotland*, Edinburgh, 1986

Language

Craigie, W. A., Aitken, A. J. and Stevenson, J. A. C.: *A Dictionary of the Older Scottish Tongue from the Twelfth Century to the end of the Seventeenth*, Chicago and Oxford, 1931–

Grant, W. and Murison, D.: *The Scottish National Dictionary, designed partly on regional lines and partly on historical principles and containing all the Scottish words known to be in use or to have been in use since c. 1700*, 10 vols., Edinburgh, 1929–76

Jamieson, J.: *An Etymological Dictionary of the Scottish Language*, Edinburgh, 1808

Graham, William: *The Scots Word Book*, Edinburgh, 1977

Warrack, A.: *A Scots Dialect Dictionary*, London, 1911

Dwelly, Edward: *The Illustrated Gaelic-English Dictionary*, 1909–11, repr. Glasgow, 1977, repr 1991

MacAlpine, Neil and Mackenzie, John: *Gaelic-English and English-Gaelic Dictionary*, 1845, repr. Glasgow 1979

Murray, J. A. H., Bradley, H., Craigie, W. A. and Onions, C. T.: *A New English Dictionary on Historical Principles*, Oxford, 1888–1933, reissued 1933 as *The Oxford English Dictionary*

Nicolaisen, W. F. H.: *Scottish Place-Names*, London, 1976, repr 1989

Jakobsen, J.: *An Etymological Dictionary of the Norn Languages in Shetland*, London and Copenhagen, 1928

Aitken, A. J. and McArthur, Tom, edd.: *The Languages of Scotland*, Edinburgh, 1979

Grant, W. and Dixon, J. M.: *Manual of Modern Scots*, Cambridge, 1921

Jackson, K.: 'The Britons in southern Scotland', *Antiquity XXIX*, 1955

——: 'Common Gaelic: the evolution of the Goedelic languages', *Proceedings of the British Academy XXXVII, 1951*

——: *The Gaelic Notes in the Book of Deer*, Cambridge, 1972

——: 'The Pictish Language', in Wainwright, F. T., ed., *The Problem of the Picts*, Edinburgh, 1955, new ed. Perth, 1981

MacDonald, K. D.: 'Gaelic Dictionary: an appeal for help', *Scottish Educational Journal*, 25 November, 1966

Marwick, H.: *The Orkney Norn*, Oxford, 1929

Mather, J. Y. and Speital, H. H.: *The Linguistic Atlas of Scotland*, vols. 1 and 2, London, 1975 and 1977, vol. 3, 1985

Murison, David D.: *The Guid Scots Tongue*, Edinburgh, 1978

Murray, J. A. H.: *The Dialect of the Southern Counties of Scotland*, London, 1873

Oftedal, Magne: 'The Gaelic of Leurbost, Isle of Lewis', *Norsk Tidsskrift for Sprogvidenskap*, 1956

Smith, G. Gregory, ed.: *Specimens of Middle Scots*, Edinburgh and London, 1902

Ternes, Elmar: *The Phonemic Analysis of Scottish Gaelic*, Hamburg, 1973

Thomson, Robert L: 'The emergence of Scottish Gaelic', in Aitken, A. J., McDiarmid, M. P. and Thomson, D. S., edd.: *Bards and Makars*, Glasgow, 1977

Traynor, M.: *The English Dialect of Donegal. A Glossary*, Dublin, 1953

Watson, G.: *The Roxburghshire Word-Book*, Cambridge, 1923

Watson, W. J.: *History of the Celtic Place-Names of Scotland*, Edinburgh, 1926

Grant, William and Murison, David D., ed.: *The Compact Scottish National Dictionary*, 2 vols., Aberdeen, 1986

Kay, Billy: *Scots: The Mither Tongue*, Edinburgh, 1986

Mackay, Charles: *The Auld Scots Dictionary*, Glasgow, 1992

Macleod, Iseabail, ed.: *The Scots Thesaurus*, Aberdeen, 1990

McClure, Derrick J.: *Scotland and the Lowland Tongue: Studies in the Language and Literature of Lowland Scotland in Honour of David D. Murison*, Aberdeen, 1983

——: *Why Scots Matters: The Scots Language is a Priceless Natural Possession*, Edinburgh, 1988

McClusky, Mike: *Dundonian For Beginners*, Edinburgh, 1990

Munro, Michael: *The Patter: A Guide to Current Glasgow Usage*, Glasgow, 1985

Robinson, Mairi, ed-in-chief: *The Concise Scots Dictionary*, Aberdeen, 1987

Stevenson, James A. C.: *Scoor-oot: A Dictionary of Scots Words and Phrases in Current Use*, London, 1989

Warrack, Alexander: *Chambers Scots Dictionary*, Edinburgh, 1987

Clyne and Thomson: *Appendix to Dwelly's Gaelic-English Dictionary*, Glasgow, 1991

Cox, Richard: *Brìgh nam Facal*, Glasgow, 1991

Ó Murchú, Máirtín: *East Perthshire Gaelic: Social History, Phonology, Texts and Lexicon*, Dublin, 1989

Thomson, Derick S.: *The New English-Gaelic Dictionary*, Glasgow, 1981

Withers, Charles W. J.: *Gaelic in Scotland 1698–1981*, Edinburgh, 1984

Literature

General

Hart, Francis: *The Scottish Novel: A Critical Survey*, London, 1978

Kinsley, J., ed.: *Scottish Poetry: A Critical Survey*, London, 1955

Lindsay, Maurice: *History of Scottish Literature*, London, 1977, rev. ed. London, 1992

Mackenzie, A. M.: *An Historical Survey of Scottish Literature to 1714*, London, 1933

MacQueen, J. and Scott, T., ed.: *The Oxford Book of Scottish Verse*, Oxford, 1965, repr. 1989

Craig, Cairns, gen. ed.: *The History of Scottish Literature*, 4 vols, Aberdeen, 1987–1988

Jack, R. D. S., ed.: *The History of Scottish Literature*, Vol. 1, *Origins to 1660 (Mediaeval and Renaissance)*, Aberdeen, 1988

Hook, Andrew, ed.: *The History of Scottish Literature*, Vol. 2, *1600–1800*, Aberdeen, 1987

Gifford, Douglas, ed.: *The History of Scottish Literature*, Vol. 3, *Nineteenth Century*, Aberdeen, 1988

Craig, Cairns, ed.: *The History of Scottish Literature*, Vol. 4, *Twentieth Century*, Aberdeen, 1987

Bold, Alan: *A Literary Guide*, London, 1989

Bruce, George and Rennie, Frank, ed.: *The Land Out There: A Scottish Land Anthology*, Aberdeen, 1991

Burgess, Moira, ed.: 'Introduction', *The Other Voice: Scottish Women's Writing Since 1808*, Edinburgh, 1987

Craig, Cairns: 'Fearful Selves: Character, Community and the Scottish Imagination', *Cencrastus* 4, Winter 1980–81, 29–32

Craig, Cairns: 'The Body in the Kit Bag: History and the Scottish Novel', *Cencrastus* 1, Autumn 1979, 18–22

Hewitt, David and Spiller, Michael, ed.: *Literature of the North*, Aberdeen, 1983

Jack, R. D. S., et al: *The History of Scottish Literature*, 4 Vols., Aberdeen, 1987–88

Morgan, Edwin: *Crossing the Border: Essays on Scottish Literature*, Manchester, 1990

Muir, Edwin: *Scott and Scotland: The Predicament of the Scottish Writer*, with Introduction by Allan Massie, Edinburgh, 1982

Royle, Trevor: *The Macmillan Companion to Scottish Literature*, London, 1983

Stewart, Karen A.: *Scottish Women Writers to 1987: A Select Guide and Bibliography*, Glasgow, 1987

Watson, Roderick: *The Literature of Scotland*, Basingstoke and London, 1984

Ballads

Bold, Alan: *The Ballad*, London, 1979

Greig, Gavin: *Last Leaves of Traditional Ballads and Ballad Airs*, Aberdeen, 1925

Buchan, David: *The Ballad and the Folk*, London, 1972

Child, F. J., ed.: *The English and Scottish Popular Ballads*, 5 vols., Boston and New York, 1882–98, repr. New York, 1965

Henderson, Hamish: 'The Ballad, the folk and the oral tradition', in Cowan, Edward J., ed., *The People's Past*, Edinburgh, 1980

Reed, James: *The Border Ballads*, London, 1973

Medieval and Renaissance

The Bannatyne Manuscript, ed. W. Tod Ritchie, 4 vols., Edinburgh, 1928–32

Barbour, John: *The Bruce: A Selection*, ed. A. M. Kinghorn, Edinburgh, 1960

Brown, P. Hume: *George Buchanan, Humanist and Reformer*, Edinburgh, 1890

The Complaynt of Scotland, ed. A. M. Stewart, Edinburgh, 1879

Douglas, Gavin: *The Aeneid*, ed. D. F. C. Coldwell, 4 vols., Edinburgh, 1961–65

Bawcutt, Priscilla: *Gavin Douglas: A Critical Study*, Edinburgh, 1976

Drummond of Hawthornden, William: *Poems and Prose*, ed. R. H. MacDonald, Edinburgh and London, 1976

Dunbar, William: *The Poems of William Dunbar*, ed. James Kinsley, Oxford, 1979

Scott, Tom: *Dunbar: A Critical Exposition of the Poems*, Edinburgh and London, 1966

Hary's Wallace, ed. M. P. McDiarmid, 2 vols., Edinburgh, 1968–9

Henryson, Robert: *The Poems of Robert Henryson*, ed. Denton Fox, Oxford, 1981

MacQueen, John: *Robert Henryson: a Study of the Major Narrative Poems*, Oxford, 1967

The Kingis Quair of James Stewart, ed. M. P. McDiarmid, London, 1973

The Poems of James VI of Scotland, ed. James Craigie, 2 vols., Edinburgh and London, 1955–58

Lewis, C. S.: *English Literature in the Sixteenth Century (Excluding Drama)*, Oxford, 1954

Lindsay of Pitscottie, Robert: *The Historie and Cronicles of Scotland*, ed. A. J. G. Mackay, 3 vols., 1899–1901

Lyndsay, Sir David: *Ane Satyre of the Thrie Estatis*, ed. James Kinsley, London, 1954

——: *Squyer Meldrum*, ed. James Kinsley, London, 1959

——: *Works*, ed. D. Hamer, 4 vols., Edinburgh, 1930–34

Mill, A. J.: *Mediaeval Plays in Scotland*, Edinburgh and London, 1927

Montgomerie, Alexander: *Alexander Montgomerie: a Selection from his Songs and Poems*, ed. Helena M. Shire, Edinburgh, 1960

Scott, Alexander: *The Poems of Alexander Scott, 1525–84*, ed. A. Scott, Edinburgh, 1952

Urquhart, Sir Thomas: *The Admirable Urquhart: Selected Writings*, ed. R. Boston, London, 1975

Bawcutt, Priscilla: *Dunbar the Makar*, Oxford, 1992

Bawcutt, Priscilla and Riddy, Felicity, ed.: *Longer Scottish Poems*, vol. 1, 1375–1650, Edinburgh, 1987

——: *Selected Poems of Henryson and Dunbar*, Edinburgh, 1992

Eighteenth Century

Boswell, James: *The Private Papers*, ed. F. A. Pottle *et al.*, London, 1950 onwards (research edition, 1966——)

Buchanan, D.: *The Treasure of Auchinleck: The Story of the Boswell Papers*, New York and London, 1975

Daiches, D.: *James Boswell and his World*, London, 1976

Burns, Robert: *Poems and Songs*, ed. James Kinsley, 3 vols., Oxford, 1968 (text without notes, 1 vol., 1970)

——: *The Merry Muses of Caledonia*, ed. J. Barke, J. D. Ferguson, and S. G. Smith, London, 1965

The Songs of Robert Burns: with their Melodies, ed. J. C. Dick, London, 1903

The Letters of Robert Burns, ed. J. D. Ferguson, 2 vols., Oxford, 1931

Crawford, Thomas: *Robert Burns: A Study of the Poems and Songs*, Edinburgh and London, 1960

Daiches, David: *Robert Burns*, London, 1950, rev. ed. 1966, repr. Edin, 1981

Ericson-Roos, C.: *The Songs of Robert Burns*, Uppsala, 1977

Lindsay, Maurice: *The Burns Encyclopaedia*, London, 1959, rev. ed. 1980

Low, Donald A., ed.: *Robert Burns: The Critical Heritage*, London and Boston, 1974

—— ed.: *Critical Essays On Robert Burns*, London and Boston, 1975

Carlyle, Alexander: *Anecdotes and Characters of the Times*, ed. James Kinsley, Oxford, 1973

Fergusson, Robert: *The Poems of Robert Fergusson*, ed. M. P. McDiarmid, Edinburgh and London, 1950–56

Poems by Allan Ramsay and Robert Fergusson, ed. A. M. Kinghorn and A. Law, Edinburgh and London, 1974

Graham, Dougal: *The Collected Writings of Dougal Graham*, 2 vols., Glasgow, 1883

Songs From David Herd's Manuscripts, ed. H. Hecht, Edinburgh, 1904

Home, John: *Douglas*, ed. G. D. Parker, Edinburgh, 1972

Mackenzie, Henry: *Anecdotes and Egotisms, 1745–1831*, ed. H. W. Thompson, Oxford, 1927

Ramsay, Allan: *The Works of Allan Ramsay*, ed. J. W. Oliver, B. Martin, A. M. Kinghorn, and A. Law, 6 vols., Edinburgh and London, 1974

Thomson, James: *The Seasons and the Castle of Indolence*, ed. J. Sambrook, Oxford, 1972

Watson, James, compiler: *Choice Collection of Comic and Serious Scots Poems*, ed. Harriet Harvey Wood, vol. 1, Edinburgh, 1977

Simpson, Kenneth: *The Protean Scot: The Crisis of Identity in Eighteenth Century Scottish Literature*, Aberdeen, 1988

Nineteenth Century

Brown, George Douglas: *The House with the Green Shutters*, ed. J. T. Low, Edinburgh, 1975

Campbell, Ian, ed.: *Nineteenth-Century Scottish Fiction: Critical Essays*, Manchester, 1979

Carlyle, Thomas: *Reminiscences*, ed. Ian Campbell, London, 1972

Clive, John: *Scotch Reviewers: The Edinburgh Review, 1802–1815*, London, 1957

Cockburn, Henry: *Memorials of his Time*, Edinburgh, 1856

——: *Circuit Journeys*, Edinburgh, 1975

Miller, Karl: *Cockburn's Millennium*, London, 1975

Davidson, John: *The Poems of John Davidson*, ed. A. Turnbull, 2 vols., Edinburgh and London, 1973

Ferrier, Susan: *Marriage*, ed. H. Foltinek, Oxford, 1971

Galt, John: *The Works of John Galt*, ed. D. S. Meldrum and W. Roughead, 10 vols., Edinburgh, 1936

——: *Selected Short Stories*, ed. I. A. Gordon, Edinburgh, 1978

Gordon, I. A.: *John Galt: The Life of a Writer*, London, 1972

Gifford, Douglas, ed.: *Scottish Short Stories 1800–1900*, London, 1977

Hogg, James: *Selected Poems*, ed. Douglas Mack, Oxford, 1970

——: *The Private Memoirs and Confessions of a Justified Sinner*, ed. John Carey, Oxford, 1969, repr. 1981

Oliphant, Caroline, Lady Nairne: *The Songs of Lady Nairne*, Edinburgh, 1911

Henderson, G.: *Lady Nairne and Her Songs*, Paisley, 1899

Scott, Sir Walter: *Minstrelsy of the Scottish Border*, ed. T. F. Henderson, 4 vols., Edinburgh and London, 1902

—— *Poetical Works*, ed. J. L. Robertson, Oxford, 1894

—— *Letters*, ed. H. J. C. Grierson, 12 vols., London, 1932–7

—— *Waverley Novels*, 48 vols., Edinburgh, 1828–33

—— *Journal*, ed. W. E. K. Anderson, Oxford, 1972

Lockhart, J. G.: *Memoirs of the Life of Scott*, 7 vols., Edinburgh, 1837–8

Hayden, John O., ed.: *Scott: The Critical Heritage*, London and Boston, 1969

Bell, A. S., ed.: *Scott Bicentenary Essays*, Edinburgh, 1973

Daiches, David: *Sir Walter Scott and His World*, London, 1971

Jeffares, A. N., ed.: *Scott's Mind and Art*, Edinburgh, 1969

Johnson, Edgar: *Sir Walter Scott: The Great Unknown*, 2 vols., London, 1970

Lukacs, George: *The Historical Novel*, trans. H. and S. Mitchell, London, 1962

Tulloch, Graham: *The Language of Walter Scott*, London, 1980

Wilson, A. N.: *The Laird of Abbotsford*, Oxford, 1980

Stevenson, Robert Louis: *Collected Works*, 35 vols., London, 1923–4

—— *Collected Poems*, ed. Janet Adam Smith, London, 1950

Calder, Jenni: *RLS, a Life Study*, London, 1980, repr, Glasgow 1990

Daiches, David: *R. L. Stevenson And His World*, London, 1973

Furnas, J. C.: *Voyage to Windward*, London, 1952

Bell, Ian: *Robert Louis Stevenson: Dreams of Exile: A Biography*, Edinburgh, 1993

Campbell, Ian: *Dr Jekyll and Mr Hyde*, York Series Notes (132), Harlow, 1981

——: *Kailyard*, Edinburgh, 1981

Twentieth Century

Brown, George Mackay: *An Orkney Tapestry*, London, 1969

Buchan, John: *The Tales and Romances of John Buchan*, 17 vols., London, 1922

Smith, Janet Adam: *John Buchan*, London, 1965

Cunninghame Graham, R. B.: *Beattock for Moffat and the Best of R. B. Cunninghame Graham*, ed. P. Harris, Edinburgh, 1979

Watts, Cedric and Davies, Laurence: *Cunninghame Graham: A Critical Biography*, Cambridge, 1979

Fulton, Robin: *Contemporary Scottish Poetry: Individuals and Contexts*, Edinburgh, 1974

Garioch, Robert: *Collected Poems*, Loanhead, 1977

Gibbon, Lewis Grassic [James Leslie Mitchell]: *A Scots Quair*, London, 1946; [a trilogy made up of *Sunset Song* 1932, *Cloud Howe*, 1933, and *Grey Granite*, 1934.]

Glen, Duncan, ed.: *Whither Scotland? A Prejudiced Look at the Future of a Nation*, London, 1971

Gunn, Neil: *Highland River*, London, 1937; *The Silver Darlings*, London, 1941; *Young Art and Old Hector*, London, 1942, etc.

Scott, A. and Gifford, D., edd.: *Neil M. Gunn: The Man and the Writer*, Edinburgh, 1973

Hutchison, David: *The Modern Scottish Theatre*, Glasgow, 1977

MacCaig, Norman: *Old Maps and New: Selected Poems*, London, 1978

MacDiarmid, Hugh [C. M. Grieve]: *Collected Poems*, ed. Michael Grieve and W. R. Aitken, 2 vols., London, 1978

Grieve, M. and Scott, A., ed.: *The Hugh MacDiarmid Anthology*, London, 1972

Buthlay, Kenneth: *Hugh MacDiarmid*, Edinburgh and London, 1964, rev. ed. 1982

Glen, Duncan: *A Bibliography of Scottish Poets from Stevenson to 1974*, Preston, 1974

——, ed.: *Hugh MacDiarmid: A Critical Survey*, Edinburgh and London, 1972

——: *Hugh MacDiarmid and the Scottish Renaissance*, Edinburgh, 1964

Morgan, Edwin: *Hugh MacDiarmid*, London, 1976

Scott, Alexander: *The MacDiarmid Makars*, Preston, 1972

Scott, P. H. and Davis, A. C.: *The Age of MacDiarmid*, Edinburgh, 1979

Miller, Karl, ed.: *Memoirs of a Modern Scotland*, London, 1970

Morgan, Edwin: *From Glasgow to Saturn*, Cheadle, 1973

Muir, Edwin: *Collected Poems*, ed. J. C. Hall and Willa Muir, 2nd ed., London, 1964

Selected Letters of Edwin Muir, ed. P. H. Butter, London, 1974

Butter, P. H.: *Edwin Muir: Man and Poet*, Edinburgh and London, 1966

Royle, Trevor, ed.: *Jock Tamson's Bairns: Essays on a Scots Childhood*, London, 1977

Smith, Sydney Goodsir: *Collected Poems 1941–1975*, London, 1975

Soutar, William: *Poems in Scots and English*, ed. W. R. Aitken, Edinburgh, 1961

Scott, A., ed.: *Diaries of a Dying Man*, Edinburgh, 1954

Wilson, Norman, ed.: *Scottish Writings and Writers*, Edinburgh, 1977

Anderson, Carol, and Norquay, Glenda: 'Superiorism', - *Cencrastus* No. 15, New Year 1984, pp. 8–10

Bold, Alan: *Modern Scottish Literature*, London, 1983

Brackenbury, Rosalind: 'Women in Fiction: How We Present Ourselves and Others', *Cencrastus* No. 15, New Year 1984, pp. 12–14.

Buthlay, Kenneth, ed.: *A Drunk Man Looks at the Thistle*, annotated ed., Edinburgh, 1987

Craig, Cairns, ed.: *The History of Scottish Literature*, Vol. 4, *Twentieth Century*, Aberdeen, 1987

Crawford, Robert and Nairn, Thomas, ed.: *The Arts of Alasdair Gray*, Edinburgh, 1991

Crawford, Robert and Whyte, Hamish, ed.: *About Edwin Morgan*, Edinburgh, 1990

Davie, George Elder: *The Crisis of the Democratic Intellect*, Edinburgh, 1986

Gifford, Douglas: *The Dear Green Place? The Novel in the West of Scotland*, Glasgow, 1985

Hart, Francis Russell: *The Scottish Novel: A Critical Survey*, London, 1978

Harvie, Christopher: *No Gods and Precious Few Heroes: Scotland 1914–18*, London, 1981

Hendry, Joy and Ross, Raymond, ed.: *Norman MacCaig: Critical Essays*, Edinburgh, 1990

Hendry, Joy, ed.: 'The State of Scotland: A Predicament for the Scottish Writer?', *Chapman* 35–6, July 1983

Linklater, Andro: *Compton Mackenzie: A Life*, London, 1987

McIlvanney, William: *Surviving the Shipwreck*, Edinburgh, 1991

Morgan, Edwin: *Nothing Not Giving Messages: Reflections on Work and Life*, Edinburgh, 1990

——: *Twentieth Century Scottish Classics*, Glasgow, 1987

Murray, Isobel and Tait, Bob: *Ten Modern Scottish Novels*, Aberdeen, 1984

Nicholson, Colin, ed.: *Iain Crichton Smith: Critical Essays*, Edinburgh, 1992

Nairn, Tom: *The Break-Up of Britain: Crisis and Neo-Nationalism*, London, 1977

Scott, P. H. and Davis, A. C., ed.: *The Age of MacDiarmid: Hugh MacDiarmid and His Influence on Contemporary Scotland*, Edinburgh, 1992

Smout, T. C.: *A Century of the Scottish People*, London, 1986

Wallace, Gavin and Stevenson, Randall: *The Scottish Novel Since the Seventies*, Edinburgh, 1993

Watson, Roderick: *The Literature of Scotland*, London, 1984

Gaelic

Bruford, Alan: *Gaelic Folk-Tales and Mediaeval Romances*, Dublin, 1969

——: 'Recitation or Re-Creation? Examples from South Uist Storytelling', *Scottish Studies* 22, 1978

Buchanan, Dugald: *Spiritual Songs*, ed. Donald Maclean, Edinburgh, 1913

Camerson, Alexander: *Reliquiae Celticae*, 2 vols., Inverness, 1892–4

Campbell, J. F.: *Popular Tales of the West Highlands*, 4 vols., 2nd ed., London, 1890, repr. 1993

Campbell, J. L., ed.: *Highland Songs of the Forty-Five*, Edinburgh, 1933

Carmichael, Alexander, ed.: *Carmina Gaedelica*, 5 vols., 2nd ed., Edinburgh, 1928–56

Delargy, J. H.: 'The Gaelic storyteller', *Proceedings of the British Academy* 31, 1945

Grimble, I. *The World of Rob Donn*, London, 1979

Hay, George Campbell: *Fuaran Sléibhe*, Glasgow, 1948

MacAulay, Donald, ed.: *Nua-bhàrdachd Ghàidhlig: Modern Scottish Gaelic Poems*, Edinburgh, 1976

MacCodrum, John: *The Songs of John MacCodrum*, ed. W. Matheson, Edinburgh, 1938

MacDonald, Alexander: *The Poems of Alexander MacDonald*, ed. A. and A. MacDonald, Inverness, 1974

MacDonald, John: *The Songs of John MacDonald, Bard of Keppoch*, ed. Annie Mackenzie, Edinburgh, 1964

Mackenzie, Annie, ed.: *Orain Iain Luim*, Glasgow, 1964, 1973

[Mackay] Rob Donn: *Rob Donn: Songs and Poems*, ed. Hew Morrison, Edinburgh, 1899

Mackinnon, Donald: *The Gaelic Bible and Psalter*, Dingwall, 1930

Maclean, Sorley: *Dàin Do Eimhir*, Glasgow, 1943

——: 'The poetry of the Clearances', *Transactions Of The Gaelic Society of Inverness* XXXVIII, 1962

Macintyre, Duncan Ban: *The Songs of Duncan Ban Macintyre*, ed. Angus Macleod, Glasgow, 1952, 1978

Smith, Iain Crichton: *Ben Dorain* [translation], Preston, 1969

Gillies, William: 'The Poem in Praise of Ben Dobhrain', *Lines Review* 63, 1977

Macleod, Angus, ed.: *Sàr Orain: Three Gaelic Poems*, Glasgow, 1933 [long poems by Mary Macleod, Alexander Macdonald, and Duncan Ban Macintyre]

Macleod, J. N.: *Memorials of Rev. Norman Macleod*, Edinburgh, 1898

Mackinnon, L., ed.: *Prose Writings of Donald Mackinnon*, Edinburgh, 1956

Macleod, Mary: *The Gaelic Songs of Mary Macleod*, ed. J. C. Watson, London and Glasgow, 1934, repr. 1965

Mactavish, Duncan C.: *The Gaelic Psalms 1694* (Introduction), repr. Loc gilphead, 1934

Meek, Donald, ed.: *Màiri Mhór nan Oran*, Glasgow, 1977

Murchison, T. M., ed.: *Prose Writings of Donald Lamont*, Edinburgh, 1960

Ross, William: *Gaelic Songs by William Ross*, ed. George Calder, London, 1937

Thomson, D. S.: *An Dealbh Briste. Gaelic poems with some translations in English*, Edinburgh, 1951

——: *The Gaelic Sources of MacPherson's 'Ossian'*, London, 1952

——: *An Introduction to Gaelic Poetry*, London, 1974

——: *The New Verse in Scottish Gaelic: A Structural Analysis*, Dublin, 1974

Watson, W. J., ed.: *Scottish Verse from the Book of the Dean of Lismore*, Edinburgh, 1937

Black, Ronald: *MacMhaighstir Alasdair: The Ardnamurchan Years*, West Highlands, 1986

——: 'Thunder, Renaissance and Flowers: Gaelic Poetry in the Twentieth Century', in Craig, Cairns, ed., *The History of Scottish Literature*, Vol. 4

Campbell, J. L.: *Hebridean Folksongs*, 3 Vols., Oxford, 1969, 1977, 1981

Gairm Publications: *Gaelic Books: A Complete List, Including New and Forthcoming Books*, Glasgow, 1990

MacDonald, Ian: *Leabhraichean Gaidhlig: A Classified Catalogue of Gaelic and Gaelic-Related Books in Print*, 4th ed., Glasgow, 1987

Gillies, William, ed.: *Gaelic and Scotland*, Edinburgh, 1989

Maclennan, Malcolm: *A Pronouncing and Etymological Dictionary of the Gaelic Language*, Aberdeen, 1979

Gillies, William: 'Gaelic: the Classical Tradition', in Jack, R. D. S., ed., *The History of Scottish Literature*, Vol. 1, Aberdeen, 1988

Thomson, Derick S.: *The Companion to Gaelic Scotland*, London, 1983, 1987

——: 'The Poetic Tradition in Gaelic Scotland', in Proc. of the Seventh International Congress of Celtic Studies, Oxford, 1986

——: 'The Earliest Scottish Gaelic Non-Classical Verse Texts', *Scottish Studies*, Vol. 4, Verlag Peter Lang, Frankfurt, 1986

Thomson, D. S.: *Creachadh na Clàrsaich / Plundering the Harp*, Glasgow, 1982

——: *European Poetry in Gaelic*, Glasgow, 1990

——: *Smeur an Dòchais / Bramble of Hope*, Edinburgh, 1992

——: 'Macpherson's "Ossian": Ballads to Epics', in Almqvist, B., ed., *The Heroic Process*, Dun Laoghaire, 1987

——: 'MacMhaighstir Alasdair's, Nature Poetry and its Sources', in Thomson, D., ed., *Gaelic and Scots in Harmony*, Glasgow, 1990

——: 'Alasdair MacMhaighstir Alasdair's Political Poetry', *Trans. Gaelic Society of Inverness*, Vol. LVI, Inverness, 1991

——: 'The Seventeenth-Century Crucible of Scottish Gaelic Poetry', *Studia Celtica* (forthcoming, 1993)

Whyte, Christopher: *An Aghaidh na Sìorraidheachd / In the Face of Eternity. Eight Gaelic Poets*, Edinburgh, 1991

Celtic

Jackson, K.: *The Gododdin, the Oldest Scottish Poem*, Edinburgh, 1969

Medicine

Chalmers, A. K.: *The Health of Glasgow*, 1818–1925, Glasgow, 1930

Comrie, J. D.: *History of Scottish Medicine*, London, 1932

Gordon, A.: *Treatise on the Epidemic Puerperal Fever of Aberdeen*, London, 1795

Lawrence, Christopher: 'The nervous system and society in the Scottish Enlightenment', in Barnes, Barry, and Shapin, Steven, ed., *Natural Order: Historical Studies of Scientific Culture*, Beverley Hills and London, 1979

Nettler, C.: *History of Medicine*, Philadelphia, 1947

Richards, R.: 'Rae of the Arctic', *Medical History* 19 (176), 1975

Shapin, Steven: 'Phrenological knowledge and the social structure of early nineteenth century Edinburgh', *Annals of Science* 32, 1975

British Congress on the History of Medicine (11th, Edinburgh, 1986), Derek Dow, ed.: *The Influence of Scottish Medicine: An Historical Assessment of its International Impact*, Carnforth, Lancs., 1988

Scottish Medicine, vol. 1, no. 1 (April 1981-), Edinburgh, Hermiston Publications, 1981

Music

Collinson, F. M.: *The Traditional and National Music of Scotland*, London, 1956

——: *The Bagpipe: The history of a musical instrument*, London, 1975

Crawford, Thomas: *Society and the Lyric: a Study of the Song Culture of Eighteenth Century Scotland*, Edinburgh, 1979

Dalyell, Sir J. G.: *Musical Memoirs of Scotland*, Edinburgh, 1849

Dow, D.: *A Collection of Ancient Scots Music*, Edinburgh, 1776

Edmonstone, A. W.: *A View of the Ancient and Present State of the Zetland Isles*, vol. II, Edinburgh, 1809

Elliott, K. and Shire, H. M., edd.: *Music of Scotland 1500–1700*, Musica Britannica XV, London, 1957

Elliott, K. and Rimmer, F., edd.: *A History of Scottish Music*, London, 1973

Emmerson, G.: *Rantin' Pipe and Tremblin' String*, London, 1971

Farmer, H. G.: *A History of Music in Scotland*, London, 1947

Flett, J. F. and T. M.: *Traditional Dancing in Scotland*, London, 1964

Fraser, Duncan: *The Passing of the Precentor*, Edinburgh, 1906

Fraser, Captain S.: *The Airs and Melodies Peculiar to the Highlands of Scotland and the Isles*, Edinburgh and London, 1816

Glen, J.: *The Glen Collection of Scottish Dance Music*, vols. 1 and 2, Edinburgh, 1891, 1895

Gow, N. and Sons: *A Complete Repository of the Original Scotch Slow Strathspeys and Dances*, Edinburgh, 1799

Harris, D. F.: *St Cecilia's Hall in the Niddry Wynd*, Edinburgh, 1899

Henderson, J. Murdoch: *Flowers of Scottish Melody*, Glasgow, 1935

Honeyman, W. C.: *Scottish Violin Makers Past and Present*, Newport on Tay, 1898

Hunter, J.: *The Fiddle Music of Scotland*, Edinburgh, 1979

Johnson, D.: 'Music publishing in 18th century Edinburgh', *The British Journal for 18th century Studies* I (I), 1978

——: *Music and Society in Lowland Scotland in the 18th Century*, London, 1972

——: 'William McGibbon: Scotland's unknown composer', *The Scotsman*, 25 March 1978

The Scots Musical Museum originally published by James Johnson (6 vols., Edinburgh, 1787–1803), repr. Hatboro, Pennsylvania, 2 vols., 1962

Lord, Albert B.: *The Singer of Tales*, London, 1965

Marshall, W.: *A Collection of Strathspey Reels*, Edinburgh, 1781

Murdoch, A. G.: *The Fiddle in Scotland*, London, Edinburgh, and Glasgow, 1888

Oswald, J.: *A Curious Collection of Scots Reels or Country Dances*, Edinburgh, c. 1740

Playford, H.: *A Collection of Original Scotch Tunes (Full of the Highland Humours) for Violin*, London, 1700

Shire, H. M.: *Song, Dance and Poetry of the Court of Scotland under King James VI*, Cambridge, 1969

Topham, Capt. E.: *Letters from Edinburgh Written in the Years 1774 and 1775*, London, 1776

Tytler, W.: 'On the fashionable amusements and entertainments in Edinburgh in the last century', *Transactions of the Society of Antiquaries of Scotland* I, 1792

Wilson, Conrad, ed.: *Music and Musicians in Scotland*, Edinburgh, 1980

Alburger, Mary Anne: *Scottish Fiddlers and Their Music*, London, 1983

Cannon, Roderick: *A Bibliography of Bagpipe Music*, Edinburgh, 1980

——: *The Highland Bagpipe and its Music*, Edinburgh, 1980

Carmichael, Alexander: *Carmina Gadelica: Hymns and Incantations Collected in the Highlands and Islands of Scotland in the Last Century*, Edinburgh, 1992

Collinson, Francis: *The Bagpipe, Fiddle and Harp*, Newtongrange, 1983

——: *The Bagpipe: the History of a Musical instrument*, London, 1975

Cooke, Peter: *The Fiddle Tradition of the Shetland Isles*, Cambridge, 1986

Davie, Cedric Thorpe: *Scotland's Music*, Edinburgh, 1980

Greig, Gavin and Duncan, Rev. James B., ed. Emily Lyle: *The Greig Duncan Folk Song Collection*, Vols. 1–4, Aberdeen, 1981–1988

Hardie, William, ed.: *The Beauties of the North: A Scots Fiddle Collection*, Edinburgh, 1987

Hardie, Alastair J.: *The Caledonian Companion*, London, 1981

Henderson, Hamish: *Alias Macalias: Writings on Songs, Folk and Literature*, Edinburgh, 1992

Johnson, David: *Scottish Fiddle Music of the 18th Century*, Edinburgh, 1984

Olson, Ian A.: *Scottish Contemporary Music and Song: An Introduction*, Heidelberg, 1989

Porter, James: *The Traditional Music of Britain and Ireland: A Research and Information Guide*, New York and London, 1989

Purser, John: *Scotland's Music: A History of the Traditional and Classical Music of Scotland From Earliest Times to the Present Day*, Edinburgh, 1992

Sanger, Keith and Kinnaird, Alison: *Tree of Strings: Crann Nan Teud: A History of the Harp in Scotland*, Shillinghill, Midlothian, 1992

Scott, Willie, McMorland, Alison, ed.: *Herd Laddie O the Glen: Songs of a Border Shepherd*, 1988

Wood, Nicola: *Scottish Traditional Music*, Edinburgh, 1991

Kane, Patrick: *Tinsel Show: Pop, Politics, Scotland*, Edinburgh, 1992

Wilkie, Jim: *Blue Suede Brogans: Scenes from the Secret life of Scottish rock music*, Edinburgh, 1992

Greig, R. W.: *The Story of the Scottish Orchestra*, Glasgow, 1945 [14 pages]

Discography
Psalms from Lewis
(2 Cassettes)
Lewis Recordings, Stornoway
J. Scott Skinner: The Strathspey King
Topic Records 12T280

Hector MacAndrew—Scots Fiddle
Scottish Records SCRN 138
The Music of Scott Skinner
Topic Records 12TS268
Scots Fiddle, high style
(Sonatas and variations written in Scotland 1735–70, by Foulis, McLean, Oswald and anon.)
Scottish Records, SR 0117, Glasgow, 1976
The King's Music (The Later Middle Ages, 1250–1550)
Scottish Records, SRSS I
(edited by K. Elliott to accompany the book *History of Scottish Music*)
Music Fyne (Songs and Dances of the Scottish Court, 1550–1625)
Scottish Records, SRSS 2
The Seventeenth Century (Music of Castle, Burgh and Countryside)
Scottish Records, SRSS 3 1972–4
Scottish Tradition Nos. 1–9 (series ed. Peter R. Cooke)
Green Trax Records
1. *Bothy Ballads*, CDTRAX/CTRAX 9001
2. *Music from the Western Isles*, CDTRAX/CTRAX 9002
3. *Waulking Songs from Barra*, CDTRAX/CTRAX 9003
4. *Shetland Fiddle Music*, CDTRAX/CTRAX 9004
5. *The Muckle Songs*, CDTRAX/CTRAX 9005
6. *Gaelic Psalms from Lewis*, CDTRAX/CTRAX 9006
7. *Calum Ruadh—Bard of Skye*, CTRAX 9007
8. *James Campbell of Kintail—Gaelic Songs*, CTRAX 9008
9. *The Fiddler & His Art*, CDTRAX/CTRAX 9009
10. *Pibroch—Pipe-Major William MacLean*, CTRAX 9010
11. *Pibroch—Pipe-Major Robert Brown*, CTRAX 9011
12. *Pibroch—Pipe-Major R. B. Nicol*, CTRAX 9012
13. *Calum & Annie Johnston*, CTRAX 9013
14. *Gaelic Stories told by Peter Morrison*, CTRAX 9014
15. *Pibroch—George Moss*, CTRAX 9015
16. *William Matheson: Gaelic Bards & Minstrels*, CTRAX 9016
(1, 2, 5, 9, 1993 rest forthcoming)

Newspapers

Barr, B. and McKay, R.: *The Story of the Scottish Daily News*, Edinburgh, 1976

Couper, W. J.: *The Edinburgh Periodical Press ... from the Earliest Times to 1800*, 2 vols., Stirling, 1908

Cowan, R. M.: *The Newspaper in Scotland: A Study of its First Expansion, 1815–1860*, Glasgow, 1946

Craig, M. E.: *The Scottish Periodical Press, 1750–1789*, Edinburgh, 1931

Ferguson, J. P. S.: *Scottish Newspapers Held in Scottish Libraries*, Edinburgh, 1956

Hams, Paul: *The D. C. Thomson Bumper Fun Book*, Edinburgh, 1977

Hutchison, D., ed.: *Headlines: The Media in Scotland*, Edinburgh, 1978

Baird, Patricia: *The General Election 1992: A Review in Cuttings and Pictures for Use in Schools and Colleges*, Glasgow, 1992

Roy, Kenneth, ed.: *The Best of Scotland on Sunday*, Ayr, 1990

Painting and Sculpture

Apted, Michael R.: *The Painted Ceilings of Scotland, 1560–1650*, Edinburgh, 1966

Bruce, George: *Anne Redpath*, Edinburgh, 1974

Buchanan, W.: *Joan Eardley*, Edinburgh, 1978

Caw, Sir James L.: *Scottish Painting 1620–1908*, Edinburgh, 1908, repr. Bath, 1975

Cunningham, A.: *The Life of Sir David Wilkie*, 3 vols., London, 1843

Dickson, T. E.: *W. G. Gillies*, Edinburgh, 1974

Firth, Jack: *Scottish Watercolour Painting*, Edinburgh, 1979

Gordon, Esme: *The Royal Scottish Academy of Painting, Sculpture and Architecture, 1826–1976*, Edinburgh, 1976

Hall, Douglas: *William Johnstone*, Edinburgh, 1980

Irwin, David and Francina: *Scottish Painters at Home and Abroad 1700–1900*, London, 1975

Lindsay, Maurice: *Robin Philipson*, Edinburgh, 1978

McLure, D.: *John Maxwell*, Edinburgh, 1976

Nasmyth, James: *An Autobiography*, ed. Samuel Smiles, London and Edinburgh, 1883

Oliver, Cordelia: *James Cowie*, Edinburgh, 1980

Raeburn Bicentenary Exhibition: catalogue by David Baxandall, Edinburgh, 1956

Armstrong, W. and Stevenson, R. A. M.: *Sir Henry Raeburn*, London, 1901

Greig, James: *Sir Henry Raeburn RA*, London, 1901

Smart, A.: *The Life and Art of Allan Ramsay*, London, 1952

Wood, H. H.: *W. McTaggart*, Edinburgh, 1974

Allen, J. Romilly: *The Early Christian Monuments of Scotland*, Edinburgh, 1903

Richardson, James S.: *The Medieval Stone-Carver in Scotland*, Edinburgh, 1964

Halliday, T. S. and Bruce, G.: *Scottish Sculpture: a record of twenty years*, Dundee, 1946

Gage, Edward: *The Eye in the Wind of Scottish Painting Since 1945*, London, 1977

Halsby, Julian and Harris, Paul: *The Dictionary of Scottish Painters 1600–1960*, Edinburgh, 1990

Halliday, Thomas S.: *Scottish Sculpture: A Record of Twenty Years*, Dundee, 1946

Hardie, William: *Scottish Painting: 1837 to the Present*, London, 1990

MacMillan, Duncan: *Painting in Scotland: The Golden Age*, Oxford, 1986

——: *Scottish Art 1460–1990*, Edinburgh, 1990

Smith, W. Gordon: *W. G. Gillies: A Very Still Life*, Edinburgh, 1991

Performing Arts

Goodwin, N.: *A Ballet for Scotland: The First Ten Years of The Scottish Ballet*, Edinburgh, 1959, repr. 1979

Hutchison, David: *The Modern Scottish Theatre*, Glasgow, 1977

Wilson, Conrad: *Scottish Opera: The First Ten Years*, London and Glasgow, 1972

Campbell, Donald: *A Brighter Sunshine: One Hundred Years of the Edinburgh Royal Lyceum Theatre*, Edinburgh, 1983

Devlin, Vivien: *Kings, Queens and People's Palaces: An Oral History of the Scottish Variety Theatre*, Edinburgh, 1991

Oliver, Cordelia: *It is a Curious Story: The Tale of Scottish Opera 1962–1987*, Edinburgh, 1987

Roy, Kenneth, ed.: *Scottish Theatre Directory*, Maybole, 1979

Philosophy

Bryson, Gladys: *Man and Society: The Scottish Inquiry of the Eighteenth Century*, Princeton, 1945

Campbell, T. D.: *Adam Smith's Science of Morals*, London, 1971

——: *The Scottish Enlightenment and early Victorian English Society*, London, 1986

Chitnis, Anand: *The Scottish Enlightenment. A Social History*, London, 1976

Davie, G. E.: 'Hume, Reid, and the passion for ideas', in Douglas Young, ed., *Edinburgh in the Age of Reason*, Edinburgh, 1967

Grave, S. A.: *The Scottish Philosophy of Common Sense*, Oxford, 1960

Mossner, E. C.: *The Life of David Hume*, Edinburgh, 1954, rev. 1972

Phillipson, N. T.: 'Towards a definition of the Scottish Enlightenment', in P. Fritz and D. Williams, *City and Society in the Eighteenth Century*, Toronto, 1973

Rendall, Jane: *The Origins of the Scottish Enlightenment*, London, 1978

Schneider, L., ed.: *The Scottish Moralists on Human Nature and Society*, Chicago, 1967

Broadie, Alexander: *The Tradition of Scottish Philosophy: A New Perspective on the Enlightenment*, Edinburgh, 1990

Davie, George E.: *The Scottish Enlightenment, and other Essays*, with foreword by James Kelman, Edinburgh, 1991

Davis, Spencer: *Scottish Philosophical History: Hume to James Mill*, Ottawa, 1981

Hope, V., ed.: *Philosophers of the Scottish Enlightenment*, Edinburgh, 1984

Jones, Peter, ed.: *Philosophy and Science in the Scottish Enlightenment: Essays*, Edinburgh, 1988

——: *The 'Science of Man' in the Scottish Enlightenment: Hume, Reid and Their Contemporaries*, Edinburgh, 1989

Stewart, M. A., ed.: *Studies in the Philosophy of the Scottish Enlightenment*, Oxford, 1990

Politics

Drucker, H. M. and Brown, Gordon: *The Politics of Nationalism and Devolution*, London, 1980

Harvie, Christopher: *Scotland and Nationalism: Scottish Society and Politics, 1707–1977*, London, 1977

Mackay, Donald, ed.: *Scotland: The Framework for Change*, Edinburgh, 1979

Maclean, Colin, ed.: *The Crown and the Thistle: The Nature of Nationhood*, Edinburgh, 1979

Daiches, David, ed.: *Fletcher of Saltoun: Selected Writings*, Edinburgh, 1979

——: *Scotland and the Union*, London, 1977

Lenman, Bruce: *The Jacobite Risings in Britain. London, 1980*

Petrie, Sir Charles: *The Jacobite Movement*, 3rd ed., London, 1959

Phillipson, N. T. and Mitchison, Rosalind: *Scotland in the Age of Improvement*, Edinburgh, 1970

Meikle, H. W.: *Scotland and the French Revolution*, Glasgow, 1912

Saunders, L. J.: *Scottish Democracy, 1815–1840*, Edinburgh, 1950

Wilson, Alexander: *The Chartist Movement in Scotland*, Manchester, 1970

Wright, L. C.: *Scottish Chartism*, Edinburgh, 1953

Johnston, T.: *History of the Working Classes in Scotland*, Glasgow, 1920

Middlemas, R. K.: *The Clydesiders*, London, 1965

Young, J. D.: *The Rousing of the Scottish working class*, London, 1979

Bealey, Frank: *The Politics of Independence: A Study of a Scottish Town* [Peterhead], Aberdeen, 1981

Beveridge, Craig and Turnbull, Ronald: *The Eclipse of Scottish Culture: Inferiorism and the Intellectuals*, Edinburgh, 1989

Brown, Alice, ed.: *Women in Scottish Politics*, Edinburgh, 1991

Donnachie, Ian; Harvie, Christopher; and Wood, Ian S., ed.: *Forward! Labour Politics in Scotland, 1888–1988*, Edinburgh, 1989

Drucker, H. M. and Brown, Gordon: *The Politics of Nationalism and Devolution*, London, 1980

Edwards, Owen Dudley, ed.: *A Claim of Right for Scotland*, Edinburgh, 1989

Fry, Michael: *Patronage and Principle: A Political History of Modern Scotland*, Aberdeen, 1987

Kellas, James G.: *The Scottish Political System*, 4th ed., Cambridge, 1989

Marr, Andrew: *The Battle for Scotland*, London, 1992

Mitchell, James: *The Myth of Scottish Dependency*, Scottish Centre for Economic and Social Research 'Forward' Series Paper no. 3, Edinburgh, 1990

Miller, William L.: *The End of British Politics? Scots and English Political Behaviour in the Seventies*, Oxford, 1981

Parry, Richard: *Scottish Political Facts*, Edinburgh, 1988

Parsler, Ron, ed.: *Capitalism, Class and Politics in Scotland*, Farnborough, Hants, 1980

Sillars, Jim: *The Case For Optimism*, Edinburgh, 1986

Scott, Paul: *Towards Independence*, Edinburgh, 1991

McCrone, David: *Understanding Scotland: The Sociology of a Stateless Nation*, London, 1992

Gray, Alasdair: *Why Scots Should Rule Scotland*, Edinburgh, 1992

Kellas, James G.: *The Scottish Political System*, 4th ed., Cambridge, 1989

Parry, Richard: *Scottish Political Facts*, Edinburgh, 1988

Maclean, I.: *The Legend of Red Clydeside*, Edinburgh, 1983

Drucker, Henry: *Breakaway: The Scottish Labour Party*, Edinburgh, 1978

Durbin, Elizabeth: *New Jerusalems: The Labour Party and the Economics of Democratic Socialism*, London, 1985

Keating, Michael and Bleiman, David: *Labour and Scottish Nationalism*, London, 1979

Knox, William, ed.: *Scottish Labour Leaders 1918–39: A Biographical Dictionary*, Edinburgh, 1984

MacDougall, Ian: *Essays in Scottish Labour History*, Edinburgh, 1978

Morgan, Kenneth O.: *Keir Hardie: Radical and Socialist*, London, 1975

Pelling, Henry: *A Short History of the Labour Party*, 6th ed., London, 1978

Shinwell, Emanuel: *Lead With the Left: My First Ninety-Six Years*, London, 1981

Behrens, Robert: *The Conservative Party: From Heath to Thatcher: Policies and Politics*, Farnborough, Hants., 1980

Lawson, Iain: *The Anti-Scottish Tories: A Record of Betrayal*, Edinburgh, 1987

Lindsay, Thomas Fanshawe and Harrington, Michael: *The Conservative Party, 1918–1979*, 2nd ed., London, 1979

Mayall, Mark: *Scotland: Reversing the Conservative Decline*, London, 1991 [published by the Monday Club]

Mitchell, James: *Conservatives and the Union: A Study of Conservative Party Attitudes to Scotland*, Edinburgh, 1990

Ward, J. T.: *The First Century: A History of Scottish Tory Organisation, 1882–1982*, Edinburgh, 1982

Brand, Jack: *The National Movement in Scotland*, London, 1978

Kauppi, Mark Veblen: *Scottish Nationalism: A Conceptual Approach*, Boulder, Colorado, 1980

Pate, C. W.: *The Place of the Scottish National Party in the Party System in Scotland*, 1986 [MSc thesis, London School of Economics]

Webb, Keith: *The Growth of Nationalism in Scotland*, rev. ed., Harmondsworth, 1978

Communist Party of Britain, Scottish Branch: *Scotland: the Fight Back*, Glasgow, 1988

Macfarlane, L. J.: *The British Communist Party: Its Origin and Development until 1929*, London, 1966

Printing, Publishing, and Libraries

Aldis, H. G.: *A List of Books Printed in Scotland before 1700* (1904), rev. ed., Edinburgh, 1970

Beattie, William: *The Scottish Tradition in Printed Books*, Edinburgh, 1949

——: *The Chepman and Myllar Prints: Nine Tracts from the First Scottish Press*, Edinburgh, 1950

Couper, W. J.: *James Watson King's Printer*, Glasgow, 1910

Gaskell, Philip: *A Bibliography of the Foulis Press*, London, 1964

Maclehose, J.: *The Glasgow University Press, 1631–1931*, Glasgow, 1931

Wyn-Evans, D.: *James Watson of Edinburgh: A Bibliography of Works from his Press 1695–1722*, Transactions of the Edinburgh Bibliographical Society, vol. 5 part 2, 1981

Macleod, R. D.: *The Scottish Publishing Houses*, Glasgow, 1953

Constable, Thomas: *Archibald Constable and his Literary Correspondents*, 3 vols., Edinburgh, 1873

Oliphant, Mrs M. and Porter, Mrs G.: *Annals of a Publishing House: Blackwood and his Sons, their Magazine and Friends*, 3 vols., Edinburgh, 1897–8

Ross, I. and Scobie, S.: 'Patriotic publishing as a response to the Union', in *The Union of 1707*, ed. T. I. Rae, Glasgow, 1974

Keir, David E.: *The House of Collins: The Story*, London, 1952

Adam and Charles Black, 1807–1957: some Chapters in the History of a Publishing House, London, 1957

Chambers, W.: *Memoir of Robert Chambers: with Autobiographic Reminiscences*, Edinburgh, 1872

Wilson, Sir Daniel: *William Nelson: a Memoir*, Edinburgh, 1889

Aitken, W. R.: *A History of the Public Library Movement in Scotland to 1955*, Glasgow, 1971

Armstrong, N. E. S.: *Local Collections in Scotland*, Glasgow, 1977

Williams, Bob: *Marketing Books in Scotland*, Edinburgh, 1985

Regional Studies

Brander: *Over the Lowlands*, London, 1965

Daiches, David: *Edinburgh*, London, 1978

——: *Glasgow*, London, 1977

Darling, F. Fraser: *West Highland Survey*, Oxford, 1955

Fenton, A.: *The Northern Isles: Orkney and Shetland*, Edinburgh, 1978

Gray, Malcolm: *The Highland Economy*, Edinburgh, 1957

Grimble, Ian and Thomson, D. S.: *The Future of the Highlands*, London, 1968

Hunter, James: *The Making of the Crofting Community*, Edinburgh, 1976

Lindsay, Maurice: *Lowland Scottish Villages*, London, 1980

Murray, W. R.: *The Islands of Western Scotland: The Inner and Outer Hebrides*, London, 1973

Simpson, W. Douglas: *Portrait of the Highlands*, London, 1969

Third Statistical Account of Scotland, Edinburgh, 1946–

Tranter, Nigel: *Portrait of the Border Country*, London, 1972

——: *Portrait of the Lothians*, London, 1979

Youngson, A. J.: *After the Forty-Five: The Economic Impact On the Scottish Highlands*, Edinburgh, 1973

Daiches, David: *Edinburgh: A Traveller's Companion*, London, 1986

Edwards, Owen Dudley and Richardson, Graham, ed.: *Edinburgh*, Edinburgh, 1983

McKean, Charles: *Edinburgh: Portrait of a City*, London, 1991

Nimmo, Ian: *Edinburgh: The New Town*, Edinburgh, 1991

Turnbull, Michael: *Edinburgh Portraits*, Edinburgh, 1987

Archer, Ian: *Glasgow: From the Eye in the Sky*, photographs by Douglas Corrance, Edinburgh, 1989

Gallagher, Tom: *Glasgow: The Uneasy Peace: Religious Tension in Modern Scotland*, Manchester, 1987

Gibb, Andrew: *Glasgow: The Making of a City*, London, 1983

Hanley, Cliff, ed.: *Glasgow: A Celebration*, Edinburgh, 1984

Lindsay, Maurice: *Glasgow*, 3rd ed. (prev. ed. published as *Portrait of Glasgow*, 1981), London, 1989

Massie, Allan: *Glasgow: Portraits of a City*, London, 1989

McPhee, John: *In the Highlands and the Islands*, London, 1986

Maitland, Alexander: *The Highland Year: A Sketchbook of the Open Road*, London, 1988

Donaldson, Gordon: *The Faith of the Scots*, London, 1990

——: *Scottish Church History*, Edinburgh, 1985

Science

Christie, John R. R.: 'The rise and fall of Scottish science', in Crosland, Maurice, ed., *The Emergence of Science in Western Europe*, New York, 1976

Clement, A. G. and Robertson, R. H. S.: *Scotland's Scientific Heritage*, Edinburgh, 1961

Davie, George E.: *The Democratic Intellect: Scotland and her Universities in the Nineteenth Century*, Edinburgh, 1961

Donovan, A. L.: *Philosophical Chemistry in the Scottish Enlightenment*, Edinburgh, 1975

Morell, J. B.: 'Reflections on the history of Scottish science', *History of Science* 12, 1974

Olson, Richard: 'Scottish philosophy and mathematics, 1750–1830', *Journal of the History of Ideas* 32, 1971

——: *Scottish Philosophy and British Physics 1750–1880*, Princeton, 1975

Shapin, Steven: 'Property, patronage and the politics of science: the founding of the Royal Society of Edinburgh', *British Journal of the History of Science* 7, 1974

——: 'The audience for science in eighteenth century Edinburgh', *History of Science* 12, 1974

Fletcher, Bill: *Great Scottish Discoveries and Inventions*, Glasgow, 1985

Scots Abroad

Burton, John Hill: *The Scot Abroad*, 2 vols., Edinburgh, 1864

Campbell, D. and MacLean, R. A.: *Beyond the Atlantic Roar: A Study of the Nova Scotia Scots*, Toronto, 1974

Donaldson, Gordon: *The Scots Overseas*, London, 1966

Dunn, C. W.: *Highland Settler: A Portrait of the Scottish Gael in Nova Scotia*, Toronto, 1953

Fischer, T. A.: *The Scots in Germany*, Edinburgh, 1902

——: *The Scots in Sweden*, Edinburgh, 1907

Gibb, Andrew Dewar: *Scottish Empire*, Glasgow, 1937

Glendennen, G. W. and Cunningham, I. C.: *David Livingstone: A Catalogue of Documents*, Edinburgh, 1979

Graham, I. C. C.: *Colonists from Scotland: Emigration to North America, 1707–83*, Ithaca, New York, 1956

Hook, Andrew: *Scotland and America: A Study of Cultural Relations 1750–1853*, Glasgow and London, 1975

Insh, G. P.: *Scottish Colonial Schemes, 1620–1686*, Glasgow, 1922

——: *Papers Relating to the Ships and Voyages of the Company of Scotland Trading to Africa and the Indies 1696–1707*, Edinburgh, 1925

Lepton, Kenneth: *Mungo Park the African Traveller*, Oxford, 1979

McCullough, John Herries: *The Scot in England*, London, 1935

MacMillan, D. S.: *Scotland and Australia, 1788–1850*, Oxford, 1967

Martell, J. S.: *Immigration to and Emigration from Nova Scotia, 1815–1838*, Halifax, Nova Scotia, 1942

Notestein, W.: *The Scot in History*, London, 1947

Reid, W. Stanford, ed.: *The Scottish Tradition in Canada*, Toronto, 1976

Shepperson, George: 'David Livingston the Scot', *The Scottish Historical Review* XXXIX (128), 1960

———: *David Livingstone and the Rovuma: a Notebook*, Edinburgh, 1965

Wall, Joseph Grazier: *Andrew Carnegie*, New York, 1970

Andrews, Allen: *The Scottish Canadians*, Toronto and London, 1981

Bumsted, J. M.: *The People's Clearance: Highland Emigration to British North America, 1770–1815*, Edinburgh, 1982

Cage, R. A.: *The Scots Abroad: Labour, Capital and Enterprise, 1780–1914*, London, 1985

McCrae, Alistar: *Scots in Burma: Golden Times in a Golden Land*, Edinburgh, 1990

Prentis, Malcolm D.: *The Scottish in Australia, Melbourne*, 1987

Sport

Crampsey, Bob: *The Scottish Footballer*, Edinburgh, 1979

Kerr, John: *History of Curling*, Edinburgh, 1890

MacDonald J. Ninian: *Shinty*, Inverness, 1932

Speedy, Tom: *The Natural History of Sport In Scotland with Rod and Gun*, Edinburgh, 1920

Thorburn, Sandy: *The History of Scottish Rugby*, London, 1980

Ward-Thomas, P.: *The Royal and Ancient*, Edinburgh, 1980

Blackstock, Dixon: *Scotland: Five in a Row: The Road to Rome*, Edinburgh, 1990

Douglas, Derek: *The Flowering of Scotland: Grand Slam '90*, Edinburgh, 1990

——— ed.: *Feet, Scotland, Feet!: The Book of Scottish Rugby*, Edinburgh, 1991

Rev. Marshall, F.: *Football – the Rugby Union Game*, London, 1892

Ward, Andrew: *Scotland: The Team*, Derby, 1987

Murray, Bill: *The Old Firm: Sectarianism, Sport and Society in Scotland*, Edinburgh, 1984

Moorhouse, H. F.: 'We're Off to Wembley', *New Edinburgh Review* No. 83 (July 1990), pp. 66–76

Leatherdale, Clive: *Scotland's Quest for the World Cup: A Complete Record 1950–1986*, Edinburgh, 1986

Crampsey, Bob: *The Scottish Football League: The First One Hundred Years*, Glasgow, 1990

——— *Mr Stein: A Biography of Jock Stein*, Edinburgh, 1986

McLauchlan, Ian and Rea, Chris: *Scotland's Grand Slam '84*, London, 1984

Pincott, H. and Davidson, J. McI.: *The Scotsman Rugby Yearbook, No. 1*, Edinburgh, 1990

Trotter, J. J.: *The Royal High School, Edinburgh*, London, 1911

Burnet, Bobby: *The St Andrews Opens*, Edinburgh, 1990

Geddes, Olive. M.: *A Swing through Time: Golf in Scotland 1457–1743*, Edinburgh, 1992

Price, Robert: *Scotland's Golf Courses*, Edinburgh, 1992

Robertson, James K.: *St. Andrews: Home of Golf*, 2nd ed. rev. by Tom Jarrett, Edinburgh, 1984

Ward Thomas, Pat: *The Royal and Ancient Golf Club*, Edinburgh, 1980

Hutchinson, Roger: *Camanachd!*, Edinburgh, 1989

Jarvie, Grant: *Highland Games: The Making of the Myth*, Edinburgh, 1991

Travellers and Transport

Mitchell, Sir Arthur and Cash, C. G.: *A Contribution to the Bibliography of Scottish Topography*, 2 vols., Edinburgh, 1917

Hancock, P. D.: *A Bibliography of Works Relating to Scotland, 1916–1950*, 2 vols., Edinburgh, 1959–60

Brown, P. Hume: *Early Travellers in Scotland*, Edinburgh, 1891, repr. 1978

Burt, Captain E.: *Letters from a Gentleman in the North of Scotland*, 2 vols., London, 1754

Gilpin, William: *Observations Relating Chiefly to Picturesque Beauty, Particularly in the Highlands of Scotland*, 2 vols., London, 1789

Johnson, Samuel: *A Journey to the Western Islands of Scotland in 1773*, London, 1775

Martin, Martin: *A Description of the Western Isles of Scotland, circa 1695*, London, 1703

Pennant, Thomas: *A Tour in Scotland and Voyage to the Hebrides*, London, 1772

Wordsworth, Dorothy: *Recollections of a Tour Made in Scotland AD 1803*, ed. J. C. Shairp, Edinburgh, 1874

Donaldson, Gordon: *Northwards by Sea*, Edinburgh, 1966

Gardiner, L.: *Stage-Coach to John-O'-Groats*, London, 1961

Haldane, A. R. B.: *The Drove Roads of Scotland*, Edinburgh, 1952

———: *New Ways through the Glens*, London, 1962

———: *Three Centuries of Scottish Posts*, Edinburgh, 1971

Holloway, J. and Errington, L.: *The Discovery of Scotland: The Appreciation of Scottish Scenery through Two Centuries of Painting*, Exhibition Catalogue, Edinburgh, 1978

Lindsay, Jean: *The Canals of Scotland*, Newton Abbot, 1968

Lindsay, Maurice: *The Discovery of Scotland: Travellers in Scotland from the thirteenth to the eighteenth centuries*, London, 1966

———: *The Eye is Delighted: Some Romantic Travellers in Scotland*, London, 1971

Nock, O. S.: *Scottish Railways*, London, 1961

Salmond, J. B.: *Wade in Scotland*, Edinburgh, 1938

Burke, John: *A Traveller's History of Scotland*, London, 1990

Cooper, Derek: *Road to the Isles: Travellers in the Hebrides, 1770–1914*, London, 1979

Crowl, Philip A.: *The Intelligent Traveller's Guide to Historic Scotland*, London, 1986

HMSO: *The Scottish Railway Story*, Edinburgh, 1992

Index

Page numbers in bold type refer to the main references

Alastair MacLeod —
  writer of short stories about
  Scottish descendants on Cape Breton